T5-BYJ-982

DISCARD
Chicago Public Library
West Pullman Branch
830 W 119th St 312 747-1425

Beyond Picture Books

Recent Titles in the
Children's and Young Adult Literature Reference Series
Catherine Barr, Series Editor

The Children's and Young Adult Literature Handbook: A Research and Reference Guide
John T. Gillespie

A to Zoo: Subject Access to Children's Picture Books. Seventh Edition
Carolyn W. Lima and John A. Lima

Best Books for Children: Preschool through Grade 6. Eighth Edition
Catherine Barr and John T. Gillespie

The Newbery/Printz Companion: Booktalks and Related Materials for Award Winners and Honor Books
John T. Gillespie and Corinne J. Naden

Books Kids Will Sit Still For 3: A Read-Aloud Guide
Judy Freeman

Classic Teenplots: A Booktalk Guide to Use with Readers Ages 12–18
John T. Gillespie and Corinne J. Naden

Best Books for Middle School and Junior High Readers: Grades 6–9. Supplement to the First Edition
John T. Gillespie and Catherine Barr

Best Books for High School Readers: Grades 9–12. Supplement to the First Edition
John T. Gillespie and Catherine Barr

War and Peace: A Guide to Literature and New Media, Grades 4–8
Virginia A. Walter

Across Cultures: A Guide to Multicultural Literature for Children
Kathy East and Rebecca L. Thomas

Best Books for Children, Supplement to the 8th Edition: Preschool through Grade 6
Catherine Barr and John T. Gillespie

Beyond Picture Books

SUBJECT ACCESS TO BEST BOOKS FOR BEGINNING READERS

Third Edition

BARBARA BARSTOW
JUDITH RIGGLE
LESLIE MOLNAR

Children's and Young Adult Literature Reference
Catherine Barr, Series Editor

Westport, Conn. London

Library of Congress Cataloging-in-Publication Data
Barstow, Barbara.
Beyond picture books : subject access to best books for beginning readers / Barbara Barstow, Judith Riggle, and Leslie Molnar. — 3rd ed.
p. cm. — (Children's and young adult literature reference)
Includes bibliographical references and index.
ISBN 978-1-59158-545-9 (alk. paper)
1. Children's literature—Bibliography. 2. Children—Books and reading—United States. 3. Children's libraries—United States—Book lists. I. Riggle, Judith. II. Molnar, Leslie, 1955- III. Title.
Z1037.B278 2008
[PN1009.A1]
011.62—dc22 2007042282

British Library Cataloguing in Publication Data is available.

Library of Congress Catalog Card Number: 2007042282
ISBN 978-1-59158-545-9

First published in 2008

Libraries Unlimited, 88 Post Road West, Westport, CT 06881
A Member of the Greenwood Publishing Group, Inc.
www.lu.com

Printed in the United States of America

The paper used in this book complies with the Permanent Paper Standard issued by the National Information Standards Organization (Z39.48–1984).

10 9 8 7 6 5 4 3 2 1

TO RALPH, AGAIN, WITH THANKS
—BARB

TO MY HUSBAND, TOM, WITH HEARTFELT APPRECIATION
—JUDY

FOR MY PARENTS, WHO WERE MY INSPIRATION INTO THE WORLD OF BOOKS
—LESLIE

CONTENTS

PREFACE

In this our third edition of *Beyond Picture Books*, we have made some changes that we hope will facilitate ease of use by librarians, teachers, and parents. A major change for us was the addition of Leslie M. Molnar, who oversees the selection of materials for children and teens for the Cuyahoga County Public Library in the suburban Cleveland area. Our combined experience with books and young children now exceeds one hundred years!

We continue to define first readers as books intended for children from kindergarten to third grade. They usually have a standard format and appear in series, have large print, short sentences, and a limited amount of text per page. For the younger end of the age range, books have one illustration per page; for the older end, there is one illustration per double-page spread. The vocabulary can be, but is not always, controlled and is generally limited to sight words, words of few syllables, and a familiar spoken vocabulary.

The following criteria were used to determine the addition or deletion of titles for the third edition of this bibliography:

1. Texts are well written
2. Information is accurate
3. Stories and subjects are of interest to the intended audience
4. Illustrations are attractive and complement and extend the text by providing visual clues
5. Out-of-print titles must show at least 100 libraries holding them (determined by checking OCLC First Search WorldCAT) before they can be kept or added

Along with local public and school libraries, *Children's Catalog* and publishers' catalogs were used as resources. Publishers were generous in their donation of titles published since the 1996 edition of *Beyond Picture Books*, and we thank them.

Some titles were not selected because they seemed to be intended for either an older or younger group than the targeted age level. Others were not included because they contained misinformation.

To make this volume easier to use, the format has been changed. Subject access is now provided in the front of the book in the Subject Guide. In determining subject assignments, we continue to use a combination of

The Sears List of Subject Headings, Library of Congress subject headings when available, and our experience with library users.

As in the second edition we continue to rely on our own experience with children and books to assign general levels of reading difficulty. Our objective is to *encourage* children to read by providing access to quality material within their reach and to help them *stretch* their reading skills by not stifling their interest.

- Reading Level A: Books have sentences with three to five single-syllable, easily recognizable words in large print. Illustrations generally take up to two-thirds of each page.
- Reading Level B: Books have a balance between text and illustrations. They have more complex sentences with more descriptors, phrases, and multi-syllabic words.
- Reading Level C: Books have more text, sentences are frequently compound, and vocabulary is more difficult. Texts may be divided under chapter headings. Illustrations take up less space and may only appear on alternating pages.

At the request of the publisher, we have also included the reading levels assigned to books by the Lexile Framework for Reading when available. We recognize that there are many other readability methods used throughout the country including Guided Reading, Reading Recovery, Fry, and Spache.

In this the third edition of *Beyond Picture Books*, there is a net gain of more than 1,265 titles. Despite our efforts to identify new books, and books overlooked in earlier editions, we know that we will have missed some.

We continue to be impressed by the quality of writing for children who are beginning to read, and we are very pleased that the Association for Library Service to Children, a division of the American Library Association, has created the Geisel Award to recognize books in this category.

THE GEISEL AWARD

BACKGROUND

In 1954, author John Hersey wrote a now-famous article for *Life* magazine, entitled "Why Do Students Bog Down on the First R?," in which he criticized the "insipid illustrations . . . [of] abnormally courteous, unnaturally clean boys and girls" featured in most early readers of the Dick-and-Jane model. As part of his call for change, Hersey suggested a list of talented illustrators, including Theodor Seuss Geisel, who might do a better job.

Geisel's publisher at Houghton Mifflin, William Spaulding, took up the challenge and asked Geisel to create "a story that first graders can't put down." Written with a restricted vocabulary of only 225 words, Geisel's response, *The Cat in the Hat,* changed juvenile literature when it was published in 1957. Its wild, original story about a mysterious, lanky cat who livens up a rainy day for a boy and girl while their parents are away was so compelling that children clamored to read it from start to finish, all by themselves.

"*The Cat in the Hat* liquidated Dick and Jane forever," wrote Clifton Fadiman in the introduction to *Six by Seuss: A Treasury of Dr. Seuss Classics* (Random House, 1991). "It . . . persuad[ed] the wee beginner that reading could be fun. No American child aware of his constitutional rights can reach the age of six without absorbing *The Cat in the Hat* and one or more of Seuss's seventeen Beginner Books that have followed it."

By 1960, the trade edition of *The Cat in the Hat* had sold nearly one million copies, and Geisel had started his Beginner Books series at Random House, which printed such early-reader classics as P. D. Eastman's *Go, Dog. Go!* (1961).

Fifty years after *The Cat in the Hat* first appeared, Geisel's work remains beloved among children and their families. Subversive, entertaining, and timeless, the Dr. Seuss books invite children to enter fantastical worlds, to laugh, and to delight in language, all while acquiring the serious skills of literacy.

Geisel's extraordinary contribution to children's books continues with the Theodor Seuss Geisel Award, first granted in 2006. According to its criteria, the annual award recognizes "the author[s] and illustrator[s] of the most distinguished American book for beginning readers published in English in the United States." Endowed by the Dr. Seuss Fund and administered by the Association for Library Service to Children (ALSC), a division of the American Library Association (ALA), the annual Theodor Seuss Geisel Award honors "literary and artistic achievements that demonstrate creativity and imagination to engage children in reading." This makes the Geisel Award unusual in two respects. It is the only ALA award to focus specifically on books for beginning readers, and it is also the first ALA award to be given to both the author and illustrator of a book, an acknowledgement of the unique importance of the interplay between words and pictures in a beginning reader. What happens in the images should reinforce the action described in the words and provide clues to children puzzling through the story independently.

"I've got a hunch," wrote Geisel to his editor at Random House just before *The Cat in the Hat* was published. "We've got a possibility of making a tremendous noise in the noisy discussion of Why Johnny Can't Read." Geisel, of course, was right, and the publication of *The Cat in the Hat* rang in a new renaissance in creative, captivating stories that convinced children that learning to read could be pleasurable and exciting.

Will the creation of the Theodor Seuss Geisel Award have a similarly inspiring effect on the field, encouraging authors, artists, and publishing houses to create more best-quality titles for beginning readers? Enthusiasm about the award, the increasing number of titles for these young readers, and the long life of some of these titles all indicate that the field is flourishing.

The Award

Since 2006, the Theodor Seuss Geisel Award has been given annually to the author(s)/illustrator(s) of the most distinguished contribution to the body of American children's literature that encourages and supports the beginning reader published in English in the United States during the preceding year. The award is restricted to citizens or residents of the United States.

The text of the book — to be between 24 and 96 pages — must be directed at readers from pre-K through grade 2. The book must also contain illustrations that function as keys or clues to the text and demonstrate the story being told. The committee considers all forms of writing — fiction, nonfiction, and poetry.

Subject matter must be intriguing enough to motivate the child to read. New words should be added slowly enough to make learning them a positive experience and words should be repeated to ensure knowledge retention. Sentences must be simple and straightforward and the story should advance from one page to the next, creating a "page-turning" dynamic. The book may or may not include short "chapters."

Winners

2007

Winner

Zelda and Ivy: The Runaways by Laura McGee Kvasnosky (Candlewick)

Honor Books

Mercy Watson Goes for a Ride written by Kate DiCamillo and illustrated by Chris Van Dusen (Candlewick)

Move Over, Rover! written by Karen Beaumont and illustrated by Jane Dyer (Harcourt)

Not a Box by Antoinette Portis (HarperCollins)

2006

Winner

Henry and Mudge and the Great Grandpas written by Cynthia Rylant and illustrated by Suçie Stevenson (Simon & Schuster Books for Young Readers)

Honor Books

Hi! Fly Guy by Tedd Arnold (Cartwheel/Scholastic)

A Splendid Friend, Indeed by Suzanne Bloom (Boyds Mills Press)

Cowgirl Kate and Cocoa written by Erica Silverman and illustrated by Betsy Lewin (Harcourt)

Amanda Pig and the Really Hot Day written by Jean Van Leeuwen and illustrated by Ann Schweninger (Dial Books for Young Readers)

OUTSTANDING FIRST READERS

The following is a selected list of 200 outstanding first readers. This list is a mix of old and new titles, fiction and nonfiction, all currently in print according to Books in Print and all worthy of purchase for school or public library collections. Many of what we considered to be the very best first readers were out of print and therefore ineligible for this list. All of these books are well written, contain accurate information when dealing with nonfiction subjects, are of interest to primary age children, and have attractive illustrations that complement the text. No attempt was made to present a balanced list of fiction and nonfiction works or of first, second, and third grade books. For books in a series — such as Lobel's Frog and Toad series and Rylant's Henry and Mudge series — only one title is listed.

Adler, David A.	*Bones and the Big Yellow Mystery*
Aliki	*My Feet*
Alphin, Elaine Marie	*A Bear for Miguel*
Armstrong, Jennifer	*The Snowball*
Arnold, Tedd	*Hi! Fly Guy*
Avi	*Abigail Takes the Wheel*
Baker, Keith	*Lucky Days with Mr. and Mrs. Green*
Bang-Campbell, Monika	*Little Rat Sets Sail*
Bauer, Marion Dane	*Bear's Hiccups*
Beaumont, Karen	*Move Over Rover!*
Bechtold, Lisze	*Buster and Phoebe: The Great Bone Game*
Benchley, Nathaniel	*George the Drummer Boy*
Berenstain, Stan, and Jan Berenstain	*The Berenstain Bears and the Spooky Old Tree*
Berger, Melvin, and Gilda Berger	*The Whole World in Your Hands*
Bonsall, Crosby	*Mine's the Best*
Branley, Franklyn M.	*The Big Dipper*
Brown, Laura Krasny	*Rex and Lilly Schooltime*
Brust, Beth Wagner	*The Great Tulip Trade*
Byars, Betsy	*The Golly Sisters Go West*
	My Brother Ant
Caple, Kathy	*Termite Trouble*
Capucilli, Alyssa Satin	*Biscuit*
Carlson, Nancy	*Harriet and Walt*
Cazet, Denys	*Minnie and Moo and the Musk of Zorro*
	A Snout for Chocolate

Author	Title
Chaconas, Dori	*Cork and Fuzz: Good Sports*
Chorao, Kay	*Up and Down with Kate*
Clements, Andrew	*Brave Norman: A True Story*
Coerr, Eleanor	*The Josefina Story Quilt*
Cohen, Caron L.	*How Many Fish?*
Cole, Joanna	*The Magic School Bus: At the Waterworks*
Cole, Joanna, and Stephanie Calmenson	*Ready . . . Set . . . Read!*
Collicott, Sharleen	*Mildred and Sam and Their Babies*
Corey, Shana	*First Graders from Mars Episode 1: Horus's Horrible Day*
Coville, Bruce, and Katherine Coville	*The Foolish Giant*
Cowley, Joy	*Agapanthus Hum and the Eyeglasses*
Coxe, Molly	*Big Egg*
Cushman, Doug	*Aunt Eater's Mystery Vacation*
	Inspector Hopper's Mystery Year
Cutler, Jane	*Rose and Riley*
Danziger, Paula	*It's Justin Time, Amber Brown*
Delacre, Lulu	*Rafi and Rosi*
dePaola, Tomie	*Cloud Book* *Hide-and-Seek All Week*
DiCamillo, Kate	*Mercy Watson to the Rescue*
Dorros, Arthur	*Follow the Water from Brook to Ocean*
Eastman, Philip D.	*Are You My Mother?*
Edwards, Michelle	*Stinky Stern Forever*
Ehrlich, Amy	*Bravo, Kazam!*
Fisher, Aileen	*The House of a Mouse*
Floyd, Lucy	*A Place for Nicholas*
Frasier, Debra	*On the Day You Were Born*
Frith, Michael K.	*I'll Teach My Dog One Hundred Words*
Fritz, Jean	*Surprising Myself*
Gage, Wilson	*My Stars, It's Mrs. Gaddy!*
Gantos, Jack	*Practice Makes Perfect for Rotten Ralph*
Gibbons, Gail	*Stargazers*
Giganti, Paul Jr.	*Each Orange Had Eight Slices: A Counting Book*
Godwin, Laura	*The Best Fall of All*
Greene, Stephanie	*Betsy Ross and the Silver Thimble*
Grimes, Nikki	*Wild, Wild Hair*
Guest, Elissa Haden	*Iris and Walter and the Birthday Party*
Hall, Katy, and Lisa Eisenberg	*Dino Riddles*
Haskins, Lori	*Too Many Dogs*
Herman, R. A.	*Pal and Sal*
Heilbroner, Joan	*This Is the House Where Jack Lives*
Hirschmann, Kris	*Glow-in-the-Dark Animals*
Hoban, Lillian	*Arthur's Loose Tooth*
Hoban, Tana	*I Wonder*
Hoban, Russell	*Tom and the Two Handles*
	A Bargain for Frances
Hoff, Syd	*Danny and the Dinosaur*

Author	Title
Holtzman, Caren	*No Fair! A Math Reader*
Holub, Joan	*The Pizza That We Made*
Hopkinson, Deborah	*From Slave to Soldier: Based on a True Civil War Story*
Hopping, Lorraine Jean	*Tornadoes!*
Howe, James	*Bunnicula: The Vampire Bunny and His Friends*
	Pinky and Rex Go to Camp
Impey, Rose	*Wanda Witch and the Stray Dragon*
Jango-Cohen, Judith	*Ben Franklin's Big Shock*
Jenkins, Steve	*Almost Gone: The World's Rarest Animals*
Jinkins, Jim	*Pinky Dinky Doo: Where Are My Shoes?*
Johnson, Crockett	*A Picture for Harold's Room*
Kaiser, Cecily	*If You're Angry and You Know It*
Karlin, Nurit	*The Fat Cat Sat on the Mat*
Katz, Bobbi	*Lots of Lice*
Kessler, Ethel, and Leonard Kessler	*Night Story*
Kessler, Leonard	*Kick Pass Run*
	The Big Mile Race
Krensky, Stephen	*All About Snow and Ice*
	Bubble Trouble
	Lionel and Louise
Kuskin, Karla	*Soap Soup: And Other Verses*
Labatt, Mary	*Sam at the Seaside*
Landau, Elaine	*Corn*
	Minibeasts as Pets
	Tropical Forest Mammals
Lauber, Patricia	*Clarence and the Cat*
LeSieg, Theo	*Ten Apples Up on Top!*
	Wacky Wednesday
	In a People House
Levinson, Nancy Smiler	*Snowshoe Thompson*
Levy, Elizabeth	*The Mystery of the Missing Dog*
Lewis, Thomas P.	*Hill of Fire*
Lexau, Joan M.	*Crocodile and Hen*
Little, Jean	*Emma's Strange Pet*
Lobel, Arnold	*Frog and Toad Are Friends*
	Mouse Soup
	Owl at Home
Low, Joseph	*Benny Rabbit and the Owl*
Luttrell, Ida	*Milo's Toothache*
Maccarone, Grace	*Pizza Party!*
	What Is That? Said the Cat
McKissack, Patricia, and Fredrick McKissack	*Frederick Douglass: Leader Against Slavery*
McMullan, Kate	*Fluffy and the Firefighters*
McNamara, Margaret	*Fall Leaf Project*
Maestro, Betsy	*Ferryboat*

Author	Title
Marshall, James	*Fox All Week*
	Fox Outfoxed
Marzollo, Jean	*I Spy a Candy Cane*
	The Counting Race
Mills, Claudia	*Gus and Grandpa*
Minarik, Else H.	*Cat and Dog*
Monjo, F. N.	*The Drinking Gourd: A Story of the Underground Railroad*
Mooser, Stephen	*Goofball Malone, Ace Detective*
Murphy, Frank	*Thomas Jefferson's Feast*
Myrick, Mildred	*Secret Three*
Oechsli, Kelly	*Mice at Bat*
Orgel, Doris	*Button Soup*
Parish, Herman	*Amelia Bedelia, Rocket Scientist*
Parish, Peggy	*Amelia Bedelia*
	Amelia Bedelia's Family Album
Paterson, Katherine	*Marvin One Too Many*
Penner, Lucille Recht	*Lights Out!*
Pilkey, Dav	*Dragon's Fat Cat*
Pomerantz, Charlotte	*The Outside Dog*
Porte, Barbara Ann	*Harry Gets an Uncle*
Prager, Annabelle	*The Spooky Halloween Party*
Prelutsky, Jack	*It's Snowing! It's Snowing: Winter Poems*
Preszler, June	*Juneteenth: Jubilee for Freedom*
Redmond, Shirley Raye	*Pigeon Hero!*
	Tentacles! Tales of the Giant Squid
Rex, Michael	*Firefighter*
Robins, Joan	*Addie's Bad Day*
Rockwell, Anne	*Who Lives in an Alligator Hole?*
Rogers, Jacqueline	*Goose On the Loose*
Roop, Peter, and Connie Roop	*Keep the Lights Burning, Abbie*
Ross, Pat	*Meet M and M*
Rubin, Mark	*The Orchestra*
Rylant, Cynthia	*Henry and Mudge: The First Book of Their Adventures*
	Annie and Snowball and the Dress-Up Birthday
	Mr. Putter and Tabby Make a Wish
Sadler, Marilyn J.	*P. J. Funnybunny's Bag of Tricks*
Samton, Sheila White	*Hurray for Rosa*
Sandin, Joan	*At Home in a New Land*
Schwartz, Alvin	*In a Dark, Dark Room and Other Scary Stories*
Scieszka, Jon	*Time Warp Trio: South Pole or Bust (an Egg)*
Selsam, Millicent E.	*Greg's Microscope*
	Big Tracks, Little Tracks
Seuss, Dr.	*The Cat In the Hat*
	Fox in Socks
	Green Eggs and Ham
	Hop on Pop
Sharmat, Marjorie W.	*Nate the Great*

Author	Title
Shea, George	*First Flight: The Story of Tom Tate and the Wright Brothers*
Showers, Paul	*Hear Your Heart*
Shub, Elizabeth	*The White Stallion*
Silverman, Erica	*Cowgirl Kate and Cocoa*
Sklansky, Amy E.	*Where Do Chicks Come From?*
Skofield, James	*Detective Dinosaur*
Slater, Teddy	*. . . 98, 98, 100! Ready or Not, Here I Come!*
Snow, Pegeen	*Eat Your Peas, Louise!*
Spirn, Michele Sobel	*I Am the Turkey*
Standiford, Natalie	*The Bravest Dog Ever: The True Story of Balto*
Staub, Frank	*Mountain Goats*
Stevens, Carla	*Anna, Grandpa, and the Big Storm*
Stevenson, James	*Heat Wave at Mud Flat*
Stille, Darlene R.	*Oceans*
Stolz, Mary	*Emmett's Pig*
Storad, Conrad J.	*Saguaro Cactus*
Sullivan, Paula	*Todd's Box*
Swain, Gwenyth	*Johnny Appleseed*
Swanson, June	*I Pledge Allegiance*
Tarcov, Edith H.	*The Frog Prince*
Thomas, Shelley Moore	*Happy Birthday, Good Knight*
Thomson, Pat	*The Treasure Sock*
Thomson, Sarah L.	*Amazing Sharks*
Tolstoy, Alexei	*The Enormous Turnip*
Van Leeuwen, Jean	*Amanda Pig and the Really Hot Day*
	Oliver and Albert, Friends Forever
Venezia, Mike	*Da Vinci*
Walker, Sally M.	*Supercroc Found*
Wells, Rosemary	*Make New Friends*
Willems, Mo	*Today I Will Fly!*
Wiseman, Bernard	*Morris the Moose*
Wyler, Rose, and Gerald Ames	*Magic Secrets*
Yolen, Jane	*Sleeping Ugly*
	Commander Toad and the Voyage Home
Ziefert, Harriet	*Jason's Bus Ride*
	The Teeny-Tiny Woman
Zion, Gene	*Harry and the Lady Next Door*
Zoehfeld, Kathleen W.	*Dinosaur Tracks*
Zolotow, Charlotte	*Seasons: A Book of Poems*

SUBJECT GUIDE

Subject heads are to nonfiction works unless designated with the word "Fiction." To make this index easier to use, "Fiction" cross-references can refer to both fiction and nonfiction headings. When a cross-reference does not have the label "Fiction," that cross-reference applies solely to nonfiction works. Numerals refer to entry numbers, not page numbers.

ANIMALS — BURROWING

Pluckrose, Henry
Under the Ground, 2427

ANIMALS — CAMOUFLAGE

Fowler, Allan
Hard-to-See Animals, 883
McDonnell, Janet
Animal Camouflage, 1833
Slater, Teddy
Animal Hide-and-Seek, 3116

ANIMALS — CAMOUFLAGE — FICTION

Skinner, Daphne
Almost Invisible Irene, 3110

ANIMALS — CLASSIFICATION

Moncure, Jane B.
Kinds of Animals, 2143
Selsam, Millicent E.
Benny's Animals and How He Put Them in Order, 2921

ANIMALS — CLIMBING

Powell, Jillian
Climbers, 2461

ANIMALS — COMMUNICATION

McDonnell, Janet
Animal Talk, 1834
Van Woerkom, Dorothy
Hidden Messages, 3468

ANIMALS — DESERT

Pearce, Q. L., and W. J. Pearce
In the Desert, 2361

ANIMALS — ENDANGERED

Jenkins, Steve
Almost Gone, 1420
Martin, Louise
Panda, 1980
Rhinoceros, 1981
Seals, 1982
Tigers, 1983
Martin, Patricia A. Fink
Chimpanzees, 1985
Lemurs, Lorises, and Other Lower Primates, 1986
Orangutans, 1989
Murray, Peter
Gorillas, 2208
Parrots, 2210
Nottridge, Rhoda
Big Cats, 2241
Royston, Angela
The Whale, 2741
Smith, Roland
Vultures, 3145
Spilsbury, Louise, and Richard Spilsbury
Save the Black Rhino, 3161
Save the Florida Manatee, 3162
Save the Giant Panda, 3163
Staub, Frank
Manatees, 3204
Stone, Lynn M.
Bats, 3257
Bears, 3258
Birds, 3261
Butterflies, 3263
Gibbons, 3279
Gorillas, 3281
Hyenas, 3284
Jaguars, 3285
Orangutans, 3293
Parrots, 3296
Prairie Dogs, 3300
Reptiles, 3303
Sandhill Cranes, 3304
Sea Turtles, 3305
Snow Monkeys, 3308
Tigers, 3310
Wild Cats, 3313
Wolves, 3314
Thomson, Sarah L.
Amazing Dolphins! 3397
Amazing Gorillas! 3398
Amazing Whales, 3401
Tigers, 3402
Walker, Sally M.
Mystery Fish, 3500
Weinberger, Kimberly
Cats That Roar! 3528

ANIMALS — EXTINCT

Aliki
Wild and Woolly Mammoths, 68

ANIMALS — FARM

Ling, Mary
Calf, 1732
Foal, 1733
Pig, 1738
Miller, Sara Swan
Chickens, 2088
Cows, 2089
Goats, 2090
Pigs, 2091
Sheep, 2092
Oppenheim, Joanne
"Uh-Oh!" Said the Crow, 2282
Pearce, Q. L., and W. J. Pearce
In the Barnyard, 2360

ANIMALS — FARM — FICTION

Edwards, Frank B.
A Crowded Ride in the Countryside, 799
Edwards, Julie Andrews, and Emma Walton Hamilton
Dumpy to the Rescue! 802
Dumpy's Apple Shop, 803
Goodman, Susan E.
What Do You Do on a Farm? 1021
McPhail, David M.
The Day the Sheep Showed Up, 1927
The Great Race, 1929
Samton, Sheila White
Hurray for Rosa! 2844
Young, James
The Cows Are in the Corn, 3664

ANIMALS — FICTION

Adler, David A.
The Carsick Zebra and Other Animal Riddles, 14
Baker, Betty
Partners, 114
Benchley, Nathaniel
Red Fox and His Canoe, 167
Berenstain, Michael
Michael Berenstain's Hop, Waddle, Swim! 177
The Panda Club's Tree House, 179
Blocksma, Mary
Yoo Hoo, Moon! 254
Blocksma, Norma
Best Dressed Bear, 255
Boegehold, Betty
Chipper's Choices, 256
Here's Pippa Again, 258
Hurray for Pippa! 260
Brown, Marc
Arthur Loses a Friend, 367
Arthur's Classroom Fib, 369
Arthur's Fire Drill, 370
Arthur's Lost Puppy, 371
Arthur's Reading Race, 372
D.W. All Wet, 373
D.W. Flips! 374
D.W. Thinks Big, 375
Glasses for D.W., 376

ANIMALS — MIGRATION

Fowler, Allan
Animals on the Move, 871

ANIMALS — NESTS

Nussbaum, Hedda
Animals Build Amazing Homes, 2249
Selsam, Millicent E., and Joyce Hunt
A First Look at Bird Nests, 2939

ANIMALS — NOCTURNAL

Moncure, Jane B.
Night Animals, 2145
Stone, Lynn M.
Opossums, 3292

ANIMALS — REPRODUCTION

Reidel, Marlene
From Egg to Bird, 2564
Selsam, Millicent E.
Egg to Chick, 2923
Shapp, Martha, and Charles Shapp
Let's Find Out About Babies, 2978
Tatham, Betty
Penguin Chick, 3353

ANIMALS — REPRODUCTION — FICTION

Ziefert, Harriet
Sam and Lucy, 3710

ANIMALS — SENSES

Fowler, Allan
How Animals See Things, 885
Pluckrose, Henry
Look at Tongues and Tasters, 2423

ANIMALS — TEETH

Labella, Susan
Beavers and Other Animals with Amazing Teeth, 1621

ANIMALS — TRACKS

Pearce, Q. L., and W. J. Pearce
In the Barnyard, 2360
In the Desert, 2361
In the Forest, 2362
Selsam, Millicent E.
Big Tracks, Little Tracks, 2922
How to Be a Nature Detective, 2925
Zoehfeld, Kathleen W.
Dinosaur Tracks, 3750

ANIMALS — TRACKS — FICTION

Penner, Lucille Recht
Bears on the Brain, 2365

ANIMALS — ZOO — FICTION

McInnes, John
Leo Lion Paints It Red, 1845
Pape, Donna L.
Count on Leo Lion, 2309
Thaler, Mike
There's a Hippopotamus under My Bed, 3379

ANTARCTICA

Fowler, Allan
Antarctica, 873
The Top and Bottom of the World, 924
Petersen, David
Antarctica, 2379

ANTARCTICA — FICTION

Scieszka, Jon
Time Warp Trio, 2912

ANTEATERS — FICTION

Cushman, Doug
Aunt Eater Loves a Mystery, 658
Aunt Eater's Mystery Vacation, 660

ANTELOPES

Stone, Lynn M.
Antelopes, 3255

ANTS

Butterworth, Christine
Ants, 414
Calder, S. J.
If You Were an Ant, 429
Dorros, Arthur
Ant Cities, 757
Fowler, Allan
Inside an Ant Colony, 888
Retan, Walter
Armies of Ants, 2568
Rowan, James P.
Ants, 2708

ANTS — FICTION

Berenstain, Stan, and Jan Berenstain
The Berenstains' A Book, 210
Brimner, Larry Dane
How Many Ants? 354
Holub, Joan
More Snacks! 1316
Myrick, Mildred
Ants Are Fun, 2213
Pollock, Penny
Ants Don't Get Sunday Off, 2433
Quackenbush, Robert
Henry's Awful Mistake, 2496

APACHE

Santella, Andrew
The Apache, 2850

APPLES

Johnston, Tony
Big Red Apple, 1459
Kurtz, Jane
Johnny Appleseed, 1606
Marzollo, Jean
I Am an Apple, 2000
Swain, Gwenyth
Johnny Appleseed, 3343

APPLES — FICTION

McMullan, Kate
Fluffy Goes Apple Picking, 1890
Ruelle, Karen Gray
Easy as Apple Pie, 2749

APRIL FOOLS' DAY

Jacobs, Leland B.
April Fool! 1397

APRIL FOOLS' DAY — FICTION

Ruelle, Karen Gray
April Fool! 2746
Stevenson, James
Mud Flat April Fool, 3225
Ziefert, Harriet
April Fool! 3672

AQUARIUMS

Richardson, Adele
Caring for Your Fish, 2584

ARCTIC

Fowler, Allan
Living in the Arctic, 900

BATS — FICTION

Knudsen, Michelle
The Case of Vampire Vivian, 1560
Quackenbush, Robert
Batbaby Finds a Home, 2488

BEACHES — FICTION

SEE ALSO Seashores — Fiction
Rylant, Cynthia
Poppleton and Friends, 2818
Smith, Janice Lee
Wizard and Wart at Sea, 3140
Spohn, Kate
Turtle and Snake's Day at the Beach, 3173

BEARS

Black, Sonia W.
Follow the Polar Bears, 247
Pollack, Pam, and Meg Belviso
Bear Cub, 2430
Robinson, Fay
Real Bears and Alligators, 2632
Ryder, Joanne
White Bear, Ice Bear, 2764
Spanjian, Beth
Baby Grizzly, 3156
Stone, Lynn M.
Bears, 3258, 3259
Brown Bears, 3262
Ziefert, Harriet
Bears Odd, Bears Even, 3673

BEARS — FICTION

Asch, Frank
Bread and Honey, 96
Baker, Barbara
One Saturday Afternoon, 108
Barr, Catherine
Bears In — Bears Out, 136
Bauer, Marion Dane
Bear's Hiccups, 144
Berenstain, Stan, and Jan Berenstain
The Bear Detectives, 180
Bear Scouts, 181
Bears in the Night, 182
Bears' Vacation, 184
The Berenstain Bear Scouts and the Search for Naughty Ned, 185
The Berenstain Bear Scouts and the Stinky Milk Mystery, 186
The Berenstain Bear Scouts and the White Water Mystery, 187
The Berenstain Bears: Big Bear, Small Bear, 188
The Berenstain Bears: That Stump Must Go, 189
The Berenstain Bears and the Big Road Race, 190
The Berenstain Bears and the Escape of the Bogg Brothers, 191
The Berenstain Bears and the Ghost of the Forest, 192
The Berenstain Bears and the Missing Dinosaur Bone, 193
The Berenstain Bears and the Missing Honey, 194
The Berenstain Bears and the Spooky Old Tree, 195
The Berenstain Bears and the Wishing Star, 196
The Berenstain Bears Blaze a Trail, 197
The Berenstain Bears by the Sea, 198
The Berenstain Bears Clean House, 199
The Berenstain Bears Down on the Farm, 200
The Berenstain Bears in the House of Mirrors, 201
The Berenstain Bears' New Kitten, 202
The Berenstain Bears' New Pup, 203
The Berenstain Bears on the Moon, 204
The Berenstain Bears Out West, 205
The Berenstain Bears Play T-ball, 206
The Berenstain Bears Ride the Thunderbolt, 207
The Berenstain Bears Seashore Treasure, 208
The Berenstains' B Book, 211
Big Honey Hunt, 213
Bike Lesson, 214
He Bear, She Bear, 215
Inside, Outside, Upside Down, 216
Old Hat, New Hat, 217
Ready, Get Set, Go! 218
Blocksma, Norma
Best Dressed Bear, 255
Brandenberg, Franz
A Fun Weekend, 298
Brinkloe, Julie
Gordon Goes Camping, 359
Christian, Mary B.
Penrod Again, 553
Penrod's Pants, 554
Penrod's Party, 555
Penrod's Picture, 556
Delton, Judy
A Birthday Bike for Brimhall, 710
Brimhall Turns Detective, 711
Brimhall Turns to Magic, 712
No Time for Christmas, 717
Two Good Friends, 718
Dewey, Ariane, and Jose Aruego
Splash! 748
Firmin, Peter
Boastful Mr. Bear, 852
Freschet, Berniece
Little Black Bear Goes for a Walk, 935
Gackenbach, Dick
Hound and Bear, 958
Gerver, Jane E.
The Big Red Sled, 984
Grindley, Sally
Friends Forever, 1077
Gruber, Suzanne
The Monster Under My Bed, 1081
Hanel, Wolfram
Old Mahony and the Bear Family, 1121
Hawkins, Colin, and Jacqui Hawkins
I'm Not Sleepy! 1144
Hoff, Syd
Bernard on His Own, 1268
Grizzwold, 1273
Holl, Adelaide
Bedtime for Bears, 1298
Small Bear and the Secret Surprise, 1302
Small Bear Builds a Playhouse, 1303
Small Bear's Birthday Party, 1304
Small Bear's Name Hunt, 1305
Wake Up, Small Bear, 1308
Jameson, Cynthia
The House of Five Bears, 1411
Janice
Little Bear Learns to Read the Cookbook, 1414
Kelley, True
Buggly Bear's Hiccup Cure, 1500

BIOGRAPHIES — AFRICAN AMERICANS

BIOGRAPHIES — WOMEN

BLACKOUTS, ELECTRIC POWER FAILURES — FICTION

BLINDNESS

BLIZZARDS — FICTION

BLUE JAYS — FICTION

BOATS AND BOATING

BOATS AND BOATING — FICTION

BOOKS AND READING

BOOKS AND READING (cont.)

Hood, Susan
Look! I Can Read! 1325
Hopkins, Lee Bennett
Good Books, Good Times! 1339
Johnson, Jean
Librarians A to Z, 1453
Mitgutsch, Ali
From Picture to Picture Book, 2133
Raatma, Lucia
How Books Are Made, 2521
Libraries, 2522

BOOKS AND READING — FICTION

Baker, Betty
Worthington Botts and the Steam Machine, 119
Bonsall, Crosby
Tell Me Some More, 276
Elliott, Dan
Grover Learns to Read, 818
Giff, Patricia Reilly
Today Was a Terrible Day, 999
Grey, Judith
What Time Is It? 1071
Gruber, Wilhelm
The Upside-Down Reader, 1082
Hall, Malcolm
Headlines, 1113
Hall, Patricia
Hooray for Reading! 1114
Hill, Susan
Stuart Little, 1205
Hoban, Lillian
Arthur's Prize Reader, 1250
Hurd, Edith T.
Johnny Lion's Book, 1377
Hutchins, Pat
The Tale of Thomas Mead, 1388
Janice
Little Bear Learns to Read the Cookbook, 1414
Jennings, Sharon
Franklin's Reading Club, 1435
Levinson, Nancy Smiler
Clara and the Bookwagon, 1703
Little, Jean
Emma's Magic Winter, 1740
Maccarone, Grace
Recess Mess, 1800
Medearis, Angela Shelf
Lucy's Quiet Book, 2060
Minarik, Else H.
No Fighting, No Biting! 2126
Numeroff, Laura J.
Beatrice Doesn't Want To, 2245
Pape, Donna L.
Leo Lion Looks for Books, 2311
Paterson, Katherine
Marvin One Too Many, 2355
Rau, Dana Meachen
My Book by Me, 2542
Seuss, Dr.
I Can Read with My Eyes Shut! 2968

BOOKSTORES — FICTION

Maitland, Barbara
The Bookstore Burglar, 1947
The Bookstore Ghost, 1948
The Bookstore Valentine, 1949
Wheeler, Cindy
Bookstore Cat, 3551

BOXES — FICTION

Rau, Dana Meachen
A Box Can Be Many Things, 2531
Stevenson, James
The Mud Flat Mystery, 3226

BRAILLE — FICTION

Rau, Dana Meachen
The Secret Code, 2545

BREAKFAST — FICTION

Stamper, Judith B.
Breakfast at Danny's Diner, 3188

BUBBLES — FICTION

Krensky, Stephen
Bubble Trouble, 1580
Packard, Mary
Bubble Trouble, 2293

BUFFALO — FICTION

Shefelman, Janice
Young Wolf's First Hunt, 3034

BUILDING — FICTION

Van Leeuwen, Jean
Oliver Pig and the Best Fort Ever, 3459

BUOYANCY

Stewart, Melissa
Will It Float or Sink? 3240

BURIED TREASURE — FICTION

Penner, Lucille Recht
X Marks the Spot! 2371

BUSES

SEE ALSO School buses
Ready, Dee
School Bus Drivers, 2558
Stamper, Judith B.
What's It Like to Be a Bus Driver, 3191

BUSES — FICTION

Cossi, Olga
Gus the Bus, 632
Ziefert, Harriet
Jason's Bus Ride, 3695
The Wheels on the Bus, 3729

BUSINESS ENTERPRISES

Pillar, Marjorie
Pizza Man, 2411

BUSINESS ENTERPRISES — FICTION

Hoban, Lillian
Arthur's Funny Money, 1244
Jennings, Sharon
Franklin and the Scooter, 1427
Ling, Bettina
Lemonade for Sale, 1731
McInnes, John
The Chocolate Chip Mystery, 1842
Pape, Donna L.
Mrs. Twitter the Animal Sitter, 2314

BUTTERFLIES AND MOTHS

Marzollo, Jean
I'm a Caterpillar, 2015
Neye, Emily
Butterflies, 2224
Saintsing, David
The World of Butterflies, 2840
Selsam, Millicent E.
Terry and the Caterpillars, 2931
Selsam, Millicent E., and Joyce Hunt
A First Look at Caterpillars, 2941

Shapiro, Karen
Butterflies, 2977
Stone, Lynn M.
Butterflies, 3263
Moths, 3291
Watts, Barrie
Butterflies and Moths, 3519
Moth, 3521
Ziefert, Harriet
Bugs, Beetles, and Butterflies, 3676

BUTTERFLIES AND MOTHS — FICTION

Lewison, Wendy Cheyette
Princess Buttercup, 1720

CACTI

Fowler, Allan
Cactuses, 878
Petersen, David
Saguaro National Park, 2386
Storad, Conrad J.
Saguaro Cactus, 3319

CAMELS

Coerr, Eleanor
Waza Wins at Windy Gulch, 582
Landau, Elaine
Desert Mammals, 1629
Waters, John F.
Camels, 3515

CAMELS — FICTION

Shaffer, Ann
The Camel Express, 2974

CAMPS AND CAMPING

Behrens, June
Juliette Low, 162

CAMPS AND CAMPING — FICTION

Berenstain, Stan, and Jan Berenstain
Bear Scouts, 181
Brinkloe, Julie
Gordon Goes Camping, 359
Carlson, Nancy
Arnie Goes to Camp, 462
Carrick, Carol
The Longest Float in the Parade, 478
Cushman, Doug
Camp Big Paw, 661
Dauer, Rosamond
Bullfrog and Gertrude Go Camping, 681
Delton, Judy
My Mom Made Me Go to Camp, 716
Duffey, Betsy
Camp Knock Knock, 776
Camp Knock Knock Mystery, 777
Dussling, Jennifer
Gotcha! 782
Eastman, Peter
Fred and Ted Go Camping, 789
Herman, Gail
The Camping Caper, 1185
Hoban, Lillian
Arthur's Camp-Out, 1242
Hoff, Syd
Danny and the Dinosaur Go to Camp, 1272
Jeffrey at Camp, 1281
Howe, James
Pinky and Rex Go to Camp, 1368
Koontz, Robin Michal
Chicago and the Cat, 1566
Parish, Peggy
Amelia Bedelia Goes Camping, 2322
Rau, Dana Meachen
Feet, 2538
Robison, Nancy
The Mystery at Hilltop Camp, 2643
Rockwell, Anne, and Harlow Rockwell
The Night We Slept Outside, 2675
Ruelle, Karen Gray
The Monster in Harry's Backyard, 2752
Rylant, Cynthia
Henry and Mudge and the Starry Night, 2792
Sadler, Marilyn J.
P. J. Funnybunny Camps Out, 2835
Spohn, Kate
Turtle and Snake Go Camping, 3172
Thaler, Mike
Camp Rotten Time, 3371
West, Colin
Moose and Mouse, 3543
Winters, Kay
Where Are the Bears? 3587
Yolen, Jane
The Giants Go Camping, 3660
Ziefert, Harriet, and Jon Ziefert
The Small Potatoes and the Sleep-Over, 3744

CANADA

Benchley, Nathaniel
Snorri and the Strangers, 172
Landau, Elaine
Canada, 1625
Wright, David
Canada Is My Home, 3634

CANALS

Landau, Elaine
Canals, 1626

CANDY — FICTION

Wallace, Karen
Albert's Raccoon, 3504

CAR RACING

SEE Sports — Car racing

CAREERS

Aliki
How a Book Is Made, 57
Berenstain, Michael
Michael Berenstain's When I Grow Up Oh, the Things I Can Be! 178
Berenstain, Stan, and Jan Berenstain
He Bear, She Bear, 215
Florian, Douglas
A Potter, 864
Henriod, Lorraine
Marie Curie, 1180
Jann, Gayle
A Day in the Life of a Construction Foreman, 1415
A Day in the Life of a Photographer, 1416
Klein, John E., and Carol Gaskin
A Day in the Life of a Commercial Fisherman, 1555
LeSieg, Theo
Maybe You Should Fly a Jet! Maybe You Should Be a Vet! 1696
Lillegard, Dee
I Can Be a Baker, 1729

CAREERS (cont.)

Martin, Claire
I Can Be a Weather Forecaster, 1977
Matthews, Morgan
What's It Like to Be a Farmer, 2033
What's It Like to Be a Postal Worker, 2034
What's It Like to Be a Railroad Worker, 2035
Matthias, Catherine
I Can Be a Police Officer, 2036
Pickering, Robert
I Can Be an Archaeologist, 2403
Poskanzer, Susan C.
What's It Like to Be a Chef, 2447
What's It Like to Be a Dairy Farmer, 2448
What's It Like to Be a Puppeteer, 2449
What's It Like to Be a Sanitation Worker, 2450
What's It Like to Be an Astronaut, 2451
Ready, Dee
Dentists, 2550
Doctors, 2551
Fire Fighters, 2553
Mail Carriers, 2555
Nurses, 2556
Police Officers, 2557
School Bus Drivers, 2558
Sipiera, Paul P.
I Can Be a Biologist, 3094
I Can Be a Chemist, 3095
I Can Be a Geologist, 3096
I Can Be a Physicist, 3097
I Can Be an Astronomer, 3098
I Can Be an Oceanographer, 3099
Stamper, Judith B.
What's It Like to Be a Bus Driver, 3191
What's It Like to Be a Dentist, 3192
What's It Like to Be a Truck Driver, 3193
What's It Like to Be a Veterinarian, 3194
What's It Like to Be a Zoo Worker, 3195
Storm, Betsy
I Can Be an Interior Designer, 3321
Swayne, Dick, and Peter Savage
I Am a Farmer, 3346
I Am a Fisherman, 3347
Tomchek, Ann Heinrichs
I Can Be a Chef, 3412
Wandro, Mark, and Joani Blank
My Daddy Is a Nurse, 3508
Wilkinson, Sylvia
I Can Be a Race Car Driver, 3570

CAREERS — FICTION

Kessler, Ethel, and Leonard Kessler
Stan the Hot Dog Man, 1515
Scarry, Richard
Frances Fix-It, 2863
Wells, Rosemary
When I Grow Up, 3541
Wilmer, Diane
Zap Zero, 3583

CARS

Kulling, Monica
Eat My Dust! 1602
Mayer, Cassie
Getting Around by Car, 2044
Royston, Angela
Cars, 2719

CARS — FICTION

Bourne, Miriam A.
Second Car in Town, 287
Feldman, Barbara
Going, Going, 838
Hazen, Barbara Shook
Road Hog, 1160
Schade, Susan, and Jon Buller
Toad on the Road, 2875

CASTLES

Gallimard Jeunesse
Castles, 968

CATERPILLARS

Selsam, Millicent E.
Terry and the Caterpillars, 2931
Selsam, Millicent E., and Joyce Hunt
A First Look at Caterpillars, 2941

CATS
SEE Pets — Cats

CAVE DWELLERS — FICTION

Schick, Alice, and Joel Schick
Just This Once, 2884

CHAMELEONS

Martin, Louise
Chameleons, 1979
Murray, Peter
Chameleons, 2206

CHANGE

Eastman, Patricia
Sometimes Things Change, 788

CHEETAHS

Hilker, Cathryn H.
A Cheetah Named Angel, 1202
Stone, Lynn M.
Cheetahs, 3264

CHEMICAL CHANGES

Young, June
Look How It Changes! 3666

CHEMISTRY AND CHEMISTS

Sipiera, Paul P.
I Can Be a Chemist, 3095

CHEROKEE

Gleiter, Jan, and Kathleen Thompson
Sequoya, 1010

CHEYENNE — FICTION

Leech, Jay, and Zane Spencer
Bright Fawn and Me, 1679

CHICKENS

Burton, Jane
Chester the Chick, 404
Miller, Sara Swan
Chickens, 2088
Potter, Tessa, and Donna Bailey
Hens, 2454
Royston, Angela
The Hen, 2728
Sklansky, Amy E.
Where Do Chicks Come From? 3112

CHRISTMAS — FICTION (cont.)

Mr. Putter and Tabby Bake the Cake, 2804
Sharmat, Marjorie W., and Craig Sharmat
Nate the Great and the Crunchy Christmas, 3010
Spohn, Kate
Turtle and Snake and the Christmas Tree, 3170
Stevenson, James
Christmas at Mud Flat, 3221
Van Leeuwen, Jean
Oliver and Amanda's Christmas, 3457
Wiseman, Bernard
Christmas with Morris and Boris, 3593
Wood, Audrey
The Horrible Holidays, 3624

CINCO DE MAYO

Palacios, Argentina
Viva Mexico! A Story of Benito Juarez and Cinco de Mayo, 2304

CIRCUSES

Denzel, Justin
Jumbo, 726
Edwards, Anne
P. T. Barnum, 798

CIRCUSES — FICTION

Berenstain, Stan, and Jan Berenstain
The Berenstains' C Book, 212
Brandenberg, Franz
What Can You Make of It? 305
Chwast, Seymour
The Twelve Circus Rings, 560
De Brunhoff, Laurent
Babar's Little Circus Star, 690
Hillert, Margaret
Circus Fun, 1208
It's Circus Time, Dear Dragon, 1214
Hoff, Syd
Barkley, 1266
Ida the Bareback Rider, 1280
Julius, 1282
McInnes, John
On with the Circus! 1846
Marzollo, Dan
I Spy a Circus, 1994
Olson, Mary C., ed.
Fly, Max, Fly! 2272
Pape, Donna L.
The Mouse at the Show, 2312
Quackenbush, Robert
Detective Mole and the Circus Mystery, 2491
Scarry, Richard
Lowly Worm Joins the Circus, 2864
Wiseman, Bernard
Morris and Boris at the Circus, 3600

CITY AND TOWN LIFE

Jacobs, Leland B.
Playtime in the City, 1402

CITY AND TOWN LIFE — FICTION

Bozzo, Maxine Z.
Toby in the Country, Toby in the City, 294
Capucilli, Alyssa Satin
Biscuit Visits the Big City, 445
Guest, Elissa Haden
Iris and Walter, 1083
Hall, Kirsten
My New Town, 1109
Hoff, Syd
Barney's Horse, 1267
Holl, Adelaide
Sylvester, 1306
Kaye, Marilyn
Will You Cross Me? 1487
McInnes, John
The Chocolate Chip Mystery, 1842
How Pedro Got His Name, 1844
McNamara, Margaret
Eloise Breaks Some Eggs, 1909
Poulin, Stephane
Have You Seen Josephine? 2458
Schick, Eleanor
Rainy Sunday, 2888
Stolz, Mary
Emmett's Pig, 3253
Wolcott, Patty
I'm Going to New York to Visit the Queen, 3614

CIVIL RIGHTS

Collard, Sneed B., III
Rosa Parks, 604
McKissack, Patricia, and Fredrick McKissack
Frederick Douglass, 1868
Ida B. Wells-Barnett, 1870
Mary Church Terrell, 1875
Paul Robeson, 1879
Sojourner Truth, 1882
Quiri, Patricia Ryon
The Bill of Rights, 2513
Ruffin, Frances E.
Martin Luther King, Jr., and the March on Washington, 2757

CLEANLINESS

Moncure, Jane B.
Caring for My Home, 2137
Monjo, F. N.
Messy Bessey's Closet, 2151
Pluckrose, Henry
Ways to Clean It! 2428

CLEANLINESS — FICTION

Bottner, Barbara
Two Messy Friends, 282
Danziger, Paula
Second Grade Rules, Amber Brown, 679
Krensky, Stephen
What a Mess! 1593
McKissack, Patricia, and Fredrick McKissack
Messy Bessey, 1877
Mayer, Gina, and Mercer Mayer
Rosie's Mouse, 2048
Packard, Mary
My Messy Room, 2299
Simon, Charnan
Wash Day, 3082
Smith, Janice Lee
Jess and the Stinky Cowboys, 3138
Ziefert, Harriet
A Clean House for Mole and Mouse, 3680

CLOCKS — FICTION

Bram, Elizabeth
Woodruff and the Clocks, 295
Danziger, Paula
It's Justin Time, Amber Brown, 677
Richards, Kitty
It's About Time, Max! 2583
Tompert, Ann
Sue Patch and the Crazy Clocks, 3414

CONCEPTS — COLORS — FICTION

Berenstain, Stan, and Jan Berenstain
The Berenstain Bears and the Big Road Race, 190
Hillert, Margaret
Happy Birthday, Dear Dragon, 1213
Kessler, Ethel, and Leonard Kessler
Pig's Orange House, 1513
Tripp, Valerie
The Penguins Paint, 3423
Wilhelm, Hans
I Love Colors! 3567

CONCEPTS — FICTION

Bowdish, Lynea
One Glad Man, 291
Matthias, Catherine
Over-Under, 2039
Sutherland, Tui T.
Meet Mo and Ella, 3342

CONCEPTS — LEFT AND RIGHT — FICTION

Stanek, Muriel
Left, Right, Left, Right! 3200

CONCEPTS — LINES

Yenawine, Philip
Lines, 3648

CONCEPTS — NUMBERS

Berenstain, Stan, and Jan Berenstain
Bears on Wheels, 183
Calmenson, Stephanie
One Little Monkey, 433
Chwast, Seymour
The Twelve Circus Rings, 560
Cohen, Caron L.
Three Yellow Dogs, 584
Dalton, Julie
Counting Money, 672
Giganti, Paul, Jr.
Each Orange Had Eight Slices, 1001
Hamsa, Bobbie
Polly Wants a Cracker, 1118
Hautzig, Deborah
It's a Secret! 1136
Kleinhenz, Sydnie Meltzer
More for Me! 1557
Koch, Michelle
Just One More, 1561
McKay, Sindy
Too Many Cats, 1857
Milios, Rita
Bears, Bears, Everywhere, 2080
Namm, Diane
Monsters, 2217

CONCEPTS — NUMBERS — FICTION

Brimner, Larry Dane
How Many Ants? 354
Chrismer, Melanie
Odd and Even Socks, 544
Cohen, Caron L.
How Many Fish? 583
deRubertis, Barbara
Count on Pablo, 739
Edwards, Frank B.
Nightgown Countdown, 800
Fernandes, Kim
Visiting Granny, 841
Glass, Dr. Julie
Counting Sheep, 1008
Hulme, Joy N.
Mary Clare Likes to Share, 1373
Kunnas, Mauri
Ricky, Rocky, and Ringo Count on Pizza, 1605
McNamara, Margaret
The Counting Race, 1907
Matthias, Catherine
Too Many Balloons, 2040
Moncure, Jane B.
The Magic Moon Machine, 2144
Numeroff, Laura J.
Monster Munchies, 2247
Pape, Donna L.
Count on Leo Lion, 2309
Ziefert, Harriet
A Dozen Dogs, 3682

CONCEPTS — OPPOSITES — FICTION

Moses, Amy
I Am an Explorer, 2187
St. Pierre, Stephanie
It's Not Easy Being Big! 2839

CONCEPTS — SHAPE

Bendick, Jeanne
Shapes, 174
Friskey, Margaret
Three Sides and the Round One, 947
Ribke, Simone T.
The Shapes We Eat, 2573
Yenawine, Philip
Shapes, 3651

CONCEPTS — SHAPE — FICTION

Pollack, Pam, and Meg Belviso
Chickens on the Move, 2431
Rau, Dana Meachen
Circle City, 2535
Rocklin, Joanne
Not Enough Room! 2652
Simon, Charnan
Pumpkin Fever, 3077

CONCEPTS — SIZE

Barrett, Judi
I'm too small, YOU'RE TOO BIG, 139
Froman, Robert
Bigger and Smaller, 951
Ribke, Simone T.
A Garden Full of Sizes, 2572
Ziefert, Harriet
How Big Is Big? 3693

CONCEPTS — SIZE — FICTION

Berenstain, Stan, and Jan Berenstain
The Berenstain Bears, 188
O'Connor, Jane
Sir Small and the Dragonfly, 2263
St. Pierre, Stephanie
It's Not Easy Being Big! 2839

CONCEPTS — SPACE — FICTION

Archbold, Tim
The Race, 85
Berenstain, Stan, and Jan Berenstain
Bears in the Night, 182
Inside, Outside, Upside Down, 216

CONCEPTS — TIME

Grey, Judith
What Time Is It? 1071
Hopkins, Lee Bennett
It's About Time! 1341
Jennings, Terry
Time, 1439
Simon, Charnan
A Busy Guy, 3069

DINOSAURS (cont.)

McMullan, Kate
Dinosaur Hunters, 1888
Maynard, Christopher
Incredible Dinosaurs, 2052
Milton, Joyce
Dinosaur Days, 2111
Moncure, Jane B.
Dinosaurs, 2141
Parish, Peggy
Dinosaur Time, 2328
Penner, Lucille Recht
Dinosaur Babies, 2366
Riehecky, Janet
Anatosaurus, 2601
Brachiosaurus, 2602
Iguanodon, 2605
Maiasaura, 2606
Robinson, Fay, and Sue Science Team of the Field Museum
A Dinosaur Named Sue, 2640
Schlein, Miriam
What the Dinosaurs Saw, 2890
Silverman, Maida
Dinosaur Babies, 3067
Spanjian, Beth
Baby Duckbill, 3155
Baby Stegosaurus, 3158
Baby Triceratops, 3159
Walker, Sally M.
Supercroc Found, 3501
Wright, J. B.
Dinosaurs, 3636
Zoehfeld, Kathleen W.
Did Dinosaurs Have Feathers? 3748
Dinosaur Babies, 3749
Dinosaur Tracks, 3750
Dinosaurs Big and Small, 3751
Terrible Tyrannosaurs, 3753

DINOSAURS — FICTION

Adler, David A.
Bones and the Dinosaur Mystery, 12
Ahlberg, Allan
Dinosaur Dreams, 32
Alphin, Elaine Marie
Dinosaur Hunter, 79
Binnamin, Vivian
The Case of the Snoring Stegosaurus, 241
Brimner, Larry Dane
Dinosaurs Dance, 353
Brown, Laura Krasny
Rex and Lilly Schooltime, 366
dePaola, Tomie
T-Rex Is Missing, 733
Hayes, Geoffrey
The Mystery of the Pirate Ghost, 1151
The Secret of Foghorn Island, 1152
Hennessy, B. G.
Busy Dinah Dinosaur, 1178
Meet Dinah Dinosaur, 1179
Hoban, Lillian
Joe and Betsy the Dinosaur, 1252
Hoff, Syd
Danny and the Dinosaur, 1271
Danny and the Dinosaur Go to Camp, 1272
Happy Birthday, Danny and the Dinosaur! 1274
Howe, James
Pinky and Rex, 1360
Klein, Howard
My Best Friends Are Dinosaurs, 1554
Kurtz, Jane
Mister Bones, 1607
Maccarone, Grace
Magic Matt and the Dinosaur, 1791
Most, Bernard
Catch Me If You Can! 2189
Nixon, Joan L.
Danger in Dinosaur Valley, 2233
Rosenbloom, Joseph
The Funniest Dinosaur Book Ever! 2693
Sharmat, Marjorie W.
Mitchell Is Moving, 2984
Nate the Great and the Sticky Case, 2997
Skofield, James
Detective Dinosaur, 3113
Detective Dinosaur Lost and Found, 3114
Vail, Rachel
Homework Trouble, 3441
The Horrible Play Date, 3442
Wells, Rosemary
Doris's Dinosaur, 3536

DISABILITIES — PHYSICAL AND MENTAL

De Fossard, Esta
Dinah the Dog with a Difference, 692
Malone, Mary
Annie Sullivan, 1951
Prall, Jo
My Sister's Special, 2469

DISABILITIES — PHYSICAL AND MENTAL — FICTION

Avi
Prairie School, 100
Carlson, Nancy
Arnie and the New Kid, 460
Caseley, Judith
Harry and Willy and Carrothead, 491
Clements, Andrew
Brave Norman, 567
Montgomery, Elizabeth R.
The Mystery of the Boy Next Door, 2156
Rau, Dana Meachen
The Secret Code, 2545
Weiss, Leatie
Funny Feet! 3532

DISEASES

Berger, Melvin
Germs Make Me Sick! 223
Gordon, Sharon
Asthma, 1026
Pinkeye, 1033
Kohlenberg, Sherry
Sammy's Mommy Has Cancer, 1562
Powell, Jillian
Becky Has Diabetes, 2460
Showers, Paul
No Measles, No Mumps for Me, 3051
Standiford, Natalie
The Bravest Dog Ever, 3198

DISEASES — FICTION

Clarke, Jane
Scratching's Catching, 563
Demuth, Patricia B.
Achoo! All About Colds, 722

DIVERSITY — FICTION

McKissack, Patricia, and Fredrick McKissack
Messy Bessey's Holidays, 1878

DIVISION — FICTION

Ziefert, Harriet
Rabbit and Hare Divide an Apple, 3709

DIWALI

Preszler, June
Diwali, 2481

DOCTORS AND NURSES

Kessler, Ethel, and Leonard Kessler
Our Tooth Story, 1512
Ready, Dee
Doctors, 2551
Nurses, 2556
Stamper, Judith B.
What's It Like to Be a Veterinarian, 3194

DOCTORS AND NURSES — FICTION

Quackenbush, Robert
Calling Doctor Quack, 2489
Scarry, Richard
Dr. Doctor, 2862
Ziefert, Harriet
Dr. Cat, 3684
Stitches, 3719

DOGS

SEE ALSO Pets — Dogs

DOGS — RACING

Seibert, Patricia
Mush! Across Alaska in the World's Longest Sled-Dog Race, 2917

DOGS, SEEING EYE

Moore, Eva
Buddy, 2162

DOLLS AND DOLLHOUSES — FICTION

Dussling, Jennifer
A Very Strange Dollhouse, 785
Earl, Janice
Jan Has a Doll, 786
Hall, Patricia
Hooray for Reading! 1114
Herman, Gail
There Is a Town, 1197
Lexau, Joan M.
The Rooftop Mystery, 1727
Schulman, Janet
The Big Hello, 2896
Wells, Rosemary
Play with Max and Ruby, 3539

DOLPHINS

Berger, Melvin, and Gilda Berger
Splash! A Book About Whales and Dolphins, 230
Morris, Robert
Dolphin, 2184
Pfeffer, Wendy
Dolphin Talk, 2393
Roop, Peter, and Connie Roop
Whales and Dolphins, 2682
Taylor, Leighton
Dolphins, 3355
Thomson, Sarah L.
Amazing Dolphins! 3397

DOLPHINS — FICTION

Benchley, Nathaniel
Several Tricks of Edgar Dolphin, 170
Winnick, Karen
Sandro's Dolphin, 3586

DOMINICAN REPUBLIC

Landau, Elaine
Dominican Republic, 1630

DONKEYS

Anders, Rebecca
Dolly the Donkey, 80

DRAGONFLIES

Harrison, Virginia
The World of Dragonflies, 1125
Rowan, James P.
Dragonflies, 2709

DRAGONS — FICTION

Agell, Charlotte
Sailor's Book, 31
Albee, Sarah
The Dragon's Scales, 38
Hillert, Margaret
Come to School, Dear Dragon, 1210
It's Circus Time, Dear Dragon, 1214
Mayer, Mercer
Herbert the Timid Dragon, 2049
Pilkey, Dav
Dragon Gets By, 2406
Dragon's Fat Cat, 2407
Dragon's Halloween, 2408
Dragon's Merry Christmas, 2409
A Friend for Dragon, 2410
Schecter, Ellen, reteller
Sim Chung and the River Dragon, 2883
Thomas, Shelley Moore
Get Well, Good Knight, 3386
Good Night, Good Knight, 3387
Happy Birthday, Good Knight, 3388

DREAMS — FICTION

Ahlberg, Allan
Dinosaur Dreams, 32
Bauer, Marion Dane
Turtle Dreams, 152
Bonsall, Crosby
Piggle, 275
Davis, Maggie S.
A Garden of Whales, 686
Feldman, Barbara
Going, Going, 838
Hillert, Margaret
Go to Sleep, Dear Dragon, 1212
Hurd, Edith T.
No Funny Business, 1382
McKay, Sindy
Too Many Cats, 1857
Neasi, Barbara
Sweet Dreams, 2218
Ziefert, Harriet
Sleepy Dog, 3712

DRUGS AND DRUG ABUSE

Super, Gretchen
Drugs and Our World, 3335
What Are Drugs? 3337
You Can Say "No" to Drugs, 3338

DUCKS

Burton, Jane
Dabble the Duckling, 405
Chittenden, Margaret
When the Wild Ducks Come, 534
Goldin, Augusta
Ducks Don't Get Wet, 1017

Maestro, Betsy
Why Do Leaves Change Color? 1942

FALL — FICTION

Herman, Emmi S.
We All Fall for Apples, 1183
Holl, Adelaide
Bedtime for Bears, 1298
Jacobs, Leland B.
Poetry for Autumn, 1403
Lapp, Eleanor J.
The Mice Came in Early This Year, 1661
McNamara, Margaret
Fall Leaf Project, 1910
Packard, Mary
Fall Leaves, 2296
Rylant, Cynthia
Henry and Mudge under the Yellow Moon, 2803
Poppleton in Fall, 2822
Stamper, Judith B.
The Wild Leaf Ride, 3196

FAMILIES, SINGLE PARENT — FICTION

Porte, Barbara Ann
Harry's Birthday, 2441
Harry's Dog, 2442
Harry's Mom, 2443
Ross, Jan
Dogs Have Paws, 2694
Schick, Eleanor
Neighborhood Knight, 2887

FAMILY LIFE

SEE ALSO Aunts and uncles, Fathers, Grandparents, Mothers, Siblings, Stepparents
Morris, Kimberly
Molly in the Middle, 2183
Simon, Norma
Why Am I Different? 3083

FAMILY LIFE — CANADA

Wright, David
Canada Is My Home, 3634

FAMILY LIFE — FICTION

Aber, Linda W.
Grandma's Button Box, 3
Adams, Florence
Mushy Eggs, 8
Alphin, Elaine Marie
A Bear for Miguel, 78
Bader, Bonnie
Graphs, 102
Baker, Barbara
One Saturday Afternoon, 108
Barrett, Joyce D.
Willie's Not the Hugging Kind, 138
Bartels, Alice L.
The Grandmother Doll, 141
Brandenberg, Franz
Aunt Nina and Her Nephews and Nieces, 296
Everyone Ready? 297
A Fun Weekend, 298
Leo and Emily's Big Ideas, 300
Leo and Emily's Zoo, 301
Brimner, Larry Dane
Lightning Liz, 355
Bulla, Clyde R.
Daniel's Duck, 387
Byars, Betsy
Ant Plays Bear, 420
My Brother Ant, 424
Calmenson, Stephanie
Where's Rufus? 434
Capucilli, Alyssa Satin
Pedro's Burro, 451
Carlson, Nancy
The Perfect Family, 474
Chorao, Kay
Here Comes Kate, 539
Up and Down with Kate, 541
Christensen, Nancy
Good Night, Little Kitten, 545
Claverie, Jean
The Picnic, 564
Collicott, Sharleen
Mildred and Sam, 606
Mildred and Sam and Their Babies, 607
Conway, Lisa
I Like Ketchup Sandwiches, 609
Cosby, Bill
The Day I Saw My Father Cry, 622
The Day I Was Rich, 623
Hooray for the Dandelion Warriors! 624
The Meanest Thing to Say, 625
My Big Lie, 626
One Dark and Scary Night, 627
Shipwreck Saturday, 628
Super-fine Valentine, 629
The Treasure Hunt, 630
The Worst Day of My Life, 631
Cresswell, Helen
The Weather Cat, 650
Dauer, Rosamond
Bullfrog Grows Up, 683
Fine, Jane
Surprise! 844
Floyd, Lucy
A Place for Nicholas, 866
Franco, Betsy
Grandpa's Quilt, 927
Grindley, Sally, ed.
A Day with Alice and Sam, 1079
Guest, Elissa Haden
Iris and Walter and Cousin Howie, 1089
Himmelman, John
The Day-Off Machine, 1225
Hoban, Russell
Tom and the Two Handles, 1262
Hooks, William H.
Where's Lulu? 1336
Howe, James
Pinky and Rex and the New Baby, 1364
Hutchins, Pat
The Best Train Set Ever, 1387
Kidd, Ronald
Tuna Surprise, 1536
Krensky, Stephen
Lionel and Louise, 1582
Lionel-at-Large, 1583
Lionel in the Spring, 1584
Leonard, Marcia
No New Pants! 1685
The Tin Can Man, 1688
Maccarone, Grace
I Shop with My Daddy, 1788
McDaniel, Becky B.
Katie Can, 1820
Katie Couldn't, 1821
Katie Did It, 1822
Manushkin, Fran
The Perfect Christmas Picture, 1954
Marx, David F.
Baby in the House, 1991
Mayer, Mercer
Little Critter's Read-It-Yourself Storybook, 2050
Minarik, Else H.
Father Bear Comes Home, 2119
Moncure, Jane B.
Caring for My Baby Sister, 2135

FAMILY LIFE — FICTION (cont.)

FAMILY LIFE — VIETNAM

FAMILY REUNIONS — FICTION

FANTASY

FANTASY — FICTION

FARM AND COUNTRY LIFE

FARM AND COUNTRY LIFE — FICTION

FATHERS

FATHERS — FICTION

FRICTION

Trumbauer, Lisa
What Is Friction? 3435

FRIENDSHIP — FICTION

Ada, Alma Flor
Daniel's Mystery Egg, 6
Albee, Sarah
My Best Friend Is Out of this World, 39
Alexander, Sue
More Witch, Goblin, and Ghost Stories, 43
Witch, Goblin, and Ghost Are Back, 45
Witch, Goblin, and Ghost in the Haunted Woods, 46
Witch, Goblin, and Sometimes Ghost, 47
Baker, Barbara
Digby and Kate, 104
Digby and Kate Again, 105
Digby and Kate and the Beautiful Day, 106
Digby and Kate 1, 2, 3, 107
Baker, Betty
Partners, 114
Bauer, Marion Dane
Frog's Best Friend, 147
Baynton, Martin
Fifty Gets the Picture, 157
Boegehold, Betty
Hurray for Pippa! 260
Pippa Pops Out! 261
Bonsall, Crosby
The Case of the Cat's Meow, 269
The Case of the Dumb Bells, 270
The Case of the Hungry Stranger, 271
The Case of the Scaredy Cats, 272
Mine's the Best, 274
Bottner, Barbara
Two Messy Friends, 282
Brandenberg, Franz
Leo and Emily's Big Ideas, 300
Leo and Emily's Zoo, 301
Nice New Neighbors, 302
Brenner, Barbara, and William H. Hooks
Lion and Lamb Step Out, 342
Ups and Downs with Lion and Lamb, 343
Bridwell, Norman
Clifford Makes a Friend, 347
Brimner, Larry Dane
Aggie and Will, 349
Summer Fun, 357
Brown, Marc
Arthur Loses a Friend, 367
Arthur's Classroom Fib, 369
Buck, Nola
Sid and Sam, 385
Bunting, Eve
My Robot, 400
Byars, Betsy
The Seven Treasure Hunts, 425
Capucilli, Alyssa Satin
Biscuit's Big Friend, 448
Carrick, Malcolm
Today Is Shrew Day, 481
Caseley, Judith
Harry and Willy and Carrothead, 491
Chaconas, Dori
Cork and Fuzz, 519
Cork and Fuzz: Good Sports, 520
Cork and Fuzz: Short and Tall, 521
Champion, Joyce
Emily and Alice, 525
Chardiet, Bernice, and Grace Maccarone
We Scream for Ice Cream, 528
Christian, Mary B.
Penrod Again, 553
Penrod's Pants, 554
Penrod's Party, 555
Penrod's Picture, 556
Cole, Joanna
Bully Trouble, 586
The Missing Tooth, 595
Coxe, Molly
The Great Snake Escape, 642
Craig, Janet
Max and Maggie in Summer, 648
Valentine's Day Mess, 649
Cutler, Jane
Rose and Riley, 667
Danziger, Paula
What a Trip, Amber Brown, 680
Dauer, Rosamond
Bullfrog Builds a House, 682
Degen, Bruce
The Little Witch and the Riddle, 693
Delton, Judy
A Birthday Bike for Brimhall, 710
Brimhall Turns to Magic, 712
Two Good Friends, 718
Dotlich, Rebecca Kai
Peanut and Pearl's Picnic Adventure, 764
Edwards, Michelle
Pa Lia's First Day, 804
Ehrlich, Amy
Leo, Zack and Emmie, 812
Leo, Zack and Emmie Together Again, 813
Elliot, David
The Cool Crazy Crickets, 816
Finch, Margo
The Lunch Bunch, 843
Firmin, Peter
Basil Brush Goes Boating, 848
Basil Brush Goes Flying, 849
Gackenbach, Dick
Hattie Rabbit, 956
Hound and Bear, 958
Giff, Patricia Reilly
Good Luck, Ronald Morgan! 996
Happy Birthday, Ronald Morgan! 997
Gordon, Jeffie R.
Muriel and Ruth, 1024
Gordon, Shirley
Crystal's Christmas Carol, 1038
Graham, Bob
Crusher Is Coming, 1039
Grindley, Sally
Friends Forever, 1077
Guest, Elissa Haden
Iris and Walter, 1083
Iris and Walter: The School Play, 1085
Iris and Walter: The Sleepover, 1086
Iris and Walter: True Friends, 1087
Iris and Walter and Baby Rose, 1088
Iris and Walter and Cousin Howie, 1089
Iris and Walter and the Birthday Party, 1090
Iris and Walter and the Field Trip, 1091
Hall, Malcolm
Edward, Benjamin and Butter, 1112
Harshman, Terry Webb
Porcupine's Pajama Party, 1128
Hautzig, Deborah
It's Easy! 1137

It's Not Fair! Featuring Jim Henson's Sesame Street Muppets, 1138
Why Are You So Mean to Me? 1141

Hays, Anna Jane
Silly Sara, 1153

Herman, Gail
Slip! Slide! Skate! 1194

Herman, R. A.
Pal and Sal, 1199
Pal the Pony, 1200

Hillert, Margaret
A Friend for Dear Dragon, 1211

Himmelman, John
Simpson Snail Sings, 1228

Hoban, Lillian
Arthur's Great Big Valentine, 1245
Mr. Pig and Sonny Too, 1254
Silly Tilly's Thanksgiving Dinner, 1256

Hoban, Russell
A Bargain for Frances, 1261
Tom and the Two Handles, 1262

Hoff, Syd
A Walk Past Ellen's House, 1291
Who Will Be My Friends? 1293
Wilfred the Lion, 1294

Holl, Adelaide
George the Gentle Giant, 1299
Small Bear Builds a Playhouse, 1303

Howe, James
Houndsley and Catina, 1359
Pinky and Rex and the Bully, 1361
Pinky and Rex and the Mean Old Witch, 1363
Pinky and Rex and the New Baby, 1364
Pinky and Rex and the Perfect Pumpkin, 1365
Pinky and Rex and the Spelling Bee, 1366
Pinky and Rex Get Married, 1367

Jennings, Sharon
Franklin's Surprise, 1437

Johnston, Tony
The Adventures of Mole and Troll, 1456
Alien and Possum, 1457
Alien and Possum Hanging Out, 1458
Night Noises and Other Mole and Troll Stories, 1462
Odd Jobs and Friends, 1464
Sparky and Eddie, 1465
Wild, Wild Rodeo! 1466

Kaye, Marilyn
Will You Cross Me? 1487

Kessler, Ethel, and Leonard Kessler
The Big Fight, 1509
The Sweeneys from 9D, 1516

Kiser, SuAnn
Hazel Saves the Day, 1548

Komaiko, Leah
Earl's Too Cool for Me, 1564

Kraus, Robert
Dance, Spider, Dance! 1576
Trouble with Spider, 1578

Kwitz, Mary D.
Little Chick's Friend Duckling, 1612

Levinson, Nancy Smiler
Prairie Friends, 1704

Lewis, Thomas P.
The Blue Rocket Fun Show, 1714

Lexau, Joan M.
Don't Be My Valentine, 1723

Lillie, Patricia
Jake and Rosie, 1730

Little, Jean
Emma's Magic Winter, 1740

Lobel, Arnold
Days with Frog and Toad, 1746
Frog and Toad All Year, 1747
Frog and Toad Are Friends, 1748
Frog and Toad Together, 1749
Mouse Tales, 1753

Luttrell, Ida
The Bear Next Door, 1777
Tillie and Mert, 1780

Macdonald, Maryann
The Pink Party, 1826

McDonald, Megan
Beezy, 1828
Beezy and Funnybone, 1829
Beezy at Bat, 1830
Beezy Magic, 1831

McKay, Sindy
Baseball Fever, 1850

McMorrow, Catherine
The Jellybean Principal, 1886

McMullan, Kate
Pearl and Wagner, 1904

Madsen, Ross M.
Perrywinkle's Magic Match, 1935
Stewart Stork, 1936

Marshall, James
Fox All Week, 1963
Speedboat, 1972
Three by the Sea, 1973
Three Up a Tree, 1974

Marzollo, Jean, and Claudio Marzollo
Ruthie's Rude Friends, 2025

Mayer, Mercer
Little Critter's Read-It-Yourself Storybook, 2050
This Is My Friend, 2051

Meister, Cari
Skinny and Fats, Best Friends, 2067

Michaels, Anna
Best Friends, 2073

Milne, A. A.
Christopher Robin Leads an Expedition, 2106
Pooh Goes Visiting, 2107
Pooh Invents a New Game, 2108
Tigger Comes to the Forest, 2109

Minarik, Else H.
Little Bear's Bad Day, 2123
Little Bear's Friend, 2124

Montgomery, Elizabeth R.
The Mystery of the Boy Next Door, 2156

Moran, Alex
Sam and Jack, 2176

Myrick, Mildred
Ants Are Fun, 2213
Secret Three, 2214

Noonan, Julia
Friends Forever, 2240

Novak, Matt
Little Wolf Big Wolf, 2242
Newt, 2243

Numeroff, Laura J.
Amy for Short, 2244

O'Connor, Jane
Lulu Goes to Witch School, 2258
Molly the Brave and Me, 2259
Nina, Nina, Copycat Ballerina, 2261
Nina, Nina, Star Ballerina, 2262

Osborne, Mary P.
Mo and His Friends, 2287
Mo to the Rescue, 2288

FRIENDSHIP — FICTION (cont.)

FROGS AND TOADS

GAMES (cont.)

Silbaugh, Elizabeth
Let's Play Cards! 3062

GAMES — FICTION

Bonsall, Crosby
The Day I Had to Play with My Sister, 273
Milios, Rita
Sneaky Pete, 2083
Ross, Pat
M and M and the Haunted House Game, 2700
Slater, Teddy
. . . 98, 99, 100! Ready or Not, Here I Come! 3121
Ziefert, Harriet
Cat Games, 3679

GARBAGE AND GARBAGE DISPOSAL

Brimner, Larry Dane
Trash Trouble, 358
Poskanzer, Susan C.
What's It Like to Be a Sanitation Worker, 2450
Showers, Paul
Where Does the Garbage Go? 3054

GARDENING

Overbeck, Cynthia
The Vegetable Book, 2291
Pfeffer, Wendy
From Seed to Pumpkin, 2394
Robinson, Fay
Vegetables, Vegetables! 2636

GARDENING — FICTION

Hautzig, Deborah
It's Easy! 1137
Holub, Joan
The Garden That We Grew, 1314
Inches, Alison
Corduroy's Garden, 1394
Monjo, F. N.
Messy Bessey's Garden, 2152
Muntean, Michaela
A Garden for Miss Mouse, 2196
Roberts, Bethany
Ogre Eats Everything, 2620
Ryder, Joanne
First Grade Ladybugs, 2761
Samton, Sheila White
The Rosa Stories, 2845
Wolcott, Patty
Super Sam and the Salad Garden, 3617

GASES

Zoehfeld, Kathleen W.
What Is the World Made Of? 3754

GEESE

Potter, Tessa, and Donna Bailey
Ducks and Geese, 2452
Selsam, Millicent E., and Joyce Hunt
A First Look at Ducks, Geese and Swans, 2942

GEESE — FICTION

Bunting, Eve
Goose Dinner, 399
Dunbar, Joyce
Gander's Pond, 778
Kwitz, Mary D.
Gumshoe Goose, Private Eye, 1610
McPhail, David M.
A Girl, a Goat, and a Goose, 1928
Miles, Miska
Noisy Gander, 2075
Rockwell, Anne
Honk Honk! 2663
Rogers, Jacqueline
Goose on the Loose, 2679
Rylant, Cynthia
Henry and Mudge and the Wild Goose Chase, 2795
Poppleton in Fall, 2822
Sharmat, Marjorie W.
Griselda's New Year, 2982
Walker, Sally M.
The 18 Penny Goose, 3498

GEOGRAPHY

Berger, Melvin, and Gilda Berger
The Whole World in Your Hands, 234
Fowler, Allan
It Could Still Be a Lake, 891
Lands of Grass, 893
Life in a Pond, 895
Life in a Tide Pool, 896
Life in a Wetland, 897
Living in the Arctic, 900
Living on the Plains, 903
The Wonder of a Waterfall, 926
Knowlton, Jack
Geography from A to Z, 1559
Landau, Elaine
Australia and New Zealand, 1624
Canada, 1625
Canals, 1626
Dominican Republic, 1630
Egypt, 1631
France, 1632
India, 1635
Israel, 1636
Korea, 1637
Norway, 1640
Peru, 1642
Lauber, Patricia
How We Learned the Earth Is Round, 1669
Petersen, David
Antarctica, 2379
Asia, 2381
Australia, 2382
Denali National Park and Preserve, 2384
North America, 2385
South America, 2387
Sapre, Reshma
Iowa, 2852
Schulte, Mary
The Amazon River, 2902
Great Salt Lake, 2903
Stille, Darlene R.
Deserts, 3244
Taylor-Butler, Christine
Hawaii, 3360
Kansas, 3361
The Missouri River, 3362
Ohio, 3363
Vermont, 3367
Trueit, Trudi Strain
Mississippi, 3427
Utah, 3429
Valzania, Kimberly
Kentucky, 3443
Tennessee, 3444
Wade, Mary Dodson
Map Scales, 3488
Types of Maps, 3490
Walker, Cynthia
Colorado, 3495
Maine, 3496
New Mexico, 3497
Zapata, Elizabeth
Puerto Rico, 3668
Zollman, Pam
Gulf of Mexico, 3757
Lake Tahoe, 3758

GRASSHOPPERS — FICTION

Lobel, Arnold
Grasshopper on the Road, 1750

GRASSLANDS

Fowler, Allan
Lands of Grass, 893
Stille, Darlene R.
Grasslands, 3246

GRASSLANDS — AFRICA

Pearce, Q. L., and W. J. Pearce
In the African Grasslands, 2359

GRAVITY

Selsam, Millicent E.
Up, Down and Around, 2933
Trumbauer, Lisa
What Is Gravity? 3436

GREED — FICTION

Wheeler, Cindy
The Emperor's Birthday Suit, 3552

GRIZZLIES

Lepthien, Emilie U.
Grizzlies, 1689

GROUNDHOG DAY

McNamara, Margaret
Groundhog Day, 1913

GROUNDHOG DAY — FICTION

Delton, Judy
Groundhog's Day at the Doctor, 714
Ruelle, Karen Gray
Great Groundhogs, 2750

GROUNDHOGS

McNulty, Faith
Woodchuck, 1923

GROWING UP

Freschet, Berniece
Moose Baby, 937
Possum Baby, 938
Goennel, Heidi
My Day, 1016
Hurd, Edith T.
Mother Kangaroo, 1381
Suhr, Mandy
I Am Growing, 3331

GROWING UP — FICTION

Benchley, Nathaniel
Running Owl the Hunter, 168
Boegehold, Betty
Here's Pippa Again, 258
Pippa Pops Out! 261
Dauer, Rosamond
Bullfrog Grows Up, 683
Eastman, Philip D.
Are You My Mother? 790
Hoban, Lillian
Arthur's Honey Bear, 1247
Krensky, Stephen
Lionel and Louise, 1582
Lionel-at-Large, 1583

GUINEA PIGS — FICTION

McMullan, Kate
Fluffy and the Firefighters, 1889
Fluffy Goes Apple Picking, 1890
Fluffy Goes to School, 1891
Fluffy Grows a Garden, 1892
Fluffy Meets the Groundhog, 1893
Fluffy Meets the Tooth Fairy, 1894
Fluffy Saves Christmas, 1895
Fluffy's Funny Field Trip, 1896
Fluffy's Lucky Day, 1897
Fluffy's 100th Day at School, 1898
Fluffy's School Bus Adventure, 1899
Fluffy's Silly Summer, 1900
Fluffy's Spring Vacation, 1901
Rocklin, Joanne
How Much Is That Guinea Pig in the Window? 2649

GYPSIES — FICTION

DeLage, Ida
Beware! Beware! A Witch Won't Share, 697

HAIRCUTTING

SEE ALSO Human body — Hair — Fiction

HAIRCUTTING — FICTION

Davis, Gibbs
Katy's First Haircut, 685
Quin-Harkin, Janet
Helpful Hattie, 2508
Robins, Joan
Addie's Bad Day, 2623
Wilhelm, Hans
Don't Cut My Hair! 3562

HALLOWEEN

Hopkins, Lee Bennett
Ragged Shadows, 1344
Steinberg, David
The Monster Mall, 3211

HALLOWEEN — FICTION

Adler, David A.
The Twisted Witch and Other Spooky Riddles, 18
Bridwell, Norman
Clifford and the Halloween Parade, 346
Carlson, Nancy
Harriet's Halloween Candy, 466
Cassedy, Sylvia
The Best Cat Suit of All, 494
Craig, Janet
The Boo-Hoo Witch, 646
Cushman, Doug
Aunt Eater's Mystery Halloween, 659
Danziger, Paula
Orange You Glad It's Halloween, Amber Brown, 678
Grambling, Lois
Miss Hildy's Missing Cape Caper, 1041
Hautzig, Deborah
Happy Birthday, Little Witch, 1135
Little Witch's Big Night, 1139
Hillert, Margaret
The Witch Who Went for a Walk, 1223
Hoban, Lillian
Arthur's Halloween Costume, 1246
Hutchins, Pat
The Best Train Set Ever, 1387
Koontz, Robin Michal
Chicago and the Cat, 1567
McCully, Emily Arnold
Grandma's Trick-or-Treat, 1819
Markham, Marion M.
The Halloween Candy Mystery, 1961

HELICOPTERS

Stille, Darlene R.
Helicopters, 3247

HEREDITY

Showers, Paul
Me and My Family Tree, 3050

HEROES — FICTION

James, B. J.
Supertwins and the Sneaky, Slimy Book Worm, 1407
Supertwins and the Tooth Trouble, 1408
Supertwins Meet Bad Dogs from Space, 1409
Peterson, Scott
The Story of Batman, 2391
Wheeler, Lisa
When Pigs Fly, 3555

HIBERNATION

SEE Animals — Hibernation

HICCUPS — FICTION

Bauer, Marion Dane
Bear's Hiccups, 144
Jennings, Sharon
Franklin Has the Hiccups, 1428
Mooser, Stephen
The Ghost with the Halloween Hiccups, 2171
Preller, James
Hiccups for Elephant, 2471
Wardlaw, Lee
Hector's Hiccups, 3510

HIDING — FICTION

Milios, Rita
Sneaky Pete, 2083

HIKING — FICTION

Berenstain, Stan, and Jan Berenstain
The Berenstain Bears Blaze a Trail, 197
Brandenberg, Franz
Leo and Emily and the Dragon, 299
Inches, Alison
Corduroy's Hike, 1395

HIPPOPOTAMI

Markert, Jenny
Hippos, 1959
Stone, Lynn M.
Hippopotamus, 3282

HIPPOPOTAMI — FICTION

French, Vivian
Mrs. Hippo's Pizza Parlor, 934
Grey, Judith
Yummy, Yummy, 1072
Mayer, Gina, and Mercer Mayer
Rosie's Mouse, 2048
Medearis, Angela Shelf
On the Way to the Pond, 2061
Morgan, Michaela
Helpful Betty Solves a Mystery, 2177
Helpful Betty to the Rescue, 2178
Thaler, Mike
Come and Play, Hippo, 3372
Hippo Lemonade, 3374
It's Me, Hippo! 3375
There's a Hippopotamus under My Bed, 3379
Ziefert, Harriet
Harry Gets Ready for School, 3690
Harry Goes to Fun Land, 3691
Harry Takes a Bath, 3692

HISPANIC AMERICANS

Head, Judith
Mud Soup, 1161

HISTORICAL FICTION

Avi
Abigail Takes the Wheel, 99
Baker, Betty
Pig War, 115
Benchley, Nathaniel
George the Drummer Boy, 164
Sam the Minuteman, 169
Snorri and the Strangers, 172
Boegehold, Betty
A Horse Called Starfire, 259
Bourne, Miriam A.
Four-Ring Three, 286
Second Car in Town, 287
Brenner, Barbara
Wagon Wheels, 340
Dewey, Ariane
Laffite, the Pirate, 747
Finsand, Mary J.
The Town That Moved, 845
Gauch, Patricia L.
Aaron and the Green Mountain Boys, 976
Lewis, Thomas P.
Clipper Ship, 1715
Hill of Fire, 1716
Lowery, Janette S.
Six Silver Spoons, 1772
Martin, C. L. G.
Day of Darkness, Night of Light, 1976
Monjo, F. N.
Indian Summer, 2150
The One Bad Thing About Father, 2153
Rappaport, Doreen
The Boston Coffee Party, 2530
Roop, Peter, and Connie Roop
Keep the Lights Burning, Abbie, 2681
Sandin, Joan
At Home in a New Land, 2846
The Long Way Westward, 2848
Schick, Alice, and Joel Schick
Just This Once, 2884
Shaffer, Ann
The Camel Express, 2974
Sharoff, Victor
The Heart of the Wood, 3019
Walker, Sally M.
The 18 Penny Goose, 3498

HISTORY

Greene, Carol
Elie Wiesel, 1047

HISTORY — MEDIEVAL

Krensky, Stephen
We Just Moved! 1592

HISTORY — UNITED STATES

Swanson, June
I Pledge Allegiance, 3345

HOLIDAYS

SEE ALSO specific holidays, as Valentine's Day
Bennett, Kelly
Flag Day, 176
Bredeson, Carmen
Labor Day, 326
Carter, Polly
Harriet Tubman and Black History Month, 486
Cotton, Jacqueline S.
Veterans Day, 634
Jacobs, Leland B.
Just Around the Corner, 1401

HUMOROUS STORIES (cont.)

Mrs. Gaddy and the Fast-Growing Vine, 963
Mrs. Gaddy and the Ghost, 964
My Stars, It's Mrs. Gaddy! 965
Squash Pie, 966
Gelman, Rita G.
More Spaghetti, I Say! 980
Gilchrist, Theo E.
Halfway Up the Mountain, 1002
Greer, Gery, and Bob Ruddick
Billy the Ghost and Me, 1069
Haskins, Lori
Too Many Dogs, 1131
Hay, Samantha
Creepy Customers, 1150
Heilbroner, Joan
Robert the Rose Horse, 1166
Hennessy, B. G.
Busy Dinah Dinosaur, 1178
Meet Dinah Dinosaur, 1179
Himmelman, John
The Great Leaf Blast-Off, 1226
Hoban, Julia
Buzby, 1237
Hoban, Lillian
Mr. Pig and Family, 1253
Hoban, Lillian, and Phoebe Hoban
Ready-Set-Robot, 1259
Hong, Lily T.
Two of Everything, 1322
Hooks, William H.
How Do You Make a Bubble? 1333
Lo-Jack and the Pirates, 1335
Hurd, Edith T.
Stop Stop, 1384
Jacobs, Leland B.
Poetry for Chuckles and Grins, 1404
Jensen, Patricia
A Funny Man, 1440
Johnston, Tony
Farmer Mack Measures His Pig, 1460
I'm Gonna Tell Mama I Want an Iguana, 1461
Odd Jobs, 1463
Odd Jobs and Friends, 1464
Keller, Beverly
When Mother Got the Flu, 1493
Kennedy, Richard
Contests at Cowlick, 1503
Kent, Jack
Hoddy Doddy, 1505
Socks for Supper, 1506
Kessler, Ethel, and Leonard Kessler
Grandpa, Witch, and the Magic Doobelator, 1510
Pig's Orange House, 1513
King, P. E.
Down on the Funny Farm, 1542
Krasilovsky, Phyllis
The Man Who Entered a Contest, 1573
Kroll, Steven
The Goat Parade, 1596
Lauber, Patricia
Clarence and the Burglar, 1667
Clarence and the Cat, 1668
LeSieg, Theo
Ten Apples Up on Top! 1698
The Tooth Book, 1699
Would You Rather Be a Bullfrog! 1701
Lobel, Arnold
Mouse Soup, 1752
Lunn, Carolyn
Bobby's Zoo, 1775
McInnes, John
Leo Lion Paints It Red, 1845
McPhail, David M.
Big Brown Bear, 1924
Big Pig and Little Pig, 1925
Madsen, Ross M.
Perrywinkle and the Book of Magic Spells, 1934
Maestro, Giulio
Leopard and the Noisy Monkeys, 1944
Leopard Is Sick, 1945
Mallett, Anne
Here Comes Tagalong, 1950
Margolis, Richard J.
Homer the Hunter, 1956
Marshall, Edward
Four on the Shore, 1962
Marshall, James
Fox All Week, 1963
Fox and His Friends, 1964
Fox at School, 1965
Fox in Love, 1967
Fox on the Job, 1969
Fox Outfoxed, 1971
Troll Country, 1975
Massie, Diane R.
The Komodo Dragon's Jewels, 2031
Medearis, Angela Shelf
We Eat Dinner in the Bathtub, 2063
Milios, Rita
The Hungry Billy Goat, 2081
Minarik, Else H.
Percy and the Five Houses, 2127
Moore, Lilian
A Pickle for a Nickel, 2165
Mooser, Stephen
Funnyman and the Penny Dodo, 2169
Funnyman's First Case, 2170
The Ghost with the Halloween Hiccups, 2171
Muntean, Michaela
Bicycle Bear, 2194
Nicklaus, Carol
Harry the Hider, 2228
Nixon, Joan L.
Bigfoot Makes a Movie, 2232
Orgel, Doris
Next Time I Will, 2285
Palmer, Helen M.
A Fish Out of Water, 2305
Pape, Donna L.
The Big White Thing, 2307
Count on Leo Lion, 2309
Leo Lion Looks for Books, 2311
Mr. Mogg in the Log, 2313
Where Is My Little Joey? 2315
Parish, Herman
Amelia Bedelia, Bookworm, 2316
Amelia Bedelia 4 Mayor, 2317
Amelia Bedelia, Rocket Scientist, 2318
Parish, Peggy
Amelia Bedelia, 2319
Amelia Bedelia and the Baby, 2320
Amelia Bedelia and the Surprise Shower, 2321
Amelia Bedelia Goes Camping, 2322
Amelia Bedelia Helps Out, 2323
Amelia Bedelia's Family Album, 2324
Come Back, Amelia Bedelia, 2327
Good Work, Amelia Bedelia, 2330

HUMOROUS STORIES (cont.)

The Friends of Abu Ali, 3466
Old Devil Is Waiting, 3470
Voigt, Cynthia
Stories About Rosie, 3485
Waddell, Martin
The Tough Princess, 3486
Wagner, Ken, and Mary C. Olson, eds.
The Lion Who Couldn't Say No, 3492
Wallace, Karen
Ooh La La Lottie! 3506
Weiss, Ellen
Lucky Duck, 3530
Millicent Maybe, 3531
West, Colin
Monty, the Dog Who Wears Glasses, 3542
Shape Up, Monty! 3544
Weston, Martha
Dr. Clock-Sicle, 3548
Space Guys! 3550
Wilmer, Diane
Nuts About Nuts, 3581
Wiseman, Bernard
Bobby and Boo, 3592
Morris Goes to School, 3601
Morris the Moose, 3605
Wood, Audrey
Three Sisters, 3625
Wright, Mildred W.
Henri Goes to the Mardi Gras, 3637
Yolen, Jane
Commander Toad and the Big Black Hole, 3653
Commander Toad and the Dis-Asteroid, 3654
Commander Toad and the Intergalactic Spy, 3655
Commander Toad and the Planet of the Grapes, 3656
Commander Toad and the Voyage Home, 3658
The Giants' Farm, 3659
The Giants Go Camping, 3660
Sleeping Ugly, 3661
York, Carol B.
The Midnight Ghost, 3663
Zemach, Harve, and Kaethe Zemach
The Princess and Froggie, 3670
Ziefert, Harriet, reteller
The Cow in the House, 3732
Ziefert, Harriet
Move Over, 3699
The Prince's Tooth Is Loose, 3708
Zion, Gene
Harry and the Lady Next Door, 3747

HUNTING — FICTION

Margolis, Richard J.
Homer the Hunter, 1956
Parish, Peggy
Ootah's Lucky Day, 2336

HYENAS

Stone, Lynn M.
Hyenas, 3284

HYENAS — FICTION

McKissack, Patricia
Monkey-Monkey's Trick, 1861

HYPNOTISM — FICTION

Underwood, Deborah
Pirate Mom, 3440

ICE CREAM — FICTION

Siracusa, Catherine
The Banana Split from Outer Space, 3102

IGUANAS

Landau, Elaine
Your Pet Iguana, 1655

ILLNESS

Berger, Melvin
Germs Make Me Sick! 223
Kohlenberg, Sherry
Sammy's Mommy Has Cancer, 1562

ILLNESS — FICTION

Aber, Linda W.
Who's Got Spots? 4
Bottner, Barbara
Marsha Makes Me Sick, 281
Cazet, Denys
The Octopus, 510
The Shrunken Head, 512
A Snout for Chocolate, 513
Gantos, Jack
Rotten Ralph Feels Rotten, 974
Guest, Elissa Haden
Iris and Walter, 1085
Hurd, Edith T.
Johnny Lion's Bad Day, 1376
Jensen, Patricia
I Am Sick, 1441
Jinkins, Jim
Pinky Dinky Doo, 1449
Keller, Beverly
When Mother Got the Flu, 1493
Lobel, Arnold
Uncle Elephant, 1756
Maccarone, Grace
Itchy, Itchy Chicken Pox, 1789
Maestro, Giulio
Leopard Is Sick, 1945
Rylant, Cynthia
Henry and Mudge Get the Cold Shivers, 2797
Mr. Putter and Tabby Catch the Cold, 2805
Sharmat, Marjorie W.
Little Devil Gets Sick, 2983
Simon, Charnan
The Good Bad Day, 3071
Thomas, Shelley Moore
Get Well, Good Knight, 3386
Wiseman, Bernard
Morris Has a Cold, 3603
Ziefert, Harriet
So Sick! 3717

IMAGINATION

Buller, Jon, and Susan Schade
The Video Kids, 396
Curtis, Matt
Elliot Drives Away, 657
Hutchins, Hazel
And You Can Be the Cat, 1386
Krensky, Stephen
Lionel in the Winter, 1586
Kwitz, Mary D.
Little Vampire and the Midnight Bear, 1614
Lopshire, Robert
How to Make Snop Snappers and Other Fine Things, 1762
McKay, Sindy
The New Red Bed, 1856

IMAGINATION — FICTION

Alexander, Sue
Marc the Magnificent, 42
Allen, Laura J.
Where Is Freddy? 72

INSECTS (cont.)

Shapiro, Karen
Butterflies, 2977
Stewart, Melissa
Insects, 3237
Still, John
Amazing Beetles, 3241
Stone, Lynn M.
Moths, 3291
Walker, Sally M.
Fireflies, 3499
Watts, Barrie
Honeybee, 3520
Moth, 3521
Wilkinson, Valerie
Flies Are Fascinating, 3571
Ziefert, Harriet
Bugs, Beetles, and Butterflies, 3676

INSECTS — FICTION

Caple, Kathy
Termite Trouble, 438
Cushman, Doug
Inspector Hopper, 663
Inspector Hopper's Mystery Year, 664
Dubowski, Cathy E., and Mark Dubowski
Snug Bug's Play Day, 774
Edwards, Frank B.
Snug as a Big Red Bug, 801
Harvey, Jayne
Busy Bugs, 1129
Hawkins, Colin, and Jacqui Hawkins
Zug the Bug, 1149
Horowitz, Ruth
Big Surprise in the Bug Tank, 1355
Breakout at the Bug Lab, 1356
Kirk, David
Miss Spider's Tea Party Reader, 1544
McKissack, Patricia, and Fredrick McKissack
Bugs! 1865
McPhail, David M.
A Bug, a Bear, and a Boy Go to School, 1926
Pollock, Penny
The Spit Bug Who Couldn't Spit, 2435
Schade, Susan
Toad Eats Out, 2868
Schade, Susan, and Jon Buller
Snug House, Bug House! 2873
Woodworth, Viki, comp.
Bug Riddles, 3629

INTERIOR DESIGN

Storm, Betsy
I Can Be an Interior Designer, 3321

INUIT

Santella, Andrew
The Inuit, 2851

INVENTORS AND INVENTIONS

Collard, Sneed B., III
Benjamin Franklin, 602
Hudson, Wade
Five Notable Inventors, 1371
Radford, Ruby
Robert Fulton, 2526
Sherrow, Victoria
Alexander Graham Bell, 3035

INVENTORS AND INVENTIONS — FICTION

Clements, Andrew
Milo's Great Invention, 569
Corbett, Scott
The Boy Who Walked on Air, 615
Firmin, Peter
Basil Brush and the Windmills, 846
Himmelman, John
The Day-Off Machine, 1225
The Great Leaf Blast-Off, 1226
Kidd, Ronald
Tuna Surprise, 1536
Leonard, Marcia
The Tin Can Man, 1688

INVERTEBRATES

Pluckrose, Henry
Minibeasts, 2424
Selsam, Millicent E., and Joyce Hunt
A First Look at Animals Without Backbones, 2937

IOWA

Sapre, Reshma
Iowa, 2852

IRELAND

Kessel, Joyce K.
St. Patrick's Day, 1508

ISRAEL

Landau, Elaine
Israel, 1636

JAGUARS

Stone, Lynn M.
Jaguars, 3285

JAPAN — FICTION

Roy, Ron
A Thousand Pails of Water, 2717

JEALOUSY — FICTION

Howe, James
Pinky and Rex and the Perfect Pumpkin, 1365
Macdonald, Maryann
The Pink Party, 1826
O'Connor, Jane
Lulu and the Witch Baby, 2257

JELLYFISH

Kite, Patricia
Down in the Sea, 1549
Stone, Lynn M.
Jellyfish, 3286
Taylor, Leighton
Jellyfish, 3356
Waters, John F.
A Jellyfish Is Not a Fish, 3517

JOKES AND RIDDLES

Adler, David A.
The Carsick Zebra and Other Animal Riddles, 14
The Twisted Witch and Other Spooky Riddles, 18
Ball, Jacqueline A.
What Can It Be? Riddles About the Senses, 126
Bishop, Ann
Merry-Go-Riddle, 242
Cerf, Bennett A.
Bennett Cerf's Book of Animal Riddles, 515
Bennett Cerf's Book of Laughs, 516
Bennett Cerf's Book of Riddles, 517
More Riddles, 518
Cole, Joanna
Get Well, Clown-Arounds! 587

JOKES AND RIDDLES — FICTION

KANGAROOS

KANGAROOS — FICTION

KANSAS

KENTUCKY

KINGS AND QUEENS

KINGS AND QUEENS — FICTION

KITES AND KITE FLYING — FICTION

KNIGHTS AND KNIGHTHOOD — FICTION

KNITTING — FICTION

KOALAS

Serventy, Vincent
Koala, 2956
Stone, Lynn M.
Koalas, 3288

KOALAS — FICTION

Armitage, Ronda, and David Armitage
Harry Hates Shopping! 87
Tripp, Valerie
Baby Koala Finds a Home, 3420

KOREA

Landau, Elaine
Korea, 1637

KWANZAA

Rau, Dana Meachen
Kwanzaa, 2540

LABOR DAY

Bredeson, Carmen
Labor Day, 326
Scott, Geoffrey
Labor Day, 2915

LADYBUGS

McClung, Robert M.
Ladybug, 1810
Rau, Dana Meachen
Look for Ladybugs, 2541
Rowan, James P.
Ladybugs, 2712
Wong, Herbert, and Matthew Vessel
My Ladybug, 3622

LAKES

Schulte, Mary
Great Salt Lake, 2903
Zollman, Pam
Lake Tahoe, 3758

LAKOTA

Bernhard, Emery
Spotted Eagle and Black Crow, 236

LANGUAGE

Gleiter, Jan, and Kathleen Thompson
Sequoya, 1010
Koch, Michelle
Just One More, 1561

LANGUAGE — FICTION

Kido, Yukiko
Pig Wig, 1537

LATCHKEY CHILDREN — FICTION

Kessler, Ethel, and Leonard Kessler
The Sweeneys from 9D, 1516
Schick, Eleanor
Home Alone, 2885

LEAVES — FICTION

Maccarone, Grace
I See a Leaf, 1787
Stamper, Judith B.
The Wild Leaf Ride, 3196

LEGENDS

SEE ALSO Native Americans — Legends
Standiford, Natalie
The Headless Horseman, 3199

LEMMINGS

Newton, James R.
The March of the Lemmings, 2223

LEOPARDS

Stone, Lynn M.
Leopards, 3289

LEPRECHAUNS

Shub, Elizabeth
Seeing Is Believing, 3059

LETTERS — FICTION

Craig, Janet
A Letter to Santa, 647

LIBRARIES AND LIBRARIANS

Raatma, Lucia
Libraries, 2522
Ready, Dee
Librarians, 2554

LIBRARIES AND LIBRARIANS — FICTION

Adler, David A.
Young Cam Jansen and the Library Mystery, 23
Alexander, Sue
World Famous Muriel and the Magic Mystery, 49
Bonsall, Crosby
Tell Me Some More, 276
Elliott, Dan
Grover Learns to Read, 818
Levinson, Nancy Smiler
Clara and the Bookwagon, 1703
Numeroff, Laura J.
Beatrice Doesn't Want To, 2245

LICE

DerKazarian, Susan
You Have Head Lice! 736
Katz, Bobbi
Lots of Lice, 1485

LIGHT

Ardley, Neil
The Science Book of Light, 86
Murata, Michinori
Water and Light, 2198
Trumbauer, Lisa
All About Light, 3431

LIGHTHOUSES — FICTION

Hoff, Syd
The Lighthouse Children, 1283
Roop, Peter, and Connie Roop
Keep the Lights Burning, Abbie, 2681

LIONS

Johnson, Sylvia A.
Lions of Africa, 1455
Stone, Lynn M.
Lions, 3290

LIONS — FICTION

Brenner, Barbara, and William H. Hooks
Lion and Lamb Step Out, 342
Ups and Downs with Lion and Lamb, 343
Hoff, Syd
Wilfred the Lion, 1294
Hurd, Edith T.
Johnny Lion's Bad Day, 1376
Johnny Lion's Book, 1377
Johnny Lion's Rubber Boots, 1378
McPhail, David M.
Snow Lion, 1932

Partridge, Elizabeth
Annie and Bo and the Big Surprise, 2352
Pearson, Mary E.
Where Is Max? 2364
Phillips, Joan
Tiger Is a Scaredy Cat, 2401
Preller, James
Wake Me in Spring, 2472
Quackenbush, Robert
No Mouse for Me, 2500
Roche, P. K.
Webster and Arnold and the Giant Box, 2646
Root, Phyllis
Mouse Goes Out, 2685
Mouse Has Fun, 2686
Schecter, Ellen
The Town Mouse and the Country Mouse, 2881
Stevens, Janet, and Susan Stevens Crummel
Shoe Town, 3219
Sutherland, Tui T.
Fun with Mo and Ella, 3341
Meet Mo and Ella, 3342
Wallace, Karen
Ooh La La Lottie! 3506
Weeks, Sarah
Drip, Drop, 3526
West, Colin
Moose and Mouse, 3543
Wolcott, Patty
Pirates, Pirates Over the Salt, Salt Sea, 3616
Wood, Audrey
Tugford Wanted to Be Bad, 3626
Ziefert, Harriet
The Big Birthday Box, 3675
Car Trip for Mole and Mouse, 3678
A Clean House for Mole and Mouse, 3680
A New House for Mole and Mouse, 3701

MICROBES

Taylor-Butler, Christine
Tiny Life in the Air, 3365
Tiny Life on Your Body, 3366
Trumbauer, Lisa
Tiny Life in Your Home, 3433

MICROSCOPES

Selsam, Millicent E.
Greg's Microscope, 2924

MISCELLANEA

Seuss, Dr.
The Cat's Quizzer, 2961

MISSISSIPPI

Trueit, Trudi Strain
Mississippi, 3427

MOLES — FICTION

Carter, Anne
Molly in Danger, 483
Firmin, Peter
Basil Brush and the Windmills, 846
Basil Brush Gets a Medal, 847
Basil Brush Goes Flying, 849
Basil Brush on the Trail, 851
Hoban, Lillian
Silly Tilly and the Easter Bunny, 1255
Johnston, Tony
The Adventures of Mole and Troll, 1456
Night Noises and Other Mole and Troll Stories, 1462
Quackenbush, Robert
Detective Mole, 2490
Detective Mole and the Circus Mystery, 2491
Detective Mole and the Seashore Mystery, 2492
Detective Mole and the Secret Clues, 2493
Detective Mole and the Tip-Top Mystery, 2494
Sharmat, Marjorie W.
Uncle Boris and Maude, 3008
Ziefert, Harriet
Car Trip for Mole and Mouse, 3678
A Clean House for Mole and Mouse, 3680
A New House for Mole and Mouse, 3701

MOLLUSKS

Fowler, Allan
Shellfish Aren't Fish, 912
Victor, Joan B.
Shells Are Skeletons, 3483

MOLLUSKS — FICTION

Stevenson, James
Clams Can't Sing, 3222

MONEY

deRubertis, Barbara
Deena's Lucky Penny, 740
Dussling, Jennifer
Fair Is Fair! 780
Glass, Dr. Julie
A Dollar for a Penny, 1009
Mitgutsch, Ali
From Gold to Money, 2131
Roberson, Erin
All About Money, 2617

MONEY — FICTION

Maccarone, Grace
Monster Money, 1796
Sadler, Marilyn J.
Money, Money, Honey Bunny! 2834
Slater, Teddy
Max's Money, 3119

MONKEYS

Martin, Patricia A. Fink
Monkeys of Asia and Africa, 1987
Stone, Lynn M.
Chimpanzees, 3266
Snow Monkeys, 3308

MONKEYS — FICTION

Gave, Marc
Monkey See, Monkey Do, 977
Gelman, Rita G.
More Spaghetti, I Say! 980
Hurd, Edith T.
Last One Home Is a Green Pig, 1379
McKissack, Patricia
Itching and Twitching, 1860
Monkey-Monkey's Trick, 1861
Who Is Coming? 1863
Perkins, Al
Hand, Hand, Fingers, Thumb, 2375
Porter, Wesley
About Monkeys in Trees, 2445
Regan, Dana
Monkey See, Monkey Do, 2563
Rockwell, Anne
No More Work, 2665
Standiford, Natalie
The Best Little Monkeys in the World, 3197

MONSTERS

Spinner, Stephanie
Snake Hair, 3164

MONSTERS — FICTION

Bottner, Barbara, and Gerald Kruglik
Pish and Posh Wish for Fairy Wings, 284
Cazet, Denys
Minnie and Moo Meet Frankenswine, 508
Christian, Mary B.
Go West, Swamp Monsters, 549
Swamp Monsters, 557
DeCesare, Angelo
Anthony the Perfect Monster, 691
Eaton, Deborah J.
Monster Songs, 794
Farber, Erica, and J. R. Sansevere
Kiss of the Mermaid, 831
No Howling in the House, 832
Roast and Toast, 834
Zoom on My Broom, 835
Florian, Douglas
Monster Motel, 863
Grindley, Sally
The Perfect Monster, 1078
Hay, Samantha
Creepy Customers, 1150
Hayward, Linda
The Biggest Cookie in the World, 1155
Heide, Florence P., and Roxanne Heide
A Monster Is Coming! A Monster Is Coming! 1164
Herman, Gail
Double Header, 1187
Maccarone, Grace
Monster Math, 1794
McCullagh, Sheila
The Vanishing Monster, 1814
McInnes, John
Have You Ever Seen a Monster? 1843
Mueller, Virginia
A Halloween Mask for Monster, 2192
Namm, Diane
Monsters, 2217
Numeroff, Laura J.
Monster Munchies, 2247
Parish, Peggy
No More Monsters for Me! 2335
Zed and the Monsters, 2342
Roberts, Bethany
May Belle and the Ogre, 2619
Ogre Eats Everything, 2620
Rockwell, Anne
Thump Thump Thump! 2668
Up a Tall Tree, 2670
Sharmat, Marjorie W.
Scarlet Monster Lives Here, 3003
Van Leeuwen, Jean
Amanda Pig and the Awful, Scary Monster, 3449

MOOSE

Freschet, Berniece
Moose Baby, 937

MOOSE — FICTION

Hoff, Syd
Santa's Moose, 1287
Kelley, True
Buggly Bear's Hiccup Cure, 1500
May, D. J.
Mr. Marble's Moose, 2041
Van Laan, Nancy
Busy Busy Moose, 3445
Moose Tales, 3446
West, Colin
Moose and Mouse, 3543
Wiseman, Bernard
Morris and Boris at the Circus, 3600
Morris Goes to School, 3601
Morris Has a Birthday Party! 3602
Morris Has a Cold, 3603
Morris Tells Boris Mother Moose Stories and Rhymes, 3604
Morris the Moose, 3605

MORNING — FICTION

Ziefert, Harriet
Say Good Night! 3711

MOTHER GOOSE — FICTION

Kessler, Leonard
Hey Diddle Diddle, 1521
Hickory Dickory Dock, 1522
Mixed-Up Mother Goose, 1525
The Mother Goose Game, 1526

MOTHERS — FICTION

Black, Sonia W.
Hanging Out with Mom, 248
Book, Rita
My Soccer Mom from Mars, 279
Collins, David R.
If I Could, I Would, 608
Eastman, Philip D.
Are You My Mother? 790
Fine, Jane
Surprise! 844
Gackenbach, Dick
Hurray for Hattie Rabbit! 959
Goode, Molly
Mama Loves, 1020
Lorian, Nicole
A Birthday Present for Mama, 1765
Simon, Charnan
Surprise, 3081
Ziefert, Harriet
Surprise! 3721

MOTHERS, WORKING — FICTION

Power, Barbara
I Wish Laura's Mommy Was My Mommy, 2465
Smith, Lucia
My Mom Got a Job, 3142

MOTHER'S DAY — FICTION

Ruelle, Karen Gray
Mother's Day Mess, 2753
Rylant, Cynthia
Henry and Mudge and the Funny Lunch, 2786
Tripp, Valerie
Happy, Happy Mother's Day! 3421

MOUNTAIN GOATS

Staub, Frank
Mountain Goats, 3205

MOUNTAINS

Bauer, Marion Dane
The Rocky Mountains, 150
Fowler, Allan
Living in the Mountains, 901
They Could Still Be Mountains, 923

Landau, Elaine
Mountain Mammals, 1639
Zoehfeld, Kathleen W.
How Mountains Are Made, 3752

MOVIES

Brooks, Laura, adapter
The Beast's Story, 363

MOVIES — FICTION

Ziefert, Harriet
Penny Goes to the Movies, 3704

MOVING, HOUSEHOLD

Krensky, Stephen
We Just Moved! 1592

MOVING, HOUSEHOLD — FICTION

Brandenberg, Franz
Nice New Neighbors, 302
What Can You Make of It? 305
Brandon, Anthony G.
Moving Day, 306
Bunting, Eve
The Robot Birthday, 401
Cassedy, Sylvia
The Best Cat Suit of All, 494
Greenwood, Pamela D.
What About My Goldfish? 1068
Hall, Kirsten
My New Town, 1109
Hoff, Syd
Who Will Be My Friends? 1293
Kessler, Ethel, and Leonard Kessler
The Sweeneys from 9D, 1516
Lexau, Joan M.
The Rooftop Mystery, 1727
Myrick, Mildred
Ants Are Fun, 2213
Nixon, Joan L.
The Mysterious Prowler, 2235
Penner, Lucille Recht
X Marks the Spot! 2371
Rinkoff, Barbara
Rutherford T Finds 21B, 2614
Robins, Joan
Addie Meets Max, 2621
Rylant, Cynthia
Henry and Mudge and Annie's Good Move, 2778
Schulman, Janet
The Big Hello, 2896
Sharmat, Marjorie W.
Mitchell Is Moving, 2984
Scarlet Monster Lives Here, 3003
Taylor, Sydney
The Dog Who Came to Dinner, 3358
Wyeth, Sharon Dennis
Tomboy Trouble, 3638
Yee, Wong Herbert
Did You See Chip? 3646
Yolen, Jane
Spider Jane on the Move, 3662
Ziefert, Harriet
A New House for Mole and Mouse, 3701

MUMMIES

Dubowski, Mark, and Cathy E. Dubowski
Ice Mummy, 775
Milton, Joyce
Secrets of the Mummies, 2116

MUMMIES — FICTION

McMullan, Kate
The Mummy's Gold, 1902
Ross, Pat
M and M and the Mummy Mess, 2701

MUSEUMS

Aliki
Fossils Tell of Long Ago, 56
Gibbons, Gail
Dinosaurs, Dragonflies and Diamonds, 986
Papajani, Janet
Museums, 2306

MUSEUMS — FICTION

Berenstain, Stan, and Jan Berenstain
The Berenstain Bears and the Escape of the Bogg Brothers, 191
Howe, James
Pinky and Rex, 1360
James, B. J.
Supertwins Meet the Dangerous Dino-Robots, 1410
Ross, Pat
M and M and the Mummy Mess, 2701
Wells, Rosemary
Doris's Dinosaur, 3536

MUSIC AND MUSICIANS

The Friendly Beasts
The Friendly Beasts, 945
Greene, Carol
John Philip Sousa, 1055
Wolfgang Amadeus Mozart, 1065
Hautzig, Deborah
The Nutcracker Ballet, 1140
Lock, Deborah
Let's Make Music, 1757
McKissack, Patricia, and Fredrick McKissack
Louis Armstrong, 1873
Marian Anderson, 1874
Rubin, Mark
The Orchestra, 2743
Tobias, Tobi
Marian Anderson, 3409

MUSIC AND MUSICIANS — FICTION

Caseley, Judith
Molly Pink, 492
Firmin, Peter
Happy Miss Rat, 854
Hoff, Syd
Arturo's Baton, 1265
Mantinband, Gerda B.
Bing Bong Bang and Fiddle Dee Dee, 1953
Mills, Claudia
Gus and Grandpa and the Piano Lesson, 2099
Robinson, Fay
Old MacDonald Had a Farm, 2630
Rylant, Cynthia
Mr. Putter and Tabby Toot the Horn, 2816
Sharmat, Marjorie W., and Craig Sharmat
Nate the Great and the Musical Note, 3011
Ziefert, Harriet
The Wheels on the Bus, 3729
Zion, Gene
Harry and the Lady Next Door, 3747

MUSICAL INSTRUMENTS

Marzollo, Jean
Musical Instruments, 2016

MUSICAL INSTRUMENTS — FICTION

Carlson, Nancy
Loudmouth George and the Cornet, 469

MYSTERY AND DETECTIVE STORIES

Ada, Alma Flor
Daniel's Mystery Egg, 6

Adler, David A.
Bones and the Big Yellow Mystery, 9
Bones and the Birthday Mystery, 10
Bones and the Cupcake Mystery, 11
Bones and the Dinosaur Mystery, 12
Bones and the Dog Gone Mystery, 13
My Dog and the Birthday Mystery, 15
My Dog and the Green Sock Mystery, 16
My Dog and the Knock Knock Mystery, 17
Young Cam Jansen and the Baseball Mystery, 19
Young Cam Jansen and the Dinosaur Game, 20
Young Cam Jansen and the Double Beach Mystery, 21
Young Cam Jansen and the Ice Skate Mystery, 22
Young Cam Jansen and the Library Mystery, 23
Young Cam Jansen and the Lost Tooth, 24
Young Cam Jansen and the Missing Cookie, 25
Young Cam Jansen and the New Girl Mystery, 26
Young Cam Jansen and the Pizza Shop Mystery, 27
Young Cam Jansen and the Spotted Cat Mystery, 28
Young Cam Jansen and the Substitute Mystery, 29
Young Cam Jansen and the Zoo Note Mystery, 30

Ahlberg, Allan
Mystery Tour, 34

Alexander, Sue
World Famous Muriel, 48
World Famous Muriel and the Magic Mystery, 49

Allen, Laura J.
Rollo and Tweedy and the Ghost at Dougal Castle, 71
Where Is Freddy? 72

Benchley, Nathaniel
A Ghost Named Fred, 165
The Strange Disappearance of Arthur Cluck, 173

Berenstain, Stan, and Jan Berenstain
The Bear Detectives, 180
The Berenstain Bear Scouts and the Search for Naughty Ned, 185
The Berenstain Bear Scouts and the Stinky Milk Mystery, 186
The Berenstain Bear Scouts and the White Water Mystery, 187
The Berenstain Bears and the Escape of the Bogg Brothers, 191
The Berenstain Bears and the Missing Dinosaur Bone, 193
The Berenstain Bears and the Missing Honey, 194
The Berenstain Bears and the Spooky Old Tree, 195

Bonsall, Crosby
The Case of the Cat's Meow, 269
The Case of the Dumb Bells, 270
The Case of the Hungry Stranger, 271
The Case of the Scaredy Cats, 272

Christian, Mary B.
Doggone Mystery, 548
Green Thumb Thief, 550
J. J. Leggett, Secret Agent, 551

Clifford, Eth
Flatfoot Fox and the Case of the Missing Eye, 571

Coerr, Eleanor
Mixed-Up Mystery Smell, 581

Cushman, Doug
Aunt Eater Loves a Mystery, 658
Aunt Eater's Mystery Halloween, 659
Aunt Eater's Mystery Vacation, 660
Dirk Bones and the Mystery of the Haunted House, 662
Inspector Hopper, 663
Inspector Hopper's Mystery Year, 664

Delton, Judy
Brimhall Turns Detective, 711

Firmin, Peter
Basil Brush on the Trail, 851

Grambling, Lois
Happy Valentine's Day, Miss Hildy, 1040
Miss Hildy's Missing Cape Caper, 1041

Hayes, Geoffrey
The Mystery of the Pirate Ghost, 1151
The Secret of Foghorn Island, 1152

Herman, Gail
The Camping Caper, 1185
Disappearing Donuts, 1186
Ghost in the Garden, 1189
Howling on the Playground, 1191
Map in the Mystery Machine, 1192
Shiny Spooky Knights, 1193
Snack Snatcher, 1195
The Thanksgiving Mystery, 1196

Hoban, Lillian
The Case of the Two Masked Robbers, 1251

Holding, James
The Robber of Featherbed Lane, 1297

Jennings, Sharon
Franklin the Detective, 1430

Kidd, Ronald
Tuna Surprise, 1536

Krensky, Stephen
The Three Blind Mice Mystery, 1591

Kwitz, Mary D.
Gumshoe Goose, Private Eye, 1610

Lawrence, James
Binky Brothers, Detectives, 1675

Levy, Elizabeth
The Creepy Computer Mystery, 1706
The Karate Class Mystery, 1707
The Mystery of the Missing Dog, 1708
Parents' Night Fright, 1709
The Schoolyard Mystery, 1710
The Snack Attack Mystery, 1711

Lewis, Thomas P.
Mr. Sniff and the Motel Mystery, 1717

Lexau, Joan M.
The Dog Food Caper, 1722
Miss Happ in the Poison Ivy Case, 1726
McInnes, John
The Chocolate Chip Mystery, 1842
Markham, Marion M.
The Halloween Candy Mystery, 1961
Mooser, Stephen
Follow That Flea! 2168
Funnyman and the Penny Dodo, 2169
Funnyman's First Case, 2170
Goofball Malone, Ace Detective, 2172
Nixon, Joan L.
The Mysterious Prowler, 2235
The Thanksgiving Mystery, 2236
The Valentine Mystery, 2237
Obrist, Jurg
Max and Molly and the Mystery of the Missing Honey, 2252
Platt, Kin
Big Max, 2418
Big Max and the Mystery of the Missing Moose, 2419
Putnam, Polly
The Mystery of Sara Beth, 2486
Quackenbush, Robert
Detective Mole, 2490
Detective Mole and the Circus Mystery, 2491
Detective Mole and the Seashore Mystery, 2492
Detective Mole and the Secret Clues, 2493
Detective Mole and the Tip-Top Mystery, 2494
Sherlock Chick and the Giant Egg Mystery, 2505
Sherlock Chick and the Peekaboo Mystery, 2506
Sherlock Chick's First Case, 2507
Robert, Adrian
The "Awful Mess" Mystery, 2618
Robison, Nancy
The Mystery at Hilltop Camp, 2643
Rocklin, Joanne
The Case of the Backyard Treasure, 2647
The Case of the Missing Birthday Party, 2648
Rockwell, Anne
Timothy Todd's Good Things Are Gone, 2669
Rylant, Cynthia
The Case of the Baffled Bear, 2768
The Case of the Climbing Cat, 2769
The Case of the Desperate Duck, 2770
The Case of the Fidgety Fox, 2771
The Case of the Missing Monkey, 2772
The Case of the Puzzling Possum, 2773
The Case of the Sleepy Sloth, 2774
The Case of the Troublesome Turtle, 2775
Sharmat, Marjorie W.
Nate the Great, 2986
Nate the Great and Me, 2987
Nate the Great and the Boring Beach Bag, 2988
Nate the Great and the Fishy Prize, 2989
Nate the Great and the Halloween Hunt, 2990
Nate the Great and the Lost List, 2991
Nate the Great and the Missing Key, 2992
Nate the Great and the Monster Mess, 2993
Nate the Great and the Mushy Valentine, 2994
Nate the Great and the Phony Clue, 2995
Nate the Great and the Snowy Trail, 2996
Nate the Great and the Sticky Case, 2997
Nate the Great and the Stolen Base, 2998
Nate the Great Goes Down in the Dumps, 2999
Nate the Great Goes Undercover, 3000
Nate the Great Saves the King of Sweden, 3001
Nate the Great Stalks Stupidweed, 3002
Sharmat, Marjorie W., and Craig Sharmat
Nate the Great and the Crunchy Christmas, 3010
Nate the Great and the Musical Note, 3011
Nate the Great and the Tardy Tortoise, 3012
Sharmat, Marjorie W., and Mitchell Sharmat
Nate the Great, 3013
Nate the Great and the Big Sniff, 3014
Nate the Great on the Owl Express, 3015
Nate the Great Talks Turkey, 3016
Sharmat, Marjorie W., and Rosalind Weinman
Nate the Great and the Pillowcase, 3017
Siracusa, Catherine
The Peanut Butter Gang, 3107
Skofield, James
Detective Dinosaur, 3113
Detective Dinosaur Lost and Found, 3114
Warner, Gertrude Chandler
Keys and Clues for Benny, 3513
York, Carol B.
The Midnight Ghost, 3663

MYTHICAL CREATURES

SEE ALSO Dragons
Spinner, Stephanie
Snake Hair, 3164
Wise, William
Monsters of the Middle Ages, 3589

MYTHICAL CREATURES — FICTION

Alexander, Sue
World Famous Muriel and the Scary Dragon, 50
Brown, Marc
The Silly Tail Book, 377
Coville, Bruce, and Katherine Coville
Sarah's Unicorn, 637
Frith, Margaret
Mermaid Island, 948
Hillert, Margaret
Come to School, Dear Dragon, 1210
A Friend for Dear Dragon, 1211
Go to Sleep, Dear Dragon, 1212
Happy Birthday, Dear Dragon, 1213

NAVAJO — FICTION

NEIGHBORS — FICTION

NEW MEXICO

NEW YEAR'S DAY

NEW YEAR'S DAY — FICTION

NEW ZEALAND

NEWSPAPERS — FICTION

NIGHT

NIGHT — FICTION

NIGHT WORK — FICTION

NOISE — FICTION

NONSENSE

NONSENSE (cont.)

Lear, Edward
Edward Lear's Nonsense, 1678
LeSieg, Theo
Please Try to Remember the First of Octember! 1697
Would You Rather Be a Bullfrog! 1701
Maccarone, Grace
"What Is That?" Said the Cat, 1804
Merriam, Eve
The Birthday Cow, 2071
Morley, Diana
Marms in the Marmalade, 2179
Oppenheim, Joanne
Follow That Fish, 2278
Pape, Donna L.
The Book of Foolish Machinery, 2308
Seuss, Dr.
Green Eggs and Ham, 2965
One Fish Two Fish Red Fish Blue Fish, 2972
Thomson, Pat
My Friend Mr. Morris, 3394

NORTH AMERICA

Fowler, Allan
North America, 906
Petersen, David
North America, 2385

NORWAY

Landau, Elaine
Norway, 1640

NUMBERS

SEE ALSO Concepts — Numbers
Schlein, Miriam
What the Dinosaurs Saw, 2890
Simon, Charnan
One Happy Classroom, 3076
Ziefert, Harriet
Bears Odd, Bears Even, 3673

NUMBERS — FICTION

Slater, Teddy
The Bunny Hop, 3117
. . . 98, 99, 100! Ready or Not, Here I Come! 3121
Ziefert, Harriet
A Dozen Dozens, 3683

NURSERY RHYMES

Oppenheim, Joanne
Eency Weency Spider, 2277

NUTRITION

DerKazarian, Susan
Dairy, 734
Fruits and Vegetables, 735
Fontes, Justine, and Ron Fontes
Proteins, 868
Seixas, Judith S.
Vitamins, 2919
Smalley, Carol Parenzan
Fats, Oils, and Sweets, 3134

OCEANS AND OCEAN LIFE

Aliki
My Visit to the Aquarium, 64
Behrens, June
Look at the Sea Animals, 163
Berger, Melvin
Dive! A Book of Deep-Sea Creatures, 222
Cartwright, Sally
The Tide, 489
Cole, Joanna
The Magic School Bus, 594
Cooper, Jason
Coral Reefs, 611
Sea Shells, 613
Dussling, Jennifer
Giant Squid, 781
Esbensen, Barbara J.
Sponges Are Skeletons, 826
Fowler, Allan
It Could Still Be Coral, 892
Stars of the Sea, 919
Gibbons, Gail
Sharks, 990
Gordon, Sharon
Guess Who Snaps? 1030
Greene, Carol
Jacques Cousteau, 1053
Hirschmann, Kris
Ocean Hunters, 1235
Kite, Patricia
Down in the Sea, 1549
Landau, Elaine
Sea Horses, 1644
Petersen, David, and Christine Petersen
The Atlantic Ocean, 2388
The Pacific Ocean, 2389
Pfeffer, Wendy
Dolphin Talk, 2393
Redmond, Shirley Raye
Tentacles! 2562
Shaw, Evelyn
Octopus, 3025
Sipiera, Paul P.
I Can Be an Oceanographer, 3099
Stille, Darlene R.
Oceans, 3248
Taylor, Leighton
Jellyfish, 3356
Ziefert, Harriet
Under the Water, 3727
Zollman, Pam
Gulf of Mexico, 3757

OCEANS AND OCEAN LIFE — FICTION

Oppenheim, Joanne
Follow That Fish, 2278

OCTOPI

Berger, Melvin
Dive! A Book of Deep-Sea Creatures, 222
Kite, Patricia
Down in the Sea: The Octopus, 1551
Lauber, Patricia
An Octopus Is Amazing, 1670
Shaw, Evelyn
Octopus, 3025

OHIO

Taylor-Butler, Christine
Ohio, 3363

OLD AGE — FICTION

Muntean, Michaela
The Old Man and the Afternoon Cat, 2197
Pomerantz, Charlotte
Buffy and Albert, 2436
Ryder, Joanne, and Harold S. Feinburg
Mr. Putter and Tabby Walk the Dog, 2765
Rylant, Cynthia
Henry and Mudge and the Great Grandpas, 2787
Mr. Putter and Tabby Feed the Fish, 2806
Mr. Putter and Tabby Fly the Plane, 2807
Mr. Putter and Tabby Make a Wish, 2808
Mr. Putter and Tabby Pick the Pears, 2810

Mr. Putter and Tabby Pour the Tea, 2811
Mr. Putter and Tabby Row the Boat, 2812
Mr. Putter and Tabby Spin the Yarn, 2813
Mr. Putter and Tabby Stir the Soup, 2814
Mr. Putter and Tabby Take the Train, 2815
Mr. Putter and Tabby Toot the Horn, 2816
Sharmat, Marjorie W.
The Story of Bentley Beaver, 3005

OLYMPICS

Sutcliffe, Jane
Babe Didrikson Zaharias, 3339
Jesse Owens, 3340

OLYMPICS — FICTION

Stevenson, James
The Mud Flat Olympics, 3227

OPOSSUMS

Freschet, Berniece
Possum Baby, 938
Mizumura, Kazue
Opossum, 2134
Stone, Lynn M.
Opossums, 3292

OPOSSUMS — FICTION

Chaconas, Dori
Cork and Fuzz, 519
Cork and Fuzz: Good Sports, 520
Cork and Fuzz: Short and Tall, 521
Glaser, Linda
Keep Your Socks On, Albert! 1006
Hooks, William H.
Little Poss and Horrible Hound, 1334
Johnston, Tony
Alien and Possum, 1457
Alien and Possum Hanging Out, 1458

ORANGUTANS

Landau, Elaine
Tropical Forest Mammals, 1649
Martin, Patricia A. Fink
Orangutans, 1989
Stone, Lynn M.
Orangutans, 3293

ORCHESTRAS — FICTION

Hoff, Syd
Arturo's Baton, 1265

ORPHANS — FICTION

Bulla, Clyde R.
Poor Boy, Rich Boy, 388

ORTHODONTICS — FICTION

Richter, Alice, and Laura J. Numeroff
You Can't Put Braces on Spaces, 2598

OSAGE

Tobias, Tobi
Maria Tallchief, 3408

OSTRICHES

Stone, Lynn M.
Ostriches, 3294

OSTRICHES — FICTION

Coxe, Molly
Big Egg, 641

OTTERS

Brownell, M. Barbara
Amazing Otters, 380
Royston, Angela
The Otter, 2732

OTTERS — FICTION

Allen, Laura J.
Ottie and the Star, 70
Benchley, Nathaniel
Oscar Otter, 166
Skurzynski, Gloria
Honest Andrew, 3115
Tompert, Ann
Little Otter Remembers and Other Stories, 3413

OTTERS, SEA

Shaw, Evelyn
Sea Otters, 3026

OWLS

Flower, Phyllis
Barn Owl, 865
Ling, Mary
Owl, 1736
Martin, Patricia A. Fink
Northern Spotted Owls, 1988
Saintsing, David
The World of Owls, 2841
Stone, Lynn M.
Owls, 3295

OWLS — FICTION

Eastman, Philip D.
Sam and the Firefly, 793
Kanno, Wendy
Henry the Owl, 1479
Lobel, Arnold
Owl at Home, 1754
Sharmat, Marjorie W., and Mitchell Sharmat
Nate the Great on the Owl Express, 3015

PAINTING — FICTION

SEE ALSO Art and artists — Fiction
Hill, Susan
Ruby Paints a Picture, 1203
Rau, Dana Meachen
Purple Is Best, 2544
Rylant, Cynthia
Mr. Putter and Tabby Paint the Porch, 2809

PANAMA — FICTION

Palacios, Argentina
A Christmas Surprise for Chabelita, 2303

PANDAS

Gross, Ruth B.
A Book About Pandas, 1080
Landau, Elaine
Mountain Mammals, 1639
Martin, Louise
Panda, 1980
Spilsbury, Louise, and Richard Spilsbury
Save the Giant Panda, 3163

PANDAS — FICTION

Dunbar, Joyce
Gander's Pond, 778

PAPAGO

Clark, Ann N.
Little Indian Basket Maker, 561

PETS — CATS — FICTION (cont.)

Buck, Nola
Oh, Cats! 383
Caple, Kathy
Starring Hillary, 437
Capucilli, Alyssa Satin
Biscuit Wants to Play, 446
Cassedy, Sylvia
The Best Cat Suit of All, 494
Chalmers, Mary
Merry Christmas, Harry, 522
Take a Nap, Harry, 523
Throw a Kiss, Harry, 524
Cresswell, Helen
The Weather Cat, 650
Cushman, Doug
Space Cat, 665
deRubertis, Barbara
Patty Cat, 743
Eugenie, and Mary C. Olson, reteller
Kittens for Keeps, 827
Fehlner, Paul
Dog and Cat, 837
Fisher, Aileen
My Cat Has Eyes of Sapphire Blue, 858
Freeman, Martha
Mrs. Wow Never Wanted a Cow, 933
Friedman, Mel, and Ellen Weiss
Kitten Castle, 940
Gantos, Jack
Best in Show for Rotten Ralph, 972
Practice Makes Perfect for Rotten Ralph, 973
Rotten Ralph Feels Rotten, 974
Rotten Ralph Helps Out, 975
Godwin, Laura
The Best Fall of All, 1011
Happy and Honey, 1013
Happy Christmas, Honey! 1014
Honey Helps, 1015
Greenwood, Pamela D.
I Found Mouse, 1067
Harvey, Jayne
Cat Show, 1130
Hasler, Eveline
Winter Magic, 1132
Hawkins, Colin, and Jacqui Hawkins
Pat the Cat, 1147
Heilbroner, Joan
Tom the TV Cat, 1168
Hill, Susan
Stuart Little: Stuart at the Library, 1205
Stuart Little: Stuart Hides Out, 1206
Hoban, Julia
Buzby to the Rescue, 1238
Hoff, Syd
Captain Cat, 1269
Holub, Joan
Scat, Cats! 1319
Howe, James
Bunnicula, 1358
Pinky and Rex and the Just-Right Pet, 1362
Rabbit-Cadabra! 1369
Hurd, Edith T.
Come and Have Fun, 1375
No Funny Business, 1382
Jeffries, Alison
Sam and the Bag, 1418
Karlin, Nurit
The Fat Cat Sat on the Mat, 1483
Keller, Holly
A Bed Full of Cats, 1494
Kettner, Christine
Oliver Cat on Planet B, 1535
Kim, Joy
Come On Up! 1540
Koontz, Robin Michal
Chicago and the Cat, 1565
Chicago and the Cat: The Camping Trip, 1566
Chicago and the Cat: The Halloween Party, 1567
Langner, Nola
Dusty, 1660
Lauber, Patricia
Clarence and the Cat, 1668
McCullagh, Sheila
Tessa and the Magician, 1812
McKay, Sindy
Too Many Cats, 1857
Maitland, Barbara
The Bookstore Burglar, 1947
The Bookstore Ghost, 1948
Matthias, Catherine
I Love Cats, 2037
Meddaugh, Susan
Too Short Fred, 2058
Miller, Sara Swan
Cat in the Bag, 2087
Three More Stories You Can Read to Your Cat, 2093
Minarik, Else H.
Cat and Dog, 2118
Moran, Alex
Come Here, Tiger! 2175
Sam and Jack, 2176
Moskin, Marietta
Lysbet and the Fire Kittens, 2188
Muntean, Michaela
The Old Man and the Afternoon Cat, 2197
Nicklaus, Carol
Harry the Hider, 2228
Ochiltree, Dianne
Cats Add Up! 2253
Packard, Mary
The Christmas Kitten, 2294
Parish, Peggy
The Cats' Burglar, 2326
Scruffy, 2338
Phillips, Joan
Tiger Is a Scaredy Cat, 2401
Pilkey, Dav
Dragon's Fat Cat, 2407
Pomerantz, Charlotte
Buffy and Albert, 2436
Poulin, Stephane
Can You Catch Josephine? 2456
Could You Stop Josephine? 2457
Have You Seen Josephine? 2458
Ridlon, Marci
Kittens and More Kittens, 2600
Rocklin, Joanne
Jake and the Copycats, 2650
One Hungry Cat, 2653
Root, Phyllis
Here Comes Tabby Cat, 2683
Hey, Tabby Cat! 2684
Ruelle, Karen Gray
April Fool! 2746
Dear Tooth Fairy, 2747
Easter Egg Disaster, 2748
Easy as Apple Pie, 2749
Great Groundhogs, 2750
Just in Time for New Year's! 2751
The Monster in Harry's Backyard, 2752
Mother's Day Mess, 2753
Snow Valentines, 2754
Spookier Than a Ghost, 2755
The Thanksgiving Beast Feast, 2756
Ryder, Joanne, and Harold S. Feinburg
Mr. Putter and Tabby Walk the Dog, 2765

PETS — DOGS

PETS — DOGS — FICTION

PETS — DOGS — FICTION (cont.)

PETS — DOGS — FICTION (cont.)

Later, Rover, 3696
No More TV Sleepy Dog, 3703
Sam and Lucy, 3710
Sleepy Dog, 3712
Zion, Gene
Harry and the Lady Next Door, 3747

PETS — FICTION

Ada, Alma Flor
Daniel's Pet, 7
Ahlberg, Allan
The Pet Shop, 35
Aliki
At Mary Bloom's, 51
Allen, Marjorie N.
One, Two, Three-Ah-Choo! 73
Arnold, Tedd
Hi! Fly Guy, 91
Shoo, Fly Guy! 92
Super Fly Guy, 93
Berenstain, Stan, and Jan Berenstain
The Berenstain Bears' New Kitten, 202
The Berenstain Bears' New Pup, 203
Bonsall, Crosby
The Amazing the Incredible Super Dog, 267
Bowdish, Lynea
A Dog for a Day, 290
Brimner, Larry Dane
The Long Way Home, 356
Bulla, Clyde R.
Singing Sam, 389
Calmenson, Stephanie
My Dog's the Best, 432
Capucilli, Alyssa Satin
Biscuit Wins a Prize, 447
Carley, Wayne
Percy the Parrot Yelled Quiet! 456
Carrick, Carol
Empty Squirrel, 477
Clements, Andrew
Tara and Tiree, Fearless Friends, 570
Cowley, Joy
Agapanthus Hum and the Major Bark, 640
Ehrlich, Amy
Buck-Buck the Chicken, 810
Falken, Linda C.
Kitty's First Airplane Trip, 830
Greenwood, Pamela D.
What About My Goldfish? 1068
Herman, Gail
What a Hungry Puppy! 1198
Hillert, Margaret
A Friend for Dear Dragon, 1211
Go to Sleep, Dear Dragon, 1212
Howe, James
Pinky and Rex and the Just-Right Pet, 1362
Rabbit-Cadabra! 1369
Lauber, Patricia
Clarence and the Burglar, 1667
Little, Jean
Emma's Strange Pet, 1741
McKay, Sindy
Ben and Becky Get a Pet, 1851
McNulty, Faith
If Dogs Ruled the World, 1922
Parish, Peggy
No More Monsters for Me! 2335
Pinkwater, Daniel
Second-Grade Ape, 2414
Rylant, Cynthia
Henry and Mudge and Annie's Perfect Pet, 2779
Mr. Putter and Tabby Row the Boat, 2812
Puppy Mudge Loves His Blanket, 2827
Schaefer, Lola M.
Follow Me, Mittens, 2878
Mittens, 2879
Simon, Charnan
Guard the House, Sam! 3072
Stamper, Judith B.
The Bowwow Bake Sale, 3187
Steinberg, David
Club Pet and Other Funny Poems, 3209
Suen, Anastasia
Willie's Birthday, 3329
Tasan, Stan
Who Will Be My Pet? 3352
Tidd, Louise Vitellaro
The Best Pet Yet, 3403
Wallace, Carol
One Nosy Pup, 3502
Weston, Martha
Cats Are Like That, 3547

PETS — FISH

Landau, Elaine
Your Pet Tropical Fish, 1656
Pfeffer, Wendy
What's It Like to Be a Fish? 2397
Richardson, Adele
Caring for Your Fish, 2584
Selsam, Millicent E.
Plenty of Fish, 2928

PETS — FISH — FICTION

deRubertis, Barbara
Bitty Fish, 737
Palmer, Helen M.
A Fish Out of Water, 2305
Rylant, Cynthia
Mr. Putter and Tabby Feed the Fish, 2806
Silver, Jody
Rupert, Polly, and Daisy, 3064
Weston, Martha
Cats Are Like That, 3547

PETS — GERBILS

Landau, Elaine
Your Pet Gerbil, 1653
Pape, Donna L.
A Gerbil for a Friend, 2310
Snell, Nigel
Nita's Gerbil, 3147

PETS — HAMSTERS

Landau, Elaine
Your Pet Hamster, 1654

PETS — HORSES

Rabinowitz, Sandy
How I Trained My Colt, 2525

PETS — IGUANAS

Landau, Elaine
Your Pet Iguana, 1655

PETS — RABBITS

Snell, Nigel
Sam's Rabbit, 3149

PETS — RABBITS — FICTION

Parish, Peggy
Too Many Rabbits, 2341

PETS — RACCOONS — FICTION

Champion, Joyce
Emily and Alice, 525

PETS — TRAINING

Saunders, Susan
Tyrone Goes to School, 2860

PETS — TRAINING — FICTION

Capucilli, Alyssa Satin
Biscuit's New Trick, 450
Rylant, Cynthia
Henry and Mudge Take the Big Test, 2802

PETS — TURTLES

Selsam, Millicent E.
Let's Get Turtles, 2926

PETS — WILD ANIMALS

Cromie, William J.
Steven and the Green Turtle, 655
Ricciuti, Edward R.
An Animal for Alan, 2577

PETS — WILD ANIMALS — FICTION

Carrick, Carol
Empty Squirrel, 477
Christian, Mary B.
Devin and Goliath, 547
Friskey, Margaret
Indian Two Feet and the Wolf Cubs, 946
Hoff, Syd
Thunderhoof, 1290
Zweifel, Frances W.
Bony, 3761

PHOTOGRAPHY AND PHOTOGRAPHERS

Gallimard Jeunesse, Claude Delafosse, and Pierre-Marie Valat
The Camera, 970

PHOTOGRAPHY AND PHOTOGRAPHERS — FICTION

Manushkin, Fran
The Perfect Christmas Picture, 1954
Rau, Dana Meachen
Family Photo, 2537
Sandin, Joan
Pioneer Bear, 2849
Ziefert, Harriet
Take My Picture! 3722

PHYSICAL FITNESS

Trier, Carola S.
Exercise, 3419

PHYSICS AND PHYSICISTS

Sipiera, Paul P.
I Can Be a Physicist, 3097

PICNICS — FICTION

Calmenson, Stephanie
Where's Rufus? 434
Claverie, Jean
The Picnic, 564
Dotlich, Rebecca Kai
Peanut and Pearl's Picnic Adventure, 764
Hurd, Edith T.
No Funny Business, 1382
Jennings, Sharon
Franklin's Picnic, 1432
Medearis, Angela Shelf
On the Way to the Pond, 2061
Rylant, Cynthia
Mr. Putter and Tabby Row the Boat, 2812
Saunders, Susan
Charles Rat's Picnic, 2858
Williams, David K.
The Picnic, 3574
Ziefert, Harriet
Let's Trade, 3697

PIGEONS, CARRIER — FICTION

Redmond, Shirley Raye
Pigeon Hero! 2561

PIGS

King-Smith, Dick
All Pigs Are Beautiful, 1543
Ling, Mary
Pig, 1738
Miller, Sara Swan
Pigs, 2091
Moon, Cliff
Pigs on the Farm, 2158
Royston, Angela
The Pig, 2734
Stone, Lynn M.
Pigs, 3299

PIGS — FICTION

Allard, Harry
There's a Party at Mona's Tonight, 69
Bishop, Claire
Truffle Pig, 246
Carlson, Nancy
Making the Team, 472
The Mysterious Valentine, 473
The Perfect Family, 474
The Talent Show, 475
Witch Lady, 476
Chorao, Kay
Oink and Pearl, 540
Ups and Downs with Oink and Pearl, 542
DeLage, Ida
ABC Pigs Go to Market, 696
DiCamillo, Kate
Mercy Watson Fights Crime, 750
Mercy Watson Goes for a Ride, 751
Mercy Watson to the Rescue, 752
Gordon, Jeffie R.
Muriel and Ruth, 1024
Hawkins, Colin, and Jacqui Hawkins
Mig the Pig, 1146
Hazen, Barbara Shook
Road Hog, 1160
Hoban, Lillian
Mr. Pig and Family, 1253
Mr. Pig and Sonny Too, 1254
Hubbell, Patricia
Pig Picnic, 1370
Johnston, Tony
Farmer Mack Measures His Pig, 1460
Kanno, Wendy
Elmo the Pig, 1477
Keller, Holly
Geraldine's Big Snow, 1495
Kessler, Ethel, and Leonard Kessler
The Big Fight, 1509
Kroll, Steven
Pigs in the House, 1597
Lobel, Arnold
Small Pig, 1755
McPhail, David M.
Big Pig and Little Pig, 1925
Mason, Margo
Go Away, Crows! 2028
Meister, Cari
Skinny and Fats, Best Friends, 2067

SCOUTS AND SCOUTING — FICTION

Berenstain, Stan, and Jan Berenstain
The Berenstain Bear Scouts and the Search for Naughty Ned, 185
The Berenstain Bear Scouts and the Stinky Milk Mystery, 186
The Berenstain Bear Scouts and the White Water Mystery, 187
Thaler, Mike
Pack 109, 3377

SEA SLUGS

Kite, Patricia
Down in the Sea, 1552

SEA TURTLES

Stone, Lynn M.
Sea Turtles, 3305

SEAHORSES

Morris, Robert
Seahorse, 2185

SEALS

SEE ALSO Sea lions
Martin, Louise
Seals, 1982

SEALS — FICTION

Hoff, Syd
Sammy the Seal, 1286

SEALS, ELEPHANT

Shaw, Evelyn
Elephant Seal Island, 3022

SEALS AND SEA LIONS

Staub, Frank
Sea Lions, 3206

SEASHORE

Fowler, Allan
Seeing Seabirds, 911
Where Land Meets Sea, 925
Pluckrose, Henry
Seashore, 2425

SEASHORE — FICTION

Adler, David A.
Young Cam Jansen and the Double Beach Mystery, 21
Berenstain, Stan, and Jan Berenstain
The Berenstain Bears by the Sea, 198
The Berenstain Bears Seashore Treasure, 208
Burt, Denise
Our Family Vacation, 402
Eugenie, and Mary C. Olson, reteller
Kittens for Keeps, 827
Frith, Margaret
Mermaid Island, 948
Labatt, Mary
Sam at the Seaside, 1617
Miller, Pam
Sand, 2085
Rylant, Cynthia
Henry and Mudge and the Forever Sea, 2785
Schick, Eleanor
Summer at the Sea, 2889
Sharmat, Marjorie W.
Nate the Great and the Boring Beach Bag, 2988
Stevenson, James
Clams Can't Sing, 3222
Ziefert, Harriet
The Best Castle Ever, 3674
The Small Potatoes' Busy Beach Day, 3714

SEASHORES — FICTION

SEE ALSO Beaches — Fiction

SEASONS

SEE ALSO specific seasons, as Fall
Branley, Franklyn M.
Sunshine Makes the Seasons, 315
Chittenden, Margaret
When the Wild Ducks Come, 534
Jacobs, Leland B.
Just Around the Corner, 1401
McKay, Sindy
About the Seasons, 1849
Milburn, Constance
The Seasons, 2074
Pluckrose, Henry
Changing Seasons, 2420
Richardson, Joy
The Seasons, 2591
Sipiera, Paul P., and Diane M. Sipiera
Seasons, 3100
Zolotow, Charlotte
Seasons, 3760

SEASONS — FICTION

Godwin, Laura
The Best Fall of All, 1011
Jacobs, Leland B.
Hello, Year! 1399
Van Laan, Nancy
Busy Busy Moose, 3445
Ziefert, Harriet
My Apple Tree, 3700

SEEDS, ROOTS, AND BULBS

Jordan, Helene J.
How a Seed Grows, 1469
Moncure, Jane B.
How Seeds Travel, 2142
Selsam, Millicent E.
Seeds and More Seeds, 2929

SELF-ESTEEM

de Saint Mars, Dominique
Max Is Shy, 746
Simon, Norma
Why Am I Different? 3083

SELF-ESTEEM — FICTION

Buss, Nancy
The Lobster and Ivy Higgins, 411
Caple, Kathy
Starring Hillary, 437
Carlson, Nancy
Harriet's Recital, 467
The Talent Show, 475
Delton, Judy
I Never Win! 715
dePaola, Tomie
Oliver Button Is a Sissy, 731
Gantos, Jack
Best in Show for Rotten Ralph, 972
Giff, Patricia Reilly
Ronald Morgan Goes to Bat, 998
Today Was a Terrible Day, 999
Graham, Bob
Crusher Is Coming, 1039
Hautzig, Deborah
Handsomest Father, 1134
Why Are You So Mean to Me? 1141

McKay, Sindy
Ben and Becky Get a Pet, 1851
McMullan, Kate
The Mummy's Gold, 1902
Mallett, Anne
Here Comes Tagalong, 1950
Marshall, Edward
Four on the Shore, 1962
Moncure, Jane B.
Caring for My Baby Sister, 2135
Petersen, P. J.
The Fireplug Is First Base, 2390
Rocklin, Joanne
Jake and the Copycats, 2650
Ruelle, Karen Gray
April Fool! 2746
Dear Tooth Fairy, 2747
Easter Egg Disaster, 2748
Easy as Apple Pie, 2749
Great Groundhogs, 2750
Just in Time for New Year's! 2751
Mother's Day Mess, 2753
Spookier Than a Ghost, 2755
The Thanksgiving Beast Feast, 2756
Ruthstrom, Dorotha
The Big Kite Contest, 2758
Sadler, Marilyn J.
Honey Bunny Funnybunny, 2832
Simon, Charnan
I Like to Win! 3073
Surprise, 3081
Siracusa, Catherine
Bingo, the Best Dog in the World, 3103
Skinner, Daphne
Henry Keeps Score, 3111
Slater, Teddy, adapter
The Littles and the Secret Letter, 3127
Stern, Maggie
George and Diggety, 3213
Udry, Janice May
Thump and Plunk, 3439
Van Leeuwen, Jean
Amanda Pig on Her Own, 3451
More Tales of Oliver Pig, 3454
Oliver and Amanda's Christmas, 3457
Oliver and Amanda's Halloween, 3458
Wallace-Brodeur, Ruth
Stories from the Big Chair, 3507
Wardlaw, Lee
Hector's Hiccups, 3510
Welch, Sheila Kelly
Little Prince Know-It-All, 3535
Wells, Rosemary
Max and Ruby Play School, 3538
Wood, Audrey
Three Sisters, 3625
Ziefert, Harriet
Let's Trade, 3697

SIBLINGS — TRIPLETS — FICTION

Dadey, Debbie, and Marcia Thorton Jones
Triplet Trouble and the Bicycle Race, 668
Triplet Trouble and the Class Trip, 669
Triplet Trouble and the Cookie Contest, 670
Triplet Trouble and the Pizza Party, 671

SIBLINGS — TWINS — FICTION

Greydanus, Rose
Double Trouble, 1073
Hope, Laura Lee
Freddie and Flossie, 1337
Markham, Marion M.
The Halloween Candy Mystery, 1961
Putnam, Polly
The Mystery of Sara Beth, 2486
Ross, Pat
M and M and the Bad News Babies, 2697

SIGNS AND SYMBOLS

Gibbons, Gail
Puff . . . Flash . . . Bang! A Book About Signals, 989

SIMPLE MACHINES

Fowler, Allan
Simple Machines, 913

SIMPLE MACHINES — FICTION

Albee, Sarah
Clever Trevor, 37

SINGLE-PARENT FAMILIES

SEE Families, single-parent

SKUNKS

Stone, Lynn M.
Skunks, 3307

SKUNKS — FICTION

Jennings, Sharon
Franklin's Surprise, 1437
Jinkins, Jim
Pinky Dinky Doo, 1448
Luttrell, Ida
Tillie and Mert, 1780
Maccarone, Grace
Magic Matt and the Skunk in the Tub, 1793
Sabin, Louis
Birthday Surprise, 2831

SLAVERY

McKissack, Patricia
Amistad, 1859
Monjo, F. N.
The Drinking Gourd, 2149

SLAVERY — FICTION

Hopkinson, Deborah
From Slave to Soldier, 1349

SLEDDING — FICTION

Stern, Maggie
George and Diggety, 3213
Weston, Martha
Jack and Jill and Big Dog Bill, 3549

SLEEP

SEE ALSO Human body — Sleep
Richardson, Joy
What Happens When You Sleep? 2597
Showers, Paul
Sleep Is for Everyone, 3052

SLEEP — FICTION

Fernandes, Eugenie
Just You and Me, 840
Glass, Dr. Julie
Counting Sheep, 1008
Maestro, Giulio
Leopard and the Noisy Monkeys, 1944
Seuss, Dr.
I Am Not Going to Get Up Today! 2967

SPORTS — BASEBALL — FICTION (cont.)

Oechsli, Kelly
Mice at Bat, 2269
Packard, David
The Ball Game, 2292
Petersen, P. J.
The Fireplug Is First Base, 2390
Prager, Annabelle
The Baseball Birthday Party, 2466
Schade, Susan, and Jon Buller
Cat at Bat, 2869
Sharmat, Marjorie W.
Nate the Great and the Stolen Base, 2998
Sharp, Paul
Paul the Pitcher, 3020
Stadler, John
Hooray for Snail! 3182
Ziefert, Harriet
Strike Four! 3720

SPORTS — BASKETBALL

Kramer, S. A.
Basketball's Greatest Players, 1570

SPORTS — BASKETBALL — FICTION

Klein, Monica
Backyard Basketball Superstar, 1556
Kramer, S. A.
Hoop Stars, 1571
Maccarone, Grace
The Gym Day Winner, 1786
Mills, Claudia
Gus and Grandpa at Basketball, 2101
Suen, Anastasia
Loose Tooth, 3328

SPORTS — CAR RACING

Kelley, K. C.
Champions! of NASCAR, 1498
Racing to the Finish, 1499
Wilkinson, Sylvia
I Can Be a Race Car Driver, 3570

SPORTS — CAR RACING — FICTION

Driscoll, Laura
Slow Down, Sara! 770

SPORTS — FICTION

Berenstain, Stan, and Jan Berenstain
Ready, Get Set, Go! 218
McKissack, Robert
Try Your Best, 1884

SPORTS — FISHING

Swayne, Dick, and Peter Savage
I Am a Fisherman, 3347
Thomas, Art
Fishing Is for Me, 3385

SPORTS — FISHING — FICTION

Brenner, Barbara
Rosa and Marco and the Three Wishes, 339
Carlson, Nancy
Loudmouth George and the Fishing Trip, 470
Firmin, Peter
Basil Brush Goes Boating, 848
Marzollo, Jean
Amy Goes Fishing, 1996
Mills, Claudia
Gus and Grandpa Go Fishing, 2103
Root, Phyllis
Mouse Goes Out, 2685
Winnick, Karen
Sandro's Dolphin, 3586
Ziefert, Harriet
Fish Wish, 3685
Wish for a Fish, 3731

SPORTS — FOOTBALL

Mathis, Sharon Bell
Red Dog Blue Fly, 2032

SPORTS — FOOTBALL — FICTION

Carlson, Nancy
Making the Team, 472
Kessler, Leonard
Kick, Pass, and Run, 1523
Murphy, Jim
Harold Thinks Big, 2204
Stadler, John
Snail Saves the Day, 3184

SPORTS — GYMNASTICS

Brown, Marc
D.W. Flips! 374

SPORTS — GYMNASTICS — FICTION

Hoban, Lillian
Arthur's Birthday Party, 1241
Nicklaus, Carol
Head Over Heels, 2229
Ross, Pat
M and M and the Superchild Afternoon, 2703
Schade, Susan, and Jon Buller
Cat on the Mat, 2870
Schulman, Janet
Jenny and the Tennis Nut, 2901

SPORTS — HORSE RACING

Dubowski, Cathy E., and Mark Dubowski
A Horse Named Seabiscuit, 771

SPORTS — HORSEBACK RIDING — FICTION

Meister, Cari
My Pony Jack at Riding Lessons, 2066

SPORTS — HUNTING — FICTION

Parish, Peggy
Good Hunting, Blue Sky, 2329

SPORTS — ICE HOCKEY — FICTION

Bianchi, John
The Bungalo Boys III, 240
Carley, Wayne
Percy the Parrot Passes the Puck, 455

SPORTS — ICE SKATING — FICTION

Adler, David A.
Young Cam Jansen and the Ice Skate Mystery, 22
Herman, Gail
Slip! Slide! Skate! 1194
O'Connor, Jane
Kate Skates, 2256

SPORTS — INLINE SKATING

Witt, Alexa
It's Great to Skate! 3607

STORIES IN RHYME (cont.)

Messy Bessey's Holidays, 1878
Maguire, Gregory
The Peace and Quiet Diner, 1946
Marzollo, Dan
I Spy a Circus, 1994
I Spy Pirate Treasure, 1995
Marzollo, Jean
I Spy, 2003
I Spy a Balloon, 2004
I Spy a Butterfly, 2005
I Spy a Candy Cane, 2006
I Spy a Dinosaur's Eye, 2007
I Spy a Penguin, 2008
I Spy a Scary Monster, 2010
I Spy a School Bus, 2011
I Spy Funny Teeth, 2012
I Spy Santa Claus, 2014
Matthias, Catherine
I Love Cats, 2037
Medearis, Angela Shelf
The 100th Day of School, 2062
Milgrim, David
Why Benny Barks, 2079
Milios, Rita
Bears, Bears, Everywhere, 2080
I Am, 2082
Miller, Pam
Sand, 2085
Monjo, F. N.
Messy Bessey's Closet, 2151
Messy Bessey's Garden, 2152
Morley, Diana
Marms in the Marmalade, 2179
Muntean, Michaela
Bicycle Bear, 2194
Bicycle Bear Rides Again, 2195
A Garden for Miss Mouse, 2196
Namm, Diane
Little Bear, 2216
Monsters, 2217
Neasi, Barbara
Sweet Dreams, 2218
Numeroff, Laura J.
Monster Munchies, 2247
Oppenheim, Joanne
Do You Like Cats? 2275
The Donkey's Tale, 2276
Eency Weency Spider, 2277
Follow That Fish, 2278
Row, Row, Row Your Boat, 2280
"Uh-Oh!" Said the Crow, 2282
Packard, David
The Ball Game, 2292
Packard, Mary
Bubble Trouble, 2293
The Christmas Penguin, 2295
Fall Leaves, 2296
My Messy Room, 2299
Parker, Marjorie Blain
Hello, Fire Truck, 2344
Hello, Freight Train! 2345
Hello, School Bus! 2346
Pearson, Mary E.
Pickles in My Soup, 2363
Perez-Mercado, Mary Margaret
Splat! 2373
Perkins, Al
The Ear Book, 2374
Hand, Hand, Fingers, Thumb, 2375
The Nose Book, 2377
Rabe, Tish
Where Is Bear? 2524
Rau, Dana Meachen
Clown Around, 2536
Feet, 2538
Regan, Dana
Monkey See, Monkey Do, 2563
Ribke, Simone T.
A Garden Full of Sizes, 2572
Robinson, Fay
Creepy Beetles, 2624
Fantastic Frogs! 2625
Great Snakes! 2628
Mighty Spiders! 2629
Pizza Soup, 2631
Rockwell, Anne
Sweet Potato Pie, 2667
Roland, Timothy
Come Down Now, Flying Cow! 2680
Sakelaris, Page
Giggle Belly, 2842
Schade, Susan, and Jon Buller
Cat at Bat, 2869
Cat on the Mat, 2870
Railroad Toad, 2871
Snow Bugs, 2872
Snug House, Bug House! 2873
Space Dog Jack, 2874
Seltzer, Eric
Doodle Dog, 2951
Four Pups and a Worm, 2952
Serfozo, Mary
A Head Is for Hats, 2954
Seuss, Dr.
The Cat in the Hat, 2959
The Cat in the Hat Comes Back, 2960
Foot Book, 2962
Fox in Socks, 2963
Great Day for Up! 2964
Green Eggs and Ham, 2965
Hop on Pop, 2966
I Am Not Going to Get Up Today! 2967
I Can Read with My Eyes Shut! 2968
Mister Brown Can Moo! Can You? 2969
Oh, the Thinks You Can Think! 2971
One Fish Two Fish Red Fish Blue Fish, 2972
There's a Wocket in My Pocket! 2973
Sharp, Paul
Paul the Pitcher, 3020
Simon, Charnan
I Like to Win! 3073
I've Lost My Hat, 3074
Mud! 3075
Wash Day, 3082
Slater, Teddy
Busy Bunnies' Five Senses, 3118
N-O Spells No! 3120
The Wrong-Way Rabbit, 3124
Snow, Pegeen
Eat Your Peas, Louise! 3150
A Pet for Pat, 3151
Stadler, John
Cat at Bat, 3180
Cat Is Back at Bat, 3181
Stevens, Janet, and Susan Stevens Crummel
Shoe Town, 3219
Stone, Rosetta (pseud.)
Because a Little Bug Went Ka-Choo! 3317
Thaler, Mike
The Teacher from the Black Lagoon, 3378
Tripp, Valerie
Baby Koala Finds a Home, 3420
The Penguins Paint, 3423
Sillyhen's Big Surprise, 3424
Weeks, Sarah
Baa-choo! 3525
Splish, Splash! 3527
Weiss, Ellen
Lucky Duck, 3530

TOOLS

Epstein, Sam, and Beryl Epstein
Pick It Up, 823

TOOTH FAIRY

Brown, Marc
Arthur Tricks the Tooth Fairy, 368
Buller, Jon, and Susan Schade
No Tooth, No Quarter! 395

TOOTH FAIRY — FICTION

Chardiet, Bernice, and Grace Maccarone
Martin and the Tooth Fairy, 527
Gunther, Louise
A Tooth for the Tooth Fairy, 1093
McMullan, Kate
Fluffy Meets the Tooth Fairy, 1894
Ross, Pat
Molly and the Slow Teeth, 2705
Ruelle, Karen Gray
Dear Tooth Fairy, 2747
Weiss, Leatie
Heather's Feathers, 3533
Wilhelm, Hans
I Lost My Tooth! 3566

TORNADOES

Hopping, Lorraine Jean
Tornadoes! 1352

TOY AND MOVABLE BOOKS

Kalish, Muriel, and Lionel Kalish
Bears on the Stairs, 1474
Who Says Moo? A Beginner's Book of Animal Sounds, 1475
Morris, Johnny
Animal-Go-Round, 2182

TOYS

Robinson, Fay
A Ghost in the Toy Box, 2627

TOYS — FICTION

Boivin, Kelly
What's in a Box? 264
Elliott, Dan
My Doll Is Lost! 819
Hillert, Margaret
Play Ball, 1217
Katschke, Judy
Howdy, Sheriff Woody, 1484
Leonard, Marcia
My Pal Al, 1684
O'Connor, Jane
Splat! 2265
Packard, Mary
I Am King! 2297
Robinson, Fay
Old MacDonald Had a Farm, 2630
Real Bears and Alligators, 2632
When Nicki Went Away, 2638
Rylant, Cynthia
Mr. Putter and Tabby Fly the Plane, 2807
Wells, Rosemary
Play with Max and Ruby, 3539

TOYS — TEDDY BEARS

Mitgutsch, Ali
From Idea to Toy, 2132
Morris, Ann
How Teddy Bears Are Made, 2180

TOYS — TEDDY BEARS — FICTION

Inches, Alison
Corduroy Makes a Cake, 1393
Corduroy's Garden, 1394
Corduroy's Hike, 1395
Kantrowitz, Mildred
Willy Bear, 1482
Milios, Rita
Bears, Bears, Everywhere, 2080
Phillips, Joan
Lucky Bear, 2399
Robinson, Fay
Old MacDonald Had a Farm, 2630

TRACTORS

Rickard, Graham
Tractors, 2599

TRACTORS — FICTION

Baynton, Martin
Fifty and the Fox, 155
Fifty and the Great Race, 156
Fifty Gets the Picture, 157
Fifty Saves His Friend, 158
Kanno, Wendy
The Farmer's Tractor, 1478

TRADING CARDS — FICTION

Jennings, Sharon
Franklin's Trading Cards, 1438

TRAINS

Chlad, Dorothy
Stop, Look, and Listen for Trains, 538
Gibbons, Gail
Trains, 994
Matthews, Morgan
What's It Like to Be a Railroad Worker, 2035
Mayer, Cassie
Getting Around by Train, 2046
Stille, Darlene R.
Trains, 3250

TRAINS — FICTION

Ahlberg, Allan
The Ghost Train, 33
Awdry, W.
Thomas the Tank Engine and the School Trip, 101
Hillert, Margaret
Little Puff, 1215
Maestro, Betsy
All Aboard Overnight, 1937
Meeks, Esther
The Dog That Took the Train, 2064
Mills, Claudia
Gus and Grandpa Ride the Train, 2104
Parker, Marjorie Blain
Hello, Freight Train! 2345
Piper, Watty
Meet the Little Engine That Could, 2415
Rylant, Cynthia
Mr. Putter and Tabby Take the Train, 2815
Schade, Susan, and Jon Buller
Railroad Toad, 2871
Sharmat, Marjorie W., and Mitchell Sharmat
Nate the Great on the Owl Express, 3015

WOLVES — FICTION

Friskey, Margaret
Indian Two Feet and the Wolf Cubs, 946
Hubbell, Patricia
Pig Picnic, 1370
Novak, Matt
Little Wolf Big Wolf, 2242
Taylor, Sean
Small Bad Wolf, 3357
Van Woerkom, Dorothy
Meat Pies and Sausages, 3469
Wheeler, Lisa
New Pig in Town, 3554
When Pigs Fly, 3555
Who's Afraid of Granny Wolf? 3556

WOMBATS

Stone, Lynn M.
Wombats, 3315

WOMEN'S RIGHTS

Hopkinson, Deborah
Susan B. Anthony, 1350

WOOD CARVING — FICTION

Bulla, Clyde R.
Daniel's Duck, 387
Sharoff, Victor
The Heart of the Wood, 3019

WOODCHUCKS

McNulty, Faith
Woodchuck, 1923

WOODCHUCKS — FICTION

Stanovich, Betty Jo
Hedgehog Adventures, 3201
Hedgehog Surprises, 3202

WOOL

Potter, Tessa, and Donna Bailey
Sheep, 2455

WORDPLAY

SEE ALSO Puns
Cassedy, Sylvia
Zoomrimes, 495
Clifford, Eth
Flatfoot Fox and the Case of the Missing Eye, 571
Cole, Joanna
Get Well, Clown-Arounds! 587
Gage, Wilson
Squash Pie, 966
Hall, Katy, and Lisa Eisenberg
Grizzly Riddles, 1101
Snakey Riddles, 1106
Hawkins, Colin, and Jacqui Hawkins
Mig the Pig, 1146
Tog the Dog, 1148
Zug the Bug, 1149
Heller, Ruth
A Cache of Jewels and Other Collective Nouns, 1172
Kites Sail High, 1173
Many Luscious Lollipops, 1174
Merry-Go-Round, 1175
Up, Up and Away, 1176
Kessler, Leonard
Old Turtle's 90 Knock-Knocks, Jokes, and Riddles, 1528
Kido, Yukiko
Snake Cake, 1538
Krinsley, Jeanette
The Cow Went over the Mountain, 1594
Lopshire, Robert
How to Make Snop Snappers and Other Fine Things, 1762
Low, Joseph
Mad Wet Hen and Other Riddles, 1770
McKay, Sindy
The New Red Bed, 1856
Parish, Herman
Amelia Bedelia, Bookworm, 2316
Amelia Bedelia 4 Mayor, 2317
Amelia Bedelia, Rocket Scientist, 2318
Parish, Peggy
Thank You, Amelia Bedelia, 2340
Tremain, Ruthven
Teapot, Switcheroo, and Other Silly Word Games, 3418

WORK — FICTION

Spohn, Kate
Turtle and Snake at Work, 3171
Stamper, Judith B.
Breakfast at Danny's Diner, 3188

WORLD WAR II — FICTION

Redmond, Shirley Raye
Pigeon Hero! 2561

WORMS — FICTION

Caple, Kathy
Wow, It's Worm! 439

WRITERS AND WRITING

Berg, Julie
The Berenstains, 219
Maurice Sendak, 220
Daugherty, Charles M.
Samuel Clemens, 684
Fritz, Jean
Surprising Myself, 950
Greene, Carol
Margaret Wise Brown, 1057
McKissack, Patricia, and Fredrick McKissack
Zora Neale Hurston, 1883
Toby, Marlene
A. A. Milne, 3410

WRITERS AND WRITING — FICTION

Delton, Judy
The Goose Who Wrote a Book, 713
Rylant, Cynthia
Mr. Putter and Tabby Write the Book, 2817

WYOMING

Zollman, Pam
Wyoming, 3759

ZEBRAS

Stone, Lynn M.
Zebras, 3316

ZOOLOGY AND ZOOLOGISTS

Schott, Jane A.
Dian Fossey and the Mountain Gorillas, 2893

ZOOS

Fowler, Allan
Animals in the Zoo, 870
Hewett, Joan
Tiger, Tiger Growing Up, 1201
Hilker, Cathryn H.
A Cheetah Named Angel, 1202
Parramon, J. M.
My First Visit to the Zoo, 2351

ZOOS (cont.)

Stamper, Judith B.
What's It Like to Be a Zoo Worker, 3195

ZOOS — FICTION

Eyles, Heather
A Zoo in Our House, 828
Jacobs, Leland B.
Hello, Pleasant Places! 1398
Kent, Jack
The Biggest Shadow in the Zoo, 1504
McInnes, John
Leo Lion Paints It Red, 1845
Matthias, Catherine
Too Many Balloons, 2040
Robison, Nancy
Izoo, 2642
Slater, Teddy
Stay in Line, 3122
Thomson, Pat
Can You Hear Me, Grandad? 3392
Ziefert, Harriet
Take My Picture! 3722

ZUCCHINI — FICTION

Siracusa, Catherine
The Giant Zucchini, 3104

ANNOTATED BIBLIOGRAPHY

A

Abbott, Roger

1 *Sniffer's Golden Nose*. Ill. by Colin West. Kingfisher, pap., 2006, ISBN 0-7534-5959-0. SERIES: I Am Reading. SUBJECTS: Behavior — Stealing — Fiction; Pets — Dogs — Fiction. RL B.

Naughty Nancy sends her dog Sniffer in search of all things gold, including the king's new crown. Nancy appears before the king with the crown stuck to her head and the king realizes he has found two treasures. Vivid watercolor cartoon illustrations add to the silliness of this golden tale.

Aber, Linda W.

2 *Carrie Measures Up*. Ill. by Joy Allen. Kane, pap., 2001, ISBN 1-57565-100-9. SERIES: Math Matters. SUBJECTS: Arts and crafts — Fiction; Concepts — Weight — Fiction; Grandparents — Fiction. RL B.

When Grandmother comes to visit, she brings along her big knitting bag and a tape measure. Carrie is busy measuring everyone for a surprise present, except Grandma. Comical ink and watercolor illustrations capture the humor of the knitting frenzy.

3 *Grandma's Button Box*. Ill. by Page Eastburn O'Rourke. Kane, pap., 2002, ISBN 1-57565-110-6. SERIES: Math Matters. SUBJECTS: Family life — Fiction; Grandparents — Fiction; Mathematics — Fiction. RL B.

A look through Grandma's button box seems the perfect quiet activity while everyone is still sleeping, until the box comes crashing down from a high shelf. Did Grandma sort them by color, size, or shape? Join in the sorting fun as colorful watercolor illustrations enhance this unexpected family activity.

4 *Who's Got Spots?* Ill. by Gioia Fiammenghi. Kane, pap., 2000, ISBN 1-57565-099-1. SERIES: Math Matters. SUBJECTS: Illness — Fiction; Mathematics — Fiction; School stories. RL B. LEXILE 250L.

An outbreak of chicken pox threatens the school Autumn Fest. Kip and the class devise a chart and graph to predict who and how many will be in their places on stage. A mathematical concept is integrated into the story of an everyday school dilemma, highlighted by bright, cartoon-like illustrations in watercolor.

Aboff, Marcie

5 *The Giant Jelly Bean Jar*. Ill. by Paige Billin-Frye. Penguin, pap., 2004, ISBN 0-14-240049-1. SERIES: Puffin Easy-to-Read. SUBJECTS: Behavior — Shyness — Fiction. RL B.

Each week Ben is too shy to answer the riddle that wins a jar of jelly beans until, on the store's first anniversary, he overcomes his shyness to become the "Grand Prize Jelly Bean King." Endearing watercolors expressively focus on a young boy's struggle and triumph.

Ada, Alma Flor

6 *Daniel's Mystery Egg*. Ill. by G. Brian Karas. Harcourt, 2000, o.p. SERIES: Green Light Readers. SUBJECTS: Friendship — Fiction; Mystery and detective stories. RL A.

What's inside the little white egg that Daniel found? That's what Daniel and his friends are trying to find out. Earth-toned pencil and watercolor illustrations follow the boys' actions as they try to "crack" the mystery.

Ada, Alma Flor (cont.)

7 *Daniel's Pet*. Ill. by G. Brian Karas. Harcourt, 2002, o.p. SERIES: Green Light Readers. SUBJECTS: Chickens — Fiction; Pets — Fiction. RL A.

Caring for his new baby chick, Daniel is surprised one day as he discovers Jen in the henhouse, surrounded by her own little chicks. This simple story for very beginning readers is extended by warm watercolor and colored-pencil illustrations.

Adams, Florence

8 *Mushy Eggs*. Ill. by Marilyn Hirsch. Putnam, 1973, o.p. SUBJECTS: Baby-sitting — Fiction; Family life — Fiction; Parents, working — Fiction. RL C.

The new baby-sitter is nice and bakes good cookies, but cannot make mushy eggs like the boys' previous baby-sitter, their beloved Fanny. Homely details warm this tale of special relationships.

Adler, David A.

9 *Bones and the Big Yellow Mystery*. Ill. by Barbara Johansen Newman. Viking, 2004, ISBN 0-670-05947-1. SERIES: Viking Easy-to-Read. SUBJECTS: Grandparents — Fiction; Lost and found possessions — Fiction; Mystery and detective stories. RL B. LEXILE 260L.

Detective Jeffrey Bones is hot on the trail of Mr. Green's missing school bus. With the help of his new detective dog, Curly, this first mystery series episode is easily solved with "just the facts." Vibrant illustrations capture the humor and action of a detective on his first case.

10 *Bones and the Birthday Mystery*. Ill. by Barbara Johansen Newman. Viking, 2007, ISBN 978-0-670-06164-8. SERIES: Viking Easy-to-Read. SUBJECTS: Birthdays — Fiction; Grandparents — Fiction; Lost and found possessions — Fiction; Mystery and detective stories. RL A. LEXILE 260L.

It's Grandpa's birthday and icing is everywhere as Jeffrey frosts the cake. But where is Grandpa's present? Lively illustrations aptly capture the actions of a sleuth on a sticky mystery trail.

11 *Bones and the Cupcake Mystery*. Ill. by Barbara Johansen Newman. Viking, 2005, ISBN 0-670-05939-0. SERIES: Viking Easy-to-Read. SUBJECTS: Lost and found possessions — Fiction; Mystery and detective stories; School stories. RL B. LEXILE 260L.

When classmate Not-Me Amy loses her spinach noodle cupcake, Detective Bones is ready to solve the case. A bit of detective powder and deduction saves the day. Colorful illustrations provide visual clues for both reader and detective.

12 *Bones and the Dinosaur Mystery*. Ill. by Barbara Johansen Newman. Viking, 2005, ISBN 0-670-06010-0. SERIES: Viking Easy-to-Read. SUBJECTS: Dinosaurs — Fiction; Lost and found possessions — Fiction; Mystery and detective stories. RL B. LEXILE 260L.

On a visit to the museum, Grandpa, Sally, and Detective Jeffrey Bones explore the dinosaur exhibit. After a snack and a visit to the moon rocks, Bones finds he has lost his blue plastic T-Rex toy and must solve the mystery of its disappearance. Expressive illustrations reflect the humor and "drama" of the young sleuth's exploits.

13 *Bones and the Dog Gone Mystery*. Ill. by Barbara Johansen Newman. Viking, 2004, ISBN 0-670-05948-X. SERIES: Viking Easy-to-Read. SUBJECTS: Lost and found possessions — Fiction; Mystery and detective stories; Pets — Dogs — Fiction. RL B. LEXILE 260L.

On a trip to the park, Detective Bones not only loses his magnifying glass but also Grandpa's dog, Curly. There are many clues to track down and, hopefully, his detective bag will help him. The warm relationship between grandfather and grandson is aptly portrayed through the brightly colored illustrations.

14 *The Carsick Zebra and Other Animal Riddles*. Ill. by Tomie dePaola. Bantam, pap., 1985, ISBN 0-8234-0479-X. SUBJECTS: Animals — Fiction; Jokes and riddles. RL B.

Wordplay employing familiar situations and animals is used in an extremely inventive manner. Line drawings are of humorous animals.

15 *My Dog and the Birthday Mystery*. Ill. by Dick Gackenbach. Holiday House, 1987, ISBN 0-8234-0632-6. SERIES: First Mystery. SUBJECTS: Birthdays — Fiction; Mystery and

detective stories; Pets — Dogs — Fiction. RL A.

Jennie's friends, having arranged a surprise party for her birthday, trick her into working on a mystery that leads her to the party. The story is accompanied by pictures with red, orange, yellow, and gray washes with black outlining.

16 *My Dog and the Green Sock Mystery*. Ill. by Dick Gackenbach. Holiday House, 1986, ISBN 0-8234-0590-7. SERIES: First Mystery. SUBJECTS: Mystery and detective stories; Pets — Dogs — Fiction. RL B.

Jennie's astute observations and My Dog's contributions help locate Andy's missing belongings. Characteristic mishaps of childhood add humor and warmth to the tale. My Dog, curious and appealingly shaggy, is the focus of the ink drawings.

17 *My Dog and the Knock Knock Mystery*. Ill. by Marsha Winborn. Holiday House, 1985, o.p. SERIES: First Mystery. SUBJECTS: Mystery and detective stories; Pets — Dogs — Fiction. RL B.

This gently humorous mystery is solved with the intuitive help of My Dog. A slightly sick shaggy white pup lying on marbleized avocado grass surrounded by the remains of the apples he has consumed — in the course of duty — is typically appealing.

18 *The Twisted Witch and Other Spooky Riddles*. Ill. by Victoria Chess. Bantam, pap., 1986, ISBN 0-8234-0571-0. SUBJECTS: Halloween — Fiction; Jokes and riddles. RL C.

Riddles include topics such as witches. Illustrations are in gray and black.

19 *Young Cam Jansen and the Baseball Mystery*. Ill. by Susanna Natti. Viking, 1999, ISBN 0-670-88481-2. SERIES: Viking Easy-to-Read. SUBJECTS: Lost and found possessions — Fiction; Mystery and detective stories; Sports — Baseball — Fiction. RL B. LEXILE 260L.

With a "click," Cam Jansen accurately remembers anything. These perceptive powers help out when she and her friends lose their ball while playing baseball in the park. All the action is captured in bright watercolor detail. A memory game picture is perfect for budding detectives.

20 *Young Cam Jansen and the Dinosaur Game*. Ill. by Susanna Natti. Viking, 1996, ISBN 0-670-86399-8. SERIES: Viking Easy-to-Read. SUBJECTS: Mystery and detective stories; Parties — Fiction. RL B. LEXILE 370L.

At a birthday party, Cam Jansen solves the mystery of the dinosaur guessing game. Her friend Eric wins all the dinosaurs and shares them with the party guests. The detailed illustrations easily allow readers to follow along with Cam's deductive trail.

21 *Young Cam Jansen and the Double Beach Mystery*. Ill. by Susanna Natti. Viking, 2002, ISBN 0-670-03531-9. SERIES: Viking Easy-to-Read. SUBJECTS: Lost and found possessions — Fiction; Mystery and detective stories; Seashore — Fiction. RL B. LEXILE 260L.

There are two mysteries to solve at the beach as Cam, Eric, and Aunt Molly try to find Mrs. Jansen and her lost papers. Illustrations that glow with the warm feeling of sand and surf provide the perfect backdrop for Cam's detective skills.

22 *Young Cam Jansen and the Ice Skate Mystery*. Ill. by Susanna Natti. Viking, 1998, o.p. SERIES: Viking Easy-to-Read. SUBJECTS: Lost and found possessions — Fiction; Mystery and detective stories; Sports — Ice skating — Fiction. RL B. LEXILE 210L.

A fun time at the ice rink leads to a mystery as Eric loses the key to their locker. Cam uses her amazing memory and "clicks" on the scene and solves the dilemma. On every page full-color illustrations illuminate the clues and the possible solutions.

23 *Young Cam Jansen and the Library Mystery*. Ill. by Susanna Natti. Viking, 2001, ISBN 0-670-89281-5. SERIES: Viking Easy-to-Read. SUBJECTS: Libraries and librarians — Fiction; Lost and found possessions — Fiction; Mystery and detective stories. RL B. LEXILE 300L.

After a trip to the library, Cam, Eric, and Mr. Jansen head for the grocery store. But the shopping list is gone! Colorful illustrations complete with thought balloons follow Cam's detective skills as she zeroes in on the hidden clues.

Adler, David A. (cont.)

24 *Young Cam Jansen and the Lost Tooth.* Ill. by Susanna Natti. Viking, 1997, o.p. SERIES: Viking Easy-to-Read. SUBJECTS: Lost and found possessions — Fiction; Mystery and detective stories; School stories. RL B. LEXILE 360L.

At Thanksgiving, as the class is making turkey puppets, Annie bites into an apple and loses her tooth. But where is it? Text and detailed illustrations follow the detective process and "take a bite" out of the mystery.

25 *Young Cam Jansen and the Missing Cookie.* Ill. by Susanna Natti. Viking, 1996, o.p. SERIES: Viking Easy-to-Read. SUBJECTS: Lost and found possessions — Fiction; Mystery and detective stories; School stories. RL B. LEXILE 360L.

Jason's cookie is missing from his lunch box, so someone in the class must have taken it! Cookie crumbs inside the lunch box are an important clue to solving the mystery. With simple lines and bright colors, the appealing children's faces reflect the everyday problems of school life.

26 *Young Cam Jansen and the New Girl Mystery.* Ill. by Susanna Natti. Viking, 2004, ISBN 0-670-05915-3. SERIES: Viking Easy-to-Read. SUBJECTS: Lost and found possessions — Fiction; Mystery and detective stories; School stories. RL B.

Jenny, the new girl at school, can't find anything. Told to go to gym after lunch, Jenny herself goes missing. Brightly colored illustrations highlight the class antics as they search the g-y-m and finally find her helping J-i-m in the lunchroom.

27 *Young Cam Jansen and the Pizza Shop Mystery.* Ill. by Susanna Natti. Viking, 2000, o.p. SERIES: Viking Easy-to-Read. SUBJECTS: Lost and found possessions — Fiction; Mystery and detective stories; Shopping — Fiction. RL B. LEXILE 310L.

At the mall, Cam, Eric, and Mr. Jansen stop for pizza. It's very busy at the restaurant and Cam's jacket goes missing. Action-packed illustrations on each page chronicle the hubbub, the search for the jacket, and the ultimate success in solving the mystery.

28 *Young Cam Jansen and the Spotted Cat Mystery.* Ill. by Susanna Natti. Viking, 2006, ISBN 0-670-06094-1. SERIES: Viking Easy-to-Read. SUBJECTS: Lost and found possessions — Fiction; Mystery and detective stories; Pets — Cats — Fiction. RL B.

On a rainy day, a white cat suddenly appears in the classroom. Who does it belong to? As Cam and Eric solve another mystery, readers can follow along with all the picture clues in the illustrations.

29 *Young Cam Jansen and the Substitute Mystery.* Ill. by Susanna Natti. Viking, 2005, ISBN 0-670-05988-9. SERIES: Viking Easy-to-Read. SUBJECTS: Lost and found possessions — Fiction; Mystery and detective stories; School stories. RL B. LEXILE 410L.

With her photographic memory, Cam Jansen helps Mr. Baker, the substitute teacher, find his coat. A call to the cell phone in its pocket quickly solves the mystery. Comical illustrations portray the humor of the absent-minded teacher.

30 *Young Cam Jansen and the Zoo Note Mystery.* Ill. by Susanna Natti. Viking, 2003, ISBN 0-670-03626-9. SERIES: Viking Easy-to-Read. SUBJECTS: Mystery and detective stories; School stories. RL B. LEXILE 260L.

Finally remembering to bring his signed permission slip for the zoo field trip, Eric loses it on the way to school. Without the slip, Eric cannot go. Follow the clues in the detailed illustrations and solve the mystery along with Cam.

Agell, Charlotte

31 *Sailor's Book.* Ill. by author. Firefly, 1991, o.p. SUBJECTS: Dragons — Fiction; Poetry. RL A.

A gentle, rhythmic, extended simile about the sea as a dragon, whose breath is the clouds, whose waves are the scales, and whose eye is the sun. Illustrations are in textured turquoise, deep purple, and orange washes.

Ahlberg, Allan

32 *Dinosaur Dreams.* Ill. by Andre Amstutz. Greenwillow, 1991, ISBN 0-688-09955-6. SERIES: Funnybones. SUBJECTS: Cumulative

tales; Dinosaurs — Fiction; Dreams — Fiction. RL B.

A slim story about the coordinated dinosaur dreams of little and big skeleton and their skeleton dog. Readers who are familiar with the characters will enjoy the text and the striking colorful graphic illustrations against a black background.

33 *The Ghost Train*. Ill. by Andre Amstutz. Putnam, 1992, ISBN 0-688-11435-0. SERIES: Funnybones. SUBJECTS: Cumulative tales; Ghost stories; Trains — Fiction. RL A.

A baby crying in the night scares the skeletons, witches, and monsters on a midnight train adventure. Striking graphic illustrations use bright colors on a black ground.

34 *Mystery Tour*. Ill. by Andre Amstutz. Greenwillow, 1991, ISBN 0-688-09957-2. SERIES: Funnybones. SUBJECTS: Cumulative tales; Mystery and detective stories; Visual perception. RL B.

Friendly skeletons — one large and one small — drive on a mystery tour to identify silhouettes: a baby in a crib, a train, a teddy in a tent. The illustrator's vivid graphic colors against a black background are well suited to a nighttime mystery adventure.

35 *The Pet Shop*. Ill. by Andre Amstutz. Greenwillow, 1990, ISBN 0-688-09905-X. SERIES: Funnybones. SUBJECTS: Humorous stories; Pets — Fiction. RL A.

Tired of their dog digging holes and barking, the skeletons trade him in for a series of pets, each larger and more troublesome than the last. Full-color illustrations with white skeletal people and pets are vivid against a black background.

36 *Skeleton Crew*. Ill. by Andre Amstutz. Greenwillow, 1992, ISBN 0-688-11436-9. SERIES: Funnybones. SUBJECTS: Humorous stories; Vacations — Fiction. RL A.

Three skeletons on vacation are set adrift by pirates, floating in and out of danger. A choppy rhythm, some wordplay, and humor are accompanied by a vividly colored seascape and white skeletons against a black background.

Albee, Sarah

37 *Clever Trevor*. Ill. by Paige Billin-Frye. Kane, 2003, ISBN 1-57565-123-8. SERIES: Science Solves It! SUBJECTS: Behavior — Bullying — Fiction; Simple machines — Fiction. RL B.

Trevor and his friends outsmart bullies on the playground by using the scientific principle of levers and a fulcrum. Cartoon-like watercolor and pencil illustrations carry the action of the story while clearly focusing on the science.

38 *The Dragon's Scales*. Ill. by John Manders. Random House, 1998, ISBN 0-679-98381-3. SERIES: Step into Reading + Math. SUBJECTS: Concepts — Weight — Fiction; Dragons — Fiction. RL B. LEXILE 400L.

A scary dragon is threatening the townspeople of Berry Town and the berries they love to grow and eat. A little girl challenges the beast to a contest of weight and measurement and wins. Lively pastel watercolor and pencil drawings comically illustrate this fantasy, watchdragon and all.

39 *My Best Friend Is Out of this World*. Ill. by Nate Evans. Golden Books, 1998, o.p. SERIES: Road to Reading. SUBJECTS: Friendship — Fiction; UFOs — Fiction. RL A.

Featuring bold, intensely colored full-page illustrations, this story of an unusual friendship unfolds. Maddy's best friend, Victor, is polite, loves meatloaf for dinner, and is an alien. When his mother picks him up in a UFO, there is the promise of inviting Maddy to their house one day. . . . Gulp!

Alexander, Ellen

40 *Llama and the Great Flood: A Folktale from Peru*. Ill. by author. HarperCollins, 1989, ISBN 0-690-04729-0. SUBJECTS: Folklore — Peru. RL C.

After a llama saves a Peruvian family from the Great Flood, llamas become very special. Appealing watercolor illustrations supply color and pattern to an account of everyday life high in the Andes.

Alexander, Liza

41 *Splish-Splashy Day: Featuring Jim Henson's Sesame Street Muppets*. Ill. by Joseph Ewers. Western, 1989, o.p. SERIES: Sesame Street. SUBJECTS: Humorous stories;

Alexander, Liza (cont.)

Stories in rhyme; Weather — Rain — Fiction. RL A.

The Sesame Street characters enjoy playing and dancing in the mud and puddles of a rainy day — and the comfort of drying off at home. Cartoon illustrations accompany the text.

Alexander, Sue

42 *Marc the Magnificent*. Ill. by Tomie dePaola. Pantheon, 1978, o.p. SUBJECTS: Imagination — Fiction; Magic — Fiction. RL C.

A boy's fantasy of fame as a magician contrasts with his first clumsy attempts at magic — but finally ends in success. Fantasy and reality are humorously contrasted through the use of language and simple pictures. Illustrations are primarily in plum, tan, and dull gold.

43 *More Witch, Goblin, and Ghost Stories*. Ill. by Jeanette Winter. Pantheon, 1978, ISBN 0-394-83933-1. SERIES: I Am Reading. SUBJECTS: Friendship — Fiction; Ghost stories; Witches — Fiction. RL C.

An indoor picnic, a faked illness, a tall tale, and a day spent observing nature all bring these three friends closer. Soft pencil drawings complement the theme well.

44 *Seymour the Prince*. Ill. by Lillian Hoban. Pantheon, 1979, o.p. SERIES: I Am Reading. SUBJECTS: Clubs — Fiction; Plays — Fiction. RL B.

Does Seymour want to be part of the Maple Street club badly enough to be laughed at as the prince in Sleeping Beauty? Soft pencil drawings are warm and appealing.

45 *Witch, Goblin, and Ghost Are Back*. Ill. by Jeanette Winter. Pantheon, 1985, ISBN 0-394-86296-1. SERIES: I Am Reading. SUBJECTS: Friendship — Fiction; Ghost stories; Witches — Fiction. RL C.

Lessons about friendship — and the consequences of eating nothing but fudge — are gently relayed in five chapters. Another book in a series about three friends. Illustrations are low-key and in soft pencil.

46 *Witch, Goblin, and Ghost in the Haunted Woods*. Ill. by Jeanette Winter. Pantheon, 1981, ISBN 0-394-84443-2. SERIES: I Am Reading. SUBJECTS: Friendship — Fiction; Ghost stories; Witches — Fiction. RL C.

Through a story, two friends help Goblin learn how to swim. Warm, supportive friends are very different from one another. Soft pencil drawings convey the feelings.

47 *Witch, Goblin, and Sometimes Ghost: Six Read-Alone Stories*. Ill. by Jeanette Winter. Pantheon, 1976, ISBN 0-394-93216-1. SERIES: I Am Reading. SUBJECTS: Friendship — Fiction; Ghost stories; Witches — Fiction. RL B.

These six tales include friends telling stories to allay fear of lightning, and collaborating to write a book. Pencil drawings underscore the relationship of the three.

48 *World Famous Muriel*. Ill. by Chris L. Demarest. Dell, pap., 1988, ISBN 0-440-40024-4. SUBJECTS: Humorous stories; Mystery and detective stories. RL B.

Muriel follows clues, including footprints, to discover who stole the decorations for the queen's party. Tongue-in-cheek humor is appropriately illustrated with comic watercolor drawings.

49 *World Famous Muriel and the Magic Mystery*. Ill. by Marla Frazee. HarperCollins, 1990, ISBN 0-690-04789-4. SUBJECTS: Humorous stories; Libraries and librarians — Fiction; Magic — Fiction; Mystery and detective stories. RL B.

World Famous Muriel, fueled with peanut butter cookies, tracks the missing magician, the Great Hokus Pokus, to the library, boning up on his less-than-perfect magic tricks. Vivid illustrations show a library full of people and activities, as well as a male children's librarian.

50 *World Famous Muriel and the Scary Dragon*. Ill. by Chris L. Demarest. Little, Brown, 1985, o.p. SUBJECTS: Humorous stories; Mythical creatures — Fiction. RL B.

When the King of Pompandcircumstance sends for Muriel to rid the neighborhood of a dragon, she takes her tightrope and her favorite peanut butter cookies. The delightful humor is immeasurably heightened with cartoon drawings in watercolors.

Aliki

51 *At Mary Bloom's*. Ill. by author. Greenwillow, 1976, ISBN 0-688-02481-5. SUBJECTS: Cumulative tales; Pets — Fiction. RL A.

Mary Bloom helps a small girl celebrate her mouse's new babies. Marvelous animal ink drawings range from tiny mice to wall-to-wall pets and a story rebus.

52 *Corn Is Maize: The Gift of the Indians*. Ill. by author. HarperCollins, pap., 1976, ISBN 0-690-00975-5. SERIES: Let's-Read-and-Find-Out Science. SUBJECTS: Food; Native Americans. RL C.

The history of Native American corn cultivation going back 5,000 years is traced, along with the ways it has been used and valued. Fascinating illustrations in gray, yellow, and green add immeasurably to the story. Illustrated instructions for making a corn husk wreath are appended.

53 *Digging Up Dinosaurs*. Ill. by author. HarperCollins, 1988, ISBN 0-690-04716-9. SERIES: Let's-Read-and-Find-Out Science. SUBJECTS: Dinosaurs; Science and scientists. RL B.

Of utmost interest in this story is the transporting of the dinosaur fossil finds to the museum and their preparation for exhibit. The dainty, soft-colored pencil drawings are augmented by cartoon comments from children, scientists, and museum buffs.

54 *Dinosaur Bones*. Ill. by author. HarperCollins, 1988, ISBN 0-690-04550-6. SERIES: Let's-Read-and-Find-Out Science. SUBJECTS: Dinosaurs; Fossils; Geology and geologists; Science and scientists. RL B.

With typically appealing colored-pencil illustrations of dinosaurs and their discoverers, and lively dialogue accompanying the text, information about several dozen dinosaurs is given.

55 *Dinosaurs Are Different*. Ill. by author. HarperCollins, pap., 1986, ISBN 0-690-04456-9. SERIES: Let's-Read-and-Find-Out Science. SUBJECTS: Dinosaurs; Science and scientists. RL C.

Exceptionally well presented information on how one can distinguish the families of dinosaurs by their teeth and hips is illustrated with accurate sketches, color-coding, and cartoons of children. Length, weight, and the name of the dinosaurs, and the cartoons, are hand-lettered.

56 *Fossils Tell of Long Ago*. Ill. by author. HarperCollins, pap., 1990, ISBN 0-06-445093-7. SERIES: Let's-Read-and-Find-Out Science. SUBJECTS: Fossils; Museums; Science and scientists. RL B.

Lively dialogue among children visiting a natural history museum adds flavor to the easy-reading information about fossils. Appealing ink and colored pencil drawings include children making their own imprints.

57 *How a Book Is Made*. Ill. by author. HarperCollins, 1985, ISBN 0-690-04498-4. SUBJECTS: Books and reading; Careers. RL C.

Aliki likes how a book feels, looks, and smells. She details the stages of a book's creation through publication. Cat characters in soft pastel cartoons even show details of color separation and printing.

58 *I'm Growing*. Ill. by author. HarperCollins, 1992, ISBN 0-06-020245-9. SERIES: Let's-Read-and-Find-Out Science. SUBJECTS: Human body — Growth. RL B.

A small Hispanic boy marks his growth by how his clothes fit, by how his measurements increase, and by looking at a photo album. Appealing presentation and illustrations.

59 *The King's Day: Louis XIV of France*. Ill. by author. HarperCollins, 1989, ISBN 0-690-04588-3. SUBJECTS: Biographies; France; Kings and queens. RL C.

The extravagant rituals of a day in the life of the Sun King are lavishly illustrated with detailed delicate watercolors and interesting text. A chronology and some French definitions are appended.

60 *Long-Lost Coelacanth and Other Living Fossils*. Ill. by author. HarperCollins, 1973, o.p. SERIES: Let's-Read-and-Find-Out Science. SUBJECTS: Fish, prehistoric; Fossils, living. RL C.

The drama of the 1938 discovery that the coelacanth was not extinct 70 million years ago is captured in simple language. Horses, starfish, algae, and horseshoe crabs are some of the other living fossils introduced. Children are asked to guess what living fossil the author does not save!

Aliki (cont.)

61 *Milk: From Cow to Carton*. Ill. by author. HarperCollins, 1974, 1992, ISBN 0-06-020435-4. SERIES: Let's-Read-and-Find-Out Science. SUBJECTS: Cows; Food; Science and scientists. RL A.

From a pastoral landscape to a cow barn, from cow anatomy to a dairy schematic, the illustrations are tidy and appealing. The wonder of the process is not lost.

62 *My Feet*. Ill. by author. HarperCollins, 1990, ISBN 0-690-04815-7. SERIES: Let's-Read-and-Find-Out Science. SUBJECTS: Human body — Feet; Science and scientists. RL A.

Anatomy, size, differences, functioning, coverings, and comfort of feet are outlined, with the author/illustrator's characteristic simple colored-pencil illustrations.

63 *My Hands*. Ill. by author. HarperCollins, 1990, 1992, ISBN 0-690-04880-7. SUBJECTS: Human body — Hands. RL A.

Appealing drawings of preschoolers working with clay, painting, sewing, buttoning, and petting a kitten illustrate the functions and usefulness of hands. Even sign language and gesturing are mentioned in this thorough and lively account for the younger set.

64 *My Visit to the Aquarium*. Ill. by author. HarperCollins, 1993, ISBN 0-06-021459-7. SUBJECTS: Fish; Oceans and ocean life; Science and scientists. RL A.

Drawings based on several aquariums narrow the field from the wider setting to individual animals in stages. Characteristics interesting to children are featured, from tidal pools to coastal streams to coral reefs.

65 *My Visit to the Dinosaurs*. 2nd ed. Ill. by author. HarperCollins, 1985, ISBN 0-690-04423-2. SERIES: Let's-Read-and-Find-Out Science. SUBJECTS: Dinosaurs; Science and scientists. RL C.

A small boy visits a natural history museum and learns about 15 common dinosaurs, as well as the work of paleontologists. Information is well presented and appealingly illustrated with ink sketches having green, turquoise, and gray washes.

66 *The Story of Johnny Appleseed*. Ill. by author. Prentice-Hall, 1963, o.p. SUBJECTS: Biographies; Trees. RL C.

The outline of Johnny Appleseed's life and legend is given in sympathetic terms. Bold, decorative sketches underline his friendly relations with Native Americans and animals.

67 *A Weed Is a Flower: The Life of George Washington Carver*. Ill. by author. Simon & Schuster, 1988, ISBN 0-671-66118-3. SUBJECTS: Biographies; Science and scientists. RL C.

A laudatory outline of this talented man's life and accomplishments.

68 *Wild and Woolly Mammoths*. Ill. by author. HarperCollins, pap., 1983, ISBN 0-690-01276-4. SERIES: Let's-Read-and-Find-Out Science. SUBJECTS: Animals — Extinct. RL C.

In 1901 a frozen 10,000-year-old woolly mammoth was found with 30 pounds of flower, pine needles, moss, and pine cones in its stomach. Facts about Stone Age culture relating to mammoths are skillfully woven into this fascinating account. Ink and pencil sketches are in turquoise and brown.

Allard, Harry

69 *There's a Party at Mona's Tonight*. Ill. by James Marshall. Doubleday, 1979, o.p. SUBJECTS: Parties — Fiction; Pigs — Fiction. RL C.

Potter Pig repeatedly tries to inveigle an invitation to Mona's party; however, he's not invited because of his lack of tact. Arched-framed solid colors in sketches are in pig-pink, black, yellow, and turquoise.

Allen, Laura J.

70 *Ottie and the Star*. Ill. by author. HarperCollins, 1979, o.p. SERIES: Early I Can Read. SUBJECTS: Otters — Fiction. RL B.

A small otter encounters a shark, a dolphin, and a starfish trying to reach a star. Watercolor washes fit the watery setting well.

71 *Rollo and Tweedy and the Ghost at Dougal Castle*. Ill. by author. HarperCollins, 1992, ISBN 0-06-020107-X.

SERIES: I Can Read. SUBJECTS: Ghost stories; Mice — Fiction; Mystery and detective stories. RL A.

Readers are challenged to decipher simple clues, false and true, to uncover the identity of the ghost impersonator at a Scottish castle. Full-color illustrations are used against an inventive, interesting castle backdrop.

72 *Where Is Freddy?* Ill. by author. HarperCollins, 1986, o.p. SERIES: I Can Read. SUBJECTS: Imagination — Fiction; Mice — Fiction; Mystery and detective stories. RL B.

When rich Mrs. Trumbly's grandson Freddy is missing, Rollo and Tweedy follow the clues of missing coat hangers, sheets, and laundry basket to track him down. This story of imagination and logic is illustrated with ink and wash drawings of expressive mouse characters.

Allen, Marjorie N.

73 *One, Two, Three-Ah-Choo!* Ill. by Dick Gackenbach. Putnam, 1980, o.p. SERIES: Break-of-Day. SUBJECTS: Allergies — Fiction; Pets — Fiction. RL B.

Because of allergies, Wally cannot have the usual furry pets. Readers learn with him about hermit crabs. Gackenbach's warm, fuzzy drawings are in pumpkin and gray.

Allen, Marjorie N., and Carl Allen

74 *Farley, Are You for Real?* Ill. by Joel Schick. Putnam, 1976, o.p. SUBJECTS: Humorous stories; Magic — Fiction. RL B.

The misadventures of an inept genie named Farley give Archie a taste of fear and wonder when he shrinks to two inches in height. Excellent pen and ink drawings give perspective, humor, and drama.

Alley, R. W. (Robert W.)

75 *Ghost in Dobbs Diner.* Ill. by author. Parents Magazine Press, 1981, ISBN 0-8193-1055-7; pap., ISBN 0-8368-0884-3. SERIES: Read Aloud Library. SUBJECTS: Ghost stories. RL B.

Samuel Sheets, ghost and world traveler, makes himself useful at Mr. Dobbs's busy diner after appearing from a dusty pickle jar, but the busboy, cook, waitress, and customers are afraid. Soft pastel washes have milkshakes for the cover border and a very friendly ghost.

Allington, Richard L.

76 *Hearing.* Ill. by Wayne Dober. Raintree, 1980, o.p. SERIES: Beginning to Learn About. SUBJECTS: Senses — Hearing; Sound. RL B.

The sounds of vehicles and animals are drawn with onomatopoeic words such as "caroo," "moo," and "crackle." Collages in soft colors draw attention to a myriad of familiar sounds.

Allington, Richard L., and Kathleen Krull

77 *Spring.* Ill. by Lynn Uhde. Raintree, 1981, ISBN 0-8172-1342-2. SERIES: Beginning to Learn About. SUBJECTS: Spring. RL B.

The reader is asked about feelings, sounds, sports, and other signs of spring. Soft watercolors show the play, flora, and fauna of the season.

Alphin, Elaine Marie

78 *A Bear for Miguel.* Ill. by Joan Sandin. HarperCollins, 1996, ISBN 0-06-024521-2. SERIES: I Can Read. SUBJECTS: El Salvador — Fiction; Family life — Fiction. RL B. LEXILE 400L.

In an El Salvador under siege, Maria and her father must trade their family possessions — even her dearly loved stuffed bear, Paco — for food and survival. A glossary of the Spanish words used within the text is included. Expressive watercolor illustrations capture the laughter and sadness of a war-torn country.

79 *Dinosaur Hunter.* Ill. by Don Bolognese. HarperCollins, 2003, ISBN 0-06-028303-3. SERIES: I Can Read. SUBJECTS: Dinosaurs — Fiction; Fossils — Fiction; United States — History — Fiction. RL B.

On his father's Wyoming ranch in the 1880s, Ned discovers a fossilized Triceratops skeleton while out looking for fences to mend. He meets up with the son of paleontologist Charles Sternberg. The skeleton is sold and displayed in a museum. Based on historical events, this story is further enhanced by earth-toned illustrations that reflect the times.

Anders, Rebecca

80 *Dolly the Donkey*. Orig. French by Anne-Marie Pajot, trans. by Dyan Hammarberg. Photos by Antoinette Barrere and drawings by L'Enc Matte. Carolrhoda, 1976, o.p. SERIES: Animal Friends. SUBJECTS: Donkeys; Pet care; Pets. RL C.

Four children acquire Dolly the donkey and her cart. They learn about the joys and aggravations of caring for a new pet. Color photographs alternate with black-and-white. Occasional drawings give close-ups of hooves or carrying baskets.

81 *Lorito the Parrot*. Orig. French by Anne-Marie Pajot, trans. by Dyan Hammarberg. Ill. by Colyann and L'Enc Matte. Carolrhoda, 1976, o.p. SERIES: Animal Friends. SUBJECTS: Parrots; Pet care; Pets. RL C.

Children visiting their neighbor who owns a parrot learn about its habits, beak, toes, diet, eyes, and native habitat. Black-and-white close-up photographs alternate with color photographs in this easy nonfiction book.

82 *Winslow the Hamster*. Orig. French by Anne-Marie Pajot, trans. by Dyan Hammarberg. Ill. by Rank and L'Enc Matte. Carolrhoda, 1977, o.p. SERIES: Animal Friends. SUBJECTS: Hamsters; Pet care; Pets. RL C.

Well-presented facts about hamster habits, history, and charm. Excellent photographs with some drawings.

Anderson, Peggy P.

83 *Time for Bed, the Babysitter Said*. Ill. by author. Houghton Mifflin, 1987, ISBN 0-395-41851-8. SUBJECTS: Baby-sitting — Fiction; Bedtime — Fiction; Frogs and toads — Fiction. RL A.

Joe is very elusive, and the baby-sitter unimaginative, when it is time for bed. A "please" finally turns the tables in this simplistic bedtime saga. Three-tone drawings have plenty of action and nice froglike touches.

Applebaum, Stan

84 *Going My Way: Nature's Hitchhikers*. Ill. by Leonard Shortall. Harcourt, 1976, o.p. SERIES: Let Me Read. SUBJECTS: Nature; Science and scientists. RL C.

Suckerfish, oxpeckers, burrs, fleas, and beeeaters are some of the hitchhikers introduced. Illustrative sketches have a hint of color.

Archbold, Tim

85 *The Race*. Ill. by author. Holt, 1988, o.p. SUBJECTS: Concepts — Space — Fiction; Stories in rhyme. RL A.

A huge dog accompanies a gloved and helmeted boy on a headlong, crazy cart ride home for dinner. This outrageous adventure is underscored by ink washed sketches of a cart whose wheels rarely touch the ground. Very limited vocabulary is expanded by the illustrations.

Ardley, Neil

86 *The Science Book of Light*. Photos by Pete Gardner. Harcourt, 1991, ISBN 0-15-200577-3. SUBJECTS: Light; Science and scientists; Science experiments. RL C.

Experiments range from objects distorted in water to shadow puppets, periscopes, and kaleidoscopes. Color photographs in primary colors against a white ground are very appealing. Ever-popular photographic paper is used to create silhouettes.

Armitage, Ronda, and David Armitage

87 *Harry Hates Shopping!* Ill. by authors. Scholastic, pap., 1993, ISBN 0-590-45886-8. SERIES: Hello Reader! SUBJECTS: Behavior — Fiction; Humorous stories; Koalas — Fiction. RL A.

With a most imaginative twist, Mother Koala convinces her children that their teasing and bickering while shopping should stop. Acceptable illustrations show Mother's satisfaction with improved behavior clearly.

Armstrong, Jennifer

88 *The Snowball*. Ill. by Jean Pidgeon. Random House, pap., 1996, ISBN 0-679-86444-X. SERIES: Early Step into Reading. SUBJECTS: Humorous stories; Stories in rhyme; Weather — Snow — Fiction. RL A. LEXILE 100L.

Follow the escapades of a snowball as it rolls down the hill, accumulating momentum, size, and people! With a perfect match of illustration and text, the result is a riotous adventure, with repetition and predictability that will have beginners reading it again and again.

89 *Sunshine, Moonshine*. Ill. by Lucia Washburn. Random House, 1997, ISBN 0-679-96442-8. SERIES: Early Step into Reading. SUBJECTS: Astronomy and astronomers; Stories in rhyme. RL A. LEXILE 380L.

From the early morning awakening of the day until the night comes to end the play, a simple repetitive rhyme shares the joy of the moon and sun. Quiet and gentle earth-toned full-page illustrations celebrate every moment of the day.

Arnold, Marsha

90 *Quick Quack Quick!* Ill. by Lisa McCue. Random House, pap., 1996, ISBN 0-679-87243-4. SERIES: Early Step into Reading. SUBJECTS: Ducks — Fiction. RL A. LEXILE 170L.

Always lagging behind, Quack is constantly reminded by mama duck to be quick. But those stops for berries to eat and places to explore eventually save the duck family's day! Bright, breezy, detailed illustrations provide the visual clues and fun for very beginning readers.

Arnold, Tedd

91 *Hi! Fly Guy*. Ill. by author. Scholastic, 2005, ISBN 0-439-63903-4. SUBJECTS: Flies — Fiction; Humorous stories; Pets — Fiction. RL B.

Looking for a pet to take to the "Amazing Pet Show," a boy meets a fly that not only can do amazing tricks but is smart and can say the boy's name, Buzz! From the attractive holographic cover to the wacky, pop-eyed Fly Guy, the comical illustrations are a great, playful match to the story.

92 *Shoo, Fly Guy!* Ill. by author. Scholastic, 2006, ISBN 0-439-63905-0. SUBJECTS: Flies — Fiction; Humorous stories; Pets — Fiction. RL B.

On the lookout for his favorite food — anything that is "brown, oozy, lumpy and smelly" — Fly Guy searches but is shooed away from people's food. Finally he spots the perfect thing at a picnic, with his friend Buzz. Illustrations flying high on fun and the "gross factor" will attract readers to the adventures.

93 *Super Fly Guy*. Ill. by author. Scholastic, 2006, ISBN 0-439-63904-2. SUBJECTS: Flies — Fiction; Humorous stories; Pets — Fiction; School stories. RL B.

At school one day, Buzz and his pet fly learn a lot, but Fly Guy's very favorite place is the lunchroom and the garbage cans. When Roz the cook is fired, Fly Guy comes to her aid and is rewarded with a special garbage soup. From the glitzy cover to the endearingly exaggerated characters, *Fly Guy* is a hit.

Arnosky, Jim

94 *Crinkelroot's Guide to Knowing the Birds*. Ill. by author. Macmillan, 1992, ISBN 0-02-705857-3. SUBJECTS: Birds; Nature. RL C.

Bearded Crinkleroot introduces some of the techniques and basics of bird-watching. Bird songs, coloring, habitat, anatomy, and life cycle are appealingly described and illustrated, as are ways to attract and feed familiar species.

95 *Crinkelroot's Guide to Knowing the Trees*. Ill. by author. Macmillan, 1991, ISBN 0-02-705855-7. SUBJECTS: Nature; Trees. RL C.

Crinkleroot, the droll, bearded naturalist, tells how a tree grows and introduces deciduous trees and conifers, the wildlife that inhabits various levels of the forest, and some of the idiosyncrasies of individual trees. Charming ink and wash sketches enhance the text.

Asch, Frank

96 *Bread and Honey*. Ill. by author. Crown, pap., 1988, ISBN 0-8193-1077-8. SERIES: Read Aloud and Easy Reading. SUBJECTS: Bears — Fiction. RL B.

Ben's picture of his mother is modified by all his animal friends until it has features taken from many animals, but his mother likes it anyway. The warm story is illustrated with large drawings in flat primary colors.

Aseltine, Lorraine

97 *First Grade Can Wait*. Ill. by Virginia Wright Frierson. Whitman, 1988, ISBN 0-8075-2451-4. SUBJECTS: Behavior; Schools. RL B.

Luke likes singing, his teacher, and art in kindergarten, but has trouble paying attention, playing cooperatively, and sharing with the class. Pencil drawings and facing blue-type text are framed in light blue.

Averill, Esther

98 *Fire Cat*. Ill. by author. HarperCollins, pap., 1960, ISBN 0-06-020196-7. SERIES: I Can Read. SUBJECTS: Pets — Cats — Fiction. RL A.

Pickles makes up for some of his mischief when he becomes a fire cat. Stylized drawings are highlighted in red, black, and sunshine yellow.

Avi

99 *Abigail Takes the Wheel*. Ill. by Don Bolognese. HarperCollins, 1999, ISBN 0-06-027662-2. SERIES: I Can Read Chapter Book. SUBJECTS: Fathers — Fiction; Historical fiction; Ships and shipping — Fiction. RL B.

On their way to school aboard a paddle-wheel freight boat, Abigail and her brother Tom must pilot the boat while their father tries to save a damaged sailing ship. With watercolor and ink illustrations that set the 1880s stage, this is the story of a courageous young girl who earns the title of Captain Abigail.

100 *Prairie School*. Ill. by Bill Farnsworth. HarperCollins, 2001, o.p. SERIES: I Can Read Chapter Book. SUBJECTS: Books and reading; Disabilities — Physical and mental — Fiction. RL B. LEXILE 410L.

In 1880s Colorado, Aunt Dora comes to the prairie to teach Noah to read and write. Confined to a wheelchair, she struggles to interest the reluctant boy until she begins teaching him about the prairie he loves. Full-page, muted illustrations reflect the family love and the vastness of their surroundings.

Awdry, W.

101 *Thomas the Tank Engine and the School Trip: Based on The Railway Series*. Ill. by Owain Bell. Random House, 1993, ISBN 0-679-94365-X. SERIES: Step into Reading. SUBJECTS: Trains — Fiction. RL A.

Thomas the Tank Engine tries to hurry through his route so he can take a group of children home from a school trip. Very limited vocabulary is illustrated with cartoons.

B

Bader, Bonnie

102 *Graphs*. Ill. by Mernie Gallagher Cole. Grosset & Dunlap, pap., 2003, ISBN 0-448-42896-2. SERIES: All Aboard Reading. SUBJECTS: Family life — Fiction; Mathematics — Fiction; Mathematics — Graphs — Fiction. RL B.

While attending the Graff Family Reunion, Gary finds many ways to complete his math homework and have fun. He graphs temperature, food choices, and even how many use a napkin! Cartoon illustrations in bright summer colors incorporate the math concept in the everyday world with humor.

Baeten, Lieve

103 *Nicky at the Magic House*. Ill. by author. Annick, pap., 1993, ISBN 1-55037-271-8. SUBJECTS: Witches — Fiction. RL B.

Nicky the witch and her cat Theodore, cruising on their broomstick late at night, find a house with all the lights on. They find a musical witch, a cooking witch, and a sleeping witch — but it is the fixing witch who sends them on their way. Wistful soft watercolor drawings set the tone.

Baker, Barbara

104 *Digby and Kate*. Ill. by Marsha Winborn. Dutton, 1988, ISBN 0-525-44370-3. SERIES: Dutton Easy Reader. SUBJECTS: Friendship — Fiction; Pets — Cats — Fiction; Pets — Dogs — Fiction. RL A.

Digby and Kate, a dog and cat respectively, are very different in temperament but still best friends. Pastel patterned drawings are somewhat stylized and romantic.

105 *Digby and Kate Again*. Ill. by Marsha Winborn. Dutton, 1989, ISBN 0-525-44477-7. SUBJECTS: Friendship — Fiction; Pets — Cats — Fiction; Pets — Dogs — Fiction. RL A.

Four chapters show the relationship between the cat and dog friends — in the garden, with a new bicycle, raking leaves, and procrastinating about letter writing. Jewel-like colored drawings show the pair's mishaps and antics.

106 *Digby and Kate and the Beautiful Day*. Ill. by Marsha Winborn. Dutton, 1998, o.p. SUBJECTS: Friendship — Fiction; Pets — Cats — Fiction; Pets — Dogs — Fiction. RL B. LEXILE 130L.

Good friends Digby the dog and Kate the cat share adventures and sometimes arguments. Taking pictures, eating pizza, and a walk in the rain with warm cocoa afterward are all portrayed in expressive illustrations that extend the text on every page.

107 *Digby and Kate 1, 2, 3*. Ill. by Marsha Winborn. Dutton, 2004, ISBN 0-525-46854-4. SUBJECTS: Friendship — Fiction; Pets — Cats — Fiction; Pets — Dogs — Fiction. RL B.

Five more stories continue the ups and downs of being best friends as Digby the dog and Kate the cat learn to compromise and work out their differences. The variety of emotions expressed in the animals' daily encounters is shown in thoughtfully detailed illustrations.

108 *One Saturday Afternoon*. Ill. by Kate Duke. Dutton, 1999, o.p. SUBJECTS: Bears — Fiction; Family life — Fiction. RL B.

On a Saturday afternoon, Mama and Papa Bear and their four cubs bake bread, play together, and have some family squabbles. Conveying warm feelings of familial love, pastel watercolors provide a lively counterpoint to the brief chapter stories.

109 *Staying with Grandmother*. Ill. by Judith B. Schachne. Dutton, 1994, ISBN 0-525-44603-6. SERIES: Dutton Easy Reader. SUBJECTS: Grandparents — Fiction; Homesickness — Fiction. RL A.

Clair feels more at home at her grandmother's after meeting a new friend, hearing her mother's favorite Alice in Wonderland story, and sleeping with her mother's old White Rabbit stuffed animal. Pencil and wash drawings supply a comfy, old-fashioned setting for grandmother's house.

Baker, Betty

110 *All-by-Herself*. Ill. by Catherine Stock. Greenwillow, 1980, o.p. SERIES: Read-Alone. SUBJECTS: Giants — Fiction. RL B.

Even after she kills the ice giant, the villagers still do not welcome All-by-Herself because she is different. Three-tone washes on ink sketches are striking.

111 *The Big Push*. Ill. by Bonnie Johnson. Putnam, 1972, o.p. SERIES: Break-of-Day. SUBJECTS: Hopi. RL B.

The Big Push was the final break between the Hopi who accepted white influence, however reluctantly, and those who did not. Sympathetic historical treatment is illustrated with shadowy pencil drawings.

112 *Little Runner of the Longhouse*. Ill. by Arnold Lobel. HarperCollins, 1962, ISBN 0-06-020341-2. SERIES: I Can Read. SUBJECTS: Cumulative tales; Native Americans — Fiction. RL B.

Little Runner tries to trade his baby brother for some adventure in imitation of his elders on New Year's Day. Lobel adds authentic details of life in the longhouse.

113 *No Help at All*. Ill. by Emily A. McCully. Greenwillow, 1978, o.p. SERIES: Read-Alone. SUBJECTS: Folklore — Mexico; Mexico — Fiction. RL B.

The West Wind puts a Mayan boy to work after rescuing him from a man-eating "thing," but returns him home when all his own efforts to escape end in disaster. Simple, expressive drawings are well suited to this Mayan legend.

114 *Partners*. Ill. by Emily A. McCully. Greenwillow, 1978, o.p. SERIES: Read-Alone. SUBJECTS: Animals — Fiction; Friendship — Fiction. RL B.

Badger and Coyote have an imperfect friendship as they hang stars, grow crops, and hunt prairie

Baker, Betty (cont.)

dogs. Themes and humor have a folktale base. Pastel pencils color the excellent ink drawings.

115 *Pig War*. Ill. by Robert Lopshire. HarperCollins, 1969, o.p. SERIES: I Can Read History. SUBJECTS: Historical fiction; United States — 1783–1865 — Fiction. RL B.
A squabble about whether Britain or America owns a Puget Sound island is settled when a pig is paid for. Three-color comic illustrations are simple yet effective.

116 *Rat Is Dead and Ant Is Sad*. Ill. by Mamoru Funai. HarperCollins, 1981, o.p. SERIES: I Can Read. SUBJECTS: Cumulative tales; Native Americans — Legends; Pueblo (Native American people). RL C.
This unusual cumulative tale includes a rat, an ant, a jay, a cottonwood tree, a sheep, a Pueblo family, and a horse. Illustrations pick up the patterns and colors of the Southwest and Pueblo culture.

117 *Three Fools and a Horse*. Ill. by Glen Rounds. Macmillan, 1975, o.p. SERIES: Ready-to-Read. SUBJECTS: Folklore — Native Americans; Humorous stories; Native Americans — Fiction. RL B.
The Apaches' Foolish People have trouble locating a buffalo, cooking food, and staying on a horse. The comic ink drawings emphasize the People's potbellies and the looks of disgust on the horses' faces. This nonsense tale is effectively told and illustrated.

118 *The Turkey Girl*. Ill. by Harold Berson. Macmillan, 1983, o.p. SERIES: Ready-to-Read. SUBJECTS: Behavior — Brave — Fiction; Turkeys — Fiction. RL B.
Elements of the Cinderella story are woven into this tale of an orphan girl's devotion to her turkeys. Her bravery, protecting them from a wolf, earns her a family at last. Berson's graceful line drawings have a folktale flavor.

119 *Worthington Botts and the Steam Machine*. Ill. by Sal Murdocca. Macmillan, 1981, o.p. SERIES: Ready-to-Read. SUBJECTS: Books and reading — Fiction; Robots — Fiction. RL C.
Worthington Botts reads all the time — until he builds a labor-saving robot. His continuing temptations to read are especially creative. Murdocca's four-color cartoon drawings complement the text perfectly.

Baker, Keith

120 *Lucky Days with Mr. and Mrs. Green*. Ill. by author. Harcourt, 2005, ISBN 0-152-16500-2. SUBJECTS: Alligators — Fiction; Humorous stories. RL B. LEXILE 400L.
In three short stories, the loving alligator couple share excitement as they solve a mystery, win a gumball guessing contest, and star in a talent show. Vibrant illustrations, with a predominance of alligator green, mirror the energy and fun that are the essence of this special relationship.

121 *More Mr. and Mrs. Green*. Ill. by author. Harcourt, 2004, ISBN 0-152-16494-4. SUBJECTS: Alligators — Fiction; Humorous stories. RL B.
Bright splashy illustrations complement the many fun-filled adventures of these two special alligators. They enjoy each other's company as they fish, paint, and take a walk in the park. And no matter what they do, good food is always included.

122 *On the Go with Mr. and Mrs. Green*. Ill. by author. Harcourt, pap., 2007, ISBN 978-0-15-205867-8. SUBJECTS: Alligators — Fiction; Humorous stories. RL B.
These special alligators do everything together. As Mr. Green tries his hand at magic, Mrs. Green whips up a batch of delicious cookies and they both catch the inventing bug. Humor abounds in both story and illustration as large lively "green-filled" drawings depict the alligator action.

123 *Sometimes*. Ill. by author. Harcourt, 2003, ISBN 0-152-04807-3. SERIES: Green Light Readers. SUBJECTS: Alligators — Fiction; Emotions — Fiction. RL B.
Whether he is cooking, playing the banjo, or ice fishing, an alligator shares his emotions about the various activities. Expressive illustrations provide contextual visual clues to an engaging story.

Balestrino, Philip

124 *Hot as an Ice Cube*. Ill. by Tomie dePaola. HarperCollins, 1970, o.p. SERIES: Let's-Read-and-Find-Out Science. SUBJECTS: Science and scientists; Science experiments. RL C.

Household items provide a way to test many concepts relating to temperature. Well-presented facts are illustrated in turquoise and cocoa.

125 *The Skeleton Inside You.* Ill. by True Kelley. HarperCollins, 1989, ISBN 0-690-04733-9. SERIES: Let's-Read-and-Find-Out Science. SUBJECTS: Human body — Skeleton. RL C.
The function, parts, and connectors of human bones are outlined in a clear, understandable way. Large colorful framed drawings enliven the text.

Ball, Jacqueline A.

126 *What Can It Be? Riddles About the Senses.* Ill. with photos. Silver Burdett, 1989, ISBN 0-671-68580-5. SUBJECTS: Jokes and riddles. RL C.
Rhyming riddles are imaginative, tickling the senses: hearing, touch, taste, smell. Bright-colored close-up photographs give the answers on the pages following the riddles, with additional facts about the subject or the riddle.

Bancroft, Catherine, and Hannah Coale Gruenberg

127 *Felix's Hat.* Ill. by Hannah Coale Gruenberg. Macmillan, 1993, ISBN 0-02-708325-X. SUBJECTS: Frogs and toads — Fiction; Hats — Fiction; Imagination — Fiction. RL B.
Felix's family tries to cheer Felix up after he loses his favorite hat while floating in his inner tube. Only his imagination relieves his sadness. Lively ink and watercolor drawings show frog family life.

Bang, Betsy

128 *Cucumber Stem.* Ill. by Tony Chen. Greenwillow, 1980, o.p. SERIES: Read-Alone. SUBJECTS: India — Fiction. RL C.
A Bengali tale of a magic cucumber and a brave man who is two fingers tall. There are stylized Indian design details.

129 *Tuntuni the Tailor Bird.* Ill. by Molly Bang. Greenwillow, 1978, o.p. SERIES: Read-Alone. SUBJECTS: Folklore — India; India — Fiction. RL C.
In the first cumulative tale, mosquitoes set off a chain of events in order to get the barber to remove a thorn from the bird Tuntuni's foot. In costume, design, characters, and vegetation, Molly Bang (daughter of the author) captures the flavor of Bengal and the humor of the tiny bird's escapades.

Bang, Molly G.

130 *Tye May and the Magic Brush.* Ill. by Molly Bang. Greenwillow, 1981, o.p. SERIES: Read-Alone. SUBJECTS: Folklore — China; Magic — Fiction. RL B.
When the emperor tries to steal Tye May's magic brush, he gets his just reward. This satisfying tale of magic is illustrated by delicate pencil and ink drawings.

131 *Wiley and the Hairy Man: Adapted from an American Folktale.* Ill. by Molly Bang. Macmillan, pap., 1976, ISBN 0-02-708370-5. SERIES: Ready-to-Read. SUBJECTS: Folklore — African Americans; Folklore — United States; Magic — Fiction. RL B.
Following his mother's instructions, Wiley tricks the powerful Hairy Man who lives in the swamp near the Tombigbee River. Based on a well-known American folktale, this version is suitable for telling. Charcoal grays of pencil and paint are superbly apt for the Tennessee tale.

Bang-Campbell, Monika

132 *Little Rat Rides.* Ill. by Molly Bang. Harcourt, 2004, ISBN 0-152-04667-4. SUBJECTS: Fear — Fiction; Horses — Fiction; Rats — Fiction. RL B.
Eager to follow in her father's footsteps, Little Rat wants to learn to ride and take part in the Fourth of July parade. She manages to overcome her fears and she and her horse Pee Wee even win a ribbon. Richly colored illustrations offer interesting perspectives that underscore the real fears the rat must face.

133 *Little Rat Sets Sail.* Ill. by Molly Bang. Harcourt, 2002, ISBN 0-152-16297-6. SUBJECTS: Fear — Fiction; Rats — Fiction; Sports — Sailing — Fiction. RL B. LEXILE 540L.
Little Rat's parents sign her up for sailing lessons despite the fact she is frightened of the water. With the help of an able instructor, Little Rat becomes a little bit braver and maybe will sail by herself next summer. Reflecting the water, ocean-drenched color illustrations gently invite the reader to share in Little Rat's adventures.

Bare, Colleen S.

134 *Never Grab a Deer by the Ear.* Ill. by author. Dutton, 1993, ISBN 0-525-65112-8. SUBJECTS: Deer; Nature. RL B.

Information about the deer's life cycle, enemies, food, and especially antlers is given in large, clear type with excellent color photographs.

Barker, Henry

135 *It Came from Outer Space.* Ill. by Barry Gott. Kane, pap., 2003, ISBN 1-57565-122-X. SUBJECTS: Science and scientists; Space. RL B.

While sleeping outside, three friends witness a bright light streaking across the night sky. What can it be? Colorful, saturated, cartoon-like illustrations show the boys' curiosity and fear while science information boxes explain the action.

Barr, Catherine

136 *Bears In — Bears Out.* Ill. by author. Henry Z. Walck, 1967, o.p. SUBJECTS: Bears — Fiction. RL C.

At Yellowstone National Park two bear cubs get a car ride unbeknownst to the family. The credible story has child appeal. Crayon and ink drawings and hand-lettered text are very effective.

137 *Gingercat's Catch.* Ill. by author. Henry Z. Walck, 1970, o.p. SUBJECTS: India — Fiction; Pets — Cats — Fiction. RL C.

The competition is fierce when Gingercat tries out for a job as a watchcat at the state office in India. Hand-lettered text goes well with the yellow and gray pencil illustrations.

Barrett, Joyce D.

138 *Willie's Not the Hugging Kind.* Ill. by Pat Cummings. HarperCollins, 1989, ISBN 0-06-020416-8. SUBJECTS: African Americans — Fiction; Family life — Fiction. RL C.

When Willie's friend Jo-Jo makes fun of hugging, Willie feels left out of the warm embraces in his family. His sister Rose lets him know that it's "them that don't get hugging who think it's silly." An effective message is reinforced by the single-page color drawings and black-and-white headers.

Barrett, Judi

139 *I'm too small, YOU'RE TOO BIG.* Ill. by David Rose. Atheneum, 1981, o.p. SUBJECTS: Concepts — Size; Fathers. RL C.

Contrasts between father and small son are pleasantly exaggerated in framed ink and wash drawings.

Barrett, Ron

140 *Hi-Yo, Fido!* Ill. by author. Crown, 1984, o.p. SUBJECTS: Humorous stories. RL C.

This modern tall tale about how dogboys and doggirls become cowboys and cowgirls has many inventive touches. Rock formations include a huge fire hydrant and a bowl for dog biscuits; dog bones are carried on the "Bony Express." Busy four-color illustrations delight the eye.

Bartels, Alice L.

141 *The Grandmother Doll.* Ill. by Farida Zaman. Annick, 1993, ISBN 1-55037-337-4. SUBJECTS: Family life — Fiction; Imagination — Fiction. RL B.

Grandmother Doll comes to the rescue when Katy and her mother are having a bad day and Katy is banished to her room. Katy ends up making a TV, a stove, and a bed for Grandmother. It seems that Mother also knows about Grandmother Doll. Framed watercolor wash drawings are lighthearted.

Bartlett, Margaret

142 *Where Does All the Rain Go?* Ill. by Patricia Collins. Putnam, 1973, o.p. SERIES: Science Is What and Why. SUBJECTS: Science and scientists; Water. RL C.

The rain cycle is simply and expertly described. Ink sketches have block-printed highlights in gold and royal blue.

Bason, Lillian

143 *Those Foolish Molboes!* Ill. by Margot Tomes. Putnam, 1977, o.p. SUBJECTS: Denmark — Fiction; Folklore — Denmark; Humorous stories. RL C.

In the first of three tales in this book, the foolish Molboes mark the watery hiding place of the village bell on the boat! Tomes's excellent illustrations have a homely folk flavor and interesting detail.

Bauer, Marion Dane

144 *Bear's Hiccups*. Ill. by Diane Dawson Hearn. Holiday House, 1998, ISBN 0-8234-1339-X. SUBJECTS: Bears — Fiction; Frogs and toads — Fiction; Hiccups — Fiction. RL B.

On the hottest day of summer, Frog and Bear dispute who owns the cool pond. A face-to-face confrontation leads to Frog's disappearance and a bad case of the hiccups for Bear. Earth-toned watercolor and ink illustrations depict the woodland home of these forest friends.

145 *Christmas in the Forest*. Ill. by Diane Dawson Hearn. Holiday House, 1998, ISBN 0-8234-1371-3. SUBJECTS: Christmas — Fiction; Mice — Fiction; Pets — Cats — Fiction. RL B.

Locked outside on a cold Christmas Eve, a hungry cat looks for supper. She lures a baby mouse with a promise to tell about Christmas but is dissuaded from eating it. Detailed, realistic drawings of the woodland creatures embrace the spirit of the evening and the hope of a Christmas baby.

146 *Clouds*. Ill. by John Wallace. Simon & Schuster, pap., 2004, ISBN 0-689-85441-2. SERIES: Ready-to-Read. SUBJECTS: Weather — Clouds. RL B. LEXILE 240L.

Basic facts introduce three kinds of clouds — cirrus, stratus, and cumulus — and their characteristics. Simple line and watercolor illustrations demonstrate the cloud formations and the types of weather they bring, using a little boy and his cat.

147 *Frog's Best Friend*. Ill. by Diane Dawson Hearn. Holiday House, 2002, ISBN 0-8234-1501-5. SUBJECTS: Friendship — Fiction; Frogs and toads — Fiction. RL B.

Turning even greener with envy, Frog wants to be Turtle's only friend. When a baby bear captures Turtle, everyone learns it's great to have lots of friends, especially when you are in trouble. Life around the pond is gently portrayed in earthy watercolors.

148 *The Grand Canyon*. Ill. by John Wallace. Simon & Schuster, 2006, ISBN 0-689-86947-9. SERIES: Ready-to-Read. SUBJECTS: United States. RL B.

Explore the history and development of the Grand Canyon in this volume in the Wonders of America series. Discover why more than five million people visit this amazing sight. Earth-toned watercolors enhance the simple text with cutaways, diagrams, and lively illustrations.

149 *Niagara Falls*. Ill. by John Wallace. Simon & Schuster, 2006, ISBN 0-689-86945-2. SERIES: Ready-to-Read. SUBJECTS: United States. RL B.

In this volume in the Wonders of America series, find out about North America's first tourist attraction. Colorful watercolor illustrations and diagrams reinforce the information on Niagara Falls, its location, and its exciting history.

150 *The Rocky Mountains*. Ill. by John Wallace. Simon & Schuster, 2006, ISBN 0-689-86949-5. SERIES: Ready-to-Read. SUBJECTS: Mountains; United States. RL B.

The backbone of America, the Rocky Mountains are more than 3,000 miles long. Learn about their history and the people and animals that live there. Brightly colored watercolors that are detailed and informative extend the text in this title from the Wonders of America series.

151 *Snow*. Ill. by John Wallace. Simon & Schuster, 2003, ISBN 0-689-85436-6. SERIES: Ready-to-Read. SUBJECTS: Weather; Weather — Snow. RL B. LEXILE 440L.

A young boy and his dog enjoy making a snowman, ice skating, and sledding; facts about snow are interspersed throughout the brief text. Diagrams of snowflakes are cleverly positioned for greater clarity.

152 *Turtle Dreams*. Ill. by Diane Dawson Hearn. Holiday House, 1997, ISBN 0-8234-1322-5. SUBJECTS: Dreams — Fiction; Turtles — Fiction; Weather — Winter — Fiction. RL B. LEXILE 240L.

With the approach of winter, Great-great-great Grandmother tells Turtle to gather dreams in preparation. But where can they be? Expressive watercolor drawings follow Turtle's determined journey from friend to friend around the pond, looking for just the right dream to last him all winter long.

Bauer, Marion Dane (cont.)

153 *Wind.* Ill. by John Wallace. Simon & Schuster, pap., 2003, ISBN 0-689-85443-9. SERIES: Ready-to-Read. SUBJECTS: Weather; Weather — Wind. RL B. LEXILE 370L.

Interspersed with simple diagrams, pastel watercolor illustrations of a young girl and her dog enliven a brief but clear explanation of wind and its force. Interesting facts about wind follow.

Baumgartner, Barbara, reteller

154 *Crocodile! Crocodile! Stories Told Around the World.* Ill. by Judith Moffatt. Dorling Kindersley, 1994, ISBN 1-56458-463-1. SUBJECTS: Folklore; Puppetry; Storytelling. RL B.

Stories from India, Puerto Rico, China, Appalachia, and Native American peoples are retold by a Pennsylvania storyteller and illustrated with bold, unusual cut-paper graphics. Stories include two about money and crocodile, "The Squeaky Old Bed," "How the Chipmunk Got His Stripes," and "Sody Soleratus."

Baynton, Martin

155 *Fifty and the Fox.* Ill. by author. Crown, 1986, o.p. SERIES: It's Great to Read. SUBJECTS: Tractors — Fiction. RL B.

When soft-hearted Wally is assigned to rid the farm of a fox, Fifty the tractor finds a creative way to help. Comic drawings are bright with sunshine and help make a tractor protagonist plausible.

156 *Fifty and the Great Race.* Ill. by author. Crown, 1987, o.p. SERIES: It's Great to Read. SUBJECTS: Fairs — Fiction; Rats — Fiction; Tractors — Fiction. RL C.

Some farmers make fun of the old-fashioned tractor, Fifty, at the fair, so it is up to Fifty to win the big tractor race to redeem himself. In a surprise ending, Fifty's friend Norris the rat saves the day. Colored pencil drawings are in pale pastels.

157 *Fifty Gets the Picture.* Ill. by author. Crown, 1987, o.p. SERIES: It's Great to Read. SUBJECTS: Friendship — Fiction; Humorous stories; Tractors — Fiction. RL C.

It turns out that Fifty the tractor has more than one talent! He gets help from his animal friends with his artistic triumphs. Intriguing perspective is relayed as much by soft pastel drawings as by text.

158 *Fifty Saves His Friend.* Ill. by author. Crown, 1986, o.p. SERIES: It's Great to Read. SUBJECTS: Pets — Cats — Fiction; Rats — Fiction; Tractors — Fiction. RL C.

Fifty the tractor's ingenious trick scares the cat away from his friend Norris the rat permanently. Sunshine yellow predominates in soft pastel drawings.

Beaumont, Karen

159 *Move Over Rover!* Ill. by Jane Dyer. Harcourt, 2006, ISBN 0-15-201979-0. SUBJECTS: Humorous stories; Pets — Dogs — Fiction; Stories in rhyme. RL B.

Rover isn't bored and alone for long in his doghouse when a storm comes. He is soon joined by cat, raccoon, squirrel, blue jay, snake, *and* skunk. Warm, cozy watercolor and acrylic illustrations follow the action of the rhythmic and repetitive text in a lively cumulative tale.

Bechtold, Lisze

160 *Buster and Phoebe: The Great Bone Game.* Ill. by author. Houghton Mifflin, 2003, ISBN 0-618-20862-3. SUBJECTS: Pets — Dogs — Fiction. RL B.

Learning how to train his bones to "stay" is a big task for new puppy Buster, but Phoebe is willing to teach him. Buster soon learns the tricks of the trade from a dog that has been around the block a few times. The comical expressions on the dogs' faces are a perfect match for the tongue-in-cheek humor.

Behrens, June

161 *How I Feel.* Photos by Vince Streano. Childrens Press, 1973, o.p. SUBJECTS: Emotions. RL B.

Examples of situations demonstrating feelings of anger, loneliness, pride, and love are given simply. Some of the situational photographs look posed, and the language is somewhat stilted.

162 *Juliette Low: Founder of the Girl Scouts of America.* Ill. with photos. Childrens

Press, 1988, ISBN 0-516-04171-1. SUBJECTS: Biographies; Camps and camping. RL C.

One of the best biographies of Juliette Low, the energetic, eccentric founder of the Girl Scouts of the United States of America. Her childhood, jet-set marriage, and later dedication to providing unique opportunities for girls are detailed. Black-and-white photographs illustrate the text.

163 *Look at the Sea Animals*. Photos by Vince Streano. Childrens Press, 1975, o.p. SUBJECTS: Animals; Nature; Oceans and ocean life. RL C.

A sea turtle, an octopus, a hermit crab, a dolphin, and a stingray are some of the sea animals introduced. Full-color photographs are faced by basic information.

Benchley, Nathaniel

164 *George the Drummer Boy*. Ill. by Don Bolognese. HarperCollins, pap., 1977, ISBN 0-06-020500-8. SERIES: I Can Read. SUBJECTS: Historical fiction; United States — Revolutionary War — Fiction. RL B.

A most unusual perspective on the beginning of the Revolutionary War told from the point of view of a British drummer boy. His feelings prior to and during the events at Concord are sketched. Red, blue, and gray drawings convey the flavor of the period.

165 *A Ghost Named Fred*. Ill. by Ben Shecter. HarperCollins, pap., 1968, ISBN 0-06-020474-5. SERIES: I Can Read Mystery. SUBJECTS: Ghost stories; Imagination — Fiction; Mystery and detective stories. RL B.

George's solitary, imaginative play directs him to a deserted house while he is still dressed as an astronaut. This leads to a treasure hunt with a gentle ghost named Fred. Four-color illustrations enhance this satisfying tale.

166 *Oscar Otter*. Ill. by Arnold Lobel. HarperCollins, pap., 1966, ISBN 0-06-020472-9. SERIES: I Can Read. SUBJECTS: Otters — Fiction. RL B.

Oscar's fancy slide takes him far from home — and his enemies spot him! He is chased by a procession of animals. Lively animal drawings are in earth tones against white.

167 *Red Fox and His Canoe*. Ill. by Arnold Lobel. HarperCollins, pap., 1964, ISBN 0-06-020476-1. SERIES: I Can Read. SUBJECTS: Animals — Fiction; Humorous stories; Native Americans — Fiction. RL B.

Red Fox is satisfied with a small canoe after three bears, two otters, a raccoon, and a moose wreck his larger one. Action illustrations concentrate on animal misadventures and add to the tongue-in-cheek humor.

168 *Running Owl the Hunter*. Ill. by Mamoru Funai. HarperCollins, 1979, o.p. SERIES: I Can Read. SUBJECTS: Growing up — Fiction; Humorous stories; Native Americans — Fiction. RL C.

When all his independent hunting schemes go astray, Running Owl is assisted by an eagle who takes pity on him. Two-tone washes warm humorous ink sketches.

169 *Sam the Minuteman*. Ill. by Arnold Lobel. HarperCollins, pap., 1969, ISBN 0-06-020479-6. SERIES: I Can Read History. SUBJECTS: Historical fiction; United States — Revolutionary War — Fiction. RL B.

A bare and unromanticized account of the unintentional beginning of the Revolutionary War. It is told from the point of view of the young son of a Minuteman, who tells of the suspense, fear, excitement, and pain of the encounter. Pencil drawings are historically accurate in feeling and detail.

170 *Several Tricks of Edgar Dolphin*. Ill. by Mamoru Funai. HarperCollins, 1970, ISBN 0-06-020468-0. SERIES: I Can Read. SUBJECTS: Dolphins — Fiction. RL B.

Edgar the dolphin escapes his captors after adding water to his shallow tank aboard a ship. The conclusion is satisfying without creating villains. Pencil drawings have two-tone washes.

171 *Small Wolf*. Ill. by Joan Sandin. HarperCollins, 1972, 1994, ISBN 0-06-020492-3. SERIES: I Can Read. SUBJECTS: Native Americans — Fiction; United States — Colonial period — Fiction. RL A.

From the perspective of a Native American boy, the consequences of European encroachment are presented. This well-researched, unsentimental view of history is illustrated with rich, detailed drawings.

Benchley, Nathaniel (cont.)

172 *Snorri and the Strangers.* Ill. by Don Bolognese. HarperCollins, 1976, o.p. SERIES: I Can Read History. SUBJECTS: Adventure stories; Canada; Historical fiction. RL B.

Snorri, the first white child born in North America, encounters some hostile natives before returning to Greenland with his family. Adventurous history is told in simple terms and illustrated with ink drawings and red and pale lemon washes.

173 *The Strange Disappearance of Arthur Cluck.* Ill. by Arnold Lobel. HarperCollins, pap., 1967, ISBN 0-06-020478-8. SERIES: I Can Read Mystery. SUBJECTS: Mystery and detective stories. RL B.

Ralph the owl identifies missing chick Arthur by the fact that he is the only chick who rides on someone's head. Wonderful animal expressions add zest to the pumpkin and green highlighted pencil drawings.

Bendick, Jeanne

174 *Shapes.* Ill. by author. Watts, 1968, o.p. SUBJECTS: Concepts — Shape. RL C.

Some shapes are flat, some three-dimensional; some names for shapes are specific and some general; shapes evoke a range of feelings. Fascinating ideas about shapes are interspersed with thought-provoking questions. Heavy ink and red drawings are somewhat dated, however.

Benjamin, Cynthia

175 *What's Going On?* Ill. by Dorothy Handelman. Millbrook, 1999, ISBN 0-7613-2070-9; pap., ISBN 0-7613-2095-4. SUBJECTS: Clowns — Fiction; Neighbors — Fiction. RL B.

As Josh follows the clues — a funny hat, a large comb, a balloon sculpture, balls, and scarves — he discovers who his new neighbor really is. Full-page color photographs of real people engaged in real-life activities entice beginning readers.

Bennett, Kelly

176 *Flag Day.* Children's Press, 2003, ISBN 0-516-22862-5. SERIES: Rookie Read-About Holidays. SUBJECTS: Flag Day; Holidays. RL B. LEXILE NC440L.

In celebration of the birthday of the American flag, cities and towns hold special parades and ceremonies on June 14th. Color photographs and maps aid in explaining the history of the flag, its symbolism, and proper flag etiquette.

Berenstain, Michael

177 *Michael Berenstain's Hop, Waddle, Swim!* Ill. by author. Western, 1992, ISBN 0-307-11578-X. SERIES: Fast Start. SUBJECTS: Animals — Fiction; Humorous stories; Stories in rhyme. RL A.

The movements of land and ocean creatures are suggested in rollicking wordplay and rhyme with a very simple vocabulary. Cartoon illustrations unfortunately show a whale whose mouth is lined with shark-like teeth.

178 *Michael Berenstain's When I Grow Up Oh, the Things I Can Be!* Ill. by author. Western, 1992, ISBN 0-307-11579-8. SERIES: Fast Start. SUBJECTS: Careers; Stories in rhyme. RL A.

Parenting is included in a series of occupations sketched with broad strokes. They range from oil rig worker, teacher, farmer, and cowboy or cowgirl to a human cannonball for the circus. Characteristic Berenstain cartoon illustrations accompany the text.

179 *The Panda Club's Tree House.* Ill. by author. Western, 1989, ISBN 0-307-11687-5. SERIES: Golden Easy Reader. SUBJECTS: Animals — Fiction. RL A.

Tiger Anne, Little Panda, Monkey Max, Rusty the Fox, and Polly — members of the Panda Club — look for the right tree in which to build a new clubhouse. Illustrations are cartoon ink in green, pink, orange, and yellow.

Berenstain, Stan, and Jan Berenstain

180 *The Bear Detectives.* Ill. by authors. Beginner Books, 1975, ISBN 0-394-93127-0. SERIES: I Can Read It All by Myself. SUBJECTS: Bears — Fiction; Humorous stories; Mystery and detective stories. RL B.

Pa and Snuff the sniff hound lead the Bear detectives astray repeatedly. Cartoon illustrations exaggerate the miscues.

181 *Bear Scouts*. Ill. by authors. Random House, 1967, ISBN 0-394-90046-4. SUBJECTS: Bears — Fiction; Camps and camping — Fiction; Stories in rhyme. RL B.

The Scouts end up rescuing boastful Pa again and again, relying on their trusty guidebook. Cartoon illustrations help point out Pa's follies.

182 *Bears in the Night*. Ill. by authors. Random House, 1971, ISBN 0-394-92286-7. SERIES: Bright and Early Books. SUBJECTS: Bears — Fiction; Concepts — Space — Fiction; Fear — Fiction. RL A.

The path through the woods to Spook Hill leads the Bear children over, under, and around obstacles in the landscape leading to nocturnal adventure. This traditionally formatted tale is written with a simple vocabulary. Illustrations are in the blue-blacks and yellow of night.

183 *Bears on Wheels*. Ill. by authors. Random House, 1969, ISBN 0-394-90967-4. SERIES: Bright and Early Counting. SUBJECTS: Bicycles and bicycling — Fiction; Concepts — Numbers; Humorous stories. RL A.

Antics on a unicycle provide a humorous backdrop to this counting book with a primer vocabulary. Acrobatic bears perform against a very plain background.

184 *Bears' Vacation*. Ill. by authors. Beginner Books, 1968, o.p. SERIES: I Can Read It All by Myself. SUBJECTS: Bears — Fiction; Safety — Fiction; Stories in rhyme. RL A.

Papa demonstrates everything not to do for safety at the beach. Cartoon drawings exaggerate the action.

185 *The Berenstain Bear Scouts and the Search for Naughty Ned*. Ill. by authors. Scholastic, pap., 1998, ISBN 0-590-56509-5. SERIES: Merit Badge Mystery. SUBJECTS: Bears — Fiction; Mystery and detective stories; Scouts and scouting — Fiction. RL B. LEXILE 470L.

Even off-duty at the amusement park, the Bear Scouts are called upon to find Naughty Ned. After looking on the roller-coaster, bumper cars, and carousel, Dr. Wise Old Owl points them in the direction of the spooky house. Cartoon illustrations follow the Bear Scouts and their clues.

186 *The Berenstain Bear Scouts and the Stinky Milk Mystery*. Ill. by authors. Scholastic, pap., 1999, ISBN 0-590-56524-9. SERIES: Merit Badge Mystery. SUBJECTS: Bears — Fiction; Mystery and detective stories; Scouts and scouting — Fiction. RL B. LEXILE 480L.

Trying to earn their "Good Neighbor" badge, the Bear Scouts help Farmer Ben and end up solving a mystery. Once again, Dr. Wise Old Owl points them to the other side of the fence and to stinky onion grass. Visual clues in the drawings help readers play detective alongside the Scouts.

187 *The Berenstain Bear Scouts and the White Water Mystery*. Ill. by authors. Scholastic, pap., 1999, ISBN 0-590-56522-2. SERIES: Merit Badge Mystery. SUBJECTS: Bears — Fiction; Mystery and detective stories; Scouts and scouting — Fiction. RL B. LEXILE 370L.

Suspenseful illustrations follow a race down through the whitewater rapids between the Bear Scouts and the Too-Tall gang. How did the gang finish first, or did they? A map of the scene helps solve the mystery for everyone.

188 *The Berenstain Bears: Big Bear, Small Bear*. Ill. by authors. Random House, 1998, ISBN 0-679-88717-2. SERIES: Early Step into Reading. SUBJECTS: Bears — Fiction; Concepts — Size — Fiction; Humorous stories. RL A. LEXILE BR.

Using two to four words and complementary drawings that underscore the concept, the Bear family demonstrates word opposites such as heavy/light, big/small, and tight/loose.

189 *The Berenstain Bears: That Stump Must Go*. Ill. by authors. Random House, 2000, o.p. SERIES: Beginner Books. SUBJECTS: Bears — Fiction; Fathers — Fiction; Humorous stories. RL A.

After stubbing his toe on a small stump, Papa Bear discovers that its roots are deep while relentlessly pursuing the challenge of digging it up. Hilarious illustrations depict the many and varied attempts to ensure that the stump must go.

190 *The Berenstain Bears and the Big Road Race*. Ill. by authors. Random House, 1987, ISBN 0-394-99134-6. SERIES: First

Berenstain, Stan, and Jan Berenstain (cont.)

Time Readers. SUBJECTS: Bears — Fiction; Concepts — Colors — Fiction; Fables. RL B.
The little red car putt-putts past the overconfident racers, including the green one with dirty tricks. Typical cartoon illustrations are in soft pastels.

191 *The Berenstain Bears and the Escape of the Bogg Brothers*. Ill. by authors. Random House, pap., 2000, ISBN 0-679-89228-1. SERIES: Step into Reading. SUBJECTS: Bears — Fiction; Museums — Fiction; Mystery and detective stories. RL B. LEXILE 250L.
When the Bogg Brothers escape from jail, the Bear Detectives track them down to the Bearsonian by following the trail of tobacco juice. The signature cartoon illustrations offer humor and suspense.

192 *The Berenstain Bears and the Ghost of the Forest*. Ill. by authors. Random House, 1988, ISBN 0-394-90565-2. SERIES: First Time Readers. SUBJECTS: Bears — Fiction; Ghost stories; Stories in rhyme. RL C.
Papa gets more than one scare himself after trying to scare the bear scouts on a camp-out by dressing as a ghost. The forced story is illustrated with typical Berenstain cartoons.

193 *The Berenstain Bears and the Missing Dinosaur Bone*. Ill. by authors. Beginner Books, 1980, ISBN 0-394-94447-X. SERIES: I Can Read It All by Myself. SUBJECTS: Bears — Fiction; Mystery and detective stories; Stories in rhyme. RL C.
With a crowd gathering to view the museum's dinosaur bones, the Bears and their hound dog scour the museum looking for a missing thigh bone. The skillfully woven tale of suspense, humor, and mystery has typical Berenstain illustrations.

194 *The Berenstain Bears and the Missing Honey*. Ill. by authors. Random House, 1987, ISBN 0-394-99133-8. SERIES: First Time Readers. SUBJECTS: Bears — Fiction; Mystery and detective stories; Stories in rhyme. RL C.
Following clues with Snuff their sniffer hound in the lead, the Bears have one disaster after another. Pastel colors catalog this humorous sleuthing.

195 *The Berenstain Bears and the Spooky Old Tree*. Ill. by authors. Random House, 1978, ISBN 0-394-93910-7. SERIES: Bright and Early Books. SUBJECTS: Bears — Fiction; Mystery and detective stories. RL B.
A well-crafted suspense story uses very basic vocabulary. The hazards are heightened in cartoon illustrations.

196 *The Berenstain Bears and the Wishing Star*. Ill. by authors. HarperCollins, 2005, ISBN 0-06-058346-0. SERIES: I Can Read. SUBJECTS: Bears — Fiction; Wishes. RL A.
Sister Bear wishes on a star and her first two wishes come true. When the third wish fails to do so, Brother Bear reminds her about working hard to achieve a goal. Larger, less-cluttered illustrations are just right for beginning readers.

197 *The Berenstain Bears Blaze a Trail*. Ill. by authors. Random House, 1987, ISBN 0-394-99132-X. SERIES: First Time Readers. SUBJECTS: Bears — Fiction; Hiking — Fiction; Stories in rhyme. RL C.
Scout Leader Jane awards Papa and the scouts merit badges despite Papa's failures to follow the guidebook. Pastel cartoons underline Papa's follies.

198 *The Berenstain Bears by the Sea*. Ill. by authors. Random House, 1998, ISBN 0-679-88719-9. SERIES: Step into Reading + Math. SUBJECTS: Bears — Fiction; Seashore — Fiction. RL A. LEXILE 160L.
Before they can swim in the sea on their shore vacation, the Bear cubs must clean their house. Simple rhyming text and cartoon illustrations aptly express the cubs' vacation frustration.

199 *The Berenstain Bears Clean House*. Ill. by authors. HarperCollins, 2005, ISBN 0-06-058334-7. SERIES: I Can Read. SUBJECTS: Bears — Fiction; Houses — Fiction. RL A.
While spring-cleaning the house from top to bottom, the Bear family gathers items for a yard sale. Large, brightly colored illustrations display the humorous actions as their favorite yard sale items are placed in the attic to be cleaned another day.

200 *The Berenstain Bears Down on the Farm*. Ill. by authors. HarperCollins, 2006, ISBN 0-06-058350-9. SERIES: I Can Read. SUBJECTS:

Bears — Fiction; Farm and country life — Fiction. RL A.

Recounting a trip to Farmer Ben's, a simple rhyming text enumerates all the jobs that need to be done daily at the farm. Each job that Farmer Ben calls "hard fun" is conveyed in vibrant cartoon illustrations that clarify the actions of the story.

201 *The Berenstain Bears in the House of Mirrors*. Ill. by authors. Random House, 1999, o.p. SERIES: Early Step into Reading. SUBJECTS: Bears — Fiction; Stories in rhyme. RL A.

Using the idea of a funhouse mirror, the Bear family demonstrates concepts such as short/tall, happy/sad, and narrow/wide. The full-page color illustrations concentrate on presenting a corresponding visual representation.

202 *The Berenstain Bears' New Kitten*. Ill. by authors. HarperCollins, 2007, ISBN 0-06-058356-8. SERIES: I Can Read. SUBJECTS: Bears — Fiction; Pets — Cats — Fiction; Pets — Fiction. RL A.

There's a surprise for the family when Brother Bear brings home a new kitten. Lively, expressive illustrations explore the kitten's adaptation to her new surroundings.

203 *The Berenstain Bears' New Pup*. Ill. by authors. HarperCollins, 2005, ISBN 0-06-058343-6. SERIES: I Can Read. SUBJECTS: Bears — Fiction; Pets — Dogs — Fiction; Pets — Fiction. RL A.

At Farmer Ben's, Mother Bear and the cubs buy a new puppy from Queenie's litter. In spite of the cubs' promises to watch and take care of Little Lady, the new puppy gets into lots of mischief. Simple sentences on each page are accompanied by the familiar, colorfully expressive cartoon illustrations.

204 *The Berenstain Bears on the Moon*. Ill. by authors. Random House, 1985, ISBN 0-394-97180-9. SERIES: Bright and Early Books. SUBJECTS: Bears — Fiction; Space travel — Fiction; Stories in rhyme. RL B.

On the moon the Bears fly their flag, take moon notes, and collect moon rocks for their moon rock totes. This light introduction to space travel suggests that the stars are next. Cartoon illustrations are typical of the Berenstains.

205 *The Berenstain Bears Out West*. Ill. by authors. HarperCollins, 2006, ISBN 0-06-058353-3. SERIES: I Can Read. SUBJECTS: Bears — Fiction; Stories in rhyme; Vacations — Fiction. RL A.

On a vacation to the B-Bar-X Ranch, the Bear family is given the grand tour of the beauty and the history of the West by Uncle Tex. The bright, golden hues of the West are resplendent as the family tours on horseback and by buggy.

206 *The Berenstain Bears Play T-ball*. Ill. by authors. HarperCollins, 2005, ISBN 0-06-058337-1. SERIES: I Can Read. SUBJECTS: Bears — Fiction; Sports — T-ball — Fiction. RL B. LEXILE 630L.

Coaching T-ball for the Cardinals and the Bluebirds, Brother and Sister Bear need to practice patience, as Mr. Gump the ump reminds them. The excitement, confusion, and frustration of the game come through clearly in the full-color illustrations.

207 *The Berenstain Bears Ride the Thunderbolt*. Ill. by authors. Random House, 1998, ISBN 0-679-88718-0. SERIES: Early Step into Reading. SUBJECTS: Amusement parks — Fiction; Bears — Fiction. RL A. LEXILE BR.

Follow the thrill of a ride on the Thunderbolt as it goes up, down, and all around. The Bear family is ready to ride again, but this time without Father Bear. Simple sentences and bold, dynamic illustrations capture the action and reactions every second of the way.

208 *The Berenstain Bears Seashore Treasure*. Ill. by authors. HarperCollins, 2005, ISBN 0-06-058340-1. SERIES: I Can Read. SUBJECTS: Bears — Fiction; Seashore — Fiction. RL B.

At their vacation home at the seashore, Papa Bear finds a treasure map that leads to a pirate's booty. After digging in several locations, the family finds the real treasure: buckets of seashells! Sun-drenched drawings aptly depict the true treasured adventure of family fun.

209 *The Berenstain Kids: I Love Colors*. Ill. by authors. Random House, 1987, o.p. SERIES: First Time Readers. SUBJECTS: Concepts — Colors; Stories in rhyme. RL B.

Berenstain, Stan, and Jan Berenstain (cont.)

Uninspired verse reviews the colors of the rainbow and what primary colors produce each color. Pictures are typical.

210 *The Berenstains' A Book.* Ill. by authors. Random House, 1997, o.p. SERIES: Bright and Early Books. SUBJECTS: Alphabet — Fiction; Ants — Fiction. RL A.

Follow an army of ants as they advance over an array of objects that begin with the letter *a*. The silly storyline is comically enhanced by a matching audacious assortment of illustrations.

211 *The Berenstains' B Book.* Ill. by authors. Random House, 1971, ISBN 0-394-92324-3. SERIES: Bright and Early Books. SUBJECTS: Alphabet — Fiction; Bears — Fiction; Nonsense. RL A.

Cumulative nonsense follows big brown bear and friends biking backward and collectively breaking baby bird's balloon. Flat, colorful cartoon illustrations add lots of noise and action.

212 *The Berenstains'* C *Book.* Ill. by authors. Random House, 1997, o.p. SERIES: Bright and Early Books. SUBJECTS: Alphabet — Fiction; Circuses — Fiction. RL A.

Clarence the clown carries a number of animals that themselves carry items beginning with the letter *c* before the inevitable crash. Cartoon characters balancing higher and higher enhance the nonsense. New, appropriately wacky, cover art is featured on this work previously published as C *Is for Clown*.

213 *Big Honey Hunt.* Ill. by authors. Beginner Books, 1962, ISBN 0-394-90028-6. SERIES: I Can Read It All by Myself. SUBJECTS: Bears — Fiction; Stories in rhyme. RL A.

Papa Bear encounters an owl, a porcupine, a skunk, and some angry bees while trying to find his own honey. Cartoon drawings are typical of the Berenstains.

214 *Bike Lesson.* Ill. by authors. Beginner Books, 1964, o.p. SERIES: I Can Read It All by Myself. SUBJECTS: Bears — Fiction; Bicycles and bicycling — Fiction. RL A.

Papa's "lessons" end disastrously until Small Bear finally gets his first turn on the new bicycle, and he rides Papa home on his handlebars. Humor is at the expense of sound bicycle safety. Drawings are typical of the Berenstains.

215 *He Bear, She Bear.* Ill. by authors. Random House, 1974, ISBN 0-394-92997-7. SERIES: Bright and Early Books. SUBJECTS: Bears — Fiction; Careers; Stories in rhyme. RL B.

Careers for both sexes are discussed and include cowboy, astronaut, and animal trainer. Far-reaching possibilities are presented in rhyme, illustrated with cartoons.

216 *Inside, Outside, Upside Down.* Ill. by authors. Random House, 1968, ISBN 0-394-91142-3. SERIES: Bright and Early Books. SUBJECTS: Bears — Fiction; Concepts — Space — Fiction; Stories in rhyme. RL A.

A small bear returns home to tell Mama about his adventures in a box in which he traveled to town inside, outside, upside down. Simple rhythmic language and pictures focusing on the yellow box give this story its appeal.

217 *Old Hat, New Hat.* Ill. by authors. Random House, 1970, ISBN 0-394-90669-1. SERIES: Bright and Early Books. SUBJECTS: Bears — Fiction; Humorous stories. RL A.

A bear shopping for a new hat finds himself most satisfied with his old one. Cartoon drawings add humor.

218 *Ready, Get Set, Go!* Ill. by authors. Random House, 1988, ISBN 0-394-90564-4. SERIES: First Time Readers. SUBJECTS: Bears — Fiction; Sports — Fiction; Stories in rhyme. RL B.

In family Olympic events, Papa is best only at sleeping. Stereotypes of Mama as timer and starter and Papa as stupid are dull. Pastel cartoons are typical of the Berenstains.

Berg, Julie

219 *The Berenstains: The Young at Heart.* Ill. with photos. Abdo, 1993, ISBN 1-56239-224-7. SUBJECTS: Biographies; Books and reading; Writers and writing. RL C.

Jan and Stan met in art school, although they didn't marry until Stan got out of the service. They began as magazine illustrators and have been successful with children's books featuring bears, while also venturing into TV and other related markets. Black-and-white photographs add little to the text.

220 *Maurice Sendak: The Young at Heart.* Ill. with photos. Abdo, 1993, ISBN 1-56239-225-5. SUBJECTS: Books and reading; Writers and writing. RL C.

Berg includes a number of direct quotations as she writes about the creative energy of a top author and illustrator of children's books. The son of Polish immigrants, Sendak apparently had a loathing for school. Illustrations consist of a few dull black-and-white photographs.

Berger, Melvin

221 *Chomp! A Book About Sharks.* Scholastic, pap., 1999, ISBN 0-590-52298-1. SERIES: Scholastic Reader. SUBJECTS: Sharks. RL B. LEXILE 420L.

In this brief introduction to sharks, readers learn about the many types, how they hunt, and how fast they can swim. Clear underwater photographs on every page offer a glimpse into the life of sharks.

222 *Dive! A Book of Deep-Sea Creatures.* Scholastic, pap., 2000, ISBN 0-439-08747-3. SERIES: Hello Science Reader! SUBJECTS: Fish; Oceans and ocean life; Octopi. RL B. LEXILE 520L.

Travel one mile beneath the water in a submarine and discover all the deep-sea creatures that live there. Highly magnified and close-up photographs interspersed with color illustrations add unique visuals to an enticing text.

223 *Germs Make Me Sick!* Ill. by Marylin Hafner. HarperCollins, pap., 1987, ISBN 0-690-04429-1. SERIES: Let's-Read-and-Find-Out Science. SUBJECTS: Diseases; Illness. RL C.

The causes and treatment of common illnesses are discussed in this book written by a former teacher. Lively, bright illustrations include some cartoon humor.

224 *Look Out for Turtles.* Ill. by Megan Lloyd. HarperCollins, 1992, ISBN 0-06-022540-8. SERIES: Let's-Read-and-Find-Out Science. SUBJECTS: Nature; Science and scientists; Turtles. RL A.

Characteristics of and differences between turtles, from the smallest three-inch mud turtle to the 600-pound Galapagos turtle, are described and illustrated with excellent soft watercolors. Berger describes how turtles' survival is being threatened by pollution and loss of habitat in this sympathetic, interesting account.

225 *Simple Science Says: Take One Mirror.* Ill. by G. Brian Karas. Scholastic, 1989, o.p. SUBJECTS: Science experiments. RL C.

Science experiments such as looking around corners, making a rainbow or a kaleidoscope, reading backward writing, and doing word magic are intriguingly presented. Pencil drawings with turquoise highlights add humor and expand the text.

226 *Switch On, Switch Off.* Ill. by Carolyn Croll. HarperCollins, 1989, ISBN 0-690-04786-X. SERIES: Let's-Read-and-Find-Out Science. SUBJECTS: Electricity; Energy; Science experiments. RL C.

Excellent, well-presented information about how electricity is generated. Bright drawings feature familiar household scenes and pets. There are also diagrams of distribution systems.

227 *Why I Cough, Sneeze, Shiver, Hiccup, and Yawn.* Ill. by Holly Keller. HarperCollins, 1983, ISBN 0-690-04254-X. SERIES: Let's-Read-and-Find-Out Science. SUBJECTS: Human body — Reflexes; Science and scientists. RL C.

Comic sketches show how and why the reflexes work, using children and a cat as models. Well-presented information, with illustrations that lighten the tone.

Berger, Melvin, and Gilda Berger

228 *Howl! A Book About Wolves.* Scholastic, pap., 2005, ISBN 0-439-80180-X. SERIES: Berger Science Readers. SUBJECTS: Wolves. RL B. LEXILE 330L.

Discover the world of wolves in four easy chapters that explain the animals' habitats, characteristics, and future. Numerous color photographs provide a sharp, clear view into the life of wolves in the wild.

229 *Snap! A Book About Alligators and Crocodiles.* Scholastic, pap., 2001, ISBN 0-

Berger, Melvin, and Gilda Berger (cont.)

439-31746-0. SERIES: Scholastic Reader. SUBJECTS: Alligators; Crocodiles. RL B. LEXILE 440L.

There are many similarities between alligators and crocodiles, but how can you tell them apart? Clear color photographs on every page give an up-close and personal "snapshot" into the animals' life and habitats around the world.

230 *Splash! A Book About Whales and Dolphins.* Scholastic, pap., 2001, ISBN 0-439-20166-7. SERIES: Scholastic Reader. SUBJECTS: Dolphins; Whales. RL B.

From their first breath of life, find out about whales and dolphins: the many different kinds and what they eat. Color photographs in double-page spreads complement a comprehensive introduction.

231 *Telephones, Televisions, and Toilets: How They Work — and What Can Go Wrong.* Ill. by Don Madden. Ideals, 1993, ISBN 0-8249-8645-8. SERIES: Discovery Readers. SUBJECTS: Telephones; Television; Toilets. RL B.

In simple language, the authors describe how these appliances work, and how using a plunger sometimes helps. Simple color cartoons include a boy and his pets.

232 *Where Are the Stars During the Day? A Book About Stars.* Ill. by Blanche Sims. Ideals, 1993, ISBN 0-8249-8644-X. SERIES: Discovery Readers. SUBJECTS: Astronomy and astronomers; Science and scientists. RL A.

An exceptional introduction to the rotation of the earth, extending to the sun as a star, the planets, the Big Dipper, the North Star, Orion, and the Milky Way. Simple illustrations make sky observation a family affair.

233 *Where Did Your Family Come From?* Ill. by Robert Quackenbush. Ideals, 1993, ISBN 0-8249-8647-4. SUBJECTS: Emigration and immigration. RL A.

Through the stories of children — Boris from Russia, Maria from Italy, Rosa from Mexico, and Chang from Korea — examples of the reasons immigrants settle in the United States are given. Typical vivid illustrations by Robert Quackenbush enhance the text.

234 *The Whole World in Your Hands.* Ill. by Robert Quackenbush. Ideals, 1993, ISBN 0-8249-8646-6. SERIES: Discovery Readers. SUBJECTS: Geography. RL A.

A masterful introduction to reading maps takes the reader successively from the map of a house to one of a neighborhood, a town, a state, a country, and the world, as well as giving a hint of what cultural habits can be inferred from a map. The text is appropriately and attractively illustrated.

Berger, Samantha, and Pamela Chanko

235 *It's Spring.* Ill. by Melissa Sweet. Scholastic, pap., 2000, ISBN 0-439-08754-6. SERIES: Hello Reader! SUBJECTS: Spring — Fiction; Stories in rhyme. RL A.

In a simple rhyme, animals tell each other the good news that spring has come. Full-page watercolors illustrate a bucolic setting warmed by the colors of the earth.

Bernhard, Emery

236 *Spotted Eagle and Black Crow: A Lakota Legend.* Ill. by Durga Bernhard. Holiday House, 1993, ISBN 0-8234-1007-2. SUBJECTS: Birds — Fiction; Folklore; Lakota. RL C.

A powerful tale of courage, love, and forgiveness in the wake of betrayal. The author and illustrator are "longtime students of traditional shamanism and tribal art." Stylized pastel illustrations are rich in Lakota imagery in close touch with the natural world.

Bernier-Grand, Carmen T.

237 *Juan Bobo: Four Folktales from Puerto Rico.* Ill. by Ernesto Ramos Nieves. HarperCollins, 1994, ISBN 0-06-023389-3. SERIES: I Can Read. SUBJECTS: Folklore; Nonsense; Spanish language. RL A.

Flaky Juan Bobo carries water in a basket, tries to dress a pig for church, tries to follow Mama's advice on table manners and goes home hungry, and "sells" syrup mistakenly to flies. Decorative illustrations are rich in texture and color.

Berry, Steve

238 *The Boy Who Wouldn't Speak.* Ill. by Deirdre Betteridge. Annick, 1992, ISBN 1-

55037-231-9. SUBJECTS: Behavior — Shyness — Fiction; Giants — Fiction. RL B.

Owen, who at five has never spoken, befriends his new giant neighbors, Fred and Lola, and finally speaks up to defend them from nervous neighbors. Bright ink and watercolor cartoon drawings with lots of red and blue and orange enhance the text.

Bethell, Jean

239 *Three Cheers for Mother Jones*. Ill. by Kathleen Garry McCord. Holt, 1980, o.p. SUBJECTS: United States — History. RL B.

Seventy-three-year-old Mary Harris Jones marched 125 miles with mill children, taking 22 days, to see President Theodore Roosevelt at his summer home to protest the conditions under which one million children under the age of 14 worked. Federal legislation took another 35 years. Text is illustrated with pen and ink drawings.

Bianchi, John

240 *The Bungalo Boys III: Champions of Hockey*. Ill. by author. Bungalo, 1989, ISBN 0-921285-18-3. SUBJECTS: Humorous stories; Sports — Ice hockey — Fiction. RL C.

In this tongue-in-cheek parody of more serious sports, Little Shorty, guided by Bungalo ghosts (from an ice floe after the ice shatters), scores the winning goal with time running out while the organ plays. Illustrations are colorful ink and watercolor cartoons.

Binnamin, Vivian

241 *The Case of the Snoring Stegosaurus*. Ill. by Jeffrey S. Nelsen. Silver Burdett, 1989, ISBN 0-671-68818-9. SERIES: Field Trip Mysteries. SUBJECTS: Dinosaurs — Fiction; Science and scientists. RL A.

A few stray facts are given about the museum exhibits Miss Whimsy's third-grade class passes on the way to visit the stegosaurus. After the children climb over and under exhibits, they figure out why the stegosaurus snores, exhibiting some good detective work despite the inappropriate behavior.

Bishop, Ann

242 *Merry-Go-Riddle*. Ill. by Jerry Warshaw. Whitman, 1973, o.p. SUBJECTS: Jokes and riddles. RL C.

Interesting wordplay uses themes from the circus and circus performers so that the humor is cumulative. Illustrations are red and black ink cartoons.

Bishop, Bonnie

243 *No One Noticed Ralph*. Ill. by Jack Kent. Doubleday, 1978, o.p. SERIES: Reading on My Own. SUBJECTS: Parrots — Fiction. RL C.

Ralph the parrot is noticed when he gives a fire alert. Lively drawings of Ralph and people are in browns and reds.

244 *Ralph Rides Away*. Ill. by Jack Kent. Doubleday, 1979, o.p. SERIES: Reading on My Own. SUBJECTS: Lost, being — Fiction; Parrots — Fiction. RL C.

Ralph gets lost in the zoo on his first adventurous picnic in the park with Mr. and Mrs. Muggs. The creative solution to his restitution to the family is matched by bright, comic four-color illustrations.

Bishop, Claire

245 *Georgette*. Ill. by Ursula Landshoff. Putnam, 1973, o.p. SERIES: Break-of-Day. SUBJECTS: Chickens — Fiction; France — Fiction. RL B.

Georgette the chicken saves her neck with her dancing abilities in a tale of romance and suspense in a Paris apartment. Ink sketches add flavor to the setting.

246 *Truffle Pig*. Ill. by Kurt Wiese. Putnam, 1971, o.p. SERIES: Break-of-Day. SUBJECTS: France — Fiction; Pigs — Fiction. RL C.

The marvelous piglet Marcel saves his skin by his ability to dig for the elusive and costly truffles. The tale is told in simple language but not a controlled vocabulary. Distinctly French in character, illustrations are in ink with blue and yellow colored pencil.

Black, Sonia W.

247 *Follow the Polar Bears*. Ill. by Turi MacCombie. Scholastic, pap., 2000, ISBN 0-439-20641-3. SERIES: Hello Reader! SUBJECTS: Animals — Growth and

Black, Sonia W. (cont.)

development; Bears; Stories in rhyme. RL A. LEXILE 140L.

Follow the growth and development of brother and sister polar bear cubs. With illustrations depicting the icy cold barrenness of the northernmost regions, a simple rhyming text tracks the cubs from birth through independence to begin their own families.

248 *Hanging Out with Mom.* Ill. by George Ford. Scholastic, pap., 2000, ISBN 0-590-86636-2. SERIES: Hello Reader! SUBJECTS: African Americans — Fiction; Mothers — Fiction; Stories in rhyme. RL A. LEXILE BR.

When Mom gets home from work, she and her son go to the park. After feeding the ducks, playing in the sand, and climbing on the playground equipment, it's time to go home. Warm illustrations in paint and pastel crayon express the love of mother and child, and the hope of another day of playing together.

Blackwood, Gary

249 *The Just-So Woman.* Ill. by Jane Manning. HarperCollins, 2006, ISBN 0-06-057727-4. SERIES: I Can Read. SUBJECTS: Humorous stories; Neighbors — Fiction. RL B. LEXILE 560L.

The Just-So Woman likes everything to be perfect but eventually finds it can actually be fun to be like the Any-Way man. Setting the scene of a bygone era, earth-toned watercolors capture the humor of the woman's frustration at her neighbor's less-than-perfect antics.

Blassingame, Wyatt

250 *Bowleg Bill, Seagoing Cowboy.* Ill. by Herman Vestal. Garrard, 1976, o.p. SUBJECTS: Folklore — United States; Humorous stories; Tall tales. RL C.

Sailing with 10,000 rabbits he has lassoed, Bowleg Bill has his hands full when they reproduce faster than the ship is moving. Bowleg Bill also discovers the thrill of whale riding. Runaway rabbits provide the most visual interest. The illustrations are in turquoise, orange, and gray.

251 *How Davy Crockett Got a Bearskin Coat.* Ill. by Mimi Korach. Garrard, 1972, o.p. SERIES: Tall Tales. SUBJECTS: Folklore — United States; Humorous stories; Tall tales. RL B.

While trying to replace his moth-eaten coat, Davy ends up being chased by his quarry, a bear. When he catches the bear and knots its tail through a hole in a tree, the bear runs on, skinless! Comic pencil drawings add to the fun of this tall tale.

252 *Pecos Bill and the Wonderful Clothesline Snake.* Ill. by Herman Vestal. Garrard, 1978, o.p. SERIES: American Folktales. SUBJECTS: Folklore — United States; Humorous stories; Tall tales. RL C.

Glass snakes that shatter and reassemble attached to other snakes, snakes with bells instead of rattles, snakes wild as broncos, and pancake snakes sunning under syrup and blueberries — these are some of the inventions of a tall tale enhanced by turquoise and gold drawings.

253 *Pecos Bill Catches a Hidebehind.* Ill. by Herman Vestal. Garrard, 1977, o.p. SERIES: American Folktales. SUBJECTS: Folklore — United States; Humorous stories; Tall tales. RL C.

After a roperite and a telescopo help Pecos Bill and Sluefoot Sue capture a hidebehind for a zoo, they feel sorry for the shy animal and send a roperite instead. Simple turquoise and orange illustrations add to the humor of this outrageous tall tale.

Blocksma, Mary

254 *Yoo Hoo, Moon!* Ill. by Patience Brewster. Bantam, 1992, ISBN 0-553-07094-0. SERIES: Bank Street Ready-to-Read. SUBJECTS: Animals — Fiction; Cumulative tales; Night — Fiction. RL A.

As the animals wake up and shout for the moon to wake up, they mistake other lights for that of the moon. Language and story line are simple, and appealing clothed animals are painted in lavender, brown, and orange against the deep blues and greens of the night world.

Blocksma, Norma

255 *Best Dressed Bear.* Ill. by Sandra C. Kalthoff. Childrens Press, 1984, o.p. SERIES: Just One More. SUBJECTS: Animals — Fiction; Bears — Fiction; Stories in rhyme. RL A.

Bear is dressed formally for a dance — but forgets his pants. Language is rhythmic and simple, but not predictable. Full-color drawings of friendly animals add humor to a tale that uses an 80-word vocabulary.

Boegehold, Betty

256 *Chipper's Choices.* Ill. by Jim Arnosky. Putnam, 1981, o.p. SUBJECTS: Animals — Fiction; Chipmunks — Fiction. RL C.

Chipper the chipmunk tells stories about his friends Mole, Jay, Toad, and Squirrel in which the animals argue about who is boss, encounter a scary noise, and share riddles and some poems. Soft pencil drawings focus on nuts and individual animals.

257 *The Fight.* Ill. by Robin Oz. Bantam, 1991, ISBN 0-553-07086-X. SERIES: Bank Street Ready-to-Read. SUBJECTS: Cumulative tales; School stories. RL A.

A rhythmic modern cumulative tale detailing the sequence of insignificant events leading to a fight on the playground. Very effective illustrations feature ink and wash action.

258 *Here's Pippa Again.* Ill. by Cyndy Szekeres. Knopf, 1975, o.p. SERIES: Read-Aloud / Read-Alone. SUBJECTS: Animals — Fiction; Growing up — Fiction; Mice — Fiction. RL B.

Pippa is often restless and ready for adventure. She wants to learn how to swim, play in the snow, find a pet, and have a party. Her animal friends' antics are shown in charming pencil drawings.

259 *A Horse Called Starfire.* Ill. by Neil Waldman. Bantam, 1990, ISBN 0-553-05861-4. SERIES: Bank Street Ready-to-Read. SUBJECTS: Historical fiction; Horses — Fiction. RL A.

A magical telling of how Native Americans came to have horses, illustrated with flowing, stylized watercolors of the Southwest. Boegehold's story reads like a legend despite its very simple vocabulary and story line.

260 *Hurray for Pippa!* Ill. by Cyndy Szekeres. Knopf, 1980, o.p. SERIES: Read-Aloud / Read-Alone. SUBJECTS: Animals — Fiction; Friendship — Fiction; Mice — Fiction. RL B.

Testing under the chin with a buttercup, cleaning out old toys, teaching a rabbit to play games, and playing dress-up occupy Pippa and her animal friends. Joyful pencil drawings suit the homely adventures.

261 *Pippa Pops Out!* Ill. by Cyndy Szekeres. Knopf, pap., 1979, ISBN 0-440-46865-5. SERIES: Read-Aloud / Read-Alone. SUBJECTS: Friendship — Fiction; Growing up — Fiction; Mice — Fiction. RL C.

Fears and feelings of inadequacy, as well as the warmth of friendship, are explored. Pencil drawings show expressive mice, squirrels, ducklings, and crickets.

262 *Small Deer's Magic Tricks.* Ill. by Jacqueline Chwast. Putnam, 1977, o.p. SERIES: Break-of-Day. SUBJECTS: Deer — Fiction; Folklore — Indonesia. RL B.

Four traditional Indonesian trickster tales about the tiny mouse deer Kanchil. In one tale he outwits a tiger, some crocodiles, a wild pig, and an elephant. Comic-style ink drawings are mediocre.

263 *Three to Get Ready.* Ill. by Mary Chalmers. HarperCollins, 1965, o.p. SERIES: I Can Read. SUBJECTS: Pets — Cats — Fiction; Sibling rivalry — Fiction; Siblings — Fiction. RL A.

Mother Cat rescues and comforts her children Gigi, George, and Ginger as they explore the world at night outside their yard. Soft drawings in gray, green, and rose accompany this reassuring tale.

Boivin, Kelly

264 *What's in a Box?* Ill. by Janice Skivington. Children's Press, 1991, ISBN 0-516-02010-2. SERIES: Rookie Reader. SUBJECTS: Toys — Fiction. RL A.

Colored pencil and watercolor washes illustrate this story about different ways boxes can be used: for mail, tools, sand, hats, and jack-in-the boxes. A limited (55-word) vocabulary is used.

265 *Where Is Mittens?* Ill. by Clovis Martin. Children's Press, 1990, ISBN 0-516-02060-9. SERIES: Rookie Reader. SUBJECTS: Pets — Cats — Fiction; Stories in rhyme. RL A.

Boivin, Kelly (cont.)

A young girl searches everywhere for her cat, finding her with new kittens in a closet. Large colorful watercolor close-ups show a worried child.

Boland, Janice

266 *A Dog Named Sam*. Ill. by G. Brian Karas. Penguin, pap., 1996, ISBN 0-14-038438-3. SERIES: Dial Easy-to-Read. SUBJECTS: Humorous stories; Pets — Dogs — Fiction. RL B. LEXILE 120L.

Poor Sam — everything he loves to do, he does wrong; even fetching, swimming, and sleeping. But thankfully his family loves him anyway. Simple, childlike illustrations outlined in ink follow the hilarious but often maddening antics of a special dog.

Bonsall, Crosby

267 *The Amazing the Incredible Super Dog*. Ill. by author. HarperCollins, 1986, ISBN 0-06-020591-1. SUBJECTS: Pets — Cats — Fiction; Pets — Dogs — Fiction; Pets — Fiction. RL A.

A yawning puppy, Super Dog, chases a butterfly while his young mistress boasts to Willy, her cat, about all the tricks Super Dog can do. Exuberant, expressive ink and watercolor drawings of the three accompany the text.

268 *And I Mean It, Stanley*. Ill. by author. HarperCollins, pap., 1974, ISBN 0-06-444046-X. SERIES: Early I Can Read. SUBJECTS: Imagination — Fiction; Pets — Dogs — Fiction. RL A.

A small boy's creations using things found in an alley are ruined when his pet, Shaggy Stanley, finally appears. Delightful ink drawings add warmth to an inventive tale.

269 *The Case of the Cat's Meow*. Ill. by author. HarperCollins, pap., 1965, ISBN 0-06-444017-6. SERIES: I Can Read. SUBJECTS: Friendship — Fiction; Mystery and detective stories; Pets — Cats — Fiction. RL A.

Four friends try to find missing cat Mildred, using cats, dogs, food, and alarms. Characters in this series are interesting individuals. Line drawings are colored with gray, red, salmon, and pumpkin.

270 *The Case of the Dumb Bells*. Ill. by author. HarperCollins, pap., 1966, ISBN 0-06-444030-3. SERIES: I Can Read. SUBJECTS: Friendship — Fiction; Mystery and detective stories. RL A.

Wizard, Skinny, Tubby, and Snitch have some difficulties with their phone system, cleverly conveyed by one-sided telephone conversations with irate parents. Excellent ink drawings convey relationships sympathetically.

271 *The Case of the Hungry Stranger*. Ill. by author. HarperCollins, 1992, ISBN 0-06-020571-7. SERIES: I Can Read. SUBJECTS: Friendship — Fiction; Mystery and detective stories. RL A.

Wizard, Tubby, Skinny, and Snitch check for blue teeth when on the trail of the blueberry pie thief. The mishaps of the friends provide gentle humor — Tubby gets tangled in a garden hose in a scary cellar and they follow false trails of their own making. Exceptional illustrations match the text.

272 *The Case of the Scaredy Cats*. Ill. by author. HarperCollins, pap., 1971, ISBN 0-06-444047-8. SERIES: I Can Read. SUBJECTS: Friendship — Fiction; Mystery and detective stories. RL A.

During a fight between the boys in the gang and the girls who try to take the clubhouse over, little scaredy-cat Annie is lost and all join in to try to find her. The warm, reassuring, realistic ending is enhanced by ink drawings with marvelous cross-hatched patterns.

273 *The Day I Had to Play with My Sister*. Ill. by author. HarperCollins, pap., 1999, ISBN 0-06-444253-5. SERIES: My First I Can Read. SUBJECTS: Games — Fiction; Siblings — Fiction. RL A. LEXILE BR.

A small sister's way of playing hide-and-seek does not satisfy her older brother. Appealing cross-hatched ink drawings with deeper, vivid colors show the antics of a devoted shaggy dog in this newly illustrated edition.

274 *Mine's the Best*. Ill. by author. HarperCollins, 1996, ISBN 0-06-027091-8. SERIES: My First I Can Read. SUBJECTS: Behavior — Argumentative — Fiction; Friendship — Fiction. RL A.

A classic argument between friends is resolved when the boys ally against a new antagonist — a girl. Boldly colored artwork highlighted with ink enhances this newly illustrated edition.

275 *Piggle*. Ill. by author. HarperCollins, 1973, ISBN 0-06-020580-6. SERIES: I Can Read. SUBJECTS: Dreams — Fiction; Imagination — Fiction; Nonsense. RL A.

Bear teaches Homer how to play "Piggle" (making nonsense rhymes) after his overtures are rejected by Duck, Rabbit, Pig, and his sisters. Charming, witty nonsense is illustrated with warm cross-hatched ink drawings during Homer's dream, and pale pink and brown while he is awake.

276 *Tell Me Some More*. Ill. by Fritz Siebel. HarperCollins, 1961, ISBN 0-06-020601-2. SERIES: I Can Read. SUBJECTS: Books and reading — Fiction; Imagination — Fiction; Libraries and librarians — Fiction. RL A.

Andrew captures Tim's imagination with tales of elephants, camels, mountains and fountains, moons and spoons, rings and kings — which can be held in the hand or carried under his arm (in books)! The boys are drawn in ink, the imaginings are in color in this captivating tale.

277 *What Spot?* Ill. by author. HarperCollins, pap., 1963, ISBN 0-06-020611-X. SERIES: I Can Read. SUBJECTS: Birds — Fiction; Walruses — Fiction. RL B.

Polar animals puzzle over a mysterious black spot in the snow. This imaginative tale is illustrated with textured tones in pencil.

278 *Who's Afraid of the Dark?* Ill. by author. HarperCollins, pap., 2002, ISBN 0-06-444071-0. SERIES: I Can Read. SUBJECTS: Fear — Fiction; Pets — Dogs — Fiction. RL A.

A little boy transfers his fear of the dark to his dog, Stella. A friend offers some advice on ways to teach Stella not to be afraid. Bright colors, warm with friendship, newly illustrate a story of childhood fears.

Book, Rita

279 *My Soccer Mom from Mars*. Ill. by Amy Wummer. Grosset & Dunlap, pap., 2001, ISBN 0-448-42599-8. SERIES: All Aboard Reading. SUBJECTS: Mothers — Fiction; Sports — Soccer — Fiction. RL B.

Ryan's Mom embarrasses him with her exuberant cheering on the soccer sideline, but other teammates wish their parents were just like her. Lighthearted illustrations very expressively depict the many emotions of the players, especially Ryan as he struggles with his mother's enthusiasm.

Boritzer, Etan

280 *What Is God?* Ill. by Robbie Marantz. Firefly, 1990, ISBN 0-920668-89-5. SUBJECTS: Religion. RL C.

Speculation about the nature of God begins with great teachers of a variety of faiths, and their holy books. The similarities between faiths and the meaning of prayer, the universality of God, and connectedness through other people are outlined in fairly simple language.

Bottner, Barbara

281 *Marsha Makes Me Sick*. Ill. by Denise Brunkus. Golden Books, 1998, o.p. SERIES: Road to Reading. SUBJECTS: Illness — Fiction; Siblings — Fiction. RL B. LEXILE 80L.

When Lulu's little sister has the chicken pox, her mother is busy taking care of Marsha. Soon Lulu will have all the attention she craves as Marsha shares her chicken pox. Expressively detailed watercolor illustrations complement the action of the story.

282 *Two Messy Friends*. Ill. by author. Scholastic, pap., 1998, ISBN 0-590-63285-X. SERIES: Hello Reader! SUBJECTS: Cleanliness — Fiction; Friendship — Fiction. RL B. LEXILE 290L.

Exact opposites, best friends Grace and Harriet sleep over at each other's houses and each somehow becomes just like the other. Large, wide-eyed characters in bold colors support a funny story about an everyday childhood experience.

Bottner, Barbara, and Gerald Kruglik

283 *Pish and Posh*. Ill. by author. HarperCollins, 2004, ISBN 0-06-051416-7. SERIES: I Can Read. SUBJECTS: Fairies — Fiction; Lost and found possessions —

Bottner, Barbara, and Gerald Kruglik (cont.)

Fiction; Magic — Fiction. RL B. LEXILE 600L.

Because she doesn't read *The Fairy Handbook* thoroughly, Posh cannot do any of the spells correctly. Even with the wand and pixie dust, disaster ensues. Boldly outlined illustrations humorously portray the magic gone awry.

284 *Pish and Posh Wish for Fairy Wings*. Ill. by author. HarperCollins, 2006, ISBN 0-06-051419-1. SERIES: I Can Read. SUBJECTS: Fairies — Fiction; Magic — Fiction; Monsters — Fiction. RL B.

With the help of Mub, the monster under the bed, Pish and Posh use their four wishes wisely and earn their fairy wings. Humorous, lively, and colorful illustrations depict the many emotional moments of the two friends as they follow *The Fairy Handbook* to the letter.

Bourgeois, Paulette

285 *Firefighters*. Ill. by Kim LaFave. Kids Can Press, 2005, ISBN 1-55337-750-8. SERIES: Kids Can Read. SUBJECTS: Fire fighters and fire fighting. RL B.

Follow the firefighters as they are called to a fire in an apartment building. Learn about how they put out fires in rural areas, at car accidents, and in forests. Detailed watercolors chronicle the work of the firefighter while providing important visuals for fire safety rules.

Bourne, Miriam A.

286 *Four-Ring Three*. Ill. by Cyndy Szekeres. Putnam, 1973, o.p. SUBJECTS: Historical fiction; Plays — Fiction; Telephones — Fiction. RL C.

Frank and his sister Martha, with her friend Jean, convince their father to get a new-fangled telephone by producing a play. Characterizations, dialogue, and historical detail all ring true. The antics of cats and children enliven the period drawings.

287 *Second Car in Town*. Ill. by Ray Burns. Putnam, 1972, o.p. SERIES: Break-of-Day. SUBJECTS: Cars — Fiction; Historical fiction. RL B.

Garbed in a duster, Ellen felt like a princess on her first car ride. A feeling for the fear, wonder, and hazards of the new contraption is conveyed. Good ink sketches capture the action and humor.

Bowden, Joan C.

288 *Bean Boy*. Ill. by Sal Murdocca. Macmillan, 1978, o.p. SERIES: Ready-to-Read. SUBJECTS: Cumulative tales. RL A.

The adventures of a child carved from a bean by a childless couple are told in original cumulative fashion. Green and orange drawings have some folk flavor.

Bowdish, Lynea

289 *The Carousel Ride*. Ill. by Patrick Girouard. Children's Press, 1998, ISBN 0-516-20967-1. SERIES: Rookie Reader. SUBJECTS: Imagination — Fiction; Siblings — Fiction. RL A. LEXILE 40L.

Bold colors and black line drawings convey the imaginary journeys of a young girl as she rides a merry-go-round. Her brother may think the ride will take him nowhere, but Mara knows better.

290 *A Dog for a Day*. Ill. by Karen Stormer Brooks. Children's Press, 2003, ISBN 0-516-22849-8. SERIES: Rookie Reader. SUBJECTS: Pets — Dogs — Fiction; Pets — Fiction; Stories in rhyme. RL A. LEXILE AD320L.

Bertha McCain has a dog for each day of the week that exhibits a special talent. The neighbors may complain, but Bertha says there is always room for more. In this simple rhyming story, pastel pencil illustrations of friendly lovable dogs parade through the days of the week.

291 *One Glad Man*. Ill. by Kristin Sorra. Children's Press, 1999, ISBN 0-516-21595-7. SERIES: Rookie Reader. SUBJECTS: Concepts — Fiction; Loneliness — Fiction. RL A.

A lonely man finds himself surrounded by an array of animals as they count their way into his home. From one to ten, dogs, cats, spiders, birds, mice, and frogs are pictured in full-page angular illustrations in a muted palette.

292 *Thunder Doesn't Scare Me!* Ill. by John Wallace. Children's Press, 2001, ISBN 0-516-22151-5. SERIES: Rookie Reader. SUBJECTS: Fear — Fiction; Pets — Dogs — Fiction; Storms — Fiction. RL A.

Childlike watercolor illustrations enrich a simple story of a young girl helping her dog cope with his fear of thunder during a storm. Love and caring exude from the well-matched text and drawings.

Boyd, Lizi

293 *Bailey, the Big Bully*. Ill. by author. Puffin, 1991, ISBN 0-14-054051-2. SUBJECTS: Behavior — Bullying. RL A.

A didactic story about a new boy who ignores a bully called Bailey, and then invites him to join the neighborhood children in building a treehouse. Ink and wash drawings are more appealing than the story.

Bozzo, Maxine Z.

294 *Toby in the Country, Toby in the City*. Ill. by Frank Modell. Greenwillow, 1982, o.p. SUBJECTS: City and town life — Fiction; Farm and country life — Fiction. RL A.

The similarities between the lifestyle of a country boy and a city boy are emphasized, from school and play to enjoyment of the seasons. Excellent comic watercolor illustrations add sparkle to the simple text.

Bram, Elizabeth

295 *Woodruff and the Clocks*. Ill. by author. Dial, 1980, o.p. SERIES: Dial Easy-to-Read. SUBJECTS: Clocks — Fiction; Pets — Cats — Fiction. RL B.

Woodruff finds out that his neglected cat, Muffin, is more important to him than his fascination with clocks, in the first of four stories in this book. Flat colors highlight simple ink drawings.

Brandenberg, Franz

296 *Aunt Nina and Her Nephews and Nieces*. Ill. by Aliki. Greenwillow, 1983, ISBN 0-688-01870-X. SUBJECTS: Birthdays — Fiction; Family life — Fiction; Pets — Cats — Fiction. RL B.

Aunt Nina's house provides more adventure than the zoo, the toy shop, the theater, the haunted house, and a treasure hunt combined when her nieces and nephews come to celebrate her cat's birthday. Lively watercolor and ink drawings add to the action.

297 *Everyone Ready?* Ill. by Aliki. Greenwillow, 1979, o.p. SERIES: Read-Alone. SUBJECTS: Family life — Fiction; Mice — Fiction. RL B.

The Fieldmouse family is so busy they have trouble catching the train at the same time. Delicate pen and ink drawings with washes of pink and green match the warmth and humor with human parallels.

298 *A Fun Weekend*. Ill. by Alexa Brandenberg. Greenwillow, 1991, ISBN 0-688-09721-9. SUBJECTS: Bears — Fiction; Family life — Fiction. RL B.

A bear family contentedly sleeps in its van when they are too late for their reservations at a lodge after a long day of stops for stretching, swimming, eating ice cream, and shopping. Alexa Brandenberg illustrates her father's story in colorful watercolor, crayon, and colored pencil drawings.

299 *Leo and Emily and the Dragon*. Ill. by Aliki. Greenwillow, 1984, ISBN 0-688-02532-3. SERIES: Read-Alone. SUBJECTS: Baby-sitting — Fiction; Hiking — Fiction; Imagination — Fiction. RL A.

Leo and Emily have a long hike, complete with picnic, cave, sleeping bags, and sunbathing. When "boring" Harold baby-sits that night, they have another exhausting and imaginative hike indoors! Lively drawings in spring green and orange capture the delights, fears, and exhaustion well.

300 *Leo and Emily's Big Ideas*. Ill. by Aliki. Greenwillow, 1982, ISBN 0-688-00755-4. SERIES: Read-Alone. SUBJECTS: Family life — Fiction; Friendship — Fiction; Play — Fiction. RL B.

Leo and Emily's escapades include dressing up to scare people and making wet tracks and "back" marks all over the garage. The imaginative text and delicate, lively illustrations capture the spirit of adventure in everyday neighborhood play.

301 *Leo and Emily's Zoo*. Ill. by Yossi Abolafia. Greenwillow, 1988, ISBN 0-688-07457-X. SUBJECTS: Family life — Fiction; Friendship — Fiction; Play — Fiction. RL B.

Leo and Emily's backyard zoo is disappointing until some "zoo animals" appear next door. This is a very refreshing story enhanced by lively watercolors of children and animals.

Brandenberg, Franz (cont.)

302 *Nice New Neighbors*. Ill. by Aliki. Scholastic, pap., 1980, ISBN 0-688-84105-8. SERIES: Read-Alone. SUBJECTS: Friendship — Fiction; Mice — Fiction; Moving, household — Fiction. RL B.

Rejected by the other children on the street, the mice children decide to put on a play to attract their new neighbors' attention. Diminutive ink and wash drawings add to the charm of this book.

303 *A Robber! A Robber!* Ill. by Aliki. Greenwillow, 1976, o.p. SUBJECTS: Fear — Fiction; Pets — Cats — Fiction. RL B.

The sound of snoring from their bottom bunk beds scares Edward and Elizabeth, who are in their respective rooms. In the morning they find out that visitors Uncle Peter and Aunt Ann were sharing their room. Darker penciled night scenes convey just enough feeling of fear.

304 *Six New Students*. Ill. by Aliki. Greenwillow, 1978, o.p. SERIES: Read-Alone. SUBJECTS: Mice — Fiction; School stories. RL B.

Ferdinand the mouse's creative first-grade teacher introduces him to all the subjects he does not expect to enjoy in first grade. Gentle humor has marvelous small pastel watercolor mouse illustrations.

305 *What Can You Make of It?* Ill. by Aliki. Greenwillow, 1977, o.p. SERIES: Read-Alone. SUBJECTS: Circuses — Fiction; Mice — Fiction; Moving, household — Fiction. RL C.

The Fieldmouse family moves in seven vans because of all their "rubbish": magazines, toilet paper tubes, milk and egg cartons, and so on. However, they find creative uses for all their treasures. Whimsical ink sketches have yellow, orange, gray, and green colored pencil highlights.

Brandon, Anthony G.

306 *Moving Day*. Ill. by Wong Herbert Yee. Harcourt, 2005, ISBN 0-15-205646-7. SERIES: Green Light Readers. SUBJECTS: Asian Americans — Fiction; Moving, household — Fiction; Pets — Dogs — Fiction. RL B.

Everyone in the Kim household is moving except Annie, who definitely does not want to! Picking up the last box, Annie discovers a puppy. The puppy is moving to the new house, and now so is she. Framed drawings in bold colors depict the mixed emotions of a family's move. Simple activities suggested at the end extend the story.

Branley, Franklyn M.

307 *Beginning of the Earth*. Rev. ed. Ill. by Giulio Maestro. HarperCollins, 1972, ISBN 0-690-04676-6. SERIES: Let's-Read-and-Find-Out. SUBJECTS: Astronomy and astronomers; Geology and geologists; Science and scientists. RL C.

Dark, abstract designs with ink and washes of black and gray with highlights of fuchsia and blue aptly illustrate Branley's speculation.

308 *The Big Dipper*. Ill. by Molly Coxe. HarperCollins, 1991, ISBN 0-06-445100-3. SERIES: Let's-Read-and-Find-Out. SUBJECTS: Astronomy and astronomers; Nature; Science and scientists. RL B.

A girl who loves to watch the night sky with her father and her dog gives information about the big (and little) dipper (s) and the North Star. She encourages the reader to take a friend outside on a still, dark night to star-watch. Simple pencil and watercolor illustrations add humor.

309 *Oxygen Keeps You Alive*. Ill. by Don Madden. HarperCollins, 1971, o.p. SERIES: Let's-Read-and-Find-Out Science. SUBJECTS: Air; Science and scientists; Science experiments — Air. RL C.

The text underlines the importance of oxygen to animals, birds, fish, and plants, but especially to people — at high altitudes, in space, or under the sea — at every moment of life. Drawings complement the text to show how the lungs work.

310 *Rain and Hail*. Ill. by Harriett Barton. HarperCollins, 1983, ISBN 0-690-04353-8. SERIES: Let's-Read-and-Find-Out. SUBJECTS: Science and scientists; Weather. RL C.

Information about both rain and hail is logically presented. Illustrations and type are in royal blue.

311 *Shooting Stars*. Ill. by Holly Keller. HarperCollins, 1989, ISBN 0-06-020512-1. SERIES: Let's-Read-and-Find-Out. SUBJECTS: Astronomy and astronomers; Nature; Science and scientists. RL C.

One hundred tons of meteoroids fall on Planet Earth every day! When they make a light streak, they are called meteors, from a Greek word meaning "something in the sky." Informative text is illustrated with lighthearted ink and watercolor illustrations.

312 *The Sky Is Full of Stars*. Ill. by Felicia Bond. HarperCollins, pap., 1983, ISBN 0-690-04123-3. SERIES: Let's-Read-and-Find-Out Science. SUBJECTS: Astronomy and astronomers; Science and scientists. RL B.

Branley takes children out at night — with pet and blanket — to observe four common constellations, and gives directions for reproducing the configurations with a coffee can and a flashlight. Blue, light green, and various shades of gray show the children and the stars.

313 *Snow Is Falling*. Rev. ed. Ill. by Holly Keller. HarperCollins, 1986, ISBN 0-690-04548-4. SERIES: Let's-Read-and-Find-Out. SUBJECTS: Science and scientists; Weather — Snow; Winter. RL B.

The benefits as well as the hardships of snow to plants, animals, and people are presented. Details of wildlife winters and playing in the snow are drawn in ink against a sparkling blue sky.

314 *The Sun: Our Nearest Star*. Rev ed. Ill. by Don Madden. HarperCollins, 1988, ISBN 0-690-04678-2. SERIES: Let's-Read-and-Find-Out. SUBJECTS: Astronomy and astronomers; Science and scientists. RL C.

Besides information about the sun, a simple plant experiment and the idea that coal and oil are stored-up solar energy are introduced. Ink drawings in sky blue, apple green, and gray highlight and lighten the text.

315 *Sunshine Makes the Seasons*. Rev. ed. Ill. by Giulio Maestro. HarperCollins, pap., 1996, ISBN 0-690-04482-8. SERIES: Let's-Read-and-Find-Out Science. SUBJECTS: Science and scientists; Seasons. RL B.

Good information about seasonal change is logically presented and related to a child's experience. Textured crayon against black is very effective.

316 *Tornado Alert*. Ill. by Giulio Maestro. HarperCollins, 1988, ISBN 0-690-04686-3. SERIES: Let's-Read-and-Find-Out. SUBJECTS: Science and scientists; Weather — Storms. RL C.

Exceptionally well presented information about tornados is included along with simple safety precautions to follow during a tornado. Softly textured colored drawings are also factual but reassuring.

317 *Volcanoes*. Ill. by Marc Simont. HarperCollins, pap., 1986, ISBN 0-690-04431-3. SERIES: Let's-Read-and-Find-Out Science. SUBJECTS: Geology and geologists; Science and scientists. RL C.

The examples of Pompeii, Krakatoa, and Mount St. Helen's provide good information about the movement of tectonic plates and associated earthquake/volcanic activity. Excellent watercolors show the above events, simple diagrams, and geologists at work.

318 *Weight and Weightlessness*. Ill. by Graham Booth. HarperCollins, 1971, o.p. SERIES: Let's-Read-and-Find-Out Science. SUBJECTS: Concepts — Weight ; Science and scientists. RL B.

Well-described concepts of weight and weightlessness are illustrated with simple, decorative ink sketches.

319 *What Happened to the Dinosaurs?* Ill. by Marc Simont. HarperCollins, 1991, ISBN 0-690-04749-5. SERIES: Let's-Read-and-Find-Out. SUBJECTS: Dinosaurs; Science and scientists. RL C.

Theories of dinosaur extinction are examined: comet collisions caused by the twin to the sun, the Nemesis star, gathering clouds of dust into comets; or a cooler sun; or dinosaur egg predators; or some sickness. Marc Simont's exceptional watercolors illustrate current dinosaur research.

320 *What Makes Day and Night*. Rev. ed. Ill. by Helen Borten. HarperCollins, 1986, ISBN 0-690-04524-7. SERIES: Let's-Read-and-Find-Out Science. SUBJECTS: Astronomy and astronomers; Science and scientists. RL B.

As a child turns in a circle before a lamp, so the earth turns in relation to the sun, creating light and dark periods we call day and night. Basic information is well illustrated with strong black prints on white or a solid color.

Branley, Franklyn M. (cont.)

321 *What the Moon Is Like*. Rev. ed. Photos. Ill. by True Kelley. HarperCollins, pap., 1986, ISBN 0-694-00205-4. SERIES: Let's-Read-and-Find-Out. SUBJECTS: Astronomy and astronomers; Science and scientists. RL C.

Updated basic information about the moon is excellent. Illustrations are cutesy pastels, smudgy sketches, and mediocre photographs.

Bredeson, Carmen

322 *Astronauts*. Children's Press, 2003, ISBN 0-516-22529-4. SERIES: Rookie Read-About Science. SUBJECTS: Astronauts; Space travel. RL B. LEXILE 450L.

How can you become an astronaut? Learn how astronauts train and the work they do on the space shuttle. Color and black-and-white photographs clearly emphasize the many and varied jobs that astronauts perform in space.

323 *Florida*. Children's Press, 2002, ISBN 0-516-22671-1. SERIES: Rookie Read-About Geography. SUBJECTS: United States. RL B. LEXILE 380L.

From the beaches and the swamps to Walt Disney World and the state capital, travel the state of Florida to learn about its exciting past and future. Brightly colored photographs focus on the most exciting places to visit.

324 *Georgia*. Children's Press, 2002, ISBN 0-516-22670-3. SERIES: Rookie Read-About Geography. SUBJECTS: United States. RL B. LEXILE 370L.

Learn about the history, people, and landmarks of the Peach State. Full-page color photographs and maps highlight the important facts about this southeastern state.

325 *Getting Ready for Space*. Children's Press, 2003, ISBN 0-516-22498-0. SERIES: Rookie Read-About Science. SUBJECTS: Astronauts; Space travel. RL B. LEXILE 450L.

As astronauts train for space travel, they learn to float, eat, work, fix equipment, and even go to the bathroom! Simulation units in water, on land, and in the air help them prepare. Detailed color photographs provide visual examples of all the training needs mentioned in the text.

326 *Labor Day*. Children's Press, 2001, ISBN 0-516-22378-X. SERIES: Rookie Read-About Holidays. SUBJECTS: Holidays; Labor Day. RL B. LEXILE 320L.

Why do we celebrate Labor Day? A brief introduction to the history and traditions of the holiday is complemented by black-and-white archival pictures as well as contemporary color photographs.

327 *Liftoff!* Children's Press, 2003, ISBN 0-516-22499-9. SERIES: Rookie Read-About Science. SUBJECTS: Space travel. RL B. LEXILE 440L.

Get ready to blast off with the space shuttle. As the shuttle is moved into place, the astronauts are being prepared by the ground crew. Framed color photographs provide a step-by-step visual guide to launch preparations.

328 *Living on a Space Shuttle*. Children's Press, 2003, ISBN 0-516-22528-6. SERIES: Rookie Read-About Science. SUBJECTS: Space travel. RL B. LEXILE 440L.

Everyday life experiences are different when you are on the space shuttle. Imagine brushing your teeth, eating, or sleeping. Lively color photographs show the astronauts as they float in the space shuttle, trying to do their jobs.

329 *Looking at Maps and Globes*. Children's Press, 2001, ISBN 0-516-22351-8. SERIES: Rookie Read-About Geography. SUBJECTS: Globes; Maps. RL B. LEXILE 410L.

Examine the different kinds of maps and globes and learn about their special features. Diagrams, sample maps, and photographs colorfully demonstrate the importance of maps and globes and how to use them.

330 *The Moon*. Children's Press, 2003, ISBN 0-516-22864-1. SERIES: Rookie Read-About Science. SUBJECTS: Astronomy and astronomers. RL B. LEXILE 560L.

Color photographs from NASA and diagrams feature the exploration, phases, and composition of the moon. A special "Words You Know" section follows the text.

Brenner, Barbara

331 *Baltimore Orioles*. Ill. by J. Winslow Higginbottom. HarperCollins, 1974, o.p. SERIES: I Can Read. SUBJECTS: Birds. RL A.

Besides mating and nesting habits, Brenner includes hazards in the lives of young orioles. Well-presented information is accompanied by appealing illustrations.

332 *Beavers Beware!* Ill. by Emily A. McCully. Bantam, 1992, ISBN 0-553-07498-9. SERIES: Bank Street Ready-to-Read. SUBJECTS: Beavers — Fiction. RL A.

A family with a house by the river find a beaver family taking over their dock. While they are discussing beaver, tree, and people rights, a storm takes the dock downstream. Vivid, full-color illustrations are by a favorite, Emily McCully.

333 *Beef Stew*. Ill. by Catherine Siracusa. Random House, pap., 1990, ISBN 0-394-85046-7. SERIES: Step into Reading. SUBJECTS: Grandparents — Fiction. RL B. LEXILE 260L.

Nicky cannot seem to get any friends to come over for a dinner of beef stew, but he gets a nice surprise. New, colorfully expressive illustrations update a favorite story.

334 *Dinosaurium: The Museum That Explores the World of Living Dinosaurs*. Ill. by Donna Braginetz. Bantam, 1993, ISBN 0-553-07614-0. SERIES: A Bank Street Museum Book. SUBJECTS: Dinosaurs; Science and scientists. RL C.

Families move through the halls and labs of a museum to learn about time periods, bones, feeding, weight, and anatomy of dinosaurs. Insets show fossils, plate tectonics, skeletal details, eggs, and important paleontologists, including several children.

335 *A Dog I Know*. Ill. by Fred Brenner. HarperCollins, 1983, o.p. SUBJECTS: Pets — Dogs — Fiction. RL B.

The special qualities of a boy's shaggy mutt are told in the first person. Brown pencil with washes focuses on the brave-with-bear, scared-of-paper beloved pet.

336 *Moon Boy*. Ill. by J. Gaban. Bantam, 1990, ISBN 0-553-05858-4. SERIES: Bank Street Ready-to-Read. SUBJECTS: Imagination — Fiction; Night — Fiction. RL A.

When a shiny dot on his windowsill turns out to be Moon Boy, shaped like a nightlight, a small boy shuts Moon Boy in his toy box to keep him. But when the gold balloon moon and the stars are dark with sadness, the boy releases Moon Boy. Illustrations are done in midnight blue and glowing white.

337 *Nicky's Sister*. Ill. by John Johnson. Knopf, 1966, o.p. SERIES: Read-Alone. SUBJECTS: Behavior — Running away — Fiction; Sibling rivalry — Fiction. RL B.

Nicky prefers a hamster to a pesky baby sister until she is threatened by a bully. Details of home life are in ink with a three-color wash.

338 *The Plant That Kept on Growing*. Ill. by Melissa Sweet. Bantam, 1996, o.p. SERIES: Bank Street Ready-to-Read. SUBJECTS: Plants — Fiction; Stories in rhyme. RL A.

Only one plant remains in the twins' 4-H garden as the neighborhood animals enjoy a feast. Full-page watercolor and ink illustrations humorously track the growth of a tomato plant that not only wins the big prize but supplies the town with tomato soup, tomato salad, and tomato sauce for 200 pizzas.

339 *Rosa and Marco and the Three Wishes*. Ill. by Megan Halsey. Macmillan, 1992, ISBN 0-02-712315-4. SUBJECTS: Magic — Fiction; Siblings — Fiction; Sports — Fishing — Fiction. RL A.

A modern child's version of "The Fisherman and His Wife" has jealous older sister Rosa forced to use the third and last wish to get a taco unstuck from her brother's nose. Soft pencil and wash drawings of the pair support the storytelling.

340 *Wagon Wheels*. Ill. by Don Bolognese. HarperCollins, pap., 1978, ISBN 0-06-020669-1. SERIES: I Can Read History. SUBJECTS: Behavior — Brave; Frontier and pioneer life; Historical fiction. RL B.

This amazing adventure story of homesteading in the Kansas Territory is based on events in the lives of the Muldie boys and their father. Their resourcefulness and courage in facing starvation, grief, and a prairie fire are depicted. Effective pencil drawings have three-tone washes.

Brenner, Barbara, and Bernice Chardiet

341 *Where's That Insect?* Ill. by Carol Schwartz. Scholastic, 1993, ISBN 0-590-45210-X. SERIES: Hide-and-Seek Science Book. SUBJECTS: Insects; Science and scientists. RL C.

Leafcutter ants, dragonflies, ladybugs, aphids, water bugs, sphinx moths, and walking sticks are some of the insects that can be identified after this introduction with full-color drawings.

Brenner, Barbara, and William H. Hooks

342 *Lion and Lamb Step Out.* Ill. by Bruce Degen. Bantam, 1990, ISBN 0-553-05860-6. SERIES: Bank Street Ready-to-Read. SUBJECTS: Friendship — Fiction; Lions — Fiction; Sheep — Fiction. RL A.

Lamb leads the way home after friend Lion's arrogance gets them lost; Lion decides his boring life is wonderful after visiting Uncle Leo at the circus; Lion learns that best friends don't give away secrets. Exuberant drawings are by Bruce Degen.

343 *Ups and Downs with Lion and Lamb.* Ill. by Bruce Degen. Bantam, 1991, ISBN 0-553-07088-6. SERIES: Bank Street Ready-to-Read. SUBJECTS: Friendship — Fiction; Lions — Fiction; Sheep — Fiction. RL A.

Lamb starts her own club when excluded from that of the other animals and finds a way to give Lion enough courage to save Lambkin from a wolf. Imagine their joy when Lion moves only across a small river, instead of across an ocean as they feared. Lively Degen animal drawings enhance the text.

Brewster, Patience

344 *Too Many Puppies.* Ill. by author. Scholastic, pap., 1997, ISBN 0-590-60276-4. SERIES: Hello Reader! SUBJECTS: Pets — Dogs — Fiction. RL B. LEXILE 420L.

When her dog has puppies, Milly wants to keep them all, but Mommy says no. Milly disagrees until the puppies get older and she has to take care of them. Playful images of frolicking puppies change into a busy work-filled portrayal of keeping seven puppies in order.

Bridges, Margaret Park

345 *Edna Elephant.* Ill. by Janie Bynum. Candlewick, 2002, o.p. SERIES: Brand New Readers. SUBJECTS: Elephants — Fiction; Humorous stories. RL A.

A lively lavender elephant dances, dresses, and bakes her way into the hearts of brand new readers in four short episodes, followed by advice to parents. Boldly colored pages with fresh pastel watercolor and ink illustrations spin and twirl right along with Edna.

Bridwell, Norman

346 *Clifford and the Halloween Parade.* Ill. by author. Scholastic, 1999, ISBN 1-59054-545-1; pap., ISBN 0-439-09834-3. SERIES: Hello Reader! SUBJECTS: Halloween — Fiction; Pets — Dogs — Fiction. RL A. LEXILE 50L.

It's Halloween and Clifford wonders what he can be. The signature illustrations of everyone's favorite big red dog will have very beginning readers guessing. Climb aboard and join Clifford the fire engine on Halloween night.

347 *Clifford Makes a Friend.* Ill. by author. Scholastic, pap., 1998, ISBN 0-590-37930-5. SERIES: Scholastic Reader. SUBJECTS: Friendship — Fiction; Pets — Dogs — Fiction. RL A. LEXILE BR.

A very simple story of a boy and a dog celebrates the joy of friendship. Uncluttered, colorful illustrations that focus on Clifford the big red dog aid beginning readers in this portrayal of friends having fun together.

348 *Clifford's Valentines.* Ill. by author. Scholastic, pap., 2001, ISBN 0-439-18300-6. SERIES: Hello Reader! SUBJECTS: Pets — Dogs — Fiction; Valentine's Day — Fiction. RL A.

On Valentine's Day, Clifford the big red dog receives many special valentines. In the park with all his friends, Clifford makes them a big valentine in the snow. With bold colors and simple lines, Clifford's actions are well illustrated and described.

Brimner, Larry Dane

349 *Aggie and Will.* Ill. by Rebecca Thornburgh. Children's Press, 1998, ISBN 0-

516-20754-7. SERIES: Rookie Reader. SUBJECTS: Friendship — Fiction. RL B. LEXILE 460L.

Two friends have trouble agreeing on food and outdoor fun, but they do agree on one thing — going to the library. Detailed vignettes in watercolor and ink elaborate on the ups and downs of friendship.

350 *Brave Mary*. Ill. by Marilyn Mets. Children's Press, 1996, ISBN 0-516-02056-0. SERIES: Rookie Reader. SUBJECTS: Behavior — Brave — Fiction; Stories in rhyme. RL A. LEXILE BR.

Lively colorful illustrations and a simple rhyming text describe Mary's courageous acts, which are appreciated by her mother, her brother, her teacher, and her preacher.

351 *Cats!* Ill. by Tom Payne. Children's Press, 2000, ISBN 0-516-22010-1. SERIES: Rookie Reader. SUBJECTS: Pets — Cats — Fiction. RL A.

A child's joy while playing with her cats is beautifully portrayed in thirty-three words and simple line and pastel watercolors. Frisky felines romp with fun.

352 *Cowboy Up!* Ill. by Susan Miller. Children's Press, 1999, ISBN 0-516-21199-4. SERIES: Rookie Reader. SUBJECTS: Cowboys — Fiction. RL A. LEXILE BR.

From the break of day to day's end, a young boy's rodeo experience is simply chronicled in thirty-nine words. Lariat-encircled illustrations and text add to the flavor of a young cowboy's adventure.

353 *Dinosaurs Dance*. Ill. by Patrick Girouard. Children's Press, 1998, ISBN 0-516-20752-0. SERIES: Rookie Reader. SUBJECTS: Dinosaurs — Fiction. RL A. LEXILE 120L.

Brightly colored cartoon dinosaurs — some complete with sunglasses — sway, hop, and clog in their own special dance. Their expressions and unique dance steps are an enticement to beginning readers.

354 *How Many Ants?* Ill. by Joan Cottle. Children's Press, 1997, ISBN 0-516-20398-3. SERIES: Rookie Reader. SUBJECTS: Ants — Fiction; Concepts — Numbers — Fiction. RL B. LEXILE 200L.

Ants go marching, increasing their numbers by ten as they search for the favorite food group — cake! Hilarious watercolor illustrations add funny tidbits of ant humor to the simple story line while cleverly reinforcing the mathematical concept.

355 *Lightning Liz*. Ill. by Brian Floca. Children's Press, 1998, ISBN 0-516-20753-9. SERIES: Rookie Reader. SUBJECTS: Family life — Fiction. RL A. LEXILE BR.

Wherever she goes, Liz races and darts her way. It's easy to see where she got her nickname of Lightning Liz. Full-page watercolor illustrations energetically follow the escapades of a little girl constantly on the go.

356 *The Long Way Home*. Ill. by Terry Sirrell. Children's Press, 2000, ISBN 0-516-22011-X. SERIES: Rookie Reader. SUBJECTS: Pets — Fiction. RL A.

While dropping some treats, a dog, cat, hog, and rat follow a young girl home. Simple rhymes and funny cartoon drawings 'tag along' for a unique and long, eventful walk home from school.

357 *Summer Fun*. Ill. by Christine Tripp. Children's Press, 2003, ISBN 0-516-22548-0. SERIES: Rookie Choices. SUBJECTS: Friendship — Fiction; Summer — Fiction. RL B. LEXILE 240L.

A trip to the water park is canceled when the car breaks down, but neighbor Mr. Price provides another way to have cool and wet summer fun. Lighthearted illustrations depict the warm relationship of three friends.

358 *Trash Trouble*. Ill. by Christine Tripp. Children's Press, 2003, ISBN 0-516-22547-2. SERIES: Rookie Choices. SUBJECTS: Garbage and garbage disposal; School stories. RL B. LEXILE 100L.

Focusing on protecting the environment, the Corner Kids and their classmates pick up litter on their nature field trip after they discover a bird trapped in a lunch bag. Energetic drawings follow the environmental mission of the second-grade class.

Brinkloe, Julie

359 *Gordon Goes Camping*. Ill. by author. Doubleday, 1975, o.p. SUBJECTS: Bears —

Brinkloe, Julie (cont.)

Fiction; Camps and camping — Fiction. RL B.

Gordon needs his friend Marvin's advice — and company — when he goes on his first camping trip. Patterned ink drawings have a green contrasting wash.

Brisson, Pat

360 *Little Sister, Big Sister*. Ill. by Diana Cain Bluthenthal. Holt, 1999, ISBN 0-805-05887-7. SERIES: Redfeather Chapter Book. SUBJECTS: Siblings — Fiction. RL B. LEXILE 310L.

In four easy-to-read chapters, Hester and her younger sister Edna share sisterly adventures. A game of "Queen" — in which Hester entices Edna to clean up her sister's bedroom — and the making of "Thunder Cookies" when a storm frightens Edna are portrayed in simple sentences and scattered black-and-white comic illustrations that get to the heart of a home.

Brodkin, Adele M.

361 *The Lonely Only Dog*. Ill. by Larry Di Fiori. Scholastic, 1998, ISBN 0-590-52280-9. SERIES: Hello Reader! SUBJECTS: Loneliness — Fiction; Pets — Dogs — Fiction. RL B. LEXILE AD460L.

With only Gwen and Greg to play with, Harry the dog thought he was lonely until Arthur came over and ate from his bowl, slept on his pillow, and played his special game with his friends. Full-color illustrations appropriately portray Harry's delight and then dismay at having a new playmate.

Bronin, Andrew

362 *Gus and Buster Work Things Out*. Ill. by Cyndy Szekeres. Putnam, 1975, o.p. SERIES: Break-of-Day. SUBJECTS: Raccoons — Fiction; Siblings — Fiction. RL B.

Squabbling over toys or the top bunk, or even how to eat properly, two brothers settle their differences by playing each other's favorite games — football and checkers. Soft pencil drawings with pale yellow warm this reassuring tale.

Brooks, Laura, adapter

363 *The Beast's Story*. Ill. by Ed Gutierrez and Serge Michaels. Western, 1992, o.p. SERIES: Golden Easy Reader. SUBJECTS: Movies. RL A.

A drastically simplified adaptation of a Disney-stripped story uses the Disney illustrations so familiar to many movie viewers. The effect is sentimental and cutesy.

Brown, Charlotte Lewis

364 *After the Dinosaurs: Mammoths and Fossil Mammals*. Ill. by Phil Wilson. HarperCollins, 2006, ISBN 0-06-053053-7. SERIES: I Can Read. SUBJECTS: Prehistoric animals. RL B.

A paleontologist shares information about the mammals that lived on after the dinosaurs. Fascinating, full-page illustrations that are detailed and clear are accompanied by a pronunciation guide and brief description.

365 *Beyond the Dinosaurs: Monsters of the Air and Sea*. Ill. by Phil Wilson. HarperCollins, 2007, ISBN 0-06-053056-1. SERIES: I Can Read. SUBJECTS: Prehistoric animals. RL B.

Prehistoric creatures such as the Pteranodon, Deinosuchus and Ichthyosaurus flew and swam. Full-page highly detailed and colorful illustrations offer new readers a glimpse into the sky and sea millions of years ago.

Brown, Laura Krasny

366 *Rex and Lilly Schooltime*. Ill. by Marc Brown. Little, Brown, 1997, ISBN 0-316-10920-7. SERIES: Dino Easy Reader. SUBJECTS: Dinosaurs — Fiction; School stories; Siblings — Fiction. RL A. LEXILE 120L.

At school, dinosaur siblings Rex and Lilly have show-and-tell, trade lunches, and practice reading. Simple line-and-watercolor cartoon-like characters in many shades of green accent the brother and sister's school-time adventures.

Brown, Marc

367 *Arthur Loses a Friend*. Ill. by author. Random House, 2006, ISBN 0-375-82974-1.

SERIES: Step into Reading. SUBJECTS: Animals — Fiction; Friendship — Fiction. RL A.

While visiting his father for a month, Buster promises to write, but everyone is getting postcards except Arthur. Fears of losing his friend are dispelled when the mail carrier delivers a bunch of letters sent to the wrong address. Uncluttered, full-page illustrations focus on providing visual clues to the beginning reader.

368 *Arthur Tricks the Tooth Fairy*. Ill. by author. Random House, 1997, ISBN 0-679-88464-5. SERIES: Step into Reading. SUBJECTS: Human body — Teeth — Fiction; Siblings — Fiction; Tooth fairy. RL B.

After Arthur has a visit from the Tooth Fairy, sister D.W. insists she will too, even though she is too young. When all else fails, D.W. places a shark tooth under her pillow. The familial love and humor are embodied in brightly colored illustrations.

369 *Arthur's Classroom Fib*. Ill. by author. Random House, pap., 2007, ISBN 0-375-82975-X. SERIES: Step into Reading. SUBJECTS: Animals — Fiction; Friendship — Fiction; School stories. RL B.

Everyone in his class seems to have had a more exciting summer vacation than Arthur, which makes him want to slightly exaggerate his own summer activities. Humorous illustrations capture the dilemma Arthur faces.

370 *Arthur's Fire Drill*. Ill. by author. Random House, 2000, ISBN 0-679-88476-9. SERIES: Step into Reading. SUBJECTS: Animals — Fiction; Safety — Fiction; Siblings — Fiction. RL A.

Growing up, Arthur has always taught D.W. safety precautions. Now in nursery school, she is learning about fire safety rules and Arthur helps. In his signature drawings, the illustrator carefully illuminates the steps to safety and the importance of practice drills.

371 *Arthur's Lost Puppy*. Ill. by author. Random House, 2000, ISBN 0-679-88466-1. SERIES: Step into Reading. SUBJECTS: Animals — Fiction; Babies — Fiction; Pets — Dogs — Fiction. RL B.

Unable to console baby Kate at the neighborhood fair, Pal the dog runs to find the one thing that will make her stop crying — a balloon. Lively illustrations show the fun of being at the fair, along with Arthur and D.W.'s loving attempts to care for their unhappy sister.

372 *Arthur's Reading Race*. Ill. by author. Random House, 1996, ISBN 0-679-96738-9. SERIES: Step into Reading. SUBJECTS: Animals — Fiction; Siblings — Fiction. RL A.

Arthur loves to read and wants to teach D.W. He challenges her to read ten words and D.W. easily wins the ice cream cone prize while teaching Arthur a few new words. Detailed humorous illustrations help both D.W. and readers identify some new words.

373 *D.W. All Wet*. Ill. by author. Little, Brown, 1988, ISBN 0-316-11077-9. SERIES: Joy Street Books. SUBJECTS: Animals — Fiction; Siblings — Fiction; Sports — Swimming — Fiction. RL A.

When older brother Arthur dumps a reluctant D.W. into the water at the beach, she finds out she loves it! Soft pastel drawings add warmth to the family story.

374 *D.W. Flips!* Ill. by author. Little, Brown, 1987, ISBN 0-316-11239-9. SERIES: Joy Street Books. SUBJECTS: Animals — Fiction; Sports — Gymnastics. RL A.

D.W., Arthur's younger sister, thinks she's in the baby class for gymnastics, but only learns how to somersault after much practice in this lighthearted, sympathetic view of childhood learning. Illustrations of animal children are in soft pastels.

375 *D.W. Thinks Big*. Ill. by author. Little, Brown, 1993, ISBN 0-316-11305-0. SUBJECTS: Animals — Fiction; Siblings — Fiction; Weddings — Fiction. RL A.

When the ring bearer, D.W.'s older brother Arthur, drops Aunt Lucy's ring down the register, only smaller D.W. can rescue the ring. Humorous story is enhanced by the author's lively pastel drawings.

376 *Glasses for D.W.* Ill. by author. Random House, 1996, ISBN 0-679-86740-6. SERIES: Step into Reading. SUBJECTS: Animals — Fiction; Eyeglasses — Fiction; Siblings — Fiction. RL B. LEXILE 100L.

Just because Arthur has glasses, D.W. wants some too, and tries to prove she can't see until she wants to play soccer with Arthur and Buster.

Brown, Marc (cont.)

Lighthearted illustrations highlight D.W.'s playful eyewear imaginings while underscoring the importance of wearing glasses for Arthur.

377 *The Silly Tail Book*. Ill. by author. Stevens, pap., 1994, ISBN 0-8368-0986-6. SUBJECTS: Mythical creatures — Fiction; Stories in rhyme. RL A.

New colored pencil illustrations of cartoon animals ranging from armadillos to camels and seals to turtles show off the variety of tails — as well as some improbable ones. Lighthearted rhyme matches the fun.

378 *There's No Place Like Home*. Ill. by author. Parents Magazine Press, 1984, ISBN 0-8193-1125-1. SUBJECTS: Houses; Stories in rhyme. RL A.

From a cave to a shell, from a spruce to a pocket, this inventive story about possible homes stretches the imagination. Friendly colored pencil drawings are by the author.

379 *Witches Four*. Ill. by author. Parents Magazine Press, 1980, ISBN 0-448-41079-6. SERIES: Read Aloud Originals. SUBJECTS: Stories in rhyme; Witches — Fiction. RL A.

The witches four brush their teeth with spider paste and eat bat-wing sandwiches. When they lose their magic hats flying upside down on their broomsticks, they have to reclaim them from four homeless cats. Rhythmic rhyme is enhanced by the author's stylistic drawings, beginning with endpapers.

Brownell, M. Barbara

380 *Amazing Otters*. Ill. with photos. National Geographic, 1989, o.p. SERIES: Books for Young Explorers. SUBJECTS: Nature; Otters. RL C.

A most attractive book liberally illustrated with excellent land and underwater photographs of sea otters at work and play. Additional information and reading suggestions, as well as a world map showing the range of river and sea otters, are appended.

381 *Busy Beavers*. Ill. with photos and drawings. National Geographic, 1988, o.p. SERIES: Books for Young Readers. SUBJECTS: Beavers; Nature. RL C.

This photoessay has good information about beavers. Especially well done are photographs of a beaver swimming in clear water and of a beaver nursing her kit.

Brust, Beth Wagner

382 *The Great Tulip Trade*. Ill. by Jenny Mattheson. Random House, pap., 2005, ISBN 0-679-86738-7. SERIES: Step into Reading. SUBJECTS: Birthdays — Fiction; Fathers — Fiction. RL B.

Trading almost all of her birthday presents for livestock, furniture, and a painting, a young girl in Holland during the 1600s will not trade the last most precious tulip bulb even for gold and diamonds. Pastel illustrations aid in explaining an unusual era in Dutch history, a time of frenzied tulip bulb buying and selling.

Buck, Nola

383 *Oh, Cats!* Ill. by Nadine B. Westcott. HarperCollins, pap., 1997, ISBN 0-679-86738-8. SERIES: My First I Can Read. SUBJECTS: Pets — Cats — Fiction; Stories in rhyme. RL A. LEXILE BR.

In a simple rhyming story of twenty-five words for very beginning readers, a young girl spots three cats and invites them to play and stay with her. Lively pastel illustrations add to the fun, providing visual support for readers who will want to read the story again and again.

384 *Santa's Short Suit and Other Christmas Tongue Twisters*. Ill. by Sue Truesdell. HarperCollins, pap., 1997, ISBN 0-679-86738-9. SERIES: I Can Read. SUBJECTS: Christmas; Tongue twisters. RL B.

Rollicking full-page cartoon illustrations accompany and extend twenty-five lively Christmas tongue-twisters. "Shy Sam Shaw saw the same Santa Sarah says she saw."

385 *Sid and Sam*. Ill. by G. Brian Karas. HarperCollins, 1996, ISBN 0-06-025371-1. SERIES: My First I Can Read. SUBJECTS: Friendship — Fiction. RL A. LEXILE BR.

Meeting in a park, two children sing and sing until finally it is time to stop. Using minimal vocabulary, large print, and colorful mixed-media illustrations that augment the story, this book will help beginners accomplish reading success.

Buckless, Andrea

386 *Too Many Cooks!* Ill. by K. A. Jacobs. Scholastic, pap., 2000, ISBN 0-439-16966-6. SERIES: Hello Math Reader! SUBJECTS: Cookery — Fiction; Mathematics — Fiction. RL B.

While baby-sitting her younger brothers, Cara decides they should make super-duper soup. Using multiplication to adjust the soup for more people, Jay adds his own unusual ingredients to the pot. Blending colorfully detailed drawings that spice up the text, this book will help readers sharpen their math skills.

Bulla, Clyde R.

387 *Daniel's Duck.* Ill. by Joan Sandin. HarperCollins, pap., 1977, ISBN 0-06-020909-7. SERIES: I Can Read. SUBJECTS: Family life — Fiction; Wood carving — Fiction. RL A.

Everyone in Daniel's family spends long winter nights making crafts for the spring fair. When Daniel's carved duck evokes laughter, he thinks, at first, that people are laughing at him. Watercolor illustrations primarily in grays and green give rich details of Tennessee Appalachian life.

388 *Poor Boy, Rich Boy.* Ill. by Marcia Sewell. HarperCollins, 1979, o.p. SERIES: I Can Read. SUBJECTS: Orphans — Fiction. RL A.

Orphaned by war, Coco is raised by a baker, Rosa, but later claimed by a rich and doting uncle. This unusual and touching story about worldly values is simply illustrated with light tones highlighting expressive ink drawings by a noted illustrator.

389 *Singing Sam.* Ill. by Susan Magurn. Random House, 1989, ISBN 0-394-91977-7. SERIES: Step into Reading. SUBJECTS: Pets — Dogs — Fiction; Pets — Fiction. RL A.

Rob only wants his former dog, Sam, when he sees him "singing" on television. Sam's new owner, Amy, doesn't care if Sam can sing or not. Rob takes Sam back, but Sam won't perform. Sam's expression when reunited with Amy is most fitting.

390 *A Tree Is a Plant.* Ill. by Stacey Schuett. HarperCollins, pap., 2001, ISBN 0-06-445196-8. SERIES: Let's-Read-and-Find-Out Science. SUBJECTS: Nature; Science and scientists; Trees. RL B. LEXILE 290L.

Children follow an apple tree through the seasons. New, full-page illustrations colorfully depict and extend the information about the growth and development of trees.

391 *What Makes a Shadow?* Ill. by June Otani. HarperCollins, 1962, ISBN 0-06-022915-2. SERIES: Let's-Read-and-Find-Out Science. SUBJECTS: Science and scientists; Shadows. RL A.

In the most simple terms, this experienced children's author introduces how shadows are formed. Warm pictures of children and their pets, homes, and cars illustrate the text.

Buller, Jon, and Susan Schade

392 *Baseball Camp on the Planet of the Eyeballs.* Ill. by authors. Random House, 1998, o.p. SUBJECTS: Fantasy; Sports — Baseball — Fiction. RL B.

Kidnapped by space aliens on his way to baseball camp, Hugo is mistaken for Agent 86. Trying to convince the CEO, Chief Eyeball Official, of his real identity, Hugo teaches the aliens the game of baseball. Zany cartoon illustrations follow the outrageously funny antics of aliens playing the game, their way.

393 *Felix and the 400 Frogs.* Ill. by authors. Random House, 1996, o.p. SERIES: Step into Reading. SUBJECTS: Frogs and toads — Fiction; Magic — Fiction. RL C. LEXILE 480L.

Was it all a dream? Practicing his future-life career skills as a mind reader, Felix meets up with a frog princess in search of a magic moonstone. This far-flung fantasy involving a grouchy neighbor and a lawn gnome is well matched with brightly bizarre cartoon illustrations.

394 *Mike and the Magic Cookies.* Ill. by authors. Putnam, pap., 1992, ISBN 0-448-40386-2. SERIES: All Aboard Reading. SUBJECTS: Fantasy — Fiction; Magic — Fiction. RL C.

A summer of boredom is broken when a wizard at the altered Shop and Spend sells animal cookies that transform Mike and his family into animals. Watercolor cartoon illustrations accompany the text.

Buller, Jon, and Susan Schade (cont.)

395 *No Tooth, No Quarter!* Ill. by authors. Random House, 1989, ISBN 0-394-94956-0. SERIES: Step into Reading. SUBJECTS: Tooth fairy. RL A.

The tooth fairy gets bad grades for not collecting enough teeth. Walter expects a quarter even though he can't find the tooth that just fell out. He goes with the tooth fairy to Tooth Fairy Land with a chance to redeem the tooth fairy's record. This slim story has mediocre cartoon illustrations.

396 *The Video Kids*. Ill. by authors. Putnam, 1994, ISBN 0-448-40181-9. SERIES: All Aboard Reading. SUBJECTS: Imagination; Science fiction; Siblings — Fiction. RL B.

Jerome and Curtis get inside their video game via their fabulous invention and are saved only by Lavinia, Jerome's little sister, known as Lump until her heroics. Cartoon illustrations accompany the text.

397 *Yo! It's Captain Yo-Yo*. Ill. by authors. Putnam, 1993, ISBN 0-448-40191-6. SERIES: All Aboard Reading. SUBJECTS: Fantasy — Fiction; Magic — Fiction. RL B.

When a boy finds a magic yo-yo in his attic, he writes the magic password in code on his library card, which he deciphers in time — as Captain Yo-Yo — to save his school from the invading Blobs from outer space. Illustrations are typical cartoon drawings.

Bunting, Eve

398 *The Big Red Barn*. Ill. by Howard Knotts. Harcourt, pap., 1979, ISBN 0-15-611938-2. SERIES: Let Me Read. SUBJECTS: Barns — Fiction; Farm and country life — Fiction; Stepparents — Fiction. RL C.

The hayloft is where a boy mourned his mother's death, so the barn fire represents a big loss to which he must adjust — with the help of an understanding grandpa. Knotts's sympathetic pencil drawings add to the feelings of home.

399 *Goose Dinner*. Ill. by Howard Knotts. Harcourt, 1981, o.p. SERIES: Let Me Read. SUBJECTS: Farm and country life — Fiction; Geese — Fiction. RL C.

Because Goose rules the barnyard, the family does not appreciate her until she — and Dad — fend off a marauding raccoon. Warm pencil drawings glow.

400 *My Robot*. Ill. by Dagmar Fehlau. Harcourt, 2000, ISBN 0-15-205593-2. SERIES: Green Light Readers. SUBJECTS: African Americans — Fiction; Friendship — Fiction; Robots — Fiction. RL B.

For his birthday, Dennis is given a robot. Cecil can do many things, but the thing he does best is be a good friend. With playful images and repetition of phrases, young readers will follow the picture clues, read the story, and enjoy the craft activity at the end.

401 *The Robot Birthday*. Ill. by Marie DeJohn. Dutton, 1980, o.p. SERIES: Smart Cat. SUBJECTS: Birthdays — Fiction; Moving, household — Fiction; Robots — Fiction. RL B.

A birthday with a new house and sitter turns out to be the most exciting one ever, thanks to a robot birthday present. Pencil drawings have a turquoise wash.

Burt, Denise

402 *Our Family Vacation*. Photos by Haworth Bartram. Stevens, 1985, o.p. SERIES: Growing Up. SUBJECTS: Seashore — Fiction; Vacations — Fiction. RL B.

Luis is shown packing for a trip; on the next page he is catching crabs on the beach, with no textual or visual transition. The full-page color photographs are somewhat posed looking, but give some feeling of sandcastles and shells.

Burton, Jane

403 *Caper the Kid*. Photos by author. Random House, 1989, ISBN 0-8368-0203-9. SERIES: How Your Pet Grows. SUBJECTS: Goats; Nature. RL C.

The growth of a pair of white-socked kids is detailed, from their food and play to exploration and climbing abilities. Excellent color photographs capture the glint of sunlight, the sparkle of an eye, and the texture of a furry coat.

404 *Chester the Chick*. Photos by author. Random House, 1988, o.p. SERIES: How Your Pet Grows. SUBJECTS: Chickens; Pets. RL C.

The first year of a chick's life is described. Exceptional photographs depict each stage in growth.

405 *Dabble the Duckling*. Photos by author. Random House, 1989, ISBN 0-8368-0205-5. SERIES: How Your Pet Grows. SUBJECTS: Ducks; Nature. RL C.

With excellent color photographs the step-by-step development of a duck from egg to adulthood is illustrated.

406 *Fancy the Fox*. Photos by author. Random House, 1988, o.p. SERIES: How Animals Grow. SUBJECTS: Foxes; Nature. RL C.

The development of three orphan kits brought up in an animal shelter is traced with excellent color photographs and interesting details of their learning to fend for themselves in the woods.

407 *Freckles the Rabbit*. Photos by author. Random House, 1988, o.p. SERIES: How Your Pet Grows. SUBJECTS: Pets; Rabbits. RL C.

The development of Freckles the rabbit is followed, from naked newborn to having her first litter. Exceptional photographs of the lop-eared black and white rabbit are included, along with pictures of the cat, dog, and wild rabbit she encounters.

408 *Ginger the Kitten*. Photos by author. Stevens, 1989, ISBN 0-8368-0213-6. SERIES: Baby Animals Growing Up. SUBJECTS: Pets — Cats. RL C.

The weekly growth and exploration of a kitten are described in words and incredibly appealing color photographs. Feast your eyes on the three backlit six-week-old ginger kittens among the ferns!

409 *Jack the Puppy*. Photos by author. Random House, 1989, ISBN 0-8368-0209-8. SERIES: How Your Pet Grows. SUBJECTS: Pets — Dogs. RL C.

Jack's monthly growth from a groping newborn to a playmate for his mother's next litter is described in words and excellent color photographs of puppies at play.

Busch, Phyllis

410 *Cactus in the Desert*. Ill. by Harriett Barton. HarperCollins, 1979, o.p. SERIES: Let's-Read-and-Find-Out. SUBJECTS: Nature; Science and scientists. RL C.

Although the text concentrates on how cacti conserve water, their uses by animals and people are touched on. Illustrations are apt.

Buss, Nancy

411 *The Lobster and Ivy Higgins*. Ill. by Kim Mulkey. Boyds Mills, 1992, ISBN 1-56397-011-2. SUBJECTS: Lobsters — Fiction; Self-esteem — Fiction. RL C.

Ivy, the butt of her classmate's jokes because she smells like her father's fish market, comes out of her shell to try to save a 27-pound lobster her father plans to raffle. This is a satisfying story rich in dialogue, feelings, and detail.

Busser, Marianne, and Ron Schroder

412 *King Bobble*. Ill. by Hans de Beer. North-South Books, 1996, o.p. SUBJECTS: Humorous stories; Kings and queens — Fiction. RL C.

Ten stories feature King and Queen Bobble, who instead of wearing crowns wear wheels on their heads. Their absurd antics and the humorously detailed illustrations will engage more-proficient readers.

Butler, Kristi T.

413 *A Big Surprise*. Ill. by Pam Paparone. Harcourt, 2005, ISBN 0-15-205142-2. SERIES: Green Light Readers. SUBJECTS: Animals — Fiction; Birthdays — Fiction; Stories in rhyme. RL A.

Simple repetition, a rhyming text, and merry illustrations celebrate Mouse's birthday. The party atmosphere, complete with craft and snack activity, will please the very beginning reader.

Butterworth, Christine

414 *Ants*. Photos and drawings by Paula Chasty. Silver Burdett, 1988, o.p. SERIES: My World — Blue. SUBJECTS: Ants; Nature. RL C.

Pastel drawings of ant tunnels augment the information given by excellent photographs in this photoessay. Several types of ants are depicted, which is a bit confusing.

Butterworth, Christine (cont.)

415 *Beavers*. Photos and drawings by Paula Chasty. Silver Burdett, 1988, o.p. SERIES: My World — Blue. SUBJECTS: Beavers; Nature. RL B.

Marvelous photographs of beavers cutting trees, building dams, defending and feeding themselves, and raising their babies are accompanied by simple text. Drawings show the interior of the lodge.

416 *Bees*. Photos by Paula Chasty. Silver Burdett, 1988, o.p. SERIES: My World — Blue. SUBJECTS: Bees; Nature. RL B.

Outstanding close-up photographs provide the best information on bees. Language and drawings are somewhat stilted.

417 *Rabbits*. Photos and drawings by Paula Chasty. Silver Burdett, 1988, o.p. SERIES: My World — Blue. SUBJECTS: Nature; Rabbits. RL A.

With exceptional photographs and some second-rate drawings, the first year of life of a young buck and doe is outlined. Habits, enemies, fast maturity, and habitat are covered.

418 *Squirrels*. Photos and drawings by Paula Chasty. Silver Burdett, 1988, o.p. SERIES: My World — Blue. SUBJECTS: Nature; Squirrels. RL B.

Some photographs are exceptional, some less sharp, and some drawings are poor. There is confusion over types of squirrels being discussed, and neither the text nor the illustrations flow smoothly.

419 *Swallows*. Photos and drawings by Paula Chasty. Silver Burdett, 1988, o.p. SERIES: My World — Blue. SUBJECTS: Nature; Swallows. RL A.

The life cycle of migrating swallows is detailed. Text is illustrated with acceptable drawings and excellent color photographs. One photograph of a swallow drinking on the fly and another photograph showing a swallow scooping up mud for a nest are exceptional.

Byars, Betsy

420 *Ant Plays Bear*. Ill. by Marc Simont. Penguin, 1997, ISBN 0-670-86776-4. SERIES: Viking Easy-to-Read. SUBJECTS: Family life — Fiction; Siblings — Fiction. RL B. LEXILE 130L.

In four short stories, Anthony and his older brother play games, discuss growing up, and allay nighttime fears. Warm, gentle illustrations evoke the true feelings of the brothers — sometimes funny, sometimes comforting, but always loving.

421 *The Golly Sisters Go West*. Ill. by Sue Truesdell. HarperCollins, 1985, ISBN 0-06-020884-8. SERIES: I Can Read. SUBJECTS: Frontier and pioneer life — Fiction; Humorous stories; Western stories. RL B.

May-May and Rose's naiveté and arguing lead to impromptu concerts, unnecessary nighttime fears, and an unmanageable dancing horse. Six zany adventures are illustrated in full color, capturing the humor and action.

422 *The Golly Sisters Ride Again*. Ill. by Sue Truesdell. HarperCollins, 1994, ISBN 0-06-021563-1. SERIES: I Can Read. SUBJECTS: Frontier and pioneer life — Fiction; Humorous stories; Siblings — Fiction. RL A.

In five brief chapters, the zany antics of the familiar Golly sisters, Rose and May-May, are resumed. Superstition about a goat in the audience, an encounter with a talking rock, a singing and dancing "holiday," and finding comfort in a storm are grist for stories with cartoon drawings.

423 *Hooray for the Golly Sisters!* Ill. by Sue Truesdell. HarperCollins, 1990, ISBN 0-06-020898-8. SERIES: I Can Read. SUBJECTS: Fear — Fiction; Frontier and pioneer life — Fiction; Humorous stories. RL A.

The bumbled navigation and magic of the entertaining Golly Sisters as they traverse the frontier west are enlivened by the zestful ink and wash drawings of Sue Truesdell. The chapter dealing with unnamed fears in the swamp is affecting.

424 *My Brother Ant*. Ill. by Marc Simont. Penguin, 1996, ISBN 0-670-86664-4. SERIES: Viking Easy-to-Read. SUBJECTS: Family life — Fiction; Siblings — Fiction. RL B. LEXILE 130L.

Whether his brother is writing a letter to Santa for Ant, complaining that Ant drew on his homework, or reading him a story, the everyday experiences of these two brothers are funny and touching. Gentle illustrations, aglow with the warmth of family love, support each story.

425 *The Seven Treasure Hunts*. Ill. by Jennifer Barrett. HarperCollins, 1991, ISBN 0-06-020886-4. SUBJECTS: Friendship — Fiction; Sibling rivalry — Fiction. RL C.

Jackson and his friend Goat hide treasures from one another with many misfires, especially when Goat's older sister, the ogre, interferes. The treasures — M & Ms, breath mints from mother's purse, bird feathers, a Match-box car with one wheel missing — give the story special appeal.

C

Calder, S. J.

426 *If You Were a Bird*. Ill. by Cornelius Van Wright. Silver Burdett, 1989, ISBN 0-671-68595-3. SERIES: First Facts. SUBJECTS: Birds; Nature. RL A.

Information about robins is given in simple language from the point of view of a young robin. Most interesting is his learning how to fly and taking a bath. Simple comparisons to other species of birds are made. Pastel illustrations complement the text.

427 *If You Were a Cat*. Ill. by Cornelius Van Wright. Silver Burdett, 1989, ISBN 0-382-24405-2. SERIES: First Facts. SUBJECTS: Pets — Cats. RL A.

The life cycle, diet, wild relatives, and habits of domestic cats are described in simple language with appealing watercolor drawings. Most interesting is the section showing how to tell whether a cat is playful or aggressive.

428 *If You Were a Fish*. Ill. by Cornelius Van Wright. Silver Burdett, 1989, ISBN 0-671-68596-1. SERIES: First Facts. SUBJECTS: Fish; Science and scientists. RL A.

The food, anatomy, types, and enemies of goldfish are described and illustrated. Sketchy instructions for starting an aquarium are included.

429 *If You Were an Ant*. Ill. by Cornelius Van Wright. Silver Burdett, 1989, ISBN 0-671-68597-X. SERIES: First Facts. SUBJECTS: Ants; Insects; Science and scientists. RL A.

The home, work, life cycle, anatomy, food, and enemies of a wood ant are described. Pencil and wash drawings cover three-fourths of each double-page spread to illustrate vocabulary that might otherwise be too difficult for young children. Directions for making an ant farm are included.

Calmenson, Stephanie

430 *The Little Witch Sisters*. Ill. by R. W. Alley. Stevens, pap., 1993, ISBN 0-8368-0970-X. SERIES: Read Aloud. SUBJECTS: Magic — Fiction; Siblings — Fiction; Witches — Fiction. RL A.

Notes to librarians, teachers, parents, and grownups precede and follow the story. Tinka, a small witch, agrees to help her sister Plinka only after she is rescued from being turned into an alligator, a bird, and an elephant. Ink and wash drawings soften the moral tale.

431 *Marigold and Grandma on the Town*. Ill. by Mary Chalmers. HarperCollins, 1994, ISBN 0-06-020813-9. SUBJECTS: Grandparents — Fiction; Rabbits — Fiction. RL A.

Marigold and her grandmother shop for a spring bonnet, make friends with the wind, and stop for a momentarily disastrous tea and for a photograph. Delightfully imaginative and affirmative story illustrated by Chalmers's usual charming drawings.

432 *My Dog's the Best*. Ill. by Marcy Dunn Ramsey. Scholastic, pap., 1997, ISBN 0-590-33072-1. SERIES: Hello Reader! SUBJECTS: Pets — Dogs — Fiction; Pets — Fiction. RL A. LEXILE BR.

Whether they are big or small, smooth or shaggy, children celebrate their special dogs. Detailed full-page illustrations express the fervor of each child's exclamation that their dog is the best.

433 *One Little Monkey*. Ill. by Ellen Appleby. Stevens, 1982, ISBN 0-8368-0988-2. SERIES: Read Aloud. SUBJECTS: Concepts — Numbers; Stories in rhyme. RL B.

This animal counting book with cross-eyed animals and forced rhyme is illustrated in watercolors. Notes to grown-ups are appended.

434 *Where's Rufus?* Ill. by Maxie Chambliss. Stevens, 1988, ISBN 0-8368-0990-4. SERIES: Read Aloud. SUBJECTS: Family life — Fiction; Picnics — Fiction. RL B.

Calmenson, Stephanie (cont.)

A slim story about a family dog, Rufus, which the reader is invited to trace as he hides all over the house to prevent the family from leaving on a picnic because rain is coming. Watercolor and ink drawings accompany the text.

Cannon, A. E.

435 *Let the Good Times Roll with Pirate Pete and Pirate Joe*. Ill. by Elwood H. Smith. Penguin, 2004, ISBN 0-670-03679-X. SERIES: Viking Easy-to-Read. SUBJECTS: Humorous stories; Pirates — Fiction. RL B.

Ahoy, Mateys! Enjoy a day of pirate adventure with the Pirate Queen and her sons. From jellyfish on toast to a ride in the Jolly Roger van, this rollicking encounter of the pirate kind finally docks at Disco Dan's. A treasure-trove of boisterous illustrations is awash with pirate paraphernalia aplenty.

Caple, Kathy

436 *The Friendship Tree*. Ill. by author. Holiday House, 2000, ISBN 0-8234-1376-4. SERIES: Holiday House Reader. SUBJECTS: Sheep — Fiction; Trees — Fiction. RL B. LEXILE 180L.

Throughout the year, two good sheep friends, Blanche and Otis, share experiences in four stories centered around their backyard trees. The gentle anecdotes of friendship are complemented by warm and loving pastel watercolors.

437 *Starring Hillary*. Ill. by author. Carolrhoda, 1999, ISBN 1-57505-261-X. SUBJECTS: Diets — Fiction; Pets — Cats — Fiction; Self-esteem — Fiction. RL B.

Thinking she has to lose weight to realize her acting aspirations, Hillary learns she's just right the way she is when her favorite actress comes to town. Framed pastel watercolors chronicle the highly emotional saga of the young cat's diet and exercise regime.

438 *Termite Trouble*. Ill. by author. Candlewick, 2005, ISBN 0-7636-2572-8. SERIES: Brand New Readers. SUBJECTS: Insects — Fiction. RL A.

Doing what he does best gets Termite in trouble as he eats his friends' houses, but his skills come in handy when he makes a log sculpture. With reading tips for parents, these humorous exploits of a small insect and his friends are equally matched by lively and enjoyable cartoon vignettes.

439 *Wow, It's Worm!* Ill. by author. Candlewick, 2001, o.p. SERIES: Brand New Readers. SUBJECTS: Worms — Fiction. RL A.

In four short stories, Worm tries to stay cool, finds out he is just right the way he is, watches television, and builds a block tower. Simple stories of everyday life from a worm's-eye-view are comically depicted. A note to parents offers reading how-to suggestions.

Capucilli, Alyssa Satin

440 *Bathtime for Biscuit*. Ill. by Pat Schories. HarperCollins, pap., 1998, ISBN 0-06-444264-0. SERIES: My First I Can Read. SUBJECTS: Bathing — Fiction; Pets — Dogs — Fiction. RL A. LEXILE 150L.

Not wanting to take a bath, Biscuit the dog and his friend Puddles play and dig their way through the mud until everyone really needs a bath. With a limited vocabulary, repetition throughout, and large illustrations of cavorting canines, this book will be eagerly read.

441 *Biscuit*. Ill. by Pat Schories. HarperCollins, 1996, ISBN 0-06-026197-8. SERIES: My First I Can Read. SUBJECTS: Bedtime — Fiction; Pets — Dogs — Fiction. RL A. LEXILE 190L.

Meet Biscuit, a little yellow dog who does not want to go to bed. The large print, short sentences, and engaging illustrations focus on a familiar childhood experience.

442 *Biscuit and the Baby*. Ill. by Pat Schories. HarperCollins, 2005, ISBN 0-06-009459-1. SERIES: My First I Can Read. SUBJECTS: Babies — Fiction; Pets — Dogs — Fiction. RL A. LEXILE 230L.

Biscuit wants to meet the new baby at his house, but must wait until naptime is over. Biscuit's expectancy and then fear of a crying child are humorously portrayed.

443 *Biscuit Finds a Friend*. Ill. by Pat Schories. HarperCollins, 1997, ISBN 0-06-027412-3. SERIES: My First I Can Read. SUBJECTS: Ducks — Fiction; Pets — Dogs — Fiction. RL A. LEXILE 80L.

After finding a lost duckling and returning him to his pond, Biscuit wants to play with his new friend and gets all wet. Contextual clues within the lighthearted drawings aid very beginning readers.

444 *Biscuit Goes to School*. Ill. by Pat Schories. HarperCollins, 2002, ISBN 0-06-028682-2. SERIES: My First I Can Read. SUBJECTS: Pets — Dogs — Fiction; School stories. RL A. LEXILE 100L.

Not supposed to go to school, Biscuit heads there anyway, much to the delight of the class and the teacher. The endearing little yellow dog's exploits are spiritedly highlighted with warm, affectionate artwork.

445 *Biscuit Visits the Big City*. Ill. by Pat Schories. HarperCollins, 2006, ISBN 0-06-074164-3. SERIES: My First I Can Read. SUBJECTS: City and town life — Fiction; Pets — Dogs — Fiction. RL A. LEXILE 230L.

There is so much to see and do in the big city, but Biscuit finds the best thing of all — a hot dog stand. The hectic pace and congestion of city life within a muted background setting serve as an effective contrast to the animated actions of the focal characters.

446 *Biscuit Wants to Play*. Ill. by Pat Schories. HarperCollins, 2001, ISBN 0-06-028069-7. SERIES: My First I Can Read. SUBJECTS: Pets — Cats — Fiction; Pets — Dogs — Fiction; Play — Fiction. RL A. LEXILE 20L.

Biscuit finds some new friends to play with: two little kittens. Engaging images focus on the whimsical and joyous moments of new friends exploring and enjoying the playful moments.

447 *Biscuit Wins a Prize*. Ill. by Pat Schories. HarperCollins, 2004, ISBN 0-06-009455-9. SERIES: My First I Can Read. SUBJECTS: Pets — Dogs — Fiction; Pets — Fiction. RL A. LEXILE 190L.

When Biscuit goes to the pet show, he is so excited about meeting all the other contestants. Hilarious drawings of the playful yellow dog augment the text, giving the reader the real story of Biscuit's pet show experience.

448 *Biscuit's Big Friend*. Ill. by Pat Schories. HarperCollins, 2003, ISBN 0-06-029167-2. SERIES: My First I Can Read. SUBJECTS: Friendship — Fiction; Pets — Dogs — Fiction. RL A. LEXILE 310L.

Biscuit wants to do everything just like his friend Sam, who is a much bigger dog. From an everyday experience, Biscuit and his reader friends will learn that everyone has something special they can do. The disparity of the dogs' sizes and their common adventures are funny and lively.

449 *Biscuit's Day at the Farm*. Ill. by Pat Schories. HarperCollins, 2007, ISBN 0-06-074167-8. SERIES: My First I Can Read. SUBJECTS: Farm and country life — Fiction; Pets — Dogs — Fiction. RL A.

While visiting a farm, Biscuit has fun meeting all kinds of animals: hens, pigs, geese, and goats. Lively, expressive illustrations follow Biscuit as he makes new friends.

450 *Biscuit's New Trick*. Ill. by Pat Schories. HarperCollins, 2000, ISBN 0-06-028067-0. SERIES: My First I Can Read. SUBJECTS: Pets — Dogs — Fiction; Pets — Training — Fiction. RL A. LEXILE BR.

It's challenging to learn a new trick, but when the ball rolls into a mud puddle, Biscuit learns to "fetch." The humor of the simple story line is extended through delightfully funny watercolors that capture those special uniquely Biscuit moments.

451 *Pedro's Burro*. Ill. by Paul Estrada. HarperCollins, 2007, ISBN 0-06-056031-7. SERIES: I Can Read. SUBJECTS: Family life — Fiction; Fathers — Fiction. RL B.

In search of the perfect burro, Pedro and his father go to market and, as luck would have it, a burro finds them. Simple and colorful illustrations exude the warmth of familial love and support.

Carley, Wayne

452 *Charley the Mouse Finds Christmas*. Ill. by Ruth Bagshaw. Garrard, 1972, o.p. SERIES: Venture. SUBJECTS: Christmas — Fiction; Mice — Fiction. RL B.

By Christmas, a mouse living in a department store has lost all his toys, food, and companions. When a child spots the mouse in a window, the child tells Santa. Appealing mouse drawings are against a watercolor background.

Carley, Wayne (cont.)

453 *Here Comes Mirium, the Mixed-Up Witch*. Ill. by Ted Schroeder. Garrard, 1972, o.p. SUBJECTS: Magic — Fiction; Witches — Fiction. RL B.

Mirium's magic leads to adventures with an over-friendly dinosaur, a knight, a mummy, and a dog in the closed museum. Black and rose drawings are pedestrian.

454 *Mixed Up Magic*. Ill. by David Stone. Garrard, 1971, o.p. SERIES: Venture. SUBJECTS: Magic — Fiction; Witches — Fiction. RL A.

Mirium's magic mistakes turn a dog show into pandemonium. Her cloak looks mysterious in black finger-painted design against the royal blue and orange of the policeman and dogs, respectively.

455 *Percy the Parrot Passes the Puck*. Ill. by Art Cumings. Garrard, 1972, o.p. SUBJECTS: Humorous stories; Parrots — Fiction; Sports — Ice hockey — Fiction. RL C.

Hockey fan Percy the Parrot appears on a television commercial for a food he dislikes in order to have a chance to see his home hockey team in action. This lively and imaginative story is simply illustrated with apple green and orange highlights.

456 *Percy the Parrot Yelled Quiet!* Ill. by Art Cumings. Garrard, 1974, o.p. SERIES: Easy Venture. SUBJECTS: Humorous stories; Parrots — Fiction; Pets — Fiction. RL B.

Percy turns out not to be the quiet pet Mrs. Gray originally wanted, but he sure was fun! Simple story is illustrated with comic watercolor drawings.

457 *Puppy Love*. Ill. by Erica Merkling. Garrard, 1971, o.p. SERIES: Venture. SUBJECTS: Pets — Dogs — Fiction; Sibling rivalry — Fiction. RL A.

Leslie discovers that looking after her new baby brother is like taking care of her puppy, Lickins. The analogy is satisfactory. Ink drawings show Leslie's pride in accomplishment.

458 *The Witch Who Forgot*. Ill. by Lou Cunette. Garrard, 1974, o.p. SUBJECTS: Magic — Fiction; Witches — Fiction. RL A.

Mirium forgets where she put her shoe, hat, cat, and coat — even where she was going with a cake. Humor comes from unlikely places, as she looks for lost items. Cartoon drawings.

Carlson, Laurie

459 *EcoArt! Earth-Friendly Art and Craft Experiences for 3-to-9-Year-Olds*. Ill. by Loretta T. Braren. Williamson, pap., 1993, ISBN 0-913589-68-3. SERIES: Williamson Kids Can. SUBJECTS: Arts and crafts; Conservation. RL C.

Despite the large ink illustrations and appealing browsing format, some of the language and the amount of text will make this difficult for even third-graders. However, the intriguing ideas range from homemade supplies to things made with natural things or throwaways.

Carlson, Nancy

460 *Arnie and the New Kid*. Ill. by Nancy L. Carlson. Viking, 1990, ISBN 0-670-82499-2. SUBJECTS: Disabilities — Physical and mental — Fiction; Pets — Dogs — Fiction. RL A.

After Arnie, a dog, falls and needs crutches, he finds a new friend, Phillip, who must use a wheelchair. As he experiences being handicapped, he learns to empathize rather than tease. Full-color illustrations have eye-catching patterns on clothing.

461 *Arnie and the Stolen Markers*. Ill. by Nancy L. Carlson. Viking, 1987, ISBN 0-670-81548-9. SUBJECTS: Behavior — Stealing — Fiction; Pets — Dogs — Fiction. RL B.

Arnie feels bad after stealing some markers until he confesses and has a chance to work off the cost. Full-color drawings accompanying this straightforward moral seem to show the shopkeeper and mother angrier than the text indicates.

462 *Arnie Goes to Camp*. Ill. by Nancy L. Carlson. Viking, 1988, ISBN 0-670-81549-7. SUBJECTS: Animals — Fiction; Camps and camping — Fiction; Pets — Dogs — Fiction. RL B.

Despite his misgivings and homesickness, Arnie enjoys the accomplishments and the camaraderie of summer camp. Bright, colored drawings show action-filled days and nights.

463 *Harriet and the Garden*. Ill. by Nancy L. Carlson. Penguin, pap., 1985, ISBN 0-87614-184-X. SUBJECTS: Behavior — Honest — Fiction; Pets — Dogs — Fiction. RL B.

After a sleepless night struggling with her conscience, Harriet, a dog, confesses to trampling Mrs. Hoozit's prize garden — and feels better. Colorful drawings focus on Harriet's long day.

464 *Harriet and the Roller Coaster*. Ill. by Nancy L. Carlson. Penguin, pap., 1984, ISBN 0-87614-183-1. SUBJECTS: Amusement parks — Fiction; Fear — Fiction; Pets — Dogs — Fiction. RL B.

Taunted by George, a rabbit, Harriet, a dog, reluctantly tries a roller coaster — and finds she likes it! Carlson's books challenge children to broaden their experiences and outlook. Bright colors convey feelings of fear and excitement.

465 *Harriet and Walt*. Ill. by Nancy L. Carlson. Penguin, pap., 1984, ISBN 0-87614-185-8. SUBJECTS: Pets — Dogs — Fiction; Siblings — Fiction. RL B.

Harriet the dog, initially burdened by her little brother when they go to play in the snow, ends up defending him against the impatience of her friend George. This quietly moral tale is illustrated with ink and colored pencil.

466 *Harriet's Halloween Candy*. Ill. by Nancy L. Carlson. Penguin, pap., 1984, ISBN 0-87614-182-3. SUBJECTS: Behavior — Sharing — Fiction; Halloween — Fiction; Pets — Dogs — Fiction. RL B.

Harriet shares her overabundance of Halloween candy only when she is sick from eating too much. Details of how she sorts her candy by color, size, and favorites add authenticity and humor. Pastel drawings have interesting patterns of clothes and candy.

467 *Harriet's Recital*. Ill. by Nancy L. Carlson. Carolrhoda, 1982, ISBN 0-87614-181-5. SUBJECTS: Dancers and dancing — Fiction; Pets — Dogs — Fiction; Self-esteem — Fiction. RL A.

Harriet, a dog, is terrified of falling or having her costume rip during her ballet recital. After a shaky start, she blossoms, later denying being scared. The straightforward message is illustrated with typical Carlson framed drawings, in pinks and lavenders onstage.

468 *Loudmouth George and the Big Race*. Ill. by Nancy L. Carlson. Penguin, pap., 1986, ISBN 0-87614-215-3. SUBJECTS: Behavior — Excuses — Fiction; Rabbits — Fiction. RL B.

George the rabbit is too tired, too full, or too busy to train for the big race that Harriet the dog ends up winning. His fatigue is graphically captured by corduroy legs and dragging limbs. Full-color illustrations are on green or royal blue backgrounds.

469 *Loudmouth George and the Cornet*. Ill. by Nancy L. Carlson. Penguin, pap., 1985, ISBN 0-87614-214-5. SUBJECTS: Behavior — Excuses — Fiction; Musical instruments — Fiction; Rabbits — Fiction. RL B.

Rabbit George thinks he is too good at playing the cornet to take lessons and, when asked to leave the band, he has excuses and a better idea — he will take up the tuba. Colored pencil drawings show his family's consternation clearly.

470 *Loudmouth George and the Fishing Trip*. Ill. by Nancy L. Carlson. Penguin, pap., 1985, ISBN 0-87614-213-7. SUBJECTS: Behavior — Bragging — Fiction; Rabbits — Fiction; Sports — Fishing — Fiction. RL B.

George the rabbit's bragging is brought up short when Harriet's family takes him fishing. She is then on hand to keep his reports of success accurate. George in sky-blue pajamas with carrots on them is a nice touch.

471 *Loudmouth George and the Sixth-Grade Bully*. Ill. by Nancy L. Carlson. Penguin, pap., 1985, ISBN 0-87614-217-X. SUBJECTS: Behavior — Bullying — Fiction; Rabbits — Fiction; School stories. RL B.

When a bully steals George the rabbit's lunch every day, George's dog friend Harriet helps him prepare an unpleasant surprise in the next day's lunch! All who have suffered at the hands of a bully will be able to identify with George's creative revenge. Pencil drawings are in full color.

472 *Making the Team*. Ill. by Nancy L. Carlson. Carolrhoda, 1985, ISBN 0-87614-281-1. SERIES: Louanne Pig. SUBJECTS: Pigs

Carlson, Nancy (cont.)

— Fiction; Sex roles — Fiction; Sports — Football — Fiction. RL B.

Louanne and Arnie, two pigs, practice together for cheerleading and football tryouts — but Louanne makes the football squad and Arnie the cheerleading. Pencil drawings are in red, blue, and green.

473 *The Mysterious Valentine*. Ill. by Nancy L. Carlson. Carolrhoda, 1985, o.p. SERIES: Louanne Pig. SUBJECTS: Pigs — Fiction; Valentine's Day — Fiction. RL C.

The reader finally figures out who Louanne the pig's secret admirer is, but Louanne never does. Familiar characters are drawn in full color with pencil.

474 *The Perfect Family*. Ill. by Nancy L. Carlson. Carolrhoda, 1985, ISBN 0-87614-280-3. SERIES: Louanne Pig. SUBJECTS: Family life — Fiction; Pigs — Fiction; Siblings — Fiction. RL C.

Louanne the pig finds out that living in a family of ten siblings is not for her when she spends the weekend at her friend George's house. Colored pencil drawings add humor.

475 *The Talent Show*. Ill. by Nancy L. Carlson. Carolrhoda, 1985, ISBN 0-87614-284-6. SERIES: Louanne Pig. SUBJECTS: Pigs — Fiction; Self-esteem — Fiction. RL C.

Louanne the pig gets involved in the talent show even though she thinks she has nothing to contribute. Bright colored drawings add to the sympathetic treatment of feeling left out.

476 *Witch Lady*. Ill. by Nancy L. Carlson. Carolrhoda, 1985, ISBN 0-87614-283-8. SERIES: Louanne Pig. SUBJECTS: Haunted houses — Fiction; Pigs — Fiction; Scary stories. RL C.

When Louanne the pig twists her ankle in the witch lady's yard, she finds out what really goes on in that scary house — but she may not tell her friends. Colored pencil drawings are in flat primary colors.

Carrick, Carol

477 *Empty Squirrel*. Ill. by Donald Carrick. Greenwillow, 1981, o.p. SERIES: Read-Alone. SUBJECTS: Pets — Fiction; Pets — Wild animals — Fiction. RL A.

Paul returns a fish he caught to the pond and a neglected toy squirrel that lost its stuffing outside over the winter to its owner, and keeps a turtle when he discovers it likes tuna. Soft pencil drawings are in brown and orange.

478 *The Longest Float in the Parade*. Ill. by Donald Carrick. Greenwillow, 1982, o.p. SERIES: Read-Alone. SUBJECTS: Camps and camping — Fiction; Parades — Fiction. RL B.

At summer camp, Jimmy and Pinky's imaginative parade entry, a Chinese dragon, rivals all others. Warmly realistic from dialogue to atmosphere and characters, the text is complemented beautifully by the soft watercolor illustrations.

Carrick, Malcolm

479 *Happy Jack*. Ill. by author. HarperCollins, 1979, o.p. SERIES: I Can Read. SUBJECTS: Folklore. RL A.

The tale of foolish Jack who wins the princess is retold in simple language. Sepia drawings have avocado and peach washes.

480 *Mr. Tod's Trap*. Ill. by author. HarperCollins, 1980, o.p. SERIES: I Can Read. SUBJECTS: Foxes — Fiction. RL C.

Mr. Tod's ingenious rabbit traps work to Weasel's advantage, so Mrs. Tod takes over hunting and Mr. Tod takes over the housework. A houseful of appealing fox kits and lumpy clever rabbits enrich the tale.

481 *Today Is Shrew Day*. Ill. by author. HarperCollins, 1978, o.p. SERIES: I Can Read. SUBJECTS: Friendship — Fiction; Frogs and toads — Fiction; Shrews — Fiction. RL B.

Bullfrog gets all sorts of advice for baby-sitting — for a doll. Unusual perspectives add interest; illustrations are in gloomy, muddy colors.

Carter, Anne

482 *Bella's Secret Garden*. Ill. by John Butler. Crown, 1986, o.p. SERIES: It's Great to Read. SUBJECTS: Nature; Rabbits. RL C.

Human paws move Bella the rabbit from a suburban garden to a field away from the danger of cats, dogs, and machinery. Full-page artwork is outstanding. From expressive eyes and fur that invites petting, down to the rabbit endpapers, there is a consistent rabbit perspective.

483 *Molly in Danger*. Ill. by John Butler. Crown, 1986, o.p. SERIES: It's Great to Read. SUBJECTS: Moles — Fiction; Nature. RL C.

When Molly the mole is forced out of her hole by floodwaters, she faces danger from a heron and an owl before finding new burrowing ground. Exceptional close-up full-page drawings give a mole's view of the world.

484 *Ruff Leaves Home*. Ill. by John Butler. Crown, 1986, o.p. SERIES: It's Great to Read. SUBJECTS: Foxes; Nature. RL A.

A year of exploration and danger in the life of a young fox is exceptionally well portrayed in language and in effective full-page drawings. Other wildlife is shown, as well as the dangers to which a fox on the fringe of a suburban area is exposed.

485 *Scurry's Treasure*. Ill. by John Butler. Crown, 1986, o.p. SERIES: It's Great to Read. SUBJECTS: Nature; Squirrels. RL B.

The content of finely drawn full-color illustrations of the world from a young squirrel's perspective is well reflected in the text, as a squirrel mistakes a brooch for a nut.

Carter, Polly

486 *Harriet Tubman and Black History Month*. Ill. by J. Brian Pinkney. Silver Burdett, 1990, ISBN 0-671-69109-0. SERIES: Let's Celebrate. SUBJECTS: Biographies — African Americans; Holidays; United States — Civil War. RL A.

In simple language, some of the most colorful events in Harriet Tubman's adventures conducting some 300 slaves north to freedom are conveyed. Brian Pinkney's scratch drawings give a dark, shadowy background to the story of this heroine.

Cartier, Wesley

487 *Marco's Run*. Ill. by Reynold Ruffins. Harcourt, 2000, o.p. SERIES: Green Light Readers. SUBJECTS: African Americans — Fiction; Imagination — Fiction. RL A.

As he runs through the park with his dad, Marco imagines himself as fast as a bobcat, a cheetah, a horse, and a rabbit. Energetic illustrations follow the father and son on their run, adding interesting backgrounds and sights along the way.

Cartwright, Sally

488 *Sunlight*. Ill. by Marylin Hafner. Putnam, 1974, o.p. SUBJECTS: Rainbows; Science experiments; Shadows. RL B.

Simple experiments with rainbows, reflections, and shadows are suggested. Visual interest is high with soft pencil drawings, varied in their use of space.

489 *The Tide*. Ill. by Marilyn Miller. Putnam, 1970, o.p. SERIES: Science Is What and Why. SUBJECTS: Oceans and ocean life; Science and scientists. RL C.

At the simplest level, Cartwright presents information about different kinds of tides and their causes. Interesting effects with printing and overlaid washes add visual appeal.

490 *Water Is Wet*. Ill. by Marylin Hafner. Putnam, 1973, o.p. SUBJECTS: Science experiments — Water; Water. RL A.

Ideas for simple science projects with water are appealingly presented. Illustrations are well suited to the text.

Caseley, Judith

491 *Harry and Willy and Carrothead*. Ill. by author. Greenwillow, 1991, ISBN 0-688-09493-7. SUBJECTS: Disabilities — Physical and mental — Fiction; Friendship — Fiction; School stories. RL B.

This story of a growing friendship among three boys focuses on what Harry, born without a left hand, can do. Full-color illustrations show details of school activities.

492 *Molly Pink*. Ill. by author. Greenwillow, 1985, o.p. SUBJECTS: Fear — Fiction; Music and musicians — Fiction. RL C.

Despite Molly's singing practice, she freezes when she has a solo on stage — until members of her family turn their backs. Framed pictures in pink and yellow are well suited to the text.

Caseley, Judith (cont.)

493 *Three Happy Birthdays*. Ill. by author. Mulberry, pap., 1993, ISBN 0-688-11699-X. SUBJECTS: Birthdays — Fiction. RL A.

Benny, his dog Charlie, and his sister Marla, take turns celebrating their birthdays. Benny's favorite gift is an umbrella; Charlie's, a bone; and Marla's, stars. The family makes paper stars, star cookies and cake, and snow stars. Whimsical pastel illustrations accompany the text.

Cassedy, Sylvia

494 *The Best Cat Suit of All*. Ill. by Rosekrans Hoffman. Dial, 1991, ISBN 0-8037-0517-4. SERIES: Dial Easy-to-Read. SUBJECTS: Halloween — Fiction; Moving, household — Fiction; Pets — Cats — Fiction. RL A.

Matthew is sick and grumpy on Halloween in his new home, where everything and everyone is different. A real black cat that matches his Halloween costume, and his parents, cheer him up. Pencil drawings have washes mainly with black, orange, and lavender.

495 *Zoomrimes: Poems About Things That Go*. Ill. by Michele Chessare. HarperCollins, 1993, ISBN 0-06-022632-3. SUBJECTS: Poetry; Transportation; Wordplay. RL B.

Poems cover topics ranging from the wondrous spring storm of maple tree "helicopters" to an escalator, from an efficient camel sedan to a zippered zeppelin. Imaginative wordplay and unusual perspectives make this anthology a delight. Lighthearted illustrations are in shades of gray.

Castiglia, Julie

496 *Jill the Pill*. Ill. by Steven Kellogg. Atheneum, 1979, o.p. SUBJECTS: Siblings — Fiction. RL B.

Jill's teenage behavior has nothing in common with her small brother's. Expressive, detailed ink drawings add authenticity to this story.

Catton, Chris, ed.

497 *Matchmaking*. Ill. by Oxford Scientific Films. Putnam, 1987, o.p. SUBJECTS: Nature. RL C.

A variety of mating activities is briefly described, from attracting mates with dramatic coloration or scent to presenting "gifts," calling mates, and fighting for them. Excellent color photographs take the reader to woods, water, the Arctic, and the garden.

Cauley, Lorinda B.

498 *Bake-Off*. Ill. by author. Putnam, 1978, o.p. SERIES: See and Read. SUBJECTS: Animals — Fiction; Bakers and baking — Fiction; Contests — Fiction. RL C.

Knowing sweets win votes, but committed to nutritious recipes, Mr. Hare wins the autumn bake-off with a surprise entry (recipe appended). Forest animals are given individual character through expressive ink drawings alternately colored in two-tone washes.

Cazet, Denys

499 *Elvis the Rooster Almost Goes to Heaven*. Ill. by author. HarperCollins, 2003, o.p. SERIES: I Can Read. SUBJECTS: Chickens — Fiction; Humorous stories. RL B. LEXILE 270L.

Elvis, King of the Coop, swallowed a bug and the sun came up without him. He has lost his "pluck" and the chickens help him find it again. Earth-toned watercolors are a perfect foil to the zany antics and slapstick humor that read like an old detective story from the fifties.

500 *Minnie and Moo: The Attack of the Easter Bunnies*. Ill. by author. HarperCollins, 2004, ISBN 0-06-000506-8. SERIES: I Can Read. SUBJECTS: Cows — Fiction; Easter — Fiction; Humorous stories. RL B.

When the farmer decides he is too old to dress up like the Easter Bunny, Minnie and Moo ask all the farmyard animals to help. What results is an Easter Parade that will long be remembered. Cavorting cows, pigs, sheep, and chickens in bunny suits paint quite a picture!

501 *Minnie and Moo: The Case of the Missing Jelly Donut*. Ill. by author. HarperCollins, 2005, ISBN 0-06-073007-2. SERIES: I Can Read. SUBJECTS: Cows — Fiction; Humorous stories; Lost and found possessions — Fiction. RL B.

Intrepid cows Minnie and Moo are hot on the trail of a jelly donut thief. Expressive illustrations add hilarious visual commentary to Minnie and Moo's latest venture into the detective business.

502 *Minnie and Moo: The Night Before Christmas*. Ill. by author. HarperCollins, 2002, o.p. SERIES: I Can Read. SUBJECTS: Christmas — Fiction; Cows — Fiction; Humorous stories. RL B. LEXILE 260L.

In a spoof of Clement Moore's Christmas classic, Rooster Rudolf and his eight tiny chickens lead Santa Cow on her appointed rounds. The rollicking details of these hysterically funny illustrations enhance a memorable Christmas moment for all.

503 *Minnie and Moo: Will You Be My Valentine?* Ill. by author. HarperCollins, 2003, ISBN 0-06-623754-8. SERIES: I Can Read. SUBJECTS: Cows — Fiction; Humorous stories; Valentine's Day — Fiction. RL B.

Love is in the air, and Minnie and Moo, adorned in Cupid's tutus, shoot love poem arrows around the barnyard. Infused with humor, watercolor illustrations in cotton candy pink and valentine heart red capture the Cupid cow chaos.

504 *Minnie and Moo and the Haunted Sweater*. Ill. by author. HarperCollins, 2007, ISBN 0-06-073016-1. SERIES: I Can Read. SUBJECTS: Cows — Fiction; Humorous stories. RL B.

As Minnie knits a sweater for the farmer's birthday, the garment seems to take on a life of its own. But where's Elvis the Rooster? Comical illustrations aptly capture the humor of the zany cow duo, providing visual clues as to Elvis's whereabouts.

505 *Minnie and Moo and the Musk of Zorro*. Ill. by author. DK, 2000, ISBN 0-789-42652-8. SUBJECTS: Chickens — Fiction; Cows — Fiction; Humorous stories. RL B. LEXILE 210L.

Where have all the heroes gone? Cows Minnie and Moo don Zorro-like costumes and go out to save the barnyard world. The dynamic duo overcome a rooster and some scary underwear. Flamboyant and funny, the bovine friends sparkle with humorously detailed images — "lipsticked" sword and all.

506 *Minnie and Moo and the Potato from Planet X*. Ill. by author. HarperCollins, 2002, o.p. SERIES: I Can Read. SUBJECTS: Cows — Fiction; Extraterrestrial beings — Fiction; Humorous stories. RL B.

When a space alien from the Universal Packaging Service crashes to earth, cow friends Minnie and Moo help him make his Anti-Bump Cream delivery on time. Creative illustrations elaborate on the outer space theme, adding just the right amount of levity to a story that is out of this world.

507 *Minnie and Moo Go to the Moon*. Ill. by author. DK, 1998, ISBN 0-789-42516-5. SUBJECTS: Cows — Fiction; Farm and country life — Fiction; Humorous stories. RL B. LEXILE 210L.

Catastrophe in the barnyard follows Minnie and Moo's test drive of the farmer's tractor. Thinking they landed on the moon, the cows are attacked by moonsters, a.k.a. very upset chickens. Colorful watercolors vividly embrace the silliness of this farmyard fiasco.

508 *Minnie and Moo Meet Frankenswine*. Ill. by author. HarperCollins, 2001, ISBN 0-06-623748-3. SERIES: I Can Read. SUBJECTS: Cows — Fiction; Humorous stories; Monsters — Fiction. RL B. LEXILE 190L.

Dark, stormy illustrations set a scary barnyard scene fraught with impending doom as Olga the pig goes missing in the thunderstorm. Where can she be? And who is that monster in the barn?

509 *Minnie and Moo Save the Earth*. Ill. by author. DK, 1999, ISBN 0-789-42594-7. SUBJECTS: Cows — Fiction; Extraterrestrial beings — Fiction; Humorous stories. RL B. LEXILE 130L.

Under a starlit sky, the cow friends laze in a hot tub and use their fly swatters to defend the earth against an alien invasion. Humorously ludicrous artwork complete with multi-eyed aliens embellishes the zany antics of the bovine duo.

510 *The Octopus*. Ill. by author. HarperCollins, 2005, ISBN 0-06-051088-9. SERIES: I Can Read. SUBJECTS: Grandparents — Fiction; Illness — Fiction; Pets — Dogs — Fiction. RL B. LEXILE 370L.

To take the itch out of chicken pox, Grandpa tells his grandpup anti-itch stories, beginning with a

Cazet, Denys (cont.)

scary swordfish fight with an octopus. Clever use of speech balloons and dramatic swashbuckling scenes from Grandpa's stories enliven the text.

511 *Saturday*. Ill. by author. Bradbury, 1985, o.p. SUBJECTS: Grandparents — Fiction; Humorous stories; Pets — Dogs — Fiction. RL C.

Grandpa is always ready to leave work to play — or do a science project — with his grandson, Barney. Grandma's pancakes, cocoa, or a pillow help when Barney is unhappy. Humorous story illustrated with gray ink drawings captures the warmth of these relationships.

512 *The Shrunken Head*. Ill. by author. HarperCollins, 2007, ISBN 0-06-073013-7. SERIES: I Can Read. SUBJECTS: Grandparents — Fiction; Illness — Fiction; Pets — Dogs — Fiction. RL B. LEXILE 300L.

Grandpa is at it again with another anti-itch chicken pox story. This new adventure features Doc Storkmeyer and Grandpa battling the Pooches on a jungle expedition. Colorful illustrations are filled with comical detail that perfectly matches the tall tale exploits.

513 *A Snout for Chocolate*. Ill. by author. HarperCollins, 2006, ISBN 0-06-051093-5. SERIES: I Can Read. SUBJECTS: Grandparents — Fiction; Illness — Fiction; Pets — Dogs — Fiction. RL B.

While washing windows, Grandpa regales Barney with another anti-itch chicken pox story. This time, Grandpa comes to the rescue of a pig whose snout is stuck to a box of frozen chocolates. The colorfully hysterical artwork is a great match for the comical escapades of Grandpa's tall tales.

Cebulash, Mel

514 *Willie's Wonderful Pet*. Ill. by George Ford. Scholastic, 1993, ISBN 0-590-45787-X. SERIES: Hello Reader! SUBJECTS: Animals; Pets; School stories. RL A.

Willie's wiggling worm stirs up all the classroom pets on Pet Day. This primer with the simplest vocabulary is enhanced by uncluttered watercolor illustrations of children and pets.

Cerf, Bennett A.

515 *Bennett Cerf's Book of Animal Riddles*. Ill. by Roy McKie. Random House, 1964, ISBN 0-394-90034-0. SERIES: All By Myself. SUBJECTS: Animals — Fiction; Jokes and riddles. RL A.

Dogs, turtles, hummingbirds, snails, and rabbits are some of the subjects of these clever, simple riddles. They are masterfully illustrated with McKie's bold line drawings.

516 *Bennett Cerf's Book of Laughs*. Ill. by Carl Rose. Beginner, 1959, ISBN 0-394-90011-1. SERIES: I Can Read It All by Myself. SUBJECTS: Jokes and riddles. RL A.

Standard jokes relying on wordplay are retold using a vocabulary of 232 words, well geared to second-grade humor. Dated drawings nevertheless illustrate the misconceptions of the words, thus adding humor.

517 *Bennett Cerf's Book of Riddles*. Ill. by Roy McKie. Random House, 1960, ISBN 0-394-90015-4. SERIES: I Can Read It All by Myself. SUBJECTS: Jokes and riddles. RL A.

Not too familiar standard riddles about dogs, cats, horses, pigs, and children are illustrated by a cartoon master of expressive line.

518 *More Riddles*. Ill. by Roy McKie. Random House, 1961, ISBN 0-394-90024-3. SERIES: I Can Read It All by Myself. SUBJECTS: Jokes and riddles. RL A.

Traditional riddles are retold simply. Comic illustrations extending the riddles are in primary colors.

Chaconas, Dori

519 *Cork and Fuzz*. Ill. by Lisa McCue. Penguin, 2005, ISBN 0-670-03602-1. SERIES: Viking Easy-to-Read. SUBJECTS: Friendship — Fiction; Opossums — Fiction. RL B. LEXILE 330L.

An unlikely friendship blossoms between an opossum who likes to eat beetles and a muskrat who enjoys the veggie stuff. Through thoughtful ink and watercolors, the characters develop, each with his own unique personality.

520 *Cork and Fuzz: Good Sports*. Ill. by Lisa McCue. Penguin, 2007, ISBN 0-670-06145-X. SERIES: Viking Easy-to-Read. SUBJECTS:

Friendship — Fiction; Opossums — Fiction. RL B.

Whether running races or playing stickball, Fuzz the opossum learns that having a good friend is better than always winning. Detailed watercolor and ink drawings show the strong emotions of winning and losing, as well as the importance of friendship.

521 *Cork and Fuzz: Short and Tall.* Ill. by Lisa McCue. Penguin, 2006, ISBN 0-670-05985-4. SERIES: Viking Easy-to-Read. SUBJECTS: Friendship — Fiction; Opossums — Fiction. RL B. LEXILE 370L.

Cork's belief that he should be taller than Fuzz because he is older challenges the friendship between the muskrat and the possum. Gentle, earth-toned illustrations convey the fun and strong bond of love friends can share.

Chalmers, Mary

522 *Merry Christmas, Harry.* Ill. by author. HarperCollins, 1992, ISBN 0-06-022739-7. SUBJECTS: Christmas — Fiction; Pets — Cats — Fiction. RL A.

Harry's the cat's desire for a baby brother is realized on Christmas, when a kitten who drinks a little milk, takes a little nap, plays a little, and sleeps a little arrives. Chalmers's simple full-color drawings hold center stage.

523 *Take a Nap, Harry.* Ill. by author. HarperCollins, 1991, ISBN 0-06-021244-6. SUBJECTS: Pets — Cats — Fiction. RL A.

Harry the cat entertains a bee and himself when he should be napping. So he gets sleepy before "helping" his mother finish baking a cake, and finishes his nap while mother finishes the cake. Outstanding expressive watercolor animals match the gentle story admirably.

524 *Throw a Kiss, Harry.* Ill. by author. HarperCollins, 1990, o.p. SUBJECTS: Pets — Cats — Fiction. RL A.

Harry a charming white kitten, goes exploring while Mother is talking to a friend, and has to be rescued from the roof of a house by a fireman. After refusing to blow the fireman a thank-you kiss, Harry sneaks back to do so. Simple pencil and wash drawings are very appealing.

Champion, Joyce

525 *Emily and Alice.* Ill. by Suçie Stevenson. Harcourt, 1993, ISBN 0-15-200588-9. SUBJECTS: Friendship — Fiction; Pets — Raccoons — Fiction. RL A.

Emily and Alice become fast friends when Alice moves in next door. They "baby-sit" Alice's pet raccoon, picnic, and play in rain puddles together despite occasional disagreements.

Chardiet, Bernice, and Grace Maccarone

526 *The Best Teacher in the World.* Ill. by G. Brian Karas. Scholastic, 1990, ISBN 0-590-43307-5. SERIES: School Friends. SUBJECTS: Behavior — Lying — Fiction; School stories. RL A.

When timid Bunny is chosen to deliver a note to another teacher, she fails but reports otherwise. After a restless night, she confesses to a forgiving teacher. Pencil and wash drawings suggest Bunny's feelings of bewilderment in a long, empty school hall particularly well.

527 *Martin and the Tooth Fairy.* Ill. by G. Brian Karas. Scholastic, pap., 1991, o.p. SERIES: School Friends. SUBJECTS: School stories; Tooth fairy — Fiction. RL C.

Martin buys his friends' teeth when they fall out, expecting to make a windfall from the Tooth Fairy, in this story with pencil and watercolor illustrations.

528 *We Scream for Ice Cream.* Ill. by G. Brian Karas. Scholastic, 1992, o.p. SERIES: School Friends. SUBJECTS: Friendship — Fiction. RL A.

One disaster after another disrupts the neighborhood children's friendships when the ice cream truck visits. Pencil and watercolor stick figures accompany the straightforward story.

Charles, Donald

529 *Calico Cat's Exercise Book.* Ill. by author. Childrens Press, 1982, o.p. SERIES: Calico Cat. SUBJECTS: Exercise; Pets — Cats. RL B.

Exuberant decorative cat drawings encourage exercise, as does the very abbreviated text.

Chase, Catherine

530 *Pete, the Wet Pet.* Ill. by Gail Gibbons. Elsevier-Dutton, 1981, o.p. SUBJECTS: Pets — Dogs — Fiction. RL A.

A simple story of the mess a big cuddly dog makes in the house when he comes in to get dry. Ink sketches with crayon and wash coloring add to the warmth of the tale.

Chenery, Janet

531 *Toad Hunt.* Ill. by Ben Shecter. Dell, pap., 1992, ISBN 0-440-40561-0. SERIES: Science I Can Read. SUBJECTS: Nature; Reptiles and amphibians; Science and scientists. RL B.

Teddy and Peter learn about turtles, salamanders, and frogs as they search for a toad. Soft colored pencil and ink drawings show humor and reverence for wild animals.

532 *Wolfie.* Ill. by Marc Simont. Dell, pap., 1991, ISBN 0-440-40496-7. SERIES: I Can Read. SUBJECTS: Nature; Spiders. RL B.

Good information about wolf spiders is spiced with a younger sister's desire to feed "Wolfie"; she turns out to be a dead shot stunning flies for Wolfie's meals with a rubber band. Two-color illustrations are plain, yet expressive.

Chislett, Gail

533 *Whump.* Ill. by Vladyana Krykorka. Annick, 1989, o.p. SUBJECTS: Bedtime — Fiction. RL B.

Jeremy feels small and lonely in his new bed. He "whumps" on his parents and brother, keeping them awake, but finds them settled in his bed instead. This slim story has illustrations in shades of blue and lavender, with a most cozy black cat, teddies, and a shaggy dog.

Chittenden, Margaret

534 *When the Wild Ducks Come.* Ill. by Beatrice Darwin. Follett, 1972, o.p. SERIES: Beginning to Read. SUBJECTS: Ducks; Seasons. RL C.

A boy observes a pair of ducks through the seasons. Colorful, impressionistic block prints are exceptional.

Chlad, Dorothy

535 *In the Water . . . On the Water.* Ill. by Lydia Halverson. Childrens Press, 1988, o.p. SERIES: Safety Town. SUBJECTS: Safety. RL B.

Some of the safety rules discussed include wearing a life jacket, not throwing sand, not jumping into a pool, using steps and railing, and not playing with faucets. Unimaginative text seems overcautious; for example, always wearing life jackets on the beach. Illustrations are done in watercolor.

536 *Matches, Lighters, and Firecrackers Are Not Toys.* Ill. by Lydia Halverson. Childrens Press, 1982, o.p. SERIES: Safety Town. SUBJECTS: Safety. RL C.

The bare facts regarding the benefits and dangers of fire are flanked by a repetition of simple rules. Bright watercolors follow the text.

537 *Playing on the Playground.* Ill. by Lydia Halverson. Childrens Press, 1987, o.p. SERIES: Safety Town. SUBJECTS: Playgrounds; Safety. RL B.

Six rules about playground safety begin with "never go alone." Following the explanations, the rules are repeated. Large drawings are of multiethnic children.

538 *Stop, Look, and Listen for Trains.* Ill. by Lydia Halverson. Childrens Press, 1983, o.p. SERIES: Safety Town. SUBJECTS: Safety; Trains. RL C.

Chlad admonishes the reader to stop, look, and listen; never play near tracks; and wait until the train is gone before crossing tracks. A little information about trains is given as well. Large colorful paintings accompany the text.

Chorao, Kay

539 *Here Comes Kate.* Ill. by author. Penguin, 2000, o.p. SERIES: Dutton Easy Reader. SUBJECTS: Elephants — Fiction; Family life — Fiction. RL B.

Kate, an elephant child, experiences the love of her parents whether she is having fun or having a tantrum. The lively art radiates with strong familial bonds and caring support.

540 *Oink and Pearl.* Ill. by author. HarperCollins, 1981, o.p. SERIES: I Can

Read. SUBJECTS: Pigs — Fiction; Siblings — Fiction. RL A.

The pigs Oink and Pearl feel frustrated, but find solace in each other's company. Elements from four chapters are skillfully woven together. Pig-pink and soft apple green color sympathetic illustrations.

541 *Up and Down with Kate.* Ill. by author. Penguin, 2002, ISBN 0-525-46891-9. SERIES: Dutton Easy Reader. SUBJECTS: Elephants — Fiction; Family life — Fiction; Grandparents — Fiction. RL B.

Whether it is learning to swim, squabbling with her brother, or waiting for Grandma to visit again, Kate enjoys the love of her family. The many ups and downs of the little elephant's moods are comically — yet realistically and empathetically — portrayed.

542 *Ups and Downs with Oink and Pearl.* Ill. by author. HarperCollins, 1986, o.p. SERIES: I Can Read. SUBJECTS: Pigs — Fiction; Sibling rivalry — Fiction. RL B.

Pearl's anger and jealousy of her little brother evaporate with laughter and sharing in this story about pig siblings. Soft pink, orange, and yellow washes warm this gentle tale.

Chrismer, Melanie

543 *Multiply This!* Scholastic, 2005, ISBN 0-516-25264-X. SERIES: Rookie Read-About Math. SUBJECTS: Mathematics — Fiction; Mathematics — Multiplication. RL B. LEXILE 400L.

Making breakfast becomes a lesson in multiplication for Tim and his Dad. Bright, uncluttered color photographs clearly demonstrate the multiplication problems described in the text.

544 *Odd and Even Socks.* Scholastic, 2005, ISBN 0-516-25265-8. SERIES: Rookie Read-About Math. SUBJECTS: Concepts — Numbers — Fiction; Mathematics — Fiction. RL B. LEXILE 470L.

Find out about odd and even numbers through the clever use of socks. Lively color photographs feature a variety of socks on children as they form groups and create numbers with their bodies.

Christensen, Nancy

545 *Good Night, Little Kitten.* Ill. by Dennis Hockerman. Childrens Press, 1990, o.p. SERIES: My First Reader. SUBJECTS: Bedtime — Fiction; Family life — Fiction. RL A.

In simplest large-print language, Mama and Papa Kitten urge Little Kitten to go to sleep instead of playing. Story is simplistic for school age. Colored pencil and watercolor drawings show cute kittens and toys.

546 *Who Am I?* Ill. by Rowan Barnes Murphy. Scholastic, 1993, ISBN 0-590-46192-3. SERIES: My First Hello Reader. SUBJECTS: Animals — Fiction; Stories in rhyme. RL A.

The rhyming riddle about someone who is not tall or small, has no spots or hat, or who doesn't swim or fly is a surprise, although a few visual clues have been given. Simple rhymes use very easy vocabulary. Flash cards and quizzes clutter the book.

Christian, Mary B.

547 *Devin and Goliath.* Ill. by Normand Chartier. Addison-Wesley, 1974, o.p. SUBJECTS: Pets — Wild animals — Fiction; Turtles — Fiction. RL B.

Devin finds that capturing a turtle named Goliath is not as satisfying as he expected. Pencil drawings with two-color highlights are especially sympathetic to animals.

548 *Doggone Mystery.* Ill. by Irene Trivas. Whitman, 1980, o.p. SERIES: First Read-Alone Mystery. SUBJECTS: Mystery and detective stories; Pets — Dogs — Fiction. RL B.

The kids' dog, Ruffles, helps them uncover a thief. Ink and turquoise washed sketches add humor and help provide clues.

549 *Go West, Swamp Monsters.* Ill. by Marc Brown. Dial, 1985, o.p. SERIES: Dial Easy-to-Read. SUBJECTS: Behavior — Manners — Fiction; Humorous stories; Monsters — Fiction. RL B.

Four swamp monsters in cowboy attire join some child campers visiting their swamp. Humor comes from the monsters' literal interpretation of camping. Brown's illustrations of the monsters make them appear *very* friendly.

Christian, Mary B. (cont.)

550 *Green Thumb Thief*. Ill. by Don Madden. Whitman, 1982, o.p. SERIES: First Read-Alone. SUBJECTS: Mystery and detective stories; Pets — Dogs — Fiction. RL C.

The undercover kids and their shedding dog, Hercules, track down a plant thief. This far-fetched mystery has ink with gray and red wash drawings.

551 *J. J. Leggett, Secret Agent*. Ill. by Jacquie Hann. Lothrop, 1978, o.p. SUBJECTS: Mystery and detective stories. RL C.

A boy's walkie-talkie unexpectedly saves the day. Humorous pencil drawings have pumpkin highlights.

552 *Lucky Man*. Ill. by Glen Rounds. Macmillan, 1979, o.p. SERIES: Ready-to-Read. SUBJECTS: Folklore. RL A.

Felix gets poorer and deeper and deeper in trouble despite all his hard work until one unexpected day in court. Ink sketches have a folk flavor.

553 *Penrod Again*. Ill. by Jane Dyer. Macmillan, 1987, o.p. SERIES: Ready-to-Read. SUBJECTS: Bears — Fiction; Friendship — Fiction; Porcupines — Fiction. RL A.

Five chapters show the trials and satisfactions of friendship between a bear and a porcupine who have very different personalities. Jewel-like watercolors of the animal characters are outstanding.

554 *Penrod's Pants*. Ill. by Jane Dyer. Macmillan, 1986, o.p. SERIES: Ready-to-Read. SUBJECTS: Bears — Fiction; Friendship — Fiction; Porcupines — Fiction. RL B.

The friendship between a bear and a porcupine is strained when they shop for pants, pull a loose tooth, and decide who is to get the last cookie. Full-color watercolors feature emerald greens, royal blues, and sunshine yellows.

555 *Penrod's Party*. Ill. by S. D. Schindler. Macmillan, 1990, o.p. SERIES: Ready-to-Read. SUBJECTS: Bears — Fiction; Friendship — Fiction; Porcupines — Fiction. RL B.

Since Penrod the Porcupine always seems to take advantage of their friendship, Griswold the Bear tries to sabotage Penrod's party when he's not invited. To his surprise, the party's really for him! The story is illustrated with appealing pastel drawings.

556 *Penrod's Picture*. Ill. by S. D. Schindler. Macmillan, 1991, o.p. SUBJECTS: Bears — Fiction; Friendship — Fiction; Porcupines — Fiction. RL B.

Penrod the Porcupine's best intentions mean disaster for Griswold the Bear's wall, and their camping trip. Penrod's misguided gardening and their garage sale end up more successfully, despite blunders. Friendly pencil and watercolor drawings add interesting details.

557 *Swamp Monsters*. Ill. by Marc Brown. Dial, 1983, o.p. SERIES: Dial Easy-to-Read. SUBJECTS: Monsters — Fiction; School stories. RL B.

Swamp monsters Fenny and Crag decide they like snail stew and their own swamp after they go to school with a group of children. Children may gain some perspective on how others might view their everyday behavior. Literal-minded humor is illustrated with watercolors in rose, lemon, and brown.

558 *The Toady and Dr. Miracle*. Ill. by Ib Ohlsson. Macmillan, pap., 1985, o.p. SERIES: Ready-to-Read. SUBJECTS: Frontier and pioneer life — Fiction; Humorous stories. RL C.

In this frontier story, Luther proves he is not dumb when he outwits an itinerant medicine man. Vivid language and pen and ink drawings complement each other to set the mood, create interesting characters, and add humor to the story.

559 *Ventriloquist*. Ill. by Mamoru Funai. Putnam, 1982, o.p. SERIES: Break-of-Day. SUBJECTS: Pets — Dogs — Fiction. RL B.

Arthur's dog Burford has marvelous gifts that go unrecognized, according to his master. Three-tone illustrations alternate with gray tones.

Chwast, Seymour

560 *The Twelve Circus Rings*. Ill. by author. Harcourt, 1993, ISBN 0-15-200627-3. SUBJECTS: Circuses — Fiction; Concepts — Numbers; Cumulative tales. RL A.

The flat pastel double-spreads fill up with the animals and performers of the circus as the tale cumulates. Attention is drawn to the rather sophisticated counting and multiplying cunningly incorporated with a series of questions at the end.

Clark, Ann N.

561 *Little Indian Basket Maker*. Ill. by Harrison Begay. Melmont, 1957, o.p. SERIES: Look Read Learn. SUBJECTS: Art and artists; Papago. RL C.

The basket making of Papago Native Americans involves hands and heart. Illustrations capture the color and texture of that culture with simply colored drawings featuring one little girl and her grandmother.

Clarke, Ginjer L.

562 *Baby Alligator*. Ill. by Neecy Twinem. Grosset & Dunlap, 2000, o.p. SERIES: All Aboard Reading. SUBJECTS: Alligators. RL B. LEXILE 300L.

Detailed, full-color paintings follow the birth, growth, and development of an alligator in Florida. Close-ups, cutaways, diagrams, and maps enhance an informative text.

Clarke, Jane

563 *Scratching's Catching*. Ill. by Jan Lewis. Kingfisher, 2007, ISBN 978-0-7534-5958-4. SERIES: I Am Reading. SUBJECTS: Diseases — Fiction; Humorous stories. RL B.

A cautionary tale about head lice features the kingdom of Hairia, with a long-haired king and his princess daughter. Lively, color cartoon illustrations add to the silliness of this story with educational undertones.

Claverie, Jean

564 *The Picnic*. Ill. by author. Crown, 1985, o.p. SERIES: It's Great to Read. SUBJECTS: Family life — Fiction; Picnics — Fiction. RL B.

A family's relaxing day in the country ends up at a fast-food joint, ketchup-spattered, but with sun-yellow balloons with hearts. Muted pastel illustrations contrast adult and child response to events. Binding is poor.

565 *Shopping*. Ill. by author. Crown, 1985, o.p. SERIES: It's Great to Read. SUBJECTS: Humorous stories; Shopping — Fiction. RL B.

A small child's adventures at the grocery store and in the television department of a store have tongue-in-cheek adult humor. Misty yellows, reds, and blues draw the reader into a child's world. Binding is poor.

566 *Working*. Ill. by author. Crown, 1985, o.p. SERIES: It's Great to Read. SUBJECTS: Fathers — Fiction; Imagination — Fiction; Parents, working — Fiction. RL B.

A small boy's explorations at his father's work place provide varied adult reactions, judging by their expressions. This tale is warmed by the snowball play and hug on the way home. Light pastel drawings have a grainy texture.

Clements, Andrew

567 *Brave Norman: A True Story*. Ill. by Ellen Beier. Simon & Schuster, 2001, ISBN 0-689-82914-0. SERIES: Ready-to-Read. SUBJECTS: Disabilities — Physical and mental — Fiction; Pets — Dogs. RL B. LEXILE 30L.

Shortly after adopting Norman the dog from an animal shelter, his family discovers he is going blind. However, at the beach, Norman jumps into the water and saves a girl from drowning. Colorful, detailed illustrations focus on Norman and his inspirational courage and bravery in all situations.

568 *Dolores and the Big Fire: A True Story*. Ill. by Ellen Beier. Simon & Schuster, 2002, ISBN 0-689-82916-7. SERIES: Ready-to-Read. SUBJECTS: Fire fighters and fire fighting; Pets — Cats. RL B.

One night Dolores the cat wakes her friend to warn him of a fire in the house. Kyle escapes unharmed but his feline hero is badly burned and slowly recovers with loving care. Full-page watercolors enhance the danger and the drama of Dolores's bravery in saving a man's life.

569 *Milo's Great Invention*. Ill. by Barbara Johansen Newman. Raintree, 1998, o.p. SUBJECTS: Food — Fiction; Inventors and inventions — Fiction. RL B. LEXILE 340L.

Everyone in the family loves peas except Milo. To solve his problem, Milo invents the Peas-Be-Gone machine. Clever full-page illustrations track the creative process, and drawn journal entries add interest.

570 *Tara and Tiree, Fearless Friends*. Ill. by Ellen Beier. Simon & Schuster, 2002, o.p. SERIES: Ready-to-Read. SUBJECTS: Pets —

Clements, Andrew (cont.)

Dogs — Fiction; Pets — Fiction. RL B. LEXILE 230L.

When Jim falls through the ice into the cold lake, Tiree tries to rescue him but falls in too. It is up to Tara to save them both. Full-page realistic illustrations capture the fear and ultimate triumph of the amazing dogs. Based on a true story.

Clifford, Eth

571 *Flatfoot Fox and the Case of the Missing Eye*. Ill. by Brian Lies. Houghton Mifflin, 1990, ISBN 0-395-51945-4. SUBJECTS: Animals — Fiction; Mystery and detective stories; Wordplay. RL B.

Flamboyant Fat Cat's beautiful sky-blue artificial eye is stolen when he serves no ice cream or cake at his birthday party because everyone is so mean to him. Ink drawings of Flatfoot Fox and his assistant, Secretary Bird, and his rabbit, pig, goat, and snake suspects add drama and humor.

Climo, Shirley

572 *King of the Birds*. Ill. by Ruth Heller. HarperCollins, 1988, o.p. SUBJECTS: Birds — Fiction; Folklore. RL C.

An appealing story of how Wren became King of the Birds by using his wits, though he never affected a topknot or a robe of bright feathers. Illustrations in browns, blacks, and lavender show the rich variety of birds; the tale tells how they acquired their habits.

Coatsworth, Elizabeth

573 *Bob Bodden and the Seagoing Farm*. Ill. by Frank Aloise. Garrard, 1970, o.p. SUBJECTS: Humorous stories; Tall tales. RL C.

This story explains how Maine sea-captain Bob Bodden's oceangoing farm caused the lakes and islands along Maine's shores. Ink sketches are a bit dated.

Cobb, Annie

574 *Wheels!* Ill. by Davy Jones. Random House, pap., 1996, ISBN 0-679-86445-8. SERIES: Early Step into Reading. SUBJECTS: Wheels — Fiction. RL A.

Everywhere you go there are wheels; on cars, trucks, grocery carts, and skates. Boldly colored, rounded illustrations focus directly on the wheels and enthusiastically demonstrate their importance.

Cocca-Leffler, Maryann

575 *Princess for a Day*. Ill. by author. Grosset & Dunlap, 1998, ISBN 0-448-41604-2. SERIES: All Aboard Reading. SUBJECTS: Imagination — Fiction; Play — Fiction. RL B. LEXILE 140L.

Each day is different, but today Jessie uses her imagination to become a princess. When her Uncle Steve comes bearing a slipper, the "Prince" and Princess go out for royal pizza. Aglow with bright color and movement, the watercolors reflect the simple fun and enjoyment of pretending.

576 *What a Pest!* Ill. by author. Putnam, 1994, o.p. SERIES: All Aboard Reading. SUBJECTS: Siblings — Fiction. RL A.

Little sister Jessie saves the day when one of the dance duo gets chicken pox. Appealing watercolor illustrations support this lighthearted story.

Coerr, Eleanor

577 *The Big Balloon Race*. Ill. by Carolyn Croll. HarperCollins, 1981, ISBN 0-06-021353-1. SERIES: I Can Read. SUBJECTS: Balloons; Biographies. RL A.

Ariel and her mother, Carlotta Myers, the most famous aeronaut of the 1880s, win a hot air balloon race by using their wits and courage. A stowaway, a thunderstorm, and an unscheduled touchdown in a pond, plus full-color drawings, add to the drama.

578 *Chang's Paper Pony*. Ill. by Deborah Kogan Ray. HarperCollins, 1988, ISBN 0-06-021329-9. SERIES: I Can Read. SUBJECTS: Horses — Fiction; United States — 1783–1865 — Fiction. RL C.

A Chinese American boy, Chang, growing up in a gold mining town, dreams of having a pony. Pencil drawings in turquoise and gold soften the harsh outlines of his life, and celebrate the realization of his dream.

579 *Jane Goodall.* Ill. by Kees de Kiefte. Putnam, 1976, o.p. SUBJECTS: Biographies; Science and scientists. RL C.

The outlines of Goodall's dreams, opportunities, and choices are given. Soft pencil sketches are appropriate.

580 *The Josefina Story Quilt.* Ill. by Bruce Degen. HarperCollins, 1986, ISBN 0-06-021349-3. SERIES: I Can Read. SUBJECTS: Frontier and pioneer life — Fiction; Quilting — Fiction; Western stories. RL B.

The hardships and satisfactions of wagon train travel are commemorated in a quilt by a young girl. Each chapter is headed with a quilt patch significant to Josefina's experience and there are pencil outline drawings.

581 *Mixed-Up Mystery Smell.* Ill. by Tomie dePaola. Putnam, 1976, o.p. SERIES: See and Read. SUBJECTS: Clubs — Fiction; Haunted houses — Fiction; Mystery and detective stories. RL B.

While hunting for a mysterious smell's source, the children nervously follow their noses to a "haunted" house, and discover the source of the delicious smell. Pale cocoa, avocado, and turquoise coloring alternates with pencil in dePaola's distinctive drawings.

582 *Waza Wins at Windy Gulch.* Ill. by Janet McCaffery. Putnam, 1977, o.p. SERIES: See and Read. SUBJECTS: Camels; Humorous stories; United States — 1783–1865 — Fiction. RL C.

A true story about the imported Camel Brigade of the 1850s that reads like a tall tale as Dirtyshirt Dan tries to get the camels in trouble to save his mules. Excellent textured drawings are in shades of brown.

Cohen, Caron L.

583 *How Many Fish?* Ill. by S. D. Schindler. HarperCollins, pap., 1998, ISBN 0-06-444273-X. SERIES: My First I Can Read. SUBJECTS: Concepts — Numbers — Fiction; Fish — Fiction. RL A. LEXILE BR.

Children and a school of fish play a counting game in this book with an effective underwater perspective. The focus on feet with colorful fish darting around them provides an enjoyable point of view.

584 *Three Yellow Dogs.* Ill. by Peter Sis. Greenwillow, 1986, o.p. SUBJECTS: Concepts — Numbers; Pets — Dogs — Fiction. RL A.

A five-word text is enlivened with dogs of all shapes and pastel colors. Some are shown close-up and others are seen from a distance.

Cole, Joanna

585 *Bony-Legs.* Ill. by Dirk Zimmer. Scholastic, pap., 1988, ISBN 0-02-722970-X. SUBJECTS: Folklore — Russia; Magic — Fiction; Russia — Fiction. RL A.

Sasha's kindness to Baba Yaga's creaking gate and a hungry cat and dog helps her escape from the Russian witch. Richly patterned illustrations embroider this simple version of a traditional tale of fear, magic, and kindness.

586 *Bully Trouble.* Ill. by Marylin Hafner. Random House, 1989, ISBN 0-394-94949-8. SERIES: Step into Reading. SUBJECTS: Behavior — Bullying — Fiction; Friendship — Fiction. RL A.

Best friends Arlo and Robby take revenge on bully Big Eddie with a hot soda concoction and a hot chili sandwich. Colored pencil and wash illustrations show the boys in action.

587 *Get Well, Clown-Arounds!* Ill. by Jerry Smath. Stevens, 1982, ISBN 0-8368-0895-9. SUBJECTS: Clowns — Fiction; Jokes and riddles; Wordplay. RL A.

Grandma Clown-Around's chicken soup and general clean-up "cures" her family of the green pox, caught when Baby paints green spots on the bathroom mirror. Games for learning are appended. Pastel drawings are busy and playful.

588 *Golly Gump Swallowed a Fly.* Ill. by Bari Weissman. Parents Magazine Press, 1981, ISBN 0-8193-1069-. SUBJECTS: Humorous stories; Tall tales. RL B.

Golly Gump's adventures lead him to cover his mouth when he yawns in a tale paralleling "I Know an Old Lady Who Swallowed a Fly." Flat pastel colors and expressive animals add to the humor.

589 *How You Were Born.* Photos by Margaret Miller. Morrow, 1993, ISBN 0-688-12059-8.

Cole, Joanna (cont.)

SUBJECTS: Human body — Birth; Nature. RL C.

This is a slightly revised edition, leaving out diagrams of the male and female reproductive systems and the statement "During labor, your mother had to work hard."

590 *The Magic School Bus: At the Waterworks*. Ill. by Bruce Degen. Scholastic, 1986, ISBN 0-590-43739-9. SERIES: Magic School Bus. SUBJECTS: School stories; Science and scientists; Water. RL C.

This imaginative class trip takes the class in a raindrop from a cloud, downstream to a water filtration plant, into a water tower, and back through water pipes to the school. Irreverent dialogue, Ms. Frizzle's outrageous dresses, and the parting notes to "serious" students add humor.

591 *The Magic School Bus: Inside the Earth*. Ill. by Bruce Degen. Scholastic, 1987, ISBN 0-590-40759-7. SERIES: Magic School Bus. SUBJECTS: Geology and geologists; School stories; Science and scientists. RL C.

Ms. Frizzle, with her zany, unpredictable clothing, leads her third-grade class into the center of the earth in their air-conditioned magic school bus. A humorous conversation between a reader and the illustrator at the end sorts out the fiction from real science.

592 *The Magic School Bus: Inside the Human Body*. Ill. by Bruce Degen. Scholastic, 1989, ISBN 0-590-72633-1. SERIES: Magic School Bus. SUBJECTS: Human body; School stories; Science and scientists. RL C.

This magic school bus field trip takes the third-graders through Arnold's body, through the blood stream to the brain, exiting with a sneeze. A humorous "test" at the end sorts out truth from fiction. Lively dialogue and fanciful illustrations add to the imaginative text.

593 *The Magic School Bus: Lost in the Solar System*. Ill. by Bruce Degen. Scholastic, 1992, ISBN 0-590-41429-1. SERIES: Magic School Bus. SUBJECTS: Astronomy and astronomers; School stories; Science and scientists. RL C.

Ms. Frizzle, third-grade teacher extraordinaire, drives her class to the planets when they find the earthly planetarium closed. Through dialogue, school essays and adventures, narrative, a humorous appendix, and spirited ink and watercolor drawings, an introduction to outer space is given.

594 *The Magic School Bus: On the Ocean Floor*. Ill. by Bruce Degen. Scholastic, 1992, ISBN 0-590-41430-5. SERIES: Magic School Bus. SUBJECTS: Oceans and ocean life; School stories; Science and scientists. RL C.

This magic school bus drives right into the ocean where the class — and the lifeguard — don diving gear to explore various ocean layers, passing the tidal pools to visit the depths and a coral reef, visit with sharks and dolphins, and go bus surfing. Lively illustrations match imaginary trip.

595 *The Missing Tooth*. Ill. by Marylin Hafner. Random House, 1988, o.p. SERIES: Step into Reading. SUBJECTS: Friendship — Fiction; Human body — Teeth — Fiction. RL B.

Arlo and Robby had the same pets, liked the same games, and looked alike, down to the same missing teeth. After a bet about which one was going to lose the next tooth, the friendship becomes strained. Full colors warm this realistic story with a satisfying resolution.

596 *Mixed-Up Magic*. Ill. by True Kelley. Scholastic, pap., 1987, o.p. SUBJECTS: Magic — Fiction; Nonsense; Stories in rhyme. RL A.

Rhyming nonsense is effectively paired with an elf's inept magic. Soft pastels warm the text.

597 *Plants in Winter*. Ill. by Kazue Mizumura. HarperCollins, 1973, o.p. SERIES: Let's-Read-and-Find-Out Science. SUBJECTS: Plants; Winter. RL B.

A child finds out how various plants survive the winter from a botanist whose theories do not cover the hardy snowdrop blossom. Pale gray and green washes most appropriately illustrate each type of plant.

598 *Who Put the Pepper in the Pot?* Ill. by R. W. Alley. Parents Magazine Press, 1989, ISBN 0-8193-1189-8. SERIES: Read Aloud Originals. SUBJECTS: Farm and country life — Fiction; Humorous stories. RL A.

Mama Sue and Papa Joe and their three kids live on hard work sweetened with love. They are nervous when their rich Aunt Tootie comes for dinner. Aunt Tootie surprises them by saving them from a disastrous stew. Illustrations suit the description of chaotic, cooperative farm life.

599 *You Can't Smell a Flower with Your Ear! All About Your Five Senses.* Ill. by Mavis Smith. Putnam, 1994, o.p. SERIES: All Aboard Reading. SUBJECTS: Human body; Senses — Sight; Senses — Smell. RL A.

The senses are introduced in ten-page chapters that give anatomy, some background, and some experiments to try. Examples given are familiar to any child. Diverse ages and races are pictured in ink and watercolor drawings.

Cole, Joanna, and Stephanie Calmenson

600 *Ready . . . Set. . . . Read!* Ill. by Anne Burgess and Chris L. Demarest. Doubleday, 1990, ISBN 0-385-41416-1. SERIES: The Beginning Reader's Treasury. SUBJECTS: Books and reading; Poetry. RL B.

Dr. Seuss, Arnold Lobel, Bernard Wiseman, and Joanna Cole are some of the authors whose stories are included in this anthology of poetry and stories with original art. Poets include Lilian Moore, Gwendolyn Brooks, David McCord, and other favorites.

Collard, Sneed B., III

601 *Abraham Lincoln: A Courageous Leader.* Marshall Cavendish, 2007, ISBN 0-7614-2162-9. SERIES: American Heroes. SUBJECTS: Biographies; Presidents — United States; United States — History. RL C.

While embroiled in the Civil War, the sixteenth president of the United States issued the Emancipation Proclamation declaring all slaves in the South to be free. Images and artwork from archives offer a unique and thoughtful addition to the biography of a heroic man.

602 *Benjamin Franklin: The Man Who Could Do Just About Anything.* Marshall Cavendish, 2007, ISBN 0-7614-2161-0. SERIES: American Heroes. SUBJECTS: Biographies; Inventors and inventions; United States — History. RL C.

A brief look into the life of Benjamin Franklin finds a scientist, statesman, printer, inventor, and Founding Father. Relevant archival art, a timeline, and glossary round out an informative biography.

603 *David Crockett: Fearless Frontierman.* Marshall Cavendish, 2007, ISBN 0-7614-2160-2. SERIES: American Heroes. SUBJECTS: Biographies; United States — History. RL C.

Archival prints and art complement the biography of the famous nineteenth-century frontiersman who became an American hero, legendary for his honesty and courage.

604 *Rosa Parks: The Courage to Make a Difference.* Marshall Cavendish, 2007, ISBN 0-7614-2163-7. SERIES: American Heroes. SUBJECTS: African Americans; Biographies; Civil rights. RL C.

On a historical day for the civil rights movement, Rosa Parks refused to give up her seat on the bus. Elegantly descriptive archival material chronicles the contributions of a courageous woman.

605 *Sacagawea: Brave Shoshone Girl.* Marshall Cavendish, 2007, ISBN 0-7614-2166-1. SERIES: American Heroes. SUBJECTS: Biographies; Explorers and exploration; Native Americans. RL C.

In this well-researched biography, the young Shoshone girl's significant contribution to the expedition of Lewis and Clark and to American history is illustrated with numerous paintings from the nineteenth century.

Collicott, Sharleen

606 *Mildred and Sam.* Ill. by author. HarperCollins, 2003, ISBN 0-06-026682-1. SERIES: I Can Read. SUBJECTS: Family life — Fiction; Houses — Fiction; Mice — Fiction. RL B.

After the arrival of eight tiny baby mice, Sam finally realizes why Mildred wanted a bigger house. A palette of warm, cheerful colors creates cozy images befitting this quaint family story.

607 *Mildred and Sam and Their Babies.* Ill. by author. HarperCollins, 2005, ISBN 0-06-058111-5. SERIES: I Can Read. SUBJECTS: Family life — Fiction; Mice — Fiction. RL B.

As the little mice grow up Mildred is always worried about them and their safety. But the little mice have big dreams. Colorfully playful illustrations of everyday life are juxtaposed with full-

Collicott, Sharleen (cont.)

page, spirited imaginings of tiny mice awaiting new adventures.

Collins, David R.

608 *If I Could, I Would*. Ill. by Kelly Oechsli. Garrard, 1979, o.p. SERIES: Imagination. SUBJECTS: Imagination — Fiction; Mothers — Fiction. RL B.

A small boy likes his mother so much he would give her lots of candy; take her for a wagon ride to the moon; give her a haunted house, lots of pets, and a castle — and even eat spinach! Gentle humor is reinforced by four-color cartoon drawings.

Conway, Lisa

609 *I Like Ketchup Sandwiches*. Ill. by author. Random House, 1991, ISBN 0-679-81719- . SERIES: Pictureback Reader. SUBJECTS: Family life — Fiction. RL A.

The 48-word vocabulary appears at the end for cutting out as flash cards. A small child likes to burp, talk, dance, make her swing set bump, hang from trees, and visit her grandma. Soft colored-pencil drawings complement the story of a world familiar to a child.

Cooke, Ann

610 *Giraffes at Home*. Ill. by Robert Quackenbush. HarperCollins, 1972, ISBN 0-690-33082-0. SERIES: Let's-Read-and-Find-Out Science. SUBJECTS: Giraffes; Nature. RL C.

Information about giraffes' mating, birth, feeding, enemies, and herd behavior is presented in an interesting fashion. Excellent four-color illustrations alternate with gray ones.

Cooper, Jason

611 *Coral Reefs*. Ill. with photos. Rourke, 1992, o.p. SERIES: The Sea. SUBJECTS: Conservation; Oceans and ocean life. RL C.

Excellent close-up photographs of coral reefs and their colorful fish are accompanied by brief information in large print. Short glossary and index are included.

612 *Magnets*. Ill. with photos. Rourke, 1992, ISBN 0-86593-165-8. SERIES: Science Secrets. SUBJECTS: Magnets; Science and scientists. RL C.

Excellent full-page color photographs illustrate the text on half of each double spread. Magnetic rocks, electromagnets, and gravity are some of the topics introduced.

613 *Sea Shells*. Photos by Lynn M. Stone. Rourke, 1992, o.p. SERIES: Discovery Library of the Sea. SUBJECTS: Conservation; Oceans and ocean life; Shells. RL C.

The text highlights difficult words, which are defined in the glossary as well as in the text. Explanations are simple but informative, and are illustrated with outstanding close-up photographs of different kinds of shells. Conservation as well as wonder is stressed.

614 *Wind*. Ill. with photos. Rourke, 1992, ISBN 0-86593-171-2. SERIES: Science Secrets. SUBJECTS: Science and scientists; Weather — Wind. RL C.

Basic concepts of the causes and effects of wind energy are introduced. Windmills, weather vanes, hurricanes, waterspouts, and tornadoes are illustrated with full-page color photographs. A brief glossary and an index are appended.

Corbett, Scott

615 *The Boy Who Walked on Air*. Ill. by Ed Parker. Little, Brown, 1974, o.p. SUBJECTS: Humorous stories; Inventors and inventions — Fiction. RL B.

Max's willpower and Morry's inventiveness have disastrous results — most of the time — as they try to become airborne. Cartoon illustrations add humor.

Corey, Dorothy

616 *Everybody Takes Turns*. Ill. by Lois Axeman. Whitman, 1980, o.p. SERIES: Self-Starters. SUBJECTS: Behavior — Sharing. RL A.

At the most basic level, the text talks about people, including children, taking turns: in line, when only one toy is available, and crossing the street. Situations have child appeal, as do illustrations with varied patterns, cherry red washes, and pets.

Corey, Shana

617 *First Graders from Mars Episode 1: Horus's Horrible Day*. Ill. by Mark Teague. Scholastic, 2001, ISBN 0-439-26220-8. SUBJECTS: Extraterrestrial beings — Fiction; Humorous stories; School stories. RL B. LEXILE 150L.

No slime table, no snooze mats! The first day of first grade on Mars is not what Horus expected until he helps Pelly, the new girl. Creatively zany images in bright Martian colors enhance the comical traumas of Horus's school day.

618 *First Graders from Mars Episode 2: The Problem with Pelly*. Ill. by Mark Teague. Scholastic, 2002, o.p. SUBJECTS: Extraterrestrial beings — Fiction; Humorous stories; School stories. RL B. LEXILE 170L.

Having a fluffernobbin instead of tentacles on her head makes Pelly feel sad and different. Creative Mars-scapes with engagingly flamboyant inhabitants effectively illustrate a story that is alive with wit and empathy.

619 *First Graders from Mars Episode 3: Nergal and the Great Space Race*. Ill. by Mark Teague. Scholastic, 2002, o.p. SUBJECTS: Extraterrestrial beings — Fiction; Humorous stories; School stories. RL B. LEXILE 80L.

Not feeling as fit as a Martian should, Nergal worries about running in the Space Race during Martian Health Week. Out-of-this-world humor is matched by the lighthearted and entertaining drawings of first-grade life on Mars.

620 *First Graders from Mars Episode 4: Tera, Star Student*. Ill. by Mark Teague. Scholastic, 2003, ISBN 0-439-26634-3. SUBJECTS: Extraterrestrial beings — Fiction; Humorous stories; School stories. RL B. LEXILE 170L.

There is no gold star at the end of the day for Tera when she does not work well within Group Earth. The fun and foibles of everyday school life are humorously related with creatively detailed pictures that add the perfect Martian touch.

Cosby, Bill

621 *The Best Way to Play*. Ill. by Varnette P. Honeywood. Scholastic, 1997, ISBN 0-590-13756-5. SERIES: Little Bill. SUBJECTS: African Americans — Fiction; Imagination — Fiction. RL B. LEXILE 360L.

When his friend gets the video game of his favorite television show, "Space Explorers," Little Bill discovers it is more fun to play outdoors and use his imagination. Playful illustrations in bright colors visually interpret the strong bonds of friendship within the group.

622 *The Day I Saw My Father Cry*. Ill. by Varnette P. Honeywood. Scholastic, 2000, ISBN 0-590-52197-7. SERIES: Little Bill. SUBJECTS: African Americans — Fiction; Death — Fiction; Family life — Fiction. RL B. LEXILE 300L.

The death of a beloved neighbor across the street makes Little Bill's family sad. Alan Mills had shown them how to make people feel good even in bad situations. Expressive drawings convey the range of emotions experienced when losing someone special.

623 *The Day I Was Rich*. Ill. by Varnette P. Honeywood. Scholastic, pap., 1999, ISBN 0-590-52173-X. SERIES: Little Bill. SUBJECTS: African Americans — Fiction; Family life — Fiction. RL B. LEXILE 490L.

Finding a huge "diamond" while playing a game of stickball hockey leads Little Bill and friends to dream of what they will do with all the money. Bright, action-filled illustrations follow the possibilities until reality sets in when they discover the diamond is a paperweight.

624 *Hooray for the Dandelion Warriors!* Ill. by Varnette P. Honeywood. Scholastic, 1999, ISBN 0-590-52191-8. SERIES: Little Bill. SUBJECTS: African Americans — Fiction; Family life — Fiction; Sports — Baseball — Fiction. RL B. LEXILE 380L.

Enthusiastic illustrations capture the team spirit and field action of the Dandelion Warriors on the baseball diamond. Afraid he wasn't going to play second base, Little Bill learns what it means to be part of a team with a very special name.

625 *The Meanest Thing to Say*. Ill. by Varnette P. Honeywood. Scholastic, 1997, ISBN 0-590-13754-9. SERIES: Little Bill. SUBJECTS: African Americans — Fiction; Family life — Fiction; School stories. RL B. LEXILE 350L.

Cosby, Bill (cont.)

With the help of his parents, Little Bill learns how to handle a bully who wants to say mean things about everyone. A warm family spirit of caring and support is mirrored in the faces of those who love Little Bill.

626 *My Big Lie*. Ill. by Varnette P. Honeywood. Scholastic, 1999, ISBN 0-590-52160-8. SERIES: Little Bill. SUBJECTS: African Americans — Fiction; Behavior — Honest — Fiction; Family life — Fiction. RL B. LEXILE 400L.

Telling a lie about why he was late getting home to dinner lands Little Bill in his room with a copy of *The Boy Who Cried Wolf*, thinking about what he did wrong. From the fun on the basketball court to the family's fear for his safety, the energetic artwork heightens the impact of the text.

627 *One Dark and Scary Night*. Ill. by Varnette P. Honeywood. Scholastic, 1999, ISBN 0-590-51475-X. SERIES: Little Bill. SUBJECTS: African Americans — Fiction; Family life — Fiction; Fear — Fiction. RL B. LEXILE 490L.

Little Bill's great-grandmother offers a magical solution to his fear of the scary things that are inside his closet at night. The dark colors of Little Bill's room effectively contrast with the brighter colors of rooms that represent security.

628 *Shipwreck Saturday*. Ill. by Varnette P. Honeywood. Scholastic, 1998, ISBN 0-590-16400-7. SERIES: Little Bill. SUBJECTS: African Americans — Fiction; Family life — Fiction. RL B. LEXILE 430L.

Proud of the boat he built, Little Bill is devastated when it is broken. Vibrant pictures effectively depict the range of Bill's emotions, which move from despair to glee when Kiku's grandmother transforms the wreckage of his boat into a kite.

629 *Super-fine Valentine*. Ill. by Varnette P. Honeywood. Scholastic, 1998, ISBN 0-590-16401-5. SERIES: Little Bill. SUBJECTS: African Americans — Fiction; Family life — Fiction; School stories; Valentine's Day — Fiction. RL B. LEXILE 430L.

It's Valentine's Day and Little Bill is reluctant to give a special valentine to Mia for fear of being teased by his classmates. Full-page, detailed drawings ably set the backdrop for Little Bill's fear of a valentine fiasco.

630 *The Treasure Hunt*. Ill. by Varnette P. Honeywood. Scholastic, pap., 1997, ISBN 0-590-95618-3. SERIES: Little Bill. SUBJECTS: African Americans — Fiction; Family life — Fiction; Storytelling. RL B. LEXILE 390L.

On a rainy day with nothing to do, Little Bill discovers that everyone but him has a special thing they care about. What can his treasure be? Rich colors in a folk art style blend energy and emotion.

631 *The Worst Day of My Life*. Ill. by Varnette P. Honeywood. Scholastic, pap., 1999, ISBN 0-590-52175-6. SERIES: Little Bill. SUBJECTS: African Americans — Fiction; Family life — Fiction; Parties — Fiction. RL B. LEXILE 580L.

It's Saturday, and Little Bill has to wear a suit and tie during his parents' party. While his friends play outside, Little Bill imagines the fun he could be having but respects his parents' wishes. Vivid illustrations aptly capture the musings of a bored young man.

Cossi, Olga

632 *Gus the Bus*. Ill. by Howie Schneider. Scholastic, 1989, o.p. SUBJECTS: Buses — Fiction. RL C.

After getting new tires, Gus, the school bus, has a day chasing a dog and horses, racing a fire truck, and attempting to take off at the airport. Pastel cartoons show the silly grin on his radiator and the wild flowers on his mirror.

Cottle, Joan

633 *Emily's Shoes*. Ill. by author. Children's Press, 1999, ISBN 0-516-21585-X. SERIES: Rookie Reader. SUBJECTS: Shoes — Fiction. RL A.

A little girl unsure of what is going to happen next imagines the different types of shoes she could wear — for soccer, for ballet, for a party. . . . Pastel watercolors allow the reader to speculate along with her.

Cotton, Jacqueline S.

634 *Veterans Day*. Children's Press, 2002, ISBN 0-516-22672-X. SERIES: Rookie Read-About Holidays. SUBJECTS: Holidays; Veterans Day. RL B. LEXILE 620L.

Color photographs highlight the history and significance of Veterans Day, celebrated on November 11. Parades, ceremonies, and proudly flying the flag are just some of ways to honor our country's veterans.

Counsel, June

635 *But Martin!* Ill. by Carolyn Dinan. Faber & Faber, 1984, o.p. SUBJECTS: Cultural diversity — Fiction; School stories. RL B.

This intriguing, upbeat story celebrating diversity, play, and cooperative learning focuses on Martin, who is green and flies to school in a saucer. Ink drawings are brightened with washes and colored pencil.

Coville, Bruce, and Katherine Coville

636 *The Foolish Giant*. Ill. by authors. HarperCollins, 1978, ISBN 0-397-31800-6. SERIES: I-Like-to-Read. SUBJECTS: Giants — Fiction. RL C.

A loving portrait of a brave, kind, and friendly giant named Harry is given, along with an explanation of his limitations and powers. All the tears are not Harry's in this evocative story illustrated with soft, detailed pencil drawings.

637 *Sarah's Unicorn*. Ill. by authors. HarperCollins, pap., 1985, ISBN 0-397-31873-1. SERIES: I-Like-to-Read. SUBJECTS: Mythical creatures — Fiction; Witches — Fiction. RL B.

Sarah's magical adventures with Oakhorn the unicorn nearly come to an end when Mag the evil witch discovers them together. Pencil drawings supply atmosphere and expressive details, especially of the forest animals.

Cowley, Joy

638 *Agapanthus Hum and the Angel Hoot*. Ill. by Jennifer Plecas. Penguin, 2003, ISBN 0-399-23344-X. SUBJECTS: Human body — Teeth — Fiction; Humorous stories. RL B.

When Agapanthus loses her first tooth she can no longer hum, but she can whistle. Her father calls it an angel hoot, and her dog Major Bark calls it fun and joins in with a howl. Alternating full-page illustrations and vignettes embrace the energy and unique spirit of this fun-loving character.

639 *Agapanthus Hum and the Eyeglasses*. Ill. by Jennifer Plecas. Penguin, 1999, ISBN 0-399-23211-7. SUBJECTS: Eyeglasses — Fiction; Humorous stories. RL B. LEXILE 570L.

As Agapanthus discovers, eyeglasses and gymnastics do not mix. A professional acrobat teaches her the secret of keeping eyeglasses safe. Bright and breezy illustrations are a perfect match to this story about a charming young girl who is a "whizzer."

640 *Agapanthus Hum and the Major Bark*. Ill. by Jennifer Plecas. Penguin, 2001, ISBN 0-399-23322-9. SUBJECTS: Humorous stories; Pets — Dogs — Fiction; Pets — Fiction. RL B.

Agapanthus and her new dog, Major Bark, enter a local dog show. Surprisingly, her "champion bitser" (a dog of many breeds) wins a blue ribbon for the dog with the smallest eyes. Lively illustrations in cheerful colors enthusiastically show the warmth and vitality of Agapanthus and her loving family.

Coxe, Molly

641 *Big Egg*. Ill. by author. Random House, 1997, ISBN 0-679-98126-8. SERIES: Early Step into Reading. SUBJECTS: Chickens — Fiction; Ostriches — Fiction. RL A. LEXILE BR.

Finding an unusually large egg in her nest, Hen tries to find the owner. Fox slyly claims it as the big "chick" hatches and saves all the little just-hatched chicks. Humorous cartoon drawings highlight a repetitive story for beginning readers.

642 *The Great Snake Escape*. Ill. by author. HarperCollins, 1994, ISBN 0-06-022869-5. SERIES: I Can Read. SUBJECTS: Animals — Fiction; Friendship — Fiction. RL A.

Friends Mirabel the goose and Maxie the frog are helped by the feared king cobra who escaped from the zoo. Simple but absorbing story is illustrated in pencil and soft pastels.

Coxe, Molly (cont.)

643 *Hot Dog*. Ill. by author. Golden Books, pap., 1998, ISBN 0-307-26101-8. SERIES: Road to Reading. SUBJECTS: Pets — Dogs — Fiction; Summer — Fiction. RL A. LEXILE BR.

Limited vocabulary and frequent repetition of words follow the comedic exploits of a hot dog in search of a cool place. Bold, expressive cartoon art hilariously enhances a story that uses less than twenty-five words.

644 *R Is for Radish*. Ill. by author. Random House, 1997, o.p. SUBJECTS: Rabbits — Fiction; School stories. RL B.

Focusing on a favorite letter, Radish R-A-P-S her spelling words, has fun at recess, and eats raspberry pie with friends. Cartoon drawings embellish the funny predicaments of an endearing rabbit.

645 *Six Sticks*. Ill. by author. Random House, 1999, o.p. SERIES: Early Step into Reading + Math. SUBJECTS: Mathematics — Fiction. RL A. LEXILE 120L.

Learn basic principles of geometry using six popsicle sticks. Collage illustrations show how two friendly mice construct swings, snowflakes, and even a clubhouse using the sticks.

Craig, Janet

646 *The Boo-Hoo Witch*. Ill. by Pat Schories. Troll, 1993, o.p. SERIES: Giant First-Start. SUBJECTS: Halloween — Fiction; Homelessness — Fiction; Witches — Fiction. RL A.

Little Witch is constantly crying because she has no home to go to. Her animal friends try to share their homes, but none works until a kitten shows her the perfect little house for the two of them. Very easy to read, the text is illustrated with colorful, though rather mediocre, pastel drawings.

647 *A Letter to Santa*. Ill. by Laura Rader. Troll, 1993, ISBN 0-8167-3252-3. SERIES: Giant First-Start. SUBJECTS: Christmas — Fiction; Letters — Fiction. RL A.

Knowing that Christmas is coming, Mike, Jill, and Scott write letters to Santa. They tell him that they have been good and what they want for Christmas. After the holidays, the three write a thank-you letter. Active, childlike watercolor and ink paintings illustrate the story.

648 *Max and Maggie in Summer*. Ill. by Paul Meisel. Troll, 1994, o.p. SERIES: Nice Mice. SUBJECTS: Friendship — Fiction; Mice — Fiction; Summer — Fiction. RL C.

Best friends Max and Maggie argue over what to do: fish or have a picnic. Friendship overcomes anger as they take turns. In the second story, Max's boredom is overcome as he watches clouds with Maggie. Humorous watercolor and ink paintings are delightful.

649 *Valentine's Day Mess*. Ill. by Deborah Morse. Troll, 1993, o.p. SERIES: Giant First-Start. SUBJECTS: Friendship — Fiction; Mice — Fiction; Valentine's Day — Fiction. RL A.

Friends Jan and Ken enjoy doing things together but when their special Valentine's Day surprises are accidentally destroyed, each blames the other. Friendship does win out though as they again do things together. Soft, carefully crafted pictures seem to be painted with an air brush.

Cresswell, Helen

650 *The Weather Cat*. Ill. by Barbara Walker. Forest House, 1990, o.p. SERIES: Quality Time. SUBJECTS: Family life — Fiction; Pets — Cats — Fiction. RL B.

Mr. Briggs the cat adopts a family and spends nice mornings hunting birds, but colder ones hunting mice and spiders. Soon there are five weather cats! Soft colored pencil drawings accompany the text.

Cresswell, Helen, and Judy Brown

651 *Almost Goodbye*. Dutton, 1990, o.p. SERIES: Speedsters. SUBJECTS: Magic — Fiction. RL A.

Gumball becomes invisible when he and his friend Susie wish on a white-elephant lamp. After a hobo picks up the lamp with one wish left, the panic and fun begin. A lighthearted twist on an old theme includes some cartoon dialogue with the ink and gray wash cartoon drawings.

Cristaldi, Kathryn

652 *Baseball Ballerina*. Ill. by Abby Carter. Random House, 1992, o.p. SERIES: Step into Reading. SUBJECTS: Dancers and dancing — Fiction; Sports — Baseball — Fiction. RL A.

A tomboy is afraid her Sharks baseball team will think she is a wimp in the ballet recital, but all ends well when she catches Princess Dandelion's flyaway crown. Text is illustrated with appealing watercolors in blue and lavender.

653 *Even Steven and Odd Todd*. Ill. by Henry B. Morehouse. Scholastic, pap., 1996, ISBN 0-590-22715-7. SERIES: Hello Math Reader! SUBJECTS: Mathematics — Fiction. RL B. LEXILE 410L.

When cousin Odd Todd comes to visit, Even Steven becomes upset at his preference for odd numbers. Detailed ink-and earth-toned watercolors ably delineate the boys' penchant for numbers, both even and odd. Math activities included.

Croll, Carolyn

654 *Too Many Babas*. Ill. by author. HarperCollins, 1979, ISBN 0-06-021384-1. SERIES: I Can Read. SUBJECTS: Cookery — Fiction. RL A.

Each of Baba Eldis's visitors adds something to her soup until it is unpalatable. With the second batch, they work as a team. Inspired by the exhibition of Russian costumes at the Metropolitan Museum of Art, the story and illustrations do have a folk flavor.

Cromie, William J.

655 *Steven and the Green Turtle*. Ill. by Tom Eaton. HarperCollins, 1970, o.p. SERIES: I Can Read Science. SUBJECTS: Nature; Pets — Wild animals; Turtles. RL B.

Steven's rescue and later release of a tiny green turtle is sympathetically treated in this easy science book. Sketches have a predominantly turquoise wash.

Curran, Eileen

656 *Life in the Meadow*. Ill. by James Watling. Troll, 1985, o.p. SUBJECTS: Animals; Insects. RL B.

A child frolics and observes the abundant life in a meadow. Textual illustrations are bright, with interesting perspectives; however, the cover is dull.

Curtis, Matt

657 *Elliot Drives Away*. Ill. by author. Children's Press, 1996, ISBN 0-516-02058-7. SERIES: Rookie Reader. SUBJECTS: Imagination; Siblings — Fiction. RL B.

Tired of vegetables, chores, and bullying brothers, Elliot makes an imaginary getaway in his toy car. Vivid illustrations create a wondrous and danger-filled world where Elliot is the size of a bug.

Cushman, Doug

658 *Aunt Eater Loves a Mystery*. Ill. by author. HarperCollins, 1987, ISBN 0-06-021327-2. SERIES: I Can Read. SUBJECTS: Anteaters — Fiction; Mystery and detective stories. RL C.

A missing suitcase, a mysterious shadow, a strange visitor next door, and a cat-sitting adventure are competently dealt with by Aunt Eater. Homey pictures are in turquoise, yellow, and forest green.

659 *Aunt Eater's Mystery Halloween*. Ill. by author. HarperCollins, 1998, ISBN 0-06-027803-X. SERIES: I Can Read. SUBJECTS: Costumes — Fiction; Halloween — Fiction; Mystery and detective stories. RL B. LEXILE 260L.

It's a good thing Aunt Eater is dressed up as her favorite detective because there are so many mysteries to solve on Halloween. Mildly spooky watercolors awash in the colors of the season complement scary mysteries just waiting to be solved.

660 *Aunt Eater's Mystery Vacation*. Ill. by author. HarperCollins, 1992, ISBN 0-06-020514-8. SERIES: I Can Read. SUBJECTS: Anteaters — Fiction; Mystery and detective stories. RL A.

Aunt Eater alternates time reading mysteries and solving them on her vacation. She finds the missing ferry boat captain and recovers hotel guests' valuables, a valuable Swinesaurus bone, and a fellow mystery-lover. Simple stories illustrated in watercolor washes are dedicated to Prelutsky.

Cushman, Doug (cont.)

661 *Camp Big Paw*. Ill. by author. HarperCollins, 1990, o.p. SERIES: I Can Read. SUBJECTS: Animals — Fiction; Behavior — Bullying — Fiction; Camps and camping — Fiction. RL A.

Cyril, the bumbling tiger camper, is bullied by weasel Nigel Snootbutter. Cyril's bird house is messed up; he stands up in the canoe during a race, overturning it; he loses the baton in a swimming relay, and gets lost in the woods. Half-page pastel drawings focus on the animal campers.

662 *Dirk Bones and the Mystery of the Haunted House*. Ill. by author. HarperCollins, 2006, ISBN 0-06-073764-6. SERIES: I Can Read. SUBJECTS: Haunted houses — Fiction; Mystery and detective stories. RL B.

As the ace reporter for *The Ghostly Tomb*, Dirk Bones investigates a haunted house with strange noises and discovers a vampire writing a cookbook. Lighthearted illustrations in watercolor and ink capture the humorous spirit of an unusual skeleton detective.

663 *Inspector Hopper*. Ill. by author. HarperCollins, 2000, o.p. SERIES: I Can Read. SUBJECTS: Insects — Fiction; Mystery and detective stories. RL B. LEXILE 150L.

Inspector Hopper, the Private Bug, and his sidekick McBugg are hot on the trail, solving mysteries that seem to revolve around McBugg's favorite hobby — eating. Creative illustrations from a bug's-eye view offer an interesting perspective.

664 *Inspector Hopper's Mystery Year*. Ill. by author. HarperCollins, 2003, ISBN 0-06-008963-6. SERIES: I Can Read. SUBJECTS: Insects — Fiction; Mystery and detective stories. RL B.

Whatever the season or time of year, Inspector Hopper and his right-hand insect, McBugg, are ready, willing, and able to solve a mystery. Each mystery features the colors of the season and humorously details the detectives' adventures.

665 *Space Cat*. Ill. by author. HarperCollins, 2004, ISBN 0-06-008966-0. SERIES: I Can Read. SUBJECTS: Pets — Cats — Fiction; Robots — Fiction; Science fiction. RL B.

Landing on King Zorp's planet when their rocket is hit by a space rock, Space Cat and Earl the Robot are in need of fuel to return to Earth. Engaging space creatures on distant planets create the enticing science fiction world of Space Cat.

666 *Uncle Foster's Hat Tree*. Ill. by author. Dutton, 1988, o.p. SERIES: Dutton Easy Reader. SUBJECTS: Aunts and uncles — Fiction; Tall tales. RL A.

Bored Merle becomes absorbed in the adventure stories attached to Uncle Foster's hats. Bright perky watercolors enliven the imaginative first-person tall tales.

Cutler, Jane

667 *Rose and Riley*. Ill. by Thomas F. Yezerski. Farrar, Straus & Giroux, 2005, ISBN 0-374-36340-4. SUBJECTS: Friendship — Fiction. RL B.

Meet good friends Rose, a vole, and Riley, a groundhog, who share fun, plan an un-birthday party, and make worry dolls. Simple adventures of friendship are illustrated in gentle earth tones.

D

Dadey, Debbie, and Marcia Thorton Jones

668 *Triplet Trouble and the Bicycle Race*. Ill. by John Speirs. Scholastic, 1997, o.p. SUBJECTS: Bicycles and bicycling — Fiction; Humorous stories; Siblings — Triplets — Fiction. RL C.

Their school is planning a bicycle race to fund more computers for the classrooms, and the triplets and friend Sam are eager to win. But who will come first? Black line drawings interspersed through the eight chapters follow the race to the finish.

669 *Triplet Trouble and the Class Trip*. Ill. by John Speirs. Scholastic, pap., 1997, ISBN 0-590-90730-1. SUBJECTS: Humorous stories; School stories; Siblings — Triplets — Fiction. RL C. LEXILE 330L.

On a trip to the museum, the triplets are sure to be in trouble as Alex decides to make it a treasure hunt. This longer chapter book filled with exciting adventures is illustrated with simple line drawings distributed at intervals through the text.

670 *Triplet Trouble and the Cookie Contest.* Ill. by John Speirs. Scholastic, 1996, o.p. SUBJECTS: Humorous stories; School stories; Siblings — Triplets — Fiction. RL C. LEXILE 410L.

Even making cookies becomes a contest between the triplets and their friend Sam. Their teacher, acting as judge, declares there is an ingredient missing — friendship. Readers looking for a longer story will find many adventures, all complemented by pen and ink drawings.

671 *Triplet Trouble and the Pizza Party.* Ill. by John Speirs. Scholastic, pap., 1996, ISBN 0-590-90729-8. SUBJECTS: Humorous stories; School stories; Siblings — Triplets — Fiction. RL C. LEXILE 350L.

To help the class behave just before the holidays, their teacher offers a pizza party as a reward. But the triplets find it's going to be difficult. Fun-filled chapters follow the adventures of the trio and their friend Sam. Simple line drawings adequately follow the fun.

Dalton, Julie

672 *Counting Money.* Scholastic, 2005, ISBN 0-516-25260-7. SERIES: Rookie Read-About Math. SUBJECTS: Concepts — Numbers; Mathematics. RL B. LEXILE 400L.

Ben opens his piggy bank and counts all the pennies, nickels, dimes, and quarters. Color photographs clearly focus on Ben counting, sorting, and playing games with his money.

673 *Patterns Everywhere.* Scholastic, 2005, ISBN 0-516-25266-6. SERIES: Rookie Read-About Math. SUBJECTS: Mathematics; Mathematics — Patterns. RL B. LEXILE 430L.

As Ella looks around, she finds patterns everywhere. Colorful photographs prominently feature patterns in quilts that Grandma makes, on wallpaper, and on stone paths.

Daniel, Claire

674 *The Chick That Wouldn't Hatch.* Ill. by Lisa Campbell Ernst. Harcourt, 1999, o.p. SERIES: Green Light Readers. SUBJECTS: Chickens — Fiction; Humorous stories. RL B. LEXILE AD20L.

Five eggs hatch in Mother Hen's nest but the sixth rolls away with all the barnyard animals in pursuit. Comical artwork follows the runaway egg straight into Mother Hen's waiting wings.

Danziger, Paula

675 *Get Ready for Second Grade, Amber Brown.* Ill. by Tony Ross. Putnam, 2002, ISBN 0-399-23607-4. SERIES: A Is for Amber. SUBJECTS: School stories. RL B. LEXILE 300L.

With a new teacher and mean Hannah in her class, Amber isn't sure she is ready for second grade. Playful watercolor illustrations and a realistic story capture the spirit of Amber and her friends on the first day of school.

676 *It's a Fair Day, Amber Brown.* Ill. by Tony Ross. Putnam, 2002, ISBN 0-613-61635-9. SERIES: A Is for Amber. SUBJECTS: Fairs — Fiction; Lost, being — Fiction. RL B. LEXILE 230L.

On vacation together in the Poconos, Amber's and Justin's families go to a county fair. As her parents argue, Amber walks away to find Justin and gets lost. Bright cheery drawings captivate the reader with action-filled scenes.

677 *It's Justin Time, Amber Brown.* Ill. by Tony Ross. Putnam, pap., 2001, ISBN 0-399-23470-5. SERIES: A Is for Amber. SUBJECTS: Birthdays — Fiction; Clocks — Fiction; Concepts — Time — Fiction. RL B. LEXILE 280L.

It's Amber's birthday and she wants a watch. Clever puns about time abound in this everyday family story. Humor and love are evidenced in the colorful and expressive watercolors.

678 *Orange You Glad It's Halloween, Amber Brown.* Ill. by Tony Ross. Putnam, 2005, ISBN 0-399-23471-3. SERIES: A Is for Amber. SUBJECTS: Halloween — Fiction; School stories. RL B.

With her parents arguing, Amber isn't sure Halloween is going to be fun this year. Capturing the wonderful Halloween spirit at school and at home, the colors of the season bedeck the cupcakes, book-character pumpkins, and clever costumes.

679 *Second Grade Rules, Amber Brown.* Ill. by Tony Ross. Putnam, 2004, ISBN 0-399-

Danziger, Paula (cont.)

23472-1. SERIES: A Is for Amber. SUBJECTS: Cleanliness — Fiction; School stories. RL B. LEXILE 420L.

It's so hard for Amber to keep her desk clean, but she really wants Deskarina the Clean Desk Fairy to leave her a blue ribbon and a special treat. Amber's everyday dilemmas are lovingly depicted in exuberant illustrations with care and humor.

680 *What a Trip, Amber Brown*. Ill. by Tony Ross. Putnam, 2001, ISBN 0-399-23469-1. SERIES: A Is for Amber. SUBJECTS: Friendship — Fiction; Vacations — Fiction. RL B. LEXILE 250L.

On a vacation with her best friend's family, Amber gets mad at Justin's pool hi-jinks, but later they all enjoy a family sleep-out with hot dog kebabs and scary stories. The many moods of Amber are portrayed with humor and wit.

Dauer, Rosamond

681 *Bullfrog and Gertrude Go Camping*. Ill. by Byron Barton. Dell, pap., 1988, ISBN 0-440-40074-0. SERIES: Read-Alone. SUBJECTS: Camps and camping — Fiction; Frogs and toads — Fiction; Snakes — Fiction. RL B.

Gertrude and Bullfrog come home a family after adopting Itsa Snake during a camping trip. Four-color framed drawings have shapeless friendly frogs and an expressive snake.

682 *Bullfrog Builds a House*. Ill. by Byron Barton. Greenwillow, 1976, o.p. SERIES: Read-Alone. SUBJECTS: Friendship — Fiction; Frogs and toads — Fiction. RL B.

Bullfrog does not enjoy his new house with the front-porch diving board until he invites Gertrude to share it. Simple humor and a feeling of home regarding these two frogs are conveyed partly through avocado, rust, and cocoa drawings.

683 *Bullfrog Grows Up*. Ill. by Byron Barton. Dell, pap., 1988, ISBN 0-440-40007-4. SERIES: Read-Alone. SUBJECTS: Family life — Fiction; Frogs and toads — Fiction; Growing up — Fiction. RL B.

Bullfrog needs a lunch, a pack of cards, and a last bath before setting off on his own from his adopted mouse family (practicing his neglected frog talk). Interesting ideas for presentation to primary-school-age children are illustrated with humor, enhancing individual characters.

Daugherty, Charles M.

684 *Samuel Clemens*. Ill. by Kurt Werth. HarperCollins, 1970, o.p. SERIES: HarperCollins Biography. SUBJECTS: Biographies; Writers and writing. RL C.

The zestful life of this famous writer is well portrayed. Werth's expressive drawings give character and flavor to Clemens's adventures.

Davis, Gibbs

685 *Katy's First Haircut*. Ill. by Linda Shute. Houghton Mifflin, 1985, o.p. SUBJECTS: Haircutting — Fiction; School stories. RL C.

A simple topic, a first haircut, is dealt with sympathetically, especially by Katy's teacher (a male) and parents, who give her free choice about how her hair is to be cut. Full-color illustrations are softened by pencil outlines and shading.

Davis, Maggie S.

686 *A Garden of Whales*. Ill. by Jennifer O'Connell. Camden House, 1993, o.p. SUBJECTS: Dreams — Fiction; Eskimos — Fiction; Whales — Fiction. RL C.

A boy dreams about danger to whales during his bath, and with other children (arriving in flying bathtubs) calls on the whales to give them tears to water their secret whale garden. Inspired by an Eskimo song, the story resonates with deep watercolors.

Day, Jenifer W.

687 *What Is a Flower?* Ill. by Dorothea Barlowe. Golden Books, 1975, ISBN 0-307-11800-2. SERIES: Child's Golden Science. SUBJECTS: Flowers; Nature. RL C.

A few sentences discuss various plants ranging from wild and garden flowers to vegetables, grasses, vines, and exotic flowers. Good information is illustrated with large, colorful watercolors.

688 *What Is a Fruit?* Ill. by Enid Kotschnig. Golden Books, 1976, o.p. SERIES: Child's Golden Science. SUBJECTS: Fruit; Nature. RL C.

Information is given about tomatoes and melons, grains, peas and berries, and the relationships between them. Word lists are appended. Large watercolor drawings add to the book's appeal.

Day, Marie

689 *Dragon in the Rocks*. Ill. by author. Firefly, 1991, o.p. SUBJECTS: Biographies; Geology and geologists; Science and scientists. RL C.

The remarkable story of young Mary Anning of Lyme Regis, England, who helped support her family after her father's death by selling the fossils she found in the sea cliffs. Cheerful watercolor washes illustrate this retelling of Mary's finds.

De Brunhoff, Laurent

690 *Babar's Little Circus Star*. Ill. by author. Random House, 1988, o.p. SERIES: Step into Reading. SUBJECTS: Circuses — Fiction; Elephants — Fiction. RL A.

Isabelle cannot climb trees, ride a bike, or go to school, and she must go to bed early. However, small as she is, she has success in the circus. Flat decorative pastel drawings present the typical Babar family.

DeCesare, Angelo

691 *Anthony the Perfect Monster*. Ill. by author. Random House, 1996, o.p. SERIES: Beginner Books. SUBJECTS: Monsters — Fiction; School stories. RL B. LEXILE 170L.

Anthony is the perfect child at home but nobody likes him at school, where he is angry and uncooperative. Cartoon illustrations employing a bright color palette ably portray the transformation of a little boy who finally learns to be himself.

De Fossard, Esta

692 *Dinah the Dog with a Difference*. Photos by Haworth Bartram. Stevens, 1985, o.p. SERIES: Dial Easy-to-Read Animal Adventures. SUBJECTS: Disabilities — Physical and mental; Pets — Dogs. RL A.

Dinah's curiosity and fearlessness set her apart from her litter mates, and make her suitable for work as a guide dog. Photograph close-ups of puppy adventures are captivating.

Degen, Bruce

693 *The Little Witch and the Riddle*. Ill. by author. HarperCollins, 1980, o.p. SERIES: I Can Read. SUBJECTS: Friendship — Fiction; Jokes and riddles; Witches — Fiction. RL B.

The Little Witch needs the help of her friend Otto Ogre to solve the riddles that open the "Book of Magic." This witty, gentle story is enhanced by framed pencil drawings of the pair. The drawings are highlighted in rose and gold.

Delacre, Lulu

694 *Rafi and Rosi*. Ill. by author. HarperCollins, 2004, ISBN 0-06-009896-1. SERIES: I Can Read. SUBJECTS: Frogs and toads — Fiction; Puerto Rico — Fiction; Siblings — Fiction. RL B. LEXILE 440L.

As brother and sister Puerto Rican tree frogs, Rafi and Rosi share magical adventures together. Full-page, detailed images illustrate the gentle family stories interspersed with Spanish words. Information at the end expands on the science and nature concepts within the text.

695 *Rafi and Rosi Carnival!* Ill. by author. HarperCollins, 2006, ISBN 0-06-073598-8. SERIES: I Can Read. SUBJECTS: Frogs and toads — Fiction; Puerto Rico — Fiction; Siblings — Fiction. RL B. LEXILE 480L.

It's carnival season, and Rafi and Rosi celebrate by creating a float for a parade and making a costume and a scary mask. Bright colors portray the festive mood of carnival for the brother and sister. Art and craft ideas at the end of the book will enable everyone to enjoy this traditional event in Ponce.

DeLage, Ida

696 *ABC Pigs Go to Market*. Ill. by Kelly Oechsli. Garrard, 1977, o.p. SERIES: Once Upon an ABC. SUBJECTS: Alphabet — Fiction; Pigs — Fiction. RL B.

Pig children at the supermarket explore the dairy, look at keys, buy an ounce and a pound of nuts, and wait for change. Although the parts of speech are inconsistent and the vocabulary is not necessarily familiar, the mischief, curiosity, and setting of watercolor drawings definitely are.

697 *Beware! Beware! A Witch Won't Share*. Ill. by Ted Schroeder. Garrard, 1972, o.p.

DeLage, Ida (cont.)

SERIES: Old Witch. SUBJECTS: Gypsies — Fiction; Witches — Fiction. RL C.
Both the farmer and the witch have trouble with the gypsies. Pencil drawings are highlighted with chartreuse and yellow.

698 *A Bunny Ride.* Ill. by Tracy McVay. Garrard, 1975, o.p. SUBJECTS: Rabbits — Fiction. RL A.
Baby bunnies want to ride to town as their raccoon and opossum friends do. However, the baby bunnies find a pony ride too bumpy. Pastel drawings of the babies are most appealing.

699 *Frannie's Flower.* Ill. by Ellen Sloan. Garrard, 1979, o.p. SUBJECTS: Imagination — Fiction. RL A.
A doll survives Frannie's milk-feeding, swinging, sleeping, and wagon-riding better than her flower. Soft pastel drawings focus on a small girl's play.

700 *Good Morning, Lady.* Ill. by Tracy McVay. Garrard, 1974, o.p. SUBJECTS: Animals — Fiction. RL A.
The possum tinker sells a pot to a mouse to use for an unusual purpose. Pastel colors show the smallest woodland creatures.

701 *Hello, Come In.* Ill. by John Mardon. Garrard, 1971, ISBN 0-8116-6708-1. SUBJECTS: Houses — Fiction. RL A.
Grandma, a witch, a pig, a ghost, a frog, a bird, a pony, a toymaker, and some children invite the reader into their abodes. The thin story line is supported by stylized, two-color drawings.

702 *Old Witch and the Crows.* Ill. by Marianne Smith. Garrard, 1983, o.p. SERIES: Old Witch. SUBJECTS: Witches — Fiction. RL C.
When Old Witch helps the crows by chasing away the owl, they return the favor by bringing creepy crawlies for her brew. Bright purple and orange, with some gray and brown, keep the setting spooky.

703 *Old Witch Finds a New House.* Ill. by Pat Paris. Garrard, 1979, SERIES: Old Witch. SUBJECTS: Witches — Fiction. RL C.
A woodcutter returns Old Witch's favor in full after she rescues him when he is trapped under a fallen tree. Comic drawings are in black, red, and green.

704 *Old Witch Goes to the Ball.* Ill. by Gustave E. Nebel. Garrard, 1969, o.p. SERIES: Old Witch. SUBJECTS: Witches — Fiction. RL B.
The clever farmer's wife distracts Old Witch from getting even when the angry witch does not win the Halloween costume contest. Gray and gold washes highlight lively ink drawings.

705 *The Old Witch's Party.* Ill. by Mimi Korach. Garrard, 1976, o.p. SERIES: Old Witch. SUBJECTS: Witches — Fiction. RL B.
Children mistake Old Witch for Grandma Petticoat twice. Turquoise and fuchsia highlight ink drawings.

706 *Pilgrim Children Come to Plymouth.* Ill. by Herman Vestal. Garrard, 1981, o.p. SUBJECTS: Pilgrims; Thanksgiving. RL B.
Written from the point of view of Pilgrim children, the book focuses on the contributions and friendship of the Native Americans, without softening the fear and hardships. Warmth is added by watercolor drawings.

707 *Squirrel's Tree Party.* Ill. by Tracy McVay. Garrard, 1978, o.p. SUBJECTS: Squirrels — Fiction. RL A.
Cute animal children celebrate in the rain, sunshine, or wind. Appealing soft watercolors of animals complement the gentle story.

708 *Weeny Witch.* Ill. by Kelly Oechsli. Garrard, 1968, o.p. SERIES: Old Witch. SUBJECTS: Fairies — Fiction; Witches — Fiction. RL C.
Weeny Witch does not fit in with those who try to darken the sky by capturing the night fairies. Some imaginative twists and rhymes give substance to the story. Drawings help set the atmosphere with lavender, blue, and pink.

709 *What Does a Witch Need?* Ill. by Ted Schroeder. Garrard, 1971, o.p. SERIES: Old Witch. SUBJECTS: Witches — Fiction. RL B.
Old Witch discovers she needs a stray dog as much as a new kitten to make her brew and protect her toadstools from the gnomes. Nice touches of expression, both verbal and facial, enliven this tale.

Delton, Judy

710 *A Birthday Bike for Brimhall.* Ill. by June Leary. Carolrhoda, 1985, o.p. SERIES: On My Own. SUBJECTS: Bears — Fiction; Bicycles and bicycling — Fiction; Friendship — Fiction. RL B.

Did Bear trick Brimhall into learning how to ride his birthday bike? (Yes, and it worked!) Finely textured ink drawings add detail and drama to this story.

711 *Brimhall Turns Detective.* Ill. by Cherie R. Wyman. Carolrhoda, 1983, o.p. SERIES: On My Own. SUBJECTS: Bears — Fiction; Humorous stories; Mystery and detective stories. RL A.

The antics of two friends who trace monster tracks have exaggerated humor. Ink drawings have sepia pencil accents.

712 *Brimhall Turns to Magic.* Ill. by Bruce Degen. Lothrop, 1979, o.p. SERIES: Fun-to-Read. SUBJECTS: Bears — Fiction; Friendship — Fiction; Magic — Fiction. RL B.

When Roger the rabbit appears in Brimhall's hat by magic, it takes special friends to make him "disappear." Soon Bear regrets his grumpiness when Roger was around. Pencil drawings in gray and brown give detailed characterizations.

713 *The Goose Who Wrote a Book.* Ill. by Catherine Cleary. Carolrhoda, 1982, o.p. SERIES: On My Own. SUBJECTS: Writers and writing — Fiction. RL B.

"Cheese Louise" says Goose when her friends want her absentminded fictional character to be a different animal. Pencil drawings are highlighted with turquoise and orange.

714 *Groundhog's Day at the Doctor.* Ill. by Giulio Maestro. Parents Magazine Press, 1981, o.p. SUBJECTS: Animals — Fiction; Groundhog Day — Fiction. RL C.

After Groundhog wakes up a day early feeling stiff and tired, he finds himself giving advice to animals he meets in the doctor's waiting room — and ends up going skiing with the doctor. Full-color drawings have a textured background.

715 *I Never Win!* Ill. by Cathy Gilchrist. Carolrhoda, 1981, o.p. SERIES: On My Own. SUBJECTS: Self-esteem — Fiction. RL B.

Although a boy does not win birthday prizes or games, he takes his frustrations out on his piano practicing and eventually gets recognition for his talent. Ink drawings with black and red highlights are expressive of feelings.

716 *My Mom Made Me Go to Camp.* Ill. by Lisa McCue. Delacorte, 1990, o.p. SUBJECTS: Camps and camping — Fiction. RL B.

This is a reassuring book for child and parent about the fears and insecurities of going to summer camp — but the children in the illustrations look more like toddlers than children who would go to overnight camp.

717 *No Time for Christmas.* Ill. by Anastasia Mitchell. Carolrhoda, 1988, ISBN 0-87614-327-3. SERIES: On My Own. SUBJECTS: Bears — Fiction; Christmas — Fiction. RL B.

Bear and Brimhall are so busy working to buy each other Christmas presents that they don't see each other. Bright watercolors warm the friendship.

718 *Two Good Friends.* Ill. by Giulio Maestro. Crown, 1974, o.p. SUBJECTS: Bears — Fiction; Ducks — Fiction; Friendship — Fiction. RL B.

What good are a clean house and wonderful nut pies without an understanding friend? Differences that seem insurmountable are resolved with love. Soft colored pencil drawings complement the mood.

Demas, Corinne

719 *The Perfect Pony.* Ill. by Jacqueline Rogers. Random House, 2000, o.p. SERIES: Step into Reading. SUBJECTS: Horses — Fiction. RL B. LEXILE 310L.

An ad for a free pony seems too good to be true, but Jamie forms a strong bond with the pony called McIntosh. Detailed watercolor illustrations aid understanding of the horse terms and the types of equipment mentioned in the story.

720 *Yuck! Stuck in the Muck.* Ill. by Laura Rader. Scholastic, pap., 2006, ISBN 0-439-79431-5. SERIES: Scholastic Reader. SUBJECTS: Humorous stories; Pets — Dogs — Fiction. RL A.

Demas, Corinne (cont.)

After chasing Duck, Dog gets stuck in the muck. Lively and colorful cartoon illustrations humorously follow the many attempts by people and animals to come to his aid. A hilarious cumulative and repetitive tale for very beginning readers.

Demers, Jan

721 *What Do You Do with a . . .* Ill. by Don Robison. Willowisp, 1985, o.p. SERIES: Predictable Read Together. SUBJECTS: Stories in rhyme. RL A.

Rhythmic questions about familiar settings are answered in short rhyming phrases. Busy, brightly colored animals illustrate the questions.

Demuth, Patricia B.

722 *Achoo! All About Colds.* Ill. by Maggie Smith. Grosset & Dunlap, 1997, o.p. SERIES: All Aboard Reading. SUBJECTS: Diseases — Fiction. RL B. LEXILE 290L.

How did Sam catch a cold? Scientific fact and medical knowledge about germs and cold remedies are interwoven in a story about a young boy playing and going to school. Lighthearted illustrations and diagrams provide an interesting introduction to colds.

723 *Inside Your Busy Body.* Ill. by Paige Billin Frye. Putnam, 1993, o.p. SERIES: All Aboard Books. SUBJECTS: Human body; Science and scientists. RL C.

Muscles, lungs (air bags), digestion, brain (big boss on top), and senses are introduced in a few sentences, and illustrated with flat cutout collages, mostly of children.

724 *Snakes.* Photos by Paul Dyer. Ill. by Judith Moffatt. Putnam, 1993, o.p. SERIES: All Aboard Reading. SUBJECTS: Science and scientists; Snakes. RL A.

The characteristics of about a dozen snakes are introduced, and illustrated with exceptional colored and patterned heavy paper cutouts. The python, boa, cobra, rat, and rattlesnake, as well as the garter, green, thread, mud, cottonmouth, and sidewinder are included.

Denton, Kady MacDonald

725 *Watch Out, William!* Ill. by author. Kingfisher, pap., 1996, ISBN 0-7534-5960-4. SERIES: I Am Reading. SUBJECTS: Pets — Dogs — Fiction; Siblings — Fiction. RL B.

William's little sister may be small but she can definitely make William do what she wants. Comical watercolor illustrations show the give-and-take of a brother-and-sister relationship that is based on love.

Denzel, Justin

726 *Jumbo: Giant Circus Elephant.* Ill. by Richard Amundsen. Garrard, 1973, o.p. SERIES: Famous Animal Stories. SUBJECTS: Circuses; Elephants. RL B.

A true story tells about a small, gentle elephant who delighted fans for twenty years on both sides of the Atlantic. Full-color illustrations show the drama of Jumbo's farewell to the circus.

dePaola, Tomie

727 *Boss for a Day.* Ill. by author. Grosset & Dunlap, pap., 2001, ISBN 0-448-42544-0. SERIES: All Aboard Reading. SUBJECTS: Pets — Dogs — Fiction; Siblings — Fiction. RL B. LEXILE 250L.

Being ten minutes older than her dog twin Morgan entitles Moffie to be the boss, even when she says it's Morgan's turn. Silly details in the playful, funny illustrations will delight readers, especially those with bossy siblings.

728 *Cloud Book.* Ill. by author. Holiday House, 1975, ISBN 0-8234-0259-2. SUBJECTS: Weather — Clouds. RL C.

An index is included in this lively presentation of information and sayings about clouds. Children, animals, and imagination abound in the simple, decorative illustrations.

729 *Hide-and-Seek All Week.* Ill. by author. Grosset & Dunlap, 2002, ISBN 0-448-42617-X. SERIES: All Aboard Reading. SUBJECTS: Pets — Dogs — Fiction; Siblings — Fiction. RL B.

Everyone wants to play hide-and-seek, but Moffie, Morgie and their classmates spend all their time deciding on rules rather than having fun. Readers will relate to the endearingly expressive faces of the animal friends sharing a common school experience.

730 *The Kids' Cat Book.* Ill. by author. Holiday House, 1979, o.p. SUBJECTS: Pet care; Pets — Cats. RL B.
Cat history and care is intriguingly presented when a boy visits Granny Twinkle. Add the author's outstanding creamy pastel illustrations to the text for a book that should be owned universally.

731 *Oliver Button Is a Sissy.* Ill. by author. Harcourt, 1979, ISBN 0-15-257852-8. SUBJECTS: Dancers and dancing — Fiction; Self-esteem — Fiction; Sex roles — Fiction. RL B.
Oliver likes to draw and read, play jump rope — and dance. Although the boys at school tease him, and his father thinks he is a sissy, Oliver revels in dance lessons and the teasing turns to admiration. Drawings are in turquoise and cocoa.

732 *The Quicksand Book.* Ill. by author. Holiday House, pap., 1977, ISBN 0-526-53582-3. SUBJECTS: Nature; Science and scientists. RL C.
Jungle Boy corrects misconceptions people have about quicksand while Jungle Girl sinks. When he falls in, she is in no hurry to help him out. Good information is presented in an arresting way and ably illustrated with hand-lettered cartoons and fact boxes.

733 *T-Rex Is Missing.* Ill. by author. Grosset & Dunlap, pap., 2002, ISBN 0-448-42870-9. SERIES: All Aboard Reading. SUBJECTS: Dinosaurs — Fiction; Lost and found possessions — Fiction. RL B. LEXILE AD60L.
After playing with their dinosaurs, Morgie notices his T-Rex is missing and accuses his friend Billy. The signature pastel watercolor illustrations convey the emotional ups and downs of friendship and the problem of jumping to conclusions.

DerKazarian, Susan

734 *Dairy.* Scholastic, 2005, ISBN 0-516-23672-5. SERIES: Rookie Read-About Health. SUBJECTS: Nutrition. RL B.
Find out about dairy products and their importance in a healthy diet. Full-color photographs show children incorporating and enjoying the recommended dairy products in their daily lives. A diagram of the food pyramid is included.

735 *Fruits and Vegetables.* Scholastic, 2005, ISBN 0-516-23673-3. SERIES: Rookie Read-About Health. SUBJECTS: Fruit; Nutrition; Vegetables. RL B.
Do you know why it is important to eat fruits and vegetables every day? Full-color photographs highlight a variety of fruits and vegetables and show how they grow and ways to ensure they are part of your daily diet. A diagram of the food pyramid is included.

736 *You Have Head Lice!* Scholastic, 2005, ISBN 0-516-25879-6. SERIES: Rookie Read-About Health. SUBJECTS: Health; Lice. RL B.
In a candid presentation, the transmission and treatment of head lice is explored. Full-color photographs clearly feature enlargements of the insect and a step-by-step sequence of treatment techniques.

deRubertis, Barbara

737 *Bitty Fish.* Ill. by Eva Vagreti Cockrille. Kane, pap., 1997, ISBN 1-57565-002-9. SERIES: Let's Read Together. SUBJECTS: Humorous stories; Pets — Fish — Fiction. RL B. LEXILE 160L.
A young boy tries to place a fish in a small aquarium but Bitty Fish wants a bigger fish bowl — and maybe a friend. Bright colors and large images attract attention. Suggested activities at the end of the story concentrate on the short *i* vowel sound.

738 *A Collection for Kate.* Ill. by Gioia Fiammenghi. Kane, pap., 1999, ISBN 1-57565-089-4. SERIES: Math Matters. SUBJECTS: Mathematics — Addition; Mathematics — Fiction. RL B. LEXILE 210L.
Kate has been watching, and everyone else in her class has a big collection. What will Kate bring to show the class? She decides on her own unique collection — a collection of collections. Bright, entertaining drawings deftly highlight the mathematical groupings demonstrated in the story.

739 *Count on Pablo.* Ill. by Rebecca Thornburgh. Kane, pap., 1999, ISBN 1-57565-090-8. SERIES: Math Matters. SUBJECTS: Concepts — Numbers — Fiction;

deRubertis, Barbara (cont.)

Grandparents — Fiction; Mathematics — Fiction. RL B. LEXILE 190L.

Helping his abuela, Pablo counts all the vegetables they will sell at the market. When the produce doesn't sell, Pablo suggests making salsa, which is a huge success. With a visual focus on counting, the realistic artwork also shows the bond of love between grandmother and grandson.

740 *Deena's Lucky Penny*. Ill. by Joan Holub and Cynthia Fisher. Kane, pap., 1999, ISBN 1-57565-091-6. SERIES: Math Matters. SUBJECTS: Birthdays — Fiction; Mathematics — Fiction; Money. RL B. LEXILE 160L.

Finding a penny is very lucky for Deena. As she describes her good fortune, everyone adds to it. Soon she has a dollar to buy a present for her mother's birthday. Bright, cheerful illustrations are highlighted by visual images of coins and the addition of their monetary worth.

741 *Lucky Ducky*. Ill. by Eva Vagreti Cockrille. Kane, pap., 1997, ISBN 1-57565-004-5. SERIES: Let's Read Together. SUBJECTS: Ducks — Fiction; Humorous stories. RL B. LEXILE 530L.

Duck is stuck in the mud but a skunk with a drum soon has him on the run. Silly illustrations and a rhyming story concentrate on the short *u* vowel sound. Suggested activities for parents and children follow the story.

742 *Lulu's Lemonade*. Ill. by Paige Billin-Frye. Kane, pap., 2000, ISBN 1-57565-093-2. SERIES: Math Matters. SUBJECTS: Concepts — Weight — Fiction; Cookery — Fiction; Mathematics — Fiction. RL B. LEXILE 120L.

On a hot summer day, what better to make than lemonade? Playful illustrations highlight the liquid measurements involved in creating a very special recipe for entry into the Kid's Cooking Contest. A measurement chart and activities follow.

743 *Patty Cat*. Ill. by Benton Mahan. Kane, 1997, o.p. SERIES: Let's Read Together. SUBJECTS: Pets — Cats — Fiction; Rats — Fiction. RL B. LEXILE 480L.

As Pat the Cat and Hal play ball, Max the Rat runs away with the bat. With repetition of sounds, short rhyming phrases, and large simple art that conveys the action, very beginning readers focus on the short *a* vowel sound.

744 *Penny Hen*. Ill. by Eva Vagreti Cockrille. Kane, pap., 1997, ISBN 1-57565-001-0. SERIES: Let's Read Together. SUBJECTS: Chickens — Fiction. RL B. LEXILE 490L.

Being Jenny's only pet hen seems best to Penny. But soon she is joined by Tess and Bess. Speech bubbles and expressive drawings effectively offer Penny's side of the story, which centers on the short *e* vowel sound.

de Saint Mars, Dominique

745 *Lily Fights with Her Brother*. Ill. by Serge Bloch and Cathy Mini. Child's World, 1993, o.p. SERIES: About Me. SUBJECTS: Behavior — Fiction; Siblings — Fiction. RL A.

Lily and Max turn the tables on their parents when they reflect their new lesson, "you are big enough and smart enough to solve your own problems, and I love both of you." Cartoon characters use very realistic dialogue and situations for significant learning.

746 *Max Is Shy*. Ill. by Serge Bloch and Cathy Mini. Child's World, 1992, o.p. SERIES: About Me. SUBJECTS: Behavior — Shyness; Self-esteem. RL B.

With exaggerated cartoons and pointed dialogue, Max's social terrors are illustrated, as well as the perceptions neighborhood children have of him. A few illustrated questions at the end point out some antidotes to shyness.

Dewey, Ariane

747 *Laffite, the Pirate*. Ill. by author. Greenwillow, 1985, o.p. SUBJECTS: Historical fiction; Pirates — Fiction; United States — 1783–1865 — Fiction. RL C.

Rousing stories of Laffite the pirate's bravado and occasional generosity and legends of treasure troves are retold by Dewey. Her colorful, decorative illustrations have clear lines and flat colors.

Dewey, Ariane, and Jose Aruego

748 *Splash!* Ill. by authors. Harcourt, 2000, o.p. SERIES: Green Light Readers. SUBJECTS: Bears — Fiction. RL B. LEXILE 170L.

Sam and Nelly, two clumsy bears, make quite a splash when they join their bear friends in search of food. The delightfully plump and pleasing bears add zest and zing to a very fishy story.

DeWitt, Lynda

749 *What Will the Weather Be?* Ill. by Carolyn Croll. HarperCollins, 1991, ISBN 0-06-021597-6. SERIES: Let's-Read-and-Find-Out Science. SUBJECTS: Science and scientists; Weather. RL C.

Descriptions of warm and cold fronts and air pressure and the way meteorologists measure them are simple and well illustrated. Information is related to predicting weather so farmers know when to plant, and people know what to wear, and when a storm is anticipated.

DiCamillo, Kate

750 *Mercy Watson Fights Crime.* Ill. by Chris Van Dusen. Candlewick, 2006, ISBN 0-7636-2590-6. SERIES: Mercy Watson. SUBJECTS: Humorous stories; Pigs — Fiction. RL B. LEXILE 390L.

The slapstick humor continues in this third adventure as a man in a ten-gallon hat robs the kitchen and steals some butter — Mercy the pig's favorite food. The silliness extends to the colorful illustrations sure to delight fans.

751 *Mercy Watson Goes for a Ride.* Ill. by Chris Van Dusen. Candlewick, 2006, ISBN 0-7636-2332-6. SERIES: Mercy Watson. SUBJECTS: Humorous stories; Pigs — Fiction. RL B. LEXILE 390L.

A surprise in the back seat sets pig Mercy and Mr. Watson on a car ride to disaster. Bright, energetic illustrations drive the humor straight home for a nice piece of buttered toast.

752 *Mercy Watson to the Rescue.* Ill. by Chris Van Dusen. Candlewick, 2005, ISBN 0-7636-2270-2. SERIES: Mercy Watson. SUBJECTS: Humorous stories; Pigs — Fiction. RL B. LEXILE 450L.

Snuggling in bed with Mr. and Mrs. Watson, Mercy the pig dreams of warm buttered toast until the bed breaks and falls through the ceiling. Lively, exaggerated illustrations aptly capture the chaos that ensues.

Dineen, Jacqueline

753 *Let's Look at Rain.* Ill. by Carolyn Scrace. Bookwright, 1989, o.p. SERIES: Let's Look At. SUBJECTS: Nature; Water. RL B.

The water cycle, collection and uses of water, weather, and storms related to the water cycle are introduced. Includes glossary and index. Acceptable pastel drawings.

Dines, Glen

754 *John Muir.* Ill. by author. Putnam, 1974, o.p. SERIES: See and Read Biography. SUBJECTS: Biographies; Nature. RL B.

Inventor and naturalist John Muir wrote lovingly about the wilderness. His work helped to save large tracts of land as parks for others to enjoy. This well-told, simple story has forest green, black, and gray colored drawings.

Dobkin, Bonnie

755 *Collecting.* Ill. by Richard Hackney. Children's Press, 1993, ISBN 0-516-02015-3. SERIES: Rookie Reader. SUBJECTS: Collectors and collecting; Stories in rhyme. RL A.

In a 96-word vocabulary, the fun of collecting — from stamps to shells, from comic books to insects, from posters to rockets — is shown. Colorful, lively illustrations accompany the text.

Donnelly, Judy

756 *Tut's Mummy: Lost and Found.* Ill. by James Watling. Random House, 1988, ISBN 0-394-99189-3. SERIES: Step into Reading. SUBJECTS: Egypt, ancient. RL C.

The drama of finding of Tutankhamen's tomb is presented factually. Full-color pastel drawings are taken from tomb paintings; the poor-quality black-and-white photographs detract.

Dorros, Arthur

757 *Ant Cities.* Ill. by author. HarperCollins, 1987, ISBN 0-690-04570-0. SERIES: Let's-Read-and-Find-Out Science. SUBJECTS: Ants; Nature. RL C.

An overview of the social organization, food, and types of ants is given, along with such details as how the antennae are used and how to build

Dorros, Arthur (cont.)

one's own ant city. Soft watercolors give cutaways and close-up views of ant cities.

758 *Elephant Families*. Ill. by author. HarperCollins, 1994, o.p. SERIES: Let's-Read-and-Find-Out Science. SUBJECTS: Elephants; Science and scientists. RL B.

Elephants weigh as much as a large truck and may walk 40 miles a day looking for food and water. The watercolor illustrations are simple and appealing. Additional facts about elephants are added in small type.

759 *Feel the Wind*. Ill. by author. HarperCollins, 1989, ISBN 0-690-04741-X. SERIES: Let's-Read-and-Find-Out Science. SUBJECTS: Science and scientists. RL C.

Beginning by introducing familiar results that demonstrate the characteristics of wind, the text continues by describing the causes and uses of wind. Soft watercolors personalize and enhance this excellent text.

760 *Follow the Water from Brook to Ocean*. Ill. by author. HarperCollins, 1991, ISBN 0-06-021599-2. SERIES: Let's-Read-and-Find-Out Science. SUBJECTS: Nature; Science and scientists; Water. RL C.

The movement of water is traced downhill from the down spouts of houses to streams and rivers, over waterfalls and through canyons to the sea. Some of the plants, animals, and even smells en route are sketched. This is an excellent replacement for the Bartlett books, now out of print.

761 *Me and My Shadow*. Ill. by author. Scholastic, 1990, o.p. SUBJECTS: Science and scientists; Shadows. RL A.

Complex ideas such as sonar and x-ray shadows and eclipses are built on a simple base of chasing one's own shadow, trying shadow puppetry, or hand shadows. Simple drawings of children at play include their own dialogue.

762 *Pretzels*. Ill. by author. Greenwillow, 1981, o.p. SERIES: Read-Alone. SUBJECTS: Humorous stories. RL C.

I Freyem Fine's biscuit dough, after being used as an anchor chain, is reconstituted as a pretzel. This tall tale is illustrated with ink and two-tone washes.

Dorsky, Blanche

763 *Harry: A True Story*. Ill. by Muriel Batherman. Prentice-Hall, 1977, o.p. SUBJECTS: Rabbits — Fiction; School stories. RL C.

Harry, the nursery school's pet rabbit, is "not himself," and it takes a trip to the vet to find out why. Delicate ink sketches are in pastel colors except for the black rabbit.

Dotlich, Rebecca Kai

764 *Peanut and Pearl's Picnic Adventure*. Ill. by R. W. Alley. HarperCollins, 2007, ISBN 0-06-054920-3. SERIES: I Can Read. SUBJECTS: Friendship — Fiction; Picnics — Fiction. RL B.

Sunshine-bright illustrations follow two friends on a picnic. Each heads off in a different direction and thinks the other is lost. The offbeat humor will be enjoyed by new readers.

Drescher, Henrik

765 *Whose Scaly Tail? African Animals You'd Like to Meet*. Ill. by author. HarperCollins, 1987, ISBN 0-397-32237-2. SUBJECTS: Animals. RL A.

Despite limited vocabulary and liberal ink and watercolor clues, the animals — aardvark, elephant, giraffe, gorilla, pangolin, redtail monkey, and porcupine — are not all easy to identify. Appealing drawings accompany the question-and-answer format.

Driscoll, Laura

766 *Apples and How They Grow*. Ill. by Tommy Smith. Grosset & Dunlap, pap., 2003, ISBN 0-448-43275-7. SERIES: All Aboard Science Reader. SUBJECTS: Fruit. RL B.

Focusing on the Rome apple, the growth of apples and the concept of grafting are explored. Full-color stylized artwork enriches the story as it shows the apple grower in the orchard, including close-ups for greater clarity.

767 *The Blast Off Kid*. Ill. by Rebecca Thornburgh. Kane, pap., 2003, ISBN 1-57565-130-0. SERIES: Math Matters. SUBJECTS: Contests — Fiction; Mathematics — Fiction. RL B.

Needing 10,000 Blast Off Bar wrappers to win a trip to space camp, Jim begins collecting them all over town. Detailed ink and watercolor artwork adeptly visually integrates the mathematical concept of place value.

768 *The Bravest Cat! The True Story of Scarlett.* Ill. by DyAnne DiSalvo-Ryan. Grosset & Dunlap, pap., 1997, ISBN 0-448-41703-0. SERIES: All Aboard Reading. SUBJECTS: Fire fighters and fire fighting; Pets — Cats. RL B. LEXILE 310L.

As firefighters battle a blaze in an abandoned building, they witness a mother cat bravely saving each of her newborn kittens. Colorful watercolors aid in chronicling the true story of the rescue and search for homes for the stray kittens and their very brave mother.

769 *Frogs.* Ill. by Judith Moffatt. Grosset & Dunlap, pap., 1998, ISBN 0-448-41839-8. SERIES: All Aboard Reading. SUBJECTS: Frogs and toads; Reptiles and amphibians. RL B. LEXILE 150L.

Follow the development of frogs, including their life cycle, habitat, and survival techniques. Intricate, cut-paper collage illustrations enhance the information and provide insight into key facts.

770 *Slow Down, Sara!* Ill. by Page Eastburn O'Rourke. Kane, pap., 2003, ISBN 1-57565-125-4. SERIES: Science Solves It! SUBJECTS: Science and scientists; Sports — Car racing — Fiction. RL B.

Sara is always the first to finish, but when she is designing her racer for the Soapbox Derby, she carefully experiments and analyzes the best alternatives. Colorful full-page illustrations with information boxes visually demonstrate the principle of friction.

Dubowski, Cathy E., and Mark Dubowski

771 *A Horse Named Seabiscuit.* Ill. by Michael Langham Rowe. Grosset & Dunlap, pap., 2003, ISBN 0-448-43342-7. SERIES: All Aboard Reading. SUBJECTS: Horses; Sports — Horse racing. RL B. LEXILE 430L.

Seabiscuit's transformation from awkward, temperamental horse to champion is recounted here. Detailed, realistic illustrations are interspersed with archival black-and-white photographs.

772 *Pirate School.* Ill. by authors. Grosset & Dunlap, 1996, o.p. SERIES: All Aboard Reading. SUBJECTS: Pirates — Fiction; School stories. RL B. LEXILE 240L.

At Pirate School, where you learn subtraction by students walking the plank, Pete and archenemy Grimy vie to find the pirate treasure. Interesting perspectives and comical facial expressions give a unique pirate aspect.

773 *Pretty Good Magic.* Ill. by Mark Dubowski. Random House, 1987, o.p. SERIES: Step into Reading. SUBJECTS: Humorous stories; Magic — Fiction; Rabbits — Fiction. RL C.

The town of Forty Winks is so quiet that Presto decides to learn a new, impressive trick to wake everyone up — and finds himself stuck with dozens of rabbits. Comical pencil and wash drawings successfully complement the text.

774 *Snug Bug's Play Day.* Ill. by authors. Grosset & Dunlap, 1997, o.p. SERIES: All Aboard Reading. SUBJECTS: Insects — Fiction; Play — Fiction. RL B.

Sleeping in a tissue box and playing on a ruler teeter-totter, Snug Bug learns to share with others during his day at play. Large type, short sentences, and humorous drawings from a bug's-eye perspective offer beginning readers a fun and successful experience.

Dubowski, Mark, and Cathy E. Dubowski

775 *Ice Mummy: The Discovery of a 5,000 Year-old-man.* Random House, pap., 1998, ISBN 0-679-85647-1. SERIES: Step into Reading. SUBJECTS: Mummies; Prehistoric man. RL B. LEXILE 510L.

While hiking in the Alps, Helmut and Erika Simon discover the body of what will be identified as the 5,000-year-old "Iceman." Numerous, clear color photographs chronicle the discovery and identification process.

Duffey, Betsy

776 *Camp Knock Knock.* Ill. by Fiona Dunbar. Bantam, 1996, o.p. SERIES: Yearling First Choice Chapter Book. SUBJECTS: Camps and camping — Fiction; Jokes and riddles — Fiction. RL B. LEXILE 160L.

Duffey, Betsy (cont.)

At camp, Willie is the knock-knock king until he is challenged by Crow, who is the best at everything. With a focus on the demeanor of the campers, action-filled illustrations capture the friendly jokester rivalry.

777 *Camp Knock Knock Mystery*. Ill. by Fiona Dunbar. Bantam, 1997, o.p. SERIES: Yearling First Choice Chapter Book. SUBJECTS: Camps and camping — Fiction; Jokes and riddles — Fiction. RL B. LEXILE 180L.

Back for another year, Willie is armed with a knock-knock book and ready to defend his knock-knock king title against Crow. When the book goes missing, Willie must follow the knock-knock clues. Entertaining watercolors follow the campers on their mystery trail.

Dunbar, Joyce

778 *Gander's Pond*. Ill. by Helen Craig. Candlewick, 1999, o.p. SERIES: Pander and Gander Stories. SUBJECTS: Behavior — Cooperative; Geese — Fiction; Pandas — Fiction. RL B.

Gander has plans to make a pond in which to cool off. Gathering enough raindrops seems impossible until Panda and Gander work together to make a pond in a tub. Quietly gentle illustrations on sky blue pages emphasize the spirit of friendship.

Dussling, Jennifer

779 *Dinosaur Eggs*. Ill. by Pamela Johnson. Golden Books, pap., 2000, ISBN 0-448-42093-7. SERIES: All Aboard Science Reader. SUBJECTS: Dinosaurs. RL B. LEXILE 320L.

Be a part of the 1997 discovery of a dinosaur nesting ground in South America. Full-page color illustrations document the find and provide detailed comparisons, diagrams, and visual enlargements of the sauropods.

780 *Fair Is Fair!* Ill. by Diane Palmisciano. Kane, pap., 2003, ISBN 1-57565-131-9. SERIES: Math Matters. SUBJECTS: Mathematics — Fiction; Money. RL B.

On a campaign to raise his allowance, Marco surveys his friends and uses bar graphs to plot the data. The concept of information gathering and creating graphs is well demonstrated through creative and colorful illustrations.

781 *Giant Squid: Mystery of the Deep*. Ill. by Pamela Johnson. Grosset & Dunlap, pap., 1999, ISBN 0-448-41995-5. SERIES: All Aboard Science Reader. SUBJECTS: Oceans and ocean life. RL B.

In 1997 off the coast of New Zealand, fishermen captured a 25-foot dead giant squid in their nets. Full-page, color artwork and archival photographs chronicle the find and the scientists' research, which provided the world with new information about this mysterious creature of the deep.

782 *Gotcha!* Ill. by John Nez. Kane, pap., 2003, ISBN 1-57565-124-6. SERIES: Science Solves It! SUBJECTS: Camps and camping — Fiction; Science and scientists. RL B.

Practical joker Pete tells a ghost story that scares his friends as he uses magnets to add authenticity to his prank. His friends reciprocate and use the magnet for their own joke. Humorous art pictorially describes the scientific principle.

783 *Slinky Scaly Snakes!* DK, 1998, ISBN 0-7894-3766-X. SERIES: DK Readers. SUBJECTS: Reptiles and amphibians; Snakes. RL B. LEXILE 550L.

Explore the world of snakes through highly dramatic and informative color photographs that examine the many varieties, habitats, and life cycle of this interesting reptile.

784 *Stars*. Ill. by Mavis Smith. Grosset & Dunlap, pap., 1996, ISBN 0-448-41148-2. SERIES: All Aboard Science Reader. SUBJECTS: Astronomy and astronomers. RL B. LEXILE 260L.

This simple introduction to stars offers a brief explanation of what they are made of, the importance of the sun, and the lore surrounding the constellations. Cartoon-style illustrations enhance the readable text with clear drawings and diagrams.

785 *A Very Strange Dollhouse*. Ill. by Sonja Lamut. Grosset & Dunlap, 1996, o.p. SERIES: Eek! Stories to Make You Shriek. SUBJECTS: Dolls and dollhouses — Fiction; Scary stories. RL B. LEXILE 220L.

Lucy, the strange new girl at school, invites a young girl to her house to play with her dollhouse. Eerie background colors and odd perspectives portray the true nature of this very unusual dollhouse and its inhabitants.

E

Earl, Janice

786 *Jan Has a Doll.* Ill. by Tricia Tusa. Harcourt, 2003, ISBN 0-15-205168-6. SERIES: Green Light Readers. SUBJECTS: Dolls and dollhouses — Fiction. RL A.

Alternating a page of very simple text and an illustration, this story of a young girl's surprise at finding a special look-alike doll made by her father unfolds. The full-page drawings in blue and gold are charmingly cozy and filled with love. Suggested craft activities follow.

Early, Bobbi

787 *Tiny Life in a Puddle.* Scholastic, 2005, ISBN 0-516-25272-0. SERIES: Rookie Read-About Science. SUBJECTS: Science and scientists; Water. RL B.

In one drop of water in a puddle live over a million examples of life called protists. Highly magnified color photographs show the many types of tiny life forms.

Eastman, Patricia

788 *Sometimes Things Change.* Ill. by Seymour Fleischman. Children's Press, 1983, o.p. SERIES: Rookie Reader. SUBJECTS: Change. RL A.

Things change: caterpillars, tadpoles, eggs, grapes, seeds, buds, babies, strangers, clouds, and so forth. Some rather complex ideas for beginning readers using a 47-word vocabulary. Simple ink and wash drawings focus on children and animals.

Eastman, Peter

789 *Fred and Ted Go Camping.* Ill. by author. Random House, 2005, ISBN 0-375-82965-2. SERIES: Beginner Books. SUBJECTS: Camps and camping — Fiction; Pets — Dogs — Fiction. RL B. LEXILE 150L.

Despite their many differences, Fred and Ted are good friends who go camping together. The bright, colorful cartoon illustrations embrace and extend the fun, including a fishing trip disaster that ends well with the help of a little birdie.

Eastman, Philip D.

790 *Are You My Mother?* Ill. by author. Beginner Books, 1960, ISBN 0-394-90018-9. SERIES: I Can Read It All by Myself. SUBJECTS: Growing up — Fiction; Mothers — Fiction; Parent and child — Fiction. RL A.

Baby Bird hatches while Mother is out digging worms. He seeks her in the barnyard and is hoisted by a snorting machine — into his own nest just in time to meet his mother. Brown pencil drawings have yellow and red highlights, complementing this reassuring tale.

791 *Best Nest.* Ill. by author. Beginner Books, 1968, ISBN 0-394-90051-0. SUBJECTS: Birds — Fiction; Houses — Fiction. RL B.

Mr. Bird's search for a better nest demonstrates that a shoe, a mailbox, and a church steeple all have their drawbacks. Simple comic illustrations underline his relief when he finds his wife safe — back in the old nest.

792 *Flap Your Wings.* Ill. by author. Random House, 1969, o.p. SERIES: Early Bird. SUBJECTS: Birds — Fiction. RL A.

Mr. and Mrs. Bird hatch a foundling egg with surprising results. A well-constructed story that is illustrated simply. This reissue includes a cassette tape.

793 *Sam and the Firefly.* Ill. by author. Random House, 1958, ISBN 0-394-80006-0. SERIES: I Can Read It All by Myself. SUBJECTS: Fireflies — Fiction; Owls — Fiction. RL A.

Gus the firefly's skill at spelling runs amok until he is saved from the consequences of his mischief by his friend Sam, an owl. Inventive humor has turquoise illustrations with yellow owl eyes and firefly writing.

Eaton, Deborah J.

794 *Monster Songs*. Ill. by Dorothy Handelman. Millbrook, pap., 1999, ISBN 0-7613-2079-2. SERIES: Real Kids Readers. SUBJECTS: Monsters — Fiction; Siblings — Fiction. RL B.

Hal has a monster who sings at night under his bed, and wants his brother Jack to make the scary creature go away. After several ingenious attempts, Jack helps his brother do this himself. Colorful, full-page photographs of "real kids" make the action accessible and immediate.

795 *My Wild Woolly*. Ill. by G. Brian Karas. Harcourt, 1999, ISBN 0-15-205148-1. SERIES: Green Light Readers. SUBJECTS: Imagination — Fiction; Play — Fiction. RL B.

His mother doesn't believe him, but all day long a little boy plays with his imaginary "Wild Woolly." Simple earth-toned illustrations portray the fun and friendship. An animal bookmark project is included at the end.

796 *The Rainy Day Grump*. Ill. by Dorothy Handelman. Millbrook, 1998, ISBN 0-7613-2018-0. SERIES: Real Kids Readers. SUBJECTS: African Americans — Fiction; Rain — Fiction; Sports — Baseball — Fiction. RL B.

It's raining and Clay can't play baseball so his sister tries to suggest other activities. Full-color photographs of children staging the action aptly capture the unhappiness, dismay, and sheer grumpiness of young boy who would rather be anyplace else than inside, playing dress-up.

Edwards, Anne

797 *The Great Houdini*. Ill. by Joseph Ciardiello. Putnam, 1977, o.p. SERIES: See and Read. SUBJECTS: Biographies; Magic. RL C.

This true story of the best-known magician ever has great drama and human interest. Ink drawings add interesting details.

798 *P. T. Barnum*. Ill. by Marylin Hafner. Putnam, 1977, o.p. SERIES: See and Read Biography. SUBJECTS: Biographies; Circuses. RL C.

Barnum's colorful career is traced — from the small boy who always had a head for sums to the flamboyant showman. Gray tone drawings capture some of the excitement.

Edwards, Frank B.

799 *A Crowded Ride in the Countryside*. Ill. by John Bianchi. Pokeweed, 1999, ISBN 1-894323-03-3. SERIES: Pokeweed Press New Reader. SUBJECTS: Animals — Farm — Fiction; Farm and country life — Fiction. RL A.

On the way to the county fair a farmer and his dog pick up all the farm animals that want to come along. Hilarious cartoon-like drawings illustrate the action of the rhyming text as pigs, cows, sheep, and a chicken all hitch a ride on the farmer's truck.

800 *Nightgown Countdown*. Ill. by John Bianchi. Pokeweed, 1999, ISBN 1-894323-05-X. SERIES: Pokeweed Press New Reader. SUBJECTS: Bedtime — Fiction; Concepts — Numbers — Fiction. RL B.

In a countdown from ten, the dancing farm animals one-by-one drop off to sleep. Against an evening sky, bright full-page illustrations carry the humor of the rhymed story and the entertaining antics of a barnyard bedtime hoe-down.

801 *Snug as a Big Red Bug*. Ill. by John Bianchi. Pokeweed, pap., 1999, ISBN 1-894323-00-9. SERIES: Pokeweed Press New Reader. SUBJECTS: Insects — Fiction. RL A.

As winter approaches where will a red bug live? Refused by all the farmyard animals, the big red bug settles into Farmer Brown's rug. A repetitive, rhymed text with humorous close-ups of the bug's prospective homes will keep readers guessing until the end.

Edwards, Julie Andrews, and Emma Walton Hamilton

802 *Dumpy to the Rescue!* Ill. by Tony Walton. HarperCollins, 2004, ISBN 0-06-052689-0. SERIES: My First I Can Read. SUBJECTS: Animals — Farm — Fiction; Farm and country life — Fiction; Trucks — Fiction. RL B.

After hauling the food for the farm animals' dinner, Dumpy the truck helps Mama Goat find her missing Baby Goat. The question-filled text, highlighted by lighthearted drawings in bright colors, invites readers to join in the search.

803 *Dumpy's Apple Shop*. Ill. by Tony Walton. HarperCollins, 2004, ISBN 0-06-052692-0. SERIES: My First I Can Read. SUBJECTS: Animals — Farm — Fiction; Farm and country life — Fiction; Trucks — Fiction. RL B.

It's time for the Apple Day Celebration in Apple Harbor and everyone in the Barnes family wants to help get ready, including Dumpy the truck. Colorfully detailed illustrations explore the family's preparations as repetitive words and phrases tell the story.

Edwards, Michelle

804 *Pa Lia's First Day*. Ill. by author. Harcourt, 1999, o.p. SERIES: Jackson Friends. SUBJECTS: Friendship — Fiction; School stories. RL B. LEXILE 390L.

Being the new girl on the first day of school is scary for Pa Lia Vang, but by the end of the day she has made two new friends. A gentle school story, told in eight chapters and illustrated throughout with black-and-white drawings from interesting perspectives.

805 *Stinky Stern Forever*. Ill. by author. Harcourt, 2005, ISBN 0-15-216389-1. SERIES: Jackson Friends. SUBJECTS: Behavior — Bullying — Fiction; Death — Fiction; School stories. RL B.

When the class bully is killed in a car accident on the way home from school, the class members honestly share their memories as they try to understand their feelings. Expressive illustrations skillfully enhance a story told with care and sensitivity.

806 *The Talent Show*. Ill. by author. Harcourt, pap., 2005, ISBN 0-15-205760-9. SERIES: Jackson Friends. SUBJECTS: Grandparents — Fiction; School stories. RL B. LEXILE 300L.

At the final rehearsal for the Jackson Magnet School talent show, Howardina experiences stage fright. With the help of her grandmother, the young girl becomes the star of her dreams. The black-and-white pen and ink illustrations offer additional insight into an emotion-filled event.

807 *Zero Grandparents*. Ill. by author. Harcourt, pap., 2005, ISBN 0-15-205754-4. SERIES: Jackson Friends. SUBJECTS: Grandparents — Fiction; School stories. RL B. LEXILE 420L.

On Grandparent's Day, wearing a shawl her grandmother made, Calliope introduces the class to her deceased grandmother, Flory Sophia Turnipseed. Realistic black-and-white drawings capture the emotion of a young girl's solution to her lack of living grandparents.

Edwards, Roberta

808 *Five Silly Fishermen*. Ill. by Sylvie Wickstrom. Random House, 1989, ISBN 0-679-80092-1. SERIES: Step into Reading. SUBJECTS: Folklore; Humorous stories; Storytelling. RL A.

A traditional tale about fishermen, each of whom forgets to count himself, is retold using very simple language. Pencil drawings with watercolor washes illustrate the large-type text.

Ehrlich, Amy

809 *Bravo, Kazam!* Ill. by Barney Saltzberg. Candlewick, 2002, ISBN 0-7636-1315-0. SERIES: Brand New Readers. SUBJECTS: Humorous stories; Magic — Fiction. RL B.

When a young girl magician tries her hand at magic, the tricks turn out with fun, unexpected results. Spirited illustrations focus on the magic trick, adding humorous touches that enliven the text. Reading tips are included.

810 *Buck-Buck the Chicken*. Ill. by R. W. Alley. Random House, 1987, o.p. SERIES: Step into Reading. SUBJECTS: Chickens — Fiction; Humorous stories; Pets — Fiction. RL B.

Won by Nancy's father at the county fair, Buck-Buck is a pampered pet who does not seem to know how to act like a chicken. This delightfully silly story is illustrated with watercolors with ink detailing.

811 *Kazam's Magic*. Ill. by Barney Saltzberg. Candlewick, 2001, o.p. SERIES: Brand New Readers. SUBJECTS: Humorous stories; Magic — Fiction. RL B.

In four short stories, Kazam performs magic tricks using her wand, a rabbit, and some coins. Simple,

Ehrlich, Amy (cont.)

engaging drawings center on the young girl magician and the humorous results of her magical attempts. Reading tips are included.

812 *Leo, Zack and Emmie*. Ill. by Steven Kellogg. Dial, 1981, ISBN 0-8037-4761-6. SERIES: Dial Easy-to-Read. SUBJECTS: Friendship — Fiction; School stories. RL B.
Emmie, as the newcomer, upsets the friendship between Leo and Zack. Four episodes of everyday experiences are warm and humorous, enhanced by delicious four-color action-filled illustrations.

813 *Leo, Zack and Emmie Together Again*. Ill. by Steven Kellogg. Dial, 1987, o.p. SERIES: Dial Easy-to-Read. SUBJECTS: Friendship — Fiction; School stories. RL B.
Four stories tell how the friendship of these three is tested at school and in the neighborhood. The drawings add to the sense of mischief and express the emotions and warmth of childhood.

Ehrlich, Fred

814 *A Class Play with Ms. Vanilla*. Ill. by Martha Gradisher. Viking, 1992, o.p. SERIES: Hello Reading. SUBJECTS: Humorous stories; Plays — Fiction; Stories in rhyme. RL A.
The hunters grab the wolf's tail and pull his paws to save Little Red Riding Hood in this charming, reproducible play in rhyme for primary age children. Cartoon characters model the simple costumes and the action for a class production.

815 *Lunch Boxes*. Ill. by Martha Gradisher. Viking, 1991, o.p. SERIES: Hello Reading. SUBJECTS: School stories; Stories in rhyme. RL A.
Although a class at Oak Hill School walks peacefully to and from the lunchroom, they turn the lunchroom into a disaster area for a while. Cartoon drawings add action.

Elliot, David

816 *The Cool Crazy Crickets*. Ill. by Paul Meisel. Candlewick, 2000, o.p. SUBJECTS: Clubs — Fiction; Friendship — Fiction. RL B.
Four friends form a club, complete with a refrigerator box clubhouse and a mascot named Noodles. Lively watercolor and ink illustrations depict realistic and everyday interactions between friends as they decide on the reason for their club.

Elliott, Dan

817 *Ernie's Little Lie*. Ill. by Joe Mathieu. Random House, 1983, ISBN 0-394-85440-3. SERIES: Start-to-Read. SUBJECTS: Behavior — Lying — Fiction. RL B.
Ernie did not originally intend to claim someone else's artwork as his own, but he certainly feels better after confessing. Straightforward drawings show "Sesame Street" characters.

818 *Grover Learns to Read*. Ill. by Normand Chartier. Random House, 1985, ISBN 0-394-97498-0. SERIES: Start-to-Read. SUBJECTS: Books and reading — Fiction; Libraries and librarians — Fiction. RL B.
Grover is not sure he wants to learn to read if he misses out on his mother's bedtime story. Bright pastel drawings are of "Sesame Street" characters.

819 *My Doll Is Lost!* Ill. by Joe Mathieu. Random House, 1984, ISBN 0-679-83953-4; pap., ISBN 0-394-96251-6. SERIES: Sesame Street Start-to-Read. SUBJECTS: Puppetry — Fiction; Toys — Fiction. RL A.
The characters of "Sesame Street" turn out to look for Herry's "beautiful" doll, but each is looking for a doll that resembles himself or herself. Sympathetic story with familiar characters.

820 *Oscar's Rotten Birthday*. Ill. by Normand Chartier. Random House, 1992, o.p. SERIES: Sesame Street Start-to-Read. SUBJECTS: Birthdays — Fiction; Puppetry — Fiction. RL A.
Oscar the Grouch surprises everyone, including himself, by enjoying his birthday party, with presents of stinkweed, broken toys, peanut shells, and a jar of mud. Illustrations are typical cartoons of "Sesame Street" puppets.

Elting, Mary, and Michael Folsom

821 *Q Is for Duck: An Alphabet Guessing Game*. Ill. by Jack Kent. Houghton Mifflin, 1980, o.p. SUBJECTS: Alphabet — Fiction; Animals — Fiction. RL C.
This alphabet book is for older readers because the letters represent verbs not nouns. "L is for

Frog Why? Because a Frog Leaps." However, the verbs used are not predictable or even logical. Drawings are charming.

Epstein, Sam, and Beryl Epstein

822 *Hold Everything*. Ill. by Tomie dePaola. Holiday House, 1973, o.p. SUBJECTS: Science and scientists. RL C.

Sewing, adhesives, saliva, icing, staples, nails, and zippers are some of the ways things are held together. Creative possibilities such as holding hands and using "and" are suggested. Three-color illustrations give detail and humor.

823 *Pick It Up*. Ill. by Tomie dePaola. Holiday House, 1971, o.p. SUBJECTS: Human body — Hands; Science and scientists; Tools. RL C.

Using familiar objects or animals as examples, the many ways things are picked up are discussed. Alternating cocoa and turquoise and black-and-white drawings add humorous touches.

824 *Who Needs Holes?* Ill. by Tomie dePaola. Hawthorn, 1970, o.p. SUBJECTS: Concepts. RL A.

Armholes, buttonholes, colanders, shower heads, drills, lifesavers, and keyholes are some of the common holes explored in this creative text using a self-discovery experimental approach. DePaola's appealing people and animal drawings alternate ink with lavender and golden brown.

Esbensen, Barbara J.

825 *Baby Whales Drink Milk*. Ill. by Lambert Davis. HarperCollins, 1994, o.p. SERIES: Let's-Read-and-Find-Out Science. SUBJECTS: Science and scientists; Whales. RL A.

Information about mammals and the birth and habits of humpback whales is introduced in very simple vocabulary, accompanied by simple drawings of whales. A few facts about other types of whales and where whales can be observed is appended.

826 *Sponges Are Skeletons*. Ill. by Holly Keller. HarperCollins, 1993, o.p. SERIES: Let's-Read-and-Find-Out Science. SUBJECTS: Oceans and ocean life; Science and scientists. RL A.

Sponges have survived 700 million years. The parallels to the skeleton of a boy and his cat are shown, as well as the life of a sponge under the sea, and how the sponges get from there to the bathtub. Simple ink and watercolor illustrations accompany the text.

Eugenie, and Mary C. Olson, reteller

827 *Kittens for Keeps*. Ill. by author. Western, 1987, ISBN 0-307-03678-2. SERIES: Step Ahead Beginning Reader. SUBJECTS: Grandparents — Fiction; Pets — Cats — Fiction; Seashore — Fiction. RL A.

Visiting her grandmother at the seashore, Meg finds two kittens and keeps them until the end of the summer when one stays with her grandmother and the other goes home to the city with Meg. Illustrated with sweet watercolor paintings.

Eyles, Heather

828 *A Zoo in Our House*. Ill. by Andy Cooke. Warner, 1988, o.p. SERIES: Early Reader. SUBJECTS: Zoos — Fiction. RL C.

One by one some zoo animals visit a little boy's house, then all come for a party! Large, colorful zany animals and the messes they create are eye-catching.

F

Faiella, Graham

829 *Whales*. Ill. by Turi MacCombie. Grosset & Dunlap, pap., 2002, ISBN 0-448-42600-5. SERIES: All Aboard Reading. SUBJECTS: Whales. RL B.

Learn how whales are born, where they live, and what they eat. Realistic, detailed illustrations focus on the unique characteristics of each type of whale. Cutaway drawings, maps, and diagrams are included.

Falken, Linda C.

830 *Kitty's First Airplane Trip*. Ill. by Lynn Adams. Scholastic, 1993, o.p. SERIES: Read with Me. SUBJECTS: Airplanes — Fiction; Pets — Fiction. RL A.

Falken, Linda C. (cont.)

A toddler lets his kitty loose during their first airplane flight. Soft ink and wash drawings.

Farber, Erica, and J. R. Sansevere

831 *Kiss of the Mermaid*. Random House, 1996, o.p. SERIES: Step into Reading. SUBJECTS: Magic — Fiction; Monsters — Fiction. RL B. LEXILE 400L.

Temporarily turned into a mermaid, fearless Thistle Howl swims into the undersea cave of the wicked sea witch to save the family of Mara the mermaid. Cartoon illustrations in vibrant colors capture the drama of a perilous underwater adventure.

832 *No Howling in the House*. Random House, 1996, o.p. SERIES: Step into Reading. SUBJECTS: Magic — Fiction; Monsters — Fiction. RL B. LEXILE 420L.

When Thistle and Jack cannot learn basic monster skills of howling and flying, they hope a magic pie will help. Humorously scary cartoon drawings ably set the scene and depict the joy of a lesson of monstrous proportions finally learned.

833 *Ooey Gooey*. Random House, 1998, o.p. SERIES: Step into Reading. SUBJECTS: Human body — Teeth — Fiction; Pirates — Fiction; Stories in rhyme. RL B.

After eating a concoction of bubble gum and tuna fish, Captain Short Bob loses his gold tooth to a sea beast and must live out his life eating stews and mush. Full-page cartoons in bold colors aptly capture the humor of this rhymed pirate adventure.

834 *Roast and Toast*. Random House, 1998, o.p. SERIES: Step into Reading. SUBJECTS: Monsters — Fiction; Stories in rhyme. RL B.

A midnight barbecue is just the thing for Axel Howl and his vampire friends. This story in rhyme is enhanced by large, detailed cartoon illustrations that add humor and excitement to the unique after-hours beach party.

835 *Zoom on My Broom*. Random House, 1998, o.p. SERIES: Step into Reading. SUBJECTS: Monsters — Fiction; Stories in rhyme. RL A. LEXILE BR.

A play date at Thistle Howl's home is very unusual — from a mother with a magic wand to a zoom around the room on a broom. Hilarious cartoon drawings vividly demonstrate the new friends' fun complete with bug juice on ice.

Feder, Paula K.

836 *Where Does the Teacher Live?* Ill. by Lillian Hoban. Dutton, 1979, o.p. SUBJECTS: School stories. RL B.

The answer to a question many children ponder — "where does teacher live?" — is discovered by the reader, but not the children of this slight story. Hoban's soft watercolors are suitable.

Fehlner, Paul

837 *Dog and Cat*. Ill. by Maxie Chambliss. Childrens Press, 1990, o.p. SERIES: My First Reader. SUBJECTS: Pets — Cats — Fiction; Pets — Dogs — Fiction. RL A.

In a text of just 20 words, the old dog chases, after a fashion, the fat cat, with disastrous results. The ink and watercolor illustrations carry most of the humor.

Feldman, Barbara

838 *Going, Going*. Ill. by author. Firefly, 1989, o.p. SERIES: Annick Toddler Series. SUBJECTS: Cars — Fiction; Dreams — Fiction. RL A.

With rich fabric appliqué, the author enriches the story of a boy whose world is enlarged when his mother learns to drive a car. Illustrations employ very detailed and inventive patterns and textures, and vivid colors.

Felton, Carol, and Amanda Felton

839 *Where's Harley?* Ill. by Page Eastburn O'Rourke. Kane, 2003, ISBN 1-57565-732-7. SERIES: Math Matters. SUBJECTS: Lost and found possessions — Fiction; Mathematics — Fiction; Rabbits — Fiction. RL B.

In search of Harley the rabbit, Mandy, Nate, and all of their friends in the apartment building use their walkie-talkies as they hunt from floor to floor. Clever illustrations combine humor, mystery, and excitement along with visual reinforcement of ordinal numbers.

Fernandes, Eugenie

840 *Just You and Me.* Ill. by author. Firefly, 1993, o.p. SUBJECTS: Babies — Fiction; Sleep — Fiction. RL A.

Neither the river nor the wind, nor the moon's story, nor the birds' lullaby, nor fishes' heads put the baby to sleep so Auntie Pearl will baby-sit so Mother and Heather can have some time together. Remarkable molded clay in crisp colors illustrates the whimsical story.

Fernandes, Kim

841 *Visiting Granny.* Ill. by author. Firefly, 1990, o.p. SUBJECTS: Concepts — Numbers — Fiction; Farm and country life — Fiction; Grandparents — Fiction. RL A.

While two children play, listen to a story, and help Granny in the kitchen, some lambs, goats, piglets, and kittens wander in and get shooed outside. Very appealing detailed molded clay scenes alternate with pages with large print.

842 *Zebo and the Dirty Planet.* Ill. by author. Firefly, 1991, o.p. SUBJECTS: Conservation — Fiction. RL B.

With very colorful dimensional clay figures and landscape, the author illustrates a slim story about Zebo, who brings pairs of animals from the dirty planet to earth. Illustrations are very appealing.

Finch, Margo

843 *The Lunch Bunch.* Ill. by Dorothy Handelman. Millbrook, pap., 1998, ISBN 0-7613-2030-X. SERIES: Real Kids Readers. SUBJECTS: Friendship — Fiction; School stories. RL B. LEXILE 170L.

Full-page photographs that focus on "real kids" effectively follow an everyday situation at school. Meg, new to school, finds two classmates to sit with at lunch. While trading lunches, the three girls become fast friends.

Fine, Jane

844 *Surprise!* Ill. by Mary Morgan. Viking, 1988, o.p. SERIES: Hello Reading. SUBJECTS: Birthdays — Fiction; Family life — Fiction; Mothers — Fiction. RL B.

Three young children get up very early and quietly prepare a tray of juice and cookies for their mother's birthday. The text is very brief, relying on the pictures of the excited children and their rambunctious cat to help tell the story. Illustrations are in bright, vibrant watercolors.

Finsand, Mary J.

845 *The Town That Moved.* Ill. by Reg Sandland. Carolrhoda, pap., 1991, ISBN 0-440-40489-4. SERIES: On My Own. SUBJECTS: Historical fiction. RL C.

In the 1920s, when iron ore was discovered under the town of Hibbing, Minnesota, the buildings were rolled one by one on logs to a nearby location. Pencil drawings show the action.

Firmin, Peter

846 *Basil Brush and the Windmills.* Ill. by author. Prentice-Hall, 1979, o.p. SUBJECTS: Foxes — Fiction; Inventors and inventions — Fiction; Moles — Fiction. RL C.

Most of Basil the fox's inventions to save money turn out disastrously, save one. Humorous ink sketches are highlighted in red.

847 *Basil Brush Gets a Medal.* Ill. by author. Prentice-Hall, 1973, o.p. SUBJECTS: Cumulative tales; Foxes — Fiction; Moles — Fiction. RL C.

This original cumulative tale recounts Basil the fox and Harry the mole's adventures getting milk for the princess's porridge before deserved medals can be awarded. Red wash highlights ink animal drawings.

848 *Basil Brush Goes Boating.* Ill. by author. Prentice-Hall, 1969, o.p. SUBJECTS: Foxes — Fiction; Friendship — Fiction; Sports — Fishing — Fiction. RL B.

Basil the fox and his friend Harry the mole manage to leave all of their equipment behind when they go fishing. Gentle humor warms this tale of friendship; blue highlights ink drawings.

849 *Basil Brush Goes Flying.* Ill. by author. Prentice-Hall, 1977, o.p. SUBJECTS: Foxes — Fiction; Friendship — Fiction; Moles — Fiction. RL B.

Irrepressible optimism fuels Basil the fox and his friend Harry the mole's flying adventures. A blue wash brightens action-filled ink drawings.

Firmin, Peter (cont.)

850 *Basil Brush in the Jungle*. Ill. by author. Prentice-Hall, 1970, o.p. SUBJECTS: Foxes — Fiction; Humorous stories; India — Fiction. RL C.

Basil the fox takes the cage he makes to India, where the butterfly, crocodile, snake, and tiger are happier in the jungle than in his cage. Humor is used in this exotic adventure; ink and green wash sketches focus on animals, an unforgettable Indian ferryman, and an umbrella man.

851 *Basil Brush on the Trail*. Ill. by author. Prentice-Hall, 1979, o.p. SUBJECTS: Foxes — Fiction; Moles — Fiction; Mystery and detective stories. RL B.

Basil the fox and Harry the mole's bungling attempts do not uncover the real thief of the silver tennis trophies until the owner returns home. Ink drawings have orange highlights.

852 *Boastful Mr. Bear*. Ill. by author. Delacorte, 1989, o.p. SERIES: The Old Tree Stories. SUBJECTS: Bears — Fiction; Behavior — Bragging — Fiction; Foxes — Fiction. RL A.

Mr. Bear rejects help from all his woodland friends — until he sits in a blackthorn bush. Typical cute pencil and watercolor illustrations depict a simplified traditional theme.

853 *Foolish Miss Crow*. Ill. by author. Delacorte, 1989, o.p. SERIES: The Old Tree Stories. SUBJECTS: Crows — Fiction; Foxes — Fiction. RL B.

Wily Mr. Fox lures vain Miss Crow with a scarf, a hat, jewelry, and his camera. Typical Firmin cartoon characters appear in illustrations.

854 *Happy Miss Rat*. Ill. by author. Delacorte, 1989, o.p. SERIES: The Old Tree Stories. SUBJECTS: Music and musicians — Fiction; Rats — Fiction. RL A.

Like Lionni's Frederick, Miss Rat plays her banjo and sings instead of preparing for winter, but shares in the harvest as she shares her songs. Typical Firmin cutesy watercolor forest animals are depicted in illustrations.

855 *Hungry Mr. Fox*. Ill. by author. Delacorte, 1989, o.p. SERIES: The Old Tree Stories. SUBJECTS: Animals — Fiction; Foxes — Fiction. RL A.

A watered-down version of "The Three Billy Goats Gruff" has the mouse, rat, and hare escaping Mr. Fox, who goes after the bigger one who follows — a warm fuzzy bear.

Fisher, Aileen

856 *Always Wondering: Some Favorite Poems of Aileen Fisher*. Ill. by Joan Sandin. HarperCollins, 1991, ISBN 0-06-022851-2. SUBJECTS: Poetry. RL C.

Appealing poems are loosely gathered into sections, and include such topics as animals, holidays, shooting stars, snails, and seasons. Pencil drawings begin each of four sections.

857 *The House of a Mouse*. Ill. by Joan Sandin. HarperCollins, 1988, ISBN 0-06-021849-5. SUBJECTS: Mice — Fiction; Poetry. RL C.

The world of different kinds of mice is explored — the dangers, tracks, nests, and habits — in lighthearted simple verse. Soft pencil drawings beautifully complement this rhythmic celebration of mice.

858 *My Cat Has Eyes of Sapphire Blue*. Ill. by Marie Angel. HarperCollins, 1973, o.p. SUBJECTS: Pets — Cats — Fiction; Poetry. RL B.

Playful, sleepy-though-alert, acrobatic, protective cats and kittens live in this book of celebratory poetry. Expressive illustrations are in colored pencil.

859 *When It Comes to Bugs*. Ill. by Chris Degen and Bruce Degen. HarperCollins, 1986, o.p. SUBJECTS: Nature; Poetry. RL B.

Beetles and dragonflies, caterpillars, spiders, and centipedes are celebrated in inventive poetry with touches of whimsy. Text is becomingly illustrated with color overlays on black scratchboard by the Degens.

Fisher, Ronald M.

860 *Cottontails: Little Rabbits of Field and Forest*. Ill. with photos. National Geographic, 1989, o.p. SERIES: Books for Young Explorers. SUBJECTS: Nature; Rabbits. RL C.

Excellent color photographs show some of the 14 kinds of cottontails at different stages of development in different habitats. A picture dictionary of appealing domestic rabbits, a bibliography, and additional facts are appended.

FitzGerald, Cathleen

861 *Let's Find Out About Words*. Ill. by Georgia Froom. Watts, 1971, o.p. SUBJECTS: English language. RL B.

FitzGerald celebrates the contributions of various cultures to the English language, as well as the history and evolution of our language. Information is well presented. Ink drawings are against a gold or orange background.

Fleischman, Sid

862 *Kate's Secret Riddle Book*. Ill. by Barbara Bottner. Watts, 1977, o.p. SERIES: Easy-Read Story. SUBJECTS: Jokes and riddles. RL B.

Riddles for young readers are woven into a story about some girls trying to find out the answer to their friend Wally's riddle. Yellow and pumpkin colors predominate in illustrations with humor (but weird faces).

Florian, Douglas

863 *Monster Motel*. Ill. by author. Harcourt, 1993, ISBN 0-15-255320-7. SUBJECTS: Monsters — Fiction; Poetry. RL C.

Shy Shegs who never come out of their eggs, Gazzygoos who touch feet and grow a daisy when they meet, and the Crim who cries a river (and luckily knows how to swim) share the spotlight with the Brilly who takes its bath in lemon Jell-O. Whimsical childlike watercolors enhance imaginative poems.

864 *A Potter*. Ill. by author. Greenwillow, 1991, o.p. SUBJECTS: Careers. RL A.

In simple rhythmic language and drawings with black felt pen, crayon, and colored pencils and watercolor washes with immense graphic appeal, the author describes the work of a female potter.

Flower, Phyllis

865 *Barn Owl*. Ill. by Cherryl Pape. HarperCollins, 1978, ISBN 0-06-021919-X. SERIES: I Can Read Science. SUBJECTS: Owls; Science and scientists. RL B.

The life cycle of a barn owlet is traced, simply and eloquently. Pencil drawings with tan and gray washes show the drama of learning to fly and the first successful hunt.

Floyd, Lucy

866 *A Place for Nicholas*. Ill. by David M. McPhail. Harcourt, 2000, ISBN 0-15-205150-3. SERIES: Green Light Readers. SUBJECTS: Family life — Fiction; Siblings — Fiction. RL B.

Looking for a special place just for him, Jeff's little brother comes up with the perfect solution. Gentle pastel watercolor and ink illustrations evoke the feelings of a young boy in search of his own space. Suggested craft projects and activities follow the story.

Fontes, Allan

867 *All the Colors of the Rainbow*. Children's Press, 1998, ISBN 0-516-20801-2. SERIES: Rookie Read-About Science. SUBJECTS: Rainbows. RL B.

Made of sunlight shining through water, the colors of the rainbow are there all the time, but you only see them once in a while. This brief introduction to the formation of rainbows is enhanced by clear diagrams and color photographs.

Fontes, Justine, and Ron Fontes

868 *Proteins*. Scholastic, 2005, ISBN 0-516-23647-4. SERIES: Rookie Read-About Health. SUBJECTS: Food; Nutrition. RL B.

What are proteins and what foods are considered proteins? Numerous, clear color photographs focus on the examples of essential proteins needed in a healthy daily diet.

Fowler, Allan

869 *Africa*. Scholastic, 2001, ISBN 0-516-22238-4. SERIES: Rookie Read-About Geography. SUBJECTS: Africa. RL B. LEXILE 340L.

As the second-largest continent, Africa is made up of more than fifty countries. Photographs in full color highlight the many animals that inhabit the continent as well as some of the extraordinary topography.

Fowler, Allan (cont.)

870 *Animals in the Zoo*. Children's Press, 2000, ISBN 0-516-21218-4. SERIES: Rookie Read-About Science. SUBJECTS: Animals; Zoos. RL B.

Explore the different types of zoos around the country and how the animals are housed and fed. Expressive color photographs of some of the many animals in zoological parks give readers a close-up experience.

871 *Animals on the Move*. Children's Press, 2000, ISBN 0-516-21589-2. SERIES: Rookie Read-About Science. SUBJECTS: Animals; Animals — Migration. RL B.

All animals move around, but in autumn and spring many animals travel great distances in search of suitable weather, food, and breeding grounds. Full-page color photographs capture the migrations of a variety of bird, insect, and animal species.

872 *Animals Under the Ground*. Children's Press, 1997, ISBN 0-516-20427-0. SERIES: Rookie Read-About Science. SUBJECTS: Animals; Animals — Hibernation; Animals — Homes. RL B. LEXILE AD690L.

Moles, woodchucks, prairie dogs, and badgers build tunnels or burrows to live underground. Their various types of homes are the focal point of sharp color photographs that feature cutaways and picture-in-pictures.

873 *Antarctica*. Children's Press, 2001, ISBN 0-516-21669-4. SERIES: Rookie Read-About Geography. SUBJECTS: Antarctica. RL B. LEXILE 520L.

Find out about the coldest continent and its geographical features, vegetation, and animal life. The many distinct color photographs center on the unique physical features that are described within the text.

874 *Arms and Legs and Other Limbs*. Children's Press, 1999, ISBN 0-516-20809-8. SERIES: Rookie Read-About Science. SUBJECTS: Animals. RL B.

Humans have four limbs while various other animals have wings, flippers, legs, fins, or tentacles. Colorful photographs on every page closely follow the text and prominently emphasize animal anatomy.

875 *Asia*. Children's Press, 2001, ISBN 0-516-22234-1. SERIES: Rookie Read-About Geography. SUBJECTS: Asia. RL B. LEXILE 360L.

As the largest continent, Asia contains many different kinds of land, from tundra and desert to rain forests and grasslands. Crisp color photographs complement the information with clear examples of landforms and indigenous animals.

876 *Australia*. Children's Press, 2001, ISBN 0-516-21670-8. SERIES: Rookie Read-About Geography. SUBJECTS: Australia. RL B.

Surrounded by water, Australia is the smallest of the continents. From aerial views to underwater close-ups, color photographs show the amazing geography and animal life.

877 *The Biggest Animal on Land*. Children's Press, 1996, ISBN 0-516-06050-3. SERIES: Rookie Read-About Science. SUBJECTS: Animals; Elephants. RL B.

Focusing on the elephant, the biggest animal on land, this brief introduction features the animal's growth, development, and habitat. Colorful photographs embellish the text with closely cropped pictures of the various types of elephants.

878 *Cactuses*. Children's Press, 2001, ISBN 0-516-21686-4. SERIES: Rookie Read-About Science. SUBJECTS: Cacti; Plants. RL B. LEXILE 440L.

Growing in dry places such as deserts, cacti can be found in North, South, and Central America. Diagrams of the root system and numerous color photographs assist in visually explaining the plants' unusual features.

879 *Cougar: Lion of the Mountains*. Children's Press, 1999, ISBN 0-516-21207-9. SERIES: Rookie Read-About Science. SUBJECTS: Animals; Cougars. RL B.

There is no difference between a puma, a mountain lion, and a cougar. They are all names for a member of the cat family that lives in the Americas. Sharp, full-page color photographs show cougars living and hunting for food.

880 *Ferns*. Children's Press, 2001, ISBN 0-516-21687-2. SERIES: Rookie Read-About Science. SUBJECTS: Plants. RL B. LEXILE 390L.

Learn about ferns — the different types, how they grow from spores, and their need for damp and shade. Color pictures using a microscope and close-up photography give a clear understanding of the topic.

881 *From Seed to Plant.* Children's Press, 2001, ISBN 0-516-21682-1. SERIES: Rookie Read-About Science. SUBJECTS: Plants. RL B.

Follow the development of a seed into a plant from pollination to fertilization and dissemination. In addition to clear, close-up photographs, numerous diagrams clarify and identify the parts of plants and the roles they play in growth.

882 *Good Mushrooms and Bad Toadstools.* Children's Press, 1998, ISBN 0-516-20808-X. SERIES: Rookie Read-About Science. SUBJECTS: Plants. RL B. LEXILE 700L.

There are more than 3,000 different types of mushrooms that come in all sizes and colors. Never eat any mushrooms found growing in the wild. Colorful photographs zoom in on the many types and characteristics of mushrooms and toadstools.

883 *Hard-to-See Animals.* Children's Press, 1997, ISBN 0-516-20548-X. SERIES: Rookie Read-About Science. SUBJECTS: Animals; Animals — Camouflage. RL B. LEXILE AD790L.

Stripes, spots, color, and shape — animals use these to blend into their surroundings. Each full-page color photograph carefully captures excellent examples of how animals use camouflage.

884 *Horns and Antlers.* Children's Press, 1998, ISBN 0-516-20806-3. SERIES: Rookie Read-About Science. SUBJECTS: Animals; Animals — Growth and development. RL B. LEXILE 580L.

Find out the differences between horns and antlers, how they grow, and why they are important to a variety of animals around the world. Close-up color photographs clearly show examples of horns and antlers as described in the text.

885 *How Animals See Things.* Children's Press, 1998, ISBN 0-516-20797-0. SERIES: Rookie Read-About Science. SUBJECTS: Animals; Animals — Senses. RL B. LEXILE 550L.

Animals may all have two eyes, but they see differently. In addition to the numerous color photographs, excellent comparative pictorial examples clearly demonstrate what dogs, cats, and insects see.

886 *How Do You Know It's Fall?* Ill. with photos. Children's Press, 1992, ISBN 0-516-04922-4. SERIES: Rookie Read-About Science. SUBJECTS: Fall; Nature. RL A.

The beginning of school and the picking of apples, the jack-o-lanterns and the football game, herald the season. Text is illustrated with photographs of landscapes, animals, and multiethnic children.

887 *How Do You Know It's Summer?* Ill. with photos. Children's Press, 1992, ISBN 0-516-04923-2. SERIES: Rookie Read-About Science. SUBJECTS: Nature; Summer. RL B.

The busy farmer and the fresh strawberries, the beach and camp, the storm and the fireworks all illustrate the joys of summer. This book has simple, large-print text with color photographs and a brief picture dictionary.

888 *Inside an Ant Colony.* Children's Press, 1998, ISBN 0-516-20804-7. SERIES: Rookie Read-About Science. SUBJECTS: Ants; Insects. RL B. LEXILE 550L.

What goes on inside an ant colony? Thousands of different kinds of ants are found all over the world. Relying on high magnification, the many color photographs offer unique views of ant life.

889 *It Could Still Be a Desert.* Children's Press, 1997, ISBN 0-516-20319-3. SERIES: Rookie Read-About Science. SUBJECTS: Deserts. RL B. LEXILE NC690L.

Discover what deserts are like and how the animals, plants, and people that live there survive. Photographs of the different kinds of deserts enhance the information offered within the text.

890 *It Could Still Be a Flower.* Children's Press, 2001, ISBN 0-516-21681-3. SERIES: Rookie Read-About Science. SUBJECTS: Flowers. RL B.

Explore the world of flowers. They may grow from the ground, stems, bushes, or trees. Beautiful close-up color photographs of the many varieties of flowers embellish this brief introduction.

891 *It Could Still Be a Lake.* Children's Press, 1996, ISBN 0-516-06051-1. SERIES: Rookie

Fowler, Allan (cont.)

Read-About Science. SUBJECTS: Geography. RL B. LEXILE 580L.

It may be called a sea, but a lake is a body of water that has land all around it. The many colorful photographs plainly demonstrate the types of lakes, how they are formed, and pollution problems and solutions.

892 *It Could Still Be Coral.* Children's Press, 1996, ISBN 0-516-20028-3. SERIES: Rookie Read-About Science. SUBJECTS: Oceans and ocean life. RL B. LEXILE NC630L.

Beautiful coral reefs all began with coral polyps that can be classified as both animal and mineral. Wondrously colorful photographs exhibit excellent examples of coral and coral reefs.

893 *Lands of Grass.* Children's Press, 2000, ISBN 0-516-21213-3. SERIES: Rookie Read-About Science. SUBJECTS: Ecology; Geography; Grasslands. RL B.

Highlighted by captioned color photographs that identify the many types of grasslands around the world, this clear introduction includes information about the environment and the animals that inhabit it.

894 *Let's Talk About Tongues.* Children's Press, 1997, ISBN 0-516-20324-X. SERIES: Rookie Read-About Science. SUBJECTS: Animals — Growth and development; Human body — Tongue. RL B.

There are many different uses for a tongue. Humans use them for tasting and speaking; animals may also use them to catch food or keep clean. Great color photographs catch the action of tongues of both man and animals.

895 *Life in a Pond.* Children's Press, 1996, ISBN 0-516-06053-8. SERIES: Rookie Read-About Science. SUBJECTS: Ecology; Geography; Pond life. RL B. LEXILE AD660L.

Visit a pond to see all kinds of life, from plankton, the very smallest lifeform, to fish, ducks, and beavers. Numerous color photographs enhance the text with clear illustration of life in and around a pond.

896 *Life in a Tide Pool.* Children's Press, 1996, ISBN 0-516-20031-3. SERIES: Rookie Read-About Science. SUBJECTS: Ecology; Geography. RL B. LEXILE 520L.

How are tide pools created? In this clear presentation, with full-page color photographic examples throughout, tidal action and the numerous sea animals that inhabit tide pools are ably described.

897 *Life in a Wetland.* Children's Press, 1998, ISBN 0-516-20799-7. SERIES: Rookie Read-About Science. SUBJECTS: Ecology; Geography. RL B. LEXILE NC660L.

There are many different types of wetlands, from swamps and marshes to bogs. Captioned color photographs identify types of wetlands around the world and the many plants and animals that call them home.

898 *Living in a Desert.* Children's Press, 2000, ISBN 0-516-21560-4. SERIES: Rookie Read-About Science. SUBJECTS: Deserts; Ecology. RL B.

Very little rain falls in desert areas, but all around the world animals and people have adapted to living and working there. A helpful map of the world deserts and many colorful photographs enable readers to better understand life in a desert.

899 *Living in a Rain Forest.* Children's Press, 2000, ISBN 0-516-21555-8. SERIES: Rookie Read-About Geography. SUBJECTS: Ecology; Rain forests. RL B.

Many unique plants and animals live below the canopies of rain forests around the world. Color photographs provide good examples of the many different kinds of life found there.

900 *Living in the Arctic.* Children's Press, 2000, ISBN 0-516-21561-2. SERIES: Rookie Read-About Geography. SUBJECTS: Arctic; Ecology; Geography. RL B.

Most of the Arctic is made up of water, but there are some people, animals, and plants that survive on the tundra. Color photographs with brief captions highlight the text and a map serves as a locator.

901 *Living in the Mountains.* Children's Press, 2000, ISBN 0-516-21563-9. SERIES: Rookie Read-About Geography. SUBJECTS: Ecology; Mountains. RL B.

In mountainous areas people live on plateaus, in valleys, or on the mountains themselves. Numerous color photographs illuminate this simple introduction to mountains around the world.

902 *Living on Farms*. Children's Press, 2000, ISBN 0-516-21564-7. SERIES: Rookie Read-About Geography. SUBJECTS: Farm and country life. RL B.

On family farms most of the food is homegrown. Today most of the country's food comes from larger farms that specialize in certain crops or animals. Color photographs visually elaborate on a variety of farms and farming techniques.

903 *Living on the Plains*. Children's Press, 2000, ISBN 0-516-21565-5. SERIES: Rookie Read-About Geography. SUBJECTS: Ecology; Geography. RL B. LEXILE 600L.

Covering most of the central United States and Canada, the plains area is rich in farmlands because of glacial activity long ago. Archival photographs, maps, and color photographs aid in the description of the Great Plains and prairie lands.

904 *A Look at Teeth*. Children's Press, 1999, ISBN 0-516-21217-6. SERIES: Rookie Read-About Science. SUBJECTS: Human body — Teeth. RL B.

Find out about human teeth and how they grow and develop, as well as the importance of teeth for animals. Pictorial examples of a variety of teeth and a demonstration of good dental hygiene enhance the information.

905 *Maple Trees*. Children's Press, 2001, ISBN 0-516-21684-8. SERIES: Rookie Read-About Science. SUBJECTS: Trees. RL B. LEXILE 600L.

With a focus on the maple, beginning readers find out how trees grow and the many products that come from them, such as maple syrup. Full-page color photographs offer close-ups of maple trees and the sugaring process.

906 *North America*. Children's Press, 2001, ISBN 0-516-21671-6. SERIES: Rookie Read-About Geography. SUBJECTS: North America. RL B.

North America is 3,000 miles wide between the Atlantic and Pacific Oceans. As the text describes the diversity of geography and climate, color photographs provide clear visual examples.

907 *Of Mice and Rats*. Children's Press, 1998, ISBN 0-516-20800-4. SERIES: Rookie Read-About Science. SUBJECTS: Animals; Mice; Rats. RL B. LEXILE NC660L.

Belonging to a group of animals called, rats and mice may be people's pets but they are also pests. Sharp color photographs allow the reader to see rats and mice up close in a variety of habitats.

908 *Pine Trees*. Children's Press, 2001, ISBN 0-516-21685-6. SERIES: Rookie Read-About Science. SUBJECTS: Trees. RL B. LEXILE 620L.

As an evergreen, a pine tree is always green and has needles for storing water. Color photographs on every page show the trees' growth and development and the useful products derived from them.

909 *Plants That Eat Animals*. Children's Press, 2001, ISBN 0-516-21683-X. SERIES: Rookie Read-About Science. SUBJECTS: Plants. RL B.

Plants such as the Venus Flytrap, Sundew, and Bladderwort do not get the minerals they need to grow from the soil, so they eat insects. From microscopic pictures to explicit color photographs showing plants eating animals, the visuals enhance the text.

910 *Raccoons*. Children's Press, 2000, ISBN 0-516-21590-6. SERIES: Rookie Read-About Science. SUBJECTS: Animals; Raccoons. RL B.

Raccoons live in the forest of North and South America and may be near your own backyard. Plentiful color photographs augment the text, which covers the birth, development, and habits of the masked animals.

911 *Seeing Seabirds*. Children's Press, 1999, ISBN 0-516-21210-9. SERIES: Rookie Read-About Science. SUBJECTS: Birds; Seashore. RL B. LEXILE NC640L.

Color photographs identify ten different seabirds, often shown with their young. Learn about nesting and feeding habits along the shores of lakes, seas, and oceans.

912 *Shellfish Aren't Fish*. Children's Press, 1998, ISBN 0-516-20802-0. SERIES: Rookie Read-About Science. SUBJECTS: Mollusks. RL B. LEXILE NC710L.

Mollusks — such as clams, mussels, oysters and scallops — are all animals with soft bodies inside a hard shell. Great underwater photography shows the bivalves living and moving within their environment.

Fowler, Allan (cont.)

913 *Simple Machines.* Children's Press, 2001, ISBN 0-516-21680-5. SERIES: Rookie Read-About Science. SUBJECTS: Simple machines. RL B.

Levers, wheels, axles, inclined planes, and pulleys are four types of simple machines that have few parts. Color photographs ably illustrate many practical examples of simple machines from everyday life.

914 *A Snail's Pace.* Children's Press, 1999, ISBN 0-516-20812-8. SERIES: Rookie Read-About Science. SUBJECTS: Snails. RL B.

Thousands of different kinds of snails live on land and in water, both fresh and salt water. Clear, crisp color photographs identify some of the varieties and show how they move and eat.

915 *South America.* Children's Press, 2001, ISBN 0-516-21672-4. SERIES: Rookie Read-About Geography. SUBJECTS: South America. RL B.

In this brief introduction to South America, learn about its geography, climate, people, and animals. Colorful photographs carefully highlight the major land areas and inhabitants of this continent.

916 *Spiders Are Not Insects.* Children's Press, 1996, ISBN 0-516-06054-6. SERIES: Rookie Read-About Science. SUBJECTS: Spiders. RL B. LEXILE 550L.

Spiders are arachnids that may live in water, trees, woods, or even in your home, and are helpful because of the many insects they eat. Close-up photography and picture-in-picture shots zoom in on the great variety of spiders and their webs.

917 *Squirrels and Chipmunks.* Children's Press, 1997, ISBN 0-516-20323-1. SERIES: Rookie Read-About Science. SUBJECTS: Chipmunks; Prairie dogs; Squirrels. RL B. LEXILE 580L.

Belonging to the rodent family, there are many types of squirrels and chipmunks around the world. Sharp color photographs aid in easy identification of the animals within their habitats.

918 *Stars in the Sky.* Children's Press, 1996, ISBN 0-516-06055-4. SERIES: Rookie Read-About Science. SUBJECTS: Astronomy and astronomers. RL B. LEXILE 570L.

The focus of this simple presentation is on stars; how we can see them, what they are they made of, and how far away they are. Photographs of far-off galaxies, star clusters, and constellations help to clarify this brief introduction.

919 *Stars of the Sea.* Children's Press, 2000, ISBN 0-516-21214-1. SERIES: Rookie Read-About Science. SUBJECTS: Oceans and ocean life. RL B.

Color photographs complement the text in this exploration of the world of sea stars by visually extending the information on the size, movement, and habitat of starfish and their relatives, the sea cucumber and sand dollar.

920 *Taking Root.* Children's Press, 2000, ISBN 0-516-21591-4. SERIES: Rookie Read-About Science. SUBJECTS: Plants. RL B.

Find out about the nature and purpose of roots, and which you have eaten lately. Captioned color photographs provide a close-up look at roots and how they grow.

921 *Telling Tails.* Children's Press, 1998, ISBN 0-516-20803-9. SERIES: Rookie Read-About Science. SUBJECTS: Animals; Animals — Growth and development. RL B. LEXILE 520L.

Animals of all kinds use their tails — short or long, curly or straight — for a variety of purposes, including swimming, balance, climbing, expressing emotion, swatting flies, and so forth. Tails of many animals are featured prominently in numerous color photographs.

922 *These Birds Can't Fly.* Children's Press, 1998, ISBN 0-516-20798-9. SERIES: Rookie Read-About Science. SUBJECTS: Birds; Penguins. RL B. LEXILE 510L.

They may not be able to fly but ostriches can run and penguins can swim very fast. Concentrating on the many birds that do not fly, captioned photographs clearly identify them within their natural surroundings.

923 *They Could Still Be Mountains.* Children's Press, 1997, ISBN 0-516-20320-7. SERIES: Rookie Read-About Science. SUBJECTS: Mountains. RL B. LEXILE 600L.

In a simple comparative analysis between the Rockies and the Appalachian Mountains, similarities and differences are identified. Closely following the text, color photographs extend the information.

924 *The Top and Bottom of the World.* Children's Press, 1997, ISBN 0-516-20321-5. SERIES: Rookie Read-About Science. SUBJECTS: Antarctica; Arctic. RL B. LEXILE 710L.

The regions around the north and south poles are very cold, with winters consisting of six months of darkness. Numerous color photographs act as a travel guide to the areas, featuring the geography, plants, and animals.

925 *Where Land Meets Sea.* Children's Press, 1997, ISBN 0-516-20322-3. SERIES: Rookie Read-About Science. SUBJECTS: Seashore. RL B. LEXILE NC610L.

There are many different types of seashores, from rocky cliffs to marshes. Specific pictorial examples of where the land meets the sea offer further insight.

926 *The Wonder of a Waterfall.* Children's Press, 1999, ISBN 0-516-20813-6. SERIES: Rookie Read-About Science. SUBJECTS: Geography. RL B.

Feel like a tourist as you travel the world learning about the spectacular waterfalls there are to see. Beautiful color photographs add interest and excitement to the description of how waterfalls are formed.

Franco, Betsy

927 *Grandpa's Quilt.* Ill. by Linda A. Bild. Children's Press, 1999, ISBN 0-516-21604-X. SERIES: Rookie Reader. SUBJECTS: Family life — Fiction; Grandparents — Fiction. RL B. LEXILE 110L.

From the bed where he stays all winter long, Grandpa reads stories to Anna, Ben, and Lilly. Because the quilt is too short, Grandpa's toes are cold and the grandchildren cut and sew to make it just right. Cozy illustrations featuring curly-haired children are warm and bright, just like Grandpa's quilt.

928 *My Pinkie Finger.* Ill. by Margeaux Lucas. Children's Press, 2001, ISBN 0-516-22221-X. SERIES: Rookie Reader. SUBJECTS: Human body — Growth — Fiction; Stories in rhyme. RL B.

Comparing the length of his pants to the charted height marks on a door frame, a young boy notices how much he is growing. Spirited drawings in lively colors reflect the joy of family life and the pride in a growing boy's accomplishments.

929 *Shells.* Ill. by Kristin Sorra. Children's Press, 2000, ISBN 0-516-22012-8. SERIES: Rookie Reader. SUBJECTS: Shells; Stories in rhyme. RL B.

From seashells and pasta shells to turtle shells and taco shells, children examine the many different types of shells. With a brief phrase about each shell, the full-page illustrations visually expand the text and depict a child's curiosity about the object.

930 *Silly Sally.* Ill. by Stacey Lamb. Children's Press, 2002, ISBN 0-516-22492-1. SERIES: Rookie Reader. SUBJECTS: Babies — Fiction; Siblings — Fiction. RL A.

Everything that her big brother does makes Sally smile. There are just two words per page, and the simple line drawings awash in color playfully embellish each scene of familial love.

Frasier, Debra

931 *On the Day You Were Born.* Ill. by author. Harcourt, 1991, ISBN 0-15-257995-8. SUBJECTS: Ecology; Human body — Growth. RL C.

A grand celebration of the wonders of the natural world told in cumulative rhythmic language with stunning graphics. The text touches on migration, the spinning earth, gravity, the sun, stars, and moon, tides and rain, trees, air, and finally singing people.

Freedman, Russell

932 *Dinosaurs and Their Young.* Ill. by Leslie Morrill. Holiday House, 1983, o.p. SUBJECTS: Dinosaurs; Science and scientists. RL C.

How the recent discovery of a duckbill dinosaur nursery by a Montana high school teacher has altered scientists' ideas about how dinosaurs lived is detailed by this 1984 Newbery Medal winner.

Freeman, Martha

933 *Mrs. Wow Never Wanted a Cow*. Ill. by Steven Salerno. Random House, 2006, ISBN 0-375-83418-4. SERIES: Beginner Books. SUBJECTS: Cows — Fiction; Pets — Cats — Fiction; Pets — Dogs — Fiction. RL B.

Initially unhappy when a cow turns up in her yard, Mrs. Wow suddenly realizes the cow will help mow the grass and will give her milk to make ice cream. Intensely colored illustrations, boldly outlined in black, add to the humor.

French, Vivian

934 *Mrs. Hippo's Pizza Parlor*. Ill. by Clive Scruton. Kingfisher, 1999, ISBN 0-7534-5823-3. SERIES: I Am Reading. SUBJECTS: Food — Fiction; Hippopotami — Fiction. RL B.

Business is slow at Mrs. Hippo's Pizza Parlor and William is worried there won't be enough money for a birthday bike. But advertising in a special way certainly pays off. Humor abounds in these exhilarating, action-filled illustrations that are right on target.

Freschet, Berniece

935 *Little Black Bear Goes for a Walk*. Ill. by Glen Rounds. Scribner, 1977, o.p. SUBJECTS: Bears — Fiction. RL B.

Little Bear's first exploration on his own introduces him to bugs, porcupines, water, bees — and honey. The expressive ink sketches add humor.

936 *Lizard Lying in the Sun*. Ill. by Glen Rounds. Scribner, 1975, o.p. SUBJECTS: Lizards; Nature; Science and scientists. RL B.

Good information about lizards is presented in an absorbing way by focusing on one lizard. Intriguing ink sketches enhance the text.

937 *Moose Baby*. Ill. by Jim Arnosky. Putnam, 1979, o.p. SERIES: See and Read Nature. SUBJECTS: Growing up; Moose; Nature. RL C.

Encounters with a skunk, a coyote, and fighting bull moose mark a baby moose's first year. The ink and wash sketches are very appealing.

938 *Possum Baby*. Ill. by Jim Arnosky. Putnam, 1978, o.p. SERIES: See and Read Nature. SUBJECTS: Growing up; Nature; Opossums. RL C.

The trials of growing up are told from the point of view of a young possum — from birth to independence. The tale is interrupted briefly to give information about other marsupials. Arnosky's black ink drawings are very appealing.

Friedman, Dawn

939 *Dance, Annie*. Ill. by Nicole in den Bosch. Children's Press, 2001, ISBN 0-516-22233-3. SERIES: Rookie Reader. SUBJECTS: African Americans — Fiction; Dancers and dancing — Fiction; Stories in rhyme. RL A.

At her recital, Annie dances her way through the entire performance. Exuberantly detailed illustrations show the intricacies of each dance step and the joy of movement.

Friedman, Mel, and Ellen Weiss

940 *Kitten Castle*. Ill. by Lynn Adams. Kane, pap., 2001, ISBN 1-57565-103-3. SERIES: Math Matters. SUBJECTS: Mathematics — Fiction; Pets — Cats — Fiction. RL B. LEXILE 280L.

Adding Streak's babies to their pet menagerie proves difficult until Anna and Tom build a castle fit for four frolicking kittens using a variety of shapes. Colorful, detailed drawings illustrate geometric shapes in an entertaining and lively presentation.

Friedman, Michael

941 *Superman's First Flight*. Ill. by Dean Motter. Scholastic, pap., 2000, ISBN 0-439-09550-6. SERIES: Hello Reader! SUBJECTS: Adventure stories; Superheroes — Fiction. RL B. LEXILE 280L.

After saving a life in a horrific explosion, Clark Kent realizes his superhuman abilities and learns the true story behind his birth. Realistic watercolors depict the life of Superman using interesting angles of perspective.

Friend, Catherine

942 *Eddie the Raccoon*. Ill. by Wong Herbert Yee. Candlewick, 2004, o.p. SERIES: Brand

New Readers. SUBJECTS: Raccoons — Fiction. RL A.

Poor Eddie. Whether he is raiding the chicken coop, eating jam, or chasing a skunk, the little raccoon always has a problem. Pastel illustrations enhance the four simple stories for beginning readers, injecting them with humor and fun.

943 *Funny Ruby*. Ill. by Rachel Merriman. Candlewick, 2000, o.p. SERIES: Brand New Readers. SUBJECTS: Sheep — Fiction. RL A.

Follow Ruby the sheep as she jumps, eats, and plays. Repetitive words and phrases are humorously augmented by playful, childlike drawings. Reading tips for parents to share are included.

944 *Silly Ruby*. Ill. by Rachel Merriman. Candlewick, 2000, o.p. SERIES: Brand New Readers. SUBJECTS: Sheep — Fiction. RL A.

Ruby the sheep has more adventures as she plays in the mud, eats cow's food, and is covered in apples after kicking the old apple tree. With humor and fun, simple pastel illustrations visually extend the four short stories for beginning readers.

The Friendly Beasts

945 *The Friendly Beasts: A Traditional Christmas Carol*. Ill. by Sarah Chamberlain. Dutton, 1991, ISBN 0-525-44773-3. SUBJECTS: Christmas; Cumulative tales; Music and musicians. RL B.

Multicolored linoleum block prints are highlighted by hand with pastels of wheat and blue to accentuate the pastoral wonder of Jesus' birth.

Friskey, Margaret

946 *Indian Two Feet and the Wolf Cubs*. Ill. by John Hawkinson. Childrens Press, 1971, o.p. SUBJECTS: Native Americans — Fiction; Pets — Wild animals — Fiction; Wolves — Fiction. RL B.

Indian Two Feet spends so much time watching the wolf family that he is included in their family circle. When he tries to adopt a cub, he is advised that other wolves will take care of any orphans. Watercolor drawings are especially good of the animals.

947 *Three Sides and the Round One*. Ill. by Mary Gehr. Childrens Press, 1973, o.p. SUBJECTS: Concepts — Shape; Mathematics; Stories in rhyme. RL B.

Creative, rhythmic language introduces shapes of ordinary objects. Striking, simple shapes stand out on bright solid backgrounds.

Frith, Margaret

948 *Mermaid Island*. Ill. by Julie Durrell. Grosset & Dunlap, 1997, o.p. SERIES: Eek! Stories to Make You Shriek. SUBJECTS: Mythical creatures — Fiction; Seashore — Fiction. RL B.

On her summer vacation at the beach, Jane befriends a young girl named Molly who wears pants even on the hottest days. Who is she really and why did she leave fish scales in the tub after her bath? Colorful cartoon-like illustrations provide visual clues for this mildly scary story.

Frith, Michael K.

949 *I'll Teach My Dog One Hundred Words*. Ill. by P. D. Eastman. Beginner Books, 1973, ISBN 0-394-82692-2. SERIES: Bright and Early Books. SUBJECTS: Humorous stories; Stories in rhyme. RL B.

Rhythmic humor teaching the reader, as well as the dog, 100 new words; accented by excellent comic drawings.

Fritz, Jean

950 *Surprising Myself*. Photos by Andrea F. Pfleger. Richard Owen, 1992, ISBN 1-878450-37-9. SERIES: Meet the Author. SUBJECTS: Biographies — Women; Books and reading; Writers and writing. RL C.

In typically refreshing style, Jean Fritz outlines how she writes — and relaxes. Photographs show her at play at Virgin Gorda, and with her grandsons, as well as at work. Lively and interesting text.

Froman, Robert

951 *Bigger and Smaller*. Ill. by Gioia Fiammenghi. HarperCollins, 1971, o.p. SUBJECTS: Concepts — Size. RL C.

The relative nature of size is emphasized and some entertaining relationships are explored. Ink and wash drawings are graphically interesting.

Fuller, Jill

952 *Springtime Addition*. Scholastic, 2004, ISBN 0-516-24422-1. SERIES: Rookie Read-About Math. SUBJECTS: Mathematics; Mathematics — Addition. RL B. LEXILE 120L.

Using the beauty of nature during springtime, learn to add. Sharp, carefully formatted color photographs offer easy and exciting ways to practice addition.

953 *Toy Box Subtraction*. Scholastic, 2004, ISBN 0-516-24423-X. SERIES: Rookie Read-About Math. SUBJECTS: Mathematics; Mathematics — Subtraction. RL B. LEXILE 380L.

With the help of his friends, a young boy empties his overflowing toy box, providing an exercise in subtraction. Fun, colorful photographs offer clear examples of subtraction problems using an incident from everyday life.

Funai, Mamoru

954 *Moke and Poki in the Rain Forest*. Ill. by author. HarperCollins, 1971, o.p. SERIES: I Can Read. SUBJECTS: Folklore — Hawaii; Hawaii — Fiction; Rainbows — Fiction. RL A.

Moke and Poki are six-inch menehunes. With the help of their friends they build a house, sing to the moon, sail a bean-pod canoe, and search for rainbows. Turquoise and rose-brown colors create a tropical setting for the wee friends.

G

Gackenbach, Dick

955 *Hattie Be Quiet, Hattie Be Good*. Ill. by author. HarperCollins, 1977, ISBN 0-06-021952-1. SERIES: Early I Can Read. SUBJECTS: Behavior — Obedient — Fiction; Rabbits — Fiction. RL A.

Hattie Rabbit's effort to please her mother by uncharacteristically spending time quietly is misinterpreted, as is her effort to help her friend Shirley feel perkier. Fat, cuddly rabbits with pumpkin coloring help portray Hattie's zest for life.

956 *Hattie Rabbit*. Ill. by author. HarperCollins, 1976, ISBN 0-06-021940-8. SERIES: Early I Can Read. SUBJECTS: Friendship — Fiction; Rabbits — Fiction. RL A.

Hattie makes two decisions: She likes her mother because she is warm, soft, and furry, and the money she won by tricking her friends is a poor substitute for their friendship. Brown and turquoise drawings are of appealing rabbits.

957 *Hattie, Tom and the Chicken Witch (a play and a story)*. Ill. by author. HarperCollins, 1980, ISBN 0-06-021959-9. SERIES: I Can Read. SUBJECTS: Easter — Fiction; Plays — Fiction; Rabbits — Fiction. RL A.

Hattie Rabbit is allowed a part in the Easter play only when Linda Chicken twists her ankle. Chickens and rabbits are important to Easter, they decide. Sympathetic animal characters are drawn in rose, beige, and gray.

958 *Hound and Bear*. Ill. by author. Houghton Mifflin, 1976, o.p. SUBJECTS: Bears — Fiction; Friendship — Fiction; Pets — Dogs — Fiction. RL B.

Hound loses out on his own birthday when he tricks Bear into sleeping too long; he loses a present when he tries another trick. Bear gets the best present of all when Hound promises not to play any more tricks. The gentle moral is illustrated with gray and rust washes.

959 *Hurray for Hattie Rabbit!* Ill. by author. HarperCollins, 1986, ISBN 0-06-021960-2. SERIES: Early I Can Read. SUBJECTS: Mothers — Fiction; Rabbits — Fiction. RL B.

The mischievous, sad, smug, and repentant expressions of two cuddly friends, Hattie Rabbit and Rosie Pig, are captivating. Their mothers find creative solutions for sleeplessness and the girls have a bet for who will get her mother to say "yes" first.

960 *Mother Rabbit's Son Tom*. Ill. by author. HarperCollins, 1977, ISBN 0-06-021947-5. SERIES: Early I Can Read. SUBJECTS: Rabbits — Fiction. RL B.

Tom's steady diet of a hamburger with onion, ketchup, and pickles on a poppy-seed roll has results even his parents do not expect. It is also clear that Tom's mother should never have consented to a dinosaur for a pet! Gentle, simple illustrations are rust and beige with a dark outline.

Gage, Wilson

961 *The Crow and Mrs. Gaddy*. Ill. by Marylin Hafner. Scholastic, pap., 1985, ISBN 0-590-44507-3. SERIES: Read-Alone. SUBJECTS: Humorous stories. RL C.

Mrs. Gaddy has a running feud with a mischievous crow. Broad humor is enhanced by detailed ink and wash drawings.

962 *Down in the Boondocks*. Ill. by Glen Rounds. Greenwillow, 1977, o.p. SERIES: Read-Alone. SUBJECTS: Humorous stories; Stories in rhyme. RL C.

This sprightly comic story of a robber scared away by the racket in the boondocks that the deaf farmer cannot hear is told in wonderfully repetitive, rhythmic style. Scratchy ink drawings colored with textured brown and avocado are marvelously appropriate.

963 *Mrs. Gaddy and the Fast-Growing Vine*. Ill. by Marylin Hafner. Greenwillow, 1985, o.p. SERIES: Read-Alone. SUBJECTS: Humorous stories. RL B.

The goat Mrs. Gaddy buys as a last resort to trim the vine that grows like lightning is almost as hard to get rid of as the vine. Comic sketches are in green and brown.

964 *Mrs. Gaddy and the Ghost*. Ill. by Marylin Hafner. Greenwillow, 1979, o.p. SERIES: Read-Alone. SUBJECTS: Ghost stories; Humorous stories. RL B.

Mrs. Gaddy's inventive devices for getting rid of a noisy ghost all fail, but she changes her mind about getting rid of the ghost when she hears it crying. Excellent illustrations are in rose and brown.

965 *My Stars, It's Mrs. Gaddy!* Ill. by Marylin Hafner. Greenwillow, 1991, ISBN 0-688-10514-9. SUBJECTS: Farm and country life — Fiction; Ghost stories; Humorous stories. RL A.

This anthology of three previously published Mrs. Gaddy stories retains the original charming illustrations by Marylin Hafner. Mrs. Gaddy finds accommodation with her resident ghost, persists in her skirmishes of mean tricks with the crow, and deals with a goat and a vine devouring her house.

966 *Squash Pie*. Ill. by Glen Rounds. Greenwillow, 1976, o.p. SUBJECTS: Humorous stories; Wordplay. RL B.

The farmer's seeing-eye potatoes, corn ears, and dogwood tree's bark do not catch the thief stealing his squash. When the farmer's wife discovers she likes squash pie, no more are stolen. Droll pen-and-ink drawings have textured light blue and orange highlights.

Galbraith, Kathryn O.

967 *Roommates*. Ill. by Mark Graham. Macmillan, 1990, o.p. SUBJECTS: Babies — Fiction; Siblings — Fiction. RL A.

When a new baby is expected, Mimi and Beth become unwilling roommates. Their quarrels and their support of one another are presented sympathetically. Soft watercolor cover in blues with pencil drawings illustrates the text.

Gallimard Jeunesse

968 *Castles*. Ill. by C. Millet and D. Millet. Scholastic, 1990, ISBN 0-590-46377-2. SERIES: First Discovery Book. SUBJECTS: Castles. RL C.

Clear overlays show inside and outside the turret, the whole family sharing a bed, and both sides of the wall during an assault. The design adds dimension and visual interest. Spiral binding is inside a traditional one. Information is provided on everyday life in a castle as well as during wartime.

Gallimard Jeunesse, and Laura Bour

969 *The River*. Ill. by Laura Bour. Scholastic, 1992, ISBN 0-590-47128-7. SERIES: First Discovery Book. SUBJECTS: Animals; Nature; Plants. RL C.

Clear overlays show the river level during flood and drought, birds swimming and diving or nesting, dragonflies molting, and riverbanks clean and polluted. Drawings of birds, fish, amphibians, people, and insects along the river are detailed and fascinating.

Gallimard Jeunesse, Claude Delafosse, and Pierre-Marie Valat

970 *The Camera: Snapshots, Movies, Videos, and Cartoons*. Ill. by Pierre-Marie Valat.

Gallimard Jeunesse, Claude Delafosse, and Pierre-Marie Valat (cont.)

Scholastic, 1993, ISBN 0-590-47129-5. SERIES: First Discovery Book. SUBJECTS: Photography and photographers. RL C.

A fascinating first look at point-and-shoot, Polaroid, and video cameras and animated cartoons using images painted on clear pages to show the front and back of the image. Pages move easily on spiral binding.

Gambrell, Linda B.

971 *Party Fun*. DK, 2003, ISBN 0-7894-9994-0. SERIES: DK Readers. SUBJECTS: Birthdays — Fiction. RL B.

From invitations and decorations to presents and party favors, readers will learn what makes a birthday party fun. Bold, close-up color photographs with a unique border and added pictures offer a surprise look into every child's favorite day.

Gantos, Jack

972 *Best in Show for Rotten Ralph*. Ill. by Nicole Rubel. Farrar, Straus & Giroux, 2005, ISBN 0-374-36358-7. SUBJECTS: Pets — Cats — Fiction; Self-esteem — Fiction. RL B.

Encouraged by Sarah to try and beat cousin Percy at the cat show, Rotten Ralph decides just to be himself and wins a prize — "The Worst at Being Best in Show." Delightfully humorous and detailed illustrations show Ralph at his rotten best.

973 *Practice Makes Perfect for Rotten Ralph*. Ill. by Nicole Rubel. Farrar, Straus & Giroux, 2002, ISBN 0-374-36356-0. SUBJECTS: Behavior — Cheating — Fiction; Pets — Cats — Fiction. RL B. LEXILE 460L.

At a carnival, Ralph's rivalry with Percy intensifies. Percy keeps winning prizes and Ralph keeps losing, until he begins cheating at the games. Comical cartoon drawings enhance the impossibly funny predicaments that challenge Ralph as he always learns a lesson . . . for the moment.

974 *Rotten Ralph Feels Rotten*. Ill. by Nicole Rubel. Farrar, Straus & Giroux, 2004, ISBN 0-374-36357-9. SUBJECTS: Illness — Fiction; Pets — Cats — Fiction. RL B.

Instead of eating the healthy food that Sarah serves, Ralph raids the neighborhood trash cans and begins to feel very rotten. Engaging colorful cartoons in framed panels embellish the humorous story with hysterically funny details.

975 *Rotten Ralph Helps Out*. Ill. by Nicole Rubel. Farrar, Straus & Giroux, 2001, ISBN 0-374-36355-2. SUBJECTS: Pets — Cats — Fiction; School stories. RL B. LEXILE 430L.

Ralph is helping again. This time with Sarah's class project about Ancient Egypt. Creative detailed illustrations extend the story by providing images of Ralph's "help" and visual clues of more fun to come.

Gauch, Patricia L.

976 *Aaron and the Green Mountain Boys*. Ill. by Margot Tomes. McDonald, 1987, o.p. SUBJECTS: Historical fiction; United States — Revolutionary War — Fiction. RL C.

Although an eager boy wants to help in the fight against the British, his part of chopping wood and washing mugs at first seems very unglamorous. A well-told history from a child's view has exceptional, authentic pen and ink drawings.

Gave, Marc

977 *Monkey See, Monkey Do*. Ill. by Jacqueline Rogers. Scholastic, 1993, ISBN 0-590-45801-9. SERIES: Hello Reader! SUBJECTS: Monkeys — Fiction; Stories in rhyme. RL A.

Playful watercolor illustrations make the best of a limited, repetitive text, adding humor, visual interest, and an appealing punch line.

Gelman, Rita G.

978 *Hey, Kid!* Ill. by Carol Nicklaus. Watts, 1977, o.p. SERIES: Easy-Read Story. SUBJECTS: Gifts and gift giving — Fiction; Stories in rhyme. RL B.

A girl's surprise box holds a friendly critter who talks and sings until she gives it to another curious child. Ink drawings have colored pencil and three-color painted background. The ghostlike visitor is defined with pencil.

979 *Mole in a Hole*. Ill. by Holly Hannon. Random House, 2000, o.p. SERIES: Step into

Reading. SUBJECTS: Animals — Fiction; Rebuses; Stories in rhyme. RL A. LEXILE NP.

Mole is lonely and invites other animals to his home, which is too small and dark for them. Stumbling upon Ms. Mole proves to be his lucky day. Gentle, full-page pastel illustrations complement a cozy animal rebus story.

980 *More Spaghetti, I Say!* Ill. by Mort Gerberg. Scholastic, 1992, ISBN 0-590-45783-7. SERIES: Hello Reader! SUBJECTS: Humorous stories; Monkeys — Fiction; Stories in rhyme. RL A.

Minnie is so busy eating spaghetti she hasn't time to play with Freddy. Lively watercolor illustrations match the light tone of the rhyme.

981 *Pizza Pat.* Ill. by Will Terry. Random House, 1999, o.p. SERIES: Step into Reading. SUBJECTS: Food — Fiction; Stories in rhyme. RL B. LEXILE NP.

In a parody of "The House that Jack Built," Pizza Pat makes a delicious pizza that is stolen by mice. Lighthearted drawings add humor and zest to the pizza-making *and* pizza-stealing process.

George, Olivia

982 *The Weather.* Ill. by Rusty Fletcher. Scholastic, 2005, ISBN 0-516-24968-1. SERIES: My First Reader. SUBJECTS: Trees — Fiction; Weather — Fiction. RL A. LEXILE 20L.

Focusing on a little girl and the tree outside her window, brightly colored full-page illustrations depict the changing seasons. A word list is included.

Geringer, Laura

983 *The Stubborn Pumpkin.* Ill. by Holly Berry. Scholastic, pap., 1999, ISBN 0-590-10850-6. SERIES: Scholastic Reader. SUBJECTS: Pumpkins. RL B. LEXILE 260L.

This variation on the story of "The Great Big Enormous Turnip" features a giant pumpkin that stubbornly refuses to come off the vine. Hilarious illustrations feature a variety of people and animals struggling to pull the pumpkin free.

Gerver, Jane E.

984 *The Big Red Sled.* Ill. by Priscilla Burris. Scholastic, 2001, ISBN 0-439-20434-8. SERIES: Hello Reader! SUBJECTS: Animals — Fiction; Bears — Fiction; Stories in rhyme. RL A. LEXILE BR.

While his parents are sleeping, a little bear sneaks outside to go sledding. After playing in the snow with all the animals, Fred thinks he is lost until he hears familiar loud snores. Playful, loving illustrations elaborate on a small one's adventure all alone.

Ghigna, Charles

985 *Oh My, Pumpkin Pie!* Ill. by Kenneth Spengler. Random House, 2005, ISBN 0-375-92945-2. SERIES: Step into Reading. SUBJECTS: Pumpkins — Fiction; Stories in rhyme. RL B.

Pumpkins come in a variety of shapes and sizes and can be used in many entertaining and delicious ways. Simple, orange-toned art complements the short sentences for beginning readers, providing visual descriptions of the assortment of pumpkins.

Gibbons, Gail

986 *Dinosaurs, Dragonflies and Diamonds: All About Natural History Museums.* Ill. by author. Macmillan, 1988, ISBN 0-02-737240-5. SUBJECTS: Dinosaurs; Museums. RL B.

The variety and development of exhibits, the many people who work behind the scenes in a museum, and the research being done are skillfully outlined and illustrated with fascinating glimpses of museum life that include child visitors.

987 *Happy Birthday!* Ill. by author. Holiday House, 1986, ISBN 0-8234-0614-8. SUBJECTS: Birthdays. RL C.

Basic information about birthdays is illustrated in full-color decorative style with bright blue predominating.

988 *The Magnificent Morris Mouse Clubhouse.* Ill. by author. Watts, 1981, o.p. SERIES: Easy-Read Story. SUBJECTS: Animals — Fiction. RL A.

Morris the mouse's long, unwieldy tail knocks over a bucket of nails and one of paint and then a

Gibbons, Gail (cont.)

ladder when he tries to help his friends build a clubhouse. With care, he finds his tail useful for measuring, lifting, and balancing when he builds his own clubhouse. Blue and yellow washes illustrate the text.

989 *Puff . . . Flash . . . Bang! A Book About Signals*. Morrow, 1993, o.p. SUBJECTS: Signs and symbols. RL C.

Familiar sight and sound signals are described, from an alarm clock to a buoy, from sign language to a lighthouse. Vivid blues and greens predominate in the author's appealing drawings.

990 *Sharks*. Ill. by author. Holiday House, 1992, ISBN 0-8234-0960-0. SUBJECTS: Oceans and ocean life; Sharks. RL B.

There are about 350 different kinds of sharks, some of which are introduced with a gray drawing highlighted with chalk against the stylized bright blue and green of the sea. Details show the egg cases or live young, teeth, gills, and fins of a variety of sharks.

991 *Spiders*. Ill. by author. Holiday House, 1993, ISBN 0-8234-1006-4. SUBJECTS: Spiders. RL B.

The author describes and illustrates the differences between spiders and insects, molting and ballooning of spiderlings, spinning, and enemies of spiders. Basic information is presented with vivid blue, green, and brown illustrations.

992 *Stargazers*. Ill. by author. Holiday House, 1992, ISBN 0-8234-0983-X. SUBJECTS: Astronomy and astronomers; Science and scientists. RL C.

A little history, the difference between a refracting and a reflecting telescope, and a few of the most prominent features to be seen with the naked eye or binoculars are included in this simple book featuring a family of stargazers.

993 *Sun up, Sun Down*. Ill. by author. Harcourt, 1983, ISBN 0-15-282781-1. SUBJECTS: Astronomy and astronomers. RL B.

The effect of the sun on the everyday life of a small girl is outlined, from the patterns of sun and shadow to the grains that she eats. Rain, storms, and rainbows are discussed briefly in a text accompanied by the author's appealing illustrations.

994 *Trains*. Ill. by author. Holiday House, pap., 1987, ISBN 0-8234-0640-7. SUBJECTS: Trains. RL C.

Information regarding trains, such as types of engines and cars, loading and unloading, and signals for engineers and drivers of cars near tracks, is given. Strong primary-color graphics add appeal.

Giff, Patricia Reilly

995 *The Almost Awful Play*. Ill. by Susanna Natti. Puffin, pap., 1985, ISBN 0-14-050530-X. SUBJECTS: Plays — Fiction; School stories. RL B.

Thespian disaster turns into triumph with Ronald Morgan's quick thinking. Colored drawings help capture the spirit of school rivalries and friendship.

996 *Good Luck, Ronald Morgan!* Ill. by Susanna Natti. Penguin, 1996, o.p. SUBJECTS: Friendship — Fiction; Pets — Dogs — Fiction. RL B. LEXILE 240L.

While unsuccessfully training Lucky, his new birthday puppy, Ronald tries to make friends with the new neighbor girl and her cat. When Lucky retrieves her special baseball cap all is well. Energetic watercolor and ink illustrations enliven the humorous attempts to teach Lucky, who has a mind of his own.

997 *Happy Birthday, Ronald Morgan!* Ill. by Susanna Natti. Viking, 1986, o.p. SUBJECTS: Birthdays — Fiction; Friendship — Fiction; School stories. RL A.

Ronald Morgan has bad news — his birthday comes after school is out, and he has lost the friendship of his best friend. His teacher encourages him to make up; he does not notice the surreptitious preparations underway for a party. Full-color drawings illustrate very real situations.

998 *Ronald Morgan Goes to Bat*. Ill. by Susanna Natti. Viking, 1988, ISBN 0-670-81457-1. SUBJECTS: Self-esteem — Fiction; Sports — Baseball — Fiction. RL A.

Ronald's enthusiasm for baseball is originally outstripped by his skill, but some tips and practice improve his confidence. Bright, lively watercolors warm the sympathetic tale.

999 *Today Was a Terrible Day*. Ill. by Susanna Natti. Puffin, pap., 1984, ISBN 0-670-71830-0. SUBJECTS: Books and reading — Fiction; School stories; Self-esteem — Fiction. RL B.
One upbeat note from his teacher turns a day full of misery into one of joy for second grader Ronald Morgan. Comic drawings underline the mishaps and teasing of a boy anxious to please.

1000 *Watch Out, Ronald Morgan!* Ill. by Susanna Natti. Puffin, pap., 1986, ISBN 0-670-80433-9. SUBJECTS: Eyeglasses — Fiction; School stories. RL B.
Ronald's teacher encourages him to have his eyes checked when he seems to be tripping and squinting, and has trouble making visual distinctions. This upbeat book has emerald greens and royal blues in lively child-centered drawings.

Giganti, Paul, Jr.

1001 *Each Orange Had Eight Slices: A Counting Book*. Ill. by Donald Crews. Greenwillow, 1992, ISBN 0-688-10429-0. SUBJECTS: Concepts — Numbers. RL B.
Using familiar objects such as fruit with seeds, flowers with bugs, ducks with ducklings, and clowns with balloons, multiplication concepts are simply introduced. Graphically striking illustrations in primary colors are by Donald Crews.

Gilchrist, Theo E.

1002 *Halfway Up the Mountain*. Ill. by Glen Rounds. HarperCollins, 1978, o.p. SUBJECTS: Folklore — United States; Humorous stories. RL C.
Vivid, colorful language spices this traditional tale of a nearly blind old woman scaring off a bandit, Bloodcoe, as she tries to salt and pepper the beef and push the garlic bits inside. Wry pen and ink drawings are masterful.

Gillham, Bill

1003 *What's the Difference?* Photos by Fiona Horne. Putnam, 1986, o.p. SERIES: Look and Talk. SUBJECTS: Concepts; Visual perception. RL B.
The reader is asked to describe the differences between such things as a girl with long hair and one with braids and a big wheel and a bicycle. Basic differentiation is easy with excellent color photographs featuring primary colors.

Ginsburg, Mirra

1004 *The Night It Rained Pancakes*. Ill. by Douglas Florian. Greenwillow, 1975, o.p. SERIES: Read-Alone. SUBJECTS: Folklore — Russia; Russia — Fiction. RL B.
Clever Ivan's trickery enables his simple brother's tale of finding gold to be discredited. The traditional tale is told and illustrated with appropriately plain ink and wash drawings.

Gise, Joanne

1005 *Dogs*. Ill. by Roseanna Pistolesi. Troll, 1990, o.p. SERIES: A Picture Book of. SUBJECTS: Pets — Dogs. RL B.
Each page is shared by background on and a drawing of a breed of dog, from the non-barking Basenji to more familiar household breeds. A line or two about why breeds developed special characteristics is included. This is a good introduction to dogs.

Glaser, Linda

1006 *Keep Your Socks On, Albert!* Ill. by Sally G. Ward. Dutton, 1992, o.p. SERIES: Dutton Easy Reader. SUBJECTS: Opossums — Fiction; Siblings — Fiction. RL A.
Albert's older sister, Shirley, tells him moral tales that are a little too scary — but Albert reciprocates when the blame shifts. Imaginative dialogue fits situations familiar to all siblings. Appealing drawings are primarily in royal blue, red, and palest green washes.

1007 *Rosie's Birthday Rat*. Ill. by Nancy Poydar. Delacorte, 1996, o.p. SERIES: Yearling First Choice Chapter Book. SUBJECTS: Birthdays — Fiction; Rats — Fiction. RL B. LEXILE 230L.
Much to her mother's chagrin, all Rosie wants for her birthday is a pet rat. After much cajoling, Midnight comes to live with them, and when she escapes, Rosie's mother rescues her. Watercolor and ink vignettes feature expressive close-ups of Midnight's journey to her new home.

Glass, Dr. Julie

1008 *Counting Sheep*. Ill. by Mike Wohnoutka. Random House, 2000, ISBN 0-375-80619-9. SERIES: Step into Reading + Math. SUBJECTS: Concepts — Numbers — Fiction; Mathematics — Fiction; Sleep — Fiction. RL A. LEXILE BR.

When a little boy cannot sleep, he begins counting sheep, one by one, then two by two. As more animals appear, he counts by threes and fours. The comical animal illustrations are well designed and effectively demonstrate the counting of sets.

1009 *A Dollar for a Penny*. Ill. by Joy Allen. Random House, pap., 2000, ISBN 0-679-88973-6. SERIES: Step into Reading + Math. SUBJECTS: Mathematics — Fiction; Money; Stories in rhyme. RL B.

Colorful, whimsical illustrations complement the lighthearted rhyming text as a young girl tries to earn money for her mother's birthday card by selling lemonade. Renderings of the coins on each page help readers learn the values.

Gleiter, Jan, and Kathleen Thompson

1010 *Sequoya*. Ill. by Tom Redman. Raintree, 1988, o.p. SUBJECTS: Biographies; Cherokee; Language. RL C.

Sequoya had the ingenuity to turn the Cherokee language into a written language — twice, as his first efforts burned up in a fire. Then he had to convince the elders that his work was not witchcraft in this simple story with watercolor illustrations.

Godwin, Laura

1011 *The Best Fall of All*. Ill. by Jane Chapman. Simon & Schuster, 2002, ISBN 0-689-84713-0. SERIES: Ready-to-Read. SUBJECTS: Pets — Cats — Fiction; Pets — Dogs — Fiction; Seasons — Fiction. RL A.

Fall is a good time for Happy the dog and Honey the cat. Apples, pumpkins, and fall leaves are wonderful to play with. Lighthearted and uncluttered acrylic illustrations provide visual clues for beginning readers.

1012 *Forest*. Ill. by Stacey Schuett. HarperCollins, 1998, o.p. SERIES: I Can Read. SUBJECTS: Animal rescue — Fiction; Deer — Fiction. RL B. LEXILE 270L.

Finding a fawn all alone in the forest, Jeannie and her family care for her overnight and then take her to a special wildlife sanctuary. Enchanting forest scenes provide a vivid background for a gentle story of love and caring.

1013 *Happy and Honey*. Ill. by Jane Chapman. Simon & Schuster, 2000, o.p. SUBJECTS: Pets — Cats — Fiction; Pets — Dogs — Fiction; Play — Fiction. RL A.

Wanting to sleep, Honey tries to wake up Happy and when she does, the dog and cat enjoying playing together. Focusing on the silly antics of the animal friends, the playful drawings follow a simple story just perfect for beginning readers.

1014 *Happy Christmas, Honey!* Ill. by Jane Chapman. Simon & Schuster, 2002, ISBN 0-689-84714-9. SERIES: Ready-to-Read. SUBJECTS: Christmas — Fiction; Pets — Cats — Fiction; Pets — Dogs — Fiction. RL A.

It's Christmas, and Honey the cat wants to help with decorations and baking. Happy the dog wants nothing to do with it, and gently encourages the cat to wait with him for Santa. Humorous and expressive acrylic illustrations capture the dog's patient understanding and the wonder of the holiday season.

1015 *Honey Helps*. Ill. by Jane Chapman. Simon & Schuster, 2000, o.p. SUBJECTS: Pets — Cats — Fiction; Pets — Dogs — Fiction. RL A. LEXILE BR.

Honey wants to help Happy bury his bone. Honey digs up the bone and gives her friend a surprise. Ample white space surrounding Honey and Happy's comical antics easily enables beginning readers to enjoy a wonderful story of friendship.

Goennel, Heidi

1016 *My Day*. Ill. by author. Little, Brown, 1988, o.p. SUBJECTS: Growing up; Play. RL B.

This tale of a girl's ordinary school day takes on special qualities because of the simple graphics of the artwork.

Goldin, Augusta

1017 *Ducks Don't Get Wet*. Ill. by Leonard Kessler. HarperCollins, 1989, o.p. SERIES:

Let's-Read-and-Find-Out Science. SUBJECTS: Ducks; Nature. RL C.

An introduction to various kinds of ducks and their characteristics. Facts include: some ducks can dive 100 feet deep and some can fly 70 miles per hour! Charming ducks and neighboring pond animals are in watercolors.

1018 *Straight Hair, Curly Hair*. Ill. by Ed Emberley. HarperCollins, 1966, o.p. SERIES: Let's-Read-and-Find-Out Science. SUBJECTS: Human body — Hair; Science experiments. RL C.

Information about hair is interspersed with simple experiments and suggested observations. Accompanying sketches have touches of humor to lighten the text.

Goldman, Susan

1019 *Grandma Is Somebody Special*. Ill. by author. Whitman, 1976, o.p. SERIES: Self-Starters. SUBJECTS: Grandparents — Fiction. RL C.

The joy and comfort in simple activities with Grandma — looking at a fire engine, photographs, and her jewelry box; cooking; playing games; telling and reading stories; and singing old songs — are clearly conveyed. Full-color watercolors also have a homey everyday appeal.

Goode, Molly

1020 *Mama Loves*. Ill. by Lisa McCue. Random House, 1999, o.p. SERIES: Bright and Early Books. SUBJECTS: Animals — Fiction; Mothers — Fiction; Stories in rhyme. RL B.

Whether they are dogs, raccoons, birds, or pandas, all mamas love their babies, care for them, and help them grow. Evocative double-page spreads in full color embrace the joy and pride of a mother's love.

Goodman, Susan E.

1021 *What Do You Do on a Farm?* Ill. by Steve Pica. Millbrook, 2002, ISBN 0-7613-2756-8. SERIES: Silly Millies. SUBJECTS: Animals — Farm — Fiction; Farm and country life — Fiction. RL A.

If you live on a farm what do you do when you want eggs or have to feed the animals? A young girl finds out what farm life is like in this book featuring comical pastel illustrations.

Gorbachev, Valeri

1022 *Ms. Turtle the Babysitter*. Ill. by author. HarperCollins, 2005, ISBN 0-06-058073-9. SERIES: I Can Read. SUBJECTS: Baby-sitting — Fiction; Frogs and toads — Fiction; Turtles — Fiction. RL B.

Ms. Turtle is the best baby-sitter ever as she keeps three little frogs happy — reading to them, making them smile, and listening to their secrets. Each of the three chapters is generously illustrated with endearing watercolor and ink artwork.

1023 *Whose Hat Is It?* Ill. by author. HarperCollins, 2004, ISBN 0-06-053434-6. SERIES: My First I Can Read. SUBJECTS: Hats — Fiction; Turtles — Fiction. RL A.

On a windy day a turtle finds a hat and goes in search of its owner. Along the way, he asks mouse, rabbit, beaver, and crocodile whose hat it is. Beginning readers will enjoy the repetition of words, fun-filled illustrations, and surprise ending.

Gordon, Jeffie R.

1024 *Muriel and Ruth: A Book about Friendship*. Ill. by Lane Yerkes. Bell Books, 1992, ISBN 1-878093-18-5. SUBJECTS: Friendship — Fiction; Pigs — Fiction; School stories. RL B.

Muriel meets Ruth the first day of school, and they become best friends. Despite a squabble when Ruth doesn't want to share her new birthday present, they remain pals. Fat, rosy-cheeked pig characters predominantly in green and orange people the story.

Gordon, Sharon

1025 *Allergies*. Children's Press, 2003, ISBN 0-516-22581-2. SERIES: Rookie Read-About Health. SUBJECTS: Allergies; Health. RL B. LEXILE 320L.

What makes you sneeze, your nose run, your skin itch, and gives you trouble breathing? A brief but clear introduction to common allergies is complemented by numerous color photographs that illustrate a variety of symptoms and causes.

Gordon, Sharon (cont.)

1026 *Asthma*. Children's Press, 2003, ISBN 0-516-22582-0. SERIES: Rookie Read-About Health. SUBJECTS: Diseases; Health. RL B. LEXILE NC320L.

An asthma attack can be triggered by allergies, exercise, or even a bad cold. Descriptive diagrams and color photographs augment the text as it addresses the nature of asthma and the common treatments.

1027 *Earaches*. Children's Press, 2003, ISBN 0-516-22584-7. SERIES: Rookie Read-About Health. SUBJECTS: Health; Human body — Ears. RL B. LEXILE 190L.

Highly magnified photographs of germs and the middle ear offer clear visuals for a better understanding of earaches and their causes, treatment, and prevention.

1028 *Exercise*. Children's Press, 2002, ISBN 0-516-22571-5. SERIES: Rookie Read-About Health. SUBJECTS: Exercise; Health. RL B. LEXILE 90L.

Helping you use all your muscles, exercise is good for your body's health. Numerous color photographs illustrate many different ways to keep physically active.

1029 *Guess Who Runs?* Benchmark, 2004, ISBN 0-7614-1763-X. SERIES: Bookworms: Guess Who. SUBJECTS: Animals; Horses. RL B.

Brief text and color photographs offer clues that enable the reader to guess which animal runs — a horse.

1030 *Guess Who Snaps?* Benchmark, 2004, ISBN 0-7614-1765-6. SERIES: Bookworms: Guess Who. SUBJECTS: Oceans and ocean life. RL B.

Clear, underwater color photographs join with the brief text to create a guessing game that serves as an introduction to lobsters.

1031 *Guess Who Spins?* Benchmark, 2004, ISBN 0-7614-1768-0. SERIES: Bookworms: Guess Who. SUBJECTS: Spiders. RL B.

High-magnification color photography zooms in on the anatomical aspects of the spider as readers use the visual and verbal clues for a fun guessing game.

1032 *Hearing*. Children's Press, 2001, ISBN 0-516-22289-9. SERIES: Rookie Read-About Health. SUBJECTS: Senses — Hearing. RL B. LEXILE 350L.

Examine the world of hearing through a brief introduction to the ear and how it works. Visual close-ups, comparative photographs, and simple diagrams augment the text.

1033 *Pinkeye*. Children's Press, 2003, ISBN 0-516-22583-9. SERIES: Rookie Read-About Health. SUBJECTS: Diseases; Health. RL B. LEXILE 190L.

The causes and treatment of pinkeye, a common childhood ailment, are described. Color photographs of infected eyes are shown and preventative measures are offered in a valuable health lesson.

1034 *Seeing*. Children's Press, 2001, ISBN 0-516-22291-0. SERIES: Rookie Read-About Health. SUBJECTS: Senses — Sight. RL B. LEXILE 360L.

One of the five senses, sight enables your eyes to see the world around you. Diagrams and color photographs identify the parts of the eye and their functions.

1035 *Tasting*. Children's Press, 2001, ISBN 0-516-22293-1. SERIES: Rookie Read-About Health. SUBJECTS: Senses; Senses — Taste. RL B. LEXILE 390L.

There are so many different things to taste, and it all begins with your tongue. Excellent diagrams of the tongue and a variety of color photographs of food extend the interesting textual information.

1036 *Touching*. Children's Press, 2001, ISBN 0-516-22290-2. SERIES: Rookie Read-About Health. SUBJECTS: Senses; Senses — Touch. RL B. LEXILE 380L.

Everywhere you have skin you can feel things through nerve endings. Children experiencing the sense of touch are exhibited in the many colorful photographs.

1037 *What a Dog!* Ill. by Deborah Sims. Troll, 1980, o.p. SERIES: First-Start Easy Reader. SUBJECTS: Pets — Dogs — Fiction. RL A.

Only 9 of the 56 words in the book have more than one syllable. Bernie walks the eager dog — or is it the other way around? Line drawings focus on a roly-poly pet.

Gordon, Shirley

1038 *Crystal's Christmas Carol.* Ill. by Edward Frascino. HarperCollins, 1989, o.p. SUBJECTS: Christmas — Fiction; Friendship — Fiction. RL C.

Susan and Sherri are embarrassed when their friend Crystal sings Christmas carols everywhere — but then they notice the happy faces of people on the street and in the mall, and join her more enthusiastically. Pen and wash drawings are expressive, featuring holiday colors.

Graham, Bob

1039 *Crusher Is Coming.* Ill. by author. Viking, 1988, o.p. SUBJECTS: Friendship — Fiction; Self-esteem — Fiction. RL B.

Peter introduces many activities to impress an older friend, Crusher, but Crusher enjoys most playing with Peter's baby sister. Excellent watercolor and ink sketches underline the contrast between how Crusher looks and how he acts.

Grambling, Lois

1040 *Happy Valentine's Day, Miss Hildy.* Ill. by Bridget Starr Taylor. Random House, 1998, o.p. SERIES: Step into Reading. SUBJECTS: Mystery and detective stories; Valentine's Day — Fiction. RL B. LEXILE 460L.

When a dozen long-legged flamingos arrive from a secret admirer, Miss Hildy tries to solve her Valentine's Day mystery. Full-page colorful illustrations focus on following the trail of clues and on the humorous cast of likely suspects.

1041 *Miss Hildy's Missing Cape Caper.* Ill. by Bridget Starr Taylor. Random House, 2000, o.p. SERIES: Step into Reading. SUBJECTS: Halloween — Fiction; Mystery and detective stories. RL B.

On Halloween someone stole Miss Hildy's detective cape and hat. With some fast legwork, she catches the thief, with chocolate on his flamingo beak. Entertaining artwork enhances the humorous bumbling escapades of a unique detective.

Graves, Charles P.

1042 *Wright Brothers.* Ill. by Fermin Rocker. Putnam, 1973, o.p. SERIES: See and Read Beginning to Read Biography. SUBJECTS: Airplanes; Biographies. RL C.

The author traces the history of the Wright brothers' determined efforts to fly. Good ink sketches give a flavor of the times.

Greene, Carol

1043 *Benjamin Franklin: A Man with Many Jobs.* Photos by Steven Dobson. Children's Press, 1988, o.p. SERIES: Rookie Biography. SUBJECTS: Biographies; United States — History. RL B.

Aided by a simple, well-illustrated format, the creative accomplishments of Benjamin Franklin are outlined. Five short chapters are augmented by a timeline and index.

1044 *Black Elk: A Man with a Vision. Drawings and.* Ill. with drawings and photos. Children's Press, 1990, o.p. SERIES: Rookie Biography. SUBJECTS: Biographies; Native Americans; United States — History. RL C.

Black Elk, an Oglala Sioux, was born in 1863 and died in 1950. Despite his recurring visions of peace, he endured the routing of the Indians from their ancestral homes, traveled in Europe with the Buffalo Bill Cody's Wild West show, and survived the Wounded Knee massacre.

1045 *Christopher Columbus: A Great Explorer.* Ill. with photos and drawings. Children's Press, 1989, o.p. SERIES: Rookie Biography. SUBJECTS: Biographies; Explorers and exploration; United States — History. RL C.

This is a very simple version of the successes and frustrations of Columbus's explorations, illustrated with lithographs, paintings, photographs, and drawings.

1046 *Daniel Boone: Man of the Forests.* Ill. with drawings and photos. Children's Press, 1990, o.p. SERIES: Rookie Biography. SUBJECTS: Biographies; Explorers and exploration; Frontier and pioneer life. RL C.

One of eleven children born to a blacksmith and his wife, Daniel Boone fathered ten. He opened Kentucky and Missouri to settlers against the active opposition of Indians, whom he befriended, fought, and escaped from after being

Greene, Carol (cont.)

captured more than once. In his eighties, he walked to Yellowstone and back.

1047 *Elie Wiesel: Messenger from the Holocaust.* Ill. with photos. Childrens Press, 1987, o.p. SUBJECTS: Biographies; History; Religion. RL C.
Elie Wiesel's acceptance speech for the 1986 Nobel Peace Prize concludes this outline of his concentration camp ordeals and later witness. A timeline is appended to this moving tribute.

1048 *George Washington: First President of the United States.* Ill. with photos. Children's Press, 1991, o.p. SERIES: Rookie Biography. SUBJECTS: Biographies; Presidents — United States; United States — History. RL C.
A pedestrian account of George Washington's career, beginning when he was a surveyor at age 16. Black-and-white photographs predominate; timeline and index are appended.

1049 *Hi, Clouds.* Ill. by Gene Sharp. Children's Press, 1983, ISBN 0-516-02036-6. SERIES: Rookie Reader. SUBJECTS: Weather — Clouds — Fiction. RL A.
Many shapes are seen in the clouds by two city children. A 27-word vocabulary and simple bright illustrations make this an appealing beginning reader.

1050 *Ice Is . . . Whee!* Ill. by Paul Sharp. Children's Press, 1983, o.p. SERIES: Rookie Reader. SUBJECTS: Winter — Fiction. RL A.
The beauty of ice and the fun of sliding on it or playing with icicles are celebrated with a 21-word vocabulary. Cartoon drawings are colorful, yet simple.

1051 *Indira Nehru Gandhi: Ruler of India.* Ill. with photos. Childrens Press, 1985, o.p. SUBJECTS: Biographies — Women; India. RL C.
Born to an Indian ruling family, Indira followed her father in becoming prime minister of India. Political issues are touched on lightly. Photographs trace the maturing political leader until her assassination.

1052 *Jackie Robinson: Baseball's First Black Major-Leaguer.* Ill. with photos. Children's Press, 1990, o.p. SERIES: Rookie Biography. SUBJECTS: African Americans; Biographies; Sports — Baseball. RL C.
Raised by his mother in a poor Pasadena neighborhood, Jackie went on to earn letters in four sports at UCLA. Branch Rickey of the Brooklyn Dodgers gave him an opportunity to play professionally. He was Rookie of the Year despite discrimination, and went on to fight racial prejudice on and off the field.

1053 *Jacques Cousteau: Man of the Oceans.* Ill. with photos. Children's Press, 1990, o.p. SERIES: Rookie Biography. SUBJECTS: Biographies; Oceans and ocean life; Science and scientists. RL C.
Cousteau discovered three wonderful things as a boy: water, machines, and film, all of which shaped his life. While in the navy, he explored the sea and sea life, all of which he shared through film, books, TV, and live appearances.

1054 *John Chapman: The Man Who Was Johnny Appleseed.* Ill. with photos and drawings. Children's Press, 1991, o.p. SERIES: Rookie Biography. SUBJECTS: Biographies; Trees. RL C.
The legend and the skimpy facts known about Johnny Appleseed are given in this interesting tale of an eccentric, Bible-toting vegetarian who "lived for others" and planted apple trees throughout Pennsylvania, Ohio, and Indiana. Lithographs, drawings, and photographs illustrate this text.

1055 *John Philip Sousa: The March King. Black and white.* Ill. with photos. Children's Press, 1992, o.p. SERIES: Rookie Biography. SUBJECTS: Biographies; Music and musicians. RL C.
The outline of John Philip Sousa's life, with his successful career composing music, especially marches, and directing the Marine Corps Band. A timeline and an index are appended to this work liberally illustrated with black-and-white photographs.

1056 *Louis Pasteur: Enemy of Disease.* Ill. with photos. Children's Press, 1990, o.p. SERIES: Rookie Biography. SUBJECTS: Biographies; Medicine; Science and scientists. RL C.
Pasteur's life is outlined in five chapters, with a timeline and an index appended. Through painstaking work he discovered microbes and developed vaccines; the Pasteur Institute was

founded as more and more people came for help. Three of his five children died in childhood. Illustrations are black-and-white photographs.

1057 *Margaret Wise Brown: Author of Goodnight Moon*. Ill. with photos and illustrations. Children's Press, 1993, o.p. SERIES: Rookie Biography. SUBJECTS: Biographies — Women; Books and reading; Writers and writing. RL C.

Margaret Wise Brown's love of cats and rabbits, woods and fields, is described, as well as her dissatisfaction with her life and the many changes in it. She died at age 42, engaged to be married. Black-and-white photographs of Brown, color photographs of the woods, and some famous book illustrations appear throughout.

1058 *Martin Luther King, Jr.: A Man Who Changed Things*. Ill. with photos. Children's Press, 1989, o.p. SERIES: Rookie Biography. SUBJECTS: African Americans; Biographies; Martin Luther King, Jr., Day. RL C.

With many black-and-white photographs and some in color, and stirring language augmenting the narrative outline of King's life, the author brings King's message and roots to the young reader.

1059 *Mother Teresa: Friend of the Friendless*. Ill. with photos. Childrens Press, 1983, o.p. SUBJECTS: Biographies. RL C.

The inspiring story of the way in which one determined, dedicated person can change the world. Mother Teresa, born in Yugoslavia, began work as a missionary in India while a young woman, and has inspired people all over the globe.

1060 *Please Wind?* Ill. by Gene Sharp. Children's Press, 1982, ISBN 0-516-02033-1. SERIES: Rookie Reader. SUBJECTS: Spring — Fiction; Stories in rhyme. RL A.

A child's wish for a brisk wind is granted, blowing clothes on the clothesline, a balloon, a hat, and even her kite. The creative story uses only 22 words and has simple watercolor drawings.

1061 *Pocahontas: Daughter of a Chief*. Ill. by Steven Dobson. Children's Press, 1988, o.p. SERIES: Rookie Biography. SUBJECTS: Biographies; Native Americans; United States — Colonial period. RL C.

A bare-bones account of Pocahontas's lasting friendship with the settlers at Jamestown, first John Smith, then John Rolfe, whom she married. While with her husband and son in England, she died and was buried at Gravesend. Paintings, lithographs, photographs, and drawings are used liberally.

1062 *Rain! Rain!* Ill. by Larry Frederick. Children's Press, 1982, ISBN 0-516-42034-8. SERIES: Rookie Reader. SUBJECTS: Stories in rhyme; Weather — Rain. RL A.

Twenty-nine words celebrate rain (especially puddles to play in). Cheerful, action-filled illustrations feature emerald green and royal blue watercolors.

1063 *Shine, Sun!* Ill. by Gene Sharp. Children's Press, 1983, ISBN 0-516-02038-2. SERIES: Rookie Reader. SUBJECTS: Play — Fiction; Summer — Fiction. RL A.

Twenty-seven words and bright watercolors focus on a little girl dancing and wading on a sunny day, as well as her admiring the flowers, butterflies, and birds singing.

1064 *Snow Joe*. Ill. by Paul Sharp. Children's Press, 1982, o.p. SERIES: Rookie Reader. SUBJECTS: Stories in rhyme; Winter — Fiction. RL A.

Remarkable interest is generated in snow play using just 15 words. Large comic illustrations are in pastels.

1065 *Wolfgang Amadeus Mozart: Musical Genius*. Children's Press, 1993, o.p. SERIES: Rookie Biography. SUBJECTS: Biographies; Music and musicians. RL C.

The difficulties and triumphs of Mozart's music-making are celebrated in this short biography with five chapters, a timeline, and an index. Photographs, lithographs, paintings, and playbills illumine the text.

Greene, Stephanie

1066 *Betsy Ross and the Silver Thimble*. Ill. by Diana Magnuson. Simon & Schuster, 2002, ISBN 0-689-84967-2. SERIES: Ready-to-Read. SUBJECTS: Biographies. RL B. LEXILE 190L.

Greene, Stephanie (cont.)

Because she was a girl, Betsy Ross couldn't help her father make furniture, but with the help of her mother and the gift of a silver thimble, she found her own true talent. Full-page colorful acrylic illustrations enliven a simple event in the life of young Betsy Ross.

Greenwood, Pamela D.

1067 *I Found Mouse.* Ill. by Jennifer Plecas. Clarion, 1994, o.p. SUBJECTS: Loneliness — Fiction; Parent and child — Fiction; Pets — Cats — Fiction. RL C.

Tessie's big brother is camping with their grandmother, her best friend has gone to visit her father, and her mother is at school in Colorado. What starts out as a very long three weeks turns into a growing experience for Tessie when she finds a stray kitten and gives it a home. Illustrated with childlike watercolors with ink definition, the story is divided into chapters and uses humor well to balance Tessie's concerns.

1068 *What About My Goldfish?* Ill. by Jennifer Plecas. Houghton Mifflin, 1993, o.p. SUBJECTS: Moving, household — Fiction; Pets — Dogs — Fiction; Pets — Fiction. RL A.

When a boy moves, he makes new friends only after he brings his goldfish, Merlin and Skunk, for show-and-tell, and has a Pond Party (since his birthday is too far away). Simple ink and watercolor drawings complement the text.

Greer, Gery, and Bob Ruddick

1069 *Billy the Ghost and Me.* Ill. by Roger Roth. HarperCollins, 1997, o.p. SERIES: I Can Read. SUBJECTS: Humorous stories; Robbers and outlaws — Fiction. RL B. LEXILE 270L.

With the help of Billy the Ghost, Sarah catches the two outlaws who robbed the bank in Cactus Junction and becomes an official deputy. The story, told in three chapters, is complemented by detailed, earth-toned illustrations.

Greve, Andreas

1070 *The Good Night Story.* Ill. by Kitty Macaulay. Annick, 1993, ISBN 1-55037-288-2. SUBJECTS: Animals — Fiction; Bedtime — Fiction; Storytelling. RL B.

A small boy finishes the bedtime story his grandfather began — with startlingly realistic results.

Grey, Judith

1071 *What Time Is It?* Ill. by Susan Hall. Troll, 1981, o.p. SUBJECTS: Animals — Fiction; Books and reading — Fiction; Concepts — Time. RL A.

A boy squirrel asks whether it is time to eat or play. Rhythmic language is used with a basic vocabulary of 25 words. Pastel washes feature cute animals, butterflies, and birds.

1072 *Yummy, Yummy.* Ill. by Joan E. Goodman. Troll, 1981, o.p. SUBJECTS: Bakers and baking — Fiction; Hippopotami — Fiction. RL A.

A hippo makes an apple-carrot-honey-chocolate cake for a yummy treat. Slight story has a 37-word vocabulary and soft pastel illustrations.

Greydanus, Rose

1073 *Double Trouble.* Ill. by Roland Rodegast. Troll, 1981, o.p. SUBJECTS: Raccoons — Fiction; Siblings — Twins — Fiction. RL B.

Jim and Tim, raccoon twins, blame each other for messes, but end up doing the cleaning together. Limited story line uses a 34-word vocabulary. Large textured drawings are in bright colors.

1074 *Let's Pretend.* Ill. by Marsha Winborn. Troll, 1981, o.p. SERIES: Giant First-Start. SUBJECTS: Imagination — Fiction. RL B.

Children "spy" on their dog and cat. A slim story line and text are expanded by attractive marbleized watercolors on white.

Gridley, Marion

1075 *Osceola.* Ill. by Lloyd E. Oxendine. Putnam, 1972, o.p. SERIES: See and Read Beginning to Read Biography. SUBJECTS: Biographies; Seminole. RL B.

The bravery and determination of one man to preserve his native culture culminates in his early death. Crude ink sketches have orange highlights.

Grimes, Nikki

1076 *Wild, Wild Hair*. Ill. by George Ford. Scholastic, 1997, ISBN 0-590-26590-3. SERIES: Hello Reader! SUBJECTS: African Americans — Fiction; Human body — Hair — Fiction; Stories in rhyme. RL B. LEXILE 400L.

Tisa hates Monday mornings when her mother braids her wild hair into twenty beautiful braids. This rhymed story with detailed pastel watercolors tells a gentle family story about a young girl who grumbles about her hair until it is beautifully plaited.

Grindley, Sally

1077 *Friends Forever*. Ill. by Penny Dann. Kingfisher, 2007, ISBN 978-0-7534-5976-8. SERIES: I Am Reading. SUBJECTS: Bears — Fiction; Foxes — Fiction; Friendship — Fiction. RL B.

Two stories feature Jefferson Bear and Figgy Twosocks the fox. Gentle, earth-toned watercolor illustrations follow the ups and downs of the very special friends.

1078 *The Perfect Monster*. Ill. by Erica-Jane Waters. Kingfisher, 2005, ISBN 0-7534-5858-6. SERIES: I Am Reading. SUBJECTS: Monsters — Fiction; School stories. RL B.

From birth, Mungus Bigfoot was the perfect monster — scary, smelly, and rude. Now, he must teach Emily Twinkletoes how to be a good monster or be expelled from school! Riotous blue and pink cartoon monsters try to learn their monster lessons with humorous results.

Grindley, Sally, ed.

1079 *A Day with Alice and Sam: Ten Stories and a Picture Dictionary*. Ill. by Maureen Galvani. Kingfisher, 1993, o.p. SERIES: Kingfisher Ready-to-Read. SUBJECTS: Family life — Fiction. RL B.

The activities of a family with three children from sunup to bedtime include teasing, pretending, planting a tree, baking cupcakes, going to a street fair, hunting for the family dog, and a bedtime story. Ink and wash drawings include a picture dictionary.

Gross, Ruth B.

1080 *A Book About Pandas*. Ill. with photos. Dial, 1972, o.p. SUBJECTS: Nature; Pandas. RL C.

Habits and characteristics of pandas learned from studying their behavior in a zoo are related in this photoessay. Black-and-white pictures are numerous, catching pandas in a variety of poses.

Gruber, Suzanne

1081 *The Monster Under My Bed*. Ill. by Stephanie Britt. Troll, 1985, o.p. SERIES: Giant First-Start. SUBJECTS: Bears — Fiction; Bedtime — Fiction. RL C.

A small bear, certain that he hears noises under his bed, calls his mother repeatedly for reassurance. He settles down only when the source of the disturbance is found — his cat, Fluffy. The reassuring tale has excellent watercolor drawings with royal blue predominating.

Gruber, Wilhelm

1082 *The Upside-Down Reader*. Ill. by Marlies Rieper-Bastian. North-South Books, 1998, o.p. SUBJECTS: Books and reading — Fiction; Siblings — Fiction. RL B.

Sitting across from his big sister as she practices her reading homework, Tim learns to read upside-down. Brightly colored full-page illustrations help readers visualize and better understand the unusual way Tim reads.

Guest, Elissa Haden

1083 *Iris and Walter*. Ill. by Christine Davenier. Harcourt, 2000, ISBN 0-15-202122-1. SUBJECTS: City and town life — Fiction; Farm and country life — Fiction; Friendship — Fiction. RL B. LEXILE 330L.

After moving from her apartment in the city to the country, Iris is sad until Grandpa helps her find a new friend named Walter. Spirited pen and ink illustrations accented with watercolor splashes in hues of blue and purple gently animate this emotion-filled story of moving.

1084 *Iris and Walter: Lost and Found*. Ill. by Christine Davenier. Harcourt, 2004, ISBN 0-15-216701-3. SUBJECTS: Babies — Fiction; Lost and found possessions — Fiction; Siblings — Fiction. RL B. LEXILE 450L.

Guest, Elissa Haden (cont.)

Baby Rose is growing up and getting into mischief; she breaks Iris's necklace and hides Walter's harmonica. This story of family and friendship is highlighted by warm, cozy watercolors that blend perfectly with the everyday adventures.

1085 *Iris and Walter: The School Play*. Ill. by Christine Davenier. Harcourt, 2003, ISBN 0-15-216481-2. SUBJECTS: Friendship — Fiction; Illness — Fiction; School stories. RL B. LEXILE 310L.

Practicing for the class bug play is exciting until Walter the dragonfly has stage fright and Iris the cricket gets sick. Reassuring watercolors follow the excitement and dread leading up to the big day.

1086 *Iris and Walter: The Sleepover*. Ill. by Christine Davenier. Harcourt, 2002, ISBN 0-15-216487-1. SUBJECTS: Friendship — Fiction; Homesickness — Fiction. RL B. LEXILE 350L.

Excited about sleeping over, Iris and Walter plan all kinds of fun things to do. But at Walter's house, Iris is suddenly homesick. Exuberant artwork mirrors the impending sleepover activities and the joyful adventures of two best friends.

1087 *Iris and Walter: True Friends*. Ill. by Christine Davenier. Harcourt, 2001, o.p. SUBJECTS: Friendship — Fiction; School stories. RL B. LEXILE 270L.

As Walter helps Iris learn to ride a horse, Iris shows Walter a way to solve his problem at school. Bright, full-page illustrations provide visual clues for readers as they learn about the meaning of friendship.

1088 *Iris and Walter and Baby Rose*. Ill. by Christine Davenier. Harcourt, 2002, ISBN 0-15-202120-5. SUBJECTS: Babies — Fiction; Friendship — Fiction; Sibling rivalry — Fiction. RL B. LEXILE 330L.

With all of Baby Rose's crying and fussiness, it's no fun being a big sister. As the seasons move from spring through to fall, everyone grows, and taking the baby for a walk is now just perfect for Iris. Expressive artwork captures the joys and trials of a new baby in the family.

1089 *Iris and Walter and Cousin Howie*. Ill. by Christine Davenier. Harcourt, 2003, ISBN 0-15-216695-5. SUBJECTS: Family life — Fiction; Friendship — Fiction. RL B. LEXILE 340L.

When Walter's favorite cousin visits, Iris is disappointed because he is bossy and doesn't teach them any magic tricks. Pen and ink drawings with vibrant watercolors follow the complex emotional ups and downs of Howie's stay in the country.

1090 *Iris and Walter and the Birthday Party*. Ill. by Christine Davenier. Harcourt, 2006, ISBN 0-15-205015-9. SUBJECTS: Birthdays — Fiction; Friendship — Fiction; Parties — Fiction. RL B. LEXILE 340L.

Everyone is excited about riding his horse at Walter's upcoming birthday party. But Rain provides a real surprise when she presents them with a foal. Energetic ink-and-watercolors in bright birthday colors ably depict the joy of a true birthday celebration.

1091 *Iris and Walter and the Field Trip*. Ill. by Christine Davenier. Harcourt, 2005, ISBN 0-15-205014-0. SUBJECTS: Friendship — Fiction; Lost, being — Fiction; School stories. RL B. LEXILE 450L.

On a field trip to the aquarium, the class has fun seeing all kinds of fish until suddenly Iris notices that Walter is not with them. He is lost! Lighthearted ink and watercolor artwork portrays the excitement of the day as well as the calm composure of the teacher facing a realistic situation.

1092 *Iris and Walter and the Substitute Teacher*. Ill. by Christine Davenier. Harcourt, 2004, ISBN 0-15-205013-2. SUBJECTS: Grandparents — Fiction; School stories; Teachers and teaching — Fiction. RL B. LEXILE 470L.

The first day Grandpa is the substitute teacher for her class is great for Iris, but by the second day she is jealous of the attention he pays to the other students. The classroom atmosphere is aptly captured in lively watercolor and ink illustrations.

Gunther, Louise

1093 *A Tooth for the Tooth Fairy*. Ill. by Jim Cummins. Garrard, 1978, o.p. SUBJECTS: Tooth fairy — Fiction. RL B.

When Rose loses her tooth in the grass at the playground and tries to substitute a fake, she finds that her trouble was not necessary. The straightforward story has full-color illustrations.

H

Haddad, Helen R.

1094 *Truck and Loader*. Ill. by Donald Carrick. Greenwillow, 1982, o.p. SERIES: Read-Alone. SUBJECTS: Trucks. RL B.

The complementary work of loader and dump truck doing road building, tree removal, and pond building is well described. Carrick's exceptional drawings are in muted orange, beige, and green.

Hall, Katy, and Lisa Eisenberg

1095 *Buggy Riddles*. Ill. by Simms Taback. Dial, 1986, o.p. SERIES: Dial Easy-to-Read. SUBJECTS: Jokes and riddles. RL B.

Each of the 41 riddles (with answers) featuring insects is given a full page. The illustrations are bold, brightly colored, and humorous.

1096 *Bunny Riddles*. Ill. by Nicole Rubel. Dial, 1997, o.p. SERIES: Dial Easy-to-Read. SUBJECTS: Jokes and riddles. RL B. LEXILE 280L.

Boldly colored, cartoon-style illustrations enhance the punch lines for 42 riddles about rabbits that abound with child appeal.

1097 *Chickie Riddles*. Ill. by Thor Wickstrom. Dial, 1997, o.p. SERIES: Dial Easy-to-Read. SUBJECTS: Jokes and riddles. RL B. LEXILE 140L.

With a focus on chickens, riddles on every page are extended by colorfully humorous illustrations that provide a visual punch line of their own.

1098 *Creepy Riddles*. Ill. by S. D. Schindler. Dial, 1998, o.p. SERIES: Dial Easy-to-Read. SUBJECTS: Jokes and riddles. RL B.

Mildly scary and funny monster riddles — "What do witches like to eat for dessert?" — are highlighted by wonderfully ghoulish pen-and-ink and watercolor illustrations.

1099 *Dino Riddles*. Ill. by Nicole Rubel. Dial, 2002, ISBN 0-8037-2239-7. SERIES: Dial Easy-to-Read. SUBJECTS: Jokes and riddles. RL B.

Everyone's favorite creatures are the center of silly humor and jokes galore. Offbeat cartoon illustrations offer a perfect match to the fun.

1100 *Fishy Riddles*. Ill. by Simms Taback. Dial, 1983, o.p. SERIES: Dial Easy-to-Read. SUBJECTS: Jokes and riddles. RL B.

The riddles all have pleasing, but not always predictable, plays on words. Fittingly illustrated in cartoon style with turquoise and orange.

1101 *Grizzly Riddles*. Ill. by Nicole Rubel. Dial, 1989, o.p. SERIES: Dial Easy-to-Read. SUBJECTS: Jokes and riddles; Wordplay. RL B.

Inventive twists on old riddles revolve around grizzly bears in school, on picnics, on airplanes, or fishing. Cartoon drawings feature grisly grizzlies and eye-catching patterns.

1102 *Kitty Riddles*. Ill. by R. W. Alley. Dial, 2000, o.p. SERIES: Dial Easy-to-Read. SUBJECTS: Jokes and riddles. RL B.

On each framed page a joke or riddle about cats is imaginatively illustrated in ink and watercolor. The creative embellishments add to the visual humor.

1103 *Piggy Riddles*. Ill. by Renee Andriani. Dial, 2004, ISBN 0-8037-2855-7. SERIES: Dial Easy-to-Read. SUBJECTS: Jokes and riddles. RL B.

Brightly colored cartoon illustrations feature plenty of pigs in jokes and riddles. Beginning readers will enjoy the porcine humor.

1104 *Ribbit Riddles*. Ill. by Robert Bender. Dial, 2001, ISBN 0-8037-2525-6. SERIES: Dial Easy-to-Read. SUBJECTS: Jokes and riddles. RL B.

A unique technique using cell-vinyl paint on layers of acetate gives a shimmery glow to an enjoyable collection of frog and toad jokes.

1105 *Sheepish Riddles*. Ill. by R. W. Alley. Dial, 1996, o.p. SERIES: Dial Easy-to-Read. SUBJECTS: Jokes and riddles. RL B. LEXILE 340L.

"What do you get if you cross a sheep with a piece of chocolate?" That is just the beginning of the sheep jokes that will tickle the funny bone and keep everyone laughing as they pore over the

Hall, Katy, and Lisa Eisenberg (cont.)

hijinks of the detailed ink and watercolor illustrations.

1106 *Snakey Riddles*. Ill. by Simms Taback. Dial, 1990, o.p. SERIES: Dial Easy-to-Read. SUBJECTS: Jokes and riddles; Snakes; Wordplay. RL B.
Delightful play with language with dozens of riddles about snakes. Watercolor drawings show richly textured snakes.

1107 *Stinky Riddles*. Ill. by Renee Andriani. Dial, 2005, ISBN 0-8037-2928-6. SERIES: Dial Easy-to-Read. SUBJECTS: Jokes and riddles. RL B.
Readers won't shy away from this wonderfully malodorous offering of stinky jokes and riddles with brightly colored illustrations that positively reek with humor.

Hall, Kirsten

1108 *Bunny, Bunny*. Ill. by Kathy Wilburn. Childrens Press, 1990, o.p. SERIES: My First Reader. SUBJECTS: Rabbits — Fiction; Stories in rhyme. RL A.
Blue-jacketed Bunny romps in the meadow with his friends all day, before returning to his hollow in tree roots to be tucked into bed by his parents. Light, playful illustrations accompany the simple rhymed text, limited to 24 words.

1109 *My New Town*. Ill. by Gerardo Suzan. Scholastic, 2005, ISBN 0-516-24877-4. SERIES: My First Reader. SUBJECTS: City and town life — Fiction; Moving, household — Fiction. RL A. LEXILE BR.
From his new teacher and barber to the dentist and mail carrier, a young boy tours his new town and introduces new friends. Full-page illustrations in earth tones aid the beginning reader in enjoying the simple family story.

Hall, Lynn

1110 *Captain: Canada's Flying Pony*. Ill. by Tran Mawicke. Garrard, 1976, o.p. SERIES: Famous Animal Stories. SUBJECTS: Horses. RL C.
A true story of a mud-colored pony and a girl who out-jumped larger horses all over the world is told with drama and humor. Watercolor drawings focus on the pony and girl.

Hall, Malcolm

1111 *CariCATures*. Ill. by Bruce Degen. Putnam, 1978, o.p. SERIES: Break-of-Day. SUBJECTS: Animals — Fiction; Jokes and riddles — Fiction; Newspapers — Fiction. RL B.
The Claws and Paws newspaper begins to thrive only when some cat cartoons and riddles are added. Excellent ink and wash drawings of the animal characters enhance the good characterizations.

1112 *Edward, Benjamin and Butter*. Ill. by Tomie dePaola. Putnam, 1981, o.p. SUBJECTS: Friendship — Fiction; Horses — Fiction; Tapirs — Fiction. RL B.
The tables are turned when Edward tries to cheer up his gloomy friend Benjamin with a trick. Pencil and yellows illustrate this story with gentle humor and unexpected twists.

1113 *Headlines*. Ill. by Wallace Tripp. Putnam, 1973, o.p. SERIES: Break-of-Day. SUBJECTS: Animals — Fiction; Books and reading — Fiction; Newspapers — Fiction. RL C.
Editor Theodore Cat's newspaper headlines come out wrong because a pack rat family steals type. Good characterization comes from text and Tripp's outstanding ink drawings.

Hall, Patricia

1114 *Hooray for Reading!* Ill. by Kathryn Mitter. Simon & Schuster, 2002, ISBN 0-689-85178-2. SERIES: Classic Raggedy Ann and Andy. SUBJECTS: Books and reading — Fiction; Dolls and dollhouses — Fiction; Fantasy. RL B.
After reading to her dolls, Marcella leaves and Raggedy Ann teaches all the other animals to read and share in the adventures. Brightly colored artwork focuses on the flash card technique that is promoted as the dolls learn to read.

Hamilton, Virginia M.

1115 *Jahdu*. Ill. by Jerry Pinkney. Greenwillow, 1980, o.p. SERIES: Read-Alone. SUBJECTS: Fantasy; Shadows — Fiction. RL B.

Accompanied by his independent shadow, Jahdu rolls up the sky to crawl behind, and sticks his finger in the cup of night to taste it. Rich language patterns and pencil drawings on palest lavender stimulate the imagination.

Hamsa, Bobbie

1116 *Dirty Larry*. Ill. by Paul Sharp. Children's Press, 1983, ISBN 0-516-02040-4. SERIES: Rookie Reader. SUBJECTS: Play — Fiction. RL C.

Larry's dirty anatomy from ears and knees to nose and neck are detailed in 32 familiar words. Cartoons show how much fun he has getting so dirty. (Beginning readers will be able to enjoy this book despite the Spache reading level assignment.)

1117 *Fast Draw Freddie*. Ill. by Susan Miller. Children's Press, 2000, o.p. SERIES: Rookie Reader. SUBJECTS: Art and artists — Fiction; Stories in rhyme. RL A.

Fast-Draw Freddie is busy drawing tall pictures, small pictures, cat pictures, and dad pictures. A brief text and detailed illustrations demonstrate the concepts.

1118 *Polly Wants a Cracker*. Ill. by Jerry Warshaw. Children's Press, 1986, o.p. SERIES: Rookie Reader. SUBJECTS: Concepts — Numbers; Parrots — Fiction; Stories in rhyme. RL B.

A simple 32-word vocabulary is used for a story counting the crackers Polly wants. Lively full-color drawings of three children and a dog pampering Polly keep the story moving.

Hancock, Sibyl

1119 *Bill Pickett: First Black Rodeo Star*. Ill. by Lorinda B. Cauley. Harcourt, 1977, o.p. SERIES: Let Me Read. SUBJECTS: African Americans; Biographies; Western stories. RL B.

The rodeo adventures of the first black international rodeo star. The close relationship he had with his horse, Spradley, is also emphasized. Sepia drawings add to the story.

1120 *Old Blue*. Ill. by Erick Ingraham. Putnam, 1980, o.p. SERIES: See and Read. SUBJECTS: Cowboys; Western stories. RL C.

The remarkable true story of a tame lead longhorn steer named Old Blue is told from the point of view of a novice on one particular drive in 1878. This tale is exceptional in its telling, as well as in its soft pencil drawings.

Hanel, Wolfram

1121 *Old Mahony and the Bear Family*. Ill. by Jean-Pierre Corderoc'h. North-South Books, 1997, o.p. SUBJECTS: Bears — Fiction; Behavior — Cooperative. RL B.

After unsuccessfully competing with a bear family as he fishes for salmon, Old Mahony sets out to capture the bears, but falls into his own trap and is rescued by the bears. Comical, detailed illustrations depict the frustration and ultimate gratitude of the poor fisherman.

Hare, Norma Q.

1122 *Wish Upon a Birthday*. Ill. by Diane Dawson. Garrard, 1979, o.p. SUBJECTS: Bakers and baking — Fiction; Birthdays — Fiction; Kings and queens — Fiction. RL B.

The cook's helper, Gabe, makes the very first birthday cake as his gift for Princess Melinda. Busy, bright cartoon-style drawings show the bustle in the castle kitchen.

Harrison, David

1123 *Wake Up, Sun*. Ill. by Hans Wilhelm. Random House, 1986, o.p. SERIES: Step into Reading. SUBJECTS: Cumulative tales; Farm and country life — Fiction. RL A.

The animals were very nice to the farmer's baby after her cries coincided with the sunrise. Appealing simple watercolors focus on friendly farm animals.

Harrison, Virginia

1124 *The World of a Falcon*. Photos by Oxford Scientific Films. Stevens, 1988, o.p. SERIES: Where Animals Live. SUBJECTS: Falcons; Nature. RL C.

The habitat, life cycle, and special characteristics of kestrels (a kind of falcon), and their adjustment to people are covered. Index and glossary are helpful. Close-up color photographs are exceptional, especially of kestrels "hovering" with feath-

Harrison, Virginia (cont.)

ers extended. Adapted from Mike Birkhead's *The Falcon Over the Town* (Stevens, 1988).

1125 *The World of Dragonflies.* Photos by Oxford Scientific Films. Stevens, 1988, o.p. SERIES: Where Animals Live. SUBJECTS: Dragonflies; Nature. RL C.

The habitat, anatomy, and life cycle of dragonflies are introduced, along with their enemies and relationships with people. Spectacular close-up photographs of dragonflies at every stage of their life cycle accompany the informative text. Adapted from Christopher O'Toole's *The Dragonfly Over the Water* (Stevens, 1988).

1126 *The World of Lizards.* Photos by Oxford Scientific Films. Stevens, 1988, o.p. SERIES: Where Animals Live. SUBJECTS: Lizards; Nature. RL C.

Information about the variety, habitats, anatomy, and life cycle of lizards, particularly their protective coloration and habits, is given. Exceptional close-up color photographs are up to Oxford Scientific Films' standards. Adapted from Mike Linley's *The Lizard in the Jungle* (Stevens, 1988).

1127 *The World of Mice.* Photos by Oxford Scientific Films. Stevens, 1988, o.p. SERIES: Where Animals Live. SUBJECTS: Mice; Nature. RL C.

The habitat, life cycle, senses, and food, as well as the enemies of mice are described. Mice as pests and pets for people are also discussed. Exceptional close-up color photographs add immeasurably to the book. Adapted from Robert Burton's *The Mouse in the Barn* (Stevens, 1988).

Harshman, Terry Webb

1128 *Porcupine's Pajama Party.* Ill. by Doug Cushman. HarperCollins, pap., 1988, ISBN 0-06-444140-7. SERIES: I Can Read. SUBJECTS: Animals — Fiction; Friendship — Fiction; Scary stories. RL A.

Porcupine invites friends Owl and Otter to a pajama party, where they watch a scary movie and bake chocolate chip cookies. The movie turns out to be a little too scary for a good night's sleep. This is a reassuring story with very appealing ink and watercolor drawings of the friends.

Harvey, Jayne

1129 *Busy Bugs: A Book About Patterns.* Ill. by Bernard Adnet. Grosset & Dunlap, pap., 2003, ISBN 0-448-43159-9. SERIES: All Aboard Math Reader. SUBJECTS: Insects — Fiction; Mathematics — Fiction; Stories in rhyme. RL B.

The mathematical concept of patterns is highlighted as insects get ready for a big show. Humorous big-eyed bugs dance and fly across the pages, demonstrating a variety of patterns for the reader.

1130 *Cat Show.* Ill. by Tamara Petrosino. Grosset & Dunlap, pap., 2003, ISBN 0-448-43112-2. SERIES: All Aboard Math Reader. SUBJECTS: Mathematics — Fiction; Pets — Cats — Fiction. RL B.

At the cat show, the children find a variety of ways to sort their ten cats. Full-page cartoon drawings aptly and humorously demonstrate the different groupings of cats.

Haskins, Lori

1131 *Too Many Dogs.* Ill. by Joe Mathieu. Random House, pap., 1998, ISBN 0-679-86443-1. SERIES: Step into Reading. SUBJECTS: Humorous stories; Pets — Dogs — Fiction. RL A. LEXILE 20L.

An unattended barbecue becomes the focus of attention for all the neighborhood dogs as they "sample" the feast before the guests arrive. Hilarious cartoon drawings dramatize the slapstick humor of doggie bedlam at an outdoor picnic gone awry.

Hasler, Eveline

1132 *Winter Magic.* Trans. of *In Winterland.* Ill. by Michele Lemieux. Morrow, 1985, o.p. SUBJECTS: Fantasy; Pets — Cats — Fiction; Winter — Fiction. RL B.

Peter takes a winter ride on his cat, Sebastian, through the caves, forest, and underground. Somewhat impressionistic paintings reinforce the dreamy qualities of his adventure.

Hatch, Shirley C.

1133 *Wind Is to Feel.* Ill. by Marilyn Miller. Putnam, 1973, o.p. SUBJECTS: Senses — Touch; Weather. RL B.

The wind is described through a variety of familiar sensory experiences and experiments. Effective pencil sketches have pale blue, yellow, and gray washes.

Hautzig, Deborah

1134 *Handsomest Father.* Ill. by Muriel Batherman. Greenwillow, 1979, o.p. SERIES: Read-Alone. SUBJECTS: Fathers — Fiction; School stories; Self-esteem — Fiction. RL B.

A child's agonies regarding his father's personal appearance are sympathetically portrayed when the father attends open house at school. Ink and wash sketches blend superbly.

1135 *Happy Birthday, Little Witch.* Ill. by Marc Brown. Random House, 1985, ISBN 0-394-97365-8. SERIES: Step into Reading. SUBJECTS: Birthdays — Fiction; Halloween — Fiction; Witches — Fiction. RL B.

When Little Witch's Halloween friends surprise her with a birthday party, she plays pin the tail on the devil, it rains black and blue jellybeans, and there are firecrackers. Expectations are gently overturned in this story illustrated with Brown's humorous drawings.

1136 *It's a Secret!* Ill. by Tom Leigh. Random House, 1988, ISBN 0-394-99672-0. SERIES: Start-to-Read. SUBJECTS: Concepts — Numbers. RL A.

Bert's feelings are hurt when Ernie tells others that Bert can't count past one hundred. The "Sesame Street" group then learns to count together. Characters are in bright colors.

1137 *It's Easy!* Ill. by Joe Mathieu. Random House, 1988, ISBN 0-394-91376-0. SUBJECTS: Friendship — Fiction; Gardening — Fiction; Puppetry — Fiction. RL A.

Big Bird finds he needs help with his sunflower garden after all to keep the birds away. Large colored drawings are of "Sesame Street" characters.

1138 *It's Not Fair! Featuring Jim Henson's Sesame Street Muppets.* Ill. by Tom Leigh. Random House, pap., 1986, ISBN 0-679-83951-8. SERIES: Start-to-Read. SUBJECTS: Friendship — Fiction. RL B.

After Bert does all the work and Ernie gets the credit, Ernie gives Bert an unusual gift — a dustpan and brush. Realistic differences are dealt with sympathetically. Colorful cartoons of familiar television characters illustrate the text.

1139 *Little Witch's Big Night.* Ill. by Marc Brown. Random House, 1984, ISBN 0-394-96587-6. SERIES: Step into Reading. SUBJECTS: Halloween — Fiction; Witches — Fiction. RL C.

Little Witch, left behind on Halloween because she had been too good, gives some trick-or-treaters a night to remember. Friendly watercolor drawings take away all fear.

1140 *The Nutcracker Ballet.* Ill. by Carolyn Ewing. Random House, 1992, ISBN 0-679-92385-3. SERIES: Step into Reading. SUBJECTS: Dancers and dancing; Fairy tales; Music and musicians. RL B.

When Marie helps break the spell on the curious nutcracker given her by her eccentric godfather, the nutcracker turns into a prince in this simple retelling with watercolor drawings.

1141 *Why Are You So Mean to Me?* Ill. by Tom Cooke. Random House, 1986, ISBN 0-394-88060-9. SERIES: Start-to-Read. SUBJECTS: Friendship — Fiction; Self-esteem — Fiction. RL B.

Grover's mother tells him he will always be good at being himself, regardless of how he plays baseball. Feelings are expressed and friends forgiven in another Henson Muppet series book, illustrated in bright pastels.

Hawes, Judy

1142 *Fireflies in the Night.* Ill. by Ellen Alexander. HarperCollins, 1990, o.p. SERIES: Let's-Read-and-Find-Out. SUBJECTS: Fireflies; Nature; Science and scientists. RL B.

The ways in which firefly light is generated, changes with the temperature, and is used by people are simply outlined, with suitable illustration of nighttime scenes. The fireflies are always released by bedtime.

1143 *Why Frogs Are Wet.* Ill. by Don Madden. HarperCollins, 1968, o.p. SERIES: Let's-Read-and-Find-Out Science. SUBJECTS: Frogs and toads; Science and scientists. RL B.

Hawes, Judy (cont.)

Frogs preceded dinosaurs by 50 million years, have 2,000 varieties, were the first animals to have a voice. Fascinating frog facts are illustrated by bright, decorative drawings with bold strokes.

Hawkins, Colin, and Jacqui Hawkins

1144 *I'm Not Sleepy!* Ill. by authors. Crown, 1985, o.p. SERIES: It's Great to Read. SUBJECTS: Bears — Fiction; Bedtime — Fiction. RL A.
Not until Mommy comes to tuck him in does Baby Bear settle down for the night. Abbreviated dialogue between mother and child is illustrated showing only the rotund baby's delaying antics.

1145 *Jen the Hen.* Ill. by authors. Putnam, 1985, o.p. SERIES: Flip-the-Page Rhyming. SUBJECTS: Birthdays — Fiction; Stories in rhyme. RL A.
Ken, Ben, Wren, and a hen called Jen meet in the glen at ten — for a birthday party. Wordplay using basic vocabulary is illustrated with rotund cartoon characters in pastels, and two tiny bookish worms.

1146 *Mig the Pig.* Ill. by author. Putnam, 1986, o.p. SERIES: Flip-the-Page Rhyming. SUBJECTS: Pigs — Fiction; Stories in rhyme; Wordplay. RL A.
The beginning consonant of "pig" changes to make "big," "wig," "twig," and five other rhyming words. Zany cartoons include "talking" scallop-edged worms.

1147 *Pat the Cat.* Ill. by authors. Putnam, pap., 1983, ISBN 0-399-20957-3. SUBJECTS: Pets — Cats — Fiction; Stories in rhyme. RL A.
Pat the fat cat has a rat named Nat and a bat named Tat in his hat on the mat. The story is as lively as vocabulary allows, brightened by scallop-edged animals and worms.

1148 *Tog the Dog.* Ill. by author. Putnam, 1986, o.p. SERIES: Flip-the-Page Rhyming. SUBJECTS: Pets — Dogs — Fiction; Stories in rhyme; Wordplay. RL A.
Jog, fog, cog, frog, bog, hog, log, and a dog named Tog are rhyming words produced by changing initial consonants and accenting them with humorous wordplay. Visual humor is added with lumpy cartoon animals.

1149 *Zug the Bug.* Ill. by author. Putnam, 1988, o.p. SERIES: Flip-the-Page Rhyming. SUBJECTS: Insects — Fiction; Stories in rhyme; Wordplay. RL A.
Seven words rhyming with bug are made by changing the initial consonant. Cartoons are enlivened by the humorous commentary of two worms.

Hay, Samantha

1150 *Creepy Customers.* Ill. by Sarah Warburton. Kingfisher, pap., 2005, ISBN 0-7534-5857-8. SERIES: I Am Reading. SUBJECTS: Humorous stories; Monsters — Fiction. RL B.
Working at his father's pharmacy during school vacation seems dull until some interesting customers come in for wart remover, a strong comb, and cough drops. Cartoon illustrations featuring humorously "creepy " customers enhance a funny story that readers are sure to enjoy.

Hayes, Geoffrey

1151 *The Mystery of the Pirate Ghost: An Otto and Uncle Tooth Adventure.* Ill. by author. Random House, 1985, o.p. SERIES: Step into Reading. SUBJECTS: Dinosaurs — Fiction; Mystery and detective stories; Pirates — Fiction. RL B.
Dinosaurs Otto and Uncle Tooth uncover a pirate "ghost" with a trumpet. The mystery is well constructed with some humor and a satisfying conclusion. Koalas, puffins, and octopi complete the cast of characters. Illustrations are in watercolor.

1152 *The Secret of Foghorn Island.* Ill. by author. Random House, 1988, ISBN 0-394-99614-3. SERIES: Step into Reading. SUBJECTS: Dinosaurs — Fiction; Mystery and detective stories. RL B.
Dinosaurs Otto and Uncle Tooth save Auntie Hicks from Sid Rat, Weasel, and the magical Doctor Ocular in an adventure with sea witches and shipwrecks. Pastel comic drawings keep the tone light.

Hays, Anna Jane

1153 *Silly Sara.* Ill. by Sylvie Wickstrom. Random House, pap., 2002, ISBN 0-375-81231-8. SERIES: Step into Reading.

SUBJECTS: Friendship — Fiction; Stories in rhyme. RL A.

With minimal vocabulary, this phonics reader focuses on Sara, who is sometimes clumsy and silly. But with her best friend Sam she is super. Lively cartoon art captures the fun adventures of two friends.

Hayward, Linda

1154 *Baker, Baker, Cookie Maker.* Ill. by Tom Brannon. Random House, 1998, o.p. SERIES: Step into Reading. SUBJECTS: Bakers and baking — Fiction; Stories in rhyme. RL B. LEXILE 250L.

Whenever Cookie Monster bakes up a batch of cookies, all his friends from "Sesame Street" come to eat them. Everyone's favorite characters are featured in colorful, lighthearted illustrations that expressively demonstrate the Cookie Monster's dilemma.

1155 *The Biggest Cookie in the World.* Ill. by Joseph Ewers. Random House, 1989, ISBN 0-394-84049-6. SERIES: Pictureback Reader. SUBJECTS: Bakers and baking — Fiction; Monsters — Fiction; Puppetry — Fiction. RL A.

While Cookie Monster — of "Sesame Street" — waits for a batch of chocolate chip cookies to bake, he dreams about the largest cookie in the world, losing track of baking time — with disastrous results. Ideas for using the 32 vocabulary words on flash cards are included on the back cover.

1156 *Cave People.* Ill. by Gabriela Dellosso. Grosset & Dunlap, 1997, o.p. SERIES: All Aboard Reading. SUBJECTS: Prehistoric man. RL B. LEXILE 330L.

A look back fifty thousand years briefly examines the Neanderthals and how they lived. Full-page earth-toned illustrations highlight the information within the text.

1157 *A Day in the Life of a Dancer.* DK, 2001, ISBN 0-7894-7370-4. SERIES: DK Readers. SUBJECTS: Dancers and dancing. RL B. LEXILE 140L.

From nine in the morning, the reader follows Lisa, a ballet dancer, as she practices in preparation for an evening performance. Color photographs chronicle a day in a young dancer's career.

1158 *Hello, House!* Ill. by Lynn Munsinger. Random House, 1988, o.p. SERIES: Step into Reading. SUBJECTS: Folklore — African Americans; Folklore — United States. RL A.

Brer Rabbit outsmarts Brer Wolf again in a classic trickster tale. Pastel drawings with expressive main characters enhance this simple, effective retelling.

Hazen, Barbara Shook

1159 *Digby.* Ill. by Barbara Phillips-Duke. HarperCollins, 1997, o.p. SERIES: I Can Read. SUBJECTS: African Americans — Fiction; Pets — Dogs — Fiction. RL B. LEXILE 160L.

An older sister explains to her younger brother that now that Digby the dog is older he can no longer run and play catch, but can watch them play and be their special dog. Boldly colored illustrations warmly express the love and devotion the children and their dog have for each other.

1160 *Road Hog.* Ill. by Davy Jones. Golden Books, 1998, o.p. SERIES: Road to Reading. SUBJECTS: Cars — Fiction; Pigs — Fiction; Stories in rhyme. RL B. LEXILE AD820L.

Much to everyone's dismay — especially that of the police officer who gives him a ticket — Road Hog likes to go fast, whether driving on the farm or on the streets. Action-packed artwork comically extends the text by illustrating the disaster Hog leaves in his wake.

Head, Judith

1161 *Mud Soup.* Ill. by Susan Guevara. Random House, pap., 2003, ISBN 0-375-81087-0. SERIES: Step into Reading. SUBJECTS: Food; Hispanic Americans. RL B.

Each time Rosa invites Gordon to try her Abuela's Mud Soup, he finds a polite excuse not to, until one day he tries it and finds it's *delicioso.* Brightly colored watercolor illustrations offer expressive facial expressions that underscore Gordon's apprehension.

Hearn, Emily

1162 *Ring Around Duffy.* Ill. by Paul Frame. Garrard, 1974, o.p. SERIES: Venture. SUBJECTS: Ducks — Fiction; Pollution — Fiction. RL B.

Hearn, Emily (cont.)

An injured duckling, rescued by a family dog, is returned to the wild, but needs to be rescued again when he gets a soda can ring stuck around his bill. Pencil and turquoise wash drawings present animals best.

1163 *TV Kangaroo.* Ill. by Tom Eaton. Garrard, 1975, o.p. SUBJECTS: Animals — Fiction; Weather — Fiction. RL B.

No matter what weather the television kangaroo announces, some animals like it and others "avoid" it. A simple text and idea, illustrated with lighthearted animal cartoons.

Heide, Florence P., and Roxanne Heide

1164 *A Monster Is Coming! A Monster Is Coming!* Ill. by Rachi Farrow. Watts, 1980, o.p. SUBJECTS: Monsters — Fiction; Television — Fiction. RL B.

Neither her younger brother, Eddie, nor a monster can distract Alice from television. Pale lemon and lavender on a strong black-and-white checked floor contrast with the fuchsia, red, and gold monster.

Heilbroner, Joan

1165 *The Happy Birthday Present.* Ill. by Mary Chalmers. HarperCollins, 1962, o.p. SERIES: I Can Read. SUBJECTS: Birthdays — Fiction; Siblings — Fiction. RL A.

Peter takes his little brother Davy shopping for Mother's birthday. With limited resources they end up with an imaginative birthday tree. Very realistic dialogue, childlike misconceptions, and soft pencil drawings add to the appeal.

1166 *Robert the Rose Horse.* Ill. by P. D. Eastman. Random House, 1962, ISBN 0-394-90025-1. SERIES: I Can Read It All by Myself. SUBJECTS: Allergies — Fiction; Horses — Fiction; Humorous stories. RL A.

Robert's allergies cause him to end several careers prematurely, but when his big sneeze captures some bank robbers, he finally finds his calling. Cartoon sketches fit the humor.

1167 *This Is the House Where Jack Lives.* Ill. by Aliki. HarperCollins, 1962, ISBN 0-06-022286-7. SERIES: I Can Read. SUBJECTS: Cumulative tales. RL A.

The very best of modern cumulative tales includes an assortment of apartment dwellers, from the maid and window-washer to a boy walking a dog and Jack taking an exuberant bath on an upper floor. Drawings are fun in gray and fuchsia.

1168 *Tom the TV Cat: A Step Two Book.* Ill. by Sal Murdocca. Random House, 1984, ISBN 0-394-96708-9. SERIES: Step into Reading. SUBJECTS: Pets — Cats — Fiction; Self-esteem — Fiction; Television — Fiction. RL A.

Tom the cat tests some television roles by imitating the song man, the strong man, superman, and a ball man — with disastrous results. Murdocca's cartoons underline the humor of Tom's antics.

Heiligman, Deborah

1169 *Mike Swan, Sink or Swim.* Ill. by Chris L. Demarest. Delacorte, 1998, o.p. SUBJECTS: Fear — Fiction; Sports — Swimming — Fiction. RL B. LEXILE 240L.

Afraid to swim, Mike is reluctant to take lessons. With the help of his father, friend Lizzie, and a peanut butter and baloney sandwich, he succeeds. Colorful watercolor and ink drawings ably express Mike's many emotions as he tries to overcome his fear.

Heling, Kathryn

1170 *Mouse Makes Words.* Ill. by Patrick Joseph. Random House, 2002, o.p. SERIES: Step into Reading. SUBJECTS: Mice — Fiction; Stories in rhyme. RL B. LEXILE 310L.

As a phonics reader, Mouse makes new words by changing the first letters. Large, playful illustrations accompany each new word printed out in oversized letters, giving a visual clue for the beginning reader who is concentrating on initial consonants.

1171 *Mouse's Hide-and-Seek Words.* Ill. by Deborah Hembrook. Random House, 2003, ISBN 0-375-92185-0. SERIES: Step into Reading + Phonics. SUBJECTS: Mice — Fiction. RL B. LEXILE 150L.

In this phonics reader, beginners seek smaller words that are "hiding" within bigger words. Simple, colorful illustrations focus on the word action and highlight the "hide-and-seek" concept by using two colors in the font.

Heller, Ruth

1172 *A Cache of Jewels and Other Collective Nouns*. Ill. by author. Putnam, 1987, o.p. SUBJECTS: English language; Wordplay. RL C.
In imaginative rhythmic, rhyming language, an array of collective nouns is presented — a gam of whales and a muster of peacocks, a parcel of penguins and a drift of swans. Double-spread, dramatic, realistic drawings show animals, fruit, flowers, and trees.

1173 *Kites Sail High: A Book About Verbs*. Ill. by author. Putnam, 1988, o.p. SUBJECTS: English language; Wordplay. RL C.
Verbs are highlighted in bold, large type in the playful rhyming text. Tenses, moods, and contractions and voices are introduced, and illustrated with bold, double-page drawings from under the sea and from fairy tales, of animals and a single peacock feather quill, to a close-up box of candy.

1174 *Many Luscious Lollipops: A Book About Adjectives*. Ill. by author. Putnam, 1989, o.p. SUBJECTS: English language; Wordplay. RL C.
Demonstratives and possessives, comparative and irregular and superlative adjectives are introduced painlessly in this introduction to grammar and language. The playful rhyming text has sweeping illustrations of animals, ice cream, mazes, tree ornaments, and space.

1175 *Merry-Go-Round: A Book About Nouns*. Ill. by author. Putnam, 1990, o.p. SUBJECTS: English language; Wordplay. RL C.
Stunning full-page thematic illustrations extend the unpatronizing vocabulary and grammar of nouns, ranging from medieval to space-age themes. The language and the format are imaginative and instructive, covering plurals and possessives, compound and collective nouns, and determiners.

1176 *Up, Up and Away: A Book About Adverbs*. Ill. by author. Putnam, 1991, o.p. SUBJECTS: English language; Wordplay. RL C.
Three large owls in a spruce illustrate the introduction of the questions adverbs ask: when, how, where, and why. Illustrations range from a monochromatic long-haired cat, to black-and-white pandas among the bright green bamboo, to the eerie purple and orange of the genies.

Helmer, Marilyn

1177 *Recess Riddles*. Ill. by Jane Kurisu. Kids Can Press, 2004, ISBN 1-55337-577-7. SERIES: Kids Can Read. SUBJECTS: Jokes and riddles. RL B.
Thirty jokes, riddles, and knocks-knocks take a funny look at the school day. Colorfully framed illustrations extend the humor.

Hennessy, B. G.

1178 *Busy Dinah Dinosaur*. Ill. by Ana Marrin Larranaga. Candlewick, 2000, o.p. SERIES: Brand New Readers. SUBJECTS: Dinosaurs — Fiction; Humorous stories. RL A.
In four short stories, Dinah is very busy playing with her friend, finding a turtle, and running away from a scary T-rex. Simply shaped illustrations outlined in black enrich the repetitive sentence structure.

1179 *Meet Dinah Dinosaur*. Ill. by Ana Marrin Larranaga. Candlewick, 2000, o.p. SERIES: Brand New Readers. SUBJECTS: Dinosaurs — Fiction; Humorous stories. RL A.
From morning to night, four stories follow Dinah as she plays in the mud, eats flowers, plays hide-and-seek, and dreams. Boldly outlined artwork expressively augments the simple repetition of words in sentences.

Henriod, Lorraine

1180 *Marie Curie*. Ill. by Fermin Rocker. Putnam, 1970, o.p. SERIES: See and Read. SUBJECTS: Biographies; Careers; Science and scientists. RL B.
In simple terms, without neglecting the hardships or hazards, the story of Marie Curie's amazing accomplishments in science is told. Ink drawings have a pale blue wash.

Henwood, Chris

1181 *Frogs*. Photos by Barrie Watts. Watts, 1988, o.p. SERIES: Keeping Minibeasts. SUBJECTS: Frogs and toads; Pets. RL C.

Henwood, Chris (cont.)

Background information about frogs is geared for the catching, caring, and feeding of frogs as pets. Exceptional color photographs give additional information about their habitat and handling.

1182 *Spiders*. Photos by Barrie Watts. Watts, 1988, o.p. SERIES: Keeping Minibeasts. SUBJECTS: Pets; Spiders. RL C.
The handling and feeding of spiders of different sizes are described and illustrated with excellent color photographs. Information on webs and the exaggerated danger to man from spiders is given.

Herman, Emmi S.

1183 *We All Fall for Apples*. Ill. by Anne Kennedy. Scholastic, pap., 2006, ISBN 0-439-83312-4. SERIES: Scholastic Reader. SUBJECTS: Fall — Fiction; Fruit. RL B.
Everyone wants to go to the farm to pick apples, go on a hayride, and drink apple cider. Colorful illustrations of the family and friends follow the simple, repetitive text as everyone has fall fun.

Herman, Gail

1184 *Buried in the Backyard*. Ill. by Jerry Smath. Kane, pap., 2003, ISBN 1-57565-126-2. SERIES: Science Solves It! SUBJECTS: Prehistoric animals — Fiction; Siblings — Fiction. RL B.
While digging in their yard to make a swimming pool, Ryan and Katie unearth a big bone. A trip to the museum reveals its origin, and soon the backyard is an excavation site. Clever illustrations seamlessly interweave fascinating facts about prehistoric animals.

1185 *The Camping Caper*. Ill. by Duendes del Sur. Scholastic, pap., 2006, ISBN 0-439-80942-8. SERIES: Scooby-Doo Readers. SUBJECTS: Camps and camping — Fiction; Mystery and detective stories; Pets — Dogs — Fiction. RL B.
When Mystery, Inc goes camping, Scooby and Shaggy look for firewood and hear creepy noises. Are the woods haunted? Colorful cartoon art as seen on the television series provides visual clues to help solve this spooky mystery.

1186 *Disappearing Donuts*. Ill. by Duendes del Sur. Scholastic, pap., 2000, ISBN 0-439-16168-1. SERIES: Scooby-Doo Readers. SUBJECTS: Food — Fiction; Mystery and detective stories; Pets — Dogs — Fiction. RL B.
With the promise of all the free donuts they can eat, Scooby and friends hide out in the shop to help solve the mystery of the disappearing donuts. Action-packed illustrations match the adventures of everyone's favorite dog, Scooby-Doo.

1187 *Double Header*. Ill. by Jerry Smath. Putnam, 1993, ISBN 0-448-40157-6. SERIES: All Aboard Reading. SUBJECTS: Monsters — Fiction; Sports — Baseball — Fiction. RL A.
Although the two heads of a double-headed boy monster almost always agree, their disagreement on the baseball diamond costs their team the game. Seeing a good scary double feature — Human Beings and Human Beings 2-at Fright Night unites the two again. Friendly colored pencil drawings complement the text.

1188 *Flower Girl*. Ill. by Paige Billin-Frye. Grosset & Dunlap, pap., 1996, ISBN 0-448-41108-3. SERIES: All Aboard Reading. SUBJECTS: Siblings — Fiction; Weddings — Fiction. RL B. LEXILE 210L.
With the help of her lucky ring, a young girl hopes to be the best flower girl ever at her sister's wedding. Expressive pastel watercolors humorously portray the young girl's hopes and fears as she walks down the aisle.

1189 *Ghost in the Garden*. Ill. by Duendes del Sur. Scholastic, 2000, o.p. SERIES: Scooby-Doo Readers. SUBJECTS: Ghost stories; Mystery and detective stories; Pets — Dogs — Fiction. RL B. LEXILE 80L.
To help catch a ghost thief in the farmer's garden, Scooby and Shaggy dress up as scarecrows. Comical cartoons help reveal the real mystery behind the mystery of the vanishing vegetables.

1190 *The Haunted Bike*. Ill. by Blanche Sims. Grosset & Dunlap, 1996, o.p. SERIES: Eek! Stories to Make You Shriek. SUBJECTS: Bicycles and bicycling — Fiction; Ghost stories. RL B.
Emma finds that her new bicycle has strange powers, and a new boy named Bobby says he used to have one just like it. Is this a strange coincidence or not? Watercolor and ink drawings

demonstrate the eerie, unique abilities of the unusual bicycle.

1191 *Howling on the Playground*. Ill. by Duendes del Sur. Scholastic, pap., 2000, ISBN 0-439-16169-X. SERIES: Scooby-Doo Readers. SUBJECTS: Mystery and detective stories; Pets — Dogs — Fiction. RL B. LEXILE 140L.

While helping to build a playground, Scooby and the gang solve the mystery surrounding its "haunting." Full-page cartoon illustrations expressively dramatize the sleuths in action.

1192 *Map in the Mystery Machine*. Ill. by Duendes del Sur. Scholastic, pap., 2000, ISBN 0-439-16167-3. SERIES: Scooby-Doo Readers. SUBJECTS: Mystery and detective stories; Pets — Dogs — Fiction. RL B.

Following an old pirate map leads the Mystery Machine down a road where a ghost warns them to travel no further. Colorful cartoons follow the "scary" adventures of Fred, Daphne, Velma, Shaggy, and Scooby.

1193 *Shiny Spooky Knights*. Ill. by Duendes del Sur. Scholastic, pap., 2000, ISBN 0-439-20227-2. SERIES: Scooby-Doo Readers. SUBJECTS: Mystery and detective stories; Pets — Dogs — Fiction. RL B. LEXILE 40L.

When the van breaks down outside a castle, the gang wants to call for help. Meeting a vampire, a witch, and a mummy they fear the worst until they are invited to share cake at a costume party. Hilarious cartoon artwork captures the scary predicaments of Mystery, Inc.

1194 *Slip! Slide! Skate!* Ill. by Paige Billin-Frye. Scholastic, pap., 1999, ISBN 0-439-09907-2. SERIES: Hello Reader! SUBJECTS: Friendship — Fiction; Sports — Ice skating — Fiction. RL B. LEXILE 10L.

After receiving her first pair of ice skates, a young girl tries to be the very best skater, but finally realizes it's more important to have fun. Lively watercolor illustrations ably portray the intensity of a girl's passion for perfectionism and her friends' enjoyment of the sport.

1195 *Snack Snatcher*. Ill. by Duendes del Sur. Scholastic, pap., 2001, ISBN 0-439-20229-9. SERIES: Scooby-Doo Readers. SUBJECTS: Mystery and detective stories; Pets — Dogs — Fiction. RL B.

Who is the monster who stole Scooby's snacks at the Coolsville Bake-Off Contest? Detailed cartoon illustrations enable the reader to follow the trail of crumbs and search for the clues to solve the mystery.

1196 *The Thanksgiving Mystery*. Ill. by Duendes del Sur. Scholastic, pap., 2005, ISBN 0-439-78359-3. SERIES: Scooby-Doo Readers. SUBJECTS: Mystery and detective stories; Pets — Dogs — Fiction; Thanksgiving — Fiction. RL B.

Frightened by the pumpkin head monsters, Scooby and Shaggy scare themselves into winning the pie-eating contest. The comical mishaps of the duo are captured in the full-page cartoon illustrations.

1197 *There Is a Town*. Ill. by Katy Bratun. Random House, pap., 1996, ISBN 0-679-86439-3. SERIES: Early Step into Reading. SUBJECTS: Birthdays — Fiction; Dolls and dollhouses — Fiction. RL B. LEXILE 390L.

In a parody of "The House that Jack Built," a young girl celebrates her birthday and receives a special dollhouse as a present. Colorful drawings of a birthday party at home and in the dollhouse are paired, providing a unique parallel experience.

1198 *What a Hungry Puppy!* Ill. by Norman Gorbaty. Putnam, 1993, o.p. SERIES: All Aboard Reading. SUBJECTS: Pets — Dogs — Fiction; Pets — Fiction. RL A.

Despite the admonition that dinner is almost ready, Lucky the puppy strays, sniffing, digging, and chewing, until chased home by a big white sheepdog, who turns out not to be threatening after all. Raggedy puppy drawings are appealing.

Herman, R. A.

1199 *Pal and Sal*. Ill. by Betina Ogden. Grosset & Dunlap, pap., 1998, ISBN 0-448-41716-2. SERIES: All Aboard Reading. SUBJECTS: Friendship — Fiction; Horses — Fiction. RL B.

The big horses at the Star Ranch don't want to play with Pal the pony, but he eventually finds a new friend named Sal. Gentle, earth-toned illustrations detail Pal's loneliness.

Herman, R. A. (cont.)

1200 *Pal the Pony*. Ill. by Betina Ogden. Grosset & Dunlap, pap., 1996, ISBN 0-448-41257-8. SERIES: All Aboard Reading. SUBJECTS: Friendship — Fiction; Horses — Fiction. RL B. LEXILE 270L.

Pal can't be like all the horses in the rodeo, but when a little girl wants to ride him, he finds he is a star to all the small children. Lively, earth-toned watercolors show the contrast between the fast action of the rodeo stars and the gentleness of Pal.

Hewett, Joan

1201 *Tiger, Tiger Growing Up*. Photos by Richard Hewett. Houghton Mifflin, 1993, o.p. SUBJECTS: Conservation; Tigers; Zoos. RL C.

The development of a newborn tiger cub, Tara, into a cat ambassador for Marine World Africa USA is traced through playful, affectionate color photographs and narrative.

Hilker, Cathryn H.

1202 *A Cheetah Named Angel*. Ill. with photos. Watts, 1992, ISBN 0-531-15252-9. SUBJECTS: Cheetahs; Conservation; Zoos. RL C.

Cathryn raises a cheetah cub from the Columbus, Ohio, zoo at her farm near Cincinnati, along with her Great Dane and, later, a mountain lion cub, Carrie. Both the cubs become TV stars and international ambassadors to lobby for preservation of habitat for wild cats. Excellent photographs accompany the text.

Hill, Susan

1203 *Ruby Paints a Picture*. Ill. by Margie Moore. HarperCollins, 2005, ISBN 0-06-008978-4. SERIES: I Can Read. SUBJECTS: Painting — Fiction; Raccoons — Fiction. RL A.

Although Ruby did not paint the wide wings, long ears, red tail, or webbed feet of her friends, she did paint their very best feature! Gentle pastels illustrate this cozy story.

1204 *Stuart Little: Stuart at the Fun House*. Ill. by Columbia Pictures. HarperCollins, 2001, ISBN 0-06-029539-2. SERIES: I Can Read. SUBJECTS: Amusement parks — Fiction; Mice — Fiction. RL B.

Tiny Stuart is too small to enjoy most of the activities at the amusement park — except when he and brother George go to the Fun House!

1205 *Stuart Little: Stuart at the Library*. HarperCollins, 2001, o.p. SERIES: I Can Read. SUBJECTS: Books and reading — Fiction; Mice — Fiction; Pets — Cats — Fiction. RL A.

Bookworm, the library owl, and Stuart become friends, and Stuart helps Bookworm learn to read.

1206 *Stuart Little: Stuart Hides Out*. HarperCollins, 2001, o.p. SERIES: I Can Read. SUBJECTS: Mice — Fiction; Pets — Cats — Fiction. RL A.

Stuart and the family cat, Snowbell, play hide-and-seek when their family is gone.

1207 *Stuart Little: Stuart Sets Sail*. Ill. by Lydia Halverson. HarperCollins, 2001, o.p. SERIES: I Can Read. SUBJECTS: Mice — Fiction. RL A.

Stuart's adventures — sailing on a lake, seeing a fish with a hook in its mouth, glimpsing a snapping turtle, and receiving waves from a motorboat and a bird — are not visible to the Littles on the shore. These adventures on a mini-scale are illustrated by Lydia Halverson.

Hillert, Margaret

1208 *Circus Fun*. Ill. by Elaine Raphael. Modern Curriculum Press, 1969, o.p. SUBJECTS: Circuses — Fiction. RL A.

Fifty words are used to tell about the circus. Watercolors focus on clowns, lions, and elephants.

1209 *Come Play with Me*. Ill. by Kinuko Craft. Follett, 1975, o.p. SERIES: Just Beginning-to-Read. SUBJECTS: Poetry. RL A.

Simple poems about familiar things, composed of 75 pre-primer words, are illustrated with imaginative watercolors in a fairy tale atmosphere.

1210 *Come to School, Dear Dragon*. Ill. by David Helton. Modern Curriculum Press, 1985, ISBN 0-8136-5133-6. SERIES: Beginning to Read. SUBJECTS: Dragons —

Fiction; Mythical creatures — Fiction; School stories. RL A.

A dragon makes himself useful when his boy takes him to school. This primer employs a 75-word vocabulary and typically cutesy Helton drawings.

1211 *A Friend for Dear Dragon*. Ill. by David Helton. Modern Curriculum Press, 1985, ISBN 0-8136-5136-0. SERIES: Beginning to Read. SUBJECTS: Friendship — Fiction; Mythical creatures — Fiction; Pets — Fiction. RL A.

Using a 67-word vocabulary, a former first grade teacher relays the moral play of a boy and his pet dragon, and the new neighbor girl and her unicorn. Cutesy drawings and unimaginative text limit the appeal of this book.

1212 *Go to Sleep, Dear Dragon*. Ill. by David Helton. Modern Curriculum Press, 1985, ISBN 0-8136-5023-2. SERIES: Beginning-to-Read. SUBJECTS: Dreams — Fiction; Mythical creatures — Fiction; Pets — Fiction. RL A.

Using a 74-word vocabulary, the author spins a tale of how the dreaming boy finds his dear dragon's egg in medieval times. This is more interesting than many Hillert books with such limited vocabularies, but has typical drawings.

1213 *Happy Birthday, Dear Dragon*. Ill. by Carl Kock. Modern Curriculum Press, 1977, ISBN 0-8136-5021-6. SERIES: Just Beginning-to-Read. SUBJECTS: Concepts — Colors — Fiction; Mythical creatures — Fiction; Valentine's Day — Fiction. RL A.

A child and a baby dragon celebrate Valentine's Day by focusing on red things familiar to children: a cardinal, a fire truck, a stop light, school, apples, and a valentine. Drawings are simple.

1214 *It's Circus Time, Dear Dragon*. Ill. by David Helton. Modern Curriculum Press, 1984, ISBN 0-8136-5132-8. SUBJECTS: Circuses — Fiction; Dragons — Fiction. RL A.

In text with a 65-word vocabulary, a boy and his pet dragon visit the circus. The book is dry and unimaginative in text and illustration, except for the dragon's mild mischief in trying the tuba or joining the parade of elephants.

1215 *Little Puff*. Ill. by Sid Jordan. Modern Curriculum Press, 1973, ISBN 0-8136-5014-3. SUBJECTS: Trains — Fiction. RL A.

Sixty words are used to tell the slight story of a train that is not wanted in town or at the zoo, only on the tracks with children as passengers. Drawings have color and pattern reminiscent of a mosaic.

1216 *Not I, Not I*. Ill. by Diana Magnuson. Modern Curriculum Press, 1981, ISBN 0-8136-5063-1. SERIES: Beginning to Read. SUBJECTS: Chickens — Fiction. RL A.

The story of the Little Red Hen is told using a 44-word vocabulary illustrated with watercolors of the animals.

1217 *Play Ball*. Ill. by Dick Martin. Follett, 1978, ISBN 0-8136-5034-8. SERIES: Just Beginning-to-Read. SUBJECTS: Play — Fiction; Toys — Fiction. RL A.

Interest and humor are generated with 58 words as two boys look for balls and equipment to play various games. There are unexpected and magical qualities to their play. Pale tans and yellows predominate in clever illustrations.

1218 *Run to the Rainbow*. Ill. by Barbara Corey. Modern Curriculum Press, 1981, ISBN 0-8136-5065-8. SERIES: Beginning-to-Read. SUBJECTS: Rainbows; Science and scientists. RL A.

The text, even though a bit choppy, introduces some interesting, commonplace ways to produce rainbows. Watercolor illustrations are a bit busy to locate the "rainbows."

1219 *Snow Baby*. Ill. by Liz Dauber. Follett, 1969, ISBN 0-8136-5065-8. SERIES: Just Beginning-to-Read. SUBJECTS: Weather — Snow — Fiction; Winter — Fiction. RL A.

Children's play in the snow leads to a surprise find in this pre-primer with a 50-word vocabulary. Full-color drawings fill the pages.

1220 *The Three Goats*. Ill. by Mel Pekarsky. Modern Curriculum Press, 1963, ISBN 1-59953-027-9. SUBJECTS: Goats — Fiction. RL A. LEXILE BR.

A dated, oversimplified version of *The Three Billy Goats Gruff*.

Hillert, Margaret (cont.)

1221 *What Is It?* Ill. by Kinuko Craft. Modern Curriculum Press, 1978, ISBN 0-8136-5056-9. SERIES: Just Beginning-to-Read My Stories in Verse. SUBJECTS: Imagination — Fiction; Stories in rhyme. RL A.

Two elflike children follow a string through an imaginary land. The rhymed text uses 55 simple words. Illustrations are stilted pastels.

1222 *Who Goes to School?* Ill. by Nan Brooks. Modern Curriculum Press, 1981, ISBN 0-8136-5075-5. SERIES: Just Beginning-to-Read. SUBJECTS: Pets — Cats; Pets — Dogs; School stories. RL A.

Circus, television commercial, and police dogs go to school, as do children. A vocabulary of 65 words is used to give very basic information about school. Folk-style illustrations add appeal.

1223 *The Witch Who Went for a Walk.* Ill. by Krystyna Stasiak. Follett, 1982, o.p. SERIES: Just Beginning-to-Read. SUBJECTS: Halloween — Fiction; Witches — Fiction. RL A.

Sixty-seven words are used to show the witch's fear of children dressed for Halloween. Some scary elements such as owls, caves, bats, and trees are shown with wide eyes in dark colors.

Himmelman, John

1224 *The Animal Rescue Club.* Ill. by author. HarperCollins, 1998, ISBN 0-613-18234-0. SERIES: I Can Read Chapter Book. SUBJECTS: Animal rescue — Fiction; Animals — Fiction. RL B. LEXILE 360L.

Anita, Mudpie, and Mike rescue a squirrel from the mud, a baby opossum from a drainpipe, and a goose with a shriveled foot. The appendix cautions children not to try rescuing wild animals by themselves. Pencil and wash drawings.

1225 *The Day-Off Machine.* Ill. by author. Small Packages, 1990, o.p. SERIES: Fix-It Family. SUBJECTS: Beavers — Fiction; Family life — Fiction; Inventors and inventions — Fiction. RL B.

Orville and Willa Wright and their children, Alexander, Graham, and Belle, can fix anything! But little Graham invents a way to give the whole family a day off. Cheerful watercolor illustrations show the buck-toothed beaver family.

1226 *The Great Leaf Blast-Off.* Ill. by author. Silver Burdett, 1990, ISBN 0-671-69634-3. SERIES: Fix-It Family. SUBJECTS: Beavers — Fiction; Humorous stories; Inventors and inventions — Fiction. RL A.

Pen and wash drawings add humor to this chapter story of inventive beavers named Wright. The brothers make unsuccessful machines to avoid raking, their parents invent new contraptions to replace appliances the boys "borrowed," but "space girl" Belle steals the day.

1227 *Ibis: A True Whale Story.* Ill. by author. Scholastic, 1990, ISBN 0-590-42848-9. SUBJECTS: Nature; Whales. RL A.

A true story about a small whale saved by scientists from net entanglement off Provincetown, Massachusetts, in 1984. Simple friendly whale illustrations accompany the text.

1228 *Simpson Snail Sings.* Ill. by author. Dutton, 1992, ISBN 0-525-44978-7. SERIES: Dutton Easy Reader. SUBJECTS: Animals — Fiction; Friendship — Fiction; Snails — Fiction. RL A.

Imaginative gentle tales of friends Simpson the Snail and Gypsy Moth are accompanied by delicate, expressive ink and wash drawings. The two share a trophy for best costume; Simpson learns to sing his own song; Simpson loses — and regains — a friend; and he and Tucker Turtle have a sleepover.

1229 *The Ups and Downs of Simpson Snail.* Ill. by author. Dutton, 1989, o.p. SERIES: Easy Reader. SUBJECTS: Snails — Fiction. RL B.

Simpson Snail gets stuck on a branch, looks for a new shell, tries flying, and looks for a friend to play with. Pen and wash drawings add humor and warmth to the story.

Hindley, Judy

1230 *Zoom on a Broom! Six Fun-Filled Stories.* Ill. by Tony Goffe. Kingfisher, 1991, ISBN 1-85697-826-5. SERIES: Kingfisher Read-Alone. SUBJECTS: Cumulative tales; Folklore. RL A.

Elements of familiar folk tales and themes are rewoven, some with more success than others. "The Magical Apple Tree" and "Tricky Tom" (royal suitor outwits giant) work well, but "The

Wonderful Turnip" and "What Do Witches Like?" are flat. Excellent lighthearted ink and wash drawings illustrate the tales.

Hirschi, Ron

1231 *Fall.* Photos by Thomas D. Mangelsen. Cobblehill, 1981, ISBN 0-525-65053-9. SUBJECTS: Birds; Fall. RL B.

Excellent photographs of a web, a flower, a squirrel eating a mushroom, salmon, an eagle, and deer are shown against the rich tapestry of fall colors. Large print is used for vividly described seasonal changes.

1232 *Spring.* Photos by Thomas D. Mangelsen. Cobblehill, 1990, ISBN 0-525-65037-7. SERIES: A Wildlife Seasons Book. SUBJECTS: Nature; Spring. RL B.

From the golden weasel to the nest of baby owls, from the marmot atop his rocky hill to a vivid mountain bluebird perched on the top of a pine tree, this photoessay celebrates the wonder and diversity at the beginning of spring.

1233 *What Is a Bird?* Photos by Galen Burrell. Walker, 1987, ISBN 0-8027-6721-4. SUBJECTS: Birds. RL B.

Short, expressive descriptions of a variety of birds are stunningly illustrated with close-up framed photo of birds against their native settings. This book is full of wonder and poetry.

Hirschmann, Kris

1234 *Glow-in-the-Dark Animals.* Ill. by Jean Cassels. Troll, 2000, ISBN 0-606-21214-0. SERIES: Planet Reader. SUBJECTS: Biology; Bioluminescence; Science and scientists. RL C.

Fireflies, cookie-cutter sharks, glowworms, and jellyfish all glow in the dark to attract a mate or prey. Fascinating details about a wide variety of animals are illustrated with simple chalk drawings.

1235 *Ocean Hunters.* Ill. by Monika Popowitz. Troll, 2000, ISBN 0-606-21361-9. SERIES: Planet Reader. SUBJECTS: Oceans and ocean life; Sharks; Whales. RL C.

Ocean predators, from orcas and moray eels to sharks and octopi, are introduced in this indexed book illustrated with paper collages.

Hiscock, Bruce

1236 *The Big Rock.* Ill. by author. Atheneum, 1988, ISBN 0-689-31402-7. SUBJECTS: Geology and geologists; Science and scientists. RL C.

The geological history of the Adirondacks is presented in an interesting and understandable way by following the movement of one rock. The watercolor illustrations complement the text well.

Hoban, Julia

1237 *Buzby.* Ill. by John Himmelman. HarperCollins, 1990, ISBN 0-06-022399-5. SERIES: I Can Read. SUBJECTS: Animals — Fiction; Humorous stories. RL A. LEXILE 300L.

When polite, clean kitten Buzby, who is also a good mouser, finds a job as a hotel busboy, he spills ice water on an opera singer and slips in the butter on the king's table. Gentle humor is enhanced by ink and wash illustrations.

1238 *Buzby to the Rescue.* Ill. by John Himmelman. HarperCollins, 1993, ISBN 0-06-021024-9. SERIES: I Can Read. SUBJECTS: Pets — Cats — Fiction. RL A.

Buzby, the proud hotel cat, saves a hotel guest, star Serena Lovejoy, from herself, and some suspected robbers. Fine, simple drawings show the innocent hotel cat and the other characters.

1239 *Quick Chick.* Ill. by Lillian Hoban. Dutton, 1989, ISBN 0-525-44490-4. SUBJECTS: Chickens — Fiction. RL B.

The littlest slow-learning chick is renamed after escaping from a cat. Friendly barnyard animals are in soft pastels.

Hoban, Lillian

1240 *Arthur's Back to School Day.* Ill. by author. HarperCollins, 1996, ISBN 0-06-024955-2. SERIES: I Can Read. SUBJECTS: Chimpanzees — Fiction; School buses — Fiction; Siblings — Fiction. RL B. LEXILE 400L.

The children's lunch boxes get mixed up when left behind at the bus stop in this inventive way to present school bus rules. Lively colored-pencil drawings.

Hoban, Lillian (cont.)

1241 *Arthur's Birthday Party*. Ill. by author. HarperCollins, 1999, ISBN 0-06-027799-8. SERIES: I Can Read. SUBJECTS: Birthdays — Fiction; Chimpanzees — Fiction; Sports — Gymnastics — Fiction. RL B. LEXILE 470L.

Arthur's gymnastic birthday party concludes with everyone getting a prize. Colored-pencil drawings of friends.

1242 *Arthur's Camp-Out*. Ill. by author. HarperCollins, 1993, ISBN 0-06-020526-1. SERIES: I Can Read. SUBJECTS: Camps and camping — Fiction; Chimpanzees — Fiction; Siblings — Fiction. RL B.

Arthur's fears and problems when he follows his younger sister's friends on a camp-out are eased when the girls feed him and keep him company. The baby-sitter welcomes the campers home with a banner and breakfast pancakes. Reassuring pencil and wash drawings accompany the text.

1243 *Arthur's Christmas Cookies*. Ill. by author. HarperCollins, 1972, ISBN 0-06-022367-7. SERIES: I Can Read. SUBJECTS: Chimpanzees — Fiction; Christmas — Fiction; Cookery — Fiction. RL B. LEXILE 390L.

Arthur again turns defeat into triumph when his Bake E-Z Christmas cookies are rock-hard. Pencil and wash drawings complement this story of childhood mishaps featuring a loving chimp family.

1244 *Arthur's Funny Money*. Ill. by author. HarperCollins, 1980, ISBN 0-06-022344-8. SERIES: I Can Read. SUBJECTS: Business enterprises — Fiction; Chimpanzees — Fiction. RL B. LEXILE 490L.

Violet finds out Arthur does not know numbers as well as he says when they go into the bike-washing business. Realistic characterization is underlined by soft pencil drawings with a four-color wash.

1245 *Arthur's Great Big Valentine*. Ill. by author. HarperCollins, 1988, ISBN 0-06-022406-1. SERIES: I Can Read. SUBJECTS: Chimpanzees — Fiction; Friendship — Fiction; Valentine's Day — Fiction. RL B. LEXILE 410L.

Arthur makes up with his friends by sending an unusual valentine. The pain and humor of childhood are shown throughout the book. Illustrations are of chimpanzee children.

1246 *Arthur's Halloween Costume*. Ill. by author. HarperCollins, 1983, ISBN 0-06-022387-1. SERIES: I Can Read. SUBJECTS: Chimpanzees — Fiction; Halloween — Fiction. RL B. LEXILE 380L.

Arthur's search for his homework in the trash can unwittingly enables him to win a costume prize after all — the Spirit of Halloween! Colored pencil and wash illustrations add to the gentle humor.

1247 *Arthur's Honey Bear*. Ill. by author. HarperCollins, pap., 1974, ISBN 0-06-022370-7. SERIES: I Can Read. SUBJECTS: Chimpanzees — Fiction; Growing up — Fiction; Siblings — Fiction. RL B.

Arthur becomes his Honey Bear's uncle when he reluctantly trades his beloved toy to Violet and regrets it. The sadness and joy of growing up are celebrated here.

1248 *Arthur's Loose Tooth*. Ill. by author. HarperCollins, 1985, ISBN 0-06-022354-5. SERIES: I Can Read. SUBJECTS: Baby-sitting — Fiction; Chimpanzees — Fiction; Human body — Teeth — Fiction. RL B. LEXILE 420L.

This cozy book has excellent dialogue, good relationships, and gentle humor. Arthur the chimp's loose tooth does not keep him from enjoying s'mores and taffy apples. The expressive chimps express children's fears and childlike misbehaviors.

1249 *Arthur's Pen Pal*. Ill. by author. HarperCollins, pap., 1976, ISBN 0-06-022372-3. SERIES: I Can Read. SUBJECTS: Baby-sitting — Fiction; Chimpanzees — Fiction; Siblings — Fiction. RL B.

Arthur decides he does not want to trade families with his pen pal after all, despite the irritations of baby-sitting for a younger sister. Good characterization and dialogue. Softly colored pencil drawings capture the feeling of everyday family life.

1250 *Arthur's Prize Reader*. Ill. by author. HarperCollins, pap., 1978, ISBN 0-06-022380-4. SERIES: I Can Read. SUBJECTS: Books and reading — Fiction; Chimpanzees — Fiction; Siblings — Fiction. RL B.

While trying to help her older brother, Arthur, with a Super Chimp Comic contest, Violet learns to read hard words. Dialogue and pencil and wash drawings capture the flavor of childhood.

1251 *The Case of the Two Masked Robbers*. Ill. by author. HarperCollins, 1986, ISBN 0-06-022299-9. SERIES: I Can Read. SUBJECTS: Mystery and detective stories; Raccoons — Fiction; Turtles — Fiction. RL B.

Raccoons Arabella and Albert, seeking the turtle-egg robber, have some nocturnal adventures and find a way to safeguard the eggs. The nighttime fears are most effectively portrayed in pencil with dusky violet, tan, and green.

1252 *Joe and Betsy the Dinosaur*. Ill. by author. HarperCollins, 1995, ISBN 0-06-024474-7. SERIES: I Can Read. SUBJECTS: Dinosaurs — Fiction. RL A.

Betsy the Dinosaur is just too big to visit her friends indoors in the wintertime, but she and her caveboy friend Joe add coziness to their cave with a fire. Typical Hoban pencil illustrations.

1253 *Mr. Pig and Family*. Ill. by author. HarperCollins, 1980, ISBN 0-06-022384-7. SERIES: I Can Read. SUBJECTS: Humorous stories; Pigs — Fiction. RL B.

Mr. Pig and his family find home wherever they are together, surrounded by their favorite things. Lazy Mr. Pig plants "vegetable soup" with all the seeds in one hole. An easy chapter book with merry colored-pencil drawings.

1254 *Mr. Pig and Sonny Too*. Ill. by author. HarperCollins, 1977, ISBN 0-06-022341-3. SERIES: I Can Read. SUBJECTS: Friendship — Fiction; Pigs — Fiction. RL B.

Mr. Pig's mishaps while skating, picnicking, and going to a wedding (his own) have amusing and loving resolutions. The pigs are drawn with lumpy detail in pastel greens and pale oranges dominating.

1255 *Silly Tilly and the Easter Bunny*. Ill. by author. HarperCollins, pap., 1989, ISBN 0-06-444127-X. SERIES: Early I Can Read. SUBJECTS: Easter — Fiction; Moles — Fiction; Rabbits — Fiction. RL A. LEXILE 390L.

Silly Tilly nearly misses the Easter Bunny's visit by her forgetful behavior. The slight story has friendly pastel, lumpy animal watercolors.

1256 *Silly Tilly's Thanksgiving Dinner*. Ill. by author. HarperCollins, pap., 1990, ISBN 0-06-444154-7. SERIES: I Can Read. SUBJECTS: Friendship — Fiction; Thanksgiving — Fiction. RL B. LEXILE 350L.

Silly Tilly's vision problems lead to a series of mistakes, which are solved when her Thanksgiving guests provide all the food. Gentle humor is amplified by the author's appealing animal drawings.

1257 *Stick-in-the-Mud Turtle*. Ill. by author. Greenwillow, 1977, o.p. SERIES: Read-Alone. SUBJECTS: Turtles — Fiction. RL C.

Fred, his wife, and their ten turtle children live simply and well until another turtle family moves into their pond. Pastel sketches with dominant green underline their contentment — shattered and then regained.

Hoban, Lillian, and Phoebe Hoban

1258 *Laziest Robot in Zone One*. Ill. by author. HarperCollins, pap., 1983, ISBN 0-06-022352-9. SERIES: I Can Read. SUBJECTS: Robots — Fiction; Science fiction. RL C.

Robots Sola and Sol's search for Big Rover leads them to rescue Power Puss and get a lot of help with their household chores. Interesting differences from and similarities to life familiar to modern children are illustrated in lavender, orange, gray, and fuchsia watercolor sketches in this science fiction story.

1259 *Ready-Set-Robot*. Ill. by author. HarperCollins, pap., 1982, ISBN 0-06-022346-4. SERIES: I Can Read. SUBJECTS: Humorous stories; Robots — Fiction; Science fiction. RL C.

Space and robot humor evolves from a messy robot's involvement in a space race, which he wins only with his robot dog's help. Interesting ideas about life for robots are illustrated in pastels.

Hoban, Russell

1260 *Ace Dragon Ltd.* Ill. by Quentin Blake. Jonathan Cape, 1980, o.p. SUBJECTS: Mythical creatures — Fiction. RL B.

John's astute observation earns him a day of high adventure with a dragon named Ace in Wellingtons. This playful and imaginative tale has some amusing twists of plot. Lively pen sketches have light orange and gray washes.

1261 *A Bargain for Frances.* Ill. by Lillian Hoban. HarperCollins, 2002, ISBN 0-7587-5999-1. SERIES: I Can Read. SUBJECTS: Badgers — Fiction; Friendship — Fiction. RL B. LEXILE 470L.

Frances finds that carefully avoiding her friend's tricks is not as much fun as being friends. Fairly sophisticated ideas are presented in a reassuring, simple manner. Soft pencil drawings maintain that tone.

1262 *Tom and the Two Handles.* Ill. by Lillian Hoban. HarperCollins, 1965, ISBN 0-06-022431-2. SERIES: I Can Read. SUBJECTS: Family life — Fiction; Friendship — Fiction. RL B.

Tom's father encourages Tom to look for the "other handle" in his scraps with his best friend, Kenny. Pencil and wash drawings.

Hoban, Tana

1263 *I Wonder.* Ill. with photos. Harcourt, pap., 1999, ISBN 0-15-204835-9. SERIES: Green Light Readers. SUBJECTS: Animals. RL B.

A child wonders about the small critters she sees in the park — from a caterpillar and a frog to ladybugs and a worm. Simple text illustrated with photographs.

Hoff, Syd

1264 *Albert the Albatross.* Ill. by author. HarperCollins, 1961, ISBN 0-06-022446-0. SERIES: Early I Can Read. SUBJECTS: Albatrosses — Fiction. RL B.

While lost from his ship, Albert encounters a parrot, a cuckoo, a woodpecker, and a weathervane bird. When he roosts on a hat belonging to a lady off on a cruise, he finds his ship again. Plain cartoons follow Albert's adventures.

1265 *Arturo's Baton.* Ill. by author. HarperCollins, pap., 1995, ISBN 0-618-19597-1. SERIES: I Can Read. SUBJECTS: Music and musicians — Fiction; Orchestras — Fiction. RL B.

Arturo's audience finds out he is a great conductor, with or without his favorite baton!

1266 *Barkley.* Ill. by author. HarperCollins, 1975, ISBN 0-06-022448-7. SERIES: I Can Read. SUBJECTS: Circuses — Fiction; Pets — Dogs — Fiction. RL B.

Barkley the dog leaves the circus as he grows old, but on his return is given the job of training new dogs — and playing with the children.

1267 *Barney's Horse.* Ill. by author. HarperCollins, 1987, ISBN 0-06-022450-9. SERIES: Early I Can Read. SUBJECTS: City and town life — Fiction; Horses — Fiction. RL B.

Barney the peddler's horse runs away — once. A warm view of city life is illustrated with cartoon drawings.

1268 *Bernard on His Own.* Ill. by author. Houghton Mifflin, 1993, ISBN 0-395-65226-X. SUBJECTS: Bears — Fiction. RL A.

Bernard has to be rescued by his parents repeatedly because he is too young to stand on his hind legs or growl. Very simple colored-pencil drawings are nevertheless comforting to a young reader.

1269 *Captain Cat.* Ill. by author. HarperCollins, pap., 1993, ISBN 0-06-444176-8. SERIES: I Can Read. SUBJECTS: Pets — Cats — Fiction. RL B. LEXILE 400L.

Soldiers, particularly one named Pete, befriend a tiger cat — soon named Captain Cat, since he has more stripes than anyone else. Captain Cat enjoys mess duty and marching — although not in the rain. Typical Hoff drawings show a very contented cat.

1270 *Chester.* Ill. by author. HarperCollins, 1986, ISBN 0-606-01822-0. SERIES: I Can Read. SUBJECTS: Horses — Fiction. RL B. LEXILE 170L.

The horse Chester's search for loving leads him to a farm, a market, a park, a carousel, and a firehouse. Simple cartoon drawings and predicaments evoke gentle humor.

1271 *Danny and the Dinosaur*. Ill. by author. HarperCollins, pap., 1958, ISBN 0-06-022466-5. SERIES: I Can Read. SUBJECTS: Dinosaurs — Fiction. RL B.

A dinosaur takes a day off from the museum to frolic with Danny. This imaginative tale is very appealing to children. Flat drawings have humor in the episodes, from the dinosaur's large size to its delighted expression.

1272 *Danny and the Dinosaur Go to Camp*. Ill. by author. HarperCollins, 1996, ISBN 0-06-444095-8. SERIES: I Can Read. SUBJECTS: Camps and camping — Fiction; Dinosaurs — Fiction. RL B. LEXILE 290L.

Danny's dinosaur becomes his rowboat and the carrier of tired hikers when they go to camp together.

1273 *Grizzwold*. Ill. by author. HarperCollins, 1963, ISBN 0-06-022481-9. SERIES: I Can Read. SUBJECTS: Bears — Fiction. RL B. LEXILE 220L.

Grizzwold the bear leaves his forest after the loggers take down the trees. He tries the zoo and the circus and goes to a masked dance before he finds a national park with lots of trees, where he poses for tourist pictures.

1274 *Happy Birthday, Danny and the Dinosaur!* Ill. by author. HarperCollins, 1995, ISBN 0-06-026438-1. SERIES: I Can Read. SUBJECTS: Birthdays — Fiction; Dinosaurs — Fiction. RL B. LEXILE 320L.

The children celebrate the dinosaur's hundred million years and one day birthday with cake and ice cream.

1275 *Happy Birthday, Henrietta!* Ill. by author. Garrard, 1983, o.p. SERIES: Imagination. SUBJECTS: Birthdays — Fiction; Chickens — Fiction. RL A.

Besides being treated to flowers, a movie, and popcorn in town, Henrietta has yet another birthday surprise in store. Watercolors make the cartoon animals appear warm.

1276 *Henrietta Goes to the Fair*. Ill. by author. Garrard, 1979, o.p. SERIES: Imagination. SUBJECTS: Chickens — Fiction; Fairs — Fiction; Farm and country life — Fiction. RL A.

Henrietta accidentally wins a blue ribbon at the fair, but her real concern is for Winthrop the pig's feelings. Simple watercolors focus on the animals.

1277 *Henrietta, the Early Bird*. Ill. by author. Garrard, 1978, o.p. SERIES: Imagination. SUBJECTS: Chickens — Fiction; Farm and country life — Fiction. RL A.

Henrietta mistakenly tries to arouse the barnyard and town in the middle of the night. Comic watercolors are simple and expressive.

1278 *Henrietta's Fourth of July*. Ill. by author. Garrard, 1981, o.p. SERIES: Imagination. SUBJECTS: Chickens — Fiction; Farm and country life — Fiction; Fourth of July — Fiction. RL A.

Henrietta carries the flag when the farm animals participate in the Fourth of July festivities. Cartoon drawings add humor.

1279 *The Horse in Harry's Room*. Ill. by author. HarperCollins, 1970, ISBN 0-06-022482-7. SERIES: Early I Can Read. SUBJECTS: Horses — Fiction; Imagination — Fiction. RL B. LEXILE 470L.

Even after a trip to the country to see real horses, Harry knows that his imaginary horse will stay in his room as long as Harry wants. Typical Hoff cartoons have either turquoise or brown wash.

1280 *Ida the Bareback Rider*. Ill. by author. Putnam, 1972, o.p. SERIES: See and Read. SUBJECTS: Circuses — Fiction. RL C.

Ida the circus bareback rider wants all the applause until a fire teaches her that teamwork is more important. A sampling of circus acts with a fairly didactic story is illustrated with typical Hoff cartoons in yellow, pink, and orange washes.

1281 *Jeffrey at Camp*. Ill. by author. Putnam, 1968, o.p. SUBJECTS: Camps and camping — Fiction. RL C.

Jeffrey's moaning from overeating scares a bear away from camp, and changes Jeffrey's eating habits permanently. Cartoon drawings have yellow highlights.

1282 *Julius*. Ill. by author. HarperCollins, 1959, ISBN 0-06-022491-6. SERIES: I Can Read. SUBJECTS: Circuses — Fiction; Gorillas — Fiction. RL B. LEXILE 210L.

Hoff, Syd (cont.)

A circus gorilla gets lost when he tries to find the people he has just scared away. Simple sketches are typical of Hoff.

1283 *The Lighthouse Children*. Ill. by author. HarperCollins, 1994, ISBN 0-06-022959-4. SERIES: I Can Read. SUBJECTS: Lighthouses — Fiction. RL B. LEXILE 440L.

Sam and Rose fed the gulls and kept the lighthouse until a storm ruined the lighthouse, forcing the couple to move away. Lonely for their gulls, they find a way to entice the gulls to follow them. Typical Hoff cartoons illustrate the story.

1284 *Little Chief*. Ill. by author. HarperCollins, 1961, ISBN 0-06-022501-7. SERIES: I Can Read. SUBJECTS: Frontier and pioneer life — Fiction; Native Americans — Fiction. RL B.

Little Chief, tired of helping his mother sweep and husk and hang out the wash, reunites a buffalo with its herd. When the children from a wagon train he's befriended are threatened by a buffalo stampede, Little Chief saves the day.

1285 *Mrs. Brice's Mice*. Ill. by author. HarperCollins, pap., 1988, ISBN 0-06-444145-8. SERIES: Early I Can Read. SUBJECTS: Mice — Fiction. RL B.

Mrs. Brice fed her 25 mice the finest cheese, and washed and dried behind their ears. One mouse is always the nonconformist. Cartoon illustrations underline the humor.

1286 *Sammy the Seal*. Ill. by author. HarperCollins, pap., 1959, ISBN 0-06-022526-2. SERIES: I Can Read. SUBJECTS: Seals — Fiction. RL A.

Despite success in learning how to read at school, Sammy the seal discovers that at the zoo he can swim and have a tasty diet more easily than in his city explorations. Cartoon illustrations are appropriate for the slight tale.

1287 *Santa's Moose*. Ill. by author. HarperCollins, 1978, ISBN 0-06-022505-X. SERIES: I Can Read. SUBJECTS: Christmas — Fiction; Moose — Fiction; Santa Claus — Fiction. RL B.

Milton the Moose needs practice landing on roofs and being patient when he leads the eight reindeer. Simple cartoon illustrations.

1288 *Soft Skull Sam*. Ill. by author. Harcourt, 1981, o.p. SERIES: Let Me Read. SUBJECTS: Sports — Soccer — Fiction. RL B.

Sam's afraid of hitting the ball with his head in soccer, but he discovers it doesn't hurt. Didactic story is illustrated with Hoff's cartoons that have gray and green washes.

1289 *Stanley*. Ill. by author. HarperCollins, 1992, ISBN 0-06-022535-1. SERIES: I Can Read. SUBJECTS: Man, prehistoric — Fiction; Self-esteem — Fiction. RL A.

A new, full-color edition of Syd Hoff's tale of a prehistoric man whose seed-planting, picture-painting, and kindness distances him from other cave-dwellers. This is a rhythmic, imaginative, simple tale.

1290 *Thunderhoof*. Ill. by author. HarperCollins, 1971, ISBN 0-06-022560-2. SERIES: Early I Can Read. SUBJECTS: Cowboys — Fiction; Horses — Fiction; Pets — Wild animals — Fiction. RL C.

Wild Thunderhoof throws every comer from his saddle, but after escaping to the range, he misses the brushing and currying, so he returns to the ranch more docile. Illustrations are very simple.

1291 *A Walk Past Ellen's House*. Ill. by author. McGraw-Hill, 1972, o.p. SUBJECTS: Behavior — Shyness — Fiction; Friendship — Fiction. RL B.

Harvey overcomes his shyness only when he forgets himself to help someone else. Comic drawings have brown and blue wash.

1292 *Walpole*. Ill. by author. HarperCollins, 1977, o.p. SERIES: Early I Can Read. SUBJECTS: Walruses — Fiction. RL B.

Big, strong Walpole does not want to be leader of the walrus pack; he is busy caring for orphan walruses. Although the language is simple, there are some nice touches and real warmth. Illustrations in brown and blue match the quality of the text.

1293 *Who Will Be My Friends?* Ill. by author. HarperCollins, pap., 1960, ISBN 0-06-022556-4. SERIES: Early I Can Read. SUBJECTS: Friendship — Fiction; Moving, household — Fiction. RL A.

Freddy's ability to play baseball gives him an entry into a new neighborhood. This simple story is illustrated with typically simple Hoff pencil drawings, alternating sepia with four colors.

1294 *Wilfred the Lion.* Ill. by author. Putnam, 1970, o.p. SUBJECTS: Behavior — Brave — Fiction; Friendship — Fiction; Lions — Fiction. RL B.

Wilfred's attempts to act as brave as his favorite animal, the lion, help him to be less fearful in the playground, but he ends up lonely — until his mother helps him become a boy again. Typical Hoff cartoons have pale blue and tan washes.

Hogrogian, Nonny

1295 *Billy Goat and His Well-Fed Friends.* Ill. by author. HarperCollins, 1972, o.p. SERIES: I Can Read. SUBJECTS: Goats — Fiction. RL B.

Together Billy Goat and four friends escape being some farmers' dinner, and they scare wolves away from their new house in the woods. In cadence and result, the tale is reminiscent of the "Musicians of Bremen." Pale pastel pencil drawings are very appealing.

Holabird, Katharine

1296 *The Best Sleepover Ever!* Ill. by Helen Craig. Grosset & Dunlap, pap., 2006, ISBN 0-448-44016-4. SERIES: Angelina Ballerina. SUBJECTS: Dancers and dancing — Fiction; Mice — Fiction; Sleepovers — Fiction. RL C.

Angelina and her dancing friends don't dance well after their all-night sleepover. Charming ink drawings of mice.

Holding, James

1297 *The Robber of Featherbed Lane.* Ill. by author. Putnam, 1970, o.p. SERIES: See and Read. SUBJECTS: Mystery and detective stories. RL B.

An imaginative cumulation of lost items includes a diamond ring, a banana cake, a monkey, a small child, and a kitten. Ink sketches are in yellow and avocado.

Holl, Adelaide

1298 *Bedtime for Bears.* Ill. by Cyndy Szekeres. Garrard, 1973, o.p. SERIES: Venture. SUBJECTS: Bears — Fiction; Fall — Fiction. RL B.

Full of curiosity, Small Bear succumbs to sleep only after finding the other animals too busy preparing for winter to have time to play. Pencil drawings with a pale blue wash give the animals a very appealing mien.

1299 *George the Gentle Giant.* Ill. by Frank Daniel. Golden Books, 1962, o.p. SERIES: Read It Yourself. SUBJECTS: Friendship — Fiction; Giants — Fiction. RL B.

George the Giant tries unsuccessfully with a picnic and singing to make friends with the village children. When his tears make a pool, friendly contact is made. Plain colored drawings have little imaginative detail.

1300 *If We Could Make Wishes.* Ill. by Judy Pelikan. Garrard, 1977, o.p. SERIES: Imagination. SUBJECTS: Imagination — Fiction. RL C.

Two children play with dragons, ghosts, mermaids, and giants — in their imaginations! They are content with being themselves in real life. Message and pastel watercolors are a bit stilted.

1301 *The Long Birthday.* Ill. by Ethel Gold. Garrard, 1974, o.p. SERIES: Venture. SUBJECTS: Birthdays — Fiction. RL B.

Jody finds a butterfly chrysalis, earns money to buy some seeds, and makes a card for her mother's birthday after giving away or losing her precious three dimes. Drawings in kelly green and pencil are static.

1302 *Small Bear and the Secret Surprise.* Ill. by Tien. Garrard, 1978, ISBN 0-8116-4455-3. SUBJECTS: Bears — Fiction. RL B.

Small Bear's secret surprise is a new baby sister, who wanders off while under his care, climbs a tree, and will not come down. This quiet, gentle adventure is suitably illustrated with soft ink drawings with a turquoise wash.

1303 *Small Bear Builds a Playhouse.* Ill. by Cyndy Szekeres. Garrard, 1978, o.p. SERIES: Small Bear Adventures. SUBJECTS: Bears — Fiction; Behavior — Sharing — Fiction; Friendship — Fiction. RL B.

Small Bear does not enjoy his new playhouse much until he invites his friends to share it. Pencil drawings of animals have a green wash.

Holl, Adelaide (cont.)

1304 *Small Bear's Birthday Party*. Ill. by Leigh Grant. Garrard, 1977, o.p. SERIES: Small Bear Adventures. SUBJECTS: Bears — Fiction; Birthdays — Fiction. RL B.

When Small Bear's friends are too busy to play, his feelings are hurt, but the party they are planning for him changes his feelings. Patterned ink drawings with a pale turquoise wash suit the gentleness of the story.

1305 *Small Bear's Name Hunt*. Ill. by Pat Bargielski. Garrard, 1977, o.p. SERIES: Small Bear Adventures. SUBJECTS: Bears — Fiction. RL A.

Small Bear's gentle encounters with other animals convince him that his own name is most appropriate. Bargielski's use of cool green detracts from the warmth of her drawings.

1306 *Sylvester: The Mouse with the Musical Ear*. Ill. by N. M. Bodecker. Golden Books, 1973, o.p. SERIES: Read It Yourself. SUBJECTS: City and town life — Fiction; Farm and country life — Fiction; Mice — Fiction. RL B.

When development encroaches on the pastoral music of his fields, Sylvester finds a home that suits his musical ear — a guitar! In delightful progression, a town-city mouse story becomes a tall tale, well underscored by delicate line drawings.

1307 *Too Fat to Fly*. Ill. by Bill Morrison. Garrard, 1973, o.p. SERIES: Venture. SUBJECTS: Elephants — Fiction; Self-esteem — Fiction. RL B.

Marco's attempts to imitate Lark, Butterfly, and Fish are disastrous, but he is just right for being an elephant. Illustrations are adequate.

1308 *Wake Up, Small Bear*. Ill. by Pat Bargielski. Garrard, 1977, o.p. SERIES: Small Bear Adventures. SUBJECTS: Bears — Fiction; Spring — Fiction. RL A.

Joyfully Small Bear greets the spring after his winter nap, as he searches for his friend Binky. Fuzzy ink animals have an apple green backdrop.

Holland, Marion

1309 *Big Ball of String*. Ill. by author. Beginner Books, 1958, ISBN 0-394-90005-7. SUBJECTS: Imagination — Fiction; Stories in rhyme. RL B.

A boy's adventures while adding to his ball of string and using it when he is confined to bed are highly creative. Red and blue colored pencil highlights the drawings.

Holtzman, Caren

1310 *No Fair! A Math Reader*. Ill. by Joan Holub. Scholastic, pap., 1997, ISBN 0-5909-2230-0. SERIES: Scholastic Reader. SUBJECTS: Mathematics — Fiction. RL B.

David and Kristy figure out whether their dice game is fair and whether the candy distribution will come out even. Lively watercolor and ink drawings.

1311 *A Quarter from the Tooth Fairy*. Ill. by Betsy Day. Scholastic, pap., 1995, ISBN 0-590-26598-9. SERIES: Scholastic Reader. SUBJECTS: Human body — Teeth — Fiction; Stories in rhyme. RL B. LEXILE 550L.

Math activities by Marilyn Burns provide a framework for the rhyming story and the activities appended.

Holub, Joan

1312 *Abby Cadabra, Super Speller*. Ill. by author. Grosset & Dunlap, 2000, ISBN 0-448-42281-6. SERIES: All Aboard Reading. SUBJECTS: Behavior — Cooperative; English language — Spelling — Fiction; Witches — Fiction. RL B.

As Abby competes with the new witch in her class, Wanda, the reader learns spelling tips. However, teamwork wins the spelling bee.

1313 *Cleopatra and the King's Enemies: Based on a True Story of Cleopatra in Egypt*. Ill. by Nonna Aleshina. Aladdin, 2006, ISBN 0-689-87196-1. SERIES: Ready-to-Read. SUBJECTS: Biographies; Egypt — Fiction. RL C.

Young Cleopatra's facility with language saves the life of her father, the king; she herself goes on to become queen. A well-told, well-illustrated story based on an actual event.

1314 *The Garden That We Grew*. Ill. by Hiroe Nakata. Viking, 2001, ISBN 0-670-89799-X. SERIES: Viking Easy-to-Read. SUBJECTS:

Gardening — Fiction; Pumpkins — Fiction. RL A.

Cheery watercolor illustrations show children patiently growing a garden, from planting the seed to harvesting the pumpkins to carve for Halloween.

1315 *The Gingerbread Kid Goes to School.* Ill. by Debbie Palen. Grosset & Dunlap, pap., 2002, ISBN 0-448-42674-9. SERIES: All Aboard Science Reader. SUBJECTS: Folklore. RL B.

After the principal bakes a gingerbread kid, he is chased by the gym teachers, three lunch ladies, four other teachers, caught — temporarily — by a student, and consumed by his dog. A pale, nonrhythmic attempt to modernize an old standby.

1316 *More Snacks! A Thanksgiving Play.* Ill. by Will Terry. Aladdin, pap., 2006, ISBN 1-4169-0954-0. SERIES: Ready-to-Read. SUBJECTS: Ants — Fiction; Stories in rhyme. RL A.

Abounding in familiar three-letter rhyming words, this is a simple story of ant "pilgrims." Very limited vocabulary and simple colored drawings.

1317 *Pajama Party.* Ill. by Julie Durrell. Grosset & Dunlap, pap., 2007, ISBN 0-448-41739-1. SUBJECTS: Parties — Fiction. RL B. LEXILE 300L.

After pizza and banana splits, six girlfriends are noisy, do each other's hair and nails, blow bubble gum bubbles, have a pillow fight — and fall asleep before dawn. Ink and wash drawings.

1318 *The Pizza That We Made.* Ill. by Lynne Woodcock Cravath. Puffin, 2001, ISBN 0-670-03520-3. SERIES: Puffin Easy-to-Read. SUBJECTS: Cookery — Fiction; Stories in rhyme. RL A.

Rhythmic rhymed instructions are provided for making pizza, with the recipe appended. Fat-cheeked youthful bakers.

1319 *Scat, Cats!* Ill. by Rich Davis. Viking, pap., 2001, ISBN 0-14-130905-9. SERIES: Viking Easy-to-Read. SUBJECTS: Pets — Cats — Fiction. RL A. LEXILE BR.

This basic reader features lots of appealing cats with scalloped outlines and light washes.

1320 *Why Do Horses Neigh?* Ill. with photos. Dial, pap., 2003, ISBN 0-142-30119-1. SERIES: Dial Easy-to-Read. SUBJECTS: Horses. RL C.

Many facts about horses are given in question-and-answer format, illustrated with sharp photographs and a few drawings.

1321 *Why Do Rabbits Hop? And Other Questions About Rabbits, Guinea Pigs, Hamsters, and Gerbils.* Ill. with photos. Puffin, pap., 2003, ISBN 0-142-30120-5. SERIES: Puffin Easy-to-Read. SUBJECTS: Gerbils; Pets; Rabbits. RL C.

A question-and-answer format, illustrated with excellent photographs, is used to cover classification, food, size, babies, communication, senses, and differences. Good information.

Hong, Lily T.

1322 *Two of Everything.* Ill. by author. Whitman, 1993, ISBN 0-8075-8157-7. SUBJECTS: Folklore — China; Humorous stories. RL B.

A wonderful retelling of a Chinese folk tale about a magic pot that makes two of everything. It even clones its owners! Striking design, color, and details are shown with appealing, roly-poly Mr. and Mrs. Haktak.

Hood, Flora

1323 *One Luminaria for Antonio.* Ill. by Ann Kirn. Putnam, 1966, o.p. SERIES: See and Read. SUBJECTS: Christmas — Fiction; Mexico — Fiction. RL C.

Antonio gets a candle for a luminaria and an accompanying blessing despite his poverty and a temptation he has trouble resisting. Earth-tone textured sand paintings have an authentic flavor.

Hood, Susan

1324 *Bad Hair Day.* Ill. by Joy Allen. Grosset & Dunlap, pap., 1999, ISBN 0-448-41996-3. SERIES: All Aboard Reading. SUBJECTS: Human body — Hair — Fiction; Stories in rhyme. RL A. LEXILE 210L.

After receiving a bad home haircut, a girl notices the variety of haircuts on other people. Ink and wash drawings.

Hood, Susan (cont.)

1325 *Look! I Can Read!* Ill. by Amy Wammer. Grosset & Dunlap, pap., 2000, ISBN 0-448-41967-X. SERIES: All Aboard Reading. SUBJECTS: Books and reading. RL A.
The progression from reading "stop" and "school" to knowing the alphabet and writing one's name to "A is for __" is presented in a lively way.

1326 *Look! I Can Tie My Shoes!* Ill. by Amy Wummer. Grosset & Dunlap, 2002, ISBN 0-448-42835-0. SERIES: All Aboard Reading. SUBJECTS: Shoes — Fiction. RL A.
"I can do it! Nothing to it!" Tie her shoes — after a long struggle — that is.

1327 *Pup and Hound.* Ill. by Linda Hendry. Kids Can Press, 2004, ISBN 1-55337-572-6. SERIES: Kids Can Read. SUBJECTS: Pets — Dogs — Fiction; Stories in rhyme. RL A.
Hound finds food for Pup, who leaves none for Hound. Textured pencil drawings are appealing.

1328 *Pup and Hound at Sea.* Ill. by Linda Hendry. Kids Can Press, 2005, ISBN 1-55337-804-4. SERIES: Kids Can Read. SUBJECTS: Pets — Dogs — Fiction; Stories in rhyme. RL A.
Pup and Hound's adventures aboard a pirate raft end with a wreck and an unexpected treasure — pizza! Again, drawings add warmth and personality to the two friends.

1329 *Pup and Hound Lost and Found.* Ill. by Linda Hendry. Kids Can Press, 2006, ISBN 1-55337-806-7. SERIES: Kids Can Read. SUBJECTS: Fairs — Fiction; Pets — Dogs — Fiction; Stories in rhyme. RL A.
Hound looks all over the fairgrounds for Pup, finding him in charge of the kissing booth! Pencil drawings have an appealing texture.

Hooks, William H.

1330 *A Dozen Dizzy Dogs.* Ill. by Gary Baseman. Bantam, 1990, ISBN 0-8368-1748-6. SERIES: Bank Street Ready-to-Read. SUBJECTS: Mathematics; Pets — Dogs — Fiction; Stories in rhyme. RL A. LEXILE AD570L.
Lively cartoon dizzy dog antics are featured in this book, counting from one to ten and back again.

1331 *Feed Me! An Aesop Tale.* Ill. by Doug Cushman. Bantam, pap., 1991, ISBN 0-5533-7023-5. SERIES: Bank Street Ready-to-Read. SUBJECTS: Birds — Fiction. RL A.
The hungry lark chicks must report danger from the farmer before their mother will feed them. They move into the woods safely before the corn is cut. Cartoons add humor and drama.

1332 *The Gruff Brothers.* Ill. by Pierre Cornuel. Bantam, 1989, ISBN 0-8368-1749-4. SERIES: Bank Street Ready-to-Read. SUBJECTS: Folklore — Norway; Rebuses. RL A. LEXILE 340L.
Rebuses for colors and nouns aid the beginning reader. The green-haired troll adds drama.

1333 *How Do You Make a Bubble?* Ill. by Doug Cushman. Bantam, 1992, ISBN 0-553-35487-6. SERIES: Bank Street Ready-to-Read. SUBJECTS: Animals — Fiction; Humorous stories; Stories in rhyme. RL A.
Humorous ink and wash cartoon animal characters help a beginning reader answer a question on each page. "How do you make a pie? You bake it. . . . Make a malted? You shake it."

1334 *Little Poss and Horrible Hound.* Ill. by Carol Newsom. Bantam, 1992, ISBN 0-553-07881-X. SERIES: Bank Street Ready-to-Read. SUBJECTS: Opossums — Fiction; Pets — Dogs — Fiction. RL B.
Little Poss escapes from Horrible Hound three times with his ingenious reworking of his father's cautions. "One a day keeps the doctor away" becomes the apple jammed into Hound's mouth giving time for Little Poss to escape. Illustrations are shallow except for Hound's expressions.

1335 *Lo-Jack and the Pirates.* Ill. by Tricia Tusa. Bantam, 1991, ISBN 0-553-07092-4. SERIES: Bank Street Ready-to-Read. SUBJECTS: Humorous stories; Pirates — Fiction. RL B.
A boy enamored of the glamorous life of pirates is hijacked by real pirates. When he takes all orders literally, he ends up saving a ship full of men, women, and children from being blown to bits for treasure. Lively illustrations add much to the humor of the misunderstandings.

1336 *Where's Lulu?* Ill. by R. W. Alley. Bantam, 1991, ISBN 0-553-07093-2. SERIES:

Bank Street Ready-to-Read. SUBJECTS: African Americans — Fiction; Family life — Fiction. RL A.

A small girl searches the house and yard for Lulu to play ball with — the reader is surprised to find that Lulu is a very playful black dog. Dad joins in the fun. Dialogue is realistic. Illustrations in pencil and wash reflect warm family life.

Hope, Laura Lee

1337 *Freddie and Flossie: The Bobbsey Twins.* Ill. by Chuck Pyle. Aladdin, pap., 2004, ISBN 1-4169-0270-8. SERIES: Ready-to-Read. SUBJECTS: Siblings — Fiction; Siblings — Twins — Fiction. RL A.

Preschool twins enjoy firefighting and tending store. The illustrations suit a primer.

Hopkins, Lee Bennett

1338 *Blast Off! Poems About Space.* Ill. by Melissa Sweet. HarperCollins, 1995, ISBN 0-06-024260-4. SERIES: I Can Read. SUBJECTS: Poetry; Space — Fiction. RL B.

Ashley Bryan and Jane Yolen are just two of the poets featured in this collection of poems about topics including black holes, meteorites, and astronauts. Very appealing poems and watercolor illustrations.

1339 *Good Books, Good Times!* Ill. by Harvey Stevenson. HarperCollins, 1990, ISBN 0-06-022528-9. SUBJECTS: Books and reading; Poetry. RL C.

Whimsical bold watercolors use unusual perspective to stimulate the imagination in this celebration of the joys of reading. Arnold Lobel, Jack Prelutsky, David McCord, and X. J. Kennedy are some of the poets lending their talent to this delightful collection.

1340 *Happy Birthday.* Ill. by Hilary Knight. Simon & Schuster, 1991, ISBN 0-671-70973-9. SUBJECTS: Birthdays — Fiction; Poetry. RL B.

Charming ink and wash drawings capture the excitement of birthdays for a young child. Familiar favorite poets such as Dr. Seuss, Aileen Fisher, Myra Cohn Livingston, Margaret Hillert, and Shakespeare create the party atmosphere.

1341 *It's About Time!* Ill. by Matt Novak. Simon & Schuster, 1993, ISBN 0-671-78512-5. SUBJECTS: Concepts — Time; Poetry. RL B.

Poems by favorites such as Charlotte Zolotow, Karla Kuskin, Gwendolyn Brooks, Harry Behn, Aileen Fisher, and Dorothy Aldis — about spaghetti, bedtime, and a new puppy — are illustrated with graphically pleasing colored pencil drawings.

1342 *More Surprises.* Ill. by Megan Lloyd. HarperCollins, 1987, ISBN 0-06-024261-2. SERIES: I Can Read. SUBJECTS: Poetry. RL C. LEXILE NP.

Poems by poets such as Aileen Fisher and Charlotte Zolotow deal with seasons, books, and nonsense. Faintly textured soft pastels give variety and humor.

1343 *Questions.* Ill. by Carolyn Croll. HarperCollins, 1992, ISBN 0-06-022413-4. SERIES: I Can Read. SUBJECTS: Poetry. RL A.

Felice Holman, Margaret Wise Brown, Eve Merriam, Christina Rossetti, and Karla Kuskin are some of the many quality poets represented in this excellent collection of poems. All ask questions, dealing with friendship, pretending, feelings, and humor.

1344 *Ragged Shadows: Poems of Halloween Night.* Ill. by Giles Laroche. Little, Brown, 1993, ISBN 0-316-37276-5. SUBJECTS: Halloween; Poetry. RL C.

Laroche uses cut-paper illustrations to create the mystery of Halloween through bare tree branches, from the inside of a jack-o'-lantern, with costumed skeletons passing the cemetery. Poems are by a variety of poets, including Valerie Worth, Nancy Willard, and Aileen Fisher.

1345 *Surprises.* Ill. by Megan Lloyd. HarperCollins, 1984, ISBN 0-06-022584-X. SERIES: I Can Read. SUBJECTS: Poetry. RL B. LEXILE NP.

Poems by the best in children's poets, including Aileen Fisher, Dorothy Aldis, Charlotte Zolotow, Eve Merriam, and Leland B. Jacobs. Pets, weather, creepy crawlies, boats, planes, and trains are familiar to children. Ink and colored pencil drawings.

Hopkins, Lee Bennett (cont.)

1346 *Weather*. Ill. by Melanie Hall. HarperCollins, 1994, ISBN 0-06-021462-7. SUBJECTS: Poetry; Weather — Fiction. RL A.

Poems about the sun, wind, rain, and snow are imaginative and lively. X. J. Kennedy has a spider making a snowflake soufflé, Isabel Glaser's lion-maned sun scorches the earth. Valerie Worth has a cat purring on a warm flat quilt made by the sun through the window panes. Pastel illustrations enhance the poems.

Hopkins, Lee Bennett, selector

1347 *Sports! Sports! Sports! A Poetry Collection*. Ill. by Brian Floca. HarperCollins, 1999, o.p. SERIES: I Can Read. SUBJECTS: Poetry; Sports. RL B.

Lively, rhythmic poems capture the fun and wonder of baseball, track, swimming, soccer, basketball, football, and ice skating. Some of the best-known poets for children are represented in this collection. Illustrations are colorful and cartoon-like. An index to first lines and authors is included.

1348 *Valentine's Hearts: Holiday Poetry*. Ill. by JoAnn Adinolfi. HarperCollins, 2005, ISBN 0-06-008057-4. SERIES: I Can Read. SUBJECTS: Poetry; Valentine's Day. RL B.

A dozen poems by a variety of poets capture the fun and the worry of Valentine's Day. The book and its childlike art are carefully designed to reflect the holiday. It includes a table of contents and author/title index.

Hopkinson, Deborah

1349 *From Slave to Soldier: Based on a True Civil War Story*. Ill. by Brian Floca. Aladdin, 2005, ISBN 0-689-83965-0. SERIES: Ready-to-Read. SUBJECTS: Slavery — Fiction; United States — Civil War — Fiction. RL B.

Young Johnny, a slave, proves himself when he joins the Union Army. Ink and wash drawings.

1350 *Susan B. Anthony: Fighter for Women's Rights*. Ill. by Amy Bates. Aladdin, 2005, ISBN 0-689-86910-X. SERIES: Ready-to-Read. SUBJECTS: Biographies; Women's rights. RL C.

"Failure is impossible." Susan B. Anthony's conducted a single-minded crusade for women's rights but the right to vote was not gained until after her death. Pencil and wash drawings are sympathetic.

Hopping, Lorraine Jean

1351 *Blizzards! Wild Weather*. Ill. by Jody Wheeler. Scholastic, pap., 1998, ISBN 0-590-39730-3. SERIES: Hello Science Reader! SUBJECTS: Weather. RL C.

Presents interesting blizzard-related facts about shipwreck rescues, school crises, avalanches, superstorms, and the impact of supercomputers on storm prediction. Effective, illustrative drawings.

1352 *Tornadoes!* Ill. by Jody Sheeler. Scholastic, 1994, ISBN 1-4242-0347-3. SERIES: Scholastic Reader. SUBJECTS: Tornadoes; Weather. RL C. LEXILE 580L.

Hopping has written a very lively account of the unpredictability of tornadoes, where they hit, and why they form. Accompanied by charts, maps, a radar picture, and drawings of the dangers tornado chasers face.

Hornblow, Leonora, and Arthur Hornblow

1353 *Insects Do the Strangest Things*. Ill. by Michael Frith. Random House, 1968, ISBN 0-394-94306-6. SERIES: Step-Up. SUBJECTS: Insects; Nature; Science and scientists. RL C.

The 17 insects shown are illustrated in four color. They range from caddis fly to flea and walking stick to termite.

1354 *Reptiles Do the Strangest Things*. Ill. by Michael Frith. Random House, 1970, ISBN 0-394-90074-X. SERIES: Step-Up. SUBJECTS: Nature; Reptiles and amphibians; Science and scientists. RL C.

Among the 25 reptiles introduced is the brontosaurus; however, the information is out of date. The wonder and variety of reptiles is stressed. Good watercolors dominate each double-page spread.

Horowitz, Ruth

1355 *Big Surprise in the Bug Tank*. Ill. by Joan Holub. Dial, 2005, ISBN 0-8037-2874-3. SERIES: Dial Easy-to-Read. SUBJECTS: Cockroaches — Fiction; Insects — Fiction; Siblings — Fiction. RL C. LEXILE 550L.

When their favorite bugs in their mother's lab — hissing cockroaches — have babies, the brothers try selling some and giving some away. They get some support from Mr. Lee, the school librarian, who has an odd pet show, and gives a home to the ones without bumps, the females. Cartoon illustrations.

1356 *Breakout at the Bug Lab*. Ill. by Joan Holub. Dial, 2001, ISBN 0-8037-2510-8. SERIES: Dial Easy-to-Read. SUBJECTS: Cockroaches — Fiction; Insects — Fiction. RL C. LEXILE 260L.

Mom's favorite bug in her lab is Max, a giant cockroach. He escapes just when a TV show is ready to begin and is recaptured in an unusual way. Cartoon drawings give Max character.

Horton, Joan

1357 *I Brought My Fat for Show-and-Tell: And Other Funny School Poems*. Ill. by Melanie Siegel. Grosset & Dunlap, 2004, ISBN 0-448-43490-3. SERIES: All Aboard Poetry Reader. SUBJECTS: Behavior — Bullying; Poetry; School stories. RL B.

Poems on topics from show-and-tell to the class play, holidays, and cafeteria food are lively and humorous.

Howe, James

1358 *Bunnicula: The Vampire Bunny and his Friends*. Ill. by Jeff Mack. Atheneum, 2004, ISBN 0-689-85724-1. SERIES: Ready-to-Read. SUBJECTS: Pets — Cats — Fiction; Pets — Dogs — Fiction; Rabbits — Fiction. RL C.

Wonderfully expressive animal faces match the delight in the story of the new vampire? pet joining Chester the cat and the doggy narrator of the story.

1359 *Houndsley and Catina*. Ill. by Marie-Louise Gay. Candlewick, 2006, ISBN 0-7636-2404-7. SUBJECTS: Friendship — Fiction. RL B. LEXILE 580L.

Houndsley and Catina decide being friends is better than being famous after failing to become a skilled writer or contest cook. Pencil and pale washes with patterned clothes enhance the text.

1360 *Pinky and Rex*. Ill. by Melissa Sweet. Atheneum, 1990, ISBN 0-689-31454-X. SUBJECTS: Dinosaurs — Fiction; Museums — Fiction; Siblings — Fiction. RL C.

Pinky gets advice from sister Amanda on what to wear to the museum, and he has to say good-bye to every one of his 27 stuffed animals. But the pink dinosaur from the museum shop has to be shared three ways! Delightful watercolor illustrations.

1361 *Pinky and Rex and the Bully*. Ill. by Melissa Sweet. Atheneum, 1996, ISBN 0-689-80834-8. SERIES: Ready-to-Read. SUBJECTS: Behavior — Bullying — Fiction; Friendship — Fiction; Self-esteem — Fiction. RL C. LEXILE 480L.

Kevin makes fun of Pinky's name, his favorite color, and his choice of best friend, a girl named Rex. Old Mrs. Morgan helps Pinky be more comfortable with himself. Expressive watercolor illustrations.

1362 *Pinky and Rex and the Just-Right Pet*. Ill. by Melissa Sweet. Atheneum, 2001, ISBN 0-689-82861-6. SERIES: Ready-to-Read. SUBJECTS: Pets — Cats — Fiction; Pets — Fiction; Siblings — Fiction. RL C. LEXILE 530L.

Although Amanda really wants a cat, the new kitty bonds with dog-lover Pinky. Six short chapters are illustrated with watercolors.

1363 *Pinky and Rex and the Mean Old Witch*. Ill. by Melissa Sweet. Macmillan, 1991, ISBN 0-689-31617-8. SUBJECTS: Friendship — Fiction; Loneliness — Fiction. RL A.

A well-crafted story of the "mean old witch" next door who chases friends Pinky and Rex and Pinky's little sister, Amanda, when they set foot in her yard. The story is suspenseful, with a satisfying ending, not overdone. Melissa Sweet's watercolor illustrations are charming.

1364 *Pinky and Rex and the New Baby*. Ill. by Melissa Sweet. Macmillan, 1993, ISBN 0-689-31717-4. SUBJECTS: Babies — Fiction;

Howe, James (cont.)

Family life — Fiction; Friendship — Fiction. RL B.

The dialogue and relationships between friends and family members is engaging and realistic. The arrival of Rex's new baby engenders a discussion of adoption as well. Seven short chapters are tightly woven and illustrated with the author's appealing watercolor paintings.

1365 *Pinky and Rex and the Perfect Pumpkin*. Ill. by Melissa Sweet. Atheneum, 1998, ISBN 0-689-81782-7. SERIES: Ready-to-Read. SUBJECTS: Friendship — Fiction; Jealousy — Fiction; Pumpkins — Fiction. RL C. LEXILE 500L.

Good-as-a-granddaughter Rex feels left out of the traditional pumpkin choosing and carving with her neighbor's grandparents, but all ends well. The drama is enhanced by watercolor and ink drawings.

1366 *Pinky and Rex and the Spelling Bee*. Ill. by Melissa Sweet. Macmillan, 1991, ISBN 1-59961-079-5. SUBJECTS: Friendship — Fiction; School stories. RL C. LEXILE 480L.

Pinky finds out there may be something worse than losing a spelling bee. Friendship overcomes all! Sweet's watercolors are marvelous.

1367 *Pinky and Rex Get Married*. Ill. by Melissa Sweet. Simon & Schuster, 1990, ISBN 0-685-58512-3. SERIES: Ready-to-Read. SUBJECTS: Weddings — Fiction; Friendship — Fiction. RL C. LEXILE 390L.

When Rex returns from a wedding, she and Pinky have their own wedding, witnessed by all their stuffed animals and presided over by pig Pretzel. Sweet's excellent drawings add flavor to this enduring friendship.

1368 *Pinky and Rex Go to Camp*. Ill. by Melissa Sweet. Atheneum, 1992, ISBN 0-689-31718-2. SUBJECTS: Camps and camping — Fiction; Homesickness — Fiction; Siblings — Fiction. RL C. LEXILE 490L.

Pinky doesn't really want to go to Camp Wackatootchee even if friend Rex is going. Only when he shares his feelings does he get the courage to go. Sweet's sympathetic watercolors enhance the story.

1369 *Rabbit-Cadabra!* Ill. by Alan Daniel. Morrow, 1993, ISBN 0-688-10403-7. SUBJECTS: Magic — Fiction; Pets — Cats — Fiction; Pets — Fiction. RL C.

Harold the dog and Chester the cat manage to turn the Amazing Karlovsky's magic show at the local elementary school into chaos. Vivid, engaging watercolor illustrations enhance the text; instructions for pulling a rabbit from a hat are appended.

Hubbell, Patricia

1370 *Pig Picnic*. Ill. by Nadine B. Westcott. Golden Books, 1999, ISBN 0-307-26108-5. SERIES: Road to Reading. SUBJECTS: Pigs — Fiction; Stories in rhyme; Wolves — Fiction. RL A.

Pig Picnic has an unexpected twist when the wolf arrives. Flat watercolors are by Westcott.

Hudson, Wade

1371 *Five Notable Inventors: Great Black Heroes*. Ill. by Ron Garnett. Scholastic, pap., 1995, ISBN 0-606-07521-6. SERIES: Scholastic Reader. SUBJECTS: Biographies; Inventors and inventions. RL C. LEXILE 620L.

African Americans Madam C. J. Walker, Jan Ernst Matzeliger, Garrett A. Morgan, Elijah McCoy, and Granville T. Wood are featured in this interesting collective biography.

Huelin, Jodi

1372 *Turtles*. Ill. by Pedro Julio Gonzalez. Grosset & Dunlap, 2002, ISBN 0-448-43143-2. SERIES: All Aboard Science Reader. SUBJECTS: Science and scientists; Turtles. RL B.

Ways in which different kinds of turtles protect themselves are illustrated in this book about both sea and land turtles. Watercolor illustrations focus on the turtles' markings.

Hulme, Joy N.

1373 *Mary Clare Likes to Share: A Math Reader*. Ill. by Lizzy Rockwell. Random House, 2005, ISBN 0-375-83421-4. SERIES: Step into Reading. SUBJECTS: Concepts —

Numbers — Fiction; Stories in rhyme. RL A.

The idea of fractions is introduced as Mary Clare shares goodies with different numbers of friends. Illustrated by simple pictures in colored pencil and watercolor.

Hunter, Sara Hoagland

1374 *Miss Piggy's Night Out*. Ill. by Tom Leigh. Viking, 1995, ISBN 0-670-86107-3. SERIES: Viking Easy-to-Read. SUBJECTS: Puppetry — Fiction; Restaurants — Fiction. RL B.

Kermit is Miss Piggy's biggest fan, even after she fluffs her big night out by parading around with whipped cream on her nose.

Hurd, Edith T.

1375 *Come and Have Fun*. Ill. by Clement Hurd. HarperCollins, 1962, ISBN 0-06-022681-1. SERIES: Early I Can Read. SUBJECTS: Mice — Fiction; Pets — Cats — Fiction. RL A.

A simple story deals with a cat chasing a mouse, incorporating some nice twists of language and cozy sketches that focus on the two animals.

1376 *Johnny Lion's Bad Day*. Ill. by Clement Hurd. HarperCollins, 2001, ISBN 0-06-444296-9. SERIES: I Can Read. SUBJECTS: Illness — Fiction; Lions — Fiction. RL A. LEXILE 200L.

Johnny Lion has bad dreams while staying in bed with a cold. Wonderful drawings of a lion family and the animals who inhabit Johnny Lion's dreams.

1377 *Johnny Lion's Book*. Ill. by Clement Hurd. HarperCollins, 2001, ISBN 0-06-029333-0. SERIES: I Can Read. SUBJECTS: Books and reading — Fiction; Lions — Fiction. RL B. LEXILE 280L.

Johnny Lion doesn't read very well, but gets lost, scared, and hungry, just like the small lion in his book. Very warm pencil-outlined drawings.

1378 *Johnny Lion's Rubber Boots*. Ill. by Clement Hurd. HarperCollins, 2000, ISBN 0-06-029337-3. SERIES: I Can Read. SUBJECTS: Lions — Fiction. RL B. LEXILE 120L.

Johnny Lion plays all sorts of imaginative games in his room on a rainy day before his father gives him some new rubber boots. An affectionate story, accented by huggable lion family illustrations.

1379 *Last One Home Is a Green Pig*. Ill. by Clement Hurd. HarperCollins, 1959, ISBN 0-06-022716-8. SERIES: I Can Read. SUBJECTS: Ducks — Fiction; Monkeys — Fiction. RL A.

Duck and Monkey have a great race, hitching rides on everything from a bicycle and a horse to a submarine and a fire engine. They even vow to race again the next day. The language is simple, but with the rhythm of a cumulative tale. Sketchy action drawings have a green wash.

1380 *Look for a Bird*. Ill. by Clement Hurd. HarperCollins, 1977, o.p. SERIES: Science I Can Read. SUBJECTS: Birds; Nature; Science and scientists. RL B.

Robins, blue jays, hummingbirds, pigeons, cardinals, and crows are some of the birds that appear on double spreads, half text and half watercolor illustrations. Tips for identifying each are included.

1381 *Mother Kangaroo*. Ill. by Clement Hurd. Little, Brown, 1976, o.p. SERIES: Mother Animal. SUBJECTS: Growing up; Kangaroos; Nature. RL C.

The growth of one "joey" is described in an intriguing fashion. Exceptional shaded block prints rivet one's attention.

1382 *No Funny Business*. Ill. by Clement Hurd. HarperCollins, 1962, o.p. SERIES: I Can Read. SUBJECTS: Dreams — Fiction; Pets — Cats — Fiction; Picnics — Fiction. RL A.

When the family goes on a picnic, their cat, Carl, is left at home. However, he has imaginary picnic adventures in his dreams. Carl's expressive, mischievous eyes are the focal point of ink and two-tone wash drawings.

1383 *Sandpipers*. Ill. by Lucienne Bloch. HarperCollins, 1961, o.p. SERIES: Let's-Read-and-Find-Out Science. SUBJECTS: Nature; Sandpipers. RL B.

In rhythmic language, the life cycle of sandpipers is lovingly recounted. Exceptional block prints in

Hurd, Edith T. (cont.)

a variety of perspectives are in khaki, gray, and blue.

1384 *Stop Stop*. Ill. by Clement Hurd. HarperCollins, 1961, ISBN 0-06-022746-X. SERIES: I Can Read. SUBJECTS: Baby-sitting — Fiction; Humorous stories. RL A.
Suzie's favorite baby-sitter Miss Mugs has an exaggerated passion for cleanliness, until the elephant at the zoo gives her a shower. Comic ink sketches add to the fun.

1385 *White Horse*. Ill. by Tony Chen. HarperCollins, 1970, o.p. SUBJECTS: Imagination — Fiction; Loneliness — Fiction. RL A.
A lonely boy, Jimmie Lee, on a class trip to the zoo, takes a magical trip on a white horse in his imagination. Evocative story has four-color drawings that focus on the boy and an unusually textured white horse.

Hutchins, Hazel

1386 *And You Can Be the Cat*. Ill. by Ruth Ohi. Annick, 1992, ISBN 1-55037-219-X. SUBJECTS: Imagination; Siblings — Fiction. RL B.
Leanna's little brother, Norman, is an increasingly disruptive cat when Neil comes to play with Leanna. But after being banished, Norman creates such a wonderful castle that he gets a better offer. Full-color illustrations show the action.

Hutchins, Pat

1387 *The Best Train Set Ever*. Ill. by author. Greenwillow, 1978, o.p. SERIES: Read-Alone. SUBJECTS: Birthdays — Fiction; Family life — Fiction; Halloween — Fiction. RL B.
Very satisfying stories are told of Peter's birthday wish coming true, little Maria creating a prize-winning Halloween costume, and a family laid low by measles saving their Christmas celebration for July. The family is drawn in avocado, pumpkin, cocoa, and lemon.

1388 *The Tale of Thomas Mead*. Ill. by author. Greenwillow, 1980, ISBN 0-688-84282-8. SERIES: Read-Alone. SUBJECTS: Books and reading — Fiction; Stories in rhyme. RL C.
Thomas discovers that not knowing how to read gets him in lots of awkward situations. The rhyming of this exaggerated story is reminiscent of Maurice Sendak's *Pierre* (HarperCollins, 1962). Pastel paintings complement the text well.

I

Impey, Rose

1389 *Wanda Witch and the Bullies*. Ill. by Katharine McEwen. Scholastic, pap., 2003, ISBN 0-439-73000-7. SERIES: Scholastic Reader. SUBJECTS: Behavior — Bullying — Fiction; Witches — Fiction. RL B.
Wanda outfoxes the bullying goblins by making them appear silly. Three sets of rhyming words used in the story are appended.

1390 *Wanda Witch and the Stray Dragon*. Ill. by Katharine McEwen. Scholastic, 2006, ISBN 1-4156-8957-1. SERIES: Scholastic Reader. SUBJECTS: Witches — Fiction. RL B.
Cat-a-bogus tries many tricks to discourage his mistress, Wanda the Witch, from adopting a stray dragon. The best illustrations are of Cat-a-bogus's jealous eyes.

1391 *Wanda Witch and the Wobbly Fang*. Ill. by Katharine McEwen. Cartwheel, pap., 2006, ISBN 0-439-78450-6. SERIES: Scholastic Reader. SUBJECTS: Human body — Teeth — Fiction; Witches — Fiction. RL B.
Wanda uses her magic to clean up prizes from the tooth fairy.

1392 *Wanda Witch and Too Many Frogs*. Ill. by Katharine McEwen. Scholastic, pap., 2003, ISBN 0-439-78451-4. SERIES: Scholastic Reader. SUBJECTS: Frogs and toads — Fiction; Magic — Fiction; Witches — Fiction. RL B.
Wanda needs to learn to read so she can get her spells to work. Victor the vulture doesn't appreciate becoming a frog — or many frogs.

Inches, Alison

1393 *Corduroy Makes a Cake*. Ill. by Allan Eitzen. Based on characters created by Don Freeman. Penguin, 2001, ISBN 0-670-88946-6. SERIES: Viking Easy-to-Read. SUBJECTS: Birthdays — Fiction; Toys — Teddy bears — Fiction. RL B.

Corduroy puts himself into a cake box for Lisa's birthday.

1394 *Corduroy's Garden*. Ill. by Allan Eitzen. Based on characters created by Don Freeman. Penguin, 2001, ISBN 0-670-03547-5. SERIES: Viking Easy-to-Read. SUBJECTS: Gardening — Fiction; Toys — Teddy bears — Fiction. RL B.

When Corduroy plants green peppers instead of beans after the puppy digs up Lisa's beans, everyone is surprised.

1395 *Corduroy's Hike*. Ill. by Allan Eitzen. Based on characters created by Don Freeman. Penguin, 2001, ISBN 0-670-88945-8. SERIES: Viking Easy-to-Read. SUBJECTS: Hiking — Fiction; Toys — Teddy bears — Fiction. RL B.

Corduroy's adventures after he falls out of Lisa's backpack are greater than Lisa realizes.

J

Jackson, Garnet

1396 *George Washington: Our First President*. Ill. by Cornelius Van Wright and Ying-Hwa Hu. Scholastic, pap., 2000, ISBN 0-439-09867-X. SERIES: Scholastic Reader. SUBJECTS: Biographies; United States — Revolutionary War. RL B. LEXILE 350L.

A 15-word vocabulary list follows basic information about our first president.

Jacobs, Leland B.

1397 *April Fool!* Ill. by Lou Cunette. Garrard, 1973, o.p. SERIES: Venture. SUBJECTS: April Fools' Day. RL B.

A series of standard April Fool's jokes played on Nancy gives her an idea on how to enjoy this holiday. Well written and illustrated with pencil and pale blue wash.

1398 *Hello, Pleasant Places!* Ill. by Kelly Oechsli. Garrard, 1972, o.p. SUBJECTS: Animals — Fiction; Poetry; Zoos — Fiction. RL A.

Inventive poetic wordplay is grouped by settings: city, park, zoo, shore, woods, and country. Includes average ink drawings with an apple green or orange wash.

1399 *Hello, Year!* Ill. by Frank Aloise. Garrard, 1972, o.p. SERIES: Venture. SUBJECTS: Holidays — Fiction; Poetry; Seasons — Fiction. RL B.

Poets such as Maurice Sendak and Aileen Fisher celebrate sensory experiences around various holidays. Bright orange and fuchsia highlight small ink sketches.

1400 *I Don't, I Do*. Ill. by Frank Carlings. Garrard, 1971, o.p. SERIES: Venture. SUBJECTS: Animals — Fiction; Poetry. RL B.

In this poem, children don't want to be fish, penguins, or camels, but they do want to play, row, or eat ice cream. Mediocre ink drawings have flat apple green highlights.

1401 *Just Around the Corner: Poems About the Seasons!* Ill. by Jeff Kaufman. Henry Holt, 1993, ISBN 0-8050-2676-2. SUBJECTS: Holidays; Poetry; Seasons. RL C.

The flowers, birds, and leaves of fall; snowprints, sneezes, and New Year's bells; the rain and flowers of spring; the shadows, shore, and sun of summer — all are celebrated in poetry. Intriguing rhyming patterns and word play are illustrated with bold graphic colors.

1402 *Playtime in the City*. Ill. by Kelly Oechsli. Garrard, 1971, o.p. SERIES: Venture. SUBJECTS: City and town life; Poetry. RL A.

Poems about swinging, playing games, blowing soap bubbles, and pretending are written by children's poets such as Aileen Fisher. Line drawings have turquoise highlights.

1403 *Poetry for Autumn*. Ill. by Stina Nagel. Garrard, 1968, o.p. SUBJECTS: Fall — Fiction; Holidays — Fiction; Poetry. RL C.

Robert Frost and David McCord are some of the poets who write about animals, voters, fall holi-

Jacobs, Leland B. (cont.)

days, and books in simple poems. Ink sketches show tiny children and animals.

1404 *Poetry for Chuckles and Grins*. Ill. by Tomie dePaola. Garrard, 1968, o.p. SERIES: Poetry. SUBJECTS: Humorous stories; Poetry. RL B.

Mary O'Neill opens this good anthology of humorous verse by such poets as Ogden Nash and Aileen Fisher. Broadly outlined humorous sketches have gold and pink coloring.

1405 *Poetry for Space Enthusiasts*. Ill. by Frank Aloise. Garrard, 1971, o.p. SUBJECTS: Imagination — Fiction; Poetry; Space travel — Fiction. RL C.

Planes, zeppelins, bubbles, planets, clouds, stars, and witches are the stuff dreams are made of. This collection of poems is illustrated with ink sketches highlighted in sky blue.

1406 *Teeny-Tiny*. Ill. by Marilyn Lucey. Garrard, 1976, o.p. SERIES: Easy Venture. SUBJECTS: Imagination — Fiction; Stories in rhyme. RL B.

An enchanting adventure of teeny-tiny children in a teeny-tiny toy store is told in rhythmic rhyme. Bright watercolor pictures focus on the children's play.

James, B. J.

1407 *Supertwins and the Sneaky, Slimy Book Worm*. Ill. by Chris L. Demarest. Scholastic, 2004, ISBN 0-439-46626-1. SERIES: Scholastic Reader. SUBJECTS: Heroes — Fiction; School stories; Siblings — Fiction. RL B.

Silliness rules as the Supertwins rescue the school library books from the book worms.

1408 *Supertwins and the Tooth Trouble*. Ill. by Chris L. Demarest. Scholastic, 2003, ISBN 0-439-46624-5. SERIES: Scholastic Reader. SUBJECTS: Heroes — Fiction; Human body — Teeth — Fiction; Siblings — Fiction. RL B.

This time the Supertwins track the Tooth Bandit to his cave and rescue the Tooth Fairy. Demarest's lively cartoons add to the fun.

1409 *Supertwins Meet Bad Dogs from Space*. Ill. by Chris L. Demarest. Scholastic, 2003, ISBN 0-439-46623-7. SERIES: Scholastic Reader. SUBJECTS: Extraterrestrial beings — Fiction; Heroes — Fiction; Siblings — Fiction. RL B.

The Supertwins banish the threatening flying poodles not once, but twice! Cartoon action.

1410 *Supertwins Meet the Dangerous Dino-Robots*. Ill. by Chris L. Demarest. Scholastic, 2003, ISBN 0-439-46625-3. SERIES: Scholastic Read. SUBJECTS: Museums — Fiction; Robots — Fiction; Siblings — Fiction. RL B.

The Supertwins defeat the evil museum robot dinosaurs. Silly, but lively.

Jameson, Cynthia

1411 *The House of Five Bears*. Ill. by Lorinda B. Cauley. Putnam, 1978, o.p. SUBJECTS: Bears — Fiction; Folklore — Russia. RL A.

An old man and an old woman seeking shelter from a blizzard stumble into the cave of five bears, who abandon the cave, thinking a dragon is there. Detailed ink drawings have royal highlights of palest gold and purple.

1412 *Winter Hut*. Ill. by Ray Cruz. Putnam, 1973, o.p. SUBJECTS: Folklore — Russia; Russia — Fiction. RL C.

In this retelling of a Russian folk tale, only by working together can the animals scare off Wolf and Bear from the shelter Bull has had to build alone. Ink drawings with beige focus on close-ups of the animals.

Jango-Cohen, Judith

1413 *Ben Franklin's Big Shock*. Ill. by Kevin Lepp. Millbrook, 2006, ISBN 1-57505-873-1. SERIES: On My Own Science. SUBJECTS: Biographies; Electricity; Science and scientists. RL B.

The author shows the experiments that preceded Franklin's proof that lightning was electricity, and his invention of lightning rods to protect buildings. Lepp's colored-pencil illustrations focus on the science.

Janice

1414 *Little Bear Learns to Read the Cookbook.* Ill. by Mariana. Lothrop, 1969, o.p. SUBJECTS: Bears — Fiction; Books and reading — Fiction; Cookery — Fiction. RL B.

Little Bear learns to read so she can bake a chocolate cake. Of course she relates the alphabet to food, as do her animal friends. Pencil drawings and washes showcase the animals.

Jann, Gayle

1415 *A Day in the Life of a Construction Foreman.* Photos by author. Troll, 1988, ISBN 0-8167-1121-6. SERIES: A Day in the Life of. SUBJECTS: Careers. RL C.

Without a glossary, readers will have to rely on good color photographs for assistance with the fairly technical language, as the work of a construction foreman supervising electricians building a skyscraper is outlined.

1416 *A Day in the Life of a Photographer.* Photos by author. Troll, 1988, ISBN 0-8167-1123-2. SERIES: A Day in the Life of. SUBJECTS: Careers. RL C.

Technical language for professional commercial photography abounds with little background given. Equipment, exposure, layout, marketing, accounting, and the personal qualities necessary for running one's own photography business are outlined.

Jaspersohn, William

1417 *How the Forest Grew.* Ill. by Chuck Eckart. Greenwillow, 1980, o.p. SERIES: Read-Alone. SUBJECTS: Nature; Science and scientists; Trees. RL C.

The life cycle of a forest and its dependent wildlife is related in rich detail. The framed ink drawings have the same wealth of detail.

Jeffries, Alison

1418 *Sam and the Bag.* Ill. by Dan Andreasen. Harcourt, 2004, ISBN 0-15-205152-X. SERIES: Green Light Readers. SUBJECTS: Pets — Cats — Fiction. RL A.

Oil-painted kittens on burnt sienna add charm to the simplest of readers.

Jenkins, Priscilla Belz

1419 *Falcons Nest on Skyscrapers.* Ill. by Megan Lloyd. HarperCollins, 1994, ISBN 0-06-021104-0. SERIES: Let's-Read-and-Find-Out Science. SUBJECTS: Birds; Conservation; Falcons. RL B. LEXILE 790L.

Researchers at the Hawk Barn were instrumental in saving the peregrine falcon from extinction by raising, banding, and releasing falcons. But only when Scarlett, living on a Baltimore skyscraper, found a mate were these birds reestablished in the wild. Detailed drawings of falcons, including the peregrine.

Jenkins, Steve

1420 *Almost Gone: The World's Rarest Animals.* Ill. by author. HarperCollins, 2004, ISBN 0-06-053598-9. SUBJECTS: Animals — Endangered. RL C. LEXILE AD1020L.

Stunning cutouts illustrate data on species with fewer than 100 animals extant, including specific kinds of iguanas, wombats, rhinos, tortoises, flying foxes, and tamarins.

Jenner, Caryn

1421 *The Journey of a Humpback Whale.* Ill. with photos. DK, 2002, ISBN 0-7894-8514-1. SUBJECTS: Whales. RL B. LEXILE IG490L.

Photographs from above and below water illustrate this informative book about a humpback whale's journey 2,000 miles from the Caribbean to the North Atlantic.

1422 *The Story of Pocahontas.* Ill. by Peter Dennis. DK, 2000, ISBN 0-7894-6636-8. SERIES: DK Readers. SUBJECTS: Biographies; Native Americans. RL B.

A simplified but factual account of Pocahontas's friendliness to the English settlers. She died in England at age 21.

1423 *Survivors: The Night the Titanic Sank.* DK, 2001, ISBN 0-7894-7374-7. SERIES: DK Readers. SUBJECTS: Shipwrecks — Fiction. RL B. LEXILE 260L.

A family is separated when the *Titanic* begins to sink; factboxes add to the realism and drama, as do the period drawings. An index is appended.

Jennings, Sharon

1424 *Franklin and the Bubble Gum.* Ill. by Sean Jeffrey. Kids Can Press, 2005, ISBN 1-55337-816-4. SERIES: Kids Can Read With Help. SUBJECTS: Behavior — Stealing — Fiction; Turtles — Fiction. RL B.
All Franklin's friends enjoy sharing his bubble gum until they find out how he got it.

1425 *Franklin and the Contest.* Ill. by Sean Jeffrey. Kids Can Press, 2003, ISBN 1-55337-491-6. SERIES: Kids Can Read With Help. SUBJECTS: Contests — Fiction; Turtles — Fiction. RL B.
Franklin can't think what to do for five straight hours to win a magazine contest until . . . .

1426 *Franklin and the Magic Show.* Ill. by Sean Jeffrey. Kids Can Press, 2002, ISBN 1-55074-990-0. SERIES: Kids Can Read With Help. SUBJECTS: Magic — Fiction; Turtles — Fiction. RL B. LEXILE BR.
Franklin the Fabulous can make most things disappear, especially the cookies given by friends as admission fees.

1427 *Franklin and the Scooter.* Ill. by Sean Jeffrey. Kids Can Press, 2003, ISBN 1-55337-493-2. SERIES: Kids Can Read With Help. SUBJECTS: Behavior — Sharing — Fiction; Business enterprises — Fiction; Turtles — Fiction. RL B.
Franklin and his friend Rabbit each find a way to get his heart's desire.

1428 *Franklin Has the Hiccups.* Ill. by Sean Jeffrey. Kids Can Press, 2005, ISBN 1-55337-802-4. SERIES: Kids Can Read With Help. SUBJECTS: Hiccups — Fiction; Turtles — Fiction. RL B.
After finally getting rid of his hiccups, Franklin gobbles his next meal and starts all over again!

1429 *Franklin Stays Up.* Ill. by Sean Jeffrey. Kids Can Press, 2002, ISBN 1-55337-371-5. SERIES: Kids Can Read With Help. SUBJECTS: Sleepovers — Fiction; Turtles — Fiction. RL B. LEXILE 130L.
Franklin is the last of his friends to fall asleep and then wants to sleep all day.

1430 *Franklin the Detective.* Ill. by Sean Jeffrey. Kids Can Press, 2004, ISBN 1-55337-497-5. SERIES: Kids Can Read With Help. SUBJECTS: Mystery and detective stories; Turtles — Fiction. RL B.
Franklin "uses his head" to retrieve the lost baseball.

1431 *Franklin's Library Book.* Ill. by Sean Jeffrey. Kids Can Press, 2004, ISBN 1-55337-712-5. SERIES: Kids Can Read With Help. SUBJECTS: Kites and kite flying — Fiction; Turtles — Fiction. RL B.
Franklin has to track down his lost library book on kite making.

1432 *Franklin's Picnic.* Ill. by Sean Jeffrey. Kids Can Press, 2004, ISBN 1-55337-715-X. SERIES: Kids Can Read With Help. SUBJECTS: Picnics — Fiction; Turtles — Fiction. RL B.
None of Franklin's friends likes the picnic he prepares when all of the offerings have flies.

1433 *Franklin's Pond Phantom.* Ill. by Sean Jeffrey. Kids Can Press, 2004, ISBN 1-55337-718-4. SERIES: Kids Can Read With Help. SUBJECTS: Turtles — Fiction. RL B.
Franklin's pond phantom turns out to be Mr. Mole's sailboat.

1434 *Franklin's Pumpkin.* Ill. by Sean Jeffrey. Kids Can Press, 2004, ISBN 1-55337-495-9. SERIES: Kids Can Read With Help. SUBJECTS: Fairs — Fiction; Pumpkins — Fiction; Turtles — Fiction. RL B.
Franklin does not win the prize he expects at the fair, even after he sculpts a coach for his sister from his really big pumpkin.

1435 *Franklin's Reading Club.* Ill. by Sean Jeffrey. Kids Can Press, 2002, ISBN 1-55337-369-3. SERIES: Kids Can Read With Help. SUBJECTS: Books and reading — Fiction; Turtles — Fiction. RL B.
His friends are so eager to read *Dynaroo and the Monster* that Franklin ends up reading it to them out loud.

1436 *Franklin's Soapbox Derby.* Ill. by Sean Jeffrey. Kids Can Press, 2005, ISBN 1-55337-818-1. SERIES: Kids Can Read With Help. SUBJECTS: Soapbox derby — Fiction; Turtles — Fiction. RL B.

With one bicycle wheel, one buggy wheel, and two shopping cart wheels, Franklin's entry wins by bumping the others off the track.

1437 *Franklin's Surprise*. Ill. by Sean Jeffrey. Kids Can Press, 2003, ISBN 1-55337-465-7. SERIES: Kids Can Read With Help. SUBJECTS: Friendship — Fiction; Skunks — Fiction; Turtles — Fiction. RL B.

Franklin isn't listening when others try to tell him that his friend Skunk isn't moving very far away. Ink and wash drawings.

1438 *Franklin's Trading Cards*. Ill. by Sean Jeffrey. Kids Can Press, 2002, ISBN 1-55337-463-0. SERIES: Kids Can Read With Help. SUBJECTS: Trading cards — Fiction; Turtles — Fiction. RL B.

Even though his friends don't like Fly Krispy cereal, they do covet Franklin's trading cards.

Jennings, Terry

1439 *Time*. Ill. by David Anstey. Gloucester, 1988, o.p. SERIES: Junior Science. SUBJECTS: Concepts — Time; Science and scientists; Science experiments. RL B.

Activities and experiments with water and candle clocks and a sundial are simply illustrated in bright watercolors.

Jensen, Patricia

1440 *A Funny Man*. Ill. by Wayne Becker. Scholastic, 1993, ISBN 0-590-46193-1. SERIES: My First Hello Reader. SUBJECTS: Humorous stories; Stories in rhyme. RL A.

In crisp, rhythmic language, the idiosyncrasies of a man who drives a teapot and has a banjo-playing crocodile and a bed with work boots and a propeller are outlined. Flash cards and quizzes detract from the fun.

1441 *I Am Sick*. Ill. by Johanna Hanatel. Children's Press, 2005, ISBN 0-516-24878-2. SERIES: My First Reader. SUBJECTS: Illness — Fiction. RL A. LEXILE BR.

A 46-word vocabulary relates a child's nervous trip to the doctor, and improvement after taking medicine. Whimsical watercolors lighten the fear.

1442 *The Mess*. Ill. by Molly Delaney. Scholastic, 1990, ISBN 0-516-22932-X. SERIES: My First Reader. SUBJECTS: Behavior — Neatness — Fiction; Stories in rhyme. RL A. LEXILE 30L.

Using a 20-word vocabulary, this story relates a child's need to clean his room before going out to play.

Jensen, Patsy

1443 *Loose-Tooth Luke*. Ill. by Dorothy Handelman. Millbrook, 1997, ISBN 0-7613-2009-1. SERIES: Real Kids Readers. SUBJECTS: Human body — Teeth — Fiction. RL C. LEXILE 130L.

Luke's tooth defies his friends' efforts to pull it out, but it falls out naturally. The posed photographs are stilted.

Jerome, Kate Boehm

1444 *Civil War Sub: The Mystery of the Hunley*. Ill. by Frank Sofo. Grosset & Dunlap, 2002, ISBN 0-613-64032-2. SERIES: All Aboard Reading. SUBJECTS: Boats and boating; United States — Civil War. RL C.

The South's experimental submarine *Hunley*, named after its creator, took 21 men to their deaths but also sank the Union's wooden ship *Housatonic*. Mysteries about its disappearance are being addressed after it was recovered in 2000. Watercolor illustrations.

Jewell, Nancy

1445 *Silly Times with Two Silly Trolls*. Ill. by Lisa Thiesing. HarperCollins, 1996, ISBN 0-606-11845-4. SERIES: I Can Read. SUBJECTS: Trolls — Fiction. RL B. LEXILE AD250L.

Nip and Tuck ponder the meaning of *here* and *there*, make poems about slipping on the ice, and wonder why their newly found timepiece always says it's 5 o'clock.

1446 *Two Silly Trolls*. Ill. by Lisa Thiesing. HarperCollins, 1992, ISBN 0-06-022830-X. SERIES: I Can Read. SUBJECTS: Siblings — Fiction; Trolls — Fiction. RL B. LEXILE 350L.

Troll friends build a house without a roof, get lost going to their own picnic, and find a new sweater just too scratchy to sleep in.

Jinkins, Jim

1447 *Pinky Dinky Doo: Back to School Is Cool!* Photos by Sandra Kress. Random House, 2005, ISBN 0-375-93237-2. SERIES: Step into Reading. SUBJECTS: Human body — Hair — Fiction; Siblings — Fiction. RL B.
The whole class is having a bad hair day on school picture day. In fact, Pinky Dinky's hairdo looked like a shady rain forest. This lively story introduces new vocabulary, well explained.

1448 *Pinky Dinky Doo: Pinky Stinky Doo.* Photos by Sandra Kress and Vinh Troung. Random House, 2006, ISBN 0-375-93511-8. SERIES: Step into Reading. SUBJECTS: Behavior — Kindness — Fiction; Skunks — Fiction. RL B.
Pinky's new name teaches her to treat her friend as she wants to be treated. Cartoon ink and colored pencil drawings.

1449 *Pinky Dinky Doo: Polka Dot Pox.* Random House, 2004, ISBN 0-375-82915-6. SUBJECTS: Illness — Fiction; Imagination — Fiction. RL B.
Colored-pencil cartoon drawings illustrate Pinky Dinky's made-up story.

1450 *Pinky Dinky Doo: Where Are My Shoes?* Random House, 2004, ISBN 0-375-92712-3. SUBJECTS: Imagination — Fiction; Shoes — Fiction. RL B.
A zany made-up story about children wearing edible shoes, with cartoon illustrations.

Johanasen, Heather, and Sindy McKay

1451 *About the Rain Forest: Designed for Shared Reading.* Treasure Bay, 2000, ISBN 1-891327-23-2. SERIES: We Both Read. SUBJECTS: Environment; Rain forests. RL B/C.
Both the parents' pages and the children's pages relay interesting information about the plants and animals of the rain forest. Excellent color photographs illustrate both pages.

Johnson, Crockett

1452 *A Picture for Harold's Room.* Ill. by author. HarperCollins, 1960, ISBN 0-606-00383-5. SERIES: I Can Read. SUBJECTS: Imagination — Fiction. RL A. LEXILE 310L.
With a magic crayon, Harold travels the world, changing size and perspective with a stroke of the crayon. Very spare drawings of a boy show his artistic creations with a purple line.

Johnson, Jean

1453 *Librarians A to Z.* Ill. with photos. Walker, 1988, ISBN 0-8027-6842-3. SERIES: Community Helpers. SUBJECTS: Alphabet; Books and reading; Community helpers. RL C.
An alphabet presents various aspects of librarianship, from cataloging, programming, videos, weeding, and zigzag books. Excellent close-up black-and-white photographs show librarianship as an active, current, and vital profession.

Johnson, Mildred

1454 *Wait, Skates!* Ill. by Tom Dunnington. Children's Press, 1983, ISBN 0-516-02039-0. SERIES: Rookie Reader. SUBJECTS: Sports — Roller skating — Fiction. RL A.
With a 30-word vocabulary, a boy is shown learning how to roller skate. Action and humor are captured well in the bright colored drawings.

Johnson, Sylvia A.

1455 *Lions of Africa.* Orig. French by Anne-Marie Pajot, trans. by Dyan Hammarberg. Ill. with photos, plus drawings by L'Enc Matte. Carolrhoda, 1977, o.p. SERIES: Animal Friends. SUBJECTS: Lions; Nature. RL C.
Uncle David shows Luke and Ted his movies of African lions, while they and the reader learn of the lions' habits. Excellent black-and-white photographs alternate with color photographs.

Johnston, Tony

1456 *The Adventures of Mole and Troll.* Ill. by Wallace Tripp. Putnam, 1972, o.p. SUBJECTS: Friendship — Fiction; Moles — Fiction; Trolls — Fiction. RL B.
The friendship of neighbors Mole and Troll survives a day at the beach, shoelaces that constantly come untied, and attempts to live like the other. Outstanding ink and wash drawings by Tripp add to the humor and appeal.

1457 *Alien and Possum: Friends No Matter What*. Ill. by Tony DiTerlizzi. Simon & Schuster, pap., 2002, ISBN 0-689-85326-2. SUBJECTS: Extraterrestrial beings — Fiction; Friendship — Fiction; Opossums — Fiction. RL B. LEXILE 160L.

The differences between the new friends are humorous and illuminating. An interesting chapter story whose illustrations add warmth to the unusual friendship.

1458 *Alien and Possum Hanging Out*. Ill. by Tony DiTerlizzi. Aladdin, 2002, ISBN 0-689-83836-0. SERIES: Ready-to-Read. SUBJECTS: Extraterrestrial beings — Fiction; Friendship — Fiction; Opossums — Fiction. RL B.

Possum and Alien reinforce that each is unique and celebrate their birthdays together, but do not both enjoy hanging upside down. Very appealing illustrations.

1459 *Big Red Apple*. Ill. by Judith Hoffman Corwin. Scholastic, pap., 1999, ISBN 0-439-09860-2. SERIES: Scholastic Reader. SUBJECTS: Apples. RL A. LEXILE 110L.

Wonderful embroidery illustrates the life cycle of an apple.

1460 *Farmer Mack Measures His Pig*. Ill. by Megan Lloyd. HarperCollins, 1986, o.p. SUBJECTS: Farm and country life — Fiction; Humorous stories; Pigs — Fiction. RL B.

Farmer Mack and Farmer Tubb compete to determine whose pig is fatter and the better jumper. Slapstick humor is delightful. Colorful comic drawings add to the spirited humor.

1461 *I'm Gonna Tell Mama I Want an Iguana*. Ill. by Lillian Hoban. Putnam, 1990, o.p. SUBJECTS: Humorous stories; Poetry. RL B.

Strong rhythm and delightful humor characterize short, memorable poems with unusual twists. Illustrated by Lillian Hoban's soft, colored-pencil children comforting a dog on the way to the vet, or watching Grandma let down her hair.

1462 *Night Noises and Other Mole and Troll Stories*. Ill. by Cyndy Szekeres. Putnam, 1977, o.p. SUBJECTS: Friendship — Fiction; Moles — Fiction; Trolls — Fiction. RL B.

Troll is Mole's rain-or-shine friend. He sneezes a tooth out after Mole's helpful schemes, such as slamming a door, fail. Chapters about this special friendship are illustrated with pencil-drawn friendly looking critters.

1463 *Odd Jobs*. Ill. by Tomie dePaola. Putnam, 1977, o.p. SERIES: See and Read. SUBJECTS: Humorous stories. RL C.

Washing an uncooperative dog, Bouncer (not once but four times!), subbing in dance class, and balloon-sitting are some of the jobs undertaken by a sometimes successful Odd Jobs. Pencil drawings are gloriously appropriate.

1464 *Odd Jobs and Friends*. Ill. by Tomie dePaola. Putnam, 1982, o.p. SERIES: See and Read. SUBJECTS: Friendship — Fiction; Humorous stories. RL C.

Odd Jobs takes on some odd tasks — protecting an arm cast from a romantic scribbler, teaching Annie how to blow bubble-gum bubbles, and keeping a new kid company until he finds a friend. Warm, expressive pencil drawings are of multiethnic friends.

1465 *Sparky and Eddie: The First Day of School*. Ill. by Susannah Ryan. Scholastic, 1992, ISBN 0-590-47978-4. SERIES: Sparky and Eddie. SUBJECTS: Friendship — Fiction; School stories. RL B. LEXILE 90L.

Next-door neighbor buddies dread being separated when they get to school after a summer of climbing trees and looking at bugs. It turns out their teachers know just what kids like.

1466 *Wild, Wild Rodeo! Sparky and Eddie*. Ill. by Susannah Ryan. Scholastic, 1998, o.p. SERIES: Sparky and Eddie. SUBJECTS: Friendship — Fiction; Rodeos — Fiction; School stories. RL B. LEXILE 290L.

Competing classes rope their teddy bears, locate their boots in a classroom pile, sail a tortilla, and find many uses for a bandana before finding out that friendship is more important than winning. Expressive faces add to the story.

Jones, Christianne C.

1467 *Beauty and the Beast*. Ill. by Amy Bailey Muehlenhardt. Parents Magazine Press, 2004, ISBN 1-4048-0981-3. SERIES: Read It! Reader. SUBJECTS: Fairy tales; Folklore. RL B.

Jones, Christianne C. (cont.)

Such simplified language depletes the romance from the familiar tale. Drawings are pedestrian.

Jones, Lynda

1468 *Five Brilliant Scientists*. Ill. by Ron Garnett. Scholastic, pap., 2000, ISBN 0-590-48031-6. SERIES: Scholastic Reader. SUBJECTS: African Americans; Biographies; Science and scientists. RL C. LEXILE 660L.

Pediatrician Susan McKinney Steward, George Washington Carver, marine biologist Ernest Everett Just, chemist Percy Lavon Julian, and nuclear scientist Shirley Ann Jackson are highlighted in this collective biography.

Jordan, Helene J.

1469 *How a Seed Grows*. Ill. by Loretta Krupinski. HarperCollins, 1991, ISBN 0-06-020104-5. SERIES: Let's-Read-and-Find-Out Science. SUBJECTS: Seeds, roots, and bulbs. RL B. LEXILE 400L.

The author suggests planting ten bean seeds and digging up one each day to understand the way in which a seed begins to develop. Sketches are accurate and visually interesting.

Judson, Clara I.

1470 *Christopher Columbus*. Ill. by Polly Jackson. Follett, 1960, o.p. SERIES: Beginning to Read. SUBJECTS: Biographies. RL A.

In 368 basic vocabulary words, the outline of Columbus's dream and the suspense of whether he would achieve it before his crew mutinied are well portrayed. Full-color drawings are a bit dated.

Justus, May

1471 *Surprise for Perky Pup*. Ill. by Mimi Korach. Garrard, 1971, o.p. SERIES: Venture. SUBJECTS: Pets — Dogs — Fiction. RL A.

When Perky Pup is hit over the head, his howling alarms all the dogs until they find the source of the blow. Delightful simple drawings are in emerald green, royal blue, and cocoa.

K

Kaiser, Cecily

1472 *If You're Angry and You Know It!* Ill. by Cary Pillo. Scholastic, pap., 2005, ISBN 0-606-33822-5. SERIES: Scholastic Reader. SUBJECTS: Emotions — Fiction; School stories. RL B. LEXILE NP.

You can tell a friend, bang a drum, or walk away if you're angry. Pen and wash drawings illustrate the message using a simple, repetitive vocabulary.

Kalbacken, Joan

1473 *Badgers*. Ill. with photos. Children's Press, 1996, ISBN 0-516-20157-3. SERIES: True Book. SUBJECTS: Badgers. RL C. LEXILE 790L.

The badger's relatives, food, burrow, daily life, and predators are detailed. *Dachshund* means "badger dog," for the hunting dog's success in unearthing badgers. Aztec Indians called badgers "coyotes of the earth."

Kalish, Muriel, and Lionel Kalish

1474 *Bears on the Stairs: A Beginner's Book of Rhymes*. Ill. by authors. Scholastic, 1993, ISBN 0-590-44918-4. SERIES: Cartwheel. SUBJECTS: Stories in rhyme; Toy and movable books. RL A.

Six rhymes about animals are completed only when the 3/4-page flap is opened. Pencil and wash drawings are large and simple.

1475 *Who Says Moo? A Beginner's Book of Animal Sounds*. Ill. by authors. Scholastic, 1993, ISBN 0-590-44917-6. SERIES: Cartwheel. SUBJECTS: Animals — Fiction; Stories in rhyme; Toy and movable books. RL A.

The sounds made by six familiar animals are uncovered as the 3/4-page flap is opened. The friendly animals are shown in simple pencil and wash drawings.

Kanno, Wendy

1476 *Clara Chicken*. Ill. by Bob Reese. Aro, 1993, ISBN 0-89868-212-6. SERIES: Funny Farm. SUBJECTS: Chickens — Fiction; Dancers and dancing — Fiction. RL A.

Clara the chicken loves to dance. This love infects all the chickens. A 20-word vocabulary is used in this slight story.

1477 *Elmo the Pig*. Ill. by Bob Reese. Aro, 1993, ISBN 0-89868-161-8. SERIES: Funny Farm. SUBJECTS: Nonsense; Pigs — Fiction. RL A.

Elmo the pig grows big-big when he gets mad. A humorous 20-word story with cartoon drawings.

1478 *The Farmer's Tractor*. Ill. by Bob Reese. Aro, 2001, ISBN 0-89868-218-5. SERIES: Funny Farm. SUBJECTS: Farm and country life — Fiction; Tractors — Fiction. RL A.

The farmer's tractor doesn't stop until it wants to — at the end of the day back at the barn. A 20-word vocabulary is used in a slight tale with cartoon drawings.

1479 *Henry the Owl*. Ill. by Bob Reese. Aro, 2001, ISBN 0-89868-216-9. SERIES: Funny Farm. SUBJECTS: Owls — Fiction; Stories in rhyme. RL A.

Henry the Owl sleeps all day and cries all night. Slight humor with cartoon illustrations.

1480 *Sampson the Horse*. Ill. by Bob Reese. Aro, 1984, ISBN 0-89868-163-4. SERIES: Funny Farm. SUBJECTS: Horses — Fiction; Stories in rhyme. RL A.

Instead of pulling, Sampson pushes carts and plows when doing his farm work. A 20-word vocabulary and cartoon drawings.

1481 *Waldo Duck*. Ill. by Bob Reese. Aro, 1984, ISBN 0-89868-157-X. SERIES: Funny Farm. SUBJECTS: Ducks — Fiction; Stories in rhyme. RL A.

A 20-word vocabulary story about Waldo's small feet and big beak, with comic drawings.

Kantrowitz, Mildred

1482 *Willy Bear*. Ill. by Nancy W. Parker. Macmillan, pap., 1989, ISBN 0-689-71345-2. SUBJECTS: School stories; Toys — Teddy bears — Fiction. RL B.

A small boy eases his anxiety about his first day at school by talking to his faithful teddy bear. Neat pastel drawings have an appropriate simplicity and comfort.

Karlin, Nurit

1483 *The Fat Cat Sat on the Mat*. Ill. by author. HarperCollins, 1996, ISBN 0-06-026673-2. SERIES: I Can Read. SUBJECTS: Pets — Cats — Fiction; Rats — Fiction; Stories in rhyme. RL A. LEXILE 220L.

Very effective repetitive 3-letter rhyming words tell the story of a fat cat. Charming drawings full of personality.

Katschke, Judy

1484 *Howdy, Sheriff Woody*. Ill. by Disney artists. Disney, pap., 1999, ISBN 0-7868-4358-6. SERIES: Toy Story. SUBJECTS: Toys — Fiction. RL B.

A plastic toy figure, Woody, awaits the monster, alias Buzz Lightyear on Bullseye. Photographs and drawings.

Katz, Bobbi

1485 *Lots of Lice*. Ill. by Steve Bjorkman. Scholastic, pap., 1998, ISBN 0-590-10834-4. SERIES: Hello Reader! SUBJECTS: Lice; Science and scientists; Stories in rhyme. RL B. LEXILE 460L.

In humorous rhyme, children learn about lice and how to get rid of them — from the lice's point of view. Cartoon illustrations underline the light humor.

1486 *Make Way for Tooth Decay*. Ill. by Steve Bjorkman. Scholastic, pap., 1999, ISBN 0-590-52290-6. SERIES: Scholastic Reader. SUBJECTS: Human body — Teeth; Stories in rhyme. RL B. LEXILE 210L.

Bacteria will always say, "Please, make way for tooth decay!" Dental care presented in a very inventive, lively way.

Kaye, Marilyn

1487 *Will You Cross Me?* Ill. by Ned Delaney. HarperCollins, 1985, o.p. SERIES: Early I Can Read. SUBJECTS: City and town life — Fiction; Friendship — Fiction. RL A.

Two friends need frequent help to cross a city street to play together. Comic details of animals and newspapers add to the picture of the busy neighborhood.

Keenan, Sheila

1488 *The Biggest Fish*. Ill. by Holly Hannon. Scholastic, 1996, ISBN 0-590-26600-4. SERIES: Hello Math Reader! SUBJECTS: Concepts — Weight — Fiction. RL B. LEXILE 150L.

The Mayor of Littleton advertises to find the biggest fish. Text and illustrations underscore that there are many different ways to measure size.

1489 *Lizzy's Dizzy Day: Math Activities by Marilyn Burns*. Ill. by Jackie Snider. Scholastic, pap., 2001, ISBN 0-439-05963-1. SERIES: Hello Math Reader! SUBJECTS: Mathematics — Fiction; Stories in rhyme. RL B. LEXILE 240L.

Addition and subtraction are used for distributing cookies at a birthday party, folding socks, blowing up balloons (counting backwards), counting peanuts and chairs, adding guests to the party, or subtracting chairs for musical chairs. The illustrations match.

1490 *What's Up With That Cup? Math Activities by Marilyn Burns*. Ill. by Jackie Snider. Scholastic, pap., 2000, ISBN 0-439-09954-4. SERIES: Hello Math Reader! SUBJECTS: Mathematics — Fiction; Stories in rhyme. RL B. LEXILE 310L.

A lively, imaginative introduction to measurement, in this case for making a pinata. The illustrations suit.

Keller, Beverly

1491 *Beetle Bush*. Ill. by Marc Simont. Putnam, 1975, o.p. SUBJECTS: Self-esteem — Fiction. RL C.

Arabella becomes an ex-failure when her garden produces snails, moles, beetles, and one overlooked melon. This story is sensitively told and illustrated sympathetically in colored pencil.

1492 *Don't Throw Another One, Dover*. Ill. by Jacqueline Chwast. Putnam, 1975, o.p. SERIES: Break-of-Day. SUBJECTS: Anger — Fiction; Grandparents — Fiction; Sibling rivalry — Fiction. RL B.

To his surprise, Dover is drawn into the daily activities of his grandmother's simple lifestyle. He is visiting her while his mother is having a baby; Grandma gets his attention by throwing her own "tantrum," since Dover has thrown some of his own while with his mother. Pencil drawings have a burnt orange wash.

1493 *When Mother Got the Flu*. Ill. by Maxie Chambliss. Putnam, 1984, o.p. SERIES: Break-of-Day. SUBJECTS: Humorous stories; Illness — Fiction. RL C.

Despite his best intentions not to bother his mother, who has the flu, a small boy breaks the knob on the television set, gets bubble gum all over the cat, melts crayons on the television, and falls into a well while chasing the cat. Black-and-white illustrations alternate with two colors, thus exaggerating the mess.

Keller, Holly

1494 *A Bed Full of Cats*. Ill. by author. Harcourt, 2003, ISBN 0-15-204876-6. SERIES: Green Light Readers. SUBJECTS: Pets — Cats — Fiction. RL A. LEXILE 180L.

Lee is sad when Flora does not appear on his bed at night, but after a while she reappears with four kittens. Simple, warm illustrations.

1495 *Geraldine's Big Snow*. Ill. by author. Greenwillow, 1988, ISBN 0-688-07514-2. SUBJECTS: Pigs — Fiction; Weather — Snow — Fiction. RL B.

During Geraldine's impatient wait for the first snow she meets neighbors preparing for a blizzard. The story is simply told and joyfully illustrated in bright watercolors.

1496 *The Hat*. Ill. by author. Harcourt, 2005, ISBN 0-15-205179-1. SERIES: Green Light Readers. SUBJECTS: Hats — Fiction. RL A.

A simple reader is enhanced by large graphic drawings of Pam and Dan and the hat, followed by some simple activities.

Kelley, Emily

1497 *Happy New Year*. Ill. by Priscilla Kiedrowski. Carolrhoda, 1984, ISBN 0-87614-269-2. SERIES: On My Own. SUBJECTS: New Year's Day. RL C.

New Year's customs in seven countries, some jokes, food, songs, and games are described. Colored-pencil drawings give some of the details of the various cultures.

Kelley, K. C.

1498 *Champions! of NASCAR*. Ill. with photos. Reader's Digest, 2005, ISBN 0-7944-0757-9. SERIES: All-Star Readers. SUBJECTS: Sports — Car racing. RL C.

A sketchy history of NASCAR racing, including such winners as Richard Petty and Cale Yarborough.

1499 *Racing to the Finish: Teamwork at 200 mph!* Ill. with photos. Reader's Digest, 2005, ISBN 0-7944-0603-3. SERIES: All-Star Readers. SUBJECTS: Sports — Car racing. RL C.

Information about the teamwork it takes to win a NASCAR race. Photographs are of mediocre quality.

Kelley, True

1500 *Buggly Bear's Hiccup Cure*. Ill. by author. Parents Magazine Press, 1982, ISBN 0-8193-1081-6. SERIES: Parents Magazine Read Aloud Original. SUBJECTS: Bears — Fiction; Moose — Fiction. RL A.

Counting, honey, tickling, eating, singing, and swimming fail to cure the hiccups. Cute animal illustrations.

Kenah, Katharine

1501 *The Best Chef in Second Grade*. Ill. by Abby Carter. HarperCollins, pap., 2007, ISBN 0-06-053561-X. SERIES: I Can Read. SUBJECTS: Cookery — Fiction; School stories. RL B.

Ollie's family doesn't have a favorite food to report when a chef visits his class — until he remembers macaroni cheese with a face. Pencil and wash drawings.

1502 *The Best Teacher in Second Grade*. Ill. by Abby Carter. HarperCollins, 2006, ISBN 0-06-053564-4. SERIES: I Can Read. SUBJECTS: School stories. RL B.

Luna, fascinated with the stars, presents good ideas for the class performance, but it takes a good teacher to blend her ideas with those of others in her new class. Illustrations capture the puzzled, focused, or giggly moods of the children.

Kennedy, Richard

1503 *Contests at Cowlick*. Ill. by Marc Simont. Little, Brown, 1975, o.p. SUBJECTS: Humorous stories; Tall tales; Western stories. RL C.

A small boy single-handedly rounds up an entire outlaw gang of 15 by trickery in this most satisfying book. Colored-pencil drawings add humor and action.

Kent, Jack

1504 *The Biggest Shadow in the Zoo*. Ill. by author. Parents Magazine Press, 1980, ISBN 0-8193-1048-4. SUBJECTS: Elephants — Fiction; Shadows — Fiction; Zoos — Fiction. RL A.

Goober the elephant refuses to give rides to zoo visitors while mourning the loss of his shadow, which fell in the moat. This charming, lighthearted story is illustrated with ink and crayon cartoon characters.

1505 *Hoddy Doddy*. Ill. by author. Greenwillow, 1979, o.p. SUBJECTS: Folklore — Denmark; Humorous stories; Nonsense. RL C.

Three Danish tales of fools are retold, one about the Norse lobster sailors, another about marking the watery hiding place of the village clock, and the final one about the human winner of a cuckoo contest. Illustrations are well suited to the simple retellings.

1506 *Socks for Supper*. Ill. by author. Crown, pap., 1988, ISBN 0-8193-0965-6. SUBJECTS: Farm and country life — Fiction; Humorous stories. RL C.

A poor farmer and his wife unravel his sweater to knit socks to trade for milk in order to make butter and cheese. The ending has a nice twist, with Kent's excellent full color drawings spicing the simple tale.

1507 *Wizard of Wallaby Wallow*. Ill. by author. Parents Magazine Press, 1971, o.p. SUBJECTS: Magic — Fiction; Mice — Fiction; Self-esteem — Fiction. RL C.

When discontented Mouse acquired one of the Wizard's unlabeled bottles containing a magic spell, he decides he likes being a mouse best. Comic illustrations underline the gentle humor.

Kessel, Joyce K.

1508 *St. Patrick's Day*. Ill. by Cathy Gilchrist. Carolrhoda, 1982, ISBN 0-87614-193-9. SERIES: On My Own. SUBJECTS: Ireland; St. Patrick's Day. RL B.

The holiday celebrating Patrick's unifying and bringing Christianity to the tribes of Ireland 1,600 years ago is outlined. Ink drawings with green accents and borders underline the seriousness of this religious holiday.

Kessler, Ethel, and Leonard Kessler

1509 *The Big Fight*. Ill. by Pat Paris. Garrard, 1981, o.p. SERIES: Begin to Read with Duck and Pig. SUBJECTS: Ducks — Fiction; Friendship — Fiction; Pigs — Fiction. RL A.

Pig and Duck both make an effort to make up after they have a name-calling fight. Comic drawings add good characterization.

1510 *Grandpa, Witch, and the Magic Doobelator*. Ill. by authors. Macmillan, 1981, o.p. SERIES: Ready-to-Read. SUBJECTS: Humorous stories; Magic — Fiction; Witches — Fiction. RL B.

When Wanda and Willy learn magic tricks for Halloween, they find that Grandpa Witch's magic sometimes has unexpected results. Ink and wash drawings feature pet cats and a fabulous fantasy machine — the Doobelator.

1511 *Night Story*. Macmillan, 1981, ISBN 0-02-750220-1. SUBJECTS: Night — Fiction; Night work — Fiction. RL B.

As a boy goes to sleep, his father begins his nightly truck run, observing all the workers doing their jobs at night, from the nocturnal animals to the hospital and emergency road crews to the police, fire crews, and diner employees. Interestingly presented. Typical Kessler pen and wash drawings.

1512 *Our Tooth Story: A Tale of Twenty Teeth*. Ill. by authors. Dodd, Mead, 1972, o.p. SUBJECTS: Doctors and nurses; Human body — Teeth. RL B.

A story for kindergartners about teeth gives simple facts from a child's perspective, as well as tips for good dental hygiene. Bold childlike line drawings extend the text.

1513 *Pig's Orange House*. Ill. by Pat Paris. Garrard, 1981, o.p. SERIES: Begin to Read with Duck and Pig. SUBJECTS: Animals — Fiction; Concepts — Colors — Fiction; Humorous stories. RL A.

When Pig's friends help him paint his house, it ends up with a most unusual effect. Full-color comic drawings are appropriate for the fun.

1514 *Slush Slush!* Parents Magazine Press, 1973, ISBN 0-8193-0675-4. SUBJECTS: Stories in rhyme; Weather — Snow — Fiction. RL A.

A child delights in the fresh snow, catching flakes on his tongue, following tracks, sledding, feeding the birds, making a snowman. Satisfying watercolor drawings.

1515 *Stan the Hot Dog Man*. HarperCollins, 1990, ISBN 1-59054-089-1. SERIES: I Can Read. SUBJECTS: Careers — Fiction; Weather — Snow — Fiction. RL B. LEXILE 310L.

Stan retires from a bakery to become a compassionate hot dog man who feeds those who are short of money or caught in a blizzard. After work, he and his wife Emma go fishing. Ink and watercolor wash drawings enhance the warm, neighborly story.

1516 *The Sweeneys from 9D*. Ill. by Leonard Kessler. Macmillan, 1985, o.p. SERIES: Ready-to-Read. SUBJECTS: Friendship — Fiction; Latchkey children — Fiction; Moving, household — Fiction. RL B.

Tommy's nervous stomach disappears after his first full day in a new school and a new apartment. Ink sketches have orange, gray, and beige washes.

1517 *What's Inside the Box?* Dodd, Mead, 1976, ISBN 0-396-07328-X. SUBJECTS: Animals — Fiction; Play — Fiction. RL B.

Seven animals find a box in the woods and scatter fearfully at each new noise or clue to the contents. Simple suspense and humor are effective, especially when matched with Kessler's three-color comic drawings.

Kessler, Leonard

1518 *The Big Mile Race*. Ill. by author. Greenwillow, 1983, ISBN 0-688-01421-6.

SERIES: Read-Alone. SUBJECTS: Animals — Fiction; Sports — Running — Fiction. RL B.

Animals with individual characteristics learn about running, and practice for the big race. The dialogue is lively, but the strength of the story is in the support and encouragement the animals provide for each other. Kessler's sketches add humor and action.

1519 *The Forgetful Pirate*. Ill. by author. Garrard, 1974, o.p. SERIES: Venture. SUBJECTS: Parrots — Fiction; Pirates — Fiction. RL C.

The cider-drinking pirate is so forgetful that only his parrot can lead the crew to gold. Simple watercolors illustrate this thin tale.

1520 *Here Comes the Strikeout*. Ill. by author. HarperCollins, 1992, ISBN 0-06-023156-4. SERIES: I Can Read. SUBJECTS: Sports — Baseball — Fiction. RL A. LEXILE 140L.

Thanks to help from his friend Willie, Bobby finds out that neither lucky bats nor helmets, only hard work, will help him learn how to improve his batting record (all strikeouts). Pen and wash illustrations have typical Kessler appeal.

1521 *Hey Diddle Diddle*. Ill. by author. Garrard, 1980, o.p. SERIES: Young Mother Goose. SUBJECTS: Mother Goose — Fiction; Nonsense; Stories in rhyme. RL C.

Inventive rhyming wordplay nonsense is illustrated with cartoon drawings of animals.

1522 *Hickory Dickory Dock*. Ill. by Doug Cushman. Garrard, 1980, o.p. SERIES: Young Mother Goose. SUBJECTS: Concepts — Time — Fiction; Mother Goose — Fiction; Stories in rhyme. RL A.

The hours of the day are celebrated with nonsense rhymes as the clock strikes each hour. Colored ink drawings focus on a cat and a mouse.

1523 *Kick, Pass, and Run*. Ill. by author. HarperCollins, 1995, ISBN 0-06-023159-9. SERIES: I Can Read. SUBJECTS: Animals — Fiction; Sports — Football — Fiction. RL B. LEXILE 140L.

Exceptionally well presented facts about football from the point of view of animals who find a football, watch the game being played, and then try to play themselves. Very simple, colorful drawings capture the humor and action.

1524 *Last One in Is a Rotten Egg*. Ill. by author. HarperCollins, 1969, ISBN 0-06-028484-6. SUBJECTS: Sports — Swimming — Fiction. RL B. LEXILE 220L.

Freddy is only able to join his friends at the deep end of the pool after Tom's instruction, and encouragement from his friends. Pen and wash illustrations.

1525 *Mixed-Up Mother Goose*. Ill. by Diane Dawson. Garrard, 1980, o.p. SERIES: Young Mother Goose. SUBJECTS: Mother Goose — Fiction; Stories in rhyme. RL C.

After a collision in which she hurts her head, Mother Goose thinks Little Bo Peep herds goats, and Little Miss Muffet is eating pink ice cream. Humor is illustrated with pastel drawings in this rhyming story.

1526 *The Mother Goose Game*. Ill. by Pat Paris. Garrard, 1980, o.p. SERIES: Young Mother Goose. SUBJECTS: Mother Goose — Fiction; Stories in rhyme. RL A.

Mother Goose makes friends with Mole, Hen, Pig, Cat, Goat, Cow, Frog, Dog, Fox, Bird, Ant, Duck, and Mouse, who introduce themselves in rhyme. Comic animal drawings suit this simple text.

1527 *Mr. Pine's Purple House: 40th Anniversary Edition*. Ill. by author. Purple House, 1993, ISBN 1-9309003-2-5. SUBJECTS: Colors — Fiction. RL A.

In an effort to distinguish his house from the look-alikes around it, Mr. Pine plants a tree; so do all his neighbors. He plants a bush with the same result, but triumphs when he paints his house (and himself and the dog and the cat) purple.

1528 *Old Turtle's 90 Knock-Knocks, Jokes, and Riddles*. Ill. by author. Greenwillow, 1991, ISBN 0-688-09586-0. SUBJECTS: Animals — Fiction; Jokes and riddles; Wordplay. RL B.

Dog, Rabbit, Mouse, Duck, Chicken, Cat, Bird, and Owl have sections on Jokes and Riddles followed by Knock-Knocks. All were apparently tested on the children at Indian Rock and East York Elementary schools, to whom the book is dedicated. Watercolors are as entertaining as the humorous text.

Kessler, Leonard (cont.)

1529 *Old Turtle's Riddle and Joke Book.* Ill. by author. Greenwillow, 1986, ISBN 0-688-05954-6. SERIES: Read-Alone. SUBJECTS: Jokes and riddles. RL B.

Standard riddles familiar to many adults, but new to children, are illustrated with apple green and pumpkin cartoons that exaggerate the humor.

1530 *Old Turtle's Soccer Team.* Ill. by author. Greenwillow, 1988, ISBN 0-688-07158-9. SERIES: Read-Alone. SUBJECTS: Animals — Fiction; Sports — Soccer — Fiction. RL B.

The no-name animals have much to learn about soccer, and about cooperation, before they become a team. Colorful comic animal drawings add to the excellent simple dialogue, interesting characterization, and humorous wordplay.

1531 *Old Turtle's Winter Games.* Ill. by author. Dell, pap., 1990, ISBN 0-440-40261-1. SERIES: Read-Alone. SUBJECTS: Animals — Fiction; Sports — Winter — Fiction. RL A.

The animals help each other out of the snowbank after a ski jump, and down the hill when there are not enough sleds. With imaginative humor beginning readers are introduced to Olympic events. Four-color comic illustrations are simple, yet expressive.

1532 *On Your Mark, Get Set, Go!* Ill. by author. HarperCollins, 1972, o.p. SERIES: Sports I Can Read. SUBJECTS: Animals — Fiction; Sports — Olympics — Fiction. RL B.

In the animal Olympics, everyone can do something and everybody learns something. Exceptionally imaginative presentation of information and values is illustrated with comic ink drawings colored in three tones.

1533 *The Pirate's Adventure on Spooky Island.* Ill. by author. Garrard, 1979, o.p. SERIES: Imagination. SUBJECTS: Parrots — Fiction; Pirates — Fiction. RL A.

An inept pirate, Captain Ben, needs his parrot's help to capture Bad Bart. Lively drawings by Kessler add to the fun.

1534 *The Worst Team Ever.* Ill. by author. Greenwillow, 1985, ISBN 0-688-04235-X. SERIES: Read-Alone. SUBJECTS: Animals — Fiction; Sports — Baseball — Fiction. RL B.

Melvin Moose, Bobo Bullfrog, and Pickles Frog improve at swampball with Old Turtle's encouragement and discipline. Clever humor lightens the lesson, as do the two-tone comic drawings.

Kettner, Christine

1535 *Oliver Cat on Planet B.* Ill. by author. Dutton, 2003, ISBN 0-525-47094-8. SERIES: Dutton Easy Reader. SUBJECTS: Cumulative tales; Pets — Cats — Fiction; Rabbits — Fiction. RL B.

Oliver Cat is always willing to play a game, is late to school when he goes to great lengths to find a replacement button, and goes fishing on an unusual fishing trip. Graphically interesting, cheery illustrations.

Kidd, Ronald

1536 *Tuna Surprise: Undercover Kid.* Ill. by Andy Sklar. Grosset & Dunlap, pap., 2006, ISBN 0-448-44128-4. SERIES: All Aboard Reading. SUBJECTS: Family life — Fiction; Inventors and inventions — Fiction; Mystery and detective stories. RL C.

Young detective Maggie uses her inventor grandfather's aging machine in her investigations. Cartoon colored-pencil illustrations.

Kido, Yukiko

1537 *Pig Wig.* Blue Apple, 2006, ISBN 1-59354-175-9. SERIES: Flip-a-Word. SUBJECTS: Language — Fiction. RL A.

Graphically interesting illustrations assist children in substituting initial vowels to build vocabulary.

1538 *Snake Cake.* Ill. by author. Blue Apple, 2006, ISBN 1-59354-176-7. SERIES: Flip-a-Word. SUBJECTS: Stories in rhyme; Wordplay. RL A.

Durable cutouts frame words in three different word families, decorated with simple stylized drawings.

Kilborne, Sarah S.

1539 *Leaving Vietnam: The True Story of Tuan Ngo.* Ill. by Melissa Sweet. Simon & Schuster, 1999, o.p. SERIES: Ready-to-Read.

SUBJECTS: Refugees — Fiction; Vietnam — Fiction. RL C.

A risky escape from Vietnam and journey to the United States are chronicled in seven chapters. This true story features the drama of escape, pirates, and rescue, and the uncertainty of life in refugee camps. Watercolors highlight the fear and relief.

Kim, Joy

1540 *Come On Up!* Ill. by Paul Harvey. Troll, 1981, ISBN 0-89375-511-7. SERIES: Giant First-Start. SUBJECTS: Pets — Cats — Fiction; Pets — Dogs — Fiction. RL A.

A small cat is afraid to climb a tree — until a dog comes along. Unfortunately the author puts the dog in the tree as well as the cat at the end. Bright comic illustrations show a rotund, timid yellow kitten and her raggedy playmate.

1541 *Rainbows and Frogs: A Story about Colors.* Ill. by Paul Harvey. Troll, 1981, ISBN 0-89375-505-2. SUBJECTS: Concepts — Colors. RL A.

Using a 35-word vocabulary, Kim asks the reader what color he or she likes and what feelings each color generates. Rich, rainbow-colored close-ups are humorous.

King, P. E.

1542 *Down on the Funny Farm: A Step Two Book.* Ill. by Alastair Graham. Random House, 1986, ISBN 0-394-97460-3. SERIES: Step into Reading. SUBJECTS: Farm and country life — Fiction; Humorous stories. RL B.

As soon as the farmer trains his animals properly, the old owner shows up to confuse them all again. This well-paced story has an open ending. Full-color comic illustrations suit the text.

King-Smith, Dick

1543 *All Pigs Are Beautiful.* Ill. by Anita Jeram. Candlewick, 1993, ISBN 1-56402-148-3. SERIES: Read and Wonder. SUBJECTS: Farm and country life; Pigs. RL B.

The author loves pigs, and, if pressed, will say that a black-and-white-spotted, medium-snouted, flop-eared Gloucestershire pig is his favorite. He imagines what his pig, Monty, is thinking when he gets his head scratched after he eats. Delightful pen and wash sketches illustrate the text.

Kirk, David

1544 *Miss Spider's Tea Party Reader.* Ill. by author. Scholastic, pap., 2006, ISBN 0-439-83305-1. SERIES: Scholastic Reader. SUBJECTS: Insects — Fiction; Spiders — Fiction; Stories in rhyme. RL B.

An unusual twist to spiders' reputation, with close-up illustrations in primary colors.

Kirk, Ruth

1545 *Desert Life.* Ill. by Ruth Kirk and Louis Kirk. Natural History, 1970, o.p. SUBJECTS: Deserts; Nature; Science and scientists. RL C.

Kirk describes the birds, mammals, reptiles, insects, weather, and plants of the desert. Colored close-up photographs are compelling.

Kirkpatrick, Rena K.

1546 *Look at Magnets.* Ill. by Ann Knight. Raintree, 1985, ISBN 0-8172-2354-1. SERIES: Look at Science. SUBJECTS: Magnets; Science and scientists; Science experiments. RL C.

Simple tests to see the power of magnets, and how to make electromagnets and a compass are shown in an elementary fashion. Children doing the experiments are in brightly colored clothing on a white background.

1547 *Look at Rainbow Colors.* Ill. by Anna Barnard. Raintree, 1985, ISBN 0-8172-2356-8. SERIES: Look at Science. SUBJECTS: Concepts — Colors; Rainbows; Science and scientists. RL C.

Ordinary sources of rainbows and some exploration of how colors change are introduced. Bright drawings show flowers and animals.

Kiser, SuAnn

1548 *Hazel Saves the Day.* Ill. by Betsy Day. Dial, 1994, ISBN 0-8037-1489-0; pap., ISBN 0-8037-1488-2. SERIES: Dial Easy-to-Read. SUBJECTS: Chickens — Fiction; Friendship — Fiction. RL A.

In four short chapters, Hazel Hen moves in, foils a thief, and makes a party — full of new animal

Kiser, SuAnn (cont.)

friends. Cheery colored pencil and watercolor drawings augment the text.

Kite, Patricia

1549 *Down in the Sea: Jellyfish.* Ill. with photos. Whitman, 1993, ISBN 0-8075-1712-7. SUBJECTS: Jellyfish; Nature; Oceans and ocean life. RL B.

Exceptional close-up photographs of a wondrous variety of jellyfish are accompanied by a rhythmic, poetic text. Jellyfish come smaller than a grape and bigger than a bed, with tentacles less than an inch to longer than a basketball court.

1550 *Down in the Sea: The Crab.* Ill. with photos. Whitman, 1994, ISBN 0-8075-1709-7. SUBJECTS: Crabs. RL B.

Using colorful photographs and short, easily understood sentences, the author introduces a great variety of true crabs (those with ten legs visible) to young readers. The format is attractive, some of the photographs are beautiful, and the text is interesting. A final page of facts about crabs brings the information together.

1551 *Down in the Sea: The Octopus.* Ill. with photos. Whitman, 1993, ISBN 0-8075-1715-1. SUBJECTS: Nature; Octopi. RL B.

Exceptionally interesting information about octopi is illustrated with appropriate close-up photographs of octopi in hiding, guarding eggs, escaping in a cloud of ink, and eating a crab.

1552 *Down in the Sea: The Sea Slug.* Ill. with photos. Whitman, 1994, ISBN 0-8075-1717-8. SUBJECTS: Sea slugs. RL B.

Through photographs of these brightly colored shell-less creatures (captioned with their scientific names) and a brief interesting text, children are offered an opportunity to learn about sea slugs, their habits, enemies, and life cycle. A final lengthier page of text brings the information together and adds to it.

Klasky, Charles

1553 *Rugs Have Naps (But Never Take Them).* Ill. by Mike Venezia. Childrens Press, 1984, o.p. SERIES: Easy Reading. SUBJECTS: English language — Homonyms. RL C.

Twenty-four homonyms include ones about knots and fillings in their double meanings. Illustrations are in watercolor cartoon format.

Klein, Howard

1554 *My Best Friends Are Dinosaurs.* Ill. by Windrow. McKay, 1965, o.p. SUBJECTS: Dinosaurs — Fiction; Stories in rhyme. RL C.

A boy's affinity for dinosaurs is conveyed in simple verse. Ink drawings of dinosaurs are paralleled by the boy's imaginative play.

Klein, John E., and Carol Gaskin

1555 *A Day in the Life of a Commercial Fisherman.* Photos by John F. Klein. Troll, 1988, ISBN 0-8167-1109-7. SERIES: A Day in the Life of. SUBJECTS: Careers. RL C.

Commercial fisherman Mark Brown is shown preparing the specialized gear on board his boat for an eight-day fishing trip with his partner, Curt. The camera follows them from port to fish house. Text is detailed for a third-grader.

Klein, Monica

1556 *Backyard Basketball Superstar.* Ill. by Nola Langner. Pantheon, 1981, o.p. SERIES: I Am Reading. SUBJECTS: Sex roles — Fiction; Sports — Basketball — Fiction. RL B.

After some mental adjustments, the Flyers, the neighborhood basketball team, vote unanimously to have Melanie join the all-male team. Excellent pencil drawings lighten the message.

Kleinhenz, Sydnie Meltzer

1557 *More for Me!* Ill. by Jerry Zimmerman. Scholastic, pap., 1997, ISBN 0-590-30877-7. SERIES: Hello Math Reader! SUBJECTS: Concepts — Numbers; Stories in rhyme. RL A.

Marilyn Burns has constructed activities to go with this rhymed story about a boy who doesn't realize that a piece of toast cut in pieces is not bigger, and that a glass of milk in a thinner, taller glass is not larger. A very interesting presentation with cartoon illustrations.

Knight, David

1558 *Let's Find Out About Sound.* Ill. by Ulrick Schramm. Watts, 1974, o.p. SUBJECTS: Science and scientists; Sound. RL C.

The variety of sources, kinds, and transmitters of sound to the human ear are introduced. Line drawings help convey the well-organized and carefully presented information.

Knowlton, Jack

1559 *Geography from A to Z: A Picture Glossary.* Ill. by Harriett Barton. HarperCollins, 1988, ISBN 0-690-04618-9. SUBJECTS: Geography. RL C.

Zones, palisade, key, and crevasse are some of the geographic terms defined and illustrated here. Large paintings are in flat primary colors. Very appealing, informative, and readable.

Knudsen, Michelle

1560 *The Case of Vampire Vivian.* Ill. by Amy Wummer. Kane, pap., 2003, ISBN 1-57565-127-0. SERIES: Science Solves It! SUBJECTS: Bats — Fiction. RL B.

Pencil and wash drawings enhance a story about a classmate who loves bats.

Koch, Michelle

1561 *Just One More.* Ill. by author. Greenwillow, 1989, ISBN 0-688-08127-4. SUBJECTS: Concepts — Numbers; Language. RL A.

Each double spread has singular and plural nouns illustrated with small, graphically pleasing soft watercolors in a box. Numbers range from 3 geese to 13 sharks or 15 sheep.

Kohlenberg, Sherry

1562 *Sammy's Mommy Has Cancer.* Ill. by Lauri Crow. Stevens, 1994, ISBN 0-8368-1071-6. SUBJECTS: Diseases; Illness. RL B.

The author is a young mother with cancer who wrote the book first for her toddler, and has added notes for parents with cancer to use with their children before, during, and after treatment. With bright affirming drawings, the text gives a child's view of changes in his mother.

Kohn, Berniece

1563 *Echoes.* Ill. by Albert Pucci. Putnam, 1965, o.p. SUBJECTS: Science and scientists; Sound. RL C.

The scientific applications for sonar properties are touched on by a scientist and science writer. The text is still useful despite dated prints and an old copyright.

Komaiko, Leah

1564 *Earl's Too Cool for Me.* Ill. by Laura Cornell. HarperCollins, pap., 1988, ISBN 0-06-443245-9. SUBJECTS: Fantasy; Friendship — Fiction. RL C.

A boy imagines that Earl has accomplished exotic feats. After making Earl's acquaintance, the boy discovers that Earl is more ordinary than he had imagined. So begins a real cool friendship. Rhythmic text has appropriately exaggerated watercolor comic illustrations.

Koontz, Robin Michal

1565 *Chicago and the Cat.* Ill. by author. Cobblehill, 1993, ISBN 0-525-65097-0. SERIES: Little Chapter Book. SUBJECTS: Pets — Cats — Fiction; Rabbits — Fiction. RL B.

A cat moves in with Chicago the rabbit, and turns out to be a really good cook — even though he ruins Chicago's garden. Their trip to the animal shelter for a protector puppy has unexpected success. Charming watercolor illustrations enhance the story.

1566 *Chicago and the Cat: The Camping Trip.* Ill. by author. Cobblehill, 1994, ISBN 0-525-65137-3. SERIES: Little Chapter Book. SUBJECTS: Camps and camping — Fiction; Pets — Cats — Fiction; Rabbits — Fiction. RL B.

Chicago the rabbit and the cat are unprepared for the rigors of camping and river rafting, and scared of the noises, the bear, and the rapids. Friendly pencil and wash drawings detail their adventures.

1567 *Chicago and the Cat: The Halloween Party.* Ill. by author. Cobblehill, 1994, ISBN 0-525-65138-1. SERIES: Little Chapter Book. SUBJECTS: Halloween — Fiction; Pets — Cats — Fiction; Rabbits — Fiction. RL B.

Chicago the rabbit and the cat have trouble coordinating their two-person horse costume and,

Koontz, Robin Michal (cont.)

scared on the way to the party, miss the costume contest. Charming pencil and wash drawings warm the tale.

Koss, Amy Goldman

1568 *Where Fish Go in Winter: And Other Great Mysteries*. Ill. by Laura J. Bryant. Penguin, 1987, ISBN 0-8037-2704-6. SERIES: Dial Easy-to-Read. SUBJECTS: Science and scientists; Stories in rhyme. RL C.

"Why does popcorn pop?" "How do birds fly?" These are some of the questions answered in seven rhyming stanzas illustrated with watercolor pastels.

Kowalczyk, Carolyn

1569 *Purple Is Part of a Rainbow*. Ill. by Gene Sharp. Children's Press, 1985, ISBN 0-516-02068-4. SERIES: Rookie Reader. SUBJECTS: Stories in rhyme. RL B.

A simple vocabulary is used to present interesting ideas about the parts that make up a whole of familiar things, such as a rainbow. Rhyming couplets are accompanied by vivid, sprightly drawings.

Kramer, S. A.

1570 *Basketball's Greatest Players*. Ill. with photos. Random House, 2002, ISBN 0-679-98112-8. SERIES: Step into Reading. SUBJECTS: Biographies; Sports — Basketball. RL C. LEXILE 660L.

Bill Russell, Wilt Chamberlain, Kareem Abdul-Jabbar, Larry Bird, and Michael Jordan are featured here, and some statistics on other great players are included. There is a photograph and a fact page on each player.

1571 *Hoop Stars*. Ill. by Mitchell Heinze. Grosset & Dunlap, pap., 1995, ISBN 0-448-40943-7. SERIES: All Aboard Reading. SUBJECTS: Biographies; Sports — Basketball — Fiction. RL B. LEXILE 600L.

The stories of O'Neal, Robinson, Barkley, and Olajuwon are told in this chapter book illustrated with colored pencils and a few dated photographs.

Krasilovsky, Phyllis

1572 *The Man Who Cooked for Himself*. Ill. by Mamoru Funai. Parents Magazine Press, 1981, o.p. SERIES: Read Aloud and Easy Reading. SUBJECTS: Food — Fiction; Sex roles — Fiction. RL C.

A lazy man living on the edge of a wood discovers he can be self-sufficient in feeding himself and his cat. The colorful pictures have a fuzzy appearance from poor reproduction.

1573 *The Man Who Entered a Contest*. Ill. by Yuri Salzman. Doubleday, 1980, o.p. SERIES: Reading on My Own. SUBJECTS: Bakers and baking — Fiction; Contests — Fiction; Humorous stories. RL B.

A man who had one last cake left from his old stove gets help from his cat to win a new stove in a contest for the most unusual cake. Two-color line drawings are original and effective in design and humor.

1574 *The Man Who Tried to Save Time*. Ill. by Marcia Sewell. Doubleday, 1979, o.p. SERIES: Reading on My Own. SUBJECTS: Behavior — Efficient — Fiction; Concepts — Time — Fiction. RL B.

A man's orderly life with his cat is disrupted by his efforts to save time by doing everything ahead of time. For example, he sleeps in his clothes, on top of the covers, and eats peculiarly. Three-color washes on ink have a folksy flavor.

Kraske, Robert

1575 *Daredevils Do Amazing Things*. Ill. by Ivan Powell. Random House, 1978, o.p. SERIES: Step-Up. SUBJECTS: Adventure stories; Biographies. RL B.

True stories about Blondin (a Niagara Falls tightrope walker), Houdini, Annie Oakley, a deep-sea fight with a 24-foot octopus, and Evel Knievel's skycycle jump over Snake River Canyon are extremely well told. Ink sketches are appropriate.

Kraus, Robert

1576 *Dance, Spider, Dance!* Ill. by author. Western, 1992, ISBN 0-307-11566-6. SERIES: Golden Easy Reader. SUBJECTS: Friendship — Fiction; Spiders — Fiction. RL A.

Spider is the hit of the dance contest when he jumps to rescue his friend — and her balloons — and lands on a banana peel. With friends Fly and Ladybug, he celebrates with a banana split. Typical wry cartoon characters are by the author.

1577 *Phil the Ventriloquist.* Ill. by author. Greenwillow, 1989, ISBN 0-688-07987-3. SUBJECTS: Ventriloquism — Fiction. RL A.

Phil's parents despair of Phil's ventriloquist jokes — until a burglar creeps in the house one night. Simple pen-and-marker cartoons add to the fun.

1578 *Trouble with Spider.* Ill. by author. HarperCollins, 1962, o.p. SUBJECTS: Flies — Fiction; Friendship — Fiction; Spiders — Fiction. RL B.

Fly overcomes his suspicion of Spider when Spider needs help. Good dialogue and excellent ink and wash drawings have a marvelous sense of scale and provide selective detail.

Krensky, Stephen

1579 *All About Snow and Ice.* Ill. by Anna DeVito. Scholastic, pap., 1994, ISBN 0-590-41449-6. SERIES: Do-It-Yourself Science. SUBJECTS: Weather; Weather — Snow. RL C.

Experiments include checking the temperatures on top of and under the snow, checking to see if the snowman or the snow around the snowman melts first, and making your own iceberg with an ice cube. Observations and information about why the phenomenon occurs are straightforward.

1580 *Bubble Trouble.* Ill. by Jimmy Pickering. Aladdin, 2004, ISBN 0-689-85711-X. SERIES: Ready-to-Read. SUBJECTS: Bubbles — Fiction; Stories in rhyme. RL A.

A delightful rhythmic story about bubbles multiplying all over town — until the sun comes out! The illustrations are most apt.

1581 *Fraidy Cats.* Ill. by Betsy Lewin. Scholastic, 1993, ISBN 0-7857-2439-7. SERIES: Scholastic Reader. SUBJECTS: Fear — Fiction. RL B. LEXILE 280L.

The Fraidy Cats — Scamper and Sorry — imagine all sorts of creatures outside on a stormy night, but settle on a vegetarian ultrasaurus as their best protection.

1582 *Lionel and Louise.* Ill. by Susanna Natti. Dial, pap., 1992, ISBN 0-606-11564-1. SERIES: Dial Easy-to-Read. SUBJECTS: Family life — Fiction; Growing up — Fiction. RL B. LEXILE 160L.

Lionel saves older sister Louise from a dragon (a fly buzzing inside her window), lets his sister build a fancy sandcastle when the waves are threatening, "helps" Louise clean up muddy footprints and handprints, and worries Louise when they leave the water. Illustrations are appealing watercolors.

1583 *Lionel-at-Large.* Ill. by Susanna Natti. Dial, 1986, ISBN 0-8037-0241-8. SERIES: Dial Easy-to-Read. SUBJECTS: Family life — Fiction; Growing up — Fiction. RL B.

Lionel finds his "vegetable shelf" (when deprived of dessert), and survives his first sleepover and a shot at the doctor's office. Familiar fears are overcome in the five humorous chapters on family life. Full-color illustrations keep the tone light.

1584 *Lionel in the Spring.* Ill. by Susanna Natti. Dial, pap., 1990, ISBN 0-606-11565-X. SERIES: Dial Easy-to-Read. SUBJECTS: Family life — Fiction; Spring — Fiction. RL B. LEXILE 340L.

Lionel plants a vegetable garden (with one pumpkin plant), fixes a tenth anniversary breakfast for his parents with his sister, refuses to drink the monster's concoction, and is reluctant to throw anything out when his family begins spring cleaning. Natti's colorful pencil and wash drawings suit the stories well.

1585 *Lionel in the Summer.* Ill. by Susanna Natti. Penguin, 1998, ISBN 0-8037-2243-5. SERIES: Dial Easy-to-Read. SUBJECTS: Summer — Fiction. RL B. LEXILE 270L.

Lionel's four summer adventures are of his imaginative activities on the longest day, the fireworks, the lemonade stand, and the car trip. Classy colored-pencil illustrations.

1586 *Lionel in the Winter.* Ill. by Susanna Natti. Dial, 1994, o.p. SERIES: Dial Easy-to-Read. SUBJECTS: Imagination; Winter — Fiction. RL B. LEXILE 330L.

Lionel's explores the Arctic in the snow, learns about New Year's resolutions, and builds a snowman facing his house. The Arctic chapter is especially enchanting. Appealing illustrations.

Krensky, Stephen (cont.)

1587 *Lionel's Birthday*. Ill. by Susanna Natti. Penguin, 2003, ISBN 0-8037-2752-6. SERIES: Dial Easy-to-Read. SUBJECTS: Birthdays — Fiction; Siblings — Fiction. RL B. LEXILE 440L.

Pencil, colored pencil, and watercolor washes make bright, appealing illustrations for the separate adventures in each of four chapters. Lionel is searching for a hidden birthday present, digging to bury a time capsule, and making a wish for his birthday.

1588 *My Loose Tooth*. Ill. by Hideko Takahashi. Random House, 1999, ISBN 0-679-88847-5. SERIES: Step into Reading. SUBJECTS: Human body — Teeth — Fiction; Stories in rhyme. RL A.

A small boy with a loose tooth wonders if the zoo animal tykes also lose teeth! Understated drawings suit the text.

1589 *Snow and Ice*. Ill. by John Hayes. Scholastic, 1989, ISBN 0-590-41449-6. SERIES: Science Is Fun. SUBJECTS: Science and scientists; Science experiments; Winter. RL C.

Besides basic information and simple experiments about snow and ice, including icicles, simple directions for making a snow fort are included. Humorous line drawings have a royal blue wash.

1590 *Striking It Rich: The Story of the California Gold Rush*. Ill. by Anna DiVito. Simon & Schuster, pap., 1996, ISBN 0-689-80803-8. SERIES: Ready-to-Read. SUBJECTS: Gold Rush; United States — History. RL C.

The story of the Gold Rush is told in five chapters illustrated in appealing pen and wash drawings.

1591 *The Three Blind Mice Mystery*. Ill. by Lynn Munsinger. Bantam, 1994, ISBN 0-385-32131-7. SERIES: Yearling First Choice Chapter Book. SUBJECTS: Mice — Fiction; Mystery and detective stories. RL B. LEXILE 340L.

A small detective tracking one mouse, and then two missing mice, finds clues involving a variety of nursery rhymes before solving the mystery. Active, imaginative animal illustrations.

1592 *We Just Moved!* Ill. by Larry Di Fiori. Scholastic, pap., 2003, ISBN 0-590-33127-2. SERIES: Scholastic Reader. SUBJECTS: History — Medieval; Moving, household. RL B. LEXILE 250L.

A new twist on the changes for a child when a family moves, as a medieval family moves from one castle to another, taking pets and household goods, and meeting new friends (including giants and dragons). Lively ink and wash drawings.

1593 *What a Mess!* Ill. by Joe Mattieu. Random House, 2001, o.p. SERIES: Step into Reading. SUBJECTS: Cleanliness — Fiction. RL A.

An inventive story line traces the muddy tracks past the kids, the dog, and the cat — to Dad, now in the tub. The repetitive language is enlivened by the illustrations, full of imaginative activities.

Krinsley, Jeanette

1594 *The Cow Went over the Mountain*. Ill. by Feodor Rojankovsky. Golden Books, 1963, o.p. SUBJECTS: Animals — Fiction; Wordplay. RL A.

Five animals conclude after exploring the next mountain that conditions are best right at home. The language is playful and the full-color drawings show friendly animals.

Kroll, Steven

1595 *Eat!* Ill. by Diane Palmisciano. Hyperion, 1995, ISBN 0-7868-0139-5. SERIES: Hyperion Chapters. SUBJECTS: School stories; Vegetarianism. RL C. LEXILE 640L.

Harry's vegetarianism becomes a political issue at school. Then better menus become government-mandated. Pencil drawings.

1596 *The Goat Parade*. Ill. by Tim Kirk. Parents Magazine Press, 1983, ISBN 0-8193-1100-6. SUBJECTS: Humorous stories; Parades — Fiction; Stories in rhyme. RL B.

Sam leads the goat parade into school — with memorable results. Lively, rhythmic, zany humor is illustrated with full-color cartoon drawings.

1597 *Pigs in the House*. Ill. by Tim Kirk. Parents Magazine Press, 1983, ISBN 0-8193-1111-1. SERIES: Read Aloud. SUBJECTS: Farm and country life — Fiction; Pigs — Fiction; Stories in rhyme. RL A.

Three pigs get into the farmhouse, wreaking havoc. Stimulated by the observation of his house, "what a pigpen"! Comic cartoon drawings fit the story.

Krulik, Nancy E.

1598 *Jar Jar's Mistake: Star Wars Episode I.* Ill. by Richard Walz. Random House, 1999, ISBN 0-375-90000-4. SERIES: Jedi Readers. SUBJECTS: Science and scientists — Fiction. RL A.

When Jar Jar helps himself to a frog from a market vendor, he doesn't anticipate the consequences. Watercolor cartoons illustrate an array of aliens.

1599 *My Picture Book of the Planets.* Photos by NASA. Scholastic, 1991, ISBN 0-590-43907-3. SUBJECTS: Astronomy and astronomers; Science and scientists. RL A.

In large type, each of the planets is described in a few sentences. Attractive format shows the position of each planet, along with a photograph of each planet's surface.

Kueffner, Sue

1600 *Our New Baby: Fisher-Price.* Ill. by Dorothy Stott. Reader's Digest, pap., 1999, ISBN 1-57584-292-0. SERIES: All-Star Readers. SUBJECTS: Babies — Fiction; Siblings — Fiction; Stories in rhyme. RL A.

A story of an older sister's perception of the new baby, using a 51-word vocabulary. Simple watercolors suit the text.

Kuller, Alison M.

1601 *An Outward Bound School.* Photos by Thomas R. Stewart. Troll, 1990, ISBN 0-8167-1731-1. SUBJECTS: Schools. RL C.

A class of ten students experience an 18-day course in sailing. Each day begins with a run and a dip in the cool Atlantic Ocean, a group meeting, possibly some rock climbing instruction, or experiencing the ropes course. Navigation, nature study, and "going solo" are all part of the project.

Kulling, Monica

1602 *Eat My Dust! Henry Ford's First Race.* Ill. by Richard Walz. Random House, 2004, ISBN 0-375-81510-4. SERIES: Step into Reading. SUBJECTS: Biographies; Cars. RL B.

Henry's first race with his horseless carriage was 10 miles for $1,000 against Alexander Winton's Daredevil, with his mechanic, Spider, on the running board as ballast. Walz's lively drawings add to the drama.

Kumin, Maxine W.

1603 *Paul Bunyan.* Ill. by Dirk Gringhuis. Putnam, 1966, o.p. SERIES: See and Read Beginning to Read. SUBJECTS: Folklore — United States; Tall tales. RL B.

Paul's antics account for the sun in the morning, the tides in the Bay of Fundy, a pancake griddle large enough to skate on, and the formation of the Rocky Mountains. Tall-tale humor shown in pencil with a blue wash.

Kumin, Maxine W., and Anne Sexton

1604 *Eggs of Things.* Ill. by Leonard Shortall. Putnam, 1963, o.p. SERIES: See and Read Beginning to Read. SUBJECTS: Frogs and toads; Nature; Spring. RL B.

Skippy and Buzz raise tadpoles secretly in a third-floor bathtub. Cowboy, a dog, and Skippy's sister, Pest, add to their difficulties in parenting. This creative presentation about spring eggs is well illustrated by Shortall's ink with two-tone wash drawings.

Kunnas, Mauri

1605 *Ricky, Rocky, and Ringo Count on Pizza.* Ill. by author. Crown, 1986, o.p. SERIES: It's Great to Read. SUBJECTS: Concepts — Numbers — Fiction; Cookery — Fiction; Rhinoceroses — Fiction. RL A.

Wheelbarrows and buckets of ingredients are assembled for a present for hungry rhino cousins on National Pizza Day. Simple counting book with riotous cartoon illustrations.

Kurtz, Jane

1606 *Johnny Appleseed.* Ill. by Mary Haverfield. Simon & Schuster, 2001, ISBN 0-689-86959-7. SERIES: Ready-to-Read. SUBJECTS:

Kurtz, Jane (cont.)

Apples; Biographies; Frontier and pioneer life. RL A.

A rhythmic simple telling of Johnny Appleseed's story, with too-sweet pencil and wash drawings.

1607 *Mister Bones: Dinosaur Hunter.* Ill. by Mary Haverfield. Aladdin, 2004, ISBN 0-689-85961-9. SERIES: Ready-to-Read. SUBJECTS: Dinosaurs — Fiction; Stories in rhyme. RL A.

Barnum Brown's discovery of a T-rex skeleton was a sensation. This very simplified version will delight the youngest of dinosaur lovers.

Kuskin, Karla

1608 *Soap Soup: And Other Verses.* Ill. by author. Celebration, 1992, ISBN 0-673-75930-X. SERIES: I Can Read. SUBJECTS: Poetry. RL B. LEXILE 500L.

Small children's exploration of the world around them includes their own bodies, the seasons, friends, and their families. Simple, playful language describes how to eat an egg, how a stew turns into you, and a stroll through clover with Granny. Very simple illustrations match.

1609 *Something Sleeping in the Hall.* Ill. by author. HarperCollins, 1982, ISBN 0-06-023634-5. SERIES: I Can Read. SUBJECTS: Poetry. RL B.

Gently humorous rhymed wordplay involves familiar animals and events. Tiny, fuzzy colored-pencil drawings are equally warm and imaginative.

Kwitz, Mary D.

1610 *Gumshoe Goose, Private Eye.* Ill. by Lisa Campbell Ernst. Dial, 1988, ISBN 0-8037-0424-0. SERIES: Dial Easy-to-Read. SUBJECTS: Geese — Fiction; Mystery and detective stories. RL A.

In four short chapters, Gumshoe Goose solves the kidnapping of baby chick. Appealing drawings and simple style make this accessible to beginning readers.

1611 *Little Chick's Breakfast.* Ill. by Bruce Degen. HarperCollins, 1983, ISBN 0-06-023674-4. SERIES: Early I Can Read. SUBJECTS: Chickens — Fiction. RL A.

Little Chick sees the whole barnyard awaken and get breakfast before she gets hers. Colored-pencil illustrations are rich in design and detail.

1612 *Little Chick's Friend Duckling.* Ill. by Bruce Degen. HarperCollins, 1992, ISBN 0-06-023638-8. SERIES: I Can Read. SUBJECTS: Chickens — Fiction; Ducks — Fiction; Friendship — Fiction. RL A.

New friends explore the barnyard with its big, scary things — a horse and a dog. To the new chicks *they* are the big, scary things. Captivating illustrations.

1613 *Little Chick's Story.* Ill. by Cyndy Szekeres. HarperCollins, 1978, ISBN 0-06-023664-7. SERIES: Early I Can Read. SUBJECTS: Chickens — Fiction. RL B.

Broody Hen sings Little Chick a bedtime story about what she will do when she grows up. Soothing pencil drawings with sand and turquoise washes mirror the language.

1614 *Little Vampire and the Midnight Bear.* Ill. by S. D. Schindler. Dial, 1995, ISBN 0-8037-1528-5. SERIES: Dial Easy-to-Read. SUBJECTS: Imagination; Vampires — Fiction. RL B.

Little Vampire forgets he can't fly when the Midnight Bear threatens his baby brother. Even the names of their snacks — and their dog, Scary Noise — are inventive. The illustrations add details, such as the bat wallpaper.

L

Labatt, Mary

1615 *A Parade for Sam.* Ill. by Marisol Sarrazin. Kids Can Press, 2005, ISBN 1-55337-787-7. SERIES: Kids Can Read. SUBJECTS: Parades — Fiction; Pets — Dogs — Fiction. RL A.

Chalk tactile drawings of a dog named Sam follow his efforts to join a parade.

1616 *Pizza for Sam.* Ill. by Marisol Sarrazin. Kids Can Press, 2003, ISBN 1-55337-329-4. SERIES: Kids Can Read. SUBJECTS: Pets — Dogs — Fiction. RL B. LEXILE 170L.

Fuzzy-haired puppy Sam is looking for anything good to eat that is not dog food. He finds it! Pencil and chalk drawings show a lovable puppy.

1617 *Sam at the Seaside*. Ill. by Marisol Sarrazin. Kids Can Press, 2006, ISBN 1-55337-876-8. SERIES: Kids Can Read. SUBJECTS: Pets — Dogs — Fiction; Seashore — Fiction. RL A.

The only fun puppy Sam has at the seashore is rolling on a smelly fish skeleton. The illustrator perfectly captures doggy smiles!

1618 *Sam Goes Next Door*. Ill. by Marisol Sarrazin. Kids Can Press, 2006, ISBN 1-55337-878-4. SERIES: Kids Can Read. SUBJECTS: Pets — Dogs — Fiction. RL A.

Sam the playful puppy finds his own ways to have fun with the new kids next door. His smug expression is priceless.

1619 *Sam Goes to School*. Ill. by Marisol Sarrazin. Kids Can Press, 2004, ISBN 1-55337-564-5. SERIES: Kids Can Read. SUBJECTS: Pets — Dogs — Fiction; School stories. RL A.

Disasters happen when Sam the chubby puppy is smuggled into school.

1620 *Sam's Snowy Day*. Ill. by Marisol Sarrazin. Kids Can Press, 2005, ISBN 1-55337-789-3. SERIES: Kids Can Read. SUBJECTS: Pets — Dogs — Fiction; Weather — Snow — Fiction. RL A.

Sam the puppy fails at many snowy activities in this simply repetitive text with fuzzy puppy illustrations.

Labella, Susan

1621 *Beavers and Other Animals with Amazing Teeth*. Ill. with photos. Scholastic, 2005, ISBN 0-516-24930-4. SERIES: News Nonfiction Readers. SUBJECTS: Animals — Teeth; Beavers. RL B. LEXILE 510L.

The teeth of walruses, snakes, crocodiles, and sharks are shown, as well as those of beavers.

Landau, Elaine

1622 *Angelfish*. Ill. with photos. Children's Press, 1999, ISBN 0-516-20660-5. SERIES: True Book. SUBJECTS: Fish; Pets. RL C.

An aerial map showing the Amazon Basin, the source of freshwater angelfish, introduces the variety and characteristics and needs of this popular and prolific pet. Books and Web sites for more information precede the index.

1623 *Apples*. Ill. with photos. Children's Press, 1999, ISBN 0-516-21024-6. SERIES: True Book. SUBJECTS: Food. RL C. LEXILE 780L.

Some of the varieties of apples are featured. Apples are 85 percent water, contain vitamins A and C and potassium, and are a good source of fiber. The recipe is for baked cinnamon apples. Grafting, the role of honeybees, and use of pesticides are discussed.

1624 *Australia and New Zealand*. Ill. with photos. Children's Press, 1998, ISBN 0-516-20981-7. SERIES: True Book. SUBJECTS: Australia; Geography; New Zealand. RL C.

The history, governments, and economies of these two countries are described, as well as unique wildlife and sights. Rare black swans and the poisonous tiger snake are pictured, as are the Great Barrier Reef, diamond miners, the Sydney Opera House, and Maori in traditional dress.

1625 *Canada*. Ill. with photos. Children's Press, 2000, ISBN 0-516-21170-6. SERIES: True Book. SUBJECTS: Canada; Geography. RL C.

Only Russia is larger than Canada. Canada's native population is mentioned, as are the many ethnic groups besides the French. Oil refining, fishing, and farming are some of the contributors to its economy.

1626 *Canals*. Ill. with photos. Children's Press, 2001, ISBN 0-513-22183-3. SERIES: True Book. SUBJECTS: Canals; Geography. RL C. LEXILE 850L.

The ancient canals are introduced, followed by information about the Erie Canal, the Suez Canal, and the Panama Canal. The construction, usefulness, and uses of canals are covered, as is the function of locks.

1627 *Corn*. Ill. with photos. Children's Press, 1998, ISBN 0-516-21026-2. SERIES: True Book. SUBJECTS: Food. RL C.

Landau, Elaine (cont.)

Half the world's corn is grown in the United States. There are thousands of different types of corn, some of which are introduced, as is the 7,000-year-old history of corn. Instructions for making popcorn and cornbread are included.

1628 *Cowboys*. Ill. with photos. Children's Press, 1990, o.p. SUBJECTS: Cowboys; Frontier and pioneer life. RL C.
With historic paintings and photographs, the author outlines the daily life of cowboys, including roundups and trail drives, hardships and hazards.

1629 *Desert Mammals*. Ill. with photos. Children's Press, 1996, ISBN 0-516-20038-0. SERIES: True Book. SUBJECTS: Animals — Mammals; Camels; Deserts. RL C. LEXILE 900L.
A map shows where antelope jackrabbits, pallid bats, kangaroo rats, addaxes, and camels live. The addax can tolerate extremely high temperatures; its wide hoofs help it travel on sand and its coloring changes with the season.

1630 *Dominican Republic*. Ill. with photos. Children's Press, 1999, ISBN 0-516-21171-4. SERIES: True Book. SUBJECTS: Dominican Republic; Geography. RL C.
This country boasts the largest lake in the Caribbean, Lake Enriquillo, home to many endangered species. Its history, people, religion, sports, housing, farm products, and dance are illustrated.

1631 *Egypt*. Ill. with photos. Children's Press, 1999, ISBN 0-516-21172-2. SERIES: True Book. SUBJECTS: Egypt; Geography. RL C.
The contrasts between ancient and modern Egypt are shown, and information about the economy and government is given. Photographs show the recovery of some artifacts from the Lighthouse of Alexandria, one of the Seven Wonders of the World.

1632 *France*. Ill. with photos. Children's Press, 2000, o.p. SERIES: True Book. SUBJECTS: France; Geography. RL C.
The geography, government, history, economy, and art and culture of the people are described. Photographs show a field of lavender, scenes along the Champs Elysees, a resort in the Alps, the World Champions of soccer, cheese, and perfume exports, and a chateau.

1633 *Grassland Mammals*. Ill. with photos. Children's Press, 1996, ISBN 0-516-20039-9. SERIES: True Book. SUBJECTS: Aardvarks; Animals — Mammals; Prairie dogs. RL C. LEXILE NC950L.
The threats to the survival of the giraffe, prairie dog, African elephant, aardvark, and kangaroo are defined. For instance, a dingo is the greatest threat to the kangaroo. The Web addresses show how to view individual giraffes at the Cheyenne Mountain Zoo.

1634 *The Homestead Act*. Ill. with photos. Children's Press, 2005, ISBN 0-516-25870-2. SERIES: True Book. SUBJECTS: Frontier and pioneer life; United States — Colonial period. RL C.
The grassy areas east and west of the Rockies were opened up to European settlers in the 1860s after treaties with the Indians were broken and Indians relocated to reservations. A man or woman head of a household who was at least 21 could claim 160 acres of free land. They had to live there for at least five years, and develop the land. The hardships and ingenuity of settlers are chronicled.

1635 *India*. Ill. with photos. Scholastic, pap., 2000, ISBN 0-516-26764-7. SERIES: True Book. SUBJECTS: Geography; India. RL C.
After an introduction to the location and people of India, other topics such as religion, food, clothing, economy, and history follow, accented by color photographs. A glossary, bibliography, and Web site references are appended.

1636 *Israel*. Ill. with photos. Children's Press, 1998, ISBN 0-516-20983-3. SERIES: True Book. SUBJECTS: Geography; Israel. RL C.
Maps and aerial and close-up photographs of food, terrain, children, peacemakers and military people, restaurants, and religious sites illustrate this informative book about Israel.

1637 *Korea*. Ill. with photos. Children's Press, pap., 1999, ISBN 0-516-26766-3. SERIES: True Book. SUBJECTS: Geography; Korea. RL C.
Prominent cities and rivers are shown on the map; photographs of cities and the border fence

and of people at home and planting rice and at worship illustrate the introductory material about this country.

1638 *Minibeasts as Pets*. Ill. with photos. Children's Press, 1997, ISBN 0-516-20388-6. SERIES: True Book. SUBJECTS: Insects; Pets. RL C.

Ants, ladybugs, crickets, and millipedes are some of the potential pets suggested. Millipedes can be between 1/8" and 11" long! There are up to 10,000 kinds of millipedes! Nine books are in the bibliography.

1639 *Mountain Mammals*. Ill. with photos. Children's Press, 1996, ISBN 0-516-20040-4. SERIES: True Book. SUBJECTS: Animals — Mammals; Mountains; Pandas. RL C. LEXILE NC940L.

Interesting facts about picas, bighorn sheep, yaks, giant pandas, and vicunas are introduced, as well as threats to their survival. Yaks live at 20,000 feet elevation and are domesticated in places such as Tibet, where every part of the animal is utilized when killed for meat.

1640 *Norway*. Ill. with photos. Children's Press, 1998, ISBN 0-516-20985-X. SERIES: True Book. SUBJECTS: Geography; Norway. RL C.

The fjords, food, fishermen, and farmers are shown, as are the country's artists, writers, and rulers.

1641 *The Oregon Trail*. Ill. with photos. Children's Press, 2005, ISBN 0-516-25871-0. SERIES: True Book. SUBJECTS: Frontier and pioneer life; United States — Colonial period. RL C.

Emphasizes the courage of early pioneers who pulled up stakes and headed west by wagon train, traveling from Independence to Forts Laramie, Bridger, and Boise and as far as Oregon City. One in ten died along the trail. The supplies taken and the hardships suffered are described. The most telling photograph is one of wagon ruts that can still be seen today.

1642 *Peru*. Ill. with photos. Children's Press, 1999, ISBN 0-516-21174-9. SERIES: True Book. SUBJECTS: Geography; Peru. RL C.

Photographs show people and places in the mountains, the rain forest, and on the coast. Annie's Peak is named after a 58-year-old American woman who climbed the highest peak in the western hemisphere, Mount Huascaran, in 1908. The rain forest is called the "world's largest pharmacy."

1643 *The Pony Express*. Ill. with photos. Children's Press, 2005, ISBN 0-531-25873-7. SERIES: True Book. SUBJECTS: Frontier and pioneer life; United States — Colonial period. RL C.

The Pony Express existed for just a year and half, carrying mail between Saint Joseph in the Kansas Territory and Sacramento, via Salt Lake City. Prior to this express service, mail traveled by sea, canoe, and mule pack, taking a month; stagecoaches took 21 days. Eighty daring Pony Express riders traveled about 75 miles, riding between 3 and 10 different horses, with relays at 153 stations that used more than 400 horses. They covered 2,000 miles in 10 days in the summer, and between 12 and 16 days in the winter.

1644 *Sea Horses*. Ill. with photos. Children's Press, 1998, ISBN 0-516-20675-3. SERIES: True Book. SUBJECTS: Oceans and ocean life. RL C.

The ways in which sea horses protect themselves and their young, how they reproduce, and how they can become pets are outlined. Several Web sites with information on the care of sea horses in aquariums are mentioned.

1645 *Stegosaurus*. Ill. with photos. Children's Press, 2007, ISBN 0-531-16830-1. SERIES: True Book. SUBJECTS: Dinosaurs. RL C.

Stegosaurus dining and defenses are introduced. The animal's range 150 million years ago is shown on a map. Its brain was the size of a walnut. The 17 bony plates along its spine may have helped it control its temperature.

1646 *Sugar*. Ill. with photos. Children's Press, 1998, ISBN 0-516-21027-0. SERIES: True Book. SUBJECTS: Food. RL C. LEXILE 780L.

The growing of sugar and its harvest, the foods in which it is used, and its effect on health are covered. Recipes for sugar cookies and for angel food candy are included.

1647 *Temperate Forest Animals*. Ill. with photos. Children's Press, 1996, ISBN 0-516-20043-7. SERIES: True Book. SUBJECTS: Animals — Mammals; Raccoons. RL C.

Landau, Elaine (cont.)

After describing temperate forest environments, there are chapters on beavers, echidnas, raccoons, koalas, and wild boars. Echidnas lay eggs, like platypuses, and have sharp spines and a long snout. A photograph shows the bare youngster in the palm of a hand.

1648 *Triceratops*. Ill. with photos. Children's Press, 2007, ISBN 0-531-16831-X. SERIES: True Book. SUBJECTS: Dinosaurs. RL C.
The fossil record of triceratops is gathered from western U.S. states, up into Alberta and Saskatchewan. From the fossils, paleontologists theorize about the animal's habits, food, and body structure. It took about one million years for all the dinosaurs to become extinct.

1649 *Tropical Forest Mammals*. Ill. with photos. Children's Press, 1996, ISBN 0-516-20044-5. SERIES: True Book. SUBJECTS: Animals — Mammals; Orangutans; Tapirs. RL C.
A map shows where the mammals featured live: the jaguar, tapir, orangutan, howler monkey, and sloth. Their young, food, and habits are outlined, as are the threats to their future.

1650 *Wheat*. Ill. with photos. Children's Press, 1999, ISBN 0-516-21029-7. SERIES: True Book. SUBJECTS: Food. RL C.
More than 30 different types of wheat are grown in the United States, brought here by European immigrants. The history of wheat cultivation is illustrated, as well as the changes in technology for its harvesting. A wheat kernel has three parts: the endosperm, the bran, and the germ. Improvements in wheat allow a more plentiful harvest.

1651 *Your Pet Cat*. Ill. with photos. Children's Press, 1997, ISBN 0-516-20381-9. SERIES: True Book. SUBJECTS: Pets — Cats. RL C.
The needs of different types of house cats are discussed, as is their requirement for more than food and water. Some ways to stimulate cats are suggested.

1652 *Your Pet Dog*. Ill. with photos. Children's Press, 2006, ISBN 0-531-16767-4. SERIES: True Book. SUBJECTS: Pets — Dogs. RL C.
Preparing, selecting, equipping, house-training, and grooming a dog are discussed. Photographs are appealingly close-up.

1653 *Your Pet Gerbil*. Ill. with photos. Children's Press, 1997, ISBN 0-516-20384-3. SERIES: True Book. SUBJECTS: Pets — Gerbils. RL C.
How to select a healthy gerbil, and keep it healthy, is shown, as well as feeding it and providing playgrounds. The safety of different kinds of wheels is covered.

1654 *Your Pet Hamster*. Ill. with photos. Children's Press, 2007, ISBN 0-531-16798-4. SERIES: True Book. SUBJECTS: Pets — Hamsters. RL C.
Any child would want a hamster after viewing the photographs in this book. Brief bibliography and Web sites and an index are appended.

1655 *Your Pet Iguana*. Ill. with photos. Children's Press, 2006, ISBN 0-531-16790-9. SERIES: True Book. SUBJECTS: Iguanas; Pets — Iguanas; Reptiles and amphibians. RL C. LEXILE 850L.
Step-by-step tips, illustrated with close-up color photographs, cover choosing, housing, and caring for this unusual pet.

1656 *Your Pet Tropical Fish*. Ill. with photos. Children's Press, 1997, ISBN 0-516-20386-X; pap., ISBN 0-516-26278-5. SERIES: True Book. SUBJECTS: Pets — Fish. RL C.
Information about which fish get along together best, how and why to equip an aquarium, and how to feed the fish is introduced. Most interesting is information about the lateral line, which enables fish to sense their environment. Web sites appended include the ASPCA.

Landshoff, Ursula

1657 *Cats Are Good Company*. Ill. by author. HarperCollins, 1983, o.p. SERIES: I Can Read. SUBJECTS: Pet care; Pets — Cats. RL B.
Care of cats, cat characteristics, and the benefits of owning a cat are given in a fascinating and humorous text. Childlike sketches match the tone perfectly.

1658 *Okay, Good Dog*. Ill. by author. HarperCollins, 1978, o.p. SERIES: I Can Read. SUBJECTS: Pet care; Pets — Dogs. RL B.
Loving training directions include housebreaking and teaching the dog to sit, come, heel, stay, and

lie down. Whimsical pencil drawings keep the tone light.

Langerman, Jean

1659 *No Carrots for Harry!* Ill. by Frank Remkiewicz. Putnam, 1992, ISBN 0-8368-0876-2. SERIES: Read Aloud. SUBJECTS: Rabbits — Fiction; Vegetables — Fiction. RL B.

Stubborn, non-carrot-eating Harry, must eat one before having his sweetgrass tart dessert. A slight story with colored pencil drawings full of rabbits and an array of carrots.

Langner, Nola

1660 *Dusty.* Ill. by author. Putnam, 1976, o.p. SERIES: Break-of-Day. SUBJECTS: Pets — Cats — Fiction. RL B.

A girl's patience in gaining a stray cat's trust leads to a friendship that warms her even after Dusty no longer appears. This affecting story is illustrated with unsentimental soft pencil drawings.

Lapp, Eleanor J.

1661 *The Mice Came in Early This Year.* Ill. by David Cunningham. Whitman, 1976, o.p. SUBJECTS: Fall — Fiction; Grandparents — Fiction. RL B.

A boy helps his grandfather prepare for winter by digging up potatoes, chopping wood, picking apples and hazelnuts, and watching a neighbor pull in his boat. Wonderful watercolors capture the atmosphere of homely seasonal preparations.

Larrick, Nancy, ed.

1662 *More Poetry for Holidays.* Ill. by Harold Berson. Garrard, 1973, o.p. SERIES: Poetry. SUBJECTS: Poetry. RL C.

Poetry about holidays, including Jewish ones, is presented chronologically with brief notes appended. One holiday included is Children's Book Week. Fanciful ink sketches enliven the space and enrich the mental images.

1663 *Poetry for Holidays.* Ill. by Kelly Oechsli. Garrard, 1966, o.p. SERIES: Poetry. SUBJECTS: Poetry. RL C.

John Ciardi, Aileen Fisher, and Henry Longfellow are among the noted poets celebrating ten holidays. This good selection has somewhat stilted tiny drawings.

Latham, Jean L.

1664 *What Tabbit the Rabbit Found.* Ill. by Bill Dugan. Garrard, 1974, o.p. SERIES: Easy Venture. SUBJECTS: Rabbits — Fiction. RL A.

Using primer vocabulary, a small rabbit finds everything except the blue ball he was looking for. Childlike drawings are appropriate.

Lattimore, Deborah N.

1665 *The Flame of Peace: A Tale of the Aztecs.* Ill. by author. HarperCollins, 1991, ISBN 0-06-023709-0. SUBJECTS: Cumulative tales; Folklore — Mexico; Peace — Fiction. RL C.

An Aztec boy braves the road past the nine demons of darkness to seek the flame of peace to reconcile his people with their enemy in this dramatic tale with a familiar cumulative rhythm. Illustrations are decorative Aztec symbols with primary colors against earth-tones.

Lauber, Patricia

1666 *Be a Friend to Trees.* Ill. by Holly Keller. HarperCollins, 1994, ISBN 0-06-021529-1. SERIES: Let's-Read-and-Find-Out Science. SUBJECTS: Science and scientists; Trees. RL B.

Holly Keller's strong graphic design and rich colors enhance the well-written basic information about trees. The fruits and nuts, the tree eaters, the uses of trees, and how to be a friend to trees are introduced.

1667 *Clarence and the Burglar.* Adapted by F. N. Monjo. Ill. by Paul Galdone. Putnam, 1973, o.p. SERIES: Break-of-Day. SUBJECTS: Humorous stories; Pets — Dogs — Fiction; Pets — Fiction. RL B.

Adapted from a chapter in Clarence the TV Dog (Putnam, 1955). Clarence, the friendliest of dogs, overwhelms a burglar by untying the burglar's shoes when he refuses to play. Fun to read, with lively ink and wash pictures.

1668 *Clarence and the Cat.* Ill. by Paul Galdone. Putnam, 1977, o.p. SERIES: Break-of-Day. SUBJECTS: Humorous stories; Pets — Cats — Fiction; Pets — Dogs — Fiction. RL B.

Lauber, Patricia (cont.)

Clarence the dog is an incredibly generous host to a visiting cat, even sharing his food and toys, his favorite chair — and his canine friends. Cat is not so bossy after their visit! Galdone captures Clarence's irrepressible friendliness and Cat's hauteur perfectly.

1669 *How We Learned the Earth Is Round.* Ill. by Megan Lloyd. HarperCollins, 1990, ISBN 0-690-04860-2. SERIES: Let's-Read-and-Find-Out Science. SUBJECTS: Explorers and exploration; Geography; Science and scientists. RL B.
Using simple language and suggested experiments, a noted science author shows how early geographers and explorers proved the Earth is round. The illustrations augment the text with simple maps, diagrams, sketches, and — finally — a photo of the Earth from space.

1670 *An Octopus Is Amazing.* Ill. by Holly Keller. HarperCollins, 1990, ISBN 0-690-04803-3. SERIES: Let's-Read-and-Find-Out Science. SUBJECTS: Octopi; Science and scientists. RL B.
A female octopus takes a week to lay her 200,000 eggs, which she glues onto stems hanging in her den. She then spends all her time guarding them and. cleaning them; when they hatch, she dies. Very light pastel line drawings give a friendly sense of the octopus world.

1671 *Snakes Are Hunters.* Ill. by Holly Keller. HarperCollins, 1988, ISBN 0-690-04630-8. SERIES: Let's-Read-and-Find-Out Science. SUBJECTS: Nature; Snakes. RL C.
This clear, factual presentation about snakes of all sizes and kinds offers information on the life cycles and physical characteristics of snakes and methods of hunting and feeding them. The spare cartoons present a non-menacing animal that is sure to engage the interest of children.

1672 *You're Aboard Spaceship Earth.* Ill. by Holly Keller. HarperCollins, 1994, ISBN 0-06-022407-0. SERIES: Let's-Read-and-Find-Out Science. SUBJECTS: Planets — Earth; Recycling; Water cycle. RL B. LEXILE 460L.
Food, water, and oxygen are all recycled on planet Earth. Pastel drawings help a child's mind encompass these large issues.

Laurence, Daniel

1673 *Captain and Matey Set Sail.* Ill. by Claudio Munoz. HarperCollins, 2001, ISBN 0-06-028957-0; pap., ISBN 0-06-445159-3. SERIES: I Can Read. SUBJECTS: Pirates — Fiction. RL B.
In four chapters, Captain and Matey acquire a parrot, create a new pirate song, get rid of a tattooed visitor, and search for treasure. Bold cartoons illustrate the nonsense.

Lawlor, Laurie

1674 *The Biggest Pest on Eighth Avenue.* Ill. by Cynthia Fisher. Holiday House, 1997, ISBN 0-8234-1321-7. SERIES: Holiday House Reader. SUBJECTS: Plays — Fiction; Siblings — Fiction. RL B. LEXILE 500L.
Little brother Tommy is a pest when the neighbor kids help Mary Lou put on a scary play — until the children find a way to include him. Watercolors capture the imaginative activities of the neighborhood children.

Lawrence, James

1675 *Binky Brothers, Detectives.* Ill. by Leonard Kessler. HarperCollins, pap., 1968, ISBN 0-694-00018-3. SERIES: I Can Read. SUBJECTS: Clubs — Fiction; Mystery and detective stories; Siblings — Fiction. RL B.
Dinky thinks he has the solution to the mystery — but has to be rescued by his younger brother, Binky, who demands full partnership in the detective business. Very simple ink drawings have orange and cocoa washes.

Lawrence, Judith

1676 *Goat for Carlo.* Ill. by Liz Dauber. Garrard, 1971, ISBN 0-8116-6709-X. SERIES: Venture. SUBJECTS: Goats — Fiction; Mexico — Fiction. RL A.
Carlo's new goat produces a surprise bonus. Red serapes, sashes, and skirts highlight the setting of this simple tale.

Lazarus, Keo F.

1677 *Billy Goat in the Chili Patch.* Ill. by Carol Rogers. University of Chicago Press, 1975, o.p. SUBJECTS: Folklore — Mexico; Mexico — Fiction. RL C.

A burro, a dog, a cock, and an ant try to help Pepito get a billy goat out of his chili patch. They discover that sometimes little and wise is better than big and strong. Simple earth-tone paintings enhance the Mexican flavor.

Lear, Edward

1678 *Edward Lear's Nonsense*. Ill. by P. Mark Jackson. Collins, 1990, o.p. SUBJECTS: Nonsense; Poetry. RL C.

The limericks of the master, Edward Lear, are printed in large type, accompanied by full page interesting, eccentric illustrations with a British look. Lear was the first children's author to delight in nonsense.

Leech, Jay, and Zane Spencer

1679 *Bright Fawn and Me*. Ill. by Glo Coalson. HarperCollins, 1979, o.p. SUBJECTS: Cheyenne — Fiction; Sibling rivalry — Fiction. RL B.

A young girl caring for her toddler sister explores a trading fair. As the toddler draws a lot of attention, the older sister experiences a wide range of emotions. Earth-tone drawings give a feeling of the Native American culture and of relationships.

Leedy, Loreen

1680 *Postcards from Pluto: A Tour of the Solar System*. Ill. by author. Holiday House, 1993, ISBN 0-8234-1000-5. SUBJECTS: Astronomy and astronomers; Science and scientists; Space. RL C.

Tour guide Dr. Quasar conducts a group of multicultural children on an abbreviated tour of the solar system. Dialogue and postcards convey facts about the tour. Vivid purple, blue, and green acrylics are set against the black background of space.

Leonard, Marcia

1681 *Dan and Dan*. Ill. by Dorothy Handelman. Millbrook, 1998, ISBN 0-7613-2003-2. SERIES: Phonic-Based Story. SUBJECTS: Grandparents — Fiction; Stories in rhyme. RL A. LEXILE BR.

Posed color photographs show the activities of Dan and his grandfather, Dan.

1682 *Dress-Up*. Ill. by Dorothy Handelman. Millbrook, 1999, ISBN 0-7613-2053-9. SERIES: Real Kids Readers. SUBJECTS: Imagination — Fiction; Stories in rhyme. RL A.

A child playing dress-up likes best to be: *Me!* Color photographs dress up the text with limited phonic vocabulary.

1683 *Get the Ball, Slim*. Ill. by Dorothy Handelman. Millbrook, 1998, ISBN 0-7613-2000-8. SERIES: Real Kids Readers. SUBJECTS: Siblings — Fiction; Stories in rhyme. RL A. LEXILE 40L.

An appealing golden retriever, Slim, retrieves the baseball that Jim hits. Posed color photographs.

1684 *My Pal Al*. Ill. by Dorothy Handelman. Millbrook, 1998, ISBN 0-7613-2001-6. SERIES: Real Kids Readers. SUBJECTS: Stories in rhyme; Toys — Fiction. RL A. LEXILE 100L.

A very simple reader with controlled rhyming vocabulary about a girl and her stuffed red pet rabbit Al, illustrated with photographs.

1685 *No New Pants!* Ill. by Dorothy Handelman. Millbrook, 1999, ISBN 0-7613-2063-6. SERIES: Real Kids Readers. SUBJECTS: Family life — Fiction; Shopping — Fiction; Stories in rhyme. RL A. LEXILE BR.

A young boy is dissatisfied with the jeans in the store, but contented with wearing his older brother's worn ones. Illustrations are posed photographs on a white background.

1686 *The Pet Vet*. Ill. by Dorothy Handelman. Millbrook, 1999, ISBN 0-7613-2050-4. SERIES: Real Kids Readers. SUBJECTS: Stories in rhyme; Veterinarians — Fiction. RL A. LEXILE 130L.

A small boy plays vet when his friends bring stuffed animals for attention — just like his dad, the vet.

1687 *Spots*. Ill. by Dorothy Handelman. Millbrook, 1998, ISBN 0-7613-2016-4. SERIES: Real Kids Readers. SUBJECTS: Siblings — Fiction; Stories in rhyme. RL A. LEXILE BR.

A small girl likes spots on clothes, balls, lamps, art work, toys — but her twin sister does not! Large, posed color photographs illustrate the rhyme.

Leonard, Marcia (cont.)

1688 *The Tin Can Man: A Phonics-Based Story for Pre-K to Grade 1*. Ill. by Dorothy Handelman. Millbrook, 1998, ISBN 0-7613-2012-1. SERIES: Real Kids Readers. SUBJECTS: Family life — Fiction; Inventors and inventions — Fiction; Stories in rhyme. RL A. LEXILE BR.

Nan and her dad make a tin can man to ride her trike in the parade. A creative idea well told.

Lepthien, Emilie U.

1689 *Grizzlies*. Ill. with photos. Children's Press, 1996, ISBN 0-516-20159-X. SERIES: True Book. SUBJECTS: Grizzlies. RL C. LEXILE 800L.

Characteristics of grizzlies, including their diet of 90 pounds of plants per day and information about their teeth, hibernation, reproduction, and play precede the difficulties they present in national parks crowded with tourists.

1690 *Llamas*. Ill. with photos. Children's Press, 1996, ISBN 0-516-20160-3. SERIES: True Book. SUBJECTS: Llamas. RL C.

Llamas have been used as pack animals for more than 4,000 years in the high Andes — the males only of course. Their padded cloven feet do not disturb the soil as hoofed animals do. Many more interesting facts about llamas are wonderfully illustrated with close-up photographs.

Lerner, Sharon

1691 *Follow the Monsters! Featuring Jim Henson's Sesame Street Puppets*. Ill. by Tom Cooke. Random House, 1999, o.p. SERIES: Step into Reading. SUBJECTS: Puppetry — Fiction; Stories in rhyme. RL A.

Simple colored-pencil drawings reflect the rhymed nonsense following the monsters "out of the country and into the town."

LeSieg, Theo

1692 *Come Over to My House*. Ill. by Richard Erdoes. Random House, 1966, ISBN 0-394-90044-8. SERIES: I Can Read It All by Myself. SUBJECTS: Cultural diversity; Houses; Stories in rhyme. RL B.

After skimming the world celebrating its diversity of housing, the tour concludes that despite the differences, houses are alike when friends are invited in. Indifferent comic illustrations keep the tone light in this rhyming story.

1693 *The Eye Book*. Ill. by Roy McKie. Random House, 1968, ISBN 0-375-90033-0. SERIES: Bright and Early Books. SUBJECTS: Human body — Eyes — Fiction; Stories in rhyme. RL A. LEXILE 140L.

Eyes that see blue, red, a bird and a bed, trees and clocks, bees and socks, are celebrated. Lively, simply outlined cartoons are in primary colors.

1694 *I Wish That I Had Duck Feet*. Ill. by B. Tobey. Random House, 1965, ISBN 0-394-80040-0. SERIES: Beginner Books. SUBJECTS: Imagination — Fiction; Stories in rhyme. RL B.

Having duck feet, antlers, a whale spout, a long tail, and long nose and a Which-What-Who all have their assets and detractions. Bold ink drawings with simple wash.

1695 *In a People House*. Ill. by Roy McKie. Random House, 1972, ISBN 0-394-92395-2. SERIES: Bright and Early Books. SUBJECTS: Houses; Stories in rhyme. RL C. LEXILE NP.

A lively, rhyming catalog of household objects is illustrated with full-color line drawings

1696 *Maybe You Should Fly a Jet! Maybe You Should Be a Vet!* Ill. by Michael J. Smollin. Random House, 1980, ISBN 0-394-94448-8. SERIES: I Can Read It All by Myself. SUBJECTS: Careers; Stories in rhyme. RL C.

Lively suggestions of career options range from teaching and preaching to being a turkey farmer. Cartoon sketches show mostly males.

1697 *Please Try to Remember the First of Octember!* Ill. by Art Cumings. Random House, 1977, ISBN 0-394-83563-8. SERIES: I Can Read It All by Myself. SUBJECTS: Nonsense; Stories in rhyme. RL B.

In this rhyming story, wonderful, magical things come true when you wish on the first of Octember. Pastel drawings are more static than those in LeSieg's other books.

1698 *Ten Apples Up on Top!* Ill. by Roy McKie. Random House, 1961, ISBN 0-394-90019-7. SERIES: I Can Read It All by Myself. SUBJECTS: Humorous stories; Stories in rhyme. RL A.

Toe-tapping rhythm, outrageous bragging, and a marvelous chase draw the reader into this story. Simple, expressive line drawings are accented with red and yellow.

1699 *The Tooth Book.* Ill. by Roy McKie. Random House, 1981, ISBN 0-394-84825-X. SERIES: Bright and Early Books. SUBJECTS: Human body — Teeth; Humorous stories; Stories in rhyme. RL C. LEXILE 400L.

Creative, humorous uses of teeth are detailed using rhyming text; the closing admonishes the readers to remember, no matter what, that the dentist is their teeth's best friend. Comic illustrations are lively and appropriate.

1700 *Wacky Wednesday.* Ill. by George Booth. Random House, 1974, ISBN 0-394-92912-8. SERIES: I Can Read It All by Myself. SUBJECTS: Mathematics — Fiction; Puzzles; Stories in rhyme. RL A.

Comic visual and rhyming puzzles intrigue the reader as well as delight the eye, as the reader is invited to identify all the errors in the cartoon pictures.

1701 *Would You Rather Be a Bullfrog!* Ill. by Roy McKie. Random House, 1975, ISBN 0-394-93128-9. SERIES: Bright and Early Books. SUBJECTS: Humorous stories; Nonsense; Stories in rhyme. RL C.

Rhymed couplets ask readers what outrageous animals or things they would like to be, from hammers and nails to minnows and whales. Humor is accentuated with McKie's usual comic drawings, with strong simple lines and bold colors.

Leverich, Kathleen

1702 *The Hungry Fox and the Foxy Duck.* Ill. by Paul Galdone. Parents Magazine Press, 1978, ISBN 0-8193-0988-5. SUBJECTS: Ducks — Fiction; Folklore; Foxes — Fiction. RL A.

Foxy Duck requires hungry Fox to bring a table, dishes, and a tablecloth before she leaves the pond to join him for breakfast. Fox finds out the pond has a fence around it for a reason in this original and clever retelling of an old tale with flowing, simple Galdone watercolors.

Levinson, Nancy Smiler

1703 *Clara and the Bookwagon.* Ill. by Carolyn Croll. HarperCollins, 1988, ISBN 0-06-023838-0. SERIES: I Can Read. SUBJECTS: Books and reading — Fiction; Farm and country life — Fiction; Libraries and librarians — Fiction. RL B. LEXILE 290L.

Though Clara works hard on the family farm, her father, who feels that books are only for rich people, will not help her learn to read — until the bookwagon librarian changes his attitude. Simple colored pencil drawings add to this moving story of a child's determination to read.

1704 *Prairie Friends.* Ill. by Stacey Schuett. HarperCollins, 2003, ISBN 0-06-028002-6. SERIES: I Can Read. SUBJECTS: Friendship — Fiction; Frontier and pioneer life — Fiction. RL A. LEXILE 480L.

Life on the prairie is lonely for Betsy until another girl settles nearby, who needs to learn how to live on the prairie. Watercolor illustrations show some of the ways in which families helped each other and entertained themselves.

1705 *Snowshoe Thompson.* Ill. by Joan Sandin. HarperCollins, 1992, ISBN 0-15-314329-0. SERIES: I Can Read. SUBJECTS: Biographies; Frontier and pioneer life. RL A. LEXILE 330L.

John Thompson earned his nickname from his many trips over the Sierra Nevadas delivering mail on homemade skis. The simple retelling focuses on a boy's desire to send a letter to his father, who is off seeking gold. His story is enhanced by appealing watercolor illustrations by Joan Sandin.

Levy, Elizabeth

1706 *The Creepy Computer Mystery: Invisible Inc.* Ill. by Denise Brunkus. Scholastic, pap., 1996, ISBN 0-590-60322-1. SERIES: Scholastic Reader. SUBJECTS: Computers — Fiction; Mystery and detective stories. RL C. LEXILE 380L.

The detective trio solves another mystery, this one involving computers that do strange things. Pen and wash illustrations.

Levy, Elizabeth (cont.)

1707 *The Karate Class Mystery: Invisible Inc.* Ill. by Denise Brunkus. Scholastic, 1996, ISBN 0-590-60323-X. SERIES: Scholastic Reader. SUBJECTS: Mystery and detective stories; Sports — Karate — Fiction. RL C. LEXILE 440L.

Invisible Chip and deaf Charlene solve mysteries, this time tracking down who stole Justin's karate belt and why. There is even an invisible dog — whose tail is not invisible.

1708 *The Mystery of the Missing Dog: Invisible Inc.* Ill. by Denise Brunkus. Scholastic, pap., 2004, ISBN 0-439-56864-1. SERIES: Scholastic Reader. SUBJECTS: Mystery and detective stories; Pets — Dogs — Fiction. RL C. LEXILE 410L.

The detective trio's pet dog Max is invisible except for his tail. When he is kidnapped at the fair, they follow several false leads before locating Max when he barks. Ink and wash drawings add humor to the story.

1709 *Parents' Night Fright: Invisible Inc.* Ill. by Denise Brunkus. Scholastic, pap., 1998, ISBN 0-590-60324-8. SERIES: Hello Reader! SUBJECTS: Mystery and detective stories; School stories. RL C.

By reading lips, the detectives think they have solved the mystery of the missing writing, but they have more detective work to do. Lively cartoons add dimension to the story.

1710 *The Schoolyard Mystery: Invisible Inc.* Ill. by Denise Brunkus. Scholastic, 2004, ISBN 0-590-47483-9. SERIES: Scholastic Reader. SUBJECTS: Mystery and detective stories; School stories. RL C. LEXILE 410L.

The fearless trio track a missing salamander.

1711 *The Snack Attack Mystery: Invisible Inc.* Ill. by Denise Brunkus. Scholastic, pap., 1995, ISBN 0-590-60289-6. SERIES: Scholastic Reader. SUBJECTS: Mystery and detective stories. RL C.

The Invisible Inc. detectives look into the strange disappearance of some of their favorite foods.

Lewis, Brenda Ralph

1712 *The Story of Anne Frank.* Ill. with photos and drawings. DK, pap., 2001, ISBN 0-7894-7379-8. SERIES: Reading Alone. SUBJECTS: Biographies; United States — World War II. RL C. LEXILE 840L.

Anne's story from her diary is followed by information about Miep Gies, who sheltered her, and about her father's publishing of her story, as the only surviving family member. Glossary and index follow.

Lewis, Hara

1713 *Cinderella.* Ill. by Barbara Lanza. Scholastic, pap., 2004, ISBN 0-439-47153-2. SERIES: Scholastic Reader. SUBJECTS: Folklore. RL B.

A pedestrian retelling is matched by pretty, soft pastel illustrations.

Lewis, Thomas P.

1714 *The Blue Rocket Fun Show: Or Friends Forever.* Ill. by Ib Ohlsson. Macmillan, 1986, o.p. SERIES: Ready-to-Read. SUBJECTS: Amusement parks — Fiction; Friendship — Fiction; Science fiction. RL B.

Leslie and Niki's summer friendship is not interrupted by surprise revelations about Niki's origin at summer's end. Well-constructed story has imaginative details and two-tone pencil highlights.

1715 *Clipper Ship.* Ill. by Joan Sandin. HarperCollins, 1978, ISBN 0-06-023808-9. SERIES: I Can Read History. SUBJECTS: Historical fiction; Sex roles — Fiction; Ships and shipping — Fiction. RL C. LEXILE 420L.

Based on true-life stories of captains' wives who took over responsibility for ships, this book details one such passage to the California gold fields via the treacherous Cape Horn. An absorbing adventure shown in gray and beige with a touch of turquoise.

1716 *Hill of Fire.* Ill. by Joan Sandin. Scholastic, 1998, ISBN 0-439-04434-0. SERIES: I Can Read History. SUBJECTS: Geology and geologists; Historical fiction; Volcanoes. RL A. LEXILE 350L.

The true story of the 1943 eruption of Particutin in a Mexican farmer's field is told from the point of view of his son Pablo. Authentic ink drawings feature earth tones.

1717 *Mr. Sniff and the Motel Mystery*. Ill. by Beth L. Weiner. HarperCollins, 1984, ISBN 0-06-023824-0. SERIES: I Can Read. SUBJECTS: Mystery and detective stories; Pets — Dogs — Fiction. RL B.

Mr. Sniff identifies the perpetrator of motel mischief as someone without hay fever, who knows where to find lipstick, chews bubble gum, and is not afraid of crabs or jellyfish. The challenging puzzle has a compassionate conclusion and illustrations in turquoise, pumpkin, and avocado.

Lewison, Wendy Cheyette

1718 *The Big Snowball*. Ill. by Maryann Cocca-Leffler. Grosset & Dunlap, pap., 2000, ISBN 0-448-42184-4. SERIES: All Aboard Reading. SUBJECTS: Rebuses; Stories in rhyme; Winter — Fiction. RL A. LEXILE NP.

This simple, imaginative story in rhyme uses rebuses and humor.

1719 *Buzzzz Said the Bee*. Ill. by Hans Wilhelm. Scholastic, 1992, o.p. SERIES: Scholastic Reader. SUBJECTS: Cumulative tales; Stories in rhyme. RL A. LEXILE 410L.

The sheep, cow, pig, hen, duck, and bee all have a part in this story with appealing watercolor illustrations.

1720 *Princess Buttercup: A Flower Princess Story*. Ill. by Jerry Smath. Grosset & Dunlap, 2001, ISBN 0-613-35619-5. SERIES: All Aboard Science Reader. SUBJECTS: Butterflies and moths — Fiction; Fairies — Fiction. RL A. LEXILE BR.

When Princess Buttercup gets lost following a butterfly, she finds her way home — on the back of a butterfly! Pastel drawings match the text.

Lexau, Joan M.

1721 *Crocodile and Hen: A Bakongo Folktale*. Ill. by Doug Cushman. HarperCollins, pap., 2001, ISBN 0-06-444263-2. SERIES: I Can Read. SUBJECTS: Animals — Folklore; Folklore — French Congo. RL A. LEXILE 120L.

Crocodile is baffled when his next meal, Hen, calls him brother, and decides that the differences matter little. Cushman's ink and wash illustrations are suitably simple for the beginning vocabulary.

1722 *The Dog Food Caper*. Ill. by Marylin Hafner. Penguin, 1987, ISBN 0-8037-0107-1. SERIES: Dial Easy-to-Read. SUBJECTS: Mystery and detective stories. RL B.

The witch on Orange Street helps Willy find out who is stealing his charge's dog food and hiding it all over the house. Gentle humor with colored-pencil drawings.

1723 *Don't Be My Valentine*. Ill. by Syd Hoff. HarperCollins, 1999, ISBN 0-06-028240-1. SERIES: I Can Read. SUBJECTS: Friendship — Fiction; School stories; Valentine's Day — Fiction. RL C. LEXILE 190L.

Even after Albert helps them make up, Sam and Amy Lou are bugging each other on Valentine's Day at school. Features realistic relationships with typical Hoff comic illustrations in strong colors.

1724 *Finders Keepers, Losers Weepers*. Ill. by Tomie dePaola. HarperCollins, 1976, o.p. SUBJECTS: Siblings — Fiction. RL B.

Max tries to cover for his sister Amanda, but he has some hardships along the way. Stylized drawings have gold, blue, and avocado coloring.

1725 *I Hate Red Rover*. Ill. by Gail Owens. Dutton, 1979, o.p. SERIES: Fat Cat. SUBJECTS: Fear — Fiction; Grandparents — Fiction; Self-esteem — Fiction. RL A.

Jill's skill at playing Red Rover at school is strengthened by her desire to help Grandpa adjust to his new dentures — neither like being laughed at. Expressive pencil drawings have a pale red wash.

1726 *Miss Happ in the Poison Ivy Case*. Ill. by Marylin Hafner. Dial, 1983, o.p. SERIES: Dial Easy-to-Read. SUBJECTS: Mystery and detective stories; Witches — Fiction. RL A.

When the magical peanut butter and grape seed concoction of Willy Nilly's neighbor, Miss Happ, fails to cure his sister's poison ivy, he discovers a cure himself. Expressive, action-filled drawings are brightened with shades of orange and turquoise.

1727 *The Rooftop Mystery*. Ill. by Syd Hoff. HarperCollins, 1968, o.p. SERIES: I Can Read. SUBJECTS: Dolls and dollhouses — Fiction; Moving, household — Fiction; Siblings — Fiction. RL B.

Lexau, Joan M. (cont.)

When Sam loses his sister's doll, for which he was responsible during a move, his detective work saves his skin. Flat comic drawings are a bit dull.

1728 *T for Tommy*. Ill. by Janet Compere. Garrard, 1971, o.p. SERIES: Venture. SUBJECTS: Storytelling. RL A.

Another version of a familiar tell-and-draw story with primary school-level vocabulary and very basic ink illustrations.

Lillegard, Dee

1729 *I Can Be a Baker*. Ill. with photos and drawings. Childrens Press, 1986, ISBN 0-516-01892-2. SERIES: I Can Be. SUBJECTS: Careers; Food. RL C.

A picture glossary and an index accompany information about machine- and hand-baking, emphasizing the necessary speed and teamwork. Excellent color photographs and a few drawings amplify the text.

Lillie, Patricia

1730 *Jake and Rosie*. Ill. by author. Greenwillow, 1989, ISBN 0-688-07624-6. SUBJECTS: Friendship — Fiction. RL B.

Jake and Rosie decide to be twins and to dress alike, well almost. They even get chicken pox at the same time. Simple pen and wash drawings complement the warm story.

Ling, Bettina

1731 *Lemonade for Sale*. Photos by Dorothy Handelman. Millbrook, 1998, ISBN 0-7613-2010-5. SERIES: Real Kids Readers. SUBJECTS: Birthdays — Fiction; Business enterprises — Fiction. RL B. LEXILE 160L.

Despite rain, a bicycle accident, and the park closing, Kate and her friends earn enough to buy Kate's father a birthday present.

Ling, Mary

1732 *Calf*. Photos by Gordon Clayton. DK, 1993, o.p. SERIES: See How They Grow. SUBJECTS: Animals — Baby; Animals — Farm; Cows. RL A.

Excellent color photographs trace the growth of a calf from birth to two years old. Calf borders and endpapers further decorate the simple text.

1733 *Foal*. Photos by Gordon Clayton. DK, 1992, o.p. SERIES: See How They Grow. SUBJECTS: Animals — Baby; Animals — Farm; Horses. RL A.

Exceptional photographs of a foal from birth to five months are further enhanced by watercolor horse borders and endpapers. The text is simple.

1734 *Fox*. Photos by Jane Burton. DK, 1992, o.p. SERIES: See How They Grow. SUBJECTS: Animals — Baby; Foxes. RL A.

Playful kits, from birth to 12 weeks old, are illustrated with excellent close-up color photographs, and a watercolor border and endpapers. The text is simple.

1735 *Giraffe*. Photos by Peter Anderson. DK, 1993, o.p. SERIES: See How They Grow. SUBJECTS: Animals — Baby; Giraffes. RL A.

A close-up look at giraffes, from birth to one year old. Simple text is dominated by excellent photographs as well as giraffe borders and endpapers.

1736 *Owl*. Photos by Kim Taylor. DK, 1992, o.p. SERIES: See How They Grow. SUBJECTS: Owls. RL A.

Color photographs show an owl from the incredibly ugly and helpless newly hatched baby to fully grown beauty at 12 weeks. Simple text has decorative borders and endpapers.

1737 *Penguins*. Photos by Neil Fletcher. DK, 1993, o.p. SERIES: See How They Grow. SUBJECTS: Penguins. RL A.

Seven stages in the growth of a penguin, from birth to two and a half years, are shown in exceptional close-up photographs, limited text, and decorative borders.

1738 *Pig*. Photos by Bill Ling. DK, 1993, ISBN 1-56458-204-3. SERIES: See How They Grow. SUBJECTS: Animals — Farm; Pigs. RL A.

Exceptional photographs of pigs against a white ground are accented by watercolor borders and endpapers of pigs, plus a simple text.

Little, Emily

1739 *David and the Giant.* Ill. by Hans Wilhelm. Random House, 2003, ISBN 0-394-98867-1. SERIES: Step into Reading. SUBJECTS: Bible stories. RL A. LEXILE 140L.

Young David and King David are shown accompanied by his eager pup.

Little, Jean

1740 *Emma's Magic Winter.* Ill. by Jennifer Plecas. HarperCollins, 1998, ISBN 0-06-025390-8. SERIES: I Can Read. SUBJECTS: Books and reading — Fiction; Friendship — Fiction; School stories. RL B. LEXILE 250L.

Emma's red "magic" boots are just like her neighbor Sally's, and their magic helps her overcome shyness in making friends and reading aloud in school. Plecas's drawings are cheery.

1741 *Emma's Strange Pet.* Ill. by Jennifer Plecas. HarperCollins, 2003, ISBN 0-06-028350-5. SERIES: I Can Read. SUBJECTS: Adoption — Fiction; Pets — Fiction; Siblings — Fiction. RL B. LEXILE 260L.

Newly adopted Max wants a strange pet just like his sister's. Simple drawings underscore the subtleties of the story.

1742 *Emma's Yucky Brother.* Ill. by Jennifer Plecas. HarperCollins, 2000, ISBN 0-06-028348-3. SERIES: I Can Read. SUBJECTS: Adoption — Fiction; Siblings — Fiction. RL B. LEXILE 200L.

The challenges of adopting a 4-year-old are presented in Jean Little's story of "Yucky Emma," Max's new sister. Acceptable watercolor and ink drawings.

Littledale, Freya

1743 *The Snow Child.* Ill. by Barbara Lavallee. Scholastic, 1989, ISBN 0-590-05398-1. SUBJECTS: Folklore — Russia; Russia — Fiction. RL C.

A childless couple makes a snow child who teaches the villagers how to make snow sculptures, but the snow child disappears with the spring thaw. This tale of renewal has the lavenders, blues, and whites of fantasy.

Livingstone, Star

1744 *Harley.* Ill. by Molly Bang. Chronicle, 2001, ISBN 1-58717-150-3. SUBJECTS: Llamas — Fiction. RL C. LEXILE 200L.

The fascinating story of an independent llama who becomes a guard llama, protecting sheep from coyotes and from being lost. Soft chalk drawings enhance this tale.

Lobel, Anita

1745 *The Straw Maid.* Ill. by author. Greenwillow, 1983, ISBN 0-517-65240-4. SUBJECTS: Folklore. RL B.

A girl escapes from three robbers by dressing a straw figure in her clothes, and dressing herself in feathers stuck on with honey. This original folk tale has a satisfying ending. Delicate ink drawings and patterns emphasize the folk flavor.

Lobel, Arnold

1746 *Days with Frog and Toad.* Ill. by author. HarperCollins, 1984, ISBN 0-06-023963-8. SERIES: I Can Read. SUBJECTS: Friendship — Fiction; Frogs and toads — Fiction. RL B. LEXILE 320L.

Procrastination, kite-flying frustrations, scary-story shivers, a too-big birthday hat, and two close friends, Frog and Toad, sitting alone together are the themes of the five chapters. Green and brown soft pencil drawings are reassuring and warm, like the friendship.

1747 *Frog and Toad All Year.* Ill. by author. HarperCollins, 1976, ISBN 0-06-023951-4. SERIES: I Can Read. SUBJECTS: Friendship — Fiction; Frogs and toads — Fiction. RL B. LEXILE 300L.

Toad needs Frog's encouragement to go sledding; they search together for spring and share chocolate ice cream cones and a late Christmas. The story and earth-tone drawings have humor and compassion.

1748 *Frog and Toad Are Friends.* Ill. by author. HarperCollins, 1970, ISBN 0-06-023958-1. SERIES: I Can Read. SUBJECTS: Friendship — Fiction; Frogs and toads — Fiction. RL B. LEXILE 400L.

Frog and Toad, as usual, support and encourage each other, in searching for spring and a lost but-

Lobel, Arnold (cont.)

ton, and in waiting for a letter. Drawings focus closely on the two friends.

1749 *Frog and Toad Together.* Ill. by author. HarperCollins, 1999, ISBN 0-694-01298-X. SERIES: I Can Read. SUBJECTS: Friendship — Fiction; Frogs and toads — Fiction. RL B. LEXILE 330L.

Toad can do nothing without his list and he finds that helping frightened seeds is very hard work. With Frog's assistance, everything becomes easier. The author's splendid illustrations help show the ways in which friends overcome irritations and frustrations.

1750 *Grasshopper on the Road.* Ill. by author. HarperCollins, 1986, ISBN 0-06-444094-X. SERIES: I Can Read. SUBJECTS: Grasshoppers — Fiction. RL B. LEXILE 310L.

Lobel writes powerfully about the joys of embracing new experiences in six small tales about Grasshopper: Grasshopper meets some small critters so involved in one narrow activity that they will not risk traveling with him. Rhythmic, imaginative language is accompanied by sympathetic drawings typical of Lobel.

1751 *Lucille.* Ill. by author. HarperCollins, 1986, ISBN 0-06-023966-2. SERIES: I Can Read. SUBJECTS: Animals — Fiction; Horses — Fiction; Self-esteem — Fiction. RL B.

Lucille considers herself dull and dirty as a workhorse, but chooses that role after she dresses up and tries to act like a lady. The lively drawings add humor and keep the tone light.

1752 *Mouse Soup.* Ill. by author. HarperCollins, 1977, ISBN 0-06-023967-0. SERIES: I Can Read. SUBJECTS: Animals — Fiction; Humorous stories; Mice — Fiction. RL B. LEXILE 240L.

A mouse's tales of bees, thorns, stones, and mud help him escape from being the weasel's soup. Imaginative and varied ideas have excellent illustrations, highlighted by the picture of bee stings on the weasel's head.

1753 *Mouse Tales.* Ill. by author. HarperCollins, 1978, ISBN 0-8085-2659-6. SERIES: I Can Read. SUBJECTS: Animals — Fiction; Friendship — Fiction; Mice — Fiction. RL B. LEXILE 440L.

Seven simple tales of friendship and kindness deal with a child mouse afraid of a cloud that looks like a cat, and a wishing well that grants every wish after being given a pillow to cushion the impact of pennies being dropped in. Some drawings are small, some open and flowing.

1754 *Owl at Home.* Ill. by author. HarperCollins, 1975, ISBN 0-06-023949-2; pap., ISBN 0-06-444034-6. SERIES: I Can Read. SUBJECTS: Birds — Fiction; Fear — Fiction; Owls — Fiction. RL B. LEXILE 370L.

Owl has Winter for an unwelcome guest, strange bumps under his blanket, and some comforting tear-water tea. Humor warms Owl's apprehensions, as do the soft pencil drawings.

1755 *Small Pig.* Ill. by author. HarperCollins, 1988, ISBN 0-8335-2818-1. SERIES: I Can Read. SUBJECTS: Farm and country life — Fiction; Pigs — Fiction. RL B. LEXILE 440L.

When the farmer's wife cleans up Small Pig's beloved mud puddle, he goes in search of a new place to wallow — and chooses unwisely. This very effective story has expressive four-color drawings.

1756 *Uncle Elephant.* Ill. by author. HarperCollins, 1981, ISBN 0-06-023980-8. SERIES: I Can Read. SUBJECTS: Elephants — Fiction; Illness — Fiction; Loneliness — Fiction. RL B. LEXILE 330L.

An old elephant helps a small, sick, lonely elephant while away the time. They share peanuts, have supper by moonlight, and trumpet in the dawn. Rose and pale green washes embellish the wrinkly pair's adventures.

Lock, Deborah

1757 *Let's Make Music.* Ill. with photos. DK, 2005, ISBN 0-7566-1423-6. SERIES: Learning to Read. SUBJECTS: Music and musicians. RL A.

In colored photographs, children are shown playing a dozen instruments, from feet, hands, and voice, to harmonica, tambourine, and recorder.

Lohf, Sabine

1758 *Things I Can Make with Buttons.* Ill. by author. Chronicle, 1990, ISBN 0-87701-

687-9. SERIES: Things I Can Make With. SUBJECTS: Arts and crafts. RL C.

Creative ideas for button craft are introduced by a child gnome cartoon figure in large colorful photographs on a white ground. One can count or paint buttons, make jewelry or animals, stitchery or collages, games, gardens, or puppets.

1759 *Things I Can Make with Leaves.* Ill. by author. Chronicle, 1990, ISBN 0-87701-763-8. SERIES: Things I Can Make With. SUBJECTS: Arts and crafts. RL C.

Imaginative leaf animals and people, cards, dolls, crowns, collages, jewelry, puppets, prints, and tea are illustrated with large color photographs against a white ground, with a Swedish child gnome making suggestions.

1760 *Things I Can Make with Paper.* Ill. by author. Chronicle, 1989, ISBN 0-87701-671-2. SERIES: Things I Can Make With. SUBJECTS: Arts and crafts. RL C.

Torn paper collage, crumbled paper pictures, greeting cards, woven paper, stars and snowflakes, play money, pinwheels, masks, and accordion animals are some of the creative ideas for paper crafts. A Swedish elf helps amplify each double spread illustrated with a color photo.

London, Sara

1761 *The Good Luck Glasses.* Ill. by Jacqueline Rogers. Scholastic, pap., 2000, ISBN 0-590-97212-X. SERIES: Scholastic Reader. SUBJECTS: Eyeglasses — Fiction. RL C. LEXILE 350L.

Nomi has trouble seeing the blackboard at school and trips on the cat at home before going to have her eyes tested. Of course, her younger siblings want glasses just like hers when she comes home.

Lopshire, Robert

1762 *How to Make Snop Snappers and Other Fine Things.* Ill. by author. Greenwillow, 1977, o.p. SERIES: Read-Alone. SUBJECTS: Imagination; Wordplay. RL B.

A tantalizing table of contents shows toys to be created, from an airboat and a sock puppet to a Ballimp (balloon-turned-blimp). Exceptionally imaginative ideas, directions, and wordplay. The illustrations are humorous, yet precise.

1763 *I Am Better Than You!* Ill. by author. HarperCollins, 1968, o.p. SERIES: I Can Read. SUBJECTS: Behavior — Bragging — Fiction; Lizards — Fiction. RL A.

In this story about two lizards, Sam tries to outdo Pete in *everything*, but oversells his abilities; perhaps he will make a new friend. Lovely lizard activities such as zapping flies and changing colors are illustrated in avocado green.

1764 *I Want to Be Somebody New!* Ill. by author. Beginner Books, 1986, ISBN 0-394-97616-9. SERIES: I Can Read It All by Myself. SUBJECTS: Animals — Fiction; Self-esteem — Fiction; Stories in rhyme. RL A.

The disadvantages of being an elephant, a giraffe, or a mouse become apparent when a zoo animal uses its magic to try different shapes. A light tone is conveyed by rhyme and comic drawings.

Lorian, Nicole

1765 *A Birthday Present for Mama: A Step Two Book.* Ill. by J. P. Miller. Random House, 1984, ISBN 0-394-96755-0. SERIES: Step into Reading. SUBJECTS: Birthdays — Fiction; Mothers — Fiction; Rabbits — Fiction. RL B.

Little Rabbit seeks help in finding a birthday present for his mother from a sheep, a frog, a cat, a fox, and a squirrel — but a hug is enough! Spring colors brighten friendly cartoon drawings.

Losi, Carol A.

1766 *512 Ants on Sullivan Street.* Ill. by Patrick Merrell. Scholastic, pap., 2006, ISBN 0-439-79854-X. SERIES: Scholastic Reader. SUBJECTS: Mathematics — Fiction; Stories in rhyme. RL C. LEXILE NP.

Marilyn Burns's math activities are enlivened by the rhythmic story of an ant invasion of a picnic. Multiplication's relationship to addition is introduced.

Low, Alice

1767 *The Witch Who Was Afraid of Witches.* Ill. by Jane Manning. HarperCollins, pap., 2000, ISBN 0-06-444255-1. SERIES: I Can Read. SUBJECTS: Siblings — Fiction; Witches — Fiction. RL B.

Low, Alice (cont.)

Wendy the Witch had two older sisters, but had to find out from a new friend that she had powers of her own. Lighthearted illustrations keep the story line on track.

1768 *Zena and the Witch Circus*. Ill. by Laura Cornell. Dial, 1990, ISBN 0-8037-0404-6. SERIES: Dial Easy-to-Read. SUBJECTS: Magic — Fiction; Witches — Fiction. RL A.

A small witch, Zena, has trouble with her magic, but succeeds in taming the witches' dragon, a dog, by shrinking him into a puppy with softly spoken magic. Whimsical, lively pen and wash sketches add dashes of color and humor.

Low, Joseph

1769 *Benny Rabbit and the Owl*. Ill. by author. Greenwillow, 1978, o.p. SERIES: Read-Alone. SUBJECTS: Fear — Fiction; Rabbits — Fiction. RL B.

Father Rabbit has an ingenious way to allay Benny's fear of an owl in his closet. The imaginative, reassuring story has expressive ink and wash drawings.

1770 *Mad Wet Hen and Other Riddles*. Ill. by author. Greenwillow, 1977, ISBN 0-688-11511-X. SERIES: Read-Alone. SUBJECTS: Jokes and riddles; Wordplay. RL B.

People, pigs, elephants, peacocks, and umbrellas are the focus of these refreshingly original riddles. Pen and wash drawings spark the imagination.

Lowery, Barbara

1771 *Mammals*. Ill. by Michael Charlton. Watts, 1976, o.p. SERIES: Easy-Read Fact. SUBJECTS: Animals; Nature; Science and scientists. RL C.

Good descriptions of mammal characteristics and behavior are accompanied by two-tone pencil illustrations and an index.

Lowery, Janette S.

1772 *Six Silver Spoons*. Ill. by Robert Quackenbush. HarperCollins, 1971, o.p. SERIES: I Can Read History. SUBJECTS: Historical fiction; United States — Revolutionary War — Fiction. RL A.

Some of the fear of the Redcoats' presence in Boston and the battle at Lexington are conveyed from a young girl's perspective. Pencil drawings with two-tone washes portray the spirit of the times.

Lowery, Linda, and Marybeth Lorbiecki

1773 *Earthwise at School: A Guide to the Care and Feeding of your Planet*. Ill. by David Mataya. Carolrhoda, 1993, ISBN 0-87614-731-7. SUBJECTS: Conservation. RL C.

Headings for this environmental action book include Cloudy Skies, Tree Treasures, Sea Sickness, Land's End (waste management), People Power, and Where Do We Go from Here? Following outlines of environmental problems, specific examples of positive action from around the world are given.

Lundell, Margo

1774 *A Girl Named Helen Keller*. Ill. by Irene Trivas. Scholastic, pap., 1995, ISBN 0-590-47963-6. SERIES: Scholastic Reader. SUBJECTS: Biographies; Blindness. RL B. LEXILE 350L.

Both Helen Keller and her teacher of fifty years always remembered the birthday of Helen's soul, when she first understood language. Watercolors illustrate the tantrums and the triumphs of small Helen.

Lunn, Carolyn

1775 *Bobby's Zoo*. Ill. by Tom Dunnington. Childrens Press, 1989, ISBN 0-516-02089-7. SERIES: Start-to-Read. SUBJECTS: Animals — Fiction; Humorous stories; Stories in rhyme. RL A.

This humorous story uses a 53-word vocabulary and bright watercolors to tell of all the wild animals who've taken over Bobby's house.

1776 *Spiders and Webs*. Ill. by Tom Dunnington. Children's Press, 1989, ISBN 0-516-02093-5. SERIES: Rookie Reader. SUBJECTS: Stories in rhyme. RL A.

Rhythmic imaginative associations of things familiar to children, from baths and bubbles and lightning and thunder to why and wonder. Watercolor illustrations are lively, of multicultural children. Text employs a 61-word vocabulary.

Luttrell, Ida

1777 *The Bear Next Door*. Ill. by Sarah Stapler. HarperCollins, 1991, ISBN 0-06-024024-5. SERIES: I Can Read. SUBJECTS: Bears — Fiction; Friendship — Fiction; Gophers — Fiction. RL A.

Arlo Gopher's sprinkler soaks the belongings of his new neighbor, Vic, in the first of three chapter stories about their budding friendship. A gentle humor infuses all three. Colorful, wry ink and watercolor illustrations match the text.

1778 *Lonesome Lester*. Ill. by Megan Lloyd. HarperCollins, 1984, ISBN 0-06-024030-X. SUBJECTS: Prairie dogs — Fiction; Solitude — Fiction. RL C.

Prairie dog Lester finds that ants, his super-clean Aunt Martha, and a crying lost baby rabbit do not make good company — you cannot be just plain peaceful with company around. Soft-colored drawings, particularly of frowning Aunt Martha, are especially effective.

1779 *Milo's Toothache*. Ill. by Enzo Giannini. Dial, 1992, ISBN 0-606-14269-X. SERIES: Dial Easy-to-Read. SUBJECTS: Animals — Fiction; Dentists — Fiction. RL B. LEXILE 420L.

Milo the pig's friends accompany him to the dentist, thinking he will be afraid. Expressive cartoon animals accompany the simple story.

1780 *Tillie and Mert*. Ill. by Doug Cushman. HarperCollins, pap., 1985, ISBN 0-06-444159-8. SERIES: I Can Read. SUBJECTS: Friendship — Fiction; Skunks — Fiction. RL B.

The strong friendship of two skunks, Tillie and Mert, survives bad judgment in their small business and Tillie's success in fortune telling. Good characterization and cozy watercolors complement the theme well.

M

Maass, Robert

1781 *Fire Fighters*. Photos by author. Scholastic, 1989, ISBN 0-590-41459-3. SUBJECTS: Fire fighters and fire fighting. RL C.

This photoessay looks at a fire station on a quiet day and follows fire fighters doing maintenance work and relaxing while on call. When an alarm sounds, readers follow the fire fighters to the scene of a fire. Clear color photographs and text explain what fire fighting is all about.

McArthur, Nancy

1782 *Pickled Peppers*. Ill. by Denise Brunkus. Scholastic, 1988, o.p. SERIES: Hello Reader! SUBJECTS: Behavior — Responsible — Fiction; Pet care — Fiction; Pets — Birds — Fiction. RL B.

Suzie wants to keep her aunt's dog, Pud, but she did not take good care of the dog when he visited and now her Mom and Dad say no. To prove that she is responsible, Suzie pet-sits for her neighbors' tongue-twister-reciting parakeet. The humorous story is illustrated with comic drawings with green accents.

Maccarone, Grace

1783 *The Classroom Pet*. Ill. by Betsy Lewin. Scholastic, 1995, ISBN 0-590-26264-5. SERIES: Hello Reader! SUBJECTS: Crabs — Fiction; School stories; Stories in rhyme. RL A. LEXILE 310L.

Sam takes home the classroom hermit crab, who eludes him several times. Good drawings show the same cast of children as in other books in this series.

1784 *Dinosaurs*. Ill. by Richard Courtney. Scholastic, pap., 2001, ISBN 0-439-20060-1. SERIES: Scholastic Reader. SUBJECTS: Dinosaurs; Fossils; Stories in rhyme. RL B. LEXILE BR.

The 15-word vocabulary list follows a gallery of 21 kinds of dinosaurs.

1785 *Graduation Day Is Here! First-Grade Friends*. Ill. by Rick Brown. Scholastic, pap., 2006, ISBN 0-439-83298-5. SERIES: Scholastic Reader. SUBJECTS: Graduations —

Maccarone, Grace (cont.)

Fiction; Stories in rhyme. RL A. LEXILE 370L.

Sam's dad just makes his graduation; his class includes a girl in a wheelchair. A 12-word vocabulary list is appended.

1786 *The Gym Day Winner*. Ill. by Betsy Lewin. Scholastic, 1996, ISBN 0-590-26263-7. SERIES: Hello Reader! SUBJECTS: School stories; Sports — Basketball — Fiction; Stories in rhyme. RL A. LEXILE 230L.

Children, including a girl in a wheelchair, run and flip and dribble. But it is Sam, usually last, who's unguarded to make the winning basketball goal. Action-filled ink and wash drawings enhance the story.

1787 *I See a Leaf: Literacy Activities by Alayne Pick*. Ill. by Laura Freeman. Scholastic, pap., 2001, ISBN 0-439-33016-5. SERIES: Scholastic Reader. SUBJECTS: Leaves — Fiction; School stories. RL A. LEXILE 70L.

Teacher Miss Hill figures out what to do with all the leaves the round-faced children collect on the way to class.

1788 *I Shop with My Daddy*. Ill. by Denise Brunkus. Scholastic, pap., 1998, ISBN 0-590-50196-8. SERIES: Hello Reader! SUBJECTS: Family life — Fiction; Shopping — Fiction; Stories in rhyme. RL A. LEXILE BR.

Daddy tells his daughter "Not today" when she wants to buy sweets at the grocery. But outside, it's a different matter!

1789 *Itchy, Itchy Chicken Pox*. Ill. by Betsy Lewin. Scholastic, 1992, o.p. SERIES: Hello Reader! SUBJECTS: Illness — Fiction; Stories in rhyme. RL A. LEXILE 80L.

Lewin's drawings capture the twitchy, itchy chicken pox. The boy is accompanied by a charming dog.

1790 *The Lunch Box Surprise*. Ill. by Betsy Lewin. Scholastic, pap., 2003, ISBN 0-590-26267-X. SERIES: Scholastic Reader. SUBJECTS: Behavior — Sharing; School stories; Stories in rhyme. RL A. LEXILE 460L.

Thanks to his friends, Sam has his best lunch ever when his mother forgets to pack his lunch.

1791 *Magic Matt and the Dinosaur*. Ill. by Norman Bridwell. Scholastic, pap., 2004, ISBN 0-439-37607-6. SERIES: Scholastic Reader. SUBJECTS: Dinosaurs — Fiction; Magic — Fiction. RL A.

Matt's magic has unexpected results when he conjures an unmanageable dinosaur instead of a turtle. Bridwell's gentle illustrations are flat, with smiley faces.

1792 *Magic Matt and the Jack-o'-Lantern*. Ill. by Norman Bridwell. Scholastic, pap., 2003, ISBN 0-439-43992-2. SERIES: Scholastic Reader. SUBJECTS: Magic — Fiction; Stories in rhyme. RL A.

The magic words begin with "j" — or "g."

1793 *Magic Matt and the Skunk in the Tub*. Ill. by Norman Bridwell. Scholastic, pap., 2003, ISBN 0-439-40570-X. SERIES: Scholastic Reader. SUBJECTS: Magic — Fiction; Skunks — Fiction. RL A. LEXILE BR.

A slim story about magic spells that go awry.

1794 *Monster Math: Math Activities by Marilyn Burns*. Ill. by Marge Hartelius. Scholastic, pap., 1995, ISBN 0-590-22712-2. SERIES: Scholastic Reader. SUBJECTS: Mathematics — Fiction; Monsters — Fiction; Stories in rhyme. RL A. LEXILE 30L.

"Twelve little monsters wake up at seven . . ."; they leave one by one — until there are zero. Friendly monsters are in yellow, orange, and apple green.

1795 *Monster Math: School Time: Math Activities by Marilyn Burns*. Ill. by Marge Hartelius. Scholastic, pap., 1997, ISBN 0-590-30859-9. SERIES: Scholastic Reader. SUBJECTS: Mathematics — Fiction; Stories in rhyme; Time — Fiction. RL A. LEXILE 330L.

In school, the twelve little monsters have a different activity every hour. Appealing child monsters are shown in ink and wash.

1796 *Monster Money: Math Activities by Marilyn Burns*. Ill. by Marge Hartelius. Scholastic, pap., 1998, ISBN 0-590-12007-7. SERIES: Hello Math Reader! SUBJECTS: Mathematics — Fiction; Money — Fiction; Stories in rhyme. RL A. LEXILE 520L.

Child monsters can buy many jiggly, giggly pets for combinations of nickels, pennies, and dimes.

Drawings show real coins, along with imaginary pets and monsters.

1797 *Mr. Rover Takes Over.* Ill. by Meredith Johnson. Scholastic, pap., 2000, ISBN 0-439-20057-1. SERIES: Hello Reader! SUBJECTS: Pets — Dogs — Fiction; School stories. RL A. LEXILE BR.

Although the children had fun when Mrs. Katz was ill, they welcome her back. Action-packed pencil and wash illustrations.

1798 *My Tooth Is About to Fall Out.* Ill. by Betsy Lewin. Scholastic, 1995, ISBN 0-590-48376-5. SERIES: Hello Reader! SUBJECTS: Human body — Teeth — Fiction; Stories in rhyme. RL A. LEXILE 410L.

Lewin's lively illustrations of a girl and her cat enhance the simple telling.

1799 *Pizza Party!* Ill. by Emily A. McCully. Scholastic, pap., 1994, ISBN 0-590-47563-0. SERIES: Hello Reader! SUBJECTS: Cookery — Fiction; Parties — Fiction. RL A. LEXILE BR.

In the simplest language, a multiethnic group of children and a dad prepare and wait suspensefully for their pizza to bake before their pizza party.

1800 *Recess Mess: First-Grade Friends.* Ill. by Betsy Lewin. Scholastic, pap., 1996, ISBN 1-59054-665-2. SERIES: Scholastic Reader. SUBJECTS: Books and reading — Fiction. RL A. LEXILE 200L.

Bold ink and wash drawings show the recess fun — and Sam's dilemma when he can't decide which restroom to use.

1801 *The Sleep Over.* Ill. by Betsy Lewin. Scholastic, pap., 2003, ISBN 0-439-38575-X. SERIES: Scholastic Reader. SUBJECTS: Sleepovers — Fiction. RL A. LEXILE AD30L.

Even with his Huggy Bear, Sam is homesick on his first sleepover.

1802 *Soccer Game!* Ill. by Meredith Johnson. Scholastic, pap., 1994, ISBN 0-5904-8369-2. SERIES: Scholastic Reader. SUBJECTS: Sports — Soccer — Fiction. RL A. LEXILE BR.

Lively watercolor illustrations show boys and girls — and their dogs — playing a soccer game.

1803 *Three Pigs, One Wolf, and Seven Magic Shapes: Math Reader.* Ill. by David Neuhaus. Scholastic, pap., 1997, ISBN 0-5903-0857-2. SERIES: Scholastic Reader. SUBJECTS: Mathematics — Fiction. RL C. LEXILE 630L.

Marilyn Burns offers basic use of tangrams in this easy story reworking the three pigs.

1804 *"What Is That?" Said the Cat.* Ill. by Jeffrey Scherer. Scholastic, pap., 1995, ISBN 0-5902-5945-8. SERIES: Scholastic Reader. SUBJECTS: Nonsense; Stories in rhyme. RL A.

An imaginative, rhythmic story about animals opening a crate, with humorous results. A 12-word vocabulary is appended.

McCauley, Jane

1805 *Animals in Summer.* Ill. with photos. National Geographic, 1988, ISBN 0-87044-738-6. SERIES: Books for Young Readers. SUBJECTS: Animals; Summer. RL C.

A potpourri of impressive color photographs has "animals" and "summer" as loose themes with the text serving mostly as captions. The book excites readers and interests them in nature rather than providing information or answering questions on nature. A brief bibliography is included.

1806 *Let's Explore a River.* Ill. by Joseph H. Bailey. National Geographic, 1988, ISBN 0-87044-741-6. SERIES: Books for Young Explorers. SUBJECTS: Nature. RL C.

A Florida park manager and his three children take a canoe trip on a river. Readers see the great diversity of nature through large color photographs and a clear simple text. A two-page addendum suggests ways for parents to make such a trip with their children. A bibliography is included.

McClintock, Mike

1807 *A Fly Went By.* Ill. by Fritz Siebel. Beginner Books, 1958, ISBN 0-394-90003-0. SERIES: I Can Read It All by Myself. SUBJECTS: Cumulative tales; Stories in rhyme. RL A. LEXILE 270L.

As he relaxes next to a lake, a little boy watches one animal after another race by. Each animal thinks it is being chased by the animal behind it. The charcoal and wash illustrations reflect the fast pace and humor of the rhyming text.

McClintock, Mike (cont.)

1808 *What Have I Got?* Ill. by Leonard Kessler. HarperCollins, 1961, o.p. SERIES: Early I Can Read. SUBJECTS: Imagination — Fiction; Stories in rhyme. RL A.

A little boy tells in rhyme about all the things he could do with what he has in his pockets. At times forced or awkward, the text is brief, easy to read, and helped by the simple line drawings with color accents.

McClung, Robert M.

1809 *Horseshoe Crab.* Ill. by author. Morrow, 1967, o.p. SUBJECTS: Horseshoe crabs. RL C.

Not really a crab but an ancient form of sea life, the horseshoe crab goes through many years of molting its shells before it becomes an adult. Watercolor pictures aid a carefully prepared text in describing this curious animal and its life cycle.

1810 *Ladybug.* Ill. by author. Morrow, 1966, o.p. SUBJECTS: Ladybugs. RL C.

The ladybug is one of the farmer's most valued insects. This book about its life cycle and habits makes fascinating reading. The illustrations are done in watercolors, and although the portraits of insects are good, larvae and eggs do not always seem to be drawn to the same scale.

McCrady, Lady

1811 *The Perfect Ride.* Ill. by Dennis Kendrick. Parents Magazine Press, 1981, o.p. SUBJECTS: Amusement parks — Fiction; Pets — Dogs — Fiction. RL B.

The Dog family spends Saturday at Play Land amusement park. With only four tickets left, they decide to take a boat ride to the "Bermuda Triangle." Scary and full of surprises, the ride is the perfect end to their day. The marker drawings show stodgy dogs finally enjoying themselves.

McCullagh, Sheila

1812 *Tessa and the Magician.* Ill. by John Lobban. Ladybird, 1985, o.p. SUBJECTS: Magic — Fiction; Pets — Cats — Fiction. RL A/B.

This book uses an unusual format, combining four-word sentences with longer text on the opposite page. Watercolor illustrations add mystery.

1813 *Tim Cathamouse.* Ill. by Tony Morris. Puddle Lane, 1985, o.p. SUBJECTS: Magic — Fiction; Mice — Fiction. RL A/B.

A mouse called Tim lives with his mother and sister under the steps of an old house. His adventures, including an encounter with a magician, are told using a very limited vocabulary.

1814 *The Vanishing Monster.* Ill. by Mark Chadwick. Puddle Lane, 1985, o.p. SUBJECTS: Imagination — Fiction; Monsters — Fiction. RL A/B.

The two green ears of Davy's monster appear first, then the eyes, and so forth. The monster disappears when others are around. The story is written in easy and also in more advanced vocabulary.

McCully, Emily Arnold

1815 *The Battle for St. Michaels.* Ill. by Emily A. McCully. HarperCollins, 2001, ISBN 0-06-028729-2. SERIES: I Can Read Chapter Book. SUBJECTS: Sports — Running — Fiction; United States — History — Fiction. RL C. LEXILE 440L.

All but two of the 30 defenders of Saint Michaels, on the Chesapeake, fled when 300 British attacked during the War of 1812. Trickery may, or may not, have saved the town. Watercolors help tell the tale from the point of view of fictional children Caroline and Robert.

1816 *The Grandma Mix-Up.* Ill. by Emily A. McCully. HarperCollins, 1988, ISBN 0-06-024201-9. SERIES: I Can Read. SUBJECTS: Baby-sitting — Fiction; Grandparents — Fiction. RL B. LEXILE 380L.

Pip and both grandmas, who've come to baby-sit, get grumpy because each of them is used to doing things differently — until Pip takes charge. An interesting story with appealing illustrations.

1817 *Grandmas at Bat.* Ill. by Emily A. McCully. HarperCollins, 1993, ISBN 0-06-021032-X. SERIES: I Can Read. SUBJECTS: Grandparents — Fiction; Sports — Baseball — Fiction. RL B. LEXILE 270L.

When the grandmas begin cheerleading, the Stings begin winning — much to the surprise of the embarrassed Pip.

1818 *Grandmas at the Lake*. Ill. by Emily A. McCully. HarperCollins, 1990, ISBN 0-06-024126-8. SERIES: I Can Read. SUBJECTS: Grandparents — Fiction; Vacations — Fiction. RL B. LEXILE 250L.

Pip and her friend Ski join Pip's constantly arguing grandmas for a lakeside vacation. Tired of the adults' arguments, the two young children attempt to teach them a lesson by refusing to bring the boat back to shore. Attractive watercolors make light of a potentially dangerous situation.

1819 *Grandma's Trick-or-Treat*. Ill. by Emily A. McCully. HarperCollins, 2001, ISBN 0-06-028730-6. SERIES: I Can Read. SUBJECTS: Behavior — Bullying — Fiction; Grandparents — Fiction; Halloween — Fiction. RL B.

Grandma Nan and Grandma Sal join together to scare away the Halloween bullies. Both text and illustrations reveal the unique personalities and relationships.

McDaniel, Becky B.

1820 *Katie Can*. Ill. by Lois Axeman. Children's Press, 1987, ISBN 0-516-02082-X. SERIES: Rookie Reader. SUBJECTS: Family life — Fiction; Siblings — Fiction. RL A. LEXILE 120L.

Katie's sister and brother come to see her teaching their dog a new trick, even though she failed the last time. This series features cartoon children with an Asian appearance.

1821 *Katie Couldn't*. Ill. by Lois Axeman. Children's Press, pap., 1985, ISBN 0-516-42069-0. SERIES: Rookie Reader. SUBJECTS: Family life — Fiction; Siblings — Fiction. RL A. LEXILE 170L.

Katie can't do many of the things her older siblings can — but she is still small enough to be picked up for a hug.

1822 *Katie Did It*. Ill. by Richard Hoit. Children's Press, 2002, ISBN 0-516-22848-X. SERIES: Rookie Reader. SUBJECTS: Family life — Fiction; Siblings — Fiction. RL A. LEXILE 290L.

As the youngest, Katie gets blamed for everything, even for bringing her mother flowers.

1823 *Larry and the Cookie*. Ill. by Clovis Martin. Children's Press, 1993, ISBN 0-516-02014-5. SERIES: Rookie Reader. SUBJECTS: Food — Fiction; Play — Fiction. RL A.

Larry puts one of his favorite cookies into the front of his overalls and goes to play football. When the game is over, Larry cannot find the cookie until he discovers crumbs. The simple colored paintings and minimal text work well together.

McDermott, Gerald

1824 *The Fox and the Stork*. Ill. by author. Harcourt, pap., 2003, ISBN 0-15-204837-5. SERIES: Green Light Readers. SUBJECTS: Fables; Foxes — Fiction; Storks — Fiction. RL B. LEXILE 250L.

Stork tricks Fox just as he has been tricked in this simple fable illustrated with pebbled colored pencil drawings.

Macdonald, Maryann

1825 *Hedgehog Bakes a Cake*. Ill. by Lynn Munsinger. Gareth Stevens, 1996, ISBN 0-8368-1619-6. SERIES: Bank Street Ready-to-Read. SUBJECTS: Animals — Fiction; Bakers and baking — Fiction; Hedgehogs — Fiction. RL B. LEXILE 270L.

Hedgehog locks his friends out of the house after their disastrous efforts to "help" bake a cake, so he can do the baking properly. Watercolor illustrations suit the gentle friendships.

1826 *The Pink Party*. Ill. by Abby Carter. Hyperion, 1994, ISBN 1-56282-620-4. SUBJECTS: Friendship — Fiction; Jealousy — Fiction. RL B.

Best friends Lisa and Amy live next door to each other and both love pink. When the two try to keep up with each other's purchases, Lisa finds herself jealous of Amy, who seems to get anything she wants. Pencil drawings with pastel washes gently support the text.

1827 *Rabbit's Birthday Kite*. Ill. by Lynn Munsinger. Bantam, 1991, ISBN 0-8368-

Macdonald, Maryann (cont.)

1779-6. SERIES: Bank Street Ready-to-Read. SUBJECTS: Hedgehogs — Fiction; Kites and kite flying — Fiction; Rabbits — Fiction. RL B.

Hedgehog decides to make a kite for his friend Rabbit's birthday. The excitable rabbit cannot restrain himself and, though he knows nothing about kite flying, decides he needs no help. Happily resolved, the story is complemented by gentle watercolors of the two good friends.

McDonald, Megan

1828 *Beezy*. Ill. by Nancy Poydar. Orchard, 1996, ISBN 0-531-30046-3. SUBJECTS: Friendship — Fiction. RL B. LEXILE 40L.

Taking shelter during a hurricane, Mr. Gumm says he knew Gran when "stones were soft." Beezy acquires a stray dog whom she names Funnybones, and Beezy and buddy Merlin find a new friend, a circus performer named Sarafina Zippy. The gouache illustrations match the creative text.

1829 *Beezy and Funnybone*. Ill. by Nancy Poydar. Orchard, 2000, ISBN 0-531-30211-3. SUBJECTS: Friendship — Fiction. RL B. LEXILE 190L.

Beezy tires of Funnybone's fetching; Gran is better than a dictionary; Funnybone accidentally becomes airborne. Again with Nancy Poydar's affectionate gouache drawings.

1830 *Beezy at Bat*. Ill. by Nancy Poydar. Orchard, 1998, ISBN 0-531-30085-4. SUBJECTS: Friendship — Fiction; Grandparents — Fiction; Jokes and riddles — Fiction. RL B. LEXILE 160L.

"Never trouble trouble till trouble troubles you" says Gran, when Beezy brings home a snake. In another chapter, Gran, Beezy, and Mr. Gumm crack riddles, and in yet another a stingray mitt is a hit. Imaginative episodes are well illustrated with gouache paintings.

1831 *Beezy Magic*. Ill. by Nancy Poydar. Orchard, 1998, ISBN 0-531-30064-1. SUBJECTS: Friendship — Fiction. RL B.

Beezy finds out her name means "honeybee," Gran's rabbit foot brings her good stories, and her dog, Funnybone, sells several key lime pies. Imaginative stories with lively gouache illustrations to match.

MacDonald, Steven

1832 *Just Clowning Around: Two Stories*. Ill. by David M. McPhail. Harcourt, 2003, ISBN 0-15-204816-2. SERIES: Green Light Readers. SUBJECTS: Bears — Fiction; Clowns — Fiction. RL A. LEXILE BR.

Very basic vocabulary is enlivened by David McPhail's appealing pen and wash drawings.

McDonnell, Janet

1833 *Animal Camouflage: Hide-and-Seek Animals*. Ill. by Diana Magnuson. Child's World, 1990, ISBN 0-89565-562-4. SERIES: Discovery World: First Steps to Science. SUBJECTS: Animals — Camouflage. RL B.

Professor Facto takes readers to different areas of the world to discover how camouflage helps animals survive. Watercolor illustrations effectively draw children in as the text asks them to find hidden animals. Camouflage activities are also included.

1834 *Animal Talk: Barks, Growls, Hisses, Howls*. Ill. by Ching. Child's World, 1990, ISBN 0-89565-558-6. SERIES: Discovery World: First Steps to Science. SUBJECTS: Animals — Communication. RL B.

Text and illustrations combine to explain how animals use body language, sound, and smell to get their messages across. Brief but very interesting text and pen and wash pictures show a dog begging, a cat with raised back, a peacock displaying feathers, and so on.

1835 *Baby Animals: Safe and Sound*. Ill. by Linda Hohag and Lori Jacobson. Child's World, 1990, ISBN 0-89565-554-3. SERIES: Discovery World: First Steps to Science. SUBJECTS: Animals — Baby. RL B.

Professor Facto takes a little boy to see the new babies at the zoo and on an imaginary trip to Antarctica to see emperor penguins. The brief information is accompanied by a pictorial listing of baby animals with their names (e.g., kid for goat). Illustrations are rather flat, lifeless.

1836 *Celebrating Earth Day*. Ill. by Diana Magnuson. Childrens Press, 1994, ISBN 0-516-00689-4. SERIES: Circle the Year with Holidays. SUBJECTS: Conservation; Earth Day; Recycling. RL C.

With Earth Day approaching, the children in Ms. Webster's class begin to learn about taking care of the earth by not polluting and by being recyclers. Useful and attractive illustrations complement the text. A section of experiments is at the end.

1837 *Space Travel: Blast-Off Day*. Ill. by Rondi Collette. Child's World, 1990, ISBN 0-89565-556-X. SERIES: Discovery World: First Steps to Science. SUBJECTS: Space travel. RL B.

From strapping in to blast-off to their return, a space shuttle crew is followed in words and pictures as they work inside and outside the spacecraft. Following the main text is a section of activities and a brief index. Illustrated with realistic color pictures.

1838 *Wind: What Can It Do?* Ill. by Gwen Connelly. Child's World, 1990, ISBN 0-89565-555-1. SERIES: Discovery World: First Steps to Science. SUBJECTS: Weather; Weather — Wind. RL B.

This is not an explanation of how winds are formed, but an exploration of the things winds do and become: tornadoes, drying the clothes, moving clouds, bringing warm or cold air, and so on. Includes an activity section, an index, and bright but hurried-looking watercolors with pencil detailing.

McEwan, Jamie

1839 *The Heart of Cool*. Ill. by Sandra Boynton. Simon & Schuster, pap., 2002, ISBN 0-689-82178-6. SERIES: Ready-to-Read. SUBJECTS: School stories; Self-esteem — Fiction. RL C. LEXILE 410L.

The new kid in school tries very hard to be the coolest student. Illustrations show Bobby on a skateboard, with sunglasses.

McGoldrick, Jane R.

1840 *Animal Clowns*. Ill. with photos. National Geographic, 1989, o.p. SERIES: Books for Young Explorers. SUBJECTS: Animals. RL C.

Animals are photographed in amusing postures or performing rituals that appear comical. A very brief and superficial text merely calls attention to and identifies the animals. A section for adults is included.

McGovern, Ann

1841 *Little Wolf*. Ill. by Nola Langner. Abelard-Schuman, 1965, o.p. SUBJECTS: Native Americans — Fiction; Self-esteem — Fiction. RL A.

Little Wolf is often ridiculed by his tribe because he cannot kill an animal. He is wise in the lore of the forest, a knowledge that he uses to save the chief's son from poisoning and gain the tribe's respect. Sepia-colored drawings are lovely and restrained, complementing the fine story.

McInnes, John

1842 *The Chocolate Chip Mystery*. Ill. by Paul Frame. Garrard, 1972, o.p. SERIES: Venture. SUBJECTS: Business enterprises — Fiction; City and town life — Fiction; Mystery and detective stories. RL A.

Forced to move, Max opens his ice cream store in a building that everyone thinks is haunted. His customers do not come and his chocolate chip ice cream starts disappearing. Max's young helper Peppino solves the mystery of the missing ice cream and finds a way to bring customers in. Realistic sketches.

1843 *Have You Ever Seen a Monster?* Ill. by Tom Eaton. Garrard, 1974, o.p. SERIES: Easy Venture. SUBJECTS: Monsters — Fiction. RL B.

On every other page there are questions about things that a monster might do that are then answered with fantastic things that the narrator claims to have seen them do. Predictable refrains build the confidence of children struggling with reading. Illustrated with energetic cartoon-like artwork.

1844 *How Pedro Got His Name*. Ill. by Edward Malsberg. Garrard, 1974, o.p. SERIES: Venture. SUBJECTS: City and town life — Fiction; Pets — Dogs — Fiction. RL A.

To earn enough money to buy a puppy, Tony works for a shoemaker. Once he has the money saved he gets sick and his physician, Dr. Pedro, promises he will buy the dog for Tony. The story has a Hispanic setting and is illustrated with full-color realistic paintings.

1845 *Leo Lion Paints It Red*. Ill. by Tom Eaton. Garrard, 1974, o.p. SERIES: Easy Venture.

McInnes, John (cont.)

SUBJECTS: Animals — Zoo — Fiction; Humorous stories; Zoos — Fiction. RL A.

When a little girl gives him red paint, clever Leo the Lion starts making signs for himself and the other zoo animals. Children respond to the signs by giving the animals what they want. Simple, colorful pictures illustrate this silly but engaging story.

1846 *On with the Circus!* Ill. by William Hutchinson. Garrard, 1973, o.p. SERIES: Venture. SUBJECTS: Circuses — Fiction. RL B.

Judy gets a chance to be a part of the circus when the littlest clown gets sick. No one knows who she is when she is dressed in Bingo's clothes and she has a wonderful time. The realistic color illustrations recreate the old Big Top ambiance.

McIntyre, Ida M.

1847 *Unicorn Magic.* Ill. by Don Hedin. Garrard, 1972, o.p. SERIES: Venture. SUBJECTS: Magic — Fiction; Mythical creatures — Fiction. RL B.

A unicorn tells a tale of sorcery, a beautiful princess made from straw, and a prince seeking a bride. It is the unicorn's magic that saves the princess from being returned to straw by the sorcerer. The lack of unicorn stories has made this book popular despite the undistinguished illustrations.

McKay, Sindy

1848 *About Dinosaurs.* Ill. by Robert Walters. Treasure Bay, 2004, ISBN 1-891327-53-4. SERIES: We Both Read. SUBJECTS: Dinosaurs. RL A/C.

A brief glossary and some root words are appended to the text introducing a number of general facts and theories about dinosaurs. Very child-friendly.

1849 *About the Seasons.* Ill. with photos. Treasure Bay, 2000, ISBN 1-891327-27-5. SERIES: We Both Read. SUBJECTS: Seasons. RL A/C.

Child-friendly photographs illustrate the dual texts intended for parent and child.

1850 *Baseball Fever.* Ill. by Meredith Johnson. Treasure Bay, 2003, ISBN 1-891327-45-3. SERIES: We Both Read. SUBJECTS: Friendship — Fiction; Sports — Baseball — Fiction. RL A/C.

Jason's cold keeps him from his baseball game, but his friend Karen keeps him up to date by cell phone. Pencil and wash illustrations focus on Jason.

1851 *Ben and Becky Get a Pet.* Ill. by Meredith Johnson. Treasure Bay, 1998, ISBN 1-891327-10-0. SERIES: We Both Read. SUBJECTS: Pets — Fiction; Siblings — Fiction; Snakes — Fiction. RL B/C.

After chasing Killer, the green snake, all over the mall, Ben and Becky settle on a more cuddly pet. Plenty of action is shown in the ink and watercolor drawings.

1852 *Ben and Becky in the Haunted House.* Ill. by Meredith Johnson. Treasure Bay, 1999, ISBN 1-891327-14-3. SERIES: We Both Read. SUBJECTS: Scary stories. RL B/C.

Grandpa doesn't account for all the mysteries when Ben and Becky stay overnight in a deserted house! Very satisfying pen and watercolor drawings.

1853 *The First Christmas.* Ill. by Mary O'Keefe Young. Treasure Bay, 1998, ISBN 1-891327-04-6. SERIES: We Both Read. SUBJECTS: Christmas. RL A/C.

Text for a parent is opposite text for a beginning reader. Basic ink and wash are used for illustration.

1854 *Happy and Healthy.* Ill. with photos. Treasure Bay, 2002, ISBN 1-891327-47-X. SERIES: We Both Read. SUBJECTS: Health. RL B/C.

Photographs of children at work and play accompany a brief text for children and a more difficult one for a parent.

1855 *My Day.* Ill. by Meredith Johnson. Treasure Bay, 2002, ISBN 0-89132-743-7. SERIES: We Both Read. SUBJECTS: Stories in rhyme. RL A/B.

Predictable rhyming words are left for the beginning reader to fill in. Colorful action illustrations of children.

1856 *The New Red Bed*. Ill. by Erin Marie Mauterer. Treasure Bay, 1999, ISBN 1-891327-12-7. SERIES: We Both Read. SUBJECTS: Imagination; Stories in rhyme; Wordplay. RL A/C.

Sam sees "green bats in hats and big fat blue cats." Cartoons illustrate the nonsense.

1857 *Too Many Cats*. Ill. by Meredith Johnson. Treasure Bay, 2003, ISBN 1-891327-49-6. SERIES: We Both Read. SUBJECTS: Concepts — Numbers; Dreams — Fiction; Pets — Cats — Fiction. RL A/C.

Suzu wants one white cat for her birthday, but dreams she has ten, all different colors. When she awakes — you guessed it — one white cat. The pen and wash illustrations are more appealing than the story.

McKie, Roy, and P. D. Eastman

1858 *Snow*. Ill. by author. Random House, 1962, ISBN 0-394-80027-3. SERIES: I Can Read It All by Myself. SUBJECTS: Stories in rhyme; Winter — Fiction. RL A.

An exuberant dog invites two children to join him in playing in the snow, skiing, making angels, making a snow house, and having a picnic. Lively illustrations are integral to the snow adventures.

McKissack, Patricia

1859 *Amistad: The Story of a Slave Ship*. Ill. by Sanna Stanley. Grosset & Dunlap, pap., 2005, ISBN 0-448-43900-X. SERIES: All Aboard Reading. SUBJECTS: Slavery; United States — History. RL C.

The story follows the fate of Cinque, a leader of a rebellion aboard a slave ship, through two years of imprisonment between trials, to his homecoming in Sierra Leone. Strong pencil and wash illustrations.

1860 *Itching and Twitching: A Nigerian Folktale*. Ill. by Laura Freeman. Scholastic, pap., 2003, ISBN 0-439-24224-X. SERIES: Hello Reader! SUBJECTS: Folklore — Nigeria; Monkeys — Fiction; Rabbits — Fiction. RL B. LEXILE 340L.

Rabbit and Monkey learn to reconcile their differences; Rabbit twitches and Monkey scratches when he itches. The illustrations are grounded in royal blue.

1861 *Monkey-Monkey's Trick: Based on an African folktale*. Ill. by Paul Meisel. Random House, 1989, ISBN 0-394-99173-7. SERIES: Step into Reading. SUBJECTS: Folklore; Hyenas — Fiction; Monkeys — Fiction. RL B. LEXILE 280L.

Monkey-Monkey tricks trickster Hyena — and gets his new house built! Delightful, simple ink and wash drawings of the African animals.

1862 *Our Martin Luther King Book*. Ill. by Helen Endres. Child's World, 1986, ISBN 0-89565-342-7. SERIES: A Special Day. SUBJECTS: African Americans; Biographies; Martin Luther King, Jr., Day. RL C.

A class of young children learns from their teacher about Martin Luther King Jr., and his commitment to equal rights for African Americans. The children role-play segregation, sing "We Shall Overcome," and have a party in King's honor. Illustrated with full-color paintings and photographs.

1863 *Who Is Coming?* Ill. by Clovis Martin. Children's Press, 1986, ISBN 0-516-02073-0. SERIES: Rookie Reader. SUBJECTS: Africa — Fiction; Animals — Fiction; Monkeys — Fiction. RL A.

Little monkey runs up, down, in, out, and always away from the large African animals until an illustration shows a tiger. Little monkey does not run away then because, as everyone knows, there are no tigers in Africa. The simple, repetitive text has sketchy but colorful pictures.

McKissack, Patricia, and Fredrick McKissack

1864 *Booker T. Washington: Leader and Educator*. Ill. by Michael Bryant. Enslow, 1992, ISBN 0-89490-314-4. SERIES: Great African Americans. SUBJECTS: African Americans; Biographies; Teachers and teaching. RL C.

Born into slavery, Booker T. Washington is shown as an individual with determination and a commitment to his people. He works his way through Hampton Institute, founds Tuskegee Institute, and begins teaching African Americans the trades necessary for independence. Black-and-white illustrations accompany the text.

McKissack, Patricia, and Fredrick McKissack (cont.)

1865 *Bugs!* Ill. by Clovis Martin. Children's Press, 1988, ISBN 0-516-21658-9. SERIES: Rookie Reader. SUBJECTS: Insects — Fiction; Mathematics — Fiction. RL A. LEXILE BR.
Two exuberant children explore the countryside and happily discover all kinds of fanciful bugs and show the numbers 1 to 5. The McKissacks and Martin successfully combine forces in their use of a very brief text and attractive watercolor pictures to tell this story.

1866 *Carter G. Woodson: The Father of Black History*. Ill. by Edward Ostendorf. Enslow, 1991, ISBN 0-89490-309-8. SERIES: Great African Americans. SUBJECTS: African Americans; Biographies; Teachers and teaching. RL B.
The founder of Black History Month is shown as a determined man who came to education at age 18 and stuck with it. He became a teacher, a principal, and an innovative educator. Well and clearly written, the text is illustrated with black-and-white pictures.

1867 *Constance Stumbles*. Ill. by Tom Dunnington. Children's Press, 1988, ISBN 0-516-02086-2. SERIES: Rookie Reader. SUBJECTS: Bicycles and bicycling — Fiction. RL A.
Prone to accidents, Constance nevertheless determines to learn to ride her bicycle. A very brief text relies on full-color pictures of an ebullient black child and a watchful owl to capture children's interest.

1868 *Frederick Douglass: Leader Against Slavery*. Ill. by Edward Ostendorf. Enslow, 1991, ISBN 0-89490-306-3. SERIES: Great African Americans. SUBJECTS: African Americans; Biographies; Civil rights. RL B. LEXILE 400L.
A stirring look at the life of the one-time slave, abolitionist, writer, and tireless worker for civil rights, this story of Douglass gives young readers a taste of his life and the evils of slavery. Illustrated in black and white, the book also contains an index and glossary.

1869 *George Washington Carver: The Peanut Scientist*. Ill. by Edward Ostendorf. Enslow, 1991, ISBN 0-89490-308-X. SERIES: Great African Americans. SUBJECTS: African Americans; Biographies; Science and scientists. RL C. LEXILE 400L.
Born into slavery, Carver worked and studied hard and became a professor at Tuskegee Institute. There he taught science and introduced many uses for the peanut and the sweet potato. Illustrated in black and white with drawings and photographs. Glossary and index are included.

1870 *Ida B. Wells-Barnett: A Voice Against Violence*. Ill. by Edward Ostendorf. Enslow, 1991, ISBN 0-89490-301-2. SERIES: Great African Americans. SUBJECTS: African Americans; Biographies; Civil rights. RL C.
Determined to stop the violence against African Americans by the Ku Klux Klan and others filled with hate, Wells-Barnett spoke out and wrote to make people — including the president — aware of lynchings and other acts of violence. Text is illustrated with black-and-white photographs and prints.

1871 *Jesse Owens: Olympic Star*. Ill. by Michael David Biegel. Enslow, 2001, ISBN 0-7660-1681-1. SERIES: Great African Americans. SUBJECTS: African Americans; Biographies; Sports — Running. RL B.
Owens was born into a poor southern family. His father moved the family north, where Jesse became a runner and a track star, ultimately becoming a member of the U.S. track and field team at the Olympics in 1936. There he won four gold medals and became an inspiration to children everywhere. Well-written, the book is illustrated with photographs and occasionally awkward pen and ink drawings. Index and glossary are appended.

1872 *Langston Hughes: Great American Poet*. Ill. by Michael David Biegel. Enslow, 2002, ISBN 0-7660-1695-1. SERIES: Great African Americans. SUBJECTS: African Americans; Biographies; Poetry. RL C. LEXILE 530L.
Inspired by African American people throughout the country, Langston Hughes wrote poetry, fiction, and plays. He traveled but spent most of his time in Harlem. A look at both the poet and his family, the book is illustrated with pen and ink drawings and photographs.

1873 *Louis Armstrong: Jazz Musician*. Ill. by Edward Ostendorf. Enslow, 2001, ISBN 0-

7660-1675-7. SERIES: Great African Americans. SUBJECTS: African Americans; Biographies; Music and musicians. RL B.

From his early years in a poor section of New Orleans, to reform school and the discovery of his musical talent, this overview covers Armstrong's life and especially his career. A substantial biography for this level, it is well organized, interesting, and illustrated with photographs and ink drawings.

1874 *Marian Anderson: A Great Singer.* Ill. by Edward Ostendorf. Enslow, 2001, ISBN 0-7660-1676-5. SERIES: Great African Americans. SUBJECTS: African Americans; Biographies; Music and musicians. RL C. LEXILE 440L.

A gifted singer, Miss Anderson sang throughout the United States and the world, breaking racial barriers in Washington and in the American opera world. The story of Anderson's rise from poverty and her commitment to music is illustrated with black-and-white pictures and photographs.

1875 *Mary Church Terrell: Leader for Equality.* Ill. by Edward Ostendorf. Enslow, 2002, ISBN 0-7660-1697-8. SERIES: Great African Americans. SUBJECTS: African Americans; Biographies; Civil rights. RL C.

Born into a wealthy Memphis family, Mary Church Terrell was a well-educated woman who dedicated her life to fighting for the civil rights of African Americans and women. Well written, her story is illustrated with black-and-white pictures and photographs.

1876 *Mary McLeod Bethune: A Great American Educator.* Ill. by Edward Ostendorf. Enslow, 2001, ISBN 0-7660-1680-3. SERIES: Great African Americans. SUBJECTS: African Americans; Biographies; Teachers and teaching. RL B.

As a small child, Bethune was determined to learn to read. She went on to graduate from college and start a school for African Americans, which earned her respect, fame, and a place in the Roosevelt administration. This well-written book has black-and-white drawings as well as photographs.

1877 *Messy Bessey.* Ill. by Richard Hackney. Children's Press, 1987, ISBN 0-516-02083-8. SERIES: Rookie Reader. SUBJECTS: Behavior — Fiction; Cleanliness — Fiction; Stories in rhyme. RL A.

Bessey's room and her clothes are a terrible mess. Finally she cleans herself and her room, stuffing most things into her closet. Attractive and colorful pictures help the very brief rhyming text tell the story.

1878 *Messy Bessey's Holidays.* Ill. by Dana Regan. Children's Press, 1998, ISBN 0-516-20829-2. SERIES: Rookie Reader. SUBJECTS: Diversity — Fiction; Holidays — Fiction; Stories in rhyme. RL A.

Messy Bessey bakes cookies to give to her friends to celebrate Christmas, Chanukah, and Kwanzaa. Simple ink-and-watercolors illustrate the rhymed text.

1879 *Paul Robeson: A Voice to Remember.* Ill. by Michael David Biegel. Enslow, 2001, ISBN 0-7660-1674-9. SERIES: Great African Americans. SUBJECTS: African Americans; Biographies; Civil rights. RL B. LEXILE 520L.

Taught to never give up, Paul Robeson fought for his education and his place in the world of music and theater. An outspoken advocate of equal rights for African Americans and all persons, Robeson is an example of courage for all children. Illustrations are pen and ink and photographs.

1880 *Ralph J. Bunche: Peacemaker.* Ill. by Edward Ostendorf. Enslow, 2002, ISBN 0-7660-1701-X. SERIES: Great African Americans. SUBJECTS: African Americans; Biographies; United Nations. RL B.

Born into a family that gave him love and determination, Ralph Bunche was the first African American to earn a Ph.D. in political science from Harvard. After his work to end fighting in Israel, Dr. Bunche became the first African American to win the Nobel Peace Prize. Black-and-white illustrations.

1881 *Satchel Paige: The Best Arm in Baseball.* Ill. by Michael David Biegel. Enslow, 2002, ISBN 0-7660-1699-4. SERIES: Great African Americans. SUBJECTS: African Americans; Biographies; Sports — Baseball. RL C.

A star of the Negro Baseball League, Satchel Paige was a great pitcher who, in his forties, was one of the first to integrate baseball. Accented with black-and-white photographs and pen and

McKissack, Patricia, and Fredrick McKissack (cont.)

ink drawings, the story of Paige's life is well written.

1882 *Sojourner Truth: A Voice for Freedom*. Ill. by Michael David Biegel. Enslow, 2002, ISBN 0-7660-1693-5. SERIES: Great African Americans. SUBJECTS: African Americans; Biographies; Civil rights. RL C.

Born into slavery in New York, Sojourner Truth fought long and hard for the rights of slaves and former slaves and the rights of women. Through charcoal drawings, photographs, reproductions of art, and a good text, the life of an unusual and brave woman is made real. Index and glossary included.

1883 *Zora Neale Hurston: Writer and Storyteller*. Ill. by Michael Bryant. Enslow, 1992, ISBN 0-89490-316-0. SERIES: Great African Americans. SUBJECTS: African Americans; Biographies; Writers and writing. RL C.

Coming from a small Florida town, Zora Neale Hurston worked hard to earn an education, graduating from college when she was 37. The story of her life, her determination to write, and her pride in her heritage makes inspirational reading. Glossary and index included.

McKissack, Robert

1884 *Try Your Best*. Ill. by Joe Cepeda. Harcourt, 2004, ISBN 0-15-205089-2. SERIES: Green Light Readers. SUBJECTS: School stories; Self-esteem — Fiction; Sports — Fiction. RL B.

After encouraging Ann to "do your best," Mr. York needs the same encouragement.

McLeod, Kate

1885 *Outback Adventure*. Ill. with photos. DK, 2004, ISBN 0-7566-0544-X. SERIES: Beginning to Read Alone. SUBJECTS: Australia. RL C.

A boy's adventures from the seacoast to the rivers to the interior are illustrated with excellent photographs and enhanced by factoids about termites, fossils, and aborigines.

McMorrow, Catherine

1886 *The Jellybean Principal*. Ill. by Amy Wummer. Random House, 1994, ISBN 0-679-94743-4. SERIES: Step into Reading. SUBJECTS: Friendship — Fiction; School stories. RL C.

After ending up in the principal's office several times, three friends resolve to stay out of trouble. Yet when they hear someone calling for help from inside the closed school, they cannot resist helping. Exaggerated situations and humor are illustrated with cartoon-like color drawings.

McMullan, Kate

1887 *The Biggest Mouth in Baseball*. Ill. by Anna DiVito. Grosset & Dunlap, pap., 1993, ISBN 0-448-40516-4. SERIES: All Aboard Reading. SUBJECTS: Jokes and riddles; Sports — Baseball — Fiction. RL C.

Although a boy's jokes help loosen up his baseball teammates, only his more serious sister, Anna, can get him focused on baseball. Lively dialog illustrated with pen and wash drawings.

1888 *Dinosaur Hunters*. Ill. by John R. Jones. Random House, 1989, ISBN 0-394-91150-4. SERIES: Step into Reading. SUBJECTS: Dinosaurs. RL C.

In lengthy chapters, this history of paleontology gives young enthusiasts good information about searching for fossils and what is done with them after they are found. Brontosaurus is not called apatosaurus. Illustrated with utilitarian paintings.

1889 *Fluffy and the Firefighters*. Ill. by Mavis Smith. Scholastic, pap., 1999, ISBN 0-439-12917-6. SERIES: Scholastic Reader. SUBJECTS: Fire fighters and fire fighting — Fiction; Guinea pigs — Fiction; School stories. RL B.

Irreverent Fluffy, the classroom pet, thinks he can be a firefighting hero until he sees what it really takes.

1890 *Fluffy Goes Apple Picking*. Ill. by Mavis Smith. Scholastic, pap., 2002, ISBN 0-439-31420-8. SERIES: Scholastic Reader. SUBJECTS: Apples — Fiction; Guinea pigs — Fiction; School stories. RL B. LEXILE 150L.

Fluffy's animated thoughts contrast with what the class is saying, but Fluffy does get to accompany them on their apple-picking field trip. Pen and wash illustrations.

1891 *Fluffy Goes to School.* Ill. by Mavis Smith. Scholastic, pap., 1997, ISBN 0-590-37213-0. SERIES: Scholastic Reader. SUBJECTS: Guinea pigs — Fiction; School stories. RL B. LEXILE 240L.

An arrogant, imaginative new classroom pet, a guinea pig whom the class names "Fluffy," has adventures in his own cage, and when introduced to a guinea pig in another classroom. Smith's illustrations enhance the humor.

1892 *Fluffy Grows a Garden.* Ill. by Mavis Smith. Scholastic, 2002, ISBN 0-439-20674-X. SERIES: Hello Reader! SUBJECTS: Guinea pigs — Fiction; School stories. RL B.

This time Fluffy reluctantly welcomes various critters he thinks might be threatening his growing carrot. Great dialog with illustrations to match.

1893 *Fluffy Meets the Groundhog.* Ill. by Mavis Smith. Scholastic, pap., 2001, ISBN 0-439-20672-3. SERIES: Scholastic Reader. SUBJECTS: Guinea pigs — Fiction; School stories. RL B. LEXILE 150L.

Fluffy, the classroom pet, stars on TV, standing in for the shy groundhog.

1894 *Fluffy Meets the Tooth Fairy.* Ill. by Mavis Smith. Scholastic, pap., 2000, ISBN 0-439-02918-4. SERIES: Scholastic Reader. SUBJECTS: Guinea pigs — Fiction; Human body — Teeth — Fiction; Tooth fairy — Fiction. RL B. LEXILE 320L.

Class pet Fluffy is determined that Wade will be visited by the Tooth Fairy. A 15-word vocabulary list is appended.

1895 *Fluffy Saves Christmas.* Ill. by Mavis Smith. Scholastic, pap., 1998, ISBN 0-5905-2308-2. SERIES: Scholastic Reader. SUBJECTS: Christmas — Fiction; Guinea pigs — Fiction. RL B. LEXILE 320L.

Fluffy expects Santa to produce a great big carrot right now; he is chagrined when his class feasts on guinea pig cookies; his big dream comes true. Ink and wash drawings.

1896 *Fluffy's Funny Field Trip.* Ill. by Mavis Smith. Scholastic, pap., 2001, ISBN 0-439-20673-1. SERIES: Scholastic Reader. SUBJECTS: Astronomy and astronomers — Fiction; Guinea pigs — Fiction. RL B. LEXILE 210L.

After sleeping through the planetarium show, Fluffy invents his own names for constellations.

1897 *Fluffy's Lucky Day.* Ill. by Mavis Smith. Scholastic, pap., 2002, ISBN 0-439-31944-7. SERIES: Hello Reader! SUBJECTS: Guinea pigs — Fiction; School stories; St. Patrick's Day — Fiction. RL C. LEXILE 160L.

Fluffy, the class guinea pig, encounters more than one leprechaun, but cannot outwit them.

1898 *Fluffy's 100th Day at School.* Ill. by Mavis Smith. Scholastic, pap., 1999, ISBN 0-5905-2309-0. SERIES: Hello Reader! SUBJECTS: Guinea pigs — Fiction; Mathematics — Fiction; School stories. RL B. LEXILE 270L.

When the class celebrates Fluffy's 100th day at school, they learn a lot about numbers at the same time. Pen and wash drawings include odd-looking guinea pigs.

1899 *Fluffy's School Bus Adventure.* Ill. by Mavis Smith. Scholastic, pap., 2000, ISBN 0-439-20671-5. SERIES: Scholastic Reader. SUBJECTS: Guinea pigs — Fiction; School stories. RL B. LEXILE 180L.

Fluffy helps save the day when the school bus breaks down. Jasmine was supposed to take him home with her, and imagines that he has had a rough day, when the opposite is true.

1900 *Fluffy's Silly Summer.* Ill. by Mavis Smith. Scholastic, pap., 1998, ISBN 0-5900-3269-0. SERIES: Scholastic Reader. SUBJECTS: Guinea pigs — Fiction. RL B. LEXILE 60L.

Fluffy saves himself from a shark and wins the pet contest because of a flea. Summer adventures of the classroom pet.

1901 *Fluffy's Spring Vacation.* Ill. by Mavis Smith. Scholastic, pap., 1998, ISBN 0-590-37217-3. SERIES: Scholastic Reader. SUBJECTS: Guinea pigs — Fiction; School stories. RL B. LEXILE 180L.

Fluffy the Brave scares the vacation family cats away, has an adventure at the barber shop, and makes it to security at the airport.

McMullan, Kate (cont.)

1902 *The Mummy's Gold.* Ill. by Jeff Spackman. Grosset & Dunlap, 1996, ISBN 0-448-41345-0. SERIES: Easy-to-Read. SUBJECTS: Mummies — Fiction; Scary stories; Siblings — Fiction. RL B.

After a scary movie, when Jake is threatened, he thinks first it is his older brother Henry, then their friend Max. Does he get a surprise! Good mummy drawings.

1903 *Pearl and Wagner: Three Secrets.* Ill. by R. W. Alley. Dial, 2004, ISBN 0-8037-2574-4. SERIES: Dial Easy-to-Read. SUBJECTS: Amusement parks — Fiction; Animals — Fiction; Birthdays — Fiction. RL B.

Friends Pearl and Wagner visit an ice cream factory and an amusement park for a birthday party, learning about secrets. Excellent pen and wash animals grace the illustrations.

1904 *Pearl and Wagner: Two Good Friends.* Ill. by R. W. Alley. Scholastic, 2003, ISBN 0-8037-2573-6. SERIES: Dial Easy-to-Read. SUBJECTS: Friendship — Fiction; Mice — Fiction; Rabbits — Fiction. RL B. LEXILE 340L.

Pearl and Wagner work on a never-quite-together science fair robot, and Wagner finds a way to apologize to his friend.

McNamara, Louise G., and Ada B. Litchfield

1905 *Your Busy Brain.* Ill. by Ruth Hartshorn. Little, Brown, 1973, o.p. SERIES: All About You. SUBJECTS: Human body — Brain; Science and scientists. RL C.

Using simple language and good, clear diagrams and pictures, the authors explain the many bodily functions that the human brain and nervous system control.

1906 *Your Living Bones.* Ill. by Patricia Grant Porter. Little, Brown, 1973, o.p. SERIES: All About You. SUBJECTS: Human body — Skeleton; Science and scientists. RL C.

A lively text discusses the function and growth of bones and encourages children to feel their own bones and pay attention to how they move. The pictures of children and bones are realistic.

McNamara, Margaret

1907 *The Counting Race: Robin Hill School.* Ill. by Mike Gordon. Aladdin, pap., 2003, ISBN 0-689-85539-7. SERIES: Ready-to-Read. SUBJECTS: Concepts — Numbers — Fiction; School stories. RL A.

The first-graders find an inventive way to count to ten in one second! Ink and wash drawings emphasize the cohesiveness of the class.

1908 *Election Day: Robin Hill School.* Ill. by Mike Gordon. Aladdin, 2004, ISBN 0-689-86426-4. SERIES: Ready-to-Read. SUBJECTS: School stories. RL B.

When a newcomer promises only to do her best if elected class president, she, surprisingly, wins. Appealing round-eyed children illustrate the story.

1909 *Eloise Breaks Some Eggs: Kay Thompson's Eloise.* Ill. by Tammie Lyon. Aladdin, pap., 2005, ISBN 0-689-87368-9. SERIES: Ready-to-Read. SUBJECTS: City and town life — Fiction. RL A.

Nanny decides Eloise will never become a cook after a disastrous trip to the chef's kitchen. Story and artwork are based on the original book by Kay Thompson, illustrated by Hilary Knight.

1910 *Fall Leaf Project: Robin Hill School.* Ill. by Mike Gordon. Aladdin, 2006, ISBN 1-4169-1538-9. SERIES: Ready-to-Read. SUBJECTS: Fall — Fiction; School stories. RL B. LEXILE 270L.

Mrs. Connor's class collects differently colored and shaped leaves, most of which they can identify, to send to her friend's class where leaves do not change color. Whimsical pen and wash drawings accompany the text.

1911 *The First Day of School: Robin Hill School.* Ill. by Mike Gordon. Aladdin, 2005, ISBN 0-689-86915-0. SERIES: Ready-to-Read. SUBJECTS: Pets — Dogs — Fiction; School stories. RL A.

Michael misses his dog, Cookie, on the first day of school. Sympathetic doggie drawings add to the emotion.

1912 *First-Grade Bunny: Robin Hill School.* Ill. by Mike Gordon. Aladdin, 2005, ISBN 0-689-86428-0. SERIES: Ready-to-Read. SUBJECTS: School stories. RL A.

Reza's afraid of rabbits, but Mrs. Connor nudges him toward helping in the class bunny's care. Appealing ink and wash drawings.

1913 *Groundhog Day: Robin Hill School*. Ill. by Mike Gordon. Aladdin, pap., 2006, ISBN 1-4169-0507-3. SERIES: Ready-to-Read. SUBJECTS: Groundhog Day; School stories. RL A. LEXILE 430L.

Chester, the class hamster, is called into service to see his shadow on February 2. Familiar round-eyed children illustrate the story.

1914 *Happy Graduation! Robin Hill School*. Ill. by Mike Gordon. Aladdin, 2006, ISBN 1-4169-0510-3. SERIES: Ready-to-Read. SUBJECTS: Graduations — Fiction; School stories. RL B.

Michael's dog, Cookie, almost wrecks the first-grade graduation. Simple pen and wash illustrations.

1915 *Happy Thanksgiving: Robin Hill School*. Ill. by Mike Gordon. Aladdin, 2005, ISBN 1-4169-0506-5. SERIES: Ready-to-Read. SUBJECTS: School stories; Thanksgiving — Fiction. RL B.

When the first-graders go outside for a fire drill, they awe the kindergartners. Simple illustrations complement the text.

1916 *The Luck of the Irish: Robin Hill School*. Ill. by Mike Gordon. Aladdin, 2007, ISBN 1-4169-1540-0. SERIES: Ready-to-Read. SUBJECTS: School stories; St. Patrick's Day — Fiction. RL B. LEXILE 420L.

When Mrs. Connor's and Katie's shamrocks look different, they check a reference book to find Katie is right. Simple, appealing illustrations.

1917 *The Playground Problem: Robin Hill School*. Ill. by Mike Gordon. Aladdin, pap., 2004, ISBN 0-689-85876-0. SERIES: Ready-to-Read. SUBJECTS: School stories. RL B.

Emma and her father devise a scheme to allow her to play soccer with all the kids in her class.

1918 *A Tooth Story: Robin Hill School*. Ill. by Mike Gordon. Aladdin, 2004, ISBN 0-689-86424-8. SERIES: Ready-to-Read. SUBJECTS: Human body — Teeth — Fiction; School stories. RL A. LEXILE 320L.

Jamie's smile is no longer toothy when the class picture is taken. Lots of untoothy children appear in Gordon's cartoon illustrations

McNulty, Faith

1919 *Dancing with Manatees*. Ill. by Lena Shiffman. Scholastic, pap., 1994, ISBN 0-590-46401-9. SERIES: Scholastic Reader. SUBJECTS: Animals; Manatees. RL B.

A girl dives with her friend, Woody, who teaches her about the gentle manatees.

1920 *The Elephant Who Couldn't Forget*. Ill. by Marc Simont. HarperCollins, 1980, ISBN 0-06-024146-2. SERIES: I Can Read. SUBJECTS: Elephants — Fiction; Memory and memorization — Fiction; Sibling rivalry — Fiction. RL B.

Congo, the youngest elephant in his family, prides himself on his extraordinary memory and tries hard not to forget anything. Unfortunately he remembers things better left forgotten. Filled with good information, this story has lovely pencil and wash illustrations.

1921 *How to Dig a Hole to the Other Side of the World*. Ill. by Marc Sirnont. HarperCollins, 1979, ISBN 0-06-024148-9. SUBJECTS: Earth; Geology and geologists. RL C.

A child takes an imaginary journey through the earth and out again on the other side. A geological adventure, the book uses humor and lots of good information to explain the construction of the earth. Attractive watercolor and pencil pictures help to make the story fun.

1922 *If Dogs Ruled the World*. Ill. by Julie Durrell. Scholastic, pap., 2002, ISBN 0-439-08752-X. SERIES: Hello Reader! SUBJECTS: Pets — Dogs — Fiction; Pets — Fiction. RL B. LEXILE NC680L.

If dogs ruled the world, there would be house people and guard people, who would have to be washed (licked), walked, and perhaps be fed dry food. Cute watercolors enhance this turnabout story.

1923 *Woodchuck*. Ill. by Joan Sandin. HarperCollins, 1974, o.p. SERIES: Science I Can Read. SUBJECTS: Groundhogs; Woodchucks. RL A.

McNulty, Faith (cont.)

Readers first meet the woodchuck when she is hibernating, then observe her meeting a male, giving birth to and raising young, and finally being alone again. There is no romanticizing here, just an honest view of animal life. Realistic and detailed pencil and wash drawings.

McPhail, David M.

1924 *Big Brown Bear.* Ill. by author. Harcourt, 1999, ISBN 0-15-202345-3. SERIES: Green Light Readers. SUBJECTS: Bears — Fiction; Humorous stories. RL A. LEXILE BR.

David McPhail draws the most huggable bears! In this story, with the most basic vocabulary, Big Bear encounters several colorful mishaps while painting his treehouse.

1925 *Big Pig and Little Pig.* Ill. by author. Harcourt, 2001, ISBN 0-15-216516-9. SERIES: Green Light Readers. SUBJECTS: Humorous stories; Pigs — Fiction. RL A. LEXILE 170L.

With the most basic vocabulary and charming, lively, expressive pen and wash drawings of the pigs, the author creates humor and action as a big pig digs a tiny pool, and the little pig digs a giant one.

1926 *A Bug, a Bear, and a Boy Go to School.* Ill. by author. Scholastic, pap., 1999, ISBN 0-439-07783-4. SERIES: Scholastic Reader. SUBJECTS: Bears — Fiction; Insects — Fiction; School stories. RL A. LEXILE 210L.

Simple, gentle text about school, the ride, kites, and the picture are enhanced by the cuddly big bear, the boy, and the cricket.

1927 *The Day the Sheep Showed Up.* Ill. by author. Scholastic, pap., 1998, ISBN 0-590-84910-7. SERIES: Scholastic Reader. SUBJECTS: Animals — Farm — Fiction; Jokes and riddles. RL A. LEXILE 230L.

The differences and likenesses between farmyard animals are explored when a new animal shows up, a sheep. McPhail's animals always delight.

1928 *A Girl, a Goat, and a Goose.* Ill. by author. Scholastic, pap., 2000, ISBN 0-439-09978-1. SERIES: Hello Reader! SUBJECTS: Geese — Fiction; Goats — Fiction. RL A. LEXILE 160L.

Three friends are not as afraid when they stay together. Together they find Goose's missing feather and together they dream. No one draws more appealing children and animals!

1929 *The Great Race.* Ill. by author. Scholastic, pap., 1997, ISBN 0-590-84909-3. SERIES: Scholastic Reader. SUBJECTS: Animals — Farm — Fiction. RL A. LEXILE 170L.

None of the animals is used to running in the mud, but the race ends in a dead heat. Irresistible McPhail animals.

1930 *Lorenzo.* Ill. by author. Doubleday, 1984, o.p. SUBJECTS: Animals — Fiction; Art and artists — Fiction; Houses — Fiction. RL B.

Tired of his life as an itinerant painter, Lorenzo moves into a deserted house in a hollow tree and paints while making friends with the woodland animals. Illustrated with appealing ink sketches that have red and brown washes.

1931 *Rick Is Sick.* Ill. by author. Harcourt, 2004, ISBN 0-15-205091-4. SERIES: Green Light Readers. SUBJECTS: Bears — Fiction; Rabbits — Fiction. RL A.

Jack the rabbit tries to help his friend Rick when he is sick, with humorous consequences. Very basic vocabulary, accompanied by McPhail's typically appealing drawings.

1932 *Snow Lion.* Ill. by author. Gareth Stevens, 1992, ISBN 0-8193-1097-2. SUBJECTS: Lions — Fiction; Weather — Snow — Fiction. RL B. LEXILE BR.

Lion, seeking relief from the heat of the jungle, discovers fluffy stuff. His jungle friends don't believe him until he takes them to play in the stuff. The lion is especially huggable.

MacQuitty, Miranda, ed.

1933 *Side by Side.* Ill. with photos. Putnam, 1988, o.p. SUBJECTS: Animals; Plants; Symbiosis. RL C.

Symbiosis and parasitism, examples of how animals or plants live side by side, are explained with excellent color photographs captioned with explanatory text showing animals and plants from around the world. An addendum offers more in-depth information on the animals and plants mentioned in the text.

Madsen, Ross M.

1934 *Perrywinkle and the Book of Magic Spells*. Ill. by Dirk Zimmer. Dial, pap., 1986, ISBN 0-8037-0243-4. SERIES: Easy-to-Read. SUBJECTS: Humorous stories; Magic — Fiction. RL B.

Perrywinkle practices spells from the wizard's books and creates havoc for everyone. His pet bird and his new friend Andromeda try to help him control his "spelling." The budding wizard's frustrations at mastering magic are apparent in the lively pencil and wash pictures.

1935 *Perrywinkle's Magic Match*. Ill. by Dirk Zimmer. Dial, 1997, o.p. SERIES: Dial Easy-to-Read. SUBJECTS: Friendship — Fiction; Magic — Fiction. RL B. LEXILE 360L.

When Perrywinkle and Andromeda compete to create magic, disastrous events follow. Illustrations show young witches with dark hair and big noses.

1936 *Stewart Stork*. Ill. by Megan Halsey. Penguin, 1993, ISBN 0-8037-1326-6. SERIES: Dial Easy-to-Read. SUBJECTS: Friendship — Fiction; Self-esteem — Fiction; Storks — Fiction. RL B.

Stewart longs to be taller, faster, and stronger, but finds out, with the help of his friends, that he is fine the way he is. Cheery drawings add humor and warmth to the story.

Maestro, Betsy

1937 *All Aboard Overnight: A Book of Compound Words*. Ill. by Giulio Maestro. Houghton Mifflin, 1992, o.p. SUBJECTS: English language — Fiction; Trains — Fiction. RL B.

While preparing for and actually taking a train trip, a little girl describes the things she does and sees, introducing many compound words. The attractive book, illustrated throughout with realistic watercolor and pencil pictures, also presents a fine look at railroad travel.

1938 *Ferryboat*. Ill. by Giulio Maestro. HarperCollins, 1986, ISBN 0-690-04520-4. SUBJECTS: Boats and boating. RL B.

Attractive watercolor paintings and a simple text tell the story of a Connecticut river crossing on the modern ferryboat *Selden III*. Readers learn how cars are loaded and how the captain and crew manage the boat. The brief text gives a good sense of what it is like to take a ferryboat trip.

1939 *How Do Apples Grow?* Ill. by Giulio Maestro. HarperCollins, 1992, ISBN 0-06-020055-3. SERIES: Let's-Read-and-Find-Out Science. SUBJECTS: Fruit; Trees. RL B. LEXILE 550L.

The development of apples — from the winter bud on a branch to the final ripened fruit in the fall — is followed through text and carefully crafted pencil and watercolor pictures. The care with which this was created makes it an especially fine nonfiction book.

1940 *In My Boat*. Ill. by Giulio Maestro. Crowell, 1976, ISBN 0-690-01255-1. SUBJECTS: Boats and boating — Fiction; Imagination — Fiction. RL A.

Rhythmic, repetitive language catalogs the imaginative surprises on a boat trip. Appealing graphic animals complement the text.

1941 *A More Perfect Union: The Story of Our Constitution*. Lothrop, 1987, ISBN 0-688-06840-5. SUBJECTS: United States — History. RL C. LEXILE AD850L.

The difficulties in writing a plan for governing the new United States are shown in the very interesting and carefully worded text and in the art. Pencil and watercolor pictures carefully re-create a post-revolutionary America in this story of the writing of the Constitution of the United States. Appended are a summary of the Constitution, a list of the signers, and pertinent dates and facts.

1942 *Why Do Leaves Change Color?* Ill. by Loretta Krupinski. HarperCollins, 1994, ISBN 0-06-022873-3. SERIES: Let's-Read-and-Find-Out Science. SUBJECTS: Fall; Plants; Trees. RL B. LEXILE 580L.

Gouache and colored-pencil pictures fill the pages and vibrantly accent and extend the text, which explores how and why leaves change color. This reads well and children will enjoy the appended activities that include appropriate safety precautions.

Maestro, Betsy, and Ellen DelVecchio

1943 *Big City Port*. Ill. by Giulio Maestro. Scholastic, pap., 1984, ISBN 0-590-41577-8.

Maestro, Betsy, and Ellen DelVecchio (cont.)

SUBJECTS: Ports and harbors; Ships and shipping. RL B.

A picture of the activity in the harbor or port of a large city is carefully drawn in ink and watercolor pictures and in the text. Use of gray tones gives the pictures a dark look.

Maestro, Giulio

1944 *Leopard and the Noisy Monkeys.* Ill. by author. Greenwillow, 1979, o.p. SERIES: Read-Alone. SUBJECTS: Animals — Fiction; Humorous stories; Sleep — Fiction. RL B.

Escaping from the noise of the 20 monkeys he has allowed to use his treehouse, Leopard goes to Crocodile's house, and Crocodile goes to Aardvark's to escape Leopard, Aardvark to Hippo's, Hippo to Leopard's. Amusing illustrations and story are silly enough to please young readers.

1945 *Leopard Is Sick.* Ill. by author. Greenwillow, 1978, o.p. SERIES: Read-Alone. SUBJECTS: Animals — Fiction; Humorous stories; Illness — Fiction. RL B.

Bored with being sick but ordered by his doctor to rest, Leopard feels better only when his three friends disguise themselves as doctors to cheer him up. Simple yet interesting paintings with gray outlining and details fit well with the funny story.

Maguire, Gregory

1946 *The Peace and Quiet Diner.* Ill. by David Perry. Parents Magazine Press, 1988, ISBN 0-8193-1176-6. SERIES: Parents Magazine Read Aloud Original. SUBJECTS: Animals — Fiction; Stories in rhyme. RL B.

Visiting Auntie Jane misses all the action; her nephew finds a way to send her on her way. Action-filled ink and wash drawings.

Maitland, Barbara

1947 *The Bookstore Burglar.* Ill. by Nadine B. Westcott. Dutton, 2001, ISBN 0-525-46684-3. SERIES: Dutton Easy Reader. SUBJECTS: Bookstores — Fiction; Pets — Cats — Fiction. RL B.

When bookstore owner Mr. Brown fails to notice his spare key is gone, Cobweb the cat and the "ghosts" scare the burglar away. Pen and wash drawings are not at all spooky.

1948 *The Bookstore Ghost.* Ill. by Nadine B. Westcott. Dutton, 1998, ISBN 0-525-46049-7. SERIES: Dutton Easy Reader. SUBJECTS: Bookstores — Fiction; Pets — Cats — Fiction. RL B. LEXILE 50L.

Mr. Brown's cat, Cobweb, finds a way to keep the mice in the bookstore out of sight, and to add to the ghostly ambiance. Cozy pen and wash illustrations.

1949 *The Bookstore Valentine.* Ill. by David LaRochelle. Penguin, 2002, ISBN 0-525-46913-3. SERIES: Dutton Easy Reader. SUBJECTS: Bookstores — Fiction; Romance — Fiction. RL B.

Mr. Brown advertises for help in his Black Cat Bookstore, the one with the ghost. Miss Button is "perfect" for the job, and romance blossoms with help from the cat, Cobweb. Pen and watercolor wash illustrations.

Mallett, Anne

1950 *Here Comes Tagalong.* Ill. by Steven Kellogg. Parents Magazine Press, 1971, o.p. SUBJECTS: Humorous stories; Loneliness — Fiction; Siblings — Fiction. RL B.

Steve does not know any children his own age so he tags along after his older brother and his friends. Finally old enough to go around the block, he makes his own friends and his younger brother becomes Tagalong. Spirited pictures catch the humor as well as Steve's initial loneliness.

Malone, Mary

1951 *Annie Sullivan.* Ill. by Lydia Rosier. Putnam, 1971, o.p. SERIES: See and Read Beginning to Read Biography. SUBJECTS: Biographies; Disabilities — Physical and mental. RL B.

Annie Sullivan's life story is told in a concise and straightforward way beginning with her childhood poverty and going through her years as "Teacher" to Helen Keller. No dates are provided, although World War I is mentioned. Illustrated with realistic ink drawings.

Mann, Rachel

1952 *Race to a Fire!* Ill. with photos. Compass Point, 2003, ISBN 0-7565-0522-4. SERIES: Phonics Readers. SUBJECTS: Fire fighters and fire fighting; Rebuses. RL A.

A word list and word bingo game are appended to a simple description of firefighters' work, complemented by rebuses.

Mantinband, Gerda B.

1953 *Bing Bong Bang and Fiddle Dee Dee.* Ill. by Anne Rockwell. Doubleday, 1979, o.p. SERIES: Reading on My Own. SUBJECTS: Farm and country life — Fiction; Marriage and wedding customs — Fiction; Music and musicians — Fiction. RL B.

To his wife's dismay, an old man buys a fiddle and tries to play it. She starts banging on pots to stop his squeaking and their music drives the animals from their farm. An affectionate reconciliation ends this story of marital discord. Simple, childlike drawings accompany the humorous story.

Manushkin, Fran

1954 *The Perfect Christmas Picture.* Ill. by Karen A. Weinhaus. HarperCollins, pap., 1980, ISBN 0-06-024069-5. SERIES: I Can Read. SUBJECTS: Family life — Fiction; Photography and photographers — Fiction. RL C.

All year Mr. Green has tried with no success to take a perfect Christmas picture of his six children. His frustrations and the children's antics will have readers laughing. The spare, humorous ink and wash drawings work very well with the story.

Margolis, Richard J.

1955 *Big Bear, Spare That Tree.* Ill. by Jack Kent. Greenwillow, 1980, o.p. SERIES: Read-Alone. SUBJECTS: Bears — Fiction; Blue jays — Fiction. RL B.

Trying to save her soon-to-hatch eggs, a blue jay screams for Bear to stop chopping down her tree. He ignores her until he sees that the eggs are hatching and then he must really come to the rescue. The conflict is handled well and Kent's humorous drawings keep the story light.

1956 *Homer the Hunter.* Ill. by Leonard Kessler. Macmillan, 1972, o.p. SERIES: Ready-to-Read. SUBJECTS: Animals — Fiction; Humorous stories; Hunting — Fiction. RL B.

Rabbit, Squirrel, and Crow initially fool Homer, a terrible hunter, into believing they are ghosts haunting him. Finally Homer decides to share in the fun and pretends that he is a ghost too. Comical sketches in gray, brown, and red complement the story.

1957 *Wish Again, Big Bear.* Ill. by Robert Lopshire. Macmillan, 1972, o.p. SERIES: Ready-to-Read. SUBJECTS: Bears — Fiction; Fish — Fiction; Wishes — Fiction. RL B.

To save himself from being eaten, Fish tells Big Bear he is magic and will grant him three wishes. Fish saves himself and Bear gets what he wished for — a friend. The humor in Fish's trickery and Bear's gullibility acts as a perfect complement to Lopshire's comic ink drawings.

Margulies, Teddy

1958 *The Runaway Rabbit.* Ill. by Carolyn Bracken. Scholastic, 2001, ISBN 0-439-21361-4. SERIES: Big Red Reader. SUBJECTS: Pets — Dogs — Fiction; Rabbits — Fiction. RL B. LEXILE 140L.

Clifford and his doggie friends find out how much trouble a rabbit can be when they are commissioned to take care of him. Typical friendly, simple drawings.

Markert, Jenny

1959 *Hippos.* Ill. with photos. Child's World, 1993, ISBN 1-56766-003-7. SUBJECTS: Hippopotami. RL C.

Sharp color photographs and a focused text show how the third largest land animal lives, protects its territory, and cares for its young. Slightly more difficult than the others in the Naturebooks series. Includes an index.

1960 *Reptiles.* Ill. with photos. Child's World, 1993, ISBN 0-89565-850-X. SERIES: Wildlife Library. SUBJECTS: Reptiles and amphibians. RL C.

Alternating pages of large, well-spaced text and striking color photographs should lure young readers into this introductory look at reptiles such

Markert, Jenny (cont.)

as the basilisk lizard, the gila monster, and the gavial.

Markham, Marion M.

1961 *The Halloween Candy Mystery*. Ill. by Emily A. McCully. Houghton Mifflin, 1982, o.p. SUBJECTS: Halloween — Fiction; Mystery and detective stories; Siblings — Twins — Fiction. RL B.

Dressed in their panda costumes and ready to go trick-or-treating, twin sisters Mickey and Kate get involved in reporting a robbery and in helping to find the missing robber. Longer than most first readers, this is entertaining and has good black-and-white drawings.

Marshall, Edward

1962 *Four on the Shore*. Ill. by James Marshall. Dial, 1994, ISBN 0-8037-0142-X. SERIES: Dial Easy-to-Read. SUBJECTS: Humorous stories; Siblings — Fiction; Storytelling — Fiction. RL B. LEXILE 210L.

Three children — Lolly, Spider, and Sam — share stories around a fire, hoping to frighten Spider's little brother, Willie, into going home. Drawn in ink with colorful washes, the pictures are simple yet comical, adding to the already delightful humor of the stories.

Marshall, James

1963 *Fox All Week*. Ill. by author. Dial, 1984, ISBN 0-8037-0066-0. SERIES: Dial Easy-to-Read. SUBJECTS: Foxes — Fiction; Friendship — Fiction; Humorous stories. RL B. LEXILE 170L.

From Monday morning to Sunday evening, Fox, his friends, and his family face situations that are sure to stir memories in adults and be very funny for children. The book is illustrated with humorous full-color ink and watercolor paintings.

1964 *Fox and His Friends*. Ill. by author. Dial, pap., 1982, ISBN 0-14-037007-2. SERIES: Dial Easy-to-Read. SUBJECTS: Baby-sitting — Fiction; Foxes — Fiction; Humorous stories. RL B. LEXILE 200L.

In each of three stories, Fox cannot seem to get away with anything. In two stories he is stuck taking care of his spunky little sister Louise and in the third his conscience gets the better of him. The first two stories are very funny and the third is hilarious, especially with the deadpan, comic illustrations.

1965 *Fox at School*. Ill. by author. Penguin, pap., 1993, ISBN 0-14-036544-3. SERIES: Dial Easy-to-Read. SUBJECTS: Foxes — Fiction; Humorous stories; School stories. RL B. LEXILE 210L.

Always wanting the easy way out, egocentric Fox is surprised that it takes hard work to act in the class play or control the class. Children are sure to identify with the imperfect but lovable Fox. Illustrated with comic ink drawings with coral and green tints.

1966 *Fox Be Nimble*. Ill. by author. Penguin, pap., 1994, ISBN 0-14-036842-6. SERIES: Puffin Easy-to-Read. SUBJECTS: Foxes — Fiction. RL B. LEXILE 210L.

Fox is a showoff, but doesn't always escape the consequences. You've never seen such self-satisfied foxy expressions!

1967 *Fox in Love*. Ill. by author. Penguin, pap., 1994, ISBN 0-14-036843-4. SERIES: Dial Easy-to-Read. SUBJECTS: Foxes — Fiction; Humorous stories; Romance — Fiction. RL B. LEXILE 170L.

Forced to take his little sister Louise to the park, Fox is surprised to meet Raisin, a lovely white fox, and is soon swooning over her as well as Millie, Rose, and Lola. Fun to read, this book has whimsical ink cartoon drawings with orange and green washes.

1968 *Fox on Stage*. Ill. by author. Penguin, pap., 1996, ISBN 0-14-038032-9. SERIES: Dial Easy-to-Read. SUBJECTS: Foxes — Fiction; Magic — Fiction; Plays — Fiction. RL B. LEXILE 80L.

In three stories, Fox continues to cause laughter as he very seriously tries to entertain his bedridden Grannie, refuses to believe in magic, and attempts to put on a scary play. The watercolor drawings are a perfect match for the stories' humor.

1969 *Fox on the Job*. Ill. by author. Penguin, pap., 1995, ISBN 0-14-037602-X. SERIES: Dial Easy-to-Read. SUBJECTS: Foxes —

Fiction; Humorous stories. RL B. LEXILE 150L.

To impress the girls, Fox shows off on his bike and ends up demolishing it. When Mom refuses to buy him a new one, Fox goes through several jobs before he finds one just right for his special talents. Story and artwork continue to be as witty and satisfying as in the earlier Fox stories.

1970 *Fox on Wheels*. Ill. by author. Penguin, pap., 1993, ISBN 0-14-036541-9. SERIES: Dial Easy-to-Read. SUBJECTS: Baby-sitting — Fiction; Bicycles and bicycling — Fiction; Foxes — Fiction. RL B. LEXILE 180L.

In three stories with surprise endings, Fox gets into more trouble than he bargained for — especially when he baby-sits for his little sister Louise or goes biking through the park. Illustrations are ink line drawings with color overlays in a whimsical style.

1971 *Fox Outfoxed*. Ill. by author. Penguin, pap., 1996, ISBN 0-14-038113-9. SERIES: Dial Easy-to-Read. SUBJECTS: Foxes — Fiction; Halloween — Fiction; Humorous stories. RL B. LEXILE 120L.

Three hilarious stories feature Fox, his little sister Louise, and his friends as they stage a race; as Fox gets tricked out of his comics; and as they go trick-or-treating and end up tricked. Marshall's text and delightfully humorous watercolors are sure winners with young readers.

1972 *Speedboat*. Ill. by author. Houghton Mifflin, pap., 1999, ISBN 0-606-16540-1. SUBJECTS: Boats and boating — Fiction; Friendship — Fiction. RL B.

Raisintoast thinks his day was more adventurous that than of his stay-at-home friends, but Tweedy-Jones knows better. An imaginative story with drawings in gray and green wash to match.

1973 *Three by the Sea*. Ill. by author. Penguin, pap., 1994, ISBN 0-14-037004-8. SERIES: Dial Easy-to-Read. SUBJECTS: Friendship — Fiction; Storytelling — Fiction. RL B. LEXILE 60L.

After a filling picnic lunch at the beach, Lolly decides to share a story from her reader with Spider and Sam. Bored, they try to create their own stories. Sure to appeal to children and adults, this book is illustrated with humorous ink and pencil drawings.

1974 *Three Up a Tree*. Ill. by author. Penguin, 1994, ISBN 0-8037-0329-5. SUBJECTS: Friendship — Fiction; Storytelling — Fiction; Treehouses — Fiction. RL B. LEXILE 160L.

To get into Spider and Sam's treehouse, Lolly promises to tell a story. Soon the other two are trying to outdo Lolly with their own storytelling. The colorful, often silly illustrations and stories are sure to evoke appreciative smiles.

1975 *Troll Country*. Ill. by author. Penguin, pap., 1996, ISBN 0-14-038110-4. SERIES: Dial Easy-to-Read. SUBJECTS: Fantasy; Humorous stories; Trolls — Fiction. RL B. LEXILE 320L.

After hearing her mother's story of her encounter with a troll, Elsie Fay is sure she will know exactly how to handle one. Droll ink drawings with colored pencil accents in gray, green, and rust are perfect for this entertaining story.

Martin, C. L. G.

1976 *Day of Darkness, Night of Light*. Ill. by Victoria M. Williams. Dillon, 1988, o.p. SERIES: It Really Happened. SUBJECTS: Fire fighters and fire fighting — Fiction; Historical fiction. RL C.

Fire breaks out and threatens to destroy Menominee, Michigan, in October 1871. After getting his mother and sisters to safety, Daniel and his grandfather help battle the blaze and save their town. Based on an actual event, this suspenseful story is effectively illustrated in pencil.

Martin, Claire

1977 *I Can Be a Weather Forecaster*. Ill. with photos. Childrens Press, 1987, ISBN 0-516-01908-2. SERIES: I Can Be. SUBJECTS: Careers; Weather. RL C.

Weather forecasting is presented as an interesting and demanding profession involving much more than is seen on a television weather report. Illustrated with color photographs and simple drawings, the text mentions weather satellites, stations, computers, and other forecasting tools.

Martin, Louise

1978 *Alligators*. Ill. with photos. Rourke, 1989, ISBN 0-86592-579-8. SERIES: Reptile

Martin, Louise (cont.)

Discovery Library. SUBJECTS: Alligators; Reptiles and amphibians. RL C.

Good photographs add appeal to a very brief text divided into nine paragraph-size sections. The various aspects of alligators' lives are mentioned. A limited glossary and an index are included.

1979 *Chameleons*. Ill. with photos. Rourke, 1989, ISBN 0-86592-576-3. SERIES: Reptile Discovery Library. SUBJECTS: Chameleons; Reptiles and amphibians. RL C.

Nine sections of text with paragraph-size bits of information are augmented by photographs. Together they offer an introduction to the life of a number of chameleons. A confusing section says the tongue is half the size of its body and shows a tongue twice the size. There is a minimal glossary and an index.

1980 *Panda*. Ill. with photos. Rourke, 1988, ISBN 0-86592-996-3. SERIES: Wildlife in Danger. SUBJECTS: Animals — Endangered; Pandas. RL B.

Martin provides interesting information to support her plea for the preservation of the panda, stressing threats to its existence such as poaching and loss of habitat. Some photographs are not matched correctly to the text but the information is good enough to compensate for that.

1981 *Rhinoceros*. Ill. with photos. Rourke, 1988, ISBN 0-86592-997-1. SERIES: Wildlife in Danger. SUBJECTS: Animals — Endangered; Rhinoceroses. RL B.

The threat of extinction is mentioned on nearly every page of this simply written and useful book. There is a good deal of information about rhinos: types, habitat, diet, poaching, protection, and horns. Color photographs are not always matched to the text and captions could be more informative.

1982 *Seals*. Ill. with photos. Rourke, 1988, ISBN 0-86592-999-8. SERIES: Wildlife in Danger. SUBJECTS: Animals — Endangered; Seals. RL B.

Using only 18 pages of alternating text and photographs, Martin presents well-documented threats to the existence of seals without presenting much information on the various species of seals. The brief information could be useful for reports on endangered animals.

1983 *Tigers*. Ill. with photos. Rourke, 1988, ISBN 0-86592-995-3. SERIES: Wildlife in Danger. SUBJECTS: Animals — Endangered; Tigers. RL B.

The emphasis here is on the threat to Asian tigers through poaching and habitat destruction rather than on the general characteristics of the largest member of the cat family. Good information and attractive color photographs are provided.

1984 *Trapdoor Spiders*. Ill. with photos. Rourke, 1988, ISBN 0-86592-963-7. SERIES: Spiders Discovery Library. SUBJECTS: Spiders. RL B.

An excellent text describes the unusual burrow and some of the habits of the trapdoor spiders that are found all over the world. The scope of information is limited and a discussion of the spider's life cycle could have been included. The photographs include two that have mismatched captions.

Martin, Patricia A. Fink

1985 *Chimpanzees*. Ill. with photos. Children's Press, 2000, ISBN 0-516-21572-/. SERIES: True Book. SUBJECTS: Animals — Endangered; Chimpanzees. RL C.

Chimpanzees' food, use of tools, social groups, and close relatives — the bonobos — are described. Names of primate protection agencies are appended.

1986 *Lemurs, Lorises, and Other Lower Primates*. Ill. with photos. Children's Press, 1999, ISBN 0-516-21575-2. SERIES: True Book. SUBJECTS: Animals — Endangered; Primates. RL C.

Prosimians have been around longer than monkeys, and range from the ring-tailed lemur to the aye-aye, loris, galago, and tarsier. The lemur and aye-aye are from Madagascar, the loris and tarsier from Southeast Asia, and the galago from Africa. Photographs capture these mostly tiny, shy animals close-up.

1987 *Monkeys of Asia and Africa*. Ill. with photos. Children's Press, 1999, ISBN 0-516-21573-6. SERIES: True Book. SUBJECTS: Monkeys. RL C.

The proboscis monkey, the Hanuman langue, the golden monkey, the baboon, and the patas monkey are featured, differentiating them from the monkeys of Central and South America. The Web sites of conservancy groups are listed at the end.

1988 *Northern Spotted Owls.* Ill. with photos. Children's Press, 2001, ISBN 0-516-22164-7. SERIES: True Book. SUBJECTS: Birds; Owls. RL C. LEXILE 640L.

Special adaptations of owls, in particular northern spotted owls, are listed. The aids to hearing and seeing at night are interesting, as is the fact that these owls mate for life.

1989 *Orangutans.* Ill. with photos. Children's Press, 2000, ISBN 0-516-21571-X. SERIES: True Book. SUBJECTS: Animals — Endangered; Orangutans. RL C.

Great apes are larger than monkeys and have no tail. Gorillas, bonobos, and chimpanzees are also great apes. Physical characteristics, food, mating rituals, and endangered status are cataloged.

Martin, Patricia M.

1990 *The Pumpkin Patch.* Ill. by Tom Hamil. Putnam, 1966, o.p. SUBJECTS: Halloween — Fiction; School stories. RL B.

Kate loves kindergarten and cannot wait for her class to go to the pumpkin patch so she can pick out her very own pumpkin. Once there she discovers that the perfect pumpkin already has an owner — a field mouse. Very sketchy drawings are busy and childlike and work well with this story.

Marx, David F.

1991 *Baby in the House.* Ill. by Cynthia Fisher. Children's Press, 1999, ISBN 0-516-21688-0. SERIES: Rookie Reader. SUBJECTS: Babies — Fiction; Family life — Fiction. RL A.

Eve is not happy with the new baby in the house until she finds ways to play with her.

1992 *Hello, Doctor.* Ill. by Mark A. Hicks. Children's Press, 1999, ISBN 0-516-22033-0. SERIES: Rookie Reader. SUBJECTS: Medicine — Fiction. RL A.

In 28 words, a boy's trip to the doctor is treated lightly; illustrated with cartoon drawings, reinforcing the light tone.

1993 *Our Raspberry Jam.* Ill. by Paul Michalak. Children's Press, 1999, ISBN 0-516-22174-4. SERIES: Rookie Reader. SUBJECTS: Food — Fiction. RL A.

Using a 112-word vocabulary, a girl tells how her family makes raspberry jam — and why she loves it!

Marzollo, Dan

1994 *I Spy a Circus.* Photos by Ward Yoshimoto and James Levin. Scholastic, 2003, o.p. SERIES: Cartwheel. SUBJECTS: Circuses — Fiction; Jokes and riddles; Stories in rhyme. RL A.

The playroom toys in the photographs end up organizing a circus.

1995 *I Spy Pirate Treasure.* Photos by Ward Yoshimoto. Scholastic, pap., 2003, ISBN 0-439-45525-1. SERIES: Cartwheel. SUBJECTS: Jokes and riddles; Pirates — Fiction; Stories in rhyme. RL A.

Spyler and CeCe dig for treasure on the beach.

Marzollo, Jean

1996 *Amy Goes Fishing.* Ill. by Ann Schweninger. Dial, 1980, o.p. SERIES: Easy-to-Read. SUBJECTS: Parent and child — Fiction; Sports — Fishing — Fiction. RL B.

On her first fishing trip with father, Amy remembers how boring her brother and sister thought fishing was. She is pleasantly surprised at how much she enjoys their day together. An understated text and quiet, soft-hued pictures blend to create an enjoyable, low-key story.

1997 *Cannonball Chris.* Ill. by Blanche Sims. Random House, 1987, ISBN 0-394-98512-5. SERIES: Step into Reading. SUBJECTS: Fear — Fiction; Parent and child — Fiction; Sports — Swimming — Fiction. RL B.

Realizing that something is wrong, Chris's father convinces Chris to say what is bothering him — a fear of diving into deep water. His father helps Chris to face his fear, name it, and finally overcome it with his support. This very well done story has lively multiracial children drawn in pencil and wash.

1998 *Happy Birthday, Martin Luther King.* Ill. by J. Brian Pinkney. Scholastic, 1993, ISBN

Marzollo, Jean (cont.)

0-590-44065-9. SUBJECTS: African Americans; Biographies; Martin Luther King, Jr., Day. RL B.

In simple words and beautiful scratchboard illustrations, the story of King's life and his commitment to understanding between races is told. Though this is in a picture-book format, the care taken in writing the text has made it very accessible to young readers.

1999 *I Am a Star*. Ill. by Judith Moffatt. Scholastic, pap., 2000, ISBN 0-439-11320-2. SERIES: Scholastic Reader. SUBJECTS: Astronomy and astronomers. RL A. LEXILE 10L.

Decorative cutouts illustrate basic information about stars.

2000 *I Am an Apple*. Ill. by Judith Moffatt. Scholastic, 1997, ISBN 0-590-37223-8. SERIES: Hello Science Reader! SUBJECTS: Apples; Trees. RL A. LEXILE 120L.

Wonderful collages show apples from tree to table.

2001 *I Am Fire*. Ill. by Judith Moffatt. Scholastic, pap., 1996, ISBN 0-590-84778-3. SERIES: Scholastic Reader. SUBJECTS: Safety. RL A. LEXILE 160L.

Illustrated with colorful cutouts, fire safety tips are offered.

2002 *I Am Water*. Ill. by Judith Moffatt. Scholastic, pap., 1996, ISBN 0-5902-6587-3. SERIES: Scholastic Reader. SUBJECTS: Water. RL A. LEXILE 30L.

Rhythmic text using basic vocabulary about water is illustrated with close-up cutouts with child-friendly details.

2003 *I Spy: Four Picture Riddle Books*. Photos by Walter Wick. Scholastic, 2005, ISBN 0-439-76309-6. SERIES: Reader Collection. SUBJECTS: Jokes and riddles; Stories in rhyme. RL B.

Photographs of objects familiar to children in bright primary colors add to the visual and vocabulary challenges of this I Spy book.

2004 *I Spy a Balloon*. Photos by Walter Wick. Scholastic, pap., 2006, ISBN 0-439-73864-4. SERIES: Scholastic Reader. SUBJECTS: Jokes and riddles; Stories in rhyme. RL A.

The photograph riddles are followed by identifying words ending with "ck" or "'s," and rhyming words.

2005 *I Spy a Butterfly*. Photos by Walter Wick. Scholastic, pap., 2007, ISBN 0-439-73865-2. SERIES: Scholastic Reader. SUBJECTS: Jokes and riddles; Stories in rhyme. RL A.

More marvelous close-up photographs of objects interesting to children, ending with practice finding words that start or end with certain letters.

2006 *I Spy a Candy Cane*. Photos by Walter Wick. Scholastic, pap., 2004, ISBN 0-439-52474-1. SERIES: Scholastic Reader. SUBJECTS: Jokes and riddles; Stories in rhyme. RL A.

Marzollo has created an imaginative story with inventive language and interesting photograph collages.

2007 *I Spy a Dinosaur's Eye*. Photos by Walter Wick. Scholastic, pap., 2003, ISBN 0-439-52471-7. SERIES: Scholastic Reader. SUBJECTS: Jokes and riddles; Stories in rhyme. RL A.

Photographs of toys of all sorts illustrate this book promoting words ending and beginning with certain letters, as well as a broader vocabulary.

2008 *I Spy a Penguin*. Photos by Walter Wick. Scholastic, pap., 1994, ISBN 0-439-73862-8. SERIES: Scholastic Reader. SUBJECTS: Jokes and riddles; Stories in rhyme. RL A.

Marzollo and Wick create another book with high interest and language challenges. Close-up photographs of toys are matched with rhyming text with practice finding words beginning or ending with certain sounds.

2009 *I Spy a Pumpkin*. Photos by Walter Wick. Scholastic, pap., 2005, ISBN 0-439-73863-6. SERIES: Scholastic Reader. SUBJECTS: Jokes and riddles. RL A.

Challenges readers to find words that begin or end with the same sound, or that rhyme, using close-up photographs of nursery toys.

2010 *I Spy a Scary Monster*. Photos by Walter Wick. Scholastic, pap., 2004, ISBN 0-439-68054-9. SERIES: Scholastic Reader.

SUBJECTS: Jokes and riddles; Stories in rhyme. RL A.

Photographs of children's toys help with vocabulary and sharpen observation and spelling skills.

2011 *I Spy a School Bus*. Photos by Walter Wick. Scholastic, pap., 2003, ISBN 0-439-52473-3. SERIES: Scholastic Reader. SUBJECTS: Jokes and riddles; Stories in rhyme. RL A.

Close-ups of a model town laid out using wooden blocks illustrate this text promoting vocabulary and spelling tips.

2012 *I Spy Funny Teeth*. Photos by Walter Wick. Scholastic, pap., 1995, ISBN 0-439-52472-5. SERIES: Scholastic Reader. SUBJECTS: Jokes and riddles; Stories in rhyme. RL A.

Some wind-up false teeth are hidden among the many close-up photographs of toys in primary colors. Rhyming words and words beginning or ending with the same sound are appended.

2013 *I Spy Lightning in the Sky*. Photos by Walter Wick. Scholastic, pap., 2005, ISBN 0-439-68052-2. SERIES: Scholastic Reader. SUBJECTS: Jokes and riddles; Weather. RL A.

Tips on words beginning or ending with certain letters, or rhymes are appended, with color photographs of childhood toys to expand vocabulary.

2014 *I Spy Santa Claus*. Photos by Walter Wick. Scholastic, pap., 2005, ISBN 0-439-78414-X. SERIES: Scholastic Reader. SUBJECTS: Jokes and riddles; Stories in rhyme. RL A.

Close-up photographs of toys with a Christmas theme, with word and vocabulary practice appended.

2015 *I'm a Caterpillar*. Ill. by Judith Moffatt. Scholastic, pap., 1997, ISBN 0-590-84779-1. SERIES: Scholastic Reader. SUBJECTS: Butterflies and moths; Insects. RL A. LEXILE 60L.

Fanciful cutouts bring the simple text to life.

2016 *Musical Instruments*. Translated from the French and rewritten. Ill. by Donald Grant. Scholastic, 1992, ISBN 0-590-47729-3. SERIES: First Discovery Book. SUBJECTS: Musical instruments. RL C.

On heavy paper with occasional transparent overlays that attract the interest of young readers, explanations are provided for how classical, popular, and folk instruments are made. Illustrations are colorful paintings set against a white background.

2017 *The Rain Forest*. Translated from the French and rewritten. Ill. by Rene Mettler. Scholastic, 1992, ISBN 0-590-47728-5. SERIES: First Discovery Book. SUBJECTS: Animals; Conservation; Rain forests. RL C.

Heavy-weight glossy paper with occasional transparent overlays displays the rain forest and its plants and animals. Colors are vibrant and the overlays add surprises and fun to an interesting subject. On darker pages, however, the text is often difficult to read.

2018 *Red Sun Girl*. Ill. by Susan Meddaugh. Dial, 1983, ISBN 0-8037-7494-X. SERIES: Easy-to-Read. SUBJECTS: Animals — Fiction; Magic — Fiction; Science fiction. RL B.

Everyone on the planet is a human during Red Sun and an animal during Blue Sun except Kiri. Tired of being laughed at, she finds a way to get her own animal shape. This is an appealing, well-paced book that is divided into chapters. Simple, cartoon-style pictures are drawn with colored pencil.

2019 *Soccer Sam*. Ill. by Blanche Sims. Random House, pap., 1987, ISBN 0-394-88406-X. SERIES: Step into Reading. SUBJECTS: Sports — Soccer — Fiction. RL B. LEXILE 370L.

Cousin Marco arrives from Mexico speaking little English, but soon learns as he coaches the second graders so they can challenge the third graders to a game. The rules of the game and the role of the players come naturally. Pleasant pencil and wash illustrations.

2020 *Whales*. Ill. by Ute Fuhr and Raoul Sautai. Scholastic, 1991, ISBN 0-590-47130-9. SERIES: First Discovery Book. SUBJECTS: Whales. RL B.

Clever plastic overlays extend an interesting text and add child appeal to an already intriguing animal. The plastic overlays give readers an opportunity to see different views and even a skeleton of a whale. One difficulty may be reading text that is set against blue.

Marzollo, Jean, and Claudio Marzollo

2021 *Blue Sun Ben.* Ill. by Susan Meddaugh. Dial, 1984, ISBN 0-8037-0063-6. SERIES: Easy-to-Read. SUBJECTS: Animals — Fiction; Magic — Fiction; Science fiction. RL B.

On Ben's planet everyone is an animal during Blue Sun and a human during Red Sun. Caught by the evil Animal Singer while in his chipmunk shape, Ben manages to escape with the help of his cousin Kiri and the Fox Woman. Colored-pencil drawings effectively delineate the exciting story.

2022 *Jed and the Space Bandits.* Ill. by Peter Sis. Dial, 1987, ISBN 0-8037-0136-5. SERIES: Science Fiction Easy-to-Read. SUBJECTS: Science fiction. RL C.

Since she is able to become invisible, Molly is not seen by the space bandits who kidnap her scientist parents. Jed, his cogs (telepathic half-dog, half-cat animals), and his robot Teddy Bear join Molly in an exciting rescue of her parents. The story is illustrated with good full-color pictures.

2023 *Jed's Junior Space Patrol.* Ill. by David Rose. Dial, 1982, ISBN 0-8037-4287-8. SERIES: Easy-to-Read. SUBJECTS: Science fiction. RL B.

Left alone while his space pilot parents work, Jed hears a call for help and rescues two cogs — telepathic half-dog, half-cat animals. Taken from Jed, the little animals use telepathy to get him to rescue them again. This time they stay with him. The futuristic pictures are done in ink and washes.

2024 *Robin of Bray.* Ill. by Diane Stanley. Dial, 1982, ISBN 0-8037-7332-3. SERIES: Easy-to-Read. SUBJECTS: Fairy tales; Magic — Fiction; Trolls — Fiction. RL B.

In this creative and appealing fairy tale, Robin is stuck being a shepherd when he has talent enough to be a magician. After rescuing a princess from trolls, he discovers his true identity. Contains suitably fanciful pointillist ink drawings with washes.

2025 *Ruthie's Rude Friends.* Ill. by Susan Meddaugh. Dial, pap., 1984, ISBN 0-8037-0116-0. SERIES: Easy-to-Read. SUBJECTS: Behavior — Manners — Fiction; Friendship — Fiction; Science fiction. RL B.

Ruthie, newly arrived from Earth, is just as rude to the strange beings she meets as she believes they are to her until they rescue her from a terrible three-headed monster. Ink line drawings with vibrant colored-pencil details carry and expand the successful science fiction theme.

Marzollo, Jean, Dan Marzollo, and Dave Marzollo

2026 *Baseball Brothers.* Ill. by True Kelley. Scholastic, pap., 1999, ISBN 0-590-38398-1. SERIES: Scholastic Reader. SUBJECTS: Sports — Baseball — Fiction. RL B. LEXILE 200L.

Timmy's inattentive on the baseball field until he inadvertently hits a home run. Even then he needs some reminding. Ink and wash drawings.

Mason, Jane

2027 *The Flying Horse: The Story of Pegasus.* Ill. by Susan Swan. Grosset & Dunlap, pap., 1999, ISBN 0-448-41980-7. SERIES: All Aboard Reading. SUBJECTS: Astronomy and astronomers; Myths. RL B. LEXILE 90L.

Magical paper cutouts are enhanced with fabric to illustrate the story of Pegasus, who, with the prince and a magic spear, killed the beast with the head of a lion, the body of a goat, and the tail of a snake.

Mason, Margo

2028 *Go Away, Crows!* Ill. by David Prebenna. Bantam, 1989, ISBN 0-553-05817-7. SERIES: Little Rooster Read-A-Story. SUBJECTS: Birds — Fiction; Pigs — Fiction. RL A.

When a bunch of crows descend on the two pigs' home, nothing Big Pig does seems to work. Finally Little Pig finds the solution — a scarecrow. Soft pencil and watercolor pictures comically illustrate this very brief story.

2029 *Good Dog, Rover.* Ill. by Sandy Hoffman. Bantam, 1989, ISBN 0-553-05814-2. SERIES: Little Rooster Read-A-Story. SUBJECTS: Pets — Dogs — Fiction. RL A.

Amy and Andy and their parents know they do not want a black or white, a large or small dog. They find Rover, a medium-size spotted dog, at the pound and he is perfect. The children begin training him and he quickly learns. Cartoonish ink and watercolor pictures augment the very brief text.

2030 *Ready, Alice?* Ill. by Catherine Siracusa. Bantam, 1990, ISBN 0-553-05816-9. SERIES: Little Rooster Read-A-Story. SUBJECTS: Behavior — Fiction. RL A.

Despite her parents' impatience and constant reminders, Alice dawdles getting up, getting dressed, eating, and, finally, getting ready for the beach. Pencil and watercolor drawings ably illustrate this very short story.

Massie, Diane R.

2031 *The Komodo Dragon's Jewels.* Ill. by author. Macmillan, 1975, o.p. SERIES: Ready-to-Read. SUBJECTS: Humorous stories; Lizards — Fiction. RL C.

The Komodo Dragon, a giant lizard, gets his chance to see the jewels shining from the mainland when he is mistaken for a passenger and is allowed aboard a tour boat. The fun found in the text is augmented by the outlandish ink and wash illustrations.

Mathis, Sharon Bell

2032 *Red Dog Blue Fly: Football Poems.* Ill. by Jan Spivey Gilchrist. Viking, 1991, ISBN 0-670-83623-0. SUBJECTS: African Americans; Poetry; Sports — Football. RL C.

The fears and glories, the coaches and parents, the cheerleaders and playoff pizza, are all a part of the pulsing, rhythmic poems about America's favorite sport. Strong illustrations are done primarily in blues and greens, with yellow and purple accents.

Matthews, Morgan

2033 *What's It Like to Be a Farmer.* Ill. by Anne Kennedy. Troll, 1990, ISBN 0-8167-1803-2. SERIES: What's It Like to Be a . . . SUBJECTS: Careers; Farm and country life. RL C.

The Smith family has a large farm with a variety of crops and animals. Readers follow the Smiths through a year as they plant, tend crops and animals, and harvest. Ink drawings with color washes effectively illustrate the text.

2034 *What's It Like to Be a Postal Worker.* Ill. by Mark A. Hicks. Troll, 1990, ISBN 0-8167-1813-X. SERIES: What's It Like to Be a . . . SUBJECTS: Careers; Mail. RL C.

Readers follow letters through the postal system and learn about the various jobs and machines involved in getting mail from place to place. Illustrations, done with pen and ink drawings with color washes, help to explain the system.

2035 *What's It Like to Be a Railroad Worker.* Ill. by Lynn Sweat. Troll, 1990, ISBN 0-8167-1815-6. SERIES: What's It Like to Be a . . . SUBJECTS: Careers; Trains. RL C.

As Jimmy and his parents travel on the passenger train, the conductor tells the boy about trains and how they operate. Ink drawings with color washes supplement the text.

Matthias, Catherine

2036 *I Can Be a Police Officer.* Ill. with photos. Childrens Press, 1984, ISBN 0-516-01840-X. SERIES: I Can Be. SUBJECTS: Careers; Police. RL B.

Supported by full-color photographs and drawings, this book gives an overview of police work in the United States and abroad. It also discusses the type of work done by American police officers and the educational requirements for entry into the force.

2037 *I Love Cats.* Ill. by Tom Dunnington. Children's Press, 1983, ISBN 0-516-02041-2. SERIES: Rookie Reader. SUBJECTS: Pets — Cats — Fiction; Stories in rhyme. RL B.

A plump little boy admits that he likes all kinds of animals but he loves cats. Like other books in the Rookie Reader series, the text here is very brief. It relies on its rhyme and humorous pictures to interest readers.

2038 *Out the Door.* Ill. by Eileen M. Neill. Children's Press, 1982, ISBN 0-516-03560-6. SERIES: Rookie Reader. SUBJECTS: School stories. RL A.

A forgetful little girl has to go back home for her lunchbox and then her umbrella as she tries to get to the school bus and a full day at school. The very brief text relies on the flat ink and wash pictures to carry the story.

2039 *Over-Under.* Ill. by Gene Sharp. Children's Press, 1984, ISBN 0-516-02048-X. SERIES: Rookie Reader. SUBJECTS: Concepts — Fiction; Playgrounds — Fiction. RL A.

Matthias, Catherine (cont.)

A young African American child demonstrates on/off, in/out, over/under, around/between, inside/outside, above/below, and up/down using playground equipment. Cheerful ink and watercolor paintings illustrate the concepts mentioned in the very brief text.

2040 *Too Many Balloons*. Ill. by Gene Sharp. Children's Press, 1982, ISBN 0-516-03633-5. SERIES: Rookie Reader. SUBJECTS: Balloons — Fiction; Concepts — Numbers — Fiction; Zoos — Fiction. RL A.
Buying one balloon to correspond to the first animal she sees at the zoo, the little girl keeps buying balloons as she visits animals until she has 55 balloons and starts to float away. The brief and simple text has full-color paintings with ink details.

May, D. J.

2041 *Mr. Marble's Moose*. Ill. by Sabra Smith. Word, 1991, ISBN 0-8499-0969-4. SERIES: Word Kids. SUBJECTS: Christian life — Fiction; Moose — Fiction. RL B.
Though Mr. Marble's moose Sam loves to express his happiness with life and his joy in God by singing, the noise bothers others. Sam learns how to "make a joyful noise" while being kind to others. Bold cartoon-like pictures fill the picture book-size reader.

Mayer, Cassie

2042 *Getting Around by Bicycle*. Ill. with photos. Heinemann, 2005, ISBN 1-4034-8391-4. SERIES: Getting Around. SUBJECTS: Bicycles and bicycling. RL B.
Photographs show a tricycle, a rickshaw, and bicycles loaded with people and goods. Primarily Asian illustrations.

2043 *Getting Around by Boat*. Ill. with photos. Heinemann, 2005, ISBN 1-4034-8389-2. SERIES: Getting Around. SUBJECTS: Boats and boating. RL B.
Some vocabulary and a picture glossary are appended to a book about the ways in which boats, primarily Asian, are used.

2044 *Getting Around by Car*. Ill. with photos. Heinemann, 2005, ISBN 1-4034-8394-9. SERIES: Getting Around. SUBJECTS: Cars. RL B.
A very basic book about cars, illustrated with photographs, with a picture glossary appended.

2045 *Getting Around by Plane*. Ill. with photos. Heinemann, 2005, ISBN 1-4034-8390-6. SERIES: Getting Around. SUBJECTS: Airplanes. RL B.
The most interesting photograph is that of a firefighting plane. Basic vocabulary is illustrated with photographs from Asia.

2046 *Getting Around by Train*. Ill. with photos. Heinemann, 2005, ISBN 1-4034-8392-2. SERIES: Getting Around. SUBJECTS: Trains. RL B.
Photographs of trains are accompanied by basic text.

2047 *Getting Around on Foot*. Ill. with photos. Heinemann, 2005, ISBN 1-4034-8393-0. SERIES: Getting Around. SUBJECTS: Walking. RL B.
The most interesting photograph is that of people crossing a busy river walking on a bamboo pole.

Mayer, Gina, and Mercer Mayer

2048 *Rosie's Mouse*. Ill. by Mercer Mayer. Western, 1992, ISBN 0-307-11468-6. SERIES: Golden Star Reader. SUBJECTS: Cleanliness — Fiction; Hippopotami — Fiction; Mice — Fiction. RL C.
Rosie, a hippo, has the neatest of houses until a little uninvited mouse moves in. Then things become very messy and the big but gentle-hearted hippo tries to find ways to get rid of the mouse. Humorous, cartoon-like paintings are done in Mayer's typical high-child-appeal style.

Mayer, Mercer

2049 *Herbert the Timid Dragon*. Ill. by author. Western, 1991, ISBN 0-307-11463-5. SERIES: Golden Star Reader. SUBJECTS: Dragons — Fiction; Fear — Fiction; Knights and knighthood — Fiction. RL C.
Herbert, a fearful dragon, thinks he is rescuing a princess and ends up with a spunky young woman who terrorizes him. When she really is in danger the dragon comes to her rescue. The busy

watercolor and ink-lined comic pictures have more child appeal than the rather forced text.

2050 *Little Critter's Read-It-Yourself Storybook: Six Funny Easy-to-Read Stories*. Ill. by author. Western, 1993, ISBN 0-307-16840-9. SUBJECTS: Family life — Fiction; Friendship — Fiction; Sibling rivalry — Fiction. RL A.

Little Critter shares his family, pets, and friends in six brief but humorous stories. The text is intentionally straightforward while the comic watercolor animal characters inject humor and fun into the stories.

2051 *This Is My Friend*. Ill. by author. Western, 1989, ISBN 0-307-11685-9. SERIES: Easy Readers. SUBJECTS: Friendship — Fiction. RL A.

The ins and outs of friendship are seen in the humorous illustrations and brief text of this story. The pictures are done in watercolors with ink definition.

Maynard, Christopher

2052 *Incredible Dinosaurs*. Ill. with photos. Covent Garden Books, pap., 1994, ISBN 1-56458-551-4. SERIES: Snap Shot. SUBJECTS: Dinosaurs. RL C.

A chatty tone and colorful photographic layout let children know that this is not only about their favorite topic but it is also fun. Most dinosaurs are given a double page spread with much of the information in captions. Table of contents and index provide access.

2053 *Incredible Flying Machines*. Ill. with photos. Covent Garden Books, pap., 1994, ISBN 1-56458-552-2. SERIES: Snap Shot. SUBJECTS: Aeronautics; Airplanes. RL C.

A light tone, creative layout of photographs, and unusual placement of some text should make this highly attractive to young readers. The brief text is helped by the captioning of pictures, which as a whole present a limited history of flight.

2054 *Incredible Little Monsters*. Ill. with photos. Covent Garden Books, pap., 1994, ISBN 1-56458-553-0. SERIES: Snap Shot. SUBJECTS: Animals; Bats; Reptiles and amphibians. RL C.

Lizards, bats, fish, turtles, and other unusual animals are given double page spreads with many photographic silhouettes to highlight their special features. The text is chatty and fun, and the entire book has much child appeal. Tight binding causes some of the text or pictures to be lost.

2055 *Incredible Mini-Beasts*. Ill. with photos. Covent Garden Books, pap., 1994, ISBN 1-56458-554-9. SERIES: Snap Shot. SUBJECTS: Animals; Insects; Spiders. RL C.

Words and phrases like "Deadly jaws . . ." and "Beware the poison fang!" are in bold type near colorful photographs and are sure to attract the interest of readers. The insects and spiders focused on include the tarantula, praying mantis, and cockroach. Format and information are guaranteed to be fun.

Mayo, Gretchen

2056 *Big Trouble for Tricky Rabbit*. Ill. by author. Walker, 1994, ISBN 0-8027-8275-2. SERIES: Native American Trickster Tales. SUBJECTS: Folklore — Native Americans; Rabbits. RL B.

Gathered from a variety of sources, the six stories in this collection are all very well done. The rhythm of the language and the subtle paintings expertly capture the spirit of these stories. After each story, sources are given and the final section of the book gives additional source information.

2057 *Here Comes Tricky Rabbit!* Ill. by author. Walker, 1994, ISBN 0-8027-8273-6. SERIES: Native American Trickster Tales. SUBJECTS: Folklore — Native Americans; Rabbits — Fiction. RL B.

Cherokee, Kickapoo, and Apache stories are the roots for three of the six tales in this volume. Carefully retold, including the sources at the end of each story, and illustrated with subtle yet effective paintings, these folktales will be entertaining for young readers and useful for storytelling.

Meddaugh, Susan

2058 *Too Short Fred*. Ill. by author. Houghton Mifflin, 1978, o.p. SUBJECTS: Pets — Cats — Fiction; Self-esteem — Fiction. RL A.

Though he constantly complains of being short, Fred's size is usually no hindrance to having fun. Pencil and chalk drawings show an assortment of

Meddaugh, Susan (cont.)

humanized cats illustrating the action in the text. Children will enjoy Fred and his friends in this well-written, well-illustrated piece.

Medearis, Angela Shelf

2059 *Here Comes the Snow*. Ill. by Maxie Chambliss. Scholastic, pap., 1996, ISBN 0-606-09407-5. SERIES: Hello Reader! SUBJECTS: Winter — Fiction. RL A. LEXILE BR.

This story captures the anticipation and joyful play of well-padded children in the snow.

2060 *Lucy's Quiet Book*. Ill. by Lisa Campbell Ernst. Harcourt, 2004, ISBN 0-15-205144-9. SERIES: Green Light Readers. SUBJECTS: Books and reading — Fiction. RL B.

Lucy finds that her six noisy brothers quiet down when she reads to them, as do the noisy preschoolers in the library.

2061 *On the Way to the Pond*. Ill. by Lorinda B. Cauley. Harcourt, 2006, ISBN 0-15-205599-1. SERIES: Green Light Readers. SUBJECTS: Hippopotami — Fiction; Picnics — Fiction; Tigers — Fiction. RL B.

Herbert the hippo can't be found when he's swimming in the pond. A recipe for a popcorn picnic snack and directions for making a book of family activities are appended.

2062 *The 100th Day of School*. Ill. by Joan Holub. Scholastic, 1996, ISBN 1-59054-394-7. SERIES: Scholastic Reader. SUBJECTS: Mathematics — Fiction; School stories; Stories in rhyme. RL B. LEXILE 340L.

On the 100th day, the students count to 100, have a 100-word spelling bee, jump rope, decorate a tree, draw and measure, and recycle, all using the number 100. Pen and wash drawings add action.

2063 *We Eat Dinner in the Bathtub*. Ill. by Jacqueline Rogers. Scholastic, pap., 1996, ISBN 0-590-73886-0. SERIES: Scholastic Reader. SUBJECTS: Humorous stories. RL A. LEXILE 270L.

Harris invites Josh to dinner, but has to explain that his family cooks in the bedroom, parks the car in the kitchen, and eats in the bathtub. Watercolors from different perspectives enhance the nonsense.

Meeks, Esther

2064 *The Dog That Took the Train*. Ill. by Ted Schroeder. Follett, 1972, o.p. SERIES: Beginning-to-Read. SUBJECTS: Lost, being — Fiction; Pets — Dogs — Fiction; Trains — Fiction. RL B.

The conductor of a train tries to find the owner of a dog that has strayed onto the passenger line. The lively full-color pictures add excitement to this book.

Meister, Cari

2065 *My Pony Jack*. Ill. by Amy Young. Viking, 2004, ISBN 0-670-05917-X. SERIES: Viking Easy-to-Read. SUBJECTS: Horses — Fiction. RL A.

A young girl grooms a pony. Descriptors and illustrations are very simple.

2066 *My Pony Jack at Riding Lessons*. Ill. by Amy Young. Viking, 2005, ISBN 0-670-05918-8. SERIES: Viking Easy-to-Read. SUBJECTS: Sports — Horseback riding — Fiction. RL A.

Pony words are appended to this brief outline of a riding lesson, including taking care of the pony. The illustrations are similarly simple.

2067 *Skinny and Fats, Best Friends*. Ill. by Steve Bjorkman. Holiday House, 2001, ISBN 0-8234-1692-5. SERIES: Holiday House Reader. SUBJECTS: Friendship — Fiction; Pigs — Fiction; Rabbits — Fiction. RL B.

A recipe for marshmallow pie follows three adventures of these best friends.

2068 *Tiny the Snow Dog*. Ill. by Rich Davis. Viking, 2001, ISBN 0-670-89117-7. SERIES: Viking Easy-to-Read. SUBJECTS: Pets — Dogs — Fiction; Weather — Snow — Fiction. RL A.

Tiny the dog is *not* tiny and is always visible to the reader, if not to his boy.

2069 *Tiny's Bath*. Ill. by Rich Davis. Viking, 1999, ISBN 0-670-87962-2. SERIES: Viking Easy-to-Read. SUBJECTS: Pets — Dogs — Fiction. RL A. LEXILE BR.

Tiny heads right back to the mud after his bath in his boy's pool. Simple drawings underscore the basic, repetitive vocabulary.

2070 *When Tiny Was Little*. Ill. by Rich Davis. Viking, 1999, o.p. SERIES: Viking Easy-to-Read. SUBJECTS: Pets — Dogs — Fiction. RL A.

Tiny, the huge dog, still thinks he is tiny, but big or small, he's his boy's best friend.

Merriam, Eve

2071 *The Birthday Cow*. Ill. by Guy Michel. Knopf, 1978, o.p. SUBJECTS: Nonsense; Poetry. RL B.

This book contains fifteen nonsensical poems about silly things that children will be familiar with and enjoy, such as birthdays, Halloween, clowns, and cows. Illustrated with suitably whimsical multicolored drawings.

Meyers, Susan

2072 *The Truth About Gorillas*. Ill. by John Hamberger. Dutton, 1980, o.p. SERIES: Smart Cat. SUBJECTS: Gorillas. RL C.

Children reading this introduction to gorillas will find that it presents the gorilla's life in an interesting way. The book is well researched and well written, and encourages its readers to care about wildlife. The realistic illustrations are done with pencil and washes.

Michaels, Anna

2073 *Best Friends*. Ill. by G. Brian Karas. Harcourt, 2001, ISBN 0-15-205136-3. SERIES: Green Light Readers. SUBJECTS: Friendship — Fiction. RL A.

Dan and Zack pick apples together, and share a discovery under a tree. Very basic vocabulary is used, accompanied by appealing colored pencil drawings and followed by some reading questions and activities.

Milburn, Constance

2074 *The Seasons*. Ill. by Ann Baum. Bookwright, 1988, ISBN 0-531-18179-0. SERIES: Let's Look At. SUBJECTS: Seasons. RL C.

Originally published in England, this book offers a clear explanation of why we have seasons and how they differ in various parts of the world. Illustrated with full-color pictures, including one that shows the Earth's rotation around the sun and how this causes the seasons.

Miles, Miska

2075 *Noisy Gander*. Ill. by Leslie Morrill. Dutton, 1978, o.p. SERIES: Unicorn Book. SUBJECTS: Farm and country life — Fiction; Geese — Fiction. RL C.

The other animals mock the little gosling's father for his constant honking at animals until his vigilance — and honking — rids the barnyard of a coyote. The story, told simply and well, has realistic pencil drawings.

2076 *Tree House Town*. Ill. by Emily A. McCully. Little, Brown, 1974, o.p. SUBJECTS: Conservation — Fiction. RL C.

As children come into the forest to build treehouses, they drive out the animals. Night after night, as the treehouses multiply during the day, the animals leave for the other side of the forest. With its expressive ink and colored pencil drawings, this story could lead to discussion of conservation.

Milgrim, David

2077 *See Pip Point*. Ill. by author. Atheneum, pap., 2004, ISBN 0-689-85140-5. SERIES: Ready-to-Read. SUBJECTS: Bees — Fiction; Mice — Fiction; Robots — Fiction. RL A. LEXILE 150L.

This imaginative story uses very few words to tell the story of Pip's balloon adventure. Boldly outlined characters support the story.

2078 *Swing Otto Swing!* Ill. by author. Atheneum, 2004, ISBN 0-689-85564-8. SERIES: Ready-to-Read. SUBJECTS: Mice — Fiction; Robots — Fiction. RL A.

Otto the robot figures out a safer way to swing than from jungle vines. Bold illustrations are as simple as the story.

2079 *Why Benny Barks*. Ill. by author. Random House, 1994, ISBN 0-679-96157-7. SERIES: Step into Reading. SUBJECTS: Pets — Dogs — Fiction; Stories in rhyme. RL A.

Milgrim, David (cont.)

A little boy tries to understand what makes his dog, Benny, bark so much. Finally, he decides that, even though he has no answer, Benny is still his friend. Cartoonish and childlike watercolors are very effective with this humorous text.

Milios, Rita

2080 *Bears, Bears, Everywhere*. Ill. by Keiko Motoyama. Children's Press, 2002, ISBN 0-516-22847-1. SERIES: Rookie Reader. SUBJECTS: Concepts — Numbers; Stories in rhyme; Toys — Teddy bears — Fiction. RL A.

A rhymed counting book features teddy bears everywhere, shown with simple lined drawings.

2081 *The Hungry Billy Goat*. Ill. by Mary C. Walters. Children's Press, 1989, ISBN 0-516-02090-0. SERIES: Rookie Reader. SUBJECTS: Goats — Fiction; Humorous stories. RL A.

A little boy describes the things a very hungry goat eats, including the child's shoe, shirt, hat, and scarf. The limited vocabulary is supported by pen and ink drawings with color washes.

2082 *I Am*. Ill. by Clovis Martin. Children's Press, 1987, ISBN 0-516-42081-X. SERIES: Rookie Reader. SUBJECTS: English language — Synonyms and antonyms — Fiction; Stories in rhyme. RL A.

Attractive full-color pictures of children with different cultural backgrounds, some with physical impairments, accompany a brief rhyming text. Together they explain opposites such as *up* and *down*, and compare and contrast words such as *say* and *do*, and *one* and *many*.

2083 *Sneaky Pete*. Ill. by Clovis Martin. Children's Press, 1989, ISBN 0-516-02092-7. SERIES: Rookie Reader. SUBJECTS: Games — Fiction; Hiding — Fiction. RL A.

No one can find Pete at home or with his friends. Pete is clever enough to be the best at hide-and-seek and at finding himself a good place to hide and read. Colorful ink and water-color pictures give clues to Pete's whereabouts while adding fun to the story.

Miller, Jay

2084 *American Indian Games*. Ill. with photos. Children's Press, 1996, ISBN 0-561-20136-0. SERIES: True Book. SUBJECTS: Games; Native Americans. RL C. LEXILE 770L.

A map shows the location of 16 tribes of Native Americans. Their toys include those intended for fun, and those for learning adult tasks. A sled made from buffalo ribs is especially interesting. Lacrosse, of course, is a Native American game.

Miller, Pam

2085 *Sand*. Ill. by Rick Stromoski. Children's Press, 1999, ISBN 0-516-22013-6. SERIES: Rookie Reader. SUBJECTS: Seashore — Fiction; Stories in rhyme. RL A.

Two cartoon children show the variety and uses of sand in this rhyming text using 61 words.

Miller, Sara Swan

2086 *Better than TV*. Ill. by Michael Chesworth. Delacorte, 1998, ISBN 0-385-32325-5. SERIES: Yearling First Choice Chapter Book. SUBJECTS: Pets — Dogs — Fiction; Play — Fiction; Television — Fiction. RL B. LEXILE 260L.

A sly dog pulls the plug on the TV, and Chris and Erin produce TV shows for the family in their basement studio.

2087 *Cat in the Bag*. Ill. by Benton Mahan. Children's Press, 2001, ISBN 0-516-22014-4. SERIES: Rookie Reader. SUBJECTS: Pets — Cats — Fiction; Travel — Fiction. RL A. LEXILE BR.

Fifty-six words relate a girl's difficulties in packing while the cat gets into her suitcase.

2088 *Chickens*. Ill. with photos. Children's Press, 1999, ISBN 0-516-21576-0. SERIES: True Book. SUBJECTS: Animals — Farm; Chickens. RL C.

There are six chickens for each human on the planet! There are more than 50 breeds in the United States alone, some of which are pictured and described. Close-ups of the combs are especially interesting.

2089 *Cows*. Ill. with photos. Children's Press, 1999, ISBN 0-516-23106-5. SERIES: True

Book. SUBJECTS: Animals — Farm; Cows. RL C.

Instructions on how to make your own butter are included, as well as Web sites for 4-H and the Dairy Council.

2090 *Goats*. Ill. with photos. Children's Press, 1999, ISBN 0-516-21578-7. SERIES: True Book. SUBJECTS: Animals — Farm; Goats. RL C.

More people around the world get milk from goats than from cows. Goats were tamed more than 9,000 years ago. There are more than 210 breeds today.

2091 *Pigs*. Ill. with photos. Children's Press, 2000, ISBN 0-516-21579-5. SERIES: True Book. SUBJECTS: Animals — Farm; Pigs. RL C.

Eight thousand years ago, wild pigs were domesticated. They have become the most popular food, except for Muslims and Jews. Crossbreeds grow faster, have more young, and stay healthier than purebreds.

2092 *Sheep*. Ill. with photos. Children's Press, 1999, ISBN 0-516-21580-9. SERIES: True Book. SUBJECTS: Animals — Farm; Sheep. RL C.

In Iran, a 6,000-year-old statue of a sheep was found. Half the land in New Zealand is given over to raising sheep. Wool, cheese, and other sheep milk products are sold all over the world. Some of the care of sheep is illustrated.

2093 *Three More Stories You Can Read to Your Cat*. Ill. by True Kelley. Houghton Mifflin, 2003, ISBN 0-618-11035-6. SUBJECTS: Birthdays — Fiction; Pets — Cats — Fiction; Weather — Snow — Fiction. RL B.

Stories for a cat feature happy and less happy birthdays, snow *not* being fun, and getting worn out trying to be fed. An inventive twist from the cat's point of view, illustrated with ink and wash illustrations showing an irritable black cat with white face and paws.

2094 *Three Stories You Can Read to Your Dog*. Ill. by True Kelley. Houghton Mifflin, 1995, ISBN 0-395-69938-X. SUBJECTS: Pets — Dogs — Fiction. RL B.

Three stories told from the dog's point of view: keeping burglars away, burying a bone in the yard, and becoming a Wild Dog rather than a House Dog. Kelley has captured the dog asleep and zooming home to be fed.

Mills, Claudia

2095 *Gus and Grandpa*. Ill. by Catherine Stock. Farrar, Straus & Giroux, 1997, ISBN 0-374-32824-2. SERIES: Sunburst. SUBJECTS: Grandparents — Fiction. RL B. LEXILE 400L.

Gus and Grandpa share secrets from Gus's parents about Grandpa's forgetfulness. Grandpa expects Gus to clean up the mess he made trying to train Grandpa's dog, Skipper, to be a circus star. Illustrations warm their friendship.

2096 *Gus and Grandpa and Show-and-Tell*. Ill. by Catherine Stock. Farrar, Straus & Giroux, 2000, ISBN 0-374-32819-6. SUBJECTS: Grandparents — Fiction; School stories. RL B. LEXILE 450L.

Gus runs out of ideas for show-and-tell in first grade — until he brings Grandpa for the one featuring Colorado history. Wonderful, warm drawings underscore the special relationship between these two.

2097 *Gus and Grandpa and the Christmas Cookies*. Ill. by Catherine Stock. Farrar, Straus & Giroux, 1996, ISBN 0-374-42815-8. SERIES: Sunburst. SUBJECTS: Christmas — Fiction; Cookery — Fiction; Grandparents — Fiction. RL B. LEXILE 560L.

Grandpa's neighbor ladies can't imagine that a man living alone can bake, so Gus and Grandpa take their excess bounty to the red kettle Santa. Decorative illustrations capture the beauty and joy of Christmas giving.

2098 *Gus and Grandpa and the Halloween Costume*. Ill. by Catherine Stock. Farrar, Straus & Giroux, 2001, ISBN 0-374-32816-1. SERIES: Sunburst. SUBJECTS: Grandparents — Fiction; Halloween — Fiction. RL B.

Gus's dad's old Mountie costume turns out to be a hit when Gus needs a costume. Stock's drawings capture the warmest hugs!

2099 *Gus and Grandpa and the Piano Lesson*. Ill. by Catherine Stock. Farrar, Straus & Giroux, 2004, ISBN 0-374-32814-5.

Mills, Claudia (cont.)

SUBJECTS: Grandparents — Fiction; Music and musicians — Fiction. RL B.

When Gus has trouble remembering his recital piece, Grandpa has a novel way to help him practice — involving the whole family.

2100 *Gus and Grandpa and the Two-Wheeled Bike.* Ill. by Catherine Stock. Farrar, Straus & Giroux, 1997, ISBN 0-374-32821-8. SUBJECTS: Bicycles and bicycling — Fiction; Grandparents — Fiction. RL B. LEXILE 430L.

Grandpa's patience helps Gus learn how to give up his training wheels.

2101 *Gus and Grandpa at Basketball.* Ill. by Catherine Stock. Farrar, Straus & Giroux, 2001, ISBN 0-374-32818-8. SUBJECTS: Grandparents — Fiction; Sports — Basketball — Fiction. RL B. LEXILE 310L.

Grandpa is very sensitive to Gus's lack of self-confidence at Gus's last game of the season.

2102 *Gus and Grandpa at the Hospital.* Ill. by Catherine Stock. Farrar, Straus & Giroux, 1997, ISBN 0-374-32827-7. SUBJECTS: Grandparents — Fiction; Hospitals — Fiction. RL B. LEXILE 410L.

Gus and Grandpa buy a lottery ticket, but decide that being together after Grandpa's heart attack is way more valuable.

2103 *Gus and Grandpa Go Fishing.* Ill. by Catherine Stock. Farrar, Straus & Giroux, 2002, ISBN 0-374-32815-3. SUBJECTS: Grandparents — Fiction; Sports — Fishing — Fiction. RL B.

Gus and Grandpa turn out to be the successful fishermen in the family, but only after a lot of persistence.

2104 *Gus and Grandpa Ride the Train.* Ill. by Catherine Stock. Farrar, Straus & Giroux, pap., 2000, ISBN 0-374-42813-1. SUBJECTS: Grandparents — Fiction; Trains — Fiction. RL B. LEXILE 440L.

When Grandpa forgets where he put the tickets for their steam train ride, Gus helps him find them. They never forget that they love one another.

Mills, J. Elizabeth

2105 *Beauty and the Beast.* Ill. by Barbara Lanza. Scholastic, 2003, o.p. SERIES: Scholastic Reader. SUBJECTS: Folklore. RL B.

This terse retelling of the classic is illustrated with pencil and wash drawings.

Milne, A. A.

2106 *Christopher Robin Leads an Expedition.* Ill. by Ernest H. Shepard. Adapted by Stephen Krensky. Dutton, 2003, ISBN 0-525-46824-2. SERIES: Dutton Easy Reader. SUBJECTS: Bears — Fiction; Friendship — Fiction. RL B.

This gentle adventure featuring small animals accompanying Christopher Robin to search for the North Pole is very faithful to the original language and mood, accented by Ernest Shepard's fine drawings.

2107 *Pooh Goes Visiting.* Ill. by Ernest H. Shepard. Adapted by Stephen Krensky. Dutton, 2002, ISBN 0-525-46821-8. SERIES: Dutton Easy Reader. SUBJECTS: Bears — Fiction; Friendship — Fiction. RL B.

When Pooh visits Rabbit and consumes all the honey, he can't get out of Rabbit's hole. Only after a week of being read to by Christopher Robin does Pooh lose enough weight to be pulled/pushed out of the hole. Shepard's marvelous ink drawings decorate the story.

2108 *Pooh Invents a New Game.* Ill. by Ernest H. Shepard. Adapted by Stephen Krensky. Dutton, 2003, ISBN 0-525-46823-4. SERIES: Dutton Easy Reader. SUBJECTS: Bears — Fiction; Friendship — Fiction. RL B.

Pooh's wonder at the pine cone reappearing on the other side of the bridge, about Eeyore and the game called Poohsticks, ending with Eeyore being bounced into the river. Very quiet story with great adventure.

2109 *Tigger Comes to the Forest.* Ill. by Ernest H. Shepard. Adapted by Stephen Krensky. Dutton, 2002, ISBN 0-525-46822-6. SERIES: Dutton Easy Reader. SUBJECTS: Bears — Fiction; Friendship — Fiction; Tigers — Fiction. RL B.

Tigger doesn't understand mirrors; he finds out he doesn't like honey, haycorns (Piglet's favorite), or thistles (Eeyore's favorite), but he does like Extract of Malt (Kanga's medicine).

Milton, Joyce

2110 *Bats: Creatures of the Night*. Ill. by Judith Moffatt. Putnam, 1993, ISBN 0-448-40193-2. SERIES: All Aboard Reading. SUBJECTS: Bats. RL B.

How bats live and raise their young, what they eat, and their relationship to humans and the environment are touched on in this carefully and interestingly written look at the only flying mammal. Excellent art is created from pictures using paper-cut figures and designs.

2111 *Dinosaur Days*. Ill. by Richard Roe. Random House, 1985, ISBN 0-394-97023-3. SERIES: Step into Reading. SUBJECTS: Dinosaurs. RL B.

Fans of dinosaurs will enjoy the brief but informative text. When a dinosaur is introduced, the pronunciation of its name is given along with a few important facts about it. The detailed drawings are in colored pencil.

2112 *Heavy-Duty Trucks*. Ill. by Richard Courtney. Random House, 2002, ISBN 0-679-88130-1. SERIES: Step into Reading. SUBJECTS: Trucks. RL B. LEXILE 470L.

Tractors, street sweepers and garbage trucks, cherry pickers, pumper and ladder trucks, bulldozers and backhoes, dump trucks, cranes, and semis for moving furniture and hauling cars, logs, or live animals are some of the vehicles highlighted. The differences are shown in the illustrations.

2113 *Honeybees*. Ill. by Pete Mueller. Grosset & Dunlap, 2003, ISBN 0-448-43142-4. SERIES: All Aboard Reading. SUBJECTS: Bees; Insects. RL B.

The life cycle and benefits of honeybees are presented; illustrated with watercolor drawings.

2114 *Pocahontas: An American Princess*. Ill. by Shelly Hehenberger. Grosset & Dunlap, pap., 2000, ISBN 0-448-42181-X. SERIES: All Aboard Reading. SUBJECTS: Biographies; Native Americans; United States — Colonial period. RL C.

The story of the relationship between Pocahontas and John Smith mirrors the unpredictable relationship between the English and the Native Americans at Jamestown. The drawings are pedestrian.

2115 *Sacajawea: Her True Story*. Ill. by Shelly Hehenberger. Grosset & Dunlap, 2001, ISBN 0-448-42616-1. SERIES: All Aboard Reading. SUBJECTS: Biographies; Native Americans. RL B.

Milton has written a very complete biography of Sacajawea using simple language. The pastel drawings are pedestrian.

2116 *Secrets of the Mummies*. Ill. by Dolores Santoliquido. Random House, 1984, o.p. SERIES: Step-Up. SUBJECTS: Egypt, ancient; Mummies. RL C.

An interesting and instructive narrative tells about mummies in general and those of ancient Egypt in particular. The description of the making of mummies is fascinating as are the sections on tombs and animal mummies. The lengthy text dominates well-chosen black-and-white photographs.

2117 *Wild, Wild Wolves*. Ill. by Larry Schwinger. Random House, 1992, ISBN 0-679-91052-2. SERIES: Step into Reading. SUBJECTS: Wolves. RL B.

Their dwindling population worldwide and their misunderstood nature are mentioned along with discussion of the life cycle and behavior of wolves and their place in nature, plus some American Indian folklore. Fine watercolor and pencil pictures beautifully capture the animal.

Minarik, Else H.

2118 *Cat and Dog*. Ill. by Fritz Siebel. HarperCollins, 1960, ISBN 0-06-074247-X. SERIES: Early I Can Read. SUBJECTS: Pets — Cats — Fiction; Pets — Dogs — Fiction. RL A. LEXILE 180L.

Imaginative mischief as Dog chases Cat, threatening all sorts of consequences, which often befall the chaser. Extremely appealing drawings enhance the text.

2119 *Father Bear Comes Home*. Ill. by Maurice Sendak. HarperCollins, pap., 1959, ISBN 0-06-024231-0. SERIES: I Can Read. SUBJECTS: Bears — Fiction; Family life — Fiction; Mythical creatures — Fiction. RL A.

Minarik, Else H. (cont.)

Father Bear is finally home from ocean fishing and Little Bear and his family now share problems with hiccups, a picnic by the river, and fantasizing about a mermaid. This delightful story is a good portrayal of a nuclear family. Detailed drawings are of dignified turn-of-the-century bears.

2120 *A Kiss for Little Bear*. Ill. by Maurice Sendak. HarperCollins, 1968, o.p. SERIES: I Can Read. SUBJECTS: Animals — Fiction; Bears — Fiction. RL B. LEXILE 100L.

As Hen says, delivering a kiss from Grandmother to Little Bear "gets all mixed up" when one animal after another is recruited to send it on. The skunks' wedding results, however. Charming Sendak animals.

2121 *Little Bear*. Ill. by Maurice Sendak. Newfield, 1957, ISBN 0-06-444004-4. SERIES: I Can Read. SUBJECTS: Bears — Fiction. RL B. LEXILE 370L.

Little Bear decides that his own fur coat will keep him warm; he makes his own birthday soup; he yearns to fly. Comfort is still in his mother's lap.

2122 *Little Bear and the Missing Pie*. Ill. by Chris Hahner. HarperCollins, 2002, ISBN 0-694-01705-1. SERIES: Maurice Sendak's Little Bear. SUBJECTS: Bears — Fiction. RL B.

Hen, Owl, Duck, and Emily are in turn suspected of stealing the freshly baked pie.

2123 *Little Bear's Bad Day*. Ill. by David T. Wenzel. HarperCollins, 2003, ISBN 1-4131-6955-4. SERIES: Maurice Sendak's Little Bear. SUBJECTS: Bears — Fiction; Friendship — Fiction. RL B.

Friends Cat and Hen cheer up Little Bear when he bumps his nose, spills his milk and his paints, and hurts his paw on a fishing hook. Expressive drawings by David Wenzel.

2124 *Little Bear's Friend*. Ill. by Maurice Sendak. HarperCollins, 1960, ISBN 0-06-024255-8. SERIES: I Can Read. SUBJECTS: Bears — Fiction; Friendship — Fiction. RL B.

Four gentle stories of a little girl and her doll, Owl, Duck, and Little Bear

2125 *Little Bear's Visit*. Ill. by Maurice Sendak. HarperCollins, 1961, ISBN 0-06-444023-0. SERIES: I Can Read. SUBJECTS: Bears — Fiction; Grandparents — Fiction. RL B. LEXILE 290L.

Little Bear's grandparents tell stories of letting a fledgling robin fly free, and a goblin. There is lots of hugging in this bear family.

2126 *No Fighting, No Biting!* Ill. by Maurice Sendak. HarperCollins, 1958, ISBN 0-06-444015-X. SERIES: I Can Read. SUBJECTS: Books and reading — Fiction; Storytelling — Fiction. RL B.

Light-foot and Quick-foot are so busy squabbling that a hungry alligator nearly eats them. These stories are made up by Cousin Joan who wants her small cousins, Rosa and Willy, to stop squabbling so she can read. Sendak's illustrations are especially expressive in showing Joan's exasperation.

2127 *Percy and the Five Houses*. Ill. by James Stevenson. Penguin, 1990, ISBN 0-688-08105-3. SUBJECTS: Beavers — Fiction; Houses — Fiction; Humorous stories. RL A.

After Percy, a beaver, finds gold in the stream, he is invited by Ferd Fox to become a member of the House of the Month Club. Percy has fun playing with each fragile dwelling he receives, but finally decides home is the best house of all. Illustrated with zany, comic watercolors.

Mitchell, Barbara

2128 *Cornstalks and Cannonballs*. Ill. by Karen Ritz. Carolrhoda, 1980, o.p. SERIES: On My Own. SUBJECTS: United States — War of 1812. RL B.

Besieged by English warships, the people of Lewes, Delaware, wait until the middle of the night and then, dressed as American soldiers, with cornstalks for guns, scare the English ships away. Based on an actual event, this story is illustrated with realistic blue ink drawings.

2129 *Hush, Puppies*. Ill. by Cherie R. Wyman. Carolrhoda, 1983, ISBN 0-87614-201-3. SERIES: On My Own. SUBJECTS: Cookery — Fiction; United States — 1783–1865 — Fiction. RL C.

Southern folk legends say that hush puppies were created by a clever slave cook to quiet the hounds at her master's fish fry. An entertaining and almost upbeat look at an unfortunate time, this book offers a good story as well as a recipe for hush puppies. Illustrated with ink drawings.

2130 *Tomahawks and Trombones*. Ill. by George Overlie. Carolrhoda, 1982, o.p. SERIES: On My Own. SUBJECTS: Delaware (Native American people); Religion; United States — French and Indian War. RL B.

Waiting for the Delaware Indians to attack on Christmas Day, the Moravians of Bethlehem, Pennsylvania, hide in their homes. Four men take their trombones and play them from a housetop — scaring away the Delaware. This interesting bit of U.S. history is illustrated with realistic paintings.

Mitgutsch, Ali

2131 *From Gold to Money*. Ill. by author. Carolrhoda, 1985, ISBN 0-87614-230-7. SERIES: Start to Finish. SUBJECTS: Money. RL C.

Starting with prehistoric times, Mitgutsch looks at the development of bartering, the use of gold, and then the minting of money. The text is clearly written with good examples and colorful, humorous illustrations that further a child's understanding of trade and money.

2132 *From Idea to Toy*. Ill. by author. Carolrhoda, 1988, ISBN 0-87614-352-4. SERIES: Start to Finish. SUBJECTS: Toys — Teddy bears. RL B.

From reading about the artist sketching live bears at the zoo to learning about the final "blowing in" of foam filling, children are presented with the rudiments of teddy bear creation. The simple, colorful paintings help to describe the process.

2133 *From Picture to Picture Book*. Ill. by author. Carolrhoda, 1988, ISBN 0-87614-353-2. SERIES: Start to Finish. SUBJECTS: Books and reading; Publishing. RL C.

One picture book is followed from an artist's idea and his interpretation of it in words and pictures through the steps leading to the book's sale in a bookstore. Simple yet colorful paintings help to explain the publishing process.

Mizumura, Kazue

2134 *Opossum*. Ill. by author. Crowell, 1974, o.p. SERIES: Let's-Read-and-Find-Out. SUBJECTS: Opossums. RL C.

After seeing an opossum playing dead in the woods, a little boy goes home to find out everything he can about the animal. The interesting information is supported by well-done watercolor pictures in soft hues.

Moncure, Jane B.

2135 *Caring for My Baby Sister*. Ill. by Clovis Martin. Child's World, 1991, ISBN 0-89565-669-8. SERIES: Growing Responsible. SUBJECTS: Behavior — Responsible — Fiction; Family life — Fiction; Siblings — Fiction. RL B.

Becoming a big brother means learning how to hold and feed and watch out for a baby sister. The child in this story positively takes on his new responsibilities and enjoys most of them. The text is illustrated with color paintings with ink definition.

2136 *Caring for My Body*. Ill. by Jodie McCallum. Child's World, 1991, ISBN 0-89565-668-X. SERIES: Growing Responsible. SUBJECTS: Health; Human body. RL B.

A little boy enthusiastically recounts how he and his classmates learned about the importance of healthy behavior: getting exercise, eating properly, and so on. Brief, useful text is illustrated with "cute" colored pictures.

2137 *Caring for My Home*. Ill. by Gwen Connelly. Child's World, 1991, ISBN 0-89565-667-1. SERIES: Growing Responsible. SUBJECTS: Behavior — Helpful; Behavior — Responsible; Cleanliness. RL B.

A child describes how she and everyone in her family pitches in to get things done. She also talks about being responsible for her own things and her room. A very brief and upbeat text, this is illustrated with textbookish color paintings.

2138 *Caring for My Kitty*. Ill. by Christina Rigo. Child's World, 1990, ISBN 0-89565-666-3. SERIES: Growing Responsible. SUBJECTS: Pet care; Pets — Cats. RL B.

A little girl explains the pleasures and the work involved in having her own kitten. The brief text

Moncure, Jane B. (cont.)

is accompanied by "cute" watercolor paintings. Information on pet care is provided to children in a positive way.

2139 *Caring for My Things*. Ill. by Rondi Collette. Child's World, 1991, ISBN 0-89565-670-1. SERIES: Growing Responsible. SUBJECTS: Behavior — Responsible — Fiction; Lost and found possessions — Fiction. RL B.

A little boy learns what it means to be responsible for his belongings as he listens to stories told by his mother and grandparents. Although definitely didactic, this is still thoughtfully written and has child appeal. Illustrations are adequate watercolors with ink definition.

2140 *A Color Clown Comes to Town*. Ill. by Linda Hohag. Child's World, 1988, ISBN 0-89565-369-9. SERIES: Magic Castle Readers. SUBJECTS: Concepts — Colors. RL A.

An imaginative child encounters a clown who introduces her to colors. The little girl insists on their proper use for painting but also learns about mixing primary colors to get secondary colors. Very limited text is accompanied by unimaginative art.

2141 *Dinosaurs: Back in Time*. Ill. by Linda Hohag and Lori Jacobson. Child's World, 1990, ISBN 0-89565-550-0. SERIES: Discovery World. SUBJECTS: Dinosaurs. RL B.

A trip to the museum to see the dinosaur models is made even better by an imaginary trip back in time to see them as they lived then. An index and two pages of activities end the book. Illustrations are childlike and done in watercolors.

2142 *How Seeds Travel: Popguns and Parachutes*. Ill. by Helen Endres. Child's World, 1990, ISBN 0-516-08116-0. SERIES: Discovery World. SUBJECTS: Seeds, roots, and bulbs. RL B.

The many ways plant seeds travel to new areas are shown by the examples of a cherry tree's fruit being eaten by birds, a squirrel burying an oak's acorn, a dandelion's seeds being carried by the wind, and so on. Brief but clear explanations are helped by full-color paintings.

2143 *Kinds of Animals: Flyers, Leapers, Crawlers, Creepers*. Ill. by Linda Hohag and Lori Jacobson. Child's World, 1990, ISBN 0-89565-567-5. SERIES: Discovery World. SUBJECTS: Animals — Classification. RL B.

The classification of animals by insect, reptile, amphibian, and other groups is reinforced as a child sees animal after animal. Distinctive physical characteristics are mentioned for each. A section of reinforcing activities and an index follow. Undistinguished color illustrations accompany the text.

2144 *The Magic Moon Machine*. Ill. by Linda Hohag. Child's World, 1988, ISBN 0-89565-410-5. SERIES: Magic Castle Readers. SUBJECTS: Concepts — Numbers — Fiction; Fantasy; Space travel — Fiction. RL B.

After he decides to join an astronaut on his way to the moon, a boy keeps delaying to gather things he wants to take with him: pets, food, and so on. He has so many things the spacecraft cannot go. A silly story with some chances for counting objects, it is illustrated with "cute" watercolors.

2145 *Night Animals: Wake Up, Little Owl!* Ill. by Lydia Halverson. Child's World, 1990, ISBN 0-89565-568-3. SERIES: Discovery World. SUBJECTS: Animals — Nocturnal. RL C.

With Grandpa as her guide, a child goes into a rural area looking for night animals, including the bat, raccoon, beaver, and owl. Good information is included in the brief but rather difficult text, illustrated with suitably dark watercolors. Index and activity section included.

2146 *Our Columbus Day Book*. Ill. by Jean Shackelford. Child's World, 1986, ISBN 0-89565-347-8. SERIES: Special-Day. SUBJECTS: Biographies; Columbus Day; Explorers and exploration. RL C.

Good ideas for introducing the explorations of Columbus and the difficulties he faced are presented in this introduction to the holiday.

2147 *Rain: A Great Day for Ducks*. Ill. by Joy Friedman. Child's World, 1990, ISBN 0-89565-553-5. SERIES: Discovery World. SUBJECTS: Science experiments — Weather; Weather. RL B.

While a little boy walks in the rain looking at ducks and frogs and plants, the text explains how rain helps things grow, keeps animals alive, and so forth. Following the text is a section of activities and experiments. An index is included. Pictures are attractive watercolor with pencil definition.

2148 *Step into Spring: A New Season*. Ill. by Jenny Williams. Child's World, 1990, ISBN 0-89565-571-3. SERIES: Discovery World. SUBJECTS: Spring. RL B.

A boy and his dog use their senses to discover that spring has finally returned. They taste strawberries, smell lilacs, touch a pussy willow, and listen to birds. Then they explore the farm for signs of the new season. Illustrations are in colored pencil. Activity section and index are included.

Monjo, F. N.

2149 *The Drinking Gourd: A Story of the Underground Railroad*. Ill. by Fred Brenner. HarperCollins, 1970, ISBN 0-06-024330-9. SERIES: I Can Read. SUBJECTS: Slavery; Underground Railroad; United States — History. RL C. LEXILE 370L.

When Tommy's mischief gets him expelled from church, he finds a slave family hiding in the loft in his barn. It is Tommy's quick thinking that saves the family from the bounty hunters later that night. A well-told, suspenseful story with good ink and wash illustrations.

2150 *Indian Summer*. Ill. by Anita Lobel. HarperCollins, 1968, o.p. SERIES: I Can Read. SUBJECTS: Frontier and pioneer life — Fiction; Historical fiction; United States — Revolutionary War — Fiction. RL C.

With their father away fighting the British, four children and their mother have to repulse an attack by Indians. Detailed ink and wash pictures show an ingenious and brave woman and her family.

2151 *Messy Bessey's Closet*. Ill. by Rick Hackney. Children's Press, 1989, ISBN 0-516-02091-9. SERIES: Rookie Reader. SUBJECTS: Behavior — Sharing; Cleanliness; Stories in rhyme. RL A.

After cleaning her room, Bessey opens the closet and all kinds of things tumble out. Then she discovers things she no longer wants and decides to give them away. A very brief rhyming text is lively enough to encourage reading. Colorful illustrations are simple and realistic.

2152 *Messy Bessey's Garden*. Ill. by Richard Hackney. Children's Press, 1991, ISBN 0-516-02008-0. SERIES: Rookie Reader. SUBJECTS: Gardening — Fiction; Stories in rhyme. RL A.

Messy Bessey plants a garden but forgets about it until it is filled with weeds. Then she works hard to earn her pumpkin harvest. A very limited text and full-color illustrations invite children into this story.

2153 *The One Bad Thing About Father*. Ill. by Rocco Negri. HarperCollins, 1970, ISBN 0-06-024334-1. SERIES: I Can Read. SUBJECTS: Family life — Fiction; Historical fiction; Presidents — United States — Fiction. RL C. LEXILE 520L.

Quentin's father, Theodore Roosevelt, could have been just about anything, but Quentin thinks that his father's being president makes life very difficult for the family. The entertaining yet informative text has pictures with detailed ink cross-hatchings and color overlays.

2154 *Poor Richard in France*. Ill. by Brinton Turkle. Holt, Rinehart, 1974, ISBN 0-03-088597-3. SUBJECTS: Biographies; United States — History. RL C.

In five chapters, 7-year-old Benjamin Franklin Bache reports on his 70-year-old grandfather's air baths en route to France, partly to escape the British. His grandson points out his grandfather's eccentricities as well as his spying and accomplishments. Highly recommended for a text with a lot of child-appeal as well as good illustrations.

2155 *The Secret of the Sachem's Tree*. Ill. by Margot Tomes. Coward, McCann, 1972, ISBN 0-698-30446-2. SUBJECTS: Halloween — Fiction; United States — History; Witches — Fiction. RL C.

The true — or untrue — story of how the Connecticut charter was secreted in an oak tree. Lively writing with excellent woodcuts.

Montgomery, Elizabeth R.

2156 *The Mystery of the Boy Next Door*. Ill. by Ethel Gold. Garrard, 1978, o.p. SERIES: For Real. SUBJECTS: Disabilities — Physical and

Montgomery, Elizabeth R. (cont.)

mental — Fiction; Friendship — Fiction. RL A.

To the children the new boy on their street seems unfriendly and intent on ignoring them. They understand his behavior and renew their offers of friendship when they discover he is deaf. An attempt to further the acceptance of the impaired, this book has realistic ink and wash drawings.

Moon, Cliff

2157 *Dairy Cows on the Farm*. Ill. by Anna Jupp. Bookwright, 1983, o.p. SERIES: Down on the Farm. SUBJECTS: Cows; Farm and country life. RL B.

At a typical modern British dairy farm, calves are taken from cows so that milk can be used for humans. The text and full-color pictures then take the reader to the milking area, where modern machinery is discussed and pictured, and finally to a local dairy where milk is bottled.

2158 *Pigs on the Farm*. Ill. by Anna Jupp. Bookwright, 1983, o.p. SERIES: Down on the Farm. SUBJECTS: Farm and country life; Pigs. RL B.

Children are introduced to pig farming in this British book. They are told in text and in full-color realistic pictures how pigs are raised and butchered, and how their meat is sold in markets. Throughout the book questions are occasionally asked so that children get involved in what they are reading.

2159 *Poultry on the Farm*. Ill. by Bill Donohoe. Bookwright, 1983, o.p. SERIES: Down on the Farm. SUBJECTS: Farm and country life; Poultry. RL B.

Both traditional and modern methods of raising poultry are discussed and shown in full-color realistic pictures in this British book. Chickens, ducks, and turkeys are shown on farms and information is provided on hatcheries and the preparation of poultry for markets.

2160 *Sheep on the Farm*. Ill. by Anna Jupp. Bookwright, 1983, o.p. SERIES: Down on the Farm. SUBJECTS: Farm and country life; Sheep. RL C.

In this British book, sheep are shown wandering fields and hills under the protection of a shepherd and his dog. The way in which sheep are shorn and dipped as well as the products that come from their wool and meat are discussed and shown in full-color realistic paintings.

Moore, Elaine

2161 *See You Later, Excavator*. Ill. with photos. Troll, 1999, ISBN 0-606-20901-8. SERIES: Planet Reader. SUBJECTS: Trucks — Fiction. RL A.

Drills, backhoes, dump trucks, bulldozers — and of course, excavators — are depicted with full-page photographs.

Moore, Eva

2162 *Buddy: The First Seeing Eye Dog*. Ill. by Don Bolognese. Scholastic, pap., 1996, ISBN 0-590-26585-7. SERIES: Scholastic Reader. SUBJECTS: Dogs, seeing eye. RL C. LEXILE 600L.

Strong pencil and wash drawings illustrate the story of Morris Frank's seeing eye dog, which he called Buddy. Frank and Buddy publicized ways in which dogs could indeed be the "eyes" for blind people, and were involved in the first school in this country, in Morristown, New Jersey.

2163 *Good Children Get Rewards: A Story of Williamsburg in Colonial Times*. Ill. by Don Bolognese and Elaine Raphael. Scholastic, pap., 2001, ISBN 0-590-92921-6. SERIES: Hello Reader! SUBJECTS: Rebuses; United States — Colonial period. RL B.

The reader gets a tour of colonial Williamsburg by tracing the path of two children making deliveries to and from various shops. Heavily outlined drawings give a flavor of the times.

Moore, Lilian

2164 *Junk Day on Juniper Street and Other Easy-to-Read Stories*. Ill. by Arnold Lobel. Parents Magazine Press, 1969, o.p. SUBJECTS: Family life — Fiction; Farm and country life — Fiction. RL B.

This is a collection of short stories with perfectly plausible happy endings. They are about families, neighbors, old married couples, a silly dog guarding a duckling, and a donkey who helps a boy find a silver mine. The gentle, whimsical stories have detailed and humorous ink drawings.

2165 *A Pickle for a Nickel.* Ill. by Susan Perl. Golden Books, 1961, o.p. SERIES: Read It Yourself. SUBJECTS: Humorous stories; Noise — Fiction; Parrots — Fiction. RL B.

Mr. Bumble likes everything quiet — his house, his car, and even his parrot. While he is working, a neighbor boy talks to the parrot who, to Bumble's consternation, begins to squawk continuously. Detailed, comic illustrations in full-color ink and wash add to the humor.

Moore, Maggie

2166 *Jack and the Beanstalk.* Ill. by Steve Cox. Picture Window, 2003, ISBN 1-4048-0059-X. SUBJECTS: Folklore. RL B.

Another simple retelling, which takes much of the magic out of the story. Illustrations feature a fiendish giant.

2167 *Little Red Riding Hood.* Ill. by Paula Knight. Picture Window, 2003, ISBN 1-4048-0064-6. SUBJECTS: Folklore. RL B.

The controlled vocabulary leaves nothing to the imagination in this retelling. The drawings are cheery.

Mooser, Stephen

2168 *Follow That Flea! Goofball Malone, Ace Detective.* Ill. by Brian Biggs. Grosset & Dunlap, 2005, ISBN 0-448-43894-1. SERIES: All Aboard Reading. SUBJECTS: Mystery and detective stories. RL C.

Following the clues, Goofball locates Dr. Fleaflicker's puppy. Ink-outlined cartoon drawings.

2169 *Funnyman and the Penny Dodo.* Ill. by Tomie dePaola. Watts, 1984, o.p. SERIES: Easy-Read Story. SUBJECTS: Humorous stories; Jokes and riddles — Fiction; Mystery and detective stories. RL C.

Detective Funnyman uses his jokes to find Putty Face Pete and reclaim valuable stolen stamps. Both the story and the jokes are enjoyable. Text is illustrated with humorous pencil drawings with beige and blue washes.

2170 *Funnyman's First Case.* Ill. by Tomie dePaola. Watts, 1981, o.p. SERIES: Easy-Read Story. SUBJECTS: Humorous stories; Jokes and riddles — Fiction; Mystery and detective stories. RL C.

Forever cracking jokes to his customers, Archie finds his job as a waiter is in jeopardy until he uses his talent to capture Big Red, a local thief. Though the jokes are old, children will enjoy them, the silly plot line, and the comical pencil drawings with pink and beige tones.

2171 *The Ghost with the Halloween Hiccups.* Ill. by Tomie dePaola. Avon, pap., 1981, ISBN 0-380-40287-4. SERIES: Easy-Read Story. SUBJECTS: Halloween — Fiction; Hiccups — Fiction; Humorous stories. RL C.

Mr. Penny's appearance in the Halloween play is a tradition that may be stopped by a bad case of hiccups. Almost scary full-color pictures of Halloween creatures trying to cure him of the hiccups add to the fun.

2172 *Goofball Malone, Ace Detective.* Ill. by Brian Biggs. Grosset & Dunlap, pap., 2005, ISBN 0-448-43893-3. SERIES: All Aboard Mystery Station Reader. SUBJECTS: Jokes and riddles; Mystery and detective stories; School stories. RL C.

Mooser has written an especially interesting school mystery, with the major clues being by smell. Cartoon characters include Pupu the clown.

Mooser, Stephen, and Lin Oliver

2173 *Tad and Dad.* Ill. by Susan Day. Warner, 1988, ISBN 1-55782-023-6. SERIES: Catch the Reading Bug. SUBJECTS: Bears — Fiction; Behavior — Fiction; Parent and child — Fiction. RL A.

In two nearly wordless stories, a small bear and his father share adventures that need the ink and wash pictures to create their rather thin plots. Meant to facilitate reading for the very beginner, this book uses four sight words and eight words with "ad" as their base.

Moran, Alex

2174 *Boots for Beth.* Ill. by Lisa Campbell Ernst. Harcourt, 2003, ISBN 0-15-204878-2. SERIES: Green Light Readers. SUBJECTS: Animals — Fiction; Pigs — Fiction. RL A.

Moran, Alex (cont.)

Beth the pig is offered boots by her friends, and finally finds a pair that fits. Ink and wash drawings are gentle and appealing.

2175 *Come Here, Tiger!* Ill. by Lisa Campbell Ernst. Harcourt, 2000, ISBN 0-15-204820-0. SERIES: Green Light Readers. SUBJECTS: Pets — Cats — Fiction. RL A. LEXILE BR.
A small girl finds a variety of other pets in her search for her cat, Tiger. Appealing ink and wash drawings

2176 *Sam and Jack: Three Stories.* Ill. by Tim Bowers. Harcourt, 2001, ISBN 0-15-204822-7. SERIES: Green Light Readers. SUBJECTS: Friendship — Fiction; Mice — Fiction; Pets — Cats — Fiction. RL A.
Sam the mouse makes friends with Jack the cat. Very spare drawings complement the text that uses the most basic vocabulary.

Morgan, Michaela

2177 *Helpful Betty Solves a Mystery.* Ill. by Moira Kemp. Carolrhoda, 1994, ISBN 0-87614-832-1. SUBJECTS: Behavior — Helpful — Fiction; Hippopotami — Fiction. RL B.
Betty the hippopotamus is an ace detective, and teaches a baby bird to fly and a baby alligator to swim after mixing up the eggs.

2178 *Helpful Betty to the Rescue.* Ill. by Moira Kemp. Carolrhoda, 1993, ISBN 0-87614-831-3. SUBJECTS: Behavior — Helpful — Fiction; Hippopotami — Fiction. RL B.
Ace detective Betty the hippopotamus hears a cry and sets off to rescue a monkey, with her usual lack of helpfulness.

Morley, Diana

2179 *Marms in the Marmalade.* Ill. by Kathy Rogers. Carolrhoda, 1984, o.p. SERIES: On My Own. SUBJECTS: English language; Nonsense; Stories in rhyme. RL C.
Poking fun at the illogical way that many English words are constructed, this rhyming book takes familiar words like caterpillar and gives logical though silly definitions for them. Children and adults will enjoy the nonsense and the attractive full-color drawings.

Morris, Ann

2180 *How Teddy Bears Are Made: A Visit to the Vermont Teddy Bear Factory.* Ill. by Ken Heyman. Scholastic, 1994, ISBN 0-590-47152-X. SUBJECTS: Toys — Teddy bears. RL B.
Three children take a tour of a factory that makes all kinds of teddy bears. Through appealing color photographs and a brief text readers are taken through most of the steps in the manufacturing of the toys.

Morris, Jennifer E.

2181 *May I Please Have a Cookie?* Ill. by author. Scholastic, pap., 2004, ISBN 0-439-73819-9. SERIES: Scholastic Reader. SUBJECTS: Alligators — Fiction; Behavior — Manners — Fiction. RL A. LEXILE 250L.
A warm cookie and a warm hug are Alfie's reward for asking his mother politely for a cookie.

Morris, Johnny

2182 *Animal-Go-Round: Turn the Wheel and See the Animals Grow.* Ill. with photos. Dorling Kindersley, 1993, ISBN 1-56458-329-5. SUBJECTS: Animals — Growth and development; Toy and movable books. RL B.
Appealing, excellent color photographs on a white ground show the growth of cuddly animals familiar to children, from chicks and puppies to butterflies and frogs. Lambs are shown from birth to 12 weeks, frogs from egg to full grown on a full-page rotating wheel revealing one stage at a time.

Morris, Kimberly

2183 *Molly in the Middle: A Story Blending Phonics and Whole Language.* Photos by Dorothy Handelman. Millbrook, 1998, ISBN 0-7613-2059-8. SERIES: Real Kids Readers. SUBJECTS: Family life; Siblings. RL B. LEXILE 340L.
Molly sees the disadvantages of being neither the oldest nor the youngest in her family, but needs help to see the advantages. Illustrated with posed photographs but realistic situations.

Morris, Robert

2184 *Dolphin.* Ill. by Mamoru Funai. HarperCollins, pap., 1975, ISBN 0-06-024342-2. SERIES: Science I Can Read. SUBJECTS: Conservation; Dolphins; Nature. RL C.

Much can be learned about the bottle-nosed dolphin in a story of the birth and growth of a baby dolphin. Illustrated with realistic watercolor paintings, the book helps to promote a concern for nature and conservation.

2185 *Seahorse.* Ill. by Arnold Lobel. HarperCollins, 1972, o.p. SERIES: Science I Can Read. SUBJECTS: Seahorses. RL A.

A carefully worded and fascinating text with lovely, detailed pencil, ink, and wash drawings explains how sea horses live, travel, bear young, and hide from predators.

Morton, Lone

2186 *Good Night, Everyone.* Ill. by Jakki Wood. World Book, 1996, o.p. SERIES: First Stories. SUBJECTS: Bedtime — Fiction. RL A.

Martha aligns her menagerie of furry animals in her bed before she squeezes in. A 16-word picture dictionary is appended to cheerful story.

Moses, Amy

2187 *I Am an Explorer.* Ill. by Rick Hackney. Children's Press, 1990, ISBN 0-516-02059-5. SERIES: Rookie Reader. SUBJECTS: Concepts — Opposites — Fiction; Explorers and exploration — Fiction; Imaginative play — Fiction. RL B.

A lively little boy imagines himself a world explorer going in and out of caves, over and under water, up and down a mountain, and so on. Along the way, through the very brief text and clear watercolor pictures, children are introduced to concepts.

Moskin, Marietta

2188 *Lysbet and the Fire Kittens.* Ill. by Margot Tomes. Putnam, 1973, o.p. SERIES: Break-of-Day. SUBJECTS: Fire fighters and fire fighting — Fiction; Pets — Cats — Fiction; United States — Colonial period — Fiction. RL C.

Left for a short time to care for the house and her cat Stuyver, who is about to have kittens, Lysbet builds a fire that accidentally sets the house ablaze while she is ice skating. After alerting her New Amsterdam neighbors, Lysbet rescues the cat and her new kittens. Ink drawings ably capture the 1662 setting.

Most, Bernard

2189 *Catch Me If You Can!* Ill. by author. Harcourt, 1999, ISBN 0-439-15326-3. SERIES: Green Light Readers. SUBJECTS: Dinosaurs — Fiction. RL A. LEXILE AD60L.

The little dinosaur is not afraid of the biggest dinosaur — who turns out to be his Grandpa. Simple drawings complement the simple text.

2190 *The Very Boastful Kangaroo.* Ill. by author. Harcourt, 2003, ISBN 0-15-204880-4. SERIES: Green Light Readers. SUBJECTS: Behavior — Bragging — Fiction; Jokes and riddles — Fiction; Kangaroos — Fiction. RL A. LEXILE 300L.

The Very Boastful Kangaroo even wins when challenged to jump higher than a tree! Very simple outlined drawings.

Mozelle, Shirley

2191 *Zack's Alligator.* Ill. by James Watts. HarperCollins, 1989, ISBN 0-06-024309-0. SERIES: I Can Read. SUBJECTS: Alligators — Fiction. RL B. LEXILE 310L.

Zack's birthday gift of an alligator on a keychain turns out to be Bridget, who requires a *lot* of tending! Zack's fight with the garden hose is the most memorable drawing.

Mueller, Virginia

2192 *A Halloween Mask for Monster.* Ill. by Lynn Munsinger. Whitman, 1986, ISBN 0-8075-3134-0. SERIES: Just-for-Fun. SUBJECTS: Halloween — Fiction; Monsters — Fiction. RL A.

The little green monster tries on human and animal masks but finds them too scary. Finally he decides to go trick-or-treating as himself. The predictable repetition of phrases in the very brief story and the delightful color pictures make this just right for the beginning reader.

Munsil, Janet

2193 *Where There's Smoke*. Ill. by Michael Martchenko. Annick, 1993, ISBN 1-55037-291-2. SUBJECTS: Behavior — Fiction. RL B.
Daisy and Dad help each other stop nail-biting and smoking, respectively. They share an inventive list of new hobbies together. The punch line is a bit forced, however. Lively watercolor drawings accompany the text.

Muntean, Michaela

2194 *Bicycle Bear*. Ill. by Doug Cushman. Stevens, 1994, ISBN 0-8368-0963-7. SERIES: Read Aloud Originals. SUBJECTS: Bears — Fiction; Humorous stories; Stories in rhyme. RL B.
Bicycle Bear delivers a moose for Ima Goose in this humorous rhyming story illustrated with funny watercolor pictures. Following the story is a section featuring advice for adults using books with young readers.

2195 *Bicycle Bear Rides Again*. Ill. by Doug Cushman. Gareth Stevens, 1989, ISBN 0-8193-1193-6. SERIES: Parents Magazine Read Aloud Original. SUBJECTS: Bears — Fiction; Stories in rhyme. RL B.
Bicycle Bear's vacation is interrupted when his substitute, his nephew Tricycle Bear, needs help moving an apartment housing 99 mice. Very simple watercolor drawings.

2196 *A Garden for Miss Mouse*. Ill. by Christopher Santoro. Parents Magazine Press, 1993, ISBN 0-8368-0891-6. SERIES: Read Aloud Library. SUBJECTS: Gardening — Fiction; Mice — Fiction; Stories in rhyme. RL B.
Miss Mouse impulsively digs up her whole yard for a huge garden. At first, it is lovely. Then it really starts to grow and Miss Mouse is a captive of her lush vegetable garden until friends join in for the harvest. Lively rhyming text is illustrated with exuberant watercolors.

2197 *The Old Man and the Afternoon Cat*. Ill. by Bari Weissman. Parents Magazine Press, 1982, ISBN 0-8193-1072-7. SERIES: Read Aloud and Easy Reading. SUBJECTS: Old age — Fiction; Pets — Cats — Fiction. RL B.
The lonely and grumpy old man looks forward to his afternoons at the park with a friendly cat. When the cat disappears, the old man begins a search that earns him friends, the cat, and a new outlook on life. This satisfying story has attractive full-color illustrations.

Murata, Michinori

2198 *Water and Light: Looking Through Lenses*. Photos by Isamu Sekido. Lerner, 1993, ISBN 0-8225-2904-1. SERIES: Science All Around You. SUBJECTS: Light; Science experiments; Water. RL C.
Clear color photographs and straightforward explanations of how light is magnified or changed through lenses and water are supported by easy-to-follow experiments.

Murdocca, Sal

2199 *Take Me to the Moon!* Ill. by author. Lothrop, 1976, o.p. SERIES: Fun-to-Read. SUBJECTS: Fantasy; Kings and queens — Fiction. RL B.
When the queen orders that she be taken to the moon, an astrologer, a carpenter, and a knight scramble to find a way to get her there, finally deciding on a dragon-propelled spaceship. Illustrated with humorous cartoon-type pictures in shades of blue and yellow.

2200 *Tuttle's Shell*. Ill. by author. Lothrop, 1976, o.p. SERIES: Fun-to-Read. SUBJECTS: Turtles — Fiction. RL B.
Louis the Rat steals Tuttle Turtle's shell while he is bathing. It takes the combined cunning of Tuttle and his friends to win it back. Comic pen and ink drawings with detailed cross-hatchings illustrate the silly but fun-to-read story.

Murphy, Frank

2201 *Ben Franklin and the Magic Squares*. Ill. by Richard Walz. Random House, 2001, ISBN 0-375-90621-5. SERIES: Step into Reading. SUBJECTS: Biographies; Mathematics. RL C. LEXILE 400L.
Ben Franklin's "most magically magical magic squares" are just one of his many inventions. Pencil and wash illustrations.

2202 *George Washington and the General's Dog*. Ill. by Richard Walz. Random House, 2003, ISBN 0-375-91015-8. SERIES: Step into

Reading. SUBJECTS: Biographies; Pets — Dogs; United States — Revolutionary War. RL C. LEXILE 380L.

When Washington returned General Howe's dog to him after a battle, his relationship with the British changed. Colored pencil illustrations.

2203 *Thomas Jefferson's Feast*. Ill. by Richard Walz. Random House, 2002, ISBN 0-613-86238-4. SERIES: Step into Reading. SUBJECTS: Biographies; Presidents — United States. RL B.

Thomas Jefferson spent as much as $50 a day on food ($750 today), promoted love apples (tomatoes, thought to be poisonous), and held famous dinner parties. An interesting way to introduce the third president to young readers. Pastel cartoon drawings.

Murphy, Jim

2204 *Harold Thinks Big*. Ill. by Susanna Natti. Crown, 1980, o.p. SUBJECTS: Pigs — Fiction; Romance — Fiction; Sports — Football — Fiction. RL A.

Smitten with Esther, a porcine cheerleader, Harold goes to lawyer Owl for advice. "Think big" is his suggestion and Harold does, with disastrous results. Comic line and wash illustrations complement this story of unrequited love that is sure to bring empathetic smiles to its readers.

Murray, Peter

2205 *Beavers*. Ill. with photos. Child's World, 1992, ISBN 0-89565-844-5. SERIES: Nature Books. SUBJECTS: Beavers. RL C.

Alternating pages of well-spaced, boldfaced type and color photographs introduce children to the many facets of the world of the beaver.

2206 *Chameleons*. Ill. with photos. Child's World, 1993, ISBN 1-56766-016-9. SERIES: Nature Books. SUBJECTS: Chameleons; Reptiles and amphibians. RL C.

Many misconceptions about chameleons and their habits are clarified by Murray through his brief text and the very well done color photographs. Among other things, readers learn that chameleons do not change color to match their environment. A great many different chameleons are pictured but not identified.

2207 *Frogs*. Ill. with photos. Child's World, 1993, ISBN 1-56766-010-X. SERIES: Nature Books. SUBJECTS: Frogs and toads; Reptiles and amphibians. RL C.

The many kinds and sizes of frogs, their life cycle, and their predators are discussed in a text complemented by attractive color photographs. The pictures would have been more effective if they had specific captioning to identify a type of frog. Index is included.

2208 *Gorillas*. Ill. with photos. Child's World, 1993, ISBN 1-56766-020-7. SERIES: Nature Books. SUBJECTS: Animals — Endangered; Gorillas. RL C.

Color photographs and a carefully worded text afford young readers a good look at some of the kinds of gorillas found in Africa. The book explains some of their habits, the foods they eat, and the danger man and the loss of the rainforest are to them.

2209 *Hummingbirds*. Ill. with photos. Child's World, 1993, ISBN 1-56766-011-8. SERIES: Nature Books. SUBJECTS: Birds; Hummingbirds. RL C.

An attractive format featuring colored pages, full-color photographs, and widely spaced lines of text will draw readers into this well-written look at hummingbirds of the Americas. Though most pictures are identified in the text, some birds are frustratingly without identification.

2210 *Parrots*. Ill. with photos. Child's World, 1993, ISBN 1-56766-015-0. SERIES: Nature Books. SUBJECTS: Animals — Endangered; Birds; Parrots. RL C.

Native to rainforest areas and attractive to man because of their plumage and ability to mimic, parrots are endangered. Murray discusses their habits, calls, and life cycle. Full-color photographs are beautiful but could use captioning. Index is included.

2211 *Porcupines*. Ill. with photos. Child's World, 1994, ISBN 1-56766-019-3. SERIES: Nature Books. SUBJECTS: Porcupines. RL C.

Good full page color photographs complement an interesting text that presents the life of the porcupine, its young, its food, and other porcupines found throughout the world. One quibble: On page 29, the author mentions two different porcupines without identifying the one pictured.

Murray, Peter (cont.)

2212 *Tarantulas*. Ill. with photos. Child's World, 1993, ISBN 1-56766-060-6. SERIES: Nature Books. SUBJECTS: Spiders. RL C.

A gentle but sometimes frightening-looking spider, the tarantula lives in the Southwest in burrows or trees. Through clear color photographs and well-spaced lines of text, children learn a great deal about the habits and lifestyle of a spider that can also be a pet.

Myrick, Mildred

2213 *Ants Are Fun*. Ill. by Arnold Lobel. HarperCollins, 1968, o.p. SERIES: I Can Read. SUBJECTS: Ants — Fiction; Friendship — Fiction; Moving, household — Fiction. RL B.

From their treehouse observatories, two boys see a new neighbor who is their age carrying a mysterious box. Later they learn it is an ant nest. Through the boys' curiosity, a great deal is discovered about ants. Charming pencil drawings with color washes add much to the story.

2214 *Secret Three*. Ill. by Arnold Lobel. HarperCollins, 1963, ISBN 0-06-024356-2. SERIES: I Can Read. SUBJECTS: Clubs — Fiction; Codes and secret messages — Fiction; Friendship — Fiction. RL B.

Finding a bottle on the beach with a secret message in it starts an exchange of coded messages and inspires the creation of the Secret Three Club. Readers will easily decipher the codes that are included in the detailed and attractive ink drawings with color washes.

N

Nagel, Karen Berman

2215 *Two Crazy Pigs*. Ill. by Brian Schatell. Scholastic, pap., 1992, ISBN 0-5904-4972-9. SERIES: Scholastic Reader. SUBJECTS: Pigs — Fiction. RL A.

The pigs tickle the hens when they are laying eggs, tie the cows' tails together, and have a mud fight. A 15-word vocabulary list is appended.

Namm, Diane

2216 *Little Bear*. Ill. by Lisa McCue. Childrens Press, 1990, ISBN 0-516-05356-6. SERIES: My First Reader. SUBJECTS: Bears — Fiction; Food — Fiction; Stories in rhyme. RL A.

A 16-word rhyming vocabulary and sweet watercolor pictures tell the story of a baby bear who refuses to be tempted by good food. Instead the little animal wants only honey. The limited vocabulary will make this accessible to the very beginning reader.

2217 *Monsters*. Ill. by Maxie Chambliss. Childrens Press, 1990, ISBN 0-516-05358-2. SERIES: My First Reader. SUBJECTS: Concepts — Numbers; Monsters — Fiction; Stories in rhyme. RL A.

Cute and colorful monsters — just out of the child's sight — gather as the child looks for them. The very brief text is sure to be fun for the child just beginning to read as it reinforces counting skills.

Neasi, Barbara

2218 *Sweet Dreams*. Ill. by Clovis Martin. Children's Press, 1987, ISBN 0-516-02084-6. SERIES: Rookie Reader. SUBJECTS: Dreams — Fiction; Stories in rhyme. RL A.

A little girl looks forward to all the different kinds of dream stories she may encounter while sleeping. The dreams she imagines she might have and the entire text are illustrated with bright comic-style watercolor and ink pictures.

Nelson, Sharlene, and Ted Nelson

2219 *Hawaii Volcanoes National Park*. Ill. with photos. Children's Press, 1997, ISBN 0-516-20623-0. SERIES: True Book. SUBJECTS: National parks; United States; Volcanoes. RL C. LEXILE 710L.

Hawaii's first people arrived about 1,600 years ago and worshipped Pele, the goddess of volcanoes. Photographs of the volcanoes are augmented by a diagram of how volcanoes are created. The wildlife is introduced, as are the scientists who study volcanoes.

2220 *Mount Rainier National Park*. Ill. with photos. Children's Press, 1997, ISBN 0-516-20624-9. SERIES: True Book. SUBJECTS: National parks; United States. RL C.

The First People who lived in the area are cataloged. The first settlers and climbers, including John Muir, are mentioned, and the vistas and wildlife visitors can expect to see are illustrated.

Newman, Alyse

2221 *It's Me, Claudia!* Ill. by author. Watts, 1981, o.p. SERIES: Easy-Read Story. SUBJECTS: Human body — Ears — Fiction; Self-esteem — Fiction. RL B.

Thinking her large ears make her look like a mouse, Claudia tries different ways to hide them, finally settling on wearing a large hat. The hat acts as a barrier to friends and fun and Claudia finally gives it up. Ink and wash drawings show a little girl coming to terms with how she looks.

Newman, Nanette

2222 *That Dog!* Ill. by Marylin Hafner. HarperCollins, 1983, ISBN 0-690-04229-9. SUBJECTS: Death — Fiction; Pets — Dogs — Fiction. RL B.

Ben and his dog Barnum are inseparable and when Barnum dies, Ben is sure he can never love another dog. With the support of loving family and friends, Ben finally does make room for a stray puppy. The gently humorous illustrations capture Ben and Barnum's very special relationship.

Newton, James R.

2223 *The March of the Lemmings.* Ill. by Charles Robinson. HarperCollins, 1976, o.p. SERIES: Let's-Read-and-Find-Out. SUBJECTS: Lemmings. RL C.

When food and room are plentiful, the lemming population of northern Norway grows continuously until both food and room are scarce. Then many of the little animals leave their homes and head westward, toward the ocean. Good information and realistic pencil drawings make this a very useful book.

Neye, Emily

2224 *Butterflies.* Ill. by Ron Broda. Grosset & Dunlap, pap., 2000, ISBN 0-448-41966-1. SERIES: All Aboard Science Reader. SUBJECTS: Butterflies and moths; Science and scientists. RL A. LEXILE 180L.

Collages illustrate the life cycle of butterflies and point out the differences between butterflies and moths.

2225 *Water.* Ill. by Cindy Revell. Grosset & Dunlap, pap., 2002, ISBN 0-448-42847-4. SERIES: All Aboard Science Reader. SUBJECTS: Science and scientists; Water. RL A.

Elflike children find out about the different forms water takes, and about the water cycle.

Nicklaus, Carol

2226 *Come Dance with Me.* Ill. by author. Silver Burdett, 1991, ISBN 0-671-73503-9. SERIES: Silver Sower Easy Reader. SUBJECTS: Animals — Fiction; Dancers and dancing — Fiction. RL A.

A group of animals expressively dance in all kinds of ways: fast, slow, together, apart, looking mean or pretty, like a snake, and so on. The few words per page combine with the cartoon-like color paintings to give children an idea of dance as a personal statement.

2227 *The GO Club.* Ill. by author. Silver Burdett, 1991, ISBN 0-671-73500-4. SERIES: Silver Sower Easy Reader. SUBJECTS: Bicycles and bicycling — Fiction; Safety — Fiction. RL A.

Animal characters ride bikes with one, two, three, and four wheels. All are heading to the park and along the way share safety tips. Few words per page are helped by cartoon-like color illustrations set against much white.

2228 *Harry the Hider.* Ill. by author. Watts, 1979, o.p. SERIES: Easy-Read Story. SUBJECTS: Humorous stories; Pets — Cats — Fiction. RL A.

Miranda thinks it is fruitless to try to enter her cat Harry in the circus — all he can do is hide. However, it is his camouflaging ability that not only wins him first prize but also intrigues the reader, who must look carefully at the ink line drawings to try to find the missing Harry.

2229 *Head Over Heels.* Ill. by author. Silver Burdett, 1991, ISBN 0-671-73506-3. SERIES: Silver Sower Easy Reader. SUBJECTS: Animals — Fiction; Sports — Gymnastics — Fiction. RL A.

Nicklaus, Carol (cont.)

With the help of an instructor, a reluctant puppy begins to learn the fun of basic gymnastic movements. By book's end the puppy is introducing others to things he has learned. Illustrated with colorful cartoon-like paintings that work with the brief text to show the power of determination.

2230 *Sidekicks*. Ill. by author. Silver Burdett, 1991, ISBN 0-671-73504-7. SERIES: Silver Sower Easy Reader. SUBJECTS: Animals — Fiction; Sports — Soccer — Fiction. RL A.
Two young animals of opposite temperament join a soccer team, learn to play by the rules, and try hard to be members of the team. The importance of teamwork is reinforced by the colorful cartoon-like artwork.

Nirgiotis, Nicholas

2231 *Volcanoes: Mountains That Blow Their Tops*. Ill. by Michael Radencich. Grosset & Dunlap, 1996, ISBN 0-448-41144-X. SERIES: All Aboard Reading. SUBJECTS: Volcanoes. RL B. LEXILE 310L.
Dramatic layered collages illustrate the origin of volcanoes and detail several notable ones, including Mount St. Helens and Pompeii.

Nixon, Joan L.

2232 *Bigfoot Makes a Movie*. Ill. by Syd Hoff. Putnam, 1979, o.p. SUBJECTS: Fantasy; Humorous stories; Mythical creatures — Fiction. RL B.
Young Bigfoot naively believes the film crew want to be his friends when they mistake him for an actor dressed as Bigfoot. The exaggerated cartoon-like illustrations are childlike and guarantee that the story is not taken seriously.

2233 *Danger in Dinosaur Valley*. Ill. by Marc Simont. Putnam, 1978, o.p. SERIES: See and Read. SUBJECTS: Dinosaurs — Fiction; Science fiction; Sports — Baseball — Fiction. RL B.
The climate is growing colder and the Diplodocus family must go south. Little Diplodocus, watching a baseball game on a Back Into Time tourist's television, learns to pitch rocks to help the family escape Tyrannosaurus Rex. Subject matter and humorous illustrations are sure to appeal to children.

2234 *Muffie Mouse and the Busy Birthday*. Ill. by Geoffrey Hayes. Seabury, 1978, o.p. SUBJECTS: Birthdays — Fiction; Family life — Fiction; Mice — Fiction. RL B.
It is mother mouse's birthday and little Muffie decides to make it extra special. She concocts a very unusual birthday breakfast, teaches Tommy Mouse to share, and stops horrible cousin Harry from scaring her. The detailed drawings show a secure, well-loved, turn-of-the-century mouse.

2235 *The Mysterious Prowler*. Ill. by Berthe Amoss. Harcourt, 1976, o.p. SERIES: Let Me Read. SUBJECTS: Behavior — Shyness — Fiction; Moving, household — Fiction; Mystery and detective stories. RL B.
Spotting someone peeking in the window and later ringing his doorbell and vanishing, Jonathan decides to track down the mysterious prowler. He discovers it is his new neighbor, a boy too shy to stay and talk. The ink drawings add to the suspense created by Nixon's careful pacing.

2236 *The Thanksgiving Mystery*. Ill. by Jim Cummins. Whitman, 1980, ISBN 0-8075-7820-7. SERIES: First Read-Alone Mystery. SUBJECTS: Mystery and detective stories; Thanksgiving — Fiction. RL B.
Positive that she has seen a ghost, Susan, with Mark and Mrs. Pickett, devises a plan to trap it during their Thanksgiving holiday. This is a longer book than most readers are used to and may be just right for youngsters wanting a "long" book. Illustrated with prosaic ink and wash pictures.

2237 *The Valentine Mystery*. Ill. by Jim Cummins. Whitman, 1979, ISBN 0-8075-8450-9. SERIES: First Read-Alone Mystery. SUBJECTS: Mystery and detective stories; Valentine's Day — Fiction. RL C.
Susan's two-year-old brother's clue to the identity of the giver of her Valentine card adds to the mystery. Children reading the book will be trying to guess how to decipher the clue as well as the mystery. Illustrated with realistic ink and wash sketches.

Nobens, C. A.

2238 *The Happy Baker*. Ill. by author. Carolrhoda, 1979, o.p. SERIES: On My Own. SUBJECTS: Bakers and baking — Fiction; Food — Fiction. RL B.

Having left his bakery and friends, Joseph travels the world sampling and refusing other countries' breads while relishing their soups. When he returns home, he reopens his bakery, adding soup to his menu. Illustrated with flat, humorous watercolor pictures in green and rust tones.

Nodset, Joan L.

2239 *Who Took the Farmer's Hat?* Ill. by Fritz Siebel. HarperCollins, 1988, ISBN 0-06-024565-4. SUBJECTS: Cumulative tales; Farm and country life — Fiction. RL A. LEXILE 210L.

The farmer gets a new brown hat, even after finding his old brown hat. Bold ink and light wash drawings.

Noonan, Julia

2240 *Friends Forever: Hare and Rabbit.* Ill. by author. Scholastic, pap., 2000, ISBN 0-439-08753-8. SERIES: Scholastic Reader. SUBJECTS: Friendship — Fiction; Rabbits — Fiction. RL B. LEXILE 190L.

A carefully controlled vocabulary includes three sets of five rhyming words that tell stories of the friendship of Hare and Rabbit. Gentle rabbit illustrations.

Nottridge, Rhoda

2241 *Big Cats.* Ill. by David Nockels. Watts, 1990, ISBN 0-531-18285-1. SERIES: Let's Look At. SUBJECTS: Animals — Endangered; Pets — Cats. RL B.

This overview of the lives of lions, cougars, tigers, and other big cats, offers general information on their size, environment, and prey. It also encourages the conservation of animal life. Illustrations are realistic color paintings Index and habitat map are included.

Novak, Matt

2242 *Little Wolf Big Wolf.* Ill. by author. HarperCollins, 1999, ISBN 0-06-027486-7. SERIES: I Can Read. SUBJECTS: Friendship — Fiction; Wolves — Fiction. RL B.

Big and Little Wolf decide to be friends despite their differences.

2243 *Newt.* Ill. by author. HarperCollins, 1996, ISBN 0-06-024502-6. SERIES: I Can Read. SUBJECTS: Friendship — Fiction. RL B. LEXILE 410L.

Newt returns his friend's flower, realizes that his bug is satisfactory after all, and finds that the moon can be afraid of dark shapes. Colored pencil drawings of the friends.

Numeroff, Laura J.

2244 *Amy for Short.* Ill. by author. Macmillan, 1976, o.p. SERIES: Ready-to-Read. SUBJECTS: Friendship — Fiction; Self-esteem — Fiction. RL C.

Amy has no problem with being the tallest in her class but she worries that her friend Mark may not like her as much now that she is taller than he is. A good depiction of a child whose family and friends help her to accept and like herself. Illustrations are in coral and black pastels.

2245 *Beatrice Doesn't Want To.* Ill. by author. Watts, 1981, o.p. SERIES: Easy-Read Story. SUBJECTS: Books and reading — Fiction; Libraries and librarians — Fiction. RL B.

Not liking books or reading, Beatrice resents her trips to the library until she hears the children's librarian read aloud. This upbeat look at non-reading children captures Beatrice's resistance to books and her reluctant capitulation. Illustrations are ink drawings and color washes.

2246 *Does Grandma Have an Elmo Elephant Jungle Kit?* Ill. by author. Greenwillow, 1980, o.p. SERIES: Read-Alone. SUBJECTS: Grandparents — Fiction. RL C.

Though Donald is afraid there will be nothing to do at Grandma and Grandpa's house, the weekend is full of fun and Donald is anxious to visit again. This positive look at active, loving grandparents is well done and has appropriate, simple ink and wash drawings.

2247 *Monster Munchies.* Ill. by Nate Evans. Random House, 1998, ISBN 0-679-89163-3. SERIES: I Can Read It All by Myself. SUBJECTS: Concepts — Numbers — Fiction; Monsters — Fiction; Stories in rhyme. RL A.

Twenty hungry monsters are looking for something to chew — the reader better be sure it isn't "you"!

2248 *The Ugliest Sweater.* Ill. by author. Watts, 1980, o.p. SERIES: Easy-Read Story.

Numeroff, Laura J. (cont.)

SUBJECTS: Gifts and gift giving — Fiction. RL B.

Grandmother's intricately designed multicolored sweater seems ugly to Peter until his teacher says the student wearing red, white, and blue may bring in their special guest from France. Outlined in heavy ink with blue and red washes, the illustrations are bold and complement the story.

Nussbaum, Hedda

2249 *Animals Build Amazing Homes*. Ill. by Christopher Santoro. Random House, 1979, ISBN 0-394-83850-5. SERIES: Step-Up. SUBJECTS: Animals — Homes; Animals — Nests. RL B.

Whether it is mound-building termites, pond-digging alligators, or tunnel-digging prairie dogs, the animals and the homes in this book make fascinating reading. The clear text is illustrated with realistic drawing with some washes.

2250 *Plants Do Amazing Things*. Ill. by Joe Mathieu. Random House, 1977, ISBN 0-394-93232-3. SERIES: Step-Up. SUBJECTS: Plants. RL B.

In brief, entertaining, and informative chapters, many unusual plants and plant characteristics are described, including lichens, flytraps, cacti, and examples of symbiosis. The two-color illustrations are cartoon-like but appear to depict natural objects accurately.

Nye, Emily

2251 *Honeybees*. Ill. by Tom Leonard. Random House, 2002, ISBN 0-307-26217-0. SERIES: Step into Reading. SUBJECTS: Bees; Insects. RL B.

Simple vocabulary and drawings show the life of honeybees.

O

Obrist, Jurg

2252 *Max and Molly and the Mystery of the Missing Honey*. Ill. by author. North-South Books, 2000, ISBN 0-7358-1267-5. SUBJECTS: Beekeeping — Fiction; Grandparents — Fiction; Mystery and detective stories. RL B.

Max and Molly have fun at Grandpa's house every August — until Grandpa becomes obsessed with his bees and accuses the children of stealing his honey. Cheerful drawings add mystery and playfulness.

Ochiltree, Dianne

2253 *Cats Add Up!* Ill. by Marcy Dunn-Ramsey. Scholastic, pap., 2006, ISBN 0-439-79853-1. SERIES: Scholastic Reader. SUBJECTS: Mathematics — Fiction; Pets — Cats — Fiction. RL A. LEXILE 480L.

Readers can practice both addition and subtraction as the number of cats fluctuates in this household. Marilyn Burns math activities are appended to this story appealingly illustrated with watercolors.

O'Connor, Jane

2254 *Dear Tooth Fairy*. Ill. by Joy Allen. Grosset & Dunlap, pap., 2002, ISBN 0-448-42849-0. SERIES: All Aboard Reading. SUBJECTS: Human body — Teeth — Fiction. RL B.

Robby has a long correspondence with the Tooth Fairy when his tooth is slow to fall out, and then he can't find it. Pencil and wash drawings are very attractive.

2255 *Eek! Stories to Make You Shriek*. Ill. by G. Brian Karas. Grosset & Dunlap, pap., 1991, ISBN 0-448-40382-X. SERIES: All Aboard Reading. SUBJECTS: Scary stories. RL B.

Colored pencil drawings enhance three stories — about a mysterious monster at a Halloween party, a new doll that seems alive, and a mysterious big black dog in the family's new house.

2256 *Kate Skates*. Ill. by DyAnne DiSalvo-Ryan. Grosset & Dunlap, pap., 1994, ISBN 0-448-40935-6. SERIES: All Aboard Reading. SUBJECTS: Sports — Ice skating — Fiction. RL B. LEXILE 170L.

A big sister meets the skating star Diana Lin, who helps her master her new skates. An easy read, illustrated with colored pencil drawings.

2257 *Lulu and the Witch Baby.* Ill. by Emily A. McCully. HarperCollins, 1986, ISBN 0-06-024627-8. SERIES: I Can Read. SUBJECTS: Jealousy — Fiction; Witches — Fiction. RL B.

Lulu tries to make Baby Witch disappear but relents when she can't find the baby.

2258 *Lulu Goes to Witch School.* Ill. by Emily A. McCully. HarperCollins, 1990, ISBN 0-06-024628-6. SERIES: I Can Read. SUBJECTS: Friendship — Fiction; School stories; Witches — Fiction. RL B.

Her first day of witch school, Lulu meets Sandy Witch, who can do everything better than Lulu. When each contracts lizard pox, the tables are turned, and the two become friends.

2259 *Molly the Brave and Me.* Ill. by Sheila Hamanaka. Random House, 1990, ISBN 0-394-94175-6. SERIES: Step into Reading. SUBJECTS: Behavior — Brave — Fiction; Friendship — Fiction. RL B.

Beth is nervous about spending the night at Molly's house, but finds that she is the brave one when they get lost in a cornfield.

2260 *Nina, Nina Ballerina.* Ill. by DyAnne DiSalvo-Ryan. Grosset & Dunlap, pap., 1993, ISBN 0-448-40511-3. SERIES: All Aboard Reading. SUBJECTS: Dancers and dancing — Fiction. RL A.

Nina's mom has no trouble finding Nina on stage during the butterfly dance as Nina sports an arm cast. Very gentle pencil and wash drawings.

2261 *Nina, Nina, Copycat Ballerina.* Ill. by DyAnne DiSalvo-Ryan. Grosset & Dunlap, 1999, ISBN 0-448-42152-6. SERIES: All Aboard Reading. SUBJECTS: Dancers and dancing — Fiction; Friendship — Fiction. RL A.

Another Nina joins dance class, and the first Nina gets tired of being copied — until they join up together for an original duet. Pencil and wash drawings.

2262 *Nina, Nina, Star Ballerina.* Ill. by DyAnne DiSalvo-Ryan. Grosset & Dunlap, 1996, ISBN 0-448-41611-5. SERIES: All Aboard Reading. SUBJECTS: Dancers and dancing — Fiction; Friendship — Fiction. RL A.

Nina doesn't want her friend Ann to come to the dance show because she is not *the* star Ann expects.

2263 *Sir Small and the Dragonfly.* Ill. by John O'Brien. Random House, 1988, ISBN 0-394-89625-4. SERIES: Step into Reading. SUBJECTS: Concepts — Size — Fiction; Fantasy; Knights and knighthood — Fiction. RL B.

Smaller even than the very small people of Pee Wee, Sir Small is the only one brave enough to try to rescue Lady Teena from the dragonfly's cave. The fanciful color pictures have sketchy ink detailing and a need for more differentiation among the characters' faces.

2264 *Snail City.* Ill. by Rick Brown. Grosset & Dunlap, pap., 2001, ISBN 0-448-42418-5. SERIES: All Aboard Science Reader. SUBJECTS: Snails — Fiction. RL A.

Gail the snail is no longer called Fast Poke after she rescues a snail baby in danger of drowning. Humorous ink and wash drawings match the story.

2265 *Splat!* Ill. by Marilyn Mets. Grosset & Dunlap, pap., 1994, ISBN 0-448-40219-X. SERIES: All Aboard Science Reader. SUBJECTS: Toys — Fiction. RL B.

The Splat Master has the biggest water gun until he meets Tim, who has a gun the same size. They agree to splat only each other. Ink and wash drawings.

2266 *Super Cluck.* Ill. by Megan Lloyd. HarperCollins, 1991, ISBN 0-06-024594-8. SERIES: I Can Read. SUBJECTS: Science fiction; Superheroes — Fiction. RL B.

Chuck Cluck looks like other chicks, but is from the planet Nestron. He is no longer called a dumb cluck after rescuing 12 eggs from a marauding rat.

2267 *The Teeny Tiny Woman.* Ill. by R. W. Alley. Random House, 1986, ISBN 0-394-88320-9. SERIES: Step into Reading. SUBJECTS: Folklore — England; Ghost stories. RL A.

The teeny tiny woman encounters a ghost in this traditional story with ink drawings and a light wash.

Oda, Hidetomo

2268 *Insect Hibernation.* Trans. by Jun Amano. Ill. by Hidekazu Kubo. Raintree, 1986, ISBN 0-8172-2551-X. SERIES: Nature Close-Ups. SUBJECTS: Animals — Hibernation. RL C.

A clear text and excellent color photographs follow a variety of insects from fall to winter, when they hibernate hidden away in trees and earth, to spring when they emerge again. Detailed captions significantly supplement the text, which was originally published in Japan.

Oechsli, Kelly

2269 *Mice at Bat.* Ill. by author. HarperCollins, 1986, ISBN 0-06-024623-5. SERIES: I Can Read. SUBJECTS: Mice — Fiction; Sports — Baseball — Fiction. RL B.

An inventive story about a big midnight ball game between the Mighty Mites and the Boomers, all mice, with Old Casey the cat as umpire. Ink drawings with orange and turquoise washes complement the epic event.

Olson, Gillia M.

2270 *Phases of the Moon.* Ill. with photos. Capstone, 2007, ISBN 0-7368-6340-0; pap., ISBN 0-7368-7541-7. SERIES: Patterns in Nature. SUBJECTS: Astronomy and astronomers. RL B.

A bibliography, with Web sites, and glossary are appended to photograph pages showing the phases of the moon.

Olson, Mary C., ed.

2271 *Elephant on Skates.* Ill. by Jerry Scott. Golden Books, pap., 1987, ISBN 0-307-03676-6. SERIES: Step Ahead Beginning Reader. SUBJECTS: Elephants — Fiction; Self-esteem — Fiction; Sports — Roller skating — Fiction. RL A.

Everyone in her family tries to convince Edna that elephants do not belong on roller skates. Undaunted, she finally manages to get her family to try roller skating too. The story is fun, as are the full-color comic drawings of the elephant family.

2272 *Fly, Max, Fly!* Ill. by Donald Leake. Golden Books, pap., 1987, ISBN 0-307-03677-4. SERIES: Step Ahead Beginning Reader. SUBJECTS: Circuses — Fiction; Pets — Dogs — Fiction. RL A.

All the human members of the family are trapeze artists and Max, their dog, longs to be up flying with them. With the help of a clown, the children of the family train Max to be a part of their troupe. Children will enjoy the story and the boldly colored pictures, each with borders and stars.

Oppenheim, Joanne

2273 *The Christmas Witch.* Ill. by Annie Mitra. Bantam, 1993, ISBN 0-553-09392-4. SERIES: Bank Street Ready-to-Read. SUBJECTS: Christmas; Folklore — Italy. RL C.

Too late, Befana, an old Italian woman, decides to follow the three kings in search of the Christ child. Not able to find him, she searches every year at Christmas, leaving gifts, according to the old Italian legend. Illustrations are simply designed, childlike watercolors.

2274 *Could It Be?* Ill. by S. D. Schindler. Bantam, 1990, ISBN 0-553-05893-2. SERIES: Bank Street Ready-to-Read. SUBJECTS: Bears — Fiction; Spring — Fiction. RL B.

None of the usual signs or sounds of spring can awaken the hibernating bear. It takes a buzzing bumblebee and its connection to honey to get the bear up. The gentle text is illustrated with watercolors with ink definition.

2275 *Do You Like Cats?* Ill. by Carol Newsom. Gareth Stevens, 1993, ISBN 0-8368-1757-5. SERIES: Bank Street Ready-to-Read. SUBJECTS: Pets — Cats; Stories in rhyme. RL A.

Simple watercolors capture some very tactile cats in a variety of activities.

2276 *The Donkey's Tale.* Ill. by Chris Demarest. Bantam, 1991, ISBN 0-553-07090-8. SERIES: Bank Street Ready-to-Read. SUBJECTS: Folklore; Stories in rhyme. RL B.

An old man and his son decide to take their donkey to market to sell. Along the way they get all kinds of advice and, trying to please everyone, take it and end up with nothing. Based on a traditional tale, the story is illustrated with humorous watercolor and ink pictures.

2277 *Eency Weency Spider*. Ill. by S. D. Schindler. Bantam, 1990, ISBN 0-553-07316-8. SERIES: Bank Street Ready-to-Read. SUBJECTS: Nursery rhymes; Spiders — Fiction; Stories in rhyme. RL A.

The Eency Weency Spider meets other nursery rhyme characters in his travels. Ink and wash drawings.

2278 *Follow That Fish*. Ill. by Devis Grebu. Gareth Stevens, 1997, ISBN 0-8368-1751-6. SERIES: Bank Street Ready-to-Read. SUBJECTS: Nonsense; Oceans and ocean life — Fiction; Stories in rhyme. RL B.

A tall tale about a small boy's encounters when he is pulled overboard while fishing. The ink and wash drawings strike a fine balance between showing some ocean critters and the tall tale.

2279 *"Not Now!" Said the Cow*. Ill. by Chris Demarest. Bantam, 1989, ISBN 0-553-05826-6. SERIES: Bank Street Ready-to-Read. SUBJECTS: Animals — Fiction; Folklore. RL B.

A variant of "The Little Red Hen," this has Crow finding corn seed and having no luck getting other animals to help him plant it and care for it. Sketchy comic paintings show Crow struggling and finally getting his reward: popcorn to eat by himself.

2280 *Row, Row, Row Your Boat*. Ill. by Kevin O'Malley. Bantam, 1993, ISBN 0-553-09498-X. SUBJECTS: Boats and boating — Fiction; Songs; Stories in rhyme. RL B.

From the rowboat to the ferry and tug, the fireboat and the submarine, a boy dreams from his own tub. Pencil and wash drawings.

2281 *The Show-and-Tell Frog*. Ill. by Kate Duke. Gareth Stevens, pap., 1997, ISBN 0-8368-1762-1. SERIES: Bank Street Ready-to-Read. SUBJECTS: Frogs and toads — Fiction; School stories. RL B.

Allie ends up with a lost and found show-and-tell frog, although the reader can always spot the wayward frog. Very pleasing ink and wash drawings.

2282 *"Uh-Oh!" Said the Crow*. Ill. by Chris L. Demarest. Gareth Stevens, 1997, ISBN 0-8368-1753-2. SERIES: Bank Street Ready-to-Read. SUBJECTS: Animals — Farm; Cumulative tales; Stories in rhyme. RL B.

A dozen farm animals deny being spooked by apples falling from a tree. Very appealing watercolors.

Orgel, Doris

2283 *Button Soup*. Ill. by Paul Estrada. Gareth Stevens, 1998, ISBN 0-8368-1761-3. SERIES: Bank Street Ready-to-Read. SUBJECTS: Folklore — France. RL B.

Rag-Tag Meg conjures up a marvelous block party when she drops a button into a soup pot and begins to chant. Marvelous illustrations in yellow, lavender, and tan with green and brown highlights.

2284 *The Mouse Who Wanted to Marry*. Ill. by Holly Harmon. Bantam, 1993, ISBN 0-553-09235-9. SERIES: Bank Street Ready-to-Read. SUBJECTS: Folklore; Mice — Fiction. RL B.

A variant of a folktale told in Asian countries, this features a lovely mouse trying to find the most steadfast husband. She tries the sun, the clouds, the wind, a wall, and finally discovers that a mouse is the strongest of them all. The story is illustrated with attractive, colorful paintings.

2285 *Next Time I Will*. Ill. by Betsy Day. Bantam, 1993, ISBN 0-553-09031-3. SERIES: Bank Street Ready-to-Read. SUBJECTS: Folklore — England; Humorous stories. RL B.

Bill, a boy who does exactly as he is told, tries to earn extra money for food. Instead he does one thing after another wrong. Finally even his mistakes are redeemed because his actions make a rich man's daughter laugh. Illustrations are colorful paintings that look stiff.

Orgel, Doris, and Ellen Schecter

2286 *The Flower of Sheba*. Ill. by Laura Kelly. Bantam, 1994, ISBN 0-553-09041-0. SERIES: Bank Street Ready-to-Read. SUBJECTS: Bible stories. RL C.

Hoping to learn from the wisest man in the world, the Queen of Sheba travels to Israel to meet King Solomon. To prove his wisdom, she gives him a great test: finding a real flower amid

Orgel, Doris, and Ellen Schecter (cont.)

thousands of false ones. The text is illustrated with dramatic full-color paintings.

Osborne, Mary P.

2287 *Mo and His Friends*. Ill. by DyAnne DiSalvo-Ryan. Dial, 1989, ISBN 0-8037-0504-2. SERIES: Easy-to-Read. SUBJECTS: Animals — Fiction; Friendship — Fiction. RL B.

In four quiet stories set in the different seasons, the value and fun of friendship is seen through Sheriff Mo (a beaver), Peewee and Pearl (mice), Chicken Lucille, and the other Smith Pond characters. The pictures are in watercolor and pencil and reflect the gentle nature of the stories.

2288 *Mo to the Rescue*. Ill. by DyAnne DiSalvo-Ryan. Dial, pap., 1987, ISBN 0-8037-0182-9. SERIES: Easy-to-Read. SUBJECTS: Animals — Fiction; Friendship — Fiction; Sheriffs — Fiction. RL A.

Kind-hearted sheriff Mo Beaver welcomes newcomers, cleverly breaks up fighting blue jays, sees monsters in the shadows, and finally gets away to just sit and read a book. The gentle, "folksy" story is illustrated with full-color pencil sketches with watercolor washes.

Otto, Carolyn

2289 *I Can Tell by Touching*. Ill. by Nadine B. Westcott. HarperCollins, 1994, ISBN 0-06-023324-9. SERIES: Let's-Read-and-Find-Out Science. SUBJECTS: Senses — Touch. RL B.

A child notices the difference in the way things around the house feel — a pet rabbit and a drawing of a rabbit, gravel, a hillside he rolls down, and more. Westcott's simple and attractive pencil drawings with watercolors add to the text. A list of supplementary activities is appended.

2290 *Our Puppies Are Growing*. Ill. by Mary Morgan. HarperCollins, 1997, ISBN 0-06-027271-6. SUBJECTS: Animals — Baby; Pets — Dogs. RL B.

Chronicles puppies' birth and first six weeks of life. The illustrations are very simple watercolors.

Overbeck, Cynthia

2291 *The Vegetable Book*. Ill. by Sharon Lerner. Lerner, 1975, o.p. SERIES: Early Nature Picture Book. SUBJECTS: Gardening; Vegetables. RL C.

In a tour of a vegetable garden, this book comments on a dozen common edibles: how they are grown and used as food. The brightly colored illustrations are semi-realistic.

P

Packard, David

2292 *The Ball Game*. Ill. by R. W. Alley. Scholastic, pap., 1993, ISBN 0-590-46190-7. SERIES: My First Hello Reader. SUBJECTS: Sports — Baseball — Fiction; Stories in rhyme. RL A.

A very young ball player describes being up at bat and hitting the winning run. Short sentences and lots of action in the watercolor illustrations give the story a "you are there" feeling. The book also includes tear-out flash-cards and a section of activities to reinforce language skills.

Packard, Mary

2293 *Bubble Trouble*. Ill. by Elena Kucharik. Scholastic, pap., 2003, ISBN 0-439-59417-0. SERIES: Scholastic Reader. SUBJECTS: Bubbles — Fiction; Stories in rhyme. RL A.

A simple story about soap and gum bubbles, with language activities appended. Colored pencil and wash illustrations.

2294 *The Christmas Kitten*. Ill. by Jenny Williams. Children's Press, pap., 1994, ISBN 0-516-05364-7. SUBJECTS: Christmas — Fiction; Pets — Cats — Fiction. RL A.

Christmas Kitten is taken in by Santa, who, on Christmas Eve, finds just the right home for it! Thirty-two words are used; the watercolor illustrations of Santa's workshop give a Scandinavian feel.

2295 *The Christmas Penguin*. Ill. by Teri Weidner. Scholastic, pap., 2001, ISBN 0-439-32102-6. SERIES: Scholastic Reader.

SUBJECTS: Christmas — Fiction; Penguins — Fiction; Stories in rhyme. RL A.

Rollie the penguin saves Santa's Christmas bundle when it falls into the water. Colored pencil and wash drawings match the gentle story.

2296 *Fall Leaves*. Ill. by Dana Regan. Cartwheel, pap., 1999, ISBN 0-439-09911-0. SERIES: Scholastic Reader. SUBJECTS: Fall — Fiction; Stories in rhyme; Trees — Fiction. RL B. LEXILE 270L.

With leaves changing color and animals scurrying for nuts, fall is a wonderful time of year. The simple, rhyming text and pencil and watercolor art work well together.

2297 *I Am King!* Ill. by Leonid Gore. Children's Press, 1994, ISBN 0-516-05365-5. SERIES: My First Reader. SUBJECTS: Toys — Fiction. RL A. LEXILE BR.

A small boy commands an army when playing on his nursery floor. Soft pastel watercolors accent this imaginative story.

2298 *The Kite*. Ill. by Benrei Huang. Children's Press, 1990, ISBN 0-516-05355-8. SERIES: My First Reader. SUBJECTS: Kites and kite flying — Fiction. RL A.

A 20-word vocabulary doesn't go very far in this book about a boy flying a kite, accompanied by bare-bones, roly-poly illustrations.

2299 *My Messy Room*. Ill. by Stephanie Britt. Scholastic, pap., 1993, ISBN 0-590-46191-5. SERIES: My First Hello Reader. SUBJECTS: Cleanliness — Fiction; Stories in rhyme. RL A.

An exuberant little girl celebrates the messiness of her room, finally admitting that no matter how much she likes it, her mother does not. Bold pictures with strong colors and black outlining have great appeal. The book also includes language-reinforcement activities and flash cards.

2300 *Surprise!* Ill. by Benrei Huang. Childrens Press, 1990, ISBN 0-516-05360-4. SERIES: My First Reader. SUBJECTS: Birthdays — Fiction. RL A.

A very young child, opening birthday gifts, is happily surprised by the last, which holds a puppy. The 16-word vocabulary briefly describes the event, which is illustrated with pastel colored watercolors featuring chubby, round-faced little children.

2301 *Where Is Jake?* Ill. by Carolyn Ewing. Childrens Press, 1990, ISBN 0-516-05361-2. SERIES: My First Reader. SUBJECTS: Concepts; Pets — Dogs — Fiction. RL A.

As two children search for their dog, they also demonstrate spatial concepts such as up/ down, in/out, and so on. Each double page spread is illustrated with attractive pencil and watercolor pictures and captioned with just three words, usually in the form of a question.

Page, Josephine, adapter

2302 *Clifford the Big Red Dog: Tummy Trouble*. Ill. by Ken Edwards. Scholastic, pap., 2000, ISBN 0-439-21358-4. SERIES: Big Red Reader. SUBJECTS: Pets — Dogs — Fiction. RL B.

Clifford, Cleo, and T-Bone all have tummy trouble after rewarding themselves with three boxes of treats in this adaptation of the TV script of Bridwell's book.

Palacios, Argentina

2303 *A Christmas Surprise for Chabelita*. Ill. by Lori Lohstoeter. BridgeWater, 1993, ISBN 0-8167-3131-4. SUBJECTS: Grandparents — Fiction; Panama — Fiction; Parent and child — Fiction. RL B.

Living with her grandparents while her mother teaches far away, Chabelita memorizes a special poem and gets to recite it at the school holiday program. Spanish phrases, explained in context, and a beautifully illustrated Panamanian setting reinforce the uniqueness of this fine book.

2304 *Viva Mexico! A Story of Benito Juarez and Cinco de Mayo*. Ill. by Howard Berelson. Raintree, 1993, ISBN 0-8114-7214-0. SERIES: Stories of America. SUBJECTS: Biographies; Cinco de Mayo; Mexico. RL C.

A Zapotec Indian, Benito Juarez worked hard for an education and then worked equally hard to help others — finally becoming president of Mexico. When the country was invaded he helped to fight off the French and make May 5 a time to remember. The text is illustrated with expressive ink and watercolor drawings.

Palmer, Helen M.

2305 *A Fish Out of Water.* Ill. by P. D. Eastman. Beginner Books, 1961, ISBN 0-394-90023-5. SERIES: I Can Read It All by Myself. SUBJECTS: Humorous stories; Pets — Fish — Fiction. RL A.

A little boy is warned that he must feed his new goldfish, Otto, no more than a spot of food, but he still feeds him the entire box. Otto grows and grows until the pet store owner, Mr. Carp, must use his magic to return him to goldfish size. Never having waned in popularity, this book remains a delight with its humorous yet simple drawings.

Papajani, Janet

2306 *Museums.* Ill. with photos. Childrens Press, 1983, ISBN 0-516-01682-2. SERIES: New True. SUBJECTS: Museums. RL C.

From a discussion of the things Alexander the Great collected to a look at the Baseball Hall of Fame, museums of all kinds are mentioned. Young people are encouraged to visit and explore a variety of museums and the good color photographs of exhibits are an extra enticement to reading and visiting.

Pape, Donna L.

2307 *The Big White Thing.* Ill. by Bill Morrison. Garrard, 1975, o.p. SERIES: Easy Venture. SUBJECTS: Humorous stories; Raccoons — Fiction. RL A.

Not until a rainstorm fills it with water do the raccoons realize what the big white bathtub might be. Then they jump right in, swimming and bathing. The pictures are a bit sweet but their comic portrayal of the woodland animals is appealingly done in colored pencil and wash.

2308 *The Book of Foolish Machinery.* Ill. by Fred Winkowski. Scholastic, 1988, ISBN 0-590-40907-7. SUBJECTS: Nonsense; Poetry. RL A.

Nearly tongue twisters with their contortions of familiar words and with their silly rhymes, these poems about nonsensical machines and how they work are ideal for reading aloud by a confident young reader. The humorous, colorful illustrations are of complex machines.

2309 *Count on Leo Lion.* Ill. by Tom Eaton. Garrard, 1973, o.p. SERIES: Venture. SUBJECTS: Animals — Zoo — Fiction; Concepts — Numbers — Fiction; Humorous stories. RL A.

Asleep in his zoo cage, Leo Lion is awakened by two monkeys squabbling over how they should divide the peanuts they have. Deciding that they need to learn to count, Leo tries all kinds of ways to teach the monkeys their numbers. Illustrated with colorful and amusing drawings.

2310 *A Gerbil for a Friend.* Ill. by Diane Martin. Prentice-Hall, 1973, o.p. SUBJECTS: Pets — Gerbils. RL B.

Mark already has a cage waiting for the little gerbil when she is finally old enough for him to take home. By following Mark's example, children will be able to provide a good home for a pet gerbil. Illustrated with expressive ink drawings.

2311 *Leo Lion Looks for Books.* Ill. by Tom Eaton. Garrard, 1972, o.p. SERIES: Venture. SUBJECTS: Books and reading — Fiction; Humorous stories; Lions — Fiction. RL A.

Leo likes reading but there is not much to read in the zoo. He leaves his cage and wanders through town, discovers a bookstore, and ends up in the library. When the zookeeper comes for him, Leo does not want to leave the books. Full-color cartoon pictures show a dramatic lion who loves books.

2312 *The Mouse at the Show.* Ill. by Gail Gibbons. Elsevier-Dutton, 1981, o.p. SUBJECTS: Animals — Fiction; Circuses — Fiction; Mice — Fiction. RL A.

One animal after another trades places with a little mouse. By the time she gets to just the right seat, the circus-like show is over. Simple sentences are repeated or paraphrased to make reading this story very easy. Good layout and attractive ink and wash drawings will appeal to children.

2313 *Mr. Mogg in the Log.* Ill. by Mimi Korach. Garrard, 1972, o.p. SERIES: Venture. SUBJECTS: Humorous stories. RL B.

Trying to retrieve a quarter he has dropped, Mr. Mogg gets stuck in a log. Mrs. Mogg and their friend Mr. Jones try pulling him loose, having a helicopter shake him free, and more until they finally find a simple but sloppy solution. Illustrated with colorful, sketchy marker drawings.

2314 *Mrs. Twitter the Animal Sitter.* Ill. by Dora Leder. Garrard, 1972, o.p. SERIES: Venture. SUBJECTS: Animals — Fiction; Business enterprises — Fiction; Pet care — Fiction. RL A.

Mrs. Twitter answers an ad for a sitter and ends up taking care of a horse. She does everything wrong until a child helps her. Next she takes care of a seal and teaches it to balance a ball on its nose. The very silly story has realistic yet comical illustrations.

2315 *Where Is My Little Joey?* Ill. by Tom Eaton. Garrard, 1978, o.p. SERIES: Imagination. SUBJECTS: Humorous stories; Kangaroos — Fiction. RL A.

After napping in a park, poor Kara Kangaroo notices her little joey is gone. She searches everywhere for him but is hampered by having her pouch used for all kinds of things whenever she stops. The humorous story has colorful, cartoon-like pictures.

Parish, Herman

2316 *Amelia Bedelia, Bookworm.* Ill. by Lynn Sweat. Greenwillow, 2002, ISBN 0-06-051890-1. SUBJECTS: Humorous stories; Jokes and riddles; Wordplay. RL B.

Amelia Bedelia is given a book mobile, after taking off with the bookmobile. Lots of library- and book-related wordplay.

2317 *Amelia Bedelia 4 Mayor.* Ill. by Lynn Sweat. Greenwillow, 2002, ISBN 0-06-001421-0. SUBJECTS: Humorous stories; Jokes and riddles; Wordplay. RL B.

Amelia Bedelia has all of Dr. Horton's patients in a frenzy with her misunderstandings when she tries to help.

2318 *Amelia Bedelia, Rocket Scientist.* Ill. by Lynn Sweat. Greenwillow, 2004, ISBN 0-06-051887-1. SUBJECTS: Humorous stories; Jokes and riddles; Wordplay. RL B.

This time Amelia Bedelia helps out at the science fair. A whole box of baking soda and a leaf blower wreak havoc with the volcano display.

Parish, Peggy

2319 *Amelia Bedelia.* Ill. by Fritz Siebel. HarperCollins, 1992, ISBN 0-06-020186-X. SERIES: I Can Read. SUBJECTS: Humorous stories. RL B.

The Rogers hire Amelia Bedelia and leave her with a list of chores. Following their instructions exactly, she "dusts" the furniture with dusting powder, "dresses" the chicken in clothes — and more. This perennial favorite is illustrated in full color.

2320 *Amelia Bedelia and the Baby.* Ill. by Lynn Sweat. Greenwillow, 1981, ISBN 0-688-00316-8. SERIES: Read-Alone. SUBJECTS: Baby-sitting — Fiction; Humorous stories. RL A.

Mrs. Rogers insists that Amelia Bedelia take care of the neighbor's baby. The child's mother leaves detailed instructions for Amelia Bedelia to follow and, to the baby's delight, Amelia follows them exactly. The ink and wash pictures add to the fun.

2321 *Amelia Bedelia and the Surprise Shower.* Ill. by Fritz Siebel. HarperCollins, pap., 1979, ISBN 0-06-024643-X. SERIES: I Can Read. SUBJECTS: Humorous stories. RL B.

Not familiar with "showers," Amelia Bedelia assumes she is to spray the bride-to-be with water. In a story filled with her literal and very funny interpretations of instructions, Amelia Bedelia's antics will keep children laughing. The book has humorous ink and wash sketches.

2322 *Amelia Bedelia Goes Camping.* Ill. by Lynn Sweat. Greenwillow, pap., 1985, ISBN 0-688-04058-6. SERIES: Read-Alone. SUBJECTS: Camps and camping — Fiction; Humorous stories. RL A.

When Mr. Rogers says to hit the road, Amelia Bedelia of course takes a stick and hits the road. After creating her usual havoc on their camping trip, Amelia Bedelia again redeems herself with her cooking. This book is illustrated with spare ink drawings and washes.

2323 *Amelia Bedelia Helps Out.* Ill. by Lynn Sweat. Greenwillow, pap., 1982, ISBN 0-688-84631-3. SERIES: Read-Alone. SUBJECTS: Humorous stories. RL B.

When Miss Emma's gardener is ill, Amelia Bedelia and her niece offer to help. They create the usual problems caused by Amelia Bedelia's

Parish, Peggy (cont.)

literal interpretation of orders. Adding to the hilarity are the ink and wash pictures.

2324 *Amelia Bedelia's Family Album.* Ill. by Lynn Sweat. Greenwillow, 1988, ISBN 0-688-07677-7. SUBJECTS: Family life — Fiction; Humorous stories. RL B.

Mr. and Mrs. Rogers decide to have a party for their silly maid, Amelia Bedelia, and want to invite her family. When she shows them her family album, her employers realize that her family is as unusual as Amelia herself. A new format and full-color pictures are used for this twenty-fifth anniversary edition.

2325 *Be Ready at Eight.* Ill. by Leonard Kessler. Macmillan, 1979, o.p. SERIES: Ready-to-Read. SUBJECTS: Birthdays — Fiction; Memory and memorization — Fiction. RL B.

Miss Molly cannot remember why she has a string tied around her finger although everybody in town is reminding her that they will see her at eight. Her forgetfulness turns her birthday party into a surprise. Simple line drawings with orange and green accents add to the fun.

2326 *The Cats' Burglar.* Ill. by Lynn Sweat. Greenwillow, pap., 1983, ISBN 0-688-01826-2. SERIES: Read-Alone. SUBJECTS: Pets — Cats — Fiction; Robbers and outlaws — Fiction. RL A.

Aunt Emma refuses to give up any of her nine cats. When a burglar breaks in, the cats gang up on the very allergic man. The independent Aunt Emma and the police know how lucky she is not to be hurt while the humorous drawings and antics of the cats keep the tone light.

2327 *Come Back, Amelia Bedelia.* Ill. by Wallace Tripp. Greenwillow, pap., 1971, ISBN 0-06-024668-5. SERIES: I Can Read. SUBJECTS: Humorous stories. RL B.

After being fired by Mrs. Rogers for her latest literal interpretation of instructions, Amelia Bedelia starts looking for work, with predictable and often hilarious results. The ink and wash drawings give Amelia Bedelia an innocence that adds to the story's humor and success.

2328 *Dinosaur Time.* Ill. by Arnold Lobel. HarperCollins, pap., 1974, ISBN 0-06-024654-5. SERIES: Early I Can Read. SUBJECTS: Dinosaurs. RL B.

Eleven dinosaurs are introduced, with the pronunciation of their names and facts about their size and lifestyle. The never-waning popularity of dinosaurs and the attractive detailed drawings and brief text make this a continuing favorite.

2329 *Good Hunting, Blue Sky.* Ill. by James Watts. HarperCollins, 1988, ISBN 0-06-024661-8. SERIES: I Can Read. SUBJECTS: Native Americans — Fiction; Sports — Hunting — Fiction. RL B.

In a good revision of *Good Hunting, Little Indian* (1962), Blue Sky goes out hunting with bow and arrow and misses everything he aims for. Walking home, he is chased by a boar and ends up riding it into his village, where his father kills it. This book is illustrated with attractive full-color drawings.

2330 *Good Work, Amelia Bedelia.* Ill. by Lynn Sweat. Greenwillow, pap., 1982, ISBN 0-688-84022-1. SERIES: Read-Alone. SUBJECTS: Humorous stories. RL B.

Amelia Bedelia's well-known literal approach to following instructions gets her in more trouble as she patches a screen with cloth, serves cracked corn as a chicken dinner, and puts pieces of sponge in batter for a sponge cake. Ink and colored pencil drawings add to the humor.

2331 *Granny and the Desperadoes.* Ill. by Steven Kellogg. Macmillan, 1970, o.p. SUBJECTS: Robbers and outlaws — Fiction; Western stories. RL B.

The threat of Granny's shotgun, which does not work, is the reason the robbers are helping Granny repair her house and capture ducks. Kellogg's hilarious pencil sketches guarantee fun.

2332 *Merry Christmas, Amelia Bedelia.* Ill. by Lynn Sweat. Greenwillow, pap., 1987, ISBN 0-688-06102-8. SERIES: Read-Alone. SUBJECTS: Christmas — Fiction; Humorous stories. RL B.

When Mrs. Rogers leaves to pick up Aunt Myra for Christmas, Amelia Bedelia is left with a list of instructions for trimming the tree, stuffing stockings, and more, all of which she interprets literally and humorously. Ink and wash sketches support the zaniness of the story.

2333 *Mind Your Manners*. Ill. by Marylin Hafner. Greenwillow, pap., 1978, ISBN 0-688-84157-0. SERIES: Read-Alone. SUBJECTS: Behavior — Manners. RL B.

This humorous, light-handed approach to manners gives children the appropriate behavior for 18 situations — from meeting new people to chewing gum. The ink and wash illustrations reinforce the importance of good manners.

2334 *Mr. Adams's Mistake*. Ill. by Gail Owens. Macmillan, 1982, ISBN 0-02-769800-9. SERIES: Ready-to-Read. SUBJECTS: Chimpanzees — Fiction; Humorous stories; School stories. RL B.

Mr. Adams, a nearsighted truant officer, mistakes a chimpanzee for a child and hurries it off to school with riotous results. Realistic full-color drawings add to the humor of the story.

2335 *No More Monsters for Me!* Ill. by Marc Simont. HarperCollins, pap., 1987, ISBN 0-06-024658-8. SERIES: I Can Read. SUBJECTS: Monsters — Fiction; Parent and child — Fiction; Pets — Fiction. RL B.

After arguing with her mother about having a pet, Minn finds a gentle baby monster and hides it in the basement. While there, it starts to grow at an alarming rate. In the end, it is taken back to its home and replaced by a more ordinary pet. Humorous ink and wash pictures show a huge but still lovable monster.

2336 *Ootah's Lucky Day*. Ill. by Mamoru Funai. HarperCollins, 1970, o.p. SERIES: I Can Read. SUBJECTS: Eskimos — Fiction; Hunting — Fiction. RL A.

With nothing to eat and no oil for a fire, little Ootah, an Eskimo boy, takes his dogs and goes hunting alone. Using all his training and courage, Ootah surprises everyone by killing a walrus, thus providing meat for all the people in his village. Simple, realistic drawings illustrate the book.

2337 *Play Ball, Amelia Bedelia*. Ill. by Wallace Tripp. HarperCollins, pap., 1978, ISBN 0-06-024656-1. SERIES: I Can Read. SUBJECTS: Humorous stories. RL B.

When the Grizzlies are short one player in their game with the Tornadoes, Amelia Bedelia volunteers to help out. Putting paper tags on players, stealing bases, and carrying boys "out" are typical of the good-natured misunderstandings depicted in the ink and wash line drawings.

2338 *Scruffy*. Ill. by Kelly Oechsli. HarperCollins, 1988, ISBN 0-06-024659-6. SERIES: I Can Read. SUBJECTS: Animal rescue — Fiction; Pets — Cats — Fiction. RL B.

Todd goes to an animal shelter to find his birthday kitten, where he has trouble finding just the right one.

2339 *Teach Us, Amelia Bedelia*. Ill. by Lynn Sweat. Scholastic, pap., 1987, ISBN 0-688-84069-8. SERIES: Read-Alone. SUBJECTS: Humorous stories; School stories. RL B.

Taking a message to the principal, Amelia Bedelia is mistaken for the new teacher and hurried into a classroom. She diligently follows a list of instructions, concocting her own hilarious way of teaching. Illustrated with funny ink, colored pencil, and wash pictures.

2340 *Thank You, Amelia Bedelia*. Ill. by Barbara Siebel Thomas. Greenwillow, 1992, ISBN 0-06-022979-9. SUBJECTS: Humorous stories; Jokes and riddles; Wordplay. RL B.

Amelia Bedelia removes the spots on her patron's dress — with scissors. She strings all the beans — on a string. Literal-minded Amelia keeps life interesting.

2341 *Too Many Rabbits*. Ill. by Leonard Kessler. Macmillan, 1974, o.p. SERIES: Ready-to-Read. SUBJECTS: Pets — Rabbits — Fiction; Rabbits — Fiction. RL A.

When the rabbit she takes in has a litter, Miss Molly decides to keep them all until they start multiplying. Humorous line drawings and a simple text tell the story of a kindhearted woman who just cannot say no to stray animals.

2342 *Zed and the Monsters*. Ill. by Paul Galdone. Doubleday, 1979, o.p. SERIES: Reading on My Own. SUBJECTS: Monsters — Fiction; Tall tales. RL B.

An offer of gold entices lazy Zed to match wits with and overcome four monsters. Humorous and good for storytelling, the story is illustrated with outlandishly funny ink and wash pictures.

Park, Margaret

2343 *Harvey and Rosie . . . and Ralph.* Ill. by Ann Iosa. Dutton, 1992, ISBN 0-525-44836-5. SERIES: Speedsters. SUBJECTS: Magic — Fiction; Pets — Dogs — Fiction; Sports — Soccer — Fiction. RL C.

Harvey is such a poor soccer player that even his dog Rosie is better. On the day of their big game, Rosie is magically transformed into a soccer-playing child who helps them win. Black-and-white pictures are scattered throughout this engaging sports story.

Parker, Marjorie Blain

2344 *Hello, Fire Truck.* Ill. by Bob Kolar. Scholastic, pap., 2004, ISBN 0-439-59890-7. SERIES: Scholastic Reader. SUBJECTS: Fire fighters and fire fighting — Fiction; Stories in rhyme. RL A.

The work of a firefighter is described in simplest terms with illustrations modeled on toy equipment.

2345 *Hello, Freight Train!* Ill. by Bob Kolar. Scholastic, pap., 2005, ISBN 0-439-59891-5. SERIES: Scholastic Reader. SUBJECTS: Stories in rhyme; Trains — Fiction. RL A.

Simple information about the cars that make up a train is followed by a 12-word vocabulary list.

2346 *Hello, School Bus!* Ill. by Bob Kolar. Scholastic, pap., 2004, ISBN 0-439-59889-3. SERIES: Scholastic Reader. SUBJECTS: School buses — Fiction; Stories in rhyme. RL A.

A 12-word vocabulary list follows the rhythmic text.

Parker, Philip

2347 *The Life Cycle of a Stickleback.* Ill. by Jackie Harland. Bookwright, 1988, o.p. SERIES: Life Cycles. SUBJECTS: Fish. RL B.

Sticklebacks are notable in that they lay eggs in a nest and then the male guards the nest and looks after the hatchlings. The tiny three-spined freshwater stickleback is seen in its habitat as readers learn about its breeding and diet. Full-color paintings accurately depict the excellent text.

2348 *The Life Cycle of a Sunflower.* Ill. by Jackie Harland. Bookwright, 1988, ISBN 0-531-18191-X. SERIES: Life Cycles. SUBJECTS: Flowers. RL B.

Using clear, carefully executed paintings that work very well with an excellent text, this book presents a good description of the growth of a sunflower from seed to maturity. Attention is also paid to clear instructions for growing a sunflower. A glossary, bibliography, and index are included.

Parramon, J. M.

2349 *My First Visit to a Farm.* Ill. by G. Sales. Barron's, 1990, ISBN 0-8120-4305-7. SERIES: My First Visit. SUBJECTS: Farm and country life; School stories. RL B.

A class visits an old-fashioned family farm where cows are milked by hand and horses are used to pull wagons of hay. Following the story is a two-page section geared to adults about domestic animals and farming. The illustrations are sweet watercolors.

2350 *My First Visit to the Aviary.* Ill. by G. Sales. Barron's, 1990, ISBN 0-8120-4303-0. SERIES: My First Visit. SUBJECTS: Birds; School stories. RL B.

A teacher takes her students to an aviary where they learn a little about the habits of some common and some exotic birds. Paintings are colorful and somewhat realistic. A section intended for parents and teachers offers additional information.

2351 *My First Visit to the Zoo.* Ill. by author. Barron's, 1990, ISBN 0-8120-4302-2. SERIES: My First Visit. SUBJECTS: School stories; Zoos. RL B.

A class visits the zoo and identifies the animals and comments on their zoo habitats. Illustrations of the animals are realistic watercolors while those of the people gazing at them are more cartoon-like. One mistake: Baboons are identified as monkeys.

Partridge, Elizabeth

2352 *Annie and Bo and the Big Surprise.* Ill. by Martha Weston. Dutton, 2001, ISBN 0-525-46728-9. SERIES: Dutton Easy Reader. SUBJECTS: Bakers and baking — Fiction; Friendship — Fiction; Mice — Fiction. RL B.

Bo and Annie each have a surprise for the other after skating on a snowy night. Simple expressive drawings depict the friends.

Patent, Dorothy H.

2353 *All About Whales*. Ill. with photos. Holiday House, 1987, ISBN 0-8234-0644-X. SUBJECTS: Conservation; Whales. RL C.

This book characterizes whales as mammals belonging to two groups (baleen and toothed) and discusses their growth, feeding, senses, and communication, and the efforts of humans to save them from extinction. An index is included. Black-and-white photographs accompany an extensive text.

Paterson, Diane

2354 *Someday*. Ill. by author. Macmillan, 1993, ISBN 0-02-770565-X. SUBJECTS: Animals — Fiction; Boats and boating — Fiction; Humorous stories. RL B.

For three clams, a shell, and a pebble, a sea gull purchases a sailboat, names it Someday, and invites his animal friends to go sailing with him. One misadventure after another fills their day with fun. Text is illustrated with watercolor paintings with much child appeal.

Paterson, Katherine

2355 *Marvin One Too Many*. Ill. by Jane C. Brown. HarperCollins, 2001, ISBN 0-06-028769-1. SERIES: I Can Read. SUBJECTS: Books and reading — Fiction. RL B.

Marvin's father discovers Marvin is a late reader like himself. A sympathetic story with appealing colored-pencil drawings of school and family life.

2356 *Marvin's Best Christmas Present Ever*. Ill. by Jane C. Brown. HarperCollins, 1996, ISBN 0-06-027159-0. SERIES: I Can Read. SUBJECTS: Farm and country life — Fiction. RL B.

Marvin and his sister, May, live in a trailer on a dairy farm. Marvin's presents are always a flop — until his sister helps him make a big Christmas wreath to hang on the end of their trailer. Soft, colored-pencil illustrations.

2357 *The Smallest Cow in the World*. Ill. by Jane C. Brown. HarperCollins, 1991, ISBN 0-06-024690-1. SERIES: I Can Read. SUBJECTS: Cows — Fiction; Farm and country life — Fiction; Imagination — Fiction. RL B.

Forced not only to move but to see Rosie, his favorite cow, sold, Marvin gets so angry that he imagines a miniature Rosie — a Rosie who does mean things until Marvin gives her a good home. The problems of moving and of having little control over anything are well handled in text and pictures.

Paul, Ann Whitford

2358 *Silly Sadie, Silly Samuel*. Ill. by Sylvie Wickstrom. Simon & Schuster, 1998, ISBN 0-689-81689-8. SERIES: Ready-to-Read. SUBJECTS: Humorous stories. RL B. LEXILE 220L.

Sadie and Samuel love each other despite their differences, which are shown in silly arguments over such topics as the correct place to hang a picture. The illustrations are appropriately silly.

Pearce, Q. L., and W. J. Pearce

2359 *In the African Grasslands*. Ill. by Delana Bettoli. Silver Burdett, 1990, ISBN 0-671-68831-6. SERIES: Nature's Footprints. SUBJECTS: Animals — Baby; Animals — Habits and behavior; Grasslands — Africa. RL A.

Mother and young of cheetah and antelope, jackal and leopard, baboon and ostrich, and two other pairs are shown and minimal information is provided about each. Realistic watercolor pictures are framed with the tracks of the animals.

2360 *In the Barnyard*. Ill. by Delana Bettoli. Silver Burdett, 1990, ISBN 0-671-68828-6. SERIES: Nature's Footprints. SUBJECTS: Animals — Farm; Animals — Habits and behavior; Animals — Tracks. RL A.

Ten farm animals in five sets (duck and cat, dog and sheep, and so on) are shown in a farm setting. The minimal text starts with the animal's sound then briefly states the animal's use. Rather sweet watercolor pictures use animal tracks to lead readers forward and introduce an animal.

2361 *In the Desert*. Ill. by Delana Bettoli. Silver Burdett, 1990, ISBN 0-671-68829-4. SERIES: Nature's Footprints. SUBJECTS: Animals —

Pearce, Q. L., and W. J. Pearce (cont.)

Desert; Animals — Habits and behavior; Animals — Tracks. RL A.

With emphasis on their tracks, five sets of animals (tortoise and vulture, roadrunner and prairie dog, and so on) are shown with tracks leading to them and tracks framing the pictures. Text merely captions the full-color realistic pictures and provides little information.

2362 *In the Forest.* Ill. by Delana Bettoli. Silver Burdett, 1990, ISBN 0-671-68830-8. SERIES: Nature's Footprints. SUBJECTS: Animals — Habits and behavior; Animals — Tracks; Forest rangers and forestry. RL A.

Five sets of woodland and pond animals (beaver and frog, owl and skunk, and so on) are pictured in their natural environment with minimal information. Readers are urged to use the tracks that frame the colorful, rather sweet, paintings to find the appropriate animal.

Pearson, Mary E.

2363 *Pickles in My Soup.* Ill. by Tom Payne. Children's Press, 1999, ISBN 0-516-21636-8. SERIES: Rookie Reader. SUBJECTS: Food — Fiction; Stories in rhyme. RL A. LEXILE 20L.

A cartoon girl with her faithful dog relates all the ways she likes to eat pickles — until . . . !

2364 *Where Is Max?* Ill. by Samantha L. Walker. Children's Press, 1999, ISBN 0-516-22019-5; pap., ISBN 0-516-27077-X. SERIES: Rookie Reader. SUBJECTS: Mice — Fiction; School stories. RL A.

Bug-eyed classmates search for the missing pet mouse, who is visible all the time to the reader in this book with a 29-word vocabulary.

Penner, Lucille Recht

2365 *Bears on the Brain.* Ill. by Lynn Adams. Kane, pap., 2003, ISBN 1-57565-121-1. SERIES: Science Solves It! SUBJECTS: Animals — Tracks — Fiction; Science and scientists — Fiction. RL B.

Gabriel, Sam, Jill, and Oscar figure out what animal(s) is into their garbage and garden by studying tracks in their library book. Expressive pen and wash drawings.

2366 *Dinosaur Babies.* Ill. by Peter Barrett. Random House, 1991, ISBN 0-679-91207-X. SERIES: Step into Reading. SUBJECTS: Dinosaurs. RL A.

Scientific in its approach to what is known about dinosaurs and their young, this book lets children know what has been verified and what is supposition with few words and realistic, well-designed pictures of the dinosaurs.

2367 *Lights Out!* Ill. by Jerry Smath. Kane, pap., 1999, ISBN 1-57565-092-4. SERIES: Math Matters. SUBJECTS: Mathematics — Subtraction. RL B.

A small girl stays up late counting the number of lights still on in the apartment building across from hers. An original way of introducing math concepts, with pencil and wash drawings.

2368 *Snakes!* Ill. by Peter Barrett. Random House, 1994, ISBN 0-679-94777-9. SERIES: Step into Reading. SUBJECTS: Reptiles and amphibians; Snakes. RL B.

Engaging, realistic paintings of snakes and their environments will attract children to this book and the well-done text will maintain their interest. The author includes information on physical aspects of snakes, their food, social behavior, and the important part they play in the balance of nature.

2369 *The True Story of Pocahontas.* Ill. by Pamela Johnson. Random House, 1994, ISBN 0-679-96166-6. SERIES: Step into Reading. SUBJECTS: Biographies; Native Americans; United States — History. RL B.

In a brief look at the life of the young American Indian woman alleged to have saved the life of John Smith, readers get a glimpse of the life of her people and her own character. The ending unfortunately says only that she spent the remainder of her life in England, not that disease killed her as she was returning to Virginia. Watercolor and pencil pictures attractively depict her life.

2370 *Where's That Bone?* Ill. by Lynn Adams. Kane, pap., 1999, ISBN 1-57565-097-5. SERIES: Math Matters. SUBJECTS: Maps — Fiction; Pets — Dogs — Fiction. RL B.

Jill draws maps of where her dog, Bingo, buries his bones when Bingo has trouble finding them. Lively pen and wash drawings.

2371 *X Marks the Spot!* Ill. by Jerry Smath. Kane, pap., 2002, ISBN 1-57565-111-4. SERIES: Math Matters. SUBJECTS: Buried treasure — Fiction; Maps — Fiction; Moving, household — Fiction. RL B.

Grandpa leaves Jake and Leo some treasure maps to get them acquainted with their new neighborhood when the family moves into Grandpa's old house. They lead to a treasure any child would covet! Watercolor illustrations.

Penny, Malcolm

2372 *Let's Look at Sharks.* Ill. by Wendy Meadway. Watts, 1990, ISBN 0-531-18308-4. SERIES: Let's Look At. SUBJECTS: Fish; Sharks. RL B.

Detailed and realistic watercolors show many different kinds of sharks — including the ray and the hammerhead — while the text explains where they live and how. There is also information on sharks dangerous to humans. A brief glossary is included.

Perez-Mercado, Mary Margaret

2373 *Splat!* Ill. by Richard L. Torrey. Children's Press, 1999, ISBN 0-516-21615-5. SERIES: Rookie Reader. SUBJECTS: Cookery — Fiction; Humorous stories; Stories in rhyme. RL A.

A lighthearted story in rhyme about frosting that lands everywhere but on the cake, illustrated with similarly zany cartoon drawings.

Perkins, Al

2374 *The Ear Book.* Ill. by William O'Brien. Random House, 1968, ISBN 0-394-91199-7. SERIES: Bright and Early Books. SUBJECTS: Human body — Ears — Fiction; Stories in rhyme. RL B.

A short, rhythmic text leads children not only to consider the many ways and things that ears hear but also offers children a chance for a successful beginning reading experience. Full-color comic paintings of people and things are arranged on a white background.

2375 *Hand, Hand, Fingers, Thumb.* Ill. by Eric Gurney. Random House, 1969, ISBN 0-394-91076-1. SERIES: Bright and Early Books. SUBJECTS: Monkeys — Fiction; Stories in rhyme. RL C.

A rhyming text introduces the reader to one monkey drumming, then more and more monkeys using their hands in a variety of ways. Finally millions of monkeys are drumming in this catchy non-story that both readers and listeners enjoy. Illustrated with detailed line drawings and washes.

2376 *Hugh Lofting's Travels of Doctor Dolittle.* Ill. by Philip Wende. Random House, 1967, ISBN 0-394-80048-6. SERIES: Beginner Books. SUBJECTS: Adventure stories; Animals — Fiction; Fantasy. RL C.

This very abbreviated version of the classic story is abridged well, and children will enjoy his taste of Doctor Dolittle's adventures. Here he travels to Africa by ship to cure the monkeys of a terrible disease. Illustrations, similar in style to Lofting's, are done in color.

2377 *The Nose Book.* Ill. by Roy McKie. Random House, 1970, ISBN 0-394-90623-3. SERIES: Bright and Early Books. SUBJECTS: Human body — Nose — Fiction; Stories in rhyme. RL A.

A brown dog explores the great variety of noses among animals and humans and notes the things noses are used for, such as holding up glasses and smelling food. The lively, rhyming text is matched to bright, bold paintings with black outlines.

2378 *Tubby and the Lantern.* Ill. by Rowland Wilson. Beginner Books, 1971, o.p. SERIES: I Can Read It All by Myself. SUBJECTS: Adventure stories; Elephants — Fiction. RL B.

Ah Mee, the son of a lantern maker, has Tubby, a small elephant, as his very special pet and friend. The two are lifted away by a huge lantern and carried out to sea and they have a great adventure. Illustrated with lively full-color pictures.

Petersen, David

2379 *Antarctica.* Ill. with photos. Children's Press, 1998, ISBN 0-516-20770-9. SERIES: True Book. SUBJECTS: Antarctica; Geography. RL C.

A satellite view, a map, and photographs show the spectacular scenery in Antarctica.

Petersen, David (cont.)

2380 *Arches National Park*. Ill. with photos. Children's Press, 1998, ISBN 0-516-20941-8. SERIES: True Book. SUBJECTS: Geology and geologists; National parks; United States. RL C.

The geology of the formation of arches is outlined, and some of the most dramatic arches are featured. The animals and plants that live in the park are described, as is the importance of cryptocrust.

2381 *Asia*. Ill. with photos. Children's Press, 1997, ISBN 0-516-20764-4. SERIES: True Book. SUBJECTS: Asia; Geography. RL C.

The geology, cultures, and wildlife of Asia are introduced. Fast Facts include the highest/lowest points, the longest river, and the largest lake.

2382 *Australia*. Ill. with photos. Children's Press, 1998, ISBN 0-516-20765-2. SERIES: True Book. SUBJECTS: Australia; Geography. RL C.

From the outback to Tasmania, from aborigines to geology and wildlife, this book gives a good overview of this country/continent.

2383 *Chaco Culture National Park*. Ill. with photos. Children's Press, 1998, ISBN 0-516-20942-6. SERIES: True Book. SUBJECTS: National parks; Native Americans; United States. RL C.

Thousands of Anasazi artifacts have been unearthed at Chaco, home of petroglyphs and pictographs. Four of its great houses have been excavated, the largest of which has 500 rooms, 16 kivas, a plaza, and four stories.

2384 *Denali National Park and Preserve*. Ill. with photos. Children's Press, 1996, ISBN 0-516-20050-X. SERIES: True Book. SUBJECTS: Geography; National parks; United States. RL C.

Denali is rich in wildlife and plants, many of which are pictured here. The books and Web pages listed provide further information on this stunning park.

2385 *North America*. Ill. with photos. Children's Press, 1998, ISBN 0-516-20768-7. SERIES: True Book. SUBJECTS: Geography; North America. RL C.

Climates and landscapes, water and sand, wildlife and people are all covered in this account that includes Central America. Web sites listed include ones on music, the Great Lakes, weather, insects, and a kids home page for Canada.

2386 *Saguaro National Park*. Ill. with photos. Children's Press, 1998, ISBN 0-516-20944-2. SERIES: True Book. SUBJECTS: Cacti; National parks; United States. RL C.

The characteristics and variety of desert life are outlined, with attention to the desert monarch, the saguaro. From a single, soaking rain, one saguaro can absorb 200 gallons of water, enough for a year. The saguaro is home to several different kinds of desert animal, and its fruit is gathered for food and to make syrups and jams.

2387 *South America*. Ill. with photos. Children's Press, 1998, ISBN 0-516-20769-5. SERIES: True Book. SUBJECTS: Geography; South America. RL C.

Chapters give information on the Amazon, the Andes, the central plains, waterfalls, and the people. The Web sites listed include ones on cybertours.

Petersen, David, and Christine Petersen

2388 *The Atlantic Ocean*. Ill. with photos. Children's Press, 2001, ISBN 0-516-22042-X. SERIES: True Book. SUBJECTS: Oceans and ocean life. RL C.

The history of exploration of the Atlantic, fairly recent, is outlined, and the ocean floor is pictured. Some of the creatures found in the ocean are described, including lobsters, jellyfish, crabs, and clams. Lesson plans from the Smithsonian are given on the Ocean Planet Web site, and the New England Aquarium is highlighted.

2389 *The Pacific Ocean*. Ill. with photos. Children's Press, 2000, ISBN 0-516-22043-8. SERIES: True Book. SUBJECTS: Oceans and ocean life. RL C.

The other three oceans could fit inside the Pacific. It is also the deepest ocean. A diagram shows the ocean floor, and the uneasy geology, the tides, kelp forests, reefs, and some sea life are described. Web sites of the Monterey Bay and Vancouver aquariums are appended.

Petersen, P. J.

2390 *The Fireplug Is First Base*. Ill. by Betsy James. Dutton, 1990, ISBN 0-525-44587-0. SERIES: Speedsters. SUBJECTS: Siblings — Fiction; Sports — Baseball — Fiction. RL B.

Joe's little brother "Flea" finally gets a chance to bat in the Big Boys' street game of baseball Through a series of mishaps, Flea gets a triple home run. Black-and-white pencil and wash pictures are lively and have balloons filled with dialogue. The format makes it appear to be aimed at older readers.

Peterson, Scott

2391 *The Story of Batman*. Ill. by Rick Burchett. Scholastic, pap., 2006, ISBN 0-439-47104-4. SERIES: Scholastic Reader. SUBJECTS: Heroes — Fiction. RL B.

Billionaire Bruce Wayne travels the world learning skills to combat crime, but lacks the intimidating costume. In this introduction, he also confronts Penguin for the first time. Illustrated with cartoons.

Petrie, Catherine

2392 *Joshua James Likes Trucks*. Ill. by Joel Snyder. Children's Press, 1999, ISBN 0-516-21639-2. SERIES: Rookie Reader. SUBJECTS: Trucks — Fiction. RL A. LEXILE BR.

Toddler Joshua James just loves trucks, of every size and color and shape.

Pfeffer, Wendy

2393 *Dolphin Talk: Whistles, Clicks, and Clapping Jaws*. Ill. by Helen K. Davie. HarperCollins, 2001, ISBN 0-06-028801-9. SERIES: Let's-Read-and-Find-Out. SUBJECTS: Dolphins; Oceans and ocean life. RL C.

A diagram shows how dolphins produce clicks and use echolocation, and theories as to when dolphins make various sounds are presented in simple text and watercolor drawings.

2394 *From Seed to Pumpkin*. Ill. by James Graham Hale. HarperCollins, 2004, ISBN 0-06-028038-7. SERIES: Let's-Read-and-Find-Out. SUBJECTS: Gardening; Pumpkins. RL B.

The life cycle of a pumpkin is enjoyed by a pair of children.

2395 *From Tadpole to Frog*. Ill. by Holly Keller. HarperCollins, 1994, ISBN 0-06-023044-4. SERIES: Let's-Read-and-Find-Out Science. SUBJECTS: Frogs and toads; Reptiles and amphibians. RL B.

Using the bullfrog as an example, the author and illustrator take a fascinating step-by-step approach to the frog's development. Watercolor illustrations are detailed and attractive. A final section, geared to older readers, provides more information on frogs. A map concludes the book.

2396 *Sound All Around*. Ill. by Holly Keller. HarperCollins, 1997, ISBN 0-06-027711-4. SERIES: Let's-Read-and-Find-Out. SUBJECTS: Science and scientists; Sound. RL B.

Information about sound begins with those children make and hear. The uses of drums and echolocation are introduced, as is the concept of measuring sound.

2397 *What's It Like to Be a Fish?* Ill. by Holly Keller. HarperCollins, 1996, ISBN 0-06-024428-3. SERIES: Let's-Read-and-Find-Out Science. SUBJECTS: Pets — Fish. RL B.

Information about how fish breathe, swim, and eat is followed by how to set up a small aquarium.

2398 *Wiggling Worms at Work*. Ill. by Steve Jenkins. HarperCollins, 2004, ISBN 0-06-028448-X. SERIES: Let's-Read-and-Find-Out Science. SUBJECTS: Earthworms; Science and scientists. RL C. LEXILE AD740L.

Through a carefully written text and colorful, realistic collage illustrations, the life cycle of the earthworm is detailed. A curious young naturalist will be fascinated by the information. The final two pages provide activities to further explore the earthworm.

Phillips, Joan

2399 *Lucky Bear*. Ill. by J. P. Miller. Random House, 1986, ISBN 0-394-97987-7. SERIES: Step into Reading. SUBJECTS: Toys — Teddy bears — Fiction. RL A.

Named Lucky by the toymaker, a teddy bear falls out of a window and into a series of adventures that earn him a friend. A very brief text with large print is complemented by soft watercolor pictures.

Phillips, Joan (cont.)

2400 *My New Boy*. Ill. by Lynn Munsinger. Random House, 1986, ISBN 0-394-98277-0. SERIES: Step into Reading. SUBJECTS: Humorous stories; Pets — Dogs — Fiction. RL A.

In this brief whimsical story a puppy teaches his boy tricks and takes care of him. Simple paintings with ink details effectively convey the humor and warmth of the story.

2401 *Tiger Is a Scaredy Cat*. Ill. by Norman Gorbaty. Random House, 1986, ISBN 0-394-98056-5. SERIES: Step into Reading. SUBJECTS: Fear — Fiction; Mice — Fiction; Pets — Cats — Fiction. RL A.

Tiger, a young cat, is afraid of dogs, trucks, the vacuum cleaner, the dark, and even mice. When a baby mouse is lost and needs help, Tiger gathers his courage and returns the mouse to its home. Pictures are simple yet bold and colorful and work with the text to create an appealing book.

Phleger, Frederick B.

2402 *Red Tag Comes Back*. Ill. by Arnold Lobel. HarperCollins, 1961, ISBN 0-06-024706-1. SERIES: Science I Can Read. SUBJECTS: Fish. RL A.

After explaining the purpose of tagging to a young boy, a naturalist tags a salmon just for him. This well-done book follows Red Tag the salmon's journey to the sea, her growth, and finally her return to the same area to spawn. Detailed ink and wash drawings realistically portray the life of the salmon.

Pickering, Robert

2403 *I Can Be an Archaeologist*. Ill. with photos. Childrens Press, 1987, ISBN 0-516-01909-0. SERIES: I Can Be. SUBJECTS: Careers. RL C.

Study, persistence, painstaking care, and curiosity are the traits most important to becoming an archaeologist according to this brief look at the profession. The text and photographs have people doing all aspects of the work in the field and in museums.

Pickett, Anola

2404 *Old Enough for Magic*. Ill. by Ned Delaney. HarperCollins, 1989, ISBN 0-06-024732-0. SERIES: I Can Read. SUBJECTS: Magic — Fiction; Sibling rivalry — Fiction. RL B.

For his birthday Peter gets a very special magic set. His older sister insists he is too young for magic. Yet she is the one who does not read the directions and gets turned into a frog and Peter comes to her rescue. Text is illustrated with cartoon-like color paintings.

Pierce, Terry

2405 *Tae Kwon Do!* Ill. by Todd Bonita. Random House, 2006, ISBN 0-375-83448-6. SERIES: Step into Reading. SUBJECTS: Sports — Tae Kwon Do. RL A.

In the simplest language with apt illustrations, the basics of tae kwon do are shown, featuring small children.

Pilkey, Dav

2406 *Dragon Gets By: Dragon's Second Tale*. Ill. by author. Orchard, 1991, ISBN 0-531-05935-9. SERIES: Dragon Tales. SUBJECTS: Dragons — Fiction; Humorous stories. RL B.

Waking up groggy, the little blue dragon proceeds to do just about everything, not only wrong, but usually backward. He sweeps his dirt floor until he has a huge hole, eats so much he cannot fit into the car, and so on. Vibrant watercolors capture the humor and are sure to attract readers.

2407 *Dragon's Fat Cat: Dragon's Fourth Tale*. Ill. by author. Orchard, 1992, ISBN 0-531-05982-0. SERIES: Dragon Tales. SUBJECTS: Dragons — Fiction; Pet care — Fiction; Pets — Cats — Fiction. RL B.

On a snowy winter day, Dragon notices a fat cat sitting near his door. After adopting the cat, Dragon finds he knows nothing about caring for it. In five brief chapters, illustrated with vividly colored paintings, the kindly but bumbling blue dragon humorously entertains readers.

2408 *Dragon's Halloween: Dragon's Fifth Tale*. Ill. by author. Orchard, 1993, ISBN 0-631-08590-2. SERIES: Dragon Tales.

SUBJECTS: Dragons — Fiction; Halloween — Fiction. RL B.

The gentle blue giant gets into the spirit of Halloween by creating a pumpkin monster that scares even him, has a great costume until he is rained on, and scares himself with his own hungry stomach rumblings. Vibrant colors and active shapes invite children into the stories.

2409 *Dragon's Merry Christmas: Dragon's Third Tale.* Ill. by author. Orchard, 1993, ISBN 0-531-05957-X. SERIES: Dragon Tales. SUBJECTS: Christmas — Fiction; Dragons — Fiction. RL B.

Four stories featuring the gentle blue dragon capture perfectly the fun and joy of the Christmas holidays. Pilkey's colors are vibrant, his comic character endearing, and the van Gogh-like starry night in the final chapter is just right.

2410 *A Friend for Dragon: Dragon's First Tale.* Ill. by author. Orchard, 1991, ISBN 0-531-05934-0. SERIES: Dragon Tales. SUBJECTS: Dragons — Fiction; Friendship — Fiction. RL B.

The lonely little blue dragon is tricked into believing an apple can talk and want to be his friend. Humorous and brightly colored watercolors help to carry the brief story and work to attract a reader's attention.

Pillar, Marjorie

2411 *Pizza Man.* Ill. with photos. HarperCollins, 1990, ISBN 0-690-04836-X. SUBJECTS: Business enterprises; Food — Pizza. RL C.

Through black-and-white photographs and a very brief text in large type, readers can follow the "pizza man" as he prepares to make pizzas. Readers should be impressed by the amount of work that goes into making this favorite food.

Pinkwater, Daniel

2412 *Big Bob and the Thanksgiving Potatoes.* Ill. by Jill Pinkwater. Scholastic, pap., 1999, ISBN 0-590-64095-X. SERIES: Hello Reader! SUBJECTS: Friendship — Fiction. RL B. LEXILE 270L.

Big Bob and Gloria, second graders, are bigger than their classmates. At first they are friends because of their size, but they discover they really like each other. Jill Pinkwater's illustrations match the story.

2413 *Big Bob and the Winter Holiday Potato.* Ill. by Jill Pinkwater. Cartwheel, pap., 1999, ISBN 0-439-04243-7. SERIES: Scholastic Reader. SUBJECTS: Holidays — Fiction; Plays — Fiction; Winter — Fiction. RL C. LEXILE 300L.

When Mr. Salami, the second-grade teacher, announces that his class will create a winter holiday play, Big Gloria and Big Bob volunteer to write it — about Potato Claus. The humorous story and even funnier play are presented in chapters with childlike illustrations.

2414 *Second-Grade Ape.* Ill. by Jill Pinkwater. Scholastic, 1997, ISBN 0-590-37261-0. SERIES: Hello Reader! SUBJECTS: Gorillas — Fiction; Pets — Fiction. RL B. LEXILE 330L.

Flash takes his pet gorilla to school with him, where he stars as a painter and climber.

Piper, Watty

2415 *Meet the Little Engine That Could.* Ill. by Cristina Ong. Grosset & Dunlap, 2001, o.p. SERIES: First Friends First Readers. SUBJECTS: Trains — Fiction. RL A.

The Little Engine That Could is rewritten in very basic vocabulary, with the addition of a story about the engine reuniting a little hippo with his parents.

Pitt, Valerie

2416 *Let's Find Out About Names.* Ill. by Patricia Grant Porter. Watts, 1971, o.p. SERIES: Let's Find Out About. SUBJECTS: Names. RL B.

Surnames, Christian names, and meanings and origins of some names are clearly and entertainingly explained. This book might inspire children to investigate the origins of their given names. Illustrated with representative black, fuchsia, and ocher sketches.

2417 *Let's Find Out About the Community.* Ill. by June Goldsborough. Watts, 1972, o.p. SERIES: Let's Find Out About. SUBJECTS: Communities; Community helpers. RL C.

A clear and simple text and watercolor pictures together define what a community is made up of

Pitt, Valerie (cont.)

— libraries, schools, community helpers, citizens, and government. The community is then examined to see how the many parts work together to run smoothly.

Platt, Kin

2418 *Big Max*. Ill. by Robert Lopshire. HarperCollins, pap., 1978, ISBN 0-06-444006-0. SERIES: I Can Read. SUBJECTS: Elephants — Fiction; Mystery and detective stories. RL B. LEXILE 200L.

The greatest detective in the world, who travels by umbrella, finds out how, where, and why the King of Pooka Pooka's prize elephant disappeared. Very simple vocabulary and illustrations.

2419 *Big Max and the Mystery of the Missing Moose*. Ill. by Robert Lopshire. HarperCollins, 1977, o.p. SERIES: I Can Read Mystery. SUBJECTS: Humorous stories; Mystery and detective stories. RL B.

Traveling by hot-air umbrella, Big Max heads for the zoo and begins his search for Marvin the missing moose. By trial and error and with plenty of humor, Max finds Marvin in Moose Land with his family. Comical pencil and wash drawings suit the text well.

Pluckrose, Henry

2420 *Changing Seasons*. Ill. with photos. Childrens Press, 1994, ISBN 0-516-08116-0. SERIES: Walkabout. SUBJECTS: Seasons. RL B.

The signs of seasonal change are noted in a brief text and full page color photographs. The changes are seen in animals, plants, and weather. Many unfamiliar animals are not named, the illustrations are grainy, and the pages seem crowded.

2421 *Flowers*. Ill. with photos. Childrens Press, 1994, ISBN 0-516-08117-9. SERIES: Walkabout. SUBJECTS: Flowers. RL B.

An appreciation of flowering plants without much detailed information about them individually, this does encourage observation and an interest in the ways in which plants grow and reproduce. Color photographs are rather grainy and layout is not always appealing.

2422 *In the Air*. Ill. with photos. Childrens Press, 1994, ISBN 0-516-08118-7. SERIES: Walkabout. SUBJECTS: Air. RL B.

A brief text set against full-color, often grainy and unappealing photographs helps children to gain an understanding of how air is a vital part of the world of animals and plants.

2423 *Look at Tongues and Tasters*. Ill. with photos. Watts, 1990, o.p. SERIES: Look At. SUBJECTS: Animals — Senses; Human body — Tongue; Senses — Taste. RL B.

Text and color photographs work together to demonstrate how tongues in humans and other animals not only provide a sense of taste but also help with speech, food gathering, grooming, and so on. Experiments and an index are also provided.

2424 *Minibeasts*. Ill. with photos. Childrens Press, 1994, ISBN 0-516-08119-5. SERIES: Walkabout. SUBJECTS: Insects; Invertebrates. RL C.

The brief text and full-page color photographs (which are often grainy and with a crowded effect) attempt to encourage children to look at the world around them and especially at insects, slugs, snails, and other invertebrates.

2425 *Seashore*. Ill. with photos. Childrens Press, 1994, ISBN 0-516-08120-9. SERIES: Walkabout. SUBJECTS: Seashore. RL C.

Tides, shells, animal life, and human use are discussed in this look at what constitutes a seashore. The text is brief but introduces many proper names for creatures found in this environment — making it somewhat more difficult. Photographs are grainy and not always attractive.

2426 *Trees*. Ill. with photos. Childrens Press, 1994, ISBN 0-516-08121-7. SERIES: Walkabout. SUBJECTS: Trees. RL B.

A brief and superficial look at trees and what they contribute, this book could encourage observation of trees and nature by young readers. The photographs are often grainy and the book design is rather crowded. A glossary would have helped for pronunciation of some words.

2427 *Under the Ground*. Ill. with photos. Childrens Press, 1994, ISBN 0-516-08122-5. SERIES: Walkabout. SUBJECTS: Animals — Burrowing; Tunnels. RL C.

A look at not only some of the kinds of animals that live underground but also the ways in which the underground areas are used by man, this brief book encourages observation. Photographs are often grainy and poorly placed or chosen.

2428 *Ways to Clean It!* Photos by Chris Fairclough. Watts, 1990, o.p. SERIES: Ways to . . . SUBJECTS: Cleanliness. RL B.

Pluckrose explains how important it is to keep things clean and free from bacteria — a child's face and hands or the dishes used for dinner. Color photographs help clarify the text. Simple experiments are also included.

2429 *Weather.* Ill. with photos. Childrens Press, 1994, ISBN 0-516-08123-3. SERIES: Walkabout. SUBJECTS: Weather. RL C.

The kinds of weather — hot, cold, windy, dry, rainy, and so on — are discussed briefly along with some information about those who forecast the weather. A glossary would have been helpful for pronunciation of some unfamiliar words. Photographs are grainy and sometimes poorly chosen.

Pollack, Pam, and Meg Belviso

2430 *Bear Cub.* Ill. by Neecy Twinem. Grosset & Dunlap, pap., 2001, ISBN 0-448-42523-8. SERIES: All Aboard Science Reader. SUBJECTS: Animals — Baby; Bears. RL B.

Two brown bears are born during hibernation and are still small when they make their first journey out of the cave. All summer the mother bear trains them in finding food. Before the next hibernation, a third cub has been added and readers watch the three grow the next summer as well. Illustrations are realistic paintings.

2431 *Chickens on the Move.* Ill. by Lynn Adams. Kane, pap., 2002, ISBN 1-57565-113-0. SERIES: Math Matters. SUBJECTS: Chickens — Fiction; Concepts — Shape — Fiction; Measurement — Fiction. RL B. LEXILE 270L.

Grandpa surprises the three children with three chickens and materials for a coop. They try one area and one shape after another until they find the perfect place for the chickens. The changing dimensions of the coop will help children understand the concept of perimeter.

2432 *Ponies.* Ill. by Lisa Bonforte. Grosset & Dunlap, pap., 2003, ISBN 0-448-42524-6. SERIES: All Aboard Science Reader. SUBJECTS: Animals — Habits and behavior; Horses. RL B.

Information about the behavior, care, and characteristics of ponies throughout the world is provided along with realistic watercolor illustrations.

Pollock, Penny

2433 *Ants Don't Get Sunday Off.* Ill. by Lorinda B. Cauley. Putnam, 1978, o.p. SERIES: See and Read. SUBJECTS: Ants — Fiction. RL C.

Anya, an old ant, is tired of constantly taking care of the nursery yet she is the first to try to rescue the eggs from flooding. Caught in the water, she is carried away on a great adventure. Facts about ants are interspersed in the text, which is complemented by clever ink and chalk pictures.

2434 *The Slug Who Thought He Was a Snail.* Ill. by Lorinda B. Cauley. Putnam, 1980, o.p. SERIES: See and Read. SUBJECTS: Self-esteem — Fiction; Slugs — Fiction; Snails — Fiction. RL C.

A forceful snail convinces Sam Slug that he is a snail who has lost his house and must find a new one. Sam does exactly as the snail tells him until he meets another slug who assures him he is fine as he is. Detailed pictures are slightly comical while the text provides accurate information on slugs.

2435 *The Spit Bug Who Couldn't Spit.* Ill. by Lorinda B. Cauley. Putnam, 1982, o.p. SERIES: See and Read. SUBJECTS: Insects — Fiction. RL C.

Ezra, a newly hatched spittlebug, has little success making spit until he grows and matures, but each step in the process is difficult for the timid little bug. Factual information about spittlebugs is included at the end of this story, which has humorous colored pencil drawings.

Pomerantz, Charlotte

2436 *Buffy and Albert.* Ill. by Yossi Abolafia. Greenwillow, 1982, o.p. SERIES: Read-Alone. SUBJECTS: Grandparents — Fiction; Old age — Fiction; Pets — Cats — Fiction. RL B.

Pomerantz, Charlotte (cont.)

The two children's grandfather complains about having to take care of his two old cats. When their grandfather has an accident and is bedridden, the younger child lovingly shows him that the cats cannot help being old any more than he can. The ink drawings with pastel accents are perfect for the story.

2437 *The Outside Dog.* Ill. by Jennifer Plecas. HarperCollins, 1993, ISBN 0-06-024783-5. SERIES: I Can Read. SUBJECTS: Grandparents — Fiction; Pets — Dogs — Fiction; Spanish language. RL B.
Marisol lives with her grandfather in a small Puerto Rican village. He says they can never have a dog, but a stray and the little girl slowly change his mind. Spanish words are nicely mixed into the text and explained in a glossary. Childlike ink drawings with color washes illustrate the story.

Poploff, Michelle

2438 *Bat Bones and Spider Stew.* Ill. by Bill Basso. Delacorte, 1998, o.p. SERIES: First Choice Chapter Book. SUBJECTS: Halloween — Fiction; Haunted houses — Fiction. RL C. LEXILE 350L.
On Halloween, Henry agrees to go to his friend Artie Doomsday's house for dinner. The house and its inhabitants at first seem scary. Artie and his family soon have Henry trading Halloween riddles and having fun. The illustrations, with green-faced Granny and Wanda and a very scary house, don't quite match the story but do add to its child appeal.

Porte, Barbara Ann

2439 *Harry Gets an Uncle.* Ill. by Yossi Abolafia. Greenwillow, 1991, ISBN 0-06-001150-5. SUBJECTS: Family life — Fiction; Marriage and wedding customs — Fiction. RL B.
Though Harry's friend Dorcas scares him with tales of terrible wedding mishaps, Aunt Rose and Uncle Leo's wedding turns out just right — even though Harry's dog gets loose. Delightful watercolor pictures are perfect. Flip through the pages and look at the bottom right for a special treat!

2440 *Harry in Trouble.* Ill. by Yossi Abolafia. Greenwillow, pap., 1989, ISBN 0-06-001153-X. SUBJECTS: Behavior — Responsible — Fiction; Humorous stories; Lost and found possessions — Fiction. RL A.
Harry is on his third library card: the first his dog ate, the second his father put in the wash, and the third he can't find. Now he has to face the librarian and tell her what he's done. Harry's humorous first person account is accompanied by warm and lively watercolor paintings.

2441 *Harry's Birthday.* Ill. by Yossi Abolafia. Greenwillow, 1994, ISBN 0-06-050355-6. SUBJECTS: Birthdays — Fiction; Families, single parent — Fiction; Parties — Fiction. RL B.
Harry keeps telling his friends and father that he hopes to get a cowboy hat for his birthday. On the big day, he has a wonderful party and gets not one but seven hats. Gentle humor, a grasp of the concerns of young children, and delightful watercolor art fill this book.

2442 *Harry's Dog.* Ill. by Yossi Abolafia. Greenwillow, 1984, o.p. SERIES: Read-Alone. SUBJECTS: Allergies — Fiction; Families, single parent — Fiction; Pets — Dogs — Fiction. RL B.
Knowing his father is allergic to dogs, Harry nonetheless accepts one. He tells outlandish stories to explain her presence and to convince his father to allow him to keep her. Aunt Rose finds the perfect solution to Harry's dilemma. Illustrated in soft colors with gentle humor.

2443 *Harry's Mom.* Ill. by Yossi Abolafia. Greenwillow, 1985, o.p. SERIES: Read-Alone. SUBJECTS: Families, single parent — Fiction; Parent and child — Fiction. RL B.
When the dictionary says an orphan is someone with one parent, Harry rushes home to his father for comfort. His dad assures him that, even though his mother is dead, he is not an orphan. Harry also gets to hear more about his sports reporter mom. Ink and pencil drawings and text are excellent.

2444 *Harry's Visit.* Ill. by Yossi Abolafia. Greenwillow, 1983, o.p. SERIES: Read-Alone. SUBJECTS: Behavior — Shyness — Fiction. RL B.
When his father's friends invite him to spend the day, Harry inaccurately predicts that he will have

a terrible time. The reluctance of this shy and very polite only child to venture beyond his territory is capably portrayed. Simple pastel colored pictures help tell the story.

Porter, Wesley

2445 *About Monkeys in Trees*. Ill. by Dominique Churchill. Watts, 1979, o.p. SUBJECTS: Folklore — Africa; Monkeys — Fiction. RL B.

This reworking of an African folktale tells how sly tortoise borrows money from monkey and, when the time comes to repay it, convinces monkey that she has thrown it away. This folktale explains why monkeys stay in trees (to search for the lost money). Illustrations are simple, uninspiring, but colorful paintings.

2446 *The Magic Kettle*. Ill. by Lynn Sweat. Watts, 1979, o.p. SUBJECTS: Folklore — Japan. RL C.

An old man finds a kettle, polishes it, and sees it transformed into a wild little animal. Once it is back in its kettle form, the old man sells it to a merchant who gets wealthy by holding shows where the kettle changes into its animal form. Expressively illustrated in bright colors and ink.

Poskanzer, Susan C.

2447 *What's It Like to Be a Chef*. Ill. by Karen E. Pellaton. Troll, 1990, ISBN 0-8167-1797-4. SERIES: What's It Like to Be a . . . SUBJECTS: Careers; Cookery. RL C.

While visiting her Uncle Peppi at the restaurant where he is chef, Casey gets to watch and help with the preparation of lunch. Some of the many duties of a professional chef are lightly touched on. Illustrated with watercolors outlined in ink, the book offers a good look at a career.

2448 *What's It Like to Be a Dairy Farmer*. Ill. by George Ulrich. Troll, 1989, o.p. SERIES: What's It Like to Be a . . . SUBJECTS: Careers; Farm and country life. RL B.

At Sunrise Dairy Farm Kira and her parents all begin work early in the morning. Her parents milk the cows as Kira fixes breakfast, then Kira has her other chores to do. This is a nonglamorized look at dairy farming as a career. The illustrations are ink and watercolor washes.

2449 *What's It Like to Be a Puppeteer*. Ill. by Diane Paterson. Troll, 1989, o.p. SERIES: What's It Like to Be a . . . SUBJECTS: Careers; Puppetry. RL C.

Two puppeteers get ready for their regular weekend performance in the park. They check their puppets and stage and allow a young boy and his grandmother to watch them practice. Lots of good information on using puppets is provided. The illustrations are well-done watercolors with ink.

2450 *What's It Like to Be a Sanitation Worker*. Ill. by Allan Eitzen. Troll, 1989, o.p. SERIES: What's It Like to Be a . . . SUBJECTS: Careers; Community helpers; Garbage and garbage disposal. RL C.

Tom, Mary, and Frank are followed through a complete day of gathering garbage from their town, taking it to the landfill, and finally returning to the garage and cleaning the truck. A positive look at this career, the book is illustrated in realistic watercolor pictures.

2451 *What's It Like to Be an Astronaut*. Ill. by Allan Eitzen. Troll, pap., 1990, o.p. SERIES: What's It Like to Be a . . . SUBJECTS: Astronauts; Careers; Space travel. RL C.

Andrew excitedly greets his mission specialist mom as she returns from a space shuttle flight. She explains to him many of the things that happen on a shuttle as well as telling him about the special training she has had in preparation for it.

Potter, Tessa, and Donna Bailey

2452 *Ducks and Geese*. Ill. by Gill Tomblin. Raintree, 1990, o.p. SERIES: Animal World. SUBJECTS: Ducks; Geese. RL B.

Good color photographs and paintings illustrate the habits of ducks and geese while a short but clear text provides basic information on these waterfowl. Index is included.

2453 *Goats*. Ill. by Gill Tomblin. Raintree, 1990, o.p. SERIES: Animal World. SUBJECTS: Farm and country life; Goats. RL B.

Using full-color realistic paintings and photographs and very short sentences providing the simplest of information, the authors introduce domestic and wild goats from different areas of the world to children. The focus is on the domestic animal and its uses.

Potter, Tessa, and Donna Bailey (cont.)

2454 *Hens*. Ill. by Gill Tomblin. Raintree, 1990, o.p. SERIES: Animal World. SUBJECTS: Chickens; Farm and country life; Poultry. RL B.

Free-range and factory-raised chickens are introduced through color photographs, drawings, and a brief text. The difference in quality of life for the animals is apparent in the illustrations and just might spark discussion. In both instances the hens are used for egg production.

2455 *Sheep*. Ill. by Gill Tomblin. Raintree, 1990, o.p. SERIES: Animal World. SUBJECTS: Farm and country life; Sheep; Wool. RL B.

After initially showing sheep grazing on a British farm and then being sheared, the book changes its focus to the use of wool in fabric production. Illustrated with full-color photographs and paintings. Index is included.

Poulin, Stephane

2456 *Can You Catch Josephine?* Ill. by author. Tundra, 1987, o.p. SUBJECTS: Humorous stories; Pets — Cats — Fiction; School stories. RL A.

When Daniel's cat Josephine sneaks into his backpack and into his school, she creates havoc as Daniel and others try to catch her. Set in Montreal, the detailed and colorful paintings show an old-fashioned school staffed by modem multiracial teachers and students.

2457 *Could You Stop Josephine?* Ill. by author. Tundra, 1988, o.p. SUBJECTS: Farm and country life — Fiction; Humorous stories; Pets — Cats — Fiction. RL A.

Thinking they have left Daniel's cat Josephine safely home in Montreal, Daniel and his father drive out to the country to visit cousins. When they arrive, the spunky Siamese who has been hiding in the car gets loose and leads them on a merry chase. Illustrated with vibrant pictures of the Quebec countryside in summer.

2458 *Have You Seen Josephine?* Ill. by author. Tundra, 1988, o.p. SUBJECTS: City and town life — Fiction; Pets — Cats — Fiction. RL A.

Daniel decides to follow his cat Josephine to see where she goes every Saturday. He chases her through his Montreal neighborhood and finally to a neighbor's for a special Saturday cat party. The colorful paintings and black-and-white sketches offer readers a chance to view French Canadian culture.

Powell, E. Sandy

2459 *Rats*. Photos by Jerry Boucher. Lerner, 1994, ISBN 0-8225-3003-1. SERIES: Early Bird Nature. SUBJECTS: Rats. RL C.

Attractive photographs of pet rats at all stages of development support a text full of facts about the animal. Also appealing to young readers is the chatty tone and the positive attitude toward rats as pets — though not toward wild rats. A glossary and index are included.

Powell, Jillian

2460 *Becky Has Diabetes*. Chelsea Clubhouse, 2005, ISBN 0-7910-8178-8. SERIES: Like Me Like You. SUBJECTS: Diseases; Human body. RL C.

Becky explains to readers what her life with diabetes is like: the blood testing, insulin shots, monitoring of her food, and more. The book is straightforward in its presentation of information and Becky is shown as a normal girl handling a difficult disease. Appended are a glossary, an index, and a list of references for further information.

2461 *Climbers*. Ill. with photos. Carolrhoda, 1991, o.p. SERIES: Things That Move. SUBJECTS: Animals; Animals — Climbing. RL B.

From cats, snakes, and snails to firefighters and children on playground equipment, this book explores the many ways that animals climb. A few sentences on each page caption full-color photographs depicting the animal in action.

2462 *Flyers*. Ill. with photos. Carolrhoda, 1992, o.p. SERIES: Things That Move. SUBJECTS: Animals — Flying; Flight. RL B.

Birds, kites, balloons, arrows, and helicopters are some of the things mentioned here that fly. Each page has color photographs and very brief information that acts almost like captioning. Very basic, this is identification rather than explanation of principles.

2463 *Jumpers*. Ill. with photos. Carolrhoda, 1992, o.p. SERIES: Things That Move. SUBJECTS: Animals — Jumping; Sports — Jumping. RL B.

Animals and insects as well as sports-minded humans are pictured jumping. The brief text acts as captioning for the color photographs. Some of those pictured are frogs, squirrels, kangaroos, parachutists, and skiers.

2464 *Swimmers*. Ill. with photos. Carolrhoda, 1992, o.p. SERIES: Things That Move. SUBJECTS: Animals — Aquatic. RL B.

Color photographs of aquatic animals dominate this book about animals and the means by which they move or swim in water. Though many different animals are looked at (beavers, otters, fish, frogs, and so on), the text concentrates on just the movement of each animal.

Power, Barbara

2465 *I Wish Laura's Mommy Was My Mommy*. Ill. by Marylin Hafner. Lippincott, 1979, ISBN 0-397-31859-6. SERIES: I-Like-to-Read. SUBJECTS: Family life — Fiction; Humorous stories; Mothers, working — Fiction. RL C.

It is not until Laura's mommy agrees to babysit for Jennifer and her two little brothers that Laura has to wash dishes and make her own bed. A good job is done showing how much work is involved in caring for children. Pencil drawings, often humorous, are a good match for the text.

Prager, Annabelle

2466 *The Baseball Birthday Party*. Ill. by Marilyn Mets. Random House, 1995, o.p. SERIES: Step into Reading. SUBJECTS: Birthdays — Fiction; Sports — Baseball — Fiction. RL B. LEXILE 450L.

New kid Billy decides to show everyone how well he can play baseball by having a baseball birthday party. It's almost a disaster when his little friend Dan puts the invitations in the wrong container. Watercolor pictures capture the frustrations and humor of the situation.

2467 *The Spooky Halloween Party*. Ill. by Tomie dePaola. Pantheon, 1981, ISBN 0-394-94370-8. SERIES: I Am Reading. SUBJECTS: Halloween — Fiction; Humorous stories; Parties — Fiction. RL B.

Albert is sure he will not be frightened at Nicky's spooky Halloween party. Once there, he is surprised that he cannot identify any of the children until he realizes he is at the wrong party. Suitably scary black-and-white illustrations and the delightful story will be enjoyed by youngsters.

2468 *The Surprise Party*. Ill. by Tomie dePaola. Random House, 1988, o.p. SERIES: Step into Reading. SUBJECTS: Birthdays — Fiction; Friendship — Fiction; Parties — Fiction. RL B.

A little boy convinces his best friend to plan a "surprise" party for his birthday. Fortunately the best friend is wise enough to really make it a surprise. The full-color pictures of multiracial children add to the warmth and humor of the story.

Prall, Jo

2469 *My Sister's Special*. Photos by Linda Gray. Childrens Press, 1985, o.p. SERIES: Real-Life Photo Stories. SUBJECTS: Disabilities — Physical and mental. RL B.

Angie cannot walk, talk, or use her arms and hands very well because she is brain damaged. However, she goes to school in a wheelchair and communicates with symbols. Black-and-white photographs of a smiling child and loving family are accompanied by a proud brother's description of his special sister.

Prather, Ray

2470 *Double Dog Dare*. Ill. by author. Macmillan, 1975, o.p. SERIES: Ready-to-Read. SUBJECTS: Dares — Fiction; Friendship — Fiction. RL B.

Finding a quarter leads Eddie and Rudy, two young black friends, on a series of "daring" adventures through town. Illustrated with pencil drawings with green and brown washes.

Preller, James

2471 *Hiccups for Elephant*. Ill. by Hans Wilhelm. Scholastic, pap., 1994, ISBN 0-590-48588-1. SERIES: Hello Reader! SUBJECTS: Animals — Fiction; Elephants — Fiction; Hiccups — Fiction. RL B. LEXILE 240L.

Preller, James (cont.)

As the other animals try to nap, elephant's hiccups wake them one by one. Each tries to cure him of the annoying noise but only mouse has the surefire solution. Watercolor art captures the frustration of the animals in a humorous manner.

2472 *Wake Me in Spring.* Ill. by Jeffrey Scherer. Scholastic, pap., 1994, o.p. SERIES: Hello Reader! SUBJECTS: Animals — Hibernation — Fiction; Bears — Fiction; Mice — Fiction. RL B.
As Bear gets ready to hibernate for the winter, his friend Mouse tries to get him to stay awake to enjoy sleigh rides, snowmen, and so on. Bear will not miss winter, but he will miss his friend. Simply designed, colored, cartoon-like pictures extend the text.

Prelutsky, Jack

2473 *It's Christmas.* Ill. by Marylin Hafner. HarperCollins, pap., 1995, ISBN 0-688-14393-8. SERIES: Read-Alone. SUBJECTS: Christmas — Fiction; Poetry. RL C.
A dozen whimsical poems reflect a child's view of the celebration of Christmas at home and in school. The illustrations of vivacious families of various races capture the humor and warmth of these holiday poems.

2474 *It's Halloween.* Ill. by Marylin Hafner. HarperCollins, pap., 1996, ISBN 0-688-14733-X. SERIES: Read-Alone. SUBJECTS: Halloween — Fiction; Poetry. RL C.
Excitement, fun, and a little bit of fear — necessary ingredients for a memorable Halloween night — are in these 13 poems and in the ink and wash pictures that accompany them. The poems are great fun for reading aloud and alone.

2475 *It's Snowing! It's Snowing: Winter Poems.* Ill. by Yossi Abolafia. HarperCollins, 2006, ISBN 0-688-01513-1. SERIES: I Can Read. SUBJECTS: Poetry; Weather — Snow; Winter. RL C.
Sixteen poems reveal many childhood feelings relating to winter and snow. Some are joyous, others thoughtful. The soft watercolor art captures the spirit of Prelutsky's poetry.

2476 *It's Thanksgiving.* Ill. by Marylin Hafner. HarperCollins, 1982, 2007, ISBN 0-06-053710-8. SERIES: I Can Read. SUBJECTS: Poetry; Thanksgiving. RL C. LEXILE NP.
Twelve warm and witty poems about the many aspects of Thanksgiving — from football to leftovers — will be fun for children to read aloud or alone. The colorful ink and wash paintings add great child appeal to this new edition.

2477 *My Parents Think I'm Sleeping.* Ill. by Yossi Abolafia. HarperCollins, 2007, ISBN 0-06-053720-5. SERIES: I Can Read. SUBJECTS: Bedtime; Night; Poetry. RL C. LEXILE NP.
This new edition of the book originally published in 1985 maintains the connection to a child's nighttime fears and joys. Abolafia's gently humorous paintings are a perfect match for the Children's Poet Laureate's poems.

2478 *Rainy Rainy Saturday.* Ill. by Marylin Hafner. Greenwillow, 1980, o.p. SERIES: Read-Alone. SUBJECTS: Poetry; Weather — Rain. RL B.
In 14 delightful poems, children's views of the fun, boredom, or disappointment caused by rainy Saturdays are presented in rhythmic and thoughtful verses. The pencil and wash comic drawings complement the poetry.

2479 *What I Did Last Summer.* Ill. by Yossi Abolafia. Greenwillow, 1984, o.p. SERIES: Read-Alone. SUBJECTS: Poetry; Summer — Fiction. RL B.
In 13 poems a little boy remembers his summer: going on a picnic, having a nasty cousin visit, being sick, being hot, and so on. His memories are humorous now that he is back at school even though some of the actual events were not so funny when they were taking place. The softly colored drawings capture the emotions — especially the humor — of the delightful poetry.

Preszler, June

2480 *Caring for Your Dog.* Capstone, 2007, ISBN 0-7368-6385-0. SERIES: First Facts. SUBJECTS: Pet care; Pets — Dogs. RL C. LEXILE 680L.
A child interested in adopting a dog will find this book not only well designed and attractive but also full of basic information on caring for a dog. Final pages include information on decoding a

dog's behavior, a glossary, a bibliography, Web sites, and an index.

2481 *Diwali: Hindu Festival of Lights.* Capstone, 2007, ISBN 0-7368-6395-8. SERIES: First Facts. SUBJECTS: Diwali; Holidays; Religion. RL C. LEXILE 690L.

Celebrated by Hindu people throughout the world, Diwali, the festival of lights, is held over five days in the fall. The history of the festival and how it's celebrated are covered, and the book includes an activity, glossary, bibliography, Web sites, and an index.

2482 *Juneteenth: Jubilee for Freedom.* Capstone, 2007, ISBN 0-7368-6396-6. SERIES: First Facts. SUBJECTS: African Americans; Holidays. RL C. LEXILE 780L.

The first official African American holiday, Juneteenth celebrates the freeing of slaves in Texas on June 19, 1865. The attractive book also includes color photographs, an activity, a glossary, a bibliography, Web sites, and an index.

2483 *St. Patrick's Day: Day of Irish Pride.* Capstone, 2007, ISBN 0-7368-6398-2. SERIES: First Facts: Holidays and Culture. SUBJECTS: Holidays; St. Patrick's Day. RL C. LEXILE 770L.

The history and cultural and religious significance of St. Patrick's Day are covered in this brief chapter book. At the end of the book are an activity, a glossary, a short bibliography, a list of Web sites, and an index. The book is colorful and full of photographs.

Pringle, Laurence

2484 *Twist, Wiggle, and Squirm: A Book about Earthworms.* Ill. by Peter Parnall. HarperCollins, 1973, o.p. SERIES: Let's-Read-and-Find-Out. SUBJECTS: Earthworms. RL C.

From why earthworms are found on sidewalks after a heavy rainfall to details of how and where they live and what they eat, this presents an interesting look at an important form of animal life. The illustrations are detailed, realistic pen and ink drawings.

2485 *Water Plants.* Ill. by Kazue Mizumura. HarperCollins, 1975, o.p. SERIES: Let's-Read-and-Find-Out Science. SUBJECTS: Plants; Pond life. RL C.

One animal after another feeds and is fed upon in this story of the food chain of a freshwater pond. Readers learn a great deal about the plants of the pond as they follow the animals. Well written and very interesting, it is illustrated with realistic watercolor paintings.

Putnam, Polly

2486 *The Mystery of Sara Beth.* Ill. by Judith Friedman. Follett, 1981, ISBN 0-8136-5116-6. SUBJECTS: Mystery and detective stories; School stories; Siblings — Twins — Fiction. RL B.

Sara Beth, the new girl, is decidedly unfriendly in spite of her classmates' attempts to welcome her. Only Becky guesses that Sara Beth is really a twin coming on different days because she and her sister share a winter coat. The multiracial class is realistically portrayed in ink and colored washes.

Q

Quackenbush, Robert

2487 *Animal Cracks.* Ill. by author. Lothrop, 1975, o.p. SERIES: Fun-to-Read. SUBJECTS: Fables; Humorous stories. RL C.

Seven short, humorous stories about animals present situations explaining well-known sayings such as "his bark is worse than his bite." All are illustrated with boldly outlined gold and black pencil sketches and are fun to read.

2488 *Batbaby Finds a Home.* Ill. by author. Random House, 2001, o.p. SERIES: Step into Reading. SUBJECTS: Animals — Habitats — Fiction; Bats — Fiction. RL B. LEXILE 170L.

When a bulldozer destroys the barn where they live, a little brown bat and his family must search for a new home. The habits and habitat of bats are introduced in the story and reinforced in an informational afterword. Illustrations are dark in tone, reflecting the nighttime world of the bat.

2489 *Calling Doctor Quack.* Ill. by author. Lothrop, 1978, o.p. SERIES: Fun-to-Read. SUBJECTS: Animals — Fiction; Doctors and

Quackenbush, Robert (cont.)

nurses — Fiction; Pollution — Water — Fiction. RL C.

Dr. Quack, a duck, is besieged by patients blaming their sudden illnesses on the bad-tempered Mr. Snapping Turtle. The poor animal is sick and disagreeable because the pond has become polluted and trash has lodged in his shell. Good pictures illustrate an amusing, pointed tale.

2490 *Detective Mole*. Ill. by author. Lothrop, 1976, o.p. SERIES: Fun-to-Read. SUBJECTS: Moles — Fiction; Mystery and detective stories. RL C.

Almost as soon as he finishes detective school, Mole begins solving mysteries. The five entertaining stories here involve the animals in Mole's community and are accompanied by bold pencil drawings.

2491 *Detective Mole and the Circus Mystery*. Ill. by author. Lothrop, 1980, o.p. SERIES: Fun-to-Read. SUBJECTS: Circuses — Fiction; Moles — Fiction; Mystery and detective stories. RL C.

Melba the tattooed cow disappears from the circus the day of her marriage to Boris the bull. Mole masterfully pieces together the clues and finds Melba in time for her wedding. The illustrations, in full color with blue outlining, are as imaginative as the story.

2492 *Detective Mole and the Seashore Mystery*. Ill. by author. Lothrop, 1976, o.p. SERIES: Fun-to-Read. SUBJECTS: Moles — Fiction; Mystery and detective stories. RL C.

Called to Land's End Island to find Captain Bill's stolen pearl, Mole carefully listens for clues and discovers the culprit — a giant clam. Humorous heavy line drawings add to the seaside flavor and to the fun of the story.

2493 *Detective Mole and the Secret Clues*. Ill. by author. Lothrop, 1977, o.p. SERIES: Fun-to-Read. SUBJECTS: Moles — Fiction; Mystery and detective stories. RL C.

A mysterious stranger hands Mole a small green pea as he sets off to help the Chicken family claim their Uncle Ebenezer's mansion. Clues are easy enough for children to work out in order to solve the mystery. Animal characters are drawn in heavy blue and black pencil.

2494 *Detective Mole and the Tip-Top Mystery*. Ill. by author. Lothrop, 1978, o.p. SERIES: Fun-to-Read. SUBJECTS: Moles — Fiction; Mystery and detective stories. RL C.

Down to their last guests, Mr. and Mrs. Goat call in Mole to stop the strange occurrences that are driving guests away from their mountain lodge. Humorous pencil drawings and a bit of suspense make this an exciting mystery.

2495 *Henry Goes West*. Ill. by author. Crown, pap., 1988, ISBN 0-8193-1090-5. SERIES: Read Aloud and Easy Reading. SUBJECTS: Ducks — Fiction; Humorous stories; Western stories. RL B.

Henry, a duck, misses Clara and decides to join her on her guest ranch vacation out west. When he arrives everyone is gone. As he waits for their return, Henry accidentally creates one catastrophe after another. A very funny story with a nice ending, it is illustrated in full color.

2496 *Henry's Awful Mistake*. Ill. by author. Robert Quackenbush Studios, 2005, ISBN 0-9712757-0-X. SERIES: Read Aloud Library. SUBJECTS: Ants — Fiction; Ducks — Fiction; Humorous stories. RL B.

Henry is cooking supper for Clara when he notices an ant. Determined to get rid of it, Henry creates havoc. He ends up bursting pipes, flooding the house, and canceling supper. Text is illustrated with energetic watercolor pictures heavily outlined in ink.

2497 *Henry's Important Date*. Ill. by author. Parents Magazine Press, 1981, ISBN 0-8193-1068-9. SERIES: Read Aloud and Easy Reading. SUBJECTS: Birthdays — Fiction; Concepts — Time — Fiction; Ducks — Fiction. RL B.

Henry, a duck, tries his best to get to Clara's birthday party on time — but he gets stuck in traffic, locks his keys in his car, and then gets on a bus that breaks down. Poor Henry's awful day is funny but one that everyone can empathize with. Illustrated in full color with bold comic drawings.

2498 *Moose's Store*. Ill. by author. Lothrop, 1979, o.p. SERIES: Fun-to-Read. SUBJECTS: Animals — Fiction; Farm and country life — Fiction; Friendship — Fiction. RL C.

When Beaver and the other animals decide to help Moose by transforming his friendly, old-fashioned store into a deli, Moose feels uncomfortable and out of place. Bold pencil drawings are a good complement to this tale of tradition versus modernization.

2499 *Mr. Snow Bunting's Secret.* Ill. by author. Lothrop, 1978, o.p. SERIES: Fun-to-Read. SUBJECTS: Animals — Fiction; Christmas — Fiction. RL C.

Only able to stay until November, Mr. Snow Bunting, a bird, opens a gift-wrapping business for the Christmas season that makes Mr. Dog jealous and suspicious. When Dog accuses Snow Bunting of being a sorcerer, Dog learns Snow Bunting's secret and is embarrassed. Illustrated with humorous heavy line drawings in red and black.

2500 *No Mouse for Me.* Ill. by author. Watts, 1981, o.p. SERIES: Easy-Read Story. SUBJECTS: Cumulative tales; Humorous stories; Mice — Fiction. RL B.

A little boy returns a mouse to the pet shop demanding his money back. He claims that a mouse would attract a cat that would attract a dog and on and on until a catastrophe would occur and, anyway, he would rather have a snake. Outrageously silly, this is illustrated with bold drawings.

2501 *Pete Pack Rat.* Ill. by author. Lothrop, 1976, o.p. SERIES: Fun-to-Read. SUBJECTS: Animals — Fiction; Robbers and outlaws — Fiction; Western stories. RL C.

Pete Pack Rat repeatedly outwits the notorious outlaw Gizzard Coyote in this old west style story with desert animals as characters. Illustrated with heavy line drawings, the book has humor and suspense that should appeal to young readers.

2502 *Pete Pack Rat and the Gila Monster Gang.* Ill. by author. Lothrop, 1978, o.p. SERIES: Fun-to-Read. SUBJECTS: Animals — Fiction; Robbers and outlaws — Fiction; Western stories. RL C.

The Gila Monster Gang not only robs the Pebble Junction Bank but also kidnaps Sheriff Sally Gopher. Only Pete Pack Rat is clever enough to rescue Sally and capture the gang. The delightful old west story has bold black and purple drawings.

2503 *The Return of Pete Packrat.* Robert Quackenbush Studios, 2005, ISBN 0-9712757-1-8. SUBJECTS: Animals — Fiction; Robbers and outlaws — Fiction; Western stories. RL C.

Three of the authors' Pete Packrat books (*Pete Pack Rat, Sheriff Sally Gopher and the Haunted Dance Hall,* and *Pete Pack Rat and the Gila Monster Gang*) are newly illustrated with color art. Pete and Sheriff Sally outwit outlaws in these stories set in a very fictionalized Old West.

2504 *Sheriff Sally Gopher and the Haunted Dance Hall.* Ill. by author. Lothrop, 1977, o.p. SERIES: Fun-to-Read. SUBJECTS: Animals — Fiction; Ghost stories; Western stories. RL C.

In spite of warnings that the old dance hall is haunted, Sheriff Sally Gopher tries to get it ready for a grand performance by dancer Lola Field Mouse. Suspense and humor combine in this story of an almost haunted hall. Illustrations are black and maroon pencil drawings.

2505 *Sherlock Chick and the Giant Egg Mystery.* Ill. by author. Parents Magazine Press, 1989, ISBN 0-8193-1178-2. SERIES: Read Aloud Originals. SUBJECTS: Chickens — Fiction; Farm and country life — Fiction; Mystery and detective stories. RL B.

When little Sherlock Chick discovers a giant egg, he quickly gets his mother hen to identify it. The egg is much too big for her to do anything but try to warm it, but mother hen sits while Sherlock figures out what is hatching from it. Humorous text and quirky colored paintings have child appeal.

2506 *Sherlock Chick and the Peekaboo Mystery.* Ill. by author. Parents Magazine Press, 1987, ISBN 0-8193-1149-9. SERIES: Read Aloud Originals. SUBJECTS: Animals — Fiction; Chickens — Fiction; Mystery and detective stories. RL B.

Mother Mouse hires Sherlock Chick to find her lost son. As the little chick searches, he notices lots of eyes in dark places and says again and again "Peekaboo! I see you . . ." before finding the mouse. Colorful paintings have much ink detailing.

2507 *Sherlock Chick's First Case.* Ill. by author. Parents Magazine Press, 1986, ISBN

Quackenbush, Robert (cont.)

0-8193-1148-0. SERIES: Read Aloud Originals. SUBJECTS: Chickens — Fiction; Mystery and detective stories. RL B.

Hatched wearing a detective hat, Sherlock Chick starts right in to solve the mystery of the missing corn. He follows a trail of corn and finds the culprits. Illustrated with heavily outlined watercolor pictures, the silly story is appealing.

Quin-Harkin, Janet

2508 *Helpful Hattie.* Ill. by Susanna Natti. Harcourt, 1983, o.p. SERIES: Let Me Read. SUBJECTS: Haircutting — Fiction; Human body — Teeth — Fiction. RL A.

Hattie has lots of ideas and little patience, which sometimes leads to trouble. She frosts her birthday cake with catsup, cuts her own hair, and disrupts her class picture-taking with her lost tooth. A funny story illustrated with droll ink line drawings.

2509 *Magic Growing Powder.* Ill. by Art Cumings. Parents Magazine Press, 1980, ISBN 0-8193-1038-7. SUBJECTS: Fairy tales; Magic — Fiction; Self-esteem — Fiction. RL B.

King Max hates being short and will do just about anything to be taller. He is ready to give away half his kingdom and his daughter to two tricksters for their growing powder. Princess Penny cleverly outwits the two tricksters and saves the kingdom. Illustrated with humorous full-color pictures.

Quinlan, Patricia

2510 *Anna's Red Sled.* Ill. by Lindsay Grater. Firefly, 1989, o.p. SUBJECTS: Parent and child — Fiction; Sports — Sledding — Fiction; Winter — Fiction. RL B.

Mom wants to sell Anna's old red sled at the bazaar but Anna refuses to let her. Instead Anna takes it to the park and starts remembering all the times she and mother shared when she was only three. Soft watercolors and a quiet text work well in this story.

Quiri, Patricia Ryon

2511 *The American Flag.* Children's Press, 1998, o.p. SERIES: True Book. SUBJECTS: United States — Flags; United States — Symbols. RL C. LEXILE 780L.

Discussion of the development of flags as national symbols leads into a history of the flag of the United States, the writing of the Pledge of Allegiance, and how flags are to be displayed. Appended to the text are lists of books, organizations, and Web sites, a glossary, and an index. Color photographs are found throughout.

2512 *The Bald Eagle.* Children's Press, pap., 1998, ISBN 0-516-26373-0. SERIES: True Book. SUBJECTS: Eagles; United States — Symbols. RL C. LEXILE 740L.

The importance of the bald eagle as a symbol of the United States and as a species is made clear as the author gives the history of its selection as a national symbol and then discusses the bird's life cycle and former endangered status. The book includes lists of books, organizations, and Web sites, a glossary, and an index.

2513 *The Bill of Rights.* Children's Press, 1998, o.p. SERIES: True Book. SUBJECTS: Civil rights; United States — Constitution. RL C. LEXILE 870L.

How there came to be a United States and a Bill of Rights is told with care despite the brevity of the text. Young readers will learn a great deal about the United States and its government in this book. The text is supported and extended through carefully chosen photographs; lists of books, organizations, and Web sites; a glossary and an index.

2514 *Congress.* Children's Press, 1998, o.p. SERIES: True Book. SUBJECTS: United States — Congress; United States — Government. RL C. LEXILE 780L.

Starting with the Declaration of Independence, the author gives readers a brief history of Congress and explains how, among other things, committees are set up and function, how the control of Congress is determined, and how to address a letter to a representative or senator. The book includes informative sidebars, a glossary, index, color photographs, and lists of books, organizations, and Web sites. A typographical error on page 6 says the Revolutionary War ended in 1883 instead of 1773.

2515 *The Declaration of Independence.* Children's Press, 1998, o.p. SERIES: True

Book. SUBJECTS: United States — Declaration of Independence; United States — Revolutionary War. RL C. LEXILE 710L.

The story of the colonies and their efforts to get equal rights with other British subjects leads up to the creation and signing of the Declaration of Independence and the Revolutionary War. The book is full of paintings set during the period and photographs of important objects. It ends with lists of books, organizations, and Web sites, a glossary, and an index. Note that on page 17 a typo names the king at the time George II instead of George III.

2516 *Ellis Island*. Children's Press, 1998, o.p. SERIES: True Book. SUBJECTS: Emigration and immigration; United States — History. RL C. LEXILE 710L.

The U.S. government opened an immigration center at Ellis Island in 1892 to deal with the large number of Europeans coming to America. Text and photographs tell the story of Ellis Island and of the people who came through it. Also included are a list of books, Web sites, a glossary, and an index.

2517 *The National Anthem*. Children's Press, 1998, o.p. SERIES: True Book. SUBJECTS: United States — Flags; United States — National anthem; United States — Symbols. RL C. LEXILE 860L.

Along with a brief history of the American flag, readers learn about the War of 1812 and the inspiration for the writing of Francis Scott Key's poem. The book also includes information on the formal designation of the song as the U.S. anthem; lists of books, Web sites, and organizations; and a glossary and an index.

2518 *The Presidency*. Children's Press, 1998, ISBN 0-516-20674-5. SERIES: True Book. SUBJECTS: Presidents — United States; United States — Government. RL C. LEXILE 810L.

Though published in 1998, the basic information on the presidency remains accurate. There is no focus on a particular president's work. The history and constitutional powers of the president are discussed and supported by photographs, sidebars of additional information, plus lists of books, groups, and Web sites, a glossary, and an index.

2519 *The Statue of Liberty*. Children's Press, 1998, o.p. SERIES: True Book. SUBJECTS: United States — Statue of Liberty; United States — Symbols. RL C. LEXILE 710L.

One of this nation's major monuments, the Statue of Liberty was a gift from the people of France. The story of the building of the statue and its erection on Bedloe's island is extended by photographs, sidebars of extra information, a glossary, an index, and lists of books, organizations, and Web sites.

2520 *The Supreme Court*. Children's Press, 1998, o.p. SERIES: True Book. SUBJECTS: United States — Government; United States — Supreme Court. RL C. LEXILE 780L.

Created in 1789, the Supreme Court and the judicial branch compose one of the three parts of the government of the United States. The history of the court, some famous chief justices, and important judicial decisions are presented here along with color photographs, lists of books, organizations, and Web sites, a glossary, and an index.

R

Raatma, Lucia

2521 *How Books Are Made*. Children's Press, 1998, o.p. SERIES: True Book. SUBJECTS: Books and reading; Publishing. RL C. LEXILE 860L.

From author to editor to designer to sales and many aspects in between, this book gives young readers an overview of publishing. Illustrated with color photographs, the book includes a sidebar of fonts; lists of books, organizations, and Web sites; a glossary; and an index.

2522 *Libraries*. Children's Press, 1998, ISBN 0-516-20672-9. SERIES: True Book. SUBJECTS: Books and reading; Libraries and librarians. RL C. LEXILE 820L.

Along with a history of writing and printing (on clay, papyrus, parchment, and finally paper), the evolution of libraries from ancient times to the present is given. The text is supported by reprints of art; photographs; lists of books, organizations, and Web sites; a glossary; and an index.

Rabe, Tish

2523 *Is a Camel a Mammal?* Ill. by Jim Durk. Random House, 1998, ISBN 0-679-97302-8. SERIES: The Cat in the Hat's Learning Library. SUBJECTS: Animals — Mammals; Mammals. RL C.

Using the familiar Seuss rhyming text and art, the Cat in the Hat gives a quick glimpse at a variety of mammals. A glossary (without pronunciation guide) and bibliography offer additional information.

2524 *Where Is Bear?* Ill. by Joseph Ewers. Beginner Books, 1999, o.p. SERIES: Bright and Early Books. SUBJECTS: Bears — Fiction; Play — Fiction; Stories in rhyme. RL B.

Bear and his animal friends fill their day with imaginative play. Illustrated with pencil and watercolor art in a cartoon-like style.

Rabinowitz, Sandy

2525 *How I Trained My Colt.* Ill. by author. Bantam, pap., 1991, ISBN 0-553-15848-1. SERIES: Reading on My Own. SUBJECTS: Horses — Training; Pets — Horses. RL B.

On the day of Sunny's birth, the colt's training begins. Told in the first person, the story shows how much patience and care go into the training of a horse during its first year. As a story or a horse-training book, this is very well done. Good watercolor illustrations.

Radford, Ruby

2526 *Robert Fulton.* Ill. by Salem Tamer. Putnam, 1970, o.p. SERIES: See and Read Beginning to Read Biography. SUBJECTS: Art and artists; Biographies; Inventors and inventions. RL B.

Trained as an artist and a craftsman, Robert Fulton invented many things, including a submarine called the Nautilus, before he gained fame with the steamboat. Although fictionalized conversations are added, a good portrait of a brilliant man is still provided. Realistic ink drawings.

The Random House Book of Easy-to-Read Stories

2527 *The Random House Book of Easy-to-Read Stories.* Dr. Seuss, Richard Scarry, et al. Random House, 2000, ISBN 0-679-83438-9. SUBJECTS: Stories — Collections. RL B.

Sixteen popular books for beginning readers by such authors as Dr. Seuss, the Berenstains, and P. D. Eastman, illustrated by artists such as Tomie dePaola and Marc Brown, are presented here either in their entirety or excerpted. Format and selections are sure to be winners.

Ransom, Candice F.

2528 *I Like Shoes.* Ill. by David LaFleur. Children's Press, 2005, ISBN 0-516-24858-8. SERIES: Rookie Reader. SUBJECTS: Shoes — Fiction. RL A.

A little girl talks about all the different kinds of shoes she likes in this very short rhyming text. Pages with one or two lines of bold text alternate with colorful full-page drawings.

2529 *Mother Teresa.* Ill. by Elaine Verstraete. Carolrhoda, 2001, ISBN 1-57505-441-8. SERIES: On My Own Biography. SUBJECTS: Biographies; India. RL B. LEXILE 390L.

Trained as a nun and teacher, Sister Teresa left her job as a teacher and went to work with the poorest in Calcutta, India. Illustrated with realistic watercolors, the book follows Mother Teresa's life from childhood until her death. A chronology is included.

Rappaport, Doreen

2530 *The Boston Coffee Party.* Ill. by Emily A. McCully. HarperCollins, 1988, ISBN 0-06-024825-4; pap., ISBN 0-06-444141-5. SERIES: I Can Read. SUBJECTS: Historical fiction; United States — Revolutionary War — Fiction. RL C.

When Thomas, a greedy merchant, locks away all his coffee until the price rises, the women of Boston decide to hold a coffee "party" and break into his warehouse. Based on an actual occurrence, this story could lead children to a discussion of ethics. Illustrated with ink and wash sketches.

Rau, Dana Meachen

2531 *A Box Can Be Many Things.* Ill. by Paige Billin-Frye. Children's Press, 1997, ISBN 0-516-20317-7. SERIES: Rookie Reader.

SUBJECTS: Boxes — Fiction; Imagination — Fiction; Play — Fiction. RL A. LEXILE 110L.

A sister and brother imagine all kinds of things as they play with a discarded box. Young readers will be able to identify with this duo and the creative way they use their old-fashioned toy.

2532 *Chanukah*. Children's Press, 2000, o.p. SERIES: True Book. SUBJECTS: Hanukkah; Holidays. RL C. LEXILE 720L.

The history and traditions relating to the celebration of Chanukah by Jewish people are explained through text and photographs and paintings. A dreidel game, book list, Web sites, glossary, and index are included.

2533 *Chilly Charlie*. Ill. by Martin Lemelman. Children's Press, 2001, ISBN 0-516-22210-4. SERIES: Rookie Reader. SUBJECTS: Parent and child — Fiction; Weather — Cold — Fiction. RL A.

Using a 27-word vocabulary and colorful art, this story tells of Charlie's quest to get warm. Only a hug from his mom does the trick.

2534 *Christmas*. Children's Press, 2000, ISBN 0-516-21513-2. SERIES: True Book. SUBJECTS: Christmas; Holidays. RL C. LEXILE 720L.

Christmas, its history, customs and their origins, and types of celebrations are explored through colored photographs, paintings, and an interesting text. The book also includes an activity, the words "Merry Christmas" in five languages, a list of books, Web sites, a glossary, and an index.

2535 *Circle City*. Ill. by Susan Miller. Children's Press, 1999, ISBN 0-516-21632-5. SERIES: Rookie Reader. SUBJECTS: Concepts — Shape — Fiction. RL A.

A little girl sees circles everywhere she goes in her city. Colorful illustrations allow children to find circles not mentioned in the text.

2536 *Clown Around*. Ill. by Nate Evans. Compass Point, 2001, ISBN 0-7565-0074-5. SERIES: Compass Point Early Reader. SUBJECTS: Clowns — Fiction; Stories in rhyme. RL B.

A rhyming text accompanied by comical art shows circus clowns doing all kinds of funny things. The bold print and very brief text can be more challenging than they appear.

2537 *Family Photo*. Ill. by Mike Gordon. Children's Press, 2007, ISBN 0-531-12469-X. SERIES: Rookie Reader. SUBJECTS: English language — Prepositions — Fiction; Family life — Fiction; Photography and photographers — Fiction. RL B.

A little boy directs each member of a family to a position for what seems to be a family photograph. Parental or adult interaction will help readers identify prepositions and their use.

2538 *Feet*. Ill. by Rick Stromoski. Children's Press, 2000, ISBN 0-516-22008-X. SERIES: Rookie Reader. SUBJECTS: Camps and camping — Fiction; Human body — Fiction; Stories in rhyme. RL A.

With a minimum of words and humorous cartoon-like illustrations, readers see what fun children and their feet have at camp.

2539 *Hands*. Ill. by Rick Stromoski. Children's Press, 2000, ISBN 0-516-22009-8. SERIES: Rookie Reader. SUBJECTS: Birthdays — Fiction; Human body — Fiction; Parties — Fiction. RL A.

Using a few words on a page plus colorful cartoon-like paintings of children getting ready for a birthday party, this book shows the many things that hands can do.

2540 *Kwanzaa*. Children's Press, 2000, ISBN 0-516-21517-5. SERIES: True Book. SUBJECTS: African Americans; Holidays; Kwanzaa. RL C. LEXILE 710L.

The holiday of Kwanzaa was begun in the 1960s to celebrate African roots and values for people of African heritage in the United States and around the world. The traditions of Kwanzaa are explained and shown in photographs. The book also includes lists of books, organizations, and Web sites; a glossary; and an index.

2541 *Look for Ladybugs*. Ill. by Christine Schneider. Children's Press, 2007, ISBN 0-531-12470-3. SERIES: Rookie Reader. SUBJECTS: English language — Prepositions; Ladybugs. RL A.

A child looks everywhere for ladybugs and finally finds one on his arm. With adult help, prepositions can be easily identified in this very brief text. Illustrations are bright and bold.

Rau, Dana Meachen (cont.)

2542 *My Book by Me*. Ill. by author. Children's Press, 2000, ISBN 0-516-22032-2. SERIES: Rookie Reader. SUBJECTS: Books and reading — Fiction. RL A.

A little girl creates her own book, filling it with anything she wants and sharing it with her friends. Collage art effectively illustrates this book.

2543 *New Year's Day*. Children's Press, 2000, o.p. SERIES: True Book. SUBJECTS: Holidays; New Year's Day. RL C. LEXILE 800L.

The history of the celebration of the new year, the ways in which people celebrate it today, and the varying times it is celebrated make interesting reading. With color photographs; paintings; lists of books, organizations, and Web sites; a glossary; and an index, this is a useful homework resource.

2544 *Purple Is Best*. Ill. by Mike Cressy. Children's Press, 1999, ISBN 0-516-21638-4. SERIES: Rookie Reader. SUBJECTS: Colors — Fiction; Painting — Fiction. RL A. LEXILE BR.

When Sue, who is painting with red, and Fred, who is painting with blue, accidentally spill their paint, everything becomes purple. The illustrations are expressive and fun.

2545 *The Secret Code*. Ill. by Bari Weissman. Children's Press, pap., 1998, ISBN 0-516-26362-5. SERIES: Rookie Reader. SUBJECTS: Braille — Fiction; Disabilities — Physical and mental — Fiction; School stories. RL B. LEXILE 330L.

While the other children in Oscar's class are learning their ABCs, Oscar is learning to recognize the letters in Braille. When he shows a classmate how to read a few of his letters, she is so excited that the teacher decides the entire class should learn Braille.

2546 *Shoo, Crow! Shoo!* Ill. by Mary Galan Rojas. Compass Point, 2001, o.p. SERIES: Compass Point Early Reader. SUBJECTS: Scarecrows — Fiction. RL A.

Two children gather clothes, draw a face on a pumpkin, and put up their scarecrow. A few words in bold type on alternating pages are supported by brightly colored, childlike illustrations.

2547 *So Many Sounds*. Ill. by Kristin Sorra. Children's Press, 2001, ISBN 0-516-22209-0. SERIES: Rookie Reader. SUBJECTS: Farm and country life — Fiction; Sound — Fiction. RL A.

Sounds on the farm are introduced through a very limited vocabulary and the briefest of texts. Full-color art is important to the telling of the story.

2548 *Thanksgiving*. Children's Press, 2000, o.p. SERIES: True Book. SUBJECTS: Holidays; Thanksgiving; United States — History. RL C. LEXILE 810L.

An interesting and factual look at the arrival of the Pilgrims and the history of Thanksgiving, this book gives details of the first feast, the subsequent celebrations, its designation as a national holiday, and today's traditions. The book ends with lists of books, organizations, and Web sites; a glossary; and an index.

2549 *Yahoo for You*. Ill. by Cary Pillo. Compass Point, 2002, ISBN 0-7565-0177-6. SERIES: Compass Point Early Reader. SUBJECTS: Fear — Fiction; Grandparents — Fiction. RL A.

An encouraging grandma helps a little girl overcome her fear of trying new things. Cartoon-like ink and watercolor pictures illustrate the text. An additional section offers hints to parents for helping their children overcome fears.

Ready, Dee

2550 *Dentists*. Bridgestone, 1998, ISBN 1-56065-558-5. SERIES: Community Helpers. SUBJECTS: Careers; Community helpers; Dentists. RL B. LEXILE 450L.

The many aspects of dental work, the education required to become a dentist, and the people who work with dentists are briefly explored in words and photographs. Included are an activity, a glossary, a short bibliography, Web sites, and an index.

2551 *Doctors*. Bridgestone, 1997, ISBN 1-56065-509-7. SERIES: Community Helpers. SUBJECTS: Careers; Community helpers; Doctors and nurses. RL C. LEXILE AD580L.

Supported by color photographs, an activity, and a glossary, index, bibliography, and Web sites, this book provides a brief look at doctors, their work, their education, and their tools.

2552 *Farmers*. Bridgestone, 1997, ISBN 1-56065-511-9. SERIES: Community Helpers. SUBJECTS: Community helpers; Farm and country life. RL B. LEXILE 430L.

Using color photographs to support the text, the work of farmers is explained and shown. The end of the book includes an activity, a glossary, a bibliography, Web sites, and an index.

2553 *Fire Fighters*. Bridgestone, 1997, ISBN 1-56065-510-0. SERIES: Community Helpers. SUBJECTS: Careers; Community helpers; Fire fighters and fire fighting. RL B. LEXILE IG520L.

Through alternating pages of text and color photographs, readers learn about a fire fighter's work, uniforms, vehicles, the station they live in, and more. The book also includes two exercises for keeping fit, a glossary, a very brief bibliography, two Web sites, and an index.

2554 *Librarians*. Bridgestone, 1998, ISBN 1-56065-559-3. SERIES: Community Helpers. SUBJECTS: Community helpers; Libraries and librarians. RL B. LEXILE 450L.

All kinds of librarians and libraries are looked at in pictures and discussed in the text. Education and work duties are included along with an activity, glossary, bibliography, Web sites, and index.

2555 *Mail Carriers*. Bridgestone, 1998, ISBN 1-56065-557-7. SERIES: Community Helpers. SUBJECTS: Careers; Community helpers; Postal service. RL B.

In alternating pages of color photographs and brief text, children learn about the work, uniforms, equipment, and importance of letter carriers. Also included are instructions for starting a stamp collection, a glossary, a short bibliography, Web sites, and an index.

2556 *Nurses*. Bridgestone, 1997, ISBN 1-56065-512-7. SERIES: Community Helpers. SUBJECTS: Careers; Community helpers; Doctors and nurses. RL B. LEXILE 520L.

A basic look at how nurses are trained, what they do, and where they do it is supplemented by an activity, glossary, bibliography, Web sites, index, and alternating pages of full-color photographs.

2557 *Police Officers*. Bridgestone, 1997, ISBN 0-516-20505-6. SERIES: Community Helpers. SUBJECTS: Careers; Community helpers; Police. RL C. LEXILE 490L.

The training and everyday duties of a police officer are seen in photographs and through the brief text. An activity that shows children how to take a fingerprint is included along with a glossary, an index, a bibliography, and a Web site list.

2558 *School Bus Drivers*. Bridgestone, 1998, ISBN 1-56065-560-7. SERIES: Community Helpers. SUBJECTS: Buses; Careers; Schools. RL B. LEXILE 430L.

Although most children are familiar with school bus drivers, this look at the work they do, the tests they take, and their responsibilities will add to their understanding of the job. The book includes an activity, glossary, bibliography, Web sites, and an index.

2559 *Veterinarians*. Bridgestone, 1997, ISBN 1-56065-514-3. SERIES: Community Helpers. SUBJECTS: Community helpers; Veterinarians. RL B. LEXILE AD560L.

The various types of vets, what they do, the education they need, and the people who help them are all a part of this book. Color photographs extend the text, which is further supported by an activity, glossary, index, and bibliography.

Redmond, Shirley Raye

2560 *The Dog That Dug for Dinosaurs: A True Story*. Ill. by Simon Sullivan. Aladdin, pap., 2004, ISBN 0-689-85708-X. SERIES: Ready-to-Read. SUBJECTS: Pets — Dogs; Prehistoric animals. RL C.

Mary Ann Anning and her dog Tray would comb the cliffs of Lyme Regis in England for fossils in the early 1800s. They found the remains of many prehistoric animals. This story of some very early fossil discoveries may need adult assistance as it gives no time period.

2561 *Pigeon Hero!* Ill. by Doris Ettlinger. Simon & Schuster, pap., 2003, ISBN 0-689-85486-2. SERIES: Ready-to-Read. SUBJECTS: Pigeons, carrier — Fiction; World War II — Fiction. RL B.

In a small town in Italy, the people have peacefully surrendered to British soldiers and the Germans have fled. Knowing that planes are to bomb the town, G.I. Joe, a carrier pigeon, is sent to tell the pilots not to raid it. The story, based on a true

Redmond, Shirley Raye (cont.)

event, is illustrated with realistic pencil and watercolor pictures.

2562 *Tentacles! Tales of the Giant Squid*. Ill. by Bryn Barnard. Random House, pap., 2003, ISBN 0-375-81307-1. SERIES: Step into Reading. SUBJECTS: Giant squids; Oceans and ocean life. RL C.

Exaggerated stories about the giant squid's strength and willingness to attack people, whales, and ships have been told for centuries. Scientists are trying to discover the truth about giant squids using a variety of methods. Illustrated with realistic paintings and photographs.

Regan, Dana

2563 *Monkey See, Monkey Do*. Grosset & Dunlap, pap., 2000, ISBN 0-448-42299-9. SERIES: All Aboard Reading. SUBJECTS: Monkeys — Fiction; Stories in rhyme. RL A. LEXILE 60L.

Little monkeys do many of the same things young children do — playing, dancing, hiding, and so forth. The simple text is illustrated with appealing pictures of childlike monkeys.

Reidel, Marlene

2564 *From Egg to Bird*. Ill. by author. Carolrhoda, 1981, o.p. SERIES: Start to Finish. SUBJECTS: Animals — Reproduction; Birds. RL B.

The process of rearing young birds, from nest-building to the time of the young birds' departure, is told very simply and nicely. Text is perfectly coordinated with the artwork, full-color paintings of birds raising their young. Paintings are somewhat stylized but clearly depict their subject.

Reit, Seymour

2565 *A Dog's Tale*. Ill. by Kate Flannagan. Gareth Stevens, 1996, ISBN 0-8368-1615-3. SERIES: Bank Street Reader Collection. SUBJECTS: Pet care — Fiction; Pets — Dogs — Fiction. RL B. LEXILE AD480L.

Ruff, a dog, tells the story of how he found his human, Wendy, and helped her learn to take good care of him. The illustrations are humorous and attractive.

2566 *The Rebus Bears*. Ill. by Kenneth Smith. Gareth Stevens, 1989, ISBN 0-8368-1750-8. SERIES: Bank Street Ready-to-Read. SUBJECTS: Folklore; Rebuses. RL A.

Picture clues behind or next to words will help beginning readers handle this very familiar Goldilocks folktale. Although this is longer than most of the very easy books for young readers, the combination of a familiar story and rather large full-color rebus illustrations makes it accessible.

2567 *Things That Go: A Traveling Alphabet*. Ill. by Fulvio Testa. Bantam, 1990, o.p. SERIES: Bank Street Ready-to-Read. SUBJECTS: Alphabet; Vehicles. RL B.

Surprisingly full of descriptive information, this alphabet book covers all kinds of land, sea, and air vehicles including an ambulance, a garbage truck, and a spaceship. The illustrations are detailed and fun, and augment the text.

Retan, Walter

2568 *Armies of Ants*. Ill. by Jean Cassels. Scholastic, pap., 1994, ISBN 0-590-47616-5. SERIES: Hello Reader! SUBJECTS: Ants; Insects. RL C.

This fascinating look at a number of ant varieties and their lives touches on food gathering and production, rearing of young, and interaction with other ant species. Watercolor art is detailed and important to the lengthy text.

Rex, Michael

2569 *Firefighter*. Cartwheel, pap., 2003, ISBN 0-439-52785-6. SERIES: Scholastic Reader. SUBJECTS: Fire fighters and fire fighting. RL A.

The pictures and their one-word captions tell the story of the men and women of a firehouse and their response to a fire. Details of their wardrobes, work in the firehouse, and response to the fire are included.

2570 *Pals*. Cartwheel, pap., 2003, ISBN 0-439-49310-2. SERIES: Scholastic Reader. SUBJECTS: Art and artists — Fiction; Extraterrestrial beings — Fiction; Friendship — Fiction. RL A.

When a space creature comes in through his window, a little boy communicates with him as they share drawings about their lives. One word per page helps to tell the story, which is illustrated in boldly colored cartoon-like pictures.

2571 *Where Can Bunny Paint?* Cartwheel, pap., 2002, ISBN 0-439-36605-4. SERIES: Word-by-Word First Reader. SUBJECTS: Art and artists — Fiction; Rabbits — Fiction. RL A.

Humorous pencil and paint pictures combine with a text consisting of one word per page to tell the story of a bunny's search for a place to paint. The newest reader will have little difficulty deciphering the text.

Ribke, Simone T.

2572 *A Garden Full of Sizes.* Children's Press, 2004, ISBN 0-516-24432-9. SERIES: Rookie Read-About Math. SUBJECTS: Concepts — Size; Mathematics; Stories in rhyme. RL B. LEXILE 320L.

Using an at times annoying rhyming text, comparisons are made between plants, their seeds, and even branches and tree trunks. The color photographs are integral to the book. A photo glossary and index are included.

2573 *The Shapes We Eat.* Children's Press, 2004, ISBN 0-516-24431-0. SERIES: Rookie Read-About Math. SUBJECTS: Concepts — Shape; Mathematics. RL B. LEXILE 470L.

Through everyday foods such as sandwiches, eggs, and cheese, children observe and learn about different kinds of shapes: squares, triangles, ovals, circles, and so forth. The brightly colored photographs and brief text are supplemented by a photo glossary and an index.

Ricci, Christine

2574 *The Halloween Cat.* Ill. by Zina Saunders. Simon & Schuster, pap., 2004, ISBN 0-689-86799-9. SERIES: Ready-to-Read. SUBJECTS: Halloween — Fiction; Rebuses. RL B.

Dora helps a black cat get back to the castle in time for the Halloween party. Along the way the two solve puzzles and use a map. Rebuses are included in the text.

2575 *Puppy Takes a Bath.* Ill. by Tom Mangano. Simon & Schuster, pap., 2006, ISBN 1-4169-1483-8. SERIES: Ready-to-Read. SUBJECTS: Bathing — Fiction; Pets — Dogs — Fiction. RL A.

Dora must first find her puppy before she can give it a bath. The familiar television character and her story are illustrated in boldly colored art.

Ricci, Christine, and Alison Inches

2576 *Dora's Ready-to-Read Adventures.* Simon & Schuster, pap., 2005, ISBN 0-689-87815-X. SERIES: Ready-to-Read. SUBJECTS: Adventure stories. RL B.

In five stories, popular television cartoon character Dora and her family and friends have adventures of all kinds. The text is repetitive, using rebuses for some objects and characters, but not as easy to read as might be expected.

Ricciuti, Edward R.

2577 *An Animal for Alan.* Ill. by Tom Eaton. HarperCollins, 1970, o.p. SERIES: Science I Can Read. SUBJECTS: Pets; Pets — Wild animals. RL B.

In trying to select the perfect pet, Alan slowly learns that most wild animals are not meant to be pets. Alan's father suggests that he might like a dog or a cat. The animals are realistically portrayed in ink and colored pencil drawings and the story has a good message for children.

2578 *Catch a Whale by the Tail.* Ill. by Geoffrey Moss. HarperCollins, 1969, o.p. SERIES: Science I Can Read. SUBJECTS: Whales. RL C.

Hoping to find a way to get Robert, a Beluga whale, to sing or whistle, his curator heads to the far north to find a mate for him. Readers are taken on a whaling expedition and given good information on the Beluga whale. Illustrated with exuberant blue and brown sketches.

2579 *Donald and the Fish That Walked.* Ill. by Syd Hoff. HarperCollins, 1974, o.p. SERIES: Science I Can Read. SUBJECTS: Conservation; Fish. RL B.

Donald thinks the walking catfish that begin to appear in his neighborhood are fun. Then Mr. Walter explains that they were brought from Asia and are driving out other fish. A thought-provok-

Ricciuti, Edward R. (cont.)

ing look at a conservation problem, this story is illustrated in a cartoon style.

Rice, Eve

2580 *Mr. Brimble's Hobby and Other Stories.* Ill. by author. Greenwillow, 1975, o.p. SERIES: Read-Alone. SUBJECTS: Family life — Fiction. RL C.

What first seems to be a very traditional family is far more. All of its members are strong individuals who value themselves and each other and together create enjoyable stories of a loving family. The simple warmth of the ink and wash drawings are a perfect complement to the text.

2581 *Once in a Wood: Ten Fables from Aesop.* Ill. by author. Greenwillow, pap., 1993, ISBN 0-688-12268-X. SERIES: Read-Alone. SUBJECTS: Fables. RL B.

The essence of Aesop is captured in Rice's adaptations of ten familiar fables. Each is carefully constructed with a final few lines devoted to a rhyming moral. The illustrations are very detailed, whimsical black-and-white drawings.

2582 *Papa's Lemonade and Other Stories.* Ill. by author. Greenwillow, 1976, o.p. SERIES: Read-Alone. SUBJECTS: Family life — Fiction; Pets — Dogs — Fiction. RL B.

Papa and Mama dog and their five pups share gentle yet whimsical adventures that include trying to find a substitute for a broken bank, going for a walk in the country, and making lemonade with oranges. Ink drawings of very humanized animals are given soft color washes.

Richards, Kitty

2583 *It's About Time, Max!* Ill. by Gioia Fiammenghi. Kane, pap., 2000, ISBN 1-57565-088-6. SERIES: Math Matters. SUBJECTS: Behavior — Tardiness — Fiction; Clocks — Fiction; Concepts — Time — Fiction. RL C. LEXILE 170L.

Only able to tell time by his digital watch, Max is lost — and very late -without it. The way in which Max's family helps him to learn to tell time by a clock may be helpful to readers and their families. The art is bright and humorous.

Richardson, Adele

2584 *Caring for Your Fish.* Capstone, 2007, ISBN 0-7368-6386-9. SERIES: First Facts: Positively Pets. SUBJECTS: Aquariums; Pet care; Pets — Fish. RL C. LEXILE 610L.

Bright colors, an enticing design, and easily understood instructions should encourage prospective fish owners to learn before purchasing. The book includes a page on decoding the behavior of fish, a glossary, bibliography, Web sites, and index.

2585 *Caring for Your Hamster.* Capstone, 2007, ISBN 0-7368-6387-7. SERIES: First Facts: Positively Pets. SUBJECTS: Hamsters; Pet care; Pets. RL C. LEXILE 700L.

Though having a hamster is a big responsibility, the instructions in this attractive, brightly colored book will give young pet owners some help. The book offers instructions on health, care of the cage/aquarium, food, and so forth, along with a glossary, bibliography, Web sites, color photographs, and index.

2586 *Caring for Your Hermit Crab.* Capstone, 2007, ISBN 0-7368-6388-5. SERIES: First Facts: Positively Pets. SUBJECTS: Crabs; Pet care; Pets. RL C. LEXILE 660L.

Any young child wanting a hermit crab for a pet would be wise to read this overview of pet care, health issues, safety, and behavior. The book also includes a glossary, bibliography, Web sites, and index.

Richardson, Joy

2587 *Air.* Ill. with photos. Watts, 1992, ISBN 0-531-14201-9. SERIES: Picture Science. SUBJECTS: Air; Science and scientists. RL C.

What air means to human beings, animals, plants, airplanes, and so on is discussed in brief chapters with one page of text and one color photograph. Occasional painted diagrams extend and help explain the text. An index is included.

2588 *Airports.* Ill. with photos. Children's Press, 1994, o.p. SERIES: Picture Science. SUBJECTS: Airports. RL C.

Although published in 1994, this look at airports is still relevant. It includes information on the layout of an airport, passenger security, air traffic controllers, and other essential components of a working airport. The book also includes diagrams, color photographs, and an index.

2589 *Day and Night.* Ill. with photos. Watts, 1991, o.p. SERIES: Picture Science. SUBJECTS: Days; Night. RL C.

First observing how day and night are experienced, the author then explains how the earth's turning creates daytime and nighttime. Clear explanations are presented in a rather dull format with color photographs. Index is included.

2590 *Rocks and Soil.* Ill. with photos. Watts, 1992, o.p. SERIES: Picture Science. SUBJECTS: Geology and geologists. RL C.

How soil, mountains, oil, coal, crystals, and other materials are formed is given brief but clear coverage. A textbookish format with grainy color photographs makes this less appealing than other books. Index is included.

2591 *The Seasons.* Ill. with photos. Watts, 1991, o.p. SERIES: Picture Science. SUBJECTS: Seasons. RL C.

Through textbookish color photographs and some explanatory diagrams, a look at how the world changes from season to season is presented along with some brief explanatory paragraphs on how the movement of the earth around the sun causes the changes. Index is included.

2592 *The Water Cycle.* Ill. with photos. Watts, 1992, o.p. SERIES: Picture Science. SUBJECTS: Science and scientists; Water. RL C.

The water cycle, water purification, and principles of water are covered without great depth, at a level suitable for most beginning readers. Format and bland color photographs have a textbookish look. Index is included.

2593 *The Weather.* Ill. with photos. Watts, 1992, o.p. SERIES: Picture Science. SUBJECTS: Weather. RL C.

The formation of rain, snow, frost, and fog; weather forecasting; and the climate are all covered in this brief look at the various aspects of weather. Rather dull format and mediocre color photographs lessen the appeal of the book.

2594 *What Happens When You Breathe?* Ill. by Colin Maclean and Moira Maclean. Stevens, 1986, o.p. SERIES: What Happens When . . . SUBJECTS: Human body — Respiration. RL C.

A clear, easily understood text helps children learn how breathing works. Simple experiments simulate or measure the lung's activities and further clarify the respiration process. An index and a bibliography are included. Illustrated with colored diagrams and drawings.

2595 *What Happens When You Eat?* Ill. by Colin Maclean and Moira Maclean. Stevens, 1986, o.p. SERIES: What Happens When . . . SUBJECTS: Human body — Digestion. RL C.

This explanation of digestion is clear and easily understood. Colored diagrams and drawings help show how food reaches the stomach and goes through the intestines. A bibliography and an index are included.

2596 *What Happens When You Listen?* Ill. by Colin Maclean and Moira Maclean. Stevens, 1986, o.p. SERIES: What Happens When . . . SUBJECTS: Human body — Ears; Senses — Hearing. RL C.

A clear, straightforward text helps children understand how ears work. A number of simple experiments are also suggested. There is an index, a bibliography, and a list of nonbook sources for additional information. Colored diagrams and drawings aid in conveying the message.

2597 *What Happens When You Sleep?* Ill. by Colin Maclean and Moira Maclean. Stevens, 1986, o.p. SERIES: What Happens When . . . SUBJECTS: Human body — Sleep; Sleep. RL B.

Basic information about how and why people sleep, dream, and wake up is conveyed in a simple writing style. A few experiments are suggested along with some questions to prod young readers. Included is a bibliography, a subject index, and an experiment and question index. Attractive full-color pictures.

Richter, Alice, and Laura J. Numeroff

2598 *You Can't Put Braces on Spaces.* Ill. by Laura J. Numeroff. Greenwillow, 1979, o.p. SERIES: Read-Alone. SUBJECTS: Human body — Teeth — Fiction; Orthodontics — Fiction. RL B.

A little boy can hardly wait for his teeth to grow in so that he can have braces like his brother and other older children. Good information on orthodontia is given as the older brother goes to have

Richter, Alice, and Laura J. Numeroff (cont.)

his braces put on. Boldly outlined pictures are flat and childlike but lively.

Rickard, Graham

2599 *Tractors.* Ill. by Clifford Meadway. Bookwright, 1988, o.p. SERIES: Let's Look At. SUBJECTS: Farm and country life; Tractors. RL C.

After presenting a brief history of the tractor, the machine's many uses and types are then looked at. Rickard also includes a thoughtful section on some of the disadvantages of modern farming methods. Illustrated with realistic watercolor paintings. Includes a brief glossary.

Ridlon, Marci

2600 *Kittens and More Kittens.* Ill. by Liz Dauber. Follett, 1967, o.p. SERIES: Beginning to Read. SUBJECTS: Pets — Cats — Fiction. RL A.

Finally old enough to own a pet, Jennifer Joan posts flyers in her neighborhood asking for a kitten and even gets into the newspaper. The inevitable donations of kittens occur and the little girl is fortunate to find someone to take them. Illustrated with colorful, attractive paintings.

Riehecky, Janet

2601 *Anatosaurus.* Ill. by Diana Magnuson. Child's World, 1989, o.p. SERIES: Dinosaur Books. SUBJECTS: Dinosaurs. RL C.

A dinosaur about which much is known because two mummified bodies have been found, the plant-eating anatosaurus is thought to have been able to swim. Carefully written, this book is illustrated with watercolor pictures of the duck-billed dinosaur.

2602 *Brachiosaurus.* Ill. by Jim Conaway. Child's World, 1989, o.p. SERIES: Dinosaur Books. SUBJECTS: Dinosaurs. RL C.

About 43 feet tall and weighing over 85 tons, the brachiosaurus was one of the biggest dinosaurs. Speculation about the animal's habits and herd life is presented as such. Information on current discoveries of dinosaurs that may have been larger is also given. Watercolor pictures accompany the text.

2603 *Cooperation.* Ill. by Kathryn Hutton. Capstone, 2005, ISBN 0-7368-3678-0. SERIES: Values to Live By. SUBJECTS: Behavior — Cooperative. RL B.

Twin boys and their Asian American family and multicultural friends demonstrate the many ways in which people can cooperate. Meant to reinforce and encourage positive values, the book is illustrated with sweet watercolor paintings with pencil definition.

2604 *Good Sportsmanship.* Ill. by Christina Rigo. Child's World, 1990, o.p. SERIES: Values to Live By. SUBJECTS: Behavior — Sportsmanship; Values. RL B.

A little girl demonstrates the many ways to be a good sport: with friends, playing a game; at school. The rather saccharine watercolor illustrations help the very brief text reinforce the book's message.

2605 *Iguanodon.* Ill. by Diana Magnuson. Capstone, 2006, ISBN 0-7368-5353-7. SERIES: Dinosaur Books. SUBJECTS: Dinosaurs. RL C.

The first dinosaur discovered (1822), the iguanodon was first thought to resemble a rhinoceros. The story of its finding and attempts to identify it make fascinating and lively reading. The tone of the book is light but scientific. Text is illustrated with watercolors.

2606 *Maiasaura.* Ill. by Diana Magnuson. Child's World, 1989, o.p. SERIES: Dinosaur Books. SUBJECTS: Dinosaurs. RL C.

A duck-billed dinosaur, the maiasaura, built nests for its young and watched over them until they could be independent. In 1978 remains of over 10,000 maiasaura were found in Montana. An interesting mix of information, the text is accompanied by watercolor pictures.

2607 *Snow: When Will It Fall?* Ill. by Joy Friedman. Child's World, 1990, o.p. SERIES: Discovery World: First Steps to Science. SUBJECTS: Weather — Snow. RL B.

The importance of snow to plants and animals, the problems it can create, the structure of snowflakes, and experiments are all included in this look at one aspect of weather. Illustrated with pencil and watercolors. Index is included.

2608 *What Plants Give Us: The Gift of Life.* Ill. by Rondi Collette. Child's World, 1990, o.p. SERIES: Discovery World: First Steps to Science. SUBJECTS: Plants. RL B.

Beautifully illustrated with detailed watercolors set into artfully designed frames, this book has a slightly more difficult and lengthier text than others in the series. It explores the ways in which plants help people and the text is followed by a section of experiments.

Ries, Lori

2609 *Aggie and Ben: Three Stories.* Ill. by Frank W. Dormer. Charlesbridge, 2006, ISBN 1-57091-594-6. SUBJECTS: Pet care — Fiction; Pets — Dogs — Fiction. RL B.

Ben doesn't know what kind of pet he wants until he sees Aggie. He takes the little dog home and in three stories they share their first day together. Expressive art in muted colors is a good match to the well-written text.

Riley, Kathryn

2610 *The Big Sale.* Ill. by Dorothy Handelman. Millbrook, 1999, ISBN 0-7613-2057-1. SERIES: Real Kids Readers. SUBJECTS: Grandparents — Fiction; Tag sales — Fiction. RL B. LEXILE BR.

Jeff and Jenna not only discover lots of wonderful old things at their grandfather's tag sale but they also sell many things of their own. The book, like others in the series, is illustrated with full-color photographs.

Rinkoff, Barbara

2611 *Guess What Rocks Do.* Ill. by Leslie Morrill. Lothrop, 1975, o.p. SERIES: Guess What . . . SUBJECTS: Geology and geologists. RL B.

An appreciation rather than a scientific look at rocks is presented. The book shows the many ways humans have used rocks — as weapons, for building, and for grinding. The illustrations give the reader a sense of time passing with realistic figures drawn against swaths of rust or olive.

2612 *Guess What Trees Do.* Ill. by Beatrice Darwin. Lothrop, 1974, o.p. SERIES: Guess What . . . SUBJECTS: Trees. RL C.

An appreciation of the many things that trees do for people rather than a botanical study of trees, the text reminds readers that trees provide oxygen, sap for maple syrup, wood for furniture, and much more. The illustrations, which add little to the text, are in turquoise, black, and olive.

2613 *No Pushing, No Ducking: Safety in the Water.* Ill. by Roy Doty. Lothrop, 1974, o.p. SUBJECTS: Boats and boating; Safety; Sports — Swimming. RL B.

A girl surprises her show-offish friend Tom with her knowledge of water safety and her swimming skill. The book offers a humorous but very effective approach to water safety — swimming or boating — and includes a list of water safety rules. It is nicely illustrated with cartoon-like pictures.

2614 *Rutherford T Finds 21B.* Ill. by Tomie dePaola. Putnam, 1970, o.p. SERIES: See and Read. SUBJECTS: Moving, household — Fiction; School stories. RL B.

Rutherford bravely heads for school alone but cannot find his room. New to the area, he asks a succession of children for directions and all of them end up helping him not only to find the room but to feel less like a newcomer. Illustrated with simple taupe and blue pictures.

Ripken, Cal, Jr., and Mike Bryan

2615 *Cal Ripken, Jr.: Play Ball!* Adapted by Gail Herman. Dial, pap., 1999, ISBN 0-14-130184-8. SERIES: Dial Easy-to-Read. SUBJECTS: Baseball players; Biographies; Sports — Baseball. RL C. LEXILE 380L.

The Baltimore Oriole who set a record for the most games played in a row tells about his life and what it took to become a professional ball player. Photographs from Orioles games and a list of Ripken's accomplishments as of 1999 are included in this adaptation of his autobiography *The Only Way I Know.*

Robbins, Ken

2616 *Make Me a Peanut Butter Sandwich and a Glass of Milk.* Ill. by author. Scholastic, 1992, o.p. SUBJECTS: Farm and country life; Food. RL B.

The production of peanut butter, bread, and milk — from farm to the store to the table — is shown in hand-tinted photographs and explained in an

Robbins, Ken (cont.)

understandable text. The attractive format will invite readers to learn just how much work is involved in the production of favorite foods.

Roberson, Erin

2617 *All About Money*. Children's Press, 2004, ISBN 0-516-24420-5. SERIES: Rookie Read-About Math. SUBJECTS: Mathematics; Money. RL B. LEXILE 510L.

A brief text and color photographs showing coins and objects that can be purchased with them attempts to explain the value of money today and in the past. The worth of one coin is compared with that of others. For example: two dimes and one nickel equal one quarter. The book also includes a photo glossary and an index.

Robert, Adrian

2618 *The "Awful Mess" Mystery*. Ill. by Paul Harvey. Troll, 1985, o.p. SUBJECTS: Clubs — Fiction; Mystery and detective stories. RL B.

After Katie tries on her mother's new bracelet, she loses it, creating an awful mess. Katie's fellow club members help her retrace her steps, and they finally find the bracelet. The detecting in this story is complex enough to interest young readers. Illustrated with very simple, childlike pictures.

Roberts, Bethany

2619 *May Belle and the Ogre*. Ill. by Marsha Winborn. Dutton, 2003, ISBN 0-525-46855-2. SERIES: Dutton Easy Reader. SUBJECTS: Friendship — Fiction; Monsters — Fiction. RL B. LEXILE AD150L.

In three brief stories May Belle encounters a very little and very furry ogre — finally making him her friend. With May Belle's independent spirit and the funny little ogre, the stories will make fun reading. The art is colorful and cartoonish.

2620 *Ogre Eats Everything*. Ill. by Marsha Winborn. Dutton, 2005, ISBN 0-525-47291-6. SERIES: Dutton Easy Reader. SUBJECTS: Friendship — Fiction; Gardening — Fiction; Monsters — Fiction. RL B.

From his friend May Belle, Ogre learns how not to eat the garden or the notes May Belle sends and to find ways to keep busy on a warm, sunny day. The adventures of May Belle and Ogre are portrayed with humor and gentleness in text and watercolor pictures.

Robins, Joan

2621 *Addie Meets Max*. Ill. by Sue Truesdell. HarperCollins, pap., 1985, ISBN 0-06-025064-X. SERIES: Early I Can Read. SUBJECTS: Friendship — Fiction; Moving, household — Fiction; Pets — Dogs — Fiction. RL A.

Addie's new neighbor Max seems unfriendly and so does his dog Ginger until Addie gets a chance to know them. Lively watercolor paintings expressively illustrate this light but realistic story of a blossoming friendship.

2622 *Addie Runs Away*. Ill. by Sue Truesdell. HarperCollins, 1989, ISBN 0-06-025080-1. SERIES: Early I Can Read. SUBJECTS: Behavior — Running away — Fiction; Friendship — Fiction. RL A.

Awakened by his dog Ginger, Max discovers that his neighbor — and friend — Addie is running away from home rather than going to camp. Max finally convinces her and himself that camp is not so bad. Expressive watercolor pictures add a light touch to a story about misunderstanding.

2623 *Addie's Bad Day*. Ill. by Sue Truesdell. HarperCollins, pap., 1993, ISBN 0-06-444183-0. SERIES: I Can Read. SUBJECTS: Birthdays — Fiction; Friendship — Fiction; Haircutting — Fiction. RL B.

Addie is mortified! Her new haircut is awful, she refuses to take off her hat and will not go to Max's birthday party. But good friend Max finds just the right way to get Addie to have fun again. Lively and realistic, this story is illustrated with sketchy, humorous ink and wash pictures.

Robinson, Fay

2624 *Creepy Beetles*. Ill. by Jean Cassels. Scholastic, 2000, o.p. SERIES: Hello Science Reader! SUBJECTS: Beetles; Insects; Science and scientists; Stories in rhyme. RL B. LEXILE 300L.

Using a rhyming text, the author shows how beetles live and act in their environments. The painted illustrations are detailed and realistic. The final three pages identify each beetle pictured in the book.

2625 *Fantastic Frogs!* Ill. by Jean Cassels. Scholastic, pap., 1999, ISBN 0-590-52269-8. SERIES: Hello Science Reader! SUBJECTS: Frogs and toads; Reptiles and amphibians; Stories in rhyme. RL B. LEXILE 190L.

The detailed illustrations of frogs of all sizes from around the world will grab the attention of budding naturalists. The brief rhyming text is descriptive of the art. The final two pages identify each frog.

2626 *A Frog Inside My Hat: A First Book of Poems*. Ill. by Cyd Moore. BridgeWater, 1993, o.p. SUBJECTS: Poetry. RL B.

Lively, attractive, full of humorous poems and sprightly illustrations, this collection is perfect for introducing beginning readers to the best of poetry and poets. Included are selections by Ciardi, McCord, Lear, Nikki Giovanni, Prelutsky, Milne, and other well-known poets.

2627 *A Ghost in the Toy Box*. Ill. by Ann Iosa. Childrens Press, 1992, o.p. SERIES: Bear and Alligator Tales. SUBJECTS: Hamsters; Toys. RL A.

When Ape hears a strange noise in the toy box, Bear and Alligator decide to investigate. Though Alligator runs away when he hears it, Bear bravely opens the lid to let Hamster out. The story is illustrated in cartoon-like watercolors with pencil definition.

2628 *Great Snakes!* Ill. by Jean Day Zallinger. Scholastic, pap., 1996, ISBN 0-590-26243-2. SERIES: Hello Science Reader! SUBJECTS: Reptiles and amphibians; Snakes; Stories in rhyme. RL B. LEXILE 110L.

Realistic and colorful pictures of snakes are captioned with a rhyming text. The final two pages identify each snake in the book. Though no real information is found here, the book may encourage children to find out more about snakes.

2629 *Mighty Spiders!* Ill. by Jean Day Zallinger. Cartwheel, pap., 1996, ISBN 0-590-26262-9. SERIES: Hello Science Reader! SUBJECTS: Science and scientists; Spiders; Stories in rhyme. RL B. LEXILE 320L.

With just a few rhyming words on each page to accompany detailed watercolor pictures, a lot of information is imparted to young readers. The final three pages identify the individual spiders on each page of the book.

2630 *Old MacDonald Had a Farm*. Ill. by Ann Iosa. Childrens Press, 1993, o.p. SERIES: Bear and Alligator Tales. SUBJECTS: Music and musicians — Fiction; Toys — Fiction; Toys — Teddy bears — Fiction. RL A.

After spending the day at school with his little girl, a teddy bear teaches the other toy animals how to sing their own special version of "Old MacDonald." The short, repetitive text has pencil and watercolor illustrations.

2631 *Pizza Soup*. Ill. by Ann Iosa. Childrens Press, 1993, o.p. SERIES: Bear and Alligator Tales. SUBJECTS: Cookery — Fiction; Stories in rhyme. RL B.

Father and daughter go shopping for ingredients for their favorite pizza soup and then make it and serve it. A lively, repetitive rhyming text and active pencil and watercolor pictures will draw children in, as will the inclusion of the recipe.

2632 *Real Bears and Alligators*. Photos. Ill. by Ann Iosa. Childrens Press, 1992, o.p. SERIES: Bear and Alligator Tales. SUBJECTS: Alligators; Bears; Toys — Fiction. RL A.

Series characters, illustrated with comic watercolor paintings, decide to find out which is better: alligators or bears. The body of the book is made up of alternating, often grainy, photographs of the two animals and comparisons of their behavior, life cycle, and food.

2633 *Recycle That!* Children's Press, 1995, o.p. SERIES: Rookie Read-About Science. SUBJECTS: Conservation; Recycling. RL B. LEXILE 530L.

Emphasizing how much waste is being accumulated and how many natural resources used, Robinson explains how recycling is done and how important it is. Illustrated with color photographs, the book also includes a photo glossary and index.

Robinson, Fay (cont.)

2634 *Sound All Around*. Ill. with photos. Children's Press, 1994, o.p. SERIES: Rookie Read-About Science. SUBJECTS: Sound. RL B.

Using a minimal number of words and full-color photographs, the concept of sound is explained in terms that a beginning reader can understand. Index is included.

2635 *The Upside-Down Sloth*. Children's Press, pap., 1993, ISBN 0-516-46018-8. SERIES: Rookie Read-About Science. SUBJECTS: Animals; Biology; Sloths. RL B.

Living in the jungles of Central and South America, the sloth lives most of its life upside-down. Through color photographs and a very short text, the ways in which a sloth moves, lives, and eats are described. A photo glossary, map, and index are included.

2636 *Vegetables, Vegetables!* Children's Press, 1994, ISBN 0-516-06030-9. SERIES: Rookie Read-About Science. SUBJECTS: Diets; Gardening; Vegetables. RL B. LEXILE AD620L.

Whether it be the leaves of a plant, its fruit, or its seeds, people eat all kinds of vegetables. The book discusses how some vegetables are prepared, shows people gardening, and encourages readers to help prepare a salad and enjoy it with family. Color photographs extend the text and a photo glossary and index complete the book.

2637 *We Love Fruit!* Children's Press, 1992, ISBN 0-516-06006-6. SERIES: Rookie Read-About Science. SUBJECTS: Biology; Fruit; Plants. RL B. LEXILE 590L.

Through color photographs and a brief text, fruits of all kinds are named and readers learn what makes a fruit a fruit and how fruits grow. A photo glossary and an index end the book.

2638 *When Nicki Went Away*. Ill. by Ann Iosa. Childrens Press, 1992, o.p. SERIES: Bear and Alligator Tales. SUBJECTS: Toys — Fiction. RL A.

With their little girl gone for a week, her toy animals have a great time playing and messing up the house. Just before she returns they all pitch in and clean the house. Text is illustrated with humorous watercolor pictures.

2639 *Where Do Puddles Go?* Children's Press, 1995, ISBN 0-516-06036-8. SERIES: Rookie Read-About Science. SUBJECTS: Science and scientists; Water; Water cycle. RL B. LEXILE 570L.

Evaporation, condensation, and the water cycle are just some of the topics discussed in this look at water on the earth. Illustrated with color photographs; an index and photo glossary are included.

Robinson, Fay, and Sue Science Team of the Field Museum

2640 *A Dinosaur Named Sue: The Find of the Century*. Ill. by Portia Sloan. Cartwheel, pap., 1999, ISBN 0-439-09983-8. SERIES: Scholastic Reader. SUBJECTS: Dinosaurs; Fossils; Science and scientists. RL C. LEXILE 690L.

Discovered in the hills of South Dakota, Sue is the most complete Tyrannosaurus Rex ever found. This book not only tells about Sue's discovery but also about the T. Rex itself, how Sue may have become a fossil, and the process used to remove her bones from rock and reassemble her. The book is illustrated with photographs and paintings.

Robinson, Marileta

2641 *Mr. Goat's Bad Good Idea: Three Stories*. Ill. by Arthur Getz. HarperCollins, 1977, ISBN 0-690-03862-3. SUBJECTS: Animals — Fiction; Navajo — Fiction. RL B.

In the first of three entertaining stories set in Navajo country, lazy Mr. Goat tries to get dirt for his hogan from other animals. Instead of less work, this cumulative tale shows he has far more. The other two stories are quiet yet fun. Illustrated with engaging ink and, wash pictures.

Robison, Nancy

2642 *Izoo*. Ill. by Edward Frascino. Lothrop, 1980, o.p. SERIES: Fun-to-Read. SUBJECTS: Science fiction; Zoos — Fiction. RL B.

On their way to a space show, Max and Charlie are picked up by aliens and transported to their ice zoo; they escape just before they are to be cloned. Comical yet suitably sinister drawings add to the fun of this science fiction adventure.

2643 *The Mystery at Hilltop Camp*. Ill. by Ethel Gold. Garrard, 1979, o.p. SERIES: Garrard Mystery. SUBJECTS: Camps and camping — Fiction; Mystery and detective stories. RL B.

Equipped with her detective's magnifying glass, Patty is sure she can solve the mystery of the camp's missing milk. Although lacking real suspense, this is still a story that children will be comfortable reading. Illustrated with realistic pencil drawings in turquoise and chartreuse.

2644 *Space Hijack!* Ill. by Edward Frascino. Lothrop, 1979, o.p. SERIES: Fun-to-Read. SUBJECTS: Science fiction. RL B.

While Mark and Ted are on their way to the moon with their prize-winning experiment, their ship is hijacked by an invisible alien who wants their atomic batteries. The two boys outwit the invisible man and finally return to Earth. Illustrated with comical ink and wash sketches.

2645 *UFO Kidnap!* Ill. by Edward Frascino. Lothrop, 1978, o.p. SERIES: Fun-to-Read. SUBJECTS: Science fiction; UFOs — Fiction. RL A.

Roy and Barney are mistaken for interplanetary jewel thieves and are taken to another planet. When the stolen gem appears, Roy is designated the new ruler of the planet. In the end the boys use the gem's power to escape and get home. Illustrated with humorously weird comic line drawings.

Roche, P. K.

2646 *Webster and Arnold and the Giant Box*. Ill. by author. Dial, 1980, o.p. SERIES: Dial Easy-to-Read. SUBJECTS: Imagination — Fiction; Mice — Fiction; Sibling rivalry — Fiction. RL B.

Two little mouse brothers find a large box and let their imaginations run wild as they play at being cave dwellers, engineers on an African train, restaurant owners, and more. The story is nicely illustrated with soft pastel drawings outlined in ink.

Rocklin, Joanne

2647 *The Case of the Backyard Treasure*. Ill. by John Speirs. Scholastic, pap., 1998, o.p. SERIES: Hello Math Reader! SUBJECTS: Codes and secret messages — Fiction; Maps — Fiction; Mystery and detective stories. RL B. LEXILE 250L.

Liz and her brother help Zack decode a series of secret messages from his friend Sam. The codes are fun to solve and just hard enough for young readers. The book concludes with additional activities.

2648 *The Case of the Missing Birthday Party*. Ill. by John Speirs. Scholastic, pap., 1996, ISBN 0-590-67359-9. SERIES: Hello Math Reader! SUBJECTS: Birthdays — Fiction; Mathematics — Fiction; Mystery and detective stories. RL B. LEXILE 290L.

After her hamster chews up her party invitation, only part of an address is left. Using their math skills, Liz and her little brother Henry are able to find the birthday party. Watercolor pictures combine with the text to create an inviting mystery.

2649 *How Much Is That Guinea Pig in the Window?* Ill. by Meredith Johnson. Scholastic, pap., 1995, ISBN 0-590-22716-5. SERIES: Hello Math Reader! SUBJECTS: Guinea pigs — Fiction; Mathematics — Fiction; Recycling — Fiction. RL C. LEXILE 420L.

With $50 from its bake sale, the class decides to buy a guinea pig. To pay for his food, they gather cans and bottles to recycle. Realistic watercolor and pencil art extends the story.

2650 *Jake and the Copycats*. Ill. by Janet Pedersen. Bantam, 1998, o.p. SERIES: First Choice Chapter Book. SUBJECTS: Behavior — Fiction; Pets — Cats — Fiction; Siblings — Fiction. RL B. LEXILE 220L.

In four stories, brothers Jake and Pete are forced to play with each other. They finally discover that they can actually have fun together. Little brother Pete's copycat behavior of big brother Jake is realistic.

2651 *Just Add Fun!* Ill. by Martin Lemelman. Scholastic, pap., 1999, ISBN 0-590-64399-1. SERIES: Hello Math Reader! SUBJECTS: Mathematics — Fiction; Parties — Fiction. RL B. LEXILE 270L.

Hank and Frank do some careful planning to determine how many treats they need and how many $10 will buy for their party. Colorful, cartoon-like art illustrates the text.

Rocklin, Joanne (cont.)

2652 *Not Enough Room!* Ill. by Cristina Ong. Scholastic, pap., 1998, ISBN 0-590-39962-4. SERIES: Hello Math Reader! SUBJECTS: Behavior — Sharing — Fiction; Concepts — Shape — Fiction. RL B. LEXILE 580L.
With a baby coming, Kris and Pat must find a way to share just one room. The sisters try different ways to divide their space. Attractive watercolor and pencil illustrations accompany the brief text.

2653 *One Hungry Cat.* Ill. by Rowan Barnes-Murphy. Scholastic, pap., 1997, ISBN 0-590-93972-6. SERIES: Hello Math Reader! SUBJECTS: Bakers and baking — Fiction; Mathematics — Fiction; Pets — Cats — Fiction. RL B. LEXILE 580L.
Unable to control his appetite, Tom, a hungry cat, keeps eating the food he has prepared for his guests. The humorous art and story line work well together as they introduce division.

2654 *This Book Is Haunted.* Ill. by JoAnn Adinolfi. HarperCollins, 2002, ISBN 0-06-028457-9. SERIES: I Can Read. SUBJECTS: Ghost stories; Halloween — Fiction; Scary stories. RL B.
Four stories and two poems will provide young readers with just enough scary reading for celebrating Halloween. The art is brightly colored and more funny than scary.

2655 *Three Smart Pals.* Ill. by Denise Brunkus. Scholastic, pap., 1994, ISBN 0-590-47431-6. SERIES: Hello Reader! SUBJECTS: Friendship — Fiction; Humorous stories. RL B.
Three smart pals are actually three very silly friends as they use their brains to conclude that Mr. Bing does not need to mention the word fish on his store sign, that green is the perfect color for lunch, and so on. Text is illustrated with cartoonish paintings.

Rockwell, Anne

2656 *A Bear, a Bobcat, and Three Ghosts.* Ill. by author. Macmillan, 1977, o.p. SERIES: Ready-to-Read. SUBJECTS: Ghost stories; Halloween — Fiction. RL B.
Three strange ghosts lead Timothy Todd, the miller and his wife, and Widow Wilson on a chase through the woods in search of three missing children. Flat, childlike ink drawings with washes of orange create a suitably "spooky" effect.

2657 *Big Bad Goat.* Ill. by author. Dutton, 1982, o.p. SERIES: Smart Cat. SUBJECTS: Animals — Fiction; Humorous stories. RL B.
In this very brief story, Tommy goes from larger to larger animal trying to get one of them to help him get Big Bad Goat out of the flower garden. When all have refused, a bee stings Goat and Goat finally leaves. The simple ink and watercolor pictures are childlike and appealing.

2658 *Big Boss.* Ill. by author. Macmillan, 1975, o.p. SERIES: Ready-to-Read. SUBJECTS: Folklore — China; Frogs and toads — Fiction; Tigers — Fiction. RL B.
A clever little frog outwits a huge tiger by claiming he is the Big Boss who eats tigers for dinner. Whimsical ink and watercolor pictures have a primitive look that fits this folk story well.

2659 *Bugs Are Insects.* Ill. by Steve Jenkins. HarperCollins, 2001, ISBN 0-06-028568-0. SERIES: Let's-Read-and-Find-Out Science. SUBJECTS: Insects; Science and scientists. RL B. LEXILE AD590L.
Though all bugs are insects, not all insects are bugs. With clear explanations extended by excellent collage illustrations, the author explains the differences and provides examples of both. A page of activities and a list of illustrations identifying insects are included.

2660 *The Bump in the Night.* Ill. by author. Greenwillow, 1979, o.p. SERIES: Read-Alone. SUBJECTS: Folklore — Spain; Ghost stories. RL B.
Based on a Spanish folktale, the story has Toby, a boy who likes to fix things, agree to spend the night in a castle and face its ghost. His courage never wanes as the ghost, appearing in pieces, tests him. Flat, childlike ink drawings with yellow and brown are well suited to the story.

2661 *The Gollywhopper Egg.* Ill. by author. Macmillan, 1974, o.p. SERIES: Ready-to-Read. SUBJECTS: Tall tales. RL C.
Timothy Todd sells a farmer a coconut telling him it is the egg of the Gollywhopper, a bird as big as a cow and as strong as a mule, which has unlimited talent. The simple, flat ink drawings

have a primitive charm and humor that is perfect for the story.

2662 *Honey in a Hive.* Ill. by S. D. Schindler. HarperCollins, 2005, ISBN 0-06-028566-4. SERIES: Let's-Read-and-Find-Out Science. SUBJECTS: Bees; Honey; Insects. RL C. LEXILE AD880L.

The story of honeybees, how they live, the work they do, the honey they produce, and how it is used, is told in an interesting and informative way. Illustrations work well with the text and are done in detailed watercolors. Two pages of interesting facts about honey end the book.

2663 *Honk Honk!* Ill. by author. Dutton, 1980, o.p. SERIES: Smart Cat. SUBJECTS: Farm and country life — Fiction; Geese — Fiction. RL B.

Gray Goose nips Billy Boy and the barnyard animals. After a chase the ornery goose flees to the pond, safe from everyone's anger. The brief text has flat, childlike pictures that are attractive and full of the story's vigor and humor.

2664 *My Pet Hamster.* Ill. by Bernice Lum. HarperCollins, 2002, ISBN 0-06-028564-8. SERIES: Let's-Read-and-Find-Out Science. SUBJECTS: Hamsters; Pet care; Pets. RL C.

A little girl tells readers about choosing and raising her pet hamster Silky. Any child considering acquiring a hamster will find plenty of useful information here. The final page includes activities to broaden understanding of domesticated animals.

2665 *No More Work.* Ill. by author. Greenwillow, 1976, o.p. SERIES: Read-Alone. SUBJECTS: Boats and boating — Fiction; Monkeys — Fiction; Mythical creatures — Fiction. RL B.

Trying to escape from hard work and boring food, the three little monkeys run away from their ship and land on an island with a dragon ready to eat them. Shipboard life has new appeal for the three as they head back. The very simple and childlike watercolor pictures are just right.

2666 *The Story Snail.* Ill. by author. Macmillan, 1974, o.p. SERIES: Ready-to-Read. SUBJECTS: Fantasy; Self-esteem — Fiction; Storytelling — Fiction. RL B.

Though kind and good, John seems to have no special talent until he meets a very unusual silver snail who gives him 100 stories to tell. Tired of repeatedly telling them, John gains confidence as he searches for other tales. The book has simple, childlike drawings with pastel washes.

2667 *Sweet Potato Pie.* Ill. by Carolyn Croll. Random House, 1996, o.p. SERIES: Step into Reading. SUBJECTS: Bakers and baking — Fiction; Farm and country life — Fiction; Stories in rhyme. RL A. LEXILE 260L.

When Grandma bakes sweet potato pie, everyone on the farm can hardly wait to eat it. The rhythmic text is accented by attractive full-color drawings.

2668 *Thump Thump Thump!* Ill. by author. Dutton, 1981, o.p. SERIES: Smart Cat. SUBJECTS: Folklore — United States; Monsters — Fiction. RL B.

Using the simplest language, the familiar story of the "hairy toe" — a monster coming to reclaim his missing toe — is nicely paced and retold. Illustrations are childlike and not too scary.

2669 *Timothy Todd's Good Things Are Gone.* Ill. by author. Macmillan, 1978, o.p. SERIES: Ready-to-Read. SUBJECTS: Mystery and detective stories. RL B.

Running from a thunderstorm, Timothy Todd takes refuge in an apparently deserted house and falls asleep. When he awakens, his pack full of goods is gone and he sets off to find it. The story is ably illustrated with Rockwell's easily recognizable, uncluttered ink and wash drawings.

2670 *Up a Tall Tree.* Ill. by Jim Arnosky. Doubleday, 1981, o.p. SERIES: Reading on My Own. SUBJECTS: Fantasy; Monsters — Fiction. RL B.

Nick, the son of poor woodcutters, discovers a bottle with a little monster inside. After setting it free, Nick is rewarded with three berries that can turn any metal into gold. This gift makes his family rich. Ink and pencil drawings show an incongruously modern family of woodcutters.

2671 *Walking Shoes.* Ill. by author. Doubleday, 1980, o.p. SERIES: Reading on My Own. SUBJECTS: Fairy tales; Houses — Fiction. RL A.

Rockwell, Anne (cont.)

Lonely, neglected, and unwanted, the little house is granted magic walking shoes and uses them to go in search of people who will really love her. The simple story has childlike line drawings with red and green washes.

2672 *Who Lives in an Alligator Hole?* Ill. by Lizzy Rockwell. Collins, 2006, ISBN 0-06-028530-3. SERIES: Let's-Read-and-Find-Out Science. SUBJECTS: Alligators; Ecology; Reptiles and amphibians. RL C. LEXILE AD780L.

A "keystone species," the alligator creates water holes in the dry season, providing a place for other animals and insects to live and reproduce. Carefully illustrated to provide support to the text, this book is a useful tool for explaining the importance of saving species and environments.

Rockwell, Anne, and David Brion

2673 *Space Vehicles.* Ill. by author. Dutton, 1994, ISBN 0-525-45270-2. SUBJECTS: Astronomy and astronomers; Space travel. RL B.

After a kitten watches a spaceship blast off, she explains some of the things done in the space program and identifies things that astronauts do and use. She ends by saying she wants to be an astronaut one day. Good childlike illustrations and simple text clearly explain the subject.

Rockwell, Anne, and Harlow Rockwell

2674 *Blackout.* Ill. by authors. Macmillan, 1979, o.p. SERIES: Ready-to-Read. SUBJECTS: Blackouts, electric power failures — Fiction; Emergencies — Fiction; Family life — Fiction. RL B.

An ice storm and broken power lines mean Dan and his family must find ways to stay warm for three days with no heat and electricity. The story realistically presents a family doing its best during very difficult times. Illustrated with simple pictures that underscore the story's seriousness.

2675 *The Night We Slept Outside.* Ill. by author. Macmillan, pap., 1983, o.p. SERIES: Ready-to-Read. SUBJECTS: Camps and camping — Fiction; Fear — Fiction; Night — Fiction. RL B.

Anxious to try out their new sleeping bags, two brothers spend the night on their deck and are frightened by the night noises and animals. Ink drawings with dark blue and gray watercolors capture the feeling of night outdoors while the story effectively shows children trying to combat fears.

2676 *Out to Sea.* Ill. by authors. Macmillan, 1980, o.p. SERIES: Ready-to-Read. SUBJECTS: Boats and boating — Fiction; Emergencies — Fiction. RL B.

Two children playing in a boat are washed out to sea. Their desperate parents get the Coast Guard to try to rescue them in this suspenseful and realistic story. The simple yet effective ink drawings have aqua and gray washes.

Rockwell, Harlow

2677 *I Did It.* Ill. by author. Macmillan, pap., 1974, ISBN 0-689-71126-3. SERIES: Ready-to-Read. SUBJECTS: Arts and crafts. RL B.

Children explain how to create something they have enjoyed making: a paperbag mask, a bean mosaic, a papier-mache fish, a paper airplane, invisible messages, and bread. Although no special safety precautions are given, the simple ink pictures show children working with adult supervision.

2678 *Look at This.* Ill. by author. Macmillan, pap., 1978, ISBN 0-689-71165-4. SERIES: Ready-to-Read. SUBJECTS: Arts and crafts. RL B.

Three children from different families explain how to make a dancing frog, applesauce, and a noisemaker. The instructions and the pictures accompanying them are clear and are easy for young children to follow.

Rogers, Jacqueline

2679 *Goose on the Loose.* Cartwheel, pap., 2006, ISBN 0-439-72501-1. SERIES: Scholastic Reader. SUBJECTS: Animals — Baby; Geese — Fiction; School stories. RL A.

When the class goes out for recess, they notice a grown goose in one spot and a baby goose in another. Despite Mrs. Miller's pleas that the children stay very still, it is nearly impossible for them to be quiet enough to allow the baby to return to its parent. All ends well in this very simply told story illustrated with ink and watercolor.

Roland, Timothy

2680 *Come Down Now, Flying Cow!* Ill. by author. Random House, 1997, o.p. SERIES: Beginner Books. SUBJECTS: Balloons, hot air — Fiction; Flying — Fiction; Stories in rhyme. RL B. LEXILE 60L.

Wanting to see more than just her field, Beth the Cow climbs aboard a hot air balloon and soars into mischief and fun. The very brief rhyming text will be fun to read although some words may prove challenging. Cartoon illustrations add humor.

Roop, Peter, and Connie Roop

2681 *Keep the Lights Burning, Abbie*. Ill. by Peter E. Hanson. Carolrhoda, 1985, ISBN 0-87614-275-7. SERIES: On My Own. SUBJECTS: Behavior — Brave — Fiction; Historical fiction; Lighthouses — Fiction. RL B.

For four weeks in 1856 a ferocious storm delays Abbie's father's return to their island lighthouse home. Young Abbie keeps the lights burning and tends to her ill mother until her father finally gets through to them.' Excellent watercolors illustrate this understated tale of bravery.

2682 *Whales and Dolphins*. Ill. by Carol Schwartz. Cartwheel, pap., 2000, ISBN 0-439-09912-9. SERIES: Scholastic Reader. SUBJECTS: Dolphins; Whales. RL A. LEXILE 70L.

Using a minimum of words, the authors give new readers an almost poetic picture of the life of these two mammals. Detailed, realistic paintings provide settings for and extend the text.

Root, Phyllis

2683 *Here Comes Tabby Cat*. Ill. by Katharine McEwen. Candlewick, 2000, o.p. SERIES: Brand New Readers. SUBJECTS: Pets — Cats — Fiction. RL A.

With a little introductory help from an accomplished reader, young children will be able to easily read these stories about a playful cat. The illustrations are bright and humorous.

2684 *Hey, Tabby Cat!* Ill. by Katharine McEwen. Candlewick, pap., 2000, ISBN 0-7636-0800-9. SERIES: Brand New Readers. SUBJECTS: Pets — Cats — Fiction. RL A.

With very simple yet humorous art and text, four Tabby Cat adventures are perfect for the emergent reader. The series encourages parents to share the book with their beginning readers.

2685 *Mouse Goes Out*. Ill. by James Croft. Candlewick, 2002, ISBN 0-7636-1351-7. SERIES: Brand New Readers. SUBJECTS: Mice — Fiction; Snowmen — Fiction; Sports — Fishing — Fiction. RL A.

In four brief and very repetitive stories, mouse has a variety of adventures. The series is meant to be shared by parents and beginning readers. The art is uncluttered, brightly colored, and extends the text.

2686 *Mouse Has Fun*. Ill. by James Croft. Candlewick, 2002, ISBN 0-7636-1357-6. SERIES: Brand New Readers. SUBJECTS: Mice — Fiction. RL A.

This clever format involves parents in a child's attempts to read. Each of four very simple stories about mouse has a paragraph for a parent to read that gives clues to the text. The art is colorful and humorous.

Rosen, Ellsworth

2687 *Spiders Are Spinners*. Ill. by Teco Slagboom. Houghton Mifflin, 1968, o.p. SUBJECTS: Spiders. RL C.

Using a rhyming text, Rosen discusses a variety of spiders and webs without much attention to detail or specifics. The verse and carefully created pencil drawings act as an invitation to further reading about arachnids and should work well with children.

Rosen, Sidney

2688 *How Far Is a Star?* Ill. by Dean Lindberg. Carolrhoda, 1992, ISBN 0-87614-684-1. SERIES: Question of Science. SUBJECTS: Astronomy and astronomers; Space. RL C.

A conversational tone using questions and answers posed by a child and answered by an adult is used to explain about stars, distance in space, supernovas, and so forth. Cartoon illustrations are combined with photographs to create a

Rosen, Sidney (cont.)

jumbled look with much child appeal. Glossary is included.

2689 *Where Does the Moon Go?* Ill. by Dean Lindberg. Carolrhoda, 1992, ISBN 0-87614-685-X. SERIES: Question of Science. SUBJECTS: Astronomy and astronomers; Space; Space travel. RL C.

Through a combination of good photographs, cartoon overlays, and questions and answers, a child's concerns about the moon, what and where it is, are explained. For more difficult concepts, simple experiments are used to clarify facts. A glossary is included.

Rosenberg, Amye

2690 *Rabbit's Rainy Day.* Ill. by author. Western, 1989, o.p. SERIES: Golden Easy Reader. SUBJECTS: Behavior — Bored — Fiction; Rabbits — Fiction; Weather — Fiction. RL A.

Forced to stay indoors on a rainy day, a restless bunny tries to find something to do. His efforts lead him into mischief and wear out the rest of the family. Full-color cartoon-like pictures capture the bunny's energy but otherwise exhibit little skill.

Rosenbloom, Joseph

2691 *Deputy Dan and the Bank Robbers.* Ill. by Tim Raglin. Random House, 1985, o.p. SERIES: Step into Reading. SUBJECTS: Humorous stories; Robbers and outlaws — Fiction; Western stories. RL C.

A literal-minded, persevering deputy, Dan accidentally uncovers clues to the identity of the notorious Scrambled Eggs Gang and captures them. Pen and wash pictures help to show the absurdity of this very funny story.

2692 *Deputy Dan Gets His Man.* Ill. by Tim Raglin. Random House, 1985, o.p. SERIES: Step into Reading. SUBJECTS: Humorous stories; Robbers and outlaws — Fiction; Western stories. RL C.

Dan, an old west version of Amelia Bedelia who does everything exactly as instructed, catches the pearl thief Shootin' Sam and foils a train robbery. The story is accompanied by humorous full-color ink and wash pictures.

2693 *The Funniest Dinosaur Book Ever!* Ill. by Hans Wilhelm. Sterling, 1987, o.p. SUBJECTS: Dinosaurs — Fiction; Jokes and riddles. RL B.

This collection of old jokes is bound to get laughs from young readers and groans from older siblings and adults who will be forced to hear them again. The jokes are arranged around and among funny and colorful pictures of dinosaurs that are in a variety of situations and their habits. A glossary and an index are included. Illustrated with full-color photographs.

Ross, Jan

2694 *Dogs Have Paws.* Ill. by Robert Masheris. Follett, 1982, o.p. SERIES: Beginning to Read. SUBJECTS: Families, single parent — Fiction; Pets — Dogs — Fiction. RL B.

When his father reminds him to wash his hands or put on boots, a little boy enviously thinks of his dog's paws, which are not washed and do not wear boots. Then he realizes that having hands means he can do many things a dog cannot do. Good realistic pictures show a close-knit single-parent family.

Ross, Katharine

2695 *Grover, Grover, Come on Over.* Ill. by Tom Cooke. Random House, 1991, o.p. SERIES: Step into Reading. SUBJECTS: Friendship — Fiction; Kites and kite flying — Fiction. RL A.

Though Grover refuses to come over when his friends ask, he does borrow one thing after another and surprises them with a kite. Muppet characters fill the story and are illustrated with pencil and watercolor pictures.

2696 *Twinkle, Twinkle, Little Bug.* Ill. by Tom Brannon. Random House, 1996, o.p. SERIES: Step into Reading. SUBJECTS: Birds — Fiction; Fireflies — Fiction. RL B. LEXILE 390L.

Big Bird captures a lightning bug, puts him in a jar, and has him twinkle for all his friends. Big Bird cannot figure out why the lightning bug stops twinkling until Grover asks just the right question and Big Bird sets the bug free.

Ross, Pat

2697 *M and M and the Bad News Babies.* Ill. by Marylin Hafner. Puffin, pap., 1985, ISBN 0-14-31851-8. SERIES: I Am Reading. SUBJECTS: Baby-sitting — Fiction; Friendship — Fiction; Siblings — Twins — Fiction. RL B.

Trying to earn money for a new fish tank, two friends, Mimi and Mandy, agree to baby-sit for the twins, Richie and Benjie. The girls' spunk and ingenuity in the face of two very lively babies make this story a lot of fun. Pencil and wash pictures of the four further the humor.

2698 *M and M and the Big Bag.* Ill. by Marylin Hafner. Pantheon, 1981, o.p. SERIES: I Am Reading. SUBJECTS: Friendship — Fiction; Shopping — Fiction. RL C.

On their first solo trip to the grocery store, two friends, Mandy and Mimi, lose their shopping list and almost buy all the wrong things. Fortunately they find the list just in time. This delightful story has humorous pencil and wash pictures.

2699 *M and M and the Halloween Monster.* Ill. by Marylin Hafner. Viking, 1991, o.p. SUBJECTS: Fear — Fiction; Friendship — Fiction; Halloween — Fiction. RL C.

Best friends Mandy and Mimi decide to win the Halloween costume prize in their building. As they search in their lockers in the basement, the two are sure they have seen a monster or a ghost. Longer and more difficult than the other books in the series, this is also illustrated in black and white.

2700 *M and M and the Haunted House Game.* Ill. by Marylin Hafner. Dell, pap., 1981, ISBN 0-14-038730-7. SERIES: I Am Reading. SUBJECTS: Fear — Fiction; Friendship — Fiction; Games — Fiction. RL C.

The haunted house game seems a perfect choice for a boring afternoon until two friends, Mimi and Mandy, accidentally scare themselves. A sense of fun — and near fear — in the characters' imaginative play is successfully created. The lively pictures add to the humor.

2701 *M and M and the Mummy Mess.* Ill. by Marylin Hafner. Puffin, pap., 1986, ISBN 0-14-130654-8. SUBJECTS: Friendship — Fiction; Mummies — Fiction; Museums — Fiction. RL C.

Too early for the Egyptian mummy show, two friends, Mandy and Mimi, sneak into the exhibit area and become fascinated by the mummies and the museum before being caught by the director. The light, humorous illustrations are in gray-toned pencil and wash.

2702 *M and M and the Santa Secrets.* Ill. by Marylin Hafner. Puffin, pap., 1987, ISBN 0-317-62234-X. SUBJECTS: Christmas — Fiction; Friendship — Fiction. RL C.

Two best friends, Mimi and Mandy, do not know what to get each other for Christmas until each hears the other tell Santa what she wants most. The story realistically captures the joys and frustrations of best friends while the illustrations depict the girls in lighthearted pencil sketches.

2703 *M and M and the Superchild Afternoon.* Ill. by Marylin Hafner. Viking, 1987, o.p. SUBJECTS: Dancers and dancing — Fiction; Friendship — Fiction; Sports — Gymnastics — Fiction. RL C.

Unable to decide which Superchild activity to join, two friends, Mimi and Mandy, try each other's choices — ballet and gymnastics — and discover hidden talents. Pencil and wash pictures effectively complement the text.

2704 *Meet M and M.* Ill. by Marylin Hafner. Puffin, pap., 1988, ISBN 0-14-038731-5. SERIES: I Am Reading. SUBJECTS: Behavior — Argumentative — Fiction; Friendship — Fiction. RL C.

Two best friends, Mandy and Mimi, seem inseparable until one day they are crabby and fight. Slowly they overcome their anger and hurt and decide to renew their friendship. The pencil and wash drawings in gray and white capture the emotions of these two little girls.

2705 *Molly and the Slow Teeth.* Ill. by Jerry Milord. Lothrop, 1980, o.p. SUBJECTS: Human body — Teeth — Fiction; Tooth fairy — Fiction. RL C.

Everyone in second grade but Molly has lost a tooth so she tries ways to fool her friends and the tooth fairy into believing that she is missing a tooth. Sketchy ink drawings with some color accents create pictures of less than pristine but very appealing children.

Rothaus, James R.

2706 *Squanto: The Indian Who Saved the Pilgrims (1500 (?) –1622)*. Ill. by John Nelson and Harold Henriksen. Creative Ed., 1988, o.p. SERIES: We the People. SUBJECTS: United States — Colonial period; Wampanoag. RL C.

Young Tisquantum lived in England for four years after being captured, only to be betrayed, and captured again. Having been befriended by John Smith, he supported the colony that sprang up on the site of his village, which had been decimated by disease in his absence. Large print and watercolors are used in this story.

Rotter, Charles

2707 *Walruses*. Ill. with photos. Child's World, 2001, ISBN 0-89565-841-0. SERIES: Nature Books. SUBJECTS: Walruses. RL C.

The life cycle, enemies, and environment of the walrus are carefully covered in alternating pages of text and color photographs. The information is interesting and the format, using a variety of colored pages for text, is also appealing.

Rowan, James P.

2708 *Ants*. Ill. with photos. Rourke, 1993, o.p. SERIES: Insect Discovery Library. SUBJECTS: Ants; Insects. RL B.

Various species of ants are shown in clear color photographs and discussed in facing text. The information is carefully presented and shows the life cycle of various ants as well as their predators and their prey. A brief book, this also includes a glossary and an index.

2709 *Dragonflies*. Ill. with photos. Rourke, 1993, o.p. SERIES: Insect Discovery Library. SUBJECTS: Dragonflies; Insects. RL B.

Dragonflies and damselflies are discussed in an interesting text alternating with full-page color photographs. The text offers information on several dragonflies and damselflies, their life cycle, habits, food, predators, and prey. This brief book also has a glossary and an index.

2710 *Grasshoppers*. Ill. with photos. Rourke, 1993, o.p. SERIES: Insect Discovery Library. SUBJECTS: Grasshoppers; Insects. RL B.

Using alternating pages of clear color photographs and a topically arranged text, the author provides young readers with solid information on the grasshopper, its growth and development, its relatives, predators, and prey, and its relationship to humans. An index and a glossary are appended.

2711 *Honeybees*. Ill. with photos. Rourke, 1993, o.p. SERIES: Insect Discovery Library. SUBJECTS: Bees; Insects. RL B.

Topically arranged text alternates with full page color photographs that help to make the book attractive to young readers. Interesting facts are included about the bees, their relatives, life cycle, jobs, and so on. The book also includes an index and an appendix.

2712 *Ladybugs*. Ill. with photos. Rourke, 1993, o.p. SERIES: Insect Discovery Library. SUBJECTS: Insects; Ladybugs. RL B.

The gardener's friend, the ladybug eats aphids, mealybugs, and scale insects. The clear color photographs alternate with interesting pages of text to offer readers a well-rounded look at a very helpful insect. Book includes a glossary and an index.

Rowland, Florence W.

2713 *Amish Boy*. Ill. by Dale Payson. Putnam, 1970, o.p. SERIES: See and Read. SUBJECTS: Amish — Fiction. RL B.

When lightning hits and destroys a barn, other Amish families come to help Jonathan's family build a new one. The text, a vehicle for information about the Amish, is readable but occasionally stilted, relying on the realistic pencil drawings to soften the tone.

2714 *Amish Wedding*. Ill. by Dale Payson. Putnam, 1971, o.p. SERIES: See and Read. SUBJECTS: Amish — Fiction; Marriage and wedding customs — Fiction. RL C.

Young Jonathan Lapp's oldest sister, Rebecca, is about to be married and it is through Jonathan's eyes that the reader sees Amish courtship and wedding customs. A good introduction to the Amish, the story has realistic charcoal pencil and wash pictures.

Roy, Ron

2715 *Awful Thursday*. Ill. by Lillian Hoban. Pantheon, 1979, o.p. SERIES: I Am Reading.

SUBJECTS: Behavior — Responsible — Fiction; Fear — Fiction. RL A.

Jack borrows a tape recorder from the school library. He puts it down, and a bus runs over it. Devastated, he cannot imagine how he can tell the librarian what happened and is afraid she will be very angry. Well written with some humorous moments, the story is illustrated with simple sketches.

2716 *Great Frog Swap*. Ill. by Victoria Chess. Pantheon, 1981, o.p. SUBJECTS: Contests — Fiction; Frogs and toads — Fiction. RL B.

Harriet defeats the neighborhood boys' best-laid plans and shady efforts at winning the frog-jumping contest. The boys' machinations are a bit convoluted but fascinating as they try to win. Illustrations are in shades of gray.

2717 *A Thousand Pails of Water*. Ill. by Vo-Dinh Mai. Knopf, 1978, o.p. SUBJECTS: Japan — Fiction; Parent and child — Fiction; Whales — Fiction. RL B.

Yukio does not like the fact that his father has to kill whales for a living when his friend's father can work in a market. Finding a whale stranded on the beach, Yukio tries to save it by pouring water over it. The quiet story has soft charcoal sketches that place it in Japan.

Royston, Angela

2718 *Birds*. Ill. with photos. Macmillan, 1992, o.p. SERIES: Eye Openers. SUBJECTS: Birds. RL C.

Colorful photographic silhouettes set against white pages and assisted by smaller descriptive paintings and a brief text offer young readers introductory information about eight birds. Included are the parrot, sparrow, kiwi, flamingo, and others. The 21-page book uses very heavy paper.

2719 *Cars*. Ill. with photos. Heinemann, 1998, ISBN 1-57572-171-6. SERIES: Eye Openers. SUBJECTS: Cars. RL C.

In 21 pages, eight varieties of cars, including sedan, jeep, sport, and racing, are shown in colorful photographic silhouettes. The text is brief and little more than a caption for the type of car.

2720 *The Cow*. Ill. by Bob Bampton. Watts, 1990, ISBN 0-531-19077-3. SERIES: Farm Animal Stories. SUBJECTS: Cows; Farm and country life. RL C.

A British farm is the home for this Holstein heifer who matures, has a calf, and becomes a milk cow. An overview of the farm animal's life, including some of the difficulties it has, this is brief and illustrated with realistic, colorful paintings. A list of other breeds and a glossary are added.

2721 *The Deer*. Ill. by Bernard Robinson. Warwick, 1988, o.p. SERIES: Animal Life Stories. SUBJECTS: Deer. RL C.

The life of a red deer fawn is told as a work of fiction as he grows into adulthood in the English forest. A two page addendum gives more information about the deer. Illustrations are in full color and detailed with occasional black-and-white drawings. A very short glossary is included.

2722 *Diggers and Dump Trucks*. Ill. with photos. Macmillan, 1991, o.p. SERIES: Eye Openers. SUBJECTS: Trucks. RL C.

Eight construction machines and trucks are given double-page spreads with illustrations featuring colorful photographic silhouettes. A brief text acts as a lengthy caption in this 21-page book with thick pages.

2723 *The Duck*. Ill. by Maurice Pledger and Bernard Robinson. Warwick, 1988, o.p. SERIES: Animal Life Stories. SUBJECTS: Ducks. RL B.

Courtship and rearing of young by mallard ducks are presented in a factual look at a year in a duck's life. The text introduces some of the dangers of life, differentiates between drakes and ducks, and is illustrated with full color, detailed, and realistic paintings.

2724 *The Fox*. Ill. by Bernard Robinson. Warwick, 1988, o.p. SERIES: Animal Life Stories. SUBJECTS: Foxes. RL B.

A young vixen leaves her mother and siblings to find her own habitat, mate, and to raise her cubs in this realistic account of a red fox's life. Lovely, full-color paintings illustrate the story along with black-and-white sketches. The glossary seems inadequate for the somewhat difficult text.

2725 *The Frog*. Ill. by Bernard Robinson. Dorling Kindersley, pap., 2001, ISBN 0-7894-7656-8. SERIES: Animal Life Stories. SUBJECTS:

Royston, Angela (cont.)

Frogs and toads; Reptiles and amphibians. RL B.

Detailed, realistic paintings and a brief text follow frog mating, laying of eggs, and growth of tadpoles to frogs. Their life, the hazards they face, as well as their winter aestivation are included. Brief facts about other frogs and a glossary are at the end.

2726 *The Goat.* Ill. by Eric Robson. Watts, 1990, o.p. SERIES: Farm Animal Stories. SUBJECTS: Farm and country life; Goats. RL C.

Life for a nanny goat on a small farm is shown in watercolor illustrations and explained clearly in the text. The book follows her for a year as she produces two kids and then becomes a milk-goat. A list of other goats and a glossary are included.

2727 *The Hedgehog.* Ill. by Maurice Pledger. Watts, 1989, o.p. SERIES: Animal Life Stories. SUBJECTS: Hedgehogs. RL B.

The European hedgehog's life is described in a brief text and realistic color pictures. The book follows a young female as she raises her young, meets predators, and continues her life. A glossary and additional facts are included.

2728 *The Hen.* Ill. by Dave Cook. Watts, 1990, o.p. SERIES: Farm Animal Stories. SUBJECTS: Chickens; Farm and country life. RL C.

A free-range Rhode Island Red chicken lives on a farm with other hens and rooster, lays eggs, and then hatches her own brood of chicks. The realistic look at life for chickens on small farms is illustrated with attractive watercolors. A list of other chickens and a glossary are appended.

2729 *Insects and Crawly Creatures.* Ill. with photos. Macmillan, 1992, ISBN 0-689-71645-1. SERIES: Eye Openers. SUBJECTS: Insects; Nature. RL B.

Double-spreads are dedicated to a snail, a spider, a butterfly, a bumblebee, a grasshopper, a wood ant, a ladybug, and a damselfly. Each is dominated by an oversize photo. Some small pastel drawings amplify and decorate the spreads, which include a few sentences about each insect.

2730 *Jungle Animals.* Ill. with photos. Simon & Schuster, 1998, ISBN 0-87628-471-3. SERIES: Eye Openers. SUBJECTS: Animals — Jungle. RL C.

In colorful photographic silhouettes, eight animals are presented with the text acting as a lengthy caption to the picture. Pages are thick and sturdy and the book is 21 pages long.

2731 *The Mouse.* Ill. by Maurice Pledger. Watts, 1989, o.p. SERIES: Animal Life Stories. SUBJECTS: Mice. RL C.

The many litters she bears and the constant hazards she faces from predators and nature fill the life of the mouse. Illustrated with realistic paintings, the story is interesting and not sentimentalized. Also included are a list of other species of mice and a glossary.

2732 *The Otter.* Ill. by Bernard Robinson. Warwick, 1988, o.p. SERIES: Animal Life Stories. SUBJECTS: Otters. RL B.

The description of the life and habitat of a river otter is spare, nearly poetic, in this story that follows its travels along the river to the sea and back from fall to summer. The full-color paintings and black-and-white drawings are realistic. Includes an addendum and short glossary.

2733 *The Penguin.* Ill. by Trevor Boyer. Warwick, 1988, o.p. SERIES: Animal Life Stories. SUBJECTS: Penguins. RL C.

The penguin's life on the ice and in the sea is described in a richly illustrated story about typical events in a year of a penguin — including the rearing of young. A two page section, "More about Penguins," defines some terms and clarifies differences among penguins. A glossary is included.

2734 *The Pig.* Ill. by Jim Channel. Watts, 1990, o.p. SERIES: Farm Animal Stories. SUBJECTS: Farm and country life; Pigs. RL C.

A female pig is followed as she grows, matures, has piglets, and weans them. Farm life for the outdoor pig is explained in text and watercolor pictures — although no mention of the butchering of pigs is made. Brief information on other breeds and a glossary are provided.

2735 *Planes.* Ill. with photos. Macmillan, 1992, o.p. SERIES: Eye Openers. SUBJECTS: Airplanes. RL B.

A small plane, a passenger plane, a fighter plane, and a helicopter are some of the planes featured in this brief, well-illustrated book. Text almost acts as a caption to the photographic silhouettes of planes and the small ink and wash pictures.

2736 *The Pony*. Ill. by Bob Bampton. Watts, 1990, o.p. SERIES: Farm Animal Stories. SUBJECTS: Farm and country life; Horses. RL C.

Readers learn about a British pony from shortly after its birth until it is over four years old and ready to be trained for riding. The brief but interesting text is accented with watercolor paintings. A list of other breeds of ponies and a glossary are appended.

2737 *The Sheep*. Ill. by Josephine Martin. Watts, 1990, o.p. SERIES: Farm Animal Stories. SUBJECTS: Farm and country life; Sheep. RL C.

A British farm in hilly country is the home for the Welsh Mountain Sheep described in this story. Readers follow her through a year, during which she has a lamb, is sheared, and heads back to the high hill country. Watercolors are used to illustrate this and other sheep. Glossary is provided.

2738 *The Squirrel*. Ill. by Maurice Pledger. Watts, 1989, o.p. SERIES: Animal Life Stories. SUBJECTS: Squirrels. RL C.

The life cycle of the red squirrel is shown through a female and her kittens. The way the animal builds its nest, prepares for and raises its young, and deals with some of its enemies are included. Additional information on squirrels and a glossary are at the end. Realistic watercolors accompany the text.

2739 *The Tiger*. Ill. by Graham Allen. Warwick, 1988, o.p. SERIES: Animal Life Stories. SUBJECTS: Tigers. RL B.

A female tiger is observed as she seeks a mate, has a litter, and, over a two year period, raises and trains her cubs. Realistic full-color paintings and black-and-white sketches ably depict this largest member of the cat family. A two page addendum and short glossary are included.

2740 *Trucks*. Ill. with photos. Heinemann, 1998, ISBN 1-57572-181-3. SERIES: Eye Openers. SUBJECTS: Trucks. RL B.

A fire engine, a tanker truck, a tow truck, and a snowplow are some of the vehicles featured here. The brief text extends well-chosen photographic silhouettes and ink and wash pictures. Paper is heavy.

2741 *The Whale*. Ill. by Jim Channel. Watts, 1989, o.p. SERIES: Animal Life Stories. SUBJECTS: Animals — Endangered; Whales. RL C.

Through the life story of one female blue whale, the endangered animal's patterns of feeding, travel and raising young are learned as well as some of the dangers (other than man) they face. Illustrated with detailed watercolors, the book also includes a glossary and facts on other whales.

Ruane, Joanna

2742 *Boats, Boats, Boats*. Ill. by Patti Boyd. Childrens Press, 1990, ISBN 0-516-22922-2. SERIES: My First Reader. SUBJECTS: Boats and boating. RL A.

Colorful comic paintings and a 16-word vocabulary use repetition and rhyming to give an introduction to some kinds of boats without identifying them in any way other than their color or age. Upbeat format and simplicity of text will make this appropriate for the newest reader.

Rubin, Mark

2743 *The Orchestra*. Ill. by Alan Daniel. Firefly, pap., 1984, ISBN 0-920668-99-2. SUBJECTS: Music and musicians. RL C.

A very good introduction to music and musical instruments, this book clearly explains some aspects of composing, identifies the instruments of the orchestra and how they are played, and tells how they all work together. Illustrations are colorful and attractive, and the design is good.

Ruchlis, Hy

2744 *How a Rock Came to Be in a Fence on a Road near a Town*. Ill. by Mamoru Funai. Walker, 1973, o.p. SUBJECTS: Geology and geologists. RL B.

Formed from fossil sediments millions of years ago, a piece of gray limestone is now part of a fence. A clear, informative narrative follows the stone from its beginnings, through different geologic eras, to the stone fence. Illustrated with line drawings with aquamarine and gray washes.

Rudeen, Kenneth

2745 *Roberto Clemente*. Ill. by Frank Mullins. HarperCollins, 1974, o.p. SERIES: HarperCollins Biography. SUBJECTS: Biographies; Sports — Baseball. RL C.

A member of the Baseball Hall of Fame, Clemente worked hard to be a professional player. The book looks back on his life in Puerto Rico, his triumphs with the Pittsburgh Pirates, and his tragic death on a humanitarian mission to Nicaragua. Illustrated with impressionistic drawings.

Ruelle, Karen Gray

2746 *April Fool!* Ill. by author. Holiday House, 2002, ISBN 0-8234-1686-0. SERIES: Holiday House Reader. SUBJECTS: April Fools' Day — Fiction; Pets — Cats — Fiction; Siblings — Fiction. RL B.

With April Fools' Day only two days away, kittens Harry and Emily are trying hard to think of tricks to play on their parents. The whole family has a good time playing tricks on each other on April Fools' Day. Childlike illustrations have warmth and gentleness.

2747 *Dear Tooth Fairy: A Harry and Emily Adventure*. Holiday House, 2006, ISBN 0-8234-1929-0. SERIES: Holiday House Reader. SUBJECTS: Pets — Cats — Fiction; Siblings — Fiction; Tooth fairy — Fiction. RL B.

With her first loose tooth, kitten Emily learns about the Tooth Fairy and the treasures she leaves. Emily writes her letters every day, and when the tooth falls out Emily is ready.

2748 *Easter Egg Disaster: A Harry and Emily Adventure*. Holiday House, 2004, ISBN 0-8234-1806-5. SERIES: Holiday House Reader. SUBJECTS: Easter — Fiction; Pets — Cats — Fiction; Siblings — Fiction. RL B.

Kittens Harry and Emily are so excited about Easter that they decorate all of the eggs. Then they hide them and chocolate eggs all over the house. Instead of an Easter egg hunt, they end up with an Easter egg disaster. But mother and father know how to make things just right.

2749 *Easy as Apple Pie: A Harry and Emily Adventure*. Ill. by author. Holiday House, 2002, ISBN 0-8234-1759-X. SERIES: Holiday House Reader. SUBJECTS: Apples — Fiction; Pets — Cats — Fiction; Siblings — Fiction. RL B.

During a weekend visit to their grandparents, kittens Harry and Emily pick apples, eat baked pie crust, and help make an apple pie. Though Emily says she doesn't like apples, even she has a piece of the pie.

2750 *Great Groundhogs: A Harry and Emily Adventure*. Ill. by author. Holiday House, 2006, ISBN 0-8234-1930-4. SERIES: Holiday House Reader. SUBJECTS: Groundhog Day — Fiction; Pets — Cats — Fiction; Siblings — Fiction. RL B.

Emily wants spring — and a groundhog — to come soon. She and her kitten brother Harry make a special groundhog feast and put it in the backyard. They watch carefully. There are no shadows but there are animals eating the feast. Finally there is a groundhog.

2751 *Just in Time for New Year's! A Harry and Emily Adventure*. Holiday House, 2004, ISBN 0-8234-1841-3. SERIES: Holiday House Reader. SUBJECTS: New Year's Day — Fiction; Pets — Cats — Fiction; Siblings — Fiction. RL B.

Though they have practiced staying up late and taken many naps, kittens Harry and little sister Emily are still having trouble staying awake on New Year's Eve. Finally they come up with just the right way to guarantee they welcome the New Year.

2752 *The Monster in Harry's Backyard: A Harry and Emily Adventure*. Holiday House, 1999, ISBN 0-8234-1417-5. SERIES: Holiday House Reader. SUBJECTS: Camps and camping — Fiction; Pets — Cats — Fiction. RL B.

After getting a tent for his birthday, Harry the kitten finally tries camping out in the backyard. When he hears noises and sees a "monster," Harry hurries back to the house. The next morning he discovers that the monster was only a raccoon.

2753 *Mother's Day Mess: A Harry and Emily Adventure*. Holiday House, 2003, ISBN 0-8234-1773-5. SERIES: Holiday House Reader. SUBJECTS: Mother's Day — Fiction; Pets — Cats — Fiction; Siblings — Fiction. RL B. LEXILE 320L.

Though she says that her kittens are the best Mother's Day present ever, Harry and Emily decide to make their mother's special day perfect. They plant seeds and grow flowers, make peanut butter pancakes, and create their own card.

2754 *Snow Valentines: A Harry and Emily Adventure*. Holiday House, 2000, ISBN 0-8234-1533-3. SERIES: Holiday House Reader. SUBJECTS: Pets — Cats — Fiction; Valentine's Day — Fiction; Weather — Snow — Fiction. RL B. LEXILE 200L.

Harry and Emily try very hard to think of the best Valentine's gift for their parents. When snow shuts their school, they find the perfect present: snow hearts and snow messages.

2755 *Spookier Than a Ghost: A Harry and Emily Adventure*. Holiday House, 2001, ISBN 0-8234-1667-4. SERIES: Holiday House Reader. SUBJECTS: Halloween — Fiction; Pets — Cats — Fiction; Siblings — Fiction. RL B.

After helping her big brother with his dinosaur costume, kitten Emily tries to create a very special costume herself. Harry convinces her that her costume is the best and most beautiful spooky costume ever.

2756 *The Thanksgiving Beast Feast: A Harry and Emily Adventure*. Holiday House, 1999, ISBN 0-8234-1511-2. SERIES: Holiday House Reader. SUBJECTS: Pets — Cats — Fiction; Siblings — Fiction; Thanksgiving — Fiction. RL B. LEXILE 300L.

After their mother explains Thanksgiving to Harry and Emily, the two kittens decide to create a special Thanksgiving for the birds, chipmunks, and squirrels.

Ruffin, Frances E.

2757 *Martin Luther King, Jr., and the March on Washington*. Ill. by Stephen Marchesi. Grosset & Dunlap, pap., 2001, ISBN 0-448-42421-5. SERIES: All Aboard Reading. SUBJECTS: African Americans; Civil rights; United States — History. RL B. LEXILE 480L.

With an audience of more than 250,000 people, Dr. King presents his "I have a dream" speech in Washington, D.C. This book provides the background information necessary to understanding the momentous nature of the gathering and is illustrated with powerful paintings and photographs.

Ruthstrom, Dorotha

2758 *The Big Kite Contest*. Ill. by Lillian Hoban. Pantheon, 1980, o.p. SERIES: I Am Reading. SUBJECTS: Kites and kite flying — Fiction; Siblings — Fiction. RL C.

Stephen is practicing for the kite contest when he trips and tears his prize kite. Unable to earn enough money to replace it, he gives up. Stephen's little sister repairs the kite and wins the contest with her brother's help. Illustrated with warm, sketchy drawings.

Ryder, Joanne

2759 *Fireflies*. Ill. by Don Bolognese. HarperCollins, 1977, ISBN 0-06-025153-0. SERIES: Science I Can Read. SUBJECTS: Fireflies. RL B.

A simple text tells how, after spending nearly two years underground as a glowworm, the firefly goes in search of a mate, using his special yellow light as a signal to attract a female. Detailed ink and colored wash illustrations.

2760 *First Grade Elves*. Ill. by Betsy Lewin. Troll, pap., 1994, ISBN 0-8167-3011-3. SERIES: First Grade Is the Best. SUBJECTS: Holidays — Fiction; School stories; Winter — Fiction. RL B.

Mrs. Lee's students decide to celebrate the winter holidays by becoming secret elves for their classmates. They leave handmade snowflakes each time they do a good deed. Lively and fun watercolor and ink art works well with the story.

2761 *First Grade Ladybugs*. Ill. by Betsy Lewin. Troll, 1993, o.p. SERIES: First Grade Is the Best. SUBJECTS: Gardening — Fiction; School stories. RL B.

The first-graders in Miss Lee's class work hard to create an outdoor garden. With the help of Gabe's grandmother, their garden flourishes until the fourth-graders damage it. All ends well when things are patched up. Illustrations are cartoon-like ink drawings.

2762 *First Grade Valentines*. Ill. by Betsy Lewin. Troll, 1993, o.p. SERIES: First Grade

Ryder, Joanne (cont.)

Is the Best. SUBJECTS: School stories; Valentine's Day. RL B.

Miss Lee manages to not only keep the children in her class excited about Valentine's Day but to make the holiday an opportunity for learning as they count hearts, send cards to an elderly woman, and make valentines. Illustrated with line drawings, the book also includes an origami craft.

2763 *Hello, First Grade*. Ill. by Betsy Lewin. Troll, 1993, o.p. SERIES: First Grade Is the Best. SUBJECTS: Rabbits — Fiction; School stories. RL B.

Miss Lee knows just how to make her new first-graders comfortable: She introduces them to her friendly lop-eared bunny, Martha. When they decide to do a quilt for First Grade Day, everyone paints Martha on a square. Cartoonlike line drawings and instructions for a paper bag puppet are included.

2764 *White Bear, Ice Bear*. Ill. by Michael Rothman. Morrow, 1989, o.p. SERIES: Just for a Day. SUBJECTS: Bears; Weather — Snow; Winter. RL B.

A boy wakes up to a snow-covered world and, as he looks out at it, he is transformed into a polar bear. For a day he is a bear — living on the ice, hunting for food, and surviving the cold. Wintry, blue-toned landscapes and a well-paced, poetic text make his transformation believable.

Ryder, Joanne, and Harold S. Feinburg

2765 *Mr. Putter and Tabby Walk the Dog*. Ill. by Arthur Howard. Harcourt, 1994, ISBN 0-15-256259-1. SERIES: Mr. Putter and Tabby. SUBJECTS: Old age — Fiction; Pets — Cats — Fiction; Pets — Dogs — Fiction. RL B.

When his neighbor is unable to walk her dog, Mr. Putter volunteers to walk Zeke for her. The determined little dog is a nightmare until Mr. Putter promises him a special treat and then all is well. Delightfully funny mixed-media illustrations reflect the quiet humor of the story.

2766 *Snail in the Woods*. Ill. by Jo Polseno. HarperCollins, 1979, o.p. SERIES: Nature I Can Read. SUBJECTS: Snails. RL C.

A tiny white-lipped snail hatches and begins to grow and explore its environment. It faces many dangers, survives them, and finally is old enough to lay its own eggs. The story provides good information about the snail's life cycle and is illustrated in watercolors.

Rylant, Cynthia

2767 *Annie and Snowball and the Dress-Up Birthday*. Ill. by Suçie Stevenson. Simon & Schuster, 2007, ISBN 1-4169-0938-9. SERIES: Ready-to-Read. SUBJECTS: Birthdays — Fiction; Parties — Fiction; Rabbits — Fiction. RL B. LEXILE 520L.

This is the first in a series featuring Henry's cousin Annie and her pet rabbit Snowball. Annie invites Henry's family to a dress-up party and they misinterpret it as a costume party.

2768 *The Case of the Baffled Bear*. Ill. by G. Brian Karas. Greenwillow, 2004, ISBN 0-06-053448-6. SERIES: The High-Rise Private Eyes. SUBJECTS: Animals — Fiction; Mystery and detective stories. RL C. LEXILE 330L.

Private Eyes Bunny, a rabbit, and Jack, a raccoon, are in the midst of playing a game of Slap Jack when Bernard Bear arrives needing help in finding his missing whistle. Although the text is brief it has some challenging vocabulary.

2769 *The Case of the Climbing Cat*. Ill. by G. Brian Karas. Greenwillow, 2000, ISBN 0-688-16310-6. SERIES: The High-Rise Private Eyes. SUBJECTS: Animals — Fiction; Humorous stories; Mystery and detective stories. RL B. LEXILE 210L.

When a cat steals a pair of binoculars from the 20th floor of their building, Bunny and Jack are hired to find him. Karas's comical art is a perfect match to the humorous text.

2770 *The Case of the Desperate Duck*. Ill. by G. Brian Karas. Greenwillow, 2005, ISBN 0-06-053451-6. SERIES: The High-Rise Private Eyes. SUBJECTS: Animals — Fiction; Mystery and detective stories. RL B. LEXILE 350L.

Bunny and Jack are out of popsicles and decide to go to Mabel's Tea Room. There they encounter Mabel, a duck, and her missing sugar cubes. Comedy and quick wits are the trademark of the detective duo. The art is cartoon-like and humorous.

2771 *The Case of the Fidgety Fox*. Ill. by G. Brian Karas. Greenwillow, 2003, ISBN 0-06-

009101-0. SERIES: The High-Rise Private Eyes. SUBJECTS: Friendship — Fiction; Mystery and detective stories. RL B. LEXILE 240L.

After a Saturday morning of yoga and cartoons, Bunny and Jack encounter a bus driver who is missing his fluffy dice. The two detectives take over and discover a young fox has taken them to help him learn to drive. Humorous art and a lively text complement each other.

2772 *The Case of the Missing Monkey*. Ill. by G. Brian Karas. Greenwillow, 2000, ISBN 0-688-16306-8. SERIES: The High-Rise Private Eyes. SUBJECTS: Animals — Fiction; Humorous stories; Mystery and detective stories. RL B. LEXILE 160L.

Detectives Bunny and Jack are asked to find out who stole the glass monkey from their favorite breakfast spot, the Grill Next Door. Cartoon-like art and a very funny text will capture the attention of mystery fans.

2773 *The Case of the Puzzling Possum*. Ill. by G. Brian Karas. Greenwillow, 2001, ISBN 0-688-16308-4. SERIES: The High-Rise Private Eyes. SUBJECTS: Animals — Fiction; Humorous stories; Mystery and detective stories. RL B. LEXILE 210L.

Detectives Bunny and Jack take on the case of the missing (then returned) trombone and discover a possum has been "borrowing" it whenever he plays with his band. Humorous illustrations and a lively text will entice more-confident readers.

2774 *The Case of the Sleepy Sloth*. Ill. by G. Brian Karas. Greenwillow, 2002, ISBN 0-06-009099-5. SERIES: The High-Rise Private Eyes. SUBJECTS: Friendship — Fiction; Humorous stories; Mystery and detective stories. RL B. LEXILE 180L.

Comical detective friends Bunny and Jack stumble onto the case of the missing lawn chair when they see a dog snooping at a dock. The culprit, a sloth, is finally uncovered. Funny and fun to read aloud, the text and pencil and wash art tell this silly story well.

2775 *The Case of the Troublesome Turtle*. Ill. by G. Brian Karas. Greenwillow, 2001, ISBN 0-688-16311-4. SERIES: The High-Rise Private Eyes. SUBJECTS: Friendship — Fiction; Mystery and detective stories. RL B. LEXILE 150L.

After Jack almost manages to sit still for Bunny to paint his portrait, the twosome gets a request from a toy store owner to solve the case of his missing balloons. They discover a small turtle has been taking them to his school games because they match his school colors. Cartoonish watercolor illustrations work well with the humorous text.

2776 *Henry and Mudge: The First Book of Their Adventures*. Ill. by Suçie Stevenson. Simon & Schuster, 1996, ISBN 0-689-81004-0. SERIES: Henry and Mudge. SUBJECTS: Friendship — Fiction; Pets — Dogs — Fiction. RL B.

Henry, an only child with no other children on his street to play with, is given a tiny puppy — Mudge — that grows into a very lovable 180-pound dog. Each chapter reinforces the close friendship that develops between the two. Illustrations are lively and colorful.

2777 *Henry and Mudge and a Very Merry Christmas*. Ill. by Suçie Stevenson. Simon & Schuster, 2004, ISBN 0-689-81168-3. SERIES: Henry and Mudge Ready-to-Read. SUBJECTS: Christmas — Fiction; Family life — Fiction; Pets — Dogs — Fiction. RL B.

Baking cookies for the relatives, caroling with Annie and Uncle Ed, and having the relatives at his house for breakfast make Christmas wonderful but his dog Mudge remains Henry's best present ever.

2778 *Henry and Mudge and Annie's Good Move*. Ill. by Suçie Stevenson. Simon & Schuster, 1998, ISBN 0-689-81174-8. SERIES: Ready-to-Read. SUBJECTS: Fear — Fiction; Moving, household — Fiction; Pets — Dogs — Fiction. RL B. LEXILE 400L.

Henry helps his cousin Annie overcome some of her fear of moving by lending her his dog Mudge for the day. Rylant portrays a supportive family in a gentle and often humorous manner that is supported by Stevenson's watercolor art .

2779 *Henry and Mudge and Annie's Perfect Pet*. Ill. by Suçie Stevenson. Simon & Schuster, pap., 2000, ISBN 0-689-83443-8. SERIES: Ready-to-Read. SUBJECTS: Pets —

Rylant, Cynthia (cont.)

Dogs — Fiction; Pets — Fiction; Rabbits — Fiction. RL B. LEXILE 180L.

Though his cousin Annie cannot have a dog for a pet, Henry is determined to help her find an animal that is just right for her — a bunny. The attractive and uncluttered illustrations are done in watercolors.

2780 *Henry and Mudge and Mrs. Hopper's House*. Ill. by Carolyn Bracken. Simon & Schuster, 2003, ISBN 0-689-81153-5. SERIES: Ready-to-Read. SUBJECTS: Baby-sitting — Fiction; Pets — Dogs — Fiction; Valentine's Day — Fiction. RL B.

When his mother and father go to a Valentine's Day dance, Henry and his dog Mudge stay at Mrs. Hopper's house. Henry is surprised by how much fun he has with her and the wonderful things she has in her house.

2781 *Henry and Mudge and the Bedtime Thumps: The Ninth Book of Their Adventures*. Ill. by Suçie Stevenson. Simon & Schuster, 1996, ISBN 0-689-80162-9. SERIES: Henry and Mudge. SUBJECTS: Family life — Fiction; Grandparents — Fiction; Pets — Dogs — Fiction. RL B.

When Henry and his big dog, Mudge, go to the country to visit his grandmother, Mudge is just too large to stay in the house. Afraid in the strange house, Henry ends up sleeping with his pet on the porch. This childlike book has a very real story and appealing illustrations.

2782 *Henry and Mudge and the Best Day of All*. Ill. by Suçie Stevenson. Simon & Schuster, pap., 1995, ISBN 0-689-81385-6. SERIES: Henry and Mudge. SUBJECTS: Birthdays — Fiction; Pets — Dogs — Fiction. RL B. LEXILE 470L.

It's Henry's birthday and both he and his dog Mudge are anticipating cake and ice cream and crackers — and a party. It is a perfect day and a perfect party — one any child would want.

2783 *Henry and Mudge and the Big Sleepover*. Ill. by Suçie Stevenson. Simon & Schuster, 2006, ISBN 0-689-81171-3. SERIES: Henry and Mudge. SUBJECTS: Pets — Dogs — Fiction; Sleepovers — Fiction. RL B. LEXILE 480L.

Henry and his big dog Mudge are invited to a sleepover where there will be games, pizza, and monster movies. Everyone — including Mudge — has a great time.

2784 *Henry and Mudge and the Careful Cousin: The Thirteenth Book of Their Adventures*. Ill. by Suçie Stevenson. Simon & Schuster, 1999, ISBN 0-689-81007-5. SERIES: Henry and Mudge. SUBJECTS: Family life — Fiction; Pets — Dogs — Fiction. RL B.

Henry's cousin Annie is too neat and clean for Mudge and Henry. The little boy worries about spending a whole day with her until they start playing frisbee and Annie forgets about staying clean. Fun to read, this story effectively captures a moment in childhood. It is well illustrated.

2785 *Henry and Mudge and the Forever Sea: The Sixth Book of Their Adventures*. Ill. by Suçie Stevenson. Simon & Schuster, pap., 1997, ISBN 0-689-81017-2. SERIES: Henry and Mudge. SUBJECTS: Humorous stories; Pets — Dogs — Fiction; Seashore — Fiction. RL B.

Henry, his father, and their dog, Mudge, pack up the car for a day at the ocean. They spend the day playing in the waves, eating hot dogs and snow-cones, and building a sand castle. Their glorious day is illustrated with whimsical pen and ink and watercolor drawings.

2786 *Henry and Mudge and the Funny Lunch*. Ill. by Carolyn Bracken. Simon & Schuster, 2004, ISBN 0-689-81178-0. SERIES: Ready-to-Read. SUBJECTS: Mother's Day — Fiction; Pets — Dogs — Fiction. RL B. LEXILE 600L.

Every Mother's Day Henry and his dad surprise Henry's mother with a very special lunch creation. This year it is a very funny pineapple sofa. The warm family relationships are captured beautifully by Rylant and Bracken (using the style of Suçie Stevenson).

2787 *Henry and Mudge and the Great Grandpas*. Ill. by Suçie Stevenson. Simon & Schuster, 2005, ISBN 0-689-81170-5. SERIES: Ready-to-Read. SUBJECTS: Grandparents — Fiction; Old age — Fiction; Pets — Dogs — Fiction. RL B. LEXILE 460L.

When Henry, his parents, and Mudge go to visit the great-grandpas, the little boy and his dog find a pond. Everyone (except Henry's mother) decides to go swimming in their underwear. Rylant and Stevenson offer an idyllic picture of country life.

2788 *Henry and Mudge and the Happy Cat: The Eighth Book of Their Adventures*. Ill. by Suçie Stevenson. Simon & Schuster, pap., 1996, ISBN 0-689-81013-X. SERIES: Henry and Mudge. SUBJECTS: Lost and found possessions — Fiction; Pets — Cats — Fiction; Pets — Dogs — Fiction. RL B.

Though the cat they find looks a lot like mashed prunes, it is so friendly and happy that Henry and Mudge hope that they do not find its owner. Unfortunately, he does turn up, thrilled to have the cat back. Pictures and text are full of life and true to a young child's feelings.

2789 *Henry and Mudge and the Long Weekend: The Eleventh Book of Their Adventures*. Ill. by Suçie Stevenson. Simon & Schuster, pap., 1996, ISBN 0-689-80885-2. SERIES: Henry and Mudge. SUBJECTS: Family life — Fiction; Pets — Dogs — Fiction. RL B.

What starts out as a dismal, boring weekend is quickly changed into an exciting, fun-filled one when Henry's mother suggests they make the stove and refrigerator boxes into a castle. Delightful watercolor pictures show a close-knit family.

2790 *Henry and Mudge and the Sneaky Crackers*. Ill. by Suçie Stevenson. Simon & Schuster, pap., 1998, ISBN 0-689-82525-0. SERIES: Ready-to-Read. SUBJECTS: Pets — Dogs — Fiction; Spies — Fiction. RL B. LEXILE 440L.

After buying a spy kit, Henry and his dog Mudge find a secret message next to a garbage can — and new friends. The lively watercolor art is a perfect complement to the text.

2791 *Henry and Mudge and the Snowman Plan*. Ill. by Suçie Stevenson. Simon & Schuster, pap., 1999, ISBN 0-689-83449-7. SERIES: Ready-to-Read. SUBJECTS: Parent and child — Fiction; Pets — Dogs — Fiction; Snowmen — Fiction. RL B. LEXILE 350L.

Henry, his father, and Henry's dog Mudge enter a very unusual creation in the Snowman Contest. The story and watercolor art are filled with the warmth of a positive and loving family and the fun of winter activities shared.

2792 *Henry and Mudge and the Starry Night*. Ill. by Suçie Stevenson. Simon & Schuster, 1998, ISBN 0-689-81175-3. SERIES: Ready-to-Read. SUBJECTS: Camps and camping — Fiction; Pets — Dogs — Fiction. RL B.

Henry, his parents, and his dog Mudge backpack to the perfect campsite on Big Bear Lake. There they build a fire, sing songs, and look at the starry night. The warm and loving family presents a very positive picture of camping.

2793 *Henry and Mudge and the Tall Tree House*. Ill. by Carolyn Bracken. Simon & Schuster, 2002, ISBN 0-689-81173-X. SERIES: Ready-to-Read. SUBJECTS: Aunts and uncles — Fiction; Pets — Dogs — Fiction; Treehouses — Fiction. RL B. LEXILE 290L.

Even though the treehouse his uncle builds is wonderful, Henry is lonely without his dog Mudge. Henry's dad and uncle find the perfect solution for Henry. The art and text work well together to tell the story.

2794 *Henry and Mudge and the Tumbling Trip*. Ill. by Carolyn Bracken. Simon & Schuster, 2005, ISBN 0-689-81180-2. SERIES: Henry and Mudge. SUBJECTS: Pets — Dogs — Fiction; Vacations — Fiction. RL B. LEXILE 420L.

Henry, his parents, and his dog Mudge pile into the car and head for a vacation out west. As they travel, the skies, the hills, and even the people (wearing cowboy boots) seem to get bigger. Along the way Mudge catches 42 tumbleweeds.

2795 *Henry and Mudge and the Wild Goose Chase*. Ill. by Carolyn Bracken. Simon & Schuster, 2003, ISBN 0-689-81172-1. SERIES: Henry and Mudge. SUBJECTS: Farm and country life — Fiction; Geese — Fiction; Pets — Dogs — Fiction. RL B. LEXILE 370L.

When his mother says she wants farm fresh eggs, blueberries, and corn, Henry knows it is time to go to a farm. All the animals they meet seem friendly until a goose decides to run Henry and his dog Mudge off the farm.

2796 *Henry and Mudge and the Wild Wind: The Twelfth Book of Their Adventures*.

Rylant, Cynthia (cont.)

Ill. by Suçie Stevenson. Simon & Schuster, pap., 1996, ISBN 0-689-80838-0. SERIES: Henry and Mudge. SUBJECTS: Family life — Fiction; Fear — Fiction; Pets — Dogs — Fiction. RL B.

When a summer storm strikes, Henry and Mudge are both afraid. It takes Henry's clever father to help the little boy overcome his fear and relax and have fun when the lights go out. The fear of thunderstorms is handled well in the text and in the watercolor illustrations.

2797 *Henry and Mudge Get the Cold Shivers: The Seventh Book of Their Adventures.* Ill. by Suçie Stevenson. Simon & Schuster, 1996, ISBN 0-689-81014-8. SERIES: Henry and Mudge. SUBJECTS: Friendship — Fiction; Illness — Fiction; Pets — Dogs — Fiction. RL B.

No one expects Henry's huge dog, Mudge, to get sick and when he does it is a major operation to get him to the vet. With loving care, the big dog is soon well again. The simple text and free-flowing watercolor pictures capture the special relationship between a child and a dog.

2798 *Henry and Mudge in Puddle Trouble: The Second Book of Their Adventures.* Ill. by Suçie Stevenson. Simon & Schuster, 1996, ISBN 0-689-81002-4. SERIES: Henry and Mudge. SUBJECTS: Humorous stories; Pets — Dogs — Fiction; Spring — Fiction. RL B.

Henry and his big dog, Mudge, enjoy spring as they discover a beautiful blue flower and try not to pick it, play in a deep puddle, and become protectors of their neighbor's five new kittens. Full-color washes with bold outlining make simple yet lively pictures for these gentle, funny stories.

2799 *Henry and Mudge in the Family Trees.* Ill. by Suçie Stevenson. Simon & Schuster, 1997, ISBN 0-689-81179-9. SERIES: Ready-to-Read. SUBJECTS: Family reunions — Fiction; Pets — Dogs — Fiction. RL B. LEXILE 460L.

Although Henry might be a bit nervous about meeting all of his relatives at the family reunion, Mudge, everyone's favorite dog, breaks the ice. Excellent writing and lighthearted pictures together tell a fine story.

2800 *Henry and Mudge in the Green Time: The Third Book of Their Adventures.* Ill. by Suçie Stevenson. Simon & Schuster, pap., 1996, ISBN 0-689-81001-6. SERIES: Henry and Mudge. SUBJECTS: Pets — Dogs — Fiction; Summer — Fiction. RL B.

Henry shares a summer picnic with his lovable dog, gives Mudge a bath, and turns Mudge into a dragon in these delightful and imaginative adventures. Bright summery watercolors capture the warmth and liveliness of the devoted friends.

2801 *Henry and Mudge in the Sparkle Days: The Fifth Book of Their Adventures.* Ill. by Suçie Stevenson. Simon & Schuster, 1996, ISBN 0-689-81018-0. SERIES: Henry and Mudge. SUBJECTS: Christmas — Fiction; Pets — Dogs — Fiction; Winter — Fiction. RL B.

After an almost interminable wait, snow finally falls and Henry and his big dog, Mudge, play in it, build forts, enjoy a special Christmas dinner, and share quiet and cozy moments at home or on special family walks. The well-written stories, helped by vibrant and colorful pictures, capture the best parts of childhood winters.

2802 *Henry and Mudge Take the Big Test: The Tenth Book of Their Adventures.* Ill. by Suçie Stevenson. Simon & Schuster, pap., 1996, ISBN 0-689-80886-0. SERIES: Henry and Mudge. SUBJECTS: Humorous stories; Pets — Dogs — Fiction; Pets — Training — Fiction. RL B.

Henry is impressed when a very well-trained collie goes by. He wants Mudge to be just as smart and decides to take him to obedience school. His hard work pays off when Mudge does pass the final test. Sketchy ink and watercolor pictures illustrate the story.

2803 *Henry and Mudge under the Yellow Moon: The Fourth Book of Their Adventures.* Ill. by Suçie Stevenson. Simon & Schuster, 1997, ISBN 0-689-81020-2. SERIES: Henry and Mudge. SUBJECTS: Fall — Fiction; Pets — Dogs — Fiction. RL B.

With his dog, Mudge, beside him, Henry finds that fall is better than ever. The ghost stories are not as frightening, and Aunt Sally's dreaded visit is actually fun. One of a series, this book continues to maintain high-quality writing along with lively, warm, and childlike illustrations.

2804 *Mr. Putter and Tabby Bake the Cake.* Ill. by Arthur Howard. Harcourt, 1994, ISBN 0-15-200205-7. SERIES: Mr. Putter and Tabby. SUBJECTS: Christmas — Fiction; Cookery — Fiction; Friendship — Fiction. RL B.

Mr. Putter enjoys giving Christmas presents and decides to bake a special cake for his friend and neighbor Mrs. Teaberry. Though he knows nothing about baking, he spends Christmas Eve baking and baking until he gets it right. The story is illustrated with gentle line and wash pictures.

2805 *Mr. Putter and Tabby Catch the Cold.* Ill. by Arthur Howard. Harcourt, 2002, ISBN 0-15-202414-X. SERIES: Mr. Putter and Tabby. SUBJECTS: Illness — Fiction; Pets — Cats — Fiction; Winter — Fiction. RL B. LEXILE 230L.

When Mr. Putter was young, it wasn't bad to have a cold and be fed soup and tea and read an adventure book. Wise Mrs. Teaberry sends her dog Zeke through the snow with everything Mr. Putter needs to get cozy and well again.

2806 *Mr. Putter and Tabby Feed the Fish.* Ill. by Arthur Howard. Harcourt, 2001, o.p. SERIES: Mr. Putter and Tabby. SUBJECTS: Old age — Fiction; Pets — Cats — Fiction; Pets — Fish — Fiction. RL B. LEXILE 340L.

Mr. Putter decides to bring a bowl of goldfish home but soon discovers that his cat Tabby cannot stop patting the bowl or staring at the fish. He tries covering the bowl but it does no good. Finally Mrs. Teaberry and Zeke take the fish. The art and text tell a laugh-out-loud story.

2807 *Mr. Putter and Tabby Fly the Plane.* Ill. by Arthur Howard. Harcourt, 1997, ISBN 0-15-256253-2. SERIES: Mr. Putter and Tabby. SUBJECTS: Old age — Fiction; Pets — Cats — Fiction; Toys — Fiction. RL C.

Mr. Putter may be old but he loves playing with toys — especially planes. He buys one but soon discovers a little boy who enjoys and needs the plane as much as he did when he was young.

2808 *Mr. Putter and Tabby Make a Wish.* Ill. by Arthur Howard. Harcourt, 2005, ISBN 0-15-202426-3. SERIES: Mr. Putter and Tabby. SUBJECTS: Birthdays — Fiction; Neighbors — Fiction; Old age — Fiction. RL B. LEXILE 570L.

Although he thinks he is too old to celebrate his birthday, Mr. Putter wants to anyway. To his surprise his neighbor Mrs. Teaberry makes it a birthday worth waiting for. Colorful illustrations capture the fun of the day.

2809 *Mr. Putter and Tabby Paint the Porch.* Ill. by Arthur Howard. Harcourt, 2000, ISBN 0-15-201787-9. SERIES: Mr. Putter and Tabby. SUBJECTS: Painting — Fiction; Pets — Cats — Fiction; Pets — Dogs — Fiction. RL B. LEXILE 440L.

His porch needs painting, and Mr. Putter gets the paint only to have his cat Tabby knock it over chasing a squirrel. The next day Mr. Putter tries again. This time Zeke, Mrs. Teaberry's dog, chases a chipmunk and knocks it over. This quiet story has some laugh-out-loud scenes.

2810 *Mr. Putter and Tabby Pick the Pears.* Ill. by Arthur Howard. Harcourt, 1995, ISBN 0-15-200245-6. SERIES: Mr. Putter and Tabby. SUBJECTS: Fruit — Fiction; Old age — Fiction; Pets — Cats — Fiction. RL B.

It's fall. The pears are ripe and Mr. Putter wants to make jelly. When his legs won't climb the ladder to get the pears, he tries shooting apples to knock them down. Instead the apples land in Mrs. Teaberry's yard and she creates a feast. Jelly will just have to wait until the pears fall.

2811 *Mr. Putter and Tabby Pour the Tea.* Ill. by Arthur Howard. Harcourt, 1994, ISBN 0-15-256255-9. SERIES: Mr. Putter and Tabby. SUBJECTS: Friendship — Fiction; Old age — Fiction; Pets — Cats — Fiction. RL B.

Though he spends his time doing things he enjoys, elderly Mr. Putter is lonely. A cat is what he needs and he finds the perfect companion in Tabby, an old cat that also enjoys flowers, food, and company. Humorous mixed-media illustrations capture the mood of the gentle story.

2812 *Mr. Putter and Tabby Row the Boat.* Ill. by Arthur Howard. Harcourt, 1997, ISBN 0-15-256257-5. SERIES: Mr. Putter and Tabby. SUBJECTS: Old age — Fiction; Pets — Fiction; Picnics — Fiction. RL B.

On a very hot summer day, Mr. Putter, his cat Tabby, Mrs. Teaberry, and her dog Zeke all head to the pond. They hire a rowboat and find a cool spot for a picnic. The color illustrations are a perfect match for the gently humorous story.

Rylant, Cynthia (cont.)

2813 *Mr. Putter and Tabby Spin the Yarn*. Ill. by Arthur Howard. Harcourt, 2006, ISBN 0-15-205067-1. SERIES: Mr. Putter and Tabby. SUBJECTS: Knitting — Fiction; Old age — Fiction; Pets — Cats — Fiction. RL B.
Concerned that he isn't a good neighbor to Mrs. Teaberry, Mr. Putter decides to serve tea to her knitting club. It takes all his charm to undo the damage done to a sweater and hat by his cat Tabby and Mrs. Teaberry's dog Zeke.

2814 *Mr. Putter and Tabby Stir the Soup*. Ill. by Arthur Howard. Harcourt, 2003, ISBN 0-15-202637-1. SERIES: Mr. Putter and Tabby. SUBJECTS: Cookery — Fiction; Old age — Fiction; Pets — Cats — Fiction. RL B.
When Bessie, Mr. Potter's old stove, doesn't work, he tries to make his soup next door at Mrs. Teaberry's. Unfortunately her dog Zeke is so playful that soup making comes to a halt. The illustrations extend the text by capturing the emotions and fun of the situations.

2815 *Mr. Putter and Tabby Take the Train*. Ill. by Arthur Howard. Harcourt, 1998, ISBN 0-15-201786-0. SERIES: Mr. Putter and Tabby. SUBJECTS: Old age — Fiction; Pets — Cats — Fiction; Trains — Fiction. RL B. LEXILE 450L.
Although his neighbor sometimes has very unusual suggestions, when she says they should take a train ride with their pets, Mr. Putter agrees. Rules have changed. Pets aren't allowed. But the neighbors find a way to take the ride with Tabby and Zeke.

2816 *Mr. Putter and Tabby Toot the Horn*. Ill. by Arthur Howard. Harcourt, 1998, ISBN 0-15-200244-8. SERIES: Mr. Putter and Tabby. SUBJECTS: Music and musicians — Fiction; Old age — Fiction; Pets — Cats — Fiction. RL B. LEXILE 340L.
Mr. Putter and his neighbor Mrs. Teaberry both love music. Even though neither of them plays an instrument, she decides they should join a band. When no band fits their interests, the two decide to create their own. Gentle humor is accompanied by expressive art.

2817 *Mr. Putter and Tabby Write the Book*. Ill. by Arthur Howard. Harcourt, 2004, ISBN 0-15-200241-3. SERIES: Mr. Putter and Tabby. SUBJECTS: Pets — Cats — Fiction; Winter — Fiction; Writers and writing — Fiction. RL B.
Everything outside is covered with snow, so Mr. Putter and his cat Tabby decide to stay indoors and write a mystery. Mr. Putter discovers that it is very hard work trying to write a book and ends up making a list of good things instead.

2818 *Poppleton and Friends*. Ill. by Mark Teague. Blue Sky, 1997, ISBN 0-590-84786-4. SERIES: Poppleton. SUBJECTS: Beaches — Fiction; Friendship — Fiction; Pigs — Fiction. RL B. LEXILE 360L.
Poppleton, a pig, and his friend Hudson, a mouse, enjoy a day together at the beach. Cherry Sue, a llama, teaches Poppleton about dry skin. And Poppleton discovers it's friends, not grapefruit that will help him live to 100. Gently humorous stories are illustrated with pencil and watercolor art.

2819 *Poppleton Everyday*. Ill. by Mark Teague. Blue Sky, 1998, ISBN 0-590-84845-3. SERIES: Poppleton. SUBJECTS: Pigs — Fiction; Sports — Sailing — Fiction; Stars — Fiction. RL B. LEXILE 250L.
Poppleton, a pig, tries looking at the night sky; shops for a new bed; and goes sailing with his friend Fillmore. The gentle humor in each story works well with the full-color illustrations in pencil and watercolor.

2820 *Poppleton Forever*. Ill. by Mark Teague. Blue Sky, 1998, ISBN 0-590-84843-7. SERIES: Poppleton. SUBJECTS: Friendship — Fiction; Pigs — Fiction. RL B. LEXILE 410L.
In three stories, Poppleton the pig tries to find out what is wrong with his dogwood tree; to get over a cold; and to wallpaper his kitchen. In each story, his friends do their best to help him. Illustrations are done in colored pencil and watercolors.

2821 *Poppleton Has Fun*. Ill. by Mark Teague. Blue Sky, 2000, ISBN 0-590-84839-9. SERIES: Poppleton. SUBJECTS: Animals — Fiction; Fun — Fiction; Pigs — Fiction. RL B. LEXILE 290L.
In three stories, Poppleton the pig discovers how much more fun it is to do things with friends than to do them alone. Colorful illustrations echo the fun of the stories.

2822 *Poppleton in Fall.* Ill. by Mark Teague. Blue Sky, 1999, ISBN 0-590-84789-9. SERIES: Poppleton. SUBJECTS: Fall — Fiction; Geese — Fiction; Pigs — Fiction. RL B. LEXILE 280L.

To Poppleton, a pig, fall means geese stopping by for cookies, a new coat for a very large pig (Poppleton), and the lions' annual pancake breakfast. The three stories, and their pencil and watercolor illustrations, capture the feelings of fall.

2823 *Poppleton in Spring.* Ill. by Mark Teague. Blue Sky, 1999, ISBN 0-590-84818-6. SERIES: Poppleton. SUBJECTS: Animals — Fiction; Pigs — Fiction; Spring — Fiction. RL B. LEXILE 330L.

Spring has come, and Poppleton the pig excitedly takes on spring cleaning, considers having a bike, and sleeps outside in a tent. The gentle stories are full of fun, especially when paired with Teague's illustrations.

2824 *Poppleton in Winter.* Ill. by Mark Teague. Blue Sky, 2001, ISBN 0-590-84837-2. SERIES: Poppleton. SUBJECTS: Birthdays — Fiction; Pigs — Fiction; Winter — Fiction. RL B. LEXILE 360L.

In three stories, Poppleton the pig finds a use for his fallen icicles, makes a bust of his friend Cherry Sue's head, and enjoys a surprise birthday celebration. Friendship is all-important in each of the stories.

2825 *Puppy Mudge Finds a Friend.* Ill. by Suçie Stevenson. Simon & Schuster, 2004, ISBN 0-689-83982-0. SERIES: Ready-to-Read. SUBJECTS: Pets — Cats — Fiction; Pets — Dogs — Fiction. RL A.

A very large puppy called Mudge finds a friend in Fluffy, a cat. An offshoot of the more challenging Henry and Mudge series, this is charming, easy to read, and has delightful illustrations done by the same illustrator.

2826 *Puppy Mudge Has a Snack.* Ill. by Isidre Mones. Simon & Schuster, 2003, ISBN 0-689-83981-2. SERIES: Ready-to-Read. SUBJECTS: Food — Fiction; Pets — Dogs — Fiction. RL A.

Mudge, Henry's very large puppy, wants Henry's snack and tries very hard to get Henry to give it to him. Large, colorful pictures and a few words per page make this a good bet for children beginning to read.

2827 *Puppy Mudge Loves His Blanket.* Ill. by Isidre Mones. Simon & Schuster, 2004, ISBN 0-689-83983-9. SERIES: Ready-to-Read. SUBJECTS: Pets — Dogs — Fiction; Pets — Fiction. RL A.

Henry's puppy Mudge cannot find his blanket and cannot sleep without it. Large watercolor and ink illustrations, large type, and a few words per page make this just right for beginning readers.

2828 *Puppy Mudge Takes a Bath.* Ill. by Isidre Mones. Simon & Schuster, 2002, ISBN 0-689-83980-4. SERIES: Ready-to-Read. SUBJECTS: Bathing — Fiction; Pets — Dogs — Fiction. RL A.

Henry's very large puppy Mudge loves mud. When Mudge gets muddy, it's time for a bath. When he is sprayed by a skunk, poor Mudge knows another bath is in the offing. This series acts as a steppingstone to the Henry and Mudge books, and the art is done in the style of their illustrator.

2829 *Puppy Mudge Wants to Play.* Ill. by Suçie Stevenson. Simon & Schuster, 2005, ISBN 0-689-83984-7. SERIES: Ready-to-Read. SUBJECTS: Pets — Dogs — Fiction; Play — Fiction. RL A.

Although Henry wants to read, his big puppy Mudge is determined to get him to play. The short, repetitive text makes this a good bet for beginning readers and a good introduction to the more difficult Henry and Mudge series.

Rylant, Cynthia, Stephen Krensky, et al.

2830 *Family Stories You Can Relate To.* Ill. by Suçie Stevenson, Susanna Natti, et al. North-South Books, 2001, ISBN 1-58717-103-1. SERIES: Reading Rainbow Readers. SUBJECTS: Family life — Fiction. RL B.

Excerpts from five well-known books for beginning readers (*Henry and Mudge in the Family Tree; Lionel and Louise; Rex and Lily Family Time; The Grandma Mix-Up; More Tales of Oliver Pig*) offer glimpses of family life.

S

Sabin, Louis

2831 *Birthday Surprise*. Ill. by John Magine. Troll, 1981, o.p. SERIES: Giant First-Start. SUBJECTS: Birthdays — Fiction; Self-esteem — Fiction; Skunks — Fiction. RL A.
Sammy, a skunk, is sure no one likes him or will remember his birthday. A huge box arrives with a birthday hat inside, and he feels more unhappy and goes to bed. Just then his many friends arrive to wish him a happy birthday. Pencil and marker drawings look hurried and too childlike.

Sadler, Marilyn J.

2832 *Honey Bunny Funnybunny*. Ill. by Roger Bollen. Random House, 1997, ISBN 0-614-28925-4. SERIES: I Can Read It All by Myself. SUBJECTS: Rabbits — Fiction; Siblings — Fiction. RL B.
Rabbit P.J. is always teasing his little sister, Honey Bunny. After she tells her parents, P.J. stops speaking to her. Honey Bunny is certain he doesn't love her any more, but P.J. has a surprise for her. Comical full-color illustrations increase the fun.

2833 *It's Not Easy Being a Bunny*. Ill. by Roger Bollen. Beginner Books, 1983, ISBN 0-394-86102-7. SERIES: I Can Read It All by Myself. SUBJECTS: Animals — Fiction; Rabbits — Fiction; Self-esteem — Fiction. RL B.
Tired of eating cooked carrots, having long ears, and being in a large family, P. J. Funnybunny tries being a variety of other animals. Finally he decides that being a bunny is just right. Full-color comic-style pictures complement the brief, humorous story.

2834 *Money, Money, Honey Bunny!* Ill. by Roger Bollen. Random House, 2006, ISBN 0-375-83370-6. SERIES: Bright and Early Books for Beginning Readers. SUBJECTS: Behavior — Generous — Fiction; Money — Fiction; Shopping — Fiction. RL A.
Honey Bunny has so much money that she buys gifts for friends and family and still has some left to save. Though the rhyming text is often forced, the cartoon-like illustrations and the simple text will be attractive to readers.

2835 *P. J. Funnybunny Camps Out*. Ill. by Roger Bollen. Random House, 1993, ISBN 0-679-93269-0. SERIES: Step into Reading. SUBJECTS: Camps and camping — Fiction; Humorous stories; Rabbits — Fiction. RL A.
P. J. and his best friends decide to go camping but refuse to allow his little sister and her friend to come. P. J. and his friends turn out to be inept campers and are easily scared by the two little girl animals. Very simple and brief text is paired with funny, cartoon-like pictures.

2836 *P. J. Funnybunny in the Great Tricycle Race*. Ill. by Roger Bollen. Western, 1988, o.p. SERIES: Golden Look-Look. SUBJECTS: Bicycles and bicycling — Fiction; Humorous stories; Rabbits — Fiction. RL A.
Against all odds P. J. and his family decide that he will win the Great Turtle Creek Tricycle Race. He practices hard and, despite a spill, manages to win the race. The silly cartoon style pictures in bold colors should appeal to many children.

2837 *P.J. Funnybunny's Bag of Tricks*. Ill. by Roger Bollen. Random House, pap., 2004, ISBN 0-375-82444-8. SERIES: Step into Reading. SUBJECTS: Magic — Fiction; Rabbits — Fiction. RL A.
With his magic kit, P.J. can do all kinds of tricks. When his friends and family don't want to see any more, P.J. is mad and magically — and temporarily — disappears. Appended is a magic trick for young readers.

2838 *The Very Bad Bunny*. Ill. by Roger Bollen. Beginner Books, 1984, o.p. SERIES: I Can Read It All by Myself. SUBJECTS: Behavior — Fiction; Rabbits — Fiction. RL B.
P. J.' s thoughtless behavior causes his family to think him a very bad bunny until cousin Binky arrives. Binky's intentionally nasty conduct leads them to change their opinion of P. J. Humorous, cartoon-like pictures in vibrant colors illustrate this very funny story.

St. Pierre, Stephanie

2839 *It's Not Easy Being Big!* Ill. by John Lund. Random House, 1998, ISBN 0-679-88810-1. SERIES: Bright and Early Books for Beginning Readers. SUBJECTS: Birds — Fiction; Concepts — Opposites — Fiction; Concepts — Size — Fiction. RL A.

Big Bird is sometimes too big. Elmo is sometimes too small. Using Sesame Street characters, this book makes comparisons between sizes and introduces opposites.

Saintsing, David

2840 *The World of Butterflies*. Ill. with photos. Stevens, 1987, o.p. SERIES: Where Animals Live. SUBJECTS: Butterflies and moths. RL C.

The different stages in the development of butterflies are presented along with a discussion of their enemies and the way butterflies protect themselves. The text, color photographs, and food-chain diagram are all well done and accessible to young readers.

2841 *The World of Owls*. Ill. with photos. Stevens, 1988, o.p. SERIES: Where Animals Live. SUBJECTS: Owls. RL C.

The habitats, prey, anatomy, and life cycles of a variety of owls are carefully documented in color photographs and clear text. Photographs are arranged to reflect exactly what is being discussed in the text and arrows are used to match captions and photographs. Excellent glossary clearly defines new terms. Adapted from Jennifer Coldrey's *The Owl in the Tree* (Gareth Stevens, 1988).

Sakelaris, Page

2842 *Giggle Belly*. Ill. by Richard L. Torrey. Children's Press, 2000, ISBN 0-516-22017-9. SERIES: Rookie Reader. SUBJECTS: Human body — Fiction; Stories in rhyme. RL A.

Taking his furry dog for a walk, a little boy mentions all the parts of his body and how they giggle, tickle, itch, wave, snap, nod, and more. Humorous illustrations work well with the rhyming text.

Saltzberg, Barney

2843 *What to Say to Clara*. Ill. by author. Atheneum, 1984, o.p. SUBJECTS: Behavior — Shyness — Fiction; School stories; Self-esteem — Fiction. RL B.

Otis wants to be his new classmate Clara's friend but cannot make up his mind how to do it. After much agonizing he decides to try the direct approach. He tries saying hello and it works! Ink line drawings shaded with dots illustrate this good story about overcoming shyness.

Samton, Sheila White

2844 *Hurray for Rosa!* Candlewick, pap., 2001, ISBN 0-7636-1127-1. SERIES: Brand New Readers. SUBJECTS: Animals — Farm — Fiction; Birthdays — Fiction; Food — Fiction. RL A.

In four very short but amusing stories, Rosa tries different things: copying the antics of farm animals; going to the beach; making a sandwich; cutting birthday cake. An adult or older child may want to read the explanatory introduction before each. The illustrations are brightly colored.

2845 *The Rosa Stories*. Candlewick, 2001, o.p. SERIES: Brand New Readers. SUBJECTS: Fish — Fiction; Gardening — Fiction; Play — Fiction. RL A.

Rosa jumps and runs; takes many walks; catches a fish; plants a tree. Each very brief story is illustrated with childlike pictures in bright colors. With the help of an adult or older child, a new reader should be able to enjoy all four stories.

Sandin, Joan

2846 *At Home in a New Land*. HarperCollins, 2007, ISBN 0-06-058077-1. SERIES: I Can Read. SUBJECTS: Emigration and immigration — Fiction; Historical fiction; United States — History. RL C.

Finally in Minnesota, Carl Erik and his family are living with his aunt and uncle while his father works to earn money to build a cabin on the land they've claimed. A new school, Ojibway neighbors, and chores aplenty fill the boy's days. The third in Sandin's series about Swedish immigrants, this is illustrated with realistic watercolor and ink pictures.

2847 *The Long Way to a New Land*. Ill. by author. HarperCollins, pap., 1981, ISBN 0-06-444100-8. SERIES: I Can Read History. SUBJECTS: Emigration and immigration — Fiction; Sweden — Fiction; United States — Fiction. RL C.

A Swedish farm family reluctantly decides to leave their drought-stricken land and emigrate to the United States. Their journey across the Atlantic is harrowing but ends with hope in the

Sandin, Joan (cont.)

United States. The moving story has detailed, realistic drawings.

2848 *The Long Way Westward*. Ill. by author. HarperCollins, pap., 1989, ISBN 0-06-444198-9. SERIES: I Can Read. SUBJECTS: Emigration and immigration — Fiction; Historical fiction; United States — History — Fiction. RL C.

Once Carl Erik's family arrives in America, they have to find their way to Minnesota, knowing little English and having little money. An exciting sequel to The Long Way to a New Land, this is illustrated in full-color, realistic watercolors.

2849 *Pioneer Bear: Based on a True Story*. Random House, pap., 1995, ISBN 0-679-86050-9. SERIES: Step into Reading. SUBJECTS: Bears — Fiction; Frontier and pioneer life — Fiction; Photography and photographers — Fiction. RL B. LEXILE 370L.

Word spreads about the orphaned bear cub that Andrew has taught to dance. Mr. Lacy, a photographer, decides to take the bear's picture. Though everyone looks for the cub, he seems to be hiding. A family picture Mr. Lacy takes reveals exactly where the cub was hiding.

Santella, Andrew

2850 *The Apache*. Children's Press, pap., 2001, ISBN 0-516-27311-6. SERIES: True Book. SUBJECTS: Apache; Native Americans. RL C. LEXILE 690L.

The Apache, a nomadic people, came from northwestern Canada and settled in the southwestern area of what is now the United States. Apache history, traditions, and culture are presented in a clear and interesting text. Illustrations are reprints and current-day color photographs. The book also contains sidebars of extra information; maps; lists of books, organizations, and Web sites; a glossary; and an index.

2851 *The Inuit*. Children's Press, pap., 2001, ISBN 0-516-27319-1. SERIES: True Book. SUBJECTS: Inuit; Native Americans. RL C. LEXILE 770L.

The Inuit people, once called Eskimo, live near the Arctic Circle in an area where the ground is always frozen. The land, wildlife, and plants of the area are discussed along with traditional and contemporary ways of life. Photographs and maps; lists of books, organizations, and Web sites; a glossary; and an index complete the book.

Sapre, Reshma

2852 *Iowa*. Children's Press, 2004, ISBN 0-516-22753-X. SERIES: Rookie Read-About Geography. SUBJECTS: Geography; Iowa; United States. RL B.

This visit to the Corn State gives readers a picture of the state's geography, its situation within the United States, its crops, wildlife, and the things residents do for fun. A map, lots of colored photographs, a photo glossary, and an index support the text.

Sargent, Brian

2853 *Can You Guess?* Children's Press, 2004, ISBN 0-516-24421-3. SERIES: Rookie Read-About Math. SUBJECTS: Mathematics. RL B. LEXILE 380L.

When it is too difficult to count something (such as peanuts in a bag), the author gives readers ways to make educated guesses. The book will be easy for most readers to understand because of the way the brief text and color photographs work together. There is a photo glossary and an index.

2854 *Everyone Uses Math*. Children's Press, 2005, ISBN 0-516-25263-1. SERIES: Rookie Read-About Math. SUBJECTS: Mathematics. RL B. LEXILE 570L.

To reinforce the importance of math in all areas of life, color photographs and a brief text show how people who are basketball players, farmers, cooks, musicians, pilots, and more use math in their work. A photo glossary and index complete the book.

2855 *How Heavy Is It?* Children's Press, 2005, ISBN 0-516-25267-4. SERIES: Rookie Read-About Math. SUBJECTS: Concepts — Weight ; Mathematics. RL B. LEXILE 480L.

What is weight? How is it measured? These and other questions are answered briefly but clearly through a carefully worded text and good illustrative color photographs. The book ends with a photo glossary and an index.

2856 *Pen Pals Compare*. Children's Press, 2005, ISBN 0-516-25262-3. SERIES: Rookie Read-About Math. SUBJECTS: Mathematics. RL B. LEXILE 580L.

Pen pals Rosa and Eric write questions to each other and the answers give them the opportunity to demonstrate math skills. The terms they use as they compare answers are those used when making mathematical comparisons. The book has color photographs, a photo glossary, and an index.

Sathre, Vivian

2857 *Leroy Potts Meets the McCrooks*. Ill. by Rowan Barnes-Murphy. Delacorte, 1997, ISBN 0-385-32192-9. SERIES: First Choice Chapter Book. SUBJECTS: Memory and memorization — Fiction; Robbers and outlaws — Fiction. RL C. LEXILE 550L.

On his way to propose to Miss Hattie Mae, Leroy Potts is struck by lightning and loses his memory. Two thieves find Leroy and convince him to join in their game of rob and run. Just in time, Leroy regains his memory and captures the two. Ink and wash pictures capture the humor of the situation.

Saunders, Susan

2858 *Charles Rat's Picnic*. Ill. by Robert Byrd. Dutton, 1983, o.p. SUBJECTS: Armadillos — Fiction; Picnics — Fiction; Rats — Fiction. RL A.

Charles Rat, intent on doing things just right, ends up very wet and without dinner when he takes Miranda Armadillo on a picnic. Illustrated with carefully drawn pictures of a nattily attired rat and armadillo.

2859 *Puss in Boots*. Ill. by Elizabeth Miles. Scholastic, pap., 1989, o.p. SERIES: Easy-to-Read Folktale. SUBJECTS: Folklore; Pets — Cats — Fiction. RL C.

The story of the wondrous cat who cleverly gains his poor master a dukedom and a princess is faithfully retold with no feeling of abridgment or oversimplification. Illustrations are appealing pencil sketches with delicate watercolor washes.

2860 *Tyrone Goes to School*. Ill. by Steve Bjorkman. Dutton, 1992, o.p. SERIES: Speedsters. SUBJECTS: Pets — Dogs — Fiction; Pets — Training; School stories. RL C.

Robert and his dog, Tyrone, have a lot in common: Neither one of them pays attention when he should. After obedience class Robert thinks it will be impossible to teach his dog until his teacher shows him the perfect solution. Text is illustrated with sketchy line drawings.

Scarry, Richard

2861 *Best Read-It-Yourself Book Ever*. Ill. by author. Western, 1990, o.p. SERIES: Golden Easy Reader. SUBJECTS: Humorous stories. RL B.

Twelve stories previously published individually are combined to make a collection featuring Scarry's well-known characters: Frances Fix-it, Chief Hound, Smokey, Katie Kitty, and so on. Though Scarry updated names of characters, the ink and wash pictures might still be thought "sexist."

2862 *Dr. Doctor*. Ill. by author. Western, 1988, o.p. SERIES: Golden Easy Reader. SUBJECTS: Doctors and nurses — Fiction. RL B.

Popular with children, this contrived story features a husband-and-wife team of doctors about to have their own family. Illustrations are familiar Scarry characters done in cartoon-like watercolors. Mrs. Dr. Doctor is dressed as a nurse, her title seeming to be a last-minute addition.

2863 *Frances Fix-It*. Ill. by author. Western, 1988, o.p. SERIES: Golden Easy Reader. SUBJECTS: Animals — Fiction; Careers — Fiction; Humorous stories. RL A.

No matter how simple or complex the job, Frances is always able to fix it. The bunny is able to repair TVs, ovens, cars, and so on. Familiar Scarry characters in bright watercolors illustrate the brief, repetitive text.

2864 *Lowly Worm Joins the Circus*. Ill. by author. Retold by Gail Herman. Simon & Schuster, 1998, o.p. SERIES: The Busy World of Richard Scarry Ready-to-Read. SUBJECTS: Animals — Fiction; Circuses — Fiction; Family life — Fiction. RL B.

Lowly Worm is asked to star in the traveling circus and joins immediately. A star, he soon realizes that he would rather be at home with the cat

Scarry, Richard (cont.)

family than traveling. Based on Richard Scarry's characters, the book is illustrated in his style.

2865 *Mr. Fixit's Magnet Machine.* Simon & Schuster, 1998, o.p. SERIES: Ready-to-Read. SUBJECTS: Animals — Fiction; Magnets — Fiction. RL B. LEXILE 160L.

Mr. Fixit forgets to turn off his new and gigantic magnet machine, and soon everyone in town is missing things made of metal. Familiar Busytown characters make this a lively story while introducing young children to magnetism.

2866 *The Worst Helper Ever!* Golden Books, 1998, ISBN 0-375-99990-6. SERIES: Road to Reading. SUBJECTS: Animals — Fiction; Farm and country life — Fiction. RL A.

In need of a helper, Farmer Pig hires Charlie Cat. But Charlie is not a good helper and makes one mistake after another. Adapted from an earlier work by Scarry, the art is easily recognizable as his.

Scary Stories to Read When It's Dark

2867 *Scary Stories to Read When It's Dark.* Ill. by Arnold Lobel, Dirk Zimmer, et al. Chronicle, pap., 2000, ISBN 1-58717-035-3. SERIES: Reading Rainbow Readers. SUBJECTS: Ghost stories; Scary stories. RL B.

In seven short stories (excerpted from other well-known books for beginning readers) children are exposed to slightly scary stories that are just perfect for sharing around a campfire, or on Halloween. Each of the authors and illustrators captures the feeling of the stories.

Schade, Susan

2868 *Toad Eats Out.* Ill. by Jon Buller. Random House, 1995, o.p. SERIES: Step into Reading. SUBJECTS: Frogs and toads — Fiction; Insects — Fiction; Restaurants — Fiction. RL A. LEXILE 130L.

For his birthday, Toad wants to eat at his favorite restaurant. He arrives to discover all his friends there, waiting to celebrate with him. The easy, repetitive text is illustrated with humorous, cartoon-like pictures.

Schade, Susan, and Jon Buller

2869 *Cat at Bat.* Random House, pap., 2000, ISBN 0-307-26211-1. SERIES: Step into Reading. SUBJECTS: Animals — Fiction; Sports — Baseball — Fiction; Stories in rhyme. RL B.

The Orange Blossoms are losing to the Sharks when Cat comes up to bat and hits a home run. The animals on each team are painted in expressive cartoon style. Though very brief, the text is more challenging that it first appears to be.

2870 *Cat on the Mat.* Random House, pap., 1999, ISBN 0-307-26207-3. SERIES: Step into Reading. SUBJECTS: Pets — Cats — Fiction; Sports — Gymnastics — Fiction; Stories in rhyme. RL B.

Everyone in her family has a special interest or talent and Cat finally discovers hers: gymnastics. She works hard to make the team. The text is very brief but occasionally challenging.

2871 *Railroad Toad.* Ill. by Jon Buller. Random House, 2004, ISBN 0-679-93934-2. SERIES: Step into Reading. SUBJECTS: Frogs and toads — Fiction; Stories in rhyme; Trains — Fiction. RL A.

A railroad enthusiast, Toad does not care where he goes as long as it's on a train. Through the smiling amphibian, readers catch a comically painted but relatively realistic picture of the different cars of a passenger train.

2872 *Snow Bugs.* Random House, 1996, ISBN 0-679-97913-1. SERIES: Bright and Early Books. SUBJECTS: Stories in rhyme; Weather — Snow — Fiction; Winter — Fiction. RL B.

Imaginative snow bugs find ways to have fun outside during very snowy weather. Cartoon-like and very colorful bugs fill the pages.

2873 *Snug House, Bug House!* Beginner Books, 1994, ISBN 0-679-85300-6. SERIES: Bright and Early Books. SUBJECTS: Houses — Fiction; Insects — Fiction; Stories in rhyme. RL A. LEXILE NP.

Bugs of all kinds create a very snug house with many kinds of rooms. Humorous full-color pictures extend the two words per page in this story.

2874 *Space Dog Jack.* Scholastic, pap., 2001, ISBN 0-439-20541-7. SERIES: Hello Reader!

SUBJECTS: Pets — Dogs — Fiction; Science fiction; Stories in rhyme. RL B. LEXILE 60L.

While exploring other planets, a problem with his spaceship forces Jack to land on planet earth. Comical cartoon-like drawings and a rhyming text add to the fun of this story.

2875 *Toad on the Road.* Ill. by Jon Buller. Random House, 2003, ISBN 0-679-92689-5. SERIES: Step into Reading. SUBJECTS: Cars — Fiction; Frogs and toads — Fiction; Travel — Fiction. RL A.

With great exuberance, Frog leaves driving school behind and heads out onto the road, picking up friends, stopping for gas, and just enjoying driving. Comic and colorful illustrations add much to the very brief rhyming text.

2876 *Toad Takes Off.* Random House, 1997, o.p. SERIES: Step into Reading. SUBJECTS: Airplanes — Fiction; Flying — Fiction; Frogs and toads — Fiction. RL B. LEXILE 200L.

Toad decides to take his friends for their first airplane ride. They swoop over familiar sites and finally the pilot lets Toad take over. The brief rhyming text with its large print is more challenging than it first appears.

Schaefer, Carole Lexa

2877 *Beeper's Friends.* Ill. by Julie Lacome. Candlewick, pap., 2002, ISBN 0-7636-1244-8. SERIES: Brand New Readers. SUBJECTS: Extraterrestrial beings — Fiction; Friendship — Fiction; Science fiction. RL A.

Parental participation makes this a good first series title for beginning readers. Beeper and his friends are extraterrestrials who enjoy having fun together. Bright colors and zany art are perfect for the subject.

Schaefer, Lola M.

2878 *Follow Me, Mittens.* Ill. by Susan Kathleen Hartung. HarperCollins, 2007, ISBN 0-06-054665-4. SERIES: I Can Read. SUBJECTS: Pets — Cats — Fiction; Pets — Fiction. RL A.

On a walk with his boy Nick, Mittens the kitten is distracted by a butterfly and wanders away. Realizing that he can't see Nick, Mittens searches for him until the little boy calls his name. A limited vocabulary, much repetition of familiar words, and watercolor pictures help the young reader decipher the text.

2879 *Mittens.* Ill. by Susan Kathleen Hartung. HarperCollins, 2006, ISBN 0-06-054659-X. SERIES: I Can Read. SUBJECTS: Pets — Cats — Fiction; Pets — Fiction. RL A.

Mittens is Nick's new kitten. Frightened by the unfamiliarity of everything, Mittens tries to find a safe place to hide. Still afraid, he is soothed by Nick. The very brief text captures a kitten's reactions to its new home. Uncluttered illustrations match the story well.

Schecter, Ellen

2880 *The Boy Who Cried "Wolf".* Retold in Rebus. Ill. by Gary Chalk. Gareth Stevens, 1997, ISBN 0-8368-1691-9. SERIES: Bank Street Ready-to-Read. SUBJECTS: Fables; Rebuses. RL B.

Accented with rebus drawings rather than told with them, the story of the boy who lied once too often is illustrated with paintings of leering wolves and villagers in nineteenth-century garb.

2881 *The Town Mouse and the Country Mouse.* Ill. by Holly Hannon. Gareth Stevens, 1995, ISBN 0-8368-1622-6. SERIES: Bank Street Ready-to-Read. SUBJECTS: Folklore — England; Mice — Fiction. RL C. LEXILE AD600L.

When the town mouse visits her country cousin, she is soon bored by her cousin's simple pleasures. When the country mouse visits the town, she soon learns how dangerous life there can be and moves happily back home. This well-known story is illustrated with lush paintings and is very nicely written.

2882 *The Warrior Maiden: A Hopi Legend.* Ill. by Laura Kelly. Gareth Stevens, 1992, ISBN 0-8368-1696-X. SERIES: Bank Street Ready-to-Read. SUBJECTS: Folklore — Native Americans; Hopi. RL C. LEXILE 530L.

Beautifully written, the story of Huh-ay-ay and the courage she showed in getting help for the people of her Hopi pueblo is illustrated with art that romanticizes the Hopi. This story is perfect for reading aloud.

Schecter, Ellen, reteller

2883 *Sim Chung and the River Dragon: A Folktale from Korea*. Ill. by June Otani. Gareth Stevens, 1997, ISBN 0-8368-1695-1. SERIES: Bank Street Ready-to-Read. SUBJECTS: Dragons — Fiction; Folklore — Korea. RL C. LEXILE 560L.

To regain her father's sight, a beautiful young girl agrees to become the bride of a dragon. After serving the dragon without complaint, she is able to return to her land, find her father, and marry. Illustrations capture the feeling of a magical Korean land.

Schick, Alice, and Joel Schick

2884 *Just This Once*. Ill. by author. HarperCollins, 1978, o.p. SERIES: I-Like-to-Read. SUBJECTS: Cave dwellers — Fiction; Historical fiction; Pets — Dogs — Fiction. RL C.

Og, Glok, and their children are the only ones in their tribe not terrified by the friendly wolf. Again and again they say "just this once" as they pet and feed her. Ultimately they make her a part of their tribe and the first domesticated "dog." Realistic drawings of the prehistoric setting have a humorous look to them.

Schick, Eleanor

2885 *Home Alone*. Ill. by author. Dial, 1980, o.p. SERIES: Dial Easy-to-Read. SUBJECTS: Latchkey children — Fiction; Self-esteem — Fiction. RL B.

On his first day home alone after school, Andy carefully follows the instructions his mother and father gave him as he passes the time waiting for them to come home. Carefully executed realistic colored pencil drawings illustrate this very common situation.

2886 *Joey on His Own*. Ill. by author. Dial, 1982, o.p. SERIES: Dial Easy-to-Read. SUBJECTS: Behavior — Responsible — Fiction; Shopping — Fiction. RL B.

Joey's little sister is sick and he must go to the store for his mother. Walking past unsavory characters on the way, Joey finally makes it to the store and returns home with a new sense of responsibility. The sympathetic text has realistic colored pencil drawings.

2887 *Neighborhood Knight*. Ill. by author. Greenwillow, 1976, o.p. SERIES: Read-Alone. SUBJECTS: Families, single parent — Fiction; Imagination — Fiction. RL B.

Since his father, the "king," has been gone a long time, the little boy pretends he is a courageous knight defending his mother and sister and their apartment "castle." Sensitively written and drawn, the story shows a small child dealing in the best way he can with anger and frustration.

2888 *Rainy Sunday*. Ill. by author. Dial, 1981, o.p. SERIES: Dial Easy-to-Read. SUBJECTS: City and town life — Fiction; Family life — Fiction; Weather — Rain — Fiction. RL B.

Everything in the city looks gray and feels cold when a little girl wakes up. As she shares a quiet day with her mother and father, the day brightens with their pleasure in one another's company. The colored pencil illustrations are spare and as clearly defined as the activities the small family shares.

2889 *Summer at the Sea*. Ill. by author. Greenwillow, 1979, o.p. SERIES: Read-Alone. SUBJECTS: Seashore — Fiction; Vacations — Fiction. RL B.

After an entire summer at the ocean spent meeting people, fishing, planting flowers, and enjoying almost every minute, it is hard for a little girl to return to her busy city life. The meticulous pencil and wash drawings are a perfect complement to the quiet text.

Schlein, Miriam

2890 *What the Dinosaurs Saw: Animals Living Then and Now*. Ill. by Carol Schwartz. Cartwheel, pap., 1998, ISBN 0-590-37128-2. SERIES: Hello Reader! SUBJECTS: Dinosaurs; Numbers; Prehistoric animals. RL B. LEXILE 480L.

Ten animals that were alive when the dinosaurs roamed the earth and are still alive today are introduced to readers using a counting format. Detailed and realistic paintings that fill each page.

Schneider, Herman, and Nina Schneider

2891 *Science Fun with a Flashlight*. Ill. by Harriet Sherman. McGraw-Hill, 1975, o.p. SUBJECTS: Science experiments; Shadows. RL B.

A clever text shows children how to have a good time experimenting with light and shadows. By using a flashlight they can discover color in light, how the angle of light affects shadows, and how color and light are reflected. The pictures are delightful.

School Stories Your Dog Didn't Eat

2892 *School Stories Your Dog Didn't Eat*. Ill. by Ann Schweninger, Lynn Sweat, et al. North-South Books, 2000, o.p. SERIES: Reading Rainbow Readers. SUBJECTS: School stories. RL B.

Amelia Bedelia and a host of other well-known characters from books for beginning readers fill stories about school and learning. The variety of styles of writing and illustrating guarantee that children are sure to find a story they will like.

Schott, Jane A.

2893 *Dian Fossey and the Mountain Gorillas*. Ill. by Ralph L. Ramstad. Carolrhoda, 2000, ISBN 1-57505-082-X. SERIES: On My Own Biography. SUBJECTS: Biographies; Gorillas; Zoology and zoologists. RL B.

The story of Fossey and her quest to study and preserve the mountain gorillas of Rwanda may inspire some young readers to take up her work. Illustrated with realistic watercolors, the book includes an afterword and a chronology of Fossey's life.

Schreiber, Anne

2894 *Magnets*. Ill. by Adrian Sinnott. Grosset & Dunlap, pap., 2003, ISBN 0-448-43149-1. SERIES: All Aboard Science Reader. SUBJECTS: Magnets; Science and scientists. RL C. LEXILE 760L.

Information on the power of magnets, how magnetism was discovered, how magnets are used, and different types of magnets is provided in this substantial book for beginning readers. It is illustrated with cartoon-like pictures and has activities and a glossary.

Schuette, Sarah L.

2895 *Consideration: Everyday Character Education*. Capstone, 2005, ISBN 0-7368-3677-2. SERIES: First Facts. SUBJECTS: Behavior; Thoughtfulness. RL B.

Opportunities for considerate behavior are everywhere: at school, at home, with friends, in the community. Situations for consideration as a positive force are shown throughout, and instruction is given in sending thank-you notes. The book includes an index, glossary, bibliography, and Web sites.

Schulman, Janet

2896 *The Big Hello*. Ill. by Lillian Hoban. Dell, pap., 1980, o.p. SERIES: Read-Alone. SUBJECTS: Dolls and dollhouses — Fiction; Fear — Fiction; Moving, household — Fiction. RL A.

A little girl comforts her doll as they fly to their new home in California. Once there the doll is lost but fortunately found by a child certain to be the little girl's hoped-for new friend. Pencil drawings help readers to empathize with the child's fear of the unknown.

2897 *The Great Big Dummy*. Ill. by Lillian Hoban. Greenwillow, 1979, o.p. SERIES: Read-Alone. SUBJECTS: Friendship — Fiction; Imagination — Fiction; Loneliness — Fiction. RL B.

When her friends are too busy to play with her, Anna decides to create a "sister" out of her clothes and play with her until her friends are free to play. The story and appealing pencil and wash drawings successfully present a child who is both imaginative and independent.

2898 *Jack the Bum and the Halloween Handout*. Ill. by James Stevenson. Greenwillow, 1977, o.p. SERIES: Read-Alone. SUBJECTS: Halloween — Fiction; Tramps — Fiction. RL A.

Wanting a cup of coffee, Jack the bum tries trick-or-treating and even using the word UNICEF as he goes door to door. Finally he follows children into a UNICEF party where he is the winner of $ 5. 00, which he donates to UNICEF. Illustrated with humorous pencil and wash drawings.

2899 *Jack the Bum and the Haunted House*. Ill. by James Stevenson. Greenwillow, 1977, o.p. SERIES: Read-Alone. SUBJECTS: Haunted houses — Fiction; Robbers and

Schulman, Janet (cont.)

outlaws — Fiction; Tramps — Fiction. RL A.

With nowhere else to go during the cold weather, Jack takes up residence in a supposedly haunted house. Jack's determination to stay there results in his capturing a jewel thief. Humorous pencil and wash drawings show a kindly but resolute "tramp" resigned to his lot.

2900 *Jack the Bum and the UFO*. Ill. by James Stevenson. Greenwillow, 1978, o.p. SERIES: Read-Alone. SUBJECTS: Tramps — Fiction; UFOs — Fiction. RL A.

When the children beg Jack the bum to stop a land developer from turning their forest and pond into a parking lot, Jack cleverly convinces the developer that the area is a haven for UFOs. The text combines humor with concern for the environment. Illustrated with comic pencil and wash sketches.

2901 *Jenny and the Tennis Nut*. Ill. by Marylin Hafner. Greenwillow, 1978, o.p. SERIES: Read-Alone. SUBJECTS: Self-esteem — Fiction; Sports — Gymnastics — Fiction; Sports — Tennis — Fiction. RL B.

Insistent that Jenny be accomplished in at least one sport, her father tries to teach her his favorite — tennis — overlooking her obvious talent in gymnastics. Imaginative pencil drawings capture the enthusiasm that father and daughter give to their respective sports.

Schulte, Mary

2902 *The Amazon River*. Children's Press, 2006, ISBN 0-516-25031-0. SERIES: Rookie Read-About Geography. SUBJECTS: Geography; Rivers. RL B. LEXILE 410L.

The source of the Amazon's water, the river's connection to the rain forest, and the animals that live in it and people who live along it are all briefly introduced. One missing element is the destruction of much of the rain forest and the need for conservation. A photo glossary and index are appended.

2903 *Great Salt Lake*. Children's Press, 2006, ISBN 0-516-25034-5. SERIES: Rookie Read-About Geography. SUBJECTS: Geography; Lakes. RL B. LEXILE 450L.

So salty that people can float in it, the Great Salt Lake, which has 11 islands and a bird sanctuary, is in Utah. Its salt is harvested to put on roads during winter and into salt blocks for animals. Illustrated with color photographs, the book is brief yet packed with facts. It includes a photo glossary and an index.

Schultz, Walter A.

2904 *Will and Orv*. Ill. by Janet Schultz. Carolrhoda, pap., 1991, ISBN 0-87614-568-3. SERIES: On My Own Books. SUBJECTS: Aeronautics; Biographies. RL B.

One of the five people who witnessed the Wright brothers' first flight, Johnny Moore is the one through whom the story of that historic event is told. A well-developed story line and good color-pencil drawings add appeal to an already fascinating story.

Schwartz, Alvin

2905 *All of Our Noses Are Here and Other Noodle Tales*. Ill. by Karen A. Weinhaus. HarperCollins, pap., 1985, ISBN 0-06-025288-X. SERIES: I Can Read. SUBJECTS: Folklore — United States; Humorous stories. RL B.

Anyone reading these five stories about the Brown family is sure to end up laughing. The Browns are typical noodles doing absolutely ridiculous things in total seriousness. The colored pencil and wash drawings give these silly folktales from around the world a special zany look.

2906 *Busy Buzzing Bumblebees and Other Tongue Twisters*. Ill. by Paul Meisel. HarperCollins, pap., 1982, ISBN 0-06-444036-2. SERIES: I Can Read. SUBJECTS: Tongue twisters. RL C.

Children and adults will have a good time with 46 phrases that are guaranteed to twist and torment tongues. The brightly colored, humorous ink and wash paintings definitely add to the fun and to an understanding of the rhymes.

2907 *Ghosts! Ghostly Tales from Folklore*. Ill. by Victoria Chess. HarperCollins, 1991, ISBN 0-06-021797-9. SERIES: I Can Read. SUBJECTS: Folklore; Ghost stories; Scary stories. RL B.

A wonderful collection of ghostly folktales sure to attract and hold the attention of young readers, this has Victoria Chess's delightfully spooky and rather zany illustrations to fill the book and lighten the stories.

2908 *I Saw You in the Bathtub and Other Folk Rhymes*. Ill. by Syd Hoff. HarperCollins, pap., 1989, ISBN 0-06-444151-2. SERIES: I Can Read. SUBJECTS: Folklore — United States; Humorous stories; Poetry. RL B.

Included here are rhymes and chants that children in the United States say or sing at play. Readers will be familiar with most of them and enjoy their familiarity. Hof's comic ink and wash drawings are in his popular sketchy and very funny and attractive style.

2909 *In a Dark, Dark Room and Other Scary Stories*. Ill. by Dirk Zimmer. HarperCollins, pap., 1984, ISBN 0-06-025271-5. SERIES: I Can Read. SUBJECTS: Folklore; Ghost stories; Scary stories. RL A.

The seven short, scary stories and lyrics from spooky songs are perfect for young readers to learn and tell at camp or on Halloween. The detailed ink pictures have red and yellow accents that blend humor into somewhat scary pictures.

2910 *Ten Copycats in a Boat and Other Riddles*. Ill. by Marc Simont. HarperCollins, pap., 1980, o.p. SERIES: I Can Read. SUBJECTS: Jokes and riddles. RL B.

Familiar yet still funny jokes and riddles get two pages each — one for the joke or riddle and the other for the answer. The ink, watercolor, and colored pencil drawings capably extend the silliness.

2911 *There Is a Carrot in My Ear and Other Noodle Tales*. Ill. by Karen A. Weinhaus. HarperCollins, pap., 1982, ISBN 0-06-025233-2. SERIES: I Can Read. SUBJECTS: Folklore — United States; Humorous stories. RL B.

The Brown family are the noodles as they swim in a waterless pool, try to hatch a "mare's egg," or mistake long underwear for an intruder. The six stories offer children an opportunity to have fun with absolutely ridiculous characters and comic illustrations in red, yellow, and gray.

Scieszka, Jon

2912 *Time Warp Trio: South Pole or Bust (An Egg)*. Retold by Catherine Hapka. HarperCollins, 2007, ISBN 0-06-111641-6. SERIES: I Can Read. SUBJECTS: Antarctica — Fiction; Humorous stories; Science fiction. RL C.

It's so hot in the car that the boys pull out their magic time-travel book, push the button, and land in 1911 Antarctica with Scott and his explorers. A bit of history is combined with humorous time travel in this brief episode. A page of additional information tells about Scott's expedition.

2913 *Time Warp Trio: The High and the Flighty*. Retold by Catherine Hapka and Lisa Rao. HarperCollins, 2007, ISBN 0-06-111644-0. SERIES: I Can Read. SUBJECTS: Aeronautics — Fiction; Earhart, Amelia — Fiction; Science fiction. RL C.

Three girls, descendants of the original Time Warp Trio, use the book to go back in time to meet Amelia Earhart. Although they arrive before her round-the-world trip, they are unable to find a way to secretly help her. The book includes a page of information on Earhart.

Scott, Geoffrey

2914 *Egyptian Boats*. Ill. by Nancy L. Carlson. Carolrhoda, 1981, o.p. SERIES: On My Own. SUBJECTS: Boats and boating; Egypt, ancient. RL B.

A vocabulary builder, this informative history of Egyptian watercraft describes different types and sizes of boats, how they were used, and for what purposes. It provides a brief glance at the social structure of ancient Egypt. Illustrated with detailed, realistic ink drawings.

2915 *Labor Day*. Ill. by Cherie R. Wyman. Carolrhoda, 1982, ISBN 0-87614-178-5. SERIES: On My Own. SUBJECTS: Labor Day. RL C.

A brief look at the first Labor Day celebration shows the difficult working conditions in the 1880s when the Central Labor Union and the Knights of Labor held the first Labor Day parade. The book, illustrated with romanticized pictures of workers, encourages pride in the labor movement.

Scott, Geoffrey (cont.)

2916 *Memorial Day*. Ill. by Peter E. Hanson. Carolrhoda, 1983, o.p. SERIES: On My Own. SUBJECTS: Memorial Day. RL C.

The origin of Memorial Day is traced to just after the Civil War and the celebration by the northern states of Decoration Day. Carefully written and providing good historical information and context, this book is illustrated with semirealistic ink drawings of historical scenes.

Seibert, Patricia

2917 *Mush! Across Alaska in the World's Longest Sled-Dog Race*. Ill. by Jan Davey Ellis. Houghton Mifflin, 1992, ISBN 0-395-64537-9. SUBJECTS: Dogs — Racing; Pets — Dogs. RL C.

Framing the text or in double-page spreads, the illustrations look at the famous Alaskan Iditarod sled-dog race and give readers a sense of the terrain, the strength of the dogs, and the mushers' determination. A well-written text conveys the excitement of the 1, 000-mile race.

Seixas, Judith S.

2918 *Allergies: What They Are, What They Do*. Ill. by Tom Huffman. Greenwillow, 1991, o.p. SERIES: Read-Alone. SUBJECTS: Allergies. RL C.

The history, identification, and treatment of allergies are covered in this very thorough discussion of the subject. Also mentioned are a number of common allergens: food, dust mites, chemicals, plants, and so on. A light touch is given to the serious topic by pictures using two colors.

2919 *Vitamins: What They Are, What They Do*. Ill. by Tom Huffman. Greenwillow, 1986, o.p. SERIES: Read-Alone. SUBJECTS: Nutrition; Vitamins. RL C.

Children reading this book will learn what vitamins are, how they were discovered, why they are added to foods, who needs supplements, and more. A section on nutrition and an easy-to-use vitamin chart are also included. Two-color ink drawings of smiling fruit and vegetables highlight the text.

2920 *Water: What It Is, What It Does*. Ill. by Tom Huffman. Greenwillow, 1987, o.p. SERIES: Read-Alone. SUBJECTS: Conservation; Pollution — Water; Water. RL C.

Using simple, straightforward language, the author discusses water's properties, its uses, and the abuses it suffers. With five interesting experiments, the text offers a relatively thorough examination of the subject. Illustrated with funny line drawings.

Selsam, Millicent E.

2921 *Benny's Animals and How He Put Them in Order*. Ill. by Arnold Lobel. HarperCollins, 1966, o.p. SERIES: Science I Can Read. SUBJECTS: Animals — Classification. RL A.

Benny's curiosity about how to classify his pictures of animals takes him, with his parents' encouragement, to the natural science museum. While there he learns about the way in which animals are classified. Sketchy ink and colored pencil drawings keep this story upbeat and entertaining.

2922 *Big Tracks, Little Tracks: Following Animal Prints*. Ill. by Marlene Hill Donnelly. HarperCollins, 1999, ISBN 0-690-14371-0. SERIES: Let's-Read-and-Find-Out Science. SUBJECTS: Animals — Tracks; Nature. RL B. LEXILE 370L.

Deer, rabbits, fox, frogs, and raccoons are just some of the animals that a good nature detective can identify by looking carefully at tracks. Text and watercolor art work closely together to help children learn about tracks and how to be more observant.

2923 *Egg to Chick*. Rev. ed. Photos. Ill. by Barbara Wolff. HarperCollins, pap., 1970, o.p. SERIES: Science I Can Read. SUBJECTS: Animals — Reproduction. RL B.

The development of a chick embryo is examined from the day of conception until 21 days later when the chick hatches. Multicolored drawings alternate with black-and-white photographs to present an accurate portrayal of the growth of the embryo.

2924 *Greg's Microscope*. Ill. by Arnold Lobel. HarperCollins, 1990, ISBN 0-06-444144-X. SERIES: Science I Can Read. SUBJECTS: Microscopes. RL B.

Soon after Greg's father gives him a microscope, the whole family becomes involved in using it to learn about the things around them. A well-done introduction to the microscope, the book has charming and informative pictures that help to explain the use of this instrument.

2925 *How to Be a Nature Detective*. Ill. by Marlene Hill Donnelly. HarperCollins, pap., 1995, ISBN 0-06-445134-8. SERIES: Let's-Read-and-Find-Out Science. SUBJECTS: Animals — Tracks; Nature. RL B. LEXILE 380L.

"What animal was there? Where did it go? What did it eat?" These are some of the questions a nature detective will ask as he or she learns about identifying animals by their tracks. Illustrations extend the text and give good examples of kinds of tracks.

2926 *Let's Get Turtles*. Ill. by Arnold Lobel. HarperCollins, 1965, o.p. SERIES: Science I Can Read. SUBJECTS: Pets — Turtles; Turtles. RL A.

Two best friends, Billy and Jerry, agree to get the same kind of pet — a turtle. Once they have them they learn how to take care of them and what to feed them. The lively ink and wash drawings add to the appeal of the book.

2927 *More Potatoes!* Ill. by Ben Shecter. HarperCollins, 1972, o.p. SERIES: Science I Can Read. SUBJECTS: Farm and country life; Vegetables. RL B.

Curious about how the grocery store gets potatoes, Sue asks questions that lead her class to a trip to a warehouse and a farm. Through the illustrations and the text, readers will quickly learn that vegetables do not just appear on the shelves of supermarkets.

2928 *Plenty of Fish*. Ill. by Erik Blegvad. HarperCollins, 1960, o.p. SERIES: Science I Can Read. SUBJECTS: Pets — Fish. RL A.

Irrepressible Willy is determined to have goldfish but must be constantly reminded to stop and find out the proper way to care for them. Willy's father patiently explains the curious world of goldfish to him. Illustrated with ink drawings showing a middle-class British family.

2929 *Seeds and More Seeds*. Ill. by Tomi Ungerer. HarperCollins, 1959, o.p. SERIES: Science I Can Read. SUBJECTS: Seeds, roots, and bulbs. RL A.

With his father's encouragement, Benny explores why seeds grow. He plants a variety of things and watches as seeds grow while other things do not. The sketchy ink drawings show a turn-of-the-century father and son in an opulent setting investigating seeds.

2930 *Strange Creatures That Really Lived*. Ill. by Jennifer Dewey. Scholastic, 1989, ISBN 0-590-40493-8. SUBJECTS: Prehistoric animals. RL B.

Not all of the creatures described in Selsam's clear style and Dewey's colored pencil, sometimes fanciful, drawings are all that strange, but all are interesting. A useful chart on the last page lists the dinosaurs, ancient mammals, insects, and birds included in the book.

2931 *Terry and the Caterpillars*. Ill. by Arnold Lobel. HarperCollins, 1962, o.p. SERIES: Nature I Can Read. SUBJECTS: Butterflies and moths; Caterpillars. RL A.

Terry finds three caterpillars and watches curiously as they eat, grow, spin cocoons, and months later become moths. The story is full of factual information and, with its detailed ink and wash pictures, continues to fascinate children.

2932 *Tony's Birds*. Ill. by Kurt Werth. HarperCollins, 1961, o.p. SERIES: Science I Can Read. SUBJECTS: Birds — Fiction. RL A.

An evening walk with his father leads Tony to an interest in birds. The well-developed relationship between father and son is the foundation of a story that introduces children to the rudiments of bird watching. The spare ink and wash sketches still appeal and do not appear dated.

2933 *Up, Down and Around: The Force of Gravity*. Ill. by Kenneth Dewey. Doubleday, 1977, o.p. SERIES: Chicago Museum of Science and Industry. SUBJECTS: Gravity. RL C.

A clearly written text accurately explains the fundamental concepts associated with gravity, using space travel and planetary systems as examples. Realistic but sketchy illustrations and diagrams do not add much to the text.

2934 *When an Animal Grows*. Ill. by John Kaufmann. HarperCollins, 1966, o.p. SERIES: Science I Can Read. SUBJECTS:

Selsam, Millicent E. (cont.)

Animals; Animals — Growth and development. RL B.

Four baby animals, two mammals and two birds, are contrasted from birth to independent living. A gorilla is compared with a lamb while a sparrow is compared with a mallard on alternating pages using different colors of ink for the text. Illustrated with gray watercolor paintings.

Selsam, Millicent E., and Joyce Hunt

2935 *Animal Mixups*. Ill. by John Wallner. Macmillan, 1992, o.p. SUBJECTS: Animals. RL A.

Where an animal lives, the young it raises, the tail it has, are all part of this exercise in observation. Readers are encouraged to look at the pictures and think about what is wrong and what would be right in mismatched art and oddly made animals. Ink-defined watercolors are humorous.

2936 *A First Look at Animals with Horns*. Ill. by Harriett Springer. Walker, 1989, o.p. SERIES: First Look At. SUBJECTS: Animals — Horned. RL B.

After identifying and defining "horns," animals with varying numbers of horns are then distinguished from one another. Accurate black-and-white pencil drawings accompany the simple text and work with it to help readers identify different varieties of animals by their characteristics.

2937 *A First Look at Animals Without Backbones*. Ill. by Harriett Springer. Walker, 1976, o.p. SERIES: First Look At. SUBJECTS: Invertebrates. RL C.

After differentiating between animals that have and do not have backbones, the book discusses a variety of invertebrates. Those covered include arthropods, echinoderms, mollusks, worms, coelenterates, sponges, and protozoa. Illustrated with detailed pencil drawings that help clarify the text.

2938 *A First Look at Bats*. Ill. by Harriett Springer. Walker, 1991, o.p. SERIES: First Look At. SUBJECTS: Bats. RL B.

Using pencil drawings and a text intent on getting readers to carefully look at similarities and differences among bats, the authors discuss bats, their habits, their lives, and how to tell them apart. A map showing where bats live and an index are also in the book.

2939 *A First Look at Bird Nests*. Ill. by Harriett Springer. Walker, 1984, o.p. SERIES: First Look At. SUBJECTS: Animals — Nests. RL C.

Basic information on the identification of nests of specific birds is offered. Also, an attempt is made to involve readers in identifying a nest, which is shown in detailed and realistic pencil drawings. Well researched, the book provides good information for school assignments or the satisfaction of curiosity.

2940 *A First Look at Birds*. Ill. by Harriett Springer. Walker, 1973, o.p. SERIES: First Look At. SUBJECTS: Birds. RL B.

Children can learn a great deal about birds and their physical characteristics by reading this clearly written and factually accurate book. Intending to hone powers of observation, Selsam and Hunt ask readers to choose the correct illustration from among detailed pencil drawings.

2941 *A First Look at Caterpillars*. Ill. by Harriett Springer. Walker, 1988, o.p. SERIES: First Look At. SUBJECTS: Butterflies and moths; Caterpillars. RL B.

Children reading this are encouraged to use the information in the text to help them in examining the pictures of caterpillars, butterflies, and moths, and detecting differences among them. The book has detailed, realistic pencil drawings with green accents.

2942 *A First Look at Ducks, Geese and Swans*. Ill. by Harriett Springer. Walker, 1990, o.p. SERIES: First Look At. SUBJECTS: Ducks; Geese; Swans. RL B.

A good introduction to the characteristics and differences of ducks, geese, and swans, this encourages young readers to look closely at these waterfowl, to note their differences and similarities. Carefully crafted pencil and wash pictures are essential to the text.

2943 *A First Look at Horses*. Ill. by Harriett Springer. Walker, 1981, o.p. SERIES: First Look At. SUBJECTS: Horses. RL B.

After a brief introduction to equine anatomy, several breeds of horses are mentioned and compared. The book emphasizes the importance of recognizing observable external differences among and between the horses pictured in detailed pencil drawings. Horse fans should enjoy this one.

2944 *A First Look at Insects*. Ill. by Harriett Springer. Walker, 1974, o.p. SERIES: First Look At. SUBJECTS: Insects. RL C.

Like others in the First Look At series, this book attempts to get readers to use the information in the well-written text to test their powers of observation. Here they are asked to distinguish detailed pencil drawings of particular insects from pictures of other animals and insects.

2945 *A First Look at Leaves*. Ill. by Harriett Springer. Walker, 1972, o.p. SERIES: First Look At. SUBJECTS: Trees. RL C.

Like others in the First Look At series, this book asks the reader to scan the illustrations on a page and match an object (a leaf) to a description. It also presents useful information about leaves and their parts. Simple line drawings are very clear and sufficiently accurate for leaf identification.

2946 *A First Look at Owls, Eagles, and Other Hunters of the Sky*. Ill. by Harriett Springer. Walker, 1986, o.p. SERIES: First Look At. SUBJECTS: Birds of prey. RL C.

Owls, eagles, falcons, and other birds of prey are pictured in lovely, realistic drawings and are compared to facilitate identification. The book further challenges the reader to identify birds' pictures based on the facts presented in the text.

2947 *A First Look at Poisonous Snakes*. Ill. by Harriett Springer. Walker, 1987, o.p. SERIES: First Look At. SUBJECTS: Snakes. RL C.

Encouraging children to notice the distinguishing marks and behavior of poisonous snakes, the book compares the snakes by body shape, especially head, and by type of fangs. Cobras, vipers, pit vipers, and sea snakes are contrasted. Illustrated with very detailed pencil drawings.

2948 *A First Look at Sharks*. Ill. by Harriett Springer. Walker, 1979, o.p. SERIES: First Look At. SUBJECTS: Sharks. RL C.

Like other books in the First Look At series, this book presents its subject, sharks, in terms of classification characteristics. It encourages the reader to distinguish sharks from bony fishes and different sharks from one another. The black-and-white pencil drawings are detailed and realistic.

2949 *A First Look at Spiders*. Ill. by Harriett Springer. Walker, 1983, o.p. SERIES: First Look At. SUBJECTS: Spiders. RL C.

Children are prompted to examine detailed black-and-white pencil drawings to learn what distinguishes a spider from an insect, one spider from another, and one web from another. Children reading this will increase their observational skills rather than gaining in-depth knowledge.

2950 *A First Look at the World of Plants*. Ill. by Harriett Springer. Walker, 1978, o.p. SERIES: First Look At. SUBJECTS: Plants. RL B.

This book gives its readers an opportunity to learn about plants in a variety of ways. It encourages children not only to read the text but to carefully examine the pencil and wash drawings for differences among fungi, gymnosperms, and other plants.

Seltzer, Eric

2951 *Doodle Dog*. Simon & Schuster, 2005, ISBN 0-689-85913-9. SERIES: Ready-to-Read. SUBJECTS: Art and artists — Fiction; Pets — Dogs — Fiction; Stories in rhyme. RL A.

Doodle Dog helps the other animals with their art projects. Along the way he loses his art supplies. Fortunately they are found and he can dream of another day of projects. Sketchy, cartoon-like pen and watercolor pictures illustrate the story.

2952 *Four Pups and a Worm*. Random House, 1996, o.p. SERIES: Beginner Books. SUBJECTS: Behavior — Problem solving — Fiction; Pets — Dogs — Fiction; Stories in rhyme. RL B. LEXILE 350L.

Although not as easy to read as most books in this series, this story of a team of problem-solving pups (and a worm) is silly enough to attract young readers. The ink and watercolor wash drawings are cartoonish and fun.

Seltzer, Meyer

2953 *Here Comes the Recycling Truck!* Photos by author. Whitman, 1992, o.p. SUBJECTS: Recycling. RL C.

Elisa, the driver of her community's recycling truck, is followed for a day and shown gathering glass, paper, cardboard, and cans. She takes everything to the recycling center and the text explains

Seltzer, Meyer (cont.)

how recycled items are used. Clear photographs and text show the importance of her work.

Serfozo, Mary

2954 *A Head Is for Hats*. Ill. by Katy Bratun. Scholastic, pap., 1999, ISBN 0-439-09909-9. SERIES: Hello Reader! SUBJECTS: Human body — Fiction; Senses — Fiction; Stories in rhyme. RL B. LEXILE 270L.

Starting with how a head holds a hat, a rhyming text describes the senses and how they are used, and shows how "When you add it all up, then it comes out to *you*!" Round-faced children are painted in bright colors.

Serventy, Vincent

2955 *Kangaroo*. Ill. with photos. Scholastic, pap., 1987, o.p. SERIES: Animals in the Wild. SUBJECTS: Kangaroos. RL B.

About five kinds of kangaroos are introduced in the brief text. Much of the book is devoted to following baby kangaroos from birth to the time that they are ready to leave the pouch. Good information is presented well, and the large full-color photographs are delightful.

2956 *Koala*. Ill. with photos. Scholastic, pap., 1987, o.p. SERIES: Animals in the Wild. SUBJECTS: Koalas. RL B.

A full-color photograph dominates each page with the brief text below it acting like a caption. The information ranges from the koala's diet and habitat to its young, its enemies, and current attempts by Australia to protect it. This appealing book is an Australian production.

2957 *Turtle and Tortoise*. Ill. with photos. Scholastic, pap., 1987, o.p. SERIES: Animals in the Wild. SUBJECTS: Turtles. RL C.

Good information and excellent full-color photographs tell about the natural habitats (land, sea, and shore) and life cycle of turtles and tortoises. The photographs dominate this book, and the text acts as captions.

Seuling, Barbara

2958 *Just Me*. Ill. by author. Harcourt, 1982, o.p. SERIES: Let Me Read. SUBJECTS: Imagination — Fiction. RL A.

Using odds and ends from around her home and a lot of imagination, a little girl tries being a horse, a dragon, and a robot but she always returns to being "just me." Ink and wash drawings are simple, uncluttered, and attractive.

Seuss, Dr.

2959 *The Cat in the Hat*. Ill. by author. Random House, 1957, ISBN 0-394-90001-4. SERIES: I Can Read It All by Myself. SUBJECTS: Humorous stories; Stories in rhyme. RL A.

With nothing to do on a cold, rainy day, two children are roused from their lethargy by the Cat in the Hat, who promises lots of good fun. Seuss's cartoon drawings and rhymed text always attract young readers and listeners.

2960 *The Cat in the Hat Comes Back*. Ill. by author. Random House, 1958, ISBN 0-394-90002-2. SERIES: I Can Read It All by Myself. SUBJECTS: Humorous stories; Stories in rhyme. RL B.

While Mother is gone, the children are busily working when the Cat in the Hat returns to create havoc and fun with his Little Cats A to Z. Seuss's absurdly funny drawings and text quickly capture the attention of young readers.

2961 *The Cat's Quizzer*. Ill. by author. Random House, 1976, ISBN 0-394-83296-5. SERIES: Beginner Books. SUBJECTS: Miscellanea; Tests. RL B.

A wild assortment of questions testing general knowledge is given the Seuss touch with zany illustrations and an offbeat tone. Children will be challenged to try their best at answering questions from natural science, history, and more. Answers are given at the end.

2962 *Foot Book*. Ill. by author. Random House, 1968, ISBN 0-394-90937-2. SERIES: Bright and Early Books. SUBJECTS: Human body — Feet — Fiction; Stories in rhyme. RL B.

The many varieties of feet and the many things they can do are amusingly described in words and lively colorful pictures in this humorous rhyming text with a total of 126 words.

2963 *Fox in Socks*. Ill. by author. Random House, 1965, ISBN 0-394-90038-3. SERIES: I Can Read It All by Myself. SUBJECTS: Humorous stories; Stories in rhyme; Tongue twisters. RL C.

Children who are about to read these wild tongue twisters are warned at the outset to take them slowly. Children will sympathize with poor Mr. Knox's attempts at tongue twisters and will enjoy his final victory over Fox. Typical zany Seuss creations illustrate the text.

2964 *Great Day for Up!* Ill. by Quentin Blake. Random House, 1974, ISBN 0-394-92913-6. SERIES: Bright and Early Books. SUBJECTS: Stories in rhyme. RL A.

This rousing, jubilant rhyme encourages everyone to get "up" in the morning — except for the narrator, who is sleeping in. The clever illustrations are lively, funny, and perfect for the rhyme.

2965 *Green Eggs and Ham*. Ill. by author. Random House, 1960, ISBN 0-394-90016-2. SERIES: I Can Read It All by Myself. SUBJECTS: Food — Fiction; Nonsense; Stories in rhyme. RL A.

Sam-I-am relentlessly pursues a furry top-hatted creature trying every way he can think of to get the creature to eat green eggs and ham. The well-known, cleverly illustrated creatures and the silly rhyming text are perpetual favorites of young children.

2966 *Hop on Pop*. Ill. by author. Random House, 1963, ISBN 0-394-90029-4. SERIES: I Can Read It All by Myself. SUBJECTS: Stories in rhyme. RL A.

Introducing the very simplest of words, usually of one syllable, Seuss puts them into a nonsensical rhyming format with humorous results. His illustrations of outlandish "things" entice children into trying to read.

2967 *I Am Not Going to Get Up Today!* Ill. by James Stevenson. Random House, 1987, ISBN 0-394-99217-2. SERIES: I Can Read It All by Myself. SUBJECTS: Humorous stories; Sleep — Fiction; Stories in rhyme. RL B.

In a rhyming story, neighbors, police, newspapers, and television attempt to get a little boy out of bed, but he refuses to get up. Illustrations are done with full-color wash and ink sketches in an amusing comic style.

2968 *I Can Read with My Eyes Shut!* Ill. by author. Random House, 1978, ISBN 0-394-93912-3. SERIES: I Can Read It All by Myself. SUBJECTS: Books and reading — Fiction; Stories in rhyme. RL B.

The Cat in the Hat gives children countless reasons for reading and learning while they involve themselves in a rousing, rhyming text. Seuss's typical free-form creatures are colorfully illustrated and will attract children.

2969 *Mister Brown Can Moo! Can You?* Ill. by author. Random House, 1970, ISBN 0-394-90622-5. SERIES: Bright and Early Books. SUBJECTS: Sound — Fiction; Stories in rhyme. RL C.

From the noises made by cows and owls to that of thunder, Mister Brown can imitate just about any sound. The humorous text and illustrations encourage children not only to try making the sounds themselves but also to decode new words.

2970 *Oh, Say Can You Say?* Ill. by author. Random House, 1979, ISBN 0-394-94255-8. SERIES: I Can Read It All by Myself. SUBJECTS: Tongue twisters. RL B.

The cover warns children that the tongue twisters inside are terrible to try to read and to try not to stumble over. The text is longer than others by Seuss and more challenging. His comic drawings of imaginative creatures will encourage children to try these creative phrases.

2971 *Oh, the Thinks You Can Think!* Ill. by author. Random House, 1975, ISBN 0-394-93129-7. SERIES: I Can Read It All by Myself. SUBJECTS: Imagination — Fiction; Stories in rhyme. RL A.

Children reading this will be encouraged to think imaginatively and to enjoy playing with words. Seuss creates outlandish word and picture combinations that should spur children to try making up some of their own. The illustrations are full-color, cartoon-like, and fun.

2972 *One Fish Two Fish Red Fish Blue Fish*. Ill. by author. Random House, 1960, ISBN 0-394-90013-8. SERIES: I Can Read It All by Myself. SUBJECTS: Humorous stories; Nonsense; Stories in rhyme. RL A.

Aided by a delightfully nonsensical rhyming text, two children explore the world of funny creatures. Seuss's silly story introduces children to

Seuss, Dr. (cont.)

wordplay and to an enjoyment of language. The illustrations are extremely entertaining.

2973 *There's a Wocket in My Pocket!* Ill. by author. Random House, 1974, ISBN 0-394-92920-9. SERIES: Bright and Early Books. SUBJECTS: Stories in rhyme. RL B.

Zany Seuss creations rhyming with the names of familiar items and common household objects are sure to inspire children to try to make up their own rhyming words. Typical Seuss illustrations.

Shaffer, Ann

2974 *The Camel Express.* Ill. by Robin Cole. Dillon, 1989, o.p. SERIES: It Really Happened. SUBJECTS: Camels — Fiction; Historical fiction; Western stories. RL C.

When the pony express rider is hurt, Grandpa and Mary Claire ride Carlos, a camel set free by the army, nearly 35 miles through storms and great danger to the next post. Loosely based on events of the times, the adventure is fast paced and nicely illustrated with pencil drawings.

Shannon, George

2975 *The Gang and Mrs. Higgins.* Ill. by Andrew Vines. Greenwillow, 1981, o.p. SERIES: Read-Alone. SUBJECTS: Frontier and pioneer life — Fiction; Robbers and outlaws — Fiction; Western stories. RL C.

The Andersons, the meanest gang in Kansas, try to rob kindly Mrs. Higgins of her gold. She tells them there is no gold, as she washes and washes clothes. They give up and leave, and she takes the gold out of the washtub. The humorous story is illustrated with comic, semirealistic pictures.

Shapiro, Irwin

2976 *Gretchen and the White Steed.* Ill. by Herman Vestal. Garrard, 1972, o.p. SERIES: Venture. SUBJECTS: Adventure stories; Frontier and pioneer life — Fiction; Horses — Fiction. RL B.

On the way to Texas with her big family, Gretchen is tied to their gentle mare when it wanders away with her. Lost on the prairie and surrounded by wild horses, the little girl is rescued by a wonderful white horse. Illustrated with detailed ink and wash drawings.

Shapiro, Karen

2977 *Butterflies.* Ill. by Jean Cassels. Scholastic, pap., 2001, ISBN 0-439-20636-7. SERIES: Hello Science Reader! SUBJECTS: Butterflies and moths; Insects; Science and scientists. RL B. LEXILE 190L.

Through a brief rhyming text and realistic full-color illustrations, the life cycle of a butterfly emerges. On the final page, all the butterflies illustrated in the book are identified.

Shapp, Martha, and Charles Shapp

2978 *Let's Find Out About Babies.* Ill. by Jenny Williams. Watts, 1974, o.p. SERIES: Let's Find Out About. SUBJECTS: Animals — Reproduction. RL B.

From egg and sperm to birth, the development of animal and human babies is discussed without great detail and in general terms. The authors stress the importance of loving, supportive families for babies. The book has realistic, full-color pictures.

2979 *Let's Find Out About Houses.* Rev ed. Ill. by Tomie dePaola. Watts, 1975, o.p. SERIES: Let's Find Out About. SUBJECTS: Houses. RL B.

Houses from around the world, the material used to construct them, and the reasons for their particular kind of construction are briefly surveyed in the text and vibrant pencil and watercolor pictures.

2980 *Let's Find Out About the Moon.* Ill. by Brigitte Hartmann. Watts, 1975, o.p. SERIES: Let's Find Out About. SUBJECTS: Astronomy and astronomers; Space travel. RL C.

In this book children learn of discoveries about the moon, how the moon's rotation affects the earth, and what the men who landed on the moon found there. The text is interesting and illustrated with detailed and informative pencil drawings.

Sharmat, Marjorie W.

2981 *Burton and Dudley*. Ill. by Barbara Cooney. Holiday House, 1975, o.p. SUBJECTS: Friendship — Fiction; Humorous stories; Walking — Fiction. RL A.

Dudley Possum has to prod his quiet friend Burton into taking a walk with him, but it is Burton who revels in the outdoors and only reluctantly comes home, determined to walk all over the world. The well-done pen and ink drawings are detailed and clever and reflect the story's humor.

2982 *Griselda's New Year*. Ill. by Normand Chartier. Macmillan, 1979, o.p. SERIES: Ready-to-Read. SUBJECTS: Geese — Fiction; Humorous stories; New Year's Day — Fiction. RL B.

Oblivious to the problems she is creating for her friends, Griselda Goose pushes forward with her New Year's resolution to make someone happy. The funny story is illustrated with detailed ink and wash drawings of semirealistic, humorous animals.

2983 *Little Devil Gets Sick*. Ill. by Marylin Hafner. Doubleday, 1980, o.p. SERIES: Reading on My Own. SUBJECTS: Devils — Fiction; Fantasy; Illness — Fiction. RL B.

When Little Devil wakes up with a terrible cold, he tries everything (hot spider soup, warm fires, nasty spells) to get rid of it. Only when he does a good deed does it go away. Illustrated with comical colored pencil drawings that are sure to appeal to children.

2984 *Mitchell Is Moving*. Ill. by Jose Aruego and Ariane Dewey. Simon & Schuster, pap., 1996, ISBN 0-689-80876-3. SERIES: Ready-to-Read. SUBJECTS: Dinosaurs — Fiction; Friendship — Fiction; Moving, household — Fiction. RL B.

After 60 years of living in his house, dinosaur Mitchell decides to move. He has not counted on missing his good friend and neighbor Margo and is ecstatic when she follows and moves next to him. Simple, humorous drawings effectively illustrate this delightful story.

2985 *Mooch the Messy*. Ill. by Ben Shecter. HarperCollins, 1976, o.p. SERIES: I Can Read. SUBJECTS: Parent and child — Fiction; Rats — Fiction; Self-esteem — Fiction. RL B.

When his father comes to visit his hole, Mooch, a rat, tries to make him more comfortable by cleaning up. Though he enjoys the time with his father, Mooch is happy to be alone and messy again. Simple pencil and wash drawings illustrate this humorous story about self-acceptance.

2986 *Nate the Great*. Ill. by Marc Simont. Random House, 2002, ISBN 0-385-73017-9. SERIES: Break-of-Day. SUBJECTS: Mystery and detective stories. RL A.

Pancake-eating child detective Nate the Great is involved in solving mysteries for his friends. Using a "Dragnet" style speech pattern, Nate tells about his sleuthing. Expressive pencil and wash pictures showing Nate in a trench coat and deer-stalker cap are a perfect match to the text.

2987 *Nate the Great and Me: The Case of the Fleeing Fang*. Ill. by Marc Simont. Random House, pap., 1998, ISBN 0-440-41381-8. SERIES: Nate the Great. SUBJECTS: Mystery and detective stories; Pets — Dogs — Fiction. RL B. LEXILE 360L.

In honor of the twenty-fifth anniversary of the Nate the Great series, Nate invites readers to help him find Annie's missing dog, Fang. Included are tips for being a detective, ideas for a secret code, and a pancake recipe.

2988 *Nate the Great and the Boring Beach Bag*. Ill. by Marc Simont. Random House, pap., 1989, ISBN 0-440-40168-2. SERIES: Break-of-Day. SUBJECTS: Mystery and detective stories; Seashore — Fiction. RL A.

Even while swimming in the ocean, Nate is asked to help solve a mystery. This time it is Oliver's beach bag that is missing. The watercolor paintings place the well-known children from this series and their pets at a crowded beach in the summer.

2989 *Nate the Great and the Fishy Prize*. Ill. by Marc Simont. Dell, pap., 1988, ISBN 0-440-40039-2. SERIES: Break-of-Day. SUBJECTS: Mystery and detective stories. RL A.

Rosamond asks Nate to find her prize tuna fish can for the smartest pet contest. After diligent detecting, Nate and his dog Sludge find it. Illustrated with amusing pencil and watercolor pictures.

Sharmat, Marjorie W. (cont.)

2990 *Nate the Great and the Halloween Hunt.* Ill. by Marc Simont. Random House, pap., 1990, ISBN 0-440-40341-3. SERIES: Break-of-Day. SUBJECTS: Halloween — Fiction; Mystery and detective stories. RL B.

At home with his dog, Sludge, on Halloween, Nate is asked to find Rosamund's black kitten, Little Hex. The search takes them out among trick-or-treaters, to a haunted house, and finally, after a pancake snack, to the solution. Funny text and suitably Halloweenish pictures work well together.

2991 *Nate the Great and the Lost List.* Ill. by Marc Simont. Random House, pap., 1991, ISBN 0-440-46282-7. SERIES: Break-of-Day. SUBJECTS: Mystery and detective stories. RL A.

Taking a well-earned break from detecting, Nate reluctantly agrees to use his detective skills to help Claude find his missing grocery list. Short, choppy sentences are perfectly suited to reading aloud and the pencil and wash illustrations are expressive and humorous.

2992 *Nate the Great and the Missing Key.* Ill. by Marc Simont. Dell, pap., 1982, ISBN 0-440-46191-X. SERIES: Break-of-Day. SUBJECTS: Mystery and detective stories. RL A.

Rosamond has put Annie's house key in a safe place leaving clues to its whereabouts in a poem. Annie turns to Nate for help and again he solves the case just in time to go to Fang's birthday party. The pencil and wash drawings capture Nate and his friends perfectly.

2993 *Nate the Great and the Monster Mess.* Ill. by Martha Weston. Delacorte, 1999, ISBN 0-385-32114-7. SERIES: Nate the Great. SUBJECTS: Lost and found possessions — Fiction; Mystery and detective stories. RL B. LEXILE 340L.

When Nate the Great's mother loses the recipe for his favorite cookies, he quickly decides to take on the case and solve it with the help of his dog Sludge. Weston's illustrations are done in the style of Marc Simont.

2994 *Nate the Great and the Mushy Valentine.* Ill. by Marc Simont. Random House, pap., 1995, ISBN 0-440-41013-4. SUBJECTS: Mystery and detective stories; Pets — Dogs — Fiction; Valentine's Day — Fiction. RL C.

Nate the Great is determined to discover who sent his dog, Sludge, a valentine as well as who took Annie's valentine. After a few false leads, the young sleuth discovers the answers to both. This has all pictures in full color.

2995 *Nate the Great and the Phony Clue.* Ill. by Marc Simont. Dell, pap., 1981, ISBN 0-440-46300-9. SERIES: Break-of-Day. SUBJECTS: Mystery and detective stories. RL A.

A strange piece of paper with "vita" on it leads Nate on a challenging hunt for the rest of the message. Adults and children will have fun reading aloud this text reminiscent of "Dragnet's" Joe Friday dialogue. Pencil and wash drawings ably capture the tongue-in-cheek humor.

2996 *Nate the Great and the Snowy Trail.* Ill. by Marc Simont. Dell, pap., 1984, ISBN 0-440-46276-2. SERIES: Break-of-Day. SUBJECTS: Mystery and detective stories. RL A.

Busy making a snow detective, Nate the Great and his dog are interrupted by Rosamund and her four cats. Rosamund wants Nate and his dog Sludge to find Nate's lost and very mysterious birthday present. Soft, humorous pencil and wash illustrations are delightful, as is the story.

2997 *Nate the Great and the Sticky Case.* Ill. by Marc Simont. Dell, pap., 1981, ISBN 0-440-46289-4. SERIES: Break-of-Day. SUBJECTS: Dinosaurs — Fiction; Mystery and detective stories. RL A.

After Claude asks him to find his missing stegosaurus stamp, Nate the Great begins searching for clues. During the search Nate learns a lot about the stegosaurus and of course finds the missing stamp. The illustrations, done in ink and wash, capture perfectly the detective and his friends.

2998 *Nate the Great and the Stolen Base.* Ill. by Marc Simont. Random House, 1994, ISBN 0-440-40932-2. SERIES: Nate the Great. SUBJECTS: Mystery and detective stories; Sports — Baseball — Fiction. RL B.

Nate's baseball team cannot practice because second base — Oliver's purple plastic octopus — is missing. As usual, Nate follows the clues and soon has the group playing ball again. Illustrated with Simont's usual delightful sketches with watercolor washes.

2999 *Nate the Great Goes Down in the Dumps*. Ill. by Marc Simont. Random House, pap., 1991, ISBN 0-440-40438-X. SERIES: Break-of-Day. SUBJECTS: Humorous stories; Mystery and detective stories. RL A.

When Rosamond cannot find her empty money box she turns to the inimitable Nate the Great for help. His search takes him to the garbage dump before he realizes just how to find the box. Lots of humor, a challenging mystery, and delightful pencil and wash pictures are sure to attract readers.

3000 *Nate the Great Goes Undercover*. Ill. by Marc Simont. Random House, pap., 1978 , ISBN 0-440-46302-5. SERIES: Break-of-Day. SUBJECTS: Mystery and detective stories. RL B.

Pesky Oliver insists that Nate find out who or what is getting into his garbage cans. Nate does a thorough job and uncovers the numerous culprits, including his own dog, Sludge. Charcoal, pencil, and wash pictures.

3001 *Nate the Great Saves the King of Sweden*. Ill. by Marc Simont. Delacorte, 1997, ISBN 0-385-32120-1. SERIES: Nate the Great. SUBJECTS: Mystery and detective stories; Sweden — Fiction. RL C.

Rosamond has lost her troll doll somewhere while visiting Sweden. She writes to Nate the Great asking him to find it — or she will go to the King of Sweden. With the help of his dog Sludge, Nate figures out exactly where the troll is.

3002 *Nate the Great Stalks Stupidweed*. Ill. by Marc Simont. Dell, pap., 1989, ISBN 0-440-40150-X. SERIES: Break-of-Day. SUBJECTS: Mystery and detective stories. RL B.

Oliver goes to Nate for help in finding his newly adopted and lost weed. With his usual panache Nate recovers it while providing great reading fun. Pencil and watercolor pictures of the familiar cast of characters add to the book's appeal.

3003 *Scarlet Monster Lives Here*. Reissued ed. Ill. by Dennis Kendrick. HarperCollins, 1988, ISBN 0-06-025527-7. SERIES: I Can Read. SUBJECTS: Monsters — Fiction; Moving, household — Fiction; Neighbors — Fiction. RL C.

When Scarlet Monster moves into a new house, she tries hard to make it inviting to her new neighbors and cannot understand why none of them have come to meet her. The ink and wash drawings show a variety of gawky, nonthreatening monsters wanting to be liked by each other.

3004 *Sophie and Gussie*. Ill. by Lillian Hoban. Macmillan, 1973, o.p. SERIES: Ready-to-Read. SUBJECTS: Friendship — Fiction; Squirrels — Fiction. RL C.

Sophie and Gussie's friendship survives misunderstandings and hurt feelings as the two squirrels visit each other, plan a party, and share special moments. The quiet story is illustrated with sketchy ink and wash drawings that are a delight.

3005 *The Story of Bentley Beaver*. Ill. by Lillian Hoban. HarperCollins, 1984, ISBN 0-06-025512-9. SERIES: I Can Read. SUBJECTS: Beavers — Fiction; Family life — Fiction; Old age — Fiction. RL B.

From his birth to loving beaver parents to his quiet death, Bentley Beaver's journey through a long and happy life is gently and affectionately recalled. The sketchy, whimsical animal pictures add to the reader's appreciation of Bentley and his family.

3006 *The Trip and Other Sophie and Gussie Stories*. Ill. by Lillian Hoban. Macmillan, 1976, o.p. SERIES: Ready-to-Read. SUBJECTS: Friendship — Fiction; Humorous stories; Squirrels — Fiction. RL B.

Although close friends Sophie and Gussie, two squirrels, sometimes disagree, they share a special friendship that sees them through occasional difficulties and their own foolish behavior. The sketchy, lighthearted drawings are in pen with gray, green, and yellow washes.

3007 *The Trolls of Twelfth Street*. Ill. by Ben Shecter. Putnam, 1979, o.p. SERIES: Break-of-Day. SUBJECTS: Fantasy; Trolls — Fiction. RL B.

Eldred Troll's curiosity leads the Troll family from their safe and comfortable home beneath the Brooklyn Bridge up to the streets of New York City. Mistaking human rudeness for Troll good behavior gets them into difficulty. The char-

Sharmat, Marjorie W. (cont.)

coal drawings have a rough and hurried but fanciful look.

3008 *Uncle Boris and Maude.* Ill. by Sammis McLean. Doubleday, 1979, o.p. SERIES: Reading on My Own. SUBJECTS: Behavior — Bored — Fiction; Moles — Fiction. RL B.
Maude tries everything to rid Uncle Boris of his apparently incurable boredom until she becomes bored too. Then it is his turn to drag her out of the dumps. The illustrations, done with humorous ink and wash drawings, show two very pleasant moles.

3009 *Who's Afraid of Ernestine?* Ill. by Maxie Chambliss. Putnam, 1986, o.p. SERIES: Break-of-Day. SUBJECTS: Fear — Fiction. RL B.
Afraid of Ernestine, Cecil imagines her as a vampire, a dragon lady, and a devil as he tries to escape her clutches. Finally the two children are forced to work together and Cecil discovers Ernestine is actually very nice. Illustrated with humorous ink and wash drawings.

Sharmat, Marjorie W., and Craig Sharmat

3010 *Nate the Great and the Crunchy Christmas.* Ill. by Marc Simont. Random House, pap., 1996, ISBN 0-440-41299-4. SERIES: Nate the Great. SUBJECTS: Christmas — Fiction; Mystery and detective stories; Pets — Dogs — Fiction. RL B. LEXILE 350L.
Annie's dog Fang can't find the Christmas card from his mother, and Nate has to locate it. With potato pancakes and a try at thinking like a dog, the case is solved.

3011 *Nate the Great and the Musical Note.* Ill. by Marc Simont. Dell, pap., 1991, ISBN 0-440-40466-5. SERIES: Break-of-Day. SUBJECTS: Music and musicians — Fiction; Mystery and detective stories. RL C.
Rosamund leaves Pip a message from his mother — but she has put it into a secret code. Nate the Great has less than an hour to come up with the musical solution to Pip's message. The adventures of the young detective continue to be expertly illustrated in pencil and watercolors.

3012 *Nate the Great and the Tardy Tortoise.* Ill. by Marc Simont. Dell, 1995, ISBN 0-385-32111-2. SERIES: Nate the Great. SUBJECTS: Mystery and detective stories; Turtles — Fiction. RL B. LEXILE 260L.
Nate the Great and Sludge spot a tortoise eating the flowers in their backyard and realize Nate has a new case: finding the tortoise's home. Using Nate's special detective skills, the two track down the tortoise's owner.

Sharmat, Marjorie W., and Mitchell Sharmat

3013 *Nate the Great: San Francisco Detective.* Ill. by Martha Weston. Delacorte, 2000, ISBN 0-385-90000-7. SERIES: Nate the Great. SUBJECTS: Mystery and detective stories. RL C. LEXILE 230L.
On a visit to his cousin Olivia in San Francisco, Nate helps to solve the case of the missing joke book. The story is done in a wonderful style reminiscent of early movie detective stories. The art is in the style of the original illustrator, Marc Simont.

3014 *Nate the Great and the Big Sniff.* Ill. by Martha Weston. Delacorte, 2001, ISBN 0-385-32604-1. SERIES: Nate the Great. SUBJECTS: Mystery and detective stories; Pets — Dogs — Fiction; Stores — Fiction. RL B. LEXILE 110L.
Nate the Great goes into a store to buy his dog Sludge a present, and when he comes out Sludge is gone. With the help of Annie and her dog Fang, he tries to track down Sludge.

3015 *Nate the Great on the Owl Express.* Ill. by Martha Weston. Delacorte, 2003, ISBN 0-385-73078-0. SERIES: Nate the Great. SUBJECTS: Mystery and detective stories; Owls — Fiction; Trains — Fiction. RL C. LEXILE 280L.
As they ride a train to Los Angeles, Nate the Great and his dog Sludge are supposedly bodyguards for his cousin Olivia's owl, Hoot. His cousin surprises him by being not only a very good detective but also a very clever guardian of her owl. Weston's illustrations are done in the style of Marc Simont, the original illustrator of the series.

3016 *Nate the Great Talks Turkey: With Help from Olivia Sharp.* Ill. by Jody Wheeler. Delacorte, 2006, ISBN 0-385-73336-4.

SERIES: Nate the Great. SUBJECTS: Mystery and detective stories; Turkeys — Fiction. RL B. LEXILE 370L.

Claude turns to Nate the Great and his dog Sludge when he finds and then loses a turkey. Later a huge turkey turns up in town, and Nate's cousin Olivia stops in to help him solve the case. The text has the rhythm of an old-fashioned detective yarn and the watercolor and pencil art is fun.

Sharmat, Marjorie W., and Rosalind Weinman

3017 *Nate the Great and the Pillowcase.* Ill. by Marc Simont. Random House, pap., 1995, ISBN 0-440-41015-0. SUBJECTS: Mystery and detective stories. RL B.

Nate the Great, detective, gets a telephone call at two o'clock in the morning from Rosamund. Big Hex, her cat, cannot sleep without his pillowcase; Nate must find it. In typical Nate fashion, the young detective gathers clues and solves the mystery. Expressive and colorful watercolors accompany the text.

Sharmat, Mitchell

3018 *Reddy Rattler and Easy Eagle.* Ill. by Marc Simont. Doubleday, 1979, o.p. SERIES: Reading on My Own. SUBJECTS: Eagles — Fiction; Self-esteem — Fiction; Snakes — Fiction. RL B.

Depressed because nobody seems to like him, Reddy Rattler is helped by his good friend Easy Eagle to find a new career as part of a desert rock band. The expressive ink, wash, and pencil drawings add humor and individualize the characters of the story.

Sharoff, Victor

3019 *The Heart of the Wood.* Ill. by Wallace Tripp. Putnam, 1971, o.p. SERIES: Break-of-Day. SUBJECTS: Historical fiction; Religion — Fiction; Wood carving — Fiction. RL C.

Isaac is torn between obeying the laws of Judaism and not carving animals and keeping his promise to carve a bowl with animals for the duke. The wood he finds enables him to obey the laws of his faith and keep his promise. Realistic ink and wash drawings place the story in medieval times.

Sharp, Paul

3020 *Paul the Pitcher.* Ill. by author. Children's Press, pap., 1984, ISBN 0-516-42064-X. SERIES: Rookie Reader. SUBJECTS: Sports — Baseball — Fiction; Stories in rhyme. RL C.

Paul has great fun pitching, unless the batter gets a hit. He hopes that someday he will be a professional baseball player. The lively, rhyming text uses 38 words and has ink and wash action drawings.

Shaw, Evelyn

3021 *Alligator.* Ill. by Frances Zweifel. HarperCollins, 1972, ISBN 0-06-025556-0. SERIES: Science I Can Read. SUBJECTS: Alligators. RL B.

A female alligator makes a nest, lays eggs, guards them, is nearly killed by hunters, and survives to care for her young. A straightforward, unsentimental account of an interesting animal's life, this book is illustrated with realistic colored pencil drawings.

3022 *Elephant Seal Island.* Ill. by Cherryl Pape. HarperCollins, 1978, o.p. SERIES: Science I Can Read. SUBJECTS: Seals, elephant. RL C.

The behavior and life cycle of elephant seals are explored in this factual, descriptive look at a young bull's birth and growth. The well-done illustrations are detailed and realistic.

3023 *A Fish Out of School.* Ill. by Ralph Carpentier. HarperCollins, 1970, o.p. SERIES: Science I Can Read. SUBJECTS: Fish. RL A.

Focusing on the plight of one fish separated from its school, the author uses a story format to explain how fish live and the dangers they face. Other fish are seen in the realistic watercolor paintings and identified as the little herring swims past them to join a new school.

3024 *A Nest of Wood Ducks.* Ill. by Cherryl Pape. HarperCollins, 1976, o.p. SERIES: Nature I Can Read. SUBJECTS: Ducks. RL B.

Two wood ducks are followed from mating season to the hatching and raising of their ducklings. Solid factual information combines with clear, realistic full-color pencil and watercolor pictures to present an interesting look at the wood duck.

Shaw, Evelyn (cont.)

3025 *Octopus*. Ill. by Ralph Carpentier. HarperCollins, 1971, o.p. SERIES: Science I Can Read. SUBJECTS: Oceans and ocean life; Octopi. RL B.

The life cycle and behavior of this eight-armed mollusk are discussed in such a way that the octopus seems less threatening and far more interesting than usually thought. The realistic illustrations add to the reader's knowledge and appreciation of the animal.

3026 *Sea Otters*. Ill. by Cherryl Pape. HarperCollins, 1980, o.p. SERIES: Nature I Can Read. SUBJECTS: Otters, sea. RL B.

Susan, a scientist, observes two sea otters, Garbo and her pup, Bo. Through Susan's eyes, children learn how this endangered mammal survives the cold Pacific waters, what it eats, and how Garbo trains Bo to be independent. Excellent realistic watercolor paintings.

Shea, George

3027 *First Flight: The Story of Tom Tate and the Wright Brothers*. Ill. by Don Bolognese. HarperCollins, 1997, ISBN 0-06-024503-4. SERIES: I Can Read. SUBJECTS: Aeronautics; Airplanes; Biographies. RL C. LEXILE 460L.

Twelve-year-old Tom Tate, a Kitty Hawk native, meets the Wright brothers in 1900 and is the second person to fly in one of their gliders. As the years pass, Tom and his father are able to help the brothers and are there to see their first successful flight with an engine. Realistic illustrations add to the drama of the true story.

Shecter, Ben

3028 *The Big Stew*. Ill. by author. HarperCollins, 1991, ISBN 0-06-025609-5. SUBJECTS: Cookery — Fiction; Witches — Fiction. RL A.

A couple get carried away adding things to their stew. They are transformed into witches as they add one strange thing after another. Then the stew explodes and all is back to normal. A minimal text counts on the sketchy yet colorful pictures to help tell the story.

3029 *Hester the Jester*. Ill. by author. HarperCollins, 1977, ISBN 0-06-025599-4. SERIES: Early I Can Read. SUBJECTS: Sex roles — Fiction. RL A.

A little girl tries being a jester, a knight, and a king and finally chooses just to be a little girl. The author's seriocomic pictures with ink cross-hatchings show a very self-confident child who manages to convince adults that she can be whatever she wishes.

Sheehan, Angela

3030 *The Duck*. Ill. by Maurice Pledger and Bernard Robinson. Warwick, 1976, o.p. SERIES: A First Look at Nature. SUBJECTS: Ducks. RL C.

This rather lengthy and detailed look at the courtship of mallards and the raising of their ducklings presents factual information in a story format. The very realistic full-color paintings give a clear idea of what the mallard looks like. This book was first published in England.

Sheehan, Cilla

3031 *The Colors That I Am*. Ill. by Glen Elliott. Human Sciences, 1981, o.p. SUBJECTS: Concepts — Colors; Emotions. RL B.

Intent on getting children to express their feelings, Sheehan chooses color as the vehicle for discussion. Emotions are related to colors. Each color is given a full page of text, the facing page contains an abstract painting. Conversational in tone, the text might stimulate discussion among children regarding their feelings.

Shefelman, Janice

3032 *A Mare for Young Wolf*. Ill. by Tom Shefelman. Random House, 1993, o.p. SERIES: Step into Reading. SUBJECTS: Horses — Fiction; Native Americans — Fiction. RL C.

When it is time for him to choose a horse, Young Wolf goes against tradition and asks for a beautiful and smart mare. Although he is laughed at for his choice, the horse and boy are ultimately redeemed when they warn the people of raiders. Colorful paintings depict Native Americans of the plains.

3033 *Young Wolf and Spirit Horse*. Ill. by Tom Shefelman. Random House, 1997, o.p. SERIES: Step into Reading. SUBJECTS: Horses

— Fiction; Native Americans — Fiction. RL C. LEXILE 350L.

When his horse called Red Wind is led away by the wild Spirit Horse, Young Wolf is determined to get her back. Even when an encounter with the stallion tells him that she won't return, Young Wolf continues to hope. The dramatic story is illustrated with watercolor art.

3034 *Young Wolf's First Hunt*. Ill. by Tom Shefelman. Random House, 1995, ISBN 0-679-96364-2. SERIES: Step into Reading. SUBJECTS: Buffalo — Fiction; Native Americans — Fiction. RL C. LEXILE 380L.

Wanting to join in the buffalo hunt, Young Wolf secretly trains himself, another young man, and their horses. No sources are given for the buffalo hunt tradition nor for the rituals of the Native American peoples depicted. The art seems to be generic rather than tied to a specific group of people.

Sherrow, Victoria

3035 *Alexander Graham Bell*. Ill. by Elaine Verstraete. Carolrhoda, 2001, ISBN 1-57505-460-4. SERIES: On My Own Biography. SUBJECTS: Biographies; Inventors and inventions; Telephones. RL C. LEXILE 460L.

Bell was well known as a teacher of the deaf and for his inventions, most notably the telephone. Illustrated with detailed realistic watercolors, and including a chronology and afterword, Bell's biography is carefully written.

3036 *Wilbur Waits*. Ill. by James Watts. HarperCollins, 1990, ISBN 0-06-025483-1. SUBJECTS: Birthdays — Fiction; Friendship — Fiction. RL B.

For his birthday Wilbur gets a sled, a kite, and a boat but the weather does not allow him to use any of them. Finally Wilbur discovers that playing with his friend is just as much fun anyway. Energetic colored pencil and wash pictures illustrate the story.

3037 *Wilma Rudolph*. Ill. by Larry Johnson. Carolrhoda, 2000, ISBN 0-8225-6260-X. SERIES: On My Own Biography. SUBJECTS: African Americans; Biographies; Sports. RL C. LEXILE 490L.

Despite having polio as a 4-year-old, Wilma Rudolph determined to overcome her disability and to run. Years later she won three gold medals at the 1960 Olympics. A page of additional information and a chronology conclude the book. The illustrations are expressive paintings.

Shores, Erika L.

3038 *Caring for Your Cat*. Capstone, 2007, ISBN 0-7368-6384-2. SERIES: First Facts. SUBJECTS: Pet care; Pets — Cats. RL C. LEXILE 680L.

Before a child or family gets a cat as a pet, there are things that everyone needs to know and that a cat needs to have. With full-color photographs, a guide to "decoding" a cat's behavior, glossary, bibliography, Web sites, and index, this book provides the basics for potential cat owners.

Shortall, Leonard

3039 *Just-in-Time Joey*. Ill. by author. Morrow, 1973, o.p. SUBJECTS: Grandparents — Fiction; Trees — Fiction. RL B.

The diseased elm trees on Joey's grandmother's street are being marked with big yellow circles of paint and then cut down. As a prank, one of the boys in the neighborhood sprays Joey's grandmother's healthy tree and Joey is just in time to save it. Illustrated with detailed ink drawings.

3040 *Steve's First Pony Ride*. Ill. by author. Morrow, 1966, o.p. SUBJECTS: Behavior — Responsible — Fiction; Farm and country life — Fiction; Horses — Fiction. RL B.

Steve's neighbor Mr. Turner gets a horse and pony and allows the little boy to help him take care of them. When Steve discovers the animals missing one day, he finds them for Mr. Turner and earns the opportunity to ride the pony. The well-written story is illustrated with realistic paintings.

3041 *Tony's First Dive*. Ill. by author. Morrow, 1972, o.p. SUBJECTS: Fear — Fiction; Self-esteem — Fiction; Sports — Swimming — Fiction. RL B.

Seeing that Tony is afraid of the water, one of the lifeguards at the beach gives him special lessons. He teaches Tony not only to swim but also to dive with a mask and flippers. A good story of

Shortall, Leonard (cont.)

overcoming fear and gaining self-esteem, it is illustrated with attractive ink drawings.

Showers, Paul

3042 *A Baby Starts to Grow*. Ill. by Rosalind Fry. HarperCollins, pap., 1986, ISBN 0-06-445044-9. SERIES: Let's-Read-and-Find-Out. SUBJECTS: Human body — Reproduction. RL B.

Drawings of siblings, mothers, and babies combine with an upbeat text to present a limited picture of how a baby develops from fertilized ovum to birth. This book does not contain information on human sexuality. Illustrations are semirealistic.

3043 *A Drop of Blood*. Ill. by Edward Miller. HarperCollins, 2004, ISBN 0-06-009108-8. SERIES: Let's-Read-and-Find-Out Science. SUBJECTS: Human body — Blood; Human body — Circulation. RL B. LEXILE 480L.

Newly illustrated in bright colors using a Dracula theme, this introduction to the study of human blood contains information on circulation, white and red blood cells, platelets, scab formation, and much more. The final two pages include advice on staying healthy and a brief bibliography.

3044 *Ears Are for Hearing*. Rev. ed. Ill. by Holly Keller. HarperCollins, 1990, ISBN 0-690-04718-5. SERIES: Let's-Read-and-Find-Out Science. SUBJECTS: Human body — Ears; Senses — Hearing. RL B.

Using a brief, clearly written text and simple, childlike ink and watercolor pictures, an explanation is given for the process of hearing. Text and pictures also depict and explain the parts of the ear and their functions.

3045 *Hear Your Heart*. Ill. by Holly Keller. HarperCollins, 2001, ISBN 0-06-025410-6. SERIES: Let's-Read-and-Find-Out Science. SUBJECTS: Human body — Heart; Science and scientists. RL C. LEXILE 500L.

The way in which the heart works is demonstrated through activities children can do on their own or with a friend. The information is carefully written and organized and the artwork consists of simply designed ink and watercolor pictures.

3046 *How Many Teeth?* Rev. ed. Ill. by True Kelley. HarperCollins, 1991, ISBN 0-06-021634-4. SERIES: Let's-Read-and-Find-Out Science. SUBJECTS: Human body — Teeth. RL B.

Through Sam, his baby sister, parents, and friends, readers learn about teeth, the number that children and adults have, and how they are used. Rhyming verses are interspersed to reinforce information. The full-color illustrations attractively augment the text.

3047 *How You Talk*. Rev ed. Ill. by Megan Lloyd. HarperCollins, 1992, ISBN 0-06-022767-2. SERIES: Let's-Read-and-Find-Out Science. SUBJECTS: Human body — Speech. RL B.

Using a conversational tone and a family situation, the book takes a look at how speech occurs, starting with babies and how they learn to make sounds. Lots of activities help to explain how particular sounds are made. Text is illustrated with lively pen and ink drawings with watercolors.

3048 *The Listening Walk*. New ed. Ill. by Aliki. HarperCollins, 1991, ISBN 0-06-021638-7. SUBJECTS: Senses — Hearing; Sound. RL B.

As a little girl, her father, and their dog take a walk they avoid talking and instead listen carefully. They hear a great many sounds: footsteps, sprinklers, bees, a baby crying, and more. Put into a new format, the illustrations are full color, energetic, and enticing.

3049 *Look at Your Eyes*. Rev. ed. Ill. by True Kelley. HarperCollins, 1992, ISBN 0-06-020188-6. SERIES: Let's-Read-and-Find-Out Science. SUBJECTS: Human body — Eyes. RL B.

A little boy uses his observation skills to see how his eyes work. He shows readers how to tell the ways in which eyes can move, how pupils enlarge or grow small, and how eyes are protected by eyebrows and eyelashes. Pen and ink and watercolor pictures add much to this well-done book.

3050 *Me and My Family Tree*. Ill. by Don Madden. HarperCollins, 1978, o.p. SERIES: Let's-Read-and-Find-Out. SUBJECTS: Heredity. RL B.

Parents, grandparents, and even great-great grandparents are seen as a part of a child's heritage in this overview of genetics. Gregor Mendel and his pioneering experiments in genetics are briefly mentioned and explained. The detailed Pentel drawings with orange and gold add appeal.

3051 *No Measles, No Mumps for Me*. Ill. by Harriett Barton. HarperCollins, 1980, ISBN 0-690-04018-0. SERIES: Let's-Read-and-Find-Out. SUBJECTS: Diseases; Vaccination. RL B.

A little boy tells how he will never have to get diseases like measles, mumps, and whooping cough because he has had the shots or drops that vaccinate him against them. The text and the simple, childlike pictures explain the way white cells act to fight bacteria and viruses.

3052 *Sleep Is for Everyone*. Ill. by Wendy Watson. HarperCollins, 1997, ISBN 0-690-01118-0. SERIES: Let's-Read-and-Find-Out Science. SUBJECTS: Biology; Human body; Sleep. RL B. LEXILE 480L.

A discussion of animals' sleep behaviors is followed by a look at humans' need for sleep and what happens when we are deprived of it. Vibrant cut-and-torn-paper collages illustrate this simple overview.

3053 *What Happens to a Hamburger?* Ill. by Edward Miller. HarperCollins, 2001, ISBN 0-06-027947-8. SERIES: Let's-Read-and-Find-Out Science. SUBJECTS: Biology; Human body — Digestion; Science and scientists. RL C. LEXILE 520L.

The story of digestion and the parts of the digestive system are carefully explained and shown. New illustrations are in bright colors and clearly support the text. The new diagram of the human body with the digestive system colorfully highlighted will attract the attention of young readers. Two activities further help to explain the workings of digestion.

3054 *Where Does the Garbage Go?* Rev ed. Ill. by Randy Chewning. HarperCollins, pap., 1994, ISBN 0-06-445114-3. SERIES: Let's-Read-and-Find-Out Science. SUBJECTS: Conservation; Garbage and garbage disposal; Recycling. RL C.

At school a class is learning about garbage and its disposal, and the need for recycling. Readers learn about landfills, waste incinerators, and recycling plants. Very well written and supported with detailed ink and watercolor pictures, this book provides good general information.

3055 *You Can't Make a Move Without Your Muscles*. Ill. by Harriett Barton. HarperCollins, 1982, o.p. SERIES: Let's-Read-and-Find-Out. SUBJECTS: Human body — Muscles. RL C.

As they learn about the kinds of muscles and their functions, children are encouraged to take part in activities that help them understand and feel how their muscles work. The text is illustrated with very simple childlike pictures, some in color.

3056 *Your Skin and Mine*. Rev. ed. Ill. by Kathleen Kuchera. HarperCollins, 1991, ISBN 0-06-022522-X. SERIES: Let's-Read-and-Find-Out Science. SUBJECTS: Human body — Skin. RL C.

A little boy discusses his skin and what it is made of, how it works to protect the body, and how melanin makes the color of skin and can help to prevent some burning from the sun. The updated text and full-color illustrations are even more appealing than in the first edition.

Showers, Paul, and Kay S. Showers

3057 *Before You Were a Baby*. Ill. by Ingrid Fetz. HarperCollins, 1968, ISBN 0-690-12882-7. SERIES: Let's-Read-and-Find-Out Science. SUBJECTS: Human body — Reproduction. RL B.

Accurate but not explicit information on human reproduction is provided through a brief text and ink and colored pencil diagrams and drawings. Any children reading this may be inspired to seek more information from other books or from their parents.

Shub, Elizabeth

3058 *Clever Kate*. Ill. by Anita Lobel. Macmillan, 1973, o.p. SERIES: Ready-to-Read. SUBJECTS: Folklore — Germany; Humorous stories. RL B.

The farmer's bride is a kindhearted simpleton who lets peddlers steal their gold. Her foolishness ultimately helps her husband to retrieve it. A well-known humorous German folktale, this version maintains the wit and charm of the Grimms' original. The detailed ink and wash drawings have a folk look.

3059 *Seeing Is Believing*. Ill. by Rachel Isadora. Greenwillow, 1979, ISBN 0-688-13647-8.

Shub, Elizabeth (cont.)

SUBJECTS: Folklore — England; Folklore — Ireland; Leprechauns. RL B.

New readers will be entranced by the new cover and larger format of these superb retellings of two folktales. In the first, Tom is tricked by a leprechaun; in the second, he makes his way home in spite of pixies. The detailed pen and ink drawings are sure to capture the attention of children.

3060 *The White Stallion*. Ill. by Rachel Isadora. Random House, pap., 1997, ISBN 0-440-91308-X. SERIES: Read-Alone. SUBJECTS: Frontier and pioneer life — Fiction; Horses — Fiction; Western stories. RL B.

Gretchen's grandmother tells her how her great-great-grandmother Gretchen was rescued by a beautiful white stallion on her family's journey west in 1845. A lovely and exciting story, it is illustrated with remarkable ink drawings using cross-hatchings and pointillism.

Sierra, Judy

3061 *Coco and Cavendish: Fire Dogs*. Ill. by Paul Meisel. Random House, 2004, o.p. SERIES: Step into Reading. SUBJECTS: Fire fighters and fire fighting — Fiction; Pets — Dogs — Fiction; Robots — Fiction. RL B.

Although two robot dogs try to cheat their way into jobs as fire dogs, real dogs Coco and Cavendish prove how important they can be when there is a fire. The illustrations are childlike paintings in full color.

Silbaugh, Elizabeth

3062 *Let's Play Cards! A First Book of Card Games*. Ill. by Jef Kaminsky. Simon & Schuster, 1996, o.p. SERIES: Ready-to-Read. SUBJECTS: Games. RL C.

With assistance from the "card shark" and humorous watercolor and ink paintings, children get instructions for playing the card games War, Go Fish, Concentration, Crazy Eights, and Clock Solitaire.

Silly Stories to Tickle Your Funny Bone

3063 *Silly Stories to Tickle Your Funny Bone*. Ill. by James Marshall, Arnold Lobel, et al. North-South Books, 2000, o.p. SERIES: Reading Rainbow Readers. SUBJECTS: Humorous stories; Poetry. RL B.

Excerpts from eight familiar children's books introduce young readers to well-known poetry and stories, including *Fox on the Job, Dragon Gets By*, and *Poppleton Forever*. All are illustrated with art from the original books.

Silver, Jody

3064 *Rupert, Polly, and Daisy*. Parents Magazine Press, 1984, ISBN 0-8193-1124-3. SERIES: Parents Magazine Read Aloud Original. SUBJECTS: Friendship — Fiction; Parrots — Fiction; Pets — Fish — Fiction. RL B.

When goldfish Daisy comes to live with parrot Polly and goat Rupert, everyone is amazed at how talented she is. Hurt and jealous, Polly tries to fly away from home. Rupert finds the perfect way to convince her to return. Though slightly flat in tone, this still manages to be a book that will inspire some conversation.

Silverman, Erica

3065 *Cowgirl Kate and Cocoa*. Ill. by Betsy Lewin. Harcourt, 2005, ISBN 0-15-202124-8. SUBJECTS: Cowgirls — Fiction; Horses — Fiction. RL C. LEXILE 400L.

In separate chapters, Kate tells her always hungry cowhorse Cocoa the story of how she found him, gets his help in counting the herd, gives him a special surprise, and tries to get a good night's sleep in the barn with him. Lewin's art is full of humor and fun.

3066 *Cowgirl Kate and Cocoa: Partners*. Ill. by Betsy Lewin. Harcourt, pap., 2006, ISBN 0-15-206010-3. SERIES: Cowgirl Kate and Cocoa. SUBJECTS: Cowgirls — Fiction; Cows — Fiction; Horses — Fiction. RL B. LEXILE 390L.

Cowgirl Kate and her horse Cocoa do everything together. They look for lost calves, practice roping, play hide and seek, and even end up in the river together. Lively and humorous watercolor and ink pictures work well with the text.

Silverman, Maida

3067 *Dinosaur Babies.* Ill. by Carol Inouye. Simon & Schuster, 1988, o.p. SUBJECTS: Dinosaurs; Prehistoric animals. RL C.
After a good introduction that attempts to differentiate between facts and speculation, Silverman presents theories about the behavior and rearing of the young of nine dinosaurs. The text is easily understood and interesting. Attractive detailed pictures do not always interpret the text well.

Silverman, Martin

3068 *My Tooth Is Loose!* Ill. by Amy Aitken. Viking, 1991, o.p. SERIES: Hello Reading. SUBJECTS: Human body — Teeth — Fiction. RL A.
Georgie has a loose tooth and does not know what to do. Each of his friends has advice that does nothing but scare him. Finally his mother advises that he just wait — and he does. The book, illustrated with watercolors, successfully captures the feelings of a timid child.

Simon, Charnan

3069 *A Busy Guy.* Ill. by Joan Holub. Children's Press, 1998, ISBN 0-516-20396-7. SERIES: Rookie Reader. SUBJECTS: Concepts — Time; Days — Fiction. RL B. LEXILE 440L.
Every day of the week Daniel finds something new to do — usually causing problems for members of his family. On Sunday he finally rests. Watercolor and ink pictures capture the energy of the story.

3070 *Come! Sit! Speak!* Ill. by Bari Weissman. Children's Press, 1997, ISBN 0-516-20397-5. SERIES: Rookie Reader. SUBJECTS: Babies — Fiction; Pets — Dogs — Fiction. RL B.
When she gets a new baby sister instead of a puppy, Ariel starts teaching her the way she would a dog. When the baby learns to talk, her first words are "I want a puppy." Cartoon-like watercolors illustrate the very brief story.

3071 *The Good Bad Day.* Ill. by Dorothy Handelman. Millbrook, 1998, ISBN 0-7613-2017-2. SERIES: Real Kids Readers. SUBJECTS: Illness — Fiction. RL B. LEXILE BR.
Pam does not like being sick. She misses her friend. Nothing is going well. After a nap, things start to get better. The book is illustrated with photographic silhouettes in full color.

3072 *Guard the House, Sam!* Ill. by Gary Bialke. Children's Press, 1998, ISBN 0-516-20796-2. SERIES: Rookie Reader. SUBJECTS: Pets — Dogs — Fiction; Pets — Fiction. RL A. LEXILE 320L.
Sam the dog is left to guard the house while Rosie goes shopping. The humorous illustrations tell the story of how Sam tears up the house as he attempts to guard it.

3073 *I Like to Win!* Ill. by Dorothy Handelman. Millbrook, pap., 1999, ISBN 0-7613-2087-3. SERIES: Real Kids Readers. SUBJECTS: Siblings — Fiction; Sportsmanship — Fiction; Stories in rhyme. RL A. LEXILE BR.
A big sister who is always determined to win soon finds that her little brother does not want to play with her. Big sister sets some new rules and the two play together again. The book is illustrated with full-color photographic silhouettes.

3074 *I've Lost My Hat.* Ill. by Rick Stromoski. Children's Press, 2007, ISBN 0-531-12088-0. SERIES: Rookie Reader. SUBJECTS: English language — Prepositions; Hats — Fiction; Stories in rhyme. RL A.
A little boy tries to recall all the places he had his hat as he searches the house for it. Prepositions are incorporated into the text and with adult help could easily be identified. The illustrations are humorous and done in a cartoon-like style.

3075 *Mud!* Ill. by Dorothy Handelman. Millbrook, 1999, ISBN 0-7613-2051-2. SERIES: Real Kids Readers. SUBJECTS: Play — Fiction; Stories in rhyme. RL A. LEXILE BR.
Though the grass is wet, the sun is out and it is a perfect day to play with friends — in the mud. The rhyming text and photographic silhouettes of three boys will appeal to young readers.

3076 *One Happy Classroom.* Ill. by Rebecca Thornburgh. Children's Press, 1997, ISBN 0-516-20318-5. SERIES: Rookie Reader. SUBJECTS: Mathematics; Numbers; School stories. RL A.
The children in a kindergarten classroom are doing all kinds of things, and the text challenges young readers to find particular numbers of things that are happening. The watercolor pictures are

Simon, Charnan (cont.)

humorous yet offer a good picture of a kindergarten classroom.

3077 *Pumpkin Fever*. Ill. by Jan Bryan-Hunt. Children's Press, 2007, ISBN 0-531-12086-4. SERIES: Rookie Reader. SUBJECTS: Concepts — Shape — Fiction; Family life — Fiction; Pumpkins — Fiction. RL B.

After going to a square field and selecting round pumpkins, a family carves its jack-o-lantern and mom makes a pumpkin pie. Vibrant collage pictures effectively illustrate the story.

3078 *Sam and Dasher*. Ill. by Gary Bialke. Children's Press, 1997, ISBN 0-516-20702-4. SERIES: Rookie Reader. SUBJECTS: Neighbors — Fiction; Pets — Dogs — Fiction. RL A. LEXILE 200L.

Best friends and lively dogs, Sam and Dasher are neighbors. They have so much fun playing with each other that Sam's human friend Rosie has a hard time keeping the screen door intact.

3079 *Sam's Pet*. Ill. by Gary Bialke. Children's Press, 1999, ISBN 0-516-21200-1. SERIES: Rookie Reader. SUBJECTS: Friendship — Fiction; Pets — Cats — Fiction; Pets — Dogs — Fiction. RL B.

Kitten Mabel steals Sam's food and his toys, and even scratches. But when Butch, a big bully of a dog, steals Sam's bone, the little cat knows just how to get it back. Full pages of watercolor art humorously illustrate the slight story.

3080 *Show-and-Tell Sam*. Ill. by Gary Bialke. Children's Press, 1998, ISBN 0-516-20945-0. SERIES: Rookie Reader. SUBJECTS: Pets — Dogs — Fiction; School stories. RL B. LEXILE 240L.

Sam is a rambunctious dog who approaches going to school with Rosie with great enthusiasm. While the text is positive in describing Sam's behavior, the pictures tell a different and very humorous story.

3081 *Surprise*. Ill. by Dorothy Handelman. Millbrook, 1999, ISBN 0-7613-2068-7. SERIES: Real Kids Readers. SUBJECTS: Birthdays — Fiction; Mothers — Fiction; Siblings — Fiction. RL B. LEXILE BR.

With dad out of town, two brothers decide to surprise their mother with some very special birthday treats. Photographs illustrate the story.

3082 *Wash Day*. Ill. by Dorothy Handelman. Millbrook, 1999, o.p. SERIES: Real Kids Readers. SUBJECTS: Cleanliness — Fiction; Housekeeping — Fiction; Stories in rhyme. RL A. LEXILE BR.

While dad takes a nap, two brothers wash the dishes, their toys, the walls — everything they see. A surprised dad wakes up to discover their work. Color photographs illustrate the story.

Simon, Norma

3083 *Why Am I Different?* Ill. by Dora Leder. Whitman, 1976, ISBN 0-8075-9074-6. SERIES: Concept Books. SUBJECTS: Family life; Self-esteem. RL B.

The ways that children and their families can differ from each other are presented from many children's perspectives, one per page. The overriding theme of the book is that it is okay to be different — everyone is. The full-page drawings are in black and yellow.

Simon, Seymour

3084 *Finding Out with Your Senses*. Ill. by Emily A. McCully. McGraw-Hill, 1971, o.p. SERIES: Let's-Try-It-Out. SUBJECTS: Science experiments; Senses. RL C.

A thoughtful text calls attention to many things in daily life that are experienced through the senses. Very simple experiments also help readers to appreciate sight, touch, hearing, taste, and smell. Well written, it has attractive black, gray, and blue drawings.

3085 *Soap Bubble Magic*. Ill. by Stella Ormai. Lothrop, 1985, o.p. SUBJECTS: Science experiments; Science experiments — Soap bubbles. RL C.

The "magic" of bubbles is explained in easily understood terms. Children are encouraged to experiment with soap and water to understand how surface tension and soap film can entrap air in a bubble. The realistic, three-color drawings are lively and enticing.

Sims, Lesley

3086 *Exploring Space*. Ill. by Jamie Medlin. Raintree, pap., 1995 , ISBN 0-8114-4947-5. SERIES: First Starts. SUBJECTS: Space travel. RL C.

A brief overview of space travel and the means by which man has attempted to explore space are included here. An attractive layout of color paintings and photographs augments the text. Glossary is included.

3087 *The Moon*. Ill. by Michael Lye. Raintree, pap., 1995, ISBN 0-8114-4924-6. SERIES: First Starts. SUBJECTS: Astronomy and astronomers; Space travel. RL C.

A brief look at the moon as a satellite of the earth and also as the site for space travel and exploration, this book has an attractive format with a good blend of paintings and photographs. Index and glossary are included.

3088 *The Sun and Stars*. Ill. by Ian Thompson. Raintree, pap., 1995, ISBN 0-8114-4946-7. SERIES: First Starts. SUBJECTS: Astronomy and astronomers. RL C.

Stars, supernovas, light, galaxies, constellations, and so on are given brief explanatory comments. The book is attractively illustrated with color photographs and paintings. Index and glossary are included.

Singer, Bill

3089 *The Fox with Cold Feet*. Ill. by Dennis Kendrick. Parents Magazine Press, 1980, ISBN 0-8193-1021-2. SERIES: Read Aloud Originals. SUBJECTS: Animals — Fiction; Foxes — Fiction; Humorous stories. RL B.

On a cold winter day, a sparrow tells fox that he needs boots to keep his feet warm. First sparrow, then beaver, then raccoon, trick fox into helping them in exchange for useless "boots." The silly story has broad enough humor to attract young readers. It is illustrated with heavily outlined paintings.

Sipiera, Diane M., and Paul P. Sipiera

3090 *Constellations*. Children's Press, 1997, ISBN 0-516-20331-2. SERIES: True Book. SUBJECTS: Astronomy and astronomers; Stars. RL C. LEXILE 760L.

Humans' ability to use the position of stars in the sky to tell the time of year and to navigate, as well as the stories inspired by groups of stars, are clearly explained here. The authors also offer a guide to identifying some constellations and explain why they are not visible during the day. A glossary; lists of books, Web sites, and organizations; an index; and many illustrations complete the book.

3091 *The Hubble Space Telescope*. Children's Press, 1997, o.p. SERIES: True Book. SUBJECTS: Astronomy and astronomers; Telescopes. RL C. LEXILE 890L.

After covering the development of the telescope and its use by astronomers, this book focuses on the creation of the Hubble Space Telescope and its observations as it orbits the earth. Sidebars of extra information; colorful photographs from the Hubble; a glossary; lists of books, organizations, and Web sites; and an index complete the book.

3092 *Project Gemini*. Children's Press, pap., 1997, ISBN 0-516-26274-2. SERIES: True Book. SUBJECTS: Space travel. RL C. LEXILE 830L.

President Kennedy challenged NASA to get a man on the moon before 1970. To do that NASA had three projects: Mercury, Gemini, and Apollo. Gemini allowed astronauts to pilot a spacecraft, walk in space, and dock with another ship. The photographs and text provide excellent information on a project that led to landing on the moon. The book also has a bibliography, list of space-related groups, Web sites, a glossary, and an index.

Sipiera, Paul P.

3093 *Earthquakes*. Children's Press, 1998, ISBN 0-516-20665-6. SERIES: True Book. SUBJECTS: Earthquakes; Geology and geologists. RL C.

Readers learn basic information about the layers of the earth, the plates that cover it, what causes earthquakes, and how scientists describe and predict them. Two pages of earthquake facts, a table of contents, a bibliography, online sites, a glossary, and an index are also included

3094 *I Can Be a Biologist*. Ill. with photos. Childrens Press, 1992, o.p. SERIES: I Can Be.

Sipiera, Paul P. (cont.)

SUBJECTS: Biology; Careers; Science and scientists. RL C.

The amount of education and hard work involved in becoming a biologist are weighed against the satisfaction of a career devoted to working with or for animals and humans. The color photographs show a variety of individuals and their work. The book has an index and a glossary.

3095 *I Can Be a Chemist*. Ill. with photos. Childrens Press, 1992, o.p. SERIES: I Can Be. SUBJECTS: Careers; Chemistry and chemists; Science and scientists. RL C.

Biochemistry, pharmacy, and environmental chemistry are just a few of the fields in which an individual interested in chemistry can work. The great variety of occupations makes the area inviting. Illustrated with color photographs, the book also has a glossary and an index.

3096 *I Can Be a Geologist*. Ill. with photos. Childrens Press, 1986, o.p. SERIES: I Can Be. SUBJECTS: Careers; Geology and geologists; Science and scientists. RL C.

Using color photographs and large, well-spaced type, the author explains the training and work required of those entering the field of geology. The great diversity of work within the field is also explored. Index and glossary are included.

3097 *I Can Be a Physicist*. Ill. with photos. Childrens Press, 1991, o.p. SERIES: I Can Be. SUBJECTS: Careers; Physics and physicists; Science and scientists. RL C.

For individuals interested in science and mathematics, the study of physics is presented as a fascinating and exciting career area with great possibilities for making discoveries. Illustrated with color photographs, the book includes an index and a glossary.

3098 *I Can Be an Astronomer*. Ill. with photos. Childrens Press, 1986, o.p. SERIES: I Can Be. SUBJECTS: Astronomy and astronomers; Careers. RL C.

The many ways astronomers help mankind — through development of calendars, predicting eclipses, and so on — as well as the satisfaction of studying the stars and planets are part of this introductory look at astronomy as a career. Color photographs accent the text as do an index and a glossary.

3099 *I Can Be an Oceanographer*. Ill. with photos. Childrens Press, 1987, o.p. SERIES: I Can Be. SUBJECTS: Careers; Oceans and ocean life. RL C.

Measuring tides, observing animal life, studying minerals in the depths of the oceans — individuals interested in the sea have a great many careers to choose from. Color photographs supplement the useful text. Index and glossary are appended.

Sipiera, Paul P., and Diane M. Sipiera

3100 *Seasons*. Children's Press, pap., 1998, ISBN 0-516-26439-7. SERIES: True Book. SUBJECTS: Concepts — Time; Seasons; Weather. RL C.

Tying the seasons into the measurement of time and weather makes the concept clearer. This book offers examples of ancient methods of telling time, color photographs; diagrams; lists of books, organizations, and Web sites; a glossary; and an index.

3101 *Thunderstorms*. Children's Press, pap., 1998, ISBN 0-516-26442-7. SERIES: True Book. SUBJECTS: Weather; Weather — Rain; Weather — Storms. RL C. LEXILE 680L.

Through color photographs, diagrams, and careful writing, the authors explain how thunderstorms develop. The information is further supplemented by a glossary, an index, and lists of books, Web sites, and organizations.

Siracusa, Catherine

3102 *The Banana Split from Outer Space*. Hyperion, 1995, ISBN 0-7868-0040-2. SERIES: Hyperion Chapters. SUBJECTS: Ice cream — Fiction; Science fiction; UFOs — Fiction. RL B. LEXILE 330L.

When a new highway is built, Stanley loses his ice cream store customers. Suddenly the store is hit by a spaceship driven by Zelmo, a Martian ice cream maker, and good things start to happen. The book is illustrated with humorous black-and-white art.

3103 *Bingo, the Best Dog in the World*. Ill. by Sidney Levitt. HarperCollins, 1991, o.p. SERIES: I Can Read. SUBJECTS: Pets — Dogs — Fiction; Siblings — Fiction. RL B.

Sam and her brother Stuart, wanting to give their dog a bath, trap her with too many dog treats. By the time they get her to the school dog show, Bingo has eaten so much that she just wants to sleep. Very childlike pen and ink drawings with watercolors add to the fun of the text.

3104 *The Giant Zucchini*. Ill. by author. Hyperion, 1993, ISBN 1-56282-286-1. SUBJECTS: Animals — Fiction; Fairs — Fiction; Zucchini — Fiction. RL B.

Two animal friends plant one giant zucchini seed and end up with one very tiny zucchini — until they start singing to it. Then it grows big enough to be guaranteed a prize at the fair, unless Humphrey Hog gets the better of them. Illustrated with humorous cartoon-like paintings.

3105 *No Mail for Mitchell*. Ill. by author. Random House, 1990, o.p. SERIES: Step into Reading. SUBJECTS: Friendship — Fiction; Mail — Fiction. RL B.

Mitchell, a dog, is a good mailman to the animal community but he wishes someone would send him mail. When he gets sick and someone else has to deliver the mail, he gets his wish: a whole bag full of get-well notes. Well done pictures with child appeal illustrate the story.

3106 *The Parrot Problem*. Ill. by author. Hyperion, 1994, ISBN 1-56282-626-3. SUBJECTS: Birds — Fiction; Humorous stories; Parrots — Fiction. RL B.

While her aunt takes a nap, Gina takes her parrot, Pepperoni, outside, lets him out of the cage, and ends up chasing him through town as he creates one near disaster after another. The bright, attractive art uses a variety of media.

3107 *The Peanut Butter Gang*. Hyperion, 1996, ISBN 0-7868-2300-3. SERIES: Hyperion Chapters. SUBJECTS: Bells — Fiction; Mystery and detective stories; Rabbits — Fiction. RL C. LEXILE 390L.

The doorbells from the Dingdong Doorbell Factory are not working. Billy, a rabbit and the chief doorbell tester, saves the day by discovering that a gang of squirrels has been filling the doorbells with peanut butter. Black-and-white pencil and wash illustrations add a bit of excitement.

Sislowitz, Marcel

3108 *Look! How Your Eyes See*. Ill. by Jim Arnosky. Putnam, 1977, o.p. SERIES: Science Is What and Why. SUBJECTS: Human body — Eyes. RL B.

Detailed information is provided on the various parts of the eye with clear explanations of how each works. The section on eye care and visual problems suggests seeing an ophthalmologist for treatment. A page on eye care, a glossary, and a brief index are included. Amusing ink drawings help clarify the text.

Sitomer, Mindel, and Harry Sitomer

3109 *Circles*. Ill. by George Giusti. HarperCollins, 1973, ISBN 0-690-00206-8. SERIES: Young Math. SUBJECTS: Mathematics. RL C.

Exercises using compass, ruler, and paper introduce the young reader to some of the terminology (radius, diameter) of circles and to many of their properties. Diagrams show the concepts and present a number of attractive geometric designs based on the circle.

Skinner, Daphne

3110 *Almost Invisible Irene*. Ill. by Jerry Smath. Kane, pap., 2003, ISBN 1-57565-129-7. SERIES: Science Solves It! SUBJECTS: Animals — Camouflage — Fiction; Behavior — Shyness — Fiction; School stories. RL B.

Irene is so shy that when the class learns about camouflage, she decides to try it for a week. She is so successful that she does her science report on the subject. Sidebars of additional information, as well as a page on thinking scientifically, extend the story.

3111 *Henry Keeps Score*. Ill. by Page Eastburn O'Rourke. Kane, pap., 2001, ISBN 1-57565-102-5. SERIES: Math Matters. SUBJECTS: Mathematics — Fiction; Sibling rivalry — Fiction; Siblings — Fiction. RL B.

Henry compares everything his sister Harriet gets to what he gets. Keeping score is important until they go to the dentist and Harriet has a cavity. Cartoon-like ink and watercolor art illustrates the book.

Sklansky, Amy E.

3112 *Where Do Chicks Come From?* Ill. by Pam Paparone. HarperCollins, 2005, ISBN 0-06-028892-2. SERIES: Let's-Read-and-

Sklansky, Amy E. (cont.)

Find-Out Science. SUBJECTS: Chickens; Chickens — Life cycles; Eggs. RL B. LEXILE AD640L.

With just the right amount of detail and information, young readers learn about how a chicken grows in an egg and hatches. Illustrations match the text perfectly and are done in carefully crafted watercolors.

Skofield, James

3113 *Detective Dinosaur*. Ill. by R. W. Alley. HarperCollins, 1996, ISBN 0-06-024908-0. SERIES: I Can Read. SUBJECTS: Dinosaurs — Fiction; Humorous stories; Mystery and detective stories. RL B. LEXILE 330L.

Bumbling Detective Dinosaur and his able assistant Officer Pterodactyl solve three silly and very simple mysteries. The text (including a pronunciation guide to dinosaur names) is clever, funny, and ably supported by Alley's watercolor art.

3114 *Detective Dinosaur Lost and Found*. Ill. by R. W. Alley. HarperCollins, pap., 1998, ISBN 0-06-444257-8. SERIES: I Can Read. SUBJECTS: Dinosaurs — Fiction; Mystery and detective stories. RL B. LEXILE 260L.

In three chapters, Detective Dinosaur and Officer Pterodactyl solve the cases of the missing baby Apatosaurus, the homeless kitten, and fogbound Detective Dinosaur. Humorous drawings and text will attract young dinosaur fans.

Skurzynski, Gloria

3115 *Honest Andrew*. Ill. by David Wiesner. Harcourt, 1980, o.p. SERIES: Let Me Read. SUBJECTS: Behavior — Honest — Fiction; Behavior — Manners — Fiction; Otters — Fiction. RL C.

Andrew, a young otter, tries hard to keep his word to his father and always tell the truth. Unfortunately, telling the truth can sometimes conflict with good manners and Andrew's honesty gets him into trouble. The humorous story is illustrated with skillful, realistic drawings.

Slater, Teddy

3116 *Animal Hide-and-Seek*. Ill. by Donna Braginetz. Gareth Stevens, 1997, ISBN 0-8368-1760-5. SERIES: Bank Street Ready-to-Read. SUBJECTS: Animals; Animals — Camouflage. RL B. LEXILE 590L.

Never using the word camouflage, this book nevertheless introduces the concept to young readers as they try to spot animals among the illustrations. The text encourages an interactive approach and the illustrations are detailed and realistic.

3117 *The Bunny Hop*. Ill. by Larry Di Fiori. Cartwheel, pap., 1992, ISBN 0-590-45354-8. SERIES: Scholastic Reader. SUBJECTS: Dancers and dancing — Fiction; Numbers — Fiction; Rabbits — Fiction. RL B. LEXILE 210L.

Buddy's feet are so big that the girl bunnies refuse to dance with him until he learns to lead the bunny hop. Along with the rhythmic bunny hop, readers will count the bunnies from one to ten. The illustrations show big-eyed bunnies with small feet and colorful clothing.

3118 *Busy Bunnies' Five Senses*. Ill. by Maggie Swanson. Scholastic, pap., 1999, ISBN 0-439-09910-2. SERIES: Hello Reader! SUBJECTS: Rabbits — Fiction; Senses — Fiction; Stories in rhyme. RL B. LEXILE BR.

A group of bunnies takes the reader through all five senses. Whether it is tasting something sweet or smelling something bad, the bunnies, illustrated in watercolors and pencil, sweetly demonstrate each.

3119 *Max's Money*. Ill. by Anthony Lewis. Scholastic, pap., 1998, ISBN 0-590-12010-7. SERIES: Hello Math Reader! SUBJECTS: Birthdays — Fiction; Mathematics — Fiction; Money — Fiction. RL C. LEXILE AD420L.

With his mother's birthday a week away, Max needs money for her present. First he tries to borrow money and then he tries to earn it. Finally, he takes the money he has saved and buys the perfect present. Activities for counting money are included in the text and at the end of the book.

3120 *N-O Spells No!* Ill. by Meredith Johnson. Scholastic, pap., 1993, ISBN 0-590-44186-8. SERIES: Hello Reader! SUBJECTS: Behavior — Argumentative — Fiction; Parent and child — Fiction; Stories in rhyme. RL B.

Katie is determined to do the opposite of anything her mother suggests — even when her mother attempts to bribe her with ice cream and a puppy. Finally Mom learns the power of reverse psychology. The pictures show an obnoxious child exhibiting behavior much too young for her age. Illustrations are ink and watercolor.

3121 *. . . 98, 99, 100! Ready or Not, Here I Come!* Ill. by Gioia Fiammenghi. Scholastic, pap., 1999, ISBN 0-590-12009-3. SERIES: Hello Reader! SUBJECTS: Games — Fiction; Numbers — Fiction. RL B.

While they wait for little sister Maggie to slowly count to 100, three girls try different ways to count: by fives, by tens, and by twenties. At the end of the book are activities for gaining proficiency in counting.

3122 *Stay in Line.* Ill. by Gioia Fiammenghi. Scholastic, pap., 1996, ISBN 0-590-22713-0. SERIES: Hello Math Reader! SUBJECTS: Arithmetic — Fiction; School stories; Zoos — Fiction. RL B. LEXILE 470L.

Twelve children and their teacher go on a field trip to the zoo. Told to stay in line, they creatively group in twos, threes, fours, sixes, and so forth. The rhyming text is at times forced but the art is humorous and will hold the attention of young readers.

3123 *Who's Afraid of the Big, Bad Bully?* Ill. by Pat Porter. Scholastic, 1995, o.p. SERIES: Hello Reader! SUBJECTS: Behavior — Bullying — Fiction; Pets — Dogs — Fiction; School stories. RL C. LEXILE 480L.

Everyone at school is afraid of Bertha, and Max is especially frightened of her. Even taking karate lessons doesn't help Max. But when he gets a puppy and Bertha demands to have it, Max gets the courage to say "no," inspiring the other children to stand up to the bully.

3124 *The Wrong-Way Rabbit.* Ill. by Diane de Groat. Scholastic, pap., 1993, ISBN 0-590-45359-9. SERIES: Hello Reader! SUBJECTS: Behavior — Fiction; Rabbits — Fiction; Stories in rhyme. RL B.

Tibbar Jack does everything backward-counting, bathing with his clothes on, putting his socks on his ears, and so on. The silly rhyming story has obvious humor suited to young readers and is illustrated with comical watercolors.

Slater, Teddy, adapter

3125 *The Littles and the Big Blizzard.* Ill. by Jacqueline Rogers. Scholastic, pap., 2001, ISBN 0-439-20303-1. SERIES: Littles First Readers. SUBJECTS: Babies — Fiction; Blizzards — Fiction; Fantasy. RL B. LEXILE 170L.

A new baby is due to arrive any time and the Littles are hoping that Aunt Lily, a nurse, will arrive soon. But a blizzard is raging and Aunt Lily falls out of her son's glider and the Littles, small as mice, must go out to rescue her.

3126 *The Littles and the Scary Halloween.* Ill. by Jacqueline Rogers. Scholastic, pap., 2001, o.p. SERIES: Littles First Readers. SUBJECTS: Fantasy; Halloween — Fiction. RL B. LEXILE 240L.

Determined to find an idea for a very scary Halloween costume, the very tiny Tom and Lucy take their tin-can elevator up to the attic. There Lucy gets caught in a spider's web and Tom must save her. Trying to get home again, the two take refuge in a jack-o-lantern.

3127 *The Littles and the Secret Letter.* Ill. by Jacqueline Rogers. Scholastic, 2001, o.p. SERIES: Littles First Readers. SUBJECTS: Birthdays — Fiction; Fantasy; Siblings — Fiction. RL B. LEXILE 270L.

With only her brother for a friend, Lucy longs to make contact with one of the very large human children in the house. Forgetting how dangerous that could be, she sends a letter. It is up to her brother to retrieve the letter and to keep their existence a secret.

3128 *The Littles Do Their Homework.* Ill. by Jacqueline Rogers. Scholastic, 2002, o.p. SERIES: Littles First Readers. SUBJECTS: Fantasy; Homework — Fiction; School stories. RL B. LEXILE 180L.

Assigned a science report about animals, Tom and Lucy Little (so small that they and their family live in the walls of a house) decide to steal an egg from the very large and frightening chickens. Adapted from the longer books for more accomplished readers, the story is illustrated with watercolors.

3129 *The Littles Go on a Hike.* Ill. by Jacqueline Rogers. Scholastic, pap., 2002, ISBN 0-439-31718-5. SERIES: Littles First

Slater, Teddy, adapter (cont.)

Readers. SUBJECTS: Adventure stories; Fantasy. RL B. LEXILE 300L.
Determined to visit her penpal, who lives a whole block away, Lucy's Cousin Dinky decides to take most of the family on the dangerous hike to Tina's house.

3130 *The Littles Make a Friend*. Ill. by Jacqueline Rogers. Scholastic, pap., 2000, ISBN 0-439-20301-5. SERIES: Littles First Readers. SUBJECTS: Fantasy; Pets — Cats — Fiction. RL B. LEXILE 180L.
When the Biggs go on vacation, a new and very messy family stays in their house. When a cat is brought in to catch the mice, the diminutive Littles have to find a way to tame the very large (to them) feline.

Slaughter, Hope

3131 *Buckley and Wilberta*. Ill. by Susan Torrence. Red Hen, 1996, ISBN 0-931093-15-5. SUBJECTS: Friendship — Fiction; Hedgehogs — Fiction; Rabbits — Fiction. RL B.
Best friends Buckley, a hedgehog, and Wilberta, a rabbit, share three stories. In the first, Buckley is awaiting Wilberta's return from a visit; in the second, he is selecting a present for her birthday; and in the third, he realizes that winter would be less lonely if she shared his house.

Sleator, William

3132 *Once, Said Darlene*. Ill. by Steven Kellogg. Dutton, 1979, o.p. SERIES: Fat Cat. SUBJECTS: Behavior — Lying — Fiction; Fantasy; Friendship — Fiction. RL A.
When Darlene tells fantastic stories about the adventures she used to have, none of her friends but Peter believe her. It is his belief that frees her to return to her magic kingdom. Children will empathize with Darlene while enjoying the fanciful illustrations, in ink and wash.

3133 *That's Silly*. Ill. by Larry Di Fiori. Dutton, 1981, o.p. SERIES: Smart Cat. SUBJECTS: Fantasy; Imagination — Fiction; Magic — Fiction. RL A.
More practical and analytical than Tom, Rachel thinks that his constant need to pretend is silly until the two children become involved with magic. Then imagination is essential to their survival. Pastel peach and gray washes with pencil and ink accent illustrate the story well.

Smalley, Carol Parenzan

3134 *Fats, Oils, and Sweets*. Children's Press, 2005, ISBN 0-516-25289-5. SERIES: Rookie Read-About Health. SUBJECTS: Food; Health; Nutrition. RL B.
Starting with a warning to not eat too many sweets and foods containing fats and oils, the author briefly mentions health concerns, cites the food pyramid, and provides information on the sources of fats, oils, and sweets. Color photographs illustrate the text and a photo glossary and index conclude it.

Smath, Jerry

3135 *But No Elephants*. Ill. by author. Parents Magazine Press, 1979, ISBN 0-8193-1007-7. SERIES: Read Aloud Originals. SUBJECTS: Animals — Fiction; Elephants — Fiction; Humorous stories. RL B.
Grandma Tildy buys one animal after another, making each welcome in her little house, and reluctantly agrees to take the elephant. When winter comes she is forced to bring it inside. Instead of creating a disaster, the elephant finds a way to get them all to a warmer climate. The story is illustrated with humorous paintings.

3136 *The Housekeeper's Dog*. Ill. by author. Parents Magazine Press, 1980, ISBN 0-8193-1023-9. SUBJECTS: Behavior — Manners — Fiction; Behavior — Selfish — Fiction; Pets — Dogs — Fiction. RL B.
While the housekeeper is away on a brief vacation, her dog is at a dog-training school becoming a vain and arrogant semihuman. On her return she gets fed up with her dog's behavior and sends him away. He returns, happy to be just a dog again. The rollicking story is illustrated in full color.

3137 *Pretzel and Pop's Closetful of Stories*. Ill. by author. Silver Burdett, 1991, o.p. SUBJECTS: Family life — Fiction; Humorous stories; Rabbits — Fiction. RL B.
When things pour out of their overstuffed closet, bunny Pretzel's father is reminded of stories about their family and friends. Longer than many

books for beginning readers, this is divided into eight stories and illustrated with humorous watercolor pictures.

Smith, Janice Lee

3138 *Jess and the Stinky Cowboys*. Ill. by Lisa Thiesing. Dial, 2004, ISBN 0-8037-2641-4. SERIES: Dial Easy-to-Read. SUBJECTS: Cleanliness — Fiction; Cowboys — Fiction; Pets — Dogs — Fiction. RL B.

When some stinky canine cowboys arrive in Dry Gulch, the smell gets so bad that even the fish can't stand it. It's up to Deputy Jess to find a way to get the cowboys to take a bath. The humorous art comically captures the flavor of the Old West.

3139 *Wizard and Wart*. Ill. by Paul Meisel. HarperCollins, pap., 1995, ISBN 0-06-444201-2. SERIES: I Can Read. SUBJECTS: Magic — Fiction; Pets — Dogs — Fiction; Wizards — Fiction. RL B.

When Wizard and his dog, Wart, move into their new home, they are sure they will get plenty of customers for their magical problem solving. After advertising works, the twosome have more problems than they want to handle. Comical situations are illustrated with cartoon-like watercolors and ink.

3140 *Wizard and Wart at Sea*. Ill. by Paul Meisel. HarperCollins, 1995, ISBN 0-06-024755-X. SERIES: I Can Read. SUBJECTS: Beaches — Fiction; Magic — Fiction; Wizards — Fiction. RL B. LEXILE 380L.

Since wizard work is hard, Wizard and his dog Wart take a break and magically arrive at the beach. When seagulls keep bothering Wart, Wizard transforms some into goats, others into whales, and more into monkeys. Vacation over, the animals are soon transformed into songbirds and everyone is happy. Comical pictures work well with the funny story.

3141 *Wizard and Wart in Trouble*. Ill. by Paul Meisel. HarperCollins, 1998, ISBN 0-06-027762-9. SERIES: I Can Read. SUBJECTS: Magic — Fiction; Wizards — Fiction. RL B. LEXILE 320L.

Zounds, the Wizard's pet bird, announces that trouble is coming and Wizard and Wart decide to get ready for any eventuality. In five brief chapters accompanied by ink and watercolor illustrations, the two encounter different types of trouble.

Smith, Lucia

3142 *My Mom Got a Job*. Ill. by C. Christian Johanson. Holt, Rinehart, 1979, o.p. SUBJECTS: Family life — Fiction; Mothers, working — Fiction. RL B.

A little girl recalls the special times she and her mother shared before she went back to work. Then she tells about the special things she does instead that have become just as important. A good look at the pros and cons of having a working mother. The detailed ink drawings have pink accents.

Smith, Mary M.

3143 *Orla's Upside Down Day*. Ill. by Jan Lewis. Forest House, 1990, o.p. SERIES: Quality Time. SUBJECTS: Imaginative play — Fiction. RL A.

All day long Orla and her friend do everything upside-down and even inspire others to have fun doing it as well. The repetitive text and funny watercolor pictures should attract young readers.

Smith, Mavis

3144 *A Snake Mistake*. Ill. by author. HarperCollins, 1991, ISBN 0-06-026909-X. SERIES: Amazing Animal Reader. SUBJECTS: Farm and country life; Snakes. RL B.

Meaning to fool his chickens into laying more eggs, a farmer puts light bulbs in their nests. The only one that is fooled is a pine snake, which swallows two of the bulbs. The kindly farmer rushes the snake to the vet. Cartoon illustrations in full color lighten this true story.

Smith, Roland

3145 *Vultures*. Ill. by Lynn M. Stone. Lerner, 1997, ISBN 0-8225-3011-2. SERIES: Early Bird Nature. SUBJECTS: Animals — Endangered; Birds; Vultures. RL C. LEXILE 640L.

This excellent text gives an overview of the types of vultures and their habitats and diet and explains why most vultures have no head feathers. Illustrated with color photographs.

Smith, Susan M.

3146 *No One Should Have Six Cats.* Ill. by Judith Friedman. Follett, 1982, o.p. SERIES: Beginning to Read. SUBJECTS: Pets — Cats — Fiction. RL A.

David rescues one homeless cat after another until his mother says no one should have six cats. While David worries about which cat to give up, Mom, as kindhearted as her son, picks up another stray. The story and humorous watercolor pictures depict a caring and responsible child.

Snell, Nigel

3147 *Nita's Gerbil.* Ill. by author. Childrens Press, 1988, o.p. SERIES: First Pet Care Book. SUBJECTS: Pet care; Pets — Gerbils. RL C.

With her parents' support Nita gets two female gerbils and learns how to take care of them. Using just the right amount of information for young readers, this book realistically presents the rigors and joys of pet ownership. Illustrations are colorful cartoon pictures.

3148 *Roy's Puppy.* Ill. by author. Childrens Press, 1988, o.p. SERIES: First Pet Care Book. SUBJECTS: Pet care; Pets — Dogs. RL C.

The fun and work of having and training a dog are seen in this good look at dog care. Though the book is directed to children, it emphasizes the importance of involving parents. Responsible pet ownership is stressed as well. Cartoon illustrations personalize and lighten the text.

3149 *Sam's Rabbit.* Ill. by author. Childrens Press, 1988, o.p. SERIES: First Pet Care Book. SUBJECTS: Pet care; Pets — Rabbits. RL C.

Solid information on caring for a pet rabbit is shown using Sam's care of his pet, Bugsie, as an example. The book discusses building a hutch, keeping it clean, providing food, water, and salt, and being responsible in handling the animal. Colorful cartoon illustrations work well with the text.

Snow, Pegeen

3150 *Eat Your Peas, Louise!* Ill. by Mike Venezia. Children's Press, 1985, ISBN 0-516-02067-6. SERIES: Rookie Reader. SUBJECTS: Food — Fiction; Stories in rhyme. RL A.

Louise seems impervious to any attempts to convince her to eat her peas until her big brother finally says please. The rough, full-color illustrations and brief rhyming text are vibrant and funny.

3151 *A Pet for Pat.* Ill. by Tom Dunnington. Children's Press, 1984, o.p. SERIES: Rookie Reader. SUBJECTS: Pets — Dogs — Fiction; Stories in rhyme. RL A.

Pat's parents take her to the pound to choose a dog. Back home with her new pet, Pat introduces it to her friend. The rhyming story is short, uses very few words, and depends on the realistic full-color paintings to help in its telling.

Solomon, Chuck

3152 *Our Little League.* Photos by author. Crown, 1988, o.p. SUBJECTS: Sports — Baseball. RL A.

The Little Mets, a little league baseball team from Brooklyn, practice batting and fielding, get pep talks, and play and win a game. Throughout the photo story the children (one girl is on the team) are encouraged to have fun. The color photographs are excellent and the text is good.

3153 *Our Soccer League.* Photos by author. Crown, 1988, o.p. SUBJECTS: Sports — Soccer. RL A.

While Solomon's text is not meant to "teach" soccer, his photostory of a game played by elementary school children does show what fun the game can be. Further, it presents in clear color photographs a multiracial melting pot of boys and girls having a good time.

Sorrells, Dorothy

3154 *The Little Shell Hunter.* Ill. by Carol Rogers. Raintree, 1961, o.p. SUBJECTS: Shells. RL B.

Realistic three-color pictures of shells in their habitats are matched to a very brief, informative text. The shell pictures are all labeled and the text includes something about the live inhabitants of the shells and how they live.

Spanjian, Beth

3155 *Baby Duckbill.* Ill. by Karel Havlicek Novosad. Western, 1990, o.p. SERIES: Golden Look-Look Nature Books. SUBJECTS: Dinosaurs. RL B.

Using a story format, the supposed life-style of a young duckbill dinosaur is presented. Following that is a page of information meant for an older reader or adult. It provides known facts about this dinosaur. Illustrations are detailed colored pencil drawings.

3156 *Baby Grizzly.* Ill. by John Butler. Childrens Press, 1988, o.p. SERIES: Little Reader. SUBJECTS: Bears. RL C.

Two grizzly bear cubs share a summer day with their mother — fishing, playing, and learning to take care of themselves. The interesting story is short, has large print, and is illustrated with full-color, realistic pictures. The text is followed by a page of facts about grizzlies.

3157 *Baby Raccoon.* Ill. by Eva Cellini. Childrens Press, 1988, o.p. SERIES: Little Reader. SUBJECTS: Raccoons. RL C.

The text tells about a family of raccoons exploring their surroundings on a quiet summer night. The brief story is interesting, has large print, and is followed by a page of facts about raccoons. Realistic full-color pictures.

3158 *Baby Stegosaurus.* Ill. by Alex Bloch. Western, 1990, o.p. SERIES: Golden Look-Look Nature Books. SUBJECTS: Dinosaurs. RL C.

After hatching, a baby stegosaurus joins its siblings in hunting for food. Hiding from a predator, they witness an adult stegosaurus defending itself. A page of more detailed information follows. It is geared to older children or adults. Illustrations are detailed watercolors.

3159 *Baby Triceratops.* Ill. by John Butler. Western, 1990, o.p. SERIES: Golden Look-Look Nature Books. SUBJECTS: Dinosaurs. RL C.

After hatching, the young triceratops stays in the nest until its mother decides to lead it out to forage and learn about danger. While the story supposes a family life for this dinosaur, the addendum gives basic known facts about the animal. Detailed watercolors illustrate the text.

3160 *Baby Wolf.* Ill. by Bob Travers. Childrens Press, 1988, o.p. SERIES: Little Reader. SUBJECTS: Wolves. RL C.

Baby Wolf is shown in the midst of his family practicing his hunting, playing, and learning from others. The brief text is followed by a page of facts about wolves and is illustrated with full-color, realistic paintings.

Spilsbury, Louise, and Richard Spilsbury

3161 *Save the Black Rhino.* Heinemann, 2006, ISBN 1-4034-7804-x. SERIES: Save Our Animals! SUBJECTS: Animals — Endangered; Conservation; Rhinoceroses. RL C.

Using photographs and a brief but useful text, the world of the black rhino and the dangers it faces from humans are presented. A glossary, index, and short bibliography are also included.

3162 *Save the Florida Manatee.* Heinemann, 2006, ISBN 1-4034-7806-6. SERIES: Save Our Animals! SUBJECTS: Animals — Endangered; Conservation; Manatees. RL C.

Through well-captioned photographs and a clear text, children are introduced to the manatee, its environment, and the dangers it faces from pollution and humans. The book also includes a glossary, index, and short bibliography.

3163 *Save the Giant Panda.* Heinemann, 2006, ISBN 1-4034-7807-4. SERIES: Save Our Animals! SUBJECTS: Animals — Endangered; Conservation; Pandas. RL C.

What giant pandas eat, where they live, and the dangers they face in today's world are all briefly explained to young readers. Well-captioned photographs, a map, glossary, index, and brief bibliography all help to extend the text.

Spinner, Stephanie

3164 *Snake Hair: The Story of Medusa.* Ill. by Susan Swan. Grosset & Dunlap, pap., 1999, ISBN 0-448-41981-5. SERIES: All Aboard Reading. SUBJECTS: Monsters; Mythical creatures; Myths. RL B. LEXILE 10L.

With a head so frightening that one look turns people to stone, Medusa is a monster feared by everyone. When the king asks Perseus to kill her, he does and brings her head home. This well-known Greek myth is told in very simple lan-

Spinner, Stephanie (cont.)

guage and illustrated with elaborate cut-paper pictures.

Spirn, Michele Sobel

3165 *I Am the Turkey*. Ill. by Joy Allen. HarperCollins, 2004, ISBN 0-06-053230-0. SERIES: I Can Read. SUBJECTS: Plays — Fiction; School stories; Thanksgiving — Fiction. RL B.

When the parts are handed out for the Thanksgiving play, Mark is assigned the Turkey. Not happy about his role, he nonetheless saves the show and becomes a star. Allen's pencil and watercolor pictures work well with the text.

3166 *A Know-Nothing Birthday*. Ill. by R. W. Alley. HarperCollins, 1997, o.p. SERIES: I Can Read. SUBJECTS: Birthdays — Fiction; Friendship — Fiction; Humorous stories. RL B. LEXILE 290L.

Boris's birthday is coming and he is sure his friends Morris, Norris and Doris will forget. All four find ways to make it a memorable and very funny celebration. Alley's cartoon-like watercolors add to the story's silliness.

3167 *A Know-Nothing Halloween*. Ill. by R. W. Alley. HarperCollins, 2000, ISBN 0-06-028185-4. SERIES: I Can Read. SUBJECTS: Friendship — Fiction; Halloween — Fiction; Humorous stories. RL B. LEXILE 260L.

Boris, Morris, Norris, and Doris, four very silly friends, decide to try to celebrate Halloween, with comical results. Alley's art captures the spirit of the nonsensical story.

3168 *The Know-Nothings Talk Turkey*. Ill. by R. W. Alley. HarperCollins, 2000, ISBN 0-06-028183-0. SERIES: I Can Read. SUBJECTS: Humorous stories; Thanksgiving — Fiction; Turkeys — Fiction. RL B. LEXILE 330L.

Not really understanding what "serving turkey" means, the Know-Nothings get a turkey at a farm and try to serve Thanksgiving dinner to it, rather than eating the turkey themselves. Children will be amused by the story and their superiority to the Know-Nothings.

Spohn, Kate

3169 *Dog and Cat Make a Splash*. Viking, 1997, o.p. SERIES: Viking Easy-to-Read. SUBJECTS: Friendship — Fiction; Pets — Cats — Fiction; Pets — Dogs — Fiction. RL B. LEXILE 330L.

In four short stories, Dog teaches his friend Cat to swim; the two hold a tag sale; they have a magic show; Cat and other friends surprise Dog with a boat for his birthday. The gentle stories and quiet illustrations ably demonstrate the joys of friendship.

3170 *Turtle and Snake and the Christmas Tree*. Viking, 2000, o.p. SERIES: Viking Easy-to-Read. SUBJECTS: Christmas — Fiction; Snakes — Fiction; Turtles — Fiction. RL A.

Bundled up for the cold and snow Turtle and Snake look for the perfect Christmas tree. They cannot find one until they get home and spot just the right one in their back yard. Child-like pictures in full color are a good match to the story.

3171 *Turtle and Snake at Work*. Viking, 1999, o.p. SERIES: Viking Easy-to-Read. SUBJECTS: Snakes — Fiction; Turtles — Fiction; Work — Fiction. RL A.

Turtle and Snake get up and go to work each day. Turtle directs traffic and Snake makes pizza. At the end of the day they get together to eat. Illustrations are childlike and comical.

3172 *Turtle and Snake Go Camping*. Viking, pap., 2000, ISBN 0-14-130670-X. SERIES: Viking Easy-to-Read. SUBJECTS: Camps and camping — Fiction; Snakes — Fiction; Turtles — Fiction. RL A.

Turtle and Snake are all prepared for a night of camping when suddenly they hear a strange noise. Afraid, they retrace their paths and end up happily at home in front of a very safe fire.

3173 *Turtle and Snake's Day at the Beach*. Viking, pap., 2003, ISBN 0-14-240157-9. SERIES: Viking Easy-to-Read. SUBJECTS: Beaches — Fiction; Contests — Fiction; Turtles — Fiction. RL B.

Good friends Turtle and Snake arrive at the beach and discover there is a sand castle contest at 3:00. Each time the twosome build a castle, the waves wash it away. Finally friends help them to create a castle that is just perfect.

3174 *Turtle and Snake's Spooky Halloween.* Viking, 2002, ISBN 0-670-03560-2. SERIES: Viking Easy-to-Read. SUBJECTS: Halloween — Fiction; Snakes — Fiction; Turtles — Fiction. RL A.

Snake and Turtle prepare for their Halloween party by making a list of things to do — including finding just the right costumes. With few words, colorful child-like illustrations, and a special punch recipe, the book will be a favorite at Halloween.

3175 *Turtle and Snake's Valentine's Day.* Viking, 2003, ISBN 0-670-03613-7. SERIES: Viking Easy-to-Read. SUBJECTS: Snakes — Fiction; Turtles — Fiction; Valentine's Day — Fiction. RL A.

Turtle searches for the perfect presents for Snake for Valentine's Day. When he takes them to Snake's home, he gets a Valentine's Day surprise as well. Childlike art in full color illustrates the very simple text.

Springstubb, Tricia

3176 *My Minnie Is a Jewel.* Ill. by Jim La Marche. Carolrhoda, 1980, o.p. SERIES: On My Own. SUBJECTS: Humorous stories; Marriage and wedding customs — Fiction. RL A.

Minnie is forever distracted and her cooking suffers because of it. To her husband, Henry, everything she does is just right. Strangers bet a casket of jewels that Henry will not like or eat the huge and ugly cake she baked and of course they lose. This humorous story is illustrated with detailed ink sketches.

Squire, Ann O.

3177 *African Animals.* Children's Press, 2001, ISBN 0-516-22187-6. SERIES: True Book. SUBJECTS: Africa; Animals; Conservation. RL C.

The differing African ecosystems support a great variety of animals and some of the most interesting are presented here. Illustrated with good color photographs, the book includes a message on saving endangered animals, lists of books, organizations, and Web sites, a glossary, and an index.

Srivastava, Jane J.

3178 *Averages.* Ill. by Aliki. HarperCollins, 1975, ISBN 0-690-00743-4. SERIES: Young Math. SUBJECTS: Mathematics. RL C.

Clear, careful explanations paired with opportunities to try out concepts help children to gain an understanding of mean, mode, and arithmetic mean. Ink and pencil drawings aid in the communication of information.

Stadler, John

3179 *The Adventures of Snail at School.* Ill. by author. HarperCollins, pap., 1995, ISBN 0-06-444202-0. SERIES: I Can Read. SUBJECTS: Fantasy; School stories; Snails — Fiction. RL B.

In three chapters, the diminutive snail eagerly volunteers to get things for his teacher. Each time he has adventures. A flood erupts from the drinking fountain, a fire extinguisher takes him to outer space, and musical instruments come to life in this humorous story with cartoon-like pictures.

3180 *Cat at Bat.* Ill. by author. Dutton, 1988, o.p. SERIES: Dutton Easy Reader. SUBJECTS: Animals — Fiction; Stories in rhyme. RL A.

Fourteen three-line, rhyming verses describe animals doing many different and very silly things. The humorous illustrations will help the beginning reader to decipher the nonsensical rhymes.

3181 *Cat Is Back at Bat.* Ill. by author. Dutton, 1991, o.p. SERIES: Dutton Easy Reader. SUBJECTS: Animals — Fiction; Stories in rhyme. RL A.

Short rhyming sentences describing silly circumstances, such as "A crab tries to grab a cab," are made funnier when accompanied by the zany watercolor illustrations.

3182 *Hooray for Snail!* Ill. by author. HarperCollins, pap., 1984, ISBN 0-06-443075-8. SUBJECTS: Snails — Fiction; Sports — Baseball — Fiction. RL A.

When Snail finally gets to bat, he hits the ball so hard it lands on the moon and bounces back. Snail barely makes it around the bases before the ball returns. Full-color illustrations show comical animal teammates shouting encouragement to the tiny runner.

Stadler, John (cont.)

3183 *Ready, Set, Go!* HarperCollins, pap., 1998, ISBN 0-06-444238-1. SERIES: I Can Read. SUBJECTS: Pets — Dogs — Fiction; Weather — Snow — Fiction. RL B. LEXILE 270L.

After big cousin Oliver beats her at making snowmen and forts and Juliet beats him, little Sasha saves the day by rescuing Juliet. The very brief text and simple watercolor art work well together.

3184 *Snail Saves the Day.* Ill. by author. Star Bright, pap., 2006, ISBN 1-59572-045-6. SUBJECTS: Animals — Fiction; Sports — Football — Fiction. RL A.

When his team of small animals is pitted against a team of bears, hippos, and other large creatures, Snail oversleeps, making it to the stadium just in time to make a winning touchdown. Bright, comic illustrations and a very brief story make this appropriate for the beginning reader.

3185 *Three Cheers for Hippo!* Ill. by author. HarperCollins, 1987, o.p. SUBJECTS: Animals — Fiction; Humorous stories. RL A.

Hippo, who is teaching Cat, Dog, and Pig to parachute, must quickly rescue them before they are eaten by alligators. The book's extremely brief text relies on humorous pencil, ink, and watercolor pictures to help tell the story.

Staenberg, Bonnie

3186 *A Present for Mama Bear.* Ill. by Katy Bratun. Scholastic, pap., 1999, ISBN 0-590-28154-2. SERIES: Hello Reader! SUBJECTS: Bears — Fiction; Gifts and gift giving — Fiction; Parent and child — Fiction. RL B. LEXILE 400L.

Edgar Bear wants to give his mother a special birthday present. While getting muddy and dirty, he tries to pick flowers, paint a picture, and bake a cake — all with no success. He finally gives her the best present of all: a clean Edgar Bear

Stamper, Judith B.

3187 *The Bowwow Bake Sale.* Ill. by Chris L. Demarest. Grosset & Dunlap, pap., 2002, ISBN 0-448-42845-8. SERIES: All Aboard Math Reader. SUBJECTS: Bake sales — Fiction; Pets — Dogs — Fiction; Pets — Fiction. RL C.

A puppy in need of a home prompts four children to hold a bake sale so that one of them can adopt the pup. Math is interwoven throughout the text as the children try to determine exactly how much money they will need both for supplies and profits. The story is told in chapters and illustrated with line and wash pictures.

3188 *Breakfast at Danny's Diner: A Book About Multiplication.* Ill. by Chris L. Demarest. Grosset & Dunlap, pap., 2003, ISBN 0-448-43210-2. SERIES: All Aboard Math Reader. SUBJECTS: Breakfast — Fiction; Restaurants — Fiction; Work — Fiction. RL C.

When two of his workers call in sick, Danny asks Tina and Tony to help him out at the diner. The two quickly learn how much multiplication is needed to make sure the tables are set and the meals are served.

3189 *Five Goofy Ghosts.* Ill. by Tim Raglin. Cartwheel, pap., 1996, ISBN 0-590-92152-5. SERIES: Hello Reader! SUBJECTS: Ghost stories; Humorous stories. RL C. LEXILE 400L.

Whether it's "The Hairy Toe" or "The Last Laugh," the stories in this collection are just scary enough for young readers. The gently scary illustrations keep the tone light.

3190 *Go, Fractions!* Ill. by Chris L. Demarest. Grosset & Dunlap, pap., 2003, ISBN 0-448-43113-0. SERIES: All Aboard Math Reader. SUBJECTS: Mathematics — Fiction; Sports — Soccer. RL C.

As four friends try out for the soccer team, their knowledge of fractions helps them follow the coach's instructions and become members of "The Fractions" soccer team. Soccer is a good vehicle for reinforcing or introducing fractions to readers. The ink and watercolor pictures are lively and well-done.

3191 *What's It Like to Be a Bus Driver.* Ill. by T. R. Garcia. Troll, 1990, o.p. SERIES: What's It Like to Be a . . . SUBJECTS: Buses; Careers. RL C.

The training, knowledge, and skill required of a bus driver and the daily routines he follows are included in an introductory look at this career. Illustrations are colorful cartoon-like pictures.

3192 *What's It Like to Be a Dentist*. Ill. by Dana Gustafson. Troll, 1990, o.p. SERIES: What's It Like to Be a . . . SUBJECTS: Careers; Dentists; Human body — Teeth. RL B.

A child's first visit to a dentist offers an opportunity to demonstrate the many tools used and the things done to keep teeth healthy. Very little career training information is provided. Simple Pentel and watercolor illustrations are used.

3193 *What's It Like to Be a Truck Driver*. Ill. by George Ulrich. Troll, 1989, o.p. SERIES: What's It Like to Be a . . . SUBJECTS: Careers; Trucks. RL C.

The kinds of trucks and the cargoes they carry, as well as the skill required of drivers, are discussed here. Also included are some trucking terms frequently used on CBs. Text is illustrated with ink drawings with color washes.

3194 *What's It Like to Be a Veterinarian*. Ill. by Marcy Dunn Ramsey. Troll, 1990, o.p. SERIES: What's It Like to Be a . . . SUBJECTS: Careers; Doctors and nurses; Pet care. RL C.

When Ben takes his sick puppy to the veterinarian, he asks her how to become a vet. Through Ben and other clients, readers learn what kind of work she does daily. Sketchy watercolors illustrate the story.

3195 *What's It Like to Be a Zoo Worker*. Ill. by Kathleen Garry McCord. Troll, 1989, o.p. SERIES: What's It Like to Be a . . . SUBJECTS: Careers; Zoos. RL C.

To make today's modern zoo run smoothly, a great many well-trained people are needed. This book briefly introduces the staff and the kinds of work they do. Illustrations are very attractive colored pencil drawings.

3196 *The Wild Leaf Ride*. Ill. by Carolyn Bracken. Scholastic, pap., 2003, ISBN 0-439-56988-5. SERIES: Scholastic Reader: The Magic School Bus. SUBJECTS: Fall — Fiction; Leaves — Fiction; School stories. RL B. LEXILE 240L.

Missing one of the fall leaves they are collecting, Ms. Frizzle decides to take the class on a Magic School Bus field trip. Smaller than squirrels, the members of the class start searching for the special leaf and learning about leaves and trees. Art and text are patterned after those of the original book series.

Standiford, Natalie

3197 *The Best Little Monkeys in the World*. Ill. by Hilary Knight. Random House, 1987, o.p. SERIES: Step into Reading. SUBJECTS: Baby-sitting — Fiction; Humorous stories; Monkeys — Fiction. RL B.

Marvin and Mary are two mischievous little monkeys whose baby-sitter is so wrapped up in her telephone conversations that she is oblivious to the mess they are creating. The colorful pencil and wash pictures are full of unexpected details and add to the humor in this funny story.

3198 *The Bravest Dog Ever: The True Story of Balto*. Ill. by Donald Cook. Random House, 1989, ISBN 0-394-99695-X. SERIES: Step into Reading. SUBJECTS: Alaska — History; Diseases; Pets — Dogs. RL B.

When medicine is urgently needed to save the people of Nome from diphtheria, Balto, a sled dog, bravely leads his team over 53 miles through heavy snow and subzero weather to get the serum to them. Good illustrations help tell this true story.

3199 *The Headless Horseman*. Ill. by Donald Cook. Random House, 1992, o.p. SERIES: Step into Reading. SUBJECTS: Ghost stories; Legends. RL C.

Ichabod Crane, the vain Sleepy Hollow schoolteacher, is certain that he will marry Katrina until the night he meets the headless horseman on his way home. Told with a sly humor, especially evident in the colorful pictures, the book is a good retelling of the classic story.

Stanek, Muriel

3200 *Left, Right, Left, Right!* Ill. by Lucy Hawkinson. Whitman, 1969, o.p. SERIES: Concept Books. SUBJECTS: Concepts — Left and right — Fiction; Self-esteem — Fiction. RL B.

Katie gets confused between left and right, turns in the wrong direction during a parade, and is humiliated. Her grandmother gives her a ring for her right hand and that solves her problem. A

Stanek, Muriel (cont.)

sensitive look at a problem faced by many children, it is illustrated in black and white and in color.

Stanovich, Betty Jo

3201 *Hedgehog Adventures*. Ill. by Chris L. Demarest. Lothrop, 1983, o.p. SUBJECTS: Hedgehogs — Fiction; Woodchucks — Fiction. RL B.

Exuberant Hedgehog takes his friend Woodchuck on three ill-fated adventures. Each time his spirits are revived by his kindly homebody friend Woodchuck. The gentle, expressive pencil drawings capture the pair's moods and the story's fun.

3202 *Hedgehog Surprises*. Ill. by Chris L. Demarest. Lothrop, 1984, o.p. SUBJECTS: Birthdays — Fiction; Hedgehogs — Fiction; Woodchucks — Fiction. RL B.

Excitable Hedgehog is saved from worry and a disastrous case of nerves by his friend Woodchuck as he tries to give Bear a perfect birthday party. Expressive colored pencil drawings are as humorous as the very funny story.

Staub, Frank

3203 *Herons*. Lerner, 1997, ISBN 0-8225-3017-1. SERIES: Early Bird Nature. SUBJECTS: Birds. RL C. LEXILE 600L.

In five chapters filled with color photographs and a map, North American herons, egrets, and bitterns - all members of the heron family — are introduced to young readers. The birds' habits and life cycle are explored. The book also includes a section for adults and an index.

3204 *Manatees*. Lerner, 1998, ISBN 0-8225-3023-6. SERIES: Early Bird Nature. SUBJECTS: Animals — Endangered; Manatees. RL C. LEXILE 580L.

The life cycle, physical characteristics, habitat, and endangered status of the West Indian manatee — which is found in Florida and the Caribbean — are covered in this chapter book. Illustrated with color photographs, the book also includes a section for adults, a glossary, and an index.

3205 *Mountain Goats*. Photos by author. Lerner, 1994, ISBN 0-8225-3000-7. SERIES: Early Bird Nature. SUBJECTS: Mountain goats. RL C.

Well organized into chapters and attractively illustrated with carefully placed photographs, this introduction to the mountain goat makes interesting reading. The life cycle, enemies, and habitat of the animal are discussed.

3206 *Sea Lions*. Lerner, 2000, ISBN 0-8225-3018-X. SERIES: Early Bird Nature. SUBJECTS: Seals and sea lions. RL C. LEXILE 670L.

With full-color photographs and a carefully written text, the life cycle of the sea lion, its habitat, and its predators and prey are introduced to confident beginning readers. The book concludes with a section for adults, a glossary, and an index.

3207 *Walruses*. Lerner, 1999, ISBN 0-8225-3039-2. SERIES: Early Bird Nature. SUBJECTS: Animals; Walruses. RL C. LEXILE 670L.

Though there are far more Pacific walruses than Atlantic, both species have similar life styles, habitat, and dangers. The book covers these and includes color photographs, charts, a section for adults, a glossary, and index.

Steinberg, David

3208 *Caveman Manners and Other Polite Poems*. Ill. by Adrian Sinnott. Grosset & Dunlap, pap., 2006, ISBN 0-448-44109-8. SERIES: All Aboard Poetry Reader. SUBJECTS: Behavior — Manners — Fiction; Poetry. RL B.

Cave children, pigs, nose-pickers, greedy kings, and Little Miss Muffet all have one thing in common: a problem with manners. The humorous poetry and illustrations will especially appeal to those who enjoy something a bit gross.

3209 *Club Pet and Other Funny Poems*. Ill. by Adrian Sinnott. Grosset & Dunlap, pap., 2005, ISBN 0-448-43773-2. SERIES: All Aboard Poetry Reader. SUBJECTS: Animals — Fiction; Pets — Fiction; Poetry. RL B.

Though Steinberg may stretch his rhymes a bit, his poems about animals at a spa, in the movies, trying to get in shape, and training an owner will get some readers smiling and even laughing. The poems are illustrated with humorous cartoon-like watercolors.

3210 *Grasshopper Pie and Other Poems.* Ill. by Adrian Sinnott. Grosset & Dunlap, pap., 2004, ISBN 0-448-43347-8. SERIES: All Aboard Poetry Reader. SUBJECTS: Poetry. RL B.

No grasshoppers in grasshopper pie? An alien in a matzo ball, a daddy who is a tickle monster, an elephant with a dangerous sneeze, and a boy who does everything upside down are the subjects of Steinberg's five very funny poems. All are illustrated with humorous ink and watercolor wash illustrations.

3211 *The Monster Mall: And Other Spooky Poems.* Ill. by Adrian Sinnott. Grosset & Dunlap, 2004, ISBN 0-448-43543-8. SERIES: All Aboard Reader. SUBJECTS: Halloween; Poetry. RL C.

In five poems (four of them lengthy), monsters of all kinds playfully amble and don't really attempt to scare anyone. The rhyme schemes are the same and at times forced but young readers will enjoy the monster subject and the humorous black-and-white illustrations.

Stern, Maggie

3212 *George.* Ill. by Blanche Sims. Orchard, 1999, ISBN 0-531-30197-4. SERIES: Orchard Chapters. SUBJECTS: School stories. RL B. LEXILE 230L.

George finds sitting still and waiting his turn difficult. Yet when the rabbit gets loose, the teacher asks for an assistant bread maker, and there are tickets for the school fair to use, George knows just what to do.

3213 *George and Diggety.* Ill. by Blanche Sims. Orchard, 2000, ISBN 0-531-30295-4. SERIES: Orchard Chapters. SUBJECTS: Pets — Dogs — Fiction; Siblings — Fiction; Sledding — Fiction. RL B. LEXILE 220L.

Though Diggety does not do well at the dog intelligence test, he is a terrific sledder and knows just what he wants for his birthday dinner. Lively and humorous illustrations and a recipe for dog biscuits add to the fun in this book.

Stevens, Carla

3214 *Anna, Grandpa, and the Big Storm.* Ill. by Margot Tomes. Houghton Mifflin, 1995, ISBN 0-395-73231-X. SUBJECTS: Emergencies — Fiction; Grandparents — Fiction; Weather — Snow — Fiction. RL B.

Grandpa changes his mind about staying in New York City after helping Anna and other stranded passengers get back home during a terrible blizzard in the late 1800s. The exciting story is illustrated with detailed realistic pen and ink drawings.

3215 *Hooray for Pig!* Ill. by Rainey Bennett. Seabury, 1974, o.p. SUBJECTS: Fear — Fiction; Pigs — Fiction; Sports — Swimming — Fiction. RL A.

Afraid of the water, Pig does not even want to try swimming until Otter patiently helps him begin to overcome his fear. A good handling of a common situation — it does not make fears magically disappear but shows how much work it takes. Illustrated with simple line drawings with washes.

3216 *Pig and the Blue Flag.* Ill. by Rainey Bennett. Seabury, 1977, o.p. SUBJECTS: Animals — Fiction; School stories; Self-esteem — Fiction. RL B.

Pig is so big and heavy that he never seems to do anything right in gym. Then Otter suggests they play Capture the Flag, and everyone is a winner. Children will empathize with Pig and be glad he finally succeeds. Illustrated with pen and ink drawings with soft blue and orange washes.

3217 *Sara and the Pinch.* Ill. by John Wallner. Houghton Mifflin, 1980, o.p. SUBJECTS: Behavior; School stories. RL B.

At school Sara is always determined to have things her own way and can be quite pesky when she does not. Reprimanded for pinching and sent into the hall, Sara is comforted by Mr. Zamatsky, the school custodian. Colored pencil and wash pictures capture Sara's feisty, independent nature.

3218 *Your First Pet and How to Take Care of It.* Ill. by Lisl Weil. Macmillan, 1974, o.p. SERIES: Ready-to-Read. SUBJECTS: Pet care; Pets. RL B.

Good advice on the care and training of eight popular animals is offered to children about to select a pet. Not the usual overview of a subject found in most books for beginning readers, this is a substantial 120 pages of good information with help from sketchy ink drawings.

Stevens, Janet, and Susan Stevens Crummel

3219 *Shoe Town.* Ill. by author. Harcourt, 1999, ISBN 0-15-204882-0. SERIES: Green Light Readers. SUBJECTS: Mice — Fiction; Shoes — Fiction; Stories in rhyme. RL B. LEXILE 450L.

A series of nursery tale characters joins a little mouse and together they create a perfect shoe town. Humorous illustrations are a perfect match to the rhyming story.

Stevens, Philippa J.

3220 *Bonk! Goes the Ball.* Ill. by Clovis Martin. Children's Press, 1990, o.p. SERIES: Rookie Reader. SUBJECTS: Sports — Soccer — Fiction. RL A.

A little girl does her best to play well in a game of soccer and finally makes a goal. Colorful watercolor illustrations add a light touch and help tell the very short story.

Stevenson, James

3221 *Christmas at Mud Flat.* Greenwillow, 2000, ISBN 0-688-17302-0. SUBJECTS: Animals — Fiction; Christmas — Fiction; Gifts and gift giving — Fiction. RL B. LEXILE 330L.

Everyone in Mud Flat is busily preparing for Christmas by wrapping presents, finding presents, repairing presents, and trying to find a way to see Santa Claus. Stevenson's illustrations capture the emotions and fun of the group with simple line and wash illustrations

3222 *Clams Can't Sing.* Ill. by author. Greenwillow, 1980, o.p. SERIES: Read-Alone. SUBJECTS: Humorous stories; Mollusks — Fiction; Seashore — Fiction. RL B.

The seashore animals confidently prepare for their concert and just as confidently tell Beatrice and Foster they are not in it because clams cannot sing. The two surprise everyone with a symphony for two clams. Hilarious text and drawings might get children to try to create their own music.

3223 *Fast Friends: Two Stories.* Ill. by author. Greenwillow, 1979, o.p. SERIES: Read-Alone. SUBJECTS: Animals — Fiction; Friendship — Fiction; Self-esteem — Fiction. RL B.

The first story has Murry, a turtle, and Fred, a snail, get plenty of friends when they find a skateboard. In the second story Clem Turtle convinces Thomas Mouse to build a house to attract friends. In both stories the humorous characters come to accept themselves. Pictures are ink and wash.

3224 *Heat Wave at Mud Flat.* Greenwillow, 1997, ISBN 0-688-14206-0. SUBJECTS: Animals — Fiction; Weather — Rain — Fiction. RL C.

It is the hottest summer the animals of Mud Flat can remember and there has been no rain for months. In nine short stories with comical illustrations and great humor, Stevenson offers the story of Mud Flat's sizzling summer and eventual rain.

3225 *Mud Flat April Fool.* Ill. by author. Greenwillow, 1998, ISBN 0-688-15164-5. SUBJECTS: Animals — Fiction; April Fools' Day — Fiction; Humorous stories. RL B.

The young animals of Mud Flat are having a great time playing April Fools' jokes. The old timers even manage to play a few themselves. Lively dialogue and humorous watercolor pictures add to the charm of this delightful book.

3226 *The Mud Flat Mystery.* Greenwillow, pap., 1997, ISBN 0-06-051181-8. SUBJECTS: Behavior — Curiosity — Fiction; Boxes — Fiction; Humorous stories. RL C. LEXILE 320L.

When a big box arrives for Duncan, the residents of Mud Flat cannot contain their curiosity. Though they try not to, they end up opening the box and discovering Duncan's big surprise.

3227 *The Mud Flat Olympics.* Ill. by author. Greenwillow, 1994, o.p. SUBJECTS: Animals — Fiction; Humorous stories; Olympics — Fiction. RL B.

The elephants, hippos, skunks, moles, and even snails of Mud Flat compete in their own special version of the Olympics. When the games are finished, everyone happily shares a picnic. The quiet but delightfully humorous stories are illustrated with droll ink and watercolor pictures.

3228 *Oh No, It's Waylon's Birthday!* Ill. by author. Greenwillow, 1989, o.p. SUBJECTS:

Animals — Fiction; Birthdays — Fiction; Humorous stories. RL B.

In three different stories, an elephant has a very unusual two-hundred and forty-ninth birthday; a hippo discovers noise can be just right for sleeping; and penguins slip and slide to the water's edge — and into it. Delightful ink and watercolor wash paintings carry through on the fun.

3229 *Which One Is Whitney?* Ill. by author. Greenwillow, 1990, o.p. SUBJECTS: Dugongs — Fiction; Humorous stories. RL B.

Of Mrs. Dugong's five children, Whitney is the one who is not so noticeably polite, funny, friendly, or cheerful — or is he? In three short stories Whitney cleverly outsmarts his sea mammal family as well as overconfident fish. Illustrations are simply drawn, humorous ink and watercolor paintings.

3230 *Winston, Newton, Elton, and Ed.* Ill. by author. Greenwillow, 1978, o.p. SERIES: Read-Alone. SUBJECTS: Penguins — Fiction; Sibling rivalry — Fiction; Walruses — Fiction. RL B.

In the first of two Antarctic stories, three little walrus brothers are so intent on upstaging each other that they lose their dinners. In the second, Ed, a penguin, is marooned on an ice floe, far from his friends. Deftly drawn humorous pictures accompany the two very funny stories.

3231 *Yard Sale.* Greenwillow, 1996, ISBN 0-688-14127-7. SUBJECTS: Animals — Fiction; Humorous stories; Tag sales — Fiction. RL C.

Wanting to get rid of things they don't use and trying to make extra money, the animals take their "treasures" to the Mud Flat yard sale. By the end of the day a party by the river brings everyone happily together.

Stevenson, Suçie, reteller

3232 *The Emperor's New Clothes.* Delacorte, 1998, o.p. SERIES: Yearling First Choice Chapter Book. SUBJECTS: Animals — Fiction; Clothing — Fiction; Fairy tales. RL C. LEXILE 230L.

The well-known tale is transformed into one featuring animals without losing the impact of Andersen's story of greed and pomposity. The illustrations are lively and humorous.

Stewart, Melissa

3233 *Amphibians.* Children's Press, 2001, ISBN 0-516-22037-3. SERIES: True Book. SUBJECTS: Frogs and toads; Reptiles and amphibians; Salamanders. RL C. LEXILE 870L.

Full-color photographs and a clearly written text provide plenty of information on the life cycle, habits, and environment of amphibians. The book also includes a glossary; lists of books, organizations, and Web sites; and an index.

3234 *Birds.* Children's Press, pap., 2001, ISBN 0-516-25954-7. SERIES: True Book. SUBJECTS: Birds. RL C.

The life cycle of birds and information on how their feathers keep them warm as well as allowing them to fly, what birds eat, and how they migrate are all here. The book also contains an activity demonstrating how birds fly; lists of books, organizations, and Web sites; a glossary; and an index.

3235 *Energy in Motion.* Children's Press, 2006, ISBN 0-516-24956-8. SERIES: Rookie Read-About Science. SUBJECTS: Energy; Science and scientists. RL B. LEXILE 310L.

Sports, swings, familiar activities, and objects along with activities teach young readers about different kinds of energy. Illustrated with color photographs, the book also includes a photo glossary and index.

3236 *Fishes.* Children's Press, 2001, ISBN 0-516-22038-1. SERIES: True Book. SUBJECTS: Fish. RL C.

How fish live, their life cycles, food, physical features, environment, and protective shape or coloration are all discussed in this brief but interesting overview. Illustrated with color photographs, the book includes lists of books, organizations, and Web sites; a glossary; and an index.

3237 *Insects.* Children's Press, 2001, ISBN 0-516-22040-3. SERIES: True Book. SUBJECTS: Insects. RL C.

After learning that insects make up 75 percent of earth's kinds of animal life, children will enjoy learning about them and seeing the color photographs of representative insects. The book ends with lists of books, organizations, and Web sites; a glossary; and an index.

Stewart, Melissa (cont.)

3238 *Mammals*. Children's Press, 2001, ISBN 0-516-22035-7. SERIES: True Book. SUBJECTS: Animals — Mammals. RL C.

All kinds of mammals — including humans — are discussed along with their commonalities. The text ends with a plea for using human intelligence to safeguard animal life. Color photographs, a glossary, an index, and lists of books, organizations, and Web sites complete it.

3239 *Reptiles*. Children's Press, pap., 2001, ISBN 0-516-25953-9. SERIES: True Book. SUBJECTS: Reptiles and amphibians. RL C. LEXILE 810L.

Snakes, crocodiles, turtles, and lizards are among the reptiles covered in the text and color photographs. Their body structure, life cycle, food, and environment are discussed. The book also includes an index, glossary, and lists of books, organizations, and Web sites.

3240 *Will It Float or Sink?* Children's Press, 2006, ISBN 0-516-24955-X. SERIES: Rookie Read-About Science. SUBJECTS: Buoyancy; Science and scientists; Water. RL B. LEXILE 370L.

Using illustrations of a variety of objects in water, the author explains why some things can float and others sink. Using maple syrup as an example, she then shows how water can float on it. An index and photo glossary are included.

Still, John

3241 *Amazing Beetles*. Ill. with photos. Knopf, 1991, o.p. SERIES: Eyewitness Juniors. SUBJECTS: Beetles; Insects. RL C.

Clear photographic silhouettes of beetles, accompanied by small watercolor paintings of additional beetles, are supported by a brief text and much captioning. The very inviting book offers a good deal of information while giving the appearance of being a "browser." Index is included.

Stille, Darlene R.

3242 *Airplanes*. Compass Point, 2001, ISBN 0-7565-0146-6. SERIES: Transportation. SUBJECTS: Airplanes. RL C. LEXILE 760L.

Through short chapters and colorful photographs and diagrams, children will learn about the different kinds of airplanes, the work they do, and the people who work on them and make it possible for the planes to fly. The book also includes lists of books, organizations and Web sites; a glossary; and an index.

3243 *The Circulatory System*. Children's Press, pap., 1997, ISBN 0-516-26261-0. SERIES: True Book. SUBJECTS: Human body — Blood; Human body — Circulation. RL C. LEXILE 760L.

Diagrams and photographs help the reader to understand how the heart, veins, arteries, and lungs work together to keep the human body alive and working well. Lists of books, organizations, and Web sites; a glossary; and an index are included.

3244 *Deserts*. Children's Press, pap., 1999, ISBN 0-516-26760-4. SERIES: True Book. SUBJECTS: Deserts; Geography. RL C. LEXILE 670L.

The many different kinds of deserts found throughout the world — from Antarctica to Africa and Asia — are compared and their commonalities explained. Photographs, a map of the world's deserts, an index, a glossary, and lists of books, organizations, and Web sites are included.

3245 *The Digestive System*. Children's Press, pap., 1997, ISBN 0-516-26262-9. SERIES: True Book. SUBJECTS: Human body — Digestion. RL C. LEXILE 700L.

Starting with taking a bite out of an apple, the way in which the digestive system works is clearly explained. Color photographs, an attractive design, and diagrams work well with the text. Additional resources include lists of books, organizations, and Web sites; a glossary; and an index.

3246 *Grasslands*. Children's Press, 1999, ISBN 0-516-21509-4. SERIES: True Book. SUBJECTS: Conservation; Grasslands. RL C.

Prairies, steppes such as the Great Plains, and savannas are examples of grasslands. The animals living in each area are discussed as is the need for conserving and restoring these areas. Illustrated with maps and color photographs, the volume closes with lists of books, organizations, and Web sites; a glossary; and an index.

3247 *Helicopters*. Children's Press, 1997, o.p. SERIES: True Book. SUBJECTS: Aeronautics; Helicopters. RL C. LEXILE 760L.

Any child at all interested in helicopters and how they fly and are piloted and used will find the answers in this well-written and interesting book. Good color and black-and-white photographs illustrate the text. Sidebars with extra information; lists of books, organizations, and Web sites; a glossary; and an index complete the book.

3248 *Oceans*. Children's Press, pap., 1999, ISBN 0-516-26768-X. SERIES: True Book. SUBJECTS: Oceans and ocean life; Water. RL C.

With undersea mountains, volcanoes, geysers, and amazing fish, the oceans of the world are fascinating. Color photographs augment the interesting text and are supported by an index, a glossary, and lists of books, organizations, and Web sites.

3249 *The Respiratory System*. Children's Press, pap., 1997, ISBN 0-516-26276-9. SERIES: True Book. SUBJECTS: Human body — Respiration. RL C. LEXILE 750L.

How we breathe, how the lungs work, how they interact with other body organs, and diseases affecting the lungs are carefully explained and supported by detailed diagrams and photographs. The book also has lists of books, organizations and Web sites; a glossary; and an index.

3250 *Trains*. Children's Press, 1997, ISBN 0-516-20342-8. SERIES: True Book. SUBJECTS: Trains. RL C. LEXILE 690L.

An attractive chapter format with an abundance of color photographs explains the different types of trains, the things trains carry, their history, and the people who work on them as well as introducing some of the newest trains. It offers lists of books, organizations, and Web sites; a glossary; and an index.

3251 *Tropical Rain Forests*. Children's Press, 1999, ISBN 0-516-21511-6. SERIES: True Book. SUBJECTS: Conservation; Ecology; Rain forests. RL C.

After discussing and showing photographs of the plants and wildlife of rain forests and their importance to all life, the author makes a plea for their preservation. The book ends with lists of books, organizations, and Web sites; a glossary; and an index.

3252 *Trucks*. Children's Press, 1997, o.p. SERIES: True Book. SUBJECTS: Trucks. RL C. LEXILE 780L.

From small pick-ups to tractor trailers, trucks are used to haul things and people. Color photographs and a detailed text give general information about many kinds of trucks. Also included are a bibliography, Web sites, truck-related groups, an index, and a glossary.

Stolz, Mary

3253 *Emmett's Pig*. Ill. by Garth Williams. HarperCollins, pap., 2006, ISBN 0-06-059714-3. SUBJECTS: City and town life — Fiction; Farm and country life — Fiction; Pigs — Fiction. RL C.

Though he lives in a city, Emmett dreams of having his own pig. A trip to the country makes this come true. With softly colored illustrations and a new format, this classic book for young readers is sure to continue to find fans.

Stone, Lynn M.

3254 *African Buffalo*. Ill. with photos. Rourke, 1990, o.p. SERIES: African Animal Discovery Library. SUBJECTS: African buffalo. RL C.

Native to Kenya and Tanzania, the African buffalo lives in herds, is a plant eater, and is often prey to the lion. The life, habits and habitat, enemies, and so on of the animal are briefly explored through alternating pages of colored photographs and text. A table of contents, glossary, and index are included.

3255 *Antelopes*. Ill. with photos. Rourke, 1990, o.p. SERIES: African Animal Discovery Library. SUBJECTS: Antelopes. RL C.

Through a brief text, alternating pages with colored photographs, readers are given an overview of life for the 70 species of African antelopes. The book also includes a table of contents, an index, and a glossary.

3256 *Baboons*. Ill. with photos. Rourke, 1990, o.p. SERIES: Monkey Discovery Library. SUBJECTS: Baboons. RL C.

Readers are given an opportunity to learn about the general characteristics, habits, and habitat of the seven species of baboons in a brief book with text alternating with full-color photographs. The

Stone, Lynn M. (cont.)

book also includes a table of contents, an index, and a glossary.

3257 *Bats*. Ill. with photos. Rourke, 1993, o.p. SERIES: Discovery Library of Nighttime Animals. SUBJECTS: Animals — Endangered; Bats. RL C.
How bats locate things, where they live, and what they eat are some of the things discussed in this brief look at an unusual mammal. Color photographs alternate with the text and offer a good introduction to the many kinds of bats. Glossary and index are appended.

3258 *Bears*. Ill. with photos. Rourke, 1990, o.p. SERIES: North American Animal Discovery Library. SUBJECTS: Animals — Endangered; Bears. RL C.
A descriptive text alternates with pages of full-color photographs to introduce general characteristics, habitat, and so on of bears such as the grizzly, polar, and black. The brief book also contains a table of contents, an index, and a glossary.

3259 *Bears*. Ill. with photos. Rourke, 1993, ISBN 0-86625-438-2. SERIES: Discovery Library of Predators. SUBJECTS: Bears. RL C.
Although only the polar bear is a full-time predator, other North American bears are at times predators as well. In alternating pages of text and color photographs, the habits, food, habitat, and so on of a selection of bears are introduced. Index and glossary are appended.

3260 *Beavers*. Ill. with photos. Rourke, 1990, ISBN 0-86593-041-4. SERIES: North American Animal Discovery Library. SUBJECTS: Beavers. RL B.
A very short book with alternating pages of text and rather muddied photographs, this shows beavers and their way of life, their environment, and their relationship to the world of people. An index and a glossary are appended.

3261 *Birds*. Ill. with photos. Rourke, 1993, ISBN 0-86625-440-4. SERIES: Discovery Library of Predators. SUBJECTS: Animals — Endangered; Birds. RL C.
The concentration here is on predator birds, especially hawks, eagles, and owls. There is also mention of egrets, herons, and pelicans. Their means of attacking and killing their prey and their status in the wild are also covered. Color photographs, a glossary, and an index add to the brief text.

3262 *Brown Bears*. Lerner, 1998, ISBN 0-8225-3029-5. SERIES: Early Bird Nature. SUBJECTS: Bears. RL C. LEXILE 490L.
Brownies, also known as grizzlies or Kodiaks, are the world's largest bears. This book focuses on the life and habitat of Alaska's brown bears. The book, illustrated with color photographs, also includes a section for adults, a glossary and an index.

3263 *Butterflies*. Ill. with photos. Rourke, 1993, o.p. SERIES: Discovery Library of Insects. SUBJECTS: Animals — Endangered; Butterflies and moths. RL C.
The development, food, and life cycle of the butterfly are introduced through alternating pages of colorful photographs and clear text. Many examples of butterfly species can be seen in the pictures. An index and a glossary are included.

3264 *Cheetahs*. Ill. with photos. Rourke, 1989, ISBN 0-86592-503-8. SERIES: Big Cats Discovery Library. SUBJECTS: Cheetahs; Pets — Cats. RL C.
An overview of the life, habitat, and enemies of the fastest mammal on earth, this look at the uncatlike cheetah uses alternating pages of topically arranged text and full-color photographs to present its information. Also included are an index, a glossary, and a table of contents.

3265 *Chickens*. Ill. with photos. Rourke, 1990, ISBN 0-86593-034-1. SERIES: Farm Animal Discovery Library. SUBJECTS: Chickens. RL C.
Here chickens, their habits, uses, and history, are introduced to readers via alternating pages of topically arranged text and full-color photographs. The book also includes an index, a table of contents, and a glossary.

3266 *Chimpanzees*. Ill. with photos. Rourke, 1990, ISBN 0-86593-064-3. SERIES: Monkey Discovery Library. SUBJECTS: Monkeys. RL C.
An overview of the life, habits, habitat, and so on of the chimpanzee is supported by full-color photographs accenting the topically arranged text. The book also contains an index and a glossary as well as a table of contents.

3267 *Cougars*. Lerner, 1997, ISBN 0-8225-3013-9. SERIES: Early Bird Nature. SUBJECTS: Cougars. RL C. LEXILE 540L.

Whether it is called a puma, a panther, a mountain lion, or a cougar, this large cat lives in different areas of the Americas, is a predator, and has its own territory. This and other information is provided along with color photographs, pages for adults, a glossary and an index.

3268 *Cougars*. Ill. with photos. Rourke, 1989, ISBN 0-86592-505-4. SERIES: Big Cats Discovery Library. SUBJECTS: Cougars; Pets — Cats. RL C.

An animal of many names, the cougar is found throughout North and South America. The animal's life-style, habits, habitat, and so on are covered in a topically arranged text alternating with color photographs. The book also includes an index, a glossary, and a table of contents.

3269 *Cows*. Ill. with photos. Rourke, 1990, ISBN 0-86593-039-2. SERIES: Farm Animal Discovery Library. SUBJECTS: Cows; Farm and country life. RL C.

Not native to North America, the domestic cow is an import from Europe and other parts of the world. This brief book is topically arranged and in alternating pages of text and color photographs shows how cows are raised, their uses, their great variety, and so on. Index and glossary are included.

3270 *Crocodiles*. Ill. with photos. Rourke, 1990, ISBN 0-86593-060-0. SERIES: Australian Animal Library. SUBJECTS: Alligators; Crocodiles; Reptiles and amphibians. RL C.

Its relatives, way of living, habitat, and physical characteristics are subjects covered in this brief look at the saltwater crocodile. Alternating pages of text and full-color photographs are supported by an index, a glossary, and a table of contents.

3271 *Deer*. Ill. with photos. Rourke, 1990, ISBN 0-86593-043-0. SERIES: North American Animal Discovery Library. SUBJECTS: Deer. RL C.

The relatives, habitat, physical characteristics, and so on of North American deer are described in a brief text and shown in full-page color photographs. The book also has an index, a glossary, and a table of contents.

3272 *Dingoes*. Ill. with photos. Rourke, 1990, ISBN 0-86593-057-0. SERIES: Australian Animal Library. SUBJECTS: Dingoes; Pets — Dogs. RL C.

A wild dog, the dingo is native to Australia and roams throughout it. The animal's habits, habitat, life cycle, and physical characteristics are some of the topics covered in this introductory look at the dingo. Full-color photographs are often grainy and dull. Index and glossary are included.

3273 *Ducks*. Ill. with photos. Rourke, 1990, ISBN 0-86593-036-8. SERIES: Farm Animal Discovery Library. SUBJECTS: Ducks. RL C.

Though this concentrates most text on the domestic duck, wild ducks such as the mallard are also mentioned. The book discusses the bird's physical characteristics, habits, habitat, food, and so on. Text alternates with full-page color photographs. Index, glossary, and table of contents are included.

3274 *Eagles*. Ill. with photos. Rourke, 1989, o.p. SERIES: Bird Discovery Library. SUBJECTS: Eagles. RL C.

Stone introduces several species of eagles and gives examples of their habitats, diet, nesting, and relationship to humans without dwelling on life cycles or any specifics. The color photographs are good. The brief book includes an index and glossary.

3275 *Fish*. Ill. with photos. Rourke, 1993, ISBN 0-86625-436-6. SERIES: Discovery Library of Predators. SUBJECTS: Fish. RL C.

The shark, lamprey, and muskellunge are a few of the fish mentioned in this look at fish as predators. The text is topically arranged and alternates with full-page colored photographs. Also included are an index, a table of contents, and a limited glossary.

3276 *Flamingoes*. Ill. with photos. Rourke, 1993, ISBN 0-86593-283-2. SERIES: Discovery Library of Unusual Animals. SUBJECTS: Birds; Flamingoes. RL C.

Found throughout the world, the flamingo is known for its pink plumage, long neck, and large bill. The large bird also builds a most unusual chimney-shaped nest of mud. Information about the various types of flamingoes and their habits is accompanied by color photographs, an index, and a glossary.

Stone, Lynn M. (cont.)

3277 *Flying Squirrels*. Ill. with photos. Rourke, 1993, ISBN 0-86593-298-0. SERIES: Discovery Library of Nighttime Animals. SUBJECTS: Flying squirrels. RL C.

Unlike tree squirrels, the flying squirrel is nocturnal and is able to glide from tree to tree. Found throughout the world, the animal has membranes that stretch between its side legs and can be used to navigate as it glides. Lifestyle, habitat, and more are included, as are color photographs.

3278 *Frogs*. Ill. with photos. Rourke, 1993, ISBN 0-86593-279-4. SERIES: Discovery Library of Unusual Animals. SUBJECTS: Frogs and toads; Reptiles and amphibians. RL C.

Good color photographs alternate with topical pages of text to give readers an introduction to some of the many species of frogs found throughout the world. The book covers generally their life cycle, food, means of protection, and so on. It also includes an index and a glossary.

3279 *Gibbons*. Ill. with photos. Rourke, 1990, ISBN 0-86593-062-7. SERIES: Monkey Discovery Library. SUBJECTS: Animals — Endangered; Gibbons. RL C.

Endangered because of deforestation, gibbons are apes that live high in trees and have few enemies. Their physical characteristics, habits, habitat, and more are introduced via text and full-color photographs. Index, glossary, and table of contents are included.

3280 *Giraffes*. Ill. with photos. Rourke, 1990, ISBN 0-86593-050-3. SERIES: African Animal Discovery Library. SUBJECTS: Giraffes. RL C.

Living in areas south of the Sahara Desert, the giraffe is in danger of losing its habitat to humans. In this introduction to the world's tallest animal, its habitat, relatives, physical characteristics, and so on are mentioned in a text that alternates pages with full-color photographs.

3281 *Gorillas*. Ill. with photos. Rourke, 1990, ISBN 0-86593-063-5. SERIES: Monkey Discovery Library. SUBJECTS: Animals — Endangered; Gorillas. RL C.

Gorillas are native to rain forest areas in Africa. The author describes this endangered animal's habitat, life cycle, food, and more. Page-length topical discussions are complemented with full-color photographs. The book also contains a table of contents, an index, and a glossary.

3282 *Hippopotamus*. Ill. with photos. Rourke, 1990, ISBN 0-86593-051-1. SERIES: African Animal Discovery Library. SUBJECTS: Hippopotami. RL C.

The life-style, habitat, predators of, and future hopes for the survival of the hippopotamus are explored in a brief, topically arranged text complemented by color photographs. The book is made more accessible by a table of contents, an index, and a glossary.

3283 *Horses*. Ill. with photos. Rourke, 1990, ISBN 0-86593-035-X. SERIES: Farm Animal Discovery Library. SUBJECTS: Horses. RL C.

Stone uses color photographs alternating with topical pages of text to give readers a glimpse of the history, uses, life, and habitat of a variety of horses. The brief book also contains a table of contents, an index, and a glossary.

3284 *Hyenas*. Ill. with photos. Rourke, 1990, ISBN 0-86593-049-X. SERIES: African Animal Discovery Library. SUBJECTS: Animals — Endangered; Hyenas. RL C.

As Stone explains, at least one species of hyena has become endangered due to loss of African habitat and too much hunting. In a topically arranged book, the author explains the physical characteristics, habitat, and life cycle of the hyena. Text is heavily illustrated with color photographs.

3285 *Jaguars*. Ill. with photos. Rourke, 1989, ISBN 0-86592-506-2. SERIES: Big Cats Discovery Library. SUBJECTS: Animals — Endangered; Jaguars; Pets — Cats. RL C.

Found most often in tropical forests, the jaguar resembles the leopard but is larger and stockier. Here readers can learn about the animal's habitat, food, life cycle, and so on. The text is accompanied by many full-color photographs, an index, a table of contents, and a glossary.

3286 *Jellyfish*. Ill. with photos. Rourke, 1993, ISBN 0-86593-284-0. SERIES: Unusual Animals. SUBJECTS: Jellyfish. RL C.

The common kinds of jellyfish found throughout the world, their habits and habitats, their prey and predators, and much more are included in this brief book. Text alternates with well-done full-page color photographs. An index and a glossary are included.

3287 *Kangaroos*. Ill. with photos. Rourke, 1990, ISBN 0-86593-058-9. SERIES: Australian Animal Library. SUBJECTS: Kangaroos; Marsupials. RL C.

Variations in size and other characteristics differentiate the 54 species of kangaroos in Australia. Here the author provides readers with introductory information on physical characteristics, habitat, and much more. The book is illustrated with many full-color photographs.

3288 *Koalas*. Ill. with photos. Rourke, 1990, ISBN 0-86593-055-4. SERIES: Australian Animal Library. SUBJECTS: Koalas; Marsupials. RL C.

Once nearly extinct from overhunting, the koala now faces difficulties from loss of habitat — especially eucalyptus trees. The life cycle, physical characteristics, habitat, and more are explained with a brief, topical text and full-color photographs. Index, table of contents, and glossary are included.

3289 *Leopards*. Ill. with photos. Rourke, 1989, ISBN 0-86592-502-X. SERIES: Big Cats Discovery Library. SUBJECTS: Leopards; Pets — Cats. RL C.

Similar to but smaller than the jaguar, the leopard is found in Africa and Asia. Its characteristics, life cycle, habitat, and so on are discussed in the brief text complemented by full-color photographs. The book also has a table of contents, an index, and a glossary.

3290 *Lions*. Ill. with photos. Rourke, 1989, ISBN 0-86592-501-1. SERIES: Big Cats Discovery Library. SUBJECTS: Lions; Pets — Cats. RL C.

Found only in Africa and India, the lion now faces diminishing habitat as land is used for farming and populations of humans increase. Stone offers readers brief information on the lion's habitat, life cycle, food, and so on. Many slightly fuzzy color photographs illustrate the text. Index and glossary are included.

3291 *Moths*. Ill. with photos. Rourke, 1993, ISBN 0-86593-297-2. SERIES: Discovery Library of Nighttime Animals. SUBJECTS: Butterflies and moths; Insects. RL C.

Related to the butterfly, the moth is explained here as usually being nocturnal and identifiable by its feathery antennae. Clear explanations of the moth's life cycle, habitat, and so on alternate with pages of good color photographs. The book also includes an index and a glossary.

3292 *Opossums*. Ill. with photos. Rourke, 1993, ISBN 0-86593-295-6. SERIES: Discovery Library of Nighttime Animals. SUBJECTS: Animals — Nocturnal; Marsupials; Opossums. RL C.

A relative of the Australian opossum and North America's only marsupial, the Virginia opossum now lives in a great part of the United States. In alternating pages of full-color photographs and topically arranged text, the opossum's life and habits are surveyed. A very brief index and a glossary are included.

3293 *Orangutans*. Ill. with photos. Rourke, 1990, ISBN 0-86593-065-1. SERIES: Monkey Discovery Library. SUBJECTS: Animals — Endangered; Orangutans. RL C.

Hunting and loss of habitat have made the orangutan of Borneo and Sumatra a rare primate. The shy animal's life cycle, habits, physical characteristics, and so on are described in this brief, topically arranged book. Illustrated with mediocre color photographs, the book includes an index and a glossary.

3294 *Ostriches*. Ill. with photos. Rourke, 1989, ISBN 0-86592-323-X. SERIES: Bird Discovery Library. SUBJECTS: Ostriches. RL B.

A simple, clear text and excellent photographs describe an ostrich's habitat, appearance, nesting, diet, and its predators. The book is small with only 18 pages of alternating text and photographs.

3295 *Owls*. Ill. with photos. Rourke, 1989, ISBN 0-86592-326-4. SERIES: Bird Discovery Library. SUBJECTS: Owls. RL B.

Examples of several species and the characteristics, habitat, and prey of owls are presented in color photographs and easily understood text. Although not a detailed study, this does provide good information in 18 pages of alternating text and photographs.

3296 *Parrots*. Ill. with photos. Rourke, 1993, ISBN 0-86593-280-8. SERIES: Discovery

Stone, Lynn M. (cont.)

Library of Unusual Animals. SUBJECTS: Animals — Endangered; Birds; Parrots. RL C.

Alternating pages of color photographs and topically arranged text give readers an introductory look at some of the many varieties of parrots from the hyacinth Macaw to the budgerigar. Brief glossary and index are included.

3297 *Penguins*. Lerner, 1998, ISBN 0-87614-907-7. SERIES: Early Bird Nature. SUBJECTS: Birds; Penguins. RL C. LEXILE 630L.

Seventeen species of penguins — weighing from 3 pounds to 90 pounds — live in the Southern Hemisphere. The seven the author discusses live on or near Antarctica. Information on life cycle, food, enemies, and habitat is provided along with a section for adults, a glossary, and an index.

3298 *Penguins*. Ill. with photos. Rourke, 1989, ISBN 0-86592-325-6. SERIES: Bird Discovery Library. SUBJECTS: Penguins. RL B.

Although information about the penguin's life cycle is not included, this book is nevertheless a nice introduction to penguin types, habitats, diets, and predators. The color photographs are quite good.

3299 *Pigs*. Ill. with photos. Rourke, 1990, ISBN 0-86593-037-6. SERIES: Farm Animal Discovery Library. SUBJECTS: Pigs. RL C.

Although an intelligent animal, the pig is most useful as food and as leather for apparel. Stone describes the animal, how it is raised, its wild ancestors and more. Several of the color photographs show pigs in mud without indicating why the usually clean animal coats itself with mud.

3300 *Prairie Dogs*. Ill. with photos. Rourke, 1993, ISBN 0-86593-282-4. SERIES: Discovery Library of Unusual Animals. SUBJECTS: Animals — Endangered; Prairie dogs. RL C.

A relative of the squirrel, the very social prairie dog lives on the western prairie in underground "towns" with connecting tunnels. With their number decreasing, some kinds of prairie dogs are facing extinction. Illustrated with color photographs, the brief text also has a glossary and an index.

3301 *Puffins*. Ill. with photos. Rourke, 1993, ISBN 0-86593-281-6. SERIES: Discovery Library of Unusual Animals. SUBJECTS: Birds; Puffins. RL C.

Cousins of the auk, puffins have unusual markings that make them quite distinct. They also nest underground, spend their winters at sea, and dive for their food — fish. Initially the text is confusing about whether puffins actually fly. Color photographs complement the topically arranged text.

3302 *Raccoons*. Ill. with photos. Rourke, 1990, ISBN 0-86593-045-7. SERIES: North American Animal Discovery Library. SUBJECTS: Raccoons. RL C.

Common throughout North America, the raccoon is discussed in terms of life-style, habitat, food, and so on in a topically arranged text. Color photographs illustrate the book, which also includes an index, a table of contents, and a glossary.

3303 *Reptiles*. Ill. with photos. Rourke, 1993, ISBN 0-86625-437-4. SERIES: Discovery Library of Predators. SUBJECTS: Animals — Endangered; Reptiles and amphibians. RL C.

North American reptiles such as the alligator, rattlesnake, and snapping turtle are introduced as creatures that feed on other animals. Some of their habits and habitats are included in the topically arranged book, which has text alternating with colored photographs. Index and glossary are included.

3304 *Sandhill Cranes*. Lerner, 1997, ISBN 0-8225-3027-9. SERIES: Early Bird Nature. SUBJECTS: Animals — Endangered; Birds; Cranes, Sandhill. RL B. LEXILE 560L.

Through clear color photographs and concise text, readers can learn about the life cycle, habitat, food, and courtship rituals of the beautiful gray crane with a red patch on its head. The book also includes a section for adults as well as a glossary and an index.

3305 *Sea Turtles*. Ill. with photos. Rourke, 1993, ISBN 0-86593-296-4. SERIES: Discovery Library of Nighttime Animals. SUBJECTS: Animals — Endangered; Reptiles and amphibians; Sea turtles. RL C.

In a very brief topical text with alternating pages of photographs, the author discusses several kinds of sea turtles, their nesting, food, homing instinct, and so on. The book also has both a brief — and not always clear — glossary and an index.

3306 *Sheep*. Ill. with photos. Rourke, 1990, ISBN 0-86593-038-4. SERIES: Farm Animal Discovery Library. SUBJECTS: Farm and country life; Sheep. RL C.

Alternating pages of grainy color photographs and topically arranged text look at the many kinds of sheep found around the world but especially the domestic breeds found in Great Britain and the United States. The book also has a glossary of limited usefulness and an index.

3307 *Skunks*. Ill. with photos. Rourke, 1990, ISBN 0-86593-046-5. SERIES: North American Animal Discovery Library. SUBJECTS: Skunks. RL C.

The various kinds of skunks are discussed in a topically arranged text that alternates pages with grainy photographs that often seem of little importance to the subject. The text will be useful for children studying this common animal. Index and glossary are included.

3308 *Snow Monkeys*. Ill. with photos. Rourke, 1990, ISBN 0-86593-066-X. SERIES: Monkey Discovery Library. SUBJECTS: Animals — Endangered; Monkeys. RL C.

A very social animal, the snow monkey, a macaque, lives in northern Japan and is related to many other types of macaques throughout the world. Adequate color photographs alternate with brief, topically arranged pages of text. Index and mediocre glossary are included.

3309 *Tasmanian Devil*. Ill. with photos. Rourke, 1990, ISBN 0-86593-056-2. SERIES: Australian Animal Library. SUBJECTS: Marsupials; Tasmanian devils. RL B.

The Tasmanian devil is the size of a small dog. Here its habits, food, habitat, and relatives are looked into in a topically arranged book with alternating pages of grainy photographs and clearly written text. An easy-to-understand glossary and an index are included in the very brief book.

3310 *Tigers*. Ill. with photos. Rourke, 1989, ISBN 0-86592-504-6. SERIES: Big Cats Discovery Library. SUBJECTS: Animals — Endangered; Pets — Cats; Tigers. RL C.

Well written and interesting with a text slightly longer than others in this series, the story of the tiger, its habitat, endangerment, wild relatives, and its rearing of young are all covered in alternating pages of text and grainy photographs. Index and glossary are included.

3311 *Toads*. Ill. with photos. Rourke, 1993, ISBN 0-86593-294-8. SERIES: Discovery Library of Nighttime Animals. SUBJECTS: Frogs and toads; Reptiles and amphibians. RL B.

Good color photographs and a brief text are on alternating pages in this short book. The toad and its relatives, its habitat, its life cycle, and more are mentioned here. A glossary and an index follow the text.

3312 *Vultures*. Photos by author. Rourke, 1989, ISBN 0-86592-324-8. SERIES: Bird Discovery Library. SUBJECTS: Vultures. RL B.

An excellent text that gives an overview of the types of vultures, habitats, and diet. Explains why most vultures have no head feathers. Illustrated with color photographs.

3313 *Wild Cats*. Ill. with photos. Rourke, 1993, ISBN 0-86625-441-2. SERIES: Discovery Library of Predators. SUBJECTS: Animals — Endangered; Pets — Cats. RL C.

Four of the North American wild cats — the lynx, cougar, jaguar, and bobcat — and their characteristics, habitat, food, and so on are explored in text and color photographs arranged topically. The book also includes an index, a glossary, and a table of contents.

3314 *Wolves*. Ill. with photos. Rourke, 1990, ISBN 0-86593-044-9. SERIES: North American Animal Discovery Library. SUBJECTS: Animals — Endangered; Wolves. RL C.

The habitat, characteristics, life-style, and so on of the North American gray wolf are discussed as is its relationship to humans. Illustrated with color photographs, the book also provides access to readers through a table of contents and an index. A glossary is also included.

3315 *Wombats*. Ill. with photos. Rourke, 1990, ISBN 0-86593-059-7. SERIES: Australian Animal Library. SUBJECTS: Marsupials; Wombats. RL C.

Stone, Lynn M. (cont.)

A plant eater, the wombat is discussed in terms of habits, characteristics, predators, and so on in a brief, topically arranged book that alternates text with full-color photographs. The straightforward book is accessed via an index and a table of contents. A glossary is included.

3316 *Zebras*. Ill. with photos. Rourke, 1990, ISBN 0-86593-048-1. SERIES: African Animal Discovery Library. SUBJECTS: Zebras. RL C.

The zebra is a herd animal similar to the horse. Here the life cycle, habitat, physical characteristics, and so on of the zebra are briefly looked at in a clearly written text, topically arranged, with alternating pages of rather grainy color photographs. The book also has a table of contents, an index, and a glossary.

Stone, Rosetta (pseud.)

3317 *Because a Little Bug Went Ka-Choo!* Ill. by Michael Frith. Beginner Books, 1975, ISBN 0-394-83130-6. SERIES: I Can Read It All by Myself. SUBJECTS: Humorous stories; Stories in rhyme. RL B.

A mere sneeze from a bug sets off a chain of events that results in a ship being airlifted into a circus parade. The silliness of this rhyming story is carried over into the zany full-color pictures.

Storad, Conrad J.

3318 *The Circulatory System*. Lerner, 2005, ISBN 0-8225-1246-7. SERIES: Early Bird Body Systems. SUBJECTS: Human body — Blood; Human body — Circulation. RL C. LEXILE 580L.

Color photographs and well-done diagrams work with the text to explain the way the heart pumps blood throughout the body with the aid of arteries, veins, and capillaries. A note to parents is followed by a bibliography, Web sites, a glossary, and an index.

3319 *Saguaro Cactus*. Photos by Paula Jansen. Lerner, 1994, ISBN 0-8225-3002-3. SERIES: Early Bird Nature. SUBJECTS: Cacti. RL C.

A good introduction not just to the saguaro but to cacti in general, this book handles most aspects of the saguaro's life cycle in a well-written text augmented by excellent color photographs. A glossary and an index add to the usefulness of the book.

3320 *Tarantulas*. Lerner, 1998, ISBN 0-8225-3024-4. SERIES: Early Bird Nature. SUBJECTS: Spiders; Tarantulas. RL C. LEXILE 600L.

There are more than 700 species of tarantulas in the world and 30 in the United States. This book provides information on their physical characteristics, life cycle, habitat, and behavior. Color photographs, diagrams, a section for adults, a glossary, and an index complete the book.

Storm, Betsy

3321 *I Can Be an Interior Designer*. Ill. with photos. Childrens Press, 1989, o.p. SERIES: I Can Be. SUBJECTS: Careers; Interior design. RL C.

The complexities of design work are shown in photographs and explained in the text. The amount of training, the interaction with clients, and the understanding of the effects of color are some of the things mentioned. The book also includes glossary and index.

Storr, Catherine

3322 *David and Goliath*. Ill. by Chris Molan. Raintree, 1985, o.p. SERIES: People of the Bible. SUBJECTS: Bible stories. RL B.

A brief text and many colorful romanticized paintings tell the story of the shepherd David and how he came to slay the giant Goliath and lead the Israelites to victory. Included is a map showing the sites mentioned in the Old Testament story.

3323 *Noah and His Ark*. Ill. by Jim Russell. Raintree, 1982, o.p. SERIES: People of the Bible. SUBJECTS: Bible stories. RL B.

The Old Testament story of Noah and the flood is retold in simple language with much dialogue. The detailed watercolor pictures set the story in biblical times. This might be useful for Sunday school classes as well as individual interest.

Streissguth, Tom

3324 *Daniel Boone*. Ill. by Loren Chantland. Carolrhoda, 2002, ISBN 1-57505-520-1. SERIES: On My Own Biography. SUBJECTS: Biographies; Frontier and pioneer life;

United States — History. RL C. LEXILE 500L.

Pioneer and frontiersman Daniel Boone led the first settlers into Kentucky. Illustrated with dramatic scratchboard pictures, this biography gives readers a surprisingly good overview of Boone's life. A chronology is included.

3325 *John Brown*. Ill. by Ralph L. Ramstad. Carolrhoda, 1999, ISBN 1-57505-334-9. SERIES: On My Own Biography. SUBJECTS: Abolition and abolitionists; Biographies; United States — History. RL C. LEXILE 420L.

Brought up with a strong religious ethic, John Brown attempted to start a war against slavery at Harper's Ferry. Unsuccessful, he was caught and hanged. Though not a hero to everyone, Brown's life is important to the history of the United States. Illustrated with realistic paintings, the book ends with a chronology of Brown's life.

Suen, Anastasia

3326 *The Clubhouse*. Ill. by Allan Eitzen. Puffin, 2002, ISBN 0-670-03537-8. SERIES: Puffin Easy-to-Read. SUBJECTS: Behavior — Cooperative — Fiction; Clubs — Fiction. RL B.

Five ethnically diverse children combine forces to build a clubhouse in a vacant lot. The characters are based on those created by Ezra Jack Keats. Eitzen's art uses the same media and style used by Keats in his picture books. Together the art and text make a successful urban story.

3327 *Hamster Chase*. Ill. by Allan Eitzen. Penguin, pap., 2001, ISBN 0-14-230134-5. SERIES: Viking Easy-to-Read. SUBJECTS: Hamsters — Fiction; School stories. RL B. LEXILE 160L.

As Peter, Archie, and Amy are putting the class hamster, Mikey, back in its cage, Amy sneezes and Mikey is loose. The three find the perfect way to lure Mikey back. The book bases its art and characters on those of Ezra Jack Keats.

3328 *Loose Tooth*. Ill. by Allan Eitzen. Penguin, pap., 2002, ISBN 0-14-250064-X. SERIES: Viking Easy-to-Read. SUBJECTS: African Americans — Fiction; Human body — Teeth — Fiction; Sports — Basketball — Fiction. RL B.

It's picture day at school and Peter is determined not to lose his loose tooth before he gets his picture. But when they have a game of basketball with Room 3, his tooth falls out. The series is based on the characters and created by Ezra Jack Keats.

3329 *Willie's Birthday*. Ill. by Allan Eitzen. Viking, 2001, ISBN 0-670-88943-1. SERIES: Viking Easy-to-Read. SUBJECTS: Birthdays — Fiction; Pets — Dogs — Fiction; Pets — Fiction. RL B. LEXILE 50L.

When Peter's friends bring their pets to Willie's birthday party, things don't go as planned. The story and art (part of the Peter's Neighborhood series) are based on the work of Ezra Jack Keats.

Suhr, Mandy

3330 *How I Breathe*. Ill. by Mike Gordon. Carolrhoda, 1992, o.p. SERIES: I'm Alive. SUBJECTS: Human body — Lungs; Human body — Respiration. RL B.

A child explains the importance of oxygen to her lungs and tells how her lungs work to help her muscles. Cartoon illustrations make this an enjoyable book and an additional section of ideas for parents reinforces the information found in the text.

3331 *I Am Growing*. Ill. by Mike Gordon. Carolrhoda, 1992, o.p. SERIES: I'm Alive. SUBJECTS: Animals — Growth and development; Growing up; Human body. RL B.

A little boy explains how he grew from a baby to a toddler to a child old enough to read. He then talks about the food and exercise that keep him healthy. Comic ink drawings with color washes humorously extend the text.

3332 *I Can Move*. Ill. by Mike Gordon. Carolrhoda, 1992, o.p. SERIES: I'm Alive. SUBJECTS: Human body — Skeleton. RL B.

Cartoon illustrations and a short but lively text explain how it is that muscles help skeletons to move. The information is easily understood and interesting. A final page of activities and information for parents reinforces the text.

Sullivan, George

3333 *Willie Mays*. Ill. by David Brown. Putnam, 1973, o.p. SERIES: See and Read Beginning to Read Biography. SUBJECTS: African Americans; Biographies; Sports — Baseball. RL C.

The story of baseball great Willie Mays's beginnings and career is written very clearly and well. One of the leading home-run hitters of all time, Mays was also one of the first black athletes to integrate major-league baseball. Illustrated with black, white, and green line drawings.

Sullivan, Paula

3334 *Todd's Box*. Ill. by Nadine B. Westcott. Harcourt, 2004, ISBN 0-15-205093-0. SERIES: Green Light Readers. SUBJECTS: Parent and child — Fiction; Walking — Fiction. RL A.

On a walk to the bus with his mother, Todd gathers objects to surprise her. Illustrated with cartoon-like watercolor and ink pictures, the book includes a variety of activities at the end.

Super, Gretchen

3335 *Drugs and Our World*. Ill. by Blanche Sims. Twenty-First Century, 1990, o.p. SERIES: Drug-Free Kids. SUBJECTS: Behavior — Responsible; Drugs and drug abuse. RL B.

Stressing that each person is a part of a larger community and the world, the book shows how drugs can hurt or cause unhappiness to others. Not intent on providing information on drugs, this instead pushes personal responsibility. Attractive illustrations complement the text.

3336 *Family Traditions*. Ill. by Kees de Kiefte. Twenty-First Century, 1992, o.p. SERIES: Your Family Album. SUBJECTS: Customs; Holidays. RL C.

Throughout the year and the world, families celebrate holidays in particular ways or establish traditions for themselves to share. Explanations of festivals, community holidays, and evolving traditions are given.

3337 *What Are Drugs?* Ill. by Blanche Sims. Twenty-First Century, 1990, o.p. SERIES: Drug-Free Kids. SUBJECTS: Drugs and drug abuse. RL B.

After explaining how the body works and how to keep it healthy, Super tells how different drugs (alcohol, nicotine, marijuana, cocaine, and crack) work and how they hurt the body. The final chapter gives advice on what to do in the face of drugs. Humorous watercolor and ink paintings help to get the message across.

3338 *You Can Say "No" to Drugs*. Ill. by Blanche Sims. Twenty-First Century, 1990, o.p. SERIES: Drug-Free Kids. SUBJECTS: Behavior — Responsible; Drugs and drug abuse. RL B.

Never saying that refusing drugs is easy, the author reminds readers that they have people they can turn to, even when peer pressure is very strong. The drugs mentioned here are alcohol, cigarettes, and marijuana. Illustrations are attractive pictures with child appeal.

Sutcliffe, Jane

3339 *Babe Didrikson Zaharias: All-Around Athlete*. Ill. by Jeni Reeves. Carolrhoda, 2000, ISBN 1-57505-421-3. SERIES: On My Own Biography. SUBJECTS: Biographies; Olympics; Sports. RL C. LEXILE 550L.

This biography of Zaharias, called the "World's Greatest Woman Athlete," begins with her passion for running as a child in Texas and continues to her three Olympic gold medals. A page of additional information and a chronology are included. Illustrations are done in detailed and realistic colored pencil.

3340 *Jesse Owens*. Ill. by Janice Lee Porter. Carolrhoda, 2001, ISBN 1-57505-451-5. SERIES: On My Own Biography. SUBJECTS: African Americans; Biographies; Olympics. RL C. LEXILE 490L.

Born in Alabama and educated in Ohio, Jesse Owens proves to be a record setting runner, high jumper, and Olympic champion. Strong, expressive paintings illustrate the biography. A chronology finishes the book.

Sutherland, Tui T.

3341 *Fun with Mo and Ella*. Ill. by Rose Mary Berlin. Grosset & Dunlap, pap., 2002, ISBN 0-448-42638-2. SERIES: First Friends First Readers. SUBJECTS: Elephants — Fiction;

Friendship — Fiction; Mice — Fiction. RL A.

A mouse and an elephant share a birthday, make presents for each other and bring a new friend into their lives. Pencil and watercolor art helps to create the two stories.

3342 *Meet Mo and Ella*. Ill. by Rose Mary Berlin. Grosset & Dunlap, 2001, o.p. SERIES: First Friends First Readers. SUBJECTS: Concepts — Fiction; Elephants — Fiction; Mice — Fiction. RL A.

Ella and Mo are best friends but their difference in size makes their friendship challenging — especially at the playground. The illustrations are done with soft colors depicting two gentle creatures.

Swain, Gwenyth

3343 *Johnny Appleseed*. Ill. by Janice Lee Porter. Carolrhoda, 2001, ISBN 1-57505-519-8. SERIES: On My Own Biography. SUBJECTS: Apples; Biographies; United States — History. RL C. LEXILE 530L.

John Chapman's life as a grower of apple trees and missionary is carefully researched, well written, and interesting. Brightly colored and expressive paintings illustrate the biography. A chronology concludes the book.

Swallow, Su

3344 *Water*. Photos by Chris Fairclough. Watts, 1990, o.p. SERIES: Starting Points. SUBJECTS: Arts and crafts; Science experiments; Water. RL C.

Experiments, crafts, and art activities combine with a photographic overview of water in its many forms throughout the world to engage a child's interest. Also included is information on water customs in a variety of cultures.

Swanson, June

3345 *I Pledge Allegiance*. Rev. ed. Ill. by Rick Hanson. Carolrhoda, 2002, ISBN 0-87614-925-5. SERIES: On My Own. SUBJECTS: Flags; History — United States. RL B.

More than just a stirring history of the creation of the pledge of allegiance, this book also explains what the words mean in relation to U. S. history and how saying the pledge grew in importance. Illustrated with expressive watercolors, the book is well done.

Swayne, Dick, and Peter Savage

3346 *I Am a Farmer*. Photos by author. HarperCollins, 1978, o.p. SERIES: I-Like-to-Read. SUBJECTS: Careers; Farm and country life. RL B.

First published in Britain, this book shows a young girl (the farmer) as she leads the reader around her farm and discusses animals and chores. The text is interesting and offers some insights into farm life. Photographs are in full color.

3347 *I Am a Fisherman*. Photos by author. HarperCollins, 1978, o.p. SERIES: I-Like-to-Read. SUBJECTS: Careers; Sports — Fishing. RL C.

A short but lively text shows a young boy on a fishing expedition with four seasoned sailors. The climax of this British story comes when the child catches a flounder almost as large as he is. Illustrated with good full-color photographs.

Szekeres, Cyndy

3348 *Things Bunny Sees*. Ill. by author. Western, 1990, o.p. SERIES: Golden Very Easy Reader. SUBJECTS: Behavior — Curiosity — Fiction; Rabbits — Fiction. RL A.

A very young bunny observes the world around him, noticing colors, the moon, and much more. The limited text is closely tied to the watercolor pictures, which make the story complete.

T

Taha, Karen T.

3349 *Hotdog on TV*. Ill. by Hideko Takahashi. Dial, 2005, ISBN 0-8037-2933-2. SERIES: Dial Easy-to-Read. SUBJECTS: Humorous stories; Pets — Dogs — Fiction; Television — Fiction. RL B.

After being adopted from the animal shelter by the Beans, Hotdog has a chance to be the star of a

Taha, Karen T. (cont.)

dog food commercial. All goes well until he sneezes eating the dog food.

Tangborn, Wendell V.

3350 *Glaciers*. Rev. ed. Ill. by Marc Simont. HarperCollins, 1988, o.p. SERIES: Let's-Read-and-Find-Out. SUBJECTS: Geology and geologists. RL C.

Children will find this look at glaciers fascinating as they discover how they are made, how they move, and what happens to them as they travel. The pencil and watercolor illustrations make the book even more interesting and will add to a child's understanding of the information.

Tarcov, Edith H.

3351 *The Frog Prince*. Ill. by James Marshall. Scholastic, pap., 1993, ISBN 0-590-46571-6. SERIES: Hello Reader! SUBJECTS: Folklore; Frogs and toads; Princes and princesses — Fiction. RL B. LEXILE 380L.

While playing with her ball, a princess accidentally knocks it into a well. When a frog retrieves it for her, she promises to share her life with him. Forced to keep her promise, the princess discovers the frog is really a prince. Comical ink and watercolor paintings are a delight.

Tasan, Stan

3352 *Who Will Be My Pet?* Ill. by Roy McKie. Western, 1992, o.p. SERIES: Golden Very Easy Reader. SUBJECTS: Pets — Fiction. RL A.

Each time a little boy gets, is given, or wins an animal, somehow it manages to get away from him. At story's end, they all manage to return — to the boy's surprise. Illustrated with bold, humorous drawings with watercolor washes, the very limited text works well.

Tatham, Betty

3353 *Penguin Chick*. Ill. by Helen K. Davie. HarperCollins, 2002, ISBN 0-06-028594-X. SERIES: Let's-Read-and-Find-Out Science. SUBJECTS: Animals — Baby; Animals — Reproduction; Penguins. RL C. LEXILE AD450L.

From the laying of the egg in the midst of the Antarctic winter to its hatching and growth, the story of the emperor penguin is told in an interesting but very basic way. The text is illustrated with lovely watercolor art and is followed by two pages of additional information and activities.

Taylor, Kim

3354 *Frog*. Ill. with photos. Dutton, 1991, o.p. SERIES: See How They Grow. SUBJECTS: Frogs and toads. RL B.

Colorful photographic silhouettes set against white backgrounds and accompanied by a brief captioning text take readers from the hatching of a frog to its maturity. The frog, in this first-person account, discusses being an egg and a tadpole, and developing into a year-old frog. In 21 thick pages, the frog goes through seven stages.

Taylor, Leighton

3355 *Dolphins*. Ill. by Norbert Wu. Lerner, 1999, ISBN 0-8225-3033-3. SERIES: Early Bird Nature. SUBJECTS: Dolphins. RL C. LEXILE 470L.

In five chapters illustrated with color photographs and diagrams, children can learn a great deal about the dolphin, one of their favorite ocean mammals. A glossary and in-context explanations allow the authors to use a broad vocabulary. A section for adults and an index complete the book.

3356 *Jellyfish*. Ill. by Norbert Wu. Lerner, 1998, ISBN 0-8225-3028-7. SERIES: Early Bird Nature. SUBJECTS: Jellyfish; Oceans and ocean life. RL C. LEXILE 460L.

Some of the many varieties of jellyfish found throughout the oceans of the world are discussed in a clearly written text supported by color photographs, diagrams, a map, a section of advice to parents, a glossary and index.

Taylor, Sean

3357 *Small Bad Wolf*. Ill. by Jan Lewis. Kingfisher, pap., 2004, ISBN 0-7534-5801-2. SERIES: I Am Reading. SUBJECTS: Humorous stories; Parent and child — Fiction; Wolves — Fiction. RL C.

Trying to raise the Small Bad Wolf to be as bad as he is, the Big Bad Wolf takes him hunting.

Dressed as a granny when they try to catch soccer-playing children, the little wolf decides he'd rather play the game than eat the children. The Big Bad Wolf's antics are funny, as are the illustrations.

Taylor, Sydney

3358 *The Dog Who Came to Dinner.* Ill. by John Johnson. Modern Curriculum Press, 1991, ISBN 0-8136-5043-7. SERIES: Beginning-to-Read. SUBJECTS: Moving, household — Fiction; Pets — Dogs — Fiction. RL B.

When a large dog comes into the Browns' home along with their new neighbors, each family assumes it belongs to the other. Both families are too polite to say anything when the dog misbehaves. The detailed illustrations are realistic yet humorous and are done in full color.

Taylor-Butler, Christine

3359 *Booker T. Washington.* Children's Press, 2007, ISBN 0-516-29842-9. SERIES: Rookie Biography. SUBJECTS: African Americans; Biographies; Teachers and teaching. RL C. LEXILE 780L.

Born into slavery Washington worked hard to get an education and to teach others. The founder of Tuskegee Institute, he quietly supported those fighting for the rights of African Americans. Illustrated with archival photographs, the book includes a picture glossary and index.

3360 *Hawaii.* Children's Press, 2007, ISBN 0-531-12571-8. SERIES: Rookie Read-About Geography. SUBJECTS: Geography; Hawaii; United States. RL B.

Made up of 132 islands, Hawaii has beautiful beaches, volcanoes, tropical rain forests, crops of pineapple and sugar cane, and even cattle ranches. Color photographs extend the brief text, which includes some of the state symbols. An index and a photo glossary are included.

3361 *Kansas.* Children's Press, 2006, ISBN 0-516-24966-5. SERIES: Rookie Read-About Geography. SUBJECTS: Geography; Kansas; United States. RL B. LEXILE 420L.

With a varied landscape of hills and plains, Kansas sits in the middle of the United States. The important cities, landmarks, vegetation, crops, and industry are illustrated with color photographs and a brief text. The book also has a photo glossary and index.

3362 *The Missouri River.* Children's Press, 2006, ISBN 0-516-25037-X. SERIES: Rookie Read-About Geography. SUBJECTS: Geography; Rivers. RL B. LEXILE 540L.

The path of the Missouri (the longest river in the United States), the people living along it, its early explorers, its dams and how they have affected the people and animals, and how the river is used recreationally are all mentioned here. A photo glossary and index end the book.

3363 *Ohio.* Children's Press, 2007, ISBN 0-531-12573-4. SERIES: Rookie Read-About Geography. SUBJECTS: Geography; Ohio; United States. RL B.

Starting with Ohio's symbols (the buckeye, cardinal, and carnation), the book then moves to its geographic regions, products, wildlife and industries, and sites to visit. Though very brief and relying on color photographs and maps to extend the text, it still provides a good overview. A photo glossary and index are included.

3364 *Thurgood Marshall.* Children's Press, 2006, ISBN 0-516-25015-9. SERIES: Rookie Biography. SUBJECTS: African Americans; Biographies; United States — Supreme Court. RL B. LEXILE 480L.

The life of the first African American member of the United States Supreme Court is examined briefly with an emphasis on his strength of character and his determination to fight segregation. Includes a picture glossary and index.

3365 *Tiny Life in the Air.* Children's Press, 2005, ISBN 0-516-25273-9. SERIES: Rookie Read-About Science. SUBJECTS: Air; Microbes; Science and scientists. RL B.

With plenty of color photographs supporting the text, the author explains about life forms such as molds, fungi, bacteria, and viruses and how they grow and travel. Also included are a photo glossary and an index.

3366 *Tiny Life on Your Body.* Children's Press, 2005, ISBN 0-516-25299-2. SERIES: Rookie Read-About Science. SUBJECTS: Human body; Microbes; Science and scientists. RL B.

Taylor-Butler, Christine (cont.)

Human cells are full of bacteria, and it is the good bacteria that destroy the bad to keep people healthy. Viruses and vaccines are also looked at as the book attempts to explain how the children can help their bodies stay well. An index and photo glossary are included.

3367 *Vermont*. Children's Press, 2007, ISBN 0-531-12593-9. SERIES: Rookie Read-About Geography. SUBJECTS: Geography; United States; Vermont. RL B.

This book provides a variety of information on the state known for its beautiful fall scenery and maple syrup, covering its symbols, descriptions of the regions within it, the work, and the animal life. Illustrated with color photographs and maps, the book also includes a photo glossary and an index.

Tchin

3368 *Rabbit's Wish for Snow: A Native American Legend*. Ill. by Carolyn Ewing. Cartwheel, 1997, o.p. SERIES: Hello Reader! SUBJECTS: Folklore — Native Americans; Rabbits — Fiction; Weather — Snow — Fiction. RL B. LEXILE 450L.

In this story of how rabbits got their short tail, split lips, and bent legs, a wish for snow transforms rabbits forever. Illustrated with ink and watercolors, the story is an abbreviation of a traditional Native American tale.

Terban, Marvin

3369 *In a Pickle and Other Funny Idioms*. Ill. by Giulio Maestro. Houghton Mifflin, pap., 1983, ISBN 0-89919-164-9. SUBJECTS: English language — Idioms. RL C.

Every right-hand page of this book presents an idiom, its definition, an explanation for it, and its origin. Each left-hand page has a funny illustration of the idiom. Definitions and illustrations do a good job of clarifying idioms while being entertaining to readers.

Tether, Graham

3370 *The Knee Book*. Ill. by Sylvie Wickstrom. Random House, 2005, ISBN 0-375-83116-9. SERIES: Bright and Early Books for Beginning Readers. SUBJECTS: Human body — Fiction. RL B.

A rhyming text in the style of Seuss but without the panache is illustrated with cartoon-like drawings typical of the series.

Thaler, Mike

3371 *Camp Rotten Time*. Ill. by Jared Lee. Troll, 1994, o.p. SERIES: Funny Firsts. SUBJECTS: Camps and camping — Fiction; Humorous stories. RL C.

A little boy imagines all kinds of humorously frightening things happening at camp. Once there he helps another, bigger boy overcome his fears. Illustrations will be the big attractions in this book as they zanily portray the boy's far-out concerns.

3372 *Come and Play, Hippo*. Ill. by Maxie Chambliss. HarperCollins, 1991, o.p. SERIES: I Can Read. SUBJECTS: Animals — Fiction; Hippopotami — Fiction; Humorous stories. RL B.

In four chapters, Hippo and his friends share hilarious times playing an unusual game, being careful about Friday the thirteenth, trying to start a band, and watching for magic. The blend of funny text and humorous, brightly colored pictures will work well for readers.

3373 *Fang the Dentist*. Ill. by Jared Lee. Troll, 1994, o.p. SERIES: Funny Firsts. SUBJECTS: Dentists — Fiction; Humorous stories. RL C.

Before his first visit to the dentist, a boy visualizes everything his relatives tell him — creating scary yet totally silly mental pictures of what he will encounter. Once there, Snarvey finds it almost fun. Illustrations are humorous ink and wash cartoon-like paintings.

3374 *Hippo Lemonade*. Ill. by Maxie Chambliss. HarperCollins, 1986, ISBN 0-06-026159-5. SERIES: I Can Read. SUBJECTS: Hippopotami — Fiction; Humorous stories. RL B.

Childlike Hippo wishes to be something else, sets up a lemonade stand in competition with Snake, gets scared telling spooky stories, and finally decides that being alone is all right but being with friends is better. Lively, humorous text and carefully drawn illustrations work well together.

3375 *It's Me, Hippo!* Ill. by Maxie Chambliss. HarperCollins, 1983, ISBN 0-06-026153-6. SERIES: I Can Read. SUBJECTS: Birthdays — Fiction; Hippopotami — Fiction; Humorous stories. RL A.

Whether he is trying to build a house, is feeling left out when everyone else is sick, is trying to paint a picture, or thinks his friends have forgotten his birthday, Hippo should appeal to young readers with his slapstick humor. Illustrated with peach and green humorous drawings.

3376 *My Cat Is Going to the Dogs.* Ill. by Jared Lee. Troll, 1994, o.p. SERIES: Funny Firsts. SUBJECTS: Humorous stories; Pets — Cats — Fiction; Veterinarians — Fiction. RL C.

When Snarvey Gooper's cat seems tired all the time, his mom says they must take it to the vet. Snarvey imagines what the vet's office will be like in this very funny continuation of Snarvey's misunderstandings of familiar situations. Illustrations are humorous ink and wash paintings.

3377 *Pack 109.* Ill. by Normand Chartier. Dutton, 1988, o.p. SERIES: Dutton Easy Reader. SUBJECTS: Animals — Fiction; Humorous stories; Scouts and scouting — Fiction. RL B.

The five scouts of Pack 109 are avid collectors of Merit Badges. In one of the stories in this book, the little woodland animals earn them even for unsuccessful attempts — cookies as hard as rocks are piled together to earn a rock-collecting badge. Good humor always reigns in these stories with delightful color illustrations.

3378 *The Teacher from the Black Lagoon.* Ill. by Jared Lee. Scholastic, 1997, ISBN 0-439-84803-2. SERIES: Scholastic Reader Collection. SUBJECTS: Fear — Fiction; School stories; Stories in rhyme. RL B.

A little boy's fears about his teacher, the new gym teacher, the principal, and the librarian all prove groundless. Plenty for children to relate to, with suitably monstrous imaginings.

3379 *There's a Hippopotamus under My Bed.* Ill. by Ray Cruz. Avon, pap., 1978, ISBN 0-380-40238-6. SERIES: Easy-Read Story. SUBJECTS: Animals — Zoo — Fiction; Hippopotami — Fiction; Humorous stories. RL A.

Followed home by a hippopotamus, the little boy lets it into his house. Because of its size, the hippo creates disaster wherever it moves until zoo keepers finally arrive to claim it. The imaginative and funny story is illustrated with humorous ink and wash paintings.

Thiesing, Lisa

3380 *The Aliens Are Coming: A Silly Thriller with Peggy the Pig.* Dutton, 2004, ISBN 0-525-47277-0. SERIES: Dutton Easy Reader. SUBJECTS: Communication — Fiction; Humorous stories; Pigs — Fiction. RL B.

For days Peggy Pig hears announcements that the aliens are coming. Fearing an invasion from outer space, she starts to prepare. But the aliens that Peggy fears are actually a famous rock group. Illustrations are done in watercolors.

3381 *All Better.* Golden Books, 2000, o.p. SERIES: Road to Reading. SUBJECTS: Clumsiness — Fiction; Pigs — Fiction. RL A.

Sally's upbeat attitude and love of Bandaids keeps her clumsiness from destroying a lovely day. By the next morning the boo-boos are gone and she immediately starts getting new ones! Brightly colored pictures capture Sally's good humor and her unfortunate penchant for accidents.

3382 *A Dark and Noisy Night: A Silly Thriller with Peggy the Pig.* Dutton, 2005, ISBN 0-525-47388-2. SERIES: Dutton Easy Reader. SUBJECTS: Halloween — Fiction; Humorous stories; Scary stories. RL B.

Peggy hears one scary noise after another — all easily explainable if she weren't so silly and so scared. Finally the doorbell rings, Peggy opens the door, and there stands a group of trick-or-treaters. It's Halloween of course.

3383 *The Scarecrow's New Clothes: A Silly Thriller with Peggy the Pig.* Dutton, 2006, ISBN 0-525-47750-0. SERIES: Dutton Easy Reader. SUBJECTS: Pigs — Fiction; Scarecrows — Fiction; Scary stories. RL B.

On the way home from shopping, Peggy finds the perfect outfit for the party on a scarecrow. She takes it and, on the night of the party, the scarecrow appears demanding the clothes. Thiesing has taken a well-known scary story and transformed it into a slightly scary and very funny tale.

Thiesing, Lisa (cont.)

3384 *The Viper: A Silly Thriller with Peggy the Pig*. Dutton, 2002, o.p. SERIES: Dutton Easy Reader. SUBJECTS: Fear — Fiction; Humorous stories; Scary stories. RL B.

Peggy gets a strange call from the "Viper" announcing that he will come in a year. As the time nears, she gets more calls. A story often told around a campfire, here it is funny rather than scary.

Thomas, Art

3385 *Fishing Is for Me*. Photos by author. Lerner, 1980, o.p. SERIES: Sports for Me. SUBJECTS: Sports — Fishing. RL C.

Kevin takes the reader on his fishing trips for bluegill, bass, and trout. He explains about the kinds of equipment and bait and about the fishing techniques that are used. He also gives instructions on how to cast, set a hook, and cook fish. Illustrated with black-and-white photographs.

Thomas, Shelley Moore

3386 *Get Well, Good Knight*. Ill. by Jennifer Plecas. Dutton, 2002, ISBN 0-525-46914-1. SERIES: Dutton Easy Reader. SUBJECTS: Dragons — Fiction; Illness — Fiction; Knights and knighthood — Fiction. RL B. LEXILE AD120L.

When the good knight discovers three sick dragons, he twice goes to the wizard for cures with no success. He finally tries his own home where mom has the perfect thing — chicken soup. Expressive, colorful and humorous pictures illustrate the text.

3387 *Good Night, Good Knight*. Ill. by Jennifer Plecas. Dutton, 2000, ISBN 0-525-46326-7. SERIES: Dutton Easy Reader. SUBJECTS: Bedtime — Fiction; Dragons — Fiction; Knights and knighthood — Fiction. RL B. LEXILE 50L.

Standing guard on the crumbly tumbly tower, the good knight hears three different noises and discovers three little dragons in need of someone to tuck them into bed. Watercolor illustrations capture the humor of the story.

3388 *Happy Birthday, Good Knight*. Ill. by Jennifer Plecas. Dutton, 2006, ISBN 0-525-47184-7. SERIES: Dutton Easy Reader. SUBJECTS: Birthdays — Fiction; Dragons — Fiction; Knights and knighthood — Fiction. RL B.

The three little dragons ask the good knight for help in finding a perfect birthday gift. They try making a cake, creating a card, and doing magic tricks. All create terrible messes for everyone to clean up. When he discovers it is his birthday the good knight decides he has gotten the best gift of all — laughter.

Thompson, Brenda, and Rosemary Giesen

3389 *Pirates*. Ill. by Simon Stern and Rosemary Giesen. Lerner, 1977, o.p. SERIES: First Fact. SUBJECTS: Pirates. RL C.

The short text of this book briefly discusses pirates, the terrors of the sea, and provides information on some of the most famous pirates. Busy ink and watercolor pictures dominate the pages.

Thompson, Gare

3390 *The Monitor: The Iron Warship That Changed the World*. Ill. by Larry Day. Grosset & Dunlap, 2003, ISBN 0-448-43283-8. SERIES: All Aboard Reading. SUBJECTS: Ships and shipping; United States — Civil War. RL C.

The north's *Monitor* and the south's *Virginia (Merrimack)* battle each other at Hampton Road, neither winning. Later one sinks (the *Monitor*) and the other is blown up. In 1974 scientists discover the *Monitor* on the ocean floor and in 2002 start to bring it up. Through a detailed and occasionally challenging text and realistic ink and watercolor pictures, the story of the ironclads, their battle, and the recovery of the *Monitor* is told.

Thompson, Vivian

3391 *The Horse That Liked Sandwiches*. Ill. by Aliki. Putnam, 1962, o.p. SERIES: See and Read. SUBJECTS: Horses — Fiction; Humorous stories. RL A.

While Tony is taking an afternoon nap, his horse Mario goes off in search of sandwiches. Poor Tony is left to deal with the angry and hungry people Mario has deprived of lunch. This humorous story has comic-style ink and wash illustrations that are lively and fun though somewhat dated.

Thomson, Pat

3392 *Can You Hear Me, Grandad?* Ill. by Jez Alborough. Delacorte, 1988, o.p. SERIES: Share-A-Story. SUBJECTS: Grandparents — Fiction; Humorous stories; Zoos — Fiction. RL A.

Silly Grandad feigns deafness, pretending to mishear everything his granddaughter tells him about a trip to the zoo. His twisting of her words and her reactions to it are hilarious. Meant to be read by an adult and child alternating pages, it is illustrated with expressive, humorous drawings and is delightful.

3393 *Good Girl Granny.* Ill. by Faith Jaques. Delacorte, 1987, o.p. SERIES: Share-A-Story. SUBJECTS: Behavior — Fiction; Grandparents — Fiction; Humorous stories. RL B.

In response to her grandchild's questions about her youth, Granny insists that in those days all children behaved well as she tells of one bit of mischief after another. Alternating pages for adult and child to read, good colorful illustrations, and great humor make this perfect for sharing.

3394 *My Friend Mr. Morris.* Ill. by Satoshi Kitamura. Penguin, pap., 1988, ISBN 0-14-038887-7. SERIES: Share-A-Story. SUBJECTS: Humorous stories; Nonsense; Shopping — Fiction. RL B.

A little boy's neighbor, Mr. Morris, looks through catalogs and muses about what he might buy: socks for his bed (bed socks), a can of food as a pet (pet food), and other silly but delightful nonsense. To be read by children and adults together, it is illustrated with watercolors.

3395 *One of Those Days.* Ill. by Bob Wilson. Dell, pap., 1987, ISBN 0-440-46646-6. SERIES: Share-A-Story. SUBJECTS: Frustrations — Fiction; Humorous stories; Parent and child — Fiction. RL B.

A little girl rushes home to tell Mom about her terrible day at school only to discover that her mother's day was far worse and far more humorous. Meant to be read alternately by adult and child, the book is delightfully silly and has colorful illustrations of people and settings.

3396 *The Treasure Sock.* Ill. by Tony Ross. Penguin, pap., 1987, ISBN 0-14-038886-9. SERIES: Share-A-Story. SUBJECTS: Clothing — Fiction; Humorous stories; Parent and child — Fiction. RL B.

Holding up a very full sock, a little girl tells her mother about all the "treasures" she has found on her way home. Mother and daughter alternate pages and reactions to the frog, pig, key, rubber band, chewing gum, false teeth, perfume, and so on. Illustrated with outrageously funny pictures.

Thomson, Sarah L.

3397 *Amazing Dolphins!* Ill. by Wildlife Conservation Society. HarperCollins, 2006, ISBN 0-06-054453-8. SERIES: I Can Read: Wildlife Conservation Society. SUBJECTS: Animals — Endangered; Dolphins. RL B. LEXILE 670L.

Through color photographs and an interesting and factual text, young readers learn about the world of dolphins — their lives, the sounds they make, and how they are threatened by human activity around the world.

3398 *Amazing Gorillas!* Photographs from the Wildlife Conservation Society. HarperCollins, 2005, ISBN 0-06-054459-7. SERIES: I Can Read. SUBJECTS: Animals — Endangered; Gorillas. RL B. LEXILE 670L.

Appealing photographs and a well-written text provide a good introduction to gorillas, their lives, and how they are threatened by man.

3399 *Amazing Sharks.* Photographs provided by the Wildlife Conservation Society. HarperCollins, 2005, ISBN 0-06-054458-9. SERIES: I Can Read. SUBJECTS: Fish; Sharks. RL B. LEXILE 570L.

Illustrated with color photographs from the Wildlife Conservation Society, the text is well-written, providing a good solid start for children interested in sharks. A plus is information on the current status of sharks.

3400 *Amazing Snakes!* HarperCollins, 2006, ISBN 0-06-054462-7. SERIES: I Can Read. SUBJECTS: Reptiles and amphibians; Snakes. RL B.

Using color photographs of all kinds and sizes of snakes (none of them identified), the author provides young readers a very basic look at snakes and their place in the world. This may lead readers to other books, especially those providing snake identification.

Thomson, Sarah L. (cont.)

3401 *Amazing Whales*. Photographs from the Wildlife Conservation Society. HarperCollins, 2005, ISBN 0-06-054466-X. SERIES: I Can Read. SUBJECTS: Animals — Endangered; Whales. RL C. LEXILE 630L.

A carefully written text provides information on the various kinds of whales and how they live. Photographs from the Wildlife Conservation Society extend the text.

3402 *Tigers*. Photographs from the Wildlife Conservation Society. HarperCollins, 2004, ISBN 0-06-054450-3. SERIES: I Can Read. SUBJECTS: Animals — Endangered; Tigers. RL B. LEXILE 590L.

This introduction to the tiger and its lifestyle is supported by well-chosen color photographs. The text is interesting and will encourage young readers to support the preservation of this beautiful animal.

Tidd, Louise Vitellaro

3403 *The Best Pet Yet*. Ill. by Dorothy Handelman. Millbrook, 1998, ISBN 0-7613-2006-7. SERIES: Real Kids Readers. SUBJECTS: Pets — Fiction. RL B. LEXILE 300L.

Jay's mom and dad take him to the pet store to select a pet. The dog he wants makes too much noise; the cat causes his dad's eyes to itch; the parrot is not for sale. Finally, wanting a pet to hug and play with, Jay chooses a pair of rabbits.

3404 *Did You Hear About Jake?* Ill. by Dorothy Handelman. Millbrook, 1999, ISBN 0-7613-2058-X. SERIES: Real Kids Readers. SUBJECTS: Communication — Fiction; School stories. RL B. LEXILE BR.

One child after another mishears what Jake is doing (learning to bake) in a story based on the game of telephone. The story is illustrated with full-color photographic silhouettes.

3405 *I'll Do It Later*. Ill. by Dorothy Handelman. Millbrook, 1999, ISBN 0-7613-2066-0. SERIES: Real Kids Readers. SUBJECTS: Behavior — Procrastination — Fiction; Homework — Fiction. RL B. LEXILE 50L.

Rick puts off drawing his map while he plays or does other homework and doesn't get it finished. Luckily it snows during the night and Rick has a second chance. The story realistically portrays the results of procrastination. Illustrated with full-color photographic silhouettes.

3406 *Let Me Help!* Ill. by Dorothy Handelman. Millbrook, 1999, ISBN 0-7613-2067-9. SERIES: Real Kids Readers. SUBJECTS: Behavior — Helpful — Fiction; Parent and child — Fiction. RL B. LEXILE 10L.

Anxious to help her father with his chores, a little girl makes one mess after another. Her patient father lets her help him clean up each one and learn a bit about helping each time. Illustrations are done with photographs.

3407 *Lost and Found*. Ill. by Dorothy Handelman. Millbrook, 1998, o.p. SERIES: Real Kids Readers. SUBJECTS: Lost and found possessions — Fiction. RL B. LEXILE 90L.

Nick is so messy and disorganized that he does not know where his belongings are. Looking for his sneaker, he finds things he thought were lost.

Tobias, Tobi

3408 *Maria Tallchief*. Ill. by Michael Hampshire. HarperCollins, 1970, o.p. SERIES: HarperCollins Biography. SUBJECTS: Biographies; Dancers and dancing; Osage. RL C.

A member of the Osage tribe, Maria Tallchief begins dancing as a child, practices hard, has good teachers, and becomes a member of the Ballet Society of New York and a world-renowned ballerina. Well written and interesting, it is illustrated with realistic sketches.

3409 *Marian Anderson*. Ill. by Symeon Shimin. HarperCollins, 1972, o.p. SERIES: HarperCollins Biography. SUBJECTS: African Americans; Biographies; Music and musicians. RL B.

One of the world's great singers, Marian Anderson fought poverty and prejudice to get recognition for her talent. This inspiring biography covers her life until her retirement. The illustrations are realistic, lovely, and often moving pencil and wash pictures.

Toby, Marlene

3410 *A. A. Milne: Author of Winnie the Pooh*. Children's Press, 1995, o.p. SERIES: Rookie

Biography. SUBJECTS: Biographies; Writers and writing. RL C.

The life of the creator of Winnie-the-Pooh is briefly written and highlighted with archival pictures, photographs and drawings by Shepard from the Winnie-the-Pooh books. An index and chronology are included. Note well: the wrong date is given on p. 45 for the year of Milne's death. It is correct in two other places.

Tolstoy, Alexei

3411 *The Enormous Turnip*. Ill. by Scott Goto. Harcourt, 2003, ISBN 0-15-204883-9. SERIES: Green Light Readers. SUBJECTS: Behavior — Cooperative; Cumulative tales. RL B. LEXILE NP.

An old man plants a turnip and it grows to a huge size. Unable to pull it out himself, he needs help from the old woman, the granddaughter, the dog, the cat, and the mouse. Vibrant paintings place the cumulative story in an era of Russian peasant farmers.

Tomchek, Ann Heinrichs

3412 *I Can Be a Chef*. Ill. with photos. Childrens Press, 1985, o.p. SERIES: I Can Be. SUBJECTS: Careers; Cookery. RL C.

Chefs of all types are introduced as well as a bit of the history surrounding their careers. The rigors of the work are not overlooked nor is the training. The book is illustrated with color photographs and small watercolor pictures. Index. and glossary are included.

Tompert, Ann

3413 *Little Otter Remembers and Other Stories*. Ill. by John Wallner. Crown, 1977, o.p. SUBJECTS: Otters — Fiction; Parent and child — Fiction. RL B.

In three stories Little Otter tries hard to find something for his mother's birthday, attempts to remember where he put his pinecone, and wants to get his friends to a coasting party. With Mother Otter's support each story ends happily. Illustrated with detailed colored pencil drawings.

3414 *Sue Patch and the Crazy Clocks*. Ill. by Rosekrans Hoffman. Dial, 1989, o.p. SERIES: Dial Easy-to-Read. SUBJECTS: Clocks — Fiction; Kings and queens — Fiction; Time — Fiction. RL B.

With no two clocks in his huge palace giving the same time, the King of Tango sends for Sue Patch and her bag of tricks. Detailed, humorous, yet zany and fantastic, the watercolor and pencil pictures extend the brief, often silly but satisfying story.

Torrey, Richard

3415 *Beans Baker's Best Shot*. Random House, 2006, ISBN 0-375-92839-1. SERIES: Step into Reading. SUBJECTS: Friendship — Fiction; Sports — Soccer — Fiction. RL C.

When Chester accidentally kicks and breaks Beans's foot, the team's chances for the soccer championship seem doomed. But with support from Beans, Chester redeems himself and helps the team win.

Towne, Peter

3416 *George Washington Carver*. Ill. by Elizia Moon. HarperCollins, 1975, o.p. SERIES: HarperCollins Biography. SUBJECTS: African Americans; Biographies; Science and scientists. RL B.

Born into slavery, George Washington Carver fights hard against bigotry and hatred to get an education. Although his research at Tuskegee Institute wins him fame, Carver has a social mission as well. Well written and interesting, this is illustrated with charcoal drawings.

Townsend, Donna

3417 *Apple Fractions*. Children's Press, 2004, ISBN 0-516-24419-1. SERIES: Rookie Read-About Math. SUBJECTS: Mathematics — Fractions. RL B. LEXILE 290L.

This introduction to fractions begins by using an apple that has been divided into halves, thirds, and fourths and then moves to numbers of things (muffins). The explanations are clearly presented and with the aid of color photographs are easily understood. A photo glossary and index complete the book.

Tremain, Ruthven

3418 *Teapot, Switcheroo, and Other Silly Word Games*. Ill. by author. Greenwillow,

Tremain, Ruthven (cont.)

1979, o.p. SERIES: Read-Alone. SUBJECTS: Wordplay. RL B.

Spoonerisms, Pig Latin, Gotcha, palindromes, secret messages, and word scrambles are just some of the "games" that help children have fun with language. Ink and wash sketches are used to give hints to the answers, which can be found at the end of the book.

Trier, Carola S.

3419 *Exercise: What It Is, What It Does.* Ill. by Tom Huffman. Greenwillow, 1982, o.p. SERIES: Read-Alone. SUBJECTS: Exercise; Physical fitness. RL B.

With the silly commentary of an omnipresent cat, this volume takes children through an assortment of exercises meant to promote good posture and strengthen the body. The instructions and the exercises themselves invite participation. Humorous ink line drawings add to the fun.

Tripp, Valerie

3420 *Baby Koala Finds a Home.* Ill. by Sandra C. Kalthoff. Children's Press, 1987, o.p. SERIES: Just One More. SUBJECTS: Koalas — Fiction; Stories in rhyme. RL A.

A mother koala and her baby go from branch to branch in search of a place to stay. Each time they stop an animal forces them to move on. Then they find just the right place for them. Rhyming, repetitive text is paired with childlike paintings.

3421 *Happy, Happy Mother's Day!* Ill. by Sandra K. Martin. Childrens Press, 1989, o.p. SERIES: Just One More. SUBJECTS: Animals — Fiction; Mother's Day — Fiction. RL A.

As giraffe heads home to plant flower seeds for Mother's Day, she generously shares with the other animals. When she arrives at home, all she has is one seed but it proves its worth. A minimal text, with repetitive phrases, is illustrated with ink drawings with watercolor washes.

3422 *The One and Only Delaney.* Ill. by Joy Allen. Pleasant Company, 2005, o.p. SERIES: Hopscotch Hill School. SUBJECTS: Comparisons — Fiction; School stories; Self-esteem — Fiction. RL B.

The boys and girls in Miss Sparks's classroom are talented in a variety of ways. Delaney, who loves music, compares herself unfavorably with others in reading, telling jokes and drawing until the teacher intervenes. The text is meant to teach words of comparison and includes a section for parents with advice for supporting their children.

3423 *The Penguins Paint.* Ill. by Sandra C. Kalthoff. Childrens Press, 1987, o.p. SERIES: Just One More. SUBJECTS: Concepts — Colors — Fiction; Penguins — Fiction; Stories in rhyme. RL A.

A family of penguins wants color in its life and goes to the new paint store to try first blue, then green, then yellow, and finally red. When they are done they have a rainbow. The rhyming verse moves well and the color reinforcement is good.

3424 *Sillyhen's Big Surprise.* Ill. by Sandra K. Martin. Childrens Press, 1989, o.p. SERIES: Just One More. SUBJECTS: Chickens — Fiction; Stories in rhyme. RL A.

Thinking her house too small, Sillyhen asks for advice from the duck next door. She advises Sillyhen to invite a chicken to share it, and when it seems worse, suggests she adds another. A variant of a Jewish folktale, this is illustrated in watercolors and pen and ink.

3425 *The Singing Dog.* Ill. by Sandra C. Kalthoff. Childrens Press, 1986, o.p. SERIES: Just One More. SUBJECTS: Animals — Fiction; Contests — Fiction; Friendship — Fiction. RL A.

Dog offers rides to one animal after another as he travels to the music show. Each wants to win first prize and together they do. The rhyming text is illustrated with framed, rather muddied watercolors.

Troughton, Joanna

3426 *How Rabbit Stole the Fire: A North American Indian Folk Tale.* Ill. by author. Peter Bedrick, 1986, o.p. SERIES: Folk Tales of the World. SUBJECTS: Folklore — Native Americans. RL B.

Rabbit the mischief maker contrives a way to steal fire from the Sky People, entering their land with a special headdress that he sets ablaze. He runs back to his own land with the Sky People chasing him and passes the fire to animal after animal. Lavish illustrations capture the excitement of the tale.

Trueit, Trudi Strain

3427 *Mississippi*. Children's Press, 2007, ISBN 0-531-12572-6. SERIES: Rookie Read-About Geography. SUBJECTS: Geography; Mississippi; United States. RL B.

The western part of Mississippi, bordering on the Mississippi River has rich farm land. The east has rolling hills and pine forests; the south is on the Gulf of Mexico, an area damaged by Hurricane Katrina. Wildlife, state symbols, industry, and crops are also mentioned. A photo glossary and index end the book.

3428 *Snakes*. Children's Press, 2003, ISBN 0-516-22650-9. SERIES: True Book. SUBJECTS: Reptiles and amphibians; Snakes. RL C. LEXILE 790L.

Perfect for the child fascinated by snakes or for a school assignment, this book includes a good amount of information arranged by topic, well-selected photographs, and a bibliography, glossary, and index.

3429 *Utah*. Children's Press, 2007, ISBN 0-531-12574-2. SERIES: Rookie Read-About Geography. SUBJECTS: Geography; United States; Utah. RL B.

One of the four corner states, Utah has the Rocky Mountains, beautiful canyons, wild animals and much more. The color photographs of the landscape and animals work with the text, maps, photo glossary, and index to give a glimpse of life in this state.

Trumbauer, Lisa

3430 *All About Heat*. Children's Press, 2004, ISBN 0-516-23608-3. SERIES: Rookie Read-About Science. SUBJECTS: Heat; Science and scientists. RL B. LEXILE 320L.

The many ways in which heat is experienced or seen are explored in this very basic text. Photographs show examples of each aspect of heat that is discussed. A brief index is included.

3431 *All About Light*. Children's Press, 2004, ISBN 0-516-23446-3. SERIES: Rookie Read-About Science. SUBJECTS: Light; Science and scientists. RL B. LEXILE 300L.

Light as a form of energy is discussed in very basic terms. The book mentions different forms of light and ways in which light is found. The book includes a photographic glossary and brief index.

3432 *All About Sound*. Children's Press, 2004, ISBN 0-516-23609-1. SERIES: Rookie Read-About Science. SUBJECTS: Science and scientists; Sound. RL B. LEXILE 260L.

Talking, singing, playing a guitar and hitting a pot with a spoon are all examples of vibrations that make sound. Through photographs and a brief text, children are introduced to very basic information about sound. Included are a photo glossary and an index.

3433 *Tiny Life in Your Home*. Children's Press, 2005, ISBN 0-516-25274-7. SERIES: Rookie Read-About Science. SUBJECTS: Microbes; Science and scientists. RL B.

Children learn that small life forms called bacteria, molds, mildew and fungus are found around a house. These life forms are shown in photographs and briefly explained. Pronunciation is given when the names of microbes are introduced. Colorful photographs, photo glossary, and an index are included.

3434 *What Is Electricity?* Children's Press, 2004, ISBN 0-516-23449-8. SERIES: Rookie Read-About Science. SUBJECTS: Electricity; Science and scientists. RL B. LEXILE 440L.

Where electricity comes from (power plants or batteries or lightning) and how it is used are discussed. This volume, illustrated with color photographs, also includes a photo glossary and an index.

3435 *What Is Friction?* Children's Press, 2004, ISBN 0-516-23447-1. SERIES: Rookie Read-About Science. SUBJECTS: Friction; Science and scientists. RL B. LEXILE 380L.

Color photographs and a factual text explain the way in which friction acts to slow or stop objects. A photo glossary and brief index are included. (Note: Grammatical errors on pages 17 and 21.)

3436 *What Is Gravity?* Children's Press, 2004, ISBN 0-516-23448-X. SERIES: Rookie Read-About Science. SUBJECTS: Gravity; Science and scientists. RL B. LEXILE 340L.

Trumbauer, Lisa (cont.)

Text and photographs work together to explain the most basic principle of gravity: what goes up, comes down. A photo glossary and an index complete the book

3437 *What Is Volume?* Children's Press, 2006, ISBN 0-516-23621-0. SERIES: Rookie Read-About Science. SUBJECTS: Concepts — Weight ; Science and scientists. RL B. LEXILE 360L.

Children need to know how to measure volume in order to use recipes. This book compares different measures of volume to weight. Carefully chosen color photographs extend the text. An index and a photo glossary are included.

Turner, Ann

3438 *Dust for Dinner*. Ill. by Robert Barrett. HarperCollins, 1995, ISBN 0-06-023377-X. SERIES: I Can Read. SUBJECTS: Family life — Fiction; Farm and country life — Fiction; United States — History — Fiction. RL B. LEXILE 390L.

After losing the farm to the Dust Bowl, Jake and his family pile into the truck and head west. Along the way Papa finds some work but it is not until they reach San Francisco that they finally have a home again. The story captures some of the hardships faced by families during the Great Depression.

U

Udry, Janice May

3439 *Thump and Plunk*. Ill. by Geoffrey Hayes. HarperCollins, 2000, ISBN 0-06-028528-1. SERIES: My First I Can Read. SUBJECTS: Ducks — Fiction; Siblings — Fiction. RL A. LEXILE 210L.

Two ducklings quickly get into an argument when one thumps the other's toy frog. With all the thumping and plunking of each other, children will be left laughing and totally unaware of how very limited the vocabulary is. Illustrations are done in watercolors.

Underwood, Deborah

3440 *Pirate Mom*. Ill. by Stephen Gilpin. Random House, 2006, ISBN 0-375-93323-9. SERIES: Step into Reading. SUBJECTS: Humorous stories; Hypnotism — Fiction; Pirates — Fiction. RL B.

At the magic show, Pete's mom is hypnotized and told she is a pirate. All the way home she acts just like a wicked pirate would: stealing clothes, demanding loot, and even calling a neighbor a bilge rat. Pete must find the magician to break the spell.

Vail, Rachel

3441 *Homework Trouble*. Ill. by Steve Bjorkman. Orchard, 2001, ISBN 0-439-40628-5. SERIES: Mama Rex and T. SUBJECTS: Dinosaurs — Fiction; Family life — Fiction; Homework — Fiction. RL C. LEXILE 390L.

T has forgotten to tell his mother that he needs to make a diorama about pigs. She takes him to the library and then to the natural history museum for diorama ideas. Working together they finally come up with just the right diorama. Longer than many other books, this has cartoon-like illustrations and chapters.

3442 *The Horrible Play Date*. Ill. by Steve Bjorkman. Orchard, 2001, ISBN 0-439-40627-7. SERIES: Mama Rex and T. SUBJECTS: Behavior — Fiction; Dinosaurs — Fiction; Friendship — Fiction. RL C. LEXILE 410L.

T and Walter are so excited about their play date that everything starts to go wrong. Mama Rex has the perfect solution to making the worst play date into the best. Illustrated with colorful cartoon-like art, this book has chapters and a longer than usual text.

Valzania, Kimberly

3443 *Kentucky*. Children's Press, 2003, ISBN 0-516-22697-5. SERIES: Rookie Read-About Geography. SUBJECTS: Geography;

Kentucky; United States. RL B. LEXILE NC310L.

The state of Kentucky and its unique regions of coal fields, blue grass, and the Appalachian Plateau are discussed and shown in color photographs. The book acts as an inviting introduction to the state and is supported by a photo glossary and brief index.

3444 *Tennessee.* Children's Press, 2003, ISBN 0-516-22699-1. SERIES: Rookie Read-About Geography. SUBJECTS: Geography; Tennessee; United States. RL B. LEXILE NC450L.

The three parts of Tennessee (the eastern includes the Great Smoky Mountains and the Cumberland Gap; the middle is a basin with caves, streams, and farmland; and the west has hills and valleys and cotton fields) make up a beautiful state with many things to see and do. Though this is an introduction to the state, it manages to give a good picture of its diversity. The text is supported by color photographs, a photo glossary, and an index.

Van Laan, Nancy

3445 *Busy Busy Moose.* Ill. by Amy Rusch. Houghton Mifflin, 2001, ISBN 0-395-96091-6. SUBJECTS: Animals — Fiction; Moose — Fiction; Seasons — Fiction. RL B.

Though Moose doesn't need to store acorns for winter or build a nest for baby birds in spring, throughout the year he helps the other animals. Gentle, child-like colored-pencil drawings illustrate the four stories.

3446 *Moose Tales.* Ill. by Amy Rusch. Houghton Mifflin, pap., 1999, ISBN 0-618-11128-X. SUBJECTS: Animals — Fiction; Moose — Fiction. RL B. LEXILE 100L.

Gentle moose gets some unexpected exercise, has to rescue beaver from under a tree, and joins his friends in making a snow creature. Comical full-color animal drawings fill the book.

Van Leeuwen, Jean

3447 *Amanda Pig and Her Best Friend Lollipop.* Ill. by Ann Schweninger. Dial, pap., 1998, ISBN 0-14-037999-1. SERIES: Dial Easy-to-Read. SUBJECTS: Behavior — Shyness — Fiction; Friendship — Fiction; Pigs — Fiction. RL B. LEXILE 240L.

When Lollipop comes to visit Amanda, they play and take their stuffed bunny "babies" for a walk. When Amanda visits Lollipop, she plays with baby Lulu and has great fun. But a sleepover in a strange bed is more than Amanda can handle and she goes home in the middle of the night. Soft, colorful pictures work well with stories of friendship.

3448 *Amanda Pig and Her Big Brother Oliver.* Ill. by Ann Schweninger. Penguin, pap., 1994, ISBN 0-14-037008-0. SERIES: Dial Easy-to-Read. SUBJECTS: Family life — Fiction; Pigs — Fiction; Sibling rivalry — Fiction. RL A.

One of a series of books about a close-knit family of pigs with very human personality characteristics, this story takes Amanda and Oliver through five everyday events common to small children. The illustrations are soft and pastel colored.

3449 *Amanda Pig and the Awful, Scary Monster.* Ill. by Ann Schweninger. Phyllis Fogelman Books, 2003, ISBN 0-8037-2766-6. SERIES: PJF Easy-to-Read. SUBJECTS: Bedtime — Fiction; Monsters — Fiction; Pigs — Fiction. RL B. LEXILE AD210L.

Amanda is having trouble sleeping because she is sure there are monsters in her bedroom. Mother and Father and Oliver all try to help her by giving her a flashlight, extra hugs, and a monster trap. Finally Amanda bravely discovers that there really are no monsters.

3450 *Amanda Pig and the Really Hot Day.* Ill. by Ann Schweninger. Dial, 2005, ISBN 0-8037-2887-5. SERIES: Dial Easy-to-Read. SUBJECTS: Family life — Fiction; Heat — Fiction; Pigs — Fiction. RL B. LEXILE 290L.

Throughout a very, very hot day Amanda tries selling lemonade, doing nothing with her friend Lollipop and finally hearing a cold story from Father as the family sits outside and looks at the stars.

3451 *Amanda Pig on Her Own.* Ill. by Ann Schweninger. Penguin, pap., 1994, ISBN 0-14-037144-3. SERIES: Dial Easy-to-Read. SUBJECTS: Family life — Fiction; Loneliness — Fiction; Siblings — Fiction. RL B.

Van Leeuwen, Jean (cont.)

When big brother Oliver goes to school, Amanda is left at home with mother. Slowly the little pig learns to enjoy doing things on her own and starts taking responsibility for herself. The four quiet chapters are illustrated with watercolors.

3452 *Amanda Pig, Schoolgirl.* Ill. by Ann Schweninger. Dial, 1997, o.p. SERIES: Dial Easy-to-Read. SUBJECTS: Friendship — Fiction; Pigs — Fiction; School stories. RL B. LEXILE 240L.

Amanda Pig is excited about finally going to school. On the bus she befriends a little pig with a lollipop who won't say a word. Together they go to Mrs. Flora Pig's class. The quiet story beautifully depicts a happy school room and the determination of Amanda to make Lollipop her friend.

3453 *More Tales of Amanda Pig.* Ill. by Ann Schweninger. Penguin, pap., 1995, ISBN 0-14-037603-8. SERIES: Dial Easy-to-Read. SUBJECTS: Family life — Fiction; Pigs — Fiction. RL A.

Amanda Pig; her brother Oliver; their good-natured parents, aunt, uncle, and cousins; and assorted stuffed animals share a variety of adventures common to small children everywhere. The illustrations are done in soft watercolors and pencil that deftly capture a loving family.

3454 *More Tales of Oliver Pig.* Ill. by Arnold Lobel. Penguin, pap., 1993, ISBN 0-14-036554-0. SERIES: Dial Easy-to-Read. SUBJECTS: Family life — Fiction; Pigs — Fiction; Siblings — Fiction. RL A.

From one spring to the next, Oliver shares gentle everyday adventures with his family. The stories are low key and quiet and present situations common to young children. The ink and wash illustrations capture the love, warmth, and frustrations of a very human family of pigs.

3455 *Oliver, Amanda, and Grandmother Pig.* Ill. by Ann Schweninger. Dial, 1987, o.p. SERIES: Dial Easy-to-Read. SUBJECTS: Family life — Fiction; Grandparents — Fiction; Pigs — Fiction. RL A.

Initially disturbed by Grandmother's inability to bend over or read without her glasses, Oliver and Amanda soon begin to cherish the time they spend with her. A gem of a story of intergenerational understanding and love, it is supported by simple yet colorful pastel drawings.

3456 *Oliver and Albert, Friends Forever.* Ill. by Ann Schweninger. Penguin, pap., 2000, ISBN 0-14-230084-5. SERIES: Easy-to-Read. SUBJECTS: Friendship — Fiction; Pigs — Fiction; School stories. RL B.

Albert is tall and smart and can even read. But he is not good at sports until Oliver befriends him and patiently shows him how to play kickball. The two become best friends forever.

3457 *Oliver and Amanda's Christmas.* Ill. by Ann Schweninger. Penguin, 1989, ISBN 0-685-29542-7. SERIES: Dial Easy-to-Read. SUBJECTS: Christmas — Fiction; Family life — Fiction; Siblings — Fiction. RL B.

Oliver and Amanda get ready for Christmas by writing letters to Santa, making presents, helping to find a Christmas tree, and hanging their stockings. A quiet and gentle look at a family holiday too often commercialized, the story has soft, colored pencil illustrations.

3458 *Oliver and Amanda's Halloween.* Ill. by Ann Schweninger. Dial, 1992, o.p. SERIES: Dial Easy-to-Read. SUBJECTS: Halloween — Fiction; Pigs — Fiction; Siblings — Fiction. RL B.

In four short chapters illustrated with gentle yet often humorous colored pencil and watercolor drawings, the brother and sister pigs prepare for and then go out trick or treating. Amanda dislikes scary things, Oliver loves them, and their parents manage to balance things beautifully.

3459 *Oliver Pig and the Best Fort Ever.* Ill. by Ann Schweninger. Dial, 2006, ISBN 0-8037-2888-3. SERIES: Dial Easy-to-Read. SUBJECTS: Building — Fiction; Pigs — Fiction. RL B.

With the help of his father and his friends, Oliver finally builds a very good and very large fort. When he and his friends decide to camp out that night, things don't turn out as they expect.

3460 *Oliver Pig at School.* Ill. by Ann Schweninger. Dial, 1990, o.p. SERIES: Dial Easy-to-Read. SUBJECTS: Pigs — Fiction; School stories. RL B.

As he rides the bus for his first day of school, Oliver is not sure he wants to go. Once he meets his teacher and makes a new friend, Oliver decides school is fun. Van Leeuwen captures the feelings of small children well and the pencil and watercolor pictures add another dimension.

3461 *Oliver the Mighty Pig.* Ill. by Ann Schweninger. Dial, 2004, ISBN 0-8037-2886-7. SERIES: Dial Easy-to-Read. SUBJECTS: Imagination — Fiction; Pigs — Fiction; Superheroes — Fiction. RL B.

For his birthday Oliver receives a Mighty Pig cape. With it he is sure he is stronger, faster, and just might be able to fly. Oliver happily plays superhero with his toys and family. Through Oliver, the author captures the way human children imaginatively play.

3462 *Tales of Amanda Pig.* Ill. by Ann Schweninger. Penguin, pap., 1994, ISBN 0-14-036840-X. SERIES: Dial Easy-to-Read. SUBJECTS: Family life — Fiction; Fear — Fiction; Pigs — Fiction. RL A.

The pig family's youngest member, Amanda, is the center of five gentle stories of everyday life with which children can identify. She faces fears, gains responsibility, and puts Mother to sleep by telling her a bedtime story. Pastel pictures add humor and warmth to a lovely book.

3463 *Tales of Oliver Pig.* Ill. by Arnold Lobel. Penguin, pap., 1993, ISBN 0-14-036549-4. SERIES: Dial Easy-to-Read. SUBJECTS: Family life — Fiction; Pigs — Fiction; Sibling rivalry — Fiction. RL A.

Oliver is a part of a very loving family of pigs. He bakes cookies on cold wet days and does not always appreciate his little sister, Amanda. The four short chapters about Oliver's family are illustrated in ink and wash pictures that bring them all to life.

Van Woerkom, Dorothy

3464 *Abu Ali: Three Tales of the Middle East.* Ill. by Harold Berson. Macmillan, 1976, o.p. SERIES: Ready-to-Read. SUBJECTS: Folklore — Turkey; Humorous stories. RL A.

Abu Ali, which is Van Woerkom's name for the foolish Hodja of Turkish folklore, has trouble keeping track of nine donkeys, gets even with his friends who try to cheat him, and gets his own comeuppance. The delightfully funny stories are illustrated with whimsical ink sketches in full color.

3465 *Becky and the Bear.* Ill. by Margot Tomes. Putnam, 1975, o.p. SERIES: See and Read. SUBJECTS: Bears — Fiction; Behavior — Brave — Fiction; United States — Colonial period — Fiction. RL B.

With only corn and berries to eat, Becky and Granny hope that Ned and father will be bringing back meat. Left alone briefly, Becky bravely and cleverly captures a bear. Based on a true story set in colonial Maine. The illustrations are done with ink, wash, and silhouettes.

3466 *The Friends of Abu Ali: Three More Tales of the Middle East.* Ill. by Harold Berson. Macmillan, 1978, o.p. SERIES: Ready-to-Read. SUBJECTS: Folklore — Turkey; Humorous stories. RL B.

The three stories of Abu Ali and his friends are ridiculously silly, like those in the Hodja stories from Turkey, and are sure to have children smiling at the men's antics. Illustrated with ink line drawings and watercolor washes.

3467 *Harry and Shellburt.* Ill. by Erick Ingraham. Macmillan, 1977, o.p. SERIES: Ready-to-Read. SUBJECTS: Friendship — Fiction; Rabbits — Fiction; Turtles — Fiction. RL A.

The title characters — Harry, a hare, and Shellburt, a tortoise — agree to rerun the race made famous by Aesop. Predictably, the tortoise wins but the two remain friends. The well-written and entertaining story has soft, detailed pencil drawings of realistic animals and settings.

3468 *Hidden Messages.* Ill. by Lynne Cherry. Crown, 1979, o.p. SUBJECTS: Animals — Communication; Science and scientists. RL B.

The experiments of Benjamin Franklin and other scientists lead to the discovery of pheromones, the odors particular to a species that provide them with a variety of nonverbal messages. The interesting narrative and realistic paintings combine to provide a good introduction to an unusual subject.

3469 *Meat Pies and Sausages.* Ill. by Joseph Low. Greenwillow, 1976, o.p. SERIES: Read-

Van Woerkom, Dorothy (cont.)

Alone. SUBJECTS: Folklore; Foxes — Fiction; Wolves — Fiction. RL A.
Three stories based on Eastern European folklore pit Fox and Wolf against one another in their quest for food. Fox cleverly outwits Wolf, leading him into trouble with humans. The humorous stories are illustrated with ink and wash pictures with an Eastern European setting.

3470 *Old Devil Is Waiting: Three Folktales*. Ill. by Jan Brett. Harcourt, 1985, o.p. SERIES: Let Me Read. SUBJECTS: Folklore; Humorous stories. RL B.
In the first two tales devils try to get a clever glassblower and wicked landlord to go back with them to hell. In the third, the Old Devil himself is outwitted by a farmer's wife. The three humorous stories, based on folklore from around the world, are tied together by Old Devil and all are illustrated with detailed black-and-white pictures.

3471 *Sea Frog, City Frog*. Ill. by Jose Aruego and Ariane Dewey. Macmillan, 1975, o.p. SERIES: Ready-to-Read. SUBJECTS: Folklore — Japan; Frogs and toads — Fiction. RL A.
In this Japanese folktale, two frogs meet at the top of a high hill on their respective journeys to see the city and the sea. They help each other to stand up and see where they are going. Their eyes point backward and each believes where he is going is just like where he comes from. Humorous ink and wash drawings.

3472 *Tit for Tat*. Ill. by Douglas Florian. Greenwillow, 1977, o.p. SERIES: Read-Alone. SUBJECTS: Behavior — Greedy — Fiction; Folklore — Latvia. RL A.
On a bitter winter night, a ragged stranger seeks shelter from a miser, who refuses him, and then from a kindly old woman, who helps him. Both are appropriately rewarded for their treatment of him. Based on a Latvian folktale, this is illustrated with stylized ink, wash, and pencil pictures.

Venezia, Mike

3473 *Da Vinci*. Ill. by author. Children's Press, 1989, ISBN 0-516-02275-X. SERIES: Getting to Know the World's Greatest Artists. SUBJECTS: Art and artists; Biographies. RL C.
The combination of lighthearted cartoons and solid information about Leonardo da Vinci and his art make this enjoyable reading for children just learning about the world of art. Changes in composition and the use of light — contributions of da Vinci — are mentioned and shown in examples of his paintings.

3474 *Edward Hopper*. Ill. by author. Childrens Press, 1989, ISBN 0-516-02277-6. SERIES: Getting to Know the World's Greatest Artists. SUBJECTS: Art and artists; Biographies. RL C.
Using comical cartoon paintings and reproductions of many of Hopper's paintings and etchings, the author is able to make the study of this major American artist accessible to beginning readers.

3475 *Mary Cassatt*. Ill. by author. Childrens Press, pap., 1991, ISBN 0-516-42278-2. SERIES: Getting to Know the World's Greatest Artists. SUBJECTS: Art and artists; Biographies. RL C.
Combining cartoon-like paintings with reproductions of Cassatt's art, the author cleverly introduces the artist's life and work. The illustrations comically bridge eras to help children understand important moments in her life.

3476 *Michelangelo*. Ill. by author. Childrens Press, 1991, ISBN 0-516-02293-8. SERIES: Getting to Know the World's Greatest Artists. SUBJECTS: Art and artists; Biographies. RL C.
As in his other books on famous artists, the author gives some information on the artist's childhood and schooling while concentrating on his great works. Cartoon art mixed with reproductions of Michelangelo's work lightens the book and makes it more accessible to youngsters.

3477 *Paul Gauguin*. Ill. by author. Childrens Press, 1992, ISBN 0-516-02295-4. SERIES: Getting to Know the World's Greatest Artists. SUBJECTS: Art and artists; Biographies. RL C.
Paul Gauguin's life before he discovered his talent as an artist and the changes he faced once he became a full-time painter are discussed here. Full of reproductions of Gauguin's art, that of his contemporaries, and cartoon commentaries on the time, the book has much to look at.

3478 *Paul Klee*. Ill. by author. Childrens Press, 1991, ISBN 0-516-02294-6. SERIES: Getting to Know the World's Greatest Artists. SUBJECTS: Art and artists; Biographies. RL C.

Through a careful combination of biography, cartoon drawings, reproductions of Klee's work, and commentary on his art, children are given a fascinating look at an unusual modern artist. Illustrated in full color with balloon-captioned cartoons and reprints of art.

3479 *Rembrandt*. Ill. by author. Childrens Press, 1988, ISBN 0-516-02272-5. SERIES: Getting to Know the World's Greatest Artists. SUBJECTS: Art and artists; Biographies. RL C.

Through reproductions of his better-known paintings and humorous cartoon illustrations, the life and work of Rembrandt are presented so that young readers can understand his significance.

3480 *Van Gogh*. Ill. by author. Childrens Press, 1988, ISBN 0-516-02274-1. SERIES: Getting to Know the World's Greatest Artists. SUBJECTS: Art and artists; Biographies. RL B.

A factual text presents an interesting picture of Van Gogh and his struggles as an artist. The reproductions of his work are carefully chosen to represent his genius.

Venn, Cecilia

3481 *That Is Not My Hat!* Ill. by Dorothy Handelman. Millbrook, pap., 1998, ISBN 0-7613-2033-4. SERIES: Real Kids Readers. SUBJECTS: Clubs — Fiction; Hats — Fiction; Lost and found possessions — Fiction. RL B. LEXILE 70L.

Sam asks his sister and her friends to help him find his hat. They make signs for the missing hat and for their Pocket Park Club. They put them up in their city neighborhood. The hat is found and their new club started. Illustrated with color photographs.

Vern, Alex

3482 *Where Do Frogs Come From?* Harcourt, 2000, ISBN 0-15-204884-7. SERIES: Green Light Readers. SUBJECTS: Frogs and toads; Reptiles and amphibians. RL B.

Through a concise text and full-color, detailed, and attractive color photographs, the story of the development of a frog from egg to adult is told.

Victor, Joan B.

3483 *Shells Are Skeletons*. Ill. by author. HarperCollins, 1977, o.p. SERIES: Let's-Read-and-Find-Out. SUBJECTS: Mollusks; Shells. RL C.

Carefully drawn pen and wash pictures of a variety of shells combine with the text to explain how shells and the mollusks they house grow, protect themselves, and eat.

Vinton, Iris

3484 *Look Out for Pirates*. Ill. by H. B. Vestal. Beginner Books, 1961, o.p. SERIES: I Can Read It All by Myself. SUBJECTS: Pirates — Fiction. RL B.

Pursued by pirates, Captain Jim's ship capsizes and his trunk of gold washes overboard. His men dive and retrieve the gold and Captain Jim finds a way to outwit the pirates. Though the sailors' use of diving gear seems odd, the story is popular. Illustrated with realistic paintings.

Voigt, Cynthia

3485 *Stories About Rosie*. Ill. by Dennis Kendrick. Atheneum, 1986, o.p. SUBJECTS: Humorous stories; Pets — Dogs — Fiction. RL A.

Rosie, a large, irrepressible spaniel, thinks Mommy, Daddy, Jessie, and Duff are meant to serve her. Rosie barks, runs, chases, and is always happy and excited in four humorous stories about her and her family. Color and ink sketches in a comic style capture Rosie's exuberance.

W

Waddell, Martin

3486 *The Tough Princess*. Ill. by Patrick Benson. Philomel, 1986, o.p. SUBJECTS: Fairy tales; Humorous stories; Sex roles — Fiction. RL C.

The king and queen want their daughter to marry a prince who will take care of them. Instead Princess Rosamund heads off on her rickety bicycle to fight monsters and rescue princes. The role reversals are splendid in this modern, humorous

Waddell, Martin (cont.)

fairy tale as are the comic illustrations of feisty Rosamund.

3487 *We Love Them*. Ill. by Barbara Firth. Lothrop, 1990, o.p. SUBJECTS: Animals — Fiction; Farm and country life — Fiction; Pet care — Fiction. RL A.

On a snowy day two children and their dog find a nearly dead rabbit and bring it home. The dog helps care for the rabbit and the two become friends. The dog dies and a puppy turns up to join the rabbit. Very short sentences and gentle pencil and watercolor pictures suit this quiet story.

Wade, Mary Dodson

3488 *Map Scales*. Children's Press, 2003, ISBN 0-516-22720-3. SERIES: Rookie Read-About Geography. SUBJECTS: Geography; Maps. RL B. LEXILE NC460L.

Using an interactive approach to teaching map reading, this volume focuses on determining distances by using the scale on a map. Good photographs and diagrams support and extend the text. A very brief index and pictorial glossary are included.

3489 *Tiny Life on the Ground*. Children's Press, 2005, ISBN 0-516-25298-4. SERIES: Rookie Read-About Science. SUBJECTS: Fungi; Science and scientists; Soil. RL B.

Through color photographs and a brief text, the ways in which bacteria and fungi help to create soil and get rid of pollution are discussed. A photo glossary and an index are included.

3490 *Types of Maps*. Children's Press, 2003, ISBN 0-516-22721-1. SERIES: Rookie Read-About Geography. SUBJECTS: Geography; Maps. RL B. LEXILE NC350L.

City, street, world, and other types of maps are mentioned and examples are given pictorially. The text is interactive, asking young readers to find objects or places. The examples of maps and the color photographs are clear and useful. Appended are a very brief photo glossary and an index.

Wadsworth, Ginger

3491 *Giant Sequoia Trees*. Ill. by Frank Staub. Lerner, 1995, ISBN 0-8225-3001-5. SERIES: Early Bird Nature. SUBJECTS: Trees. RL C. LEXILE 650L.

While focusing on the giant sequoia trees and their cousins the redwoods, this book also provides good general information about trees. Information is presented clearly and supported by color photographs, two pages of advice to parents, a glossary, and index.

Wagner, Ken, and Mary C. Olson, eds.

3492 *The Lion Who Couldn't Say No*. Ill. by Don Page. Golden Books, 1976, o.p. SERIES: Step Ahead Beginning Reader. SUBJECTS: Behavior — Generous — Fiction; Humorous stories; Lions — Fiction. RL A.

Leo the lion is so generous with the hair in his mane, allowing the birds to use it for nests, that he is soon almost bald. When nothing helps his hair grow back, the birds create a mane for him out of greenery. Comically illustrated in watercolors with attractive borders.

Wahl, Jan

3493 *Drakestail*. Ill. by Byron Barton. Greenwillow, 1978, o.p. SERIES: Read-Alone. SUBJECTS: Ducks — Fiction; Folklore — France. RL A.

On his way to get his money from the king, Drakestail is joined by four friends who shrink and hop into his gizzard. They reappear just in time to save him from disaster. A marvelous retelling of a French folktale, it is illustrated in green, gold, and orange with black outlining.

3494 *The Teeny, Tiny Witches*. Ill. by Margot Tomes. Putnam, 1979, o.p. SUBJECTS: Witches — Fiction. RL C.

Too tiny to do much magic and always driven from their homes by animals, Ma, Pa, and Sam Witch finally find a little cottage with a friendly old mouse who welcomes them. The gentle and whimsical pen and ink drawings are carefully created with red and brown accents.

Walker, Cynthia

3495 *Colorado*. Children's Press, 2004, ISBN 0-516-22735-1. SERIES: Rookie Read-About Geography. SUBJECTS: Colorado; Geography; United States. RL B. LEXILE 370L.

The land of the Rocky Mountains, the Continental Divide, and the mile-high capital city of Denver is introduced along with Colorado's state symbols and the lifestyle of its residents. There are color photographs, a brief text, a map, a photo glossary, and an index.

3496 *Maine*. Children's Press, 2005, ISBN 0-516-25255-0. SERIES: Rookie Read-About Geography. SUBJECTS: Geography; Maine; United States. RL B.

A rocky coastline, mountains, and beautiful scenery make Maine an inviting state for people who like to hike, sail, or climb. The important aspects of the state are mentioned and illustrated with color photographs. A photo glossary and index are appended.

3497 *New Mexico*. Children's Press, 2004, ISBN 0-516-22755-6. SERIES: Rookie Read-About Geography. SUBJECTS: Geography; New Mexico; United States. RL B.

"The Land of Enchantment" is filled with wonderful things to see: Carlsbad Caverns, mountains, canyons, and even desert. The culture and people are diverse. Color photographs extend the text and make the state inviting. The book concludes with a photo glossary and an index.

Walker, Sally M.

3498 *The 18 Penny Goose*. Ill. by Ellen Beier. HarperCollins, 1998, ISBN 0-06-027557-X. SERIES: I Can Read. SUBJECTS: Geese — Fiction; Historical fiction; United States — Revolutionary War — Fiction. RL B. LEXILE 370L.

The British are fast approaching and Letty and her family are trying to escape. Unable to take her beloved goose Solomon, Letty leaves a letter asking the soldiers not to take him. Based on a true story, the book is filled with suspense and drama. Illustrations are done in watercolors.

3499 *Fireflies*. Lerner, 2001, ISBN 0-8225-3047-3. SERIES: Early Bird Nature. SUBJECTS: Fireflies; Insects. RL C. LEXILE 600L.

The habitat, life cycle, and physical characteristics of the lightning bug or firefly — found all over the world — are explored in photographs, charts, and a text divided into chapters. Included are a section for adults, a glossary, and an index.

3500 *Mystery Fish: Secrets of the Coelacanth*. Ill. by Shawn Gould. Millbrook, 2006, ISBN 1-57505-638-0. SERIES: On My Own Science. SUBJECTS: Animals — Endangered; Fish; Prehistoric animals. RL C.

Since its discovery in 1938, scientists have studied this rare, living prehistoric fish. The book follows the studies and searches of scientists throughout the world. The book includes a timeline, glossary, and bibliography.

3501 *Supercroc Found*. Ill. by Philip Hood. Millbrook, 2006, ISBN 1-57505-760-3. SERIES: On My Own Science. SUBJECTS: Dinosaurs; Prehistoric animals; Science and scientists. RL C.

From studying bones and a skull of what came to be called a "supercroc," paleontologists have pieced together what this huge crocodile might have looked like. The story of the find and the subsequent work is fascinating. Illustrated with charts and color photographs, the book also includes a glossary, bibliography, and Web sites.

Wallace, Carol

3502 *One Nosy Pup*. Ill. by Steve Bjorkman. Holiday House, 2005, ISBN 0-8234-1917-7. SUBJECTS: Hamsters — Fiction; Pets — Dogs — Fiction; Pets — Fiction. RL B. LEXILE 280L.

Poky, a dog, likes his new house but discovers that a hamster left by the last family is eating his food. When Poky's humans, thinking the hamster may be a rat, try to trap the hamster, the little dog comes to the rescue. All ends well with the hamster gaining a new cage and food of his own.

3503 *Turkeys Together*. Ill. by Jacqueline Rogers. Holiday House, 2005, ISBN 0-8234-1895-2. SERIES: Holiday House Reader. SUBJECTS: Pets — Dogs — Fiction; Turkeys — Fiction. RL B.

Hunting for quail, a pointer spots Mother Turkey and discovers that she and another turkey are losing their eggs to opossum. The dog finds the perfect solution — to put all the eggs together so there is always a turkey guarding them. Realistic watercolor paintings illustrate the story.

Wallace, Karen

3504 *Albert's Raccoon.* Ill. by Graham Percy. Kingfisher, 2004, ISBN 0-7534-5354-1. SERIES: I Am Reading. SUBJECTS: Candy — Fiction; Raccoons — Fiction. RL C.

After Albert's pet raccoon Rocky destroys their kitchen, his mother threatens to give him away. That's when Albert decides to sneak him into his father's candy factory. Rocky causes as much trouble there but he also seems to be a genius at making candy. Illustrated with colored-pencil drawings.

3505 *I Can Swim!* DK, 2004, ISBN 0-7566-0274-2. SERIES: DK Readers. SUBJECTS: Parent and child — Fiction; Sports — Swimming — Fiction. RL B.

With each swimming lesson, George gains confidence. Finally he no longer needs his water wings and can swim across the pool. Illustrated with photographs of father and son during their lessons.

3506 *Ooh La La Lottie!* Ill. by Garry Parsons. Kingfisher, pap., 2004, ISBN 0-7534-5716-4. SERIES: I Am Reading. SUBJECTS: Humorous stories; Mice — Fiction; Pets — Dogs — Fiction. RL B.

Lottie loves playing with her dog Patrick and decides to eat only what Patrick likes: bread and cheese. After weeks of this diet, Lottie becomes a mouse, shrinks, and after a near-fatal encounter decides to be a little girl again. Illustrated with humorous pictures in full color.

Wallace-Brodeur, Ruth

3507 *Stories from the Big Chair.* Ill. by Diane de Groat. Macmillan, 1989, ISBN 0-689-50481-0. SUBJECTS: Sibling rivalry — Fiction; Siblings — Fiction. RL A.

When Molly tells Mama she wishes she were an only child, Mama suggests she tell stories about it. Every night when Molly tells her story she finds that somehow her little sister appears in it in a positive role. This well-written and honest portrait of siblings has charming charcoal drawings.

Wandro, Mark, and Joani Blank

3508 *My Daddy Is a Nurse.* Ill. by Irene Trivas. Addison-Wesley, 1981, o.p. SUBJECTS: Careers; Sex roles. RL C.

Ten fathers are seen in occupations usually associated with women, such as flight attendant, nurse, ballet dancer, preschool teacher, librarian, and telephone operator. The brief text is illustrated with black-and-white cartoon drawings.

Wang, Mary Lewis

3509 *The Good Witch: A Charles Perrault Tale Retold.* Ill. by Melodye Rosales. Childrens Press, 1989, o.p. SERIES: Start-Off Stories. SUBJECTS: Folklore — France; Sibling rivalry. RL A.

A very abbreviated version of a well-known folktale, the story of two sisters, one hard-working and generous, the other vain and selfish, is told more through the pictures than the text. In the story the good sister is rewarded with jewels while the bad sister receives snakes and toads.

Wardlaw, Lee

3510 *Hector's Hiccups.* Ill. by Joan Holub. Random House, 1999, o.p. SERIES: Step into Reading. SUBJECTS: Hiccups — Fiction; Siblings — Fiction. RL B. LEXILE 100L.

Hector's older brother and sister try every trick they can think of to cure Hector's hiccups. Nothing seems to work until they find his old teddy bear and tell him soothing stories. Wide-eyed characters painted in watercolors illustrate the story.

Warner, Gertrude Chandler

3511 *Benny's Boxcar Sleepover.* Ill. by Kay Life. Whitman, pap., 2004, ISBN 0-8075-0636-2. SERIES: A Boxcar Children Early Reader. SUBJECTS: Fear — Fiction; Sleepovers — Fiction. RL B.

Benny, his big brother Henry, and two of Benny's friends spend the night in the boxcar. Strange noises make the four a bit nervous but with Benny's dog Watch to guard them, they finally fall asleep. Illustrated with realistic pencil and watercolor pictures.

3512 *Benny's Saturday Surprise.* Ill. by Kay Life. Whitman, pap., 2001, ISBN 0-8075-0642-7. SERIES: A Boxcar Children Early Reader. SUBJECTS: Contests — Fiction; Pets — Dogs — Fiction; Teachers and teaching — Fiction. RL B. LEXILE BR.

Finished with his homework, Benny, his brother, sisters, and dog Watch go to town. Benny runs into his teacher and discovers she can be fun — especially when she helps him win a poster. Illustrated with realistic watercolor pictures.

3513 *Keys and Clues for Benny*. Ill. by Kay Life. Whitman, pap., 2004, ISBN 0-8075-4172-9. SERIES: A Boxcar Children Early Reader. SUBJECTS: Locks and keys — Fiction; Lost and found possessions — Fiction; Mystery and detective stories. RL B.

By looking carefully at the objects on the key ring, Benny is finally able to find the person who lost her keys at the library. The familiar Boxcar Children characters are illustrated with realistic watercolor pictures.

3514 *The Secret Under the Tree*. Ill. by Kay Life. Whitman, pap., 2001, ISBN 0-8075-0643-5. SERIES: A Boxcar Children Early Reader. SUBJECTS: Grandparents — Fiction; Pets — Dogs — Fiction; Treasures — Fiction. RL B. LEXILE 20L.

Using an old map provided by his grandfather, Benny starts digging for what may be treasure. All day he digs until he finds an old box with another box inside it and a glass bottle inside that. Inside the bottle is a picture of his grandfather and his dog after they have finished digging a hole in the same place.

Waters, John F.

3515 *Camels: Ships of the Desert*. Ill. by Reynold Ruffins. HarperCollins, 1974, o.p. SERIES: Let's-Read-and-Find-Out. SUBJECTS: Camels. RL C.

By comparing the camel's physiology to that of humans, Waters is able to explain the camel's suitability for desert life. He also does away with myths surrounding the animal's hump while presenting a very interesting and factual book. Pencil and wash pictures are well done.

3516 *Hungry Sharks*. Ill. by Ann Dalton. HarperCollins, 1973, o.p. SERIES: Let's-Read-and-Find-Out. SUBJECTS: Sharks. RL C.

The shark is a subject of perennial interest to children. Shark behavior and physiology is briefly explained without placing undue emphasis on its predatory nature. Expressive rather than realistic drawings suggest the shark, possibly making this book less attractive to many young readers.

3517 *A Jellyfish Is Not a Fish*. Ill. by Kazue Mizumura. HarperCollins, 1979, ISBN 0-690-03888-7. SERIES: Let's-Read-and-Find-Out. SUBJECTS: Jellyfish. RL B.

Found all over the world, jellyfish come in all sizes. Some are harmless while others, such as the sea wasp of Australia, are poisonous and deadly. Children will find the text and realistic watercolor paintings attractive.

Watson, Jane W.

3518 *The First Americans: Tribes of North America*. Ill. by Troy Howell. Pantheon, 1980, o.p. SERIES: I Am Reading. SUBJECTS: Native Americans. RL C.

A look at customs and life-styles among the Native Americans of the plains, eastern woodlands, far north, northwest coast, and the southwest places some emphasis on the role of children in these cultures. Black-and-white illustrations realistically depict the clothing, artifacts, and so on.

Watts, Barrie

3519 *Butterflies and Moths*. Ill. with photos. Watts, 1991, o.p. SERIES: Keeping Minibeasts. SUBJECTS: Butterflies and moths; Pet care. RL C.

Following a section providing basic information on butterflies and moths, instructions for capturing and keeping the insects are given. Good color photographs of the insects as well as the cage for keeping them make this a useful tool for the budding scientist. Index is appended.

3520 *Honeybee*. Photos by Helen Senior. Silver Burdett, 1989, o.p. SERIES: Stopwatch. SUBJECTS: Bees; Insects. RL B.

Clear color photographs and black-and-white paintings depict the stages in the development of worker and queen bees. The text is succinct, easily understood, and an index is included.

3521 *Moth*. Ill. with photos. Silver Burdett, 1990, o.p. SERIES: Stopwatch. SUBJECTS: Butterflies and moths; Insects. RL B.

The growth and development of a moon moth is followed from the laying of an egg to its hatching

Watts, Barrie (cont.)

from a cocoon and flying. The text and occasional descriptive drawings work with fine color photographs to clearly provide an explanation of the life of a moth.

3522 *Mouse*. Ill. with photos. Dutton, 1992, o.p. SERIES: See How They Grow. SUBJECTS: Animals — Growth and development; Mice. RL B.
Very well designed color photographic silhouettes are placed against a white background and framed with a watercolor border showing a mouse's development. The text, done in first person, tells about the things a mouse can do at each stage of development.

3523 *Potato*. Photos. Ill. by Helen Senior. Silver Burdett, 1988, o.p. SERIES: Stopwatch. SUBJECTS: Plants; Vegetables. RL B.
A straightforward, clearly written text takes the reader through the different stages of growth for the potato plant. The photographs, many of them cutaways of underground growth, and the line drawings work well with the text to explain the plant's life cycle.

3524 *Rabbit*. Ill. with photos. Dutton, 1991, o.p. SERIES: See How They Grow. SUBJECTS: Animals — Growth and development; Rabbits. RL B.
In seven stages, color photographic silhouettes set against a white background and accented with watercolor borders show the development of a white rabbit from birth to six weeks of age. The brief text is written in the first person as if told by the rabbit.

Weeks, Sarah

3525 *Baa-choo!* Ill. by Jane Manning. HarperCollins, 2004, ISBN 0-06-029236-9. SERIES: I Can Read. SUBJECTS: Sheep — Fiction; Sneezing — Fiction; Stories in rhyme. RL B. LEXILE 580L.
Sam, a lamb, asks one animal after another to help him finish his sneeze. Nothing works until they all get together and Sam produces an amazing sneeze. Comical watercolor pictures work well with the story.

3526 *Drip, Drop*. Ill. by Jane Manning. HarperCollins, 2000, ISBN 0-06-028523-0. SERIES: I Can Read. SUBJECTS: Mice — Fiction; Weather — Rain — Fiction. RL A. LEXILE BR.
Poor mouse finds one leak after another during a storm. The brief and repetitive text is accompanied by brightly colored and humorous art.

3527 *Splish, Splash!* Ill. by Ashley Wolff. HarperCollins, 1999, ISBN 0-06-027892-7. SERIES: My First I Can Read. SUBJECTS: Animals — Fiction; Stories in rhyme. RL A. LEXILE BR.
Chub the fish is taking a bath when one animal after another comes up and asks to join him. Soon the tub is filled with all kinds of animals. The very brief and repetitive text will be useful for beginning readers.

Weinberger, Kimberly

3528 *Cats That Roar!* Ill. by Turi MacCombie. Scholastic, 1999, o.p. SERIES: Hello Reader! SUBJECTS: Animals — Endangered; Pets — Cats. RL C. LEXILE 740L.
Lions, tigers, leopards, and other large cats are described; their endangered status is discussed at the end of the book. Illustrations are realistic watercolors.

3529 *The Stormy Day Rescue*. Ill. by Del Thompson and Dana Thompson. Scholastic, pap., 2001, ISBN 0-439-21360-6. SERIES: Clifford the Big Red Dog. SUBJECTS: Pets — Dogs — Fiction; Weather — Storms — Fiction. RL B. LEXILE 150L.
Cartoon character Clifford has a big bone to bury and finds all the wrong places to dig. When a storm is imminent, Clifford's digging ability is used to safeguard the library.

Weiss, Ellen

3530 *Lucky Duck*. Ill. by Brian Lies. Aladdin, pap., 2004, ISBN 0-689-86029-3. SERIES: Ready-to-Read. SUBJECTS: Ducks — Fiction; Humorous stories; Stories in rhyme. RL A.
Out for a walk and a trip to an amusement park, a jauntily attired wood duck barely misses one catastrophe after another. The pictures tell the story of the duck's adventures and are extended by a very brief text.

3531 *Millicent Maybe.* Ill. by author. Watts, 1979, o.p. SERIES: Easy-Read Story. SUBJECTS: Behavior — Decisive — Fiction; Humorous stories. RL B.

Unable to make choices, Millicent fills her home with things she does not need. She buys a large number of parrots to make decisions for her. They lead her into more trouble and finally into taking responsibility for herself. This funny story is illustrated with humorous ink drawings with blue, yellow, and green.

Weiss, Leatie

3532 *Funny Feet!* Ill. by Ellen Weiss. Watts, 1978, o.p. SUBJECTS: Disabilities — Physical and mental — Fiction; Penguins — Fiction; Self-esteem — Fiction. RL B.

Priscilla Penguin is supposed to wear corrective shoes and take ballet lessons because she is pigeon-toed. She loves ballet lessons but not her klunky shoes. At her recital someone takes her ballet slippers but Priscilla soars with her clod-hoppers. Illustrated with comic sketches.

3533 *Heather's Feathers.* Ill. by Ellen Weiss. Watts, 1976, o.p. SERIES: Easy-Read Story. SUBJECTS: Birds — Fiction; Self-esteem — Fiction; Tooth fairy — Fiction. RL B.

The only bird in her class, Heather is happy and popular until her classmates start losing their teeth. Heather feels left out when they talk of the Tooth Fairy but when she starts molting she feels like one of the crowd again. Well written, this is illustrated with soft yet playful paintings.

Weiss, Nicki

3534 *Menj.* Ill. by author. Greenwillow, 1981, o.p. SERIES: Read-Alone. SUBJECTS: Frogs and toads — Fiction; Sibling rivalry — Fiction. RL B.

To rile Francine, her older sister Norma uses the word Menj repeatedly and refuses to tell its meaning. Finally Francine wises up and ignores the teasing. This story about two frog sisters and the book's other similar stories are fun, recall the rivalry between children, and are delightfully illustrated with simple, homey pictures.

Welch, Sheila Kelly

3535 *Little Prince Know-It-All.* Ill. by Lynne Woodcock Cravath. Golden Books, 1998, o.p. SERIES: Road to Reading. SUBJECTS: Parrots — Fiction; Princes and princesses — Fiction; Siblings — Fiction. RL C. LEXILE 490L.

Prince Caleb's younger brother Prince Omar is spoiled and truly a know-it-all. Omar decides they should have pets and is sure his will be the best. Omar gets a puppy and Caleb a parrot. Finally it's the parrot that gets the best of Omar. Illustrated with bright colors and fanciful settings.

Wells, Rosemary

3536 *Doris's Dinosaur.* Hyperion, 2001, ISBN 0-7868-0726-1. SERIES: Yoko and Friends: School Days. SUBJECTS: Dinosaurs — Fiction; Museums — Fiction; School stories. RL B.

While the other children paint pictures of dinosaurs, Doris draws swirls of color. She claims she cannot paint or draw. On a trip to a museum, the class discovers the paintings of Matisse and a new appreciation for Doris. Wells's animal paintings and text capture the diverse nature of a classroom.

3537 *Make New Friends.* Hyperion, 2003, ISBN 0-7868-0730-X. SERIES: Yoko and Friends: School Days. SUBJECTS: Animals — Fiction; Friendship — Fiction; School stories. RL B. LEXILE AD200L.

Yoko is asked to be captain of the Friend Ship and to take care of new student Juanita. Yoko takes her job seriously and makes sure that Juanita has a friend. Juanita is overwhelmed by everyone's talent until Yoko shows her that she, Juanita, also is special. Wells offers a good picture of a kindergarten classroom.

3538 *Max and Ruby Play School.* Grosset & Dunlap, pap., 2003, ISBN 0-448-43182-3. SERIES: All Aboard Reading Picture Reader. SUBJECTS: Play — Fiction; School stories; Siblings — Fiction. RL B.

Though Max would rather play with his car, Ruby insists that he play school with her. She tries teaching him his ABCs and counting but relents on teaching him to tell time. Rebuses help to entice readers into the story.

Wells, Rosemary (cont.)

3539 *Play with Max and Ruby*. Grosset & Dunlap, pap., 2002, ISBN 0-448-42854-7. SERIES: All Aboard Reading Picture Reader. SUBJECTS: Dolls and dollhouses — Fiction; Rebuses; Toys — Fiction. RL A.

The story of Max's desire to have Ruby's doll Emily is told with the help of rebuses. Max can't keep his eyes off Emily and can't really focus on his own toys.

3540 *The School Play*. Hyperion, 2001, ISBN 0-7868-0721-0. SERIES: Yoko and Friends: School Days. SUBJECTS: Human body — Teeth — Fiction; Plays — Fiction; School stories. RL B. LEXILE 360L.

The kindergarten class is doing a play about dental health and Yoko gets the only non-speaking role: a cavity. Disappointed at first, she and her mother find the perfect way to make her part very interesting. Yoko's reaction to her assigned part is genuine and reflects what many children experience.

3541 *When I Grow Up*. Hyperion, 2003, ISBN 0-7868-0731-8. SERIES: Yoko and Friends: School Days. SUBJECTS: Animals — Fiction; Careers — Fiction; School stories. RL B.

Yoko comes to school dressed as what she plans to be when she grows up: a Japanese teacher. She has on a kimono and carries her family's precious netsuke collection. Later the collection is taken and Yoko is devastated. It finally is returned. Situations and feelings are realistically portrayed.

West, Colin

3542 *Monty, the Dog Who Wears Glasses*. Ill. by author. Dutton, 1990, o.p. SERIES: Speedsters. SUBJECTS: Humorous stories; Pets — Dogs — Fiction. RL C.

Monty's owner gives him lensless glasses hoping they will improve his behavior. In six short chapters illustrated with comical ink sketches, Monty causes mischief and induces laughter.

3543 *Moose and Mouse*. Kingfisher, pap., 2004, ISBN 0-7534-5715-6. SERIES: I Am Reading. SUBJECTS: Camps and camping — Fiction; Mice — Fiction; Moose — Fiction. RL C.

Moose loves the outdoors and Mouse prefers his snug house. Their two stories highlight their differences and their friendship. Illustrated with humorous ink and wash pictures.

3544 *Shape Up, Monty!* Ill. by author. Dutton, 1990, o.p. SERIES: Speedsters. SUBJECTS: Humorous stories; Pets — Dogs — Fiction. RL C.

Monty is still clumsy and nearly always in trouble despite his lensless glasses, and his appetite and eavesdropping ways cause confusion. Illustrated with many line drawings that humorously break up the text.

West, Tracey

3545 *Me and My Robot*. Ill. by Cindy Revell. Grosset & Dunlap, 2003, o.p. SERIES: All Aboard Reading. SUBJECTS: Lost and found possessions — Fiction; Pets — Cats — Fiction; Robots — Fiction. RL A.

A little boy and his robot agree to help Lucy find her kitten but the two children have a difficult time explaining to Robot exactly what a kitten is. Childlike art in full color matches the story well.

3546 *Me and My Robot #2: The Show-and-tell Show-off*. Ill. by Cindy Revell. Grosset & Dunlap, 2003, ISBN 0-448-43282-X. SERIES: All Aboard Reading. SUBJECTS: Friendship — Fiction; Robots — Fiction; School stories. RL A.

Reese takes Robot to school for show-and-tell and gets into a rivalry with Ben and his parrot. The teacher wisely intervenes and offers all of them a chance to be friends. Illustrations are comical and the story should have great child appeal.

Weston, Martha

3547 *Cats Are Like That*. Holiday House, 1999, ISBN 0-8234-1419-1. SERIES: Holiday House Reader. SUBJECTS: Pets — Cats — Fiction; Pets — Fiction; Pets — Fish — Fiction. RL B. LEXILE 180L.

Dot brings her three new fish home and her cat Fuzzy immediately shows an interest in eating them. Cats are like that. The refrain follows each of Fuzzy's mishaps. Illustrations are lively and capture the cat very well.

3548 *Dr. Clock-Sicle*. Holiday House, 2004, ISBN 0-8234-1825-1. SERIES: Holiday House Reader. SUBJECTS: Humorous stories;

Prehistoric animals — Fiction; Time travel — Fiction. RL B.

Dr. Clock's baby sneaks a ride on the time machine and lands in the Ice Age with his father — who never notices him. The two look for interesting things, discover some, and end up back home just in time to NOT be a saber-toothed tiger's lunch.

3549 *Jack and Jill and Big Dog Bill.* Random House, 2002, ISBN 0-375-91248-7. SERIES: Step into Reading: Early. SUBJECTS: Pets — Dogs — Fiction; Sledding — Fiction; Stories in rhyme. RL A.

With a minimum of words, this rhyming text and illustrations feature two children and a dog sledding on a very snowy day.

3550 *Space Guys!* Holiday House, 2000, o.p. SERIES: Holiday House Reader. SUBJECTS: Extraterrestrial beings — Fiction; Humorous stories; Science fiction. RL A. LEXILE BR.

When three space travelers land in a tree and jump in his window, a little boy's parents think he is dreaming. The next morning the house is a mess and the little boy has a picture to prove that it was three space guys who did it. The lively illustrations extend the humor and help tell the story.

Wheeler, Cindy

3551 *Bookstore Cat.* Ill. by author. Random House, 1994, ISBN 0-679-94109-6. SERIES: Step into Reading. SUBJECTS: Birds — Fiction; Bookstores — Fiction; Pets — Cats — Fiction. RL B.

Mulligan, a black and white cat, spends his days watching over a bookstore. When a pigeon accidentally gets in, Mulligan jumps right into action, creating havoc everywhere, but finally getting rid of it. The humorous story and light watercolor pictures will attract readers.

3552 *The Emperor's Birthday Suit.* Ill. by R. W. Alley. Random House, 1996, o.p. SERIES: Step into Reading. SUBJECTS: Greed — Fiction; Vanity — Fiction. RL B. LEXILE 330L.

Loosely based on the Hans Christian Andersen story of the emperor who is tricked by two scoundrels into wearing nothing for a parade, this story has a happy ending with the scoundrels punished and the emperor with a new adviser.

Wheeler, Lisa

3553 *Invasion of the Pig Sisters.* Ill. by Frank Ansley. Atheneum, 2006, ISBN 0-689-84953-2. SERIES: Ready-to-Read. SUBJECTS: Friendship — Fiction; Pigs — Fiction; Play — Fiction. RL B. LEXILE 290L.

The Saturday plans of Fitch, a very amiable wolf, and his friend Chip, a fun-loving pig, change when Chip must bring his three little sisters to the playground. At first afraid of Fitch, the girls soon gain confidence in him and everyone has fun. Pictures are done very simply in ink and watercolor.

3554 *New Pig in Town.* Ill. by Frank Ansley. Atheneum, 2003, ISBN 0-689-84950-8. SERIES: Ready-to-Read. SUBJECTS: Pigs — Fiction; School stories; Wolves — Fiction. RL B. LEXILE 160L.

The improbable friendship between Fitch, a wolf, and Chip, a pig, begins when Chip determines to find out all about the shy little wolf. Convinced that Fitch has no intention of eating him, Chip decides to make Fitch his friend. This is the first in a series about their friendship.

3555 *When Pigs Fly.* Ill. by Frank Ansley. Atheneum, 2003, ISBN 0-689-84951-6. SERIES: Ready-to-Read. SUBJECTS: Heroes — Fiction; Pigs — Fiction; Wolves — Fiction. RL B.

It's hero day at school and Chip and most of the others dress up as TV hero Hyper Hog. Fitch comes dressed in a t-shirt with a tree on it in honor of his real hero — Timberwolf. Before school starts, even Chip is convinced that a real hero is better than a TV hero. Comical watercolor illustrations are used throughout the book.

3556 *Who's Afraid of Granny Wolf?* Ill. by Frank Ashley. Atheneum, 2004, ISBN 0-689-84952-4. SERIES: Ready-to-Read. SUBJECTS: Houses — Fiction; Pigs — Fiction; Wolves — Fiction. RL B.

On his way to Fitch's granny's house, Chip (a pig) suddenly thinks about what a wolf might eat (a pig?). Once there Chip realizes that Fitch's house and his granny are very much like his own house and himself.

Wheeler, M. J.

3557 *Fox Tales*. Ill. by Dana Gustafson. Carolrhoda, 1984, o.p. SERIES: On My Own. SUBJECTS: Folklore — India; Foxes — Fiction. RL A.

Based on folk tales from India, these three stories have a fox outwitting a rascal of a farmer and a hungry tiger and being made foolish by his own ignorance. Well written and suitable for storytelling, the stories are illustrated with line drawings and watercolor pictures.

White, Diana

3558 *Ballerina Dreams*. Ill. by Jacqueline Rogers. Scholastic, pap., 1998, ISBN 0-439-83302-7. SERIES: Hello Reader! SUBJECTS: Biographies; Dancers and dancing. RL C. LEXILE 570L.

Diana White, a member of the New York City Ballet Company, tells the story of her childhood and her great desire to become a dancer. Her voice is clear and her passion obvious. The book is illustrated with watercolor paintings and ends with photographs of White and two activities.

White, Laurence B.

3559 *Science Toys and Tricks*. Ill. by Marc Brown. Addison-Wesley, 1975, o.p. SUBJECTS: Science experiments. RL B.

Twenty-three very simple and enticing science activities or crafts introduce children to scientific principles without giving lengthy explanations. Pencil drawings are clear and should help children to duplicate the activities.

Wilder, Laura Ingalls

3560 *Dance at Grandpa's*. Ill. by Renee Graef. HarperCollins, pap., 1995, ISBN 0-06-443372-2. SERIES: My First Little House Books. SUBJECTS: Dancers and dancing — Fiction; Family life — Fiction; Frontier and pioneer life — Fiction. RL B.

When Grandma and Grandpa have a party, Laura and her family all get dressed up and pile into the sleigh, traveling to Grandpa's. There they dance, eat, and enjoy seeing neighbors and friends. The warmth and honesty of the original stories are captured in the text and the pictures.

3561 *Winter Days in the Big Woods: Adapted from the Little House Books*. Ill. by Renee Graef. HarperCollins, 1994, ISBN 0-06-023014-2. SERIES: My First Little House Books. SUBJECTS: Family life — Fiction; Frontier and pioneer life — Fiction; Winter — Fiction. RL B.

Adapted from Wilder's Little House in the Big Woods, the brief text and warm pencil and watercolor pictures effectively capture the closeness of Laura's family as they do their chores and spend time together. The art is based on that of Garth Williams.

Wilhelm, Hans

3562 *Don't Cut My Hair!* Scholastic, 1997, o.p. SERIES: Hello Reader! SUBJECTS: Haircutting — Fiction; Pets — Dogs — Fiction. RL A. LEXILE BR.

The little white dog is embarrassed by his new, very short haircut. At first he refuses to play with his friends but then he tries a new approach and soon has his friends jealous. Illustrated with pencil and watercolor washes.

3563 *I Am Lost!* Scholastic, pap., 1997, ISBN 0-590-30699-5. SERIES: Hello Reader! SUBJECTS: Lost, being — Fiction; Pets — Dogs — Fiction. RL A. LEXILE BR.

Determined to catch a leaf, a little dog becomes lost. With the help of a policeman and the tag on his collar, the dog is happily home again. The very easy to read story is illustrated with pencil and watercolors.

3564 *I Can Help!* Cartwheel, pap., 2003, ISBN 0-439-46621-0. SERIES: Scholastic Reader. SUBJECTS: Behavior — Helpful — Fiction; Pets — Dogs — Fiction. RL A. LEXILE BR.

The little white dog first tries to help baby then tries to help clean the house and plant flowers. He is not good at any of these tasks but finally decides that practice may help. A very limited vocabulary and watercolor pictures will make this attractive to the new reader.

3565 *I Hate My Bow!* Cartwheel, 1995, o.p. SERIES: Hello Reader! SUBJECTS: Pets — Dogs — Fiction; Play — Fiction. RL A. LEXILE 90L.

After his bath and new bow, a little white dog seems to hate everything. Then he discovers that the cat and the baby can help him have a good time in the mud. The story is told with expressive watercolor illustrations and a minimum of words.

3566 *I Lost My Tooth!* Scholastic, pap., 1999, ISBN 0-590-64230-8. SERIES: Hello Reader! SUBJECTS: Pets — Dogs — Fiction; Tooth fairy — Fiction. RL A. LEXILE BR.
Excited about his first loose tooth, a little white puppy loses it while he is eating. Instead of a tooth under his pillow, he puts a picture of himself without his tooth.

3567 *I Love Colors!* Scholastic, pap., 2000, ISBN 0-439-19288-9. SERIES: Scholastic Reader. SUBJECTS: Concepts — Colors — Fiction; Pets — Dogs — Fiction. RL A. LEXILE BR.
A little white dog plays with red, yellow, and blue paint by dipping parts of his bottom into it. Soon his body also includes orange, green, and purple. With a quick dip in the wading pool, he is back to white.

3568 *I'm Not Scared!* Cartwheel, pap., 2002, ISBN 0-439-44334-2. SERIES: Scholastic Reader. SUBJECTS: Fear — Fiction; Halloween — Fiction; Pets — Dogs — Fiction. RL A. LEXILE BR.
A little dog excitedly tries on different costumes looking for the perfect one for Halloween. When the doorbell rings and ghosts appear, he is at first frightened then realizes they are only his friends in their costumes. Limited text is tied inextricably to the watercolor art.

3569 *It's Too Windy!* Scholastic, pap., 2000, ISBN 0-439-10849-7. SERIES: Hello Reader! SUBJECTS: Pets — Dogs — Fiction; Weather — Wind — Fictions. RL A. LEXILE BR.
A little dog who complains about everything and does not want to take his walk becomes a hero when he saves the baby's runaway stroller. A minimum of words is accompanied by expressive watercolor illustrations.

Wilkinson, Sylvia

3570 *I Can Be a Race Car Driver.* Ill. with photos. Childrens Press, 1986, o.p. SERIES: I Can Be. SUBJECTS: Careers; Sports — Car racing. RL C.
Beginning with a picture dictionary, this survey of the world of car racing repeats dictionary entries in the margins as the words appear in the text. Facts on go — carts, cars, trucks, drivers, dangers, safety, and so on are included along with full-color photographs, a glossary, and an index.

Wilkinson, Valerie

3571 *Flies Are Fascinating.* Ill. with photos. Children's Press, 1994, o.p. SERIES: Rookie Read-About Science. SUBJECTS: Flies; Insects. RL B.
Flies of all kinds are very briefly introduced through a limited and slightly more difficult than expected text and supporting color photographs. The names of flies and their order have no pronunciation guide or glossary to help young readers.

Willems, Mo

3572 *My Friend Is Sad.* Hyperion, 2007, ISBN 1-4231-0297-7. SERIES: Elephant and Piggie. SUBJECTS: Elephants — Fiction; Friendship — Fiction; Pigs — Fiction. RL A.
When Piggie's friend Gerald the elephant is sad, Piggie tries all sorts of ways to make him happy. Clever line drawings, a brief text, and great design make this a good bet for young readers.

3573 *Today I Will Fly!* Hyperion, 2007, ISBN 1-4231-0295-3. SERIES: Elephant and Piggie. SUBJECTS: Elephants — Fiction; Flying — Fiction; Pigs — Fiction. RL A.
Though Elephant Gerald is sure Piggie will never fly, she is certain she can. Imaginative drawings and the briefest of texts tell the story.

Williams, David K.

3574 *The Picnic.* Ill. by Laura Ovresat. Harcourt, 2006, ISBN 0-15-205776-5. SERIES: Green Light Readers. SUBJECTS: Picnics — Fiction; Stories in rhyme. RL A.
Mom gathers Todd, Kim, Mick, and Rick for a special picnic. Few words per page and bright illustrations with round-faced children illustrate the story.

3575 *Tick Tock.* Ill. by Laura Ovresat. Harcourt, 2006, ISBN 0-15-205581-9. SERIES: Green Light Readers. SUBJECTS: Concepts — Time — Fiction; Housekeeping — Fiction; Stories in rhyme. RL A.

Williams, David K. (cont.)

Four children hurriedly clean up the house as the clock's ticking warns them that mom will be home soon. Illustrated in lively, full-color paintings, the book also includes activities to supplement the story.

Williams, John

3576 *The Life Cycle of a Swallow*. Ill. by Jackie Harland. Bookwright, 1989, o.p. SERIES: Life Cycles. SUBJECTS: Birds. RL B.

Realistically illustrated with full-color paintings, the book clearly describes the major events in the swallows' breeding season and its habits, habitat, and diet. The book also includes an invitation to observe other birds. A glossary, index, bibliography, and table of contents are included.

3577 *The Life Cycle of a Tree*. Ill. by Jackie Harland. Bookwright, 1989, o.p. SERIES: Life Cycles. SUBJECTS: Trees. RL B.

A clear, simple text and accurate color paintings depict the stages in the development of a chestnut tree from buried nut to mature plant. With an emphasis on explanation in the text and pictures, this is an inviting science book with a glossary, bibliography, index, and table of contents.

Williams, Suzanne

3578 *Emily at School*. Ill. by Abby Carter. Hyperion, 1996, ISBN 0-7868-0149-2. SERIES: Hyperion Chapters. SUBJECTS: Friendship — Fiction; School stories. RL C.

Emily is finally in second grade and faces challenges that are portrayed realistically. A longer text with black-and-white illustrations makes this a good transition book to more challenging chapter books.

Williamson, Stan

3579 *The No-Bark Dog*. Ill. by Tom O'Sullivan. Modern Curriculum Press, 1991, ISBN 0-8136-5042-9. SERIES: Beginning-to-Read. SUBJECTS: Pets — Dogs — Fiction. RL A.

Everyone keeps asking Timothy why his new dog does not bark. His mother and father tell him to be patient but Timothy worries. Illustrated with full-color realistic paintings, this is a quiet story with a humorous and satisfying ending.

Willner-Pardo, Gina

3580 *Natalie Spitzer's Turtles*. Ill. by Molly Delaney. Whitman, 1992, o.p. SUBJECTS: Friendship — Fiction; School stories; Turtles — Fiction. RL C.

On the first day of second grade, Jess learns what it means to be left out when only she and Natalie Spitzer are not included in a new girl's games. Jess and Natalie become friends and Jess learns the importance of being herself. Longer than most readers, this has attractive watercolors.

Wilmer, Diane

3581 *Nuts About Nuts*. Ill. by Paul Dowling. Forest House, 1990, ISBN 1-878363-09-3. SERIES: Quality Time. SUBJECTS: Humorous stories; Trees — Fiction. RL B.

Mr. Conker loves fall because of the huge horse chestnut tree planted by his great-grandfather. The neighbors think he is bonkers because of his obsession with the tree's nuts but Mr. Conker does not care — he loves nuts. Illustrations are zany ink and wash pictures.

3582 *The Playground*. Ill. by Margaret Chamberlain. Forest House, 1986, ISBN 1-878363-10-7. SERIES: Quality Time. SUBJECTS: Friendship — Fiction; School stories. RL B.

Dan, the new boy at school, is reluctant to join in at recess. Then Jack decides to get his friends to include Dan in their fun. Upbeat and illustrated with childlike sketchy ink and watercolor pictures, this book has the potential for breaking barriers when used by a teacher with a class.

3583 *Zap Zero: The Delivery Man*. Ill. by Paul Dowling. Forest House, 1989, ISBN 1-878363-11-5. SERIES: Quality Time. SUBJECTS: Careers — Fiction; Noise — Fiction. RL B.

Zap, a London delivery man, is sent with a package to Scotland. As he rides his motorcycle north, the package starts making strange noises. Only when he gets to Scotland does he realize how perfect the noise is. Text is illustrated with sketchy, vibrant drawings with color washes.

Wilson, Beth

3584 *Martin Luther King, Jr*. Ill. by Floyd Sowell. Putnam, 1971, o.p. SERIES: See and

Read Beginning to Read Biography. SUBJECTS: African Americans; Biographies. RL B.

Opening with King's funeral in 1968, the text looks back on King's life and especially notes the Montgomery bus boycott, his winning the Nobel Peace Prize, and his "I have a dream" speech. The writing style is good, giving a sense of the times. Illustrated with very effective sketches.

Wilson, Lynn

3585 *Sharks!* Ill. by Courtney Studios, Inc., staff. Penguin, pap., 1992, ISBN 0-448-40300-5. SERIES: All Aboard Books. SUBJECTS: Sharks. RL C.

Detailed, realistic pictures help to explain the kinds of sharks, their size, habits, and difference from other fish. The text is clearly written, interesting, and full of unusual bits of information (e. g., a set of armor was found in a shark's stomach). It mentions the endangered status of the shark.

Winnick, Karen

3586 *Sandro's Dolphin.* Ill. by author. Lothrop, 1980, o.p. SUBJECTS: Dolphins — Fiction; Sports — Fishing — Fiction. RL B.

The mullet are becoming scarce and the fishermen in Sandro's village often come back with none at all. Young Sandro is befriended by a dolphin that seems to understand the village's problem and with other dolphins comes to the villagers' rescue. Illustrated with ink drawings with blue accents.

Winters, Kay

3587 *Where Are the Bears?* Ill. by Brian Lies. Delacorte, 1998, ISBN 0-385-32291-7. SERIES: Yearling First Choice Chapter Book. SUBJECTS: Bears — Fiction; Camps and camping — Fiction. RL C.

Warned to beware of human campers, two bear cubs watch as parents and son set up a tent and leave. The bear cubs investigate and wreak havoc. Only the boy realizes bears have damaged their belongings and are responsible for subsequent problems — and no one believes him. The humorous contrasts between the bears and the human campers are extended in the illustrations.

Wise, William

3588 *Booker T. Washington.* Ill. by Paul Frame. Putnam, 1968, o.p. SERIES: See and Read Beginning to Read Biography. SUBJECTS: African Americans; Biographies. RL A.

Born into slavery, Booker T. Washington does whatever is necessary to earn an education. He then begins a lifelong career as a teacher and educator at Tuskegee Institute. Well written and factual, the book does not overlook the controversy surrounding Washington. Illustrated with sketches.

3589 *Monsters of the Middle Ages.* Ill. by Tomie dePaola. Putnam, 1971, o.p. SERIES: See and Read. SUBJECTS: Mythical creatures. RL B.

The 14 fantastic creatures of medieval lore that are presented here are by no means all fearful monsters. They include a race of one-legged people, centaurs, unicorns, and giants, to mention a few. Entertainingly written, the book is fancifully illustrated in black line with red highlights.

Wiseman, Bernard

3590 *Barber Bear.* Little, Brown, pap., 1987, ISBN 0-316-94859-4. SERIES: Puntown Book. SUBJECTS: Bears — Fiction; Puns — Fiction. RL B.

It's the day of the dance and punster Barber Bear trims, cuts, and shampoos a succession of animals while responding to their requests with silly puns. Humorous illustrations extend the fun of the word play.

3591 *The Big Yellow School Bus.* Ill. by Ed Rodriguez. Disney, 1992, o.p. SERIES: Disney First Reader. SUBJECTS: English language — Spelling — Fiction; Safety — Fiction; School stories. RL A.

Familiar Disney characters — Mickey, Goofy, Donald, Minnie, and Daisy — ride the school bus together. The text is divided into two chapters. The first features a humorous attempt by Mickey to get Goofy to put on his seat belt. The second has the group try arithmetic. Text is illustrated in Disney cartoon style.

3592 *Bobby and Boo.* Ill. by author. Holt, Rinehart, 1978, o.p. SUBJECTS: Humorous stories; Science fiction. RL A.

Wiseman, Bernard (cont.)

Bobby is playing spaceman when Boo arrives in a flying saucer. The amazing visitor spends the day with Bobby. He eats lunch, does tricks, and plays ball while Mom and Dad think he is the new boy on the street. Illustrated with heavily outlined, comic pictures in yellow and gray.

3593 *Christmas with Morris and Boris*. Ill. by author. Little, Brown, 1983, o.p. SERIES: Morris and Boris. SUBJECTS: Animals — Fiction; Christmas — Fiction; Friendship — Fiction. RL A.

Though infuriated by Morris's constant interruptions, Boris the bear still attempts to introduce the silly moose to Christmas and Santa Claus. Morris's misunderstandings and Boris's impatience are very funny, as are the heavily outlined brown, red, and green pictures.

3594 *Don't Make Fun!* Ill. by author. Houghton Mifflin, 1982, o.p. SUBJECTS: Behavior — Manners — Fiction; Pigs — Fiction. RL B.

The way Bobby, a boar, constantly makes fun with words irritates his father, but when obnoxious, ill-mannered relatives arrive, his parents rely on Bobby's special wit to drive them away. Funny drawings and a humorous text have readers rooting for Bobby.

3595 *Halloween with Morris and Boris*. Ill. by author. Dodd, Mead, 1975, o.p. SERIES: Morris and Boris. SUBJECTS: Animals — Fiction; Friendship — Fiction; Halloween — Fiction. RL A.

Boris takes Morris on a Halloween adventure filled with costumes, trick-or-treating, a party, and their own brand of slapstick humor. Popular with many children, the silly but appealing characters and settings are illustrated in brown, orange, and blue.

3596 *Handy Hound*. Little, Brown, 1987, o.p. SERIES: Puntown Book. SUBJECTS: Pets — Dogs — Fiction; Puns — Fiction. RL B.

Handy Hound, an irrepressible punster who prefers fishing to working, fixes bikes, fences, washers, clocks, and just about everything else. Whether working or fishing, he never misses a chance to pun. Comical illustrations work well with the play on words.

3597 *Little New Kangaroo*. Ill. by Theresa Burns. Houghton Mifflin, 1993, o.p. SUBJECTS: Animals — Fiction; Australia — Fiction; Kangaroos — Fiction. RL A.

Baby Kangaroo invites four other Australian animals — a koala, a wombat, a bandicoot, and a platypus — to join him for a ride in his mother's pouch. The rhyming text is often awkward but the unusual animals and the humorous situation will appeal to readers.

3598 *The Lucky Runner*. Ill. by author. Garrard, 1979, o.p. SERIES: For Real. SUBJECTS: Sports — Running — Fiction; Superstitions — Fiction. RL A.

Buddy practices hard and is a good runner but he thinks he wins races because of his lucky socks. At the big track meet he accidentally puts on the wrong pair and still wins — reinforcing his coach's message about hard work, not luck, making winners. Illustrated in gray and coral.

3599 *Morris and Boris: Three Stories*. Ill. by author. Dodd, Mead, 1974, o.p. SUBJECTS: Animals — Fiction; Jokes and riddles — Fiction; Tongue twisters — Fiction. RL A.

Serious, impatient Boris the bear tries to get the good-natured but very dense Morris the moose to try riddles, tongue twisters, and games. Children will laugh at the pair's antics and enjoy the comical green and brown illustrations.

3600 *Morris and Boris at the Circus*. Ill. by author. HarperCollins, pap., 1990, ISBN 0-06-444143-1. SERIES: I Can Read. SUBJECTS: Bears — Fiction; Circuses — Fiction; Moose — Fiction. RL A.

Ever-patient Boris the bear takes Morris the moose to the circus. When he sees no moose in the show, Morris joins in with predictably funny results. The text is illustrated in three colors with comical drawings.

3601 *Morris Goes to School*. Ill. by author. HarperCollins, 1970, ISBN 0-06-026548-5. SERIES: I Can Read. SUBJECTS: Humorous stories; Moose — Fiction; School stories. RL A.

After going to the wrong store and being unable to count his money, Morris the moose decides he needs to go to school. At school, he has a great time and learns enough to read store names and count his change. Children will enjoy the funny story and the humorous illustrations.

3602 *Morris Has a Birthday Party!* Ill. by author. Little, Brown, 1983, o.p. SUBJECTS: Bears — Fiction; Birthdays — Fiction; Moose — Fiction. RL A.

Morris the moose knows nothing of birthdays until Boris the bear gives him a party. Morris's predictable misunderstandings of common words continue to plague poor, impatient Boris and entertain the reader. The comic-style illustrations are amusingly drawn in orange, green, and brown.

3603 *Morris Has a Cold.* Ill. by author. Dodd, Mead, 1978, o.p. SUBJECTS: Bears — Fiction; Illness — Fiction; Moose — Fiction. RL A.

Boris the bear nearly loses his patience when he tries to help literal-minded Morris the moose get over a cold. Everything Boris suggests is misinterpreted by the moose in this very silly and very funny story. The cartoon-style pictures capture the two characters well.

3604 *Morris Tells Boris Mother Moose Stories and Rhymes.* Ill. by author. Dodd, Mead, 1979, o.p. SUBJECTS: Bears — Fiction; Moose — Fiction; Sleep — Fiction. RL A.

Trying to help Boris the bear get to sleep, Morris the moose tells him other Moose stories. Boris's constant interruptions and his demands for changes in the stories are great fun for the reader. The two friends are comically illustrated in brown, black, and green.

3605 *Morris the Moose.* Rev. ed. Ill. by author. HarperCollins, 1989, ISBN 0-06-026475-6. SERIES: Early I Can Read. SUBJECTS: Humorous stories; Moose — Fiction. RL A.

When Morris the Moose meets a cow, he tries to convince her that she is a moose, too. Unsuccessful he asks two other "moose" — a cow and a deer — who turn out to be as silly as he is. New, more colorful illustrations as well as a revised text make this more attractive than the original.

3606 *Quick Quackers.* Ill. by author. Garrard, 1979, o.p. SERIES: Easy Venture. SUBJECTS: Ducks — Fiction; English language — Pronunciation — Fiction; Parrots — Fiction. RL A.

Polly, a parrot, cannot pronounce r so her request for a "quacker" brings on a trio of ducks. After much frustration and many hijinks, the ducks finally decipher her request and provide crackers. The simple story is illustrated with full-color humorous paintings.

Witt, Alexa

3607 *It's Great to Skate! An Easy Guide to Inline Skating.* Ill. by Nate Evans. Simon & Schuster, 2000, o.p. SERIES: Ready-to-Read. SUBJECTS: Sports — Inline skating. RL B. LEXILE 180L.

Equipment, safety instructions, and tips galore are sure to help guarantee a positive first experience for the child wanting to try in-line skating. Expressive, cartoon illustrations work well with the instructive text.

Wittman, Sally

3608 *Pelly and Peak.* Ill. by author. HarperCollins, 1978, o.p. SERIES: I Can Read. SUBJECTS: Friendship — Fiction; Peacocks — Fiction; Pelicans — Fiction. RL A.

Sharing April Fool's Day jokes and fishing together are just two of the special things that Pelly Pelican and Peak Peacock do to bring smiles to young readers. Ink, colored pencil, and paint are used to create the simple, almost childlike illustrations.

3609 *Plenty of Pelly and Peak.* Ill. by author. HarperCollins, 1980, o.p. SERIES: I Can Read. SUBJECTS: Friendship — Fiction; Peacocks — Fiction; Pelicans — Fiction. RL B.

In four stories, Pelly Pelican and Peak Peacock try adopting an egg, learn the earth is round, help each other fly a kite, and lose a birthday — February 29th. The simple illustrations are done with ink, colored pencils, and paint and are appealing and humorous.

Wolcott, Patty

3610 *Beware of a Very Hungry Fox.* Ill. by Lucinda McQueen. HarperCollins, 1975, ISBN 0-201-14250-3. SERIES: First Read-By-Myself. SUBJECTS: Behavior — Brave — Fiction; Chipmunks — Fiction; Foxes — Fiction. RL A.

Wolcott, Patty (cont.)

Professing not to be afraid of a very hungry fox, the chipmunks change their minds when they see one and flee leaving the fox to eat crabapples. The very limited and repetitious text relies on the vibrant illustrations to create a sense of story.

3611 *The Cake Story*. Ill. by Lucinda McQueen. HarperCollins, 1974, ISBN 0-201-14244-9. SERIES: First Read-By-Myself. SUBJECTS: Animals — Fiction; Food — Fiction. RL A.

Bear excitedly announces to the other animals that he has baked a cake. While he naps they eat the entire cake, but they make another to replace it. The ten words in this story are constantly repeated and rely on the expressive and colorful pictures to actually create the story.

3612 *Eeeeeek!* Ill. by Ned Delaney. Random House, 1981, o.p. SERIES: 10-Word Readers. SUBJECTS: Animals — Fiction. RL A.

Using ten words, and relying on the brightly colored pictures to really tell the story, the author relates the tale of Lynx and his capture of Fox, Hare and Woodpecker. The captured three foil lynx's attempt to make them into stew.

3613 *The Forest Fire*. Ill. by Robert Binks. HarperCollins, 1974, ISBN 0-201-14247-3. SERIES: First Read-By-Myself. SUBJECTS: Animals — Fiction; Flowers — Fiction. RL B.

Using a 10-word text and much repetition, a story is told through colorful illustrations more than words. In the story animals mistake flame-colored flowers for a forest fire. Although the words are not all easy or familiar, the repetition may make them a part of a reading vocabulary.

3614 *I'm Going to New York to Visit the Queen*. Ill. by Blair Drawson. HarperCollins, 1974, ISBN 0-201-14248-1. SERIES: First Read-By-Myself. SUBJECTS: Boats and boating — Fiction; City and town life — Fiction. RL A.

Two little girls walk through New York City on their way to visit the queen — the Queen Elizabeth II steamship. Full-color pictures show well-known New York attractions and provide a brief tour of the ship. The 10-word text is repetitious and very dependent on the illustrations.

3615 *Pickle Pickle Pickle Juice*. Ill. by Blair Dawson. HarperCollins, 1975, ISBN 0-201-14252-X. SERIES: 10-Word Readers. SUBJECTS: Food — Fiction. RL A.

Peter picks pickles until, with more than a million, they pop and form a pickle juice pond. Comical, brightly colored pictures give the story a medieval setting while being essential to the very brief text.

3616 *Pirates, Pirates Over the Salt, Salt Sea*. Ill. by Bill Morrison. HarperCollins, 1981, ISBN 0-201-08335-3. SERIES: First Read-By-Myself. SUBJECTS: Mice — Fiction; Pirates — Fiction; Whales — Fiction. RL A.

The ten words of this text are rearranged and repeated throughout. The text is popular with beginning readers and the repetition helps to introduce new words. The story, told in detailed and colorful drawings, is of a small sailboat of mice that are rescued from pirates by a friendly whale.

3617 *Super Sam and the Salad Garden*. Ill. by Marc Brown. HarperCollins, 1975, ISBN 0-201-14253-8. SERIES: First Read-By-Myself. SUBJECTS: Gardening — Fiction; Pets — Dogs — Fiction. RL A.

A boy and a girl plant a garden only to have it vandalized by other children. When Sam, a dog, is left in the yard, the next planting is safe and grows to be harvested. The 10-word text relies on the brightly colored pictures to tell the story.

3618 *Tunafish Sandwiches*. Ill. by Hans Zander. HarperCollins, 1975, ISBN 0-201-14245-7. SERIES: 10-Word Readers. SUBJECTS: Fish — Fiction; Food chains — Fiction. RL A.

In a text that uses only ten words and relies almost totally on the brightly colored pictures, the child reader quickly sees how a food chain operates. Plants are eaten by small fish, small fish are eaten by larger fish, and so on up to the human predator.

3619 *Where Did That Naughty Little Hamster Go?* Ill. by Rosekrans Hoffman. HarperCollins, 1974, ISBN 0-201-14245-7. SERIES: 10-Word Readers. SUBJECTS: Hamsters — Fiction; Lost and found possessions — Fiction; School stories. RL A.

In a classroom, children search for their hamster and finally find him, first in the dollhouse and then among their books. The intentionally limited text relies on the amusing watercolor pictures to tell the story.

Wolff, Barbara

3620 *Evening Gray, Morning Red: A Handbook of American Weather Wisdom*. Ill. by author. Macmillan, 1976, o.p. SERIES: Ready-to-Read. SUBJECTS: Folklore — Weather; Weather. RL C.

A potpourri of weather rhymes and lore is given historical context and meanings are explained. This interesting book is illustrated with detailed ink and colored wash pictures.

Wolff, Frieda

3621 *Watch out for Bears! The Adventures of Henry and Bruno*. Ill. by Brad Sneed. Random House, 1999, o.p. SERIES: Step into Reading. SUBJECTS: Bears — Fiction; Friendship — Fiction. RL B. LEXILE 230L.

After Henry sets up his bee hive, a bear comes out of the forest and, as all bears would, Bruno is thinking about honey. Humorous adventures bring the two together in Henry's house and on a camping trip.

Wong, Herbert, and Matthew Vessel

3622 *My Ladybug*. Ill. by Marie N. Bohlen. Addison-Wesley, 1969, o.p. SERIES: Science Series for the Young. SUBJECTS: Ladybugs. RL A.

The narrator of this investigation of ladybugs talks about what they look like, their diet, the different stages in their development, and how helpful they are to farmers. The illustrations are detailed and lovely, and demonstrate the many different varieties of ladybugs.

3623 *Plant Communities: Where Can Cattails Grow?* Ill. by Michael Eagle. Addison-Wesley, 1970, o.p. SERIES: Science Series for the Young. SUBJECTS: Plants. RL A.

By following cattail seeds into different natural areas, readers learn about various kinds of habitats and the plant life they support. Ink drawings are sometimes so full of things that it is difficult to distinguish the plants being discussed.

Wood, Audrey

3624 *The Horrible Holidays*. Ill. by Rosekrans Hoffman. Dial, 1988, o.p. SERIES: Dial Easy-to-Read. SUBJECTS: Christmas — Fiction; Family life — Fiction; Thanksgiving — Fiction. RL B.

Tormented by his horrible cousin Mert, Alf does not enjoy the holidays. Worse, when he tries to get even with her, he is the one punished. Funny and a very real view of just how horrible holidays can be (family fights, bickering children), this has humorous illustrations done in pencil and watercolors.

3625 *Three Sisters*. Ill. by Rosekrans Hoffman. Dial, 1986, o.p. SERIES: Dial Easy-to-Read. SUBJECTS: Humorous stories; Pigs — Fiction; Siblings — Fiction. RL B.

Three exuberant porcine sisters unabashedly create their own version of French, anxiously await stardom for the dancing member of the trio, and finally confront Uncle George about his smelly cigars. The softly colored pictures have confident pigs creating inoffensive mischief.

3626 *Tugford Wanted to Be Bad*. Ill. by author. Harcourt, pap., 1983, ISBN 0-15-291084-0. SERIES: Let Me Read. SUBJECTS: Behavior — Fiction; Family life — Fiction; Mice — Fiction. RL C.

Inspired by movie outlaws, Tugford, a mouse, takes a can full of shiny coins and buries it. When his father says his money is missing, Tugford mistakenly confesses to stealing it and promises to reform. The lush 1940s setting in the illustrations is perfect for Tugford's misadventure.

Woodson, Jacqueline

3627 *Martin Luther King, Jr.* Ill. by Floyd Cooper. Silver Burdett, 1990, o.p. SERIES: Let's Celebrate. SUBJECTS: African Americans; Biographies; Martin Luther King, Jr., Day. RL B.

King is shown as a dynamic and forceful man determined to bring about social change. The text is very brief and jumps from event to event. Full-color illustrations will draw readers into the biography.

Woodworth, Viki, comp.

3628 *Animal Jokes*. Ill. by author. Child's World, 1993, o.p. SUBJECTS: Animals — Fiction; Jokes and riddles. RL B.

Hippos, snakes, sheep, ocean creatures, dogs, birds, mice, and cats are topics for worn and forced jokes and riddles, with an occasional winner. Wavy ink and watercolor pictures of clothed animals adorn the pages. Jokes are in dark type, answers are in standard type with an unimaginative format.

3629 *Bug Riddles*. Ill. by author. Child's World, 1993, o.p. SUBJECTS: Insects — Fiction; Jokes and riddles. RL B.

Worn jokes are refitted or forcefully adapted to fit the insect theme. Centipedes, spiders, flies, caterpillars, ants, and other insects, the topics of the poems, grace the illustrations in wobbly ink sketches awash with violet, green, brown, and orange.

Woolfitt, Gabrielle

3630 *Blue*. Ill. with photos. Carolrhoda, 1992, o.p. SERIES: Colors. SUBJECTS: Concepts — Colors. RL C.

Blue is looked at not just as a color but as what it means in a culture and where the color is found: music, art, religion, space, nature, and so forth. Useful for discussion and for extending awareness of color, this is illustrated with textbook-like arrangements of photographs.

3631 *Green*. Ill. with photos. Carolrhoda, 1992, o.p. SERIES: Colors. SUBJECTS: Concepts — Colors. RL C.

Far beyond the color identification books associated with younger children, this book looks at how the word green is used as well as things that are green or might have been. A page of activities is included along with the full-color photographs.

3632 *Red*. Ill. with photos. Carolrhoda, 1992, o.p. SERIES: Colors. SUBJECTS: Concepts — Colors. RL C.

Red is looked at in symbols, emotions, food, nature, and more in a book designed to get young readers to observe and think about the color around them and its uses. Illustrated with photographs and a few paintings, the book also includes activities.

Worth, Bonnie

3633 *A Great Day for Pup: All About Wild Babies*. Ill. by Aristides Ruiz. Random House, 2002, ISBN 0-375-81096-X. SERIES: The Cat in the Hat's Learning Library. SUBJECTS: Animals — Baby — Fiction; Stories in rhyme. RL B.

The Cat in the Hat takes Dick and Sally on a trip round the world to see baby animals. Things One and Two help by providing signs with additional information. The rhyming text and the glossary are often not as clear as intended in the information they provide. Still, many children will use this as a starting point for finding out more about animals.

Wright, David

3634 *Canada Is My Home*. Photos by author. Stevens, 1992, o.p. SERIES: My Home Country. SUBJECTS: Canada; Family life — Canada. RL C.

An aspiring young gymnast, Rachel is moving from an upper-middle-class Toronto area to rural Nova Scotia. Photographs and text combine to present a picture of life in school, at practice, and at home for an eleven-year-old girl.

3635 *Vietnam Is My Home*. Photos by Vu Viet Dung. Stevens, 1993, o.p. SERIES: My Home Country. SUBJECTS: Family life — Vietnam; Vietnam. RL C.

Eleven-year-old Chau is the focus of this look at a child's life in Vietnam. Readers learn about family life, school, work, play, and more. Full-color photographs extend the text. A section of additional facts about Vietnam, a map, and an index complete the book, which is adapted from Patricia Norland's *Children of the World: Vietnam*.

Wright, J. B.

3636 *Dinosaurs*. Ill. by Gene Biggs. Western, 1991, o.p. SERIES: Star Reader. SUBJECTS: Dinosaurs. RL C.

Carefully written with an emphasis on the many different kinds of dinosaurs and their characteristics, this book also gives information on the discovery of the reptiles and their reconstruction. Colorful paintings and black-and-white sketches add information. A glossary is included.

Wright, Mildred W.

3637 *Henri Goes to the Mardi Gras*. Ill. by Syd Hoff. Putnam, 1970, o.p. SUBJECTS: Bears — Fiction; Humorous stories; Mardi Gras — Fiction. RL C.

Looking for honey, Henri the bear leaves the swamp for New Orleans during Mardi Gras. Everyone thinks he is in costume and treats him to all kinds of food until Henri slips away, surprised that no one was afraid of him. The cartoon-style pictures in brown and blue fit this story well.

Wyeth, Sharon Dennis

3638 *Tomboy Trouble*. Ill. by Lynne Woodcock Cravath. Random House, 1998, o.p. SERIES: Step into Reading. SUBJECTS: Moving, household — Fiction; Self-esteem — Fiction; Sex roles — Fiction. RL B. LEXILE 180L.

With a new very short haircut and a love for sports, the kids in her new school think Georgia is a boy. It isn't easy but she manages to stay true to herself and find friends with equal strengths. The book might be useful for discussion of self-acceptance and tolerance of others.

Wyler, Rose

3639 *Science Fun with Mud and Dirt*. Ill. by Pat Stewart. Simon & Schuster, pap., 1987, ISBN 0-317-56794-2. SERIES: Science Fun. SUBJECTS: Science experiments. RL C.

From a brief narrative and easily performed experiments, children learn that the makeup of dirt determines what can be done with it and whether plants will grow in it. The realistic brown and rust drawings help to clarify the instructions and the narrative sections.

3640 *What Happens If . . .? Science Experiments You Can Do by Yourself*. Ill. by Daniel Nevins. Walker, 1974, o.p. SUBJECTS: Science experiments. RL B.

A variety of simple experiments teach children about air pressure, chemical solutions, batteries, shadows, and the properties of ice cubes. The projects are interesting and the instructions easy to follow. The illustrations are sketchy but informative.

Wyler, Rose, and Gerald Ames

3641 *Magic Secrets*. Rev. ed. Ill. by Arthur Dorros. HarperCollins, pap., 1990, ISBN 0-06-444153-9. SERIES: I Can Read. SUBJECTS: Magic. RL B.

Children will enjoy trying the tricks included in this new edition. Instructions are clear and are helped by the watercolor paintings. Wyler and Ames even include ways to divert audience attention from the actual "magic" to make it seem more believable.

3642 *Prove It!* Ill. by Talivaldis Stubis. HarperCollins, 1963, o.p. SERIES: Science I Can Read. SUBJECTS: Science experiments. RL B.

By trying these very simple experiments, children at home or in the classroom can have fun learning the properties of water, air, sound, and magnets. The illustrations are simple and help to explain the procedures.

3643 *Spooky Tricks*. Newly illustrated ed. Ill. by S. D. Schindler. HarperCollins, 1968, o.p. SERIES: I Can Read. SUBJECTS: Magic. RL C.

For aspiring magicians, this sequel to Magic Secrets (see above) has more easy-to-do tricks that will need some practice but should be within the capabilities of seven- and eight-year-olds. Suitably spooky, brightly colored paintings of costumed characters maintain the ghostly ambience.

Y

Yanuck, Debbie L.

3644 *The Star-Spangled Banner*. Capstone, 2004, o.p. SERIES: American Symbols. SUBJECTS: United States — Flags; United States — National anthem; United States — Symbols. RL B.

Made in 1813, the flag that hung over Fort McHenry and was immortalized in the song by Francis Scott Key was 42 feet long and 30 feet high. The history of the flag and the song that became the national anthem of the U.S. is here along with a timeline, an activity, a glossary, bibliography, Web sites, and index.

Yanuck, Debbie L. (cont.)

3645 *Uncle Sam*. Capstone, 2004, ISBN 0-7368-2295-X. SERIES: American Symbols. SUBJECTS: United States — History; United States — Symbols. RL B.

Since the War of 1812 Uncle Sam has been a well-known symbol of the United States. The book contains a history of the symbol's development, an activity, glossary, bibliography, Web sites, index and timeline.

Yee, Wong Herbert

3646 *Did You See Chip?* Ill. by Laura Ovresat. Harcourt, 2004, ISBN 0-15-205095-7. SERIES: Green Light Readers. SUBJECTS: Lost and found possessions — Fiction; Moving, household — Fiction; Pets — Dogs — Fiction. RL A.

Lonely because they have just moved to the city, Kim and her father decide to take their dog Chip for a walk. He gets loose and a succession of friendly people helps them find him. Questions and activities follow and reinforce the story.

Yenawine, Philip

3647 *Colors*. Ill. with art from the Museum of Modern Art. Distributed Art, 2006, ISBN 0-87070-176-2. SUBJECTS: Art and artists; Concepts — Colors. RL B.

Through depictions of art by well-known modern artists, young readers are shown how expressive art can be as they learn about how color is used.

3648 *Lines*. Ill. with art from the Museum of Modern Art. Distributed Art, 2006, ISBN 0-87070-175-4. SUBJECTS: Art and artists; Concepts — Lines. RL B.

Through a simple text and well-chosen examples of art, children are shown how to see "line" within a work of art. Some of the works included are by Picasso, Klee, and Van Gogh.

3649 *People*. Ill. with art from the Museum of Modern Art. Distributed Art, 2006 , ISBN 0-87070-174-6. SUBJECTS: Art and artists. RL B.

Portraits and group paintings by artists such as Degas, Cezanne, and Rivera are used as examples of how people are depicted in art and what the pictures tell about them.

3650 *Places*. Ill. with art from the Museum of Modern Art. Delacorte, 2006, ISBN 0-87070-173-8. SUBJECTS: Art and artists. RL B.

Real and imaginary places are looked at in the works of great artists like Thomas Hart Benton, Ben Shahn, and Jacob Lawrence. Children are encouraged to carefully observe the art to see what is happening in it.

3651 *Shapes*. Ill. with art from the Museum of Modern Art. Delacorte, 2006 , ISBN 0-87070-177-0. SUBJECTS: Art and artists; Concepts — Shape. RL B.

Observing shapes used in paintings by artists such as Gauguin, Mondrian, and Dali, children are shown how shapes are used to create interesting effects and to represent objects.

3652 *Stories*. Ill. with art from the Museum of Modern Art. Delacorte, 2006, ISBN 0-87070-178-9. SUBJECTS: Art and artists. RL B.

Yenawine shows children how to imaginatively look at a work of art and pick out the story it is telling. Examples used include work by Magritte, Miro, and Wyeth.

Yolen, Jane

3653 *Commander Toad and the Big Black Hole*. Ill. by Bruce Degen. Penguin, pap., 1996 , ISBN 0-698-11403-5. SERIES: Break-of-Day. SUBJECTS: Frogs and toads — Fiction; Humorous stories; Science fiction. RL C.

What appears to be a black hole is actually an extraterrestrial toad whose long pink tongue has taken hold of Commander Toad's ship, Star Warts. The brave and bright commander ingeniously finds a way to free it. The story and the pencil drawings of the zany crew are delightfully funny.

3654 *Commander Toad and the Dis-Asteroid*. Ill. by Bruce Degen. Penguin, pap., 1996, ISBN 0-698-11404-3. SERIES: Break-of-Day. SUBJECTS: Frogs and toads — Fiction; Humorous stories; Science fiction. RL C.

Heroic Commander Toad leads his crew on a rescue mission after receiving a cryptic message about bad beans. The droll, mock science fiction story is accompanied by carefully drawn, comic illustrations.

3655 *Commander Toad and the Intergalactic Spy*. Ill. by Bruce Degen. Penguin, pap., 1997, ISBN 0-698-11418-3. SERIES: Break-of-Day. SUBJECTS: Frogs and toads — Fiction; Humorous stories; Science fiction. RL C.

The crew of the spaceship Star Warts is sent to the planet Eden to pick up Space Fleet's most famous spy (0007 1/2), a master of disguise who happens to be Commander Toad's cousin. The commander has great difficulty finding him in this funny spoof illustrated with pencil drawings.

3656 *Commander Toad and the Planet of the Grapes*. Ill. by Bruce Degen. Penguin, pap., 1996 , ISBN 0-698-11353-5. SERIES: Break-of-Day. SUBJECTS: Frogs and toads — Fiction; Humorous stories; Science fiction. RL C.

In a hilarious parody of "Star Trek," Commander Toad takes his bored and tired crew to a planet where purple grapes mysteriously engulf them. Good old Doc Peeper finds a way to free them all. The carefully drawn illustrations are done in pencil and have a zany humor of their own.

3657 *Commander Toad and the Space Pirates*. Ill. by Bruce Degen. Penguin, pap., 1997, ISBN 0-698-11419-1. SERIES: Break-of-Day. SUBJECTS: Frogs and toads — Fiction; Pirates — Fiction; Science fiction. RL C.

After a long journey taking them where no spaceship has ever gone before, the crew of the Star Warts is tired and bored. They are caught off guard by a shipload of pirate salamanders who try to take over the ship. A terrific parody of "Star Trek," this farce is illustrated in pencil.

3658 *Commander Toad and the Voyage Home*. Ill. by Bruce Degen. Penguin, pap., 1998, ISBN 0-698-11602-X. SUBJECTS: Frogs and toads — Fiction; Humorous stories; Science fiction. RL C. LEXILE 530L.

Instead of setting the dial for Planet X, Commander Toad sets it for HOME and back they go to the original amphibian home planet. Full of puns and humorous allusions to Star Wars and Star Trek, the text and illustrations will be great fun for better readers.

3659 *The Giants' Farm*. Ill. by Tomie dePaola. Seabury, 1977, o.p. SUBJECTS: Farm and country life — Fiction; Giants — Fiction; Humorous stories. RL B.

Five giants, very different in size and temperament, decide to build a farm and live together on it. In five chapters the work and fun they share help them to care about each other and become a family. Muted pencil drawings are well matched to the story. A recipe for candy is also included.

3660 *The Giants Go Camping*. Ill. by Tomie dePaola. Seabury, 1979, o.p. SUBJECTS: Camps and camping — Fiction; Giants — Fiction; Humorous stories. RL B.

The five friendly giants of Fe-Fi-Fo Farm decide to go camping together and have a much better time than any of them expected. Huge Grizzle adopts a bear as his dog; they fish, play, and do not want to go home. The delightful story is illustrated with amusing multicolored drawings.

3661 *Sleeping Ugly*. Ill. by Diane Stanley. Houghton Mifflin, 1995, ISBN 0-395-73227-1. SERIES: Break-of-Day. SUBJECTS: Behavior — Manners — Fiction; Fairy tales; Humorous stories. RL B.

A wise fairy is forced to put herself and kindly Plain Jane under a sleeping spell to stop the nasty antics of Princess Miserella. Years later a prince, wise to the ways of princesses, finds them and kisses the first two, but lets Princess Miserella, the "lying princess" sleep. Delightful, humorous text and illustrations.

3662 *Spider Jane on the Move*. Ill. by Stefen Bernath. Putnam, 1980, o.p. SERIES: Break-of-Day. SUBJECTS: Moving, household — Fiction; Spiders — Fiction. RL C.

Argumentative Spider Jane is helped by her ever-faithful friend Bluebottle Burt to make a new web, have a party, and finally relax. The pictures are slightly humorous and appropriate to the story.

York, Carol B.

3663 *The Midnight Ghost*. Ill. by Charles Robinson. Putnam, 1973, o.p. SERIES: Break-of-Day. SUBJECTS: Humorous stories; Mystery and detective stories. RL C.

With his new detective kit, Andrew determines to solve the mystery of a ghost that appears

York, Carol B. (cont.)

around midnight and leaves clues and gifts. Realistic pencil drawings capture the humor and suspense of the story.

Young, James

3664 *The Cows Are in the Corn*. Scholastic, 1995, o.p. SERIES: Hello Reader! SUBJECTS: Animals — Farm — Fiction; Farm and country life — Fiction; Stories in rhyme. RL B. LEXILE 290L.

Brother wakes up to discover that the cows won't come out of the corn. From that point on, with two large type lines per double page spread, one animal after another is where it should not be. Illustrated with watercolor and ink comical drawings.

Young, June

3665 *Energy Is Everywhere*. Children's Press, 2006, ISBN 0-516-25902-4. SERIES: Rookie Read-About Science. SUBJECTS: Energy; Matter; Science and scientists. RL B. LEXILE 50L.

Whether seeing it, hearing it, or feeling it, energy is everywhere and the brief text and photographs give some examples of the way in which energy appears and works. A photo glossary and index are included.

3666 *Look How It Changes!* Children's Press, 2006, ISBN 0-516-25901-6. SERIES: Rookie Read-About Science. SUBJECTS: Chemical changes; Science and scientists. RL B. LEXILE 10L.

Chemical changes occur when a fire is lit, when an animal's fur changes color, when trees change, when things rust and in many other ways. Color photographs extend the text. An index and photo glossary are included.

Young, Robert

3667 *Christopher Columbus and His Voyage to the New World*. Ill. by Arvis Stewart. Silver Burdett, 1990, o.p. SERIES: Let's Celebrate. SUBJECTS: Biographies; Explorers and exploration. RL B.

As a boy in Italy, Columbus is shown longing to sail. The book follows him to Portugal where he is educated, through a long search for backers, and finally to his sighting of the New World in 1492. A good look at the man and the time, this is illustrated in color.

Z

Zapata, Elizabeth

3668 *Puerto Rico*. Children's Press, 2007, ISBN 0-516-25387-5. SERIES: Rookie Read-About Geography. SUBJECTS: Geography; Puerto Rico; United States. RL B. LEXILE 650L.

An island filled with mountains, rain forests, exotic plants and animals, Puerto Rico is an American Commonwealth whose people speak Spanish and often English as well. The brief text, colorful photographs, and maps give young readers a glimpse of the island. Also included are a photo glossary and an index.

Zarins, Joyce A.

3669 *Toasted Bagels*. Ill. by author. Putnam, 1988, o.p. SERIES: Break-of-Day. SUBJECTS: Animals — Fiction; Bakers and baking — Fiction; Friendship — Fiction. RL B.

Pleased at how his bagels have turned out, P. C. invites his animal friends for a special treat. Instead of attending a party, they all battle a fire in the bakery. The gentle and satisfying story is illustrated with cartoon-like ink and watercolor and black-and-white pictures.

Zemach, Harve, and Kaethe Zemach

3670 *The Princess and Froggie*. Ill. by Margot Zemach. Farrar, Straus & Giroux, 1975, o.p. SUBJECTS: Fantasy; Frogs and toads — Fiction; Humorous stories. RL A.

In each of three stories, when things seem to be going poorly for the little princess, Froggie appears to save the day and earn himself a lollipop. The princess appears as a rather disheveled and very likable child and Froggie as comic and appealing in the lively pictures.

Ziefert, Harriet

3671 *Andy Toots His Horn.* Ill. by Sanford Hoffman. Viking, 1988, o.p. SERIES: Hello Reading. SUBJECTS: Family life — Fiction; Noise — Fiction. RL A.

Andy gets out his horn and starts making noise until other family members complain. Frustrated, he leaves and toots his horn outside until his family misses him. The very brief text has large print and is illustrated with humorous, childlike paintings in full color.

3672 *April Fool!* Ill. by Chris L. Demarest. Viking, pap., 2000, ISBN 0-14-130582-7. SERIES: Viking Easy-to-Read. SUBJECTS: April Fools' Day — Fiction; Elephants — Fiction; Stories in rhyme. RL B. LEXILE BR.

On his way to school on April 1, a boy tells his friends a fantastic story about an elephant. At first they believe him but then call him a liar. Finally, he gets the best of everyone by shouting, "April Fool!" Expressive and very lively art illustrates the story.

3673 *Bears Odd, Bears Even.* Ill. by Andrea Baruffi. Viking, pap., 1997, ISBN 0-14-038539-8. SERIES: Viking Math Easy-to-Read. SUBJECTS: Bears; Mathematics; Numbers. RL B. LEXILE AD280L.

Using two sets of bears, one brown, one white, concepts of odd and even are demonstrated. While most will be easy to understand, addition of odd and even numbers may challenge some children. Illustrations use the bears in lively situations to demonstrate the math concepts.

3674 *The Best Castle Ever.* Ill. by Carol Nicklaus. Random House, pap., 1989, o.p. SERIES: Pictureback Reader. SUBJECTS: Pets — Cats — Fiction; Sandcastles — Fiction; Seashore — Fiction. RL A.

Three cats help build a sandcastle, each adding a special feature. Each of them tries to take credit for how good it is, causing some shoving, which knocks it down. The three decide to work together to build another. A slim paperback, this has colorful, cartoon-like paintings.

3675 *The Big Birthday Box.* Ill. by Laura Rader. Random House, pap., 1989, o.p. SERIES: Pictureback Reader. SUBJECTS: Birthdays — Fiction; Mice — Fiction. RL A.

A little mouse wakes up to her fifth birthday and a special present from her grandmother — a bicycle. With a very brief text and reinforcing repetition of words, the easy story is accompanied by watercolor pictures and bound in a stapled paperback binding.

3676 *Bugs, Beetles, and Butterflies.* Ill. by Lisa Flather. Puffin, pap., 1998, ISBN 0-14-038691-2. SERIES: Science Easy-to-Read. SUBJECTS: Beetles; Butterflies and moths; Insects. RL A.

A rhyming text introduces a variety of insects and their characteristics. Illustrated in gentle pencil and watercolor pictures, the book also includes an alphabetical identification chart of mentioned insects and a page of activities.

3677 *Can You Play?* Ill. by Mavis Smith. Random House, pap., 1989, ISBN 0-394-82001-0. SERIES: Pictureback Reader. SUBJECTS: Friendship — Fiction; Pets — Dogs — Fiction. RL A.

When Jon cannot play, Jessie decides to play with her dog and teach it some new tricks. Jon finally comes to play and it is his turn to be taught. Brief text is helped by lively, cartoon-like color illustrations.

3678 *Car Trip for Mole and Mouse.* Ill. by David Prebenna. Viking, 1991, o.p. SERIES: Hello Reading. SUBJECTS: Mice — Fiction; Moles — Fiction; Travel — Fiction. RL A.

Friends Mole and Mouse decide to take a trip to a flea market. Mole drives as Mouse very cautiously reads a map and very slowly gives directions. Text is illustrated with pencil sketches with watercolor washes.

3679 *Cat Games.* Ill. by Claire Schumacher. Puffin, pap., 1995, ISBN 0-14-037857-X. SERIES: Hello Reading. SUBJECTS: Games — Fiction; Pets — Cats — Fiction. RL A.

Pat and Matt, two cats, play a game of hide-and-seek in a tree in Chapter 1. In Chapter 2 they chase each other until a friendly dog intrudes on their game. The text is very brief and repetitive, is in large type, and is easy enough for beginners. Simple but engaging color pictures.

3680 *A Clean House for Mole and Mouse.* Ill. by David Prebenna. Viking, 1988, o.p. SERIES: Hello Reading. SUBJECTS: Cleanliness

Ziefert, Harriet (cont.)

— Fiction; Mice — Fiction; Moles — Fiction. RL B.

Mole and Mouse work hard to clean their home and then, not wanting to dirty it, go outside to shower, nap, and eat. The very brief and humorous story has large print and is illustrated with comical pencil and wash pictures in full color.

3681 *Clown Games*. Ill. by Larry Stevens. Sterling, 2005, ISBN 1-4027-2724-0. SERIES: I'm Going to Read! SUBJECTS: Clowns — Fiction. RL A.

A very simple and repetitive text is interpreted by the illustrator as games played by clowns. An example of the text is: "Pancakes need syrup. Syrup needs pancakes." Art is boldly drawn and painted in vibrant colors.

3682 *A Dozen Dogs: A Read-and-Count Story*. Ill. by Carol Nicklaus. Random House, 1985, o.p. SERIES: Step into Reading. SUBJECTS: Concepts — Numbers — Fiction; Pets — Dogs — Fiction. RL A.

The story starts with a dozen dogs cavorting on the beach, but their number changes as they swim, dive, fish, or play. Children will want to count them as they read the simple text. The illustrations are done in full color and tell more of a story than does the very brief text.

3683 *A Dozen Dozens*. Ill. by Chris L. Demarest. Viking, 1998, o.p. SERIES: Viking Math Easy-to-Read. SUBJECTS: Numbers — Fiction; Stories in rhyme. RL B. LEXILE NP.

The rhyming text and lively watercolor and ink pictures reinforce the fact that twelve of anything equals a dozen and six is half a dozen. The final two pages provide questions and activities to further support the story.

3684 *Dr. Cat*. Ill. by Suzy Mandel. Viking, 1989, o.p. SERIES: Hello Reading. SUBJECTS: Doctors and nurses — Fiction. RL B.

Patient Dr. Cat cleverly finds ways to gain the trust of two kittens. A very brief text is illustrated with humorous yet reassuring pictures done in bold shapes with good clear contrasts.

3685 *Fish Wish*. Ill. by Elliot Kreloff. Sterling, pap., 2005, ISBN 1-4027-2095-5. SERIES: I'm Going to Read! SUBJECTS: Sports — Fishing — Fiction. RL A.

Drawn in a child-like manner and using a very limited and repetitive vocabulary, the text tells the story of a bear's unsuccessful attempts to catch a big fish.

3686 *Follow Me!* Ill. by Laura Rader. Viking, 1990, o.p. SERIES: Hello Reading. SUBJECTS: Pets — Dogs — Fiction; Shopping — Fiction. RL A.

Lee, a young dog, joins his mother on a shopping trip for a baby gift. When the elevator closes without him, the resourceful pup uses his reading skills to find his mother. A very brief text with much repetition, illustrated with watercolor pictures.

3687 *Good Luck Bad Luck*. Ill. by Lillie James. Viking, 1991, o.p. SERIES: Hello Reading. SUBJECTS: Superstitions. RL A.

Stepping on cracks in the sidewalk, walking under ladders, finding a four-leaf clover, and seeing the new moon over your shoulder are some of the superstitions mentioned and illustrated with pencil and watercolor.

3688 *Goody New Shoes*. Ill. by Laura Rader. Viking, 1991, o.p. SERIES: Hello Reading. SUBJECTS: Pigs — Fiction; Shopping — Fiction. RL A.

Daddy pig takes his two young children for haircuts and shoes. At the end of the day, he takes them to a bookstore, where each buys a book. Illustrated with lively watercolors.

3689 *Halloween Parade*. Ill. by Lillie James. Viking, 1992, o.p. SERIES: Hello Reading. SUBJECTS: Halloween — Fiction; School stories. RL A.

Allie is very busy preparing for Halloween and her school's holiday costume parade. The spirited and very simple text catches the fun of Halloween with few words and lively pencil and watercolor pictures.

3690 *Harry Gets Ready for School*. Ill. by Mavis Smith. Penguin, pap., 1993, ISBN 0-14-036539-7. SERIES: Hello Reading. SUBJECTS: Hippopotami — Fiction; School stories. RL A.

Harry the hippo gets ready for school by shopping for clothes, going to the doctor, getting a haircut, and more. He experiences the nervousness that most children do but quickly makes friends on the first day. Text is attractively illustrated.

3691 *Harry Goes to Fun Land*. Ill. by Mavis Smith. Viking, 1989, o.p. SERIES: Hello Reading. SUBJECTS: Amusement parks — Fiction; Grandparents — Fiction; Hippopotami — Fiction. RL A.

Little hippo Harry goes with his grandfather to an amusement park. Each time he takes a ride, he reassures himself that he is not scared — yet when Grandpa is gone for a long time, Harry really has to convince himself he is not afraid. Attractive, colorful paintings accompany the text.

3692 *Harry Takes a Bath*. Ill. by Mavis Smith. Penguin, pap., 1993, ISBN 0-14-036537-0. SERIES: Hello Reading. SUBJECTS: Bathing — Fiction; Hippopotami — Fiction. RL A.

Hippopotamus Harry gathers his things and heads for the bathroom for a good cleanup and some fun. Afterward the bathroom is a mess and Harry cleans it up. The very limited vocabulary and large type with clearly drawn, colorful illustrations are good for a child just starting to read.

3693 *How Big Is Big?* Ill. by Andrea Baruffi. Penguin, pap., 1995, ISBN 0-14-037653-4. SERIES: Hello Reading. SUBJECTS: Concepts — Size. RL A.

Each double page spread uses comparisons to show the relative nature of size. An example would be a picture showing an elephant larger than a man and another showing a man larger than a baby elephant. Text is easy to understand and well illustrated.

3694 *I Hate Boots*. Ill. by Laura Rader. Sterling, 2005 , ISBN 1-4027-2071-8. SERIES: Stickerbook Reader. SUBJECTS: Pigs — Fiction; Weather — Snow — Fiction. RL A.

A little pig says she hates each article of clothing her mother insists she wear before going out into the snow. Once outside she appreciates them. Illustrated with childlike watercolor paintings, the heavy paper pages and the reusable stickers should have both child and parent appeal.

3695 *Jason's Bus Ride*. Ill. by Simms Taback. Penguin, 1993, ISBN 0-14-036536-2. SERIES: Hello Reading. SUBJECTS: Buses — Fiction; Emergencies — Fiction. RL A.

Jason gets on the bus expecting an uneventful ride. Instead he becomes a hero when he is the only one able to get a dog to move out of the path of the bus. The bold, full-color pictures are marvelous, offering a variety of perspectives of the bus and its riders.

3696 *Later, Rover*. Ill. by David Jacobson. Penguin, pap., 1996 , ISBN 0-14-038000-0. SERIES: Hello Reading. SUBJECTS: Behavior — Bored; Pets — Dogs — Fiction. RL A.

Again and again Andy asks his busy parents and sister to play with him and the answer is always "Later, Andy." Finally Andy begins tossing a stick for the dog. When he tires of the game, it is Andy's turn to say "Later, Rover." Text is illustrated with cartoon-like full-color paintings.

3697 *Let's Trade*. Ill. by Mary Morgan. Viking, 1989, o.p. SERIES: Hello Reading. SUBJECTS: Picnics — Fiction; Siblings — Fiction. RL A.

Meg, Sam, and Jo take their lunches and go to the park for a picnic. Once there they begin trading each other for what they want to eat and then what they need to play ball. Realistic situations are handled well in text and in the full-color illustrations.

3698 *Mike and Tony: Best Friends*. Ill. by Catherine Siracusa. Viking, 1987, o.p. SERIES: Hello Reading. SUBJECTS: Friendship — Fiction. RL B.

Mike and Tony do everything together — walk to school, ride bikes, play on the same team. They even spend Friday nights at one or the other's home until they have a fight that takes some effort to settle. The vibrant full-color pictures are a good match to the story of a common situation.

3699 *Move Over*. Ill. by Laura Rader. HarperCollins, pap., 1991, ISBN 0-06-107421-7. SERIES: Stickerbook Reader. SUBJECTS: Boats and boating — Fiction; Friendship — Fiction; Humorous stories. RL A.

Five friends start out in an inflatable boat and one after another other animals ask to be let in. When the number climbs to ten, they sink. Heavy paper pages, reusable stickers, humorous illustrations in full color, and repetitive lines will all be attractive to children.

Ziefert, Harriet (cont.)

3700 *My Apple Tree*. Ill. by Laura Rader. HarperCollins, pap., 1991, ISBN 0-06-107420-9. SERIES: Stickerbook Reader. SUBJECTS: Food — Fiction; Seasons — Fiction; Trees — Fiction. RL A.

A little dog tells how his tree looks through the year and how much he loves it and its apples. Gentle and childlike watercolors support and extend the text. Reusable word stickers reinforce the vocabulary for new readers and the heavy pages guarantee a long life for this paperback.

3701 *A New House for Mole and Mouse*. Ill. by David Prebenna. Penguin, pap., 1997, ISBN 0-14-037387-X. SERIES: Easy-to-Read. SUBJECTS: Mice — Fiction; Moles — Fiction; Moving, household — Fiction. RL B.

After Mouse and Mole move into their new home, the two decide to try everything in it. Muted pictures of two friendly little animals and their very cozy home accompany the story.

3702 *Nicky Upstairs and Down*. Ill. by Richard Brown. Penguin, pap., 1994, ISBN 0-14-036852-3. SERIES: Hello Reading. SUBJECTS: Pets — Cats — Fiction. RL A.

Nicky, a kitten, and his mother are pets in a household with an upstairs and a downstairs. Nicky runs from floor to floor when his mother calls until he decides he wants to stay in the middle. The pictures to this very brief story are bright and childlike; the cats have expressive faces.

3703 *No More TV Sleepy Dog*. Ill. by Norman Gorbaty. Random House, pap., 1989, o.p. SERIES: Pictureback Reader. SUBJECTS: Bedtime — Fiction; Pets — Dogs — Fiction. RL A.

Just as small children do, a puppy begs to stay up later and tries one delaying tactic after another. He finally falls asleep after being read a story. Using very few words and with good reinforcement of the message from the simply drawn humorous pictures, the story will succeed with readers.

3704 *Penny Goes to the Movies*. Ill. by Laura Rader. Viking, 1990, o.p. SERIES: Hello Reading. SUBJECTS: Movies — Fiction; Pigs — Fiction. RL A.

On a rainy afternoon, a little pig and her mother decide to go to a movie. Shortly after it begins, the little pig notices a space child in the theater but everyone hushes her. The pictures and very brief text combine to make this warm story with a twist easy to read.

3705 *Please Let It Snow*. Ill. by Amy Aitken. Viking, 1989, o.p. SERIES: Hello Reading. SUBJECTS: Weather — Snow — Fiction. RL A.

With all kinds of new clothes for snow, a little boy anxiously awaits the first snowfall. Day after day he watches for snow until finally he gives up and — of course — it snows. The very brief text works well with the colorful yet simply drawn illustrations.

3706 *A Polar Bear Can Swim: What Animals Can and Cannot Do*. Ill. by Emily Bolam. Viking, pap., 1998, ISBN 0-14-038692-0. SERIES: Viking Science Easy-to-Read. SUBJECTS: Animals — Habits and behavior. RL B.

While a polar bear can do many things, it can't sleep upside down like a bat. A bat cannot fly backwards but a hummingbird can. One animal after another is shown doing things that others cannot in this quick look at the habits of eight animals from around the world. Cartoon-like illustrations add humor and appeal to the text.

3707 *The Prince Has a Boo-boo!* Ill. by R. W. Alley. Random House, pap., 1989, o.p. SERIES: Pictureback Reader. SUBJECTS: Injuries — Fiction; Kings and queens — Fiction; Princes and princesses — Fiction. RL A.

When the little prince bumps his head, everyone in the castle gets involved in helping him. Lively, humorous watercolor pictures help tell the story. Cutout vocabulary cards are useful for reinforcing vocabulary. This is a good purchase for the home collection.

3708 *The Prince's Tooth Is Loose*. Ill. by R. W. Alley. Random House, pap., 1990, o.p. SERIES: Pictureback Reader. SUBJECTS: Human body — Teeth — Fiction; Humorous stories; Princes and princesses — Fiction. RL A.

When the young prince has a loose tooth, the whole court jumps into action to find an apple for him to bite into. Humorous watercolor pictures extend the repetitive text. The vocabulary cards make this book attractive for home purchase and use.

3709 *Rabbit and Hare Divide an Apple*. Ill. by Emily Bolam. Viking, pap., 1998, ISBN 0-14-038820-6. SERIES: Viking Math Easy-to-Read. SUBJECTS: Behavior — Sharing — Fiction; Division — Fiction; Mathematics — Division — Fiction. RL B. LEXILE 80L.

Rabbit and Hare are tricked out of their shares of a mushroom by Raccoon. When they find an apple they decide to do the dividing themselves. This brief introduction to division provides an opportunity for discussion of math with an adult.

3710 *Sam and Lucy*. Ill. by Claire Schumacher. HarperCollins, 1992, ISBN 0-06-026913-8. SUBJECTS: Animals — Reproduction — Fiction; Pets — Dogs — Fiction. RL B.

Sam, a gray terrier, decides to wander away from home and meets Lucy, a tan poodle. They play, mate, and ultimately have four puppies. Hardly likely to instill responsible pet ownership habits, the story is nevertheless well done with colorful pictures with much child appeal.

3711 *Say Good Night!* Ill. by Catherine Siracusa. Viking, 1988, o.p. SERIES: Hello Reading. SUBJECTS: Morning — Fiction; Night — Fiction; Sleep — Fiction. RL A.

A little girl has to be convinced that night and morning are "good." Her parents oblige, and she goes to sleep and gets up happily. The very short text is accompanied by simple, colorful, and attractive pictures.

3712 *Sleepy Dog*. Ill. by Norman Gorbaty. Random House, pap., 1984, ISBN 0-394-86877-3. SERIES: Step into Reading. SUBJECTS: Bedtime — Fiction; Dreams — Fiction; Pets — Dogs — Fiction. RL A. LEXILE 80L.

A very tired puppy goes to bed and dreams, finally awakening to an alarm clock and the sun. Art and very short, repetitive text together provide a story.

3713 *The Small Potatoes and the Snowball Fight*. Ill. by Richard Brown. Dell, pap., 1986, o.p. SERIES: Small Potatoes. SUBJECTS: Clubs — Fiction; Friendship — Fiction; Weather — Snow — Fiction. RL C.

After the first heavy snowfall, the Small Potatoes Club gets together to play. They build a tunnel in a drift, cause an accident throwing snowballs, and, after cocoa and donuts, end up making snow people. Illustrated with cartoon-like ink drawings, the stories are fun.

3714 *The Small Potatoes' Busy Beach Day*. Ill. by Richard Brown. Dell, pap., 1986, o.p. SERIES: Small Potatoes. SUBJECTS: Clubs — Fiction; Friendship — Fiction; Seashore — Fiction. RL C.

The members and Molly's dog spend the day at the seashore collecting shells, swimming, playing games, and having a good time. Illustrated with black-and-white pictures, the good natured stories are just right for readers almost ready for chapter books.

3715 *The Small Potatoes Club*. Ill. by Richard Brown. Dell, pap., 1984, o.p. SERIES: Small Potatoes. SUBJECTS: Clubs — Fiction; Friendship — Fiction. RL C.

Six friends and one's dog, Spot, get together to build a clubhouse, play soccer, visit the museum, and generally have fun together. A good introduction to longer chapter books, this is illustrated with cartoon-like ink drawings.

3716 *So Hungry!* Ill. by Carol Nicklaus. Random House, 1987, o.p. SERIES: Step into Reading. SUBJECTS: Food — Fiction; Lions — Fiction. RL B.

Hungry and unable to find cookies, Kate and Lewis, lions, decide to make great big sandwiches and race to finish them. With a very limited and repetitive but not necessarily easy vocabulary, the bold, full-color cartoon-like illustrations carry the story.

3717 *So Sick!* Ill. by Carol Nicklaus. Random House, 1985, o.p. SERIES: Step into Reading. SUBJECTS: Illness — Fiction; Lions — Fiction. RL A.

After finally getting well, Lewis, a lion, plays doctor with his friend Angel. When Angel eats too many cookies in spite of Lewis's warnings, he gets sick. Full-color pictures of "cute" animals accompany a very brief, bold-type text.

3718 *Sometimes I Share*. Ill. by Carol Nicklaus. HarperCollins, pap., 1991, ISBN 0-06-107425-X. SERIES: Stickerbook Reader.

Ziefert, Harriet (cont.)

SUBJECTS: Behavior — Selfish — Fiction; Behavior — Sharing — Fiction; Sibling rivalry — Fiction. RL A.

A little girl honestly mentions how sometimes she does share with her little brother but other times she does not want to and then she becomes selfish. Lively charcoal pencil drawings have colorful washes. Heavy pages guarantee little tearing and the reusable stickers reinforce word knowledge.

3719 *Stitches*. Ill. by Amy Aitken. Viking, 1990, o.p. SERIES: Hello Reading. SUBJECTS: Accidents — Fiction; Doctors and nurses — Fiction. RL A.

When Jon falls off his bike, he cuts his head, is taken to the doctor, and has six stitches. Although far from happy during the ordeal, Jon proudly shows off his bandage and tells his story of the stitches. Easy to read the book has colorful illustrations.

3720 *Strike Four!* Ill. by Mavis Smith. Viking, 1988, o.p. SERIES: Hello Reading. SUBJECTS: Behavior — Bored — Fiction; Family life — Fiction; Sports — Baseball — Fiction. RL A.

With nothing to do, Debbie tries tossing her ball in the house until she is told to do it elsewhere. She finally takes her ball and bat outside and practices hitting — until she breaks a window. A good, brief story and simple, colorful pictures combine to create an easy yet appealing book.

3721 *Surprise!* Ill. by Mary Morgan. Sterling, pap., 2006, ISBN 1-4027-3410-7. SERIES: Hello Reading. SUBJECTS: Birthdays — Fiction; Family life — Fiction; Mothers — Fiction. RL B.

Three young children get up very early and quietly prepare a breakfast tray of juice and cookies for their mother on her birthday. The text is very brief, relying on the pictures of the excited children and their rambunctious cat to help tell the story.

3722 *Take My Picture!* Ill. by Amy Aitken. HarperCollins, 1991, ISBN 0-06-107424-1. SERIES: Stickerbook Reader. SUBJECTS: Photography and photographers — Fiction; Sibling rivalry — Fiction; Zoos — Fiction. RL A.

When they visit the zoo, a little boy's older sister takes lots of pictures of the animals but none of him until the very end of their visit. Humorous watercolor pictures extend the brief text. Heavy pages and reusable word stickers should have appeal for home purchase.

3723 *The Teeny-Tiny Woman*. Ill. by Laura Rader. Penguin, pap., 1995, ISBN 0-14-037625-9. SERIES: Easy-to-Read. SUBJECTS: Folklore; Ghost stories. RL B. LEXILE 580L.

The bone the Teeny-Tiny woman finds turns out to have belonged to someone. This well-known ghost story is perfect for sharing at Halloween, around the campfire, or at a sleepover. Illustrations are watercolors and only very slightly scary.

3724 *Three Wishes*. Ill. by David Jacobson. Viking, 1993, o.p. SERIES: Viking Easy-to-Read. SUBJECTS: Wishes — Fiction. RL A.

A little boy's three wishes are to fish until he catches two hundred fish, to eat whatever he wants, to pick fruit from a tree at night and to grab a piece of the moon. Illustrations are pen and ink with watercolor.

3725 *Tic and Tac Clean Up*. Ill. by Elliot Kreloff. Sterling, pap., 2007, ISBN 1-4027-4243-6. SERIES: I'm Going to Read! SUBJECTS: Housekeeping — Fiction; Pets — Cats — Fiction. RL B.

Cats Tic and Tac tire themselves out cleaning the whole house. When they are finished, Tic refuses to let Tac get anything dirty again. Bright colors, clean lines and geometric shapes are eye-appealing.

3726 *Tim and Jim Take Off*. Ill. by Suzy Mandel. Viking, 1990, o.p. SERIES: Hello Reading. SUBJECTS: Airplanes — Fiction; Airports — Fiction. RL A.

Two kitten brothers are taken to the airport for their flight to visit their grandparents. At the airport and on the plane, they see and do the things that all passengers do. A good introduction to flying for young travelers, this has colorful illustrations.

3727 *Under the Water*. Ill. by Suzy Mandel. Puffin, pap., 1993, ISBN 0-14-036535-4. SERIES: Hello Reading. SUBJECTS: Oceans and ocean life; Sports — Snorkeling. RL B.

Readers are introduced to life in the ocean and a snorkeler's view of it. Expressive mixed-media pictures show a variety of ocean fish and plants. Good advice is also given for would-be snorkelers.

3728 *Wait for Us!* Ill. by Amy Aitken. Random House, pap., 1989, o.p. SERIES: Pictureback Reader. SUBJECTS: Cumulative tales; Sports — Running — Fiction. RL A.

As Jenny and her dog Buffy run, they attract a crowd of other children — no one knowing where Jenny is heading. When they arrive, they all excitedly scream for ice cream. Very limited vocabulary effectively works with colorful pictures to give a sense of story.

3729 *The Wheels on the Bus.* Ill. by Andrea Baruffi. Random House, pap., 1990, o.p. SERIES: Pictureback Reader. SUBJECTS: Buses — Fiction; Music and musicians — Fiction. RL A.

The repetitive children's song "The Wheels on the Bus" is illustrated with appropriate pencil and watercolor pictures. Though the music is not included, the song is familiar enough and the rhythm catchy enough to get children singing. Vocabulary cards make this a useful home purchase.

3730 *When the TV Broke.* Ill. by Mavis Smith. Puffin, pap., 1993, ISBN 0-14-036540-0. SERIES: Hello Reading. SUBJECTS: Television — Fiction. RL A.

When the TV breaks, Jeffrey finds a whole world of things to do with his time. When it returns, the little boy is too busy playing to be bothered. Simple color-pencil and watercolor pictures and a very short text are combined effectively.

3731 *Wish for a Fish.* Ill. by Argus Childers. Random House, pap., 1989, o.p. SERIES: Pictureback Reader. SUBJECTS: Sports — Fishing — Fiction. RL A.

A little boy is determined to catch the biggest fish in the lake. Instead he manages to catch an umbrella, a swimsuit, a tube, and finally a very feisty minnow. A repetitive and very brief text is supported by humorous and colorful pictures.

Ziefert, Harriet, reteller

3732 *The Cow in the House.* Ill. by Emily Bolam. Viking, pap., 1997, ISBN 0-14-038349-2. SERIES: Viking Easy-to-Read. SUBJECTS: Folklore; Humorous stories; Noise — Fiction. RL B. LEXILE 60L.

Annoyed by squeaks and other noises in his house, a man asks advice from the wise man. The wise man tells him to bring into the house first a cow, then a donkey, then other animals. When the noise is unbearable, he has the man remove them. The house — squeaks and all — suddenly seems quiet.

3733 *Henny-Penny.* Ill. by Emily Bolam. Viking, pap., 1997, ISBN 0-14-038188-0. SERIES: Viking Easy-to-Read. SUBJECTS: Chickens — Fiction; Folklore. RL B.

When something hits her on the head, Henny-Penny decides she must hurry to tell the king that the sky is falling. Along the way other animals join her and all but Henny-Penny end up in Foxy-Loxy's den. Vibrant illustrations capture the silliness and drama of this old story.

3734 *The Little Red Hen.* Ill. by Emily Bolam. Viking, pap., 1995, ISBN 0-14-037817-0. SERIES: Viking Easy-to-Read Classic. SUBJECTS: Behavior — Laziness — Fiction; Folklore. RL B. LEXILE 200L.

When neither the dog nor the goose nor the cat is willing to help the little red hen to plant, grow, harvest, grind, or make the wheat into bread, the little red hen does it all herself. Then eats it all herself. Ziefert gives a faithful retelling of this classic story and Bolam humorously illustrates it.

3735 *Little Red Riding Hood.* Ill. by Emily Bolam. Viking, pap., 2000, ISBN 0-14-056529-9. SERIES: Viking Easy-to-Read. SUBJECTS: Folklore — Germany; Strangers — Fiction. RL B. LEXILE 200L.

Little Red Riding Hood is taking cupcakes to grandma in this version of the well-known folk tale, and by story's end has learned the danger of talking to strangers. Illustrations put the story in a contemporary setting with Little Red wearing a red hooded sweatshirt and mother in slacks.

3736 *The Magic Porridge Pot.* Ill. by Emily Bolam. Viking, 1997, o.p. SERIES: Viking Easy-to-Read. SUBJECTS: Folklore; Magic — Fiction. RL B. LEXILE 190L.

After she gives an old man her last cracker, a little girl receives a magic cooking pot and the words to tell it to fill and to stop. When her mother tries the pot, she forgets the words for stopping and

Ziefert, Harriet, reteller (cont.)

soon her house and the road and the town are filled with porridge. Children unfamiliar with many folk tales may be inspired to tell this one themselves.

3737 *The Princess and the Pea.* Ill. by Emily Bolam. Viking, pap., 1996, ISBN 0-14-038083-3. SERIES: Easy-to-Read. SUBJECTS: Princes and princesses — Fiction. RL B.

A very abbreviated version of Hans Christian Andersen's story, this captures its basic components in an easy-to-read format. Illustrations are in bright colors and extend the story.

3738 *The Snow Child.* Ill. by Julia Zanes. Viking, pap., 2000, ISBN 0-14-130577-0. SERIES: Viking Easy-to-Read. SUBJECTS: Folklore — Russia; Weather — Snow — Fiction. RL B.

An old couple who have always wanted a child of their own create a snow child who comes to life and spends the winter with them. With warm weather she disappears. When winter comes again, she returns. The story is illustrated with collage art.

3739 *The Three Little Pigs.* Ill. by Laura Rader. Viking, pap., 1995, ISBN 0-14-037624-0. SERIES: Viking Easy-to-Read. SUBJECTS: Folklore; Pigs — Fiction. RL B. LEXILE 200L.

Ziefert offers young readers a more traditional version of the three little pigs' story. In this, the first two pigs are eaten by the wolf and the wolf meets his demise when falling into a pot of boiling water at the third pig's house. Lively pen and watercolor art illustrates the story.

3740 *The Turnip.* Ill. by Laura Rader. Viking, 1996, o.p. SERIES: Viking Easy-to-Read. SUBJECTS: Folklore — Russia. RL A. LEXILE 180L.

The old man carefully raises the turnip and when it is time to pull it up, it is so big that the old woman, the girl, the dog, the cat, and the mouse must all help him. Sketchy ink and watercolor pictures add to the folksy humor.

3741 *The Ugly Duckling.* Ill. by Emily Bolam. Puffin, pap., 1997, ISBN 0-14-038352-2. SERIES: Puffin Easy-to-Read. SUBJECTS: Fairy tales; Swans — Fiction. RL A. LEXILE 40L.

Using the simplest vocabulary with much repetition, Ziefert abbreviates Andersen's story of the ugly duckling who is actually a beautiful swan. The pictures are done in muted colors with strong outlines.

Ziefert, Harriet, and Jon Ziefert

3742 *The Small Potatoes and the Birthday Party.* Ill. by Richard Brown. Dell, pap., 1985, o.p. SERIES: Small Potatoes. SUBJECTS: Birthdays — Fiction; Clubs — Fiction; Friendship — Fiction. RL C.

The members of the Small Potatoes Club decide to surprise Molly's dog, Spot, with a birthday party while adding a porch onto their clubhouse. They buy Spot his own Pet, a guinea pig, and end the day with a ball game. The book's line drawings and chapters make it appear harder than it is.

3743 *The Small Potatoes and the Magic Show.* Ill. by Richard Brown. Dell, pap., 1984, o.p. SERIES: Small Potatoes. SUBJECTS: Clubs — Fiction; Friendship — Fiction; Magic — Fiction. RL C.

The members of the club spend the day having a picnic, playing games, and coming up with a password for their club. When it is time to think about making money, they decide on a magic show. The show is a success. The book is illustrated with cartoon-like pictures.

3744 *The Small Potatoes and the Sleep-Over.* Ill. by Richard Brown. Dell, pap., 1985, o.p. SERIES: Small Potatoes. SUBJECTS: Camps and camping — Fiction; Clubs — Fiction; Friendship — Fiction. RL C.

The six members of the club and Molly's dog, Spot, camp out in the clubhouse. They play games, use a telescope to look at the sky, almost tell scary stories, and wake up the next day very tired. Black-and-white line drawings add to the fun and make this seem geared to older readers.

Ziegler, Sandra

3745 *Understanding.* Ill. by Jenny Williams. Child's World, 1989, o.p. SERIES: What Is It. SUBJECTS: Behavior — Understanding — Fiction. RL B.

A middle child demonstrates to readers the many ways to show understanding to family and friends and how to treat them as she would like to be treated. Meant to reinforce positive patterns of behavior, this brief text is nicely illustrated with pencil sketches and watercolors.

Zinnemann-Hope, Pam

3746 *Time for Bed, Ned.* Ill. by Kady MacDonald Denton. Macmillan, 1986, o.p. SUBJECTS: Bedtime — Fiction. RL A.

With difficulty, a patient mother corrals a toddler for bath and bed. This preprimer has warm watercolor washes, which include the family pets.

Zion, Gene

3747 *Harry and the Lady Next Door.* Ill. by Margaret B. Graham. HarperCollins, 1960, ISBN 0-06-026852-2. SERIES: I Can Read. SUBJECTS: Humorous stories; Music and musicians — Fiction; Pets — Dogs — Fiction. RL A.

Harry, a white dog with black spots, tries one thing after another to get the lady next door to stop her terrible high-pitched singing. A popular picture-book character, Harry is familiar to most children. This good story is combined with simple humorous pictures.

Zoehfeld, Kathleen W.

3748 *Did Dinosaurs Have Feathers?* Ill. by Lucia Washburn. HarperCollins, 2004, ISBN 0-06-029026-9. SERIES: Let's-Read-and-Find-Out Science. SUBJECTS: Birds; Dinosaurs; Feathers. RL C.

Through fossils discovered in Germany and China, scientists learned that theropod dinosaurs may have had some form of feathers. Carefully drawn illustrations help to tell the story of the earliest form of feathered animals and how they might have evolved into today's birds. The final two pages provide activities to help readers learn more about feathers.

3749 *Dinosaur Babies.* Ill. by Lucia Washburn. HarperCollins, 1999, ISBN 0-06-027141-8. SERIES: Let's-Read-and-Find-Out Science. SUBJECTS: Animals — Baby; Dinosaurs; Science and scientists. RL C. LEXILE 770L.

Did dinosaurs look after their hatchlings? Carefully done illustrations and an interesting text focus on the Maiasaurus and the Oviraptor and the work scientists have done in discovering how they cared for their young. Two final pages have children create their own fossil eggs. Adult supervision is not suggested and may be required.

3750 *Dinosaur Tracks.* Ill. by Lucia Washburn. Collins, 2007, ISBN 0-06-029024-2. SERIES: Let's-Read-and-Find-Out Science. SUBJECTS: Animals — Tracks; Dinosaurs; Fossils. RL C.

Whether they were meat eaters, plant eaters, or giant plant eaters, dinosaurs left tracks in sand or mud. The tracks tell scientists about the animals and the way they lived. Detailed illustrations add to the appeal of this carefully written book.

3751 *Dinosaurs Big and Small.* Ill. by Lucia Washburn. HarperCollins, pap., 2002, ISBN 0-06-445182-8. SERIES: Let's-Read-and-Find-Out Science. SUBJECTS: Concepts — Weight ; Dinosaurs; Science and scientists. RL B.

How scientists determine the size and weight of a dinosaur, the smallest and the largest dinosaurs, and how they relate in size to people and animals today are all a part of this colorfully illustrated book. Two pages of basic facts about the dinosaurs mentioned also include the pronunciation of their names.

3752 *How Mountains Are Made.* Ill. by James Graham Hale. HarperCollins, pap., 1995, ISBN 0-06-445128-3. SERIES: Let's-Read-and-Find-Out Science. SUBJECTS: Geology and geologists; Mountains; Science and scientists. RL C. LEXILE 620L.

A carefully written, easily understood text explains how mountains were formed over millions of years. An explanation of plate tectonics is included and illustrated. The illustrations are done in detailed watercolors and provide good examples of topics discussed in the text.

3753 *Terrible Tyrannosaurs.* Ill. by Lucia Washburn. HarperCollins, 2001, ISBN 0-06-027933-8. SERIES: Let's-Read-and-Find-Out Science. SUBJECTS: Dinosaurs; Fossils; Science and scientists. RL C. LEXILE 980L.

Inspired by fossil finds in the early 1900s, paleontologists put together what became of Tyrannosaurus rex. Showers writes about the animal's size, possible diet (other dinosaurs?), and what the scientists base their theories upon. The book is illustrated with detailed and attractive watercolor and pencil pictures.

Zoehfeld, Kathleen W. (cont.)

3754 *What Is the World Made Of? All About Solids, Liquids, and Gases.* Ill. by Paul Meisel. HarperCollins, pap., 1998, ISBN 0-06-445163-1. SERIES: Let's-Read-and-Find-Out Science. SUBJECTS: Gases; Liquids; Solids. RL C. LEXILE 560L.

Forms of matter, liquids, solids, and gases and their properties are explained in a way that young readers will understand. Simple experiments help to demonstrate the properties discussed.

3755 *What Lives in a Shell?* Ill. by Helen K. Davie. HarperCollins, 2001 , ISBN 0-06-000305-7. SERIES: Let's-Read-and-Find-Out Science. SUBJECTS: Shells; Snails. RL B.

With most of its focus on snails and shells found in the sea, this book provides good information about animals living in shells as well as fine realistic watercolor pictures of animals and their shells. Factual information is presented in an interesting and attractive manner.

3756 *What's Alive?* Ill. by Nadine B. Westcott. HarperCollins, 1995, ISBN 0-06-000306-5. SERIES: Let's-Read-and-Find-Out Science. SUBJECTS: Animals; Biology; Plants. RL B. LEXILE 430L.

As a little girl explores her world, she discovers that living things need food, water, and air. She then goes on to differentiate between living and non-living things. Illustrations are done in a child-like watercolor and ink style and work well with the text.

Zollman, Pam

3757 *Gulf of Mexico.* Children's Press, 2006, ISBN 0-516-25035-3. SERIES: Rookie Read-About Geography. SUBJECTS: Geography; Oceans and ocean life. RL B. LEXILE 490L.

Land and water animals, ports, oil rigs, and even hurricanes can all be found in the Gulf of Mexico. Clear language, well-chosen photographs, a photo glossary, and an index combine to make this a very informative though brief book.

3758 *Lake Tahoe.* Children's Press, 2006, ISBN 0-516-25036-1. SERIES: Rookie Read-About Geography. SUBJECTS: Geography; Lakes; United States. RL B. LEXILE 440L.

One of the deepest lakes in the United States, Tahoe is situated along the California-Nevada border between two mountain ranges. The lake has lots of things to see, including many wild animals. The book includes a photo glossary and an index.

3759 *Wyoming.* Children's Press, 2007, ISBN 0-516-25389-1. SERIES: Rookie Read-About Geography. SUBJECTS: Geography; United States; Wyoming. RL B. LEXILE 620L.

The first state to give women the vote, Wyoming has plains, mountain, and basin areas. Known for cold winters, beautiful scenery, wildlife, and Yellowstone National Park, the state also has many cattle ranches and farms. Though the text is brief, the information, color photographs, and maps are sure to inspire readers to want to visit. A photo glossary and index are included.

Zolotow, Charlotte

3760 *Seasons: A Book of Poems.* Ill. by Erik Blegvad. HarperCollins, 2002, ISBN 0-06-026698-8. SERIES: I Can Read. SUBJECTS: Poetry; Seasons. RL C.

Perfect for reading aloud, these poems evoke the feeling of each season in short verse. Poet Zolotow and award-winning artist Blegvad are perfectly matched and guaranteed to gain new fans for poetry.

Zweifel, Frances W.

3761 *Bony.* Ill. by Whitney Darrow. HarperCollins, 1977, o.p. SERIES: I Can Read. SUBJECTS: Pets — Wild animals — Fiction; Squirrels — Fiction. RL B.

Kim rescues an orphaned baby squirrel, names her Bony, and raises her in his home. Finally grown and behaving like the wild animal she is, Bony is reintroduced to the wild. Whimsical pencil drawings add humor to a situation that does not always end so happily.

3762 *Pickle in the Middle and Other Easy Snacks.* Ill. by Frances Zweifel. HarperCollins, 1979, ISBN 0-06-027072-1. SERIES: I Can Read. SUBJECTS: Cookery. RL C.

Without having to cook, children can use this recipe book to create 26 snacks. The instructions occasionally call for expensive items like sweetened condensed milk or dates. Many of the recipes are very sweet but most are nutritious. Appealing illustrations help to explain the instructions.

TITLE INDEX

Numerals refer to entry numbers, not page numbers.

ILLUSTRATOR INDEX

Numerals refer to entry numbers, not page numbers.

READABILITY INDEX

Titles have been categorized by range of difficulty for beginning readers: low (Reading Level A), middle (Reading Level B), and high (Reading Level C). Using the criteria established for including a title (see Preface) and relying on our experience and judgment, rather than strict adherence to readability levels, allowed for inclusion of books such as *The Berenstains' B Book,* which tested beyond the first and second grade levels. Numerals refer to entry numbers, not page numbers.

READING LEVEL A

READING LEVEL A (cont.)

READING LEVEL A (cont.)

READING LEVEL A (cont.)

READING LEVEL A (cont.)

READING LEVEL A/B

READING LEVEL A/C

READING LEVEL B

READING LEVEL B (cont.)

READING LEVEL B (cont.)

READING LEVEL B (cont.)

READING LEVEL B (cont.)

READING LEVEL B (cont.)

READING LEVEL B (cont.)

READING LEVEL B (cont.)

READING LEVEL B (cont.)

READING LEVEL B/C

READING LEVEL C

READING LEVEL C (cont.)

READING LEVEL C (cont.)

READING LEVEL C (cont.)

READING LEVEL C (cont.)

SERIES INDEX

Under each series, title entries are arranged by author, then title and entry number. No distinction has been made where publishers share the same series title.

Early Bird

Early Bird Body Systems

Early Bird Nature

Early I Can Read

Early Nature Picture Book

Early Reader

Early Step into Reading

Early Step into Reading + Math

Easy-Read Fact

Easy-Read Story

Easy Reader

Easy Readers

I Can Be

I Can Read

I Can Read: Wildlife Conservation Society

I Can Read Chapter Book

I Can Read History

I Can Read It All by Myself

My First Visit

My Home Country

My World — Blue

Nate the Great

Native American Trickster Tales

Nature Books

Nature Close-Ups

Nature I Can Read

Nature's Footprints

New True

News Nonfiction Readers

Nice Mice

North American Animal Discovery Library

The Old Tree Stories

Old Witch

On My Own

Read-Alone

Read Aloud

Read-Aloud / Read-Alone

Read Aloud and Easy Reading

Read Aloud Library

Read Aloud Originals

Read and Wonder

Read It! Reader

Read It Yourself

Read with Me

Reader Collection

Reading Alone

Reading on My Own

Reading Rainbow Readers

Ready-to-Read

Real Kids Readers

Real-Life Photo Stories

Redfeather Chapter Book

Reptile Discovery Library

Road to Reading

Rookie Biography

Rookie Choices

Rookie Read-About Geography

Rookie Read-About Health

Rookie Read-About Holidays

Rookie Read-About Math

Rookie Read-About Science

Rookie Reader

Safety Town

Save Our Animals!

Scholastic Read

Scholastic Reader

Scholastic Reader: The Magic School Bus

Scholastic Reader Collection

School Friends

Science All Around You

Science Easy-to-Read

Science Fiction Easy-to-Read

Science Fun

Science I Can Read

Science Is Fun

Science Is What and Why

Science Secrets

Science Series for the Young

Science Solves It!

Scooby-Doo Readers

The Sea

See and Read

See and Read Beginning to Read

See and Read Beginning to Read Biography

See and Read Biography

See and Read Nature

See How They Grow

Self-Starters

Sesame Street

Step into Reading: Early

Unicorn Book

Unusual Animals

Values to Live By

Venture

Viking Easy-to-Read

ABOUT THE AUTHORS

BARBARA BARSTOW, retired Head of Youth Services, Cuyahoga County (Ohio) Public Library, is the author of previous editions of this book and has published articles in major professional journals. She was president of the Association for Library Service to Children (a division of the American Library Association) in 1990–1991 and has served as chair of the Newbery Committee (2006) and the Caldecott Committee (1999).

JUDITH RIGGLE is a storyteller, former children's librarian, and retired director of the Avon Lake (Ohio) Public Library; she was named Ohio's Outstanding Librarian in her year of retirement. She is coauthor of previous editions of this book.

LESLIE MOLNAR, Youth Services Assistant Manager and Selection Head at Cuyahoga County Public Library, is a former children's librarian and teacher. She has served as chair of the Association for Library Service to Children's Notable Children's Books Committee.